Handbook of

ORGANIZATION
STUDIES

EDITORIAL BOARD

Handbook of
ORGANIZATION STUDIES

edited by

STEWART R. CLEGG,
CYNTHIA HARDY
AND WALTER R. NORD

SAGE Publications
London • Thousand Oaks • New Delhi

First published 1996

SAGE Publications Ltd
6 Bonhill Street
London EC2A 4PU

SAGE Publications Inc
2455 Teller Road
Thousand Oaks, California 91320

SAGE Publications India Pvt Ltd
32, M-Block Market
Greater Kailash – I
New Delhi 110 048

British Library Cataloguing in Publication data

A catalogue record for this book is available from the British Library

ISBN 0 7619 5132 6
ISBN 0 7619 5133 4 (pbk)

Library of Congress catalog record available

Typeset by Mayhew Typesetting, Rhayader, Powys
Printed in Great Britain by Butler & Tanner Ltd, Frome and London

Contents

Contributors

Mats Alvesson is a Professor at the Department of Business Administration at Lund University, Sweden. He is interested in critical theory, organizational culture and symbolism, gender and philosophy of science. Empirical work has mainly been conducted especially in professional service and knowledge-intensive companies. He is a co-editor of the journal *Organization*. Recent books include *Corporate Culture and Organizational Symbolism* (1992, with P.O. Berg), *Cultural Perspectives on Organizations* (1993), *Gender, Managers and Organizations* (1994, with Yvonne Billing), *Making Sense of Management: a Critical Introduction* (1996, with Hugh Willmott) and *Management of Knowledge-Intensive Companies* (1995).

Jay B. Barney is a Professor of Management and holder of the Bank One Chair for Excellence in Corporate Strategy at the Max M. Fisher College of Business, the Ohio State University. After completing his education, Professor Barney joined the faculty at the Anderson Graduate School of Management at UCLA. He moved to Texas A&M University in 1986, then joined the faculty at Ohio State in 1994. In his research, Professor Barney focuses on the relationship between idiosyncratic firm skills and capabilities and sustained competitive advantage. He has published over thirty journal articles. He has served on the editorial boards of several journals, and is currently senior editor at *Organization Science*. Professor Barney has published three books: *Organizational Economics* (with William G. Ouchi), *Managing Organizations: Strategy, Structure, and Behavior* (with Ricky Griffin) and *Gaining and Sustaining Competitive Advantage*. He won the College of Business Distinguished Research Award at Texas A&M in 1992, and presented the Holger Crafoord Memorial Lecture at the University of Lund, Sweden, in 1993. In addition, he has consulted with a wide variety of public and private organizations, focusing on implementing large-scale organizational change and strategic analysis.

Joel A.C. Baum is currently Associate Professor of Management in the Division of Management and Economics at the University of Toronto. His research focuses on ecological, institutional, and evolutionary processes in organizational populations and industries. Joel is currently studying managers' (mis)categorization of competitors (with Theresa K. Lant), multiunit organizations (with Paul L. Ingram), and spatial evolution (with Heather A. Haveman) in the Manhattan hotel industry. He is now starting a research project that will examine the evolutionary dynamics of the nursing home industry in Ontario, Canada from 1971 to 1995. He is co-editor (with Jitendra V. Singh) of *Evolutionary Dynamics of Organizations* (1994) and co-editor (with Jane E. Dutton) of *Embeddedness of Strategy* (forthcoming), and is also a member of *Administrative Science Quarterly's* editorial board.

Max H. Bazerman is the J. Jay Gerber Distinguished Professor of Dispute Resolution and Organizations at the Kellogg Graduate School of Management at Northwestern University. His research focuses on decision making, negotiation, fairness, social comparison processes and, most recently, environmental decision making and dispute resolution. He is the author or co-author of over ninety research articles, and the author, co-author, or co-editor of seven books, including *Judgement in Managerial Decision Making* (1994, 3rd edn), *Cognition and Rationality in Negotiation* (1991, with M.A. Neale), and *Negotiating Rationally* (1992, with M.A. Neale).

Alan Bryman is Professor of Social Research in the Department of Social Sciences, Loughborough University, England. His main research interests lie in research methodology and leadership studies, though he is currently co-director of a research project on the portrayal of social science research in the British mass media. He is the author of a number of books, including *Quantity and Quality in Social Research* (1988), *Charisma and Leadership in Organizations* (1992), and *Disney and his Worlds* (1995). He is editor or co-editor of *Doing Research in Organizations* (1988), *Analyzing Qualitative Data* (1994), and *Social Scientists Meet the Media* (1994).

Gibson Burrell is Professor of Organizational Behaviour at Warwick Business School and Chair of the Faculty of Social Studies, University of Warwick. He is editor of the journal *Organization* and is currently completing a book entitled *Pandemonium* which explores some undeveloped themes in organization theory.

Marta B. Calás is Associate Professor of Organization Studies and International Management at the School of Management of the University of Massachusetts–Amherst. She was born in Cuba and has lived and worked in various countries. Prior to her current position she was Professor and Associate and Acting Dean of the School of Business at the University of Puerto Rico–Mayagüez. The exile experience has facilitated for her a nomadic position from which to write and teach about the intersections between organization studies and postmodern, feminist and postcolonial theorizing.

In their collaborative scholarly work Marta B. Calás and Linda Smircich apply perspectives from cultural studies and feminist theories to question current understandings of organizational topics such as leadership, business ethics, and globalization. They are the Americas' co-editors of the new journal *Organization*. Their articles and book chapters have appeared in several national and international publications. They are the editors of two forth-coming volumes, *Critical Perspectives on Organization and Management Theory* and *Post-Modern Management Theory*.

Pamela Chapman is a doctoral student in organizational communication at Purdue University. She received her BA in communication from Rutgers University. Her research focuses on gender and organizational communication and is guided by critical and postmodern feminist perspectives. Her current interests include the discursive construction of sexual harassment and institutionalized sexism.

Stewart R. Clegg took up a Post-Doctoral Research Fellowship with EGOS (European Group for Organization Studies) in 1974. He moved to Australia for a job in 1976 and has been there ever since, apart from an interregnum in Scotland in the early 1990s. He has held a Chair in Sociology at the University of New England, 1985–9; a Chair in Organization Studies at the University of St Andrews, 1990–3; and the Foundation Chair of Management at the University of Western Sydney, Macarthur, since 1993. He was Reader at Griffith University, where he worked from 1976 to 1984. He was a founder of APROS (Asian and Pacific Researchers in Organization Studies) in the early 1980s, and has been the co-editor of *The Australian and New Zealand Journal of Sociology*, as well as editor of a leading European journal, *Organization Studies*. He serves on the editorial boards of many other leading journals. Amongst the fifteen books that he has published are *Power, Rule and Domination* (1975), *Organization, Class and Control* (1980, with David Dunkerley), *Frameworks of Power* (1989), *Organization Theory and Class Analysis* (1989), *Modern Organizations: Organization Studies in the Post-modern World* (1990), and *Capitalism in Contrasting Cultures* (1990). He has published widely in the journals. He researched the leadership and management needs of embryonic industries for the Taskforce on Leadership and Management in the Twenty First Century commissioned by the Federal Government of Australia, which reported in 1995.

Taylor Cox Jr is Associate Professor in the Organization Behavior and Human Resource Management Department of the School of Business at the University of Michigan. He is also founder and President of Taylor Cox & Associates, a research and consulting firm specializing in organization change and development work for employers with culturally diverse workforces. His work history includes nine years of management experience and twelve years of college and executive teaching. In addition to his work at the University of Michigan, he has held faculty appointments at Duke University and with the Industrial and Labor Relations School of Cornell University. He is author or co-author of more than twenty published articles on a variety of management topics including manufacturing strategy, performance appraisal, promotion systems and managing cultural diversity. His book *Cultural Diversity in Organizations: Theory, Research and Practice* (1993) was co-winner of the 1994 George R. Terry Book Award. His consulting practice has included education programmes, research, strategic planning and organization development work with more than a dozen organizations including Ford, Exxon and Philips.

Stanley Deetz is a Professor of Communication at Rutgers University, New Brunswick, New Jersey where he teaches courses in organizational theory, organizational communication and communication theory. He is author of *Transforming Communication, Transforming Business: Building Responsive and Responsible Workplaces* (1995), *Democracy in an Age of Corporate Colonization: Developments in Communication and the Politics of Everyday Life* (1992), and editor or author of eight other books. He has published numerous essays in scholarly journals and books regarding stakeholder representation, decision-making, culture, and communication in corporate organizations and has lectured widely in the US and Europe. In 1994 he was a Senior Fulbright Scholar in the Företagsekonomiska Institutionen, Göteborgs Universitet, Sweden, lecturing and conducting research on managing knowledge-intensive work. He has served as a consultant on culture, diversity, and participatory decision-making for several major corporations. He will also serve as President of the International Communication Association in 1996–7.

Lex Donaldson is Professor of Organization Design at the Australian Graduate School of Management in the University of New South Wales. His interest is theories of organization, especially of structure. Books include *In Defence of Organization Theory: a Reply to the Critics* (1985), *American Anti-Management Theories of Organization: a Critique of Paradigm Proliferation* (1995) and *For Positivist Organization Theory: Proving the Hard Core* (1996). He is also publishing a book for managers (with Frederick G. Hilmer), *Management Redeemed: Debunking the Fads that Undermine Corporate Performance*. He has also edited a collection of key articles by classic contributors in *Contingency Theory* (1995), and published widely in the journals.

Deborah Dougherty, after working in the trenches of several large bureaucracies for ten years, returned to school to study the prospects of innovation in large bureaucracies. She is now Associate Professor at McGill University, Faculty of Management, where she teaches policy and innovation management. Deborah also taught at the Wharton School, University of Pennsylvania, for five years, and at the Graduate School of Management, University of Melbourne. Her research papers on product innovation, understanding new markets, and organizing for innovation have been published in various journals. In addition to the review chapter in this handbook, she has contributed six other book chapters. Her current research concerns whether and how large, long-established organizations can transform to be more effectively innovative.

Colin Eden is Professor and Head of the Department of Management Science at the University of Strathclyde, Glasgow, Scotland. Following an early career as a construction engineer, he moved to the University of Bath where he developed the use of cognitive mapping as the basis of a group decision support system for organizational problem solving. Since moving to

Strathclyde, Colin's work has focused on strategy development and implementation and he has worked extensively with teams of senior managers in public, private and community sector organizations. His research in group decision support is widely known and accessed across the world. He is co-author of *Thinking in Organizations* (1979) and *Messing About in Problems* (1983) and is co-editor of *Tackling Strategic Problems* (1990).

Carolyn P. Egri is an Assistant Professor in the Faculty of Business Administration at Simon Fraser University. Her research and writing have primarily been concerned with innovation, organizational power and politics, organizational change and development, as well as environmental and social issues in society and organizations. Recent publications concerning environmental issues include being guest co-editor (with P.J. Frost) of the *Leadership Quarterly* special issue on 'Leadership for environmental and social change', and a chapter in *Resistance and Power in Organizations: Agency, Subjectivity and the Labor Process* (eds J.M. Jermier et al.).

Stephen Fineman is Professor of Organizational Behaviour at the School of Management, University of Bath. His background is in occupational psychology, but he has for many years been researching in social constructionist perspectives on issues of emotion in organization, stress, work meanings and unemployment. He is currently directing two major projects on the greening of management – how organizations are responding to pressures to be environmentally 'responsible'. His recent books include *Emotion in Organization* (1993), *Organizing and Organizations: an Introduction* (1993) and *Experiencing Organizations* (1996).

Suzy Fox is currently a doctoral student in industrial/organizational psychology at the University of South Florida. Her research interests include emotions, affective and behavioural responses to organizational frustration, and employees' responses to new technology in the workplace. She holds the primary dependent variable of interest to be employee well-being.

Peter Frost holds the Edgar F. Kaiser Chair in Organizational Behavior in the Faculty of Commerce and Business Administration at the University of British Columbia. He is currently a senior editor for *Organization Science*. He has published individually and collaboratively a number of books and journal articles on the topics of organizational culture, innovation and politics and on the sociology of science. Recent works include *Reframing Organizational Culture* (with Larry Moore, Meryl Louis, Craig Lundberg and Joanne Martin), *Doing Exemplary Research* (with Ralph Stablein) and a second edition of *Publishing in the Organizational Sciences* (with Larry Cummings). He has recently completed a monograph *Rhythms of Academic Life* with Susan Taylor, and is exploring new ways to think about leadership in organizations.

Pasquale Gagliardi is Director of ISTUD (Istituto Studi Direzionali, an Italian management institute at Stresa, on Lake Maggiore) and Professor of Organization Theory at the Catholic University in Milan. His research focuses on the relationship between culture and organizational order. He has published books and articles on this topic in Italy. In English, he has edited *Symbols and Artifacts: Views of the Corporate Landscape* (1990) and co-edited *Studies of Organizations in the European Tradition* (1995). Professor Gagliardi is a consultant to many large Italian corporations.

Tiffany L. Galvin is a PhD student in organization behaviour at the J.L. Kellogg Graduate School of Management at Northwestern University. Her research interests can be classified into two areas: understanding organizational change as influenced by social-structural and institutional processes and understanding organizational change within institutional environments. In the first area, Tiffany has worked on understanding corporate restructuring activity (e.g. divestitures and downsizing) through both economic and social influence/embeddedness processes. In the second area, Tiffany is pursuing questions surrounding how firms change and how new organizational forms emerge, particularly within institutional environments like health care and education. Her work seeks to explore organizational actions traditionally explained by economic-based rationales through more socially influenced explanations.

Martha Grabowski served as a shipboard merchant marine officer for El Paso Marine Company, Exxon Shipping Company, and Hvide Shipping. She subsequently spent ten years at GE, as a marketing and advanced programmes manager within GE Aerospace. Most recently, she was a programme integration manager for information systems and artificial intelligence research programmes at GE's Corporate Research and Development Center in Schenectady, New York. Currently, she is the Joseph C. Georg Chaired Professor at Le Moyne College in Syracuse, New York, and Research Associate Professor in the Department of Decision Sciences and Engineering Systems at Rensselaer Polytechnic Institute. Dr Grabowski also serves as a member of the National Research Council Marine Board, and as a member of the Secretary of Transportation's Navigation Safety Advisory Council. In 1993–4 she chaired the Marine Board study which investigated advances in marine navigation and piloting; that study report, *Minding the Helm: Advances in Marine Navigation and Piloting*, was released in October 1994. Over the past six years, she has developed a shipboard piloting expert system for oil tankers in Prince William Sound, which is an intelligent software module within an integrated ship's bridge system. She is currently developing similar systems for the St Lawrence Seaway and San Francisco Bay. Dr Grabowski's research interests include human and organizational error in large-scale systems; real-time knowledge-based systems; development methods for advanced information technology systems; and the organizational impacts of information technology.

Cynthia Hardy is Professor of Policy in the Faculty of Management, McGill University, Montreal, Canada. Her research interests have spanned organizational power and politics; managing strategic change; retrenchment and downsizing; strategy making in universities; and interorganizational collaboration. She has published a number of books, including *Managing Strategic Action: Mobilizing Change* (1994), *Strategies for Retrenchment and Turnaround: the Politics of Survival* (1990), *Managing Strategy in Academic Institutions: Learning from Brazil* (1990), and *Managing Organizational Closure* (1985). An edited volume on *Power and Politics in Organizations* was published in 1995, and a book on retrenchment in Canadian universities in 1996. Dr Hardy has also published over forty articles in scholarly journals and books.

John Hassard is Professor of Organizational Behaviour at the University of Keele, England. Before joining Keele, he was Fellow in Organizational Behaviour at the London Business School. His recent books include *Time, Work and Organization* (1989), *The Sociology of Time* (1990), *The Theory and Philosophy of Organizations* (1990), *Sociology and Organization Theory* (1993), *Postmodernism and Organizations* (1993) and *Towards a New Theory of Organizations* (1994). Professor Hassard is currently researching organizational change in manufacturing companies in China and the Czech Republic, and compiling a historical analysis of *cinéma vérité* studies of work and occupations.

William Hesterly is Associate Professor of Management in the David Eccles School of Business at the University of Utah. His current research interests are emerging organizational forms, interfirm networks, and vertical integration. He has authored and co-authored various articles on organizational economics, most recently in the journals *Organization Science* and *Academy of Management Review*.

David J. Hickson is Research Professor of International Management and Organization at Bradford Management Centre, England. His principal research interests are how societal culture affects managerial decision-making in different nations, and what influences the success of major decisions. His previous research has included processes of managerial decision-making, power in organizations and bureaucratization. He was founding editor-in-chief of the international research journal *Organization Studies* from 1979 to 1990, and was a founder of the European research association in his field, EGOS (European Group for Organizational Studies). He has held appointments in university business schools and research institutes in Canada, the United States and The Netherlands, has an Honorary PhD from the University of Umeå in Sweden, and has lectured widely around the world. He has published numerous research journal papers and book chapters and is author or editor of eight books, most recently *Management in Western Europe* (1993) and *Management Worldwide: the Impact of Societal Culture on Organizations around the Globe* (1995, with Derek Pugh). Prior to becoming an academic, David Hickson worked in financial administration, and qualified professionally as a Chartered Secretary and in personnel management.

Chris Huxham is Senior Lecturer in the Department of Management Science and Chair of MBA Programmes in the Graduate Business School at the University of Strathclyde, Glasgow, Scotland. Developed from a background of research at the Universities of Sussex and Aston in the analysis of conflict and in group decision support, Chris has been researching interorganizational collaboration for the past six years. In this time she has worked in a variety of collaboration contexts in the public and community sectors. Particular focuses have been with groups concerned with collaboration for economic and social development and for anti-poverty initiatives.

Richard Marsden is an Associate Professor of Industrial Relations in the Centre for Economics, Industrial Relations and Organization Studies (CEIROS) at Athabasca University, Canada's open and distance university, where he is Director of its national Industrial Relations program. He holds a PhD from the University of Warwick. His interests focus on the uses of social theory for understanding IR-HRM and the politics of work, and his work appears in *Sociology*, *Journal of Historical Sociology*, *Organization Studies* and the *Electronic Journal of Radical Organization Theory*. He is currently working on using critical realism to develop a chronological-bibliographic reading of Marx and on marrying this with the work of Foucoult.

Joanne Martin is the Fred H. Merrill Professor of Organizational Behavior at the Graduate School of Business and, by courtesy, in the Department of Sociology, Stanford University, California. She has been at Stanford since 1977. Her current research interests include organizational culture, with particular emphasis on subcultural identities and ambiguities, and gender and race in organizations, focusing on subtle barriers to acceptance and advancement. Her most recent books are *Reframing Organizational Culture* (1991, co-edited and co-written with Peter Frost, Larry Moore, Meryl Louis and Craig Lundberg) and *Cultures in Organizations* (1992).

Susan J. Miller is currently Lecturer in Organizational Behaviour and Strategic Management at Durham University Business School, England. Her research interests include the making and implementation of strategic decisions in organizations, particularly focusing on reasons for decision success. She is also involved in the health sector, and recent work in this area has concentrated on the managerial/clinical interface, looking at the ways in which clinicians' contribution to the strategic direction of health service organizations can be identified and developed.

Margaret A. Neale is Professor of Organization Behavior at Stanford Graduate School of Business. Her research interests include: negotiation and dispute resolution, identifying a series of cognitive mechanisms such as the use of cognitive biases that systematically reduce the quality of potential agreements; the impact of cognitive biases on decision-making in the human resource management arena; factors that influence the cognitions of the decision-maker, such as relationships among the parties, what is being allocated (burdens or benefits), and the selection of allocation norms within

xvi   HANDBOOK OF ORGANIZATION STUDIES

groups; and *how* people collaborate, the selection of collaborative partners and the cognitive and affective mechanisms that enhance collaboration among successful teams. She is the co-author of three books: *Organizational Behavior: the Managerial Challenge* (1994, 2nd edn), *Cognition and Rationality in Negotiation* (1991), and *Negotiating Rationally* (1992).

Stella M. Nkomo is Professor of Management in the Belk College of Business Administration at the University of North Carolina at Charlotte. She is a former Bunting Fellow at the Mary Ingraham Bunting Institute at Radcliffe College. Her research has focused on human resource management practices in organizations with a special emphasis on strategic human resource planning. Her current research examines race, gender and diversity in the workplace. She and her colleague Dr Ella L. Bell are writing a book on the life and career experiences of black and white women managers in private sector corporations. She is also observing and evaluating diversity initiatives in eight not-for-profit organizations in the Southeast. Dr Nkomo is the past Chair of the Women and Management Division of the Academy of Management. Her research and writing have appeared in several journals. She is the co-author of the text *Applications in Human Resource Management*.

Walter R. Nord is currently Professor of Management at the University of South Florida. Previously he was at Washington University–St Louis (1967–89). His current interests centre on developing a critical political economics perspective of organizations, organizational innovation, and organizational conflict. He has published widely in scholarly journals and edited/authored a number of books. His recent books include *The Meanings of Occupational Work* (with A. Brief), *Implementing Routine and Radical Innovations* (with S. Tucker), *Organizational Reality: Reports from the Firing Line* (with P. Frost and V. Mitchell), and *Resistance and Power in Organizations* (with J. Jermier and D. Knights). He is currently co-editor of *Employee Responsibilities and Rights Journal* and a recent past book review editor for the *Academy of Management Review*. He has served as consultant on organizational development and change for a variety of groups and organizations.

Barbara Parker is an associate professor of management in the Albers School of Business and Economics, Seattle University, USA. Following a PhD in strategic management from the University of Colorado in 1985 she has taught and conducted research in a broad range of interest areas including managing diversity, gender roles, expatriate adjustment and managing small businesses in an international context. Teaching areas include strategy, international management, diversity management and globalization. She has published widely in various journals. Seattle University offers a required course in Globalization and Business Practices; writing the text for that course is a current project for Barbara Parker. Some of the ideas found in this contributed chapter emerged from the text project.

Nelson Phillips is an Assistant Professor in the Faculty of Management at McGill University. He completed a PhD in Organizational Analysis at the

University of Alberta. He has published articles in the Academy of Management Journal, *Organization Science* and *Organization Studies*. His research interests include organizational legitimacy, organizational collaboration and a general interest in the intersection of cultural studies and organizational analysis.

Lawrence T. Pinfield is a Professor in the Faculty of Business Administration at Simon Fraser University, Burnaby, BC, Canada. His study of the internal labour market of a large forestry firm, *The Operation of Internal Labor Markets: Staffing Activities and Vacancy Chains*, was published by Plenum in 1995. Current interests include extensions of findings from his studies of ILMs: how patterns of vacancy chains support processes of organizational adaptation; how stock-flow models of human resources create and are modified by corporate cultures; what rules managers use to create and modify jobs; and how careers may be managed in organizations characterized by dynamic patterns of jobs.

Linda L. Putnam is Professor and Head of the Department of Speech Communication at Texas A & M University. Her current research interests include negotiation and organizational conflict, and language analysis in organizations. She has published over 60 articles and book chapters in management and communication journals. She is the co-editor of *Communication and Negotiation* (1992), *Handbook of Organizational Communication* (1987) and *Communication and Organization: An Interpretive Approach* (1983). She is the 1993 recipient of the Charles H. Woolbert Research Award for a seminal article in the communication field and is a Fellow of the International Communication Association.

Michael Reed is Professor of Organization Theory in the Department of Behaviour in Organizations at Lancaster University, UK. His research interests include theoretical development in organization analysis, changes to the expert division of labour and their implications for organizational forms, and the emergence of 'disorganized organizations' in high/postmodernity. His previous publications include *Redirections in Organizational Analysis* (1985), *The Sociology of Management* (1989), *The Sociology of Organizations* (1992), *Rethinking Organization* (1992, co-edited with M. Hughes) and *Organizing Modernity* (1994, co-edited with L. Ray). He is currently working on a book provisionally entitled *Beyond the Iron Cage?* which will be published in 1997. He is the joint editor with Professor Gibson Burrell of the journal *Organization*.

Karlene H. Roberts is Professor of Business Administration at the University of California, Berkeley. Her research and teaching interests have been in organizational communication, research methodology, and cross-national management. More recently she has researched the design and management of organizations in which errors can lead to catastrophic consequences. She has studied organizations that both succeeded and failed at this challenge. In the last three years she has devoted much of her time to investigating management issues in the marine industry.

Arthur D. Shulman has over twenty-five years' experience as a teacher, researcher and international consultant on organizational communication planning and management. Art is concurrently Reader in the Graduate School of Management, University of Queensland, and the Principal Research Fellow of the Communication Research Institute of Australia. He is the author or co-author of over 90 scholarly publications. His current research activities focus on ways of improving R&D team management in the health, environmental, and information technology sectors. His prior academic appointments include Associate Professor and Director of the Interdisciplinary PhD Program in Organizational Psychology and Organizational Behavior, Washington University, and Associate Professor and Coordinator of Organizational Communication, Bond University.

Linda Smircich is Professor of Organization Studies and was Acting Chair of the Management Department at the School of Management of the University of Massachusetts–Amherst. Originally from Long Island, New York, she was always interested in anthropology, but instead of going off to some distant locale, she stayed in the Northeast and has ended up studying some interesting natives: organizations and their management. The collaborative work of Linda Smircich and Marta B. Calás is described in the biography of the latter.

Ralph Stablein is currently employed in the Management Department at the University of Otago in Dunedin, New Zealand. His teaching and research interests revolve around notions of knowledge: what gets labelled as knowledge, how it is 'produced' and used, and so on.

Ann E. Tenbrunsel is an Assistant Professor in the Management Department at the University of Notre Dame. Her interests are concentrated in two research streams: one stream that aims at understanding why people engage in desirable versus undesirable behaviours, and another that investigates how decisions and behaviours are influenced by other people. In the first area, Ann has focused on understanding the factors that drive unethical behaviour, the influence of rules or standards on behaviour, strategic approaches to corporate philanthropy and the conceptual differences between the allocation of burdens and benefits. In the second area, Ann has examined the role that social comparison plays in job choice decisions, the influence of friendships in a matching market context, the transmission of sunk costs across negotiation partners, and the dual influence of family and work involvement.

Pamela S. Tolbert is currently an Associate Professor and Chair of the Department of Organizational Behavior in the School of Industrial and Labor Relations at Cornell. She has taught graduate and undergraduate courses in organization theory, occupations and professions, organizations and environmental change, and stratification. Much of her research has focused on professionals in organizations, and includes studies of career choices among engineers and engineering students, systems of decision-making within corporate law firms, and determinants of compensation and promotion of university faculty members. She was awarded the American Sociological Association's prestigious EGOS award in 1987 for a research study of the development of administrative offices in public and private universities. Among her current research projects are a study of the effects of work at home on engineering employees' careers and work attachment, and an analysis of the processes of curriculum change in higher education institutions.

Barbara Townley taught industrial relations and human resource management at the Universities of Lancaster and Warwick, in the UK, before moving to Canada, where she is Associate Professor in the Department of Organizational Analysis at the University of Alberta. Her research interests include using Foucault to reconceptualize human resource management, a theme developed in her book *Reframing Human Resource Management: Power, Ethics and the Subject at Work* (1994).

Karl E. Weick is the Rensis Likert Collegiate Professor of Organizational Behavior and Psychology at the University of Michigan. He is also a former editor of *Administrative Science Quarterly*. Dr Weick has been associated with faculties at Purdue University, the University of Minnesota, Cornell University, and the University of Texas. He has also held short-term appointments at the University of Utrecht in The Netherlands, Wabash College, Carnegie-Mellon University, Stanford University, and Seattle University. In 1990 Weick received the highest honour awarded by the Academy of Management, the Irwin Award for Distinguished Lifetime Scholarly Achievement. In the same year, he also received the award for the Best Article of the Year in the *Academy of Management Review*. Dr Weick studies such topics as how people make sense of confusing events, the social psychology of improvization, high-reliability systems, the effects of stress on thinking and imagination, indeterminacy in social systems, social commitment, small wins as the embodiment of wisdom, and linkages between theory and practice. Weick's writing about these topics is collected in four books, including *The Social Psychology of Organizing* and the co-authored *Managerial Behaviour, Performance and Effectiveness*. In addition, he has written widely in the journals and elsewhere. Weick has also consulted with a variety of organizations in the public and private sector.

Frances Westley is Associate Professor of Strategy in the Faculty of Management at McGill University. She has published numerous articles on the subject of managing strategic change and is currently involved in research and teaching in the area of sustainable development.

Richard Whipp is Professor of Human Resource Management at Cardiff Business School, University of Wales, and the Deputy Director of the School responsible for research. He has taught and researched at Aston and

Warwick Business Schools, the University of Uppsala and the Helsinki School of Economics. His book publications include: *Innovation and the Auto Industry* (with P. Clark), *Patterns of Labour: Managing Change for Competitive Success* (with A. Pettigrew) and *Competition and Chaos*. His current research centres on the relationship between the organization and strategy fields and the problem of time.

David C. Wilson is Professor of Organization Studies and Director of Research at the University of Aston Business School, Birmingham, UK. Prior to this appointment in 1993, he was at the University of Warwick Business School for eight years in the Centre for Corporate Strategy and Change. His research interests include decision-making, strategy and change. He has published five books on these topics, the most recent of which include *A Strategy of Change* (1992) and *Strategy and Leadership* (1994, with B. Leavy). He was an original member of the Bradford Research Group studying decision-making in the 1970s and continues to research the processes and implementation of strategic decisions. He has also conducted research in the UK voluntary sector, assessing to what extent organization theory can apply to charitable and non-profit activities. He is Deputy Editor of the journal *Organization Studies*.

Lynne G. Zucker is Professor of Sociology (since 1989) and Director (since 1986) of the Organizational Research Program at the Institute for Social Science Research at UCLA. Concurrently she holds appointments as Research Associate with the National Bureau of Economic Research and as Consulting Sociologist with the American Institute of Physics, and is a member of the affiliated faculty of the UCLA School of Education. Zucker is the author of four books and monographs and numerous journal and other articles on organizational theory, analysis, and evaluation, institutional structure and process, trust production, civil service, government spending and services, unionization, science and its commercialization, and permanently failing organizations. She serves or has served as associate editor or editorial board member on several journals. She has also served on the NSF Young Presidential Scholar Award Panel and the NSF Sociology Panel and as Acting Director of the UCLA Institute for Social Science Research. Zucker has had a variety of university and other appointments since 1974, including Economist with the Statistics of Income Division of the US Internal Revenue Service (1989–94), and visiting appointments in the Department of Sociology of the University of Chicago (1982), the Program on Non-Profit Organizations of the Institute for Social and Policy Studies at Yale University (1986), and the PhD Program in Organizational Behavior at the Harvard Business School (1987).

Preface

To engage in the study of organizations once involved a relatively restricted range of approaches deemed legitimate by crucial gatekeepers such as key journal editors. Principally, they emphasized survey research methods, statistical analyses, and the occasional case study or purely theoretical argument. The more 'scientific' approaches to the analysis of organizations, using larger samples, more complex statistics, and more formal hypothesis testing, were in vogue. Today, however, organization studies has opened up in ways that might once have seemed unimaginable. Editors of a handbook have a choice in their approach to the project: to exercise strict gatekeeper control or commit themselves to free trade. They may identify with regulatory authorities such as 'customs officers', 'state censors' and 'border guards' or can find affinities with 'merchants' and 'smugglers'. Our intention, in this *Handbook*, was to trade freely, smuggle widely, and disregard the security of borders. We sought to affirm a cosmopolitan rather than a provincial coverage, to encourage diversity as both principle and practice, to reflect the ways in which studies of organizations have expanded, broadened, and diversified.

OUR AIMS

Initially, we conceptualized the *Handbook* as a project in which the 'terrain' that constituted organization studies would be mapped. We wanted to show the landmarks that characterized the present, and identify the signposts that signalled possible futures. We wanted to present a panoramic vista in which many different scenes would be noted, in different ways, by many different observers. Hence, we chose our chapters and our contributors to achieve breadth, depth and multiplicity. We left our contributors to develop, from their particular perspectives and insights, their own strategies for mapping the part of the terrain for which they felt responsible, and to report on those features, the scenery, the aesthetics, the cartography, the geology, the ecology, the history, the spirituality, which they felt to be important.

We wanted the *Handbook* not only to illuminate variety and proliferation, but also to address some of the problems they present. As diversity blossoms, boundaries develop around the various methods and modes of research in which we engage: scholars start to specialize in attempts to focus their efforts, hone their skills, master their material, and colonize new worlds. Consequently, it becomes increasingly difficult for any individual to do justice to the wealth of extant material: whether in writing or editing, scholars can profess only a passing acquaintance with the vast majority of the literature.

Yet students continue to demand a comprehensive foundation; researchers continue to be drawn into unknown areas; practitioners continue to wrestle with new and often multidisciplinary challenges. Thus there are considerable benefits of a *Handbook* that offers an entrée into different areas and goes beyond past specializations. To date, there has been no attempt to represent organization studies as it stands at the *fin de siècle*, to take stock of where it has come from, where it might be going; to offer an account of the major paradigms, histories, issues, debates of concern to organization researchers, practitioners and students. Our contributors provide insights into the many pathways to knowledge of organizations. Thus, this *Handbook* provides an accounting, a stock-taking of the diversity of current and emergent approaches, not available elsewhere despite the many excellent journals and textbooks.

As the chapters were submitted, we became the first consumers of the project we had initiated. We gained from the depth, breadth and distinctiveness of our contributors' insights and, in particular, the presence and absence of links between them. We learned that some chapters overlapped; some informed others; some missed each other completely. As we engaged with the chapters, we realized that they were more than just maps, they were conversations. We began to think of the conversations we had, with each other, with the contributors, with the editorial board members. We thought of engagement rather than estrangement; of opening up rather than closing down; of complexity rather than simplicity: we thought of continuing, challenging *conversations* between *people*. It was through and out of countless, connected, contentious conversations, by listening and learning, that we realized our own practice: we wanted to initiate conversations, to draw parallel conversations, to bring in previously silent partners and offer arenas in which they might give voice.

So our aim is to map the terrain *and* open up multiple, engaging conversations. Maps *are* important. The maps are where we start: they provide understanding; raise questions; suggest some answers; offer possible routes of passage to other, very different kinds of map, other perspectives, other ways of looking and seeing. The chapters in this *Handbook* thus present diverse views of the terrain which we need to understand before we can move forward. So, these maps were our starting point. But we also wanted to engage in *conversations* with the people who created these maps, even those, perhaps especially those, with whom we disagree. These conversations are not intended to pull everything together in a nice, neat package; they are not intended to provide the illusory comfort of consensus. They are intended to be 'controversial' – controversial because they are replete with political conflict among participants proposing alternative courses of action. And as we engage in these conversations, we remember that they are the middle, not the beginning. As readers also engage with this project, we hope they, too, will bring up new interpretations, and add new voices to new conversations.

OUR TITLE

Our title, *Handbook of Organization Studies*, reflects our aims. We rejected 'organization theory' because we do not believe there is a theory, in the singular, of organizations. Instead, there are several competing and closely fought theories. To render as singular that which is clearly contested and plural encourages the elevation of one or other of the contesting theories to the status of legitimate claimant for the sovereign position. To do this, even by implication, is not part of our project in editing this *Handbook*.

We rejected 'organization science' because 'science', in the singular, is a term surrounded by cultishness and talismanic recitation as to who has it, what it is, and what it isn't. It defies definition in terms other than the most loosely empirical or the dubiously prescriptive: at one extreme, science is what 'scientists' do when they do whatever they constitute as 'science'; at the other, claims of science allow one to favour preferred projects while delegitimating those of hostile camps.

So we chose 'organization studies', aware as we did so of the possible pitfalls: after all, this is the name of a leading European journal. Given that 'organization science' is the name of a leading American journal, and 'organization' is the title of a major British journal, would this choice be construed as partiality? Between us, we have published in, review for, and sit on the editorial boards of all three journals, so that in this sphere at least we can claim disinterest. Our nomenclature is intended not as a political endorsement but as the utilization of a term sufficiently broad that none would sit too uneasily within its gloss. So, not 'organization', not 'organization theory', not 'organization science' (although our contributors use each and every one of them), but 'organization studies' in order to embrace the many and varied approaches to the study of organizations.

OUR HANDBOOK

Ideally, this *Handbook* should pass the 'Desert Island Discs' test. 'Desert Island Discs' is the name of a long-running BBC Radio programme. Each week a 'castaway', usually a moderately famous person, is asked to choose eight records and one book they would want if they were marooned on a desert island. We think of the *Handbook* in these terms. Cast into the 'field' to do research, marooned without other resources, we would want it to function as an invaluable guide; an indispensable resource to steer the way, to find out where one 'is', where one might be going, to identify and interpret salient features of the organizational landscape. Accordingly, the *Handbook* consists of a series of coordinates of the terrain of organization studies which revolves around: *organizations* as empirical objects; *organization* as theoretical discourse; and *organizing* as social process. Hence our metaphor of mapping the terrain, one which acknowledges existing landmarks as well as envisioning possible futures.

To talk of landmarks and futures presumes a context of not only space but also time. What time defines our conception of organization studies? It is now a time where there is space for multiple conversations and dialogues, a space ironically cleared by the proliferation of new and different approaches to the study of organizations. With more contestants and contenders for knowledge, more divisions, gaps and spaces open up. Emerging in and from these spaces are a set of discourses, reflected in and constitutive of the themes and arguments of organization studies. This is where we come to our second metaphor: the task of this *Handbook* is to stimulate and engage conversations at the intersection of multiple narratives, multiple sites, multiple practices.

Within this context, naturally, we made a series of choices. The choice of some chapters was straightforward: for example, any *Handbook of Organization Studies* today must address gender and diversity. Why? Because societal change and political activism have made such issues part of the 'normal' discourse of academic and organizational life. Today gender is implied in all organizing because of heightened awareness by significant institutions and agents of its salience as an aspect of social life. The inclusion of other chapters stems from more longstanding traditions. We wanted consolidation of current and developing theoretical frameworks, such as population ecology, contingency theory, institutional theory, psychological and cognitive approaches, as well as organizational economics. We wanted to represent central substantive topics, such as power, strategy, leadership, decision-making, groups, communications, technology, organization learning and innovation. The ebbs and flows of academic debate dictated still more contributions as new academic developments and interests suggested the inclusion of such topics as globalization and the ecological environment, to take us into the twenty-first century.

We also wanted to use the *Handbook* to draw attention to areas which we thought were, or ought to be, significant. Consequently, many of the chapters derive from our convictions concerning 'critical' issues for both organization scholars and organization members: critical because they remain under-developed, and are not yet central to existing definitions, classifications, practices. Hence we wanted chapters on culture in the non-prescriptive, non-managerialist sense of the term; on critical theory and postmodernism; on recently emerging issues such as emotion, aesthetics, and time; on problematizing the taken-for-granted such as data and research; on cross-cutting issues concerning paradigms, practice, and representation. Such an agenda, we believed, would not only consolidate the state of the art in organization studies: it would extend it.

We canvassed widely to develop the final list of chapters that comprise this *Handbook*. An initial list of areas was drawn up in consultations between the editors and the publisher. A list of potential topics was specified and circulated to the members of the editorial board whom we invited to work with us. Their advice became incorporated in the planning: some topics were added; some were cut – not, we should note, because they were unimportant, but because we were constrained by the limits and logistics of publishing a single volume, despite it being a large book. So, armed with an eventual list of topics, we sought, in conjunction with the editorial board members, to identify contributors. Having chosen the authors, we asked them to consider an initial brief not only to review but also, in the parlance of the day, to 'add value'. Initial ideas and early drafts were circulated to members of the editorial board who, in most cases, offered additional suggestions and ideas. The contributors then got down to the task of writing. We believe they do, indeed, add value. It takes a variety of forms: a critique of the past; an innovative way of reconceptualizing the present; a new vision for the future.

So this volume is in every sense a collaboration. It began with Sage and the editors; it grew to incorporate the editorial board; as contributors were recruited, it encompassed them and brought them into the fold of what, on occasions, became a lively debate between editors, board members and contributors. The *Handbook* bears many names: it is, in every respect, the result of a collective enterprise.

OUR STORY

The project began in October 1992, when Suzana Rodrigues, Clóvis Machado and Roberto Venosa, colleagues from Brazil, suggested a project to Stewart: they wanted to edit a *Handbook of Organizations* in Portuguese, and asked Stewart to be a partner. Stewart then had another idea: what about an English book as well? Maybe Sue Jones at Sage would be interested.

Stewart phoned Sue to discuss the idea and was surprised to learn that she had been trying to reach him with a similar suggestion. At the ensuing meeting between Stewart, Sue and other Sage editors, more concrete proposals were put on the table. The type of project that Sue envisaged also needed editorial involvement from senior people in North America, clearly a major market, and it required an editorial team whose first language was English to manage the complexity that such a project would entail. Sue knew that a project of this size could not be managed successfully by one person. Reluctantly at the time (although he was later to be grateful for her insistence), Stewart was enrolled into Sue's way of thinking and the search began for appropriate collaborators.

Sue and Stewart both drew up a short-list of potential co-editors for the envisaged three-year period. They wanted colleagues who had academic standing, covered a range of potential contributor knowledge bases and, last but definitely not least, would be fun to work with. It didn't take long to come up with Walt and Cynthia. Cynthia and Stewart had met at the Academy of Management meetings in San Francisco. Cynthia and Walt had also met at these meetings when Walt participated in a showcase session on power that Cynthia organized. Stewart and Walt had met in 1991, when Stewart visited John Jermier at the University of South Florida. Each of the editors contributed something different to the project: Walt, trained and working in the US, has a particular interest in the psychology of organizations; Stewart, who has a background in the sociology of organizations grounded in education in the UK, has worked in Europe, Asia and Australia; Cynthia, trained in organization theory in an English university, now works in the strategy area of a Canadian business school.

At the Academy of Management meetings in Las Vegas in 1992, we met to discuss the initial structure of the *Handbook* that you are reading today. Some of the editorial board members were already in place. We wanted a mixture of people both on the board and as contributors: established names and new names; men and women; North Americans and non North Americans; critics and custodians of traditions. Eventually we arrived at a reasonably balanced list, given the constraints of our professional networks, and the fact that the English language was our medium of communication. Most of the names fell into place at that meeting. Dinners were held and deals done; contributors were canvassed and agreements made. There was some urgency to get the ball rolling: Stewart had accepted an offer to return to Australia after a brief period in Scotland, and it would be difficult for the four of us to meet together again. In fact, we didn't, until the 1995 Academy meeting in Vancouver. So, most of the collaboration was managed by fax, e-mail, and the odd long-distance phone call when we thought our deans would wear it.

Letters were sent, phones buzzed, faxes were transmitted, outlines came in, suggestions went out. The book began to take shape. Then we received the awful news that Walt had been taken seriously ill and would be out of action for some time. Luckily Walt confounded the dire predictions, recovering sooner rather than later – something we were all delighted about.

Stewart and Cynthia met in the 1993 EGOS meeting in Paris to talk further with Sue and start work on their chapter on power. At this point, Stewart was *en route* back to Australia via EGOS and by air. Unfortunately, the *Handbook* materials were mistakenly sent by sea, leaving Cynthia holding the fort in Montreal with incomplete files and incompatible computer systems.

By August 1993, Walt was back in action, meeting up with Cynthia at the Atlanta Academy meetings. Sue, Walt and Cynthia held cocktails, courtesy of Sage, for contributors and editorial members (those who had survived the various filing and computer problems, and actually received invitations) to bring them up to date. In February 1994, Cynthia spent a few days in Florida at Walt's invitation, where they discussed the *Handbook*. Walt offered to write the chapter on psychological approaches to organization studies, a gap that needed filling; he made helpful comments regarding an early draft of the power chapter, and even came up with a title for it. All in all, a productive meeting.

Meanwhile deadlines came and went. Some contributors were exemplary, sending us great copy on time. Others were somewhat more 'recalcitrant'. Exhortations were made and occasionally a few impolite words were sent through cyberspace. We editors were not blameless and sometimes forgot to acknowledge receipt of a chapter. Despite these 'hiccups', the final versions accumulated and the book started to reach its final form.

In January 1995, having planned a sabbatical sojourn in the southern hemisphere to escape the Montreal winter, Cynthia made her way to Sydney to begin work with Stewart on the introduction and conclusions. Cynthia started the writing and countless drafts passed between her and Stewart. Then, having the basic ideas in place, they worked together (using two and sometimes three computers) to craft the final versions. They argued forcibly but amicably. Stewart thought Cynthia more stubborn than he, pushing him to make more transparent those ideas that seemed perfectly clear to him (and, therefore, why not to others?). She thought he was more stubborn than her, as well as prone to underestimating the work involved in incorporating new ideas into the body of an increasingly complex text. He thought her control-oriented by insisting on precision, writing endless lists of 'things to do', and refusing to go with the flow; she thought him control-oriented by physically colonizing the space of the keyboard so she couldn't get near it, tinkering with the various versions of the text so they lost track of which was which, and jumping out of his seat when she suggested changing his words. They argued over maggots, holes and humanism, engaging in discourse that bemused listeners who overheard their conversations. In spite of all this, or perhaps because of it, they both could see the work improving, developing, evolving. Their ideas took shape which they were then able to share with Walt and Sue who made their input. Copies of an early draft were also sent to Peter Frost, John Gray and Eduardo Ibarra-Colado, who provided affirmative and helpful feedback. We thank all these people for their invaluable ideas and encouragement (even if it did mean several more revisions).

Cynthia left Sydney in late May. In August 1995, the four of us finally met as planned (for only the second time) at the Academy of Management in Vancouver where we were able, finally, to tell our contributors that the manuscript was now entering the production stage.

OUR REGRETS

There were, inevitably, disappointments and aborted plans. Perhaps the greatest regret is our inability to involve fully voices from outside our geographic and linguistic mainstream. Originally, we had planned a section at the end of each of the three parts of the *Handbook* where we would invite 'other voices' to comment on the contributions. The idea was received enthusiastically at Sage and by many of the members of our editorial board.

It was an interesting idea, made with the best of intentions, but, as the project unfolded, we began to see some of the drawbacks.

We were initially going to identify those voices among colleagues (and colleagues of colleagues) whose first language was other than English and who worked in countries not normally represented in the majority of journals and publications found in organization studies. We thought that they would bring different languages, traditions, contexts and values to our project and illuminate its geographical, linguistic and cultural parameters. This idea never materialized, however, for a number of reasons. First there was the simple question of time: the project, which took four years as it was, would have been greatly extended. Since some of our contributors delayed delivery of their chapters to the last possible minute in terms of the production schedule allotted at Sage, we could not have sent the manuscript out for comment without postponing the publication date by at least another year. This in turn would also have put the chapters at risk from criticism that they were out of date and, ironically, the material that had been submitted on time (in some cases, as much as a year earlier) would be particularly vulnerable. Second, and most importantly, we realized that by designating scholars, who did not speak English as a first language or reside in the 'developed' world, as 'other' voices, we ran the risk of marginalizing and patronizing them.

So, while disappointed that we could not do more to provide space to voices not normally heard, we realized that we could not condemn them to peripheral commentary. Our experiences are typical of the mainly Anglo-Saxon centred world of which we are a part. The terrain that we have charted is the one that is visible to us, the one populated by visible subjects. In this regard, we are no exception (even postmodernist work has focused on 'advanced' societies with its interest in the post-industrial, post-Fordist, information society of disorganized capitalism). Our map is an incomplete one, like those of European monarchs before the voyages of Christopher Columbus, and our discovery of the 'invisible' threatens similar conquest and colonization. The irony is that many voices in Latin America, Asia and Africa are not heard because they are not audible from the vantage point of our institutions; yet once they become audible, become visible, tendencies towards integration and assimilation make them no longer what they were. They are seen and heard only in so far as they are refracted through the lenses of our languages, cultures, traditions, and institutions because *we* have no other way of seeing. (We are grateful for the comments and insight of Eduardo Ibarra-Colado in educating us in this respect.)

OUR ACKNOWLEDGEMENTS

Our debts require acknowledgement. The positive affirmations include many people and many places. The entire editorial board and, of course, the authors should be mentioned. We also wish to acknowledge the special reviewers we called on to help us with this volume. At short notice and with great insight, these colleagues provided us with emergency support. They include Shona Brown, Urs Gatticker, Steve Jaros, David Saunders, Anne Smith, Paul Spector.

Stewart wishes to make the following acknowledgements:

In many small and positive ways members of the University of Western Sydney, Macarthur, helped to make the realization of this project possible. Another debt is due to Loyola University, Los Angeles, and to David Boje's generosity and kindliness. It was through their good graces that I was able to be at the crucial Academy Meeting where much of the work was done to finalize the shape of the volume. Good colleagues, graduate students, faculty and friends graciously put up with a supervisor, colleague and friend whose life was increasingly devoured by 'the' *Handbook*. Without Sue Jones the project would never have happened. Constantine Kallas, Dirk Bunzel, Carol Tokley, Leanne Sharp and Olga Underwood aided the administration of the project in Sydney. Frattini's Restaurant, one of the finest Italian eateries in Sydney, provided relief from the heavy compositional tasks, and occasional bottles of Mountadam dissolved the stresses of the working day.

Cynthia wishes to acknowledge the following people and institutions:

Nancy Charbonneau handled much of the administrative work associated with the book, often at long distance, and always carrying out my countless lists of things to do with alacrity and good humour. Sue Jones was, as always, magnificent as both friend and colleague. The members of my 'Area' at McGill University deserve a special mention, not just for being good colleagues, but for contributing to the *Handbook* in ways both visible and invisible. The Social Sciences and Humanities Research Council of Canada and McGill University have provided continued support for my research over the years, without which I would never have been in a position to contribute to this volume. I fully concur with Stewart's salute to Frattini's, not to say the Mountadam.

Walt's acknowledgements follow:

Norma Walker did an outstanding job in handling the paper and computer disk processing for the portions I was responsible for. Stewart and Cynthia were especially understanding and accommodating to me when my illness slowed me down (even though it meant that a much heavier burden fell on them). Sue Jones was a great editor during the entire project.

Finally, so that we do not usurp the roles that readers play in constituting this *Handbook*, our last acknowledgement is to the readers of this volume: it is to them that we dedicate it in the hope that they find it useful.

Introduction

Organizations, Organization and Organizing

STEWART R. CLEGG AND CYNTHIA HARDY

In this *Handbook* we intended, at the outset, to provide a map to help discerning teachers and students navigate their own route around organization studies. In so doing, we had some selection rules for inclusion. We tried to review the old as well as the new; to cover more 'mainstream' work as well as some less well established areas; and to include established authors as well as relative newcomers. Nevertheless, some areas and contributions do not feature. While we apologize for what some readers may see as missing components and people, our choices have not been unreflective. Our aim was to incorporate the diverse changes in the practice and knowledge of organizations that have occurred in recent years, but not to dwell on 'esoterica' or 'exotica' for its own sake. We also cover the 'mainstream' in order to understand, challenge and, where appropriate, move beyond it. So, this *Handbook* is an reaffirmation of the dominant streams of thought in organization studies as well as a celebration of some newer modes of inquiry. In presenting this diversity, we also hope to capture and stimulate conversations within and between the different approaches to organization studies. As new perspectives have proliferated, increased opportunities present themselves for starting new conversations: more diversity, more disagreement; but also more points of intersection, and more reason for dialogue, debate and dispute.

In this introduction we will set the scene for the *Handbook*. We first provide an overview of how the theory and practice have changed over the last thirty years. We then define what we take organization studies to be in the light of

those changes. We revisit some key theoretical debates in more detail since many of the chapters refer to them. We also draw attention to some of the major changes that have marked organizational practices, to which, if it is to have any application, theory must refer. It is within this theoretical and practical context that the chapters were written and, by drawing out some important themes, we hope to orient readers, especially those who are new to organization studies. We then explain the substance of the *Handbook*: why it is organized the way it is and why it contains the chapters it does. Finally, we will turn our attention to the readers: who they are and how they might make sense of the project.

CHANGES

What is the world like today? How has it changed? What does it mean for the study of organizations? If we cast our minds back to the mid 1960s,[1] we remember that the Vietnam War was starting to heat up while the Cold War was still frigid; in Europe the Berlin Wall had only recently gone up, while in Asia and the Caribbean the dominoes were threatening to come down; in the USA, the civil rights movement was in full swing and the Berkeley Free Speech Movement was gaining momentum; in Asia, Mao's 'Cultural Revolution' was imminent and India and Pakistan were at war; in Africa, Rhodesia's 'Unilateral Declaration of Independence' broke colonial ranks, while to the south, Nelson Mandela had just started a prison sentence that would last a quarter of a century. Most organizations were still premised on instruction and surveillance through personal, written or verbal, communication, and relied on professional discretion to monitor the less routinizable areas of organization life. Hierarchies were the norm, personal computers had not been invented, and the only mode of instantaneous communication was the telephone. The new technologies that were to challenge radically accepted organization designs seemed unthinkable.

Since that time, things have changed. Consider the implosion of communism, the explosion of neo-conservativism, the eradication of apartheid, the advance of feminism, the erosion of US commercial dominance and the rise of East Asian economic power. Note the emergence of the virtual, the network, the global and the postmodern organization. There are, as we approach a new millennium, many new phenomena, new conditions, new entities, even new organizations, for organization theorists to explore.

The last thirty years have not only changed the terrain, they have also produced new approaches and concepts. Three decades ago, an 'orthodox consensus' (Atkinson 1971) seemed to be emerging in organization theory concerning the role of functionalism, by which we mean an approach premised on assumptions concerning the unitary and orderly nature of organizations. Functionalist research emphasizes consensus and coherence rather than conflict, dissensus and the operations of power. The key concept is that of the organization as a 'system' which is functionally effective if it achieves explicit goals formally defined through rational decision-making. Management's task, according to this view, is to define and achieve these goals; the researcher's task is to collect objective data concerning the way in which the organization functions around goal orientation and maintenance. Typically, the research method follows the normal science model, in which the nature of organizational reality is represented and expressed through a formal research design; quantitative data facilitate validation, reliability, and replicability; a steady accumulation and building of empirically generated knowledge derives from a limited number of theoretical assumptions.

Different theoretical approaches, such as population ecology, organizational economics, contingency theory, among others, have evolved under the dual umbrella of functionalism and normal science, both of which remain driving forces in organization studies today. Meanwhile, a plethora of alternative approaches emerged, which directly challenge the supremacy of functionalism and normal science. Marsden and Townley (Chapter 3.9) call these approaches 'contra' science since they aim at critiquing and replacing the assumptions, approaches, and methods of normal science.

One important trigger of these alternative approaches in the British context was the publication of David Silverman's (1971) *The Theory of Organisations*, whose interpretative emphasis countered the functionalist view. It opened a Pandora's Box, releasing actors as opposed to systems; social construction as opposed to social determinism; interpretative understanding as opposed to a logic of causal explanation; plural definitions of situations rather than the singular definition articulated around organizational goals. In the USA, Karl Weick's (1969) book *The Social Psychology of Organizing* provided another impetus for alternative work by focusing attention on the processes of organizing, rather than those entities called organizations, using similar phenomenological resources to Silverman (1971). The publication of Braverman's (1974) study of 'the labour process' brought the concerns of Marxist thinking on to the organization studies agenda, reinforcing concerns with conflict, power and resistance (Clegg and Dunkerley 1980; Littler 1982; Burawoy 1979; Knights and Willmott 1990). The framework offered by Burrell and Morgan (1979) in *Sociological Paradigms and Organizational Analysis* identified functionalist, interpretativist, radical humanist and radical structuralist paradigms. It provided a sense-making device to account for and locate these new approaches, as well as carving out legitimate spaces in which they could flourish.

Elsewhere, in the broader realms of social theory, a radical change in social and political thought was taking place under the rubric of 'postmodernism' (Laclau 1988). One of the first sightings of the 'post' phenomenon occurred when Leslie Fiedler (1967) tied the term to a series of radical antitheses to 'modern' trends in aesthetics. Huyssen (1984) later identified it as the primogenesis of postmodernism. While resistant to definition (Jencks 1989), postmodernism has been identified as that which is marked by discontinuity, indeterminacy and immanence (Hassan 1985). Building on the pioneering work of intellectuals like Lyotard (1984), postmodern critiques coalesced around an antipathy to 'modernist' tendencies emphasizing grand narrative; the notion of totality; and essentialism.

The object of early postmodernist critiques clearly was Marxism. Here was a master narrative *par excellence*, the sweep of class struggle delivering a teleological 'end of history' in communist society; few categories could be more 'totalizing' than the notion of the 'mode of production' which was the key to explaining all social change everywhere. At the core of this theoretical project was 'class struggle', the essential fulcrum on which social and economic development occurred; individuals were visible only in so far as they were bearers of identities that their class position either ascribed, in which case their consciousness was 'authentic'; or denied, in the case of 'false' consciousness.

Postmodern approaches challenge and invert each one of these assumptions: no grand narrative marks the unfolding of human histories. They are histories, not history: one must attend to local, fragmented specificities, the narratives of everyday lives. Any pattern that is constituted can only be as a series of assumptions framed in and by a historical context. The great totalities like 'the economy' are merely theoretical artifacts. The evolution of dominant discourses from Christian religions, to sciences of the social, to histories of their constitution (Foucault 1972) show only the contemporary vanity of humankind in placing the 'individual', a relatively recent and culturally specific category, at the centre of the social, psychological, economic, and moral universe. The subject, decentred, relative, is acknowledged not as a stable constellation of essential characteristics, but as a socially constituted, socially recognized, category of analysis. For example, no necessarily essential attributes characterize 'men' or 'women'. Instead the subjectivity of those labelled as such is culturally and historically variable and specific.

As the status of the subject is challenged so, too, is that of the researcher. No longer all-knowing, all-seeing, objective or omnipotent, the researcher is forced to re-examine, in a reflexive mode, his or her relation to the research process and the 'knowledge' it produces. No longer a disinterested observer, acutely aware of the social and historical positioning of all subjects and the particular intellectual frameworks through which they are rendered visible, the researcher can only produce knowledge already embedded in the power of those very frameworks. No privileged position exists from which analysis might arbitrate (see Chapter 1.7 by Alvesson and Deetz).[2]

Despite some defensive ploys by the establishment to weed them out, these new, different, and alternative arenas, modes, and perspectives of research are expanding, multiplying and overlapping. It would appear that diversity is here to stay, and we hope to continue the trend in a *Handbook* that celebrates, rather than denies, variation, diversity and difference.

WHAT ARE ORGANIZATION STUDIES?

These changes have major implications for our understanding of what organization studies constitute. Gone is the certainty, if it ever existed, about what organizations are; gone, too, is the certainty about how they should be studied, the place of the researcher, the role of methodology, the nature of theory. Defining organization studies today is by no means an easy task. Our approach is to conceptualize organization studies as a series of conversations, in particular those of organization studies researchers[3] who help to constitute organizations through terms derived from paradigms, methods and assumptions, themselves derived from earlier conversations.

But what are these conversations, what are they about and why do they exist? We believe they are evolving conversations, with emergent vocabularies and grammars, and with various degrees of discontinuity. Sometimes they are marked by voices from the centre of analysis and practice, sometimes they seem to come from left field, out of the blue. They reflect, reproduce and refute both the traditions of discourse that have shaped the study of organizations and the practices in which members of organizations engage. They relate to *organizations* as empirical objects, *organization* as theoretical discourse, and *organizing* as social process, and to the intersections and gaps between and within them.

Let us explain by starting with a premise: *organizations* are empirical objects. By this we mean that we see something when we see an organization, but each of us may see something different. For instance, we can refer to 'the World Bank' as an 'organization', one with specific resources and capacities, with rules that constitute it; with a boundedness that defines it more or less loosely; with a history; with employees, clients, victims and other interested agents. These boundaries, these rules, this history, these agents must be enacted and interpreted, however, if they are to form a basis for action. For example, a rule has to be represented as something enforceable and obligatory before it means anything, and it may mean nothing or it may mean many things, to members and their experience of everyday organizational life.

As researchers, we participate in these enactment and interpretation processes. We choose what empirical sense we wish to make of organizations by deciding how we wish to represent them in our work. Representation, by any device, always involves a choice concerning what aspects of the 'organization' we wish to represent and how we will represent it. For example, some see organizations as characterized by dimensions like formalization, standardization and routinization; others as exhibiting variation, selection, retention and competition; or incurring transaction costs; or distinguished by institutionalized cultures, or whatever. That organizations achieve representation in particular terms is always an effect of theoretical privilege afforded by certain ways of seeing, certain terms of discourse, and their conversational enactment. At the same time, these terms of representation are already ways of not seeing, ways of not addressing other conversational enactments, and hence, ways of not acknowledging other possible attributes of organizations. How aspects of organizations are represented, the means of representation, the features deemed salient, those features glossed and those features ignored, are not attributes of the organization. They are an effect of the reciprocal interaction of multiple conversations: those that are professionally organized, through journals, research agendas, citations and networks; those that take place in the empirical world of organizations. The dynamics of reciprocity in this mutual interaction can vary: some conversations of practice inform those of the profession; some professional talk dominates practice; some practical and professional conversations sustain each other; others talk past, miss and ignore each other.

Consider, again, the example of the World Bank: it shows that there is no artificial separation between the conversations in, of and around organizations. It is not the case that one discourse belongs to science and another to everyday life, that one can inform or reform the other in some determinate way. 'The World Bank' implies conversations lodged within diverse discourses with different emphases about, among other things, the scientific efficacy and adequacy of various models of economic and social development. The strategies of science are integral to its strategies of organization but its strategies of organization are more than merely this one restricted conversation. There are also the conversations that constitute the work of the members of the organization, conversations which implicate formal disciplinary knowledges, such as 'marketing', 'research and development', and all those other terms that provide a lexicon of 'management'. Such conversations and their associated practices arrange the organizational arena as a contested terrain: one where scenes are configured, agencies enrolled, interests translated, and work accomplished, a space in which the empirical object is constituted. Such conversations, derived from the disciplines, as well as from more local knowledges and their reciprocal interaction, shape the object, the *organization*.

So, whether located in the organization of an academic specialism such as ours, or applied in the constitution of actions that become the analytical subject of such specialisms, the insights of conversation, as a public phenomenon, something intersubjective and shared, involve *organizing* as a social process. By this we refer to the embeddedness of organizing within distinct local practices, of language, of culture, of ethnicity, of gender. There is always someone who speaks and engages in conversation in order for a conversation to occur. These individuals have identities that are implicated in what is said, or not said. Speech is never disembodied: there is always a subject who speaks, even behind the most reifying organization theorist or desiccated bureaucrat.

Organizations are thus sites of situated social action more or less open both to explicitly organized and formal disciplinary knowledges such as marketing, production, and so on, and also to conversational practices embedded in the broad social fabric, such as gender, ethnic and other culturally defined social relations, themselves potential subjects for formally organized disciplinary knowledges, such as anthropology, sociology, or, even, organization studies. Similarly, this *Handbook of Organization Studies* is a collection of voices involved in the analysis of organizations, as real objects, where the 'reality' of these objects is constituted through diverse conversations, those of both the analysts and the analysands, and where both practices are embedded socially in ways of being, ways of organizing.

With this conceptualization of organization studies, one can strive for reflexivity, by which we allude to ways of seeing which act back on and reflect existing ways of seeing. For instance, feminism is both a social movement and an intellectually organized discourse with many conversations contained within it. The conversations inform each arena: sometimes they constitute aspects of the other arena, and they can be used to reveal lacunae in that 'other' arena represented. Many research possibilities reside in these reflexive relations. For example, in studying organizations concerned with equal employment opportunity, one might want to address its impact from within feminist discourse; or one might want to address the impact of equal employment opportunity legislation on the further bureaucratization of the human resource management function within a sample of organizations; or one might be interested in the politics of implementation. None is a more 'correct' analysis than any other: they are different possibilities. Like any good conversation, the dialectic is reflexive, interlocutive and oriented, not to ultimate agreement, but to the possibilities of understanding of, and action within, these contested terrains. Contestation occurs not only in the scenes of action in organizations as empirical objects, for example around gender relations, but also in the conflicting interpretations of these scenes afforded by different theoretical, as well as 'lay' or 'practical', conversations. Where desired, this contestation and associated reflexivity generate difference, although frequently, both theorists and practitioners have a practical interest in closure, not in the continual iteration of further choice. Practical foreclosure does not resolve reflexivity: it suspends it, until the next dissenting interpretation.

Readers are interpreters: to read is an active, sense-making process. Through texts such as this the reader has an opportunity to rethink his or her own conversational practices as an organization member. The dialectic moves to that between text and the reader: readers make (and change the) sense of the words and make their own representations, a theme to which we return in the concluding chapter. Ultimately, the text is important for what the reader gives to it, not in how its various authors use it to reaffirm their own subjectivity. Through their particular reading, readers will find ways to employ aspects that enable them to speak for themselves in terms of their choosing.[4]

In promoting the stimulation and engagement of multiple conversations at the intersection of multiple narratives, multiple sites, multiple practices, we are obviously claiming a privileged position. But not, we hope, by constituting a narrowly defined, tightly constrained 'obligatory passage point' (Callon 1986) – the eye of the needle through which all contributors must pass. Our privilege is inclusive, not exclusive. We exercise our power in constituting the points of passage through which multiple, free-flowing narratives might flow, contest and engage. Consequently, we sought to constitute the *Handbook* in such a way that the reader can read the diversity of organization studies as something other than a parallel set of unrelated options, different menus, disconnected conversations.

PARADIGMS AND POLITICS

The idea that organization studies should comprise a parallel set of unrelated options, different menus, and disconnected conversations, became part of an extremely influential debate during the 1980s, in which the publication of *Sociological Paradigms and Organizational Analysis* (Burrell and Morgan 1979) was a first step. At the time, the framework, which classified research on organizations according to functionalist, interpretative, radical humanist and radical structuralist paradigms, may have seemed just a relatively straightforward way to catalogue a limited number of available options for the study of organizations. But *Paradigms* was not proposed merely as a theory of knowledge: it was a means to carve out a protected niche where 'alternative' researchers could do their thing, protected from the criticisms of functionalists, free from what they saw as the necessity of having to try to explain their work to them. The key to this defensive strategy lay in the 'incommensurability' of the paradigms and the language differences that precluded communication among them.

> For those who see in Functionalist science an exercise in intellectual imperialism, dominating organization studies both epistemologically and politically, the paradigmatic understanding of organization theory offers a way of legitimating approaches whose probity would be denied by functionalism ... What it [incommensurability] implies is that each paradigm must, logically, develop separately, pursuing its own problematic and ignoring those of other paradigms as paradigmatically invalid and that different claims about organizations, in an ideal world, be resolved in the light of their implications for social praxis. (Jackson and Carter 1991: 110)

Paradigms thus issued a Janus-headed challenge to those interested in taking it up. On the one hand, *could* one bridge the language 'problem' to allow paradigms to communicate? On the other, *should* one bridge or would it allow imperialists to invade and dominate the weaker territories?

The result was a frenzy of discussion on the subject in a three-cornered debate. One group of supporters of alternative paradigms felt the relativism of incommensurability too hard to bear. Academics trained in rational debate and the search for truth sought solutions to the incommensurability 'problem' through the use of sophisticated philosophical and linguistic discourse (e.g. Reed 1985; Hassard 1988; 1991; Gioia and Pitre 1990; Parker and McHugh 1991; Marsden 1993; Willmott 1993a; 1993b). A second group, including its creators (Burrell and Morgan 1979; also Jackson and Carter 1991; 1993), maintained a hard line on any bridge between the paradigms, requiring quasi-religious Paulinian conversion as the only way to move between them. The third group in the paradigm wars were the defenders of the 'orthodox' faith of functionalism and normal science (e.g. Donaldson 1985; Aldrich 1988). Polemics flourished between defenders and detractors (e.g. Clegg 1990; also see the debate in *Organization Studies* 1988).

Most of the discussion, both incisive and accusatory, occurred between members of the 'alternative' paradigms who share a discontent with the imperialistic tendencies of the dominant 'orthodoxy'. This debate kindled such a degree of heat that the protagonists appear less like different voices in one broad community separated by minor spats about doctrine, such as Catholics and Protestants debating the rite of communion, and more like Catholics and Protestants during the Protestant Reformation when heretics, Catholic and Protestant alike, were tortured, killed and consumed by fire. Crusades, jihads and fatwahs are the very stuff of historical encounters between religions, where incommensurability flourishes as a matter of course. An extreme example, perhaps (at least in many societies), but observers might see parallels in organization studies because, as Burrell points out in this book (Chapter 3.8), the paradigm reformists missed the point. The issue is not one of epistemology, logic or linguistic theory, it is one of politics: those defending incommensurability believe it to be the best way to protect alternative approaches from the continuing onslaught of mainstream approaches in their various and evolving forms; while many of those who attack it believe it to be counterproductive in such a defence. The main battles thus took place *between* the rebels.

In contrast, the engagement of most members of the 'orthodox' faith in the paradigm wars was muted; most inhabitants of the functionalist paradigm simply continued with business as usual. Perhaps they did not consider that *Paradigms* signalled a state of crisis, as heralded by the rebels (for example, Hassard 1988; Burrell, Chapter 3.8 in this book). Certainly, most of the United States journals ignored the upstart newcomers (Aldrich 1988) although whether this was because they were upstarts, newcomers, or aliens is not clear. Most adherents of the dominant paradigm saw little threat to their privileged position, quite possibly because the nature of the institutionalized practices of the academic and publishing arena in the US made inroads by 'alternative' researchers extremely difficult. The one defender of normal science who did enter the fray with gusto was Lex Donaldson (1985; 1988; 1995). He certainly felt an attack had been mounted, which is, presumably, one of the reasons behind his engagement with opponents he later claimed to have 'routed' (1988: 28), although the contents of this *Handbook* would indicate otherwise.

Donaldson's position notwithstanding, most adherents of functionalist, normal science approaches pursued a strategy of isolationism, known in political economy as 'protectionism',

as opposed to 'free trade'. At its extreme, however, it can lead to autarchy: where trade occurs only between those within the common boundaries. Such overdeveloped protectionism rarely springs forth from some notion of 'pure' commerce: usually there is a religious or some other ideological imperative about the profanity of exchange with the 'enemy'. Protectionism involves a political strategy of creating and policing borders; its claims to purity and morality are strengthened by something visibly 'dangerous' threatening those borders, as evidenced by Donaldson's (1985; 1995) strategies of defence.

Pfeffer (1993), for more pragmatic reasons, makes a similar plea for paradigm consensus.[5] It represents an overt attempt to re-establish the old elite's dominance over organization science (while denying any such elite exists). Pfeffer acknowledges that what constitutes consensus in a scientific field is a political affair:

> My sense is that such consensus [was] developed by a group of individuals forming a dense network of connections and unified view, who then intentionally and systematically took over positions of power and imposed their views, at times gradually and at times surreptitiously. There seems to be nothing in the natural order of things that suggests that mathematical rigor should be valued over empirical richness or realism. Rather, the criteria, the status hierarchy, and the enforcement of rules were and are very much political processes. (1995: 618)

Nonetheless, in order to attain consensus, which he believes is necessary to protect organization studies from 'hostile takeover' (1995: 618), Pfeffer advocates the establishment of a nexus of powerful gatekeepers (or perhaps 'bouncers' would be a better term) to screen out undesirable elements.

> Pfeffer requires blind faith and unquestioning adherence to a dogma decreed to be 'true' by the elites of organization studies. Even when surrounded by evidence that theory is incomplete, Pfeffer would have us ignore the evidence until it overwhelms us . . . Conformity to a central paradigm would require that we train ourselves and our students to ignore any work that strayed from the established [path] . . . Further, although Pfeffer's solution (restricting the entry of ideas decreed to be 'different') doubtless would increase the comfort level of those who are already established, it will also increase the costs of entry for new scholars and restrict innovative results on the output side. (Cannella and Paetzold 1994: 337–8)

Pfeffer argues that paradigm consensus facilitates communication which, in turn, furthers knowledge development. Such a position is ironic when you consider that he ignores most of the discussion of communication and language in that 'other' paradigm debate to which he does not refer. Pfeffer (1993) cites only Burrell and Morgan (1979); Donaldson (1985); and Marsden (1993); not Reed (1985); Hassard (1988; 1991); *Organization Studies* (1988); Clegg (1990); Gioia and Pitre (1990); Jackson and Carter (1991; 1993); Parker and McHugh (1991); or Willmott (1993a; 1993b). Evidently, what we have here is 'protectionism' for those intellectually and powerfully entrenched, designed to preserve the intellectual capital that forms the basis of their power. No surprise: collusion between traders, even in ideas, is rarely advanced for the benefit of any but the colluders, as Adam Smith (1904) was wont to observe.

Protectionism is not atypical of the broader intellectual establishment in the US, where the rationalist, quantitative, normative approaches associated with functionalism and normal science have gained their strongest foothold. For example, a comparison of the different citation patterns found in *Organization Studies* and *Administrative Science Quarterly* for a matched period of co-terminous publication found that the only European amongst 103 sources that received three or more citations in *ASQ* was Max Weber, who has been dead for most of the twentieth century. The European-based journal, *Organization Studies*, on the other hand, was found to be far more catholic, with cites of scholars based both in North America and elsewhere (Üsdiken and Pasadeos 1995). Aldrich's (1988) finding that critical theorists had made a minimal impact on leading North American journals might be interpreted as an unwillingness of parts of the United States intellectual 'establishment' in organization theory to welcome new, contradictory and challenging ideas (Marsden 1993), especially when written by overseas scholars. It appears, then, that the heartland's response to incursions from further afield, both geographically and intellectually, has, at least in the past, been to deny either the reality or, if necessary, the legitimacy of the intruders' aspirations.

Protectionism is, however, a strategy of diminishing returns in these days of European, Pan-American and Asian free trade blocks. Today, while it cannot be said that normal science is an endangered species (or even a singular species), new ways of doing and thinking about research are emerging. For example, John Van Maanen's condemnation of the tyranny of the 'Pfefferdigm' at the subsequent Academy of Management meeting is a case in point (also see Van Maanen 1995). Van Maanen (1979) edited a special issue of *Administrative Science Quarterly* on qualitative methodologies as early as 1979. Karl Weick was, and Steve Barley now is, editor

of *Administrative Science Quarterly*, neither of whom can be called practitioners of 'orthodoxy'.

Moreover, the pace to include work that falls outside narrower confines is increasing. Qualitative articles appear in the quantitative sanctum of the *Academy of Management Journal* (e.g. Dutton and Dukerich 1991; Elsbach and Sutton 1992; a special issue of which (vol. 36 no. 6, 1993) included such exotica as hermeneutics (Phillips and Brown 1993), symbolic interactionism (Prasad 1993) and textual deconstructionism (Gephart 1993). The winner of the Annual Conference of the Academy of Management's best paper award in 1994 was an ethnomethodological piece with a distinctly critical edge (Barker 1993). *Administrative Science Quarterly* plans a special issue on critical theory, while the *Academy of Management Review* has already had one (vol. 17 no. 3, 1992). Compare this with the picture represented by Aldrich's (1988) analysis of citations. It would appear that there is no denying the alternative theorists; they are emerging as new tenants in the citadels of power.

To understand the paradigm debate, we must see it as a jostling for academic space by individuals with very different values, assumptions and agendas in a metaphorical joust: there are winners and losers, broken lances and deflected blows, colours and favours, queens and kings, knights and squires, barons and retainers, grand speeches and empty gestures. Paradigm protectionists advocate a deliberately political strategy to define organization studies by investing the old elite with the necessary power to screen out alternative approaches. Others, regardless of which side of the commensurability divide they happen to be on, try to carve out new space for these alternatives. We ally with the latter, since it informs our view of how organization studies are constituted, both empirically and normatively; we reflect the thinking of those chapters that emphasize ambiguity, contradiction and difference rather than those that herald resolution, conformity and closure. Our methods thus hinge on a fundamental value of bringing in, not screening out, alternative views of organizations. Such 'agnosticism' (Nord and Connell 1993) challenges the possibility of ultimate knowledge in an area of study. Agnostics value conversation, discourse, and open, cooperative inquiry across boundaries. Starting from one's own stream of consciousness and recognizing that others start from theirs, one attends to the context in which one's own experience and that of others are embedded. What is crucial to the agnostic view is the 'sense of accurate reception' (Nord and Connell 1993). We do not, therefore, wish to eradicate the practice of what passes for normal science or functionalism (even if it were possible), but we do believe that there are other significant approaches to the study of organizations to which we want to expose our readers.

It is in the struggle between different approaches that we learn (see Zald 1994), and from the diversity and ambiguity of meaning; not through the recitation of a presumed uniformity, consensus, and unity, given in a way that requires unquestioning acceptance. Many of the more fascinating debates have arisen in the interpretation of writers who have been notoriously difficult to interpret: for example the radical and functional divergences of Weberian writings stem from the difficulties in translating, both literally and metaphorically, key concepts; discussions that follow from what Foucault may or may not have said. These are occasions for revision, not reason for exclusion. Fragmentation creates a space for weaker voices (Hardy 1994) marginalized by institutionalization, centralization and concentration. Even the paradigm warriors risk simply multiplying one orthodoxy and one hierarchy by four. There will be room for more at the top, but there will also be more space to dominate. There lies only more orthodoxy, a changing of the guard perhaps, but the same old politics of glittering prizes and exclusion, as others who have clawed their way up to find *Room at the Top* (Braine 1957) have already noted.

We also question whether any favoured elite would make the correct choices in designating the areas to be researched and problems solved. Given that processes of choice inherently premise received assumptions, as well as what we know about resistance to change, elite members of the community are as likely to send us down the 'wrong' path as anyone else. Witness the lack of success of management theorists in solving contemporary business problems (e.g. Eccles and Nohria 1993). Researchers seeking professional legitimacy could quite easily be press-ganged into learning more and more about problems that are increasingly uninteresting or irrelevant; or investing more and more in solutions that do not work. In this way, even from a functionalist view, the management project would be doomed to failure because of an inability to function effectively from the point of view of the client. The positivist approach has not guaranteed success, even for the managers it purportedly serves, as Marsden and Townley point out in Chapter 3.9. The correctness of choice is something decided not by elite agendas (and more than one *ancien régime* has toppled as a result of such arrogance), but by the unfolding of both practical and political relevancies in changing contexts.

In summary, we resist strongly the notion of unity and singular direction and stand firmly apart from any attempt to screen out. Let us

make clear, though, that our *Handbook* is, of course, a political statement. To pretend otherwise would be either naive or duplicitous. Where we differ from more protectionist approaches is in our aim to illuminate and elaborate (notwithstanding the inevitable limits to our vision).

While celebrating diversity, we should point out the limits to struggle, such as that of the paradigm wars. No 'solution' will ever satisfactorily bridge the paradigms: as theories become ever more sophisticated in attempts to bridge the yawning chasm, the very basis of the theorizing becomes more vulnerable to criticism. For example, Kuhn, as Burrell points out in this book (Chapter 3.8), used the term 'paradigm' in at least twenty different ways: other writers debate whether critiques of *Paradigms* should draw on Kuhn at all, since the authors did not intend to use a Kuhnian version of 'paradigm' (e.g. Jackson and Carter 1993 critiquing Willmott 1993a). Still others level charges of misrepresenting or misunderstanding Kuhn (e.g. Cannella and Paetzold 1994 with respect to Pfeffer 1993) and point to differences between the earlier and later Kuhn (e.g. Hassard 1988; Burrell, Chapter 3.8 in this book). Given that the emphasis on language games as barrier or bridge draws on Wittgenstein and Derrida, the possibilities for reinterpretation are endless. These are theoretical resources conducive not to definitive resolution so much as to sophisticated debate, a 'speech conversation' (Habermas 1979) whose ideal is not closure but an infinite horizon of possibilities.

It is not to say that we will not learn from such erudite discussion but we are unlikely to find a 'solution' to the 'problem' of paradigm incommensurability. Even if we did find a 'solution', there is no guarantee that it would be accepted, not if it let down the defences that some individuals believe necessary to protect 'alternative' work. So, for these reasons we do not believe that the paradigm debate can be resolved here, or anywhere else for that matter. The paradigm debate may, then, have run its course. Perhaps it is time to move on. The genie is out of the lamp, with new shadows and light, new refractions, but perhaps ready to grant new wishes not previously thought of before.

FROM BUREAUCRACY TO FLUIDITY: NEW ORGANIZATIONAL FORMS

Having considered some of the important changes in the world of academics, let us now turn to the world of organizations. Once upon a time, not so long ago chronologically, but at a considerable intellectual distance, the theme of bureaucracy dominated organization studies. Weber (1978) systematized the concept of bureaucracy as a form of organization characterized by centralization, hierarchy, authority, discipline, rules, career, division of labour, tenure. It was the staple of the typological studies of the 1950s (see Clegg and Dunkerley 1980); it represented one of the most common archetypes of organization design (e.g. Chandler 1962; Mintzberg 1979); and it was the site of key case material for subsequent critiques (Silverman 1971; Reed 1985).

While none would deny the continued relevance and existence of bureaucracies for organizational life, and some have questioned the pervasiveness of postmodernity (e.g. Latour 1993), few would fail to acknowledge the emergence of new forms of organization. On the outside, the boundaries that formerly circumscribed the organization are breaking down as individual entities merge and blur in 'chains', 'clusters', 'networks' and 'strategic alliances', questioning the relevance of an 'organizational' focus. On the inside, the boundaries that formerly delineated the bureaucracy are also breaking down as the empowered, flat, flexible post-Fordist organization changes or, to be more accurate, *loses* shape. For some writers at least, these new organizational forms are sufficiently different from the bureaucratic features of modern organization to suggest the appellation of 'postmodern' (e.g. Clegg 1990).

The newly found fluidity in the external appearance of organizations rests on the assumption that the interorganizational relations into which an organization enters may be a more important source of capacity and capability than internal features such as 'size' or 'technology'. As a result, collaboration between organizations has become increasingly interesting to researchers. While not new (for example, Blackford and Kerr 1994: 203 note that 3,000 collaborative associations had been formed by US businesses by 1900), interorganizational collaboration has taken on growing significance as a potential way to solve both business (e.g. Astley 1984; Bresser and Harl 1986; Bresser 1988; Carney 1987) and social problems (e.g. Gray 1989; Waddock 1989). It takes a variety of forms: from 'collective' strategy (Bresser and Harl 1986) based on the formation of cooperative arrangements such as joint ventures (Harrigan 1985) and alliances (Kanter 1990); to network organizations (Powell 1990; Alter and Hage 1993); to modular corporations (Tully 1993; Winkleman 1993), where all non-core activities, from the cafeteria to all information technology and computer operations, are subcontracted to outsiders; to the virtual corporation (Byrne 1993) which exists only as a transient collection of 'superhighway' linkages between ephemeral entities that donate their core competences to a temporary collaboration.

One new form of interorganizational relations is linear chains that connect disparate organizations as, for example, where a lead firm imposes strict quality controls on subcontractors and sub-subcontractors in the supply chains, as do many Japanese firms. Critical linkages can pressure management to improve innovation, as in the construction of supply chains (McKinsey Report 1993: 42). Competition combined with cooperation, an idea with far reaching implications, is the normal form of relation in such linkages. Creative use and shaping of the market through production linkages might focus, for instance, on consultative buyer/vendor relations, inter-firm associations and extra-firm agencies that facilitate continuous improvement in production (Best 1990: 19–21). Value enhancement comes through a 'virtuous circle' of pressures in the chain, such as demands that suppliers meet quality standards. Governments may play a role in these relationships by institutionalizing 'best practices' and 'industry standards'.

Clusters often occur in industrial districts, where many small and medium sized enterprises cooperate at a local level, specializing in phases that are all part of the same production cycle (Bianchi 1993; Pyke and Sengenberger 1992). Well established within industrial and artisanal traditions, these districts have also developed as a consequence of local state interventions, such as industrial districts in northern Italy (Weiss 1988) and Germany (Herrigel 1993). They may also result from government decisions to site a key industry in a particular area to establish an 'incubator' to encourage localized high-technology clustering as in technology parks, where organizations with related technologies, competences, markets etc. are able to benefit from synergistic collaboration. Sometimes, incubators act as catalysts for small-business generated developments in a tightly focused geographical area and have a valuable role to play in regional programs; in other cases they facilitate the transfer of technology and ideas from large organizations such as universities, government research bodies and large corporations to the marketplace by aiding the development of new business ventures.

Networks (e.g. Clegg 1990; Powell 1990; Alter and Hage 1993; Nohria and Eccles 1993) encompass a loosely coupled cellular structure of value-adding activities that constantly introduce new material and elements. They can take many different forms ranging from the formal to the informal; they may exist simply to exchange information or be involved in an array of joint activities; they may be explicitly mediated by network 'brokers' or emerge from the initiatives of the firms themselves. Networks appear to have a number of advantages as a form of organizing, including: risk spreading and resource sharing to avoid costly duplication of independent effort; enhanced flexibility compared to other forms of integration, such as a take-over or merger, particularly where product life-cycles are short; increased access to know-how and information through collaborative relations before the formal knowledge stage.

Strategic alliances, as Barney and Hesterly note in Chapter 1.4, are increasingly becoming mechanisms to enter new markets, domestic and global. Due to the substantial financial resources needed to develop new technology, more organizations are entering strategic alliances, often with competitors, while others are turning to their government to secure support. Strategic alliances often link multiple partners on an international basis. They offer more staid partners access to leading edge technical developments in new fields; while emerging organizations secure external assets crucial to bringing an innovation to a marketplace where 'size and financial muscle are critical for the long pull in an increasingly global economy' (Amara 1990: 145). Other important benefits include shared risks, accelerated technical progress, established market linkages and resources for subsequent product development. Such is the pattern in biotechnology (see, for example, Barley et al. 1993; Powell and Brantley 1993). Start-ups like Celltech and Genentech pioneered the application of novel recombinant-DNA technologies, while bringing such innovation to market was achieved through 'dynamic complementarity', the pairing of organizationally separate resources and skills.

Through a variety of ways and in a number of guises, argue advocates, these new organizational forms offer opportunities for more radical innovation, allowing organizations to 'reinvent the future' (Hamel and Prahalad 1994).

> [M]ore radical innovations require new organizational forms. It appears that new forms, initially, are better adapted to exploit new techno/market regimes, breaking out from existing regimes within which established corporations for historical, cultural and institutional reasons, might be rather strongly bound. (Rothwell 1992: 234)

By maintaining, modifying and transforming multifaceted interorganizational relationships, organizations can construct their own environments, their own markets (e.g. Daft and Weick 1984) as they seek allies to which they can bond for periods of mutual benefit (Fairtlough 1994).

To be successful, however, new external relations require new internal ones. Consider a firm like Semco (Semler 1989), where the whole 'architecture' of the firm and the knowledge embedded in it was reconfigured in radically different ways. New relationships between existing organizations provide the comparative advantage of a clean slate, which enables them to manage 'transilience' (Abernathy and Clark 1985) or radical innovation more effectively. Established organizations, on the other hand, face far greater difficulty in overhauling what they do and how they do it (Cooper and Kleinschmidt 1986; Anderson and Tushman 1990) since radical innovation, by definition, involves an overthrow of existing competencies. So, to offset the disadvantages of size even large, apparently bureaucratic, organizations are having to reconfigure their internal relationships.

Companies must also have both the mind-set and organizational structures (or, sometimes, the lack thereof) to actively encourage cross-disciplinary teamwork, collaboration, and thus learning. And it is not only interdepartmental barriers which must be demolished; the firm's outer boundaries also need to be radically redefined so that suppliers, customers, and strategic alliance partners can become insiders and be tapped systematically for ideas and insight (Kiernan 1993: 9).

Consequently, the resulting 'postmodern' organization (Clegg 1990) looks a lot different from the traditional bureaucracy. First, it is decentralized:

> Competitive pressures, total quality management, the trend towards knowledge work, and time based competition are all business forces that create a need for decision making and staff support to be closer to customers and products . . . Businesses have to move from single profit centres to multiple profit-measurable units. In business units, general management decisions have to move to teams with direct product, project, or customer contact. As decision power moves to teams, the teams need additional knowledge, information and rewards that are tied to the businesses they manage. Finally, in work units employee involvement must move decisions to work teams. In all cases, faster decision making, control of quality at the point of origin, and delivery of service at the point of customer contact require that decisions be moved to lower levels, which in turn leads to a focus on new, more distributed organizational structures, smaller organizations, and the decline of hierarchy. (Galbraith et al. 1993: 285–6)

Second, such organizations are designed increasingly on a 'distributed' model (named in an analogy with distributed computing). Essentially, they consist of an internal network where activities which, in the old-style modern organizations, were centralized at corporate headquarters, are distributed around an internal network of divisions or units, linked through electronic forms of communication in a 'very communication-intensive organization . . . facilitated by modern information technology' (1993: 290). To guard against fissiparous tendencies a mutuality of interests has to be designed into the network. They advocate that leadership in the new organizational forms be team based, which will require skills in team building, conflict resolution and problem solving. Moreover, information, traditionally available only at the highest levels, must now be made available through decentralized circuits to lower-level employees (1993: 297), relying on both 'hard' technological networks and 'soft', relational networking competence in and between organizations.

A third change concerns the nature of hierarchy: not its elimination; but in its signification as a social order of rank, status and privilege that serves as 'impediments and barriers' preventing 'the flow of information, co-operation, decision making, and learning' (1993: 293). Instead, hierarchies become one means among many to coordinate and control actions across people, knowledge, time and space. The development of 'groupware' means that there now exist more immediate and interactive bases for coordination than simple hierarchy. Within hierarchical layers, pressures lead to increasing teamwork, premised less on jobs and job requirements and more on competencies. Such lateral organization depends on communication. These organizations are characterized by openness, trust, empowerment and commitment (Dodgson 1993; Fairtlough 1994). Once in motion, 'virtuous circles' have a multiplier effect: collaborative, open decision-making eliminates the inefficiency of traditional hierarchical styles of secrecy, sycophancy and sabotage. Decisions are based upon expertise, openly elicited and listened to in the organization.

The result is a very different organization compared to the bureaucracy and even to the matrix organization (Galbraith 1973) and adhocracy (Mintzberg 1979). Such postmodern, networked forms are fast 'becoming the organization of choice for many companies', raising 'the question of whether large size is necessary or desirable' (Galbraith et al. 1993: 290) now that networks generate a potency that stems from being big and small simultaneously. These changes pose a very different set of research questions to those that informed and stimulated past theoretical practices. The conception of the contingent relation between the size of an organization and its structural characteristics ceases to hold if the organization is a multi-headed, networked hydra. Japanese organizations such as Mitsubishi, with their different

conditions of existence for legal ownership, have, since their inception, provided a model for these hydras. In this sense they were never 'modern' in the way that the organizations of Anglo-American-based business systems were (Whitley 1992). Ironically the latter, which provided the manna for 'universal' theories of organizations, have been revealed by both comparative analysis and changing organizational practice to be neither universal nor necessarily effective.

A USER'S GUIDE TO THE *HANDBOOK OF ORGANIZATION STUDIES*

Both the theory and practice of organizations have changed substantially in recent years. In both cases, the changes have led to increasing diversity and fluidity, and decreasing certainty and structure. As academics, we are less certain of what we do: there are more ways to do it; many of those new ways raise questions about how and, indeed, whether we should do it. In observing organizations, we are beset with a moving target: questions concerning what *is* the organization exist today in ways not envisaged thirty years ago. Such is the context in which the authors prepared their contributions for this *Handbook*.

In noting and responding to these changes, we made choices concerning both the subjects and the authors we wished to include in this project. This *Handbook*, ultimately, is *our* view of the terrain. Think of our 'map' of the terrain as being based on a series of more or less detailed photographs of the landscape. Nooks and crannies will appear (or fail to appear) as one surveys from different perspectives. The contributions in this book expose different aspects of the terrain chosen for inclusion in this portfolio of possible maps. It goes without saying that different editors would have made (some) different choices: their maps would be based on different photographs and emphasize different aspects of the landscape. They might miss some of the interesting formations that we see; conversely, they might see potential buried in the land that we have not. For example, we did not include a chapter on change because we cannot imagine any theory of, or chapter on, organizations that is *not* about change. Nor is there a chapter devoted to ethics because we did not want to isolate ethics as some kind of discrete subject: rather we see it woven as a thread through many different chapters notably, but not exclusively, in the discussions of power and critical theory, of ethnicity and diversity, and of the relation between theory and practice. While organization design and structure are not directly addressed, readers can consult chapters on contingency theory, innovation, and power which incorporate these themes. The omissions aside, any book with thirty chapters by some fifty contributors addresses most of the major themes in organization studies.

The *Handbook* moves from the past to the present, from the general to the specific, and then from the specific to the new questions that the *fin de siècle* poses for organizations and for us. Part One identifies some of the major contemporary forms of theoretical practices in organization studies, both in major relief and in some of the more specific features.

Contingency theory is one of the most widely appropriated approaches in organization studies because of the analytical economy of a perspective that deals with a finite but flexible set of variables, such as environment, technology, and size, to account for variations in organizational design and effectiveness. While there are alternative claimants for the status of normal science, perhaps none is promoted so fiercely as contingency theory. Contingency theory, at root, is an organic analogy: the organization develops depending on features of its organic form and the environment that sustains them. It is not the only major research program to take the organic analogy seriously. Organizational (including population) ecology, for instance, has been a major research program in the last decade and particularly influential in the United States. It seeks explicit inspiration by drawing on biological and ecological models to explain organizational founding and failing, and matters of organizational change.

If biological and ecological models have been imported into organization studies, other sources of inspiration derived from economics and psychology. Hence, it is appropriate that economic and psychological approaches are also considered as part of the general framework of organization studies. There is a long history to their importation into organization studies, such as the early studies of the researchers into the Hawthorne Electric Plant (Mayo 1947; Roethlisberger and Dickson 1939), who sought to meld both 'psychological' and 'economics' variables in their understanding of the behaviour first of individuals and then groups in organizations. Psychological approaches focus on the centrality of the individual to the organization; organizational economics addresses why organizations exist, how they should be managed and why some organizations outperform others.

From sociological traditions comes institutional theory, which has been an organizing device for a considerable programme of work which can be traced as far back as Selznick's (1957) classic case study of the TVA. Institutional theory shows how symbolic properties of organizations help them to secure support from external interests. Interpretive approaches owe much to anthropological traditions, offering considerable potential to areas of empirical enquiry. Subjectivist and humanistic assumptions mark interpretive approaches as pre-modern. Postmodernist approaches, which question the existence of grand theory, the centrality of the subject, and the ontological status of the social world, have a more recent pedigree, especially in so far as organization studies are concerned. Critical theories, which seek to reveal structures and processes of power and domination hidden in the legitimate and taken-for-granted aspects of our social world, can be traced back to the influential work of the Frankfurt School. Together, critical and postmodern approaches, which draw from themes that also concern the humanities, supply a creative tension that makes an important contribution to organization studies.

The final approach that we consider in the first part of the *Handbook*, feminism, presents a particularly diverse research agenda with which organization studies are engaging only slowly. Here, more than anywhere else, we have a good example of the way that knowledge and practice interact, as issues of feminism as articulated in the form of interdisciplinary concerns within a broad social movement have been brought on to the agenda of organizations and organization studies. Feminist approaches also point the way forward: the concerns and insights that comprise the final chapter in this part represent the future of organization studies far more than its past.

The major theoretical traditions addressed in Part One represent a general level of enquiry within which more specific research topics have emerged. Part Two offers more specific insight into these subjects as we move to a consideration of the following: strategy; leadership; decision-making; cognition; groups; communications; technology; innovation; organization learning; diversity; the ecological environment; and globalization. Again, some of these issues are well established, although none of the contributors treat them in a particularly conventional way. Others, such as organization learning, diversity, ecologies and the environment, and globalization, are more recent themes which have developed in responses to changes and challenges found in the contemporary, empirical world of organizations.

In Part Three, we asked our contributors to reflect on research, theory and practice in organization studies and, in particular, on the relationship between them. The connection of theory and practice invariably draws on particular conceptions of what is to count and not to count as data. It is through data that we mediate between the concerns of members of organizations and members of organization studies. All the central issues of reliability and validity presume this relationship: what is to count as what kind of data?

From the practitioner's point of view, a great deal of research probably seems arcane and esoteric, but action research is one area which directly confronts the theory/practice relationship. Any investigation of the relation of theory to practice should consider the protocols of 'action research'. Action research requires some emotional investment in the organization being studied: to want to make a difference to the way the organization operates. Yet, traditionally, the emotional attachments of the researcher and the emotional life of organizations have rarely been central topics of organization research. As a part of our brief to open up issues made critical by their relative neglect we chose to focus on emotions in organizations. We also consider aesthetics in a similar way. That organizations display aesthetics and that aesthetics enter into the very fabric of organizations are evident: in the physical structure; spatial layout; architecture and design; the dress codes that are encouraged or sanctioned; body styles that are promoted or relegated. In both subtle and overt ways organizations display a complex of aesthetic dimensions. Similarly, time is the essence of organization life. From scientific management to just-in-time, much of what organization achieves is accomplished through the increasing imposition of mechanical and abstract chronology on the rhythms of everyday life. Yet, typically, time has been taken for granted by the majority of organization theorists.

Culture has been a 'hot' topic in organization theory for a decade or so now. However, much of the interest has been prescriptive. The idea that a strong, unified culture is a 'good thing' has become widely accepted. However, when the 'culture wars' are unpacked, the certainties of this view dissolve: such treatments of this topic obscure more than they illuminate. The same might be said of power. Indeed, power is still widely regarded as something one does not talk about in polite company, like religion or sex. Perhaps it is the association with politics that generates this aura? Again, power is a topic whose relative neglect makes it critical, not only a negative but also a positive aspect of organization life.

For many organization theorists the explosion of reflexive awareness about paradigms, metaphors, discourse and genealogies has been the most significant event of the last decade or so. Paradigms are implicit, tacit and unremarked;

metaphors are used unselfconsciously as literal devices; discourse is a term that few would utter easily. Such genealogies of analysis would strike most practitioners as both irrelevant and bizarre, even though they have significant implications for practice. The final two contributions go to the heart of the theory/practice nexus. They argue that conceptions of organization theory clustered around various positivist and functionalist conceptions have not been particularly successful in their application in practice. Perhaps ironically, a different way forward lies with some of these approaches that are still relatively unfamiliar to the practitioners who might benefit from, as well as contribute to, them.

In our conclusion to this book, we revisit some of the themes that have engaged our authors and, we hope, will engage our readers. In particular, we focus on the status of representation: on how representation occurs, and what it is that is being represented. We believe that by illuminating processes of representation of both the individual and the organizational subject, we can carry out research that meshes theory and practice.

The following brief summaries introduce the readers to the individual chapters that follow. Obviously, they represent *our* reading of them, not necessarily what someone else might read or, for that matter, what the authors necessarily think they wrote. Broadly speaking, two alternative approaches can be seen. Many contributors are interested in the 'development' of organization studies and how theory building shapes it. A sense of fragility nuances the discussions which accompanies the 'realization' that knowledge about organizations is not 'right' or 'wrong', but shaped by the underlying assumptions and values of the investigators. Moving targets preoccupy these authors, for example, as the bureaucratic staple has metamorphosed into a plethora of different organizational forms, and the once assured ideal of normal, positivistic science is increasingly challenged by alternative and contradictory views. Other authors experience more certainty. Comfortable in the belief that the parameters that define their subject are secure, their language is more concrete; their confidence more evident; their documentation of 'progress' more assured. The contrasts between these two approaches bear witness to a larger struggle that engages organization studies, to which we return in our conclusions.

Frameworks for Analysis

Michael Reed's chapter provides an overview that frames the *Handbook*. He rediscovers the analytical narratives and ethical discourses shaping the historical development of organization theory. In so doing, Reed wishes to carve out a new road between 'intellectual surfing or free riding on the rising tide of relativism [and] retreating into the cave of orthodoxy'. As with many of the contributors, he locates theory building within its historical and social context, highlights the contradictory claims within different branches of organization studies, and shows how they provide the grammar, the symbolic and technical resources, as well as the texts and discourses, which shape the various academic debates.

He traces organization theory from roots in Saint-Simon and Weber through branches that reach to the modern day. The view of organizations as rational instruments shaped the early days of the formal study of organizations. Subsequently, the rediscovery of community as the organic, humanistic side of organizations, Reed suggests, led to functionalist systems and contingency theories. A third narrative, one that emphasizes the market, characterizes organizational economics and population ecology. In the fourth narrative, Reed reveals the many faces of power concealed in its less visible mechanisms and devices. The melding of knowledge and power, in the fifth narrative, illuminates the institutional biases that characterize all narratives and all theorizing. It highlights the disciplinary power embedded in micro-level routines and structures and shows how the meanings that shape our identities, as observers of organizational life as much as participants in it, emanate from these micro-systems of power. The sixth narrative focuses on the societal, institutional structures that surround and penetrate organizations, as in institutional theory and globalization, allowing us to reconnect the local and the global. Reed then discusses how these rival explanatory claims deal with, and lead to, contests between agency and structure, epistemological battles, and conflicting demands for local or global levels of analysis.

Debate emerges at points of intersection between the narratives. But, as Burrell also elaborates in his chapter, while these narratives illuminate the intersection, they also cast into shadow other themes, such as gender, ethnicity, technoscience, and disparities in global development. Reed discusses how we might bring some light to those areas. Finally, he offers his own contribution to the 'incommensurability thesis' which is one of the enduring debates that mark academic discourse.

To emphasize the contested nature of the terrain surveyed by this *Handbook*, the second chapter adopts a very different voice: when Lex Donaldson talks of structural contingency theory, he advocates paying more attention to

'normal science'. Eschewing the proliferation of paradigms, he argues that structural contingency theory provides a coherent approach to the study of organizations, one in which the accumulation of empirical results offers the prospect of consensus around the ways in which organizations structure and adapt to their environments. Donaldson discusses the origins of structural contingency theory, showing how different contingency variables have been studied, as well as introducing the model developed as a result of this work. The characteristics of the underlying research paradigm which Donaldson associates with normal science in organization theory are those of sociological functionalism. Donaldson argues that the rigorous and disciplined application of one 'scientific' approach to research enables development. Accordingly, Donaldson calls for a more focused approach to organization theory, one that revolves around structural contingency theory. Not for him the pursuit of newer theories, whatever they may contribute, because they can never supplant core theory applied to the key theme of organizational structure. This concept of organization structure is conceived in terms of variation around classical themes whose dimensions are redolent of 'bureaucratic' refrains, according to the Aston researchers (also see Donaldson 1995).

In his chapter, Joel Baum covers organizational ecology, by broadening the population ecology perspective to encompass related approaches. He first clarifies what organizational ecology is and is not, thus exposing some of the myths and misconceptions that have arisen. The focus is on recent work, especially with regard to organizational founding and failing, and to matters of organizational change. Like structural contingency theory, this approach to the study of organizations is one based on a normal science conception of the steady accumulation and building of empirically generated knowledge derived from a limited number of theoretical assumptions shared between a community of scholars. In a comprehensive review, Baum tracks recent results and thinking and notes the caveats and polemics characterizing this subject. Organizational ecology, as a recent development, represents an example of the proliferation resisted by some theorists (e.g. Pfeffer 1993; Donaldson 1985; 1995). While Baum clearly makes a case for a self-contained, growing field of inquiry or 'subdiscipline', as he calls it, he also communicates with other approaches, such as institutional theory, to show how one might complement the other.

Organizational economics, according to Jay Barney and William Hesterly, addresses four key questions: why organizations exist; how the firm should be managed; why some organizations outperform others; how firms can cooperate. Transaction cost theory has examined the relative costs of markets and hierarchies of alternative forms of governance. Managerial fiat offers distinct possibilities to counteract bounded rationality and opportunism. In the case of high uncertainty and transaction specific investment the organization offers advantages over the market. Applications of these ideas are to be found in the work on vertical integration and the multidivisional form. Agency theory examines differences between the principal (often shareholders) and the agent (usually management) concerning how the organization should be managed. Conflicting interests between these two groups open up possibilities for opportunism, especially on the part of the agent who often has recourse to information and knowledge. Work has examined the delegation of authority, monitoring mechanisms, and bonding and incentives. Strategic management concerns why some organizations outperform others. Work has focused on the effects of industry structure (turning the original intent, which was to help government regulators increase competition within an industry, on its head by focusing on how firms can develop strategies to reduce competition and earn above normal profits) and the resources and capabilities controlled by the firm. Finally, Barney and Hesterly examine cooperation between firms, including tacit collusion and strategic alliances. The latter are the more common and are becoming an increasingly important feature of many economies as new organizational forms evolve as effective means to enter new markets.

Psychological approaches assume the central focus of Walter Nord and Suzy Fox's chapter. Noting that the study of psychological factors is, perhaps, more typical of organizational analysts in North America than elsewhere, they explore the work that has been carried out under the rubric of psychological approaches, tracing the origins in Taylorism and the human relations school, which took the individual as the unit of analysis, through to more recent variations in the form of human resource management, which emphasizes context. Despite the substantial interest in the essentialist characteristics and the traditional view of the human as a purposeful being who attempts to know and cope with an external reality, Nord and Fox find clues in a deeper analysis of this literature which support a more 'postmodern' reading of the individual. An emphasis on the centrality of 'the' individual has been countered by research that has focused on contextual factors that determine, or at least influence and constrain, individual behaviour; while feminist work has forced a rethinking of the psychology of gender. Such work questions the privileged place of the individual who apparently, even in psychological or 'micro' approaches, seems to be the subject of a 'great disappearing act', to the lamentation of some researchers, and apparent glee of others. Nord and Fox argue, however, that the disappearing act is itself a trick: the individual has not disappeared but continues to be a prime issue for some; while for others, through consideration of the context, the individual has been transformed. In fact, the move to reflexivity in organization studies offers possibilities for individuals to (re)create themselves in a variety of ways. The authors trace the move towards context-based analyses in industrial organization psychology, organizational behaviour and some portions of mainstream psychological literatures.

Institutional theory, reviewed by Pamela Tolbert and Lynne Zucker, is the theme of the next chapter. Ironically, they note the low degree of institutionalization of this theory as they describe the different techniques and approaches that characterize institutional theory. Contemporary institutional theory derives from an article by Meyer and Rowan (1977) that highlighted the symbolic properties of organization structure. Institutional theory draws from functionalist approaches that study how symbolic properties produce support from external interests which, in turn, help to safeguard organizational survival. The issue of institutional *processes* (rather than the characteristics or features of institutionalization) has become an important focus of research in this area, and a number of researchers have turned their attention to how organizational domains become institutionalized. In addition, some researchers have examined the role of 'champions' in promoting and shaping processes of institutionalization. In this way, some institutionalists attribute more voluntarism and less determinism to these complex dynamics. Institutional theory is thus concerned with broadening its scope by tackling the issue of agency and the process of institutionalization, as well as accumulating and consolidating research on institutionalization as a property of a social system.

Mats Alvesson and Stanley Deetz take on a formidable body of work when they review both critical theory and postmodern approaches. They note their relatively recent adoption in organization studies. Using a model that classifies different theoretical perspectives according to the degree to which they emphasize dissensus or consensus, and the degree to which they privilege the local and emergent or the elite and *a priori*, the authors locate postmodernist and critical approaches in the broader context of organization studies. Both differ from normative and interpretative studies in terms of their emphasis on dissensus rather than consensus; they differ from each other in terms of post-modernism's local, and hence plural, focus against the elitist tendencies of critical theory. By breaking these dimensions into their constituent characteristics Alvesson and Deetz provide a helpful device for readers trying to make sense of these broad and multifaceted perspectives, as well as detailing some of the tensions that both divide and integrate them. Through their reading of more 'traditional' work on organizations, these contributors show how critical and postmodern approaches offer alternative and distinctive contributions to organization studies. Critical theory and post-modernism are both 'alike and different'. Both draw attention to the social, historical and political construction of knowledge, people and social relations. Alvesson and Deetz point to a future path that organization studies might tread, where critical theory and postmodernism go side by side, if not hand in hand. Without postmodernism, they counsel, critical theory becomes elitist and unreflective; without critical theory, postmodernism becomes esoteric. Together, with a renewed emphasis on empirical work, both offer new insights for emancipating people working in organizations.

Marta Calás and Linda Smircich provide a comprehensive review of a variety of feminist theories, showing how these approaches illuminate how both organizational practice and organizational theorization cloud our understanding of 'gender'. Feminist theories are not new: the authors trace liberal feminism back to the 1700s. But neither this lengthy tradition, nor the resurgence in interest in feminism since the 1960s, has solved the 'problems' that women face as members of society and organizations. As the authors point out, there remains sufficient inequity to justify a continuation of study into the role that women play and the challenges they face. There is, however, more to feminist approaches than this; feminist theories encompass more than women's 'problems'. Recent developments in feminist theorization help to surface the taken-for-granted assumptions that characterize organization theory and render gender and gendered identities invisible.

Calás and Smircich present seven different perspectives. Starting with liberal and psycho-analytic feminist theories, the authors argue convincingly that they are not enough. These approaches take the system of production for granted, make maleness the norm, and treat gender as a universal category. Marxist, radical and socialist feminist theory propose a more transformational overhaul of social institutions. Poststructuralist and postmodern approaches call into question not just 'society' but the very way we study it. They raise questions concerning essentialist notions of gender and offer insight into how gendered identities are crafted by individuals' experiences in organizational settings. Finally, Calás and Smircich draw our attention to (post)colonial feminist theorizations that seek to give voice to those who fall outside the parameters set by the predominantly white, often elite members of the developed world who dominate the world of organizations and of organization theory. This perhaps is the way forward for organization studies, as our interest in globalization draws us deeper into cultures and countries not normally visited and, consequently, closer to the people who populate them.

Current Issues in Organization Studies

An analysis of the pervasive use of the term 'strategy' opens Richard Whipp's chapter. He argues that we need to deconstruct and problematize the strategy concept. Noting the tensions between US and European and between economic and sociological approaches to strategy, he discusses how the term, and arena of study, has evolved. One of the earlier incarnations derived from classical economics and concerned issues of competition, efficiency, and performance. Later, sociologists and political scientists entered the fray. Whipp, like Reed in his chapter, shows how different conceptualizations not only provide insight and illumination, but also produce silences around certain issues and themes, particularly issues pertaining to levels of analysis; the problem of strategic change and time; the non-reflexive nature of most strategy authors. Documenting the way the study of strategy has evolved over the years and the different approaches that comprise this subject, Whipp notes that strategy is far less reflexive and critical than organization theory. He calls for a melding of the two and more cross-disciplinary endeavour, particularly the use of insights derived from organization theory to deconstruct and challenge the assumptions that characterize strategy research. Finally, Whipp looks to the future, arguing that strategy research must consider more thoroughly the collective and interorganizational nature of 'industries' that exist today; the implications of new technology; the effects of globalization; the application of strategy to public sector contexts.

Alan Bryman addresses the subject of leadership in organizations. Previous work divides into four broad categories. The trait approach dominated the scene until the late 1940s; the style approach held sway from then until the late 1960s; the contingency approach had its heyday from the late 1960s; and the New Leadership approach revitalized the research in the 1980s. As Bryman points out, these time periods represent the ascendance of one particular approach, rather than the demise of all the others, since different approaches co-existed in the past and continue to do so today.

The New Leadership approach has provided a 'shot in the arm' by offering an antidote to the waning interest in leadership research in the 1980s with its focus on those transformational, charismatic and visionary leaders thought to be responsible for major organizational change and success. It differs from earlier work in that the focus is on leaders of organizations rather than leaders of groups. The tendency to extol the virtues of transformational leadership heralds more universalistic thinking than that associated with the earlier contingency approach, although as Bryman points out, recent work has sought to combat this trend with a renewed interest in organizational context. This Super Leadership approach emphasizes helping others to lead themselves. Other writers have focused on leadership practices, rather than on formally designated leaders, showing how practices may constitute the leader, rather than the leader carrying out the practices.

Susan Miller, David Hickson and David Wilson examine decision-making in organizations, pointing out its practical and theoretical attraction. They start by exploring the concept of managerial rationality and the early critique of Simon's (1945) work on bounded rationality. Arguing that rational choice models have been the target of sustained criticism for over forty years, the authors then turn their attention to conceptions of decision-making as the enactment of power. They show how rational models break down and discuss both visible and less visible power dynamics. Covert aspects of decision-making raise methodological questions: if power is hidden, how can it be studied? The authors turn to a variety of empirical approaches to examine this issue.

Pointing out that an understanding of decision-making is incomplete without some consideration of implementation, the authors turn to work on how decisions are put into practice. Research has uncovered different approaches to implementation from top-down 'commander' interventions to bottom-up 'crescive' implementation. The authors conclude their chapter by classifying work on decision-making in two ways. Perspectives can be categorized in terms of whether they conceptualize decision-making as coherent or chaotic and as problem-solving or political, which helps readers to make sense of the plethora of views that constitute this domain. The authors also

provide a geographic analysis of the authors and research sites that comprise this body of work. The clear Northern/Western geographic bias of the work serves to remind us of the limitations of organization studies and the distance we must travel before we can call ourselves international.

The chapter by Anne Tenbrunsel, Tiffany Galvin, Margaret Neale and Max Bazerman focuses on how work on cognition draws from disciplines outside organization theory, especially the social cognitive psychology literature. The authors describe the way this area has grown as a result of developments elsewhere as well as through management interest in decision making. This chapter reveals the permeability of organization studies, shaped both by other disciplines and the world of practice. The emergence of negotiation as a central topic and the dominance of a cognitive orientation are key sites of these influences. The authors also outline the underlying assumptions of work on cognition: that researchers should understand the world as it is, not as how they would like it to be, and that people are not rational. They discuss the tensions between theory and practice, warning against those who make recommendations without the necessary empirical evidence, but also arguing that application strengthens descriptive research.

At the heart of this chapter is a detailed and comprehensive review of social cognition and behavioural decision theory that tracks new developments and recent findings. It provides readers with the substance of the subject: what one needs to know in order to understand where the research and theory on cognition stand today in the broader arena of organization studies. At a second level, the 'story' of cognition also shows how internal and external influences have a bearing on its research, discussion, practice and teaching. Thus, this chapter provides insight into the constitution of the subject that is 'organizational behaviour' and the colonization of the space that it occupies within organization studies. At a third level, the chapter provides insight into a particular subdiscipline: the problems that researchers see; how they define solutions; what their perceptions of progress are; and how they think the area will develop. In this regard, the approach used in this chapter is very similar to that used in the chapter on structural contingency and population ecology: both share a normal science perspective.

Increasingly, diversity has reached the organizational agenda. Stella Nkomo and Taylor Cox highlight a number of important issues that have emerged around this theme. They point out the tendency, especially among practitioners, to construe diversity as a 'problem', one that requires 'managing'. They also point to the lack of theoretical development that exists in this area. Nkomo and Cox expose some of the struggles that face 'new' areas of research, in this case, one that tries to give voice to identities that have, for most of the history of organization studies, remained nameless, faceless, genderless and colourless. The authors discuss potential contributions from two very different research traditions which can, in the terms provided by Marsden and Townley's chapter, be called 'normal' and 'contra' science.

The authors first discuss the potential contribution of normal science. They review the work on social identity theory, embedded intergroup relations theory, organizational democracy, racioethnicity and gender, and ethnology. By drawing together the insights of these bodies of literature, and building on their empirical findings, the authors indicate ways to construct more sophisticated models of diversity and identity. The authors also discuss a very different approach to diversity, one that could be constituted as contra science. This approach challenges the idea that there are objective, essentialist characteristics that define gender, race, etc. Issues of measurement and scaling become irrelevant because there is nothing to measure, other than various ideological constructs. The production of such socially constituted categories occurs in a specific time, a specific space, and a specific location, serving to create identities into which people are forced to 'fit'. The language we use and the categories we create reflect power relations which permeate us to the extent that we can see no other way of being (also see the discussion of race and gender in Reed's chapter). Accordingly, this chapter mirrors some of the important themes that weave their way through this *Handbook*. In particular, it reflects an increased interest in the individual and in identity, and it shows the alternative routes available to researchers of diversity (the normal and the contra) and the different challenges and contributions offered by each.

Arthur Shulman's chapter focuses on work group performance in relation to information technologies. Information technology is important not only in its impact on group performance, the dynamics of which relation are little understood, but also in surfacing those underlying assumptions about communication within the organizations in which work groups are partially embedded. A more informed view of work group performance emerges when these additional factors are included. The chapter suggests major implications for the conceptualization of the relation between technologies and the work groups that use them. These implications are related to a misunderstanding, not so much of group performance or of technology, but of the differences between information and communication. It is through communication that we negotiate the meanings of technological infrastructure. These negotiations are not neutral but morally based. It is within these moral frames that one understands good work group performance. Even seemingly technical and instrumental issues are not innocent of ethical dimensions.

Linda Putnam, Nelson Phillips and Pamela Chapman examine metaphors of communication and organizations. They point out that no other construct pervades organization behaviour more than the term 'communication'. Yet, opinions differ as to whether organizations determine the type and flow of communication; whether communication shapes the nature of organizing; or whether, and in what ways, the two processes co-construct each other. This confusion regarding the nature of the relationship between organizations and communication calls into question the traditional metaphors that we use to study organizations: our images of organizations are largely shaped by the metaphors that represent organizing, not the way communicating and organizing co-produce each other. The authors suggest new metaphors to deal with this dilemma. They draw on seven clusters of metaphors from communication theory and show how those clusters centre on different approaches to communication, recasting our images of organizations by viewing communicating and organizing as co-terminous. After providing an overview of the history and development of organization communication, the chapter describes these clusters of related metaphors in the organizational communication literature. By exploring these metaphors, Putnam, Phillips and Chapman are able to demonstrate their implications for new insights about organizing.

Karlene Roberts and Martha Grabowski present a descriptive picture of what technology is and examine the relations between technology and organization. They note that technology is both a process and a product and, using a selection of definitions, show how authors vary in their approach to technology, and use different theories, scientific, economic and political, to explain technological developments. The authors argue that technology is a source of stochastic, continuous and abstract events which, together, involve a variety of challenges for organizational members. They examine three perspectives on technology. First, the technological imperative sees technology as an independent influence on human behaviour and organizational properties. Second, strategic choice views technology as a product of ongoing human interaction. It encompasses socio-technical systems, shared interpretations, and Marxist labour process approaches. Third, the authors explore the link between technology and structural/organizational change. Drawing on structuration theory, they conclude that technology is both a cause and a consequence of structure. Roberts and Grabowski conclude their chapter by drawing up a research agenda for those interested in technology and organization.

Deborah Dougherty writes about innovation, specifically, how organizations can learn to innovate. The evidence, so far, is that organizations have difficulty in doing so, despite the wealth of research on this subject (Weick and Westley note a similar observation in their chapter). Dougherty argues that to address the shortcomings of practice, we need to address the shortcomings of research by confronting directly the difficulties that complex organizations have in innovating. Research which is grounded in the concrete activities of innovation, rather than focused on abstractions, and which connects the individual innovation project to the larger organization, offers a possible way forward. By locating the study of innovation within the broader context of organization studies, we can start to draw theory and practice closer together.

Dougherty uses these insights to draw attention to four tensions that arise when modern organizations attempt to innovate. These are the tensions, first, between an internal and an external focus in the attempt to link technology to market needs; second, between the old and the new, as would-be innovators struggle with creative decision making; third, between directing strategy and allowing it to emerge while monitoring and evaluating innovations; fourth, between freedom and responsibility, in seeking to build a commitment for innovation. Such tensions aid creativity, so the aim is to 'manage' them not eradicate them. Innovative success comes from managing the routine and the mundane as much as the risky and the creative. The chapter offers some ideas for reconciling these tensions creatively by focusing on the microdynamics of culture. In this way, individuals can forge identities that provide them with capacities to bridge and manage the tensions.

Karl Weick and Frances Westley tackle organizational learning. They point to the oxymoron that is organizational learning: to learn is to disorganize and increase variety; to organize is to forget and reduce variety. Consequently, in a similar manner to Dougherty's chapter on innovation, these contributors draw our attention to a series of tensions between organization and disorganization; exploration and exploitation; order and disorder; seeing and not seeing; forgetting and remembering. The authors note the importance of balancing these tensions, not eradicating them: it is *in* the paradox that learning occurs. The authors also relate the issue of learning to the broader context of organization studies: images of organization based on culture and its artifacts are particularly helpful to researchers trying to understand more about learning. Not only do the authors problematize the concept of organization, they also show the difficulties that accompany the term 'learning'. The idea of collective learning is both more than and different to a straightforward accumulation of individual learning. This analysis also illuminates the central role that language plays in learning, as all learning occurs through social interaction in which language is both the tool and the repository of learning. Finally, Weick and Westley discuss some of the facilitators that can help encourage and nurture organizational learning, such as humour, improvization, and small wins.

Carolyn Egri and Lawrence Pinfield address the place of the natural environment in organization studies. They show how the meaning of the 'environment' has changed in recent years and still has different meanings in different parts of the world. The authors trace the roots of environmentalist theory and contrast different approaches to the natural environment in ecological theory. They contrast and critique the underlying assumptions of the dominant social paradigm with its strong anthropocentric values, various forms of radical environmentalism, and the reform environmentalism perspective. In the second half of the chapter, Egri and Pinfield examine the role of the 'environment' in organization theory and show, for the most part, the environment has meant other organizations rather than referring to the natural environment.

In integrating perspectives on eco-environments and organizations the authors offer two possible directions for the future. If the eco-environment is to take a more central place in organization studies the deep structure of society requires change. They show how a political perspective that focuses on self-interest might be a way to ensure change. In this respect, reform environmentalism offers considerable potential. A second prospect is a reconceptualization of systems theory that incorporates social, technical and ecological aspects. In this chapter, the authors review organization studies in the light of the pressing new demands of our world: notably a demand for appropriate and sustainable management of the natural environment.

Barbara Parker reminds us that the revolutionary aspects associated with globalization come from a variety of sources, occurring simultaneously and interactively. Despite the multiplicity, variety and complexity of these sources of globalization, she points out that business plays a unique role in globalization: business activities stimulate, sustain and extend globalization; the various globalization processes lead to unanticipated needs for alteration and adaptation on the part of business enterprises. Consequently, organizations both instigate global change and are on the receiving end of the global change process. Yet, despite the magnitude of the global 'revolution' and the degree to which business is implicated in it, business activities are, by no means, effectively organized for globalization. There are disagreements concerning the sources of globalization; about where global change is likely to lead; even about whether globalization is a phenomenon worth paying any attention to. Because writers cannot agree on how to define globalization, the ability to 'act global, think local' and become part of the 'global village' worldwide is hindered. If we are confused about what globalization means now, small wonder that we are perplexed about what it will mean for the future.

In her chapter, Parker describes how globalization has emerged from international business practices and research, showing how 'global' business comprises a very different set of activities than 'international' business. She then explores different aspects of globalization: the global economy; global politics; global culture; global technology; and the globalization of natural resources. Only by understanding the complexity of globalization are we in a position to address some of the difficult questions that it raises, particularly those that relate to whether globalization offers potential and promise, or simply offers global opportunities for exploitation and abuse. Optimists argue that business centrality will create worldwide opportunities for growth and development; pessimists worry that business centrality will only lead to increased exploitation. The fact is that we do not even know what many of the effects, good or bad, of globalization are likely to be; hence the need for an intensified research agenda on this phenomenon.

Reflections on Research, Theory and Practice

Ralph Stablein examines different kinds of data in organization studies. He notes that while data are central to our professional activities, agreement on what data are range from the dismissal of ethnographic data as stories, to the disparaging of survey data as simplistic and distorted, to the rejection of experimental data

as unrealistic. He argues that we need a common definition of acceptable data which transcends the strictures of the qualitative/quantitative divide and which still does justice to the diversity of data that researchers collect and analyze. Stablein argues that confusion between ontology and epistemology has hindered our ability to theorize about data. Data represent the empirical world, the one that we invent, rather than discover, through our research. Collecting data is, then, an epistemological project to find ways to represent the object of research, not an ontological question concerning the metaphysical world. The empirical world that we try to represent through the collection of data is what we, as a human scholarly community, understand and communicate at a particular point in space and time.

Having established data as central to epistemology, the key question becomes 'how do we (through data) know our world?' This process of representing the empirical world requires a two-way correspondence between it and the symbolic system used to represent it, regardless of whether those symbols are numbers to plug into a statistical package, words recorded from in-depth interviews, or pictures taken of artifacts scattered across the corporate landscape. In this regard, the set of symbols chosen is less important than agreement about investigation of the organizational phenomena. The first correspondence plots a particular part of the organization into a symbol system that reduces the complexity of the organizational phenomena under investigation. The researcher then uses the already understood, abstracted relationships between the symbols to learn about the organizational phenomena. The second correspondence thus requires, following such analysis, plotting *back* the rearranged symbols on to the original organizational phenomena. From the quantitative side, it means that researchers must provide evidence of validity, that respondents replied to questions in the way that the researcher intended, if they want to be sure of their data. From a qualitative perspective, it means that case studies written from ethnographic data convey the same meaning to interviewees. This model allows Stablein to compare many different kinds of data to evaluate whether or not they further the epistemological project regardless of the particular paradigm to which the research belongs.

Action research, suggest Colin Eden and Chris Huxham, represents a major bridge between theory and practice. They trace the historical context of this approach to research and develop a series of qualities that characterize exemplary action research. Included is the purpose of organizational change as well as the goals of generalization, theory development and pragmatic research. The authors also discuss the action research process and offer guidelines for designing and validating action research. Action research draws our attention to the role of the researcher, in a way not unlike the tenets more recently associated with postmodernism. It positions the researcher as investigator, subject and consumer: the researcher is an active person with values, hopes, and goals, as one involved in the research. Although there is no myth of neutrality, the contributors warn against becoming seduced, at least unthinkingly, by managerial agendas.

Action research also emphasizes reflexivity, which here refers to 'some means of recording the reflection itself and the method for reflecting'. At the same time, the authors differentiate action research from postmodernism by dismissing the idea that any form of writing is acceptable. They maintain that the conventions discussed in the chapter are integral to what they constitute as action research. By respecting these conventions, action research can resist attempts by the academic 'marketplace' to co-opt it, for example, by demands for business sponsorship or the mingling of consultancy and research.

Stephen Fineman discusses emotion and organizing, pointing out that writers have been slow to incorporate emotions into their scholarly work. Fineman traces the historical work on emotion in psychology and organization studies (the latter usually using terms other than emotion). The overwhelming perspective in organization theory is that emotion is something to be 'managed' and suppressed. Some writers explore how emotions interfere with rationality, thus putting the organization on the couch, so to speak, to reveal and explain its shortcomings. Other writers have studied how emotional processes can serve rationality. A third approach explores how rational self-interest is thoroughly imbued with emotion.

Fineman goes on to clarify the concept of emotion and explores what it *feels* like. He then turns to emotions and organizational order, arguing that, if organizations are socially constructed, emotions are central to their construction. He discusses some of the emotions that are expressed in organizational contexts; shows how organizational culture might be 'emotionalized'; and discusses the link between stress and emotion. Fineman also illuminates how corporations often prescribe emotion, such as the smile at Walt Disney Productions, the cheery 'hello' of the flight attendant. Such emotional labour is built into many professional jobs where people are paid to be 'serious', 'sympathetic', 'objective', or 'friendly'. It can wreak considerable psychological damage but,

at the same time, should the mask crack, as between say a doctor and a patient, the professional relationship is damaged. Consequently, there are often emotional 'zones', such as the galley in the aircraft, where protagonists are able to resist by expressing forbidden emotions. Fineman concludes his chapter with a discussion of some of the directions that the relatively recent interest in emotion might take and some of the challenges it faces.

In many respects, the chapter by Pasquale Gagliardi is an interesting companion to that by Stephen Fineman. Both seek to bring the 'whole' person to the centre stage of organizational analysis. As Fineman brings emotion to the research agenda, so Gagliardi brings the aesthetic side to life. He argues eloquently how organizations cultivate all of our senses: we don't just 'see' or 'know' organizations, we feel and experience them (also see the chapter by Weick and Westley). Gagliardi makes claims for very different types of knowledge than conventionally considered: sensory knowledge (rather than intellectual knowledge); expressive forms of action; and forms of communication other than speech. He asks why we are reluctant to change our focus, and traces our silence on these matters back as far as Newton, who divided the stuff of the primary qualities of the physical world from the secondary qualities of the sensory, subjective world.

Pasquale Gagliardi draws on disciplines 'far' from the realm of traditional organization studies, such as history and aesthetics. He draws our attention to corporate landscapes, and the artifacts that are part of them, to show how sensory perception is an integral part of our life in organizations and how it can help us to reformulate the relations between ideas, images, identity, meaning and sensation. Gagliardi offers us an alternative to the analysis, calculation and logic with which we are probably most familiar; an alternative that relies more on synthesis, the recognition of the global context, and the overall form. As Gagliardi points out, it is not completely describable but, nonetheless, such ideas are integral to many of the new directions undertaken in organization studies, such as emotion (see the chapter by Fineman) or time (see the chapter by Hassard). There is, however, an inherent paradox in such an approach: 'can we study the products of the right side of the brain with the left?' Perhaps lessons present themselves from the study of art? Perhaps we must be more responsive to our own feelings if we are to comment on the feelings of others?

John Hassard examines how organization studies portray time and temporality. Many of us take time (or the lack of it) for granted, but the examination of the images and metaphors of time that emerge from social philosophy remind us that time is an elusive phenomenon. Time not only appears as objective, measurable, divisible, it is also valuable. Time is money! The apparent scarcity of time enhances its perceived value. Such a temporal concept of value is the link between time, pay, and the early time and motion studies of scientific management. One legacy of the modern organization is the reification and commodification of time, whether in the form of flexi-time or other time-structuring practices. Hassard argues that this linear-quantitative view of time requires closer scrutiny and that working time is a far richer, more complex phenomenon than is often portrayed. He revisits some of the more nuanced approaches to time in the work of Durkheim (1976), Sorokin and Merton (1937), and Gurvitch (1964) that provide a basis for cyclic-qualitative studies of time.

Classical studies of organization time exist: Hassard makes reference to studies such as Roy's (1960) 'Banana Time', Ditton's (1979) 'Baking Time', and Cavendish's (1982) 'Doing Time' to probe more deeply into the complexity of temporal structure and meaning. All these accounts draw our attention to the emptiness of time for employees and their attempts to fill this vacuum of boredom with something more meaningful. A discussion of Clarke's (1978) work on temporal repertoire shows how time frames in two different industries relate to the structures and cultures of the firm. In the final part of his chapter, Hassard looks at how we learn the meaning of time and uses the time frame of a career as an example. He then examines the three main time problems that organizations must solve: the reduction of temporal uncertainty; conflict over time; and scarce time.

The chapter by Joanne Martin and Peter Frost is not simply a summary of the work carried out on culture. Rather than promote a developmental argument showing how our understanding of culture has 'progressed' over the years, building and improving on earlier work, these authors tell a different story. It revolves around struggles that occur under the auspices of theoretical development and empirical testing. Accordingly, this chapter provides an example of some of the dynamics of theory building described in the earlier chapter by Reed, as well as the later ones by Burrell and by Marsden and Townley.

Martin and Frost argue that initial work on culture represented an opportunity to break with the constraints of dominant quantitative and positivistic approaches. 'Culture' allowed qualitative, ethnographic methodologies to acquire legitimacy. However, as the authors point out, these forays into new territory evoked new struggles: managerialist-oriented work was criticized for selling out; some qualitative work was proclaimed insufficiently 'deep'; the hermeneutic tradition was called into question for its neglect of political issues; and quantitative researchers began to reassert their control of empirical research. These different approaches to the study of organizational culture contributed much, but there is no clear, linear pattern of progress. More recently, postmodernism advises not bothering to look for progress. Yet, ironically, postmodernism offers a way forward, whether we call it progress or not. While many of its advocates are as unequivocal in their support as its detractors are in their scepticism, others adopt a middle road (cf. Parker 1992). They see, as do we, that those developments labelled as 'postmodern' inject fresh insight, new ideas, and some excitement into organization studies. Martin and Frost agree and offer creative (although, for the afficionados, possibly modernist) suggestions as to how scholars of organization studies might expropriate postmodernism. As the authors show, the study of organizational culture could be (and in some cases already is) greatly enriched by postmodern thinking.

Cynthia Hardy and Stewart Clegg discuss the role of power in organizations. They contend that the plethora of conceptualizations of power has in many respects served to restrict our understanding. As Reed says in the opening chapter: power is the 'least understood concept in organization analysis'. Hardy and Clegg seek to clarify this confusion. Like other authors in the *Handbook*, such as Burrell, and Marsden and Townley, they locate the classical heritage of power in the work of Marx and Weber, and note diverse readings of Weber proposed by different theories. In the context of functionalist organization theory, power vested in hierarchy is considered 'legitimate', 'formal' and functional. It disappears from the gaze of researchers who are much more interested in the dysfunctional, 'informal' and 'illegitimate' power that operates outside the hierarchy. In contrast to these functionalist researchers, who saw hierarchical power as non-problematic and in no need of explanations, critical theorists labelled the same phenomenon 'domination'. Both approaches could refer to different readings of Weber. The cleavage between focusing on power as illegitimate or legitimate continued as the former concentrated their study on strategies to defeat conflict, while the latter analyzed strategies of domination. Researchers with the means to bridge the chasm seemed either to draw back at the precipice or find their voices too frail to be heard on the other side.

More recently, the two-way split has become a three-way break as the work of Foucault challenged the foundations of both critical and functional approaches. The result, argue the authors, is a curiously inactive conceptualization: we know more and more about the way power works *on* us but less and less about how we might make it work *for* us. Like Alvesson and Deetz, then, Hardy and Clegg see the way forward in a melding of critical and postmodernist thinking.

Gibson Burrell was a partner in a project that marks many of the chapters in this book, as co-author of *Sociological Paradigms and Organizational Analysis*. He revisits his earlier work in his chapter. He opposes those authors for whom the 'fragmentation' of organization studies warrants replacement by a nostalgic unity and argues that fragmentation has always characterized organization studies, contrasting different readings of Weber to illustrate the point. One reading of Weber, associated with Parsons and his colleagues in the United States, saw bureaucracy as an ideal, efficient form of organizing. It was this conceptualization, according to Burrell, that gave rise to the epistemological and methodological basis of the normal science approach. However, a second reading of Weber offered a more radical interpretation and provided, from the outset, an 'alternative' view of organizations. Hence, there was always a politics implicitly at work in any reading of Weber (as, for instance, in the sociological tradition that saw Weber's work as a counterpoint to that of Marx, one to which much organization theory seemed blind).

Burrell argues that the apparent consensus associated with the heyday of the Aston Studies, when the so-called dominant 'orthodoxy' prevailed on both sides of the Atlantic, was unusual. At that time, transatlantic convergence existed around a belief in welfarism, Keynesian economics, and defence spending spurred by the Cold War. They were the result of centrally planned, coordinated activities, which provided sustenance for normal science but which were unique to that particular historical period. Since then, things have changed. The nature of organizing moved from the bureaucratic to more exotic forms; the paradigm debate legitimated alternative modes of inquiry, and the work of Foucault and other postmodernists started to influence organizational scholars. Fragmentation is back for all to see.

Some contributors in this book try to build bridges over the troubled waters of fragmentation, while others, once warriors, seek always to be warriors. Unlikely bed-fellows thus emerge. Donaldson and Burrell, for instance, are paradigm warriors both. Whereas Donaldson believes that virtue, identified with those 'truths'

that he holds dear, will triumph, Burrell restates his support for paradigm incommensurability and for the continuance of the fragmentation with which it is associated. A debate characterizes the political strategies of many 'marginalized' groups: should one communicate with adversaries and try to influence them, or is dialogue, as Burrell argues, simply a weapon of the powerful? If so, should one exclude others? If the latter, then warfare, incommensurability and fragmentation are virtues in their own right. Oddly, both paradigm warriors seem to follow the same combat strategy, even though the terms that they defend differ so markedly.

Richard Marsden and Barbara Townley mirror some of Michael Reed's concerns, bringing the book to a full circle. They consider the link between theory and practice which, as they point out, is not as antithetical as might appear. Organization theory matters because it not only reflects organizational practice, but helps constitute it. In addition, as for many of our other contributors, there exists an academic politics of theory as there is a politics of organizational practice. They show how theory, even the sometimes esoteric discourse of postmodernism, nonetheless has important implications for organizational practice.

Marsden and Townley trace organizational theory back to Marx and Weber because their work is the 'stage upon which practitioners perform'. They show that both struggled with problems of modernity, such as the creation of the abstract citizen, which continue to occupy contemporary organization theorists. Like Burrell they show how theorizing and abstraction serve to divide our world up into the seen and the unseen; also, like Burrell, they point to the particularity in Weber's work that helped produce not only the Aston Studies, but also other traditions of normal science in the United States. The authors argue that these traditions of normal science do not serve practitioners well: research methods, rather than the problems and needs of managers, much less workers, drive the research agenda. They then introduce contra organization science, drawing on Silverman's early work, through Lukes's radical view of power, to the work of Foucault. This work, according to Marsden and Townley, has some potential for practice, although its aversion to anything tainted by empiricism has steered it away from organizational settings and into the relative safety of theoretical discourse. The potential, for both theory and practice, resides in our ability to transcend the debate between normal and contra science and to engage with the duality and ambiguity of organizational life. They point to the contradiction of modernity: how it enriches as well as impoverishes,

empowers and represses, organizes and atomizes, emphasizing the importance of understanding what it means to the person. As these
authors conclude, the way forward is the ethical
interrogation of experience in terms of what our
practices mean to us and to others.

Finally, the *Handbook* concludes with a
chapter on representation. We do not attempt
to pull thirty diverse chapters together in a neat
package of conclusions. Even if this were
desirable, it would not be possible. Instead, we
explore some particular themes that emerged
from the chapters and engaged us. We are
particularly interested in the way organization
studies represent the subject: as individual and
organization. By exploring issues of representation, we believe we can draw some insights for
research, theory and practice in organization
studies as we move into the next century.

IMAGINATIVE CONSUMERISM

Handbooks are often criticized for not 'bringing
the field together'. There is, however, no
coherence to bind these chapters into a meaningful whole. Nor should readers expect it since
the very nature of such an enterprise obviates it.
Taken together, thirty topics and nearly fifty
authors (many of whom are known for their
contribution to controversy as well as to the
craft) provide no recipe for consensus. As a
result, we are reluctant to force the breadth and
diversity of organization studies into the type of
'procrustean bed' alluded to by Gibson Burrell.
Plenty of bland, homogenized textbooks already
exist, offering certainties enough for those who
require them and converting the anxieties of
their readers into easy formulae and conventions, to be recycled on ritual occasions of
examination.

This is not to say that no themes emerge from
the variety contained in this book. Far from it:
certain issues gained our attention and raised
questions that we explore in the final chapter. In
this regard, as initial readers of the text, we were
the original consumers. Certainly, we have tried
to be imaginative in our consumption of it in
identifying and discussing the themes that
engaged us. It is easy to see how, as editors
and editorial writers, we produced and were
produced by this enterprise: certainly we now
know and think things that would not have been
possible without it. We are, however, a
particular kind of reader, one immersed in the
project in ways that most other readers are
unlikely to be. We must not forget that the text
is also constituted by all its readers through a
project of 'imaginative consumerism' (Linstead
and Grafton-Small 1992). So, in these days of

consumerism and customer service, let us think
of these other readers. Different readers will
naturally expose images different to those we
expose. While we should not prescribe or
proscribe their vision, we can muse on what
they might see or, more accurately, what we
hope they will see.

Students reading this book, for example,
might be overwhelmed at the sheer immensity
and dynamic development of organization
studies (and wondering how they will ever
survive their initiation in it). For these readers,
we hope to provide a starting point, a stepping
stone, to their studies. By providing a range
found in few other texts, we can offer a useful
map to those struggling to understand particular
subjects or trying to bring the broader arena of
organization studies into perspective. For those
who have successfully endured the rites of
academic passage, we hope to achieve a
number of other things. For those preparing
courses, we hope to provide a map that
individuals can use to navigate those areas
with which they are less familiar. For those
struggling with new domains of research and
theory, we hope to provide an entrée to the
unknown and a means of rendering the
unknown slightly more familiar. We do not,
however, wish simply to provide a user-friendly
rendition of what is already known about
organization studies and how it has changed.
We have loftier aspirations as, we are sure, do
the contributors. Within and across chapters,
spaces and intersections have arisen in which
conversations might be established that mark the
way forward, that push the frontiers of organization studies. Some of those themes we will take
up again in the conclusion. In the meantime, we
hope that readers will see some of the futures as
well as some of the pasts in the individual
contributions. Now let us turn to those
contributions and, with the help of our readers,
let them speak for themselves.

NOTES

We acknowledge the substantive comments that
Walter Nord, Eduardo Ibarra-Colado, Peter Frost,
John Gray and Sue Jones made on an earlier draft of
this chapter.

1 Our comparison with the world thirty years ago is
not coincidental: *The Handbook of Organizations*
edited by James G. March was published in 1965.
We do not consider this volume to be a successor,
natural or otherwise, to March's book or other
handbooks (e.g. Dunnette 1976; Nystrom and
Starbuck 1980; Lorsch 1987), but we have often been
asked how our *Handbook* compares with March's

book. In most respects, we can only say that it does not, precisely because of the changes we mention here.

2 It is useful to differentiate between postmodernism as social theory, as described here, and the more empirically grounded hypothesis that characteristics associated with the 'modern' era are being superseded by phenomena that are radically discontinuous and sufficiently distinct to be termed 'postmodern', thus constituting a new epoch of postmodernity (see Parker 1992). Some writers also distinguish between poststructuralism and postmodernism, seeing the former as particular approaches, within the broader arena of postmodernism, which focus on the link between language, subjectivity, social organization and power. Poststructuralism counters the idea that language *reflects* social reality, arguing that, by producing meaning, it *creates* social reality. Different languages and different discourses categorize the world and give it meaning. Thus language defines, constructs and contests social organization, power and our sense of selves, our subjectivity (see Richardson 1994: 518).

3 To be more specific, we refer to a community of researchers whose engagement in and exposure to conversations revolves around the concerns of various journals and institutions. Among the journals are *Administrative Science Quarterly, The Academy of Management Review, The Academy of Management Journal, Organization Studies, Organization Science, The Journal of Management Studies* and *Organization*. The institutions include the European Group for Organization Studies (EGOS), the Standing Conference on Organization Symbolism (SCOS), Asia Pacific Researchers in Organization Studies (APROS), the Organization and Management Theory (OMT) group of the (American) Academy of Management, Research Committee 17, Sociology of Organizations, of the International Sociological Association (ISA), and the 'Organizations and Occupations' Committee of the American Sociological Association. It is from the debates, scholars and community that comprise this 'invisible college' that we have woven the threads that bind this volume.

4 We would like to thank Eduardo Ibarra-Colado for helping to clarify the ideas in this paragraph.

5 Pfeffer (1995) appears to perceive a threat not from contra science but from rational choice theory, which we would classify as one among a number of normal sciences, while viewing Pfeffer as a practitioner of another. Interestingly, Donaldson (1995), an advocate of yet another form of normal science, contingency theory, makes a similar attack on other normal science approaches, notably organizational economics; population ecology; resource dependency; institutional theory. It may be that adherents of the different 'orthodox' approaches are starting to engage more directly in a struggle amongst themselves, somewhat like the paradigm warriors. There is a difference, however, in that the original paradigm warriors entered combat around the question of communication between their paradigms; they never disputed that alternative paradigms should exist, only whether they could or should talk to each other. The signs from these more recent battles suggest that orthodox warriors want *all* alternatives, save their own, closed out, even variations on the theme of normal science if they do not correspond to the chosen path. If Donaldson and Pfeffer have their way, there won't be anything left to constitute 'orthodoxy'!

REFERENCES

Abernathy, W. and Clark, K. (1985) 'Innovation: mapping the winds of creative destruction', *Research Policy*, 14: 3–22.

Aldrich, H. (1988) 'Paradigm warriors: Donaldson versus the critics of organization theory', *Organization Studies*, 9(1): 19–25.

Alter, C. and Hage, J. (1993) *Organizations Working Together*. Newbury Park, CA: Sage.

Amara, R. (1990) 'New directions for innovation', *Futures*, 22(2): 142–52.

Anderson, P. and Tushman, N.L. (1990) 'Technological discontinuities and dominant designs: a cyclical model of technological change', *Administrative Science Quarterly*, 35: 604–33.

Astley, W.G. (1984) 'Toward an appreciation of collective strategy', *Academy of Management Review*, 9(3): 526–35.

Atkinson, M. (1971) *Orthodox Consensus and Radical Alternative: a Study in Sociological Theory*. London: Heinemann.

Barker, J.R. (1993) 'Tightening the iron cage: concertive control in self-managing teams', *Administrative Science Quarterly*, 38: 408–37.

Barley, S.R., Freeman, J. and Hybels, R.C. (1993) 'Strategic alliances in commercial biotechnology', in N. Nohria and R.G. Eccles (eds), *Network and Organizations: Structure, Form and Action*. Boston: Harvard Business School. pp. 311–47.

Best, M. (1990) *The New Competition*. Cambridge: Polity Press.

Bianchi, P. (1993) 'The promotion of small firm clusters and industrial districts: European policy perspectives', *Journal of Industry Studies*, 1(1): 6–29.

Blackford, M.G. and Kerr, K.A. (1994) *Business Enterprise in American History*. Boston: Houghton Mifflin.

Braine, J. (1957) *Room at the Top*. London: Eyre & Spottiswoode.

Braverman, H. (1974) *Labor and Monopoly Capital*. New York: Monthly Review Press.

Bresser, R.K. (1988) 'Matching collective and competitive strategies', *Strategic Management Journal*, 9: 375–85.

Bresser, R.K. and Harl, J.E. (1986) 'Collective strategy: vice or virtue?', *Academy of Management Review*, 11: 408–27.

Burawoy, M. (1979) *Manufacturing Consent*. Chicago: Chicago University Press.

Burrell, G. and Morgan, G. (1979) *Sociological Paradigms and Organizational Analysis*. London: Heinemann.

Byrne, J.A. (1993) 'The virtual corporation', *Business Week*, 8 February: 98–103.

Callon, M. (1986) 'Some elements of a sociology of translation: domestication of the scallops and the fishermen of St Brieuc Bay', in J. Law (ed.), *Power, Action and Belief*. London: Routledge. pp. 196–233.

Cannella, A.A. and Paetzold, R.L. (1994) 'Pfeffer's barriers to the advance of organizational science: a rejoinder', *Academy of Management Review*, 19(2): 331–41.

Carney, M.G. (1987) 'The strategy and structure of collective action', *Organization Studies*, 8(4): 341–62.

Cavendish, R. (1982) *Women on the Line*. London: Routledge and Kegan Paul.

Chandler, A.D. (1962) *Strategy and Structure*. Cambridge, MA: MIT Press.

Clarke, P.A. (1978) 'Temporal innovations and time structuring in large organizations', in J.T. Fraser, N. Lawrence and D. Park (eds), *The Study of Time*, vol. 3. New York: Springer.

Clegg, S.R. (1990) *Modern Organizations: Organization Studies in the Postmodern World*. London: Sage.

Clegg, S.R. and Dunkerley, D. (1980) *Organization, Class and Control*. London: Routledge and Kegan Paul.

Cooper, R. and Kleinschmidt, E. (1986) 'An investigation into the new product process: steps, deficiencies, and impact', *Journal of Product Innovation Management*, 3: 71–85.

Daft, D.L. and Weick, K.E. (1984) 'Towards a model of organizations as interpretation systems', *Academy of Management Review*, 9 (2): 284–95.

Ditton, J. (1979) 'Baking time', *Sociological Review*, 27: 157–67.

Dodgson, M. (1993) 'Organizational learning: a review of some literatures', *Organizational Studies*, 14(3): 375–94.

Donaldson, L. (1985) *In Defence of Organization Theory: a Response to the Critics*. Cambridge: Cambridge University Press.

Donaldson, L. (1988) 'In successful defence of organization theory: a routing of the critics', *Organization Studies*, 9(1): 28–32.

Donaldson, L. (1995) *American Anti-Management Theories of Organization*. Cambridge: Cambridge University Press.

Dunnette, M.D. (ed.) (1976) *Handbook of Industrial and Organizational Psychology*. Chicago: Rand McNally.

Durkheim, E. (1976) *The Elementary Forms of the Religious Life*, 2nd edn. London: Allen and Unwin.

Dutton, J.E. and Dukerich, J.M. (1991) 'Keeping an eye on the mirror: image and identity in organizational adaptation', *Academy of Management Journal*, 34(3): 517–54.

Eccles, R. and Nohria, N. (1993) *Beyond the Hype*. Boston: Harvard Business School.

Elsbach, K.D. and Sutton, R.I. (1992) 'Acquiring organizational legitimacy through illegitimate action: a marriage of institutional and impression management theories', *Academy of Management Journal*, 35(4): 699–738.

Fairtlough, G. (1994) *Creative Compartments: a Design for Future Organisations*. London: Adamantine Press.

Fiedler, F.E. (1967) *A Theory of Leadership Effectiveness*. New York: McGraw-Hill.

Foucault, M. (1972) *The Archeology of Knowledge*. London: Tavistock.

Galbraith, J.R. (1973) *Designing Complex Organizations*. Reading, MA: Addison-Wesley.

Galbraith, J.R., Lawler E.E. and Associates (1993) *Organizing for the Future: the New Logic for Managing Complex Organizations*. San Francisco: Jossey-Bass.

Garfinkel, H. (1967) *Studies in Ethnomethodology*. Englewood Cliffs, NJ: Prentice-Hall.

Gephart, R.P. (1993) 'The textual approach: risk and blame in disaster sensemaking', *Academy of Management Journal*, 36(3): 1465–514.

Gioia, D.A. and Pitre, E. (1990) 'Multiparadigm perspectives on theory building', *Academy of Management Review*, 15(4): 584–602.

Gray, B. (1989) *Collaborating: Finding Common Ground for Multiparty Problems*. San Francisco: Jossey-Bass.

Gurvitch, G. (1964) *The Spectrum of Social Time*. Dordrecht: D. Reidel.

Habermas, J. (1979) *Communication and the Evolution of Society*. London: Heinemann.

Hamel, G. and Prahalad, C.K. (1994) *Competing for the Future*. Boston: Harvard Business School.

Hardy, C. (1994) 'Understanding interorganizational domains: the case of refugee systems', *Journal of Applied Behavioral Science*, 30(3): 278–96.

Harrigan, K.R. (1985) *Strategies for Joint Ventures*. Lexington, MA: D.C. Heath/Lexington Books.

Hassan, I. (1985) 'The culture of postmodernism', *Theory, Culture and Society*, 2(3): 119–32.

Hassard, J. (1988) 'Overcoming hermeticism in organization theory: an alternative to paradigm incommensurability', *Human Relations*, 41(3): 247–59.

Hassard, J. (1991) 'Multiple paradigms and organizational analysis: a case study', *Organization Studies*, 12(2): 275–99.

Herrigel, G.B. (1993) 'Power and the redefinition of industrial districts: the case of Baden-Württemberg', in G. Graber (ed.), *The Embedded Firm: on the Socioeconomics of Industrial Networks*. London: New York. pp. 227–51.

Huyssen, A. (1984) 'Mapping the postmodern', *New German Critique*, 33.

Jackson, N. and Carter, P. (1991) 'In defence of paradigm incommensurability', *Organization Studies*, 12(1): 109–27.

Jackson, N. and Carter, P. (1993) '"Paradigm wars": a response to Hugh Willmott', *Organization Studies*, 14(5): 721–5.

Jencks, C. (1989) *What is Post-Modernism?* London: Academy.

Kanter, R.M. (1990) 'When giants learn cooperative strategies', *Planning Review*, 18(1): 15–25.

Kiernan, M.J. (1993) 'The new strategic architecture: learning to compete in the twenty-first century', *Academy of Management Executive*, 7(1): 7–21.

Knights, D. and Willmott, H. (1990) *Labour Process Theory*. London: Macmillan.

Laclau, E. (1988) 'Politics and the limits of modernity', in A. Ross (ed.), *Universal Abandon: the Politics of Postmodernism*. Minneapolis: University of Minnesota Press. pp. 63–82.

Latour, B. (1993) *We Have Never Been Modern*. Hemel Hempstead: Harvester Wheatsheaf.

Linstead, S. and Grafton-Small, R. (1992) 'On reading organizational culture', *Organization Studies*, 13: 331–55.

Littler, C. (1982) *The Labour Process in Capitalist Societies*. London: Tavistock.

Lorsch, J.W. (ed.) (1987) *Handbook of Organizational Behavior*. Englewood Cliffs, NJ: Prentice-Hall.

Lyotard, J. (1984) *The Postmodern Condition*. Manchester: Manchester University Press.

March, J.G. (ed.) (1965) *Handbook of Organizations*. Chicago: Rand McNally.

Marsden, R. (1993) 'The politics of organizational analysis', *Organization Studies*, 14(1): 92–124.

Mayo, E. (1947) *The Social Problems of an Industrial Civilization*. London: Routledge and Kegan Paul.

McKinsey Report (1993) *Emerging Exporters: Australia's High Value-Added Manufacturing Exporters*. Final Report of the Study by McKinsey and Co. for the Australian Manufacturing Council, Melbourne.

Meyer, J. and Rowan, B. (1977) 'Institutionalized organizations: formal structure as myth and ceremony', *American Journal of Sociology*, 83: 340–63.

Mintzberg, H. (1979) *The Structuring of Organizations*. Englewood Cliffs, NJ: Prentice-Hall.

Nohria, N. and Eccles, R.G. (eds) (1993) *Network and Organizations: Structure, Form and Action*. Boston: Harvard Business School.

Nord, W.R. and Connell, A.F. (1993) 'From quicksand to crossroads: an agnostic perspective on conversation', *Organization Science*, 4(1): 108–20.

Nystrom, P.C. and Starbuck, W.H. (1980) *Handbook of Organizational Design*. Oxford: Oxford University Press.

Organization Studies (1988) 'Offence and defence', *Organization Studies*, 9(1): 1–32.

Parker, M. (1992) 'Post-modern organizations or postmodern organization theory?', *Organization Studies*, 13(1): 1–17.

Parker, M. and McHugh, G. (1991) 'Five texts in search of an author: a response to John Hassard's "Multiple paradigms and organizational analysis"', *Organization Studies*, 12(3): 451–6.

Pfeffer, J. (1993) 'Barriers to the advance of organizational science: paradigm development as a dependent variable', *Academy of Management Review*, 18(4): 599–620.

Pfeffer, J. (1995) 'Mortality, reproducibility, and the persistence of styles of theory', *Organization Science*, 6(6): 681–6.

Phillips, N. and Brown, J. (1993) 'Analyzing communication in and around organizations: a critical hermeneutic approach', *Academy of Management Journal*, 36(6): 1547–76.

Powell, W.W. (1990) 'Neither market nor hierarchy: network forms of organization', in B.M. Staw and L.L. Cummings (eds), *Research in Organizational Behavior*. Greenwich, CT: JAI Press.

Powell, W.W. and Brantley, P. (1993) 'Competitive cooperation in biotechnology: learning through networks?', in N. Nohria and R.G. Eccles (eds), *Network and Organizations: Structure, Form and Action*. Boston: Harvard Business School. pp. 366–94.

Prasad, P. (1993) 'Symbolic processes in the implementation of technological change: a symbolic interactionist study of work computerization', *Academy of Management Journal*, 36(6): 1400–29.

Pyke, F. and Sengenberger, W. (eds) (1992) *Industrial Districts and Inter-Firm Co-operation in Italy*. Geneva: International Institute of Labour Studies.

Reed, M. (1985) *Redirections in Organization Analysis*. London: Tavistock.

Roethlisberger, F.G. and Dickson, W.J. (1939) *Management and the Worker*. Cambridge, MA: Harvard University Press.

Richardson, L. (1994) 'Writing: a method of inquiry', in N.K. Denzin and Y.S. Lincoln (eds), *Handbook of Qualitative Research*. Thousand Oaks, CA: Sage.

Rothwell, R. (1992) 'Successful industrial innovation: critical factors for the 1990s', *R and D Management*, 22(3): 221–39.

Roy, D.F. (1960) 'Banana time: job satisfaction and informal interaction', *Human Organization*, 18: 156–68.

Selznick, P. (1957) *Leadership in Administration: a Sociological Interpretation*. New York: Harper and Row.

Semler, R. (1989) 'Managing without managers', *Harvard Business Review*, 67(5): 76–84.

Silverman, D. (1971) *The Theory of Organisations: a Sociological Framework*. London: Heinemann.

Simon, H.A. (1945) *Administrative Behaviour*, 2nd edn. New York: Free Press.

Smith, A. (1904) *An Inquiry into the Nature and Causes of the Wealth of Nations*. London: Methuen.

Sorokin, P.A. and Merton, R.K. (1937) 'Social time: a methodological and functional analysis', *American Journal of Sociology*, 42: 615–29.

Tully, S. (1993) 'The modular corporation', *Fortune*, 8 February: 106–15.

Üsdiken, B. and Pasadeos, Y. (1995) 'Organizational analysis in North America and Europe: a comparison of co-citation networks', *Organization Studies*, 16(3): 503–26.

Van Maanen, J. (1979) 'Reclaiming qualitative methods for organisational research: a preface', *Administrative Science Quarterly*, 24(4): 520–6.

Van Maanen, J. (1995) 'Fear and loathing in organization studies', *Organization Science*, 6(6): 687–92.

Waddock, A. (1989) 'Understanding social partnerships: an evolutionary model of partnership organizations', *Administration and Society*, 21: 78–100.

Weber, M. (1978) *Economy and Society: An Outline of Interpretive Sociology*. Berkeley: University of California Press.

Weick, K. (1969) *The Social Psychology of Organizing*. Reading, MA: Addison-Wesley.

Weiss, L. (1988) *Creating Capitalism: the State and Small Business since 1945*. Oxford: Blackwell.

Whitley, R. (1992) *Business Systems in East Asia: Firms, Markets and Societies*. London: Sage.

Willmott, H. (1993a) 'Breaking the paradigm mentality', *Organization Studies*, 14(5): 681–719.

Willmott, H. (1993b) 'Paradigm gridlock: a reply', *Organization Studies*, 14(5): 727–30.

Winkleman, M. (1993) 'The outsourcing source book', *Journal of Business Strategy*, 15(3): 52–8.

Zald, M.N. (1994) 'Organization studies as a scientific and humanistic enterprise: toward a reconceptualization of the foundations of the field', *Organization Science*, 4(4): 513–28.

Part One
FRAMEWORKS FOR ANALYSIS

1.1

Organizational Theorizing: a Historically Contested Terrain

MICHAEL REED

Organization studies has its proximate historical roots in the socio-political writings of nineteenth century thinkers, such as Saint-Simon, who attempted to anticipate and interpret the nascent structural and ideological transformations wrought by industrial capitalism (Wolin 1961). The economic, social and political changes that capitalist-led modernization brought in its wake created a world that was fundamentally different from the relatively small-scale and simple forms of production and administration which had dominated earlier phases of capitalist development in the eighteenth and early nineteenth centuries (Bendix 1974). The late nineteenth and early twentieth centuries witnessed the growing dominance of large-scale organizational units in economic, social and political life as the complexity and intensity of collective activity moved beyond the administrative capacity of more personal and direct forms of coordination (Waldo 1948). Indeed, the rise of the 'administrative state' symbolized a new mode of governance in which rational, scientific organization transformed human nature:

> Organization as power over things – that was the lesson taught by Saint-Simon. The new order would be governed not by men but by 'scientific principles' based on the 'nature of things' and therefore absolutely independent of human will. In this way, organizational society promised the rule of scientific laws rather than men and the eventual disappearance of the political element entirely . . . [organization] is the 'grand device' for transforming human irrationalities into rational behaviour. (Wolin 1961: 378–83)

Thus, the historical roots of organization studies are deeply embedded in a body of writing which gathered momentum from the second half of the nineteenth century onwards and confidently anticipated the triumph of science over politics and the victory of rationally designed collective order and progress over human recalcitrance and irrationality (Reed 1985).

The growth of an 'organizational society' was synonymous with the inexorable advance of reason, liberation and justice and the eventual eradication of ignorance, coercion and poverty. Organizations were rationally designed to solve permanently the conflict between collective needs and individual wants that had bedevilled social progress since the days of Ancient Greece (Wolin 1961). They guaranteed social order and personal freedom by fusing collective decision-making and individual interest (Storing 1962) through the scientific design, implementation and maintenance of administrative structures that subsumed sectional interests within institutionalized collective goals. The perennial conflict between 'society' and 'individual' would be permanently overcome. Whereas Hegel had relied on the dialectic of history to eradicate social conflict (Plant 1973), organization theorists put their faith in modern organization as the universal solution to the problem of social order.

> [T]he organizationists looked upon society as an order of functions, a utilitarian construct of integrated activity, a means for focusing human energies in combined effort. Where the symbol of community was fraternity, the symbol of organization was power . . . organization signifies a method of social control, a means for imparting order, structure and regularity to society. (Wolin 1961: 363–4)

Viewed from the historical vantage point of the late twentieth century, however, the practice and study of organization look very different today. The earlier metanarratives of collective order and individual freedom through rational organization and material progress have fragmented and frayed into a cacophony of querulous 'voices' totally lacking in general moral force and analytical coherence (Reed 1992). The once seemingly cast-iron guarantee of material and social progress through sustained technological advance, modern organization and scientific administration now looks increasingly threadbare. Both the technical effectiveness and moral virtue of 'formal' or 'complex' organization are called into question by institutional and intellectual transformations which push inexorably towards social fragmentation, political disintegration and ethical relativism. Who amongst us can afford to ignore Bauman's argument that 'the typically modern, techno-logical-bureaucratic patterns of action and the mentality they institutionalize, generate, sustain and reproduce' (1989: 75) were the socio-psychological foundations of and organizational preconditions for the Holocaust?

In short, contemporary students of organization find themselves at a historical juncture and in a social context where all the old ideological 'certainties' and technical 'fixes' that once underpinned their 'discipline' are under attack and seemingly on the retreat in the current debate over the nature of organization and the intellectual means most appropriate to its understanding (Reed and Hughes 1992). Underlying assumptions about the inherently rational and ethical quality of modern organization are challenged by alternative voices that radically undermine 'taken-for-granted' objectivity and goodness (Cooper and Burrell 1988). While key texts published in the 1950s and early 1960s bridled with self-confidence concerning their 'discipline's' intellectual identity and rationale (see Haire 1960; Argyris 1964; Blau and Scott 1963), this self-confidence simply drained away in the 1980s and 1990s, replaced by uncertain, complex and confused expectations concerning the nature and merits of organization studies.

In Kuhnian terms, we seem to be in a phase of 'revolutionary' rather than 'normal' science (Kuhn 1970). Normal science is dominated by puzzle-solving activity and incremental research programmes carried out with generally accepted and strongly institutionalized theoretical frameworks (Lakatos and Musgrave 1970). Revolutionary science occurs when 'domain assumptions' about subject matter, interpretative frameworks and knowledge are exposed to continuous critique and re-evaluation (Gouldner 1971). Research and analysis are shaped by the search for anomalies and contradictions within prevailing theoretical frameworks, generating an internal intellectual dynamic of theoretical struggle. It signifies a discipline racked by internal conflict and dissension over ideological and epistemological fundamentals whose various supporters occupy and represent different paradigmatic 'worlds' between which communication, much less mediation, becomes impossible (Kuhn 1970; Hassard 1990). Fragmentation and discontinuity become the dominant features of a field's identity and rationale, rather than the relative stability and cohesion characteristic of 'normal science' (Willmott 1993).

One, very potent, response to the divisive impact of the break with the functionalist/positivist orthodoxy is the retreat into a nostalgic yearning for past certainties and the communal comfort they once provided (Donaldson 1985). This 'conservative' reaction may also demand an enforced and tightly policed political consensus within the field to repair intellectual tissue scarred by decades of theoretical infighting and to re-establish the theoretical hegemony of a particular research paradigm (Pfeffer 1993). Both 'nostalgic' and 'political' forms of conservatism aim to resist the centripetal trends set in motion by intellectual struggle and to return to ideological and theoretical orthodoxy. A robust combination of 'back to basics' and 'paradigm enforcement' can be a very attractive option for those unsettled by the intellectual fermentation taking place in organization studies.

Rather than 'paradigm enforcement', others look towards 'paradigm proliferation' through the separate intellectual development and nurturing of distinctive approaches within different domains, uncontaminated by contact with competing, and often more entrenched, perspectives (Morgan 1986; Jackson and Carter 1991). This response to social change and intellectual upheaval provides intellectual sustenance for a 'serious playfulness' in organization studies where postmodern irony and humility replace the sanctimonious platitudes typical of a rational modernism that is incapable of seeing that 'objective truth is not the only game in town' (Gergen 1992).

If neither conservatism nor relativism appeals, a third option is to retell organization theory's history in ways that rediscover the analytical narratives and ethical discourses that shaped its development and legitimated its character (Reed 1992; Willmott 1993). Such approaches question both a return to fundamentals and an unrestrained celebration of discontinuity and diversity: neither intellectual surfing or free riding on the rising tide of relativism, nor retreating into the cave of orthodoxy, are attractive futures for the study of organization. The former promises unrestrained intellectual freedom, but at the price of isolationism and fragmentation. The latter falls back on a worn and outmoded consensus, sustained through continuous intellectual surveillance and control.

This chapter adopts the third response. It attempts to reconstruct the history of organization theory's intellectual development in a way that balances social context with theoretical ideas, and structural conditions with conceptual innovation. It offers the prospect of rediscovering and renewing a sense of historical vision and contextual sensitivity which gives both 'society' and 'ideas' their just deserts. Neither the history of organization studies nor the way in which that history is told are neutral representations of past achievement. Indeed, any telling of history to support reconstructions of the present and visions of the future is a controversial and contested interpretation that is always open to refutation. Thus, the purpose of this chapter is to map organizational theory as a historically contested terrain within which different languages, approaches and philosophies struggle for recognition and acceptance.

The next section examines theory making and development in organization studies as an intellectual activity which is necessarily implicated in the social and historical context in which it is made and remade. The chapter then examines six interpretative frameworks that have structured the field's development over the last century or so and the socio-historical contexts in which they attained a degree of, always contested, intellectual dominance. The penultimate section considers the most significant exclusions or silences that are evident in these major narrative traditions. The chapter concludes with an evaluation of future intellectual developments, set within the context provided by the narratives outlined earlier.

THEORIZING ORGANIZATION

This conception of organizational theorizing is based on Gouldner's view that both the process and the product of theorizing should be seen as a 'doing and a making by persons caught up in some specific historical era' (1980: 9). The theoretically informed analysis of and debate about organizations and organizing are outcomes of a precarious combination of individual vision and technical production located within a dynamic socio-historical context. As such, theory making is always liable to subvert institutionalized conventions that have petrified into unreflectively

accepted orthodoxies that can never be contained completely within established cognitive frames and conceptual parameters. However, the probability of specific theoretical initiatives metamorphosing into much more significant conceptual 'paradigm shifts' is largely dependent on their cumulative impact on the particular intellectual communities and traditions through which they are mediated and received (Willmott 1993). Thus, while theory making is always *potentially* subversive of the intellectual status quo, its actual impact is always refracted through existing knowledge/power relationships and the 'contextual receptiveness' of particular socio-historical conditions to specific intellectual developments (Toulmin 1972).

In short, theory making is a historically located intellectual practice directed at assembling and mobilizing ideational, material and institutional resources to legitimate certain knowledge claims and the political projects which flow from them. The intellectual and social contexts in which theoretical debate is embedded have a crucial bearing on the form and content of particular conceptual innovations as they struggle to attain a degree of support within the wider community (Clegg 1994; Thompson and McHugh 1990). As Bendix maintains, 'A study of ideas as weapons in the management of organizations could afford a better understanding of the relations between ideas and actions' (1974: xx).

It does not mean, however, that no recognized, collective basis exists on which contradictory knowledge claims can be evaluated. At any point in time, organization studies is constituted through shared lines of debate and dialogue which establish intellectual constraints and opportunities within which new contributions are assessed. Negotiated rules and norms are generated through which collective judgements concerning new and old work are made and a vocabulary and a grammar of organizational analysis emerge. This 'grounded rationality' (Reed 1993) may lack the universality associated, however mistakenly (Putnam 1978), with the 'hard' sciences but it nonetheless establishes an identifiable framework of procedures and practices 'that provide for their own relevant discourse about proof' (Thompson 1978: 205–6). Thus, organization theory is subject to shared, although revisable, methodological procedures through which reasoned judgements of competing interpretative frames and explanatory theories are negotiated and debated. The interaction and contestation of rival intellectual traditions imply the existence of negotiated, historicized, and contextualized understandings that make rational argumentation possible (Reed 1993).

Table 1   *Analytical narratives in organization analysis*

Meta-narrative interpretative framework	Major problematic	Illustrative/exemplary/ perspectives	Contextual transitions
Rationality	Order	Classical OT, scientific management, decision theory, Taylor, Fayol, Simon	*from* nightwatchman state *to* industrial state
Integration	Consensus	Human relations, neo-HR, functionalism, contingency/ systems theory, corporate culture, Durkheim, Barnard, Mayo, Parsons	*from* entrepreneurial capitalism *to* welfare capitalism
Market	Liberty	Theory of firm, institutional economics, transaction costs, agency theory, resource dependency, population ecology, liberal OT	*from* managerial capitalism *to* neo-liberal capitalism
Power	Domination	Neo-radical Weberians, critical/structural Marxism, labour process, institutional theory, Weber, Marx	*from* liberal collectivism *to* bargained corporatism
Knowledge	Control	Ethnomethod, organizational culture/symbol, poststructuralist, post-industrial, post-Fordist/ modern, Foucault, Garfinkel, actor-network theory	*from* industrialism/modernity *to* post-industrialism/postmodernity
Justice	Participation	Business ethics, morality and OB, industrial democracy, participation theory, critical theory, Habermas	*from* repressive *to* participatory democracy

The interpretative frameworks in Table 1 constitute the historically contested intellectual terrain on which organization analysis developed – a terrain which must be mapped and traversed in relation to the interplay between the procedural and contextual factors that shape the debates around and through which 'the field' emerged (Morgan and Stanley 1993). These frameworks have shaped the development of organization studies for a century or more by providing a grammar through which coherently structured narratives can be built and communicated; symbolic and technical resources through which the nature of organization can be debated; and a communal store of texts and discourses which mediate these debates for both specialist and lay audiences. They develop in a dialectical relationship with historical and social processes as loosely structured and contested ways of conceptualizing and debating key features of organization. Each is defined in relation to the central problematic around which it developed and the socio-historical context in

which it was articulated. The discussion thus provides a grounded appreciation of the strategic analytical narratives through which the field of organization studies is constituted as a dynamic intellectual practice, permeated by theoretical controversies and ideological conflicts concerning the ways in which 'organization' can and ought to be.

RATIONALISM TRIUMPHANT

As Stretton argued, 'we take in rationality with our mother's milk' (1969: 406). Yet this belief in the naturalness of calculated ratiocination has definite historical and ideological roots. Saint-Simon (1958) has a very strong claim to being the first 'theorist of organization' to the extent that he 'was probably the first to note the rise of modern organizational patterns, identify some of their distinctive features, and insist on their prime significance for the emerging society . . .

the ground rules of modern society had been deeply altered and the deliberately conceived and planned organization was to play a new role in the world' (Gouldner 1959: 400–1). The belief that modern society is dominated by a 'logic of organization' recurs throughout the history of organization studies, promoting a principle of social organization in which rationally assigned technical function defines the socio-economic location, authority and behaviour of every individual, group and class. According to Saint-Simon, it provides a cast-iron defence against social conflict and political uncertainty in so far as it establishes a new structure of power based on technical expertise and its contribution to the smooth functioning of society, rather than on randomly allocated or 'anarchic' market advantages or birth privileges.

The organization as a rationally constructed artifice directed to the solution of collective problems of social order and administrative management is reflected in the writings of Taylor (1912), Fayol (1949), Urwick and Brech (1947) and Brech (1948). Such work advocates that the theory of organization 'has to do with the structure of co-ordination imposed upon the work division units of an enterprise . . . Work division is the foundation of organization; indeed, the reason for organization' (Gulick and Urwick 1937: 3). It legitimates the idea that society and its constituent organizational units will be managed through scientific laws of administration from which human emotions and values can be totally excluded (Waldo 1948). Epistemological principles and administrative techniques translate highly contestable, normative precepts into universal, objective, immutable, and hence unchallengeable, scientific laws. The 'rational individual is, and must be, an organized and institutionalized individual' (Simon 1957: 101–2). Human beings became 'raw material' transformed by modern organizational technologies into well-ordered, productive members of society unlikely to interfere with the long-term plans of ruling classes and elites. Thus social, political and moral problems could be transformed into engineering tasks amenable to technical solutions (Gouldner 1971). Modern organizations heralded the triumph of rational knowledge and technique over seemingly intractable human emotion and prejudice.

This model insinuated itself into the ideological core and theoretical fabric of organization studies in such a pervasive and natural manner that its identity and influence were virtually impossible to ascertain, much less question. As Gouldner (1959) argued, it prescribed a 'blueprint' for an authority structure where individuals and groups were required to follow certain laws. Principles of efficient and effective functioning were promulgated as an axiom to direct all forms of organizational practice and analysis. It provided a universal characterization of the 'reality' of formal organization irrespective of time, place and situation. Once this blueprint was accepted, it legitimated a view of organizations as autonomous and independent social units, above and beyond the purview of moral evaluation and political debate (Gouldner 1971).

Although the 'age of organization' demanded a new professional hierarchy to meet the needs of a developing industrial society, superseding the claims of both moribund aristocracy and reactionary entrepreneurs, this view was profoundly anti-democratic and anti-egalitarian. A technically and administratively determined conception of hierarchy, subordination and authority had no truck with rising socio-political agitation based on notions of universal suffrage in either workplace or polity (Wolin 1961; Mouzelis 1967; Clegg and Dunkerley 1980). Rational bureaucratic organization was socially and morally legitimated as an indispensable form of organized power, based on objective technical functions and necessary for the efficient and effective functioning of a social order founded on rational-legal authority (Frug 1984; Presthus 1975).

These principles are deeply embedded in the epistemological and theoretical foundations of those analytical perspectives that constitute the conceptual core of organization studies. Taylor's 'scientific management' is directed towards a permanent monopolization of organizational knowledge through the rationalization of work performance and job design. As Merkle argues: 'Evolving beyond its technical and national origins, Taylorism became an important component of the philosophical outlook of modern industrial civilization, defining virtue as efficiency, establishing a new role for experts in production, and setting parameters for new patterns of social distribution' (1980: 62). As both ideology and practice, Taylorism was extremely hostile towards entrepreneurial theories of organization which focused on the legimatory and technical needs of a small elite (Bendix 1974; Rose 1975; Clegg and Dunkerley 1980). As Bendix stresses, 'the managerial ideologies of today are distinguished from the entrepreneurial ideologies of the past in that managerial ideologies are thought to aid employers or their agents in controlling and directing the activities of workers' (1974: 9).

Fayol's principles of organization, although modified by a perceptive awareness of the need for contextual adaptation and compromise, were driven by the need to construct an architecture of coordination and control to contain the inevitable disruption and conflict caused by 'informal' behaviour. 'Classical' organization theory is founded on the underlying belief that organization provides a principle of structural design and a practice of operational control which can be rationally determined and formalized in advance of actual performance. Indeed, it assumed that the latter automatically follows the design rationale and control instrumentation entailed in the organization's formal structure (Massie 1965).

While Simon's (1945) concept of 'bounded rationality' and theory of 'administrative behaviour' flow from a stinging critique of the excessive rationalism and formalism of classical management and organization theory, his ideas are framed within an approach which sees rational choice between clearly delineated options as the basis of all social action (March 1988). It reduces the vital 'interpretative work', done by individual and organizational actors, to a purely cognitive process dominated by standardized rules and operating programmes. Politics, culture, morality and history are significant by their absence from this model of 'bounded rationality'. Treated as random, extraneous variables beyond the influence, much less control, of rational cognitive processes and organizational procedures, they become analytically marginalized, left outside the conceptual parameters of Simon's preferred model.

Rationalism exerted a profound influence over the historical and conceptual development of organization analysis. It established a cognitive frame and research agenda which could not be ignored, even by those who wished to take a radically different line (Perrow 1986), and ideologically resonated with the development of political institutions and economic structures during the early and mid twentieth century, rendering the corporation and political state 'knowable'. It provided a representation of emerging organizational forms that legitimated their increasing power and influence as inevitable features of a long-term historical trajectory through discourses of rational technocratic administration and management (Ellul 1964; Gouldner 1976). It also 'lifted' the theory and practice of organizational management from an intuitive craft into a codified and analyzable body of knowledge that traded on the immensely powerful cultural capital and symbolism of 'science'.

Considered in these terms, rationalism established a conception of organization theory and analysis as an intellectual technology geared to the provision of a 'mechanism for rendering reality amenable to certain kinds of action . . . it involves inscribing reality into the calculations of government through a range of material and rather mundane techniques' (Rose and Miller 1990: 7). The 'organization' becomes a tool or instrument for the authorization and realization of collective goals through the design and management of structures directed to the administration and manipulation of organizational behaviour. Organizational decision-making rests on a rational analysis of all the options available, based on certified expert knowledge and deliberately oriented to the established legal apparatus. This 'logic of organization' became the guarantor of material advance, social progress and political order in modern industrial societies as they converged around a pattern of institutional development and governance through which the 'invisible hand of the market' was gradually replaced by the 'visible hand of organization'.

Despite the primary position of the rational framework in the development of organization theory, its ideological and intellectual dominance was never complete. It is always open to challenge by alternative narratives. Challengers often shared its ideological and political 'project', that of discovering a new source of authority and control within the processes and structures of modern organization, but used different discourses and practices to achieve it. In particular, many saw the rational framework's inability to deal with the dynamism and instability of complex organizations as a major failure. This growing sense of its conceptual and practical limitations and the utopian nature of the political project which it supported provided organicist thought with a intellectual and institutional space where it could prosper in a field of study previously held in the sway of mechanistic forms of discourse.

THE REDISCOVERY OF COMMUNITY

The substantive issue which most perplexed critics, from the 1930s and 1940s onwards, was the failure of rationalistic organization theory to address the problem of social integration and the implications for the maintenance of social order in a more unstable and uncertain world. This approach remained blind to the criticism that authority is ineffective without 'spontaneous or willing co-operation' (Bendix 1974). Critics, uneasy about the highly mechanistic and deterministic character of rationalism, emphasized both a practical and a theoretical need for an alternative foundation of contemporary managerial power and authority to that provided by formal organization design. Organicist thinking was also concerned with how modern organizations combine authority with a feeling of community among their members.

The mission of the organization is not only to supply goods and services, but fellowship as well. The confidence of the modern writer in the power of organization stems from a larger faith that the organization is man's rejoinder to his own mortality . . . In community and in organization modern man has fashioned substitute love-objects for the political. The quest for community has sought refuge from the notion of man as a political animal; the adoration of organization has been partially inspired by the hope of finding a new form of civility. (Wolin 1961: 368)

This issue is at the forefront of the emergence of a human relations perspective in organization analysis that sets itself apart, in terms of solutions if not problems, from the rational model.

The *Management and the Worker* monograph (Roethlisberger and Dickson 1939) and the writings of Mayo (1933; 1945) thus accuse the rational tradition of ignoring the natural and evolutionary qualities of the new social forms which industrialization generated. The whole thrust of the human relations perspective is a view of social isolation and conflict as a symptom of social pathology and disease. The 'good' society and the effective organization are defined in relation to their capacity to facilitate and sustain the socio-psychological reality of spontaneous cooperation and social stability in the face of economic, political and technological changes that threaten the integration of the individual and group within the wider community.

Over a number of years, this conception of organizations as the intermediate social units which integrate individuals into modern industrial civilization, under the tutelage of a benevolent and socially skilled management, became institutionalized in such a way that it began to displace the predominant position held by exponents of the rational model (Child 1969; Nichols 1969; Bartell 1976; Thompson and McHugh 1990). It converged in more abstract and sociologically oriented theories of organization which held an elective affinity with the naturalistic and evolutionary predilections of the human relations school (Parsons 1956; Merton 1949; Selznick 1949; Blau 1955). Thus, the origins of organicist thought in organization studies lay in a belief that rationalism provided an extremely limited and often misleading vision of the 'realities' of organizational life (Gouldner 1959; Mouzelis 1967; Silverman 1970). It stressed mechanically imposed order and control instead of integration, interdependence and balance in organically developing social systems, each with a history and dynamic of its own. 'Interference' by external agents, such as the planned design of organizational structures, threatens the system's survival.

The organization as a social system facilitates the integration of individuals into the wider society and the adaptation of the latter to changing, and often highly volatile, sociotechnical conditions. This view is theoretically anticipated, in embryonic form, by Roethlisberger and Dickson, who talk of the industrial organization as a functioning social system striving for equilibrium with a dynamic environment (1939: 567). This conception draws on Pareto's (1935) theory of equilibrating social systems in which disparities in the rates of socio-technical change and the imbalances which they generate in social organisms are automatically counteracted by internal responses that, over time, re-establish system equilibrium.

Organizational structures are viewed as spontaneously and homeostatically maintained. Changes in organizational patterns are considered as the result of cumulative, unplanned, adaptive responses to threats to the equilibrium of the system as a whole. Responses to problems are thought of as taking the form of crescively developed defence mechanisms and being importantly shaped by shared values which are deeply internalized in the members. The empirical focus is thus directed to the spontaneously emergent and normatively sanctioned structures in the organization. (Gouldner 1959: 405–6)

In this way, emergent processes, rather than planned structures, ensure long-term system stability and survival.

By the late 1940s and early 1950s, this conception of organizations as social systems geared to the integrative and survival 'needs' of the larger societal orders of which they were constituent elements established itself as the dominant theoretical framework within organization analysis. It converged with theoretical movements in 'general systems theory', as originally developed in biology and physics (von Bertalanffy 1950; 1956), which provided considerable conceptual inspiration for the subsequent development of socio-technical systems theory (Miller and Rice 1967) and 'soft system' methodologies (Checkland 1994). It was, however, the structural-functionalist interpretation of the systems approach which assumed the intellectual 'pole position' within organization analysis and which was to dominate theoretical development and empirical research within the field between the 1950s and 1970s (Silverman 1970; Clegg and Dunkerley 1980; Reed 1985). Structural functionalism and its progeny, systems theory, provided an 'internalist' focus on organizational design with an 'externalist' concern with environmental uncertainty (Thompson 1967). The former highlighted the need for a minimum degree of stability and security in long-term system survival; the latter exposed the underlying indeterminacy of organizational action in the face of environmental demands and threats beyond the organization's control. The key research issue which emerges from this synthesis of structural and environmental concerns is to establish those combinations of internal designs and external conditions which will facilitate long-term organizational stability and growth (Donaldson 1985).

Structural functionalism and systems theory also effectively 'depoliticized' the decision-making processes through which the appropriate functional fit between organization and environment was achieved. Certain 'functional imperatives', such as the need for long-term system equilibrium for survival, were assumed to impose themselves on all organizational actors, determining the design outcomes which their decision-making produced (Child 1972; 1973; Crozier and Friedberg 1980). This theoretical sleight of hand consigns political processes to the margins of organization analysis. In keeping with the wider ideological resonances of systems theory, it converts conflicts over valued means and ends into technical issues which can be 'solved' through effective system design and management. As Boguslaw (1965) indicates this conversion relies on a theoretical façade, not to say utopia, of value homogeneity in which the political realities of organizational change, and the strains and stresses they inevitably cause, are glossed as frictional elements in an otherwise perfectly functioning system. It also gels with the ideological and practical needs of a rising group of systems designers and managers who aspire to overall control within an increasingly differentiated and complex society.

Thus, the general enthusiasm with which systems theory was received by the organization studies community in the 1950s and 1960s reflected a wider renaissance of utopian thinking which presumed that the functional analysis of social systems would provide the intellectual foundations for a new science of society (Kumar 1978). The process of socio-organizational differentiation, perhaps with a helping hand from expert social engineers, would solve the problem of social order through naturally evolving structures capable of handling endemic, escalating tensions between institutional demands and individual interests. The conceit that society itself would solve the problem of social order depended on a 'domain assumption' that 'the whole of human history has a unique form, pattern, logic or meaning underlying the multitude of seemingly haphazard and unconnected events' (Sztompka 1993: 107). Functional systems analysis provided the theoretical key to

unlock the mysteries of this socio-historical development, enabling social and organizational scientists to predict, explain and control both its internal dynamics and its institutional consequences. While this view traded on a form of socio-organizational evolutionism and functionalism which had its roots in the writings of Comte, Saint-Simon and Durkheim (Weinberg 1969; Clegg and Dunkerley 1980; Smart 1992), it reached its apogee in the work of those social scientists who contributed to the development of the theory of industrial society in the 1950s and 1960s, and who displayed little, if any, of the historical circumspection and political sensitivity of their academic predecessors.

Consequently, the functionalist/systems orthodoxy which came to dominate, or at least structure, the intellectual practice and development of organization analysis between the 1940s and 1960s was merely one part of a much broader movement that resurrected the evolutionary form of the nineteenth century (Kumar 1978: 179–90). In organization theory, it reached its theoretical consummation in the development of 'contingency theory' between the late 1960s and early 1970s (Thompson 1967; Lawrence and Lorsch 1967; Woodward 1970; Pugh and Hickson 1976; Donaldson 1985). This approach exhibited all the intellectual virtues and vices of the larger theoretical tradition on which it drew for ideological and methodological inspiration. It also reinforced a managerialist ethic which presumed to solve, through expert social engineering and flexible organizational design (Gellner 1964; Giddens 1984), the fundamental institutional and political problems of modern industrial societies (Lipset 1960; Bell 1960; Galbraith 1969).

Yet, as the 1960s progressed the virtues of organicist thought were eclipsed by a growing appreciation of its vices, especially as social, economic and political realities refused to conform to the explanatory theories promulgated by this narrative. In time, alternative interpretative frameworks, grounded in very different historical and intellectual traditions, would emerge to challenge functionalism. Before we can consider these perspectives, however, we need to take stock of market-based theories of organization.

ENTER THE MARKET

Market-based theories of organization seem a contradiction in terms: if markets operate in the way specified by neo-classical economic theory, as perfectly functioning 'clearing mechanisms' balancing price and cost, there is no conceptual role or technical need for 'organization'. As

Coase (1937) realized in his classic paper, if markets are perfect, then firms (and organizations) should not develop in perfectly regulated market transactions based on voluntary exchange of information between equal economic agents. Coase was, however, forced to recognize the reality of firms as collective economic agents, accounting for them as 'solutions' to market failure or breakdown. As mechanisms for 'internalizing' recurring economic exchanges, firms reduce the cost of individual transactions through standardization and routinization and increase the efficiency of resource allocation within the market system as a whole by minimizing transaction costs between economic agents who are naturally distrustful and suspicious of their partners.

Coase unintentionally borrows a great deal from the rational framework in assuming that behaviour is primarily motivated by the goal of minimizing market costs and maximizing market returns. Both rationalistic and economistic traditions in organization analysis rest on a conception of 'bounded rationality' to explain and predict individual and social action; both subscribe to theories that account for organization in terms of efficiency and effectiveness; both pay intellectual homage to the organic framework by emphasizing the 'natural' evolution of organizational forms that optimize returns within environments whose competitive pressures restrict strategic options. Economic theories of organization also trade on elements of the organicist tradition in focusing on organizations as an evolutionary and semi-rational product of spontaneous and unintended consequences (Hayek 1978). Organizations are an automatic response to (and a reasonable price to pay for) the need for formally free and equal economic agents to negotiate and monitor contracts in complex market transactions which cannot be accommodated in existing institutional arrangements.

Such economic theories of organization emerged in response to the inherent analytical and explanatory limitations of classical and neoclassical theories of the firm (Cyert and March 1963). They demand that a more serious consideration be accorded to resource allocation as a primary determinant of organizational behaviour and design (Williamson and Winter 1991). This focus on the 'micro-economics of organization' (Donaldson 1990; Williamson 1990) and a theory of firm behaviour that is more sensitive to the institutional constraints within which economic transactions are conducted encouraged the formulation of a research agenda emphasizing corporate governance structures and their link to organizational functions (Williamson 1990). This framework also draws

intellectual inspiration from Barnard's conception of organization as cooperation 'which is conscious, deliberate and purposeful' (1938: 4), and which can only be explained as the outcome of a complex interaction between formal and substantive rationality or technical requirements and moral order (Williamson 1990). Barnard's original attempt to provide a conceptual synthesis of 'rational' and 'natural' systems conceptions of organization provides the foundations of market-based theories of organization which flourished in the 1970s and 1980s, such as transaction cost analysis (Williamson 1975; Francis 1983) and population ecology (Aldrich 1979; 1992; Hannan and Freeman 1989).

While there are significant theoretical differences between these approaches, particularly in relation to the form and degree of environmental determinism in which they engage (Morgan 1990), both subscribe to a set of domain assumptions that unify internal administrative forms and external market conditions by means of an evolutionary logic which subordinates collective and individual action to efficiency and survival imperatives largely beyond human influence. Transaction cost theory concerns itself with the adaptive adjustments which organizations need to make in the face of pressures for maximizing efficiency in their internal and external transactions. Population ecology highlights the role of competitive pressures in selecting certain organizational forms over others. Both perspectives are based on a model of organization in which its design, functioning and development are treated as the direct outcomes of universal and immanent forces which cannot be influenced or changed through strategic action.

What is conspicuous by its absence in the market framework is any sustained interest or concern with social power and human agency. Neither the markets/hierarchies approach or population ecology or, indeed, Donaldson's (1990; 1994) 'liberal theory of organization' take much interest in how organizational change is structured by power struggles between social actors and the forms of domination which they legitimate (Francis 1983; Perrow 1986; Thompson and McHugh 1990). These approaches treat 'organization' as constituting a unitary social and moral order in which individual and group interests and values are simply derived from overarching 'system interests and values' uncontaminated by sectional conflict and power struggles (Willman 1983). Once this unitary conception is taken for granted as an 'accepted', 'natural', and virtually invisible feature of organization, power, conflict and domination can be safely ignored as being 'outside' the framework's field of analytical vision and empirical concern.

This unitary conception of organization is entirely in keeping with a wider ideological and political context dominated by neo-liberal theories of organizational and societal governance which raise 'impersonal market forces' to the analytical status of ontological universals determining the chances of individual and collective survival (Miller and Rose 1990; Rose 1992; Silver 1987). From neo-liberal or Darwinian ideologies in the last century (Bendix 1974) to more recent doctrines emphasizing the 'survival of the fittest', such ideologies advocate the progressive expansion of the market, private enterprise and economic rationality at the expense of increasingly residual and marginalized conceptions of community, public service and social concern. Through globalization, nations and enterprises engage in an expanding economic struggle which will be won by those organizations and economies that single-mindedly adapt themselves to market demands (Du Gay and Salaman 1992; Du Gay 1994). In this respect, market-based theories of organization trade on cyclical movements within the encompassing socio-economic, political and ideological context of which they are a part (Barley and Kunda 1992). Nevertheless, they remain consistently silent on the power structures and struggles in and through which organizations respond to putatively 'objective' and 'neutral' economic pressures.

FACES OF POWER

Power remains the most overused and least understood concept in organization analysis. It provides the ideological foundations and epistemological scaffolding for a theory of organization that stands in sharp contrast to the analytical narratives and interpretative frameworks previously discussed. It proffers a logic of organization and organizing analytically rooted in strategic conceptions of social power and human agency which are sensitive to the dialectical interplay between structural constraint and social action as it shapes the institutional forms reproduced and transformed through social practice (Giddens 1985; 1990; Layder 1994). It rejects the environmental determinism inherent in market-based theorizations of organization with their unremitting emphasis on the efficiency and effectiveness imperatives that secure the long-term survival of certain organizational forms rather than others. It also calls into question the unitarist assumptions that underpin the rational, organic and market frameworks by conceptualizing the organization as an arena of conflicting interests and values constituted through power struggle.

The power framework in organization analysis is grounded in Weber's sociology of domination and the analysis of bureaucracy and bureaucratization which flows from it (Weber 1978; Ray and Reed 1994). More recently, this Weberian tradition has been complemented by theorizations of power that draw their inspiration from Machiavelli's interest in the micro-politics of organizational power and its contemporary expression in the work of Foucault (Clegg 1989; 1994). Weberian-based analyses emphasized the relational character of power as a differentially distributed capacity or resource which, if deployed with the appropriate degree of strategic and tactical skill by social actors, produces and reproduces hierarchically structured relationships of autonomy and dependence (Clegg 1989; Wrong 1978). This tends to prioritize the institutional forms and mechanisms through which power is achieved, routinized and struggled over. The 'emphasis is on wider constraints and the determinants of behaviour – principally the forms of power derived from structures of class and ownership, but also the impact of markets and occupations, and of increasing interest lately the normative structures of gender' (Fincham 1992: 742). Thus, Weber's analysis of the dynamics and forms of bureaucratic power in modern society highlights the complex interaction between societal and organizational rationalization as it reproduces institutionalized structures controlled by 'experts' or 'specialists' (Silberman 1993).

This structural or institutional conception of organizational power has been complemented by a more concentrated focus on the micro-political processes through which power is attained and mobilized in opposition or in parallel to established regimes and the domination structures through which they rule. This approach resonates very strongly with Foucault's work on the mosaic of cross-cutting coalitions and alliances mobilizing particular disciplinary regimes (Lyon 1994) which provides a 'bottom-up', rather than a 'top-down', perspective on the detailed organizational practices through which power 'over others' can be temporarily secured. This processual interpretation of the concept of organizational power tends to concentrate on the detailed tactical manoeuvrings which generate a shifting balance of advantage between contending socio-political interests (Fincham 1992). But it is less convincing when attempting to explain the broadly based organizational mechanisms which become institutionalized as accepted structures and rhetorics legitimating more permanent and taken-for-granted 'imperatively coordinated associations'. Thus, the more recent research focus on the interactional processes or 'micro-politics' through which power relationships are temporarily sedimented into relatively more permanent and stable authority structures deflects attention away from the 'hierarchical mechanisms that sustain the reproduction of power' (Fincham 1992: 742).

This dialogue between Weberian/institutional and Machiavellian/processual conceptions of power led to a much more sophisticated understanding of the multi-faceted nature of power relations/processes and their implications for the structuring of organizational forms. Lukes's (1974) analysis of the multiple 'faces of power' has become the major reference point for contemporary research on the dynamics and outcomes of organizational power. His differentiation between three faces or dimensions of power, between the 'episodic', 'manipulative' and 'hegemonic' conceptions of power (Clegg 1989), results in a considerable broadening of the research agenda for the study of organizational power and the theoretical frameworks through which it is approached.

The 'episodic' conception of power concentrates on observable conflicts of interest between identifiable social actors with opposing objectives in particular decision-making situations. The 'manipulative' view concentrates on the 'behind the scenes' activities through which already powerful groups manipulate the decision-making agenda to screen out issues which have the potential to disturb, if not threaten, their domination and control. The 'hegemonic' interpretation emphasizes the strategic role of existing ideological and social structures in constituting, and thus selectively limiting, the interests and values – and hence action – available to social actors in any particular decision arena. As we move from the 'episodic' through the 'manipulative' to the 'hegemonic' conceptions of power there is a progressive analytical and valuational movement from the role of human agency in constituting power relations to that of material and ideological mechanisms in determining the structures of domination and control through which the latter are institutionalized (Clegg 1989: 86–128). There is also an increasing explanatory emphasis on the macro-level structures and mechanisms that determine the organizational designs through which micro-political power struggles are mediated and a corresponding downgrading of the organizationally specific practices that produce and reproduce institutional forms.

Researchers (e.g. Fincham 1992; Clegg 1994; Knights and Willmott 1989) attempted to overcome this potential split between institutional/ structural and processual/agency conceptions by focusing on the general but 'localized' organizational practices through which patterns of domination and control are sustained. They attempted to synthesize a Weberian-based concern with the institutional reproduction of domination structures and a Foucauldian interest in the micro-practices generating changing forms of disciplinary power. The focal point, both analytically and empirically, is the 'expert' discourses through which particular patterns of organizational structuring and control are established in different societies or sectors (Abbott 1988; Miller and O'Leary 1989; Powell and DiMaggio 1991; Larson 1979; 1990; Reed and Anthony 1992). These discourses create specific types of disciplinary regimes at an organizational or sectoral level that mediate between strategic governmental policies formulated by centralized agencies and their tactical implementation within localized domains (Miller and Rose 1990; Johnson 1993; also see some of the recent work on labour process theory, e.g. Burawoy 1985; Thompson 1989; Littler 1990; and total quality management, e.g. Reed 1995; Kirkpatrick and Martinez 1995).

This kind of research tries to account for the decay and breakdown of 'corporatist' structures within the political economies and organizational practices of advanced industrial societies by focusing on their internal contradictions and failure to respond to external ideological and political initiatives led by a resurgent neo-liberal right (Alford and Friedland 1985; Cerny 1990; Miller and Rose 1990; Johnson 1993). It also raises questions about the analytical coherence and explanatory range of a power framework with limited capacity to deal with the material, cultural and political complexities of organizational change.

KNOWLEDGE IS POWER

The knowledge-based framework is deeply suspicious of the institutional and structural bias characterizing the analytical frameworks previously reviewed. It rejects their various forms of theoretical and methodological determinism and the 'totalizing' logic of explanation on which they trade. Instead, this approach treats all forms of institutionalized or structured social action as the temporary patterning of a mosaic of tactical interactions and alliances which form relatively unstable and shifting networks of power always prone to internal decay and dissolution. It explains the development of modern 'systems' of organizational discipline and governmental control in terms of highly contingent and negotiated power mechanisms and relationships whose institutional roots lie in the capacity to exert effective management of 'the means of production of new forms of power itself' (Cerny 1990: 7).

In this context, the cultural and technical mechanisms through which particular fields of human behaviour, such as health, education, crime and business, are colonized as the preserves of certain specialist or expert groups emerge as the strategic focus of analysis. These mechanisms take on a far greater explanatory significance than sovereign political and economic powers such as the 'state' or 'class'. Knowledge, and the power which it potentially confers, assume a central role by providing the key cognitive and representational resource for the application of a set of techniques from which disciplinary regimes, however temporary and unstable, can be constructed (Clegg 1994). Highly specialized and seemingly esoteric knowledge, which can potentially be accessed and controlled by any individual or group with the required training and skill (Blackler 1993), provides the strategic resource from which the appropriation of time, space and consciousness can be realized. Thus the production, codification, storage and usage of knowledge relevant to the regulation of social behaviour become strategic considerations in the mobilization and institutionalization of a form of organized power which facilitates 'control at a distance' (Cooper 1992).

Reworked within this problematic, 'organization' becomes a portable carrier of the socio-technical knowledge and skills through which particular patterns of social relationships emerge and reproduce themselves in specific material and social circumstances (Law 1994a). It has neither inherent ontological status nor explanatory significance as a generalizable, monolithic structure or entity. Contingency, rather than universality, reigns, both in the localized and constrained knowledge which makes organizations possible, and in the power relationships they generate. The research focus lies in the 'interactional order' which produces 'organization' and the locally embedded stocks of knowledge through which agents engage in the situational practices constitutive of the structures through which 'organization' is reproduced (Goffman 1983; Layder 1994).

A number of specific theoretical approaches draw on this general orientation to develop a research agenda for organization analysis which takes the knowledge production processes through which 'organization' is reproduced as its strategic interest. Ethnomethodology (Boden 1994), postmodernist approaches to organization culture and symbolism (Calás and Smircich 1991; Martin 1992), neo-rationalist decision-making theory (March and Olsen 1986; March 1988), actor-network theory (Law 1991; 1994a) and poststructuralist theory (Kondo 1990;

Cooper 1992; Gane and Johnson 1993; Clegg 1994; Perry 1994) collectively contribute to a shift of focus in organization analysis away from macro-level formalization or institutionalization and towards micro-level social ordering or routinization. In their different ways, these approaches, many of which are represented in this book (see Chapters 1.8 by Calás and Smircich, 3.7 by Clegg and Hardy, and 1.7 by Alvesson and Deetz), attempt to reformulate the concept of organization as a socially constructed and sustained 'order' necessarily grounded in the localized stocks of knowledge, practical routines and technical devices mobilized by social actors in their everyday interaction and discourse.

Taken as a whole, contemporary studies of the knowledge/power discourses through which organizational members engage in organizational ordering to generate dynamic and ambiguous relational networks reinforce a view of organizations as 'the condensation of local cultures of values, power, rules, discretion and paradox' (Clegg 1994: 172). They resonate with the images and prejudices of a 'post-industrial' or 'postmodern' Zeitgeist in which organization is deconstructed into 'localized, decentred, on-the-spot decision-making . . . transformations and innovation in organizations occur at the intersection of information and interaction' (Boden 1994: 210). This is entirely in keeping with theories of flexible specialization (Piore and Sabel 1984) and disorganized capitalism (Lash and Urry 1987; 1994) in which the institutional forms or structures once deemed constitutive of 'political economy' dissolve into fragmented information flows and networks.

There is, however, a lingering doubt as to what is lost in this 'localization' of organization analysis, and its seeming obsession with micro-level processes and practices, which makes these approaches seem strangely disengaged from the wider issues of justice, equality, democracy and rationality. What of the classical sociological concern with the macrostructural features of modernity (Layder 1994) and their implications for how we 'ought' to lead our organizational lives?

SCALES OF JUSTICE

The analytical retreat into the local aspects of organizational life takes the study of organizations a long way, theoretically and epistemologically, from the normative themes and structural issues which shaped its historical development and intellectual rationale. At the very least, it radically redefines the 'intellectual mission' away from ethical universals and conceptual abstractions towards cultural relativities and interpretative schema that are inherently resistant to historical and theoretical generalization. Yet, the turn towards 'the local' in organization analysis and the disinclination to engage with wider ideological and structural issues have not gone unremarked. A number of commentators have attempted to redirect the study of organizations back towards institutional forms and the analytical and normative questions they raise.

One relatively obvious example of this development is to be found in the 'new institutionalism' (Powell and DiMaggio 1991; Meyer and Scott 1992; Whitley 1992; Perry 1992). Another can be seen in the resurgence of interest in the political economy of organization and its implications for the extension, in a complex range of institutional practices and forms, of bureaucratic surveillance and control in 'late modernity' (Alford and Friedland 1985; Giddens 1985; 1990; Cerny 1990; Wolin 1988; Thompson 1993; Silberman 1993; Dandeker 1990). Finally, debates about the immediate and longer-term prospects for organizational democracy and participation within the corporate governance structures which developed in political economies dominated by neo-liberal ideologies and policies during the 1980s and 1990s (Lammers and Szell 1989; Morgan 1990; Fulk and Steinfield 1990; Hirst 1993) have reawakened interest in the 'global' issues which organization analysis must address.

Each of these bodies of literature raises fundamental questions about the types of corporate governance and control prevailing in contemporary organizations and their grounding in moral and political judgements concerning justice and fairness, as measured against certain preferred interests and values. They also reassert the centrality of issues relating to the institutionalized distribution of economic, political and cultural power in developed and developing societies that tend to be marginalized in postmodernist and poststructuralist discourses centred on local representational and interpretative practices. These approaches revivify a conception of the organization as an institutionalized structure of power and authority 'over and above' the localized micro-practices of organizational members.

DiMaggio and Powell argue that 'new institutionalism' entails a 'rejection of rational-actor models, an interest in institutions as independent variables, a turn towards cognitive and cultural explanations, and an interest in properties of supraindividual units of analysis that cannot be reduced to aggregations or direct consequences of individuals' attributes or motives' (1991: 8). They focus on organizational structures and

practices found across different institutional sectors, the 'rationality myths' which legitimate and routinize prevailing arrangements, and 'the ways in which action is structured and order made possible by shared systems of rules that both constrain the inclination and capacity of actors to optimize as well as privilege some groups whose interests are secured by prevailing rewards and sanctions' (1991: 11). Their emphasis on practices which penetrate organizational structures and processes, such as the state, social class, professions and industry/sector recipes, reveals the strategic role played by power struggles between institutional actors over 'the formation and reformation of rule systems that guide political and economic action' (1991: 28).

While recognizing that the generation and implementation of institutional forms and practices 'are rife with conflict, contradiction and ambiguity' (1991: 28), institutional theory takes its central concern to be the cultural and political processes through which actors and their interests/values are institutionally constructed and mobilized in support of certain 'organizing logics' rather than others. In this way, the macro-level contexts which shape organizational behaviour and design assume explanatory primacy, given that they are constituted by and through 'supra-organizational patterns of activity through which human beings conduct their material life in time and space, and symbolic systems through which they categorize that activity and infuse it with meaning' (Friedland and Alford 1991: 232). As institutionalized forms of social practice, organizations are seen as 'structures in which powerful people are committed to some value or interest' and that 'power has a great deal to do with the historical preservation of patterns of values' (Stinchcombe 1968: 107). Thus, the historical, structural and contextual positioning of collective actors' values and interests, rather than their local (re)production through micro-level practices, emerges as the analytical and explanatory priority for institutional theory.

This focus on the historical development and structural contextualization of organizations characteristic of the 'new institutionalism' is reflected in recent work on the changing 'surveillance and control' capacities of modern organizations which, as Giddens suggests, takes the theme of 'institutional reflexivity' as its strategic concern. This is

> institutionalization of an investigative and calculative attitude towards generalized conditions of system reproduction; it both stimulates and reflects a decline in traditional ways of doing things. It is also associated with the generation of power

(understood as transformative capacity). The expansion of institutional reflexivity stands behind the proliferation of organizations in circumstances of modernity, including organizations of global scope. (1993: 6)

The rise of modern organizational forms and practices is seen to be intimately tied to the growing sophistication, scope and variety of bureaucratic systems of surveillance and control that can be adapted to very different socio-historical circumstances (Dandeker 1990). The emergence and institutional sedimentation of the nation state and professional administrative structures play a crucial role in advancing the material and social conditions in which organizational surveillance and control can be extended (Cerny 1990; Silberman 1993). Relatively new technological, cultural and political changes encouraged the creation and diffusion of more unobtrusive surveillance systems which are much less dependent on direct supervision and control (Zuboff 1988; Lyon 1994). The growing technical sophistication and social penetration of control systems also serve to reassert the continuing relevance of Weber's concern about the long-term prospects for meaningful individual involvement in a social and organizational order that seems increasingly close to, yet remote from, everyday lives (Ray and Reed 1994).

Organization analysis seems, then, to have come full circle, both ideologically and theoretically, in that the perceived threat to freedom and liberty presented by 'modern', bureaucratic organizational forms at the beginning of the twentieth century is echoed in debates over the prospects for meaningful participation and democracy in the sophisticated and unobtrusive 'surveillance and control regimes' emerging at the end of the century (Webster and Robins 1993). In so far as the 'postmodern' organization becomes a highly dispersed, dynamic and decentred mechanism of socio-cultural control (Clegg 1990) which is virtually impossible to detect, much less resist, questions relating to political responsibility and citizenship are as important now as they were a hundred years ago. As Wolin (1961: 434) so elegantly argued, organization and political theory 'must once again be viewed as that form of knowledge which deals with what is general and integrative to man [sic]; a life of common involvements'.

This aspiration to retrieve an 'institutional vision' in organization analysis which speaks to the relationship between the citizen, organization, community and state in modern societies (Etzioni 1993; Arhne 1994) is a potent theme. Research on organizational democracy and participation suggests that efforts to develop more open, participative and egalitarian organiz-

ational designs have had an extremely difficult time over the last fifteen years or so (Lammers and Szell 1989). Long-term prospects for democracy seem equally pessimistic in an increasingly globalized and fragmented world which destabilizes, if not destroys, established socio-political and cultural identities, corroding the cognitive security and ideological certainty they once bestowed (Cable 1994).

The combination of neo-libertarian policies and sophisticated surveillance has not succeeded, however, in eradicating a continuing challenge to unobtrusive and self-reinforcing forms of organizational discipline and control (Lyon 1994). As Cerny argued in relation to institutional changes at the turn of this century:

Individuals and groups must define themselves strategically and manoeuvre tactically in the context of the logic of the state, whether conforming to legal rules, competing for resources distributed or regulated by the state, or attempting to resist or avoid the influence of control of other state and non-state actors . . . the state itself is constituted by a range of middle-level and micro-level games, which are also characterized by contrasting logics, interstitial spaces, structural dynamics and ongoing tensions. (1990: 35–6)

Within these overlapping, and often contradictory, political games new organizing principles and practices are emerging which require a fundamental reconsideration of the rapidly changing relationship between the individual and the community in a socio-political context where the 'agenda for identity politics' has become much more diverse, unstable, fragmented and contested (Cable 1994: 38–40). Lyon's (1994) survey of the social movements, interest groups and political coalitions challenging centralized and undemocratic regimes of surveillance and control indicates that there are options available other than 'postmodern paranoia' and the extreme political pessimism that it seems to encourage. Similarly, writers such as Hirst (1993) and Arhne (1994; 1996) rediscovered civil society and the diverse range of 'associative' forms of social and economic governance that it continues to generate and support, even in the teeth of socio-technical pressures for enhanced centralized power and control.

Thus, this narrative demands that we reconnect, analytically and politically, the local with the global; organizationally situated practices and processes with institutional rationalities and structures; negotiated order with strategic power and control. In short, we must address the fact that:

We live in a massively but unevenly, unequally, interconnected and interdependent world, where 'organization' (and disorganization), and particular kinds of organizations, represent fundamental 'nodes', conceptually, practically, but where a dominant big business vision, for example, can only be blinkered and imperialistic, conceptually, practically. Seeking to understand and analyze such complex intersections and their ramifications must, it seems to me, represent a key component for the future development of the field if it is to meet the intellectual and practical challenges posed by such. (Jones 1994: 208)

The analytical structured narrative of organizational justice and democracy seeks to reconnect the study of locally contextualized discourses and practices with institutionalized orders of power, authority and control which have a societal rationale and historical dynamic that cannot be understood, much less explained, through a limited focus on 'everyday' interaction and events (Layder 1994). It forces us to re-discover the vital link between the practical demands and intellectual needs of the study of organizations, the 'points of intersection' between the normative and the analytical, which must be reforged if the latter is to retain its relevance and vitality in a world where long-established structures are under extreme pressure to change, indeed metamorphose, into very different institutional forms.

POINTS OF INTERSECTION

A number of interconnected themes provide the 'analytical spine' around which the six narrative frames reviewed in this chapter can be interpreted as historically contested attempts to represent and control our understanding of such a strategic institutionalized social practice as 'organization'. As with the discourse of political theory, the discourse of organization theory must be considered as a contestable and contested network of concepts and theories which are engaged in a struggle to impose certain meanings rather than others on our shared understanding of organizational life in late modernity.

To say that a particular network of concepts is contestable is to say that the standards and criteria of judgement it expresses are open to contestation. To say that such a network is essentially contestable is to contend that universal criteria of reason, as we now understand them, do not suffice to settle these contests definitely. The proponent of essentially contestable concepts charges those who construe the standards operative in their own way of life to be fully expressive of God's will or reason or nature with transcendental provincialism; they treat the

standards with which they are intimately familiar as universal criteria against which all other theories, practices and ideals are assessed. They use universalist rhetoric to protect provincial practices ... The phrase 'essentially contestable concepts', properly interpreted, calls attention to the internal connection between conceptual debates and debates over the form of the good life, to the reasonable grounds we now have to believe that rational space for such contestation will persist into the future, to the values of keeping such contests alive even in settings where a determinate orientation to action is required, and to the incumbent task for those who accept the first three themes to expose conceptual closure where it has been imposed artificially. (Connolly 1993: 225–31)

Connolly develops this argument to sustain a critique of the 'rational universalism' and 'radical relativism' which dominates political analysis in the arenas of Anglo-American analytic philosophy and continental deconstructionism (1993: 213–47). He is particularly critical of the artificial and unwarranted 'conceptual closure' of Foucauldian accounts of knowledge/power discourses that construe social actors as artifacts, rather than agents, of power. According to this view, the 'thesis of essential contestation gives way to the practice of total deconstruction' (1993: 233). He conceives of political theory as an essentially contested domain or space in which rival interpretations of political life can be analytically identified and rationally debated by responsible agents without recourse to the 'transcendental provincialism' characteristic of either epistemological universalism or cultural relativism. Such a conception can be used to survey the underlying themes which emerge from the historical account of organization theory provided in this chapter.

These themes can be summarized as follows: a theoretical debate concerning the rival explanatory claims of the concepts of 'agency' and 'structure' as they are deployed to account for key features of organization; an epistemological debate between 'constructivism' and 'positivism' and their implications for the nature and status of the knowledge which organization studies produces; an analytical debate between the relative priority to be attached to the 'local' as opposed to the 'global' level of analysis in organization studies; a normative debate between 'individualism' and 'collectivism' as competing ideological conceptions of the 'good life' in late modern societies. Each of the six narratives contributes to and participates within the contested intellectual spaces which these debates open up.

The Agency/Structure Debate

Layder argues that the 'agency/structure' debate in social theory 'concentrates on the question of how creativity and constraint are related through social activity – how can we explain their co-existence?' (1994: 4). Those who emphasize agency focus on an understanding of social and organizational order that stresses the social practices through which human beings create and reproduce institutions. Those located on the 'structure' side highlight the importance of the objectified external relations and patterns that determine and constrain social interaction within specific institutional forms.

In relation to the narrative frames above, a theoretical fault line appears between a concept of organization that refers to determinate structures which condition individual and collective behaviour and a concept that is a theoretical shorthand for consciously fabricated interactional networks through which such structures are generated and reproduced as temporary and constantly shifting ordering mechanisms or devices. The rational, integrationist and market narratives come down firmly in favour of the structural conception of organization; while researchers working within the power, knowledge and justice traditions support the agency conception of organization. Much effort has been expended in trying to overcome, or at least reconcile, this theoretical duality through approaches which emphasize the mutually constituted and constituting nature of agency and structure in the reproduction of organization (e.g. Giddens 1984; 1993; Boden 1994); but the underlying conflict between competing explanatory logics remains a source of creative tension within organization studies.

There is always the danger that agency-oriented conceptions will detach the organization from its surrounding societal context and be unable to deal with major shifts in dominant institutional forms. On the other hand, structure-oriented views tend towards a highly deterministic explanatory logic in which society crushes agency through monolithic force (Whittington 1994: 64). Whittington's conclusion is that organization analysis needs a 'theory of strategic choice adequate to the importance of managerial agency in our society' (1994: 71). His rejection of the theoretical extremes of individualistic reductionism and collectivist determinism is well taken. The need to develop explanatory theories in which 'agency derives from the simultaneously enabling and contradictory nature of the structural principles by which people act' (1994: 72) constitutes one of the central issues on the research agenda for organization analysis.

The Constructivist/Positivist Debate

Epistemological concerns have played a strategic role in the development of organization theory, especially during the last twenty-five years or so as positivist orthodoxy has given way to various schools of interpretative, realist and critical methodology (Hassard 1990; Willmott 1993; Donaldson 1985; 1994; Aldrich 1992; Gergen 1992). This debate relates to the representational forms through which the 'knowledge claims' made by organization theorists can be evaluated and legitimated. While the rational, integrationist and market narratives developed on the basis of a realist ontology and a positivist epistemology, the power, knowledge and justice traditions are more favourably disposed to a constructivist ontology and a conventionalist epistemology. The former treats 'organization' as an object or entity existing in its own right which can be explained in terms of the general principles or laws governing its operation. The latter promotes a conception of organization as a socially constructed and dependent artifact which can only be understood in terms of highly restricted and localized methodological conventions that are always open to revision and change.

These radically opposed epistemologies legitimate very different procedures and protocols for assessing the 'knowledge claims' which organization researchers make. Positivistic epistemology severely restricts the range of 'knowledge claims' allowable in organization studies to those who pass a rigorous 'trial by method' and the law-like generalizations that it sanctions. Constructivism takes a much more liberal, not to say relativistic, stance and falls back on the restricted communal norms and practices associated with specific research communities as they develop over time (Reed 1993). Various attempts to follow a middle course between these epistemological polarities have been made (Bernstein 1983), but the contested terrain mapped out by constructivism/relativism and positivism/objectivism continues to haunt the study of organizations.

The Local/Global Debate

The agency/structure debate raises fundamental questions about the logics of explanation which organization analysts should follow and the constructivism/positivism debate highlights deep-seated controversy over the representational forms through which the knowledge should be developed, evaluated and legitimated. The localism/globalism debate that emerges from the narratives focuses on questions relating to the level of analysis at which organizational research and analysis should be pitched. As Layder (1994) maintains, questions relating to levels of analysis crystallize around different models of social reality and the analytic properties of entities or objects located at different levels within those models. Thus, the 'micro/macro' debate relates to whether the emphasis should be on 'intimate and detailed aspects of face-to-face conduct [or] more impersonal and large-scale phenomena' (1994: 6).

Within organization studies, theoretical approaches developed under the auspices of the power, knowledge and justice frameworks tend to favour a focus on local/micro organizational processes and practices; while the rational, integrationist and market narratives take a more global/macro conception of the 'reality of organization' as their starting point. Ethnomethodological and poststructuralist approaches take the local focus the furthest; while population ecology and institutionalism have a more well-developed global level of analysis. Approaches fixated with the local/micro level of analysis in organization studies run the risk of basing their research on 'flat ontologies' which makes it very difficult, if not impossible, to go beyond everyday practices in which members are engaged (Layder 1994: 218–29). As a result, their theoretical capability to perceive, much less explain, the intricate and complex intermeshing of local practices – in all their variability and contingency – and institutionalized structures is severely compromised (Smith 1988). The corresponding danger with 'stratified ontologies' is that they never see the dialectic between and mutual constituting of social structures and social practices.

The prevailing tendency in organization analysis to shift the analytical focus so far towards the local/micro level risks losing sight of the wider structural constraints and resources which shape the process of organizational (re)production or 'ordering'. Some studies, however, manage to keep the highly intricate, but absolutely vital, intermeshing of the local and the global; agency and structure; construction and constraint; constantly in view. Indeed, by far the most significant recent research in the study of organizations is to be found in Zuboff's (1988) work on information technology, Jackall's (1988) analysis of the 'moral mazes' to be discovered in large American business corporations, and Kondo's (1990) research on the 'crafting of selves' in Japanese work organizations. These studies rediscover and renew the mutual constituting of situated practices and institutional forms that lies at the core of any type of organization analysis which reaches beyond the boundaries of everyday understanding to connect with the historical, social and organizational dynamics which structure a society's development.

The Individualism/Collectivism Debate

The final analytical vertebra making up the theoretical backbone of this brief history of organization studies is the ideological debate between individualistic and collectivist visions of organizational order. Individualistic theories of organization are grounded in an analytical and normative outlook which sees the former as an aggregated outcome of individual actions and reactions that are always potentially reducible to their component parts. Thus, market-based theories of organization, and the rich vein of decision-making theorizing that is woven around this individualistic perspective (Whittington 1994), deny that collective concepts, such as 'organization', have any ontological or methodological status beyond shorthand code for the behaviours of individual actors. The ideological justification for this ontological/methodological precept lies in the belief that forms of social organization that go beyond direct interpersonal association can only be justified in terms of their positive contribution to the protection of individual freedom and autonomy.

Collectivism lies at the opposite end of the ideological/methodological spectrum in that it refuses to recognize individual actors as constituent components of formal organization; they simply become ciphers for the cognitive, emotional and political programming provided by larger structures. If individualism offers a vision of organization as the unintended creation of individual actors following the dictates of their particular instrumental and political objectives, then collectivism treats organization as an objective entity that imposes itself on actors with such force that they have little or no choice but to obey its commands (Whittington 1994). The integrationist narrative relies on this view most strongly in so far as it identifies a logic of organizational functioning and development which goes on 'behind the backs' of individuals and narrowly constrains the decision-making options available to the latter virtually to the point of extinction. While it has become much less fashionable of late, such collectivism continues to offer a conception of organization and organization analysis that directly challenges the dominance of analytical perspectives which are grounded in an individualist/reductionist programme.

POINTS OF EXCLUSION

Each of the four points of intersection that emerged out of the history narrated in this chapter structures the contested terrain on which organization theory has taken shape as an identifiable and viable intellectual endeavour. They establish a set of parameters within which a dialogue between competing and conflicting interpretations of organization has been engaged for the best part of a century, as social scientists attempt to account for the rise and significance of such a strategic social practice. However, the points of intersection between the narratives are also relevant for what they exclude, for the points of exclusion or 'silences' which they reveal.

The analytical structured narratives which constitute the historically contested terrain of organization theory are stories that selectively filter and mediate an extremely diverse and complex socio-historical reality. They omit, or at the very least marginalize, aspects of organizational life which may seem of strategic significance viewed from a different angle. The narration which they provide is far from innocent; indeed, it is mired in assumptions about the reality of organization and the intellectual means most appropriate to its excavation that finds little favour in other quarters.

Our awareness of and sensitivity to these omissions or 'absences' has grown in recent years, but they remain relatively underdeveloped and understated realities in the study of organizations, with which we are only now beginning to come to terms. Four themes are crucial elements of this 'latent agenda' in organization analysis: the issue of gender and its implications for the way in which we conceptualize, analyze and practise organization; the theme of ethnicity and race and its relevance for our understanding of organizational inequality; the subject of technoscience and its potential to transform both organizational structures and the theoretical means through which they are intellectually interrogated; finally, the process of global development and underdevelopment, and its impact on forms of world-wide institutional and organizational governance.

Gender

The 'gender-blindness' of organization theory and analysis is well documented elsewhere and does not need to be rehearsed yet again (Hearn et al. 1989; Calás and Smircich 1992; Witz and Savage 1992; Mills and Tancred 1992; Ferguson 1994; Martin 1994; also see Chapter 1.8 by Calás and Smircich). The basic point here is that the fundamental categories, concepts and theories on which organization analysis trades usually fail to provide any recognition of the fact that organizational structures and processes are permeated by gender-based power relations and practices. This leads to an extreme form of institutionalized intellectual and ideological myopia in which the vital contribution which organizational theories and practices make to the production and reproduction of 'gendered persons' (Mills and Tancred 1992), as well as the structures of inequality and control through which their subordination is routinely secured (Witz and Savage 1992), are excluded from the research agenda.

Race and Ethnicity

While the feminist critique of the innate 'gender-blindness' of organization theory has gathered pace and momentum over the last ten years or so, the issue of the racial and ethnic foundations of organizational power and control is only just beginning to emerge within the literature as an acceptable topic of investigation and debate (Nkomo 1992; Reed 1992; Ferguson 1994; also see Chapter 2.5 by Nkomo and Cox).

> [C]olouring organizational studies requires thinking about what colour might mean, taking apart the complex grammar of race, which routinely mixes biological (e.g. 'black', 'white'), geographical (e.g. 'African American', 'Asian American') and historical (e.g. 'Native American', 'indigenous') signifiers to track racial identity. Race, like gender, offers itself as a kind of performance, a set of practices, languages and self-understandings so dense and freighted that history is able to masquerade as nature. (Ferguson 1994: 93)

Ferguson concludes that 'colouring' organization analysis would encourage us 'to think of race, not as a static property adhering to individuals, but as a set of practices and identities produced through complex interactions between geography, history and power' (1994: 95). In this way, both the 'gendering' and the 'colouring' of organization theory would make way for 'a much expanded definition of the constituency and objectives of organizational studies' (1994: 97) and would force us to engage in a more searching, and hence dangerous, interrogation of our basic analytical categories and ideological commitments.

Technoscience

The socio-technical processes and practices through which 'organizational ordering' takes place is a perennial theme in organization studies and re-emerges as a strategic research interest in contemporary approaches which draw on knowledge-based theories of organization such as actor-network theory (Law 1991; 1994a). However, the dynamic interplay between culture and technology attracts more attention from those researchers focusing on the development of new information technologies which seem to entail 'a fundamental transformation in the structure and meaning of modern society and culture' (Escobar 1994: 211). Scarbrough and Corbett maintain that new information technologies are generating more complex and innovative 'circuits' of control, meaning and design in that the 'transformational power of technological knowledge may escape the intentions of the powerful and undermine, and not simply reproduce, existing social and economic structures' (1992: 23). There is much talk of a neo-Taylorite strategy of organizational control as the economic and political driving force behind contemporary technological change (Webster and Robins 1993). Yet, a more nuanced reading would seem to suggest that the new sites of struggle and circuits of control opening up around advanced technologies make predictions about long-term trends in power structures more difficult.

Escobar's (1994) work on the emergence of a new 'cyberculture' in high/postmodern societies raises fundamental questions about the role of technology as both agent and product of social and cultural production. He argues that new developments in artificial intelligence and biotechnology, which radically transform the relationship between machines, bodies and behaviour, destabilize the conventional division of labour between science, technology and society. Instead of the traditional categorical distinctions between 'nature' and 'society', 'a new order for the production of life, nature and the body through biologically-based technological interventions' (1994: 214) is taking shape. It radically reconfigures the organizational practices and discourses which revolve around technoscientific developments. Escobar further maintains that these developments will lead to 'profound changes in capital accumulation, social relations, and divisions of labour at many levels . . . The shift to new information technologies marked the appearance of more flexible, decentralized labour processes highly stratified by gender, ethnic, class and geographic factors' (1994: 120).

Considered in these terms, the concept of 'technoscience' begins to sensitize organizational researchers to the new organizational sites and institutional settings in which scientific and technological development combine to form novel forms of appropriation and mechanisms of ruling. This is particularly the case in relation to Third World development where transnational corporations are engaged in biotechnological research and development in plant genetics, industrial tissue culture and genetically manipulated micro-organisms which is likely to result in a 'biorevolution' driven by the imperatives of capital accumulation rather than indigenous growth. It is in these terms that the relative silence over the cultural and political implications of biotechnology dovetails with a consistent neglect of Third World interests and traditions in organization studies.

Global Development and Underdevelopment

Researchers such as Castells (1989) and Smith (1993) have begun to recognize the 'new dependencies' between 'technology rich' and 'technology poor' countries which result from First World domination of such innovations as computers, information and biological technologies, as well as their systematic coordination through the organizational mechanisms associated with 'technoscience'. The cultural practices and political forms through which these new relationships of exploitation and dependency are mediated are also beginning to attract the attention of organizational researchers (Escobar 1994; Ramirez 1994). Yet the whole area of Western dominated cultural, economic and political globalization, and its impact on the new organizational forms emerging in both First and Third World countries, remains a seriously underdeveloped theme in contemporary organization analysis (Calás 1994).

This brief review of some of the silences exhibited by theoretical traditions reveals the inherently limited capacity for critical self-reflexivity which they display. Any analytically structured narrative, and the particular theoretical approaches and research programmes that it facilitates, excludes and marginalizes at the same time that it includes and frames. However, the dynamic interaction within and between rival traditions creates the room for rational dialogue and creative reflection through which the study of organization develops, or 'progresses', as an identifiable and coherent intellectual practice. Rational dialogue between competing traditions and critical self-reflection on their inherent limitations are ever-present characteristics of the field. They are likely to become even more prominent features when debate within and between rival narratives opens up the contradictions and tensions found in any intellectual community and the wider audiences to which it speaks. The study of organization has been going through a protracted debate about its identity, rationale and purpose for three decades or more. This debate has released a veritable torrent of new approaches which speak to a much wider range of audiences and relate to a much broader set of issues than was ever the case when the technical needs and political interests of a relatively narrow policy-making elite dominated the scene. It has also raised some very basic questions about the most appropriate ways in which the study of organization can develop in the future.

NARRATING THEORETICAL FUTURES

Law has suggested that over the last two decades organization studies has gone through a 'bonfire of the certainties' in relation to its ontological foundations, theoretical commitments, methodological conventions and ideological predilections (1994b: 248–9). Domain assumptions relating to the analytical dominance of 'order' over 'disorder', 'structure' over 'process', 'internalities' over 'externalities', 'boundaries' over 'ecologies' and 'rationality' over 'emotion' have been put to the flames in a coruscating critique of innate theoretical hubris and methodological pretentiousness. He outlines two possible responses to this situation: 'carry on regardless' or 'let a thousand flowers bloom'. The first option suggests a retreat back into, appropriately refurbished, intellectual fortifications that offer protection against the radically destabilizing effects of continuing critique and deconstruction. It supports a general regrouping around an accepted theoretical paradigm and core research programme that counteracts the fragmentary dynamic let loose by approaches that have broken with orthodoxy. The second calls for a further proliferation of 'more questions and uncertainties and . . . more narratives that generate questions' (1994b: 249). It need not necessarily result in organization studies slipping into a vortex of anarchic and uncontrollable relativism, Law argues, because it sensitizes us to the need to preserve and build on the intellectual pluralism that critique has made possible and to reveal 'the processes by which story-telling and ordering produce themselves' (1994b: 249).

As has already been intimated in earlier sections of this chapter, the urge to retreat and regroup back into reheated intellectual orthodoxy is a powerful tendency within the field at the present time. In their different ways, Donaldson (1985; 1988; 1989; 1994) and Pfeffer (1993) attempt to revive the narrative of organization studies as a scientific enterprise that speaks directly to the technical needs and political interests of policy-making elites, an aspiration and leitmotiv which has dominated the field's development since the early decades of this century. Their call for paradigmatic consensus and discipline around a dominant theoretical and methodological orthodoxy to deliver, cumulatively, codified bodies of knowledge that are 'user-friendly' to policy-making elites resonates with the current desire to re-establish intellectual order and control in an increasingly fragmented and uncertain world. They are intellectual and ideological heirs to the technocratic scientism that pervades the rational, integrationist and market narrative traditions reviewed earlier. Their call for intellectual closure around a refurbished theoretical paradigm and ideological consensus over the restrictive technocratic needs that organization analysis should serve rests on the assumption that a return to orthodoxy is a viable political project.

The alter ego of the 'return to orthodoxy' vision is the 'incommensurability thesis' into which new intellectual life has been pumped by the growing influence of poststructuralist and postmodernist approaches as represented in Foucauldian-inspired discourse theory and actor-network theory (Jackson and Carter 1991; Willmott 1993; 1994; Alvesson and Willmott 1992). Supporters of the 'incommensurability thesis' luxuriate in epistemological, theoretical and cultural relativism. They reject the possibility of shared discourse between conflicting paradigmatic positions in favour of an unqualified relativism that completely politicizes intellectual debate and adjudication between rival traditions. Relations of mutual exclusivity between paradigms offer polarized visions of organization and languages of organization analysis which cannot be reconciled. Thus the rival narratives which constitute 'our' field are locked into a struggle for intellectual power with no hope of mediation. A transcendental Nietzschean 'will to power' and a geopolitical Darwinian 'survival of the fittest' impose intellectual and institutional parameters within which this struggle has to be fought. There is no question of sustaining a narrative through argument, logic and evidence; there is simply the power of a dominant paradigm and the disciplinary practices that it generates and legitimates. There is neither recognition of negotiated ground rules within which contestation can rationally proceed (Connolly 1993: 233–4), nor a shared interest in mediating mutual suspicion and rivalry. The conception of organization studies as a historically contested and contextually mediated terrain thus gives way to the practice of total deconstruction and the unqualified relativism on which it rests.

This 'Hobson's choice' between revamped orthodoxy and radical relativism is not the only option: greater sensitivity to the socio-historical context and political dynamics of theory development need not degenerate into unreflective and total deconstruction as the only viable alternative to a resurgent orthodoxy. Willmott's (1993) reworking of Kuhn's approach to the process of theoretical development within natural and social science offers a way out of the intellectual cul-de-sac in which both orthodoxy and relativism terminate. His focus on the communal processes and practices of critical reflection required to identify anomalies within existing theories offers a more attractive alternative to both the hubris of 'carry on regardless' and the despondency of 'anything goes'. Willmott (1993) resists the dogma of paradigm incommensurability, while highlighting the crucial role of institutionalized academic politics in determining access to the resources and infrastructure (appointments, grants, journals, publishers etc.) that shape the conditions under which different paradigms of knowledge production are legitimated. However, this sensitivity to the 'production practices' that facilitate the acceptance of certain theories of organization and marginalize or exclude others does not go far enough. Willmott's analysis reveals little awareness of the ways in which these production practices mesh with adjudicatory practices, built up over a protracted period of intellectual development, to form the negotiated rules through which competing approaches and traditions can be evaluated. We need to develop greater awareness of the subtle and intricate ways in which material conditions and intellectual practices intermesh to generate and sustain the inherently dynamic narrative traditions and research programmes that constitute the field of organization studies over time.

'Institutional reflexivity' (Giddens 1993; 1994) is not only the defining feature of the phenomena to which organizational researchers attend; it is also a constitutive feature of the intellectual trade they practise. The study of organization is both progenitor of and heir to this institutionalized reflexivity in that it necessarily depends on and systematically cultivates a critical and questioning attitude to its concerns, as mediated through a dynamic interaction within and between the narrative traditions that constitute its intellectual inheritance. Students of organization cannot avoid this inheritance: it sets the background assumptions and moral context which informs the decisions that researchers make concerning ideology, epistemology and theory. These choices are made within an inheritance that is not simply 'handed down', but is constantly revisited, re-evaluated and renewed as it passes through the critical debate and reflection which is the intellectual life-blood of organization studies.

Reflexivity and criticality are institutionalized within the intellectual practices that constitute the study of organization. The specific criteria through which these 'generalized mandates' are defined and the particular socio-economic and political conditions under which they are activated vary across time and space. The material and symbolic power mobilized by different academic communities clearly affects the survival of rival narrative traditions. Nevertheless, the indelible link between practical reasoning, within and between competing analytically structured narratives, and theory development in a dynamic socio-historical context, can be erased by neither conservative orthodoxy nor radical relativism. It is the confrontation between rival narrative traditions, particularly when their internal tensions and contradictions or anomalies are most clearly and cruelly exposed, that provides the essential intellectual dynamism through which the study of organization rediscovers and renews itself. As Perry argues, 'we cannot escape from either history or the game of culture. All theorizing is therefore partial; all theorizing is selective' (1992: 98). But this is not a rationalization for a forced paradigmatic consensus or for unrestrained paradigm proliferation. Instead, it calls for a more sensitive appreciation of the complex interaction between a changing set of institutional conditions and intellectual forms as they combine to reproduce the reflexivity and criticality that is the hallmark of contemporary organization studies.

The underlying thrust of the chapter is to suggest that organization theorists have developed, and will continue to develop, a network of critical debates within and between narrative traditions that will indelibly shape their field's evolution. Three debates seem particularly intense and potentially productive at the present time. The first is the perceived need to develop a 'theory of the subject' which does not degenerate into the simplicities of reductionism or the absurdities of determinism. The second is a general desire to construct a 'theory of organization' that analytically and methodologically mediates between the restrictions of localism and the blandishments of globalism. The third is the imperative of nurturing a 'theory of (intellectual) development' that resists the constrictions of conservativism and the distortions of relativism. In so far as this chapter has made some contribution to advancing the cause of a more historically informed and intellectually coherent pursuit of these issues, it will have done its job.

REFERENCES

Abbott, A. (1988) *The System of Professions*. Chicago: University of Chicago Press.

Aldrich, H. (1979) *Organizations and Environments*. Englewood Cliffs, NJ: Prentice-Hall.

Aldrich, H. (1992) 'Incommensurable paradigms? Vital signs from three perspectives', in M. Reed and M. Hughes (eds), *Rethinking Organization: New Directions in Organization Theory and Analysis*. London: Sage. pp. 17–45.

Alford, R. and Friedland, R. (1985) *Powers of Theory: Capitalism, the State and Democracy*. Cambridge: Cambridge University Press.

Alvesson, M. and Willmott, H. (1992) *Critical Management Studies*. London: Sage.

Argyris, C. (1964) *Integrating the Individual and the Organization*. New York: Wiley.

Arhne, G. (1994) *Social Organizations*. London: Sage.

Arhne, G. (1996) 'Civil society and civil organizations', *Organization*, 3(1): 109–20.

Barley, S.R. and Kunda, G. (1992) 'Design and devotion: surges of rational and normative ideologies of control in managerial discourse', *Administrative Science Quarterly*, 37(3): 363–99.

Barnard, C. (1938) *Functions of the Executive*. Cambridge, MA: Harvard University Press.

Bartell, T. (1976) 'The human relations ideology', *Human Relations*, 29(8): 737–49.

Bauman, Z. (1989) *Modernity and the Holocaust*. Cambridge: Polity Press.

Bell, D. (1960) *The End of Ideology*. New York: Collier Macmillan.

Bendix, R. (1974) *Work and Authority in Industry*. California: University of California Press.

Bernstein, B. (1983) *Beyond Objectivism and Relativism*. Oxford: Basil Blackwell.

Bertalanffy, L. von (1950) 'The theory of open systems in physics and biology', *Science*, 3.

Bertalanffy, L. von (1956) 'General systems theory', *General Systems*, 1: 1–10.

Blackler, F. (1993) 'Knowledge and the theory of organizations: organizations as activity systems and the reframing of management', *Journal of Management Studies*, 30: 863–84.

Blau, P. (1955) *The Dynamics of Bureaucracy*. Chicago: University of Chicago Press.

Blau, P. and Scott, W.R. (1963) *Formal Organizations: a Comparative Approach*. London: Routledge and Kegan Paul.

Boden, D. (1994) *The Business of Talk: Organizations in Action*. Cambridge: Polity Press.

Boguslaw, R. (1965) *The New Utopians: the Study of System Design and Social Change*. Englewood Cliffs, NJ: Prentice-Hall.

Brech, E. (1948) *Organization: the Framework of Management*. New York: Collier Macmillan.

Burawoy, M. (1985) *The Politics of Production*. London: Verso.

Burrell, G. and Morgan, G. (1979) *Sociological Paradigms and Organizational Analysis*. London: Heinemann.

Cable, V. (1994) *The World's New Fissures*. London: Demos.

Calás, M. (1994) 'Minerva's owl? Introduction to a thematic section on globalization', *Organization*, 1(2): 243–8.

Calás, M. and Smircich, L. (1991) 'Voicing seduction to silence leadership', *Organization Studies*, 12(4): 567–601.

Calás, M. and Smircich, L. (1992) 'Re-writing gender into organizational theorizing: directions from feminist perspectives', in M. Reed and M. Hughes (eds), *Rethinking Organization: New Directions in Organization Theory and Analysis*. London: Sage. pp. 227–53.

Castells, M. (1989) *The Informational City: Information Technology, Economic Restructuring and the Urban–Regional Process*. Oxford: Basil Blackwell.

Cerny, P. (1990) *The Changing Architecture of Politics*. London: Sage.

Checkland, P. (1994) 'Conventional wisdom and conventional ignorance: the revolution organization theory missed', *Organization*, 1(1): 29–34.

Child, J. (1969) *British Management Thought*. London: Allen and Unwin.

Child, J. (1972) 'Organization structure, environment and performance: the role of strategic choice', *Sociology*, 6(1): 163–77.

Child, J. (1973) 'Organization: a choice for man', in J. Child (ed.), *Man and Organization*. London: Allen and Unwin. pp. 234–57.

Clegg, S. (1989) *Frameworks of Power*. London: Sage.

Clegg, S. (1990) *Modern Organizations: Organization Studies in the Postmodern World*. London: Sage.

Clegg, S. (1994) 'Weber and Foucault: social theory for the study of organizations', *Organization*, 1(1): 149–78.

Clegg, S. and Dunkerley, D. (1980) *Organization, Class and Control*. London: Routledge.

Coase, R. (1937) 'The nature of the firm', *Economica*, new series, 386–405.

Connolly, W. (1993) *The Terms of Political Discourse*, 3rd edn. Oxford: Basil Blackwell.

Cooper, R. (1992) 'Formal organization as representation: remote control, displacement and abbreviation', in M. Reed and M. Hughes (eds), *Rethinking Organization: New Directions in Organization Theory and Analysis*. London: Sage. pp. 254–72.

Cooper, R. and Burrell, G. (1988) 'Modernism, postmodernism and organizational analysis: an introduction', *Organization Studies*, 9(1): 91–112.

Crozier, M. and Friedberg, M. (1980) *Actors and Systems: The Politics of Collective Action*. Chicago: University of Chicago Press.

Cyert, R. and March, J. (1963) *A Behavioural Theory of the Firm*. Englewood Cliffs, NJ: Prentice-Hall.

Dandeker, C. (1990) *Surveillance, Power and Modernity*. Cambridge: Polity Press.

DiMaggio, P.J. and Powell, W.W. (1991) 'Introduction', in W.W. Powell and P.J. DiMaggio (eds), *The New Institutionalism in Organizational Analysis*. Chicago: University of Chicago Press. pp. 1–38.

Donaldson, L. (1985) *In Defence of Organization Theory: a Response to the Critics*. Cambridge: Cambridge University Press.

Donaldson, L. (1988) 'In successful defence of organization theory: a routing of the critics', *Organization Studies*, 9(1): 28–32.

Donaldson, L. (1989) 'Review article: *Redirections in Organizational Analysis* by Michael Reed', *Australian Journal of Management*, 14(2): 243–54.

Donaldson, L. (1990) 'The ethereal hand: organizational economics and management theory', *Academy of Management Review*, 15: 369–81.

Donaldson, L. (1994) 'The liberal revolution and organization theory', in J. Hassard and M. Parker (eds), *Towards a New Theory of Organizations*. London: Routledge. pp. 190–208.

Du Gay, P. (1994) 'Colossal immodesties and hopeful monsters: pluralism and organizational conduct', *Organization*, 1(1): 125–48.

Du Gay, P. and Salaman, G. (1992) 'The cult(ure) of the customer', *Journal of Management Studies*, 29(5): 615–34.

Ellul, J. (1964) *The Technological Society*. New York: Vintage Books.

Escobar, A. (1994) 'Welcome to Cyberia: notes on the anthropology of cyberculture', *Current Anthropology*, 35(3): 211–23.

Etzioni, A. (1993) *The Spirit of Community*. Chicago: University of Chicago Press.

Fayol, H. (1949) *General and Industrial Management*. London: Pitman.

Ferguson, K. (1994) 'On bringing more theory, more voices, more politics to the study of organization', *Organization*, 1(1): 81–100.

Fincham, R. (1992) 'Perspectives on power: processual, institutional and "internal" forms of organizational power', *Journal of Management Studies*, 26(9): 741–59.

Francis, A. (1983) 'Markets and hierarchies: efficiency or domination?', in A. Francis, J. Turk and P. Willman (eds), *Power, Efficiency and Institutions*. London: Heinemann. pp. 105–16.

Friedland, R. and Alford, R. (1991) 'Bringing society back in: symbols, practices, and institutional contradictions', in P. DiMaggio and W. Powell (eds), *The New Institutionalism in Organizational Analysis*. Chicago: University of Chicago Press. pp. 232–66.

Frug, G.E. (1984) 'The ideology of bureaucracy in American law', *Harvard Law Review*, 97(6): 1276–388.

Fulk, J. and Steinfield, C. (1990) *Organizations and Communication Technology*. California: Sage.

Galbraith, J.K. (1969) *The New Industrial State*. Harmondsworth: Penguin.

Gane, M. and Johnson, T. (1993) *Foucault's New Domains*. London: Routledge.

Gellner, E. (1964) *Thought and Change*. London: Weidenfeld and Nicholson.

Gergen, K. (1992) 'Organization theory in the postmodern era', in M. Reed and M. Hughes (eds), *Rethinking Organization: New Directions in Organization Theory and Analysis*. London: Sage. pp. 207–26.

Giddens, A. (1984) *The Constitution of Society*. Cambridge: Polity Press.

Giddens, A. (1985) *The Nation State and Violence*. Cambridge: Polity Press.

Giddens, A. (1990) *The Consequences of Modernity*. Cambridge: Polity Press.

Giddens, A. (1993) *New Rules of Sociological Method*, 2nd edn. Cambridge: Polity Press.

Giddens, A. (1994) 'Living in a post-traditional society', in U. Beck, A. Giddens and S. Lash, *Reflexive Modernization: Politics, Tradition and Aesthetics in the Modern Social Order*. Cambridge: Polity Press. pp. 56–109.

Goffman, E. (1983) 'The interaction order', *American Sociological Review*, 48: 1–17.

Gouldner, A. (1959) 'Organizational analysis', in R. Merton, L. Broom and L. Cottrell (eds), *Sociology Today: Problems and Prospects*. New York: Basic Books. pp. 400–28.

Gouldner, A. (1971) *The Coming Crisis of Western Sociology*. London: Heinemann.

Gouldner, A. (1976) *The Dialectic of Ideology and Technology*. London: Macmillan.

Gouldner, A. (1980) *The Two Marxisms*. London: Macmillan.

Gulick, L. and Urwick, L. (1937) *Papers on the Science of Administration*. New York: Columbia University Press.

Haire, M. (1960) *Modern Organization Theory*. New York: Free Press.

Hannan, M. and Freeman, J. (1989) *Organizational Ecology*. Cambridge, MA: Harvard University Press.

Hassard, J. (1990) 'An alternative to paradigm incommensurability in organization theory', in J. Hassard and D. Pym (eds), *The Theory and Philosophy of Organizations: Critical Issues and New Perspectives*. London: Routledge. pp. 219–30.

Hayek, F. (1978) *The Road to Serfdom*. London: Routledge.

Hearn, J., Sheppard, D., Tancred-Sheriff, P. and Burrell, G. (1989) *The Sexuality of Organization*. London: Sage.

Hirst, P. (1993) *Associative Democracy: New Forms of Economic and Social Governance*. Cambridge: Polity Press.

Jackall, R. (1988) *Moral Mazes: the World of Corporate Managers*. Oxford: Oxford University Press.

Jackson, N. and Carter, P. (1991) 'In defence of paradigm incommensurability', *Organization Studies*, 12(1): 109–27.

Johnson, T. (1993) 'Expertise and the state', in M. Gane and T. Johnson (eds), *Foucault's New Domains*. London: Routledge. pp. 139–52.

Jones, S. (1994) 'Many worlds – or, La ne sont pas des morts', *Organization*, 1(1): 203–17.

Kirkpatrick, I. and Martinez, M. (eds) (1995) *The Politics of Quality Management*. London: Routledge.

Knights, D. and Willmott, H. (1989) 'Power and subjectivity at work: from degradation to subjugation in social relations', *Sociology*, 23: 535–58.

Kondo, D. (1990) *Crafting Selves: Power, Gender, and Discourses of Identity in a Japanese Workplace*. Chicago: University of Chicago Press.

Kuhn, T. (1970) *The Structure of Scientific Revolutions*, 2nd edn. Chicago: University of Chicago Press.

Kumar, K. (1978) *Prophecy and Progress: the Sociology of Industrial and Post-Industrial Society*. London: Allen Lane.

Lakatos, I. and Musgrave, A. (1970) *Criticism and the Growth of Knowledge*. Cambridge: Cambridge University Press.

Lammers, C. and Szell, G. (eds) (1989) *International Handbook of Participation in Organizations*. Oxford: Oxford University Press.

Larson, M.S. (1979) *The Rise of Professionalism: a Sociological Analysis*. Berkeley: University of California Press.

Larson, M.S. (1990) 'In the matter of experts and professionals', in R. Torstendahl and M. Burrage (eds), *The Formation of Professions*. London: Sage. pp. 24–50.

Lash, S. and Urry, J. (1987) *The End of Organized Capitalism*. Cambridge: Polity Press.

Lash, S. and Urry, J. (1994) *Economies of Signs and Space*. London: Sage.

Law, J. (ed.) (1991) *A Sociology of Monsters: Essays on Power, Technology and Domination*. London: Routledge.

Law, J. (1994a) *Organizing Modernity*. Oxford: Blackwell.

Law, J. (1994b) 'Organization, narrative and strategy', in J. Hassard and M. Parker (eds), *Towards a New Theory of Organizations*. London: Routledge. pp. 248–68.

Lawrence, P. and Lorsch, J. (1967) *Organization and Environment*. Cambridge, MA: Harvard University Press.

Layder, D. (1994) *Understanding Social Theory*. London: Sage.

Lipset, S.M. (1960) *Political Man*. London: Macmillan.

Littler, C. (1990) 'The labour process debate: a theoretical review', in D. Knights and H. Willmott (eds), *Labour Process Theory*. London: Macmillan.

Lukes, S. (1974) *Power: a Radical View*. London: Macmillan.

Lyon, D. (1994) *The Electronic Eye: the Rise of Surveillance Society*. Cambridge: Polity Press.

March, J.G. (1988) *Decisions and Organizations*. Oxford: Basil Blackwell.

March, J.G. and Olsen, J.P. (1986) *Ambiguity and Choice in Organizations*. Bergen: Universitetsforlaget.

Martin, J. (1992) *Cultures in Organizations: Three Perspectives*. Oxford: Oxford University Press.

Martin, J. (1994) 'The organization of exclusion: institutionalization of sex inequality, gendered faculty jobs and gendered knowledge in organizational theory and research', *Organization*, 1(2): 401–31.

Massie, J. (1965) 'Management theory', in J.G. March (ed.), *Handbook of Organizations*. New York: Rand McNally.

Mayo, E. (1933) *The Human Problems of an Industrial Civilization*. London: Routledge.

Mayo, E. (1945) *The Social Problems of an Industrial Civilization*. London: Routledge.

Merkle, J. (1980) *Management and Ideology*. Berkeley: University of California Press.

Merton, R. (1949) *Social Theory and Social Structure*. New York: Collier Macmillan.

Meyer, J.W. and Scott, W.R. (1992) *Organizational Environments: Ritual and Rationality*. California: Sage.

Miller, E.J. and Rice, A.K. (1967) *Systems of Organizations*. London: Tavistock.

Miller, P. and O'Leary, T. (1989) 'Hierarchies and the American ideals, 1900–1940', *Academy of Management Review*, 14(2): 250–65.

Miller, P. and Rose, N. (1990) 'Governing economic life', *Economy and Society*, 19: 1–31.

Mills, A. and Tancred, P. (1992) *Gendering Organizational Analysis*. California: Sage.

Morgan, D. and Stanley, L. (1993) *Debates in Sociology*. Manchester: Manchester University Press.

Morgan, G. (1986) *Images of Organization*. California: Sage.

Morgan, G. (1990) *Organizations in Society*. London: Macmillan.

Mouzelis, N. (1967) *Organization and Bureaucracy*. London: Routledge and Kegan Paul.

Nichols, T. (1969) *Ownership, Control and Ideology*. London: Allen and Unwin.

Nkomo, S.M. (1992) 'The emperor has no clothes: rewriting "Race in Organizations"', *Academy of Management Review*, 17: 487–513.

Pareto, V. (1935) *The Mind and Society*. Cambridge, MA: Harvard University Press.

Parsons, T. (1956) 'Suggestions for a sociological approach to the theory of organization, I and II', *Administrative Science Quarterly*, 1(1/2): 63–85, 225–39.

Perrow, C. (1986) *Complex Organizations: a Critical Essay*, 3rd edn. New York: Random House.

Perry, N. (1992) 'Putting theory in its place: the social organization of organizational theorizing', in M. Reed and M. Hughes (eds), *Rethinking Organization: New Directions in Organization Theory and Analysis*. London: Sage. pp. 85–101.

Perry, N. (1994) 'Travelling theory/nomadic theorizing', *Organization*, 2(1): 35–54.

Pfeffer, J. (1993) 'Barriers to the advance of organizational science: paradigm development as a dependent variable', *Academy of Management Review*, 18(4): 599–620.

Piore, M. and Sabel, C. (1984) *The Second Industrial Divide*. New York: Basic Books.

Plant, G. (1973) *Hegel*. London: Allen and Unwin.

Powell, W.W. and DiMaggio, P.J. (eds) (1991) *The New Institutionalism in Organizational Analysis*. Chicago: University of Chicago Press.

Presthus, R. (1975) *The Organizational Society*, 2nd edn. New York: Random House.

Pugh, D. and Hickson, D. (eds) (1976) *Organizational Structure in its Context: the Aston Programme I*. Farnborough, Hants: Saxon House.

Putnam, H. (1978) *Meaning and the Moral Sciences*. London: Routledge and Kegan Paul.

Ramirez, M. (1994) 'The political economy of privatization in Mexico 1983–92', *Organization*, 2(1): 87–116.

Ray, L. and Reed, M. (1994) 'Max Weber and the dilemmas of modernity', in L. Ray and M. Reed (eds), *Organizing Modernity: Neo-Weberian Perspectives on Work, Organization and Society*. London: Routledge. pp. 158–97.

Reed, M. (1985) *Redirections in Organizational Analysis*. London: Tavistock.

Reed, M. (1992) *The Sociology of Organizations*. Hemel Hempstead: Harvester.

Reed, M. (1993) 'Organizations and modernity: continuity and discontinuity in organization theory', in J. Hassard and M. Parker (eds), *Postmodernism and Organizations*. London: Sage. pp. 163–82.

Reed, M. (1995) 'Managing quality and organizational politics: total quality management as a governmental technology', in I. Kirkpatrick and M. Martinez (eds), *The Politics of Quality Management*. London: Routledge.

Reed, M. and Anthony, P. (1992) 'Professionalizing management and managing professionalization: British management in the 1980s', *Journal of Management Studies*, 29(5): 591–614.

Reed, M. and Hughes, M. (eds) (1992) *Rethinking Organization: New Directions in Organization Theory and Analysis*. London: Sage.

Roethlisberger, F.J. and Dickson, W.J. (1939) *Management and the Worker*. Cambridge, MA: Harvard University Press.

Rose, M. (1975) *Industrial Behaviour: Theoretical Developments since Taylor*. London: Allen and Lane.

Rose, N. (1992) *Governing the Soul*. London: Routledge.

Rose, N. and Miller, P. (1990) 'Governing economic life', *Economy and Society* (1): 1–31.

Saint-Simon, H. (1958) *Social Organization, the Science of Man, and other Writings*. New York: Harper Torch.

Scarbrough, H. and Corbett, M.J. (1992) *Technology and Organization*. London: Routledge.

Selznick, P. (1949) *The TVA and the Grass Roots*. New York: Harper and Row.

Silberman, B.S. (1993) *Cages of Reason: the Rise of the Rational State in France, Japan, the United States, and Great Britain*. Chicago: University of Chicago Press.

Silver, J. (1987) 'The ideology of excellence: management and neo-conservativism', *Studies in Political Economy*, 24 (August): 105–29.

Silverman, D. (1970) *The Theory of Organizations*. London: Heinemann.

Simon, H. (1945) *Administrative Behaviour*. New York: Macmillan.

Simon, H. (1957) *The New Science of Management Decision*. New York: Harper.

Smart, B. (1992) *Modern Conditions, Postmodern Controversies*. London: Routledge.

Smith, D. (1988) *The Everyday World as Problematic*. Milton Keynes: Open University Press.

Smith, D. (1993) *The Rise of Historical Sociology*. Oxford: Polity Press.

Stinchcombe, A.L. (1965) 'Social structure and organizations', in J.G. March (ed.), *Handbook of Organizations*. Chicago: Rand McNally. pp. 142–93.

Stinchcombe, A.L. (1968) *Constructing Social Theories*. New York: Harcourt Brace.

Storing, H. (1962) 'The science of administration', in H. Storing (ed.), *Essays on the Scientific Study of Politics*. New York: Holt, Reinhart and Winston.

Stretton, H. (1969) *The Political Sciences*. London: Routledge.

Sztompka, P. (1993) *The Sociology of Social Change*. Oxford: Basil Blackwell.

Taylor, F.W. (1912) *Principles of Scientific Management*. New York: Harper.

Thompson, E.P. (1978) *The Poverty of Theory and Other Essays*. London: Merlin.

Thompson, J.D. (1967) *Organizations in Action*. New York: McGraw-Hill.

Thompson, P. (1989) *The Nature of Work*, 2nd edn. London: Macmillan.

Thompson, P. (1993) 'Postmodernism: fatal distraction', in J. Hassard and M. Parker (eds), *Towards a New Theory of Organizations*. London: Routledge. pp. 183–203.

Thompson, P. and McHugh, D. (1990) *Organizations: a Critical Introduction*. London: Macmillan.

Toulmin, S. (1972) *Human Understanding*, vol. 1. Princeton: Princeton University Press.

Urwick, L. and Brech, E. (1947) *The Making of*

Scientific Management. London: Management Publications.

Waldo, D. (1948) *The Administrative State*. New York: Knopf.

Weber, M. (1978) *Economy and Society: an Outline of Intepretative Sociology*. Vols 1 and 2. Berkeley: University of California Press.

Webster, F. and Robins, K. (1993) 'I'll be watching you: comment on Sewell and Wilkinson', *Sociology*, 27(2): 243–52.

Weinberg, I. (1969) 'The problem of convergence of industrial societies: a critical look at the state of a theory', *Comparative Studies in Society and History*, 11(1): 1–15.

Whitley, R. (ed.) (1992) *European Business Systems*. London: Sage.

Whittington, R. (1994) 'Sociological pluralism, institutions and managerial agency', in J. Hassard and M. Parker (eds), *Towards a New Theory of Organizations*. London: Routledge. pp. 53–74.

Williamson, O.E. (1975) *Markets and Hierarchies: Analysis and Antitrust Implications*. New York: Free Press.

Williamson, O.E. (1990) *Organization Theory: from Chester Barnard to the Present and Beyond*. New York: Oxford University Press.

Williamson, O.E. and Winter, S.G. (1991) *The Nature of the Firm*. New York: Oxford University Press.

Willman, P. (1983) 'The organizational failures framework and industrial sociology', in A. Francis, J. Turk and P. Willman (eds), *Power, Efficiency and Institutions*. London: Heinemann. pp. 117–36.

Willmott, H. (1993) 'Breaking the paradigm mentality', *Organization Studies*, 14(5): 681–719.

Willmott, H. (1994) 'Bringing agency (back) into organizational analysis: responding to the crisis of postmodernity', in J. Hassard and M. Parker (eds), *Towards a New Theory of Organizations*. London: Routledge. pp. 87–130.

Witz, A. and Savage, M. (1992) 'The gender of organizations', in M. Savage and A. Witz (eds), *Gender and Bureaucracy*. Oxford: Basil Blackwell. pp. 3–64.

Wolin, S. (1961) *Politics and Vision*. London: Allen and Unwin.

Wolin, S. (1988) 'On the theory and practice of power', in J. Arac (ed.), *After Foucault: Humanistic Knowledge, Postmodern Challenges*. New Brunswick, NJ: Rutgers University Press. pp. 179–201.

Woodward, J. (1970) *Industrial Organization: Behaviour and Control*. Oxford: Oxford University Press.

Wrong, D. (1978) *Power: its Forms, Bases and Uses*. Oxford: Basil Blackwell.

Zuboff, S. (1988) *In the Age of the Smart Machine*. London: Heinemann.

1.2

The Normal Science of Structural Contingency Theory

LEX DONALDSON

Within organization studies, contingency theory has provided a coherent paradigm for the analysis of the structure of organizations. The paradigm has constituted a framework in which research progressed leading to the construction of a scientific body of knowledge. The task of this chapter is to outline the contingency theory of organizational structure and show how research within this paradigm has proceeded in a normal science mode.

The recurrent set of relationships between organizational members can be considered to be the structure of the organization. This includes, but is not restricted to: the authority relationships, the reporting relationships as signified in the organization chart, the behaviours required by organizational rules, the patterns in decision-making such as decentralization, patterns of communication and other behaviour patterns. It embraces both the officially prescribed formal organization and the *de facto*, unofficial, informal organization (Pennings 1992). There is no definition of organizational structure that tightly circumscribes its subject matter *a priori*; rather the research projects each look at various, different aspects of organizational structure without claiming their focus to be exhaustive.

Contingency theory states that there is no single organizational structure that is highly effective for all organizations. It sees the structure that is optimal as varying according to certain factors such as organizational strategy or size. Thus the optimal structure is contingent upon these factors which are termed the *contingency* factors. For example, a small-sized organization, one that has few employees, is optimally structured by a centralized structure in which decision-making authority is concentrated at the top of the hierarchy, whereas a large organization, one that has many employees, is optimally structured by a decentralized structure in which decision-making authority is dispersed down to lower levels of the hierarchy (Child 1973; Pugh et al. 1969). There are several contingency factors: strategy, size, task uncertainty and technology. These are characteristics of the organization. However, these organizational characteristics in turn reflect the influence of the environment in which the organization is located. Thus, in order to be effective, the organization needs to fit its structure to the contingency factors of the organization and thus to the environment. Hence the organization is seen as adapting to its environment.

Each of the different aspects of the organizational structure is contingent upon one or more of the contingency factors. Thus the task of contingency research is to identify the particular contingency factor or factors to which each particular aspect of organizational structure needs to fit. This involves the construction of theoretical models of fits between contingency and structural factors and their testing against empirical data. The empirical data usually consist of data comparing different organizations as to their contingencies and structures. The contingency theory of organizational structure will be termed here 'structural contingency theory' (Pfeffer 1982).

Kuhn (1970) argues that scientific research proceeds within the framework of a paradigm, which specifies the core theoretical ideas, the assumptions, language, method and conventions. The growth of a body of knowledge is marked by paradigm revolutions, when one paradigm is overthrown and replaced by another. Such discontinuous changes are radical and infrequent. Most of the time science proceeds in a normal science phase guided by the ruling paradigm. In such a phase research works on problems within the body of work, such as resolving anomalies, while leaving the paradigm itself unquestioned.

The study of organizational structure witnessed a paradigm change when the classical management school was overthrown by the new paradigm of contingency theory, as will be seen below. This inaugurated an era of normal science research within the contingency paradigm. However, other paradigms arose subsequently that sharply question the contingency paradigm (Scott 1992). Thus the study of organizational structure is presently pluralistic with conflict between paradigms and normal science within the paradigms (Aldrich 1992; Donaldson 1985a, 1995a; Pfeffer 1993). Since other chapters in this *Handbook* deal with other paradigms we will here concentrate on the contingency paradigm. The normal science that has been pursued within the contingency paradigm is probably the largest single normal science research stream in the study of organizational structure to date. Thus in discussing the contingency paradigm there is a considerable volume of normal science research to report. Hence the concept of normal science in organizational studies is quite well illustrated by the work within the contingency theory of organizational structure (see also Donaldson 1996).

ORIGINS OF STRUCTURAL CONTINGENCY THEORY

Up until about the late 1950s academic writing about organizational structure was dominated by the classical management school. This held that there was a single organizational structure that was highly effective in organizations of all kinds. This structure was distinguished by a high degree of decision-making and planning at the top of the hierarchy so that the behaviour of lower hierarchical levels and of operations was specified in detail in advance by senior management, through job definitions, work study and the like (Brech 1957).

The classical management school held sway for the first half of this century, but was challenged increasingly from the 1930s onwards by the human relations school. This approach focused on the individual employee as possessing psychological and social needs. An understanding of these would allow an appreciation of how

work organization emerged from the interplay of group dynamics (Roethlisberger and Dickson 1939). This would enable managers to adopt a more considerate approach that would elicit employee cooperation. The focus here was on the bottom-up processes of organizing and the benefits of participation in decision-making by employees from lower levels of the hierarchy (Likert 1961). There were attempts to bring together these two antithetical approaches of classical management and human relations by arguing that each approach had its place. Thus contingency theories developed in the 1950s and 1960s on topics such as small-group decision-making and leadership (see Vroom and Yetton 1973). Around the end of the 1950s scholars began to apply this contingency idea to organizational structures.

The key idea in the small group literature was that group problem-solving was accomplished effectively in a centralized structure when the task was relatively certain but required a less centralized and more richly joined structure where the task was uncertain in order to generate and communicate the larger amount of knowledge and communications needed (Pennings 1992: 276). Applied to whole organization structures this is equivalent to a hierarchy which centralizes expertise, communications and control for tasks low in uncertainty and a flexible, participatory team network for tasks which are high on uncertainty. A major way to have a low uncertainty task is to do the same thing repeatedly by avoiding innovation. Thus innovation becomes a major underlying contingency factor of the task uncertainty contingency. Increasing scale can lead to low task uncertainty, in that scale often involves repetition, such as mass production.

Scale also leads to increasing numbers of employees which in turn leads to specialization. This narrows the scope of each job so that it becomes less varied and complex, which in turn lowers the uncertainty of the task. These low uncertainty, repetitive tasks are amenable to bureaucratic formalization such that they are pre-specified in job descriptions, standard operating procedures, rules and training. This bureaucratization further reduces the uncertainty of those performing the tasks. Thus task uncertainty is the core contingency concept that has implications for second-order contingency concepts such as innovation and size.

Much of the significance of task uncertainty resides in the insight that the more uncertain the task the more information that has to be processed and this in turn shapes the communications and control structures (Galbraith 1973). The more uncertain the task, the less the work activities can be scheduled in advance and the more the reliance on ad hoc arrangements. Moreover, organizations often have to deal with uncertainty by utilising diverse bodies of expertise and this requires departure from deference to hierarchy as some of the expertise may be possessed by those at lower hierarchical levels. Some part of these experts may be professionals and this tends to amplify the shift away from hierarchical control of employees.

The core assumption of structural contingency theory is that low uncertainty tasks are most effectively performed by centralized hierarchy since this is simple, quick and allows close coordination cheaply. As task uncertainty increases, through innovation or the like, then the hierarchy needs to loosen control somewhat and be overlain by participatory, communicative structures. This reduces structural simplicity and raises costs but is rewarded by the benefits from innovation. As size increases the compact, simple centralized structure is replaced by a bureaucracy featuring a tall hierarchy and extensive specialization. This bureaucracy allows decentralization because employees are increasingly controlled through formalization (e.g. rules) and decentralization is increasingly required because the increase in scale, internal structural complexity and length of hierarchy makes centralization infeasible. Bureaucracy brings disbenefits through rigidity, dysfunctions and some loss of control, but these are more than out-weighed by the increase in predictability, lower average wages, reduction in managerial overhead and increasing computerization which bureaucratization also brings. As the organization increases the range and complexity of its outputs, that is products or services, or increases its geographical extensiveness, such as through becoming a multinational, so it further increases its structural complexity and decentralization, through adoption of a divisional or matrix structure.

This then is the framework that provides the underlying theoretical unity of the ideas composing structural contingency. Such a totalizing vision is possible in retrospect, but the theory was developed in more piecemeal fashion, through breakthroughs that identified a connection between a particular contingency factor or factors and a structural factor or factors. These theoretical insights were typically advanced in studies that offered empirical support through field studies of actual organizations.

The seminal statement that pioneered the contingency approach to organizational structure was by Burns and Stalker (1961). They distinguished between the mechanistic structure in which organizational roles were tightly defined by superiors who had the monopoly of organizational knowledge, and the organic structure in which organizational roles were loosely defined and arrived at by mutual discussion between employees, with knowledge being dispersed among the employees who possessed varieties of expertise germane to the organizational mission. Burns and Stalker (1961) argued that where an organization faces a stable environment then the mechanistic structure is effective but where the organization faces a high level of technological and market change then the organic structure is required. The mechanistic structure becomes counter-productive where a high rate of innovation is needed; the resulting high uncertainty of the environment and of the tasks in the organization means that spontaneous cooperation within teams of experts, that is, the organic structure, is more effective.

The Burns and Stalker (1961) theory was advanced in a book that gave extensive illustrations from qualitative case studies of the electronics industry. This is probably the most widely received contribution in the structural contingency theory literature. It provided in one stroke a synthesis between classical management and human relations schools in the mechanistic and organic structures, respectively. It resolved the debate between them with the compromise that each was valid in its own place. It also gave primacy to task uncertainty, driven by innovation, as the contingency factor.

At about the same time as Burns and Stalker, Woodward (1958; 1965) conducted a comparative survey study of one hundred manufacturing organizations. She examined their organizational structures and found them to be unrelated to the size of their organizations. Operations technology emerged as the key correlate of organizational structure (Woodward 1965). Where production technology was primitive, with single articles or small batches being made, often mainly by hand and involving craft skills, for example, musical instruments, the organization was fairly informal and organic. Where production technology had advanced to large-batch and mass production using more specialized machinery, such as in automobile assembly, work organization was more formalized and mechanistic and more according to the prescriptions of classical management. However, with further technological advance to more capital intensive and automated production so that product flowed continuously, such as oil in an oil refinery, the regimentation of mass production gave way to work teams run on organic and human relations lines. The progressively greater predictability of the technical system and the smoothness of production as technology advanced led first to more mechanistic and then to more organic structures.

The Woodward (1965) model was more

complex than that of Burns and Stalker (1961), being of three rather than two stages. However, it shared a similar conceptualization of structure, as mechanistic or organic, and had some similarity in contingency factor in that technologically induced uncertainty was a commonality. Moreover, Woodward, like Burns and Stalker, held that the future belonged to the organic, human relations, style of management and that this would be forced upon management by technological change. The task of research and academic writing in this approach was to bring these models and findings to the attention of managers so that they could avoid the inefficiencies that both Woodward (1965) and Burns and Stalker (1961) depicted resulted from failure to adapt organizational structure to technological change rapidly enough.

Unlike Burns and Stalker (1961), Woodward (1958; 1965) used quantitative measures of organizational structure, such as the span of control of the first line supervisor, the number of levels of management in the hierarchy and the ratio of direct to indirect labour. Woodward (1965) gives many quantitative results showing associations between operations technology and various aspects of organizational structure. There is also one table (1965: 69, Table 4) which shows not only an association between technology and an aspect of organizational structure (average span of control of the first line supervisor), but also that organizations which conform to the association had high performance and organizations which deviated had lower performance. Woodward (1965) argued that where the organizational structure fits the organizational technology this caused superior performance to those organizations whose organizational structure is in misfit to the technology.

Burns and Stalker and Woodward worked in the UK. Pioneering contributions came also from the US. Lawrence and Lorsch (1967) have been credited with initiating the term 'contingency theory' to identify the then fledgling approach to which they made a major contribution. They theorized that the rate of environmental change affected the differentiation and integration of the organization. Greater rates of environmental change require certain parts of the organization, such as the R&D department, to face high levels of uncertainty relative to other parts, such as the production department. This leads to large differences in structure and culture between departments, with R&D being more organic internally and production being more mechanistic. This greater differentiation makes coordination between these two departments, for instance to innovate a new product, more problematic. The solution is higher levels of integration provided by more integrating personnel in project teams and the like, coupled with interpersonal processes that defuse conflict through taking a problem-solving approach. Lawrence and Lorsch (1967) advanced their theory in a comparative study of different organizations in three industries: containers, processed foods and plastics. They demonstrated also that organizations whose structures fitted their environments had higher performance.

Hage (1965) advanced an axiomatic theory of organizations, similar to Burns and Stalker, in which centralized, formalized organizations produced high efficiency but low innovation rates while decentralized, less formalized organizations produced low efficiency but high innovation rates. Thus which structure was optimal depended upon whether efficiency or innovation was the organizational objective. Hage and Aiken (1967; 1969) demonstrated the validity of the theory in a study of health and welfare organizations.

Perrow (1967) argued that knowledge technology was a contingency of organizational structure. The more codified the knowledge used in the organization and the fewer the exceptions encountered in operations, the more the organization could be centralized in decision-making.

Thompson (1967) advanced a book-length theory of organizations containing many theoretical ideas and propositions. He distinguished closed system organizations versus organizations which are open systems transacting with their environments. He argued that organizations attempt to insulate their core production technologies into a closed system to render them efficient through buffering the core from the environment. External perturbations are dealt with by forecasting, inventories and other mechanisms. Thompson (1967) distinguished also three different technologies: long-linked, mediating and intensive. Moreover, he distinguished three different levels of interdependence between activities in the workflow – pooled, sequential and reciprocal – and identified the differing coordination mechanisms to handle each interdependency. He theorized that interdependencies between activities in the organizational workflow had to be handled at different hierarchical levels, thus generating the design of the organization. Thompson (1967) further argued that the environment directly shaped the organizational structure, with different parts of the organizational structure being specialized to conform to the requirements of different parts of the environment. Thompson theorized also about organizational politics, as had Burns and Stalker and Perrow. The main focus of contingency theory, however, remained upon the way the organizational structure was shaped so as to meet the needs of the environment and the resulting tasks (see Donaldson 1996).

In the US, Blau (1970) advanced a theory of structural differentiation. This asserted that as an organization grows in size (employees) so it structures itself more elaborately into increasingly numerous sub-units, such as more divisions, more sections per division, more levels in the hierarchy and so on. He also argued that organizational growth leads to greater economies of scale with the proportion of employees who are managers or support staff declining.

Weber (1968) argued that organizations were becoming increasingly bureaucratic structures, characterized by impersonal administration, fostered in part by their increasing size. In the UK, the Aston Group (named after their university) argued the need to improve the measurement of organizational structure (Pugh et al. 1963). They developed a large number of quantitative measures of different aspects of organizational structure, with attention to reliability (Pugh et al. 1968; Pugh and Hickson 1976). The Aston Group surveyed organizations of diverse types, spanning manufacturing and service organizations and public and private sectors. They empirically distinguished two main dimensions of organizational structure: structuring of activities (how far the organization adopts specialization by function, rules and documents) and concentration of authority (centralization of decision-making) (Pugh et al. 1968). They examined a large number of contingency factors and used multiple regression to identify the distinct set of predictors of organizational structure. For structuring the main contingency was organizational size (number of employees): larger organizations are more structured (Pugh et al. 1969). For centralization the main contingencies were organizational size and whether or not the organization under study was a subsidiary of a parent organization: decentralization is higher in larger organizations which are independent (Pugh et al. 1969).

A further structural contingency theory focuses on the implications of the contingency of corporate strategy for the organizational structure of business corporations. Chandler (1962) showed historically that strategy leads to structure. Corporations need to maintain a fit between their strategy and their structure otherwise they suffer lower performance. Specifically, a functional structure fits an undiversified strategy, but is a misfit for a diversified strategy where a multidivisional structure is required for effective management of the complexity of several distinct product markets (Chandler 1962). Other researchers analysed the significance for its structure of an organization going from

operating only domestically to being a multinational (Stopford and Wells 1972; Egelhoff 1988; Ghoshal and Nohria 1989). This leads to adoption of structures such as area divisions and product-area matrices. Egelhoff (1988), in particular, advances a formal contingency theory based on the underlying information-processing requirements.

Other contingency factors, such as environmental hostility (Khandwalla 1977) and product life-cycle (Donaldson 1985b), have been identified, and their implications for organizational structure theorized. For a model prescribing the optimal organization design required by the combination of the strategy and innovation contingencies see Donaldson (1985a; 171).

THE STRUCTURAL CONTINGENCY THEORY MODEL

Increases in the innovation rate of a firm may reflect competition from other firms through new products, so the ultimate cause is the environment. For this reason the contingency approach is often termed 'the organization in its environment approach'. However, the environmental innovation leads the organization to raise its rate of intended innovation which is the immediate cause of the adoption of an organic structure. Thus the structure is caused directly by the internal factor and only indirectly by the environment. Both the internal and the environmental factors are referred to as contingencies but a more parsimonious statement of structural contingency theory would need refer only to the internal factor. Therefore, many contingency factors of structure such as organizational size or technology are internal to the organization, though they reflect the environment such as population size or commercially available technologies. Thus while it is correct to include the environmental factors as contingencies shaping structure a sufficient explanation may be obtained by considering only the internal factors as contingencies.

The import of the contingency theory may be summarized briefly in the following way. A small organization, one with few employees, is organized effectively in a simple structure (Mintzberg 1979) in which there are few levels in the hierarchy. Decision-making authority is concentrated in the top manager (who is often the owner in a small firm) who exercises power directly over the lower-level employees by directly instructing them. Thus there is little delegation of authority and there is also little specialization among the employees. As the organization grows in size, especially in the number of employees, the structure becomes more differentiated. Many more levels are added in the hierarchy, creating tiers of middle managers. Some of the decision-making authority of the top managers is delegated down to them, commensurate with their greater knowledge of local, operational matters, such as direction of lower-level personnel and some decisions on production. This delegation is to a degree forced upon senior managers by the increasing burden of decisions that they are facing as organizational size and complexity increases. Again the growth of hierarchy and the geographic spread of personnel makes senior management remote from 'the firing line' and so it becomes infeasible for them to access all the required information. However, senior managers retain decision-making over strategy, policy and large decisions, including capital allocation and budget amounts.

Throughout the organization there is a greater division of labour as operations are broken down into their components and allocated to specific departments and work-groups. Administration is also increasingly broken into specializations each handled by distinct staff roles such as accounting, production planning, records, personnel and so on. Behaviour is increasingly regulated by written job descriptions, plans, procedures and rules. These constitute an impersonal web regulating organizational members, so that control shifts from direct, personal supervision to impersonal devices. At the extreme in the large organization, its structure is a machine bureaucracy (Mintzberg 1979). The increase in scale and specialization means that the work of any one individual becomes more routine and this facilitates its bureaucratic formalization, which in turn heightens the routineness and predictability of the work. The greater formalization and predictability of employee behaviour encourages the senior levels to increase their delegation of authority down to lower levels as they can do so with more confidence that such discretion will be used as the senior levels intend, though such control is imperfect as bureaucratic dysfunctions arise (Gouldner 1954; Merton 1949). The greater specialization of personnel increase their competence, which again fosters delegation, though again with some hazards (Selznick 1957).

As organizations seek to innovate, in products or services or production processes, so this entails more uncertain tasks. These tasks cannot be formalized by the bureaucracy i.e. the tasks cannot be pre-specified in advance in a rule or procedure because this would require knowledge that the bureaucrats do not possess. Thus there is recourse to trial and error learning often accompanied by employment of more educated and higher trained employees such as professionals. The organization has to allow them discretion and encourage them to use their initiative, with the actual division of labour involving team elements and emerging through discussion between employees rather than being imposed by hierarchical superiors. This means that the R&D departments are structured more organically than the typical production department. While R&D design the new offering, the production operations department makes it and sales sells it. The dove-tailing of these requirements means that successful innovation needs coordination across these departments and this is achieved by cross-functional project teams or matrices or product divisions (depending upon the other contingencies such as the degree of strategic diversification, see Donaldson 1985b).

As the firm diversifies from a single product or service to multiple products or services, so the original functional structure becomes overwhelmed by the complexity of decision-making. A multidivisional structure allows this complexity to be factored down so that each division makes the decisions for its own product-market. This improves the expertise and speed of the decision-making and relieves the top management of overload, allowing them to concentrate on strategic decisions and more selective interventions in the divisions. The centre retains overall control through treating the divisions as profit centres and creating a corporate staff to monitor divisional performance and plan corporate strategy. Thus the organization, if large and diversified, becomes even more bureaucratic and more decentralized.

This in brief is the contingency theory model of the way organizational structure changes as the contingencies change through growth.

THE STRUCTURAL CONTINGENCY RESEARCH PARADIGM

Almost all of this pioneering structural contingency research was published between 1960 and 1970 and was the fruit of a burst of research conducted mainly in the 1960s. Thus by 1970 there was a well-established research paradigm.

The theory is sociological functionalism (Burrell and Morgan 1979). Just as biological functionalism explains the way the organs of the human body are structured so as to contribute to human well-being, so sociological functionalism explains social structures by their functions, that is their contributions to the well-being of society (Merton 1949; 1975; Parsons 1951; 1964). The organizational sociological branch of functionalism posits that organizational structures are shaped so as to provide for effective functioning by the organization (Pennings 1992). Structural functional organizational theory proceeds in the following way. Variations in organizational structures are identified. These are explained by each different organizational structure functioning effectively in its situation. The structure fits the contingency which in turn fits the environment. Fit is the underlying key. Organizations move into fit by adjusting their structure to their contingencies and this produces the observed association between contingency and structure. The emphasis on the adaptation by the organization to its environment makes structural contingency theory part of adaptive functionalism.

The functionalist theoretical base has meant that the contingency paradigm can be pursued both by sociologists interested only in the explanation of organizational structure, for whom the functionality of a structure is purely a cause, and management theorists for whom the effectiveness outcomes of structures inform their prescriptive advice to managers. In the history of contingency theory both values have motivated researchers (Hickson, personal communication).

The method used in contingency research tended to follow that used by Woodward (1965). A comparative study is made across a number of different organizations (or across different subunits within the same organization if they are the object of theoretical interest). Each contingency and structural factor is measured, either as a quantitative scale or as a series of ordered categories. Each organization is allotted a score on each contingency and structural factor. The cross-distribution of scores of the organizations on a pair of contingency and structural factors is then examined to see whether there is an association; this is done by cross-tabulation or correlation. The theory that associations between contingency and structure reflect an underlying fit is then tested. Organizations conforming to the association are contrasted with those that deviate. If the conforming organizations outperform the deviant organizations then this signifies that the association is a fit between contingency and structure. Thus in much research the empirical association is taken as approximating the fit (Child 1975; Drazin and Van de Ven 1985; Woodward 1965); however in other research the fit model is derived from theory (Alexander and Randolph 1985; Donaldson 1987). It is desirable to unite the empirically and theoretically derived fit models over the course of the research programme.

As the research progressed it became more sophisticated in at least four senses. Firstly, increasing attention was paid to the operational definitions of concepts. For example, Woodward (1965) measured organizational performance in a vague way. Later researchers were more precise and recorded their definitions more explicitly, for example Child (1974). Secondly, there was increasing attention to reliability of measurement. Woodward (1965) did not report the reliability of her measurements and used approaches that yield low reliability, such as single item measures. Later researchers sought to boost reliability by using multiple item measures, for example the Aston Group (Pugh et al. 1968). It is now commonplace among research reported in the better journals to report the reliabilities of variables. Thirdly, the theoretical models used to explain any particular aspect of organizational structure went from using one contingency factor, for example technology in Woodward (1965), to using several, such as in Pugh et al. (1969), that is from mono-causality to multi-causality. Fourthly, the analysis of data uses more sophisticated statistics. Woodward (1965) used only simple statistics whereas, by the late 1960s, multivariate statistics and statistics that took account of sample size were being used (e.g. Pugh et al. 1969).

Pioneering structural contingency theory work often used surveys of organizations at one point in time, that is a cross-sectional method. From these data inferences were made that causation flowed in particular ways, that is from contingency to structure. This adaptive functionalist interpretation is a convention in structural contingency research. Nevertheless, the correlational method left room for other causal interpretations. For example, Aldrich (1972) re-analysed the Aston data and argued the correlations were compatible with a model in which structure caused size – the opposite of the causal interpretation advanced by the Aston Group (Pugh et al. 1969). These alternative interpretations constitute challenges to the paradigm. There has been some progress in resolving some of these questions of causality in favour of contingency determinism, as will be seen below.

The theory and empirical evidence deployed in the structural contingency theory paradigm are positivist. The organization is seen as being forced to adjust its structure to material factors such as size and technology. Ideas and values do not figure prominently as causes. Moreover, little scope is seen for choice or human volition. There is little information in most contingency analyses about who exactly makes the structural decisions or what their motives are or how the structures are implemented (Pugh et al. 1969; Blau and Schoenherr 1971). Thus the analysis is depersonalized and at the level of the organization as a collective entity pursuing its objectives. There is thus the absence of an analysis at the level of the human actors (Pennings 1992). Such an analysis would identify actors in the processes of redesigning organizations, their beliefs, ideals, values, interests, power and tactics. Much of the criticism from outside of the paradigm revolves around the perceived neglect of an action-level analysis in structural contingency theory research (Silverman 1970). Indeed the validity of talking about 'the organization' rather than the individuals that compose the organization has been challenged sociologically and philosophically (Silverman 1970). However, Donaldson (1985a) has offered a defence of organizational-level constructs, arguing that they are cogent and indispensable in organization theory. Key phenomena such as organizational centralization and organizational performance cannot even be discussed unless a collectivity-level analysis of the organization as a system is made (see also Donaldson 1990).

The adaptive functionalism, contingency-fit model and comparative method constitute the core of the paradigm of structural contingency theory. They provide a framework in which subsequent researchers work.

THE NORMAL SCIENCE PHASE: REPLICATION AND GENERALIZATION

By about 1970 there was an established contingency theory paradigm and those coming afterward could orientate their efforts within this tradition and contribute to its evolving literature (for a collection see Donaldson 1995b).

The pioneering contingency studies had produced evidence of connections between contingencies and organizational structure, but these might be flukes or idiosyncrasies or reflect biases of their authors. Therefore there was a need for replication, that is for studies by other, independent researchers to see whether or not they found the same phenomena. Replication studies are seldom on the same organizations, so the studies provide also a test of generalization, that is whether the original findings hold in studies of new organizations, in settings that differ in some way, such as type of organization or country, from the pioneering studies (Fletcher 1970). For instance, during the 1970s there arose an interest in whether different national cultures require different forms of organizational structure that render the general structural contingency theories false (Hickson et al. 1974;

Lammers and Hickson 1979; Mansfield and Poole 1981; McMillan et al. 1973). This interest continues through to the 1990s and has spawned a great deal of research in the intervening period (as examples, Conaty et al. 1983; Hickson and McMillan 1981; Routamaa 1985). The initial orientation of most researchers is that they expect that they may find the contingency–structure relations of the pioneering studies but that such general assertions are to be treated cautiously until verified empirically in each particular, new setting. The studies of replication and generalization constitutes much of the normal science research in the structural contingency literature.

The Aston Group gave emphasis to replication (Child 1972a; Hinings and Lee 1971; Inkson et al. 1970). The multiple dimensions of organizational structure found in the pioneering study were not found in some replication studies, some of which found a single main dimension (Child 1972a; Grinyer and Yasai-Ardekani 1980; 1981; Hinings and Lee 1971). This is a major difference in the Aston Group literature and there have been attempts to resolve it, through examination of method issues, such as the measurement of the variable and whether the status of the organization (as between independent or dependent) affects the results (Donaldson et al. 1975; Greenwood and Hinings 1976; Mansfield 1973; see also Reimann 1973; Starbuck 1981). The different findings are seen as supporting different theoretical views and as refuting or confirming Weber (1968).

In contrast, the main contingency–structure findings of the original study have been supported: size is the major contingency of the bureaucratic structuring of the activities aspect of organizational structure. Replication studies bear this out (Pugh and Hinings 1976). Further studies show that this finding generalizes across organizations of many types and nations in diverse locations. For example, Donaldson (1986: 74) reviews thirty-five studies of the relation between the contingency of organizational size and the structural variable of degree of specialization by function; all the studies found a positive correlation. The studies include organizations from fifteen countries: Algeria, Canada, Egypt, Finland, France, Germany, India, Iran, Japan, Jordan, Poland, Singapore, Sweden, the UK and the USA (respectively, Zeffane 1989; Hickson et al. 1974; Badran and Hinings 1981; Routamaa 1985; Zeffane 1989; Child and Kieser 1979; Shenoy 1981; Conaty et al. 1983; Azumi and McMillan 1981; Ayoubi 1981; Kuc et al. 1981; Tai 1987; Horvath et al. 1981; Bryman et al. 1983; Blau et al. 1976). Thus the size-functional specialization relationships generalizes globally and is not confined to Anglo-

Saxon nations such as the UK or the USA where these sorts of relationship were originally identified (for a review see Donaldson 1996).

Causal Dynamics

The discussion thus far has concentrated on the results mainly from cross-sectional studies that correlate contingency and structure at the same point in time. The contingency literature interprets these associations according to its own theoretical paradigm of adaptive functionalism and contingency determinism. The question arises as to whether this interpretation is correct.

Each of the major theories in structural contingency theory focuses on only certain couplings of contingency and structural factors (for example, size and bureaucracy or strategy and structure); indeed, critics object that there is no singular contingency theory, only a collection of contingency theories that constitute at best a contingency approach. However, it is possible to abstract from these disparate offerings one common, underlying theory. This may be termed the structural adaptation to regain fit (SARFIT) theory (Donaldson 1987). This holds that there is fit between each contingency and one (or more) aspect of organizational structure such that fit positively affects performance and misfit negatively affects performance. An organization initially in fit changes its contingency and thereby moves into misfit and suffers declining performance: this causes adoption of a new structure so that fit is regained and performance restored. Hence the cycle of adaptation is: fit, contingency change, misfit, structural adaptation, new fit. This causal model underlies many structural contingency theories (Burns and Stalker 1961; Lawrence and Lorsch 1967; Williamson 1970; 1971; Woodward 1965).

Commentators have argued against the SARFIT type of idea and have contested each component part. They reason that the correlations between contingencies and structure signify causal processes different to those in the SARFIT model (Aldrich 1972). The errors or uncertainties in theoretical interpretation are seen as made possible by limitations in the cross-sectional method. The call is made by commentators for structural contingency theory studies to move beyond cross-sectional or synchronic research designs into those that study organizational change through time, that is longitudinal or diachronic studies (Mansfield and Poole 1981; Galunic and Eisenhardt 1994). Thus part of normal science has been the move to make studies through time in order to reveal the actual causal paths.

The topic area of strategy and structure has been studied in greater detail and so is a suitable one to examine for causality.

Dynamics of Strategy and Structure

The explanation of the correlations between strategy and structure is the functionalist theory that there is a fit between certain strategies and certain structures (Chandler 1962). Research into performance has initially focused on whether divisional structures outperform functional structures (for example, Armour and Teece 1978). However, this is not the same as contingency theory, which holds that it is not the structure *per se* but rather whether or not it fits the strategy, that is salient for performance. This requires the operationalization of a model that specifies certain combinations of strategy and structure as fits and other combinations as misfits. Donaldson (1987) advanced such a model drawing on the work of Chandler (1962) and others.

Corporations in fit are shown to outperform those in misfit, providing empirical validation (Donaldson 1987). Moreover, fit is at a period prior to performance, adding confidence that fit is a cause and performance an effect. Hamilton and Shergill (1992; 1993) have also empirically validated a very similar fit model by showing that it relates positively to performance. Organizations in fit for a number of years have superior growth in performance during those years to those in misfit over the same period. This means that being in fit leads to increasing performance and so fit should be seen as a cause and performance as a consequence. Hill et al. (1992) have also shown that the fit of strategy and structure is positively related to performance. Thus the proposition that the fit between strategy and structure affects performance receives support and some of this is from research in which the temporal dimension lends support to the causal inference that fit affects performance. The functionalist theory that corporations align their structure with their strategy because of the underlying fit is supported empirically.

Some studies of organizational change have sought for a correlation between contingency change and structural change, during the same time period or the immediately following time period. Their results have been mixed and have tended to throw into doubt structural contingency theory (Dewar and Hage 1978; Dyas and Thanheiser 1976; Inkson et al. 1970; Meyer 1979). While contingency theory states that contingency causes structure, this is the long-run effect which flows through intermediary stages such as misfit. Thus contingency change initially only leads to misfit which eventually leads to structural change and new fit. This more elongated and closely specified causal model better represents structural contingency theory. This should be the subject of empirical tests in studies of organizational change.

Donaldson (1987) combined data from studies of strategy and structure in five countries (France, Germany, Japan, the UK and the USA). First the data were analysed in the traditional way: an association was sought between change in the contingency of strategy and change in structure in the immediately following period. There was no positive strategy–structure association (1987: 13), thus reproducing the null finding of previous studies of organizational change.

Then the data were analysed by examining each of the separate stages of the SARFIT model and this was confirmed. Of the 87 corporations that moved from fit into misfit, 83 per cent did so by changing their level of the contingency of strategy, typically by diversifying (1987: 14). Thus the cycle of structural adaptation is initiated by contingency change, as SARFIT holds. Turning to the second step in the SARFIT model, the data were analysed to see whether misfit led to structural change. Of those corporations in misfit 39 per cent subsequently changed their structure, whereas of those in fit only 9 per cent did so (1987: 14). This confirms that misfit causes structural change. Of the corporations that changed their structure, 72 per cent moved from misfit into fit and only 5 per cent moved from fit into misfit (1987: 14). Thus the structural change was overwhelmingly adaptive, that is, adoption of the divisional structure to fit with the more diversified corporate strategy. Hence the misfit causes structural adaptation as SARFIT holds. Thus each separate stage of the SARFIT model was validated.

When organizational change is examined by a model that more accurately captures the full processes involved in structural adaptation then structural contingency theory is confirmed. Where the simplistic model that contingency change leads to structural change is used to analyse data it leads to the erroneous conclusion that structural contingency theory is not supported. This is normal science at work: resolving findings contrary to theory by showing that the empirical testing procedure was erroneous, in this case by not examining a properly articulated model of the theory.

Contingency theory holds that strategy leads to structure. However, Hall and Saias (1980) argue that structure leads to strategy. Bourgeois (1984) criticizes contingency research for failing to consider reverse causation in which the presumed contingency factor actually results from the structure. The possibility arises, therefore, that the positive correlations between strategy and structure arise through structure causing strategy. However, Donaldson (1982) examined this and found no effect of divisionalization on subsequent diversification. The correlation between strategy and structure does not arise through structure causing strategy. This adds confidence that the causal dynamics are those identified in the SARFIT model.

STRATEGIC CHOICE

Structural contingency theory is deterministic in that contingency causes structure (albeit with time lags). The organization bows to the imperative of adopting a new structure that fits its new level of the contingency factor in order to avoid loss of performance from misfit. This determinism has been much criticized. Some authors reject such situational determinism, asserting instead that organizational managers have a free choice (Whittington 1989) and some speak of 'free will' (Bourgeois 1984). Child (1972b) argues, more moderately, that the contingencies have some influence but that there is a substantial degree of choice, which he terms 'strategic choice' (see also Reed 1985; Pennings 1992).

Child (1972b) argues that choice for managers and other organizational controllers arises from several sources. He points out the decision-making process that intervenes between contingency and structure, so beginning to sketch an action-level analysis. Managers (and other organizational controllers) vary in their response to the contingency according to their perceptions, their implicit theories, preferences, values, interests and power (Child 1972b). The pioneering structural contingency theorists make some mention of these factors but nevertheless assert the contingency imperative (Woodward 1965).

For Child (1972b) these action-level factors gain strength from the room for manoeuvre afforded by weaknesses in the systems imperatives. An organization in misfit may suffer performance loss, but this may be of small degree relative to other causes of performance. A corporation in a dominant market position, such as monopoly or oligopoly, or a corporation in a protected industry, has sufficient excess profit, or organizational slack, that it can absorb a decrement in performance, due to structural misfit, without the profit level becoming unsatisfactory, that is, dropping below the satisficing level. Thus managers of such organizations may retain a misfitting structure that they prefer for a long time. Again, Child (1972b) argues that when a misfit is no longer tolerable and fit must be restored this can be done by retaining the structure and altering the contingency to fit the structure. Thus there is no imperative to adapt structure to contingency for there is an alternative route to regain fit. In these ways the imperative to adopt a structure for a given contingency is softened considerably and a larger role for choice is seen. The strategic choice theory has been widely received and constitutes a considerable challenge to structural contingency theory. It thereby becomes a candidate for refutation in the normal science program of structural contingency theory.

The argument of Child (1972b) that the systems imperatives are weaker than pioneering structural contingency theory supposed has been examined and is not as valid as generally presumed. Commentators point out that in the Aston research into bureaucratic structure, the contingency factors accounted for only about half the variance in structure, so that much variance may be due to strategic choice. However, the variance in structure explained by contingencies is understated due to measurement error. Donaldson (1986: 89) showed that the true correlation between size and functional specialization after correcting for measurement error is 0.82. This means that 67 per cent of variance in structural specialization is accounted for by size, which is well over half. Of the remaining 33 per cent of the variance in structure, some will be due to other contingency variables and some will be due to time-lags in adaptation of structure to size and the other contingencies. Thus the proportion of structural variance available to be explained by choice is under 30 per cent at best. And it may well be less than 30 per cent because of any other causes of structure that might exist.

Research into strategy and structure shows that organizations in misfit may delay adoption of a new, fitting structure for lengthy periods, up to decades (Channon 1973; Donaldson 1987; Dyas and Thanheiser 1976). Structural adaptation empirically tends to occur when the organization in misfit has low performance (Donaldson 1987). This is consistent with the strategic choice argument (Child 1972b). However, the study that reveals this phenomenon (Donaldson 1987; Rumelt 1974) is of large *Fortune* 500 corporations, that is, the pillars of American capitalism. Many of the studies of structural adaptation to changing contingencies are of large corporations (Channon 1973; Donaldson 1987; Dyas and Thanheiser 1976; Fligstein 1985; Mahoney 1992; Palmer et al. 1987; 1993; Pavan 1976; Rumelt 1974; Suzuki

1980). It is therefore false to see large corporations as seldom having to make structural adaptations. For example, Fligstein (1985: 386, Table 2) shows that, among the largest 100 US corporations, 71 adopted the multidivisional structure, over the years 1919 to 1979. Even large, wealthy corporations can face performance downturns that lower their performance below the satisficing level. This may arise in part through an economic recession, increased international competition, deregulation of industry and so on.

Critics assert that, whereas contingency theory depicts the organization as having to respond to the environment, the organization may alter the environment to make it more munificent for the organization (Perrow 1986; Pfeffer and Salancik 1978). This makes it easier for the organization to be profitable and thus to avoid having to make structural alterations. Perrow (1986) draws on the analysis of Hirsch (1975) which shows that organizations enjoyed greater profitability in the pharmaceutical than the phonograph industry, because the greater government regulation of pharmaceuticals is a barrier to entry that reduces competition. Presumably such a benign environment would be attractive to many organizational managements, yet they have not all succeeded in bringing such a favourable alteration of the environment into place. This indicates the resilience of the environment and of powerful institutions such as the government. The degree of regulation of the US pharmaceutical industry is atypical, reflecting public concern about drugs being more harmful than pop records. In fact, governmental policy in several countries (Australia, New Zealand, the UK and the US) is increasingly to deregulate industries in order to increase competition with the intent of curbing organizational slack and forcing organizational adaptations. Thus the idea that environmental re-engineering is a ready alternative to organizational adaptation is overstated and becoming less feasible with time.

A misfitting structure is seen as tolerable, given a modicum of organizational slack, because the negative effects of misfit on performance are seen as minor, especially for a wealthy organization enjoying market dominance such as an oligopoly (Child 1972b). However, a study by Hamilton and Shergill (1992; 1993) compared the performance effect of structural misfit with that of industry concentration, an index of market domination or oligopoly. Industry concentration accounted for 28 per cent of profitability, and structural fit (to strategy) accounted for 16 per cent (1993: 79). Thus the effect of organizational structural misfit is similar in magnitude to that of market domination. Structural misfit is not trivial in its performance effect relative to market domination. For most firms, the degree of organizational slack enjoyed through market domination would be almost exhausted by structural misfit so that performance would decline below the satisficing level, leading to structural adaptation.

Strategic choice theory argues that an organization in misfit can regain fit by altering its contingency to fit its structure, thereby avoiding the necessity of changing a structure that the managers prefer. In fact, empirical research shows that 95 per cent of corporations that move from misfit to fit do so by changes involving structural adaptations (Donaldson 1987). Corporations overwhelmingly attain fit by adapting structure to the contingency of strategy. Only 5 per cent of corporations move from misfit into fit by altering just their strategy contingency to attain fit with their existing structure. Corporations do not in reality use the contingency adjustment route to fit. The difference is so marked as to raise doubts that contingency adaptation is an alternative route. Where strategy change produces a new fit, such as by the corporation reducing its level of diversification and thereby moving from misfit into fit with its existing functional structure, this may be caused by very poor performance forcing the sell-off of non-core businesses rather than be motivated by the search for fit with a preferred structure. Instead of alternative routes to fit and choice, the research supports the view that corporations select a strategy and then tailor the structure to fit (Chandler 1962; Christensen et al. 1978).

Thus the normal science programme of solving deficiencies identified in extant work in the paradigm of structural contingency theory has been able to answer to a substantial degree the criticisms advanced from the strategic choice camp. The systems imperatives are strong and constrain to a high degree the choice open to managers and others deciding upon organizational structures. Organizations, even large and wealthy ones, bow to the dictate of having to fit structure to contingency in order to avoid intolerable performance loss. If there is much choice it is mostly restricted to timing of structural changes (see also Donaldson 1996).

There have been some moves towards demonstrating the role of individuals in the shaping of organizational structure, through showing that characteristics of individuals add to the explanation of structure by the contingencies. For instance, Miller and his colleagues show that structure is affected by the personality of the CEO (Miller et al. 1988; Miller and Droge 1986; Miller and Toulouse 1986). However, the Miller et al. (1988) study is of small organizations wherein the effect of the CEO is probably greater than in larger organizations, where the CEO has less influence, sharing it with staff specialists, and decision-making is more bureaucratized (as the authors accept (1988: 564)). Moreover, the effect of the size contingency variable is restricted in a study just of small organizations. Thus the Miller et al. (1988) study likely overstates the impact of CEO personality and understates the effect of the size contingency that would typically apply in organizations in general. Indeed Miller and Droge (1986: 552) found no relationship between CEO personality and organizational structure in large firms. Similarly, Miller and Toulouse (1986: 1397) found more numerous effects of CEO personality on organizational structure in small than in large firms. Thus the effect of CEO personality on organizational structure that is present in small firms fails to generalize completely to larger firms. Thus the effects of CEO personality is mainly restricted to small firms rather than the large corporations where institutionalization of the organizational structure means that impersonal contingency factors hold sway.

Fligstein (1985) shows that the functional background of the CEO affects structure. However, the functional background of the CEO is itself affected by the structure and by the corporate strategy, that is by a contingency of structure (Fligstein 1987). Thus it is not clear that CEO background is a cause of structure that itself is independent of structure and of the structural contingencies. Many of the individual-level factors that Child (1972b) and others see as shaping structural decisions may themselves be affected by organizational structure, strategy, size, or other contingency. For instance, power to affect selection of structure is presumably itself affected by the existing organizational structure; similarly, the interest of a manager would be affected by their position in the structure (see also Donaldson 1996).

The main attempt by Child (1973) to forge an actor-level theory of structure holds that bureaucratic formalization is affected by the degree of specialization and qualifications among the administrative staffs who are the architects of bureaucratization – specialization leads to formalization. Thus the theory is itself structural, explaining structure by structure. This adds to our knowledge yet is not a replacement of structural by an action-level analysis.

The strategic choice theory has provided the stimulus for a closer examination of several issues in structural contingency theory. The results support structural theory in its original form with the determinism intact.

Strategic choice theory often has a negative aspect in that it seeks to assert a role of managerial choice by showing that managers select structures that are less than optimal for the situation (Child 1972b), thereby exercising a capriciousness for which they should be held morally culpable (see especially Whittington 1989). Thus choice is manifested by selecting a structure different from that which the contingencies determine to be most effective. However, a second, more positive, sense of choice is that managers select the structure which moves the organization into fit with the contingencies thereby increasing organizational effectiveness through bowing to the system imperatives. Thus they exercise choice and are the human actors making the system respond but the outcome is beneficial for the organization and in conformity with contingency theory.

Support for this positive view of managerial choice is provided in research by Palmer et al. (1993). They show that the adoption of the multidivisional structure in large US corporations was greater among corporations whose CEO had a graduate degree from an elite business school. Palmer et al. (1993) argue that such CEOs would have acquired the idea of the multidivisional structure through such education. The adoption of the multidivisional structure by large US corporations was overwhelmingly rational adaptation to changes in the strategy contingency. They adopted the multidivisional structure to bring themselves into fit between strategy and structure (Donaldson 1987). Thus the effect of business education on divisionalization is encouraging evidence that the education of managers in the results of structural contingency research hastens their adoption of more effective organizational structures, as the pioneering researchers hoped (Woodward 1965).

FIT AND PERFORMANCE

As has already been pointed out, contingency theory centrally holds that there is a fit between the organizational structure and the organizational contingency that affects organizational performance. There has been renewed interest in the conceptualization and operational measurement of fit during the 1980s and subsequently. This is quite marked among researchers in the US. Such developments include the critical work of Schoonhoven (1981). Others have sought to investigate the empirical relationship between their operational definition of fit and organizational performance, assessed in various ways (Alexander and Randolph 1985; Argote 1982; Drazin and Van de Ven 1985; Gresov 1989; Gresov et al. 1989; Van de Ven and Drazin 1985).

Drazin and Van de Ven (1985) have modelled fit as a line of iso-performance and have measured the degree of misfit between a contingency variable and several different structural variables of each organization. This brings out the desirability of considering fit not just between a contingency and a structural variable, but between a contingency variable and all of the structural variables for which it is a contingency. Such a multistructural concept of fit more fully reflects the underlying fit notion and so is to be welcomed. In turn, it opens the door to a more fully multivariate model in which all the contingency factors and all the structural variables for which they are contingencies are considered simultaneously for each organization (Randolph and Dess 1984). This multidimensional model of fit would more richly capture the idea of fit. It would be more complex, but not too complex, as each structural variable has in practice only a limited number of contingencies. Many structural variables have as their contingencies only a limited set of contingency variables, mostly restricted to one or a few out of the variables of size, strategy, task uncertainty and public accountability. Clarifying the exact few contingencies that apply to each different aspect of structure and including them in multivariate models that exhaustively capture fit and then measuring this multivariate fit and its impact on performance is the next step in fit research. It constitutes an important agenda item for future contingency research.

THE CHALLENGE OF OTHER PARADIGMS

As part of the growing pluralism in the study of organizations, since about the mid 1970s new paradigms have arisen in sociology and economics which offer explanations of organizational structure additional to those available in structural contingency theory (Pennings 1992; Davis and Powell 1992). These include resource dependence (Pfeffer and Salancik 1978), institutional (Powell and DiMaggio 1991), population-ecology (Hannan and Freeman 1989) and agency (Jensen and Meckling 1976) theories and transaction cost economics (Williamson 1985). Some of these theories are outlined in other chapters of this *Handbook*. Elsewhere a detailed discussion and critique is offered of each of these organization theories and arguments in favour of contingency theory are presented (Donaldson 1995a). Our view is that while these newer organization theories have something to contribute that supplements contingency theory it remains the core explanatory theory of organizational structure (see Donaldson 1995a).

REFLECTIONS ON THE STRUCTURAL
CONTINGENCY THEORY PARADIGM

The normal science of structural contingency theory has been pursued by a number of scholars, as we have seen. However, it is not popular in all quarters and has probably declined in popularity since 1970. There have arisen many new and different approaches, for example, institutional theory in the US (Meyer and Scott 1983) and action theory in the UK (Silverman 1970). The US has witnessed a particular profusion of new organizational theories (see Donaldson 1995a). Much organizational structural research has been conducted under their ambit. It has been suggested that career incentives lie more in innovating a new paradigm than in persevering with an older paradigm (Aldrich 1992; Mone and McKinley 1993). Moreover, awareness of alternative views has combined with specific negative findings within the structural contingency research so that some researchers interpret their findings as challenges to the paradigm and advance fundamental changes. For example, Cullen et al. (1986) restudied the Blau (1970) theory and variables across time; they interpret their negative findings as meaning that Blau's theory needs to be seen only as a theory of static scale rather than the size change dynamics that Blau claimed. In such cases, the researchers are not treating negative findings as puzzles to be solved, as is the way in normal science mode.

Thus the normal science of structural contingency theory has been pursued only by some students of organization. Nevertheless their results have indicated that considerable progress has now been made in solving puzzles and advancing a strengthened structural contingency theory. Moreover, while structural contingency theory is but one of several theories in the research literature, the teaching literature is quite opposite. Books on organizational structure and design continue to rely greatly on structural contingency theory and findings (Bedeian and Zammuto 1991; Child 1984; Daft 1986).

Given the increasing theoretical pluralism of the field of organizational structure studies, many contemporary empirical researchers take the contingency-structure relationship as basic and then add on variables and interpretations from the newer structural paradigms, such as institutional theory, in eclectic fashion (for examples, Fligstein 1985; Palmer et al. 1993). In this way the contingency theory endures in the mainstream of research among researchers who maintain allegiances to more than one organization theory. This eclecticism between theories marks the breakdown of each as a distinct theoretical paradigm. Such eclecticism is to a degree resisted by the hard-core adherents of each of the organization theory paradigms (see Aldrich 1992). However, the more typical contemporary researchers seek to accommodate these differing ideas within their research models (Fligstein 1985; Palmer et al. 1993). While there are difficulties in realising integration between the diverse contemporary paradigms (see Donaldson 1995a), the attempt to re-integrate the field is greatly to be commended. This eclectic use may be becoming the largest use of structural contingency theory.

Since structural contingency theory began as a synthesis between the opposed ideas of the classical management and human relations schools, it is not inappropriate that it in turn should become synthesized with other organization theories in a wider model. The issue then becomes whether structural contingency theory is to be a minor or major part of that new synthesis. Proponents of structural contingency theory will see it as providing the major component of the new synthesis (Donaldson 1995a). Proponents of the other organization theories will see structural contingency theory as providing only a minor part and their own preferred theory as providing the major component of the new synthesis. This may well be one of the main debates in the immediate future of organization studies.

BIBLIOGRAPHY

Aldrich, Howard E. (1972) 'Technology and organizational structure: a re-examination of the findings of the Aston Group', *Administrative Science Quarterly*, 17: 26–43.
Aldrich, Howard E. (1992) 'Incommensurable paradigms? Vital signs from three perspectives', in Michael Reed and Michael Hughes (eds), *Rethinking Organization: New Directions in Organization Theory and Analysis*. London: Sage.
Alexander, Judith W. and Randolph, W. Alan (1985) 'The fit between technology and structure as a predictor of performance in nursing sub-units', *Academy of Management Journal*, 28: 844–59.
Argote, Linda (1982) 'Input uncertainty and organizational coordination in hospital emergency units', *Administrative Science Quarterly*, 27: 420–34.
Argyris, Chris (1972) *The Applicability of Organizational Sociology*. London: Cambridge University.
Armour, Henry Ogden and Teece, David J. (1978) 'Organizational structure and economic performance: a test of the multidivisional hypothesis', *Bell Journal of Economics*, 9(1): 106–22.
Ayoubi, Z.M. (1981) 'Technology, size and organization structure in a developing country: Jordan', in

D.J. Hickson and C.J. McMillan (eds), *Organization and Nation: the Aston Programme IV*. Farnborough, Hants: Gower. pp. 95–114.

Azumi, K. and McMillan, C.J. (1981) 'Management strategy and organization structure: a Japanese comparative study', in D.J. Hickson and C.J. McMillan (eds), *Organization and Nation: the Aston Programme IV*. Farnborough, Hants: Gower. pp. 155–72.

Badran, M. and Hinings, C.R. (1981) 'Strategies of administrative control and contextual constraints in a less developed country: the case of Egyptian public enterprise', in D.J. Hickson and C.J. McMillan (eds), *Organization and Nation: the Aston Programme IV*. Farnborough, Hants: Gower. pp. 115–31.

Bedeian, A.G. and Zammuto, R.F. (1991) *Organization Theory and Design*. Chicago: Dryden Press.

Beyer, J.M. and Trice, H.M. (1979) 'A reexamination of the relations between size and various components of oganizational complexity', *Administrative Science Quarterly*, 24: 48–64.

Blau, Peter M. (1970) 'A formal theory of differentiation in organizations', *American Sociological Review*, 35(2): 201–18.

Blau, Peter M. (1972) 'Interdependence and hierarchy in organizations', *Social Science Research*, 1: 1–24.

Blau, Peter M. and Schoenherr, P.A. (1971) *The Structure of Organizations*. New York: Basic Books.

Blau, Peter M., Falbe, Cecilia McHugh, McKinley, William and Tracy, Phelps K. (1976) 'Technology and organization in manufacturing', *Administrative Science Quarterly*, 21(1): 21–40.

Bourgeois III, L.J. (1984) 'Strategic management and determinism', *Academy of Management Review*, 9: 586–96.

Brech, E.F.L. (1957) *Organisation: the Framework of Management*. London: Longmans, Green.

Bryman, A., Beardsworth, A.D., Keil, E.T. and Ford, J. (1983) 'Research note: organizational size and specialization', *Organization Studies*, 4(3): 271–7.

Burns, Tom and Stalker, G.M. (1961) *The Management of Innovation*. London: Tavistock.

Burrell, Gibson and Morgan, Gareth (1979) *Sociological Paradigms and Organizational Analysis: Elements of the Sociology of Corporate Life*. London: Heinemann.

Capon, N. and Christodolou, C. (1987) 'A comparative analysis of the strategy and structure of United States and Australian corporations', *Journal of International Business Studies*, 18 (Spring): 51–74.

Chandler, Alfred D. Jr (1962) *Strategy and Structure: Chapters in the History of the American Industrial Enterprise*. Cambridge, MA: MIT Press.

Channon, Derek F. (1973) *The Strategy and Structure of British Enterprise*. London: Macmillan.

Channon, Derek F. (1978) *The Service Industries: Strategy Structure and Financial Performance*. London: Macmillan.

Chenhall, Robert H. (1979) 'Some elements of organizational control in Australian divisionalized firms', *Australian Journal of Management*, Supplement to 4(1): 1–36.

Child, John (1972a) 'Organization structure and strategies of control: a replication of the Aston Study', *Administrative Science Quarterly*, 17: 163–77.

Child, John (1972b) 'Organizational structure, environment and performance: the role of strategic choice', *Sociology*, 6: 1–22.

Child, John (1973) 'Predicting and understanding organization structure', *Administrative Science Quarterly*, 18: 168–85.

Child, John (1974) 'Managerial and organizational factors associated with company performance. Part 1', *Journal of Management Studies*, 11: 175–89.

Child, John (1975) 'Managerial and organizational factors associated with company performance. Part 2: A contingency analysis', *Journal of Management Studies*, 12: 12–27.

Child, John (1984) *Organization: a Guide to Problems and Practice*, 2nd edn. London: Harper and Row.

Child, John and Kieser, Alfred (1979) 'Organizational and managerial roles in British and West German companies: an examination of the culture-free thesis', in C.J. Lammers and D.J. Hickson (eds), *Organizations Alike and Unlike*. London: Routledge and Kegan Paul. pp. 251–71.

Child, John and Mansfield, Roger (1972) 'Technology, size and organization structure', *Sociology*, 6(3): 369–93.

Christensen, C. Roland, Andrews, Kenneth R. and Bower, Joseph L. (1978) *Business Policy: Text and Cases*, 4th edn. Homewood, IL: Richard D. Irwin.

Collins, Paul D. and Hull, Frank (1986) 'Technology and span of control: Woodward revisited', *Journal of Management Studies*, 32(2): 143–164.

Conaty, J., Mahmoudi, H. and Miller, G.A. (1983) 'Social structure and bureaucracy: a comparison of organizations in the United States and prerevolutionary Iran', *Organization Studies*, 4(2): 105–28.

Crawford, Michael (1983) 'The character, determinants and performance effects of inter-unit interactions within organisations: a disaggregated systems approach'. PhD thesis, University of New South Wales, Australia.

Crawford, Michael (1985a) 'Performance loss as an outcome of aggregate inter-unit strain within organisations'. Paper presented at the Academy of Management National Meeting, San Diego, California.

Crawford, Michael (1985b) 'Style, effort and outcome: relationships between boundary spanning effort, conflict style, appreciation and inter-unit dissonance'. Paper presented at the Academy of Management National Meeting, San Diego, California.

Cullen, J.B., Anderson, K.S. and Baker, D.D. (1986) 'Blau's theory of structural differentiation revisited:

a theory of structural change or scale', *Academy of Management Journal*, 29(2): 203–29.

Daft, Richard L. (1986) *Organization Theory and Design*, 2nd edn. St Paul: West.

Davis, Gerald F. and Powell, Walter W. (1992) 'Organization-environment relations', in Marvin Dunnette and Laetta M. Hough (eds), *Handbook of Industrial and Organizational Psychology*, 2nd edn. Palo Alto, CA: Consulting Psychologists Press. pp. 316–75.

Dewar, Robert and Hage, Jerald (1978) 'Size, technology, complexity, and structural differentiation: toward a theoretical synthesis', *Administrative Science Quarterly*, 23(1): 111–36.

Donaldson, Lex (1976) 'Woodward, technology, organizational structure and performance – a critique of the universal generalization', *Journal of Management Studies*, 13(3): 255–73.

Donaldson, Lex (1982) 'Divisionalization and diversification: a longitudinal study', *Academy of Management Journal*, 25(4): 909–14.

Donaldson, Lex (1985a) *In Defence of Organization Theory: a Reply to the Critics*. Cambridge: Cambridge University Press.

Donaldson, Lex (1985b) 'Organization design and the life-cycles of products', *Journal of Management Studies*, 22(1): 25–37.

Donaldson, Lex (1986) 'Size and bureaucracy in East and West: a preliminary meta-analysis', in S.R. Clegg, D. Dunphy and S.G. Redding (eds), *The Enterprise and Management in East Asia*. Hong Kong: University of Hong Kong Press.

Donaldson, Lex (1987) 'Strategy and structural adjustment to regain fit and performance: in defence of contingency theory', *Journal of Management Studies*, 24(1): 1–24.

Donaldson, Lex (1990) 'The ethereal hand: organizational economics and management theory', *Academy of Management Review*, 15(3): 369–81.

Donaldson, Lex (1995a) *American Anti-Management Theories of Organization: a Critique of Paradigm Proliferation*. Cambridge: Cambridge University Press.

Donaldson, Lex (1995b) *Contingency Theory*, vol. IX, in D.S. Pugh (ed.), *History of Management Thought*. Aldershot: Dartmouth Press.

Donaldson, Lex (1996) *For Positivist Organization Theory: Proving the Hard Core*. London: Sage.

Donaldson, Lex, Child, John and Aldrich, Howard (1975) 'The Aston findings on centralization: further discussion', *Administrative Science Quarterly*, 20: 453–60.

Drazin, Robert, and Van de Ven, Andrew H. (1985) 'Alternative forms of fit in contingency theory', *Administrative Science Quarterly*, 30: 514–39.

Dyas, Gareth P. and Thanheiser, Heinz T. (1976) *The Emerging European Enterprise: Strategy and Structure in French and German Industry*. London: Macmillan.

Egelhoff, William G. (1988) *Organizing the Multi-national Enterprise: an Information Processing Perspective*. Cambridge, MA: Ballinger.

Faas, F.A.M.J. (1985) 'How to solve communication problems on the R and D interface', *Journal of Management Studies*, 22(1): 83–102.

Fletcher, Colin (1970) 'On replication: notes on the notion of a replicability quotient and a generalizability quotient', *Sociology*, 4(January): 51–69.

Fligstein, Neil (1985) 'The spread of the multidivisional form among large firms, 1919–1979', *American Sociological Review*, 50: 377–91.

Fligstein, Neil (1987) 'The intraorganizational power struggle: rise of finance personnel to top leadership in large corporations, 1919–1979', *American Sociological Review*, 52: 44–58.

Ford, Jeffrey D. and Slocum, John W. Jr (1977) 'Size, technology, environment and the structure of organizations', *Academy of Management Review*, 2(4): 561–75.

Fry, Louis W. (1982) 'Technology–structure research: three critical issues', *Academy of Management Journal*, 25(3): 532–52.

Fry, Louis W. and Slocum, John W. Jr (1984) 'Technology, structure, and workgroup effectiveness: a test of a contingency model', *Academy of Management Journal*, 27(2): 221–46.

Galbraith, Jay R. (1973) *Designing Complex Organizations*. Reading, MA: Addison-Wesley.

Galunic, R. Charles and Eisenhardt, Kathleen M. (1994) 'Renewing the strategy-structure-performance paradigm', in B.M. Staw and I.I. Cummings (eds), *Research in Organizational Behavior*, 16: 215–55.

Gerwin, Donald (1977) 'Relationship between structure and technology', in Paul Nystrom and William Starbuck (eds), *Handbook of Organizational Design*. Amsterdam: Elsevier.

Gerwin, Donald (1979a) 'Relationships between structure and technology at the organizational and job levels', *Journal of Management Studies*, 16(1): 70–9.

Gerwin, Donald (1979b) 'The comparative analysis of structure and technology: a critical appraisal', *Academy of Management Review*, 4(1): 41–51.

Gerwin, Donald and Christoffel, Wade (1974) 'Organizational structure and technology: a computer model approach', *Management Science*, 20(12): 1531–42.

Ghoshal, Sumantra and Nohria, Nitin (1989) 'Internal differentiation within multinational corporations', *Strategic Management Journal*, 10(4): 323–37.

Gouldner, Alvin (1954) *Patterns of Industrial Bureaucracy*. Glencoe, IL: Free Press.

Greenwood, Royston and Hinings, C.R. (1976) 'Centralization revisited', *Administrative Science Quarterly*, 21(1): 151–5.

Gresov, C. (1989) 'Exploring fit and misfit with multiple contingencies', *Administrative Science Quarterly*, 34: 431–53.

Gresov, C., Drazin, R. and Van de Ven, A. H. (1989)

'Work-unit task uncertainty, design and morale', *Organization Studies*, 10(1): 45–62.

Grinyer, Peter H. and Yasai-Ardekani, Masoud (1980) 'Dimensions of organizational structure: a critical replication', *Academy of Management Journal*, 23: 405–21.

Grinyer, Peter H. and Yasai-Ardekani, Masoud (1981a) 'Research note: some problems with measurement of macro-organizational structure', *Organization Studies*, 2(3): 287–96.

Grinyer, Peter H. and Yasai-Ardekani, Masoud (1981b) 'Strategy, structure, size and bureaucracy', *Academy of Management Journal*, 24(3): 471–86.

Grinyer, Peter H., Yasai-Ardekani, Masoud and Al-Bazzaz, Shawki (1980) 'Strategy, structure, the environment, and financial performance in 48 United Kingdom companies', *Academy of Management Journal*, 23(2): 193–220.

Hage, Jerald (1965) 'An axiomatic theory of organizations', *Administrative Science Quarterly*, 10(4): 289–320.

Hage, Jerald and Aiken, Michael (1967) 'Program change and organizational properties: a comparative analysis', *American Journal of Sociology*, 72: 503–19.

Hage, Jerald and Aiken, Michael (1969) 'Routine technology, social structure and organizational goals', *Administrative Science Quarterly*, 14(3): 366–76.

Hage, Jerald and Dewar, Robert (1973) 'Elite values versus organizational structure in predicting innovation', *Administrative Science Quarterly*, 18(3): 279–90.

Hall, D.J. and Saias, M.D. (1980) 'Strategy follows structure!', *Strategic Management Journal*, 1: 149–63.

Hamilton, R.T. and Shergill, G.S. (1992) 'The relationship between strategy–structure fit and financial performance in New Zealand: evidence of generality and validity with enhanced controls', *Journal of Management Studies*, 29(1): 95–113.

Hamilton, R.T. and Shergill, G.S. (1993) *The Logic of New Zealand Business: Strategy, Structure, and Performance*. Auckland, New Zealand: Oxford University Press.

Hannan, Michael T. and Freeman, John (1989) *Organizational Ecology*. Cambridge, MA: Harvard University Press.

Harvey, Edward (1968) 'Technology and the structure of organizations', *American Sociological Review*, 33: 247–59.

Hickson, David J. and McMillan, C.J. (eds) (1981) *Organization and Nation: the Aston Programme IV*. Farnborough, Hants: Gower.

Hickson, David J., Pugh, D.S. and Pheysey, Diana G. (1969) 'Operations technology and organization structure: an empirical reappraisal', *Administrative Science Quarterly*, 14(3): 378–97.

Hickson, David J., Hinings, C.R., McMillan, C.J. and Schwitter, J.P. (1974) 'The culture-free context of

organization structure: a trinational comparison', *Sociology*, 8(1): 59–80.

Hill, Charles W.L. and Pickering, J.F. (1986) 'Divisionalization, decentralization and performance of large United Kingdom companies', *Journal of Management Studies*, 23(1): 26–50.

Hill, Charles W.L., Hitt, Michael A. and Hoskisson, Robert E. (1992) 'Cooperative versus competitive structures in related and unrelated diversified firms', *Organization Science*, 3(4): 501–21.

Hinings, C.R. and Lee, Gloria (1971) 'Dimensions of organization structure and their context: a replication', *Sociology*, 5: 83–93.

Hinings, C.R., Ranson, S., and Bryman, A. (1976) 'Churches as organizations: structure and context', in D.S. Pugh and C.R. Hinings (eds), *Organizational Structure: Extensions and Replications: the Aston Programme*. Farnborough, Hants: Saxon House.

Hirsch, Paul (1975) 'Organizational effectiveness and the institutional environment', *Administrative Science Quarterly*, 20(3): 327–44.

Hirst, Mark H. (1984) 'A partial meta-analysis of the relationship between organisational structure and production technology', *Australian Journal of Management*, 9(2): 35–42.

Horvath, D., McMillan, C.J., Azumi, K. and Hickson, D.J. (1981) 'The cultural context of organizational control: an international comparison', *International Studies of Management and Organization*, 6: 60–86.

Inkson, J.H.K., Pugh, D.S. and Hickson, D.J. (1970) 'Organization context and structure: an abbreviated replication', *Administrative Science Quarterly*, 15(13): 318–29.

Jelinek, Mariann (1977) 'Technology, organizations and contingency', *Academy of Management Review*, 2(1): 17–26.

Jensen, Michael C. and Meckling, William H. (1976) 'Theory of the firm: managerial behavior, agency costs and ownership structure', *Journal of Financial Economics*, 3(4): 305–60.

Khandwalla, Pradip N. (1973) 'Viable and effective organizational designs of firms', *Academy of Management Journal*, 16(3): 481–95.

Khandwalla, Pradip N. (1974) 'Mass output orientation of operations technology and organizational structure', *Administrative Science Quarterly*, 19(1): 74–97.

Khandwalla, Pradip N. (1977) *The Design of Organizations*. New York: Harcourt Brace Jovanovich.

Kuc, B., Hickson, D.J. and McMillan, C.J. (1981) 'Centrally planned development: a comparison of Polish factories with equivalents in Britain, Japan and Sweden', in D.J. Hickson and C.J. McMillan (eds), *Organization and Nation: the Aston Programme IV*. Farnborough, Hants: Gower. pp. 75–91.

Kuhn, Thomas S. (1970) *The Structure of Scientific Revolutions*, 2nd enlarged edn. Chicago: University of Chicago Press.

Lammers, C.J. and Hickson, D.J. (eds) (1979)

Organizations Alike and Unlike: International and Inter-Institutional Studies in the Sociology of Organization. London: Routledge and Kegan Paul.

Lawrence, Paul R. and Lorsch, Jay W. (1967) *Organization and Environment: Managing Differentiation and Integration*. Boston: Division of Research, Graduate School of Business Administration, Harvard University.

Leatt, Peggy and Schneck, Rodney (1982) 'Technology, size, environment, and structure in nursing subunits', *Organization Studies*, 3(2): 221–42.

Likert, Rensis (1961) *New Patterns of Management*. New York: McGraw-Hill.

Lincoln, J.R., Hanada, M. and McBride, K. (1986) 'Organizational structures in Japanese and U.S. manufacturing', *Administrative Science Quarterly*, 31: 338–64.

Lioukas, S.K. and Xerokostas, D.A. (1982) 'Size and administrative intensity in organizational divisions', *Management Science*, 28(8): 854–68.

Lorsch, Jay W. and Allen, Stephen A. (1973) *Managing Diversity and Inter-dependence: an Organizational Study of Multidivisional Firms*. Boston: Division of Research, Graduate School of Business Administration, Harvard University.

Mahoney, Joseph T. (1992) 'The adoption of the multidivisional form of organization: a contingency model', *Journal of Management Studies*, 29(1): 49–72.

Mahoney, Thomas A. and Frost, Peter J. (1974) 'The role of technology in models of organizational effectiveness', *Organizational Behavior and Human Performance*, 11: 122–38.

Mansfield, Roger (1973) 'Bureaucracy and centralization: an examination of organizational structure', *Administrative Science Quarterly*, 18: 477–88.

Mansfield, Roger and Poole, Michael (1981) *International Perspectives on Management and Organization*. Aldershot, Hampshire: Gower.

Marsh, Robert M. and Mannari, Hiroshi (1976) *Modernization and the Japanese Factory*. Princeton, NJ: Princeton University Press

Marsh, Robert M. and Mannari, Hiroshi (1980) 'Technological implications theory: a Japanese test', *Organization Studies*, 1(2): 161–83.

Marsh, Robert M. and Mannari, Hiroshi (1981) 'Technology and size as determinants of the organizational structure of Japanese factories', *Administrative Science Quarterly*, 26(1): 33–57.

McMillan, Charles J., Hickson, David J., Hinings, Christopher R. and Schneck, Rodney E. (1973) 'The structure of work organizations across societies', *Administrative Science Quarterly*, 16: 555–69.

Meadows, Ian S.G. (1980) 'Organic structure and innovation in small work groups', *Human Relations*, 33(6): 369–82.

Merton, R.K. (1949) *Social Theory and Social Structure*. Chicago, IL: Free Press.

Merton, R.K. (1975) 'Structural analysis in sociology',

in P.M. Blau (ed.), *Approaches to the Study of Social Structures*. New York: Free Press.

Meyer, John W. and Scott, W. Richard with the assistance of Rowan, B. and Deal, T.E. (1983) *Organizational Environments: Ritual and Rationality*. Beverly Hills, CA: Sage.

Meyer, Marshall W. (1979) *Change in Public Bureaucracies*. Cambridge: Cambridge University Press.

Miller, Danny and Droge, Cornelia (1986) 'Psychological and traditional determinants of structure', *Administrative Science Quarterly*, 31(4): 539–60.

Miller, Danny and Toulouse, Jean-Marie (1986) 'Chief executive personality and corporate strategy and structure in small firms', *Management Science*, 32(11): 1389–409.

Miller, Danny, Droge, Cornelia and Toulouse, Jean-Marie (1988) 'Strategic process and content as mediators between organizational context and structure', *Academy of Management Journal*, 31(3): 544–69.

Miller, George A. (1987) 'Meta-analysis and the culture-free hypothesis', *Organization Studies*, 8(4): 309–26.

Mintzberg, H. (1979) *The Structuring of Organizations: a Synthesis of the Research*. Englewood Cliffs, NJ: Prentice-Hall.

Mone, Mark A. and McKinley, William (1993) 'The uniqueness value and its consequences for organization studies', *Journal of Management Inquiry*, 2(3): 284–96.

Palmer, Donald A., Friedland, Roger, Jennings, P.D. and Powers, Melanie E. (1987) 'The economics and politics of structure: the multidivisional form and large U.S. corporations', *Administrative Science Quarterly*, 32: 25–48.

Palmer, Donald A., Jennings, P. Devereaux and Zhou, Xueguang (1993) 'Late adoption of the multidivisional form by large U.S. corporations: institutional, political, and economic accounts', *Administrative Science Quarterly*, 38: 100–31.

Parsons, T. (1951) *The Social System*. Chicago, IL: Free Press.

Parsons, T. (1964) 'Suggestions for a sociological approach to the theory of organizations', in Amitai Etzioni (ed.), *Complex Organizations: a Sociological Reader*. New York: Holt.

Pavan, Robert J. (1976) 'Strategy and structure: the Italian experience', *Journal of Economics and Business*, 28(3): 254–60.

Pennings, Johannes M. (1992) 'Structural contingency theory: a reappraisal', in B.M. Staw and I.I. Cummings (eds), *Research in Organizational Behavior*, 14: 267–309.

Perrow, Charles (1967) 'A framework for the comparative analysis of organizations', *American Sociological Review*, 32(3): 194–208.

Perrow, Charles (1986) *Complex Organizations: a Critical Essay*, 3rd edn. New York: Random House.

Pfeffer, Jeffrey (1982) *Organizations and Organization Theory*. Boston: Pitman.

Pfeffer, Jeffrey (1993) 'Barriers to the advance of organizational science: paradigm development as a dependent variable', *Academy of Management Review*, 18(4): 599–620.

Pfeffer, Jeffrey and Salancik, Gerald R. (1978) *The External Control of Organizations: a Resource Dependence Perspective*. New York: Harper and Row.

Powell, Walter W. and DiMaggio, Paul J. (1991) *The New Institutionalism in Organizational Analysis*. Chicago: University of Chicago Press.

Pugh, D.S. and Hickson, D.J. (1976) *Organizational Structure in its Context: the Aston Programme I*. Farnborough, Hants: Saxon House.

Pugh, D.S. and Hinings, C.R. (1976) *Organizational Structure: Extensions and Replications: the Aston Programme II*. Farnborough, Hants: Saxon House.

Pugh, D.S., Hickson, D.J., Hinings, C.R., Macdonald, K.M., Turner, C. and Lupton, T. (1963) 'A conceptual scheme for organizational analysis', *Administrative Science Quarterly*, 8(3): 289–315.

Pugh, D.S., Hickson, D.J., Hinings, C.R. and Turner, C. (1968) 'Dimensions of organization structure', *Administrative Science Quarterly*, 13(1): 65–105.

Pugh, D.S., Hickson, D.J., Hinings, C.R. and Turner, C. (1969) 'The context of organization structures', *Administrative Science Quarterly*, 14(1): 91–114.

Randolph, W. Alan and Dess, Gregory G. (1984) 'The congruence perspective of organization design: a conceptual model and multivariate research approach', *Academy of Management Review*, 9(1): 114–27.

Reed, Michael (1985) *Redirections in Organizational Analysis*. London: Tavistock Publications.

Reeves, Kynaston T. and Turner, Barry A. (1972) 'A theory of organization and behaviour in batch production factories', *Administrative Science Quarterly*, 17(1): 81–98.

Reimann, Bernard C. (1973) 'On the dimensions of bureaucratic structure: an empirical reappraisal', *Administrative Science Quarterly*, 18: 462–76.

Reimann, Bernard C. (1977) 'Dimensions of organizational technology and structure: an exploratory study', *Human Relations*, 30(6): 545–66.

Reimann, Bernard C. (1980) 'Organization structure and technology in manufacturing: system versus work flow level perspectives', *Academy of Management Journal*, 23(1): 61–77.

Reimann, Bernard C. and Inzerilli, Giorgio (1979) 'A comparative analysis of empirical research on technology and structure', *Journal of Management*, 5(2): 167–92.

Richards, V.G. (1980) 'Research note: the Aston Databank', *Organization Studies*, 1(3): 271–8.

Roethlisberger, Fritz J. and Dickson, William J. (1939) *Management and the Worker*. Cambridge, MA: Harvard University Press.

Rousseau, Denise M. (1979) 'Assessment of technology in organizations: closed versus open systems approaches', *Academy of Management Review*, 4(4): 531–42.

Routamaa, Vesa (1985) 'Organizational structuring: an empirical analysis of the relationships and dimensions of structures in certain Finnish companies', *Journal of Management Studies*, 22(5): 498–522.

Rumelt, Richard P. (1974) *Strategy, Structure and Economic Performance*. Boston: Division of Research, Graduate School of Business Administration, Harvard University.

Sathe, V. (1978) 'Institutional versus questionnaire measures of organizational structure', *Academy of Management*, 21: 227–38.

Schoonhoven, Claudia Bird (1981) 'Problems with contingency theory: testing assumptions hidden within the language of contingency "theory"', *Administrative Science Quarterly*, 26(3): 349–77.

Scott, W. Richard (1992) *Organizations: Rational, Natural and Open Systems*, 3rd edn. Englewood Cliffs, NJ: Prentice-Hall.

Selznick, P. (1957) *Leadership in Administration*. New York: Harper and Row.

Shenoy, S. (1981) 'Organization structure and context: a replication of the Aston study in India', in D.J. Hickson and C.J. McMillan (eds), *Organization and Nation: the Aston Programme IV*. Farnborough, Hants: Gower. pp. 133–54.

Silverman, David (1970) *The Theory of Organizations*. London: Heinemann.

Singh, Jitendra V. (1986) 'Technology, size, and organizational structure: a reexamination of the Okayama Study data', *Academy of Management Journal*, 29(4): 800–12.

Starbuck, William H. (1981) 'A trip to view the elephants and rattlesnakes in the Garden of Aston', in A. Van de Ven and W. Joyce (eds), *Perspectives on Organization Design and Behavior*. New York: Wiley.

Stopford, J.M. and Wells, L.T. Jr (1972) *Managing the Multinational Enterprise*. New York: Basic Books.

Suzuki, Y. (1980) 'The strategy and structure of the top 100 Japanese industrial enterprises 1950–1970', *Strategic Management Journal*, 1(3): 265–91.

Tai, Elizabeth (1987) 'Adaptability and organizational effectiveness: a study of thirty manufacturing firms in Singapore'. PhD thesis, University of New South Wales, Sydney, Australia.

Tauber, I. (1968) 'A yardstick of hospital organization'. Diploma thesis, University of Aston, Birmingham, England.

Thompson, James D. (1967) *Organizations in Action*. New York: McGraw-Hill.

Van de Ven, Andrew H. and Delbecq, A.L. (1974) 'A task contingent model of work-unit structure', *Administrative Science Quarterly*, 19(2): 183–97.

Van de Ven, Andrew H. and Drazin, Robert (1985) 'The concept of fit in contingency theory', in B.M. Staw and L.L. Cummings (eds), *Research in Organizational Behaviour*, vol. 7. Greenwich, CT: JAI Press.

Van de Ven, Andrew and Ferry, Diane L. (1980) *Measuring and Assessing Organizations.* New York: Wiley.

Van de Ven, Andrew H., Delbecq, A.L. and Koenig, R. Jr. (1976) 'Determinants of coordination modes within organizations', *American Sociological Review*, 41: 322–38.

Vroom, Victor H. and Yetton, Philip W. (1973) *Leadership and Decision-Making.* Pittsburgh: University of Pittsburgh Press.

Weber, Max (1968) *Economy and Society: an Outline of Interpretive Sociology*, edited by Guenther Roth and Claus Wittich. New York: Bedminster Press.

Whittington, R. (1989) *Corporate Strategies in Recession and Recovery: Social Structure and Strategic Choice.* London: Unwin Hyman.

Williamson, Oliver E. (1970) *Corporate Control and Business Behavior: an Inquiry into the Effects of Organization Form on Enterprise Behavior.* Englewood Cliffs, NJ: Prentice-Hall.

Williamson, Oliver E. (1971) 'Managerial discretion, organization form, and the multidivision hypoth-esis', in Robin Marris and Adrian Woods (eds), *The Corporate Economy: Growth, Competition and Innovative Potential.* Cambridge, MA: Harvard University Press.

Williamson, Oliver E. (1985) *The Economic Institutions of Capitalism: Firms, Markets, Relational Contracting.* New York: Free Press.

Woodward, Joan (1958) *Management and Technology.* London: HMSO.

Woodward, Joan (1965) *Industrial Organization: Theory and Practice.* London: Oxford University Press.

Woodward, Joan (1970) *Industrial Organization: Behaviour and Control*, London: Oxford University Press.

Zeffane, Rachid M. (1989) 'Organization structures and contingencies in different nations: Algeria, Britain, and France', *Social Science Research*, 18: 331–69.

Zwerman, William L. (1970) *New Perspectives on Organization Theory: an Empirical Reconsideration of the Marxian and Classical Analyses.* Westport, CT: Greenwood.

1.3

Organizational Ecology

JOEL A.C. BAUM

WHAT ORGANIZATIONAL
ECOLOGY IS AND ISN'T

Until the mid 1970s, the prominent approach in organization and management theory emphasized adaptive change in organizations. In this view, as environments change, leaders or dominant coalitions in organizations alter appropriate organizational features to realign their fit to environmental demands. Since then, an approach to studying organizational change that places more emphasis on environmental selection processes, introduced at about that time (Aldrich and Pfeffer 1976; Aldrich 1979; Hannan and Freeman 1977; McKelvey 1982), has become increasingly influential. The stream of research on ecological perspectives of organizational change has generated tremendous excitement, controversy, and debate in the community of organization and management theory scholars.

Inspired by the question, 'Why are there so many kinds of organizations?' (Hannan and Freeman 1977: 936), organizational ecologists seek to explain how social, economic, and political conditions affect the relative abundance and diversity of organizations and attempt to account for their changing composition over time. Although differences exist among individual investigators, ecological research typically begins with three observations: (1) diversity is a property of aggregates of organizations, (2) organizations often have difficulty devising and executing changes fast enough to meet the demands of uncertain, changing environments, and (3) the community of organizations is rarely stable – organizations arise and disappear continually. Given these observations, organizational ecologists pursue explanations for organizational diversity at population and community levels of

organization, and focus on rates of organizational founding and failure and creation and death of organizational populations as key sources of increasing and decreasing diversity.

Organizations, populations, and communities of organizations constitute the basic elements of an ecological analysis of organizations. A set of organizations engaged in similar activities and with similar patterns of resource utilization constitutes a population. Populations form as a result of processes that isolate or segregate one set of organizations from another, including technological incompatibilities and institutional actions such as government regulations. Populations themselves develop relationships with other populations engaged in other activities that bind them into organizational communities. Organizational communities are functionally integrated systems of interacting populations; the outcomes for firms in any one population are fundamentally intertwined with those for firms in other populations in the same community.

Organizational Ecology and
Environmental Determinism

Although organizational ecology is currently a prominent subfield of organization studies, many critics and skeptics remain. *Why?* The debate centers primarily on assumptions about the relative influences of organizational history, environment, and strategic choice on patterns of organizational change advanced by structural inertia theory (Hannan and Freeman 1977; 1984). Structural inertia theory asserts that existing organizations frequently have difficulty changing strategy and structure quickly enough to keep pace with the demands of uncertain, changing environments, and emphasizes that major organizational innovations often occur early in the life-histories of organizations and populations. Organizational change and variability are thus regarded to reflect primarily relatively inert (i.e. inflexible) organizations replacing each other. To organizational ecology's critics and skeptics this means environmental determinism and loss of human agency (Astley and Van de Ven 1983; Perrow 1986).

Do ecological approaches imply that the actions of particular individuals do not matter for organizations? The answer is no, of course. One part of the confusion is that *determinism* is mistakenly contrasted with *probabilism* (Hannan and Freeman 1989; Singh and Lumsden 1990). Leaving aside whether their actions are intelligent or foolish, carefully planned or seat-of-the-pants, individuals can clearly influence their organization's future – but under conditions of uncertainty there are severe constraints on the ability of individuals to conceive and implement correctly changes that improve organizational success and survival chances reliably in the face of competition. Thus, 'in a world of high uncertainty, adaptive efforts . . . turn out to be essentially random with respect to future value' (Hannan and Freeman 1984: 150). A second part of the confusion has to do with the level of analysis. The actions of individuals matter more to their organization than they do to their organization's population as a whole: there are limits on the influence of individuals' actions for variability in organizational properties. The actions of particular individuals may thus not explain much of the diversity in organizational populations.

Ecological Approaches to Organizational Change

Changes in organizational populations reflect the operation of four basic processes: *variation, selection, retention,* and *competition* (Aldrich 1979; Campbell 1965; McKelvey 1982). Variations are human behaviors. Any kind of change, intentional or blind, is variation. Individuals produce variations in, for example, technical and management competencies, constantly in their efforts to adjust their organization's relation to the environment. Some variations prove more beneficial than others in acquiring resources in a competitive environment and are thus selected positively – not by the *environment*, but by managers inside organizations and by investors, customers, and government regulators in the external environment (Burgelman 1991; Burgelman and Mittman 1994; McKelvey 1994; Meyer 1994; Miner 1994).

When successful variations are known, or

when environmental trends are identifiable, individuals can attempt to copy and implement these successful variations in their own organization, or they can attempt to forecast, anticipate, plan, and implement policies in the context of the predictable trends (DiMaggio and Powell 1983; McKelvey 1994; Nelson and Winter 1982). But when successful variations are unknown, because, for example, the behavior of consumers and competitors is unpredictable, the probability of choosing the correct variation and implementing it is very low. Even when successful variations are identifiable, ambiguity in the *causes* of success may frustrate attempts at imitation. Under such conditions, variations can be viewed as experimental trials, some consciously planned and some accidental, some successful and some failures (McKelvey 1994; Miner 1994).

Whether or not they are known, over time, successful variations are retained as surviving organizations come to be characterized by them. If the survival odds are low for organizations with a particular variant, it does not mean that these organizations are destined to fail. Rather, it means the capacity of individuals to change their organizations successfully is of great importance (Hannan and Freeman 1989). Thus, ecological theory does not remove individuals from responsibility for control (influence, at least) over their organization's success and survival: *individuals do matter.* Ecological theory does, however, assume that individuals cannot always (or often) determine in advance which variations will succeed or change their organizations' strategies and structures quickly enough to keep pace with the demands of uncertain, changing environments. Consequently, in contrast to adaptation approaches, which explain changes in organizational diversity in terms of the cumulative strategic choices and changes to existing organizations, ecological approaches highlight the creation of new organizations and the demise of old ones.

This Chapter

My goal in this chapter is to assess and consolidate the current state-of-the-art in organizational ecology. To accomplish this I review major theoretical statements, empirical studies, and arguments that are now being made. Although I attempt to survey the domain of inquiry in organizational ecology comprehensively, because ecological research now constitutes a large body of work, and because other extensive reviews are available (Aldrich and Wiedenmayer 1993; Carroll 1984a; Wholey and Brittain 1986; Singh and Lumsden 1990), I focus on recent work. The remainder of the chapter is organized in two main sections. I review theory and research on rates of organizational founding and failure in the first section and rates of organizational change in the second. In both sections, I emphasize contemporary issues and debates, identify central questions that remain unanswered, and highlight new and emerging directions for future research that appear promising.

ORGANIZATIONAL FOUNDING AND FAILURE

Ecological approaches to founding and failure constitute radical departures from traditional approaches, which focus on individual initiative, skills, and abilities. The traditional *traits* approach to founding assumes that there is something about an individual's background or personality that leads him or her to found an organization (Gartner 1989). Similarly, traditional business policy research typically attributes organizational failure to managerial inexperience, incompetence, or inadequate financing (Dun and Bradstreet 1978). Ecological approaches to organizational founding and failure, by comparison, emphasize contextual or environmental causes – social, economic, and political – that produce variations in organizational founding and failure rates over time by influencing opportunity structures that confront potential organizational founders and resource constraints that face existing organizations (Aldrich and Wiedenmayer 1993; Carroll 1984a; Romanelli 1991). In broad terms, ecological theory and research on founding and failure focuses on three themes summarized in Table 1: (1) demographic processes, (2) ecological processes, and (3) environmental processes.

DEMOGRAPHIC PROCESSES

Whereas founding processes are attributes of a population since no organization exists prior to founding, failure processes occur at organizational and population levels: existing organizations have histories and structures that influence their failure rates. Thus, studying organizational failure is complicated by the need to consider processes at both organizational and population levels. Demographic analysis examines the effects of organizational characteristics on failure rates in organizational populations.

Age and Size Dependence

A central line of inquiry in ecological research has been the effect of organizational aging on failure.

The predominant view is the *liability of newness* (Stinchcombe 1965: 148–9), the propensity of young organizations to have higher failure rates. Underlying this argument is the assumption that young organizations are more vulnerable because they have to learn new roles as social actors and create organizational roles and routines at a time when organizational resources are stretched to the limit. New organizations are also assumed to lack bases of influence and endorsement, stable relationships with important external constituents, and legitimacy. In a complementary viewpoint, Hannan and Freeman (1984) suggest that selection pressures favor organizations capable of demonstrating their reliability and accountability. Reliability and accountability require organizations to be highly reproducible. This reproducibility, and the structural inertia that it generates, increase as organizations age. Since selection processes favor highly reproducible structures, older organizations are less likely to fail than young organizations.

Closely related to the liability of newness is the *liability of smallness*. Larger organizations are assumed to be less likely to fail for a variety of reasons. Since large size increases inertial tendencies in organizations, and since selection pressures favor structurally inert organizations for their reliability, large organizations are proposed to be less vulnerable to the risk of failure (Hannan and Freeman 1984). The propensity of small organizations to fail is also argued to be the consequence of problems of raising capital, recruiting and training a workforce, meeting higher interest rate payments, and handling the administrative costs of compliance with government regulations (Aldrich and Auster 1986). Large size also tends to legitimate organizations, to the extent that large size is interpreted by stakeholders as an outcome of an organization's prior success and an indicator of future dependability.

Since new organizations tend to be small, if, as the liability of smallness predicts, small organizations have higher failure rates, then liabilities of newness and smallness are confounded and must be separated empirically (Freeman et al. 1983). Thus, what appears as negative age dependence may actually be a confounding of unmeasured size (Levinthal 1991a). Although numerous early ecological studies support the liability of newness hypothesis consistently (Carroll 1983; Carroll and Delacroix 1982; Freeman et al. 1983), as Table 2 shows, recent studies find that, after controlling for contemporaneous organizational size, failure rates do not decline with age. Since much of the original support for the liability of newness comes from studies in which organizational size is not controlled, the early supportive findings may simply reflect specification bias. In

Table 1   *Major ecological approaches to organizational founding and failure*

	Key variables	Key predictions	Key references
Demographic processes			
Age dependence	Organizational age	Liability of newness: organizational failure rates decline with age as roles and routines are mastered, and links with external constituents established	Freeman et al. 1983
		Liability of adolescence: organizational failure rates rise with initial increases in age, reach a peak when initial buffering resource endowments are depleted, then decline with further increases in age	Bruderl and Schussler 1990; Fichman and Levinthal 1991
		Liability of obsolescence: organizations' failure rates increase with age as their original fit with the environment erodes	Baum 1989a; Ingram 1993; Ranger-Moore 1991; Barron et al. 1994
Size dependence	Organizational size	Liability of smallness: organizational failure rates decline with size, which buffers organizations from threats to survival	Freeman et al. 1983
Ecological processes			
Niche-width dynamics	Specialist strategy	Specialists exploit a narrow range of resources and are favored in fine-grained and concentrated environments	Freeman and Hannan 1983; 1987; Carroll 1985
	Generalist strategy	Generalists tolerate widely varying environmental conditions and are favored in coarse-grained, high-variability environments	
Population dynamics	Prior foundings	Initial increases in prior foundings signal opportunity, stimulating new foundings, but further increases create competition for resources, suppressing new foundings. Increases in prior foundings that signal organizational differentiation lower the failure rate	Carroll and Delacroix 1982; Delacroix and Carroll 1983; Delacroix et al. 1989
	Prior failures	Initial increases in prior deaths free up resources, stimulating new foundings, but further increases signal a hostile environment suppressing new foundings. Resources freed up by prior deaths lower the failure rate	
Density dependence	Population density (i.e. a number of organizations in a population)	Initial increases in density increase the institutional legitimacy of a population, increasing foundings and lowering failures, but further increases produce competition, suppressing foundings and increasing failures	Hannan and Freeman 1987; 1988; 1989; Hannan and Carroll 1992
Community interdependence	Population density	Examines cross-population density effects. Competitive (mutualistic) populations suppress (stimulate) each other's founding rates and raise (lower) each other's failure rates	Hannan and Freeman 1987; 1988; Barnett 1990; Brittain 1994

Table 1 *(continued)*

	Key variables	Key predictions	Key references
Environmental processes			
Institutional processes	Political turmoil	Political turmoil affects patterns of founding and failure by shifting social alignments, disrupting established relationships between organizations and resources, and freeing resources for use by new organizations	Carroll and Delacroix 1982; Delacroix and Carroll 1983; Carroll and Huo 1986
	Government regulation	Government policies affect patterns of founding and failure by, for example, enhancing legitimacy, stimulating demand, providing subsidies, and regulating competition	Tucker et al. 1990a; Baum and Oliver 1992; Barnett and Carroll 1993
	Institutional linkages	Linkages to legitimated community and public institutions confer legitimacy and resources on organizations, lowering the failure rate	Singh et al. 1986b; Baum and Oliver 1991
Technological processes	Technology cycles	Technology cycles affect patterns of founding and failure by, for example, changing the relative importance of various resources, creating opportunities to establish new competitive positions, and rendering competencies of existing organizations obsolete	Tushman and Anderson 1986; Anderson 1988; Suárez and Utterback 1992

contrast, studies in Table 2 strongly support the liability of smallness prediction that organizational failure rates decline with increased size.

Bigger May Be Better But is Older Wiser?

These findings have prompted two alternative theoretical perspectives on age dependence that question the basic liability of newness argument.[1] The *liability of adolescence hypothesis* (Bruderl and Schussler 1990; Fichman and Levinthal 1991) predicts an inverted U-shaped relationship between age and failure. This model begins with the observation that all new organizations start with an initial stock of assets, including goodwill, positive prior beliefs, psychological commitment, and investment of financial resources, that buffer new organizations from failure during an initial honeymoon period – even when early outcomes are unfavorable. The larger the initial stock of assets, the longer the time period in which the organization is buffered. As the original stock of assets is depleted, organizations face a liability of adolescence; and those organizations fail that are unable to generate needed resource flows because, for example, they were unable to establish necessary roles and routines or develop stable relationships with important external constituents. However, after adolescence, the

future probability of failure declines since surviving organizations have been able to acquire sufficient ongoing resources.

The liability of newness and adolescence arguments provide divergent accounts of age dependence for young organizations, but both agree that rates of failure decline monotonically for older organizations. Yet, processes underlying these models (e.g. learning and creating new roles and routines, establishing relationships with external constituents, and depleting initial endowments) occur early in organizational life. The *liability of aging hypothesis* predicts an increasing rate of failure for older organizations as a result of processes that occur later in organizational life (Barron et al. 1994; Baum 1989a; Ingram 1993; Ranger-Moore 1991). Thus, the liability of aging hypothesis complements and extends the liability of newness and adolescence hypotheses (Baum 1989a).

The liability of aging argument begins with another insight from Stinchcombe's (1965: 153) essay: 'the organizational inventions that can be made at a time in history depend on the social technology available at that time.' Organizations reflect the environment at the time of their founding. As the environment into which an organization is founded changes, the fit between organizations and their environments erodes as

Table 2   *Age and size dependence studies, 1989–1994*

Population	Age[1]	Size	Size variable	References
US labor unions, 1836–1985[2]	−	+	Membership at founding	Hannan and Freeman 1989; Carroll and Hannan 1989a; 1989b; Carroll and Wade 1991; Hannan and Carroll 1992
US brewers, 1633–1988	−	na		
Argentina newspapers, 1800–1900	−	na		
Ireland newspapers, 1800–1975	−	na		
San Francisco newspapers, 1800–1975	−	na		
Little Rock newspapers, 1815–1975	−	na		
Springfield newspapers, 1835–1975	−	na		
Shreveport newspapers, 1840–1975	−	na		
Elmira newspapers, 1815–1975	−	na		
Lubbock newspapers, 1890–1975	−	na		
Lafayette newspapers, 1835–1975	−	na		
California wineries, 1940–85	0	−	Storage capacity	Delacroix et al. 1989; Delacroix and Swaminathan 1991
Iowa telephone companies, 1900–29	0	0	Subscribers	Barnett 1990; Barnett and Amburgey 1990
Pennsylvania telephone companies, 1879–1934	+	0		
West German business organizations, 1980–9	+/−	−	Employees at founding	Bruderl and Schussler 1990
Bavarian brewers, 1900–81	0	−	Small firm dummy	Swaminathan and Wiedenmayer 1991
Toronto day care centers, 1971–89	+	−	Licensed capacity	Baum and Oliver 1991; 1992;
Toronto nursery schools, 1971–87	−	−	Licensed capacity	Baum and Singh 1994b
US immigrant newspapers, 1877–1914	−	na		Olzak and West 1991
African-American newspapers, 1877–1914	−	na		
NY State life insurance companies, 1813–1935	+/0	−	Assets	Ranger-Moore 1991
Manhattan banks, 1840–1976	0	−	Assets	Banaszak-Holl 1992; 1993
Manhattan hotels, 1898–1990	+	−	Number of rooms	Baum and Mezias 1992
California S&Ls, 1970–87	0	0	Assets	Haveman 1992; 1993a
US mutual S&Ls, 1960–87	+/−	0	Assets	Rao and Neilsen 1992
US stock S&Ls, 1960–87	+/−	0	Assets	
US cement producers, 1888–1982	0/−	na		Anderson and Tushman 1992
US minicomputer manufacturers, 1958–82	+/−	na		
US group HMOs, 1976–91	0	−	Enrollment	Wholey et al. 1992
US independent practice Assn HMOs, 1976–91	+	−	Enrollment	
Finnish newspapers, 1771–1963	−	na		Amburgey et al. 1993
US brewers, 1878–1988	+	−	Production in 1878 and 1879	Carroll et al. 1993
US microcomputer manufacturers, 1975–86	+	−	Units sold	Ingram 1993
US integrated circuit manufacturers, 1971–81	0	−	Employees	Loree 1993
Medical diagnostic imaging firms, 1953–89	+/−	0	Corporate sales	Mitchell and Singh 1993
US trade associations, 1901–90	0/−	−	Membership	Aldrich et al. 1994
US credit unions, 1980–89[3]	+	−/+/−	Assets	Amburgey et al. 1994
US hotel chains, 1896–1980	0	−	Number of hotels	Ingram 1994
New York City credit unions, 1914–90	+	−	Log real total assets	Barron et al. 1994

[1] X/Y gives the signs of significant ($p<0.05$) linear and squared terms, respectively, when estimated. X gives the sign of the effect of initial increases in age, Y gives the sign of the effect for later increases.

[2] See Hannan and Freeman (1989: 257–9) for an interpretation of this positive size effect.

[3] Amburgey et al. (1994) test a cubic effect of size to examine the failure risk of mid-sized organizations.

incomplete information, bounded rationality, and inertial tendencies make it difficult, if not impossible, for individuals to keep their organizations aligned with environmental demands. Environmental change also creates opportunities for new organizations to enter and undermine the competitive positions of established organizations. Ironically, attempts to realign the organization with its environment may carry additional hazards that result from constraints on the ability of individuals to conceive and implement changes successfully and the potential for major change attempts to lower organizational performance reliability and disrupt key external relationships (Hannan and Freeman 1984). Thus, encountering a series of environmental changes that decrease the alignment of organizations and environments exposes aging organizations to an increased risk of failure.

Research Findings and Future Directions

Two sample-selection bias problems may contribute to the weak support for the liability of newness in Table 2. First, the new organizations studied may be *old* new organizations, that is, late in the process of emergence (Katz and Gartner 1988). If researchers were able to obtain data earlier in the founding process (e.g. prior to formal incorporation), liability of newness findings might be much stronger. Second, left-censored organizations, that is, those founded before the start of the observation period, are included in several analyses. Because they are already *survivors*, these organizations tend to be low-risk cases. Consequently, treating left-censored organizations as standard subjects can lead to an underestimation of failure rates at shorter durations (Guo 1993).

While the liability of newness may commonly be underestimated, the liability of aging may commonly be overestimated. If age coincides with the amount of environmental change experienced by an organization, and if the risk of failure increases with cumulative environmental change, then the probability of failure will increase, spuriously, with age if accumulated environmental change is uncontrolled (Carroll 1983: 313). Thus, in the same way that negative age dependence can result spuriously from uncontrolled size, positive age dependence (after controlling for size) may result spuriously from uncontrolled exposure to environmental change. Of course, this implies that after controlling for size and environmental change, *no* age dependence should be found.

The limited support for the liability of adolescence hypothesis may have a simpler explanation: tests of the liability of adolescence hypothesis are infrequent. Notably, five of seven studies in Table 2 that permit nonmonotonic age dependence find a liability of adolescence.

Research on age dependence must move beyond the use of age as a surrogate for all constructs underlying the various age dependence models and begin to test the models' assumptions directly. For example, the liability of newness hypothesis assumes that a lack of social approval, stability, and sufficient resources typifies recent entrants into a population and that these shortcomings increase their risk of failure, but organizational variation in these factors is rarely measured directly. Of course, if young organizations are capable of obtaining early legitimacy and access to resources through the formation of institutional attachments to community and public constituents, a liability of newness may not be observed (Baum and Oliver 1991). A further benefit of this approach is that liabilities of newness, adolescence, and obsolescence can be treated as complementary rather than as competing organizational processes. Thus, although we still know very little about *how* aging lowers organizational failure, or the *conditions* under which one, the other, or some combination of these models will predominate (the same is true for organizational size, of course), recent advances offer promise for future progress.

ECOLOGICAL PROCESSES

Niche-Width Dynamics

In the initial statement of organizational ecology, Hannan and Freeman (1977) use niche-width theory to formulate a model of the differential survival capabilities of *specialist* organizations, which possess few slack resources and concentrate on ways to exploit a narrow range of potential customers, and *generalist* organizations, which attempt to appeal to the average consumer who occupies the middle of the market and exhibit adaptive tolerance for more widely varying environmental conditions. Building on *fitness-set theory* (Levins 1968), Hannan and Freeman focus on two aspects of environmental variation to explain the relative prevalence of specialists and generalists. The first, *variability*, refers to the variance in environmental fluctuations about their mean over time. The second, *grain*, refers to the patchiness of these variations, with many, small periodic variations being *fine*-grained and few large, periodic variations being *coarse*-grained. Table 3 summarizes the dominant organizational forms predicted by niche-width theory. The key prediction (for concave fitness sets, in which the average magnitude of environmental variation is large relative to organizational tolerances) is that in fine-grained

Table 3   *Niche-width theory predictions of favored forms*

	Uncertain environment		Certain environment	
	Fine-grained	Coarse-grained	Fine-grained	Coarse-grained
Concave fitness set	Specialist	Generalist	Specialist	Specialist
Convex fitness set	Generalist	Generalist	Specialist	Specialist

Source: adapted from Hannan and Freeman 1989: 311

environments specialists dominate generalists regardless of the level of environmental uncertainty. This occurs because specialists ride out the environmental fluctuations, while generalists are unable to respond quickly enough to attain any degree of production efficiency (but see Herriott 1987). Thus, under specific conditions of fine-grained environments, fitness-set theory challenges conventional organizational contingency theory predictions that uncertain environments always favor generalist organizations because they spread out their risk (Lawrence and Lorsch 1967; Pfeffer and Salancik 1978; Thompson 1967).

Carroll (1985) advances an alternative model of niche-width dynamics designed to explain the differential survival capabilities of specialists and generalists in environments characterized by economies of scale. In contrast to fitness-set theory, which predicts that for a given population one optimal strategy exists, Carroll proposes that competition among large, generalist organizations in a population to occupy the center of the market frees peripheral resources that are most likely to be used by small, specialist members of the population. Carroll refers to the process generating this outcome as *resource partitioning*. The resource-partitioning model implies that, in concentrated markets with a few large generalists, small specialists may be able to exploit more resources without engaging in direct competition with larger, generalist organizations. This yields the prediction that increasing market concentration increases the failure rate of large, generalist organizations and lowers the failure rate of small specialist organizations.

Research Findings and Future Directions

Although the distinction between specialists and generalists is now used commonly in ecological research as a strategic distinction, recent studies of populations' niche dynamics do not make use of niche-width theory and frequently attend to *spatial* as well as temporal environmental variation (Baum and Mezias 1992; Baum and Singh 1994b; 1994c; Carroll and Wade 1991; Haveman 1994; Lomi 1995). Tests of the specific predictions of niche-width and resource-parti-

tioning theories are limited. Studies of California restaurant failure (Freeman and Hannan 1983; 1987) and US semiconductor firm failure (Hannan and Freeman 1989) do not support the basic hypothesis that (for concave fitness sets) in fine-grained environments specialists dominate over generalists regardless of the level of environmental uncertainty, and thus fail to distinguish niche-width theory from orthodox organizational contingency theory. Resource-partitioning theory is supported in studies of newspaper organization failure (Carroll 1985; 1987) as well as two more recent studies of founding and failure of American breweries (Carroll and Swaminathan 1992) and founding of rural cooperative banks in Italy (Freeman and Lomi 1994), which offer partial support. Studies that compare the predictions of these two models and studies that contrast ecological models with traditional contingency predictions are needed. Current formulations of niche-width theory, which focus exclusively on temporal environmental variation, also need to be linked to recent approaches that consider spatial environmental variation. Finally, the possibility of organizational polymorphism (e.g. unrelated diversification for temporal variation, related diversification for spatial variation), an alternative strategy to specialism and generalism, must also be incorporated within existing frameworks (Usher 1994).

Population Dynamics and Density Dependence

Recent research on founding and failure in organizational ecology has paid considerable attention to intrapopulation processes of *population dynamics*, the number of prior foundings and failures in a population, and *population density*, the number of organizations in a population.

Previous patterns of organizational founding and failure in a population can influence current rates of founding (Delacroix and Carroll 1983). Initially, prior foundings signal a fertile niche to potential entrepreneurs, encouraging foundings. But as foundings increase further, competition for resources increases, discouraging foundings. Prior failures are predicted to have a similar curvilinear effect on foundings. At first, failures release resources that can be reassembled into new foundings. But further failures signal a hostile environment, discouraging foundings. Prior foundings and failures can also lower failure rates. The resources freed up by prior failures enhance the viability of established organizations, lowering the failure rate in the next period (Carroll and Delacroix 1982). Waves of organizational founding, which reflect differentiation that segments organizations' resource requirements, lower the failure rate by reducing direct competition for resources (Delacroix et al. 1989).

Density-dependent explanations for founding and failure are similar though not identical. Initial increases in population density can increase the institutional legitimacy of a population. The capacity of a population's members to acquire resources increases greatly when those controlling resources take the organizational form for granted. However, as a population continues to grow, the interdependence among a population's members becomes competitive. When there are few organizations in a population, competition with others for scarce common resources can be easily avoided. But, this becomes more difficult as the number of potential competitors grows. Combined, the mutualistic effects of initial increases in density and the competitive effects of further increases suggest curvilinear effects of population density on founding and failure rates (Hannan and Carroll 1992; Hannan and Freeman 1989).

Hannan and Freeman (1989), Hannan and Carroll (1992), and others provide substantial empirical support for the curvilinear relationships predicted by the density dependence model. By comparison, although often significant, population dynamics findings are mixed (Aldrich and Wiedenmayer 1993; Singh and Lumsden 1990). Moreover, as illustrated in Table 4, when population dynamics and population density are modeled together, recent studies find population dynamics effects are generally weaker and less robust. Even Delacroix and Carroll's (1983) original Argentina and Ireland newspaper population findings do not hold up when density is introduced in a reanalysis of their data (Carroll and Hannan 1989b).

One possible explanation for the apparent dominance of density dependence processes over population dynamics processes is the more systematic character of density relative to the transitory nature of changes in density that result from ongoing foundings and failures. A related explanation is that the effects of foundings and failures are more transitory than the yearly data that are typically available are able to detect (Aldrich and Wiedenmayer 1993). A third explanation is the greater sensitivity of estimates

for quadratic specifications of prior foundings and failures to outliers. These issues need to be researched more thoroughly before population dynamics effects are abandoned, which is clearly the trend in recent research.

Elaborations of the Density Dependence Model

Although support for density dependence theory is quite strong, it has not been without its critics. Density dependence theory has received some critical attention for its proposed integration of ecological and institutional perspectives (Baum and Powell 1995; Delacroix and Rao 1994; Zucker 1989). Some authors have questioned the implicit assumption that each organization in a population influences and is influenced by competition equally (Baum and Mezias 1992; Baum and Singh 1994a; 1994b; Winter 1990). In a methodological critique, Petersen and Koput (1991) argue that the negative effect of initial increases in population density on the failure rate may result from unobserved heterogeneity in the population (but see Hannan et al. 1991). Singh (1993) observes that some of the debate about density dependence stems from the model's main strength, its generality, which may have been achieved at the expense of precision of measurement and realism of context. Singh concludes that 'we may do well to sacrifice some generality, provided it moves the research toward greater precision and realism' (1993: 471). Density effects are clear empirically but the specific conditions that generate legitimacy and competition are more ambiguous – defined by outcomes rather than by substance. Thus, the precise interpretation of the extensive density dependence findings need to be explored further.

Several elaborations, respecifications, and new measures have been advanced recently to address questions raised by the initial density dependence formulation. Although Hannan and Carroll have questioned some of these developments (e.g. 1992: 38–9, 71–4), these new directions appear to hold real promise for improving precision and realism with respect to both legitimation and competition. These developments, summarized in Table 5, are reviewed below.

Accounting for Concentration

The growth trajectories of diverse organizational populations appear to follow a common path. The number of organizations grows slowly initially, then increases rapidly to a peak. Once this maximum is reached, there is a decline in the number of population members and increased concentration. In organizational ecology, the

Table 4   *Population dynamics and density dependence studies,[1] 1989–1995*

Population	Prior foundings	Prior failures	Population density	References
Founding studies				
US labour unions, 1836–1985	+/−	na	+/−	Hannan and Freeman 1989;
US brewers, 1633–1988	+/−	0	+/−	Carroll and Hannan 1989a; 1989b;
San Francisco newspapers, 1800–1975	0/0	−/+	+/−	Carroll and Swaminathan 1991;
Argentina newspapers, 1800–1900	−/+	0/−	+/−	Hannan and Carroll 1992
Ireland newspapers, 1800–1975	+/−	0/0	+/−	
Little Rock newspapers, 1815–1975	0/0	0/+	+/−	
Springfield newspapers, 1835–1975	0/+	0/+	+/−	
Shreveport newspapers, 1840–1975	0/0	0/0	+/−	
Elmira newspapers, 1815–1975	+/0	0/0	+/0	
Lubbock newspapers, 1890–1975	0/0	0	0/0	
Lafayette newspapers, 1835–1975	na	0	0/0	
Pennsylvania telephone cos, 1879–1934	+	−	−/+	Barnett and Amburgey 1990
Metro Toronto day care centers, 1971–89	+	0	+/−	Baum and Oliver 1992
US State life insurance cos, 1759–1937	+/−	na	+/−	Ranger-Moore et al. 1991
Manhattan banks, 1840–1976	+/0	na	+/−	Banaszak-Holl 1992; 1993
Manhattan fax transmission cos, 1965–92				Baum et al. 1993; 1995
Pre-dominant design cohort	−/+	0	+/−	
Post-dominant design cohort	−/+	0	+/−	
NY State life insurance cos, 1842–1904	−	−	0/+	Budros 1993; 1994
German breweries, 1861–1988	−/0	na	+/−	Carroll et al. 1993
US trade associations, 1901–90	0/0	0/0	+/−	Aldrich et al. 1994
Belgian automobile industry	+/−	na	+/−	Hannan et al. 1995
British automobile industry	+/0	na	+/−	
French automobile industry	+/0	na	+/−	
Italian automobile industry	0/0	na	+/−	
German automobile industry	+/0	na	+/−	
Failure studies				
US labor unions, 1836–1985	na	0	−/+	Hannan and Freeman 1989;
US brewers, 1633–1988	+	−	−/+	Carroll and Hannan 1989a; 1989b;
San Francisco newspapers, 1800–1975	0/0	+/−	−/+	Carroll and Swaminathan 1991;
Argentina newspapers, 1800–1900	0/0	+/0	−/+	Hannan and Carroll 1992
Ireland newspapers, 1800–1975	0/0	+/−	−/+	
Little Rock newspapers, 1815–1975	+/−	0/0	0/0	
Springfield newspapers, 1835–1975	0/0	0/0	0/+	
Shreveport newspapers, 1840–1975	+/0	0/0	0/0	
Elmira newspapers, 1815–1975	+/0	0/0	0/0	
Lubbock newspapers, 1890–1975	0/0	0	0/−	
Lafayette newspapers, 1835–1975	0/0	0	0/0	
California wineries, 1940–85	−	−	0/0	Delacroix et al. 1989
US semiconductor firms	−/+	+/−	−/+	Freeman 1990
Metro Toronto day care centers, 1971–89	0	−	−/+	Baum and Oliver 1992
Manhattan fax transmission cos, 1965–92				Baum et al. 1993; 1995
Pre-dominant design cohort	−	−	+/0	
Post-dominant design cohort	0	0	−/+	
US trade associations, 1901–90	+	−	−/+	Aldrich et al. 1994

[1] Includes only analyses that estimate both population dynamics and density dependence effects. X/Y gives the signs of significant ($p<0.05$) linear and squared terms, respectively.

density dependence model is used to account for the shape of the growth trajectory to its peak (Hannan and Carroll 1992). Since no organization or small group of organizations is allowed to dominate (each organization in a population is assumed to contribute to and experience competition equally), the density dependence model predicts logistic growth in numbers to an equilibrium level. But it does not account for the later decline in numbers and increase in

Table 5   *Elaborations of the density dependence model, 1989–1995*

Model	Key variables	Nature of elaboration	References
Density delay	Population density at founding	Adds an imprinting effect of density at founding to the original formulation. Helps explain the commonly observed decline in population density in older populations	Carroll and Hannan 1989a; Hannan and Carroll 1992
Mass dependence	Population mass (population density weighted by organizational size)	Respecifies competition effect of population density by allowing larger organizations to generate stronger competition. Helps explain the tendency toward concentration in organizational populations	Barnett and Amburgey 1990
Institutional embeddedness	Relational density (number of linkages between a population and the institutional environment)	Attempts to explain the legitimation of an organizational form in terms of endorsements by powerful actors and organizations	Baum and Oliver 1992; Hybels et al. 1994
Non-density-based measures of legitimacy	Certification contests and media-based content measures	Models legitimation effects with non-density-based measures of institutionalization	Rao 1994; Hybels 1994
Early versus late low density	Population density × population age	Separates early legitimation from later market power and resource partitioning effects of low population density in populations that have evolved beyond their peak density	Baum 1995
Level of analysis	City density, state density, regional density, national density (population density at various levels of geographic aggregation)	Attempts to uncover the appropriate level of analysis to study density-dependent processes by comparing patterns of density dependency across multiple levels of analysis	Carroll and Wade 1991; Swaminathan and Wiedenmayer 1991; Hannan and Carroll 1992
Localized competition	Size similarity, price similarity, location similarity (population density weighted by the size of differences in various organizational features)	Respecifies competition effect of population density by allowing more similar organizations to compete at a greater level of intensity	Hannan et al. 1990; Baum and Mezias 1992
Organizational niche overlap	Overlap density, non-overlap density (population density weighted by the degree of overlap and non-overlap in resource requirements between organizations)	Respecifies population density by disaggregating it into competitive and mutualistic components using information on the overlap and non-overlap of resource requirement of population members	Baum and Singh 1994b; 1994c

concentration (Carroll and Hannan 1989a; Hannan and Carroll 1992). Two elaborations of the original formulation have been advanced to address this question.

Density Delay   In the density dependence model it is *contemporaneous* population density, density at particular historical times, that is the focus. Carroll and Hannan (1989a) propose a refine-

ment of the model to include an additional, *delayed* effect of population density that helps explain the decline of populations from their peak density. They suggest that organizations' survival chances are sensitive to population density levels at the time of their founding. Specifically, organizations founded in high-density conditions are proposed to experience persistently higher failure rates. High density at founding creates a *liability of resource scarcity* that prevent organizations from moving quickly from organizing to full-scale operation. High density also results in *tight niche packing*, forcing newly founded organizations, which cannot compete head-to-head with established organizations, to use inferior or marginal resources. These conditions imprint themselves on organizations, affecting their viability throughout their existence. Carroll and Hannan show that population density at the time of organizational founding is positively related to failure rates in six of the seven populations they analyze (Carroll and Hannan 1989a; Hannan and Carroll 1992). This means that organizations entering high-density populations have persistently elevated failure rates, contributing to an explanation for a decline in population density from its peak. However, several other studies failed to replicate this finding (Aldrich et al. 1994; Wholey et al. 1992). Moreover, *density delay* effects appear to produce an oscillating equilibrium, not a definite, singular downturn in population density (Hannan and Carroll 1992: 183).

Mass Dependence Various perspectives in organization and management theory suggest that larger organizations generate stronger competition than their smaller rivals as a result of their superior access to resources, greater market power, and economies of scale and scope. If large organizations generate stronger competition, then ecological models of population dynamics should reflect their greater significance. Barnett and Amburgey (1990) advance an elaboration of the density dependence model that incorporates this possibility. They do this by modeling the effects of *population mass*, the sum of the sizes of all organizations in the population, or, in other words, population density weighted by organizational size. If large organizations are stronger competitors, then, after controlling for population density, increases in population mass should have a competitive effect, slowing the founding rate and increasing the failure rate of smaller organizations.

By permitting the competitive strengths of organizations to vary as a function of their size, the mass dependence model permits larger organizations in a population to dominate by generating stronger competition than smaller organizations, displacing their population's size in numbers and increasing concentration. Large organizations may therefore play a central role in organizational ecology not because they are affected individually by selection pressures, but because they have a disproportionate influence on population dynamics (Barnett and Amburgey 1990). Unfortunately, mass dependence findings are mixed. Some studies find the predicted effects

(Banaszak-Holl 1992; 1993; Baum and Mezias 1992). Others find either no or mixed effects (Hannan and Carroll 1992), or mutualistic effects (Barnett and Amburgey 1990). Although non-supportive findings appear to be attributable to data limitations (Hannan and Carroll 1992: 130–1) or significant features of the study population (Barnett and Amburgey 1990: 98–9), a more general explanation may be found in strategic groups theory (Caves and Porter 1977), which suggests that industry-wide inferences of market power cannot be made when strategic groups characterize competition since mobility barriers differentially protect strategic groups.

Density and Institutional Processes

Drawing on the neo-institutional literature (DiMaggio and Powell 1983; Meyer and Rowan 1977; Zucker 1977), organizational ecologists draw a distinction between *cognitive* and *socio-political* legitimacy (Aldrich and Fiol 1994). From a cognitive perspective, an organizational form is legitimate 'when there is little question in the minds of actors that it serves as the natural way to effect some kind of collective action' (Hannan and Carroll 1992: 34). The socio-political approach emphasizes how embeddedness in relational and normative contexts influences an organizational form's legitimacy by signalling its conformity to social and institutional expectations. Although institutionalists view these two facets of legitimation as complementary and fundamentally interrelated, density dependence theory emphasizes *only* cognitive legitimacy. Although cognitive legitimacy may be achieved without socio-political approval, socio-political legitimacy is a vital source of, or impediment to, cognitive legitimacy. Indeed, since contemporary organizational populations rarely operate in isolation from the state, the professions, and broader societal influences, socio-political legitimacy cannot be ignored (Baum and Oliver 1992; Baum and Powell 1995).

Institutional Embeddedness and Socio-political Legitimacy In her provocative commentary, Zucker (1989) takes Hannan and his colleagues to task for invoking the concept of legitimation *ex post facto* to explain the effects of density on founding and failure rates, and suggests that density estimates are proxies for other effects (see also Miner 1993; Petersen and Koput 1991). She advocates the use of more direct measures of the underlying institutional processes. Her critique led to the density-as-process argument, in which legitimation is no longer a variable to be measured but a process that relates density to founding and failure. Hannan and Carroll claim that 'growth in density *controls* . . . [legitimation] processes – it does not reflect them' (1992: 69). These competing proxy and process views suggest different effects of adding covariates (Hannan and Carroll 1992). If density is an indirect indicator, measuring legitimation more directly would dampen first-order density effects or lead them to disappear altogether. But from the density-as-process view, inclusion of such covariates implies a sharpening and strengthening of density's legitimation effects.

Baum and Oliver (1992) address exactly this question. They argue that an important limitation of the density dependence model is that it neglects the evolution of a population's interdependencies with surrounding institutions. However, where relations with community and government are dense, these institutional actors may exert considerable influence over the conditions that regulate competition for scarce resources and legitimacy in the population. Baum and Oliver (1992) propose an alternative hypothesis in which legitimation is explained in terms of the embeddedness of a population in its institutional environment. They model institutional embeddedness with *relational density*, the number of relationships between the population's members and community organizations and government agencies in its institutional environment. While initial estimates in a study of day care centers support the curvilinear density dependence predictions for both founding and failure, inclusion of relational density altered both relationships to be purely competitive. These results support Zucker's measurement critique. Hybels et al. (1994) replicated these findings in a study of founding of American biotechnology firms in which vertical (input and output) strategic alliances are used to measure industry embeddedness in relational and institutional contexts. These studies suggest that the density-as-proxy formulation of legitimacy was more accurate, and, in addition, that population density may be a proxy for sociopolitical as well as (or instead of) cognitive legitimacy (Baum and Powell 1995). Future research incorporating both population and relational densities may provide further clarification of the role of institutional processes in population dynamics.

NON-DENSITY-BASED MEASURES OF LEGITIMACY

Several other promising *non*-density-based alternatives to studying legitimation have recently been examined. In many industries, special purpose organizations institute certification contests to evaluate products or firms and rank-order participants according to their performance on preset criteria. Certification contests offer a common social test of products and organizations that serve as a social diffusion mechanism. Rao (1994) argues that cumulative victories in such certification contests enhance organizational reputations in the eyes of risk-averse consumers and financiers, improving their access to resources and their survival chances. Moreover, Rao argues that by increasing opportunities for certification and diffusing knowledge about organizations and their products, these contests establish the identity and legitimacy of a product and its producers, lowering the risk of producer failure. His analysis of the early American automobile industry supports these ideas, demonstrating that winning heavily publicized road races improved the survival chances of individual automobile manufacturers and, in addition, that the cumulative prevalence of contests lowers the aggregate failure rate. In addition to certification contests, a wide range of accreditation, certification, and credentialing activities signal reliability, raising the sociopolitical legitimacy of organizational forms, as well as contributing to their cognitive legitimacy by spreading knowledge about them (Baum and Powell, 1995).

Another basic source of information diffusion about the activities of an organizational form are the print media. Detailed archives of media coverage exist for many industries and content analyses of these public records offer a potentially powerful technique for operationalizing legitimation. Measurement of this kind is used widely in social movement research (e.g., Olzak, 1992; Tilly, 1993). Content-based measures promise high comparability across settings covered by the business press as well as temporal comparability within a given context. Hybels (1994) successfully employed media-based measures of legitimacy in an analysis of foundings of American biotechnology firms.

Early Versus Late Low-Density Conditions Although, as noted earlier, density dependence theory only predicts logistic growth of populations to their peak size, it is frequently tested in populations that have evolved well beyond their peak density. This complicates density-dependent legitimacy interpretations. Although early low density has a specific meaning (i.e. legitimation) in density dependence theory, late low density has no meaning at all (Baum 1995). Notably, early and late low-density conditions seem likely to have analogous effects on vital rates that are not distinguished in the estimates: the few large organizations that dominate substantial segments of the market are unlikely to fail, and increasing concentration may free up resources creating opportunities for new entrants that do not require them to engage in direct competition with larger, well-established organizations (Carroll 1985). First-order density coefficients may thus mean late market power and resource partitioning, *not* early legitimation. Baum and Powell (1995) found that support for density dependence is far stronger in studies that include late low-density conditions. Thus, the findings of numerous studies supporting density-dependent legitimacy may be undermined by incorporating information on periods of population decline, which density dependence theory is not designed to explain. Consequently, future studies that estimate separate early and late linear density effects are needed (Baum 1995).

Density and Competitive Processes

Density dependence theory assumes that the intensity of competition depends on the number of organizations in a population. Some researchers, however, question the assumption implicit in this approach that all members of a population are equivalent, with each member assumed to compete for the same scarce resources and to contribute to and experience competition equally (Winter 1990: 286). Although research demonstrates that this assumption may be a reasonable starting approximation, theory in organizational ecology suggests that the intensity of competition between organizations in a population is largely a function of their similarity in resource requirements: the more similar the resource requirements, the greater the potential for intense competition (McPherson 1983; Hannan and Freeman 1977; 1989). If all organizations in a population are not equal competitors, population density may not provide the most precise measure of the competition faced by different organizations in a population. This suggests that density dependence theory can be enriched by incorporating population microstructures. Recently, several ecological models have been examined that incorporate organizational differences explicitly to specify competitive processes within organizational populations more precisely.

Level of Analysis In its original formulation, density dependence theory implicitly assumes that geographically organizations compete with each other at an intensity equal to neighboring organizations. Researchers have begun to refine this assumption by disaggregating population density according to level of analysis (i.e. spatial aggregation) to explore the geographic boundaries on competitive (and institutional) processes. For example, Hannan and Carroll (1992), Carroll and Wade (1991), and Swaminathan and Wiedenmayer (1991) analyzed density dependence in the founding rates of American

and German brewers at city, state, region, and national levels of analysis. These studies estimate the density dependence model separately for each level of analysis and then compare coefficients across levels. They reveal that local and diffuse competitive effects differ much more than comparable legitimation effects in the American and German brewing industries. Lomi (1995) obtained parallel findings in an analysis of founding rates of Italian rural cooperative banks. Recently, Hannan et al. (1995) estimated models of organizational founding in the European automobile industry in which density-dependent legitimation and competition were operationalized at *different* levels of analysis. They found stronger country-level competition and stronger European-level legitimation.

These and other recent studies (Amburgey et al. 1993; Baum and Singh 1994a; 1994b; Rao and Neilsen 1992) support Zucker's (1989: 543) speculation that 'smaller geographical areas should theoretically involve more intense competition since they are more tightly bounded resource areas.' At the same time, they also support the idea that institutional processes operate at a broader level (Hannan et al. 1995), serving to contextualize ecological processes (Scott 1992; Tucker et al. 1992). Thus, competitive processes may often be heterogeneous, operating most strongly in local environmental arenas, while institutional processes may often be homogeneous, revealing themselves most strongly at higher levels of spatial aggregation. More research is needed to support or refute this speculation.

Localized Competition Hannan and Freeman (1977: 945–6) propose that organizations of different sizes use different strategies and structures; and, as a result, that although organizations of different sizes are engaged in similar activities, large and small organizations depend on different mixes of resources. This implies that organizations compete most intensely with similarly sized organizations. For example, if large and small organizations depend on different resources (e.g. large hotels depend on conventions while small hotels depend on individual travelers), then patterns of resource use will be specialized to segments of the size distribution. Consequently, competition between large and small organizations will be less intense than competition among large or small organizations. Although size-localized competition did not receive empirical attention until recently (Hannan et al. 1990), studies of Manhattan banks (Banaszak-Holl 1992), Manhattan hotels (Baum and Mezias 1992), and US health maintenance organizations (Wholey et al. 1992) now provide empirical evidence of size-localized competition. These findings demonstrate that the intensity of competition faced by organizations in a population depends not only on the number of other organizations, but on their relative sizes as well. Baum and Mezias (1992) generalize the size-localized model to other organizational dimensions, and show that in addition to similar-sized organizations, competition within a population can be more intense for organizations that are geographically proximate and charge similar prices.

Future research on localized competition can offer direct insights into the dynamics of organizational diversity. Localized competition models imply a pattern of disruptive or segregating selection (Baum 1990b; Amburgey et al. 1994) in which competition between like entities for finite resources leads eventually to differentiation (Durkheim 1933; Hawley 1950: 201–3). This mode of selection tends to increase organizational differentiation by producing gaps rather than smooth, continuous variation in the distribution of the members of a population on some organizational dimension.

Organizational Niche Overlap Baum and Singh (1994b; 1994c) test a resource overlap model in which the potential for competition between any two organizations is directly proportional to the overlap of their targeted resource bases, or *organizational niches*. Potential competition for each organization is measured using *overlap density*, the aggregate overlap of an organization's resource requirements with those of all others in the population (i.e. population density weighted by the overlap in resource requirements). Baum and Singh define a complementary variable, *nonoverlap density*, which aggregates the resource nonoverlaps with all others in the population. Together, overlap and nonoverlap densities disaggregate competitive and noncompetitive forces for each organization in a population. Entrepreneurs are predicted to be unlikely to target or to be capable of founding organizations in parts of the resource space where overlap density is high. Organizations operating in high overlap density conditions are also predicted to be less sustainable. Conversely, entrepreneurs are predicted to be likely to target and be capable of founding organizations in parts of the resource space where nonoverlap density is high because of the absence of direct competition for resources and the potential for complementary demand enhancement. For these reasons, high nonoverlap density is also expected to lower failure rates. Baum and Singh found support for these predictions in a population of day care centers in metropolitan Toronto for which resource requirements were defined in terms of the ages of the children they had the capacity to enroll. These studies indicate that organizations

have different likelihoods of being established and endure different survival fates after founding as a function of the locations they target in a multidimensional resource space. Generalization of this disaggregation of population density into overlap and nonoverlap densities may help clarify the role of population heterogeneity in interpretations of the nonmonotonic density dependence findings (Petersen and Koput 1991; Hannan et al. 1991).

Community Interdependence

Relations among organizational populations are central to ecological theories of organization. Populations develop relationships with other populations engaged in diverse activities that bind them into organizational communities (Astley 1985; Fombrun 1986; Hawley 1950). Organizational communities are formed as competition leads to the creation of new populations that fulfill complementary roles in which they are dependent on, but noncompetitive with, established populations. In this way, competition leads to the emergence of a complex system of functionally differentiated populations linked by mutualistic interdependencies. The growth of internal complexity fosters community stability, slowing the formation of new populations. However, increasing internal complexity also sets the stage for community collapse. If complex systems experience disturbances (e.g. technological innovation, regulatory change) beyond a certain threshold level, they may disintegrate as the result of a domino effect.

When an evolving population interacts with other populations, the success and survival of its members depends on the nature and strength of its ecological interactions with organizations in other populations. Consequently, it is often difficult to understand the behavior of organizations in a single population in isolation because the fates of populations are commonly linked (Fombrun 1988). Community ecology attends explicitly to the structure and evolution of these interactions among organizational populations and considers the system-level consequences of these interactions for the dynamics of co-acting sets of populations. Brittain and Wholey (1988) identify the following possible types of interactions between two populations, j and k, where the signs are for α_{jk} and α_{kj}, respectively: $(-,-)$ *full competition*, $(-,0)$ *partial competition*, $(+,-)$ *predatory competition*, $(0,0)$ *neutrality*, $(+,0)$ *commensalism*, and $(+,+)$ *symbiosis*. Studying the effects of such interactions on the dynamics of organizational communities is now emerging as an important area of inquiry (Singh and Lumsden 1990). Findings of some recent studies of community interaction are summarized in Table 6.

Research Findings and Future Directions

Among the studies in Table 6, the applications of community interaction models to *strategic groups* appear particularly promising (Brittain 1994; Carroll and Swaminathan 1992). Although the strategic groups construct captures the idea that the force of competition on an organization's performance depends on the location of its various rivals in the resource environment, empirical research examining the effects of strategic groups on competition is quite limited (McGee and Thomas 1986; Thomas and Venkatraman 1988). Community interdependence models, which highlight interactions among multiple organizational (sub)populations, provide a way to analyze competition within and between the multiple strategic groups comprising an industry. An ecological approach to strategic groups informs research in strategic management by providing a model of the effects of organizational strategies and strategic group membership in dynamic populations.

Although studies such as those in Table 6 provide empirical evidence of the existence, structure, and potential influence of organizational communities on population dynamics, they barely scratch the surface of the Pandora's box of community ecology (DiMaggio 1994). To date, the organizational communities studied have been limited in their scale and scope to single social or economic sectors of organizational activity (but see Baum and Korn 1994; Korn and Baum 1994). Moreover, because few studies attempt to predict the form of specific interpopulation interactions, we know very little about when competition or mutualism will exist between organizations. Unfortunately, within organizational communities, populations affect each other's fates not only through direct relationships between them but also through indirect interactions and feedback flowing through the community (Baum and Singh 1994d). Thus, community dynamics involve nonlinear feedback among interacting populations: such nonlinearities can complicate substantially attempts to derive community-level predictions (Carroll 1981: 587; Puccia and Levins 1985: Chapter 3). For this reason, Baum and his colleagues (Baum and Korn 1994; Baum and Singh 1994d; Korn and Baum 1994) have advocated use of an analytical technique called *loop analysis* (Puccia and Levins 1985) for modeling complex community systems. Loop analysis permits derivation of community-level predictions that account for the effects of indirect interactions and feedback processes in the community system.

More fundamentally, however, although Hannan and Freeman (1977) called for research at the population level as a first step toward the study of community-level phenomena, research in organizational ecology remains focused primarily at the population level. Thus, the original question of organizational ecology – why are there so many kinds of organizations? – has yet to be pursued seriously. If, however, the current diversity of organizations is to be conceived as a reflection of the 'cumulative effect of a long history of variation and selection' (Hannan and Freeman 1989: 20), then an explanation of how organizational populations form, become different, and remain different through time is required. Progress on this problem seems unlikely without attention to the development of a theory of *organizational evolution* (Baum and Singh 1994a; but for different views see Carroll 1984a; Hannan and Freeman 1989). Organizational evolution involves complex interplays between ecological and historical processes. It begins with the differential proliferation of variations within populations, that leads ultimately to foundings, the product of entrepreneurial thought, that jump out of established populations to create new populations, and ends with the extinction of the last member of the population that imitation creates around the founding organization (Lumsden and Singh 1990). Few researchers have addressed the emergence and disappearance of organizational populations (for exceptions see Aldrich and Fiol 1994; Astley 1985; Lumsden and Singh 1990; Romanelli 1991). Consequently, we still know very little about the structures of organizational inheritance and transmission. Yet, a theory of organizational evolution must consider historical processes of information conservation and transmission (i.e. genealogical processes) by which production and organizing routines, organizations, and populations are carried (i.e. replicated) through time (Baum 1989b; McKelvey 1982; Nelson and Winter 1982).

Studying these genealogical processes involves tracing out the evolutionary lines of descent of organizations from their ancestors for the purpose of discovering populations of organizations and explaining their origins. Whereas biological inheritance is primarily based on the propagation of genes, inheritance processes for social organizations appear very different and suggest evolutionary dynamics strikingly different from those expected with purely genetic transmission. Baum and Singh (1994a) anticipate an approach to organizational genealogical processes that embodies a preponderance of Lamarckian inheritance mechanisms in the sense that production and organizing competence acquired through learning can be *retransmitted*.

Table 6   *Community interdependence studies, 1989–1995*

Community	Community interactions	References
US craft and industrial labor unions, 1836–1985	Partial competition $(-,0)$: increasing density of craft unions both suppress founding and increase failure of industrial unions, but industrial union density does not affect either craft union founding or failure	Hannan and Freeman 1989
Worker, marketing and consumer cooperatives in Atlantic Canada, 1900–87	Commensalism $(+,0)$: increasing density of worker coops stimulates founding of marketing coops; increasing density of marketing coops stimulates founding of consumer coops; increasing density of consumer coops stimulates founding of worker coops	Staber 1989
Early Pennsylvania telephone companies, 1879–1934: magneto and common battery technologies; single- and multi-exchange common battery companies	Partial competition $(-,0)$: increasing density of magneto companies increase failure of common battery companies but common battery company density does not affect magneto company failure	Barnett 1990
	Symbiosis $(+,+)$: increasing density of single-exchange companies lowers failure of multi-exchange companies and increasing density of multi-exchange companies lowers failure of single-exchange companies in return	
Day care centers and nursery schools in Metropolitan Toronto, 1971–87	Full competition $(-,-)$: increasing density of day care centers stimulates failure of nursery schools and increasing density of nursery schools stimulates failure of day care centers in return	Baum and Oliver 1991
Commercial and savings banks in Manhattan, 1792–1980	Neutrality $(0,0)$: densities of commercial and savings banks are unrelated to each other's founding rates	Ranger-Moore et al. 1991
Mutual and stock life insurance companies in New York State, 1760–1937	Commensalism $(+,0)$: increasing density of stock companies stimulates founding of mutual companies, but mutual company density does not affect stock company founding	
US brewing industry, 1975–90: microbreweries, brewpubs, and mass producers[1]	Commensalism $(+,0)$: increasing density of brewpubs stimulates founding of microbreweries, but microbrewery density does not affect brewpub founding	Carroll and Swaminathan 1992
	Partial competition $(-,0)$: increasing density of mass producers stimulates failure of microbreweries, but microbrewery density does not affect mass producer failure	
US HMOs, 1976–91: group HMOs and independent practice associations	Neutrality $(0,0)$: densities of group and IPA HMOs are unrelated to each other's failure rates	Wholey et al. 1992
US electronics components producers, 1947–81: r-specialists, K-specialists, r-generalists, K-generalists[2]	Full competition $(-,-)$: founding, none; failure, r-specialists and r-generalists, K-specialists and K-generalists	Brittain 1994
	Partial competition $(-,0)$: founding, r-generalists and K-specialists; failure, r-generalists and K-generalists	
	Predatory competition $(+,-)$: founding, none; failure, r-specialists and K-specialists	
	Neutrality $(0,0)$: founding, none; failure, r-generalists and K-generalists	
	Commensalism $(+,0)$: founding, r-specialists and r-generalists, r-generalists and K-generalists; failure, r-specialists and K-generalists	
	Symbiosis $(+,+)$: founding, r-specialists and K-specialists, r-specialists and K-generalists, K-specialists and K-generalists; failure, none	
Manhattan fax transmission cos, 1965–92: pre- and post-dominant design cohorts	Partial competition $(-,0)$: pre-dominant design fax transmission firms suppress founding and increase failure of post-dominant design fax transmission firms	Baum et al. 1995

[1] All other possible interactions are neutral $(0,0)$
[2] See Brittain (1994) for a more detailed discussion of these findings

Although some work in evolutionary economics (Nelson and Winter 1982; Winter 1990), organization theory (Van de Ven and Grazman 1994; Zucker 1977) and organizational learning (Levinthal 1991b) is concerned with genealogical processes of organizations, the research agenda on organizational inheritance remains wide open.

ENVIRONMENTAL PROCESSES

In their review of organizational ecology, Singh and Lumsden (1990: 182) identified the convergence of ecological and institutional perspectives on organizations 'as an exciting research development in organization theory'. Institutional and ecological theories have converged mainly around the question: how do institutional environmental variables (e.g. government policy, political conditions, and sanctioning relations) influence population dynamics? Since then, a second, equally exciting, convergence has emerged with technology cycle theory. Pursuing such convergence is central to advancing organizational ecology. Environmental processes such as institutional change and technological evolution that shape appropriate organizational forms and condition historical-structural relationships (e.g. the basis of competition among organizations) need to be integrated fully into ecological theory and research. Recent developments in these areas of convergence are reviewed below.

Institutional Processes

Organizational environments are more than simply 'sources for inputs, information, and knowhow for outputs' (Scott and Meyer 1983: 158). Institutionalized rules and beliefs about organizations also figure prominently (DiMaggio and Powell 1983; Meyer and Rowan 1977). Institutional theory emphasizes that organizations must conform to these rules and requirements if they are to receive support and be perceived as legitimate. The role of such normative constraints has figured with increasing prominence in recent ecological theory and research. Some view the relationship between ecological and institutional theory as complementary, and propose their synthesis into a single explanatory framework (Hannan and Carroll 1992; Hannan and Freeman 1989). Others conceive institutional theory as contextual to ecological theory: the relationship between them is not only complementary, it is also hierarchical (Tucker et al. 1992). From this point of view, the institutional environment constitutes the broader social context for ecological processes: the institutional environment may prescribe the environmental selection criteria for judging whether an organization or entire population is worthy of continued survival (Barnett and Carroll 1993; Baum and Oliver 1991; 1992; Fombrun 1988). Ecological research on institutional processes typically compares founding and failure rates across organizational populations or across time as the institutional arena of a particular population changes in terms of its political turbulence, government regulations, or institutional embeddedness.

Political Turbulence

Political turbulence affects organizational founding and failure by disrupting social alignments and established relationships between organizations and resources, freeing resources for use by new organizations. Supporting this argument, Delacroix and Carroll (1983) show that cycles of newspaper foundings in Argentina and Ireland reflect political turbulence in addition to population dynamics. Years of political turbulence were marked by founding rate increases in both countries. Carroll and Huo (1986) replicate this finding and also show that political turbulence increases newspaper failure rates in an analysis of newspaper foundings in the San Francisco Bay area. Amburgey and his colleagues also find evidence that political turbulence raises newspaper failure rates in Finland (Amburgey et al. 1988). Notably, newspapers founded during years of political turmoil are short lived compared to those formed during more stable years (Carroll and Delacroix 1982). To explain this finding, Carroll and his colleagues argue that newspapers founded in politically turbulent years are opportunists that thrive on resources freed in periods of social disruption but then either become obsolete or are outcompeted when the environment restabilizes. In other words, newspapers are part of the political environment. Do political processes affect other kinds of organizations? Carroll et al. (1988) provide a theoretical argument that generalizes the predictions to other kinds of organizations but it remains untested.

Government Regulation

From an ecological standpoint, government regulations are viewed as important constraints on organizing and resource acquisition that affect organizational diversity (Barnett and Carroll 1993; Hannan and Freeman 1977). By increasing (decreasing) the number and/or variety of constraints, regulation increases (decreases) environmental heterogeneity, expanding (contracting) the number of potential niches and increasing (decreasing) overall organizational diversity possible in an organizational community. Although institutional theorists agree, the central issue from their perspective is the level of fragmentation in the structure of the regulatory institutional environment (Scott and Meyer 1983). When influence in the regulatory environment is centralized, institutional demands are easily coordinated and imposed on organizations. In contrast, fragmented regulatory structures suffer from ambiguity and conflict, and coordinated action to influence organizations is difficult. Thus, consistent with ecological expectations, the greater the fragmentation of regulatory structures in an organizational field (i.e. the greater the number of distinct institutional resources and constraints), the greater the diversity of organizations that can be sustained.

Ecological research on regulatory effects focuses on how changes in government regulation influence patterns of organizational founding and failure. Some regulatory changes embody routine processes or events whose cumulative effects are substantial. For example, over time, through coercive, mimetic, and normative processes, institutional expectations of government regulations become embedded in the practices and features of organizations (DiMaggio and Powell 1983). These institutionalized features, which provide assurance that organizations can be trusted to function reliably, produce ecological consequences by, for example, constraining the range of possible competitive behaviors (Freeman and Lomi 1994). Others are more dramatic and disrupt established ties between organizations and resources, freeing resources for use by new organizations (Carroll et al. 1988).

Because regulatory contexts vary widely, ecological research often formulates hypotheses about regulatory effects for particular research settings. However, recent research identifies four basic ways in which government regulation influences founding and failure rates (see Table 7). Consistent with a view of ecological processes as nested hierarchically within institutional processes, this research shows how government regulation acts to constrain and enable organizational behavior as well as condition ecological relationships among organizations. The next logical step in this research area is to study how government regulation, and institutional processes more broadly, condition ecological processes directly by examining interactions between institutional and ecological variables (Baum and Oliver 1991; Tucker et al. 1990a; Singh et al. 1991; Tucker et al. 1988).

Institutional Linkages

Institutional theorists propose that an organization is more likely to survive if it obtains legitimacy, social support, and approval from actors in the surrounding institutional environment (DiMaggio and Powell 1983; Meyer and Rowan 1977). This external legitimation elevates the organization's status in the community, facilitates resource acquisition, deflects questions about an organization's rights and competence to provide specific products or services, and permits the organization to demonstrate its conformity to institutionalized norms and expectations. Although research on institutional embeddedness of organizations is still limited, consistent with the prediction of institutional theory, the results of existing studies indicate that the development of ties to important state and community institutions, as well as other organizations operating in the same institutional field, plays a very significant role in increasing an organization's chances of survival.

Singh et al. (1986) found that listing of a voluntary social service agency in a community registry and possession of a charitable registration number decreased the liability of newness in a population of voluntary social service organizations. Miner et al. (1990) found that Finnish newspapers affiliated with political parties had significantly lower failure rates than newspaper organizations without such an affiliation. Baum and Oliver (1991) found that day care centers and nursery schools with institutional linkages to community organizations (e.g. schools, community centers, and religious organizations) and a municipal government agency exhibited a survival advantage over those without these linkages and that this advantage also increased significantly with the intensity of competition. They also showed that young, small, and specialist child care organizations benefited from institutional linkages to a greater extent than older, larger, and generalist organizations. In a study of integrated circuit producers, Loree (1993) found that failure rates fell initially after approval for military-grade manufacture but then increased over time as the linkage aged. Uzzi (1993) also shows how firms' survival chances in the New York apparel industry increase with their levels of transactional and social interconnectedness. Overall, these studies suggest that linkages of organizations to a broader institutional context may alter basic causal relationships advanced in organizational ecology. This strongly suggests the need for additional research on institutional linkages.

Technological Processes

Technological innovation has the potential to influence organizational populations profoundly because it can disrupt markets, change the

Table 7   *Government regulation and population dynamics*

Regulatory effect	Examples	References
Barriers to entry	The national labor union founding rate increased after the Wagner Act, which provided legal protection to unions and union organizing campaigns, but declined after the Taft-Hartley Act, which repealed some protections of the Wagner Act	Hannan and Freeman 1989
	The founding rate in the US airline industry increased for several years after deregulation made it easier for airlines to enter and exit markets	Kelly 1988; Kelly and Amburgey 1991
Resources and constraints	The introduction of the Ontario government's Restraint Program lowered the founding rate and increased the failure rate of voluntary social service organizations in Metropolitan Toronto	Singh et al. 1991
	Increases in the value of the Metropolitan Toronto Children's Services Division annual budget increased the founding rate and lowered the failure rate of day care centers in the city	Baum and Oliver 1992
	State regulations that require a deposit to be filed by health maintenance organizations (HMOs) with the state insurance commissioner increases failure rates of small HMOs, but lowers failure rates of large HMOs	Wholey et al. 1992
	States with more fragmented local government boundaries (i.e. larger numbers of constraints) exhibited more limited competition among telephone companies, increasing their numbers	Barnett and Carroll 1993
	Relaxing the National Credit Union Administration's policies eroded the boundaries between credit unions and banks (i.e. reduced the number of constraints), increasing competition between them	Amburgey et al. 1994
	Regulatory constraints imposed on Italian rural cooperative banks and core national banks resulted in resource partitioning that enabled rural cooperative banks to draw on the resource base freed at the periphery of the system without engaging in direct competition with the larger generalist core banks	Freeman and Lomi 1994
Monitoring, certifying, authorizing and endorsing	The Canadian federal government's endorsement of the legitimacy of local community groups engaging in independent organizational activity to achieve collective ends through the Opportunities for Youth program increased the founding rate of voluntary social service organizations in Metropolitan Toronto	Tucker et al. 1990a; Singh et al. 1991
	Increasing involvement of the Metropolitan Toronto Children's Services Division in monitoring, certifying, authorizing, and endorsing the activities of day care centers in the city enhanced the credibility and legitimacy of the population, increasing foundings and lowering failures of day care centers	Baum and Oliver 1991; 1992
Nature of competition	The Canadian federal government's Opportunities for Youth program altered the density dependence of specialist foundings among voluntary social service organizations in Metropolitan Toronto	Tucker et al. 1990a; Singh et al. 1991
	The Kingsbury Commitment, a regulation intended to constrain the competitive activity of a dominant firm, Bell, triggered a process of competitive release, altering the relationship between large and small telephone companies from symbiotic to competitive	Barnett and Carroll 1993

relative importance of various resources, challenge organizational learning capabilities, and alter the nature of competition (Cohen and Levinthal 1990; Tushman and Anderson 1986). Technological innovation creates opportunities to found new organizations as existing sources of competitive advantage decay and new opportunities for establishing competitive positions emerge. It also creates uncertainties and risks for incumbents because its outcomes can be only imperfectly anticipated. On the one hand, the impact of an innovation may not be known until it is too late for incumbents using older technologies to compete successfully with new competitors. On the other hand, gambling too early on a given innovation may jeopardize an incumbent's survival chances if that technology turns out not to become dominant. Thus, the competitive structures of populations reflect their underlying technologies and technological innovation may profoundly influence the competitive dynamics and evolution of populations over time (Barnett 1990; Brittain and Freeman 1980; Dosi 1984; Utterback and Suárez 1993).

Technology Cycles and Population Dynamics

Supporting Schumpeter's (1934; 1950) characterization of technological evolution as a process of creative destruction, research supports the idea that technologies evolve over time through cycles of long periods of incremental change, which enhance and institutionalize an existing technology, punctuated by *technological discontinuities* in which new, radically superior technologies displace old, inferior ones, making possible order-of-magnitude or more improvements in organizational performance (Dosi 1984; Tushman and Anderson 1986). Technological discontinuities generate competition as technologically superior organizations displace outdated ones. The new technology can be either *competence enhancing*, which builds on know-how embodied in the existing technology, or *competence destroying*, which renders the skills required to operate and manage the existing technology obsolete (Tushman and Anderson 1986). This distinction helps specify whether incumbents or newcomers are likely to become technologically superior competitors as a result of technological change. Technological discontinuities are followed by *eras of ferment* in which competition for dominance among multiple variants of a new technology as well as the incumbent technology creates high uncertainty (Anderson and Tushman 1990). Technological ferment ends with the emergence of a *dominant design*, a single architecture that establishes dominance in a product class (Abernathy 1978). Once a dominant design emerges,

technological advance returns to incremental improvements and elaborations of the dominant technology. Although there is some debate about the universality of this *technology cycle*, it has proven illuminating in a wide variety of industries (Nelson 1994).

Research Findings and Future Directions

How do technology cycles influence patterns of organizational founding and failure? Available research findings relating technology cycles to organizational founding and failure appear largely supportive of the major predictions (see Table 8). Although this research provides promising initial links between technology cycles and population dynamics, it needs to be extended in at least three important ways. First, although theory suggests incumbent and newcomer failure rates differ significantly, studies of the effects of technology cycles on organizational failure do not typically differentiate between cohorts of organizations founded before and after technological discontinuities or dominant designs (Baum et al. 1993; 1995; Suárez and Utterback 1992). Second, and more fundamentally, studies rarely incorporate organization-specific measures of technology. Incorporating organization-specific information on technology extends existing research in at least three major ways. One, the patterns of interdependence among firms operating with different technologies during eras of ferment can be examined, permitting the creative destruction process to be modeled directly and in a fine-grained way (Barnett 1990). Two, the performance implications of firm-specific innovation (e.g. adopting a new technology) and conditions influencing whether and when firm-specific innovation will be rewarded can be modeled directly (Barnett 1990; Mitchell 1991). Three, patterns of interdependence among organizations using pre- and post-discontinuity or pre- and post-dominant design technologies can be examined, permitting the competitive superiority of technologies to be modeled directly (Baum et al. 1993; 1995). Third, research typically examines how changes in technology influence ecological processes. However, more research is needed that examines how ecological dynamics influence technological change. Wade (1993; 1995) provides some important first steps in this direction. His analyses of technological change in the US microprocessor market show that new entrants are the source of most design introductions, that density-dependent processes influence patterns of entry of design sponsors as well as the rate at which new designs gain organizational support, and that the emergence of a dominant design stimulates the entry of new design sponsors.

Table 8 *Technology cycles and population dynamics*

Variable	Predictions	Examples	References
Competence-enhancing discontinuity	A competence-enhancing discontinuity consolidates incumbents' competitive positions by strengthening their competencies, increasing their competitive advantage over new organizations, discouraging potential entrants	Entry-to-exit ratios declined (i.e. foundings were suppressed) in the five years after competence-enhancing discontinuities in the US cement and airline industries[1]	Tushman and Anderson 1986
	Incumbents' advantage erodes over time as inertia makes it difficult for them to take full advantage of the enhanced technology. This protects incumbents from moving too quickly to the new technology, but it also creates openings for new entrants to develop specialized assets, market knowledge, and reputation	The competence-enhancing shift from analog to digital facsimile transmission technology lowered founding and failure rates of facsimile transmission service organizations initially, but both rates increased as the discontinuity receded into the past	Baum et al. 1993
Competence-destroying discontinuity	A competence-destroying discontinuity undermines incumbents' competitive positions by rendering their competencies obsolete, permitting organizations that exploit the new technology to enter and establish positions in previously impenetrable markets at the expense of incumbents burdened with the legacy of the older technology	Semiconductor manufacturers exit rates increased after the integrated circuits competence-destroying continuity	Freeman 1990
		Leading firms in the photolithographic alignment equipment industry were supplanted successively by new entrants exploiting new technologies	Henderson and Clark 1990
Era of ferment	Technological ferment produces a succession of technological regimes that create new markets and dramatic performance improvement. Organizations must choose a new technology or defend the existing regime – but which technological regime or technical variant within competing regimes will dominate is profoundly uncertain	Organizational failure rates increased during technological ferments in the US cement, glass container, and minicomputer industries	Anderson 1988; Anderson and Tushman 1992
Dominant design	A dominant design creates a competitive advantage for incumbents by allowing realization of production and other economies, produces a wave of failures among firms that have not mastered the dominant technology, creates barriers to entry for newcomers, leading to a sharp decline in the number of organizations, and industry restabilization	Organizations founded before dominant designs in US automobile, transistor, electronic calculator, and TV industries had lower age-specific failure rates after dominant designs then those founded afterward	Suárez and Utterback 1992
		Waves of failures occurred in the period immediately after the emergence of dominant designs in cement, glass container, and window glass industries, but failure rates declined over time as the industry restabilized	Anderson 1988
		The emergence of the DOS standard was followed by a wave of failures in the US minicomputer industry but failure rates declined over time as the industry restabilized	Ingram 1993

[1] Although Tushman and Anderson (1986) interpret their original finding that entry-to-exit ratios declined in the five years after competence-destroying discontinuities in the US cement and microcomputer industries as contradictory to predictions, since entry and exit rates are *both* expected to increase after a competence-destroying discontinuity, a comparison of pre- and post-discontinuity entry-to-exit ratios is a confounded test.

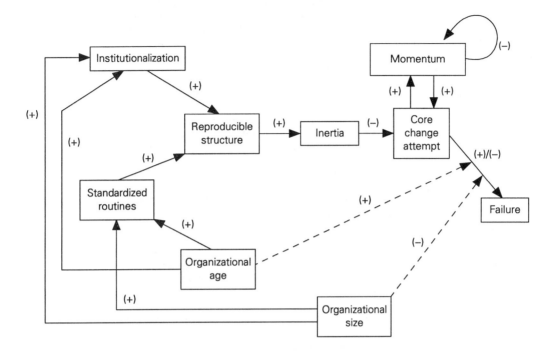

Figure 1 *Structural inertia theory* (adapted from Kelly and Amburgey 1991: 593)

ORGANIZATIONAL CHANGE: STRUCTURAL INERTIA THEORY

Although ecological researchers have assembled a wealth of studies concerning rates of organizational founding and failure, until recently, few systematic studies of rates of organizational change were available. This inattention may be traced at least in part to structural inertia theory (Hannan and Freeman 1977; 1984). Structural inertia theory depicts organizations as relatively inert entities for which adaptive response is not only difficult and infrequent, but hazardous as well. Consequently, change in individual organizations is viewed as contributing considerably less to population-level change than demographic processes of organizational founding and failure. Despite the centrality of this theoretical position to ecological approaches, until recently, its veridicality had been taken for granted. Organizational ecologists have now begun to examine the assumptions of structural inertia theory, the influence of organizational and environmental factors on rates of change in individual organizations, and the adaptiveness (i.e. survival consequences) of different kinds of organizational changes.

Organization and management theory frequently focuses on the relative advantages of alternative configurations of organizational features. Consequently, a great deal of research on organizational change has concentrated on the content of changes: a change to a more advantageous configuration is considered adaptive, while a switch to a less advantageous configuration is considered detrimental (Amburgey et al. 1993). Complementing this focus, Hannan and Freeman's (1984) structural inertia theory offers a model of the process of organizational change that considers both internal and external constraints on change. Structural inertia theory addresses two main questions: how changeable are organizations, and is change beneficial for organizations? Figure 1 presents an overview of structural inertia theory.

How Changeable Are Organizations?

Hannan and Freeman (1977) pointed out that organizations face both internal and external constraints on their capacity for change and that given these constraints, selection processes are an appropriate explanation for change in organizational populations. Building on their earlier argument, Hannan and Freeman (1984) adopt a somewhat different approach that takes seriously the potential for organizational change by viewing inertia as a *consequence* rather than *antecedent* of selection processes. They hypothesize that, although some kinds of organizational changes occur frequently in organizations and sometimes these can even be radical changes, the nature of selection processes is such that organizations with inert features are more likely to survive (1984: 149).

Structural inertia theory assumes that organizations experience pressures for reliable performance and accountability for their actions. It also assumes that both reliability and accountability require that organizational structures be highly reproducible (i.e. stable over time). Reproducibility of structure is accomplished by institutionalization of organizational purposes and standardization of organizational routines. Institutionalization and standardization offer the advantage of reproducibility but they also produce strong inertial pressures against change (1984: 154–5).

The *structure* in structural inertia theory refers to some, but not all, of the features of organizations. Hannan and Freeman (1984: 156) emphasize *core* features of organizational structure, which are related to 'the claims used to mobilize resources for beginning an organization and the strategies and structures used to maintain flows of scarce resources'. Core features include the organizational goals, forms of authority, core technology, and marketing strategy of organizations. *Peripheral* features protect an organization's core from uncertainty by buffering it and by broadening the organization's connections to its environment. Peripheral features include numbers and sizes of subunits, number of hierarchical levels, spans of control, communication patterns, and buffering mechanisms. Hannan and Freeman (1984: 156) propose that core features have higher levels of inertia than peripheral features.

Hannan and Freeman (1984) propose that in addition to varying by facet of organizational structure, inertial pressures vary with organizational age and size. Because older organizations have had time to formalize more thoroughly internal relationships, standardize routines, and institutionalize leadership and power distributions, as well as develop rich networks of dependencies and commitments with other social actors, reproducibility of structure and inertia should increase with age. Thus, older organizations should be most limited in their ability to adapt to changing environmental demands. Consequently, the probability of attempting change in core features declines with age (1984: 157). Organizational size is also associated with resistance to change. As organizations increase in size, they emphasize predictability, formalized roles, and control systems and their behavior becomes predictable, rigid, and inflexible. Moreover, by buffering organizations from failure, large size may reduce the impetus for change (Levinthal 1994). Consequently, the probability of attempting change in core features declines with size (Hannan and Freeman 1984: 159).

Is Change Beneficial?

Perhaps the most striking aspect of structural inertia theory is the relationship hypothesized between change in core features and the liability of newness, the propensity of young organizations to have higher failure rates (Stinchcombe 1965). Hannan and Freeman (1984: 160) propose that attempting core change produces a renewed liability of newness by robbing an organization's history of survival value. Attempting change in core features lowers an organization's performance reliability and accountability back to that of a new organization by destroying or rendering obsolete established routines and competencies and by disrupting relations with important environmental actors. It also undermines an organization's acquired legitimacy by modifying its visible mission. Since organizational stakeholders favor organizations that exhibit reliable performance and accountability for their actions, Hannan and Freeman (1984: 160) conclude that, frequently, attempts to change core features to promote survival – even those that might eventually reduce the risk of failure by better aligning the organization with its environment – expose organizations to a short-run increased risk of failure. Thus, structural inertia theory predicts that organizations may often fail as a direct result of their attempts to survive.

In addition to their effects on reproducibility and inertia, organizational age and size also both affect the likelihood of surviving the short-run shock of a core change attempt. Because their internal structures and routines are more institutionalized and their external linkages are better established, older organizations are especially likely to experience disruption as a result of core change (1984: 157). In contrast, larger organizations, although less likely to attempt core changes in the first place, are less likely to die during a core change attempt (1984: 159). Large size can buffer organizations from the disruptive effects of core change by, for example, helping to maintain both old and new ways of doing things during the transition period or to overcome short-term deprivations and competitive challenges that accompany the change attempt.

If an organization manages to survive the short-run shock of a core change, Hannan and Freeman (1984: 161) predict the risk of failure will decline over time as performance reliability is re-established, external relationships are restabilized, and organizational legitimacy is reaffirmed. However, the rate of decline in the failure rate after a core change is not specified by the structural inertia model. If the rate of decline in the death rate subsequent to the change continues at a rate identical to that before the change, the organization will face the short-term risk of change without any long-term benefit. If the rate of decline in the death rate following the change is slower than before, the organization will increase both its short-term and its long-term risk of failure. If, however, the rate of decline is faster than the original rate of decline, the organization will benefit in the long run from taking on the short-term risks of change. Thus, although structural inertia theory views core change as disruptive in the short run, it may, ultimately, be adaptive if the organization manages to overcome the hazards associated with the initial disruption.

Thus, structural inertia theory frames the question of whether organizational change occurs at the population level or at the level of individual organizations as an issue of the rate of change of organizations relative to the rate of change in the environment. Organizations may be unable to respond to environmental change either because they are unwilling or unable to change or because they fail prior to the realization of their change efforts.

Tests of Structural Inertia Theory

Age and Size Dependence in Rates of Change

Tests of age and size dependence in rates of organizational change are presented in Table 9. The findings are mixed and, overall, appear to offer little support for structural inertia theory's predictions. In their review of organizational ecology, Singh and Lumsden (1990: 182) use the core–periphery distinction to interpret the mixed findings available to them. They speculate that rates of core feature change decrease with age, while rates of peripheral feature change increase with age. Unfortunately, this distinction does not help account for the mixed age (and size) dependence findings in Table 9. For example, diversification – the development of new products or services, often for new clients and frequently requiring implementation of new administrative, production, or distribution technologies (Haveman 1993a) – is one core change that has been studied across multiple populations. Unfortunately, Table 9 reveals little evidence that diversification is related negatively to either age or size.

Fluidity of Age and Size Is structural inertia theory wrong? In contrast to structural inertia arguments, some theoretical views suggest that organizations become more fluid with age (Singh et al. 1988). Although selection processes favor organizations that are fit with their environment, the match between organizations and their environments is constantly eroding as managerial bounded rationality, informational constraints, and inertial pressures prevent organizations from keeping pace with constantly changing environments. Thus, 'through a cumulative history of having been alive, the stresses and strains of living through multiple environmental changes cumulate in organizations, increasing the pressure on organizations to change' (1988: 6).

Some theoretical views also support the idea that larger organizations are more fluid. Internal complexity, differentiation, specialization, and decentralization, all features of large organizations, have each been associated with the adoption of innovations (Haveman 1993a). The slack resources available to larger organizations may enable them to initiate change in response to environmental change (Cyert and March 1963). Greater size relative to other actors also increases market power (Bain 1956), lowering barriers to entry stemming from scale economies and reducing external political considerations (Pfeffer and Salancik 1978).

Age and size estimates in Table 9 support fluidity and inertia predictions with approximately equal frequency. However there are good reasons to doubt some of the fluidity findings. Most studies that find evidence of fluidity include left-censored organizations. Because left-censored organizations, founded before the observation period begins, are not observed when they are youngest and smallest, including these organizations can lead to an underestimation of rates of change at younger ages and smaller sizes. Moreover, if large organizations are buffered by their resources from the risks of change, support for the fluidity of size may reflect sample selection bias resulting from right censoring: small organizations are not observed changing because they fail prior to the realization of their efforts.

Repetitive Momentum Although Hannan and Freeman (1984) do not include prior changes in their theoretical model, Amburgey and his colleagues (Amburgey and Kelly 1985; Amburgey et al. 1993; Amburgey and Miner 1992; Kelly and Amburgey 1991) suggest a complete understanding of organizational change requires consideration of an organization's *history of changes*. From an organizational learning perspective, making a change furnishes an organization with the opportunity to routinize the change (Levitt and March 1988; Nelson and

Table 9　*Rate of organizational change studies*

Population	Type of change	Age[1]	Size	No. of prior changes	Time since last change	References
US business periodicals, 1774–1865	Ownership	−	0	+	na	Amburgey and Kelly 1985
	Editor	−	0	+	na	
	Name	−	0	0	na	
	Layout	−	0	+	na	
	Content	0	0	0	na	
Voluntary social service organizations, 1970–82	Name	+	+	na	na	Singh et al. 1988; 1991; Tucker et al. 1990b
	Sponsor	0	0	na	na	
	Location	+	0	na	na	
	Service area	+	0	na	na	
	Goals	+	0	na	na	
	Client groups	0	0	na	na	
	Service conditions	0	0	na	na	
	Chief executive	+	+	na	na	
	Structure	+	0	na	na	
Silicon Valley semiconductor producers[2]	Change in initial strategy	+	na	na	na	Boeker 1989
US medical diagnostic imaging firms, 1959–88	Entry to emerging subfield	na	0	na	na	Mitchell 1989
Metro Toronto day care centers, 1971–87	Specialist to generalist	+	−	na	na	Baum 1990a
	Generalist to specialist	+/−	0	na	na	
US health maintenance organizations[2]	For-profit to nonprofit	+	0	na	na	Ginsberg and Buchholtz 1990
US airlines, 1962–85	Business-level specialism	−	0	+	na	Kelly and Amburgey 1991; see also Kelly 1988
	Business-level generalism	0	−	+	na	
	Corporate-level specialism	0	0	+	na	
	Corporate-level generalism	0	−	+	na	
Gasoline stations, 1959–88	Domain enlargement	0	na	na	0	Usher 1991
	Domain contraction	0	na	na	+	
	Niche migration	+/−	na	na	na	
California wineries, 1946–84	Brand portfolio	0	−	+	−	Delacroix and Swaminathan 1991
	Product line	−	−	+	0	
	Land ownership status	0	0	+	0	
Fortune 500 companies, 1949–77	Product-extension mergers	na	−	+	na	Amburgey and Miner 1992; Amburgey and Dacin 1994
	Conglomerate mergers	na	0	+	na	
	Horizontal mergers	na	0	+	na	
	Vertical integration	na	0	+	na	
	Product market diversification	na	0	−	0	
	Structural decentralization	na	−	0	−	
Finnish newspapers, 1771–1963	Content	−	na	+	−	Amburgey et al. 1993; Miner et al. 1990
	Publication frequency	−	na	+	−	
State bar associations, 1918–50	Unification attempt	−	−	na	na	Halliday et al. 1993
Private liberal arts colleges, 1972–86	Change to coed	+	0	na	na	Zajac and Kraatz 1993
	Add graduate program	−	+	na	na	
	Add business program	0	+	na	na	
Bank holding companies, 1956–88	Related acquisition	−	na	+	−	Ginsberg and Baum 1994
	Unrelated acquisition	0	na	+	0	

Table 9 (continued)

Population	Type of change	Age[1]	Size	No. of prior changes	Time since last change	References
California S&Ls, 1977–87	Real estate (entry rates)	0	+	na	na	Haveman 1994;
	Nonresidential mortgages	0	0	na	na	see also
	Mortgage-backed securities	0	0	na	na	Haveman 1992;
	Consumer lending	0	0	na	na	1993a; 1993b
	Commercial lending	0	0	na	na	
	Service companies	–	0	na	na	
US trade associations, 1900–80	Change in organizing domain or goals	0/0	0	na	na	Aldrich et al. 1994
California airlines, 1979–84	Route entry	+	–	na	na	Baum and
	Route exit	–	+	na	na	Korn 1996
Metro Toronto day care centers, 1971–89	Market entry	+	–	–	+	Baum and
	Market exit	0	0	0	0	Singh 1996

[1] X/Y gives the signs of significant ($p<0.05$) linear and square terms, respectively, when estimated.
[2] Observation period dates not given.

Winter 1982). Each time an organization engages in a particular kind of change it increases its competency at that change. The more experienced an organization becomes with a particular change, the more likely it is to repeat the change – because it knows how to make it. If a particular change becomes causally linked with success in the minds of organizational decision-makers – irrespective of whether such a link in fact exists – reinforcement effects will make repetition even more likely. Thus, once change is initiated, the change process itself may become routinized and subject to inertial forces. This creates *repetitive momentum*, that is, the tendency to maintain direction and emphasis of prior actions in current behavior (Miller and Friesen 1980). Experience with change of a particular type is therefore predicted to increase the likelihood that the change will be repeated in the future.

To reconcile the idea that organizational change is propelled by repetitive momentum with evidence that organizations move from periods of change to periods of inactivity, Amburgey et al. (1993) propose that effects of prior change are dynamic. Since organizational search processes begin with the most recently utilized routines (Cyert and March 1963), the likelihood of repeating particular changes should be highest immediately after their occurrence, but decline as time since the changes were last made increases. Combined, the main and dynamic effects of prior change imply that the likelihood of repeating a particular change jumps immediately after a change of that type, the size of the jump increasing after each additional change, but declines with increases in the time since that type of change last occurred.

Support for repetitive momentum in organizational change is strong: among the estimates in Table 9, rates of change increase with the number of prior changes of the same type in eighteen of twenty-four tests. Estimates for the dynamic effect, however, are more mixed. Notably, studies that control for one or both prior change effects account for most of the support for structural inertia theory: nine of twelve negative age coefficients and seven of ten negative size coefficients occur in these studies. Thus, support for the fluidity of age and size may reflect a specification bias: older and larger organizations may be more likely to change not because they are older and larger but because they have accumulated experience with change. Overall, these findings suggest strongly the need for a broader view of inertial forces in organizations – one that includes momentum in the change process as well as inertia.

Although addressing left-censoring, right-censoring, and specification bias issues can improve our understanding of organization-level change processes incrementally, larger gains are possible if researchers begin to test the underlying arguments directly. Because age and size coefficients reveal little about the underlying organizational processes of interest, we still know very little about *how* age and size affect rates of change, or the *conditions* under which fluidity, inertia, and momentum will predominate. To learn what is really going on, studies using more direct measures of the underlying organizational processes are needed. Fluidity and inertia arguments are not necessarily competing, they can be complementary – indeed, fluidity of aging arguments rely in part on inertia to create a gap between organizations and environments – and the underlying relationships they predict can potentially exist simultaneously.

Organizational Change and Failure

While ecological research indicates that inertia and momentum often constrain organizational change, this is, of course, not necessarily harmful: in addition to promoting performance reliability and accountability, in an uncertain environment inertia and momentum can keep organizations from responding too quickly and frequently to environmental changes. But whether or not inertia and momentum are harmful ultimately depends on the hazardousness of organizational change.

Table 10 presents findings of studies investigating the survival consequences of organizational change. Organizations in the study populations do not necessarily fail as a result of their efforts to change – but they do not necessarily improve their organizational survival chances either. Do organizations operate in a world so uncertain that adaptive efforts turn out to be essentially random with respect to future value (Hannan and Freeman 1984: 150)? Unfortunately, only six studies in Table 10 separate short-run and long-run effects of change, and only three of these also test for age and/or size variation in the disruptive effects of change. Any conclusions drawn at this point would thus be premature. It is notable, however, that support for structural inertia theory predictions is strong in the three most fully specified studies (Amburgey et al. 1993; Baum and Singh 1996; Haveman 1993c), for all but one of the changes examined (i.e. market entries by day care centers).

Future Directions

In addition to the need for more research on the adaptiveness of organizational change that specifies structural inertia theory predictions fully, future research may also benefit by considering the following issues.

Left and Right Censoring Left-censored organizations, founded before the start of the observation period, are not observed when they are youngest and smallest, and, according to structural inertia theory, when they are both most likely to change and most vulnerable to the hazards of change. Including these organizations in the analysis can lead to underestimation of the overall hazard of change as well as variation in the hazard for organizations of different ages and sizes. Moreover, if core organizational change is as perilous in the short term as structural inertia arguments assert, unless data are fine-grained, core changes may frequently not be observed

because organizations fail prior to the realization of their efforts. For example, if some core changes prove fatal within a year, these deadliest changes will not be detected in the yearly data typically available. This right-censoring problem lowers estimates of the hazardousness of change because the most hazardous changes are not identified in the analysis.

Organizational Performance Although poor and superior performing organizations are likely to experience different risks of failure as well as rates and kinds of change (Hambrick and D'Aveni 1988; Haveman 1992; 1993a; 1993b; 1994), ecological analyses of the effects of change on organizational failure do not typically include measures of ongoing organizational performance. This creates two problems. First, cause and effect logic is blurred because some changes or types of change are symptoms of organizational decline rather than causes of failure. Second, model estimates are prone to specification bias: if rates of organizational change and failure are both influenced by recent performance, a spurious link between change and failure will be observed if prior performance is not controlled. Although it is unlikely that organization-specific indicators of performance can be obtained for entire populations over time, one way to cope with this problem is to use organizational growth and decline as a proxy performance measure (Baum 1990a; Baum and Singh 1996; Haveman 1993c; Scott 1992: 342–62).

Transformational Shields A closely related issue is that all organizations are assumed to be equally susceptible to the effects of change on failure. Hannan and Freeman (1984) have identified age and size as factors that alter the exposure of organizations to the liabilities of change. However, to date, only three studies (see Table 10) have accounted for this variability (Amburgey et al. 1993; Baum and Singh 1996; Haveman 1993c). Institutional linkages (i.e. ties to important state and community institutions) may also provide such a transformational shield by conferring extra resources and legitimacy on organizations (Miner et al. 1990; Baum and Oliver 1991). Like unmeasured performance, unmeasured variation in susceptibility to the risks of change can cause specification bias in model estimates.

Within-Type Variation The ecological emphasis on change processes has resulted in less attention being given by ecological researchers to change content. Although broad categories of change are differentiated according to their content (see Tables 9 and 10), all instances of a particular

Table 10 *Organizational change and failure studies*

Population	Type of change	Prior change[1]	Time since last change	Change × age	Change × size	References
US newspapers, 1800–1975	Editor	+	0	na	na	Carroll 1984b
US business periodicals, 1774–1865	Ownership	+	na	na	na	Amburgey
	Editor	0	na	na	na	and Kelly
	Name	0	na	na	na	1985
	Layout	0	na	na	na	
	Content	0	na	na	na	
Voluntary social service organizations, 1970–82	Sponsor	+	na	na	na	Singh et al.
	Location	−	na	na	na	1986
	Service area	+	na	na	na	
	Goals	0	na	na	na	
	Client groups	+	na	na	na	
	Chief executive	−	na	na	na	
	Structure	0	na	na	na	
US airlines, 1962–85	Business-level specialism	0	na	na	na	Kelly and
	Business-level generalism	0	na	na	na	Amburgey
	Corporate-level specialism	0	na	na	na	1991; see also
	Corporate-level generalism	0	na	na	na	Kelly 1988
	Peripheral change	0	na	na	na	
Gasoline stations, 1959–88	Domain enlargement or contraction	0	+	na	na	Usher 1991
California wineries, 1946–84	Brand portfolio increase	0	0	na	na	Delacroix and
	Brand portfolio decrease	0	0	na	na	Swaminathan
	Product line increase	−	0	na	na	1991; see also
	Product line decrease	0	0	na	na	Swaminathan
	Land acquisition	−	0	na	na	and Delacroix
	Land divestment	0	0	na	na	1991
Finnish newspapers, 1774–1963	Content	+	−	+	na	Amburgey et
	Frequency	+	−	+	na	al. 1990; 1993
	Layout	0	−	+	na	
	Location	0	−	+	na	
	Name	+	−	+	na	
California S&Ls, 1977–87	Residential mortgages	−	na	na	na	Haveman
	Real estate (+ invest)	0	na	na	na	1992
	Nonresidential mortgages	−	na	na	na	
	Mortgage-backed securities	0	na	na	na	
	Cash and investment securities	−	na	na	na	
	Consumer lending	0	na	na	na	
	Commercial lending	0	na	na	na	
	Service companies	0	na	na	na	
Iowa telephone companies, 1900–17	Presidential succession	+	−	0	na	Haveman
	Managerial succession	+	−	0	na	1993c
US medical diagnostic imaging firms, 1954–89	Expand and survive in new subfield	+	na	na	na	Mitchell and Singh 1993
	Expand and exit subfield	−	na	na	na	
Metro Toronto day care centers, 1971–87	Market entry	0	0	−	+	Baum and
	Market exit	+	−	+	−	Singh 1996

[1] X gives the signs of significant ($p<0.05$) coefficients.

category of change are typically considered equivalent. While this assumption may provide a reasonable starting approximation, for many kinds of change, there may be significant within-type differences with substantial survival implications. One such difference is within-type variation in the effect of changes on the intensity of competition (Baum and Singh 1996). For example, depending on how an organization's specific actions alter the size of its domain relative to the number of organizations competing over its domain, the organization's diversification activities can increase, decrease, or leave unchanged the intensity of competition the organization faces. Baum and Singh (1996) show that the effects of market domain changes (both expansion and contraction) on the survival of day care centers depend on how the changes affect the intensity of competition: changes that lower the intensity of competition improve organizational survival chances, while those that increase the intensity of competition lower survival chances. Thus, incorporating within-type variation in the effects of change may help account for some earlier mixed results in studies of the adaptive consequences of organizational change.

Reconciling Adaptation and Selection

Although adaptationist and ecological views are frequently presented as mutually exclusive alternatives with very different implications for organization studies, these views are not fundamentally incompatible. While ecological theory emphasizes the predominance of selection over adaptation, the complementarity of adaptive and ecological effects is clearly reflected in the research reviewed here. Research in Tables 8 and 9 does not appear to support strong ecological arguments: organizations change frequently in response to environmental changes, and often without any harmful effects. Moreover, rates of change are often not constrained by age and size as predicted by structural inertia theory. At the same time, however, in contrast to a strong adaptation view, survival consequences of change appear more consistent with random groping than calculated strategic action (Baum and Singh 1996; Delacroix and Swaminathan 1991). Taken together, the findings suggest a complex relationship between adaptation and selection: because organizational change can affect organizational failure, the population-level result of combined adaptation and selection is not the simple aggregate of each process separately. Studying the transformation of organizational populations during periods of rapid environmental change may provide win-

dows of opportunity to examine the links between adaptation and selection perspectives on organizational change more closely (Levinthal 1994; McKelvey 1994). Too few analyses of organizational-level change exploit such natural experiments (for an exception, see Ginsberg and Buchholtz 1990).

As Hannan and Freeman (1977: 930) point out, a full treatment of organization–environment relations must cover both adaptation and selection. *Now* is the time to expand the boundaries of ecological and adaptationist perspectives to create a combined approach that sees processes of adaptation and selection as complementary and interacting. Expanding the study of organizational change in this way will create a framework that takes seriously the occurrence of selection processes and combines it with the systematic study of organization-level changes that may, under certain conditions, be adaptive.

PROGRESS, PROBLEMS, AND FUTURE DIRECTIONS

As this review shows, organizational ecology is a vital subdiscipline within organization studies, with research proliferating and increasing in methodological sophistication constantly. *But what does organizational ecology contribute to progress in organization studies?* One way to answer this question is to examine the problems organizational ecology solves (Lauden 1984; Tucker 1994). According to Lauden (1984: 15), scientific theories must solve two kinds of problems: (1) *empirical problems*, which are substantive questions about the objects (i.e. organizations) that constitute the domain of inquiry; and (2) *conceptual problems*, which include questions about internal logical consistency and conceptual ambiguity of theories advanced to solve empirical problems, as well as the methodological soundness of tests of theoretical arguments. From this perspective, organizational ecology's contribution to progress can be defined in terms of its capacity to accumulate *solved* empirical problems while minimizing the scope of unsolved empirical problems and conceptual problems.

As revealed in this review, the primary emphasis of organizational ecology is the development of theoretical explanations for specific empirical problems. Although organizational ecology has advanced knowledge about a wide range of empirical problems, few (if any) of these can be considered solved conclusively. Of course, other organization studies subdisciplines have not solved these problems either. From a conceptual standpoint, while examples of internal logical inconsistencies are uncommon in ecological theory (but see Young 1988), instances of conceptual ambiguity abound. Questions are frequently raised about the meaning and definition of central concepts such as organization, population, founding, failure, and legitimacy (Astley 1985; Carroll 1984a; Rao 1993; 1994; McKelvey 1982; Young 1988). To be fair, these ambiguities are not unique to organizational ecology, but endemic to organization studies (Tucker 1994). Another recurrent source of conceptual problems is the methodological soundness of tests of theoretical arguments. One area of frequent debate is the appropriateness of inferring processes of legitimation from population density estimates instead of measuring the underlying construct more directly (Baum and Powell 1995; Delacroix and Rao 1994; Hannan and Carroll 1992; Zucker 1989). In part, this problem stems from organizational ecology's use of large-scale, historical databases in which, by necessity, measures are frequently removed from concepts. Research on age dependence, and to a lesser degree size dependence, also suffer from this problem.

Although unsolved empirical problems and conceptual problems are not uncommon in new and emerging areas of scientific inquiry, the longer these problems – especially conceptual problems – remain unresolved, the greater their importance becomes in debates about the veracity of the theory that generated it (Lauden 1984: 64–6). What produces organizational ecology's problems? Although organizational ecologists would like their theories to maximize generality across organizational populations, realism of context, and precision in measurement of variables, in fact, no theory can be general, precise, and realistic all at the same time (McGrath 1982; Puccia and Levins 1985; Singh 1993). Theories must therefore sacrifice on some dimensions to maximize others. For example, realistic theories may apply to only a limited domain, while general theories may be inaccurate or misleading for specific applications. Organizational ecologists appear to favor a trade-off of precision and realism for generality. For example, precision and realism are clearly sacrificed for generality in density dependence theory and structural inertia theory. This is less true of niche-width theory and the resource-partitioning model.

On the one hand, this research strategy produces organizational ecology's main strength: the accumulation of a wealth of comparable empirical evidence from diverse organizational settings on a range of empirical problems unparalleled in organization studies. On the other hand, it also creates a major weakness: the large pool of coefficients for indirect measures, such as age, size, and population density, reveals

little about theoretical explanations designed to account for the empirical problems of interest. This creates conceptual problems by fostering skepticism regarding the veracity of inferred underlying processes because conforming findings cannot be interpreted precisely, and creates unsolved empirical problems by making it difficult to account for nonconforming findings on theoretical grounds.

Thus, the sacrifice of contextual realism and measurement precision for generality may underlie several key problems in organizational ecology. Consequently, by sacrificing some generality for more precision and realism, organizational ecologists may be able to begin resolving some of these problems. Research that adopts this problem-solving strategy has already contributed to the literature in at least three ways. First, elaborations of the density dependence model (see Table 5) all help increase either measurement precision, for example, by measuring underlying processes of competition and legitimation either differently or more directly (Baum and Oliver 1992; Baum and Singh 1994b; 1994c), or contextual realism, for example, by incorporating population-specific features such as organizational size distributions or market niche structures into the model (Barnett and Amburgey 1990; Baum and Mezias 1992; Baum and Singh 1994b; 1994c). Second, ecological analyses that incorporate institutional and technological processes help improve contextual realism by linking ecological processes in organizational populations to historical processes in the surrounding environment (Barnett 1990; Barnett and Carroll 1993; Tucker et al. 1990a; Singh et al. 1991). Third, research emphasizing greater measurement precision sheds light on the underlying causes of age and size dependence in organizational failure rates (Singh et al. 1986; Baum and Oliver 1991). More robust organization-level measures are necessary to establish more firmly the micro-foundations of ecological theory.

My view is that we now have more than enough indirect tests of the general theories and that problem solving and progress in organizational ecology can be enhanced by a move toward greater precision and realism in theory and research. This means getting closer to research problems. Proximity can add realism by revealing important aspects of the phenomena that distanced ecological researchers typically cannot detect. This also means focusing more on anomalies. Results that are inconsistent with each other or with theoretical explanations are common in organizational ecology. Understanding these anomalies is crucial to specifying the conditions under which various predictions hold and increasing precision. It also means asking new kinds of research questions that develop links with other research streams in organization theory and tie together micro and macro processes. One such linkage on which work has already begun is specification of the impacts of ecological dynamics of organizations on jobs and people (Haveman and Cohen 1994; Korn and Baum 1994). Lastly, this means letting research problems drive the choice of research design and methodology rather than vice versa. For some specific questions, an organizational history will be more appropriate than an entire population's history. Organizational ecologists need to start designing studies and using methods that best enable research questions to be answered. In some cases, this may require the use of multiple methods – qualitative as well as quantitative. Altering the ecological research orientation in these ways may help realize more of the great potential contribution of organizational ecology to theory and research in organization studies, as well as to practice in public policy, management, and entrepreneurship.

NOTES

For helpful discussions, conversations, and comments, I would like to thank Howard Aldrich, Terry Amburgey, Jack Brittain, Charles Fombrun, Raghu Garud, Heather Haveman, Kathy Hick, Paul Ingram, Helaine Korn, Walter Nord, Jim Ranger-Moore, Woody Powell, Huggy Rao, Lori Rosenkopf, Kaye Schoonhoven, Jitendra Singh, Bill Starbuck, and Anand Swaminathan. This chapter was written, in part, while the author was Associate Professor of Management at the Stern School of Business, New York University.

1 I am grateful to Jim Ranger-Moore for the use of the heading for this section, which is the title of his 1991 manuscript.

REFERENCES

Abernathy, William (1978) *The Productivity Dilemma.* Baltimore, MD: Johns Hopkins University Press.

Aldrich, Howard E. (1979) *Organizations and Environments.* Englewood Cliffs, NJ: Prentice-Hall.

Aldrich, Howard E. and Auster, Ellen R. (1986) 'Even dwarfs started small: liabilities of age and size and their strategic implications', *Research in Organizational Behavior*, 8: 165–98. Greenwich, CT: JAI Press.

Aldrich, Howard E. and Fiol, Marlene C. (1994) 'Fools rush in? The institutional context of industry creation', *Academy of Management Review*, 19: 645–70.

Aldrich, Howard E. and Pfeffer, Jeffrey (1976) 'Environments of organizations', *Annual Review of Sociology*, 2: 79–105.

Aldrich, Howard E. and Wiedenmayer, Gabriele (1993) 'From traits to rates: an ecological perspective on organizational foundings', *Advances in Entrepreneurship, Firm Emergence, and Growth*, 1: 145–95. Greenwich, CT: JAI Press.

Aldrich, Howard E., Zimmer, Catherine R., Staber, Udo H. and Beggs, John J. (1994) 'Minimalism, mutualism, and maturity: The evolution of the American trade association population in the 20th century', in J.A.C. Baum and J.V. Singh (eds), *Evolutionary Dynamics of Organizations.* New York: Oxford University Press. pp. 223–39.

Amburgey, Terry L. and Dacin, Tina (1994) 'As the left foot follows the right? The dynamics of strategic and structural change', *Academy of Management Journal*, 37: 1427–52.

Amburgey, Terry L. and Kelly, Dawn (1985) 'Adaptation and selection in organizational populations: a competing risk model'. Paper presented at Academy of Management Meetings, San Diego, CA.

Amburgey, Terry L. and Miner, Anne S. (1992) 'Strategic momentum: the effects of repetitive, positional, and contextual momentum on merger activity', *Strategic Management Journal*, 13: 335–48.

Amburgey, Terry L., Dacin, Tina and Kelly, Dawn (1994) 'Disruptive selection and population segmentation: interpopulation competition as a segregating process', in J.A.C. Baum and J.V. Singh (eds), *Evolutionary Dynamics of Organizations.* New York: Oxford University Press. pp. 240–54.

Amburgey, Terry L., Kelly, Dawn and Barnett, William P. (1990) 'Resetting the clock: the dynamics of organizational change and failure', in J.L. Wall and L.R. Jauch (eds), *Academy of Management Proceedings.* San Francisco, CA: Academy of Management. pp. 160–4.

Amburgey, Terry L., Kelly, Dawn and Barnett, William P. (1993) 'Resetting the clock: the dynamics of organizational change and failure', *Administrative Science Quarterly*, 38: 51–73.

Amburgey, Terry L., Lehtisalo, Marjo-Riitta and Kelly, Dawn (1988) 'Suppression and failure in the political press: government control, party affiliation, and organizational life chances', in G.R. Carroll (ed.), *Ecological Models of Organizations.* Cambridge, MA: Ballinger. pp. 153–74.

Anderson, Philip (1988) 'The population dynamics of creative destruction', in F. Hoy (ed.), *Academy of Management Best Papers Proceedings.* Anaheim, CA: Academy of Management. pp. 150–4.

Anderson, Philip and Tushman, Michael L. (1990) 'Technological discontinuities and dominant designs: a cyclical model of technological change', *Administrative Science Quarterly*, 35: 604–33.

Anderson, Philip and Tushman, Michael L. (1992) 'Technological, ecological and economic determinants of industry exit: a longitudinal study of the American cement (1888–1980) and minicomputer

(1958–1982) industries'. Unpublished manuscript, Johnson Graduate School of Management, Cornell University.

Astley, W. Graham (1985) 'The two ecologies: population and community perspectives on organizational evolution', *Administrative Science Quarterly*, 30: 224–41.

Astley, W. Graham and Van De Ven, Andrew H. (1983) 'Central perspectives and debates in organizational theory', *Administrative Science Quarterly*, 28: 245–73.

Bain, Joe S. (1956) *Barriers to New Competition*. Cambridge, MA: Harvard University Press.

Banaszak-Holl, Jane (1992) 'Historical trends in rates of Manhattan bank mergers, acquisitions, and failures'. Unpublished manuscript, Center for Health Care Research, Brown University.

Banaszak-Holl, Jane (1993) 'Avoiding failure when times get tough: changes in organizations' responses to competitive pressures'. Unpublished manuscript, Center for Health Care Research, Brown University.

Barnett, William P. (1990) 'The organizational ecology of a technological system', *Administrative Science Quarterly*, 35: 31–60.

Barnett, William P. and Amburgey, Terry L. (1990) 'Do larger organizations generate stronger competition?', in J.V. Singh (ed.), *Organizational Evolution: New Directions*. Newbury Park, CA: Sage. pp. 78–102.

Barnett, William P. and Carroll, Glenn R. (1993) 'How institutional constraints affected the organization of early American telephony', *Journal of Law, Economics, and Organization*, 9: 98–126.

Barron, David N., West, Elizabeth and Hannan, Michael T. (1994) 'A time to grow and a time to die: growth and mortality of credit unions in New York City, 1914–1990', *American Journal of Sociology*, 100: 381–421.

Baum, Joel A.C. (1989a) 'Liabilities of newness, adolescence, and obsolescence: exploring age dependence in the dissolution of organizational relationships and organizations', *Proceedings of the Administrative Sciences Association of Canada*, 10(5): 1–10.

Baum, Joel A.C. (1989b) 'A population perspective on organizations: a study of diversity and transformation in child care service organizations'. Unpublished PhD dissertation, Faculty of Management, University of Toronto.

Baum, Joel A.C. (1990a) 'Inertial and adaptive patterns in the dynamics of organizational change', in J.L. Wall and L.R. Jauch (eds), *Academy of Management Proceedings*. San Francisco, CA: Academy of Management. pp. 165–9.

Baum, Joel A.C. (1990b) 'Why are there so many (few) kinds of organizations? A study of organizational diversity', in C. Kirchmeyer (ed.), *Proceedings of the Administrative Sciences Association of Canada*, 11(5): 1–10.

Baum, Joel A.C. (1995) 'The changing basis of competition in organizational populations: the Manhattan hotel industry, 1898–1990', *Social Forces*, 74: 177–204.

Baum, Joel A.C. and Korn, Helaine J. (1994) 'The community ecology of large Canadian companies, 1984–1991', *Canadian Journal of Administrative Sciences*, 11: 277–94.

Baum, Joel A.C. and Korn, Helaine J. (1996) 'Competitive dynamics of interfirm rivalry', *Academy of Management Journal*, 39: 255–91.

Baum, Joel A.C. and Mezias, Stephen J. (1992) 'Localized competition and organizational failure in the Manhattan hotel industry, 1898–1990', *Administrative Science Quarterly*, 37: 580–604.

Baum, Joel A.C. and Oliver, Christine (1991) 'Institutional linkages and organizational mortality', *Administrative Science Quarterly*, 36: 187–218.

Baum, Joel A.C. and Oliver, Christine (1992) 'Institutional embeddedness and the dynamics of organizational populations', *American Sociological Review*, 57: 540–59.

Baum, Joel A.C. and Powell, Walter W. (1995) 'Cultivating an institutional ecology of organizations: Comment on Hannan, Carroll, Dundon, and Torres', *American Sociological Review*, 60: 529–38.

Baum, Joel A.C. and Singh, Jitendra V. (1994a) 'Organizational hierarchies and evolutionary processes: some reflections on a theory of organizational evolution', in J.A.C. Baum and J.V. Singh (eds), *Evolutionary Dynamics of Organizations*. New York: Oxford University Press. pp. 3–22.

Baum, Joel A.C. and Singh, Jitendra V. (1994b) 'Organizational niches and the dynamics of organizational founding', *Organization Science*, 5: 483–501.

Baum, Joel A.C. and Singh, Jitendra V. (1994c) 'Organizational niches and the dynamics of organizational mortality', *American Journal of Sociology*, 100: 346–80.

Baum, Joel A.C. and Singh, Jitendra V. (1994d) 'Organization–environment coevolution', in J.A.C. Baum and J.V. Singh (eds), *Evolutionary Dynamics of Organizations*. New York: Oxford University Press. pp. 379–402.

Baum, Joel A.C., Korn, Helaine J. and Kotha, Suresh (1994) 'Dominant designs and population dynamics in telecommunications services: founding and failure of facsimile service organizations, 1965–1992', *Social Science Research*, 24: 97–135.

Baum, Joel A.C., Korn, Helaine J. and Kotha, Suresh (1995) 'Technological discontinuities and the competitive dynamics of an organizational population: founding and failure of facsimile service organizations, 1965–1992'. Presented at the Academy of Management, Organizational and Management Theory Division, Atlanta, GA.

Baum, Joel A.C. and Singh, Jitendra V. (1996) 'Dynamics of organizational responses to competition', *Social Forces*, 74(4).

Boeker, Warren (1989) 'Strategic change: the effects of

founding and history', *Academy of Management Journal*, 32: 489–515.

Brittain, Jack W. (1994) 'Density-independent selection and community evolution', in J.A.C. Baum and J.V. Singh (eds), *Evolutionary Dynamics of Organizations*. New York: Oxford University Press. pp. 355–78.

Brittain, Jack W. and Freeman, John H. (1980) 'Organizational proliferation and density dependent selection', in J. Kimberly and R. Miles (eds), *The Organizational Life Cycle*. San Francisco, CA: Jossey-Bass.

Brittain, Jack W. and Wholey, Douglas H. (1988) 'Competition and coexistence in organizational communities: population dynamics in electronics components manufacturing', in G.R. Carroll (ed.), *Ecological Models of Organizations*. Cambridge, MA: Ballinger. pp. 195–222.

Bruderl, Jossef and Schussler, Rudolf (1990) 'Organizational mortality: the liabilities of newness and adolescence', *Administrative Science Quarterly*, 35: 530–47.

Budros, Art (1993) 'An analysis of organizational birth types: organizational start-up and entry in the nineteenth-century life insurance industry', *Social Forces*, 70: 1013–30.

Budros, Art (1994) 'Analyzing unexpected density dependence effects on organizational births in New York's life insurance industry, 1842–1904', *Organization Science*, 5: 541–53.

Burgelman, Robert A. (1991) 'Intraorganizational ecology of strategy-making and organizational adaptation: theory and field research', *Organization Science*, 2: 239–62.

Burgelman, Robert A. and Mittman, Brian S. (1994) 'An intraorganizational ecological perspective on managerial risk behavior, performance, and survival: individual, organizational, and environmental effects', in J.A.C. Baum and J.V. Singh (eds), *Evolutionary Dynamics of Organizations*. New York: Oxford University Press. pp. 53–74.

Campbell, Donald T. (1965) 'Variation and selective retention in socio-cultural evolution', in H.R. Barringer, G.I. Blanksten and R.W. Mack (eds), *Social Change in Developing Areas: A Reinterpretation of Evolutionary Theory*. Cambridge, MA: Schenkman. pp. 19–48.

Carroll, Glenn R. (1981) 'Dynamics of organizational expansion in national systems of education', *American Sociological Review*, 46: 585–99.

Carroll, Glenn R. (1983) 'A stochastic model of organizational mortality: review and reanalysis', *Social Science Research*, 12: 303–29.

Carroll, Glenn R. (1984a) 'Organizational ecology', *Annual Review of Sociology*, 10: 71–93. Palo Alto, CA: Annual Reviews.

Carroll, Glenn R. (1984b) 'Dynamics of publisher succession in newspaper organizations', *Administrative Science Quarterly*, 29: 93–113.

Carroll, Glenn R. (1985) 'Concentration and specialization: dynamics of niche width in populations of organizations', *American Journal of Sociology*, 90: 1262–83.

Carroll, Glenn R. (1987) *Publish and Perish: the Organizational Ecology of Newspaper Industries*. Greenwich, CT: JAI Press.

Carroll, Glenn R. and Delacroix, Jacques (1982) 'Organizational mortality in the newspaper industries of Argentina and Ireland: an ecological approach', *Administrative Science Quarterly*, 27: 169–98.

Carroll, Glenn R. and Hannan, Michael T. (1989a) 'Density delay in the evolution of organizational population: a model and five empirical tests', *Administrative Science Quarterly*, 34: 411–30.

Carroll, Glenn R. and Hannan, Michael T. (1989b) 'Density dependence in the evolution of newspaper organizations', *American Sociological Review*, 54: 524–41.

Carroll, Glenn R. and Huo, Y. Paul (1986) 'Organizational task and institutional environments in ecological perspective: findings from the local newspaper industry', *American Journal of Sociology*, 91: 838–73.

Carroll, Glenn R. and Swaminathan, Anand (1991) 'Density dependent organizational evolution in the American brewing industry from 1633 to 1988', *Acta Sociologica*, 34: 155–76.

Carroll, Glenn R. and Swaminathan, Anand (1992) 'The organizational ecology of strategic groups in the American brewing industry from 1975–1990', *Corporate and Industrial Change*, 1: 65–97.

Carroll, Glenn R. and Wade, James B. (1991) 'Density dependence in the evolution of the American brewing industry across different levels of analysis', *Social Science Research*, 20: 271–302.

Carroll, Glenn R., Delacroix, Jacques and Goodstein, Jerry (1988) 'The political environments of organizations: an ecological view', *Research in Organizational Behavior*, 10: 359–392. Greenwich, CT: JAI Press.

Carroll, Glenn R., Preisendoerfer, Peter, Swaminathan, Anand and Wiedenmayer, Gabriele (1993) 'Brewery and *Brauerei*: the organizational ecology of brewing', *Organization Studies*, 14: 155–88.

Caves, Richard E. and Porter, Michael E. (1977) 'From entry barriers to mobility barriers', *Quarterly Journal of Economics*, 90: 241–61.

Cohen, Wesley M. and Levinthal, Daniel A. (1990) 'Absorptive capacity: a new perspective on learning and innovation', *Administrative Science Quarterly*, 35: 128–52.

Cyert, Richard M. and March, James G. (1963) *A Behavioral Theory of the Firm*. Englewood Cliffs, NJ: Prentice-Hall.

Delacroix, Jacques and Carroll, Glenn R. (1983) 'Organizational foundings: an ecological study of the newspaper industries of Argentina and Ireland', *Administrative Science Quarterly*, 28: 274–91.

Delacroix, Jacques and Rao, Hayagreeva (1994) 'Externalities and ecological theory: unbundling density dependence', in J.A.C. Baum and J.V. Singh (eds), *Evolutionary Dynamics of Organizations*. New York: Oxford University Press.

Delacroix, Jacques and Swaminathan, Anand (1991) 'Cosmetic, speculative, and adaptive organizational change in the wine industry: a longitudinal study', *Administrative Science Quarterly*, 36: 631–61.

Delacroix, Jacques, Swaminathan, Anand and Solt, Michael E. (1989) 'Density dependence versus population dynamics: an ecological study of failings in the California wine industry', *American Sociological Review*, 54: 245–62.

DiMaggio, Paul J. (1994) 'The challenge of community evolution', in J.A.C. Baum and J.V. Singh (eds), *Evolutionary Dynamics of Organizations*. New York: Oxford University Press. pp. 444–50.

DiMaggio, Paul J. and Powell, Walter W. (1983) 'The iron cage revisited: institutional isomorphism and collective rationality in organizational fields', *American Sociological Review*, 48: 147–60.

Dosi, Giovanni (1984) *Technical Change and Industrial Transformation*. New York: St Martin's Press.

Dun and Bradstreet (1978) *The Failure Record*. New York: Dun and Bradstreet.

Durkheim, Emile (1933) *The Division of Labor in Society* (1893). Glencoe, IL: Free Press.

Fichman, Mark and Levinthal, Daniel A. (1991) 'Honeymoons and the liability of adolescence: a new perspective on duration dependence in social and organizational relationships', *Academy of Management Review*, 16: 442–68.

Fombrun, Charles J. (1986) 'Structural dynamics within and between organizations', *Administrative Science Quarterly*, 31: 403–21.

Fombrun, Charles J. (1988) 'Crafting an institutionally informed ecology of organizations', in G.R. Carroll (ed.), *Ecological Models of Organizations*. Cambridge, MA: Ballinger. pp. 223–39.

Freeman, John (1990) 'Ecological analysis of semiconductor firm mortality', in J.V. Singh (ed.), *Organizational Evolution: New Directions*. Newbury Park, CA: Sage. pp. 53–77.

Freeman, John H. and Hannan, Michael T. (1983) 'Niche width and the dynamics of organizational populations', *American Journal of Sociology*, 88: 1116–45.

Freeman, John H. and Hannan, Michael T. (1987) 'The ecology of restaurants revisited', *American Journal of Sociology*, 92: 1214–20.

Freeman, John and Lomi, Alessandro (1994) 'Resource partitioning and foundings of banking cooperative in Italy', in J.A.C. Baum and J.V. Singh (eds), *Evolutionary Dynamics of Organizations*. New York: Oxford University Press. pp. 269–93.

Freeman, John H., Carroll, Glenn R. and Hannan, Michael T. (1983) 'The liability of newness: age dependence in organizational death rates', *American Sociological Review*, 48: 692–710.

Gartner, William B. (1989) 'Some suggestions for research on entrepreneurial traits and characteristics', *Entrepreneurship: Theory and Practice*, 14: 27–37.

Ginsberg, Ari and Baum, Joel A.C. (1994) 'Evolutionary processes and patterns of core business change', in J.A.C. Baum and J.V. Singh (eds), *Evolutionary Dynamics of Organizations*. New York: Oxford University Press. pp. 127–51.

Ginsberg, Ari and Buchholtz, Anne (1990) 'Converting to for-profit status: corporate responsiveness to radical change', *Academy of Management Journal*, 33: 447–77.

Guo, Guang (1993) 'Event history analysis for left-truncated data', *Sociological Methodology*, 23: 217–44.

Halliday, Terrence, Powell, Michael J. and Granfors, Mark W. (1993) 'After minimalism: transformations of state bar associations, 1918–1950', *American Sociological Review*, 58: 515–35.

Hambrick, Donald C. and D'Aveni, Richard A. (1988) 'Large corporate failures as downward spirals', *Administrative Science Quarterly*, 33: 1–23.

Hannan, Michael T. and Carroll, Glenn R. (1992) *Dynamics of Organizational Populations: Density, Competition, and Legitimation*. New York: Oxford University Press.

Hannan, Michael T. and Freeman, John H. (1977) 'The population ecology of organizations', *American Journal of Sociology*, 83: 929–84.

Hannan, Michael T. and Freeman, John H. (1984) 'Structural inertia and organizational change', *American Sociological Review*, 49: 149–64.

Hannan, Michael T. and Freeman, John H. (1987) 'The ecology of organizational founding: American labor unions, 1836–1985', *American Journal of Sociology*, 92: 910–43.

Hannan, Michael T. and Freeman, John H. (1988) 'The ecology of organizational mortality: American labor unions, 1836–1985', *American Journal of Sociology*, 94: 25–52.

Hannan, Michael T. and Freeman, John H. (1989) *Organizational Ecology*. Cambridge, MA: Harvard University Press.

Hannan, Michael T., Barron, David and Carroll, Glenn R. (1991) 'On the interpretation of density dependence in rates of organizational mortality: a reply to Peterson and Koput', *American Sociology Review*, 56: 410–15.

Hannan, Michael T., Carroll, Glenn R., Dundon, Elizabeth A. and Torres, John C. (1995) 'Organizational evolution in a multinational context: entries of automobile manufacturers in Belgium, Britain, France, Germany, and Italy', *American Sociological Review*, 60: 509–28.

Hannan, Michael T., Ranger-Moore, James and Banaszak-Holl, Jane (1990) 'Competition and the evolution of organizational size distributions', in J.V. Singh (ed.), *Organizational Evolution: New Directions*. Newbury Park, CA: Sage. pp. 246–68.

Haveman, Heather A. (1992) 'Between a rock and a hard place: organizational change and performance under conditions of fundamental environmental transformation', *Administrative Science Quarterly*, 37: 48–75.

Haveman, Heather A. (1993a) 'Organizational size and change: diversification in the savings and loan industry after deregulation', *Administrative Science Quarterly*, 38: 20–50.

Haveman, Heather A. (1993b) 'Follow the leader: mimetic isomorphism and entry into new markets', *Administrative Science Quarterly*, 38: 593–627.

Haveman, Heather A. (1993c) 'Ghosts of managers past: managerial succession and organizational mortality', *Academy of Management Journal*, 36: 864–81.

Haveman, Heather A. (1994) 'The ecological dynamics of organizational change: density and mass dependence in rates of entry into new markets', in J.A.C. Baum and J.V. Singh (eds), *Evolutionary Dynamics of Organizations*. New York: Oxford University Press. pp. 152–66.

Haveman, Heather A. and Cohen, Lisa E. (1994) 'The ecological dynamics of careers: the impact of organizational founding, dissolution, and merger on job mobility', *American Journal of Sociology*, 100: 104–52.

Hawley, Amos H. (1950) *Human Ecology: A Theory of Community Structure*. New York: Ronald.

Henderson, Rebecca M. and Clark, Kim B. (1990) 'Architectural innovation: the reconfiguration of existing product technologies and failure of established firms', *Administrative Science Quarterly*, 35: 9–30.

Herriott, Scott R. (1987) 'Fitness-set theory in the population ecology of organizations: comment on Freeman and Hannan', *American Journal of Sociology*, 92: 1210–14.

Hybels, Ralph C. (1994) 'Legitimation, population density, and founding rates: the institutionalization of commercial biotechnology in the US, 1971–89'. Unpublished PhD dissertation, Cornell University.

Hybels, Ralph C., Ryan, Alan R. and Barley, Stephen R. (1994) 'Alliances, legitimation, and founding rates in the U.S. biotechnology field, 1971–1989'. Paper presented at the Academy of Management National Meetings, Dallas, TX.

Ingram, Paul L. (1993) 'Old, tired, and ready to die: the age dependence of organizational mortality reconsidered'. Paper presented at the Academy of Management Meetings, Atlanta, GA.

Ingram, Paul L. (1994) 'Endogenizing environmental change: the evolution of hotel chains, 1896–1980'. Unpublished manuscript, Johnson Graduate School of Management, Cornell University.

Katz, Jerome and Gartner, William B. (1988) 'Properties of emerging organizations', *Academy of Management Review*, 13: 429–41.

Kelly, Dawn (1988) 'Organizational transformation and failure in the US airline industry, 1962–1985'. Unpublished PhD dissertation, Graduate School of Business, Northwestern University.

Kelly, Dawn and Amburgey, Terry L. (1991) 'Organizational inertia and momentum: a dynamic model of strategic change', *Academy of Management Journal*, 34: 591–612.

Korn, Helaine J. and Baum, Joel A.C. (1994) 'Community ecology and employment dynamics: a study of large Canadian firms', *Social Forces*, 73: 1–32.

Lauden, Larry (1984) *Progress and its Problems*. Berkeley, CA: University of California Press.

Lawrence, Paul R. and Lorsch, Jay W. (1967) *Organizations and Environments: Managing Differentiation and Integration*. Boston, MA: Harvard Business School Press.

Levins, Richard (1968) *Evolution in Changing Environments*. Princeton, NJ: Princeton University Press.

Levinthal, Daniel A. (1991a) 'Random walks and organizational mortality', *Administrative Science Quarterly*, 36: 397–420.

Levinthal, Daniel A. (1991b) 'Organizational adaptation and environmental selection – interrelated processes of change', *Organization Science*, 2: 140–5.

Levinthal, Daniel A. (1994) 'Surviving Schumpeterian environments: an evolutionary perspective', in J.A.C. Baum and J.V. Singh (eds), *Evolutionary Dynamics of Organizations*. New York: Oxford University Press. pp. 167–78.

Levitt, Barbara and March, James G. (1988) 'Organizational learning', *Annual Review of Sociology*, 14: 319–40.

Lomi, Alessandro (1995) 'The ecology of organizational founding: location dependence and unobserved heterogeneity', *Administrative Science Quarterly*, 40: 111–44.

Loree, David W. (1993) 'Organizational mortality: the price paid for institutional linkages in the semiconductor industry'. Paper presented at the Academy of Management Meetings, Atlanta, GA.

Lumsden, Charles J. and Singh, Jitendra V. (1990) 'The dynamics of organizational speciation', in J.V. Singh (ed.), *Organizational Evolution: New Directions*. Newbury Park, CA: Sage. pp. 145–63.

McGee, John and Thomas, Howard (1986) 'Strategic groups: theory, research, and taxonomy', *Strategic Management Journal*, 7: 141–60.

McGrath, Joseph E. (1982) 'Dilemmatics: the study of research choices and dilemmas', in J.E. McGrath, J. Martin and R.A. Kulka (eds), *Judgement Calls in Research*. Beverly Hills, CA: Sage. pp. 69–102.

McKelvey, Bill (1982) *Organizational Systematics*. Berkeley, CA: University of California Press.

McKelvey, Bill (1994) 'Evolution and organizational science', in J.A.C. Baum and J.V. Singh (eds), *Evolutionary Dynamics of Organizations*. New York: Oxford University Press. pp. 314–26.

McPherson, J. Miller (1983) 'An ecology of affiliation', *American Sociological Review*, 48: 519–32.

Meyer, John W. and Rowan, Brian (1977) 'Institutionalized organizations: formal structure as myth and ceremony', *American Journal of Sociology*, 83: 340–63.

Meyer, Marshall W. (1994) 'Turning evolution inside the organization', in J.A.C. Baum and J.V. Singh (eds), *Evolutionary Dynamics of Organizations*. New York: Oxford University Press. pp. 109–16.

Miller, Danny, and Friesen, Peter H. (1980) 'Momentum and revolution in organizational adaptation', *Academy of Management Journal*, 22: 591–614.

Miner, Anne S. (1993) 'Review of *Dynamics of Organizational Populations: Density, Competition, and Legitimation*, by Michael T. Hannan and Glenn R. Carroll', *Academy of Management Review*, 18: 355–67.

Miner, Anne S. (1994) 'Seeking adaptive advantage: evolutionary theory and managerial action', in J.A.C. Baum and J.V. Singh (eds), *Evolutionary Dynamics of Organizations*. New York: Oxford University Press. pp. 76–89.

Miner, Anne S., Amburgey, Terry L. and Stearns, Timothy (1990) 'Interorganizational linkages and population dynamics: buffering and transformational shields', *Administrative Science Quarterly*, 35: 689–713.

Mitchell, Will (1989) 'Whether and when? Probability and timing of entry into emerging industrial subfields', *Administrative Science Quarterly*, 34: 208–30.

Mitchell, Will (1991) 'Dual clocks: entry order influences on incumbent and newcomer market share and survival when specialized assets retain their value', *Strategic Management Journal*, 12: 85–100.

Mitchell, Will and Singh, Kulwant (1993) 'Death of the lethargic: effects of expansion into new technical subfields on performance in a firm's base business', *Organization Science*, 4: 152–80.

Nelson, Richard R. (1994) 'The coevolution of technology, industrial structure, and supporting institutions', *Industrial and Corporate Change*, 3: 47–64.

Nelson, Richard R. and Winter, Sidney G. (1982) *An Evolutionary Theory of Economic Change*. Cambridge, MA: Harvard University Press.

Olzak, Susan (1992) *Dynamics of Ethnic Competition and Conflict*. Stanford, CA: Stanford University Press.

Olzak, Susan and West, Elizabeth (1991) 'Ethnic conflict and the rise and fall of ethnic newspapers', *American Sociological Review*, 56: 458–74.

Perrow, Charles (1986) *Complex Organizations: a Critical Essay*, 3rd edn. New York: Random House.

Petersen, Trond and Koput, Kenneth W. (1991) 'Density dependence in organizational mortality: legitimacy or unobserved heterogeneity', *American Sociological Review*, 56: 399–409.

Pfeffer, Jeffery and Salancik, Gerald R. (1978) *The External Control of Organizations*. New York: Harper and Row.

Puccia, Charles J. and Levins, Richard (1985) *Qualitative Modeling of Complex Systems*. Cambridge, MA: Harvard University Press.

Ranger-Moore, James (1991) 'Bigger may be better but is older wiser? Age dependence in organizational death rates'. Unpublished manuscript, Department of Sociology, University of Arizona.

Ranger-Moore, James, Banaszak-Holl, Jane J. and Hannan, Michael T. (1991) 'Density-dependent dynamics in regulated industries: founding rates of banks and life insurance companies', *Administrative Science Quarterly*, 36: 36–65.

Rao, Hayagreeva (1993) 'An ecology of emerging organizations: incorporation and operational startup in the American automobile industry, 1893–1915'. Unpublished manuscript, Emory Business School, Emory University.

Rao, Hayagreeva (1994) 'The social construction of reputation: certification contests, legitimation and the survival of organizations in the American automobile industry, 1895–1912', *Strategic Management Journal*, 15(S2): 29–44.

Rao, Hayagreeva and Neilsen, Eric H. (1992) 'An ecology of agency arrangements: mortality of savings and loan associations, 1960–1987', *Administrative Science Quarterly*, 37: 448–70.

Romanelli, Elaine (1991) 'The evolution of new organizational forms', *Annual Review of Sociology*, 17: 79–103.

Schumpeter, Joseph A. (1934) *The Theory of Economic Development*. Cambridge, MA: Harvard University Press.

Schumpeter, Joseph A. (1950) *Capitalism, Socialism and Democracy*, 3rd edn. New York: Harper and Row.

Scott, W. Richard (1992) *Organizations: Rational, Natural, and Open Systems*, 3rd edn. Englewood Cliffs, NJ: Prentice-Hall.

Scott, W. Richard and Meyer, John W. (1983) 'The organization of societal sectors', in J.W. Meyer and W.R. Scott (eds), *Organizational Environments: Ritual and Rationality*. Beverly Hills, CA: Sage. pp. 1–16.

Singh, Jitendra V. (1993) 'Review essay: density dependence theory – current issues, future promise', *American Journal of Sociology*, 99: 464–73.

Singh, Jitendra V. and Lumsden, Charles J. (1990) 'Theory and research in organizational ecology', *Annual Review of Sociology*, 16: 161–95. Palo Alto, CA: Annual Reviews.

Singh, Jitendra V., House, Robert J. and Tucker, David J. (1986) 'Organizational change and organizational mortality', *Administrative Science Quarterly*, 31: 587–611.

Singh, Jitendra V., Tucker, David J. and House, Robert J. (1986) 'Organizational legitimacy and the liability of newness', *Administrative Science Quarterly*, 31: 171–93.

Singh, Jitendra V., Tucker, David J. and Meinhard, Agnes G. (1988) 'Are voluntary social service organizations structurally inert? Exploring an assumption in organizational ecology'. Paper presented at Academy of Management Meeting, Anaheim, CA.

Singh, Jitendra V., Tucker, David J. and Meinhard, Agnes G. (1991) 'Institutional change and ecological dynamics', in W.W. Powell and P.J. DiMaggio (eds), *The New Institutionalism in Organizational Analysis.* Chicago, IL: University of Chicago Press. pp. 390–422.

Staber, Udo H. (1989) 'Age dependence and historical effects on the failure rates of worker cooperatives', *Economic and Industrial Democracy,* 10: 59–80.

Stinchcombe, Arthur L. (1965) 'Social structure and organizations', in J.G. March (ed.), *Handbook of Organizations.* Chicago, IL: Rand McNally. pp. 153–93.

Suárez, Fernando F. and Utterback, James M. (1992) 'Dominant designs and the survival of firms'. Unpublished manuscript, International Center for Research on the Management of Technology, MIT.

Swaminathan, Anand and Delacroix, Jacques (1991) 'Differentiation within an organizational population: additional evidence from the wine industry', *Academy of Management Journal,* 34: 679–92.

Swaminathan, Anand and Wiedenmayer, Gabriele (1991) 'Does the pattern of density dependence in organizational mortality rates vary across levels of analysis? Evidence from the German brewing industry', *Social Science Research,* 20: 45–73.

Thomas, Howard and Venkatraman, N. (1988) 'Research on strategic groups: progress and prognosis', *Journal of Management Studies,* 25: 537–55.

Thompson, James D. (1967) *Organizations in Action.* New York: Academic Press.

Tilly, Charles (1993) *European Revolutions, 1492–1992.* Cambridge, MA: Blackwell.

Tucker, David J. (1994) 'Progress and problems in population ecology', in J.A.C. Baum and J.V. Singh (eds), *Evolutionary Dynamics of Organizations.* New York: Oxford University Press. pp. 327–36.

Tucker, David J., Baum, Joel A.C. and Singh, Jitendra V. (1992) 'The institutional ecology of human service organizations', in Y. Hasenfeld (ed.), *Human Service Organizations.* Newbury Park, CA: Sage. pp. 47–72.

Tucker, David J., Singh, Jitendra V. and Meinhard, Agnes G. (1990a) 'Organizational form, population dynamics, and institutional change: the founding patterns of voluntary organizations', *Academy of Management Journal,* 33: 151–78.

Tucker, David J., Singh, Jitendra V. and Meinhard, Agnes G. (1990b) 'Founding characteristics, imprinting, and organizational change', in J.V. Singh (ed.), *Organizational Evolution: New Directions.* Newbury Park, CA: Sage. pp. 182–200.

Tucker, David J., Singh, Jitendra V., Meinhard, Agnes G. and House, Robert J. (1988) 'Ecological and institutional sources of change in organizational populations', in G.R. Carroll (ed.) *Ecological Models of Organizations.* Cambridge, MA: Ballinger. pp. 127–51.

Tushman, Michael L. and Anderson, Philip (1986) 'Technological discontinuities and organizational environments', *Administrative Science Quarterly,* 31: 439–65.

Usher, John M. (1991) 'Exploring the effects of niche crowding on rates of organizational change and failure'. Unpublished manuscript, Faculty of Business, University of Alberta.

Usher, John M. (1994) 'Niche width theory revisited: polymorphism and competitive strategy', in B. Dyck (ed.), *Proceedings of the Administrative Sciences Association of Canada,* 12: 90–9.

Utterback, James M. and Suárez, Fernando F. (1993) 'Innovation, competition, and industry structure', *Policy Studies,* 22: 1–21.

Uzzi, Brian (1993) 'The network effect: structural embeddedness and firm survival'. Unpublished manuscript, Kellogg Graduate School of Management, Northwestern University.

Van de Ven, Andrew H. and Grazman, David N. (1994) 'Generation to generation: a genealogy of Twin Cities health care organizations, 1853–1993'. Unpublished manuscript, Strategic Management Research Center, University of Minnesota.

Wade, James (1993) 'Organizational sources of technological designs in the microprocessor market'. Unpublished manuscript, College of Commerce and Business Administration, University of Illinois at Urbana-Champaign.

Wade, James (1995) 'Dynamics of organizational communities and technological bandwagons: an empirical investigation of community evolution in the microprocessor market', *Strategic Management Journal,* 16(S1): 111–34.

Wholey, Douglas R. and Brittain, Jack W. (1986) 'Organizational ecology: findings and implications', *Academy of Management Review,* 11: 513–33.

Wholey, Douglas R., Christianson, Jon B. and Sanchez, Susan M. (1992) 'Organizational size and failure among health maintenance organizations', *American Sociological Review,* 57: 829–42.

Winter, Sidney G. (1990) 'Survival, selection, and inheritance in evolutionary theories of organization', in J.V. Singh (ed.), *Organizational Evolution: New Directions.* Newbury Park, CA: Sage. pp. 269–97.

Young, Ruth C. (1988) 'Is population ecology a useful paradigm for the study of organizations?', *American Journal of Sociology,* 94: 1–24.

Zajac, Edward J. and Kraatz, Matthew S. (1993) 'A diametric forces model of strategic change: assessing the antecedents and consequences of restructuring in the higher education industry', *Strategic Management Journal,* 14(S): 83–102.

Zucker, Lynne G. (1977) 'The role of institutionalization in cultural persistence', *American Sociological Review,* 42: 726–43.

Zucker, Lynne G. (1989) 'Combining institutional theory and population ecology: no legitimacy, no history', *American Sociological Review,* 54: 542–5.

1.4

Organizational Economics: Understanding the Relationship between Organizations and Economic Analysis

JAY B. BARNEY AND WILLIAM HESTERLY

The field of organizational economics can be defined in a variety of ways. Some have argued that organizational economics is distinguished from other types of organizational analysis by its reliance on equilibrium analysis, assumptions of profit maximizing managers, and the use of abstract assumptions and models. In fact, some organizational economists do engage in these kinds of analyses and build models of organizations using these kinds of tools. However, not all organizational economists apply all the tools, all the time. For example, both evolutionary economic theory (Nelson and Winter 1982) and Austrian economics (Jacobson 1992) are explicitly non-equilibrium in nature. Models of risk shifting (Arrow 1985), decision-making (March and Simon 1958), and transaction economics (Williamson 1975) do not assume perfect rationality. Agency theory (Jensen and Meckling 1976), and theories of tacit collusion (Tirole 1989) and strategic alliances (Kogut 1988) do not assume that all managers, all the time, adopt profit maximizing objectives in their decision-making. Finally, a great deal of organizational economics is neither very mathematical nor highly technical – although questions of how abstract a model is are usually matters of taste.

Indeed, organizational economics, as a way of thinking about organization analysis, seems to have only two things in common. The first is an abiding interest in organizations, or firms (as economists usually call organizations). Unlike most economists, who are interested in the structure, functioning, and implications of markets, organizational economists are interested in the structure, functioning, and implications of firms.

Second, most organizational economists have an unflagging interest in the relationship between competition and organizations. Even organizational economists that study organizations under conditions of monopoly (where, presumably, there is relatively little competition) tend to focus on competitive processes that increase competition for monopolists over time (see the discussion of 'contestable market theory' below). For organizational economists, organizations exist in 'seething caldrons' of competition, where other firms, individuals, institutions, and governments are all seeking to obtain some part of the success that a particular firm may enjoy.

It is interesting to note that other forms of organizational analysis share this interest in organizations and competition. For example, the population ecology model (Hannan and Freeman 1977), in organization theory, has a well developed notion of competition, although (some might argue) a somewhat underdeveloped appreciation for the complexity of modern firms. Resource dependence theory discusses organizational responses to more or less munificent environments (Pfeffer and Salancik 1978). Even institutional theory (DiMaggio and Powell 1983) discusses the importance of legitimacy for an organization's survival. The probability of organizational survival is also of major interest in organizational economics. Organizational economics is hardly divorced from this broader organizational literature.

Incidentally, the focus on competition in organizational economics does not preclude discussions of cooperation within and between firms. As will be discussed later, intra-firm cooperation is one of the core issues in agency theory, and inter-firm cooperation (in the form of tacit collusion or strategic alliances) is an important topic in organizational economics as well. However, the role of cooperation in the Organizational Economic models is generally to enable a firm to more effectively respond to its competitive threats (Kogut 1988).

This twin focus on organizations, their origins and consequences, and on competition has generated a very large and ever growing literature. This huge literature can be conveniently divided into four major streams, each stream focusing on a slightly different, though related, central research question. These four research streams and their associated research questions are: (1) transactions cost economics (why do organizations exist?), (2) agency theory (do those associated with a firm agree about how it should be managed?), (3) strategic management theory (why do some organizations outperform others?), and (4) cooperative organizational economics (how can organizations cooperate?). These four research streams, and their associated research questions, are discussed in subsequent sections of this chapter.

WHY DO ORGANIZATIONS EXIST?

This question is, in many ways, the most central to organizational economics, in particular, and to organizational analysis more generally. To many, the question, 'why do organizations exist?' may sound odd. After all, it is pretty obvious that organizations do exist. Why go to such great effort to explain the existence of such a common phenomenon? However, this question becomes important in the context of neo-classical microeconomic theory.

Classical and neo-classical theory, beginning with Adam Smith, point to the amazing ability of markets to coordinate economic production and exchange at very low cost and without government planning. Simply stated, Smith's fundamental proposition was that an economy could be coordinated by a decentralized system of prices (the 'invisible hand'). Indeed, much of economics since the publication of *The Wealth of Nations* has involved formalizing this proposition, identifying the necessary conditions for the effective use of the invisible hand, and designing changes in those settings where the conditions are lacking (Demsetz 1990: 145). In most economics textbooks, this work is called the

theory of the firm – although the theory actually focuses exclusively on the structure and operation of markets and is unable to explain the existence of firms. Given that markets are so effective in coordinating economic exchanges, it has always been a bit of a mystery why not all exchanges are managed through markets, i.e. why economic exchanges would ever be managed through firms (Coase 1937).

Remarkably, the answer to the question 'why do organizations exist?' was formulated by Ronald Coase while he was a twenty-one-year-old student at the London School of Economics. It was Coase's great insight – published in his 1937 article 'The nature of the firm' – that the reason organizations exist is that, sometimes, the cost of managing economic exchanges across markets is greater than the cost of managing economic exchanges within the boundaries of an organization. The cost of using the price system involves such activities as discovering what prices are, negotiating contracts, renegotiating contracts, inspections, and settling disputes. The most lasting contribution of Coase's (1937) article was to place transaction costs at the center of analysis of the questions of why firms exist and to suggest that markets and organizations are alternatives for managing the same transactions. However, by Coase's (1972: 63) own admission, 'The nature of the firm' was 'much cited and little used'. This early lack of influence stems largely from Coase's failure to operationalize his approach and his lack of precision about which transactions will be left to the market and which will be internalized within firms. Later theorists addressed these deficiencies by developing a more complete model of the costs of using a market to manage economic exchanges. This work has come to be known as transaction cost theory (TCT).

The Alchian-Demsetz Approach

The first influential extension of Coase's reasoning emphasized measurement or metering problems as the reason firms exist (Alchian and Demsetz 1972). Measurement problems occur as a result of team production. Team production typically involves gains from cooperation where complex production processes are involved. The members of the team can produce more working cooperatively with one another than separately. Thus, they have an incentive to cooperate. This incentive to cooperate, however, declines as the potential for shirking among team members increases. Shirking includes behaviors that range from outright cheating to merely giving less than one's best effort. While the interdependence between team members yields potentially greater production, it also makes it more difficult to assess the contribution of each individual member. With no mechanism to monitor or measure each team member's efforts, the team cannot reward members based on individual productivity. If team members know that their individual efforts are only imperfectly connected to their individual rewards, then they have an incentive to work less diligently. The team may seek another way to reward members for their efforts.

One alternative is to split the income generated by the team equally among members. However, this equal sharing arrangement does not remove the incentive of team members to shirk. This incentive occurs because individuals know that the costs of any additional efforts on their part will be theirs alone, while the rewards that come from these efforts will be split among the team. Since each team member has this same incentive to shirk, team production will fall. Indeed, the possibility of shirking also may discourage high-output individuals from joining the team in the first place. When high-output individuals do join the team, they may become shirkers once they become members.

The firm emerges to meet the need to monitor the efforts of those individuals that make up a team. Monitoring each individual reduces the likelihood of shirking. As individuals are assigned to monitoring roles, a hierarchy emerges. Shirking is not completely eliminated by the hierarchy, however. Because monitoring is costly, it is efficient to monitor only to the point where the marginal benefits from reduced shirking equal the marginal costs of monitoring. It is typically neither reasonable nor efficient to completely remove shirking, even when technically possible.

Assigning someone the task of monitoring the performance of individuals on a team creates yet another problem. Specifically, who will monitor the monitor? As with other team members, the monitor has an incentive to shirk unless contrary incentives exist. Alchian and Demsetz's (1972) solution to this problem is to have the monitor bear the cost of her shirking by giving this person the right to negotiate contracts with all team members, to monitor their productive efforts, and (most importantly) to claim any residual value created by a team, after team members receive their expected compensation. The monitor then pays team members based on their individual productivity and keeps the remaining portion as income. This arrangement leaves the monitor with a strong incentive to monitor the efforts of each team member. The results are reduced incentives for shirking and increased team productivity that is shared between the team members and the monitor. In

the modern corporation, this ultimate 'monitor of monitors' is a firm's stockholders. Just as Alchian and Demsetz expect, stockholders have a claim on a firm's residual profits, i.e. profits that remain after all other legitimate claims on a firm have been satisfied.

Williamson's Formulation of Transaction Cost Theory

The Alchian-Demsetz approach to explaining the existence of organizations has several strengths. For example, it does explain the existence of managerial hierarchies and the existence of stockholders as a firm's residual claimants. However, many organizational economists have found that Alchian and Demsetz's exclusive focus on team production obscures some important issues associated with understanding the nature of the firm. The most highly developed alternative to the Alchian and Demsetz approach can be found in the work of Oliver Williamson. Indeed, it can be said that Williamson's answers to why organizations exist are now considered to be the core of transaction cost economics.

A basic assertion of Williamson's TCT is that markets and hierarchies are alternative instruments for completing a set of transactions (Williamson 1975: 8). As instruments for completing a set of transactions, markets and hierarchies are often also called 'governance mechanisms'. In general, market forms of governance rely on prices, competition, and contracts to keep all parties to an exchange informed of their rights and responsibilities. Hierarchical forms of governance, on the other hand, bring parties to an exchange under the direct control of a third party (typically called 'the boss'). This authoritative third party then attempts to keep all parties to an exchange informed of their rights and responsibilities. Moreover, this third party has the right to directly resolve any conflicts that might emerge in an exchange. Williamson calls the exercise of this right 'managerial fiat'.

Behavioral Assumptions

TCT rests on two essential assumptions about economic actors (be they individuals or firms) engaged in transactions: bounded rationality and opportunism. Bounded rationality means that those who engage in economic transactions are 'intendedly rational, but only limitedly so' (Simon 1947: xxiv). Within economics, this assumption is an important departure from the traditional omniscient hyperrationality of *homo economicus* (Simon 1947; Hesterly and Zenger

1993). Without cognitive limits, all exchange could be conducted through planning (Williamson 1985). People could write contracts of unlimited complexity that would specify all possible contingencies in an economic exchange (Williamson 1975). However, given bounded rationality, complex contracting breaks down in the face of uncertainty. Economic actors simply cannot foresee all possible outcomes in an exchange relationship or formulate contractual or other responses to those (unforeseeable) eventualities.

Opportunism is also a departure from the behavioral assumptions used in mainstream economics.[1] While traditional economics assumes simply that economic actors behave out of self-interest, TCT assumes the possibility of self-interest seeking with guile (Williamson 1975: 26). For Williamson (1985: 47), opportunism includes lying, stealing, and cheating, but it more generally 'refers to the incomplete or distorted disclosure of information, especially to calculated efforts to mislead, distort, disguise, obfuscate, or otherwise confuse' partners in an exchange. TCT does not assume that all economic actors are always opportunistic. Rather, all it assumes is that some of these actors may behave opportunistically and that it is costly to distinguish those who are prone to opportunism from those who are not. The threat of opportunism is important because in a world without opportunism, all economic exchange could be done on the basis of promise. Parties in such a transaction would simply pledge at the outset to perform their part of an exchange fairly (1985: 31). Given, however, that some are prone to opportunism, people and firms must design safeguards so they will not be victimized by others.

The Choice of Governance

The governance decision, as characterized in TCT, is straightforward. Economic actors will choose that form of governance (market or hierarchy) that reduces any potential exchange problems created by bounded rationality, on the one hand, and by the threat of opportunism, on the other, at the lowest cost. The governance of economic transactions is costly. However, as suggested by Adam Smith and many others, markets have lower fixed costs compared to hierarchical forms of governance. If a market form of governance enables parties to an exchange to reduce potential exchange problems created by bounded rationality and the tendency towards opportunism, then a market form of governance will be preferred over a hierarchical form of governance. However, if market governance does not solve these exchange problems,

then more costly forms of hierarchical governance may have to be employed.

Put differently, if all economic actors had to worry about was minimizing the cost of governing their economic exchanges, then they would always choose market forms of governance. Market governance is the least costly way of managing economic exchanges ever devised by human beings. Alternatively, if all economic actors had to worry about was minimizing the effects of bounded rationality and opportunism on their exchanges, then they would always choose hierarchical forms of governance. In hierarchical governance, there is always a third party whose sole responsibility is to manage an exchange in ways that minimize problems created by bounded rationality and opportunism. Of course, economic actors need to be concerned both about the problems created by bounded rationality and opportunism *and* about the cost of governing economic exchanges.

When Will Bounded Rationality and Opportunism Create Exchange Problems?

Given this characterization of the governance decisions facing economic actors, it is important to understand the attributes of transactions that will make bounded rationality and opportunism problematic. While this aspect of TCT has evolved some over the years, two attributes of transactions are now widely seen as creating the most problems for economic actors in transactions: uncertainty and transaction specific investment.

Without uncertainty, bounded rationality is irrelevant. If parties to a transaction could anticipate precisely how this transaction will evolve over time, and how rights and responsibilities in a transaction will evolve, then managing that transaction over time is very simple. All that has to be done is for parties to an exchange to write a contract that specifies all current and future states in an exchange, and the rights and responsibilities of all actors in those future states. Of course, under conditions of uncertainty, this is not possible. In general, the greater the level of uncertainty in a transaction, the more difficult it will be to use contracts and other forms of market governance to manage that transaction, and the more likely that hierarchical forms of governance will be adopted. Under hierarchical governance, a third party can decide how unanticipated problems in a transaction can be resolved. Moreover, parties in a transaction need not anticipate what these problems might be (they cannot do so), nor do they need to anticipate what the third party will do in response to these problems (they cannot do so). Rather, all they need to do is agree that, if such problems arise in the future, a third party will mediate and solve those problems.

As important as uncertainty in a transaction is for exchange partners to choose hierarchical forms of governance, the level of transaction specific investment in a transaction is generally seen as being even more important. It is often the case that parties in a transaction will need to make investments in that transaction in order to facilitate its completion. These investments can take many forms. For example, it may be the case that parties to a transaction will need to modify some of their physical technology to expedite the exchange (e.g. a firm may have to change the height of its loading docks to accommodate another firm's trucks). In many transactions, parties may need to modify some of their operating policies and procedures to expedite the exchange (e.g. a firm may have to simplify its order entry procedures to ensure more timely delivery of critical supplies). In other transactions, individuals involved may learn the special language, the informal working style, and the business practices of transaction partners, all to facilitate a transaction.

All these investments have value in the particular transaction where they were originally made. Some of these investments may have value in other transactions as well. For example, a sales person may need to learn a new word processing language in order to efficiently interact with a group of new customers who already use this language in their work. However, this word processing language may also be used by numerous other potential customers. Thus, the investment in this new language is valuable in the transaction between this sales person and her new set of customers, but it may also be valuable in possible transactions between this sales person and another set of potential customers.

On the other hand, certain investments in a transaction are only valuable in that particular transaction and have little or no value in any other transaction. Such investments are trans-action specific. Formally, transaction specific investments are investments that are much more valuable in a particular transaction compared to any other transaction. The greater the difference in value between this investment's first best use (in the current transaction) and the second best use (in some other transaction), the more specific the investment.

The existence of transaction specific investments increases the threat of opportunism. For example, suppose that a firm A is a supplier to firm B. Also, suppose that firm A has totally revised its manufacturing, sales, and distribution processes to fit firm B's needs, that firm B's needs are completely unique, and that firm A has not had to make any special investments in firm B. Also, suppose firm A has several alternative suppliers, besides firm B. In this situation, firm A has made significant transaction specific investments in its relationship with firm B. It may be the case that firm B decides to exploit firm A by, say, insisting on a lower price for firm A's supplies than what had been agreed to in the original supply contract. What can firm A do? If firm A refuses to give in to firm B's demand, it loses the economic value of its investment in A. As long as the price reductions demanded by firm B are not as costly as entirely abandoning its investment in firm B, firm A will acquiesce to firm B's demands. The specific investment made by firm A creates an opportunity for firm B to behave opportunistically.

The greater the level of transaction specific investment in an exchange, the greater the threat of opportunism. The greater the threat of opportunism, the less likely that market govern-ance will effectively reduce this threat and the more likely that hierarchical forms of govern-ance will be chosen – despite their additional costs. In the simple example discussed above, hierarchical governance would imply that firm A and firm B would be brought together into a single corporation and that a corporate manager ('the boss') would mediate the relationship between what would then be division A and division B. With this mediator in place, division A could make the transaction specific invest-ments it needs to facilitate its supply relationship with division B, relying on the mediator to make sure that division B did not take unfair advantage of these specific investments.

In short, Williamson's answer to the question 'why do organizations exist?' is that hierarchy arises to resolve the problems of market governance with transaction specific investments under conditions of uncertainty. Once under common ownership, the two parties in the exchange have less incentive to seek advantage over each other. Disputes are less likely to occur because the hierarchy is able to establish joint goals which lead to convergent expectations between those in a transaction. Additionally, hierarchy facilitates the development of codes and language that are unique to a firm which allow for more accurate and efficient commu-nication (Arrow 1974; Williamson 1975).

While hierarchy provides a resolution to the problem of transaction specific investments under uncertainty, there are, however, limits to using hierarchy. Firms are prone to important incentive and bureaucratic disabilities that limit their size. The high-powered incentives of the market are not easily duplicated within firms, particularly large ones.

Applications of Transaction Cost Theory

Vertical Integration

The most researched application of TCT, vertical integration, is the most direct examination of the question 'why do organizations exist?' (see Joskow 1988; Mahoney 1992 for reviews). TCT studies approach vertical integration differently than much of the previous work in economics (see Blair and Kaserman 1983 for review). Instead of viewing vertical integration as an aggregate measure of value added for an entire firm, TCT scholars typically use the transaction as their level of analysis. This research, which examines what in mundane terms is labeled make or buy decisions, finds consistent support for the proposition that transaction specific investment increases the likelihood that a transaction will be internalized. This finding is repeated whether transaction specific investment is operationalized as capital intensity (MacDonald 1985; MacMillan et al. 1986; Caves and Bradburd 1988), human asset specificity or firm specific skills (Armour and Teece 1980; Anderson and Schmittlein 1984; Anderson 1985; John and Weitz 1988; Masten et al. 1991), site specificity (Stuckey 1983; Joskow 1985), or small numbers bargaining (Levy 1985; MacDonald 1985; Caves and Bradburd 1988). Uncertainty has a less consistent effect on the decision to integrate (Walker and Weber 1984; 1987).

The Multidivisional Form

Another important extension of TCT to internal organization focuses on the multidivisional (M-form) firm, which Williamson (1985: 279) regards as the 'most significant organizational innovation of the twentieth century'. Chandler's (1962) historical study of strategy and structure in large American firms documented the rise of the M-form. Superimposing transaction costs logic over Chandler's findings, Williamson sees bounded rationality and opportunism at the root of the M-form's broad diffusion among US firms. He argues that as functionally organized firms (U-forms) expand in size and diversity, it becomes increasingly difficult for the top managers to deal with the myriad of operating problems faced by the company. Moreover, combining greater diversity with the interdependence between functional units makes it difficult to assign responsibility for successes and failures for a product or line of business. Thus, the complexity of the enterprise overwhelms the information processing capacity – or, in TCT terms, the bounded rationality – of top managers. Additionally, increased complexity makes it more difficult to tie the goals of functional units to the goals of the firm as a whole. This inability to operationalize functional goals causes managers to pursue functional subgoals in sales, manufacturing, etc. often at the expense of firm performance – or in TCT terms, the problem of opportunism.

The M-form resolves these difficulties by organizing firms into either product or geographic divisions where operational decisions and accountability for performance are placed on a division manager. A typical M-form structure is presented in Figure 1. Ideally, this structure separates strategic and operational decisions. Strategic decisions are limited to senior managers in the corporate office. Operational decisions are delegated to senior managers within operating divisions. By limiting their responsibility to strategic decision-making, the M-form reduces the bounded rationality problem faced by top managers in the corporate office. Dividing the firm into quasi-autonomous divisions facilitates clearer performance goals at lower levels of the organization. Responsibility for the performance of a business line is fixed upon a single divisional manager.

Ultimately, the M-form structure also allows the firm to function as a miniature capital market where the corporate office monitors division performance, assigns cash flows to their highest yield uses, and engages in diversification, acquisition, and divestiture activities (Williamson 1970; 1975; 1985). From the TCT perspective, the M-form possesses important advantages over the external capital market: (1) it has access to more accurate information about divisions; (2) it can manipulate incentives and replace poorly performing managers more easily; and (3) it can exercise control over the strategies pursued by divisions.

Empirical evidence tends to support Williamson's contention that the M-form outperforms the functional structure in large, diversified firms (see Hoskisson et al. 1993 for review). In their seminal study of M-form adoption in the oil industry, Armour and Teece (1978) found that early adopters enjoyed performance advantages over the rest of the industry. As expected, though, these performance advantages disappeared as other firms adopted the M-form structure. Several other studies offer at least some support for the M-form hypothesis (Harris 1983; Grinyer et al. 1980; Hill 1985; Hoskisson and Galbraith 1985; Hoskisson et al. 1991; Ollinger 1993; Steer and Cable 1978; Teece 1981; Thompson 1981). A few studies of non-US firms found no evidence that firms with an M-form structure enjoyed superior performance (Cable and Dirrheimer 1983; Cable and Yasuki 1985; Hill 1988; Holl 1983). Reliance upon archival data sources suggests, however, that many of these studies may not have accurately classified

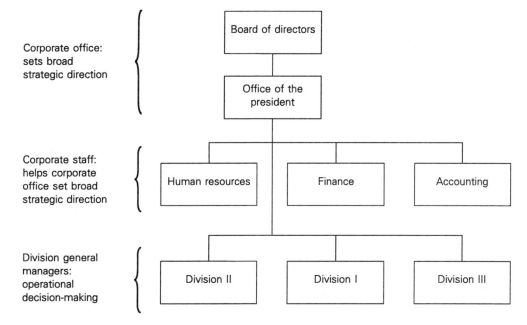

Figure 1   *Typical multidivisional (M-form) structure*

M-form structures (Hill 1988). Thus, some debate remains as to what can be learned from these empirical tests (Hoskisson et al. 1993).

Criticisms of the M-form tend to focus on its effectiveness as an internal capital market. The emergence of more powerful, concentrated, institutional investors in recent years has greatly reduced the advantages enjoyed by top managers over external investors. Arguably, the informational asymmetries between managers and outside investors has been reduced. Anecdotal accounts also suggest that external investors are much more effective at displacing top executives and even influencing strategy than in the past. Assuming these changes are true, the governance advantages of the M-form over the external capital market have eroded. Thus, according to this reasoning, the M-form hypothesis may have been true when it was formulated, but it is likely outdated (Bettis 1991: 315–16; Bartlett and Ghoshal 1993). This criticism, however, remains to be tested (Hoskisson et al. 1993: 275).

Other criticisms of the M-form are based on the notion that it does not adequately align the interests of top managers with those of shareholders. In short, it assumes away the agency problem (Hoskisson and Turk 1990 and the discussion below). While the M-form assumes strong incentives on the part of divisional managers to maximize performance, there is no explicit mechanism that motivates top managers to do the same for the firm. Thus, top managers

are able to pursue inefficient diversification. The M-form, with its decomposed structure of quasi-firms, only facilitates this excessive diversification. Incentive problems at the divisional level are not completely eliminated either. With the M-form's emphasis on financial evaluation, division managers may choose to focus on risk averse, short-term profit maximization while sacrificing activities such as R&D investment that are critical to long-term success. Research supporting these criticisms is somewhat equivocal, however, since it typically fails to disentangle the effects of strategy (diversification) from structure (the M-form).

Markets, Bureaucracies, and Clans

Ouchi (1979; 1980) extended the transactions cost framework to explain alternative ways of coordinating activities within firms. He argued that firms rely on three basic forms of control: markets, bureaucracies, and clans. Markets coordinate through prices, bureaucracies coordinate through authority and rules, and clans combine authority with shared values and beliefs to effect cooperation. As with Williamson's general formulation of TCT, the efficiency of these mechanisms varies depending on the conditions of the exchange. In these conditions of exchange, however, Ouchi departs from Williamson by emphasizing goal incongruence and performance ambiguity as the crucial dimensions of exchanges. Transaction costs in

Ouchi's (1980: 130) framework arise from a demand for equity and include 'any activity which is engaged in to satisfy each party to an exchange that the value given and received is in accord with his or her expectations'.

For Ouchi (1980), markets are efficient when goal incongruence is high and performance ambiguity is low. Prices adequately convey the information necessary to coordinate activity and the parties need not share congruent goals. As performance becomes more ambiguous and the need for congruent goals increases, firms will find bureaucratic governance more efficient than market exchange. Bureaucracy uses authority and rules which allow the firm to resolve performance ambiguity problems through monitoring employees and constrains goal incongruence through rules and other operating procedures (Ouchi 1979). When performance ambiguity reaches very high levels, then neither the measurement of market mechanisms nor bureaucratic monitoring can insure that employees' efforts will be directed towards the organization's goals. Under these circumstances, clan governance is most efficient. Clan governance requires intensive people processing (Ouchi 1979) or socialization (Ouchi 1980) and long-term associations within the firm to serve as an effective means of control. These activities are more costly than market and bureaucratic control, however. Thus, an investment in clan control is not warranted when performance ambiguity is low or moderate. Ouchi's theory of markets, bureaucracies and particularly clans was influential in stimulating interest in the topic of organizational culture.

The Multinational Enterprise

TCT perhaps found its earliest and most complete acceptance among international business and economics scholars. The internalization school (Buckley and Casson 1976; Rugman 1981; Hennart 1982) applied TCT to understanding where multinational enterprises (MNEs) would internalize transactions within the firm and where they would rely upon market exchange. The explanation for MNEs centered around market imperfections. Markets for different assets, particularly some types of knowledge (Buckley and Casson 1976: 39), are subject to market imperfections. The main conclusion of this early work was that markets will tend to be more efficient when there are a large number of buyers and sellers. Transactions characterized by high uncertainty and complex, heterogeneous products between a small number of buyers and traders, on the other hand, favor internalization (Buckley and Casson 1976: 167–8).

Teece (1986) extended Casson and Buckley's reasoning on the role of knowledge in determining firm boundaries. He argued that when knowledge is difficult to trade – either because doing so would give away that knowledge or because the necessary infrastructure of capabilities, communication codes, or culture is absent – firms will internalize those transactions. Empirical evidence (see Teece 1986 for review) supports the transaction cost theory of the MNE. Though fairly distinct literatures on vertical integration and MNEs have emerged, there is little in the TCT theory of the MNE that is distinctly international. The MNE from a TCT perspective is largely a special case of the vertical integration problem. In essence, this literature is a simple restatement of the question 'why do organizations exist?' to become 'why do MNEs exist?'

Hybrid Forms of Organization

Early TCT focused on the polar opposites of markets and hierarchies for organizing economic activity. Alternatives to markets other than hierarchies were acknowledged, but how these intermediate forms are viewed has shifted over time. Initially, Williamson (1975) saw them as unstable, then later acknowledged that they might occur as often as markets and hierarchies (Williamson 1985). TCT labels these intermediate forms hybrids. Hybrids include governance structures that are neither hierarchy nor market. Research on hybrids has focused on long-term contracting (Joskow 1985), joint ventures (Hennart 1991), and franchises (Brickley and Dark 1987; Brickley et al. 1991; Fladmoe-Lindquist and Jacque 1995). More recently, network organizations – production among a set of firms with continuing ties – have received much attention (Thorelli 1986; Powell 1987). Scholars have observed such networks in areas as diverse as the US film industry (Baker and Faulkner 1991), publishing (Powell 1987), construction (Eccles 1981), Italian textiles (Mariotti and Cairnarca 1986), the Japanese auto industry (Fruin 1992; Nishiguchi 1994) and Silicon Valley (Saxenian 1994).

The existence of hybrids extends Coase's original question: 'Why do hybrids exist?' The most general answer is that hybrids have stronger incentives and adaptive capabilities than hierarchies while offering more administrative control than markets (Williamson 1991a: 281). Thus, for transactions that require a mix of incentives, adaptation, and control, hybrids are well-suited (Williamson 1991a).

Debate remains, however, about whether hybrid governance structures are discrete mechanisms or consist of a continuum of forms ranging from pure market to pure hierarchy (Bradach and Eccles 1989). On the one hand,

Williamson (1991c: 165, 176) argues that the 'impossibility of selective intervention' (i.e. the problem of infusing market attributes into hierarchies and hierarchical features into markets) precludes a continuum of governance forms. According to this logic, differences in contract law also drive governance towards discrete forms (Masten 1988; Williamson 1991c). Conversely, others view hybrid governance structures as a continuum of plural forms that combine the features of hierarchy and market (Bradach and Eccles 1989; Hennart 1993).

Other Applications of Transaction Cost Theory

TCT has been used to address a variety of other topics including: (1) the internal organization of Congress (Weingast and Marshall 1988), (2) the organization of public administration (Moe 1991), (3) the role of trust in economic exchanges (Williamson 1993a), (4) the functions of corporate governance (Williamson 1985), and (5) how firms are financed (Williamson 1991b). It seems likely that TCT will continue to be applied to a wide range of organizational phenomena.

Criticisms of Transaction Cost Theory

Transaction cost theory has attracted its share of critics (see, for example, Perrow 1986; Putterman 1984; Robins 1987; Demsetz 1988). Of the many criticisms directed at TCT, three are particularly central: (1) TCT focuses on cost minimization; (2) it understates the cost of organizing; (3) it neglects the role of social relationships in economic transactions.

TCT focuses on cost minimization as the organizational imperative. Or, as Williamson (1991b: 76) argues, 'economizing is more fundamental than strategizing – or, put differently, *economy is the best strategy*.' Resource-based theory (discussed below), particularly, takes exception to this emphasis. As we shall see, resource-based logic suggests that creating and exploiting transaction specific investments under conditions of uncertainty is essential if firms are to gain long-term success (Conner 1991; Kogut and Zander 1992). Avoiding opportunism and minimizing governance costs are a secondary consideration. Minimizing transaction costs is of relatively little benefit if a firm has no transaction specific assets (including knowledge) that are highly valued by the market.

A second criticism of TCT is that it tends to understate the costs of organizing transactions within the firm (Jones and Hill 1988). The use of authority is assumed to resolve internal disputes

more efficiently than the market. Clearly, this is not always the case. Lengthy and costly haggling may often be more severe within a firm than between firms, as Eccles's (1985) study of transfer pricing shows. Indeed, internal organization is often susceptible to costly bargaining and influence behavior (Dow 1985; Milgrom and Roberts 1988). Even where authority may efficiently resolve some disputes, it also may be abused opportunistically (Dow 1987).

Another criticism of TCT is that it understates the role of social and cultural forces in economic activity (Granovetter 1985). While TCT seeks to adopt realistic assumptions of human nature, it does take a decidedly calculative view (Williamson 1993a) of humans that discounts the impact of social relationships and culture. Granovetter pointed out that contrary to this atomistic view of economic exchange, transactions are embedded within networks of social relationships. These transactions are influenced by expectations that are formed by the history of the relationship. Abstract transaction dimensions such as asset specificity and uncertainty do not alone determine the governance arrangements that we observe. Close friends, for example, may trade co-specialized assets without hierarchy, a formal contract, or other tangible credible commitments because they trust one another. Though certainly underappreciated in earlier work, TCT scholars are focusing more attention to understanding social forces such as trust on economic exchange (Ring and Van de Ven 1992; Williamson 1993a).

Despite these criticisms, TCT's answer to the fundamental question of why firms exist has been undeniably influential. Historically, economic theory viewed the organization as irrelevant and unworthy of economic science (Stiglitz 1991: 15) while organization theory took the existence of organization for granted. TCT has provided an approach that provoked economists to look inside the black box of the firm at the same time that it opened up a new approach for organization theorists.

DO THOSE ASSOCIATED WITH THE FIRM AGREE ABOUT HOW IT SHOULD BE MANAGED?

Given that traditional neo-classical economics did not look inside the firm, it is not surprising that it did not address the possibility of intra-firm conflict over the way a firm should be managed. Neo-classical economics assumed a monolithic goal for the firm: profit maximization. Firms that behaved contrary to this assumption were thought to have little chance of survival. Thus, there was little need to look inside the firm, since once one could explain why a firm was created, what happened inside a firm's boundaries did not really aid in scientific prediction (Stiglitz 1991). In neglecting conflict within organizations, economics ran parallel to early organization theory, which also long neglected the topic (Mintzberg 1983; Perrow 1986).

Early Departures from the Neo-Classical Firm

The neglect of intra-firm conflict ended, to some extent, with the research of a multidisciplinary group of scholars at Carnegie-Mellon University (March and Simon 1958; Cyert and March 1963; Simon 1964). Their work was an important departure for both economics and organization theory in looking more explicitly at conflicts over goals and means within organizations. Cyert and March's (1963) book *A Behavioral Theory of the Firm* addressed most directly the problems with the neo-classical theory of the firm. They rejected basic components of the neo-classical firm such as profit maximization and perfect information. In place of a single actor focused exclusively on maximizing profits (in many ways, analogous to Alchian and Demsetz's monitors), Cyert and March saw goals within the firm emerging and changing over time as coalitions formed and shifted among organizational members. Ironically, this and related work (e.g. March and Simon 1958; Simon 1964), was much more influential in organization theory than in economics. This was ironic, since many of those associated with the Carnegie-Mellon research group were economists. A few economists focused on potentially conflicting goals within the firm and argued that managers may pursue objectives other than profit maximization (e.g. they may pursue growth (Marris 1964): they may pursue discretion and perquisites (Williamson 1964)). Nevertheless, the traditional view of the firm remained the mainstream perspective.

Transactions cost theory is of surprisingly little help in analyzing conflicting goals of those associated with a firm. TCT explains why organizations exist; it fails to address how or if those affiliated with the firm agree on its goals. The implicit assumption in TCT is that agreement on how the firm should be managed is non-problematic. However, just because economic exchange partners find it in their mutual self-interest to form an organization does not mean that differences in interests, tastes, and preferences cease. Indeed, Williamson seems to argue that the problems of opportunism and bounded rationality that so plague transactions across markets almost magically disappear when transactions are internalized into an organization (Grossman and Hart 1986). This assertion seems unrealistic, at best, and is particularly ironic given Williamson's (1964) early work that examined managers' propensity to pursue their own goals at the expense of corporate profits. This lack of appreciation for the variety and complexity within organizations highlights the acknowledged incompleteness of TCT (Williamson 1985; 392, 402).

Agency Theory

A literature in organization economics, agency theory, seeks to understand the causes and consequences for organizations of these goal disagreements. It draws heavily from the property rights literature (Alchian and Demsetz 1972) and to a lesser extent from transaction cost. Like TCT, agency theory assumes that humans are boundedly rational, self-interested and prone to opportunism (Eisenhardt 1989). The theories are also similar in their emphasis on information asymmetry problems in contracting and on efficiency as the engine that drives the governance of economic transactions (Barney and Ouchi 1986; Eisenhardt 1989). Agency theory, however, differs from TCT in its emphasis on the risk attitudes of principals and agents (Eisenhardt 1989: 64).

As it originally developed, agency theory research focused on the relationship between managers and stockholders (Jensen and Meckling 1976). In this form, the theory has been used to analyze corporate governance, including issues such as the role of boards of directors and the role of top management compensation. More recently, agency theory has been applied to relationships between many stakeholders in a firm such as those between different managers within the same firm, between employees and customers (Grinblatt and Titman 1987), and between employees and different groups of stockholders and debt holders (Copeland and Weston 1983). All these conflicts have important effects on a variety of attributes of organizations, including corporate governance, compensation, and organizational structure.

Agency relationships occur whenever one partner in a transaction (the principal) delegates authority to another (the agent) and the welfare of the principal is affected by the choices of the agent (Arrow 1985). An obvious example is the relationship between outside investors in a firm and its managers. The investors delegate management authority to managers who may or may not have any equity ownership in the firm. The delegation of decision-making authority from principal to agent is problematic in that: (1) the interests of principal and agent will typically diverge; (2) the principal cannot perfectly and costlessly monitor the actions of the agent; and (3) the principal cannot perfectly and costlessly monitor and acquire the information available to or possessed by the agent. Taken together, these conditions constitute the agency problem – the possibility of opportunistic behavior on the agent's part that works against the welfare of the principal. Jensen and Meckling view the agency problem as central to both economics in general and to organization theory specifically:

> It is worthwhile to point out the generality of the agency problem. The problem of inducing an 'agent' to behave as if he were maximizing the 'principal's' welfare is quite general. It exists in all organizations and in all cooperative efforts – at every level of management in firms. . . . The development of theories to explain the form which agency costs take in each of these situations (where the contractual relations differ significantly), and how and why they are born will lead to a rich theory of organizations which is now lacking in economics and the social sciences generally. (1976: 309)

To protect the principal's interests, attempts must be made to reduce the possibility that agents will misbehave. In this attempt, costs are incurred. These costs are called agency costs. Total agency costs are the monitoring expenditures by principals, the bonding expenditures by agents, and the residual loss of the principal. The residual loss acknowledges that in many situations it will simply be too costly for principals to completely monitor agents and too costly for agents to completely assure principals that interests do not diverge (Jensen and Meckling 1976).

Assuming that agency costs exist, it is clear that principals have a strong incentive to minimize these costs (i.e. to minimize the sum of monitoring, bonding, and residual agency costs). However, agents also have an incentive to minimize these costs. Where significant savings in agency costs are possible, these benefits may be shared between agents and principals. Thus, the principal and agent have common interests in defining a monitoring and incentive structure that produces outcomes as close as possible to what would be the case if information exchange was costless (Pratt and Zeckhauser 1985).

Arrow (1985) notes two essential sources of agency problems: moral hazard, which he equates to hidden actions, and adverse selection, which he equates to hidden information. Moral hazard involves situations in which much of the agent's actions are either hidden from the principal or are costly to observe. Thus, it is either impossible or costly for the principal to fully monitor the agent's actions. Stockholders or even directors, for example, might find it prohibitively costly to fully monitor the behavior of their top management team. Indeed, the employment relation in general is one in which effort and ability are difficult to observe.

Agency problems may also involve adverse selection. In adverse selection, the agent possesses information that is, for the principal, unobservable or costly to obtain. Consequently, principals cannot fully ascertain whether or not their interests are best served by agents' decisions. For example, a lower-level manager may submit proposals to the CEO (in this instance, the principal) even though, based on information possessed by the manager and not the CEO, these proposals are unlikely to generate economic value. By doing so, the lower-level manager may be able to gain some private benefits (e.g. broader experience that may be useful in other firms). Obviously, the CEO is at an informational disadvantage. This disadvantage is only exacerbated as the number of agents with similar incentives and advantages multiplies.

At the most general level, principals and agents resolve agency problems through monitoring and bonding. Monitoring involves observing the behavior and/or the performance of agents. Bonding refers to arrangements that penalize agents for acting in ways that violate the interests of principals or reward them for achieving principals' goals. The contracts between agents and principals specify the monitoring and bonding arrangements. Indeed, contracts are central in agency theory. Jensen and Meckling (1976: 310) argue that most 'organizations are simply legal fictions which serve as a nexus for a set of contracting relationships among individuals'. Within this nexus, however, firms adopt rules about monitoring and bonding.

Given this general description of agency problems and their costly solutions, three important questions come to mind. First, why do principals delegate authority to agents, when they know that such delegation of authority will inevitably lead to agency problems? Second, what specific monitoring mechanisms can principals put in place to minimize these agency problems? Finally, what specific bonding mechanisms can agents use to reassure principals? Each of these questions is discussed in subsequent sections.

Delegating Authority

Given agency costs, principals will not delegate authority to agents unless they find compelling reasons to do so. Sometimes, there are no compelling reasons, and single economic actors engage in a full range of economic activities. For example, in proprietorships, small partnerships, and closed corporations that operate on a small scale, it may be possible for a single individual to engage in the full range of economic activities, from conceiving of a business opportunity to obtaining funding for that opportunity to making and implementing all business decisions in exploiting that opportunity. Moreover, given the small size and relative simplicity of these business operations, a single individual may be quite effective in accomplishing these numerous tasks. In such settings, there will be no delegation of authority to agents and thus no agency costs.

However, the situation facing larger, more complex business enterprises is not so simple. In these settings, a single individual may be unable to engage in all these business activities in a timely and effective way. This inability does not reflect, necessarily, a lack of will to accomplish all these tasks. Rather, individual bounded rationality and real constraints on time and energy may make it impossible to conduct business without significant delegation of authority. Such delegation always implies agency costs.

Fama and Jensen (1983) observe that the process of making most business decisions can be divided into two large categories: (1) decision management (i.e. how a decision possibility is originally initiated, and how that decision is implemented) and (2) decision control (i.e. how a decision is ratified and how performance relative to a decision is monitored). As suggested above, it may not be necessary to assign decision management and decision control responsibilities to different agents in relatively less complex business settings. However, in more complex settings, Fama and Jensen (1983a) argue that delegating decision management to one group and decision control to a second group may, on average, lead to higher-quality decisions. The management group's task is simplified, and they are able to focus on questions concerning the initiation and implementation of decisions. The control group's task is also simplified, and they are able to focus on questions concerning the ratification and monitoring of decisions. Put differently, in settings where the decision-making situation is likely to overwhelm the cognitive capacity of a single individual, assigning different groups different parts of the decision-making process is likely to improve the quality of decisions. Of course, this delegation also implies the existence of agency costs.

Monitoring

Given the existence of agency costs, principals will find it in their self-interest to try to monitor agents (Eisenhardt 1985). One way that principals can try to monitor agents is by collecting relatively complete information about an agent's decisions and actions – an agent's behavior. From this behavioral information, principals can then form judgments about the underlying goals and objectives of agents. In particular, principals can attempt to judge how similar their agents' goals and objectives are to their own goals and objectives.

Of course, monitoring agent behavior will rarely generate perfect information about an agent's decisions and actions, let alone about an agent's goals and objectives. This is especially unlikely if agents are engaging in relatively complex, highly unstructured tasks. For example, suppose that it was possible for a principal to directly observe the behavior of a group of research scientists she hired to conduct research for new products. It may well be the case that this principal would observe her scientists spending at least part of their day sitting in comfortable chairs, staring out a window. What can the principal conclude from this behavior – that the scientists are shirking? Perhaps. On the other hand, the scientists may also be thinking about some fundamental research problem, the solution to which will generate a string of very valuable products. Given this behavior, by itself, it is not possible to deduce the scientists' goals and objectives.

This limitation of behavioral monitoring is not limited to just scientists. Managerial behavior at the top levels of an organization, for example, is notoriously difficult to monitor and even more difficult to interpret. This does not mean that behavioral monitoring does not, or should not, take place at these high levels in an organization. Institutional investors monitor critical strategic decisions made by senior managers; boards of directors monitor major policy changes implemented by senior management teams; and corporate management teams monitor the decisions and strategic plans of division general managers. However, these efforts at monitoring the behavior of agents can only imperfectly reduce agency costs.

As an alternative (or supplement) to monitoring agent behavior, principals can also monitor the consequences of (only partially observed) agent behavior. Thus, instead of monitoring actions and decisions, principals may elect to monitor the performance implications of those actions and decisions. In general, monitoring performance (or output) is more efficient when tasks are not highly programmable (Eisenhardt 1985; Mahoney 1992). Output measurement, however, is not without problems. It becomes more problematic where team production is involved (Alchian and Demsetz 1972). Interdependence between agents creates ambiguity about how much each agent contributed to the final output. Thus, measuring the output of different agents is imprecise at best.

A large segment of the agency theory literature examines the abilities of owners (stockholders) to monitor shareholders (Hill and Snell 1989). Since large shareholders have a greater incentive and more resources to monitor management behavior and performance, the information asymmetries between investors and firms' managers are reduced. Thus, with the increasing presence of institutional shareholders and large shareholders, we should see less evidence of certain types of agency problems. Firms with more concentrated ownership are less likely to engage in wealth-destroying activities such as inefficient diversification (Hill and Snell 1989) but are more likely to undertake wealth-enhancing actions such as restructuring (Bethel and Liebeskind 1993).

Another mechanism that agency theory prescribes for monitoring managerial behavior and performance is the use of independent directors on corporate boards. The independent board members provide objectivity as the board ratifies and monitors the decisions of management.

A number of studies have examined the occurrence of firm policies that are thought to have negative consequences for the shareholders of a firm, including such anti-takeover amendments as greenmail and poison pills. These studies have yielded mixed support of agency theory (Kosnik 1987; Weisbach 1988; Mallette and Fowler 1992). However, recent studies suggest that the adoption of these policies may, in fact, not always signal agency problems in a firm (Mahoney and Mahoney 1993; Brickley et al. 1994). Instead, this more recent work suggests that these policies, while they can often entrench managers to the detriment of shareholders, may also increase the bargaining power of the target firm in takeover contests. The existence of outside directors has been shown to be the primary determinant of whether these policies are used to hurt or help a firm's shareholders.

Bonding and Incentives

The existence of agency costs suggests that principals have an incentive to monitor agents. However, agents also have an incentive to assure principals that they are behaving in ways consistent with the principals' interests. Recall that, in many situations, principals and agents both absorb some agency costs associated with the delegation of authority. In general, principals can use bonding mechanisms to reassure principals. Frequently, bonding mechanisms take the form of incentives that agents create for themselves – incentives that make it in their

self-interest to behave in ways consistent with the interests of principals.

Perhaps the most common form of incentive bonding focuses on the compensation package of agents. If agent compensation depends, to a significant extent, upon behaving and performing in ways consistent with a principal's interests, then – assuming that agents value financial rewards – they will behave in ways consistent with those interests. Put differently, the willingness of an agent to accept this form of compensation can be understood as a bond, a bond that reassures principals that their interests will be considered when decisions are made.

A large part of the agency theory literature examines the incentives firms use to induce agents to work in the best interests of principals. Ideally, principals would prefer an incentive scheme that fully penalizes agents for shirking and opportunism. This, however, is extremely difficult to achieve without exposing agents to risks they will find unacceptably high. Often these risks are tied to conditions beyond the agents' control. On the other hand, policies that allow agents to be compensated in ways that are independent of the principals' interests insure that an agent's earnings will not fluctuate with conditions outside of the agent's control, but provide weak inducements against opportunism. Thus, though principals prefer schemes that emphasize incentives, they must design compensation systems in ways that sometimes compromise between pure incentives and fixed compensation plans (Winship and Rosen 1988).

Research in agency theory has examined a variety of compensation plans, including bonuses and stock options for executives (Murphy 1986), salary versus commissions (Eisenhardt 1985; 1988), the effect of incentive pay on turnover (Zenger 1992), the impact of firm size on incentive intensity (Zenger 1994), choices between piece rates and time rates (Lazear 1986), and promotion contests (McLaughlin 1988). Other studies examine managerial ownership in the firm. This research (see Eisenhardt 1989, for review) indicates managers with a significant ownership interest in their firm are less likely to engage in conglomerate diversification (Amihud and Lev 1981; Argawal and Mandelker 1987), resist takeover bids (Walking and Long 1984), and use golden parachutes to the benefit of shareholders (Singh and Harianto 1989).

Rewards other than financial compensation also serve to link the welfare of principals and agents. Managers may receive promotions or other forms of recognition which may enhance their reputations and the probability of increased future income. Even if firms do not explicitly tie performance to rewards, market forces may work to reduce agency problems (Fama 1980). The managerial labor market, for instance, views the previous associations of managers with success and failure as information about their talents (Fama 1980: 292). Managers in more successful firms may not receive any immediate gain in wages, but the success of their firm may increase their value in the managerial labor market. In contrast, the managers of failing firms may not see a reduction in wages, but will be disciplined as the managerial labor market attaches less value to their services.

The Role of Market Discipline

Market discipline plays an important role in determining the arrangements and outcomes predicted by agency theory. Such a focus presupposes that markets, particularly capital markets, are efficient. Indeed, agency theory adopts at least a semi-strong form assumption of capital market efficiency (Fama 1970). Semi-strong capital market efficiency maintains that the value of a firm's assets mirrors completely and immediately all public information concerning the value of those assets (Barney and Ouchi 1986). This differs from the strong-form assumption which asserts that asset prices reflect all information regardless of whether it is public or private. It also varies from weak-form capital market efficiency which avers that asset prices reflect only the historically available information about the firm's assets.

Perhaps the most obvious example of market discipline as it is used in agency theory is the market for corporate control. Generally, this market is assumed to be semi-strong efficient, i.e. the value of a firm in the market for corporate control reflects all publicly available information about the value of that firm. If the agents (managers) of a firm take actions that are viewed by the market as adversely affecting the value of the firm's assets, then the price of these assets (i.e. the stock price) will likely drop. Managers in other firms, believing that they can more profitably manage the assets of the under-performing firm, may engage in a contest for control of the firm and a takeover battle may ensue. Barring outside interference, the troubled firm's management will eventually lose control of the firm, and old high agency cost managers will be replaced by new low agency cost managers.

In other instances, market discipline may take more subtle forms. Managerial labor markets, for example, will attach less value to the services of managers in less successful firms (Fama 1980). Or, boards of directors may replace high agency cost managers with others hired from outside the firm (Faith et al. 1984).

Empirical evidence on the wealth effects of takeovers is largely consistent with the market discipline argument in agency theory. The shareholders of takeover targets receive, on average, significant wealth gains (Jensen and Ruback 1983; Ruback 1988; Jarrell et al. 1988). These wealth gains reflect, at least in part, reductions in agency costs thought likely to occur after an acquisition is completed.

Paradoxically, the agency cost creating behavior that is most often subject to market discipline is the indiscriminate acquiring of other firms. For example, many managers of large US firms initiated programs of conglomerate diversification in the 1970s. These programs resulted directly in growth for the firm and perhaps indirectly in greater wealth and status for the managers who initiated them. The acquired units, though, typically did not perform as well under the control of a management team from an unrelated industry (Ravenscraft and Scherer 1987). Consequently, the market for corporate control eventually recognized that these firms were not maximizing the value of their assets, and they were the object of unfriendly takeovers. Indeed, there is substantial empirical evidence which indicates that the takeover, merger, and acquisition activity that refocused large firms in the last fifteen years was a correction of this earlier 'empire building' (Bhagat et al. 1990; Shleifer and Vishny 1991; Hoskisson and Johnson 1992). Although this is cited as an example of market discipline, the question has been raised as to why the market took so long to respond to this detrimental over-diversification (Shliefer and Vishny 1991; Bethel and Liebeskind 1993).

While economics was slow to recognize conflicts within the firm, and between the firm and its numerous stakeholders, the influence of agency theory in organization economics is difficult to overstate. It has spawned literally hundreds of empirical studies. While these studies examine a vast array of topics, the underlying question is the same: how do organizations deal with conflicting goals between those who delegate authority and those to whom authority has been delegated? The theory addresses this question in only a few fundamental propositions.

Criticisms of Agency Theory

Though the empirical evidence is on balance supportive of agency theory, important questions have been raised about this set of ideas. Foremost among these is that agency theory seems to adopt an unrealistic view of humans and organizations (Hirsch et al. 1990). In agency theory, humans are primarily motivated by financial gain. Much of the early research, particularly, ignored the other behavioral sciences. Studies combining agency theory with ideas from other disciplines such as institutional theory (Eisenhardt 1988), equity theory (Zenger 1992), and social influence (Wade et al. 1990; Davis 1991) have yielded additional insights and questions about the theory.

Another criticism of agency theory is more philosophical. Perrow and others (Hirsch et al. 1990) argue that agency theory has an inherent investor focus. This criticism is true of most research in the area, but may not be inherent in the theory. The framework of agency theory is, in itself, neutral. It could just as well be used to examine issues that focus on the concerns of agents (Hesterly et al. 1990). This is essentially what Shleifer and Summers (1988) have done in their review of much of the corporate control research. They argue that much of the gains to shareholders from merger and acquisition activity result from redistributing wealth from other stakeholders such as employees to owners.

WHY DO SOME ORGANIZATIONS OUTPERFORM OTHERS?

Taken together, transaction cost economics and agency theory constitute a powerful theory of the firm. Transaction cost economics explains the conditions under which economic exchanges can be most efficiently managed using hierarchical forms of governance. If a firm is, in essence, a bundle of interrelated transactions managed through hierarchical forms of governance, then transactions cost economics is a theory of the firm. Agency theory extends this theory of the firm by enabling a researcher to examine, in more detail, linkages among these different transactions. It does this by focusing attention on the effects of compensation, corporate governance, capital structure, and other attributes of firm governance on agency problems within the firm, and between a firm and its external stakeholders.

While transaction cost economics and agency theory can be used to explain why firms exist, they cannot be used to explain why some firms might outperform others. These models both assume that firms are essentially homogeneous in their transaction and agency governance skills. Put differently, these models assume that two or more firms, facing similar kinds of economic exchanges, will develop similar governance solutions. When a group of competing firms all choose similar approaches to solving similar transactions cost and agency theory problems, these common approaches cannot be sources of competitive advantage, or superior performance, for any one firm. To explain why some firms might outperform other firms, substantially greater levels of heterogeneity must be introduced into the analysis.

Of course, transaction cost economics and agency theory are not alone in being unable to explain why some firms are able to outperform others. Indeed, a major implication of neo-classical microeconomic theory is that, barring artificial barriers to competition (e.g. government regulations that limit competition), the performance of firms in an industry will converge to a common level. This level of firm performance is called 'normal economic performance' (Tirole 1989). Normal economic performance is a level of performance just large enough to enable a firm to pay all of its suppliers, including suppliers of capital, labor and technology, the return they expect. Firms that earn normal economic performance are able to survive, although they will not prosper. In neo-classical theory, firms earning above normal economic performance must be protected by artificial barriers to competition. Any superior firm performance that is not attributable to such barriers is difficult to explain using neo-classical theory.

None of this would be problematic if the performance of firms was not very heterogeneous. However, both casual observation and empirical research suggest that it is: some firms, in fact, do outperform others (Jacobson 1988). For example, while most firms in the US airline industry have struggled to break even, Southwest Airlines has made substantial economic profits (Hallowell and Heskett 1993). Some firms in the discount retail industry have been unable to survive. Others have just been able to survive, by earning normal economic profits. However, WalMart has been massively successful, generating over $3 billion in wealth for its founder, Sam Walton (Ghemawat 1986). Also, while virtually every integrated steel company in the world has experienced losses in economic value over the last thirty years, Nucor Steel has seen its economic value consistently increase (Ghemawat and Stander 1993). Transaction cost economics, agency theory, and neo-classical microeconomics cannot explain this level of performance heterogeneity.

Understanding why some firms outperform others is the primary research topic of strategic management (Rumelt et al. 1991). As this field of inquiry has evolved, two basic explanations of the performance heterogeneity of firms have been proposed. The first builds on what has come to be known as the structure-conduct-performance (SCP) paradigm in industrial organization economics, and focuses on the structure of the industries within which a firm operates to explain heterogeneity in firm performance. The second builds on a variety of research traditions in economics and organization theory, including Penrosian economics (Penrose 1959), Austrian economics (Jacobson 1992), and the evolutionary theory of the firm (Nelson and Winter 1982), and focuses on attributes of firms to explain heterogeneity in performance. This second approach has come to be known as the resource-based view of the firm (Wernerfelt 1984; Barney 1991). These two approaches to explaining why some firms outperform others are reviewed below.

The SCP Paradigm and Firm Performance

Original work on the SCP paradigm can be traced to Mason (1959) and Bain (1956). The original purpose of this framework was to assist government regulators in identifying industries that were less than perfectly competitive, and thus where firms were earning greater than normal economic performance. Traditionally, it was thought that when firms in an industry were earning above normal economic performance, customers were paying too high prices for the goods and services they purchased, the level of innovation was below what it should have been, and the quality of goods or services was less than it should have been – in short, that social welfare was not being maximized (Bain 1956). Once these non-competitive industries were discovered, regulators could then implement a variety of remedies to increase the level of competition in them, and thereby increase social welfare.

Industry Structure and Firm Performance

As suggested earlier, the primary explanation of heterogeneity in firm performance in the SCP paradigm is industry structure. The critical performance-enhancing attributes of industry structure, isolated by SCP theorists, are: (1) industry concentration, (2) level of product differentiation, and (3) barriers to entry. Industry concentration was thought to enhance performance in one of two ways. First, in highly concentrated industries, a relatively small number of firms could collude – either explicitly or tacitly – and reduce industry output below a competitive level, and thus prices above the competitive level (Tirole 1989). As long as the cost of this collusion was less than the economic profits it created, firms that operated in highly concentrated and collusive industries would outperform firms that operated in less highly concentrated and thus not collusive industries.

The implicit assumption in these assertions is that the difficulty of implementing tacit collusion strategies increases as the number of firms in an industry increases (Scherer 1980). This assumption will be discussed in more detail in later sections of this chapter.

Industry concentration can also lead to performance heterogeneity through the operation of economies of scale. Economies of scale exist when there is a close relationship between a firm's economic costs and its volume of production. In concentrated industries, where economies of scale are operating, only relatively few firms will be able to take full advantage of these economies. These few firms will, all things being equal, have lower economic costs than smaller firms in the industry, thus leading to performance heterogeneity (Scherer 1980).

Product differentiation can also enable some firms to gain above normal performance in an industry. As first discussed by Chamberlain (1933) and Robinson (1933), firms that implement product differentiation strategies are able to enhance the perceived value of the products or services they sell. In effect, these firms become monopolists for those consumers who are attracted to a firm's differentiated products. Indeed, Chamberlain first described competition in industries with product differentiation as 'monopolistic competition'. Like all monopolists (Tirole 1989), these firms are able to charge greater than the fully competitive price for their products or services. Assuming the cost of differentiating their products is less than the extra revenue created by charging greater than the competitive price, product differentiation can also be a source of above normal economic profits.

By themselves, industry concentration and product differentiation should be sources of only the very briefest above normal economic profits. The SCP paradigm suggests that any profits earned by firms in an industry will instantly lead to entry, either by new firms coming into an industry or by firms already in that industry modifying their strategies to duplicate the strategies of profitable firms (Bain 1956). Entry will continue until all profits in an industry are competed away. If entry into an industry, or entry into new industry segments, is costless, then there will be no performance heterogeneity in an industry.

A particularly strong form of this entry argument has been developed by Baumol et al. (1982), called 'contestable market theory'. These authors argue that actual entry is not required to ensure that firms do not make above normal profits. Indeed, all that is required to ensure that firms in an industry will not earn above normal profits is the *threat* of low-cost entry.

Of course, if entry into an industry is not free, then profit reducing entry may not occur. In general, if the cost of entry is greater than or equal to the value that a firm will obtain from entry, entry will not occur. The value that a firm will obtain from entry depends on the structure within that industry, i.e. the higher the level of concentration and the greater the product differentiation, the greater the potential economic value of entry. On the other hand, the cost of entry depends on the existence of barriers to entry; the more significant the barriers to entry, the more costly (and thus the less likely) that entry will actually occur (Bain 1956).

Several barriers to entry have been identified by SCP researchers, including: (1) economies of scale, (2) product differentiation, (3) cost advantages independent of scale, (4) contrived deterrence, and (5) government imposed restrictions on entry (Porter 1980). The way that each of these barriers to entry acts to deter entry is discussed, in detail, elsewhere (Bain 1956; Barney 1995).

Strategic Management and the SCP Paradigm

Strategic management researchers have turned the original intent of the SCP paradigm upside-down (Porter 1981; Barney 1986a). Where traditional SCP research was designed to help government regulators to increase competition in an industry, strategic management researchers have used SCP insights to suggest strategies firms can implement that have the effect of reducing competition in an industry, and thus enabling firms in an industry to earn above normal profits.

While several people have contributed to the SCP-based strategic management research, no one has been more influential than Michael Porter. In a series of books (Porter 1980; 1985; 1990) and articles (Porter 1974; 1979a; 1979b), Porter and his colleagues have developed a powerful model firms can use to choose and implement strategies that will generate above normal economic performance. Among the frameworks and tools Porter has developed out of the SCP tradition are: (1) the five-forces model of environmental threats, (2) a model of generic industry structure and environmental opportunities, and (3) the strategic groups concept.

The five-forces model of environmental threats, as developed by Porter, is presented in Figure 2. Based on earlier SCP research, Porter isolated five sets of threats to the profits of a firm in an industry: the threat of rivalry, the threat of entry, the threat of substitutes, the threat of suppliers, and the threat of buyers. All these

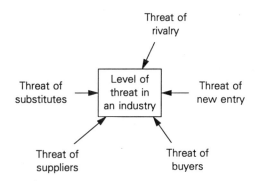

Figure 2 *The five-forces model of environmental threats* (Porter 1980)

threats act to either reduce a firm's revenues (rivalry, entry, substitutes, and buyers) or increase a firm's economic costs (suppliers) until a firm earns only normal economic performance. Porter (1980) describes, in detail, the attributes of industries that reduce the level of each of these threats. Most of these industry attributes are completely consistent with earlier SCP research, e.g. to reduce the threat of entry, firms should implement barriers to entry. They implement barriers to entry (1) by exploiting economies of scale, (2) by differentiating their products, (3) by exploiting cost advantages independent of scale, (4) by implementing contrived deterrence strategies, or (5) by encouraging the government to impose barriers to entry.

Porter's model of generic industry structures and opportunity identified five types of industries and the opportunities typically associated with them. These five industry types and associated opportunities are: (1) emerging industries (first mover advantages), (2) fragmented industries (consolidation), (3) mature industries (emphasis on service, process innovation), (4) declining industries (lead, niche, harvest, divest), and (5) global industries (multinational organization, global integrated organization). Detailed definitions of these industry types, of the opportunities associated with them and examples of each are presented in Table 1.

As suggested earlier, firm profits can motivate entry from at least two sources: from firms entering an industry from the outside, or from firms that are already in an industry entering into a new segment of that industry. This second form of entry led Porter, in cooperation with Richard Caves, to develop the concept of 'strategic groups' (Caves and Porter 1977). A strategic group is a set of firms in an industry pursuing similar strategies. Strategic groups may, or may not, be protected from entry by firms already in an industry by what Caves and

Table 1 *Industry structure and opportunities*

Industry type	Definition	Opportunities	Examples of firms exploiting these opportunities
Emerging industries	Recent changes in demand or technology; new industry standard operating procedures have yet to develop	First mover advantages	Intel in microprocessors
Fragmented industries	Large numbers of firms of approximately equal size	Consolidation	McDonald's in fast food
Mature industries	Slow increases in demand, numerous repeat customers, limited product innovation	Emphasis on service and process innovation	GE in light bulbs
Declining industries	Consistent reduction in industry demand	Leadership Niche Harvest Divest	General Dynamics in defense
Global industries	Significant international sales	Multinational Global	Nestlé; Ciba-Geigy

Porter call 'mobility barriers'. Mobility barriers are like barriers to entry, except they are applied to strategic groups of firms within an industry, not to an industry as a whole. Thus, entry into an industry is deterred by barriers to entry; entry into a strategic group is deterred by mobility barriers.

This SCP-based approach to understanding heterogeneity in firm performance has numerous important research and managerial implications. A great deal of research has been conducted testing the SCP foundations of this model of firm performance (see Scherer 1980 for an extensive review). Additional research has also been conducted examining the empirical implications of the strategic management versions of this SCP framework. Some of this work supports the theories and frameworks developed by Porter and his colleagues. For example, the five-forces model has been shown to be a reasonably accurate predictor of the overall competitiveness of an industry. On the other hand, some of the other parts of the Porter framework have not fared as well, empirically. For example, while extensive research has been conducted on the existence and performance implications of strategic groups in industries, some have argued that most of this work has been badly flawed, and that the essential elements of this concept remain untested (Barney and Hoskisson 1989). Interest in strategic group research has waned significantly, although some impressively creative strategic group research continues (e.g. Reger and Huff 1993).

Criticisms of the SCP Paradigm in Strategic Management

While research continues on the theory underlying SCP-based models of firm performance, at least two important questions have arisen concerning the managerial implications of these models. The first of these questions revolves around the appropriateness of the unit of analysis in these models – the industry or the strategic group. These models assert that the primary determinant of firm performance is the industry (or strategic group) within which a firm operates. However, research has shown that there is often more heterogeneity in the performance of firms within a single industry than there is heterogeneity in the performance of firms across industries (Rumelt 1991). Indeed, each of the examples of heterogeneous firm performance cited previously focused on performance heterogeneity of firms within an industry, i.e. Southwest Airlines in the airline industry, WalMart in the discount retail industry, and Nucor Steel in the steel industry. By adopting the industry (strategic group) as the unit of analysis, SCP-based models cannot explain intra-industry (intra-group) heterogeneity in performance.

Put differently, SCP explanations of heterogeneous firm performance continue to assume that firms within an industry, or within a strategic group, are homogeneous. In this framework, only differences between industries/groups can explain differences in firm performance. While there is more heterogeneity in these SCP models than in transaction cost, agency theory, or neo-classical theory, many have argued that there still is not enough heterogeneity in these SCP models, i.e. that the appropriate unit of analysis for the study of heterogeneous firm performance is the firm (Barney and Hoskisson 1989).

The limitations of the industry/group focus are brought into relief by examining their managerial implications. SCP logic suggests that firms seeking to earn above normal economic performance should enter and operate only in 'attractive' industries. An attractive industry is one characterized by low levels of threat, and high levels of opportunity, as defined by Porter (1980). However, the attractiveness of an industry cannot be evaluated independently of the unique skills and abilities that a firm brings to that industry (Barney 1994). Thus, while the airline industry has been unattractive for many airlines, it has been quite attractive for Southwest Airlines; while the discount retail industry has been unattractive for many firms, it has been quite attractive for WalMart; while the steel industry has been unattractive for many firms, it has been quite attractive for Nucor Steel. While the level of threat and opportunity in an industry is obviously an important component of any model of firm performance, a more complete model of performance must necessarily also include some discussion of a firm's unique resources and capabilities.

A second question about the managerial implications of SCP-based models of firm performance concerns the social welfare implications of these models. Recall that the original purpose of the SCP paradigm was to isolate industries that were not maximizing social welfare, and to correct this problem. Strategy researchers have turned this objective upside down, by trying to help firms discover settings that are less than fully competitive. By implication, this suggests that firms that implement SCP-based strategies will reduce competition below the socially optimal level. Many academics find research that may have the effect of reducing overall social welfare morally unacceptable.

The Resource-Based View of the Firm and Firm Performance

Several authors have recognized the limitations of SCP-based models of firm performance and have developed a complementary approach. This approach builds on other traditions in economics, rather than on the SCP framework, including work by Edith Penrose (1959), Joseph

Schumpeter (1934), and Michael Ricardo (Scherer 1980), among others, and is known as the resource-based view of the firm. Work on the resource-based view of the firm in strategic management began with the publication of three articles, one each by Richard Rumelt (1984), Birger Wernerfelt (1984), and Jay Barney (1986b). Other early resource-based work in strategic management includes Teece (1982) and Prahalad and Bettis (1986).

The Unit of Analysis, and Basic Assumptions of Resource-Based Logic

Unlike SCP-based models of firm performance, the resource-based view of the firm adopts, as its primary unit of analysis, the resources and capabilities controlled by a firm. A firm's resources and capabilities include all those attributes of a firm that enable it to conceive of and implement strategies. A firm's resources and capabilities can conveniently be divided into four types: financial resources (e.g. equity capital, debt capital, retained earnings, etc.), physical resources (e.g. the machines, factories, and other tangibles used by a firm), human resources (e.g. the experience, intelligence, training, judgment, and wisdom of individuals associated with a firm), and organizational resources (e.g. the teamwork, trust, friendship, and reputation of groups of individuals associated with a firm) (Barney 1991).

The resource-based view of the firm builds on two basic assumptions about a firm's resources and capabilities: (1) that resources and capabilities can vary significantly across firms (the assumption of firm heterogeneity), and (2) that these differences can be stable (the assumption of resource immobility). These assumptions differ significantly from neo-classical economic assumptions, where firms within an industry are assumed to be essentially identical, and where any differences that do emerge are quickly destroyed as firms without certain resources and capabilities move quickly to acquire or develop them (Scherer 1980). These assumptions also differ significantly from the assumptions adopted in the SCP paradigm. In this paradigm, it is assumed that firm resources and capabilities may vary across industries (or strategic groups) and that these differences can only be sustained if important barriers to entry (or mobility barriers) are in place. In resource-based logic, not all firms are assumed to be heterogeneous with respect to their resources and capabilities, nor is it assumed that all these differences will be sustained over time. Rather, it is only assumed that resources and capabilities *can* be heterogeneously distributed over time, and that heterogeneity can last, not simply because of barriers to entry, but because of the essential attributes of some of a firm's resources and capabilities.

Firms' Resources and Sustained Competitive Advantage

To turn these assumptions into testable propositions, Barney (1991) has suggested that, in order for a firm's resources and capabilities to be sources of superior performance they must be (1) valuable (in the sense of enabling a firm to exploit its environmental opportunities and/or neutralize its threats), (2) rare among its current or potential competitors, (3) costly to imitate, and (4) without close strategic substitutes. One resource or capability is a strategic substitute of another resource or capability if they both address approximately the same environmental opportunities and threats in about the same way and at about the same cost.

Imitability is an important component of the resource-based view of the firm. If other firms can acquire or develop the same, or substitute, resources as a firm that already possesses these resources, and can do so at approximately the same cost as the firm that already possesses them, then they cannot be a source of competitive advantage for any firm. Several researchers have suggested reasons why a firm's resources and capabilities may be costly to imitate (Dierickx and Cool 1989; Peteraf 1993). Barney (1991) divides these sources of costly imitation into three categories: the role of history, the role of causal ambiguity, and the role of socially complex resources and capabilities.

Sometimes, firms are able to acquire certain resources or capabilities at low cost because of their unique path through history. Dierickx and Cool (1989) suggest that these types of resources and capabilities have 'time compression diseconomies'. Arthur et al. (1987) suggest that these types of resources and capabilities accrue in a 'path dependent' way, i.e. their development depends upon a unique series of events in a firm's history. Of course, firms that have not passed through these same historical circumstances will face a significant cost disadvantage in developing or acquiring these resources, compared to firms that have passed through these circumstances. History is a linear process. Once it endows a few firms with special resources and capabilities, firms without these resources and capabilities face high cost imitation.

Sometimes it is not clear exactly why a firm with superior performance enjoys that performance advantage. This can happen whenever two or more competing hypotheses about the determinants of a firm's performance exist and

when these hypotheses cannot be tested. Both Lippman and Rumelt (1982) and Reed and DeFillippi (1990) emphasize the importance of this 'causal ambiguity' in increasing the cost of imitation. When competing firms cannot know, with certainty, what enables a particular firm to enjoy its superior performance, these firms cannot know, with certainty, which of that firm's resources and capabilities it should imitate. This uncertainty effectively increases the cost of imitation.

Finally, sometimes the resources and capabilities that enable a firm to gain superior performance are socially complex. Examples of these types of resources include a firm's culture, teamwork among its employees, its reputation with suppliers and customers, and so forth. In this context, there may be little or no uncertainty about why a firm is able to enjoy high levels of performance, and imitation can still not occur. While managers can describe these socially complex resources, their ability to manage and change them rapidly are limited (Barney 1986c). The importance of these socially complex resources as potential sources of sustained competitive advantage has led several resource-based theorists to call for increased cooperation between strategic management researchers, and those who study organizational behavior. In an important sense, the dependent variables of organizational behavior and organization theory are potentially important independent variables in resource-based models of firm performance.

The empirical implications of the resource-based view of the firm are beginning to be examined in the strategic management literature. Thus far, most results are consistent with resource-based expectations, although this empirical work is early in development. Thus, for example, Rumelt (1991) found that the unique attributes of a firm are more important determinants of its performance than the industry within which it operates. In a similar way, Hansen and Wernerfelt (1989) have shown that a firm's culture is a more important determinant of firm performance than the structure of the industry within which it operates.

Managerial Implications

The managerial implications of the resource-based view of the firm stand in marked contrast to more traditional SCP-based strategic management models. In particular, where the SCP-based models would have managers choose to enter and conduct businesses in 'attractive' industries, resource-based logic suggests that firms should look inward, discover their own valuable, rare, and costly to imitate resources and capabilities, and then discover markets where those resources can be exploited. While a particular industry may be very unattractive based on SCP criteria, it may be very attractive to a firm with just the right set of valuable, rare, and costly to imitate resources and capabilities (Barney 1991).

The social welfare implications of resource-based strategies are also very different from the social welfare implications of SCP-based strategies. SCP-based strategies are designed to reduce competition below the competitive level and thus reduce the level of general social welfare in favor of a few firms earning above normal profits. Resource-based strategies suggest that firms should discover those business activities for which they are uniquely well suited. Exploiting a firm's special resources and capabilities can, in this sense, enhance social welfare. Put differently, superior firm performance in the SCP framework suggests that firms have effectively protected themselves from competition. Superior firm performance of firms in the resource-based framework suggests that firms have discovered those business activities that they can conduct more efficiently than any current or potentially competing firms.

How Can Firms Cooperate?

All the organizational economic models discussed so far assume that firms can be analyzed as if they were independent economic entities. The picture painted, in most of these models, is of individual firms making transactions-cost vertical integration and boundary choices, solving their important agency problems, and competing against other independent firms for competitive advantage. And, indeed, there are many times when this 'independent firm' approach to economic analysis is appropriate.

However, over the last several years, scholars have come to recognize the importance of sets of cooperating firms as major players in competitive settings (Tirole 1989). Competition is still important in these settings. However, more and more frequently, competition seems to manifest itself between groups of cooperating firms rather than simply between firms.

Organizational economic models of cooperation between firms have a common form and structure (Barney 1995). First, these models examine the economic incentives otherwise independent firms have to cooperate in some way. It can be shown that firms have such incentives in a wide variety of settings. Once these cooperative incentives are understood, these economic models of cooperation then examine the incentives that cooperating firms

have to 'cheat' on their cooperative agreements. It is, perhaps, ironic, but each of the economically valuable reasons that firms can find to cooperate generally imply economically valuable ways that firms can cheat on those cooperative agreements. Finally, these models focus on activities that firms can engage in to monitor potential cheating in their cooperative relationships. If this monitoring is done well, then the incentives to cheat on cooperative agreements can be reduced, and cooperation can continue. This form of analysis has been applied to two major forms of cooperation in organizational economics: tacit collusion and strategic alliances.

Tacit Collusion as Cooperation

Traditional economics has long recognized the importance of cooperation among firms in an industry (Scherer 1980). The most common way this cooperation has been analyzed is as collusion, either explicit or tacit. A set of firms is said to be colluding when they cooperate to reduce the total output of products or services in an industry below what would be the case if they were competing in that industry (Tirole 1989). Of course, assuming that demand for an industry's products remains relatively stable, these reductions in supply will be reflected in increased prices. These increased prices can generate levels of performance much greater than what would be expected in a more competitive industry.

Incentives to Cooperate

Consider, for example, a hypothetical industry with six firms. Imagine, for simplicity, that these firms sell undifferentiated products, and that the cost of manufacturing these products is $3 per unit. Also, imagine that total demand for these products is fixed, equal to 10,000 units, but that these six firms have agreed to restrict output below this level. Again, for simplicity, suppose that each of these firms has agreed to restrict output to only 1,000 units. Since demand (10,000 units) is much greater than supply (6,000), there are a large number of customers chasing after a relatively small number of products, and prices will rise. In a fully competitive industry, these firms would only be able to charge about $3 per unit. However, in this collusive industry, they may be able to charge as much as $10 per unit. Where in the competitive case, these firms would all about 'break even', in the colluding case they could each earn substantial economic profits of $7,000 (($10 × 1,000) − ($3 × 1,000)). That $7,000 economic profit is the economic incentive for these firms to cooperate in the form of collusion.

Incentives to Cheat on
Cooperative Agreements

However, whenever there is an incentive to cooperate, there is also an incentive to cheat on those cooperative agreements. This incentive can be seen by what happens to the profits of one of our hypothetical firms if it violates the agreement to sell 1,000 units at $10, and instead sells 3,000 units at $9. In this situation, the five firms that stick with the collusive agreement still earn their $7,000 profit, but the cheating firm earns a much larger profit of $18,000 (($9 × 3,000) − ($3 × 3,000)). The $11,000 difference between the $7,000 that is earned if collusion is maintained, and the $18,000 the one firm earns if it cheats on this collusive agreement, is the economic incentive to cheat on collusion.

Cheating on these collusive agreements usually spreads rapidly. Once other firms discover that a particular firm is cheating on a collusive agreement, they may begin cheating on this agreement, and collusive cooperation in this industry will cease (Scherer 1980). This can be seen in the simple case depicted in Figure 3. In this case, there are just two firms in the industry (I and II), who have agreed to collude, restrict output, and set a price equal to P^*. P^* is greater than the price these firms could charge in a non-collusive setting. Also, to simplify this example, assume that the products or services these two firms sell are undifferentiated, and that customers face no costs switching back and forth from firm I to firm II (this roughly approximates competition between, say, two gas stations across the street from each other).

Now suppose firm I decides to cheat on this collusive agreement and charge a price $P_1 < P^*$. As soon as this happens, all those customers who had been purchasing products from firm II will instantly switch to firm I for the lower price. Firm II will have to respond by lowering its price to P_2. P_2 must be less than P_1 or customers would have no incentive to shift back from firm I to firm II. When firm II sets its price at P_2, all of firm I's customers will instantly switch to firm II, and firm I will have to readjust its price to P_3. P_3 must be less than P_2, and so forth. This competition will continue until the prices these firms charge exactly equal their economic costs, at which time any superior performance that could have been obtained from collusion will have been competed away.

Much of what has come to be known as game theory is dedicated to understanding interactions like those depicted in Figure 3. This particular game was originally studied by Bertrand (1883) and examines what happens when colluding firms cheat on their agreements by lowering their prices. It can be easily demonstrated that such

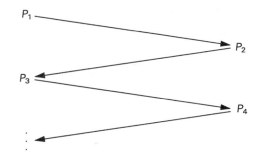

Figure 3 *Cheating on collusive agreements*

'Bertrand cheating' will lead firms to earn rates of return equal to that of firms in perfectly competitive markets (Tirole 1989). Another early, and very influential, game of this sort was studied by Cournot (1897). Cournot analyzed what will happen to prices and performance if firms cheat on their collusive agreements by increasing their output beyond agreed levels. Such 'Cournot cheating' will lead to performance somewhere between that which fully colluding firms could have earned and what firms in a perfectly competitive market will earn (Tirole 1989). Hundreds of other game theoretic models examine different types of interactions between firms and the implications of such interactions on the performance of firms in an industry (Scherer 1980; Tirole 1989). The conclusion of many of these models is that the economic incentives to cheat on collusive arrangements, despite the increased competition such cheating almost always creates, is often larger than the economic incentives firms have to maintain their collusive arrangements.

Of course, much of this problem with cheating on collusive arrangements could be resolved if managers in colluding firms could sit down together, face to face, and work out their problems. However, such direct, face to face negotiations about the level of output in an industry and prices is, in most developed economies, illegal. Such explicit collusion can lead to very real negative consequences for managers and firms, including large fines and time in prison. Most governments actively discourage explicit collusion because the lower levels of production and the higher prices it creates, while they may improve the profits of colluding firms, are generally very bad for consumers, and for society as a whole (Scherer 1980). Indeed, as was suggested earlier, the effort to eliminate collusion was one of the primary policy objectives of the SCP framework.

Given the risks associated with explicit collusion, firms seeking to engage in this form of cooperation must use, instead, tacit collusion. In tacit collusion, there again is an agreement to reduce output below, and prices above, the competitive level. However, these agreements are not directly negotiated. Rather, firms seeking to implement tacit collusion must interpret the intent of other firms to collude through the behaviors and signals these other firms send out (Spence 1974). Such interpretation of intentions to collude can be difficult. For example, suppose a firm that has been able to reduce its economic costs does not pass these lower costs along to customers in the form of lower prices. Does this mean that this firm is interested in developing some collusive relationships, or does it mean that this firm believes that demand for its highly differentiated product is sufficient to increase sales without price reductions?

One tactic suggested for sustaining tacit collusion is to punish those that either raise their output level or reduce their prices. For example, Axelrod (1984) suggests that tit-for-tat strategies where such non-cooperative behavior is immediately punished through some sort of retaliation (in this case increased output and price reductions) by competitors will discourage such behavior in the future. The effectiveness of tit-for-tat strategies in assuring collusion, however, depends upon the ability of those involved to perceive one another's moves with a high degree of certainty. As Axelrod (1984) found in his simulations, cooperative outcomes are more difficult to sustain when there is uncertainty about the moves made by players in a game. Moreover, tit-for-tat can lead to an escalation in competition as has been the case in price wars among US airlines.

Industry Structure and the Ability to Collude

The ability to interpret intentions to collude varies with several important attributes of industries and of the firms in those industries. For example, in general, tacit collusion is easier when there are relatively few firms in an industry (Scherer 1980). In such industries, firms need only receive and interpret signals of intentions to collude from a small number of firms, rather than from a large number of firms. Also, tacit collusion is typically easier in industries where all firms have about the same economic costs and sell undifferentiated products. When firms have about the same economic costs, they have about the same optimal level of production (Scherer 1980). If collusion reduces production below this optimal level, all these firms will absorb about the same extra production costs. They will also all earn about the same level of economic profits. In this setting, no one firm has a strong incentive to cheat on collusion, since no

one firm is obtaining a disproportionately smaller level of benefit from colluding. The lack of product differentiation helps maintain collusion by limiting the ways that firms can cheat on collusive arrangements. If firms can differentiate their products, they can increase demand for their own products in ways that are less obvious than by simply lowering their prices. However, if product differentiation is difficult to do, then any cheating on collusive agreements will be reflected in a firm's prices. Prices are relatively easy to monitor, and thus cheating on prices will typically lead to quick retaliation against the cheating firm. Quick retaliation, in turn, reduces the time period during which a cheating firm will be able to earn extra economic performance from cheating, and thus reduces the incentives to cheat (Scherer 1980).

Scherer (1980) describes several other industry attributes that tend to enhance the ability of firms to interpret signals of intention to collude, and thus enhance the ability of tacit collusion to emerge and remain. However, none of these other industry attributes is more important than high barriers to entry. As suggested earlier, barriers to entry increase the cost of entry into an industry. Firms that are successfully implementing tacit collusion will be earning substantial economic profits. Such profits, other things being equal, should motivate entry into an industry. New entrants, in turn, are less likely to be part of the collusive agreements in an industry and thus more likely to 'cheat' on these agreements. Such cheating will almost always have the effect of increasing competition in an industry and reducing the probability that tacit collusion agreements can be maintained. Thus, in order for colluding firms to continue in their colluding ways, they must be protected from new entry by substantial barriers to entry. These barriers to entry were discussed previously in the context of the SCP-based approach to understanding heterogeneity in firm performance.

In general, those attributes of firms and industries that have an effect on the ability of firms to interpret signals of intentions to collude can be thought of as part of the monitoring process firms engage in to reduce the probability of cheating in this form of cooperation. As suggested earlier, while there are often substantial incentives to cooperate, there are also substantial incentives to cheat on these cooperative agreements. By monitoring the behavior of their partners in collusion, the probability of cheating can be reduced, and the extra economic performance promised by collusion can be realized. The easier it is to monitor a colluding firm's behavior, the less likely cheating will occur, and the more likely that collusion will continue.

Strategic Alliances and Cooperation

Previous work suggests that tacit collusion, as a form of cooperation, is possible. However, given the difficulties associated with interpreting signals of intent to collude, most organizational economists expect this form of collusion to be relatively rare. Strategic alliances, as a form of cooperation, are, on the other hand, much more common than tacit collusion. Indeed, the number of international strategic alliances entered into by US firms has grown dramatically over the last several years (Harrigan 1986; Kogut 1988). Firms like IBM, AT&T, and Corning have, literally, hundreds of strategic alliances (Kogut 1988). One of Corning's alliances, with Dow Chemical (Dow Corning), is, itself, a *Fortune* 500 company. Thus, strategic alliances are a much more common, and economically important, form of cooperation than tacit collusion (Barney 1995). Moreover, strategic alliances usually have none of the social welfare reducing side effects of collusion (Kogut 1988).

Types of Alliances

In general, there are two broad classes of strategic alliances: contractual alliances and joint ventures (Hennart 1988). A contractual alliance is any form of cooperative relationship between two or more firms, the purpose of which is to develop, design, manufacture, market, or distribute products or services, and where a separate firm is *not* created to manage this relationship. Rather, this relationship is managed through some sort of contract. Notice that, unlike tacit collusion, the effect of contractual strategic alliances is to increase economic activity, not to reduce economic activity below the competitive level. Common examples of contractual strategic alliances include: long-term supply relationships, licensing arrangements, distribution agreements, and so forth.

Joint ventures are also cooperative relationships between two or more firms with the purpose of developing, designing, manufacturing, marketing, or distributing products or services. However, unlike contractual alliances, joint ventures always involve the creation of a separate firm (the joint venture) to manage this relationship. Partners in this joint venture provide capital and other resources to this separate firm, which is typically managed by its own management team reporting to a board of directors consisting of representatives of the joint venture partners. Partners in this joint venture are compensated for their investment from the profits that are generated by this firm. Financial interests may be equally distributed across joint venture partners, or some partners may have larger financial interest in a joint venture than other partners. For example, Dow and Corning each own 50 per cent of the Dow Corning joint venture; Corning owns over 60 per cent of its television glass joint venture with Asahi (Nanda and Bartlett 1990).

Incentives to Cooperate in Alliances

The primary economic incentive for engaging in strategic alliances is to exploit resource complementarity (Kogut 1988; Hennart 1988). The resources controlled by two or more firms are complementary when their economic value combined is greater than their economic value separately. Obviously, when firms have complementary resources, an important economic synergy among these firms exists. A strategic alliance is one way that synergy can be realized.

While economic complementarity is a general requirement for firms to pursue strategic alliances, this complementarity can come from numerous different sources. Some of the most important of these sources of complementarities between firms are listed in Table 2. For example, firms may engage in an alliance to realize economies of scale that cannot be realized by each firm on its own (Kogut 1988). In the aluminum industry, the minimum efficient scale of bauxite mining is much greater than the maximum efficient scale of aluminum smelting. Individual smelting companies, on their own, could never operate an efficient bauxite mining operation. Any smelting operation large enough to absorb all the bauxite mined in an efficient mine would be terribly inefficient and lead to high smelting costs; a mine small enough to supply just an efficient smelting operation would also be terribly inefficient and lead to high mining costs. One solution to this problem would be for a single firm to operate an efficient (i.e. very large) mine and an efficient (i.e. relatively small) smelting operation, and then to sell excess bauxite on the open market. Unfortunately, bauxite is not a homogeneous ore, and refining bauxite purchased from a large

Table 2 *Motivations for entering strategic alliances*

---

1 Exploit economies of scale
2 Low-cost entry into new markets
3 Low-cost entry into new industry segments and new industries
4 Learning from competition
5 Managing strategic uncertainty
6 Managing costs and sharing risks
7 To facilitate tacit collusion

---

mine would require a smelting firm to make enormous transaction specific investments in that mine. Such investments put these firms at risk of opportunistic behavior (see the discussion of transaction cost economics earlier), and thus these refiners would prefer not to have to purchase an independent efficient mining firm's excess bauxite (Hennart 1988). Thus, to simultaneously exploit the economies of scale associated with a large mining operation, while maintaining relatively small and efficient aluminum smelting operations, and not requiring smelting firms to make high levels of transaction specific investments across market exchanges, most bauxite mines are owned by joint ventures, where joint venture partners are smelting firms (Scherer 1980).

Another important economic motivation for entering into a strategic alliance is to reduce the cost of entry into a new market (Kogut 1988). In a global economy, many firms are beginning to recognize the importance of selling their products and services in markets around the world. However, entry into these markets can be costly and difficult. New market entrants often have to build costly new distribution networks. Moreover, new market entrants often do not have the local expertise they need to respond to customer needs in these new markets. In this setting, cooperating with a firm in a local market can be a very effective way to enter that market. Instead of building a new distribution network, market entrants can exploit the already existing distribution networks of their partner in that new market. That partner is also more likely to have the local expertise that will be necessary to be successful in that new market. On the other hand, the local partner may gain access to valuable new products and technologies that it can distribute in its traditional market. For these reasons, low-cost entry into new markets is, perhaps, one of the most common motivations behind strategic alliances (Harrigan 1986).

Alliances can also facilitate low-cost entry into new industries, or new segments of an industry (Kogut 1988). For example, Dow Chemical believed that it had some resources and capabilities that might be valuable in the electronics industry. However, as a chemical firm, they had relatively little experience in this industry. Rather than trying to enter on their own, Dow formed a strategic alliance with Philips Electronics. This alliance uses Dow's chemical expertise, and Philips' electronics expertise, to manufacture compact disks for sale in North America. It was almost certainly less costly for Dow to enter into this segment of the electronics industry with Philips as a partner than it would have been for Dow to enter into this industry by itself (Barney 1995).

Alliances can also be used to learn from competitors (Kogut 1988). Since the early 1980s, General Motors has consistently lost market share in the US automobile industry. Much of this share loss can be traced to poor quality manufacturing, especially among GM's small car lines. GM has been trying to learn how to manufacture high-quality automobiles, especially high-quality small automobiles, while still making a profit. In 1983, GM formed a strategic alliance with Toyota. Called NUMMI, this Fremont, California, assembly operation has given GM an opportunity to directly observe how Toyota builds high-quality small cars at a profit. GM has transferred much of the knowledge they gained from NUMMI, and other of their strategic alliances, to its Saturn division – a division that has been very successful at manufacturing high-quality cars (although still not at a profit).

Alliances can also be used by firms to manage strategic uncertainty (Kogut 1991). Sometimes, a firm may have several strategic options, but be unable to choose which of those options promises the most economic success. For example, after the US federal government broke up AT&T, AT&T was not completely sure what its long-term strategy should be. To be sure, it had numerous options and substantial financial and other resources at its disposal, but the best path forward was not obvious. In this context, AT&T invested in a very large number (almost 400 at one time) of strategic alliances (Kogut 1991). Each of these alliances gave AT&T some insight into the competitive and economic potential of a different business activity. In financial terms, these numerous alliances can be thought of as real options (Kogut 1991). Once the actual economic potential of different strategies becomes clear (i.e. once uncertainty is reduced), a firm can either divest itself of an option (by backing out of the alliance) or exercise an option (by, say, purchasing its alliance partner, and thus entering into an industry). In this uncertain context, multiple alliances can be thought of as a way a firm keeps its 'options open'. Once AT&T decided that the telecommunications industry and the computer industry were likely to come together in an economically valuable way, AT&T exercised some of its earlier strategic alliance options by purchasing several computer firms, including NCR.

Alliances can also be used by firms to reduce their costs and manage their risk (Barney 1995). Some potentially valuable investments are so large, or so risky, that individual firms would literally 'bet the company' if they made these investments on their own. In this case, an alliance of some sort can help a firm reduce the costs it bears from an investment, thereby reducing the risks of this investment. This is one reason why most deep water drilling platforms (typically, very risky investments) are owned by alliances of oil and gas companies and not just a single firm (Scherer 1980; Kogut 1988).

A final reason that firms may enter into strategic alliances is to facilitate the development of tacit (or even explicit) collusion (Kogut 1988). Indeed, for many years, the development of tacit collusion was seen as one of the primary motivators of strategic alliances. After all, firms that are able to directly communicate through a strategic alliance may be able to transfer this relationship to other of their businesses, where collusion may be forthcoming. For this reason, the alliance between GM and Toyota was subjected to intense regulatory scrutiny, to ensure that GM and Toyota would not use this alliance to develop collusion in the automobile industry. While alliances may, in principle, help facilitate the development of tacit collusion, most organizational economists now believe that, given the enormous economic potential of alliances from other sources, the development of tacit collusion is a relatively unimportant motivation for the creation of most alliances (Kogut 1988).

In all of the above incentives to enter into strategic alliances, resource complementarity is the central motivation for firms entering into an alliance. However, the institutional context also affects the feasibility of alliances (Williamson 1993b). It may either facilitate or inhibit the formation of alliances. In Italy, for example, one argument for the reliance on extensive networks of small firms in some industries is that labor laws provide an incentive for firms to stay small and rely on extensive cooperation. Another example of the impact of institutional conditions is Japanese subcontracting (Williamson 1985; Fruin 1992). Multiple factors – such as cross-ownership, the legal system, and culture – contribute to a greater willingness to enter into alliances than was historically the case in some countries. Cross-ownership patterns contribute to ease in entering into alliances. Firms often hold a mutual equity interest in one another which leads to a perception that they have a 'common destiny' (Williamson 1985: 121). Culture may also contribute to alliance patterns. In Japan, greater importance is attached to maintaining harmony than in some other cultures. Such a focus on harmony likely engenders less risk in entering into alliances with others who share that focus. Though institutional context clearly makes it either more or less difficult to successfully enter into alliances, organizational economics nevertheless views this as secondary to resource complementarity in explaining strategic alliances. In all of the above examples, firms also have clear resource complementarity reasons for entering into alliances and, indeed, it is potential complementarities that discriminate between firms that are potential alliance partners and those that are not.

Incentives to Cheat in Alliances

While there are significant economic incentives for firms to cooperate in strategic alliances, there are also significant economic incentives to cheat on those alliances once they are formed. Such cheating can take at least three forms: adverse selection cheating, moral hazard cheating, and hold-up cheating (Barney and Ouchi 1986). Each of these types of cheating in alliances can be thought of as specific examples of opportunistic behavior – of the sort described in transaction cost economics and agency theory. Indeed, adverse selection and moral hazard have already been discussed as problems in agency relationships; hold-up, as a function of transaction specific investments, has already been discussed as a problem in transaction cost economics.

Adverse selection exists when an alliance partner misrepresents the resources and capabilities they can bring to an alliance (Barney and Hansen 1995). For example, suppose firm I needs political contacts in a particular country in order to facilitate entry into a new market. If firm II informs firm I that it possesses these contacts, when it really does not possess them, firm II has engaged in adverse selection. In this case, firm II will be able to appropriate whatever resources and capabilities firm I makes available to the alliance, without providing any of its own resources and capabilities to the alliance.

Moral hazard exists when an alliance partner really does possess the resources and capabilities it says it possesses, but simply does not make them available to the alliance (Barney and Hansen 1995). For example, suppose that firm I and firm II are cooperating in a joint research and development effort. Also, suppose that, as part of this agreement, both firms promise to assign only their best engineering talent to this alliance. Firm I may, in fact, fulfill its part of the agreement and send top-level engineering talent to the alliance. Firm II, on the other hand, may decide to keep its best engineering talent in the parent company, where it can be used in other development projects. Rather than sending the best engineering talent, firm II might send engineers who are just well-enough-trained to learn everything that firm I's engineers can teach them, but not sufficiently well-trained to actually contribute to the alliance. In this case, firm II has engaged in moral hazard. It has been able to gain significant value from the alliance (it has learned a great deal from firm I's engineers), and it has been able to do so at very low cost (it retained its best engineers to continue working on its own development projects).

Hold-up exists when an alliance is characterized by high levels of transaction-specific investment, and where those that have made these investments are exploited by those who have not made them. In the discussion of transaction cost economics, it was suggested that high levels of transaction specific investment can subject a firm to significant threats of opportunistic behavior and may motivate vertical integration (Williamson 1975). This argument holds in the case of alliances as well: alliances characterized by high levels of specific investment may not be stable, and may have to be replaced by vertically integrated exchanges (Kogut 1988).

Reducing the Threat of Cheating

Just as different industry and firm attributes can facilitate the monitoring of cheating by partners in collusive arrangements, firms in strategic alliances can engage in activities designed to reduce the probability of adverse selection, moral hazard, and hold-up. These monitoring devices fall into two broad categories: governance and trust.

The role of governance in strategic alliances precisely parallels the role of governance in transaction cost economics. In general, the greater the value of cheating in a strategic alliance, the greater the threat of cheating. The greater the threat of cheating, the more elaborate the governance that will be required to manage an alliance. When the threat of cheating is small, simple market forms of governance (e.g. simple contracts) can reduce the threat of cheating and do so at low cost. As the threat of cheating increases, more elaborate – and costly – forms of governance will have to be implemented (e.g. contractual alliances). At even higher levels of threat, joint ventures may have to be used to manage a cooperative relationship. By creating a joint venture, parties in an alliance create a new firm to manage a relationship. Since compensation for investing in this firm depends entirely on its profits, parties in this form of alliance have incentives to not behave opportunistically when creating the joint venture. However, sometimes even joint ventures cannot efficiently reduce the threat of cheating in an exchange, and that exchange will have to be integrated into a single firm, to be managed through hierarchical forms of governance (Kogut 1988; Hennart 1988). In general, firms will prefer that form of governance that minimizes the probability of opportunism, but does so at the lowest governance cost possible (Williamson 1975).

A second approach to managing cheating in alliances builds on the trust that can develop between parties to an alliance. Over a period of time, parties to an alliance may discover that they can all be trusted to not behave opportunistically in this relationship. With this trust in place, normal governance mechanisms can be dismantled. In this sense, trust among alliance partners may be a low-cost substitute for costly governance (Barney and Hansen 1995).

However, not only can trust be a low-cost substitute for governance, but firms that trust each other may be able to explore exchange opportunities that are not available to firms that cannot trust each other. If, as transactions cost theorists suggest, governance is costly, there may well be potentially valuable economic exchanges whose value cannot be realized. This can happen in at least two ways. First, the potential gains from these exchanges may only be modest, but the threat of opportunism sufficient, such that the cost of governance is greater than the gains from trade. Second, the potential gains from these trades may be enormous. However, the threat of opportunism in these exchanges may be so large that no cost effective governance mechanism can be created. Even vertical integration may not be able to solve all the problems of opportunism that might plague these exchanges (Grossman and Hart 1986). In the absence of efficient governance, the exchanges will not occur – despite their economic potential. However, if parties in an alliance trust each other, these firms will be able to explore these exchange opportunities, and, perhaps, realize their economic potential. Moreover, if relatively few sets of alliance partners trust one another in this manner, and if this trust is costly for other sets of firms to imitate, then the resource-based view of the firm suggests that firms that are able to trust each other may be able to gain sustained competitive advantages from their cooperative efforts.

CONCLUSION

Organization economics has been, and will continue to be, an important set of theoretical tools for the analysis of organizations and organizational phenomena. It addresses some of the most fundamental issues in all of organizational research, including the four questions around which this chapter is organized. Progress in answering these questions, both theoretically and empirically, has been impressive although, clearly, much work remains.

Of course, organization economics is not alone in addressing these, and related, fundamental questions of organizational analysis. Both organizational behavior and organization theory are also concerned with understanding why organizations exist, the implications of interest conflicts among those associated with an organization, why some organizations outperform others, and how organizations can cooperate with one another. Given this overlapping set of interests, one might expect that these three literatures should build on each other, should inform work done in these different research streams – in short, that a theoretical integration of organizational economics, organizational behavior, and organization theory should be emerging.

Most observers would agree, however, that despite the potential for integration and cross-fertilization, relatively little of this integrative work has occurred. At best, cross-disciplinary work of this sort takes the form of public debates about the assumptions of economics, the quality of behavioral research, and so forth (e.g. Hirsch et al. 1990 versus Hesterly and Zenger 1993; Donaldson 1990 versus Barney 1990; Williamson and Ouchi 1981a and 1981b versus Perrow 1981). At worst, these sets of disciplines ignore each other.

There is little doubt that both organizational economists, on the one hand, and organizational behavior and theory scholars, on the other, bear responsibility for the limited integration that has developed between these fields so far. More behaviorally oriented scholars have often adopted an overly simplistic view of organizational economics, asserting that organizational economists all assume perfect rationality (which they don't), perfect information (which they don't), and equilibrium (which they don't). Economically oriented scholars criticize the 'fuzzy' and 'ill-defined' assumptions of behavioral research, despite applying many of those same assumptions (e.g. imperfect information, bounded rationality) in their own research.

One can only hope that discourse among these organizational scholars will continue, and that the real opportunities for bringing behavioral research into organizational economics, and an economic orientation into organizational behavior and organization theory, will be fully realized.

NOTE

1 The assumption of opportunism may be new to economics, but as Douglas (1990) notes, it is more familiar to organization theorists. Indeed, notions of opportunism are central to resource dependence theory in particular and to power theories in general.

REFERENCES

Alchian, A.A. and Demsetz, H. (1972) 'Production, information costs, and economic organization', *American Economic Review*, 62: 777–95.

Amihud, Y. and Lev, B. (1981) 'Risk reduction as a managerial motive for conglomerate mergers', *Bell Journal of Economics*, 12: 605–16.

Anderson, E. (1985) 'The salesperson as outside agent or employee', 4: 234–54.

Anderson, E. and Schmittlein, D. (1984) 'Integration of the sales force: an empirical examination', *Rand Journal of Economics*, 15: 385–95.

Argawal, A. and Mandelker, G. (1987) 'Managerial incentives and corporate investment and financing decisions', *Journal of Finance*, 42: 823–37.

Armour, H.O. and Teece, D.J. (1978) 'Organizational structure and economic performance', *Bell Journal of Economics*, 9: 106–22.

Armour, H.O. and Teece, D.J. (1980) 'Vertical integration and technological innovation', *Review of Economics and Statistics*, 60: 470–4.

Arrow, K.J. (1974) *The Limits of Organization*. New York: W.W. Norton.

Arrow, K.J. (1985) 'The economics of agency', in *Principals and Agents: the Structure of American Business*. Boston: Harvard Business School Press.

Arthur, W., Ermolieve, U. and Kaniovsky, Y. (1987) 'Path dependent processes and the emergence of macro structure', *European Journal of Operations Research*, 30: 294–303.

Axelrod, R. (1984) *The Evolution of Cooperation*. New York: Basic Books.

Bain, J.S. (1956) *Barriers to New Competition*. Cambridge, MA: Harvard University Press.

Baker, W.E. and Faulkner, R.R. (1991) 'Role as resource in the Hollywood film industry', *American Journal of Sociology*, 97: 279–309.

Barney, J.B. (1986a) 'Types of competition and the theory of strategy', *Academy of Management Review*, 11: 791–800.

Barney, J.B. (1986b) 'Strategic factor markets: expectations, luck, and business strategy', *Management Science*, 42: 1231–41.

Barney, J.B. (1986c) 'Organizational culture: can it be a source of sustained competitive advantage?', *Academy of Management Review*, 11: 656–65.

Barney, J.B. (1990) 'The debate between traditional management theory and organizational economics: substantive differences or inter-group conflict?', *Academy of Management Review*, 15: 382–93.

Barney, J.B. (1991) 'Firm resources and sustained competitive advantage', *Journal of Management*, 17: 99–120.

Barney, J.B. (1994) 'What is an attractive industry?', *Praktisk Okonomi og Ledelse*: 71–81.

Barney, J.B. (1995) *Advanced Strategic Management*. Reading, MA: Addison-Wesley.

Barney, J.B. and Hansen, M. (1995) 'Trustworthiness

as a source of competitive advantage', *Strategic Management Journal*, 15: 175–90.

Barney, J.B. and Hoskisson, R.E. (1989) 'Strategic groups: untested assertions and research proposals', *Managerial and Decision Economics*, 11: 187–98.

Barney, J.B. and Ouchi, W.G. (1986) *Organizational Economics: Toward a New Paradigm for Understanding and Studying Organizations*. San Francisco: Jossey-Bass.

Bartlett, C.A. and Ghoshal, S. (1993) 'Beyond the M-form: toward a managerial theory of the firm', *Strategic Management Journal*, 14(S2): 23–46.

Baumol, W.J., Panzar, J.C. and Willig, R.P. (1982) *Contestable Markets and the Theory of Industry Structure*. San Diego, CA: Harcourt Brace Jovanovich.

Bertrand, J. (1883) 'Theorie mathematique de la richesse sociale', *Journal des Savants*: 499–508.

Bethel, J.E. and Liebeskind, J. (1993) 'The effects of ownership structure on corporate restructuring', *Strategic Management Journal*, 14: 15–32.

Bettis, R.A. (1991) 'Strategic management and the straightjacket: an editorial essay', *Organization Science*, 2: 315–19.

Bhagat, S., Shleifer, A. and Vishny, R. (1990) 'Hostile takeovers in the 1980s: the return to corporate specialization', *The Brookings Papers on Economic Activity: Microeconomics*: 1–84.

Blair, R.D. and Kaserman, D.L. (1983) *Law and Economics of Vertical Integration and Control*. New York: Academic Press.

Bradach, J.L. and Eccles, R.G. (1989) 'Price, authority, and trust: from ideal types to plural forms', *Annual Review of Sociology*, 15: 97–118.

Brickley, J.A. and Dark, F. (1987) 'The choice of organizational form: the case of franchising', *Journal of Financial Economics*, 18: 401–20.

Brickley, J.A., Dark, F. and Weisbach, M. (1991) 'The economic effects of franchise termination laws', *Journal of Law and Economics*, 34: 101–32.

Brickley, J.A., Coles, J.L. and Terry, R.L. (1994) 'The board of directors and the enactment of poison pills', *Journal of Financial Economics*, 35: 371–90.

Buckley, P.J. and Casson, M. (1976) *The Future of the Multinational Enterprise*. London: Longman.

Cable, J. and Dirrheimer, M.J. (1983) 'Hierarchies and markets: an empirical test of the multidivisional hypothesis in West Germany', *International Journal of Industrial Organization*, 1: 43–62.

Cable, J. and Yasuki, H. (1985) 'Internal organization, business groups and corporate performance: an empirical test of the multidivisional hypothesis in Japan', *International Journal of Industrial Organization*, 3: 401–20.

Caves, R.E. and Porter, M.E. (1977) 'From entry barriers to mobility barriers: conjectural decisions and contrived deterrence to new competition', *Quarterly Journal of Economics*, 91: 241–62.

Caves, R.E. and Bradburd, R.M. (1988) 'The empirical determinants of vertical integration', *Journal of Economic Behavior and Organization*, 9: 265–79.

Chamberlain, E.H. (1933) *The Theory of Monopolistic Competition*. Cambridge, MA: Harvard University Press.

Chandler, A.D. (1962) *Strategy and Structure: Chapters in the History of the American Industrial Enterprise*. Cambridge, MA: MIT Press.

Coase, R.H. (1937) 'The nature of the firm', *Economica*, 4: 386–405.

Coase, R.H. (1972) 'Industrial organization: a proposal for research', in *Policy Issues and Research Opportunities in Industrial Organization*. New York: National Bureau of Economic Research.

Conner, K.R. (1991) 'A historical comparison of resource-based theory and five schools of thought within industrial organization economics: do we have a new theory of the firm?', *Journal of Management*, 17: 121–54.

Copeland, T.E. and Weston, J.F. (1983) *Financial Theory and Corporate Policy*. Reading, MA: Addison-Wesley.

Cournot, A. (1897) *Research into the Mathematical Principles of the Theory of Wealth*. New York: Macmillan.

Cyert, R.M. and March, J.G. (1963) *A Behavioral Theory of the Firm*. Englewood Cliffs, NJ: Prentice-Hall.

Davis, G.F. (1991) 'Agents without principles? The spread of the poison pill through the intercorporate network', *Administrative Science Quarterly*, 36: 583–613.

Demsetz, H. (1988) 'The theory of the firm revisited', *Journal of Law, Economics, and Organization*, 4: 141–62.

Demsetz, H. (1990) *Ownership, Control, and the Firm*. Oxford: Basil Blackwell.

Dierickx, I. and Cool, K. (1989) 'Asset stock accumulation and sustainability of competitive advantage', *Management Science*, 35: 1504–11.

DiMaggio, P. and Powell, W. (1983) 'The iron cage revisited: institutional isomorphism and collective rationality in organizational fields', *American Sociological Review*, 48: 147–60.

Donaldson, L. (1990) 'The ethereal hand: organizational economics and management theory', *Academy of Management Review*, 15: 369–81.

Douglas, M. (1990) 'Converging on autonomy: anthropology and institutional economics', *Organization Theory: From Chester Barnard to the Present and Beyond*. Oxford: Oxford University Press.

Dow, G.K. (1985) 'Internal bargaining and strategic innovation in the theory of the firm', *Journal of Economic Behavior and Organization*, 6: 301–20.

Dow, G.K. (1987) 'The function of authority in transaction cost economics', *Journal of Economic Behavior and Organization*, 8: 13–38.

Eccles, R.G. (1981) 'The quasifirm in the construction industry', *Journal of Economic Behavior and Organization*, 2: 335–58.

Eisenhardt, K.M. (1985) 'Control: organizational and economic approaches', *Management Science*, 31: 134–49.

Eisenhardt, K.M. (1988) 'Agency and institutional theory explanations: the case of retail sales compensation', *Academy of Management Journal*, 31: 488–511.

Eisenhardt, K.M. (1989) 'Agency theory: as assessment and review', *Academy of Management Review*, 14: 57–74.

Faith, R.L., Higgins, R.S. and Tollison, R.D. (1984) 'Managerial rents and outside recruitment in the Coasian firm', *American Economic Review*, 74: 660–72.

Fama, E.F. (1970) 'Efficient capital markets: a review of theory and empirical work', *Journal of Finance*, 25: 383–417.

Fama, E.F. (1980) 'Agency problems and the theory of the firm', *Journal of Political Economy*, 88: 288–307.

Fama, E.F. and Jensen, M.C. (1983) 'Separation of ownership and control', *Journal of Law and Economics*, 26: 301–26.

Fladmoe-Lindquist, K. and Jacque, L. (1995) 'Control modes in international service operations: the propensity to franchise', *Management Science*, 41.

Fruin, W.M. (1992) *The Japanese Enterprise System: Competitive Strategies and Cooperative Structures*. Oxford: Oxford University Press.

Ghemawat, P. (1986) 'WalMart Stores' discount operations', Harvard Business School Case no. 9–387-018.

Ghemawat, P. and Stander, H. (1993) 'Nucor at a crossroads', Harvard Business School Case no. 9–793-039.

Granovetter, M. (1985) 'Economic action and social structure', *American Journal of Sociology*, 91.

Grinblatt, M. and Titman, S. (1987) 'How clients can win the gaming game', *Journal of Portfolio Management*, 13: 14–20.

Grinyer, P.H., Yassai-Ardekani, M. and Al-Bazza, S. (1980) 'Strategy, structure, the environment, and financial performance in 48 United Kingdom companies', *Academy of Management Journal*, 23: 193–220.

Grossman, S. and Hart, O. (1986) 'The costs and benefits of ownership: a theory of vertical and lateral integration', *Journal of Political Economy*, 94: 691–719.

Hallowell, R. and Heskett, J. (1993) 'Southwest Airlines', Harvard Business School Case no. 9–694-023.

Hannan, M. and Freeman, J. (1977) 'The population ecology of organizations', *American Journal of Sociology*, 82: 929–64.

Hansen, G.S. and Wernerfelt, B. (1989) 'Determinants of firm performance: the relative importance of economic and organizational factors', *Strategic Management Journal*, 10: 399–411.

Harrigan, K. (1986) *Money for Joint Venture Success*. Lexington, MA: Lexington Books.

Harris, B.C. (1983) *Organization: the Effect of Large Corporations*. Ann Arbor, MI: University of Michigan Press.

Hennart, J.-F. (1982) *A Theory of Multinational Enterprise*. Ann Arbor, MI: University of Michigan Press.

Hennart, J.-F. (1988) 'A transactions cost theory of equity joint ventures', *Strategic Management Journal*, 9: 361–74.

Hennart, J.-F. (1991) 'The transaction cost theory of joint ventures: an empirical study of Japanese subsidiaries in the United States', *Management Science*, 37: 483–97.

Hennart, J.-F. (1993) 'Explaining the swollen middle: why most transactions are a mix of "Market" and "Hierarchy"', *Organization Science*, 4: 529–47.

Hesterly, W.S., Liebeskind, J. and Zenger, T.R. (1990) 'Organizational economics: an impending revolution in organization theory', *Academy of Management Review*, 15: 402–20.

Hesterly, W.S. and Zenger, T.R. (1993) 'The myth of a monolithic economics: fundamental assumptions and the use of economic models in policy and strategy research', *Organization Science*, 4: 496–510.

Hill, C.W.L. (1985) 'Internal organization and enterprise performance', *Managerial and Decision Economics*, 6: 210–16.

Hill, C.W.L. (1988) 'Internal capital market controls and financial performance in multidivisional firms', *Journal of Industrial Economics*, 37: 67–83.

Hill, C.W.L. and Snell, S.A. (1989) 'Effects of ownership structure and control on corporate productivity', *Academy of Management Journal*, 32: 25–46.

Hirsch, P.M., Friedman, R. and Koza, M.P. (1990) 'Collaboration or paradigm shift? *Caveat emptor* and the risk of romance with economic models for strategy and policy research', *Organization Science*, 1: 87–98.

Holl, P. (1983) 'Discretionary behaviour and the M-form hypothesis in large UK firms'. Paper presented at the annual conference of the European Association for Research in Industrial Economics. Bergen, Norway.

Hoskisson, R.E. and Galbraith, C.S. (1985) 'The effect of quantum versus incremental M-form reorganization: a time series exploration of intervention dynamics', *Journal of Management*, 11: 55–70.

Hoskisson, R.E., Harrison, J.S. and Dubosky, D.A. (1991) 'Capital market evaluation of M-form implementation and diversification strategy', *Strategic Management Journal*, 12: 271–9.

Hoskisson, R.E. and Johnson, R.E. (1992) 'Corporate restructuring and strategic change: the effect of diversification strategy and R&D intensity', *Strategic Management Journal*, 13: 625–34.

Hoskisson, R.E. and Turk, T.A. (1990) 'Corporate restructuring: governance and control limits of the internal market', *Academy of Management Review*, 15: 459–77.

Hoskisson, R.E., Hill, C.W.L. and Kim, H. (1993) 'The multidivisional structure: organizational fossil or source of value?', *Journal of Management*, 19: 269–98.

Jacobson, R. (1988) 'The persistence of abnormal returns', *Strategic Management Journal*, 9: 415–30.

Jacobson, R. (1992) 'The "Austrian" school of strategy', *Academy of Management Review*, 17: 782–807.

Jarrell, G.A., Brickley, J.A. and Netter, J.M. (1988) 'The market for corporate control: the empirical evidence since 1980', *Journal of Economic Perspectives*, 2: 49–68.

Jensen, M.C. and Meckling, W.H. (1976) 'Theory of the firm: managerial behavior, agency costs and ownership structure', *Journal of Financial Economics*, 3: 305–60.

Jensen, M.C. and Ruback, R.S. (1983) 'The market for corporate control: the scientific evidence', *Journal of Financial Economics*, 11: 5–50.

John, G. and Weitz, B.A. (1988) 'Forward integration into distribution: an empirical test of the transaction cost analysis', *Journal of Law, Economics, and Organization*, 4: 337–55.

Jones, G.P. and Hill, C.W.L. (1988) 'Transaction cost analysis of strategy-structure choice', *Strategic Management Journal*, 9: 159–72.

Joskow, P.L. (1985) 'Vertical integration and long term contracts: the case of coal-burning electric generating plants', *Journal of Law, Economics, and Organization*, 1: 33–80.

Joskow, P.L. (1988) 'Asset specificity and the structure of vertical relationships', *Journal of Law, Economics, and Organization*, 4: 95–117.

Kogut, B. (1988) 'Joint ventures: theoretical and empirical perspectives', *Strategic Management Journal*, 9: 319–32.

Kogut, B. (1991) 'Joint ventures and the option to expand and acquire', *Management Science*, 37: 19–33.

Kogut, B. and Zander, U. (1992) 'Knowledge of the firm, combinative capabilities, and the replication of technology', *Organization Science*, 3: 383–97.

Kosnik, R.D. (1987) 'Greenmail: a study of board performance in corporate governance', *Administrative Science Quarterly*, 32: 163–85.

Lazear, E.P. (1986) 'Salaries and piece rates', *Journal of Business*, 59: 405–31.

Levy, D.T. (1985) 'The transactions cost approach to vertical integration: an empirical investigation', *Review of Economics and Statistics*, 67: 438–45.

Lippman, S. and Rumelt, R. (1982) 'Uncertain imitability: an analysis of interfirm differences in efficiency under competition', *Bell Journal of Economics*, 13: 418–38.

MacDonald, J.M. (1985) 'Market exchange or vertical integration: an empirical analysis', 67: 327–31.

MacMillan, I., Hambrick, D.C. and Pennings, J.M. (1986) 'Uncertainty reduction and the threat of supplier retaliation: two views of the backward integration decision', *Organization Studies*, 7: 263–78.

Mahoney, J.T. (1992) 'The choice of organizational form: vertical financial ownership versus other methods of vertical integration', *Strategic Management Journal*, 13: 559–84.

Mahoney, J.M. and Mahoney, J.T. (1993) 'An empirical investigation of the effect of corporate charter antitakeover amendments on stockholder wealth', *Strategic Management Journal*, 14: 17–31.

Mallette, P. and Fowler, K. (1992) 'Effects of board composition and stock ownership on the adoption of poison pills', *Academy of Management Journal*, 35: 1010–35.

March, J.G. and Simon, H.A. (1958) *Organizations*. New York: Wiley.

Mariotti, S. and Cairnarca, G.C. (1986) 'The evolution of transaction governance in the textile clothing industry', *Journal of Economic Behavior and Organization*, 7: 351–74.

Marris, R. (1964) *The Economic Theory of Managerial Capitalism*. Glencoe, IL: Free Press.

Mason, E.S. (1959) *The Corporation in Modern Society*. Cambridge, MA: Harvard University Press.

Masten, S.E. (1988) 'A legal basis of the firm', *Journal of Law, Economics, and Organization*, 4: 181–98.

Masten, S.E., Meehan, J.W. and Snyder, E.A. (1991) 'The costs of organization', *Journal of Law, Economics, and Organization*, 7: 1–25.

McLaughlin, K.J. (1988) 'Aspects of tournament models: a survey', in *Research in Labor Economics*. Greenwich, CT: JAI Press.

Milgrom, P. and Roberts, J. (1988) 'An economic approach to influence activities in organizations', *American Journal of Sociology*, 94 (Supplement): S154–79.

Mintzberg, H. (1983) *Power in and around Organizations*. Englewood Cliffs, NJ: Prentice-Hall.

Moe, T.M. (1991) 'Politics and the theory of organization', *Journal of Law, Economics, and Organization*, 7: 106–30.

Murphy, K.J. (1986) 'Incentives, learning, and compensation: a theoretical and empirical investigation of managerial labor contracts', *Rand Journal of Economics*, 17: 59–76.

Nanda, A. and Bartlett, C. (1990) 'Corning Incorporated: a network of alliances'. Harvard Business School Case no. 9–391–102.

Nelson, R.R. and Winter, S.G. (1982) *The Evolutionary Theory of the Firm*. Cambridge, MA: Harvard University Press.

Nishiguchi, T. (1994) *Strategic Industrial Sourcing: the Japanese Advantage*. Oxford: Oxford University Press.

Ollinger, M. (1993) *Organizational Form and Business Strategy in the U.S. Petroleum Industry*. Lanham: University Press of America.

Ouchi, W.G. (1979) 'A conceptual framework for the design of organizational control mechanisms', *Management Science*, 25: 838–48.

Ouchi, W.G. (1980) 'Markets, bureaucracies, and clans', *Administrative Science Quarterly*, 25: 129–41.

Penrose, E. (1959) *The Theory of the Growth of the Firm.* Oxford: Basil Blackwell.

Perrow, C. (1981) 'Markets, hierarchies, and hegemony: a critique of Chandler and Williamson,' in A. Van de Ven and J. Joyce (eds), *Perspectives on Organization Design and Behavior.* New York: Wiley. pp. 347–70.

Perrow, C. (1986) *Complex Organizations: A Critical Essay.* New York: Random House.

Peteraf, M.A. (1993) 'The cornerstones of competitive advantage: a resource-based view', *Strategic Management Journal*, 14: 179–92.

Pfeffer, J. and Salancik, G. (1978) *The External Control of Organizations.* New York: Harper and Row.

Porter, M.E. (1974) 'Note on the structural analysis of industries'. Harvard Business School Case no. 9–376–054.

Porter, M.E. (1979a) 'How competitive forces shape strategy', *Harvard Business Review*, 57: 137–56.

Porter, M.E. (1979b) 'The structure within industries and companies' performance', *Review of Economics and Statistics*, 61: 214–27.

Porter, M.E. (1980) *Competitive Strategy.* New York: Free Press.

Porter, M.E. (1981) 'The contributions of industrial organization to strategic management', *Academy of Management Review*, 6: 609–20.

Porter, M.E. (1985) *Competitive Advantage.* New York: Free Press.

Porter, M.E. (1990) *The Competitive Advantage of Nations.* New York: Free Press.

Powell, W.W. (1987) 'Hybrid organizational arrangements', *California Management Review*, 30 (Fall): 67–87.

Prahalad, C.K. and Bettis, R.A. (1986) 'The dominant logic: a new linkage between diversity and performance', *Strategic Management Journal*, 7: 484–502.

Pratt, J.W. and Zeckhauser, R.J. (1985) 'Principals and agents: an overview', in *Principals and Agents: the Structure of American Business.* Boston: Harvard Business School Press.

Putterman, L. (1984) 'On recent explanations of why capital hires labor', *Economic Inquiry*, 22: 171–87.

Ravenscraft, D.M. and Scherer, F.M. (1987) *Mergers, Sell-offs, and Economic Efficiency.* Washington, DC: Brookings Institution.

Reed, R. and DeFillippi, R. (1990) 'Causal ambiguity, barriers to imitation, and sustainable competitive advantage', *Academy of Management Review*, 15: 88–102.

Reger, R. and Huff, A. (1993) 'Strategic groups: a cognitive perspective', *Strategic Management Journal*, 14: 103–24.

Ring, P.S. and Van de Ven, A.H. (1992) 'Structuring cooperative relationships between organizations', *Strategic Management Journal*, 13: 483–98.

Robins, J.A. (1987) 'Organizational economics: notes on the use of transaction-cost theory in the study of organizations', *Administrative Science Quarterly*, 32: 68–86.

Robinson, J. (1933) *Economics of Imperfect Competition.* London: Macmillan.

Ruback, R.S. (1988) 'An overview of takeover defenses', *Mergers and Acquisitions.* Chicago: University of Chicago Press.

Rugman, A.M. (1981) *Inside the Multinationals.* London: Croom Helm.

Rumelt, R.P. (1984) 'Toward a strategic theory of the firm', in *Competitive Strategic Management.* Englewood Cliffs, NJ: Prentice-Hall.

Rumelt, R.P. (1991) 'How much does industry matter?', *Strategic Management Journal*, 12: 167–86.

Rumelt, R.P., Schendel, D. and Teece, D. (1991) 'Strategic management and economics', *Strategic Management Journal*, 12: 5–29.

Saxenian, A. (1994) *Regional Advantage.* Cambridge, MA: Harvard University Press.

Scherer, F.M. (1980) *Industrial Market Structure and Economic Performance.* Boston: Houghton Mifflin.

Schumpeter, J. (1934) *The Theory of Economic Development.* Cambridge, MA: Harvard University Press.

Shleifer, A. and Summers, L.H. (1988) 'Breach of trust in hostile takeovers', in *Corporate Takeovers: Causes and Consequences.* Chicago: University of Chicago Press.

Shleifer, A. and Vishny, R.W. (1991) 'Takeovers in the 60's and the 80's: evidence and implications', *Strategic Management Journal*, 12: 51–9.

Simon, H.A. (1947) *Administrative Behavior.* New York: Free Press.

Simon, H.A. (1964) 'On the concept of organizational goal', *Administrative Science Quarterly*, 9: 1–22.

Singh, H. and Harianto, F. (1989) 'Management–board relationships, takeover risk and the adoption of golden parachutes: an empirical investigation', *Academy of Management Journal*, 32: 7–24.

Spence, M. (1974) 'Competitive and optimal responses to signals', *Journal of Economic Theory*, 7: 298–315.

Steer, P. and Cable, J. (1978) 'Internal organization and profit: an empirical analysis of large U.K. companies', *Journal of Industrial Economics*, 27: 13–30.

Stiglitz, J. (1991) 'Symposium on organizations and economics', *Journal of Economic Perspectives*, 5: 15–24.

Stuckey, J. (1983) *Vertical Integration and Joint Ventures in the Aluminum Industry.* Cambridge, MA: Harvard University Press.

Teece, D.J. (1981) 'Internal organization and economic performance: an empirical analysis of the profitability of principal firms', *Journal of Industrial Economics*, 30: 173–99.

Teece, D.J. (1982) 'Towards an economic theory of the

multiproduct firm', *Journal of Economic Behavior and Organization*, 3: 39–63.

Teece, D.J. (1986) 'Transaction cost economics and the multinational enterprise: an assessment', *Journal of Economic Behavior and Organization*, 7: 21–45.

Thompson, R.S. (1981) 'Internal organization and profit: a note', *Journal of Industrial Economics*, 30: 201–11.

Thorelli, H.B. (1986) 'Networks, between markets and hierarchies', *Strategic Management Journal*, 7: 37–51.

Tirole, J. (1989) *The Theory of Industrial Organization*. Cambridge, MA: MIT Press.

Wade, J., O'Reilly, C.A. and Chandratat, I. (1990) 'Golden parachutes: CEOs and the exercise of social influence', *Administrative Science Quarterly*, 35: 587–603.

Walker, G. and Weber, D. (1984) 'A transaction cost approach to make-or-buy decisions', *Administrative Science Quarterly*, 29: 373–91.

Walker, G. and Weber, D. (1987) 'Supplier competition, uncertainty, and make-or-buy decisions', *Academy of Management Journal*, 30: 589–96.

Walking, R. and Long, M. (1984) 'Agency theory, managerial welfare, and takeover bid resistance', *Rand Journal of Economics*, 15: 54–68.

Weingast, B.R. and Marshall, W. (1988) 'The industrial organization of congress', *Journal of Political Economy*, 96: 132–63.

Weisbach, M.S. (1988) 'Outside directors and CEO turnover', *Journal of Financial Economics*, 20: 431–60.

Wernerfelt, B. (1984) 'A resource-based view of the firm', *Strategic Management Journal*, 5: 171–80.

Williamson, O.E. (1964) *The Economics of Discretionary Behavior: Managerial Objectives in a Theory of the Firm*. Englewood Cliffs, NJ: Prentice-Hall.

Williamson, O.E. (1970) *Corporate Control and Business Behavior*. Englewood Cliffs, NJ: Prentice-Hall.

Williamson, O.E. (1975) *Markets and Hierarchies: Analysis and Antitrust Implications*. New York: Free Press.

Williamson, O.E. (1985) *The Economic Institutions of Capitalism: Firms, Markets, Relational Contracting*. New York: Free Press.

Williamson, O.E. (1991a) 'Comparative economic organization: the analysis of discrete structural alternatives', in *Administrative Science Quarterly*, 36: 269–96.

Williamson, O.E. (1991b) 'Strategizing, economizing, and economic organization', *Strategic Management Journal*, 12 (Special Winter): 75–94.

Williamson, O.E. (1991c) 'Economic institutions: spontaneous and intentional governance', *Journal of Law, Economics, and Organization*, 7: 159–87.

Williamson, O.E. (1993a) 'Calculativeness, trust, and economic organization', 36: 453–86.

Williamson, O.E. (1993b) 'Transaction cost economics and organization theory', *Industrial and Corporate Change*, 2: 107–56.

Williamson, O.E. and Ouchi, W. (1981a) 'The markets and hierarchies program of research: origins, implications, prospects', in A. Van de Ven and J. Joyce (eds), *Perspectives on Organization Design and Behavior*. New York: Wiley.

Williamson, O.E. and Ouchi, W. (1981b) 'A rejoinder', in A. Van de Ven and J. Joyce (eds), *Perspectives on Organization Design and Behavior*. New York: Wiley.

Winship, C. and Rosen, S. (1988) 'Introduction: sociological and economic approaches to the analysis of social structure', *American Journal of Sociology*, 94: S1–16.

Zenger, T.R. (1992) 'Why do employers only reward extreme performance? Examining the relationships among performance, pay, and turnover', *Administrative Science Quarterly*, 37: 198–219.

Zenger, T.R. (1994) 'Understanding organizational diseconomies of scale: the allocation of engineering talent, ideas, and effort by firm size', *Management Science*, 40.

1.5

The Individual in Organizational Studies: the Great Disappearing Act?

WALTER R. NORD AND SUZY FOX

This chapter reviews major developments about psychological factors and processes in organizational studies. We suggest that a profound but until now under-recognized change has taken place in this component of organizational studies. This change concerns assumptions about the appropriate primary level of analysis from the individual (psychological) level to the meso level.

Traditionally, the domain of psychology has been the individual and the quest to uncover the essential properties and universal features of the typical human being. Under this domain major areas of interest included: personality, motivation, attitudes and learning. Since to a considerable extent, organization studies, especially its micro component, was founded on psychology, these topics and the methodologies associated with them became central to organizational studies. While these topics continue to serve as headings for structuring knowledge in organization studies, emphasis has shifted from viewing individuals independently of context to consideration of the interplay between individuals and their contexts.

Before going further, we emphasize that this conclusion was reached inductively through review of the recent literature on the micro side of organizational studies and psychology proper. We did not set out with a conscious purpose of documenting such a reorientation. Rather we set out to review the literature and more or less were bombarded by information that made this reorientation appear to be the major movement in the field.

When we began, we expected that the chapter would provide a comprehensive summary of what is known about the major characteristics of a typical human being – centering on the traditional dimensions of personality, motivation, attitudes and learning. In short, we were directed to what Simon (1990) called a search for invariants. However, we soon realized that a search for invariants would not be a fruitful approach for making sense of the recent literature in the field, because the individual as viewed traditionally was disappearing in the field. Indeed it was this realization that we advance as the major contribution of this chapter about psychological factors in contemporary organization studies.

The chapter consists of three major sections and a conclusion. The first section summarizes the evidence supporting the 'disappearance' of the individual and the parallel growth of attention to mutually determining processes. The second section considers possible objections to the thesis that the individual has disappeared and attempts to refute that thesis by advancing an opposite one – i.e. 'The individual is alive and well.' The third section examines trends in psychology and the social sciences more generally that also suggest the individual's disappearance.

THE INDIVIDUAL'S DISAPPEARANCE IN INDUSTRIAL AND ORGANIZATIONAL PSYCHOLOGY AND BEHAVIOR

Recent publications in organizational psychology and behavior reveal that the individual has become less central in these fields. This section starts with a historical review of the individual's position, beginning with the centrality of psychology in the development of organizational behavior and ending with the recent growth in attention to context. The centerpiece of this review is a longitudinal study of relevant chapters published during the two most recent decades in the *Annual Review of Psychology* (*ARP*).[1] This review indicates a clear decline in the centrality of the individual's role. Since the magnitude of this development surprised us, in the next subsection we summarize our search for confirmation of this finding by seeing if others have noticed the disappearance of the individual. Since this exploration supported our finding, we turn in the final subsection to describing the major view that appears to be emerging, a view that studies the individual and context as components of mutually determining processes.

From Individual to Context

Psychological Basis for OB and this Research

At least in America, the individual had long been central in the study of organizations, even though for some time organizational sociologists had advanced the idea that the 'subject is organizations' (Scott 1992). This qualification aside, major streams of thought about organizations including both Taylorism and the human relations movement were founded on special views of and assumptions about human nature. Moreover, psychologists such as Hugo Munsterberg played an important role in early efforts to help organizational leaders most effectively utilize the human beings they employed. Then, as the fields of personnel and management moved towards a more scientific foundation and American schools of business began to teach organization behavior instead of personnel or human relations, psychology was one of the first disciplines to be tapped. As the emerging field consciously drew on American psychology for personnel as well as ideas and categories, it unconsciously took American psychology's assumptions as organizational behaviorists employed concepts and categories (e.g. motivation, perception, cognition, emotions) borrowed from psychology to structure their knowledge. Indeed the early pioneers of OB such as Douglas McGregor and Chris Argyris built directly on assumptions borrowed from psychology.

Consequently we initiated our study of the individual in organization studies in the psychologically oriented literature. We began with mainstream publications: specifically, the progression of reviews in the *Annual Review of Psychology* (ARP), the *Handbook of Industrial and Organizational Psychology*, particularly Raymond Katzell's overview of the contributions in the second edition, and the special issue on organizational psychology of the *American Psychologist* edited by Offerman and Gowing (1990). We expected that these major reviews would provide a good reading of what was playing in the major theaters – reviews of the shows 'On Broadway' so to speak.

One trend is clear: from the late 1970s to date, in OB and I/O psychology the individual had lost much of its traditional status – contextual dimensions had become much more salient. By context we mean attributes of the physical and social systems in which individuals exist. Those attributes may be analyzed at a number of levels including: physical stimuli that directly impact the individual, and social and political levels that affect the presence of the physical stimuli and the interpretation of them and the events they compose. For example, in introducing the special issue on organizational psychology in the *American Psychologist*, Offerman and Gowing (1990) noted the heightened importance of such dimensions as cohort size, sex, and age for dealing with the 'changing work force'. They wrote: 'The notion of America as a melting pot is giving way to a view of America as a rich assortment of different talents to be preserved rather than homogenized. The traditional organizational focus on conformity through assimilation needs to be replaced by a true understanding of integration' (1990: 98). Although the large inflow of immigrants in the late nineteenth and early twentieth century meant that the American workforce had long been diverse, Offerman and Gowing's call revealed that these differences could no longer be swept under the rug of 'invariant' principles promised by academic psychology. Using Gestalt terms, in I/O psychology the variations introduced by context had increasingly become part of the figure and not merely the ground.

Several signs of figure/ground reversal were evident in this issue. First, Offerman and Gowing's call for greater interdisciplinary training for I/O psychologists was particularly noteworthy. Similarly, Schein observed: 'I do not see a unique role for the traditional industrial/ organizational psychologist, but I see great potential for the psychologist to work as a team member with colleagues who are more ethnographically oriented' (1990: 118). Furthermore, writing on work motivation, Katzell and Thompson pointed to the overly simplistic theories of work motivation that dominated the field and called for greater attention to approaches dealing with 'problems of matching motivational practices to the needs and values of diverse groups of employees' (1990: 144).

Similarly, Morrison and Von Glinow (1990) observed that psychologically driven inquiries have inappropriately emphasized person-centered variables to explain women's low job status.

Longitudinal study of the *Annual Review of Psychology* (*ARP*) revealed even stronger evidence for the displacement of the individual in the OB and I/O psychology literature.

Individual in ARP: a Longitudinal View

Initially we studied *ARP* to obtain a broad picture of the field, not to examine a particular question such as what had happened to the individual. As we have noted, that question and our answer to it emerged inductively, as we progressed. Unfortunately using *ARP* for such a longitudinal study is complicated by the fact that the chapters dealing with topics in organizational studies have appeared under a variety of titles: industrial psychology, industrial and organizational psychology, human resources, organizational behavior, to name a few. Still, looking at these topics together reveals an amazingly clear trend of deemphasizing the individual and giving increasing emphasis to context.

This trend is evidenced in the changing chapter titles and definitions of the subject matter. Beginning at the end, the major theme of Jackson and Schuler's (1995) chapter entitled 'Understanding human resource management in the *context* of organizations and their environments' (italics added) was a call to recognize context. Jackson and Schuler conceptualized HRM as 'an umbrella term encompassing (a) specific human resources practices such as recruitment, selection, and appraisal; (b) formal human resource policies, which direct and partially constrain the development of specific practices; and (c) overarching human resource philosophies' (1995: 238). In addressing these somewhat traditional concerns while guided by their belief that 'To understand HRM in context we must consider how these three components of HRM are affected by the internal and external environments of organizations' (1995: 238) Jackson and Schuler proposed broadening the scope for HRM substantially.

Viewed historically, Jackson and Schuler's call for context was part of a long chain in *ARP* that is most easily traced to Cummings's (1982) chapter which explicitly tried to bring the macro side of the field into focus. However, the trend predated Cummings's chapter. Mitchell (1979) had discussed a number of comments about the lack of context in the field. Even earlier, Meltzer (1971) had noted a broadening trend in *ARP*'s industrial psychology chapters during the 1960s. Meltzer pointed to a growing interdisciplinary emphasis, as indicated by a decrease in the percentage of references to the two most frequently cited journals *Personnel Psychology* and the *Journal of Applied Psychology*.

During the 1960s Quinn and Kahn (1967) exemplified this trend, entitling their annual review chapter 'Organizational psychology'. Stating that this was not simply another name for industrial psychology, Quinn and Kahn stressed the importance of general systems theory and drew far more heavily than previous reviewers on the sociological literature. Still, industrial psychology as portrayed in *ARP* and elsewhere was quite narrow. Meltzer and Nord (1973) observed that even Quinn and Kahn's more broadly based review and Vroom's (1974) chapter entitled 'Industrial social psychology' in the second edition of Lindzey and Aronson's *Handbook of Social Psychology* had remarkably psychological orientations, at least by comparison to the interdisciplinary study of organizations reflected in March's (1965) *Handbook of Organizations*. Still, a broadening trend in *ARP* had begun in the 1960s.

Soon after, in their chapter on personnel and human resources Heller and Clark (1976) took an important next step. They proposed an open systems model and located the personnel function at the boundary between the organization and the external environment. Despite this move, they concluded that while 'The literature relevant to the personnel function reflects a diversity of approaches ... *the unit of study is characteristically the individual*' (1976: 428, italics added).

In the period following this chapter, the broadening trend was only gradual. In fact, Mitchell writing the first *ARP* chapter entitled 'Organizational behavior', even though agreeing with the field's critics that insufficient attention had been given to contextual matters and that 'our theories are often too narrow in focus' (1979: 271), adopted a primarily psychological framework and featured major sections on personality and individual differences, job attitudes, motivation. After 1979, however, emphasis on context progressed more rapidly. In order to capture the developments between 1977 and 1981 which had given organizational behavior a macro flavor, Cummings (1982) needed to employ new concepts. He concluded by calling for even more attention to the context of individual behavior and the study of linking processes, i.e. 'the processes that link individual and social system levels of analysis' (1982: 571). Notably, in the following decade linking processes received so much attention that Mowday and Sutton (1993) subtitled their *ARP* chapter on organizational behavior '*Linking individuals and groups to organizational contexts*' (italics added).

However, between 1982 and 1993, the field seemed to need to digest the changes. Staw's (1984) and Schneider's (1985) *ARP* chapters reflected this digestion. Staw recognized that organization behavior was now both micro and macro; micro OB was broader than I/O psychology. However, micro and macro had not been interwoven. Staw wrote: 'most research is still distinctly psychological or sociological in its approach to variables and levels of analysis' (1984: 628). Staw recognized the possible benefits of moving to the study of processes, but he explicitly focused on the micro or psychological side of things and called for reformulation of the field's dependent variables through recognition of the restricted set of assumptions on which existing research had been based. Staw urged the field to move beyond the traditional polarizing question of whether micro or macro factors explained the most variance in favor of finding how to bring the two sides of the field together. He suggested such approaches as dissecting sociological constructs so as to specify their intermediate mechanisms in psychological terms, and conducting research focused on truly interdisciplinary topics such as organization innovation. He concluded that multi-level research is 'where the future of the field lies' (1984: 659).

Schneider (1985) too appeared to sense the need for the field to digest the new developments more completely. Since Schneider used historical works from the field as a framework for interpretation, his chapter provides an exceptionally helpful examination of organizational behavior's digestion of the smorgasbord before it in the early 1980s. Beginning by noting the ongoing tensions over levels of analysis (e.g. whether the proper focus should be on individuals and groups or the organization) Schneider attributed much of the problem to the lineage of I/O psychology on the one hand and of organization and management theory on the other. He suggested treating the reciprocity across the levels by recognizing that topics studied at one level of analysis are 'embedded in, *and affected by*, at least the next level of analysis' (1985: 597). However, 'affected by' did not mean moderated by; rather different levels of analysis have direct or linear effects on behavior. For example, group effectiveness is a direct function of characteristics of the group and also the larger context of the group itself.

Significantly, Schneider's conclusion stemmed from analysis of research on traditional OB topics: individual motivation, job attitudes, groups, leadership, climate and culture. Consider his discussion of motivation. Schneider observed that the early OB researchers on worker motivation assumed that universal theories of

motivation were possible, were very individually oriented and focused attention on individual differences. Ultimately, however, the researchers became disillusioned about universalistic motivation theories. 'The universal motivation theories of Argyris and McGregor are not thought of as motivation theories any longer; now they are theories of organization design, perhaps included under Quality of Work Life (QWL) rubric' (1985: 578). Schneider lamented: 'Without a macro-motivation construct, comparative organization behavior becomes *person-less*' (italics added); 'One could ask "What happened to motivation research?"' (1985: 578). Even on the one traditional motivation topic where research had continued – equity theory – attention had shifted to reflect awareness of context, reflecting Cosier and Dalton's (1983) observation of the failure of traditional equity research to take history into account.

Such trends extended beyond motivation. So many diverse relationships were found in job satisfaction research that Schneider bypassed trying to integrate them into a framework about individual wants. Instead he called for the more general study of person–environment fit. Furthermore, studies of role stress had moved towards understanding the linkages between organizations and member reactions, and had been broadened to include life–job relationships. Parallel broadening had occurred in the study of commitment with the addition of organizational citizenship (behavior beyond conventional job descriptions) to the research agenda.

Further, growing use of macro or organizational outcomes such as market and industry competitiveness as dependent variables had forced research on groups and leadership to attend to context. These shifts meant that less fine-grained micro data on individuals were required and new perspectives were needed. Schneider wrote: 'we change what we look at and how we look at it. We look at planets not atoms with a telescope' (1985: 587). Schneider noticed parallel changes in the study of leadership: 'as with motivation, 1983 was not a good year for more traditional topics of research: no papers appeared on behavior trait approaches' (1985: 588). He also recalled Leavitt's (1975) invitation to take groups not individuals as the assumed building blocks of organizations.

Despite these changes, the individual still received some attention; in fact, Schneider reported that the trait approach remained strong in assessment center research. However, the outlook for the traditional quest for predicting leadership and managerial behavior across settings was bleak. Schneider advised thinking about leader attributes guided by interactional psychology in order to recognize the role of personal dispositions while simultaneously expecting the same person will behave differently in different situations.

In sum, without saying so explicitly Schneider seemed to sense that the individual was disappearing. Schneider attributed the changes to a historical fluke: early research on motivation and leadership that was focused on the enterprise, 'somehow yielded research at the individual level of analysis' (1985: 590).

While this was true, it was not the whole truth. We suggest that some of the developments Schneider reviewed represented fundamental discontinuities, as the field moved to a more collective level of analysis and away from emphasis on the individual that is embedded in the American value system. Pfeffer's (1983) introduction of the demographic view with its provocative proposition that generational cohort differences were more important than other individual attributes was a big step away from tradition. Also, importantly in view of what the future would hold, Schneider noted the replacement of 'climate' by 'culture' in organizational research. This change was especially significant because it entailed greater emphasis on the study of meaning. While meaning is held by individuals, study of meaning directs attention to *transmission*, which is a property of systemic processes. In this vein, Schneider wrote: 'organizations are a viable behavioral unit of analysis' (1985: 597). Consequently, conducting research 'on individuals *as individuals* as the unit of analysis is important and interesting but not when trying to understand and predict an organization's behavior' (1985: 597). Thus, Schneider's chapter showed how the field was digesting the changes moving in a more macro direction.

Two years later in the next *ARP* chapter entitled 'Organizational behavior' House and Singh (1987) moved the individual further from the traditionally privileged position. Noting that previous *ARP* chapters had stressed the micro over the macro side, House and Singh emphasized cross-level effects, but warned that their emphasis was speculative and called for more research of this sort. They noted that while cross-level research was evident in the areas of management succession and decision-making, little such work had appeared in important segments of the power and leadership literatures. They called for more emphasis on historical and evolutionary study of organizational behavior, going beyond traditional efforts to establish empirical regularities. They held out special hope for study of macro-level processes of selection, imitation, learning and institutionalization to help answer the why and how of these cross-level relationships. Taken as a whole, their

chapter was a call to use certain macro-level processes to explain micro-level events. If this course were followed, the individual would not have disappeared, but would seem to have become more of a dependent than an independent variable.

In the succeeding review Ilgen and Klein (1988) dealt with the multi-level issue differently, seemingly giving more prominence to the individual, by drawing on the so-called[2] 'cognitive revolution' to place the multiple levels of organizations in individuals' minds. They advanced the qualified suggestion that the essences of organizations may be seen as products of the thoughts and actions of their members. They seemed to return the individual to center stage by asserting: 'All cognitive views share the assumption that people think and that their thoughts play a major role in human behavior' (1988: 329). Building on this assumption, Ilgen and Klein synthesized a wide variety of social and organizational topics into cognitive schemata that individuals use to interpret stimuli in organizations.

Despite their successful use of the cognitive perspective, Ilgen and Klein cautioned that the demonstrated strengths of the cognitive framework lay only in a few areas of the field, particularly person perception and leadership, and that 'the "cognitive revolution" has influenced very few topics in the field of OB and has often had a narrow impact within those that have been studied' (1988: 345). Moreover, even where the cognitive influence had been felt, so far the research had been primarily *demonstrative*, showing that the cognitive variables made sense for interpreting events that occur in organization settings. They warned, unless work moves beyond this demonstrative stage, cognitive processes will become little more than another passing fad. Thus, the return of the individual to center stage appeared tenuous.

Indeed, in the next OB chapter in *ARP*, O'Reilly (1991) revealed that the comeback of the individual had failed. Among other things, most frequently cited journals had shifted from the almost total reliance on psychological publications noted by Meltzer (1971) to the *Administrative Science Quarterly* and to journals published by the Academy of Management. O'Reilly observed an increased intersection of micro and macro interests, especially through the Academy of Management. Whereas in 1979, 70 per cent of the studies published in the *Academy of Management Journal* were on micro topics, by 1989 the comparable figure was only 38 per cent. Although O'Reilly's chapter still focused on micro OB, it revealed that these changes had diminished the individual's starring role. Most notable were changes in research on the topics that had guided Mitchell's (1979) *ARP* chapter – job attitudes, motivation, and leadership. O'Reilly reported that under the headings of goal setting and equity theory, intrinsic motivation continued to be heavily researched. For the most part goal setting research seemed to have followed its traditional course. However, equity research had broadened considerably to encompass procedural as well as distributive justice. Growing emphasis on how decisions about distribution were made represented a clear move towards context. At first glance, increased interest in intrinsic motivation based on Deci's (1975) work seemed to indicate that the individual was back. However, O'Reilly observed that much of this interest centered around Deci and Ryan's (1987) extension of their theory to consideration of the context of the situation, namely the circumstances under which extrinsic rewards impair intrinsic motivation.

A similarly mixed verdict about the individual's role appeared with respect to work attitudes. Although Avery et al. (1989) had indicated that genetic factors accounted for a considerable amount of the variance in job satisfaction and Staw et al. (1986) had made a strong case for the view that job satisfaction was dispositional, others such as Gerhart (1987) and Davis-Blake and Pfeffer (1989) had challenged Staw's conclusion. Broadening was also evidenced with respect to job commitment, especially by expansion of application of the concept from commitment to just the work organization, to include commitment to unions and careers and to consideration of organizational contexts as antecedents of commitment.

With respect to leadership, however, the individual was still the star although a slightly dimmer one. O'Reilly suggested that much of the leadership research represented useful refinements to previously accepted theories; the broadening included topics such as charisma and transformational aspects of executive leadership, and greater interest in organizational consequences of leaders. Still, the negative side of the debate about whether or not leadership was a useful construct had received strong impetus from Meindl and Ehrlich's (1987) research supporting their earlier conclusion that the tendency of people to view leadership as a likely explanation for organizational performance stemmed from the existence of values and ideology that engendered a propensity to romanticize leadership.

Although O'Reilly suggested that leadership was a promising topic for the future, his overall conclusion about the individual's role was discouraging. Pointing to the growing recognition of the potential contribution of economic and sociological approaches to OB, O'Reilly

predicted some broadening due to changes in societal-level demographics. He concluded:

> Micro-OB is in a fallow period. Useful micro-OB work is being done, but more excitement and attention are currently being generated by macro-OB. The areas of micro-OB that Mitchell considered dominant – job attitudes, motivation, leadership and individual differences – remain the most frequently researched areas, though today they may generate less intellectual excitement. (1991: 445)

In the following *ARP* chapter on OB, Mowday and Sutton (1993) seemed to cement trends of the previous decade, through including the *linking* of individuals and organizations in their title. Their chapter provided a mixed picture concerning the position of the individual. After beginning by commenting on the micro–macro bifurcation in the field, the review focused explicitly on the micro material, suggesting that the individual had the same central role as always. However, then they echoed Cappelli and Sherer's (1991) concern that the field had sacrificed attention to context in order to stay in touch with its psychological roots.

Then, they took four steps which showed how the field had moved away from the individual. First, they broke with the tradition of earlier review chapters which were organized around psychological variables of motivation, work attitudes, job design, turnover and absenteeism, and leadership. Second, they agreed with O'Reilly (1991) that these topics had lost their intellectual excitement. Third, they devoted an entire section to the question 'How can we put organizations back into organizational behavior?' (1993: 220). And fourth, they substituted context for psychological variables as the fundamental organizing theme for their chapter.

In essence the fourth step substituted contextual dimensions for individual attributes to explain behavior. This substitution facilitated interesting theoretical work on the role of context, featuring reciprocal influence and the view that appropriate theorizing about context must include the opposing possibilities that some contexts have little influence and sometimes individuals create contexts. In the latter instances the individual would of course have center stage.

At the time we wrote this chapter, the latest available *ARP* chapter on OB was Wilpert's (1995). He adopted a systemic or macro focus and, as the first European to write an OB chapter for *ARP*, emphasized non-US sources. The individual did not fare well here, as Wilpert focused on the growth of symbolic and social construction approaches and on the difficulties the field is apt to meet in overcoming its widely acknowledged lack of attention to context. He suggested that previous inattention to context stemmed from (1) the conservative role of the dominant paradigm, (2) the consistency principle in science which pressures new theories to be consistent with accepted knowledge, and (3) a dominant focus on the individual as the unit of analysis in combination with the current cognitivist bias. Wilpert argued that these forces have helped make macro and micro theories incommensurate. He also provided clues about what the individual's future role might be. He advised establishing bridges between the macro and the micro and following Cappelli and Scherer's (1991) mesoscopic-level approach. He also observed that we need to clarify what 'context' means, noting that traditionally in OB context has been the environment that is outside the individual. In contrast, organizational context is the environment external to the organization including socioeconomic changes occurring in the world. Therefore, treatment of the external environment needs to incorporate variations across nation states.

Wilpert suggested that much of the conflict between micro- and macro-level approaches stems from unnecessary battles over intellectual turf, observing that the growth in the role played by symbolism and social construction 'does not make extant traditions extinct' (1995: 83). Moreover, 'The choice of a theoretical basis frequently is a function of the question to be answered' (1995: 83) and we have existing studies that have combined the various orientations successfully. Although Wilpert did not point specifically to which existing studies he had in mind, it would seem that his prime examples would include the following: Weick and Roberts's (1993) treatment of organizations as intersubjectively shared meanings through the idea of heedful interrelations that are constructed and reconstructed by individuals; Drazin and Sandelands's (1992) concept of autogenesis describing the self-organizing capacities of individuals interacting in social fields; Yammarino and Bass's (1991) multiple-level perspective of leadership including the person, the situation and person–situation; and Amburgey et al.'s (1993) treatment of organizational learning that showed how an organization's history and its position in its life cycle affect environmental impacts and organizational learning. Clearly, the individual has an important role in all of these processes but is not the whole show. In other words, the individual may continue to be important but this importance will emerge as researchers look at other problems, rather than study the state of the individual *per se*. Thus while the individual will be part of a larger plot, the play will not be a biography.

Extrapolating the trend from the last quarter-century of the *ARP* chapters, we can say that the individual will not totally disappear from the stage, but people who attend the play are more apt to pay attention to the stage setting and less likely than before to have come just to see the individual.

Finally we return to Jackson and Schuler's (1995) call to move the individual to a less visible position in HRM and to give greater attention to context. They wrote:

> Contributions will not come through research as usual. Several shifts in approach will be required: from treating organizational settings as sources of error variance to attending as closely to them as we have traditionally attended to individual characteristics; from focusing on individuals to treating social systems as the target for study; from focusing on single practices or policies to adopting a holistic approach to conceptualizing HRM systems. . . . These shifts in perspective are fundamental in many respects. In other respects, however, they require little more than a change from defining the essential features of situations as jobs (as industrial-organizational psychology often does) to a recognition that jobs are merely the first level of context in a many-level complex system of contexts. By extension, we would argue that future HRM research should elevate organization analysis (and perhaps extra-organization analysis) to a status equal to that currently enjoyed by job analysis. (1995: 256)

Jackson and Schuler took the idea of context very seriously and moved it to the second level noted by Wilpert, to include the external environment of the organization. Key elements of this context included laws and regulations, culture, politics, unions, labor markets and industry characteristics.

Summary

In short, our study of the last two decades' overviews published in mainstream sources in American organizational psychology and behavior revealed, unexpectedly, that the individual seemed to be either disappearing or changing substantially. Although the disappearance of the individual seemed pretty clear to us, we remained skeptical until we took a further look to see if others had recognized a similar trend. If the individual has been disappearing, surely missing person reports and perhaps reports of occasional 'sightings' would have been filed. We reasoned that the existence of such reports would provide evidence that others had noted the individual's disappearance, thereby lending support to our interpretations. Review of the literature indicated that indeed several missing person reports had been filed and several 'sightings' reported.

Missing Person Reports
and Occasional Sightings

Benjamin Schneider's 1985 presidential address to the Society for Industrial and Organizational Psychology (see Schneider 1987) was clearly a missing person report filed in the hope that refocus on the individual would take place. Schneider, distressed by the individual's absence, chastised his psychological colleagues for being seduced into believing that situations determine behavior.

While many of Schneider's central concerns could equally well have appeared in a debate among students of personality on the situationist position advanced by social learning theories, he directed his plea to students of organizations: 'organizations are the people in them . . . the people make the place' (1987: 450). He concluded: 'We are psychologists and behavioral scientists; let us seek explanation in people not in the results of their behavior' (1987: 451).

Other missing person reports had also been filed, although not all of them wanted the individual to return. Perhaps Salancik and Pfeffer (1977) were the first to call attention to the individual's disappearance. They wrote: 'the field has very nearly eliminated individual-level variables from the study of job attitudes. The field is no longer interested in what the individual brings to the work setting in terms of behavioral tendencies, traits, and personality' (1977: 57). Salancik and Pfeffer's sentiment, in contrast to Schneider's distress, could well be described as 'good riddance'. They took special issue with the concept of needs in previous job satisfaction studies, arguing that since people having similar or dissimilar needs when confronting similar or dissimilar job characteristics can have either the same or different attitudinal reactions, the concepts of need and need satisfaction are based on an outdated view of the individual and should be abandoned: 'Need models assume that individuals react to external realities in the context of relatively unchanging needs. Need-satisfaction models do not allow for the possibility that instead of reacting to environments which include job characteristics, individuals enact environments . . . need-satisfaction models imply that individuals are tightly linked to their environments' (1977: 440). Based on the evidence they suggested that persons are not that tightly linked to an objective environment and critiqued the concept of needs because it is very difficult to distinguish between needs and cultural expectations.

About a year later Salancik and Pfeffer (1978) dealt with the individual's disappearance in a somewhat different way, indicating that they intended not to dismiss the language of needs but rather to use it metaphorically, viewing a need as an attribution made by a person or an observer to explain a behavior that could not be explained readily by observed external demands. Believing this view provided a necessary corrective for the failure of many need-satisfaction models to adequately take the social context into account, they proposed a social information processing perspective, combining the social context of work and the presence of consequences from previous actions, as a more adequate approach. They argued that 'one can learn most about individual behavior' not by study of the individual but by 'studying the information and social environment within which the behavior occurs and to which it adapts' (1978: 226). Although recognizing that the key issues they raised about the need models had not been proven empirically, they concluded that social information processing provided a better account. Similarly in a later paper Davis-Blake and Pfeffer (1989) critiqued the dispositional approach. They began by defining the essence of the dispositional approach as follows: 'that individuals possess stable traits that significantly influence their affective and behavioral reactions to organization settings' (1989: 386). Believing that some of the apparent lack of support for the dispositional view stemmed from research design, Davis-Blake and Pfeffer explicitly stopped short of asserting that there are no dispositional effects. However, they proposed ending the search for dispositional factors, observing that even if the dispositional researchers could solve the major problems currently plaguing their research, important costs entailed by the approach (e.g. expensive selection procedures and the ease with which managers can blame individuals for poor performance) would remain.

More sympathetic missing person reports were also filed primarily by writers who were saddened by the individual's absence. For example, Katzell and Thompson, in assessing knowledge on work motivation, called on their colleagues to pay more attention to individual differences – 'habitual or even biological dispositions of the individual' (1990: 151). Other evidence of the missing individual took the form of joyful 'sightings'.

Sightings

The most notable joyful sighting was Staw et al.'s (1986) report of their longitudinal research on the dispositional approach to job attitudes. Lamenting that the individual had nearly disappeared in the wake of the job enrichment and social information processing debate, Staw et al. took heart from finding that affective dispositions predicted job attitudes over people's lifetimes.

Alderfer (1977) reported another sighting, noting that the individual had never been away and that Salancik and Pfeffer's initial missing person report was a false alarm based on misinterpretation of need theory. Similarly, Staw (1991) suggested humorously that the individual had been there all the time but had been 'dressing up like an organization', because so-called organizational actions could be explained by psychological theories.

Efforts to make light of the individual's disappearance aside, the seriousness of the concern about the individual's whereabouts was reflected in the fact that in July 1989, Mitchell and James co-edited a special issue of *The Academy of Management Review* on situational versus dispositional factors, which helped to place reports of the individual's disappearance, and the sightings, in perspective. Mitchell and James (1989a) pointed out that the whole incident was another manifestation of a long line of debates (e.g. nature versus nurture) in social science and philosophy. Similarly Pervin (1989) noted that in the history of psychology a number of perspectives had exaggerated the role of the environment and others had exaggerated the importance of the individual. Other articles in the special issue added perspective by advancing an inter-actionist framework. Pervin, for example, commented that most personality psychologists are interactionists: 'they emphasize both person and situation variables when defining behavior' (1989: 352). However, he added that the current debate had reformulated the interactionist perspective productively by calling attention to the dynamic processes through which people influence situations while also being influenced by them. Two models reveal the nature of these processes: first, Cantor and Kihlstrom's (1987) social intelligence model postulated that individuals have knowledge about social situations and that they use that knowledge to deal with specific tasks in life; and second, the goals model emphasizes that people are goal directed and that their behavior in situations depends on their goals and their perceptions of the operative reward structure. In short, people are active agents in formulating goals and plans and they are engaged in dynamic, interpretative processes, not static and descriptive ones.

By linking individual attributes and interpretative processes Pervin outlined a promising path. The individual is still around, but a person's static traits are not of central interest; more crucial are the person's goals and self-perceived competencies that influence how he/she interprets particular situations. In Pervin's words: 'it is desirable to focus on relationships between person characteristics and task demands or environmental characteristics, rather than traits desired across tasks or environments that are desirable for all people and for all circumstances' (1989: 357). Also, it must be remembered that people shape their environments by selecting them and then modifying them. Even Pfeffer, writing with Davis-Blake (Davis-Blake and Pfeffer 1989), after seemingly filing yet another missing person report by entitling a paper appearing in the special issue 'Just a mirage: the search for dispositional effects', came to a similarly interactionist position. They were comfortable talking about individuals' dispositions as long as it is recognized that the dispositions are not static and that individuals adapt to different types of situation. They wrote: 'Empirical research . . . has revealed that, over time, individuals' dispositions are significantly affected by the organizations in which they participate' (1989: 389). Mitchell and James (1989b) concluded the special issue with a very instructive paper concerning the situational versus dispositional debate, which is especially helpful for revealing the individual's new role. They observed that the traditional research paradigm in interactional psychology had changed from being concerned with partitioning behavioral variance into static entities such as persons versus situations to a paradigm '*in which reciprocally interacting person–environment relations are viewed as being simultaneously consistent and variable (adaptable)*' (1989b: 405, italics added). They called for research guided by the premise of dynamic reciprocal causality.

In our view general systems theory had long been a potential framework for such work, but its contribution was limited by the mechanistic ways in which it was first employed with a focus on inputs and outputs rather than the mutually determining processes that it could have highlighted. Currently the field is moving to serious consideration of mutually determining processes; Karl Weick's work appears to be at the forefront.

Towards a New Role for the Individual: Mutually Determining Processes

Help in thinking through the complexities of mutually determining processes is available in the social constructionist view advanced and developed by Karl Weick. Weick's (1979) influential book *The Social Psychology of Organizing* (second edition) and his more recent work have helped the field to conceptualize mutual causality across levels by providing both a system for and the spirit to focus on process. The individual is still important to Weick: his 1979 book was clearly psychologically based. However, Weick's concern was the *process of organizing*, and he advanced a new fundamental unit for organizational analysis – the double interact. Although the individual was still important, the individual's most salient features were not the traditional ones that helped the person to know his/her environment objectively. Rather, a person acts and then responds to and attempts to make sense of what he/she has done. Through this process individuals are active in creating the environments to which they respond. Although not often explicitly labeled as such, Weick's work represented a major postmodern move, leading the field away from the assumed concrete entities from the past, i.e., individuals and organizations.

From this perspective traditional ways of thinking about individuals and about larger social systems unravel. Interestingly, in some of Weick's more recent work (Weick and Roberts 1993) a concept previously used to account for individual behavior – the mind – was reformulated as the 'collective mind' to describe complex coordinated behavior among individuals. This transplant of the individual's most celebrated property (the mind) to the collective is a dramatic shift. Historically social psychologists have been highly critical of the idea of a group mind. However, Weick and Roberts's use of the term was qualitatively different than before. They began with the realization that they needed to develop 'a [new] language of organizational mind that enables us [them] to describe collective mental processes' (1993: 357). This language helps to locate the individual's new role, by permitting focus on both individuals and the collective simultaneously. As they put it: 'only individuals can contribute to a collective mind.' However, 'a collective mind is distinct from an individual mind because it inheres in the pattern of interrelated activities among many people' (1993: 360). Weick and Roberts treated the concept of 'mind' as a disposition to act with heed. Heed captures a 'set of qualities of mind that elude the more stark vocabulary of cognition' (1993: 361). Space limitations prevent a more complete summary of Weick and Roberts's conceptualization except to add that it led them to see the collective mind '"located" in the process of interrelating just as the individual mind for Ryle was "located" in . . . activities' (1993: 365). The interrelations are constructed and reconstructed by individuals. Although Weick and Roberts did not focus on a changed role for the individual, their ideas can be usefully extended to this end. They observed: 'The mindset . . . implicit in the preceding

analysis has little room for heroic, autonomous individuals. A well developed organization mind . . . is thoroughly social' (1993: 378).[3] The individual still has a role but he/she is part of a play – a play produced by individuals heedfully interacting with others. The play is the unit of interest.

Importantly, in Weick's most recent book, the individual is also thoroughly social: 'Identities are constituted out of the process of interaction' (1995: 20). Weick put the gist of this point in easily remembered prose in the question: 'How can I know who I am until I see what *they* do?' (1995: 23, italics added).

Weick's view of the thoroughly social individual seems to capture well what appears to be the emerging role of the person. The individual still plays an important role, but that role is defined by the context; the individual's essentialist properties are of less interest than before.

As we concluded our review of contemporary American industrial psychology and organizational behavior publications with Weick, we were taken by the parallels between the emerging contextual view and that of the French historian Michel Foucault, who seems to have become an intellectual hero of many European students of organizations.

The European parallel is well illustrated in Clegg's (1994) discussion of Foucault. Clegg's treatment of Foucault's concept of rule is especially pertinent. Clegg argued that Foucault's use of rule helps to transcend 'the limits of individualist accounts of "interpretative understanding" as a type of privileged access to the subjectivity of the other' (1994: 159). According to Clegg, Foucault's notion of the disciplinary gaze focuses attention on why historical subjectivities come into existence. From this vantage point, it is easier for the analyst to gain the benefits of Granovetter's (1985) embeddedness perspective, thereby avoiding the trappings of both understructuralized and overstructuralized accounts.

Similarly, Townley observed the value of Foucault for human resources management: 'Traditional approaches in personnel have taken the individual as a self-evident phenomenon . . . possessing an essential personal identity' (1994: 11). In contrast, Townley observed, Foucault offers 'a relational and dynamic model of identity. This individual is continuously constituted and constructed through social relationships, discourses and practices' (1994: 11). 'A Foucauldian analysis of the individual subject does not therefore, assume an uncovering of a given essential identity of skills, abilities, and personality traits. Rather its focus is on the processes involved in rendering the individual knowable'

(1994: 12). She also noted that Foucauldian analysis stresses organizing, not organization.

Of the European writers we reviewed, we found the strongest attack on the individual's privileged position in *Changing the Subject* by Henriques et al., who called for rejecting 'psychology's individualistic concept of the subject' (1984: 11) and for showing 'how individuals are constituted through the social domain' (1984: 17). They indicated that psychology has been plagued by dualistic conceptions (e.g. biological versus social) that make it difficult to conceptualize the individual in a fully social way. They called for reconceptualizing terms such as biology and society to avoid the implicit dualism 'in favor of stressing the relational character of their mutual effects' (1984: 21). This view challenges some fundamental and long-standing thought patterns which are embedded in our modes of discourse.

In short, there may be a basis for a *rapprochement* concerning the individual's role between American organizational and psychology behavior and a growing trend in European organizational scholarship. Both seem to be adopting a nonessentialist view of the individual and emphasizing the reciprocal relationship between the individual and social processes.

SOME POSSIBLE OBJECTIONS ABOUT THE DISAPPEARANCE OF THE INDIVIDUAL

This section was motivated both by a desire to present a balanced picture and quite frankly by our own skepticism about what we presented in the first section. Here we consider two possible objections to the thesis, developed in the first section, that the individual is disappearing.

Thoughtful readers might object that the trends we discovered are misrepresentations for at least three reasons. First, locating a trend depends on the point in time that one begins analysis. We began ours with the late 1960s. One could argue that by the 1960s, even traditional I/O psychology was far from asocial. A second objection is almost the opposite of the first. It suggests that even today there continues to be a great deal of research featuring a relatively traditional view of the individual. A third objection is that we relied very heavily on one publication – *ARP* – in developing our thesis. We consider these in order.

I/O Psychology was not Asocial as Implied

With respect to the first criticism, we agree that both industrial psychology and organization behavior have long had a social component. In fact, the social component was recognized with the famous Hawthorne studies, if not before (see Mathewson 1931). Also behind much of F.W. Taylor's work was a desire to overcome the group phenomenon he called 'soldiering'. Thus, clearly for a long time, the social system had not been totally ignored. However, we would counter that developments in the last two decades represent a qualitative change in the relationship between the individual and the social component. Earlier treatments of the social system were troubled by its role, seeing it as something that corrupted the individual or as an expression of people's lower level, nonrational instincts. Consequently, the individual was treated as signal and the social relationships were treated more as noise. Further, although we acknowledge that the spotting of a trend is a function of an often arbitrary starting point and that social relationships were recognized in organization studies long before Cummings's (1982) *ARP* chapter, we would maintain, for the reasons just stated, that things are quite different now than in the 1960s.

The Individual is Alive and Well in I/O Psychology and OB

The second objection would imply that it is possible to write an extensive story under the heading 'the individual is alive and well and starring on many stages.' Being American psychologists we were predisposed towards this possibility; we took it seriously and studied the psychological literature to see if a strong case could be made for the position that 'the individual is alive and well.'

We found that the individual retains a strong, starring role in many legitimate theaters. Indeed we found quite a renaissance of interest in a number of personality, cognitive, and affective variables in describing the experience and behavior of individuals in organizations. However, even in these places, the individual doesn't have the same role as in the past.

Personality

A resurgence of interest in personality was one of Katzell's (1994) meta-trends in his *I/O Handbook* chapter. Among the hottest topics in I/O psychology are studies of the role of the big five personality factors (see Digman 1990) in accounting for and predicting organizational performance (Hogan 1991); the role of a general intelligence factor or *g*; and other dispositional variables such as positive and negative affectivity (Brief et al. 1988; Spector et al. 1995), locus of control (Storms and Spector 1987; Perlow and Latham 1993) and impulsivity (Latham 1995). Emotions in the workplace are of increasing interest, with increasing emphasis on the underlying cognitive structure of the experience of work-related affect (Warr 1987; 1994). However, even in this traditionally psychological area, as Fineman's chapter on emotion and organizing in this volume reveals (Chapter 3.3), sociological perspectives have become increasingly important. Most notably, the recent resurgence of interest in emotions has included the association between affective responses to work and behavioral outcomes that go beyond prescribed performance criteria: behavioral role choices along a pro-role, in-role, anti-role continuum. A similar broadening of focus is evident in research examining cognitive associates of behavioral role choices, including assessments of organizational fairness and justice and psychological contracts.

The Big Five In organizational psychology some consensus is emerging about the role of personality for understanding people's behavior in organizations. The consensus is that individuals can be characterized by a number of enduring dispositional qualities, and that these characterizations can provide useful information for the theory and practice of employee development and organizational effectiveness (Hogan 1991). One predominant theory, known as the five-factor theory of personality, has evolved out of fifty years of research on the underlying structure of personality based on the trait vocabulary used to describe observed behavior. A large body of factor analytic studies of peer and self-ratings of trait vocabulary, replicated across many different languages and populations, have converged on five primary factors describing personality. These are neuroticism, extroversion, openness to experience (or culture), conscientiousness, and agreeableness. Hogan (1991) described these factors as representations of cognitive prototypes or schemata which people seem to use when observing others' behaviors. They are the basis of people's reputations, serving a social function as 'prewired categories of social cognition used to sort the behavior of others and to give some predictability to social life' (1991: 879). Based on the preponderance of evidence which 'shows that individuals who are dependable, reliable, careful, thorough, able to plan, organized, hardworking, persistent, and achievement oriented tend to have higher job performance in most if not all occupations' (1991: 272), Mount et al. (1994) observed that conscientiousness has emerged as the most important trait motivation variable in personnel psychology. Moreover, their own research, which supported

the position that ratings by observers (e.g. supervisors and coworkers) of these attributes add incrementally to the variance in performance explained by self-ratings, suggested that previous research that has relied almost exclusively on one's self-reports to measure personality may have understated the validity of personality as a predictor of job performance.

Although factor analytic methodology, and its appropriateness for uncovering an underlying structure of personality, have received some criticism (see Block 1995), most scholars in the area agree that the big five theory of personality provides a robust framework for understanding human nature and its relationship to task and interpersonal behaviors (Hogan 1991; Mount et al. 1994). However, the term 'personality' entails an inherent lack of clarity and is actually used in two very different ways. One meaning of personality is a person's social reputation as seen by others, which Hogan described as 'public, relatively objective, and describable in terms of a common vocabulary – that is in terms of trait words' (1991: 875). The personality as reputation is based on the observer's experience with the target person's past behavior, and as such may be usefully applied to projections of the person's future performance. A second meaning of personality refers to the internal structures and processes within a person, inaccessible to an observer. At best we may obtain indications of this personality construct by means of self-report, projective techniques, and the like, although their reliability is questionable. The usefulness of self-reports of personality is limited by the confound of self-presentation with issues of self-knowledge and self-concept.

Industrial psychologists have looked extensively at the relevance of the five-factor model for prediction of job performance. As noted, conscientiousness consistently appears to be a valid predictor across occupational groups and job-related criteria. A second factor, extroversion (describing sociability, talkativeness, assertiveness, ambition, and activity), appears to be a valid predictor for jobs with a large interpersonal or social component. Significantly, Mount et al.'s (1994) preference for supervisor, coworker and customer ratings over self-reports of personality traits in predicting job-related criteria, is consistent with Hogan's preference for the construct of personality as social reputation opposed to personality as reflection of internal structures and processes.[4]

Despite the various methodological and conceptual issues involved in the big five research, it is certainly one stage where the individual's star is still bright, but emphasis is given to the perceptions held by others.

General Intelligence (g) The individual continues to be the focus of attention in the growing body of research supporting the validity of a number of dispositional and general intelligence factors in prediction of job performance. This research continues to raise perplexing ethical questions, e.g. what do we do with this knowledge? Do we accept disposition as a basis of employee selection and development, in the same way as we have traditionally used requisite job-related KSAs (knowledge, skills, abilities)? At least in the US these ethical questions are linked to legal issues. Also, there is the question that in 'selecting out' candidates whose personalities do not conform with organizational performance requirements, might we be depriving organizations of important sources of creativity, renewal, and transformation? Above all, what are the human implications of 'discarding' a large portion of our potential workforce merely for possessing personality structures that do not conform with the immediate needs of the marketplace?

Summary It is clear that in the area of personality, the individual is alive and well. However, even here, macro issues raised by ethical and legal concerns threaten to rob the person's centrality. However, there is a second area where the individual seems to be thriving. This is in the study of emotions and work.

Emotions in the Workplace

Locke, in his review of a monumental body of literature, defined job satisfaction as 'a pleasurable emotional state resulting from the appraisal of one's job or job experiences' (1976: 1300). Recognizing that satisfaction is an emotional reaction, obviously emotions have been a central part of organizational studies for some time. However, contemporary interest in emotions in organizations expands traditional approaches to job satisfaction in two important respects. First, satisfaction has typically represented a very narrow component of the complex interplay of perceptions, appraisals, arousals, and responses experienced as emotions in the workplace. Second, while researchers have traditionally been concerned with satisfaction as an independent variable affecting performance and productivity (see Nord's 1974 critique of the satisfaction literature), the health and well-being of organization members as people are increasingly seen as important outcome variables in their own right (Katzell 1994).

Affective States Warr's (1994) work on job-related affective well-being exemplifies this new focus on the health and well-being of organiz-

ation members. Warr defined five components of mental health in Western societies: affective well-being, competence, aspiration, autonomy, and integrated functioning. In organizational research, affective well-being has traditionally been studied as a one-dimensional, undifferentiated construct, ranging from feeling bad to feeling good. As a result, Fineman (1993) observed, the typical presentations of job-related well-being have depicted an 'emotionally anorexic' individual in possession of a narrow range of pale human emotions – satisfactions and alienations. Organ and Near (1985) suggested that this narrow focus may partially explain the persistent lack of empirical support for a satisfaction–performance relationship, in part because traditional measures of 'performance' may fail to tap into certain types of constructive (or destructive) work behaviors; Organ has developed this theme in his body of work on altruistic or pro-social organizational behavior. More to the point, however, is the extent to which measures of job satisfaction and other job attitudes have privileged the cognitive dimension. Thus the concept of 'satisfaction' maps to an appraisal or evaluation of composite external circumstances, rather than to the 'happiness' experienced. Organ and Near cited Campbell's (1976) findings that while aggregated cognitive measures of 'satisfaction' are positively correlated with affective measures of 'happiness' ($r = 0.57$), the two sets of measures showed different patterns of relationship with a number of antecedent and consequent variables. For example, age has been found to be the most consistent positive correlate of job satisfaction; however age correlated negatively with measures of 'happiness' (Campbell 1976).

Warr (1994) further pinpointed interest in emotions as 'context-specific' affective well-being, providing a basis for investigating the relationships of a wide range of affective states to antecedent and consequent organizational events and behaviors. By examining this range of emotions specifically anchored in the job experience ('My job makes me feel' from furious to ecstatic: Van Katwyk et al. 1995) we may better understand the relationships between affective and behavioral responses to work (e.g. the range of behavioral choices that influence an organization's functioning above and beyond perfunctory performance). Similarly, emotion plays a major role in research concerning frustration and stress at work.

Organizational Frustration and Stress One model of the affective basis of organizational aggression (Spector 1975; Spector 1978; Storms and Spector 1987; Chen and Spector 1992), based on the classic (Dollard et al. 1939) frustration–aggression theory, views aggression as a consequence of frustration. Spector and colleagues examined the sequence in organizational work of situational constraints blocking individuals from achieving valued work goals, emotional reactions to frustration, and behavioral reactions. Affective reactions included job dissatisfaction and feelings of stress, frustration, anxiety and anger (Chen and Spector 1992). Organizational frustration affected job performance, absenteeism, turnover, organizational aggression, and interpersonal aggression and included withdrawal of efforts to achieve organizational goals (e.g. turnover, absenteeism) and interpersonal hostility or aggression. These behaviors may interfere with the organization's task performance, climate, or effectiveness and consequently may be thought of as counterproductive, anti-role, or anti-social behaviors.

Clearly, the individual has a starring role in this work on emotions, much as before when satisfaction and attitudes were studied in the past. The slight changes are represented by the spotlight on the less rational features of the individual, e.g., moods, emotions and affect.

Behavioral Role Continuum: Extra-Role Choices
Although research on role choices continues to focus on the individual, growing attention has been given to the possibility that the success of the postmodern, post-industrial organization may increasingly depend upon employees' behavioral role choices. Employees may choose roles that go beyond the performance requirements defined by the job role itself: pro-role (McLean Parks and Kidder 1994); pro-social (Brief and Motowidlo 1986); organizational citizenship behavior (Organ 1990). Conversely they may choose roles that covertly or overtly harm the organization: anti-role (McLean Parks and Kidder 1994); anti-social (Hogan and Hogan 1989); counterproductive (Storms and Spector 1987); deviant (Robinson and Bennett 1975); maladaptive (Perlow and Latham 1993); and sabotage (Jermier 1988). The organizational consequences of employees' extra-role behavior may be amplified by combination with a heightened competitive environment and the growing importance of computer-intensive technologies. On the one hand, the enormous capital expenditures on technology require optimal utilization of technological investments. On the other hand, computer-intensive technologies make organizations more vulnerable to employee aggression in the form of computer sabotage. According to LaNuez and Jermier (1994), in these newer organizations, changes in class relations make it more likely than before that higher-level employees, such as managers and technocrats, will be saboteurs.

Organizational Citizenship Behavior (OCB)
Perhaps OCB has received more research attention than any other topic in the role choice area. OCB researchers stress that organization members may choose to perform only the behaviors required by their jobs (or by their psychological contracts as mutually understood by employee and supervisor). Alternatively, employees may choose to exceed the requirements of their job roles and make extra-role contributions to benefit the organization.

A widely studied formulation of this latter extra-role behavior is organizational citizenship behavior (OCB), defined as organizationally helpful, constructive gestures exhibited by organization members and valued or appreciated by managers, but neither directly related to individual productivity nor inhering in the enforceable or formal requirements of the individual's role. OCB includes such behaviors as: cooperation, supporting the supervisor, helping coworkers, enhancing the reputation of the work unit, suggesting improvements, training new people, punctuality and attendance beyond required levels, and abstaining from negative behaviors.

Organ distinguished OCB from the broader notion of pro-social organizational behavior (POB), which is behavior directed at improving the welfare of the person(s) to whom it is directed. Recent advances in OCB include Graham's (1986) introduction of principled organization dissent to describe individuals' efforts in the workplace to change the organization because of their conscientious objection to a policy or practice, and Van Dyne et al.'s (1994) test of a reconceptualized notion of OCB derived from political philosophy, adding the idea of civic citizenship to the traditional elements of organizational citizenship, to conceptualize organizational citizenship as a global concept that includes all positive organizationally relevant behaviors.

Anti-Role or Counterproductive Behavior Another range on the behavior choice continuum is anti-role behavior. The growing concern with such aggressive or anti-social behaviors in both the scholarly and popular press stems from awareness that annual losses from employee theft in the United States are high (estimated at over $40 billion) and that homicide is the third leading cause of occupational death in the American workplace (McLean Parks and Kidder 1994). Frameworks employed in the study of anti-social behavior include: the organizational frustration model discussed above, the psychological contract and organizational justice.

Psychological Contract The psychological contract is the individual's belief in a reciprocal exchange agreement, and doesn't necessarily correspond to the agreement assumed by the employer or other organization members. Subjectively it is characterized by perceptions, interpretations, and sense-making (Rousseau and McLean Parks 1993). From the contractual perspective, employees and employers enter into an employment relationship with sets of expectations of reciprocal obligations that go beyond the formal, explicit agreements made in the hiring process (Rousseau and McLean Parks 1993; Rousseau 1989; Shore and Tetrick 1994; McLean Parks and Kidder 1994).

According to Shore and Tetrick (1994) the core of the typical psychological contract of the industrial age organization member was the belief that the organization will provide job security and promotional opportunities in return for hard work and loyalty. With the dissolution of the job boundary, the dismantling of the internal labor market, and the movement toward a contingent workforce, it is precisely this aspect of the psychological contract which is profoundly challenged in the post-industrial workplace.

As organizations continue to downsize, the violation of the psychological contract becomes a central issue for the survivors. If organizations move toward a more explicitly short-term, contingent, virtual model, we may expect the psychological contract to move increasingly toward the transactional end of the continuum, reducing commitment and trust, moving away from the socio-emotional aspects to focus on the purely pecuniary benefits of the relationship (McLean Parks and Kidder 1994). Thus the effects of violations on surviving 'core' members, as well as the creation of a new genre of psychological contract for the contingent labor force, will be a major issue in our study of organizations.

Organizational Justice The notion of the psychological contract is closely related to research on organizational justice (Brockner and Greenberg 1989; Greenberg 1990). Equity theory and social exchange theory were perhaps the most direct parents of current justice research. Following these theories we would expect the perception that the organization is *not* behaving in the employee's interests (organizational injustice, violation of psychological contract) to be associated with increased anti-role behavior.

Such violations of the psychological contract can cause strong affective reactions (Rousseau 1989) as well as reevaluation of the contract itself. The employee may reevaluate the relational contract, with its emphasis on long-term, interpersonal relationships and organizational commitment, to a transactional contract, or may respond affectively and evaluatively by moving down the continuum from pro-role behavior to in-role behavior. This is consistent with both the organizational frustration–aggression model and the early work of Organ (1988) linking the fairness component of job satisfaction to prosocial behavior.

Similarly, the employee's perceptions of procedural justice in the organization (the perceived fairness of processes and procedures used to make decisions, particularly interpersonal treatment) can be examined in relationship to contract evaluation, satisfaction, and ultimately behavioral response and role choice. These relationships are the core of much of the research on survivor syndrome after downsizing, the influence of fairness perceptions on survivors' work behaviors and attitudes (Greenberg 1990; Brockner and Greenberg 1989).

Due to their social psychological heritage, studies of contracts and justice have placed the individual at their cores. Consequently, the growth of current research about them supports the 'individual is alive and well' position.

Motivation

Another area where the individual continues to star stems from the continuing interest I/O psychologists have in motivation (see Pinder 1984 and Kanfer 1990 for comprehensive reviews of this work). Despite the trend that Kanfer noted towards reconceptualizing needs as flexible personal goals that vary with cognitive constructions of the environment, the individual remains at center stage.

Specifically, the individual continues to star in the monumental body of research on goal setting, pioneered by Locke (see Locke et al. 1981 for an excellent overview). More recently, the individual was highlighted in Wood and Locke's (1990) use of control theory to theorize about why goals work.

Individual Differences

The tradition of individual differences is alive and well. As we observed earlier, quite recently Ackerman and Humphreys (1990) placed individual differences at the core of I/O psychology. They wrote: 'A major purpose of industrial psychology is to categorize individuals' (1990: 224).

The individual also is at the center of a slightly different approach to the study of individual differences, the biological approach centering on genetics. Avery and Bouchard (1994) highlighted the present interactionist course of this approach. While focusing on genetic influence, however, they did not take a polar position on the nature–nurture issue, concluding that both genetic and environmental influences were important.

Leadership

There continues to be strong interest in leadership, an area where we should expect the individual to do well. The persuasive argument of House (1988) and the monumental research program of McClelland and associates (see McClelland and Boyatzis 1982) have provided a much stronger case for the role of personality on leadership than one would have imagined possible following reaction to the publication by Stogdill (1974) which was widely interpreted (misinterpreted according to some – see Lord et al. 1986) as suggesting that personality characteristics were not important for leadership.

Of course interpreting the degree to which these developments have restored the individual requires keeping other simultaneous developments in mind. When this is done, and we tie all the strands together, the leadership area does not bode as well for the role of the individual as the previous paragraph might imply. We have already noted the work of Meindl and his colleagues (see Meindl et al. 1985) on the romance of leadership that suggested the importance of leaders may be overstated in our contemporary thinking.

Even in the currently popular study of transformational leadership, where the individual appears to be prominent, there is a long-standing debate over the competing person versus situation models of leadership, corresponding to the person view ('great men [sic]') versus situation view ('great times') of history (Yammarino and Bass 1991). Clearly transformational leadership theory, with its emphasis on the charismatic qualities and behaviors of leaders, would seem to come down on the side of the individual. Charisma, whether based on Weber's innate personal attributes or a more modern behavioral approach, is seen as the basis of the transformational leader's intense normative influence over others, the ability to manipulate symbolism, rewards, and visions in order to engage and energize followers in carrying out the leader's agenda (Bryman 1992).

However, this approach to transformational leadership, with its unidirectional focus on the agency of the individual leader, has come under increasing criticism as leadership scholars have reexamined the leader in the context of the group and the organization. Bryman, for instance, noted the depth of the schism between leadership research with its emphasis on

rationality, and the postmodernist approach of much of the field of organization studies. He pointed to the need to address the reciprocal relationship between leaders and followers, the dependence of the charismatic leader on continual validation and maintenance by followers, the social formation of charisma itself, and the dangers inherent in charismatic leadership (arrogance, obsession, poor judgment, abuse of power, authoritarianism, disempowerment of subordinates, absence of moral safeguards). These issues highlight the inextricability of social context from the issues of individual leadership. Interestingly, recent research by Gaines (1993) on one well known charismatic leader indicated that Anita Roddick's style is much better captured by the idea of servant leadership than the dominating hero/heroine of the past.

Another view on leadership that threatens the individual's position by looking to the group or organizational context rather than the persona of the leader as the source of 'leadership' is implicit leadership theory. Implicit leadership theory is related to Calder's (1977) attribution theory of leadership, which focused interest on the interpersonal perceptions and inferences people use in attributing 'leadership' to another person rather than on some set of traits or behaviors embedded in an individual 'leader'. In this view actions taken to be evidence of leadership are behaviors typically expected to be performed by leaders as distinct from behaviors of most group members. Leadership is attributed when observations of the focal person's behaviors are matched against the observer's implicit theories of leadership (i.e. expectations of how leaders should act). Leadership, then, is not a quality in the person of the leader, but rather a cognitive construction by 'followers'. To the extent that leader prototypes are developed by members in a group context, these collective cognitive processes represent a strongly social constructionist model of leadership requiring consideration of several levels of analysis.

Yammarino and Bass (1991) offered an approach to researching leadership at multiple levels of analysis. Their research addressed the full range of combinations of person effects, situation effects, person–situation interactions and joint effects, from person, group, and collective levels of analysis. At each level, effects were viewed both from a wholistic perspective (a focus on differences between entities), and a parts perspective (a focus on differences within entities). A methodology was offered for testing empirically interrelationships at these multiple levels – the within and between analysis (WABA) of Dansereau et al. (1984). The

WABA design represents a breakthrough in empirical research, integrating levels of analysis in such research areas as leadership and teams, and as such is a valuable approach for understanding the individual in a rich social context.

Thus, it appears that the individual is still a star on the leadership stage; however, the role has been transformed to give larger parts to other cast members.

Summary

Clearly then, the individual has not disappeared. A good case can be made that there are areas where the individual seems to be starring, but even in many of these the individual's past glory has diminished and the new script focuses attention on context, the surroundings and the supporting cast. Still our skepticism about the individual's disappearance persuaded us to consider other possible objections.

Nonrepresentativeness of ARP

A third set of objections concerning the individual's disappearance in the OB and I/O fields might argue that our conclusions stemmed from sampling problems involving such a heavy reliance on the longitudinal study of one major publication, even one as prestigious as *ARP*. How representative of the field is *ARP*? To explore this concern, we studied other major publications in the field. Based on the results of this study (summarized below) we concluded that the individual's seeming disappearance was not limited to *ARP*. Recent major publications in OB and I/O psychology, most notably Dunnette and Hough's multivolume *Handbook of Industrial and Organizational Psychology*, and numerous chapters in the highly regarded annual series *Research in Organizational Behavior*, edited by Cummings and Staw, confirmed the results of our *ARP* study: the subject matter of the field had become wider and more concerned with context. Of course, the content of these volumes is *not* independent of *ARP*. In fact, many of the same authors published in both sets of sources; moreover, the raw materials for the annual review chapters are often these other publications and vice versa. Still, the commonality concerning the individual's disappearance was noteworthy.

Of particular note was the emphasis in recent volumes of the Cummings and Staw series on the meso theme we had encountered in several of the more recent *ARP* chapters. An especially thoughtful and potentially fruitful answer to the calls to move beyond using the individual as the unit for analysis appeared in House et al.'s (1995) treatment of the meso paradigm. This was a valuable addition to Rousseau and House's earlier outline of a meso framework for encompassing 'the effects of context on individual and group behavior' (1994: 16). This proposal was more than simply a critique of micro-level analysis; a purely macro-level analysis was also rejected. In their more recent paper, House et al. (1995) expressed concern that micro researchers apply general psychological theories to the study of behavior as though behavior is context-free. They added: 'Until general psychological theories are linked to organizational contextual variables they will remain inadequate to explain what goes on in organizations' (1995: 77).

The Cummings and Staw series also contained an important chapter by Cappelli and Sherer (1991). As we noted earlier, in calling for mesoscopic-level work Cappelli and Sherer wrote:

> research in OB has systematically abandoned contextual arguments in order to remain consistent with theoretical developments in the field of psychology. The abandonment of context comes despite substantial and wide-spread evidence of important relationships between contextual factors and the behavior of individual employees in organizations. The rise of cognitive approaches in OB research which systematically exclude considerations of the external environment leave the field with some interesting choices. If it continues on its current cognitive path, the field of OB is likely to miss the chance to establish any independent identity. What is unique about behavior in organizations is presumably that being in the organization – the context of the organization – somehow shapes behavior, and it is impossible to explore that uniqueness without an explicit consideration of context. (1991: 97)

Katzell (1994) expressed similar notions in his monumental overview chapter on the field's meta-trends in the second edition of the *Handbook of Industrial and Organizational Psychology*, although he left more room in center stage for the individual. Katzell described a continuum of embeddedness, extending from the individual and dyad to social/economic environment and national levels of analysis. He suggested that at a theoretical level, cross-level formulation enables us to understand both the cognitive/social construction of organizational properties and the dynamic patterns of person–situation interaction in the construction of personality. At an applied level, cross-level formulation can help practitioners identify interventions at the appropriate level(s) of analysis. In sum, Katzell's meta-trends revealed a mixed picture of the individual's role. On the one hand, many of the meta-trends (e.g. the growing interest that organizational psychologists have shown in how things change over time, i.e. history; in using complex and integrative systems theories, concepts, and models; and in advancing the belief that the whole is more than the sum of its parts) are consistent with the decrease in the centrality of the individual. On the other hand, Katzell observed other meta-trends, such as the growth of the cognitive perspective and the 'revival of personality' (1994: 3), that are inconsistent with that picture.

Then too, study of many of the chapters in the *Handbook* suggested that the individual had not been displaced at all. For example, Hogan (1991) criticized Mischel's (1968) argument that had advanced the situationist perspective over the traditional role of personality in accounting for human behavior. Hogan observed: 'personality and personality assessment, despite occasional rumors to the contrary, are alive and well' (1991: 877). On the other hand, Dunnette (1990), editor of the first edition of the *Handbook* and co-editor of the second, indicated that he sensed the field had moved towards context and away from the individual. He wrote:

It is obvious from the 1980 portrayal of the field that fairly heavy emphasis was placed on individual issues, though it is also apparent that group issues and organizational issues were emerging as critical areas of concern. In contrast, the picture portrayed in 1990 is one of needing to face and solve challenges related not only to these concerns, but also to many others brought by radical changes in organizations, the nature of workforces. (1990: 6)

Thus, it is clear that there are major areas of study where the individual is still starring. However, it is noteworthy that writers such as Hogan (1991), who maintained that the individual is alive and well, were writing, in part, in rebuttal to others who had suggested the individual's role was dwindling.

This review of other prestigious publications suggested that the *ARP* chapters had represented things quite well and that although the individual had not disappeared entirely in organizational and industrial psychology, the individual's star had been falling; even those who would like to have ignored the fact were unable to do so. Despite the growing support about the individual's disappearance in I/O psychology and OB, we were still skeptical.

What other evidence might help resolve our remaining doubts? Certainly if this were a major trend, given the ties between I/O psychology, OB and psychology in general we would find a similar trend in general psychology. Accordingly we explored that literature for traces of the individual's disappearance. Our findings are summarized in the next section.

CHANGING ROLE OF THE INDIVIDUAL IN GENERAL PSYCHOLOGY

Since the micro side of organizational studies had long been influenced by assumptions about human nature made in psychology and the social sciences more generally, we looked to see if the emphasis on context was crowding out the individual elsewhere in the social sciences. Exploration of the general psychological and related literatures revealed that here too, *the traditional privileged position of the individual had waned and the role of social contexts had gained in importance.* We present the evidence supporting this assertion in the next section on assumptions about human beings in modern social science.

Assumptions about Human Beings in Modern Social Science

We reviewed discussions of assumptions about human beings in major psychological publications and then explored the biological literature briefly. The original psychological theorists on whom early organizational behaviorists had drawn heavily (e.g. Maslow 1943 and White 1959) made rather essentialist assumptions about individuals (e.g. attributing fixed patterns of needs).

Interestingly, psychological essentialism has retreated in much of the recent psychological literature in favor of emphasis on how philosophical and social factors, by affecting assumptions about human nature, influence what human nature is taken to be. For example, the esteemed psychologist Gordon W. Allport (1985) described how characteristics attributed to human social nature, such as hedonism, egoism, and sympathy, were all consequences of a prevailing social ethos. He concluded: 'Like all behavioral science, social psychology rests ultimately upon broad metatheories concerning the nature of man [sic] and the nature of society' (1985: 42).

In a similar vein, another renowned psychologist, Albert Bandura, observed: 'Conceptions of human nature . . . focus inquiry on selected processes and are, in turn, strengthened by findings of research paradigms embodying the particular point of view. . . . As psychological knowledge is put into practice, the conceptions on which social technologies rest have even greater implications. . . . In this way, theoretical conceptions of human nature can influence what people actually become' (1986: 1–2).

Conclusions such as these by such great psychologists suggested a strong movement in mainstream psychology away from the assumption of the essentialist individual.

Significantly we found a similar trend in other

human sciences. In sociobiology, for instance, we found a less strong essentialist view than we had expected. For example, the famous socio-biologist Edward O. Wilson, writing the fore-word to David P. Barash's (1977) *Sociobiology and Behavior*, advanced a surprisingly nones-sentialist position, commenting that while there is very strong evidence that a human biogram (i.e. a pattern of potentials built into the heredity of the species as a whole) exists for many traits, 'In other traits human beings are . . . much more variable. . . . Human behavior is dominated by culture in the sense that the greater part, perhaps all, of the variation between societies is based on differences in cultural experience' (1977: xiv). He added: 'To understand that evolutionary history and the contemporary biogram that it produced is to understand in a deeper manner the construction of human nature. . . . An exciting collaboration between biologists and social scientists appears to have begun' (1977: xv).

Following Wilson's foreword, Barash (1977) noted the potential for social psychology, sociology and anthropology to contribute to sociobiology. This potential stems from the view of human nature that Barash attributed to sociobiology – a view that human behavior is the product of adaptive predispositions, 'A flexible, modifiable and perhaps rather fragile set of inclinations' (1977: 286). He added: 'Practitioners of sociobiology . . . do *not* necessarily advocate biological determinism of human behavior. The difference between deter-minism and genetic *influence* is the difference between shooting a bullet at a target and throwing a paper airplane; the paper airplane is acutely sensitive to environmental influences such as wind, and its ultimate path is not entirely predictable by the thrower.' Humans may be animals but, Barash warned, it does not follow that we are 'nothing but animals' (1977: 287).

Further exploration led us to a feminist critique of sociobiology in Janet Sayers's (1982) book entitled *Biological Politics: Feminist and Anti-Feminist Perspectives*, which provided a further challenge to biological essentialism. According to Sayers, feminists are divided on how biology shapes women's social status. On the one hand there is social constructionism which maintains that the influence of biology on women's status is indirect, being mediated by the way that their biology is interpreted and construed within a given society. In contrast, biological essentialism argues that biology does affect women directly through the endowment of a particular 'feminine' character. Sayers ad-vanced a third position: 'biological essentialism wrongly overestimates the biological determi-nants of women's social status at the expense of neglecting its social and historical determinants'

(1982: 3). Sayers also criticized social construc-tionism for underestimating the biological roots of women's social status, suggesting that such status has been 'determined directly by biologi-cal as well as social and historical factors' (1982: 3–4). Later she noted that the 'natural' condition of humankind, such as that advanced by Hobbes and some sociobiologists, is not given by nature but depends on specific historical contingencies.

Sayers's work moved us to further exploration of feminist writings in the psychological litera-ture. Here too, there were strong challenges to traditional ways of thinking about the individual. Marecek, for example, called for rethinking the psychology of gender, particularly the view which 'holds that the categories of "man" and "women" are natural, self-evident, and unequivocal' (1995: 162). Marecek argued for 'alternative meanings of gender [that] de-center the meaning that prevails in psychology, namely individual differ-ence' and for shifting 'the focus of analysis away from matters internal to the individual to the interpersonal and institutional arenas' (1995: 162). Such views do not deny 'biological differ-ence, but they do deny that such differences have a single, fixed meaning and salience whether from one culture to another, one historical period to another, one social group to another, or even from time to time in an individual's experience' (1995: 162). Marecek stressed the need to consider how social location, which is a function of such things as race, ethnicity and social class, mediates the significance of gender.

Other recent social science literature revealed additional concerns about the individual's position. Edward E. Sampson (1985; 1988; 1989) published a series of articles in the *American Psychologist* challenging traditional conceptions of the individual. Sampson distin-guished *self-contained* individualism character-istic of traditional American psychology, which emphasizes both firmly drawn self–other boundaries and personal self-control, from *ensembled* individualism 'that emphasizes more fluidly drawn self–nonself boundaries and field control' (1988: 16). Sampson concluded that even though all cultures must deal with the human being as an embodied entity, 'individu-alism is a sociohistorical rather than a natural event' (1988: 18). In a later article, Sampson (1989) developed the historical origins of the self-contained individual, locating them in the modern era beginning in the fifteenth and sixteenth centuries. He observed that under the historical conditions of the modern era, in which the individual became the central unit of society, studying the individual was sensible. However, we are now experiencing a transfor-mation in the central organizing principle of society away from the individual toward a more globally conceptualized entity. In this new world, individualism leaves center stage and 'understanding the individual *qua* individual is no longer relevant to understanding human life' (1989: 916). Accordingly, Sampson (1989) proposed a revised mission for psychology: 'A psychology for tomorrow is a psychology that begins actively to chart out a theory of the person that is no longer rooted in the liberal individualist assumptions, but is reframed in terms more suitable to resolving the issues of a global era.' A number of other psychologists have expressed similar thoughts.

Many were evident in a debate centering around the charge that the emphasis on the individual in American psychology is a product of a set of culture bound premises. Betancourt and Lopez (1993), for example, charged that for a long time psychologists had ignored culture. In response, Lee (1994) suggested that the problem was even deeper and located it in the individual orientedness or *individuocentrism* characteristic of mainstream American psychology. In a related response, Reid (1994) suggested that Betancourt and Lopez had identified some important issues but misdiagnosed the cause. The problem was not that culture had been ignored but that in the mainstream research, culture 'has been assumed to be homogeneous' (1994: 525), i.e. based on a standard set of values and expectations.

Additional questioning of the concept of the essentialist individual that has dominated American psychology presumes that there are some misguided assumptions about the 'self' as traditionally conceived in American psychology. Baumeister's (1987) historical account of 'How the self became a problem' was a noteworthy example. Baumeister argued that the interest in the self held by contemporary psychologists and laypersons, and the idea of self as something hidden, abstract and within the individual causing visible behavior, are very recent in history. He observed that this concept of self emerged gradually and in contrast with the earlier view of the self as 'equated with observable behavior and commitments' (1987: 165). According to Baumeister, the modern view contrasts sharply with the medieval one which denied that the person existed apart from his or her position in society. Baumeister's work suggested that the idea of the self commonly accepted in modern psychology should be viewed as the product of a specific historical stream rather than as a generalized concept.

Recently, there appears to have been some movement back towards the medieval view noted by Baumeister. Writing in the pages of the prestigious *Psychological Review*, Markus and Kitayama provided an insightful reformulation of the idea of self by contrasting the *independent* view of self, which construes the self 'as an autonomous, independent person' (1991: 226), with the *interdependent* construal. Even though in the interdependent construal the 'self also possesses and expresses a set of internal attributes, such as abilities, opinions, judgments, and personality characteristics', in this view 'these internal attributes are understood as situation specific, and thus sometimes elusive and unreliable. ... The interdependent self cannot be properly characterized as a bounded whole, for it changes structure with the nature of the particular social context. ... What is focal and objective about an interdependent self . . . is not the inner self, but the *relationships* of the person to other actors' (1991: 227).

Just as Markus and Kitayama (1991) distinguished between the independent and interpersonal views of the self, Hogan (1991) described a similar shift in the construct of personality toward a more interpersonal, relational interpretation. Hogan distinguished between two very different definitions of personality. First, he described an internal, boundaried concept that refers to 'the structures, dynamics, processes, and propensities inside a person that explain why he or she behaves in a characteristic way' (1991: 875). Second, Hogan found more organizational relevance and scientific applicability in a conceptualization of personality that refers to 'a person's social reputation and to the manner in which he or she is perceived by friends, family, co-workers, and supervisors' (1991: 875).

Treatments of the experience of emotions provides another example of the trend toward a social, relational interpretation of a phenomenon traditionally viewed as the private possession of the individual. Gergen and Gergen (1988) critiqued both the traditional biological view of emotions and the more recent cognitive view. In critiquing 'biological reductionism', they pointed to the dramatic differences in the vocabularies of emotion and patterns of emotional expression across cultures. They questioned 'cognitive reductionism' for privileging rational processing to the exclusion of values, preferences, feelings, caring. Gergen and Gergen developed a view of emotion as social performance. In this view, emotions as possessions of individuals make no sense if not understood in social context, i.e. 'related to preceding and/or anticipated events (essentially a narrative account)'. Emotional performances then are to be understood 'as constituents of larger or more extended patterns of interaction' (1988: 44).

Once more we see the reinterpretation of the individual emerging to give greater emphasis to social, relational context. The movement toward this interpretation is becoming evident in studies of personality, emotions, leadership, mental processing, schemata, attitudes – many of the fundamental psychological constructs that have played central roles in the view of the individual in organization studies. Gergen and Gergen summarized this transformation:

> narratives of the self are not fundamentally possessions of the individual; rather they are products of social interchange – possessions of the socius . . . the traditional concept of individual selves is fundamentally problematic. What have served as individual traits, mental processes, or personal characteristics can promisingly be viewed as constituents of relational forms. The form of these relationships is that of the narrative sequence. Thus, by the end of our story we shall find that the individual self has all but vanished into the world of relationship. (1988: 18)

Yet another move in mainstream American psychology against the traditional view of the individual was advanced by Simon (1990). Simon's work also appeared to be a fundamental critique of the form of psychological science, dominated by a search for invariants about human behavior that are similar to the laws of classical physics, such as those governing the speed of light. Simon argued that the quest for laws of these sorts in sciences such as biology and psychology is apt to be futile: any invariants that are to be found in these sciences are apt to be laws of qualitative structure, not quantitative ones. Simon's argument is intriguing. He asserted that biological knowledge is extremely specific, resting on the diversity of millions of species of plants and animals, and most of its invariants apply only to single species. Simon argued that in biological (including human) realms, the process is one where systems change adaptively to their environments over time. Consequently, the nature of such systems at any given time is a function of past and/or present environments, making it difficult to identify true invariants of the systems themselves. Consequently, we are dealing with 'artificial' systems – i.e. systems that are only what they are because they have responded to the shaping forces of the environment, to which they must adapt in order to survive. Part of the problem may stem from the assumptions we have made about human beings. Simon argued that the failure of psychologists to recognize the fact 'that *Homo sapiens* shares important psychological properties with nonbiological systems (e.g. computers) . . . perhaps stems from the reluctance of human beings to view themselves as "mere machines"' (1990: 4). He concluded that since many of the invariants we see in behavior are social invariants, 'social variables must be introduced to set the boundaries of our generalizations' (1990: 16).

A most recent move away from the essentialist individual in the psychological literature was present in the cognitive-affective *system* theory of personality of Mischel and Shoda (1995). They attempted to reconcile the conflicting approaches of the invariant character of the individual with social information processing. They wrote:

> When personality is conceptualized as a stable system that mediates how the individual selects, construes, and processes social information and generates social behaviors, it becomes possible to account simultaneously for both the invariant qualities of the underlying personality and the predictable variability across situations in some of its characteristic behavioral expressions. (1995: 246)

In this view, the context becomes an integral part of the system of processes that comprise the individual's personality. Both cognitive and affective processes are set off in systematic and predictable ways by features of situations, based on an individual's prior history of experience. At the same time, the situation does not represent some objective, empirical reality 'out there'. The situation as perceived by and responded to by the individual is a function of her/his constructs and subjective maps, a selective process of encoding and activation. The active and goal-directed processes by which the individual constructs the situations lend consistency to her/his pattern of responses. Mischel and Shoda observed that this theory 'accounts both for individual differences in overall average levels of behavior and for stable *if . . . then . . .* profiles of behavior variability across situations, as essential expressions of the same underlying personality system' (1995: 252).

Mischel and Shoda's approach parallels Weick's view of the double interact as the fundamental unit for organizational analysis.

Summary

The trend we found in organizational literature of giving greater emphasis to context and less to the essentialist individual is very similar to one occurring in psychology more generally. The individual has not disappeared in either place, but his/her starring role has been challenged. Challenges have come from quite diverse sources including: American social psychologists and social learning theorists, sociobiologists, feminist psychologists, leading mainstream American psychological journals, and an economics Nobel Laureate.

Some Related Topics

Comparison of psychological research conducted in America with that conducted in other cultures suggests that American psychologists may have mistaken properties of the self revealed in American research for universal attributes. The assumption that people are inherently self-interested and nonaltruistic may be a prime example, stemming from a failure to recognize how strongly social norms can affect behavior. As Markus and Kitayama observed: 'The view that altruistic behaviors are only seemingly altruistic and that they are public actions without any subjective, private foundation can perhaps be traced to the insistence of Western psychologists on the internal attributes (feeling, thought, and traits) as universal referents for behavior' (1991: 248). They asserted that 'in some cultures, on certain occasions the *individual*, in the sense of a set of significant inner attributes of the person, may cease to be the primary unit of consciousness. Instead the sense of belongingness to a social relation may be so strong that it makes better sense to think of the *relationship* as the functional unit of conscious reflection' (1991: 226); this represents additional support for our suspicion that the traditional view of the individual has been displaced and/or sharply transformed.

A look at European developments in social psychology supported the suspicion that the privileging of the self-contained individual in psychology and organization studies was in part a function of the dominance of indigenous American psychology. The European movement toward a more social, relational conceptualization of the self predated the trend we see today in American studies by about twenty years. Henri Tajfel described the 'social dimension of European social psychology' that has played an increasing role since the early 1960s, with its 'constant stress on the social and interactive aspects of our subject' (Tajfel et al. 1984: 1).

> The study of attitudes and opinions of individuals has begun to give way to research on social representations of social reality. It has become more and more clear that such representations are not just expressions of acquired behavioural dispositions, but are important reflections of the social reality in which we live and have a shared and collective nature. (1984: 2)

A slightly broader search of European writers revealed even more provocative challenges to the individual's traditional position. The British scholar Anthony Giddens (1992) observed that the move to reflexivity in modern social life has been associated with a growing tendency for individuals to create themselves. Specifically, via diets, psychotherapy, self-help, and surgery, people can create themselves in ways that were hardly imagined in other eras. Giddens observed that 'responsibility for the development and appearance of the body' (1992: 31–2) has been placed squarely in the hands of its possessor.[5] Even more recently, the spirit of these critiques of self has appeared in the organizational literature. Hoskin (1995), for instance, observed that the primacy given to the self in the modern world needs to be and can be explained historically.

Conceptual Changes

Much has been happening regarding psychological factors in organization studies. The field is bursting at the seams in several respects. First, changes (especially the move to incorporate context) in perspective about the traditional fundamental unit of analysis – the individual – have been dramatic. At times, the traditional unit of analysis seems to have been disappearing, at least in the sense that the search for essential properties of individuals is no longer assumed without qualification to be worthwhile. Second and closely related, many of the headings borrowed from psychology (e.g. motivation and satisfaction), that traditionally had been used to structure the field, although not totally obsolete, have become less useful for capturing what is going on.

Still, in many places the traditional psychological categories continue to be employed. However, even when they are used, they seem to need to be stretched considerably to cover a highly diverse set of inquiries. Major treatments of the topic of motivation illustrate this stretching. For example, in her outstanding chapter on motivation theory, Kanfer (1990), after explicitly ignoring biological and psychophysiological theories of motivation, still had to cover an enormous range of material, including distinctions between behavior and performance, as well as three sets of paradigms about motivation: need-motive-value, cognitive choice, and self-regulation metacognition theories. Since each of these in turn spanned a broad array of research, her chapter dealt with research on justice, goal setting, intrinsic motivation and so on. And, as we have noted above, many of these same topics have themselves expanded to encompass the influence of context, and become less centered on the essentialist individual and more concerned with the study of complex processes. At the end of her review, Kanfer acknowledged that substantial changes in the field had occurred. She wrote: 'Motivational psychology is entering a new phase of growth. In this phase, persons are viewed not only as processors of information but as sources of influence on behavior' (1990: 151).

In a similar vein, at the end of his excellent book on motivation, Pinder (1984) advocated inclusion of the systematic study of contexts into the study of work motivation. Pinder recognized that the need to incorporate context had complicated the study of motivation – so much so, that we should change our theoretical aspirations to developing middle range rather than universalistic theories. At this point we will not evaluate this solution; we point to it only to show how even those committed to traditional psychological categories derived from essentialist individualism feel the categories need to be stretched and/or qualified.

CONCLUSION

Our process of exploration led us through the following progression of linkages between psychology and organization studies:

1   Traditionally the domain of psychology has been the individual. Psychology has sought to uncover the essential properties and universal dimensions of the typical human being. Within this domain centered around the individual emerged major areas of interest, such as personality, motivation, attitudes, and learning.

2   Organization studies, at least in America, were founded on psychology. Thus the early concerns of organization studies, and the methodologies to study them, fell comfortably within the general paradigm of psychology.

3   Since the late 1960s, organization studies have leaned increasingly toward sociology, literature, communications, and other disciplines consistent with a more macro conceptual orientation.

4   As a result, there developed a major schism regarding the overall conceptual framework, questions asked and methodologies employed (that is a major paradigmatic discontinuity, in the Kuhnian sense) between I/O psychologists and sociologically oriented scholars in organization studies.

5   What we found, to our surprise, was that a substantial decentering of the individual has been taking place in many of the most mainstream areas of psychology, including I/O psychology. Even the most traditional strongholds of the individual in psychology, the self, identity, and personality, appear to be increasingly viewed as inseparable from their social contexts.

6   As a result, we found psychologically based micro OB to be moving conceptually in a direction consistent with the broader field of organization studies. This is reflected in the call for a meso level of analysis.

There is a curious mixture of thought and action on the psychological side of organization studies. On the one hand, we see many leading scholars have moved from the study of the essentialist individual. On the other we see many working successfully within the bounds of traditional psychological categories. This mixture may be interpreted as a manifestation of the postmodern tide, washing unevenly over and eroding the categories of the modernist era. Given the politics of social science, the different parts of the mixture could coexist for some time and coexist productively, with quite different sets of assumptions being employed in different contexts – with the postmodern frame being most useful in settings (e.g. types of organizations) in which the modernist patterns have been severely disturbed.

In any case, we conclude that with respect to psychological factors relating to organizational studies, the previous uniform assumptions of an essentialist individual have lost much of their privileged position. Moreover, the change is not confined to organizational studies; there appears to be a parallel growing discomfort with traditional assumptions about human beings in the social (and perhaps biological) sciences in general. In all these areas, when the individual appears he/she increasingly does so only in context.

Still, we found considerable evidence that inquiry concerned with properties of the individual still exists. We suggest that in the future this research will be most valuable if it is reported in ways that permit readers to locate the research in the full context in which the data were collected.

NOTES

We want to thank Ann Connell, Stewart Clegg and Paul Spector for their helpful and insightful comments on earlier versions of this chapter.

1 The *Annual Review of Psychology* is a series of reviews of topics in psychology, with the topics selected according to a master plan. The editors, editorial committee and authors are highly distinguished members of their respective psychological subfields.

2 We use 'so-called' to reflect the work of Friman et al. (1993) which suggested that while cognitive psychology was in ascendancy, it constituted nothing like a Kuhnian revolution.

3 See Klimoski and Mohammed (1994) for a review of the proliferation in I/O psychology of research in 'group-mind' constructs, such as shared mental models, common cause maps, collective cognitive mapping, shared frames, teamwork schemata, transactional memory, intersubjectivity, shared meaning,

collective interpretation, negotiated belief structure, collective mind, sociocognition, group affect, collective efficacy, group level integrative complexity, and group pro-social behavior.

4 Paul Spector (personal communication, 1995) has pointed out that supervisor ratings of performance can be thought of as essentially the person's image or reputation with the supervisor. Thus it is hard to separate supervisor performance ratings from supervisor ratings of the trait conscientiousness. 'Do I see employees as conscientious because they perform well, or do I think they perform well because they are conscientious?' This is another example of how characteristics and behaviors traditionally viewed on an inherently individual level have come to acquire a social, relational meaning.

5 In the context of Giddens's thoughts, Haraway's seemingly science fiction idea of cyborgs – 'creatures simultaneously animal and machine' (1991: 149) – seemed to be less extreme. Although Haraway noted that currently cyborgs are most common in science fiction, she did observe that modern medicine is also 'full of cyborgs, of couplings between organism and machine' (1991: 150). Although we are reluctant to go much further with Haraway's idea at this point, her observation that even today, some individuals are in part machines, would seem to represent another nail in the coffin of the essentialist individual.

REFERENCES

Ackerman, P. and Humphreys, L.G. (1990) 'Individual differences in industrial and organizational psychology', in M.D. Dunnette and L.M. Hough (eds), *Handbook of Industrial and Organizational Psychology*, 2nd edn, vol. 1. Palo Alto, CA: Consulting Psychologists Press. pp. 223–82.

Alderfer, Clayton P. (1977) 'A critique of Salancik and Pfeffer's examination of need–satisfaction theories', *Administration Science Quarterly*, 22: 658–69.

Allport, G.W. (1985) 'The historical background of social psychology', in Gardner Lindzey and Elliot Aronson (eds), *The Handbook of Social Psychology*, 3rd edn, vol. 1. Random House.

Amburgey, T.L., Kelly, D. and Barnett, W.P. (1993) 'Resetting the clock: the dynamics of organizational change and failure', *Administrative Science Quarterly*, 38, 51–73.

Avery, R.D. and Bouchard, T.J. Jr (1994) 'Genetics, twins, and organizational behavior', in Barry M. Staw and L.L. Cummings (eds), *Research in Organizational Behavior*, vol. 16. JAI Press. pp. 47–82.

Avery, R.D., Bouchard, T.J. Jr, Segal, N.L. and Abraham, L.M. (1989) 'Job satisfaction: environmental and genetic components', *Journal of Applied Psychology*, 74: 187–92.

Bandura, A. (1986) *Social Foundations of Thought and Action: A Social Cognitive Theory*. Englewood Cliffs, NJ: Prentice-Hall.

Barash, David P. (1977) *Sociobiology and Behavior*. Elsevier.

Baumeister, Roy R. (1987) 'How the self became a problem: a psychological review of historical research', *Journal of Personality and Social Psychology*, 52(1): 162–76.

Betancourt, Hector and Lopez, Steve Regesser (1993) 'The study of culture, ethnicity, and race in American psychology', *American Psychologist*, 48(6): 629–37.

Block, Jack (1995) 'A contrarian view of the five-factor approach to personality description', *Psychological Bulletin*, 117: 187–215.

Brief, A.P. and Motowidlo, S.J. (1986) 'Prosocial organizational behaviors', *Academy of Management Review*, 10: 710–25.

Brief, A.P., Burke, M.J., George, J.M. and Robinson, B.S. (1988) 'Should negative affectivity remain an unmeasured variable in the study of job stress?', *Journal of Applied Psychology*, 73: 193–8.

Brockner, J. and Greenberg, J. (1989) 'The impact of layoffs on survivors: an organizational justice perspective', in J. Carroll (ed.), *Applied Social Psychology and Organizational Settings*. Hillsdale, NJ: Lawrence Erlbaum.

Bryman, A. (1992) *Charisma and Leadership in Organizations*. London: Sage.

Calder, B.J. (1977) 'An attribution theory of leadership', in B.M. Staw and G.R. Salancik (eds), *New Directions in Organizational Behavior*. Chicago: St Clair Press.

Campbell, A. (1976) 'Subjective measures of well-being', *American Psychologist*, 31: 117–24.

Cantor, Nancy and Kihlstrom, John F. (1987) 'Personality and social intelligence', in *Personality and Social Intelligence*. Prentice-Hall.

Cappelli, P. and Sherer, P.D. (1991) 'The missing role of context in OB: the need for a meso-level approach', *Research in Organizational Behavior*, 13: 55–110.

Chen, P.Y. and Spector, P.E. (1992) 'Relationships of work stressors with aggression, withdrawal, theft and substance use: an exploratory study', *Journal of Occupational and Organizational Psychology*, 65: 117–84.

Clegg, Stewart (1994) 'Weber and Foucault: social theory for the study of organizations', *Organizations*, 1(1): 149–78.

Cosier, R.A. and Dalton, D.R. (1983) 'Equity theory and time: a reformulation', *Academy of Management Review*, 8(2): 311–19.

Cummings, L.L. (1982) 'Organizational behavior', *Annual Review of Psychology*, 33: 541–79.

Dansereau, F., Alutto, J.A. and Yammarino, F.J. (1984) *Theory Testing in Organizational Behavior: the Variant Approach*. Englewood Cliffs, NJ: Prentice-Hall.

Davis-Blake, Alison and Pfeffer, Jeffrey (1989) 'Just a mirage: the search for dispositional effects in organizational research', *Academy of Management Review*, 14(3): 385–400.

Deci, E.L. and Ryan, R.M. (1987) 'The support of autonomy and the control of behaviour', *Journal of Personnel Soc. Psychology*, 53: 1024–37.

Digman, John M. (1990) 'Personality structure: emergence of the five-factor model', in Mark R. Rosenzweig and Lyman W. Porter (eds), *Annual Review of Psychology*, 41: 417–40.

Dollard, J., Doob, L.W., Miller, N.E., Mowrer, O.H. and Sears, R.R. (1939) *Frustration and Aggression*. New Haven, CT: Yale University Press.

Drazin, R. and Sandelands, L. (1992) 'Autogenesis: a perspective on the process of organizing', *Organization Science*, 3: 230–49.

Dunnette, Marvin D. (1990) 'Blending the science and practice of industrial and organizational psychology: where are we and where are we going?', *Handbook of Industrial and Organizational Psychology*, 2nd edn, volume 1. Palo Alto, CA: Consulting Psychologists Press. p. 27.

Fineman, S. (1993) 'Organisations as emotional arenas', in S. Fineman (ed.), *Emotion in Organizations*. London: Sage.

Friman, Patrick C., Allen, Keith D., Kerwin, Mary Louise E. and Larzelere, Robert (1993) 'Changes in modern psychology: a citation analysis of the Kuhnian Displacement Thesis', *American Psychologist*, 48(6): 658–64.

Gaines, Jeannie (1993) 'You don't necessarily have to be charismatic . . .: an interview with Anita Roddick and reflections on charismatic processes in the Body Shop International', *Leadership Quarterly*, 4(3/4): 347–59.

Gergen, K.J. and Gergen, M.M. (1988) 'Narrative and the self as relationship', in L. Berkowitz (ed.), *Advances in Experimental Social Psychology*, vol. 21. San Diego: Academic Press. pp. 17–56.

Gerhart, B. (1987) 'How important are dispositional factors as determinants of job satisfaction? Implications for job design and other personnel programs', *Journal of Applied Psychology*, 72: 366–73.

Giddens, Anthony (1992) *The Transformation of Intimacy*. Stanford, CA: Stanford University Press.

Graham, Jill W. (1986) 'Principled organizational dissent: a theoretical essay', in Barry M. Staw and L.L. Cummings (eds), *Research in Organizational Behavior*, vol. 8. JAI Press. pp. 1–52.

Granovetter, M. (1985) 'Economic action and social structure: the problem of embeddedness', *American Journal of Sociology*, 91: 481–510.

Greenberg, J. (1990) 'Organizational justice: yesterday, today and tomorrow', *Journal of Management*, 16: 399–432.

Haraway, Donna J. (1991) *Simians, Cyborgs, and Women*. London: Routledge.

Heller, Frank A. and Clark, Alfred W. (1976) 'Personnel and human resources development', in

Mark R. Rosenzweig and Lyman W. Porter (eds), *Annual Review of Psychology*, 27: 405–35.

Henriques, Julian, Hollway, Wendy, Urwin, Cathy, Venn, Couze and Walkerdine, Valerie (1984) *Changing the Subject*. Methuen.

Hogan, J. and Hogan, R. (1989) 'How to measure employee reliability', *Journal of Applied Psychology*, 74: 273–9.

Hogan, Robert T. (1991) 'Personality and personality measurement', in Marvin D. Dunnette and Leaetta M. Hough (eds), *Handbook of Industrial and Organizational Psychology*, 2nd edn, vol. 2. Palo Alto, CA: Consulting Psychologists Press. pp. 873–919.

Hoskin, Keith (1995) 'The viewing self and the world we view: beyond the perspectival illusion', *Organization*, 2(1): 141–62.

House, Robert J. (1988) 'Power and personality in complex organizations', in *Research in Organizational Behavior*, vol. 10. JAI Press. pp. 305–57.

House, Robert J. and Singh, Jitendra V. (1987) 'Organizational behavior: some new directions for I/O psychology', *Annual Review of Psychology*, 38: 669–718.

Ilgen, Daniel R. and Klein, Howard J. (1988) 'Organizational behavior', *Annual Review of Psychology*, 40: 327–51.

Jermier, J.M. (1988) 'Sabotage at work: the rational view', *Research in the Sociology of Organizations*, 6: 101–34.

Kanfer, Ruth (1990) 'Motivation theory and industrial and organizational psychology', in *Handbook of Industrial & Organizational Psychology*, 2nd edn, vol. 1. Palo Alto, CA: Consulting Psychologists Press. pp. 75–170.

Katzell, Raymond A. (1994) 'Contemporary metatrends in industrial and organizational psychology', in Harry C. Triandis, Marvin D. Dunnette and Leaetta M. Hough (eds), *Handbook of Industrial and Organizational Psychology*, 2nd edn, vol. 4. Palo Alto, CA: Consulting Psychologists Press. pp. 1–88.

Katzell, Raymond A. and Thompson, Donne E. (1990) 'Work motivation: theory and practice', *American Psychologist*, 45(2): 144–53.

Klimoski, R. and Mohammed, S. (1994) 'Team mental model: construct or metaphor?', *Journal of Management*, 20: 403–37.

LaNuez, D. and Jermier, J.M. (1994) 'Sabotage by managers and technocrats: neglected patterns of resistance at work', in J.M. Jermier, D. Knights and W.R. Nord (eds), *Resistance and Power in Organizations: Critical Perspectives on Work and Organization*. London: Routledge. pp. 219–51.

Latham, L.L. (1995) Presentation at Society of Industrial and Organizational Psychologists Conference.

Leavitt, Harold J. (1975) 'Suppose we took groups seriously', in Eugene L. Cass and Frederick G.

Zimmer (eds), *Man and Work in Society*. Western Electric Company. pp. 410–20.

Lee, Yueh-Ting (1994) 'Why does American psychology have cultural limitations?', *American Psychologist*, 49(6): 524.

Locke, Edwin A. (1976) 'The nature of causes of job satisfaction', in Marvin D. Dunnette (ed.), *Handbook of Industrial and Organizational Psychology*. Rand McNally. pp. 1297–349.

Locke, E.E., Shaw, K.N., Saari, L.M. and Latham, G.P. (1981) 'Goal setting and task performance: 1969–1980', *Psychological Bulletin*, 90: 125–52.

Lord, R.G., de Vader, C.L. and Alliger, G.M. (1986) 'A meta-analysis of the relation between personality traits and leadership perceptions: an application of validity generalization procedures', *Journal of Applied Psychology*, 71: 402–10.

March, J.G. (ed.) (1965) *Handbook of Organizations*. Chicago: Rand NcNally.

Marecek, Jeanne (1995) 'Gender, politics, and psychology's ways of knowing', *American Psychologist*, 50(3): 162–3.

Markus, H.P. and Kitayama, S. (1991) Culture and the self: implications for cognition, emotion, and motivation', *Psychological Review*, 98: 224–53.

Maslow, A.H. (1943) 'A theory of human motivation', *Psychological Review*, 50: 370–96.

Mathewson, Stanley B. (1931) *Restriction of Output among Unorganized Workers*. Southern Illinois University Press.

McClelland, D.C. and Boyatzis, R.E. (1982) 'Leadership motive pattern and long-term success in management', *Journal of Applied Psychology*, 67: 737–43.

McLean Parks, J. and Kidder, D.L. (1994) '"Till death us do part . . .": changing work relationships in the 1990s', in C.L. Cooper and D.M. Rousseau (eds), *Trends in Organizational Behavior*. Wiley.

Meindl, James R. and Ehrlich, Sanford B. (1987) 'The romance of leadership and the evaluation of organizational performance', *Academy of Management Journal*, 30(1): 91–109.

Meltzer, H. (1971) 'Scope of industrial psychology references in the annual review, 1960–1969', *Personnel Psychology*, 24: 77–98.

Meltzer, H. and Nord, Walter (1973) 'The present status of industrial and organizational psychology', *Personnel Psychology*, 26: 11–29.

Mischel, W. (1968) *Personality and Assessment*. New York: Wiley.

Mischel, W. and Shoda, Y. (1995) 'A cognitive-affective system theory of personality: reconceptualizing situations, dispositions, dynamics, and invariance in personality structure', *Psychological Review*, 102: 246–68.

Mitchell, Terrence R. (1979) 'Organizational behavior', in M.R. Rosenzweig and L.W. Porter (eds), *Annual Review of Psychology*, 30: 243–81.

Mitchell, Terrence R. and James, Lawrence R. (1989a)

'Introduction and background', *Academy of Management Review*, 14(3): 331–2.

Mitchell, Terrence R. and James, Lawrence R. (1989b) 'Improving interactional organizational research: a model of person–organization fit', *Academy of Management Review*, 14(3): 333–49.

Morrison, A.M. and Van Glinow, M.A. (1990) 'Women and minorities in management', in special issue *Organizational Psychology of American Psychologist*, 45: 200–8.

Mount, M.K., Barrick, M.R. and Strauss, J.P. (1994) 'Validity of observer ratings of the big five personality factors', *Journal of Applied Psychology*, 79: 272–80.

Mowday, Richard T. and Sutton, Robert I. (1993) 'Organizational behavior: linking individuals and groups to organizational contexts', in Lyman W. Porter and Mark R. Rosenzweig (eds), *Annual Review of Psychology*, 44: 195–229.

Nord, Walter (1974) 'The failure of current applied behavioral science – a Marxian perspective', *Journal of Applied Behavioral Science*, 10(4).

Offerman, Lynn R. and Gowing, Marilyn K. (1990) 'Organizations of the future: changes and challenges', *American Psychologist*, 45(2): 95–108.

O'Reilly, Charles A. III (1991) 'Organizational behavior: where we've been, where we're going', in Lyman W. Porter and Mark R. Rosenzweig (eds), *Annual Review of Psychology*, 42: 427–58.

Organ, Dennis W. (1988) 'A restatement of the satisfaction–performance hypothesis', *Journal of Management*, 14: 547–57.

Organ, D.W. (1990) 'The motivational basis of organization citizenship behavior', *Research in Organizational Behavior*, 12: 43–72.

Organ, D.W. and Near, J.P. (1985) 'Cognition vs affect in measures of job satisfaction', *International Journal of Psychology*, 20: 241–53.

Perlow, R. and Latham, L.L (1993) 'Relationship of client abuse with locus of control and gender: a longitudinal study in mental retardation facilities', *Journal of Applied Psychology*, 78: 831–4.

Pervin, Lawrence A. (1989) 'Persons, situations, interactions: the history of a controversy and a discussion of theoretical models', *Academy of Management Review*, 14(3): 350–60.

Pinder, Craig C. (1984) *Work Motivation: Theory, Issues, and Applications*. Scott, Foresman.

Quinn, R.P. and Kahn, R.L. (1967) 'Organizational psychology', *Annual Review of Psychology*, 18: 437–66.

Reid, P.T. (1994) 'The real problem in the study of culture', *American Psychologist*, 49: 524–5.

Robinson, S.L. and Bennett, R.J. (1975) 'A typology of deviant workplace behaviors: a multidimensional scaling study', *Academy of Management Journal*, 38: 555–72.

Rousseau, Denise M. (1989) 'Psychological and implied contracts in organizations', *Employee Responsibilities and Rights Journal*, 2: 121–39.

Rousseau, D.M. and House, R.J. (1994) 'Meso organizational behavior: avoiding three fundamental biases', in C.L. Cooper and D.M. Rousseau (eds), *Trends in Organizational Behavior*, vol. 1. Chichester, England: Wiley. pp. 13–30.

Rousseau, Denise M. and Parks, Judi McLean (1993) 'The contracts of individuals and organizations', *Research in Organizational Behavior*, 15: 1–43.

Salancik, G.R. and Pfeffer, J. (1977) 'An examination of need–satisfaction models of job attitudes', *Administrative Science Quarterly*, 22: 427–56.

Salancik, G.R. and Pfeffer, J. (1978) 'A social information processing approach to job attitudes and task design', *Administrative Science Quarterly*, 23: 224–53.

Sampson, Edward E. (1985) 'The decentralization of identity: toward a revised concept of personal and social order', *American Psychologist*, 40: 1203–11.

Sampson, Edward E. (1988) 'The debate on individualism: indigenous psychologies of the individual', *American Psychologist*, 43(1): 15–22.

Sampson, Edward E. (1989) 'The challenge of social change for psychology', *American Psychologist*, 44(6): 914–21.

Sayers, Janet (1982) *Biological Politics: Feminist and Anti-feminist Perspectives*. Tavistock.

Schein, Edgar H. (1990) 'Organizational culture', *American Psychologist*, 45(2): 109–19.

Schneider, Benjamin. (1985) 'Organizational behavior', *Annual Review of Psychology*, 36: 573–611.

Schneider, Benjamin (1987) 'The people make the place', *Personnel Psychology*, 40: 437–53.

Scott, W. Richard (1992) *Organizations: Rational, Natural, and Open Systems*, 3rd edn. Prentice-Hall.

Shore, Lynn McFarlane and Tetrick, Lois E. (1994) 'The psychological contract as an explanatory framework in the employment relationship', in C.L. Cooper and D.M. Rousseau (eds), *Trends in Organizational Behavior*, vol. 1. Wiley.

Simon, H.A. (1990) 'Invariants of human behaviour', in Mark R. Rosenzweig and Lyman W. Porter (eds), *Annual Review of Psychology*, 41: 1–19.

Spector, P.E. (1975) 'Relationships of organizational frustration with reported behavioral reactions of employees', *Journal of Applied Psychology*, 60: 635–7.

Spector, P.E. (1978) 'Organizational frustration: a model and review of the literature', *Personnel Psychology*, 31: 815–29.

Spector, P.E., Jex, S.M. and Chen, P.Y. (1995) 'Relations of incumbent affect-related personality traits with incumbent and objective measures of characteristics of jobs', *Journal of Organizational Behavior*, 16: 59–65.

Staw, Barry M. (1984) 'Organizational behavior: a review and reformation of the field's outcome variables', *Annual Review of Psychology*, 35: 627–66.

Staw, Barry M. (1991) 'Dressing up like an organization: when psychological theories can explain organizational action', *Journal of Management*, 17(4): 805–19.

Staw, Barry M., Bell, Nancy E. and Clausen, John A. (1986) 'The dispositional approach to job attitudes: a lifetime longitudinal test', *Administrative Science Quarterly*, 31: 56–77.

Stogdill, R.M. (1974) *Handbook of Leadership: a Survey of Theory and Research*. New York: Free Press.

Storms, P.L. and Spector, P.E. (1987) 'Relationships of organizational frustration with reported behavioural reactions: the moderating effect of locus of control', *Journal of Occupational Psychology*, 60: 227–34.

Tajfel, H., Jaspars, J.M.F. and Fraser, C. (1984) 'The social dimension in European social psychology', in H. Tajfel (ed.), *The Social Dimension: European Developments in Social Psychology*, vol. 13. Cambridge: Cambridge University Press.

Townley, Barbara (1994) *Reframing Human Resource Management: Power, Ethics, and the Subject at Work*. London: Sage.

Van Dyne, Linn, Graham, Jill W. and Dienesch, Richard M. (1994) 'Organizational citizenship behavior: construct redefinition, measurement, and validation', *Journal of Management Journal*, 37(4): 765–802.

Van Katwyk, P., Spector, P.E., Fox, S. and Kelloway, K. (1995) 'How does my job make me feel? The development of the job-related affective well-being scale (JAWS)'. Poster presentation at Society of Industrial and Organizational Psychologists Conference.

Vroom, Victor H. (1974) 'Leadership', in Marvin D. Dunnett (ed.), *Handbook of Industrial and Organizational Psychology*. Rand McNally. pp. 1527–51.

Warr, P. (1987) *Work, Unemployment, and Mental Health*. Oxford: Oxford University Press.

Warr, P. (1994) 'A conceptual framework for the study of work and mental health', *Work and Stress*, 8: 84–97.

Weick, K.E. (1979) *The Social Psychology of Organizing*, 2nd edn. Reading, MA: Addison-Wesley.

Weick, K.E. (1995) *Sensemaking in Organizations*. Thousand Oaks, CA: Sage.

Weick, K.E. and Roberts, K.H. (1993) 'Collective mind in organizations: heedful interrelating on flight decks', *Administrative Science Quarterly*, 38: 357–81.

White, Robert W. (1959) 'Motivation reconsidered: the concept of competence', *Psychology Review*, 66: 297–334.

Wilpert, B. (1995) 'Organizational behavior', *Annual Review of Psychology*, 46: 59–90.

Wood, Robert E. and Locke, Edwin A. (1990) 'Goal setting and strategy effects on complex tasks', in Barry M. Staw and L.L. Cummings (eds), *Research in Organizational Behavior*, vol. 12. JAI Press. pp. 73–109.

Yammarino, F.J. and Bass, B.M. (1991) 'Person and situation views of leadership: a multiple levels of analysis approach', *Leadership Quarterly*, 2: 121–39.

1.6

The Institutionalization of Institutional Theory

PAMELA S. TOLBERT AND LYNNE G. ZUCKER

Since the publication of Meyer and Rowan's (1977) classic article, organizational analyses based on an institutional perspective have proliferated. Work sharing the banner of institutional theory has investigated a wide range of phenomena, from the spread of specific personnel policies (Tolbert and Zucker 1983; Baron et al. 1986; Edelman 1992) to the fundamental redefinition of organizational missions and forms (DiMaggio 1991; Fligstein 1985) to the development of domestic and international policies by government organizations (Strang 1990; Zhou 1993). Ironically, however, the institutional approach has yet to become institutionalized. There is very little consensus on the definition of key concepts, measures or methods within this theoretic tradition. Unlike population ecology and its standard measures of density, institutional theory has developed no central set of standard variables, nor is it associated with a standard research methodology or even a set of methods. Studies have relied on a variety of techniques, including case analysis, cross-sectional regression, longitudinal models of various types, and so forth (see also Davis and Powell 1992; Scott and Meyer 1994). Our review of the literature suggests one important source of such variation in approach: despite the sizeable body of work defined as part of this tradition, there has been surprisingly little attention given to conceptualizing and specifying the *processes* of institutionalization (though see DiMaggio 1991; Strang and Meyer 1993; and Rura and Miner 1994 for recent progress in this direction).

As noted in Zucker's (1977) early research, which focused on consequences of varying levels of institutionalization, institutionalization is

both a process and a property variable. Perhaps because her work was cast in a small groups setting, however, a process-based approach to institutionalization has not been followed in most organizational analyses. Instead, institutionalization is almost always treated as a qualitative state: structures are institutionalized, or they are not. Consequently, important questions of the determinants of variations in levels of institutionalization, and of how such variation might affect the degree of similarity among sets of organizations, have been largely neglected.

In this chapter, we address these questions by offering a theoretical specification of institutionalization processes. We begin by presenting a brief historical overview of sociological theorizing and research on organizations through the mid 1970s. This overview is intended both to clarify the links between institutional theory and previous traditions of sociological work on organizational structure, and to provide some context for understanding the receptivity of organizational researchers in the late 1970s to institutional theory as an explanatory framework. The next section reviews the initial exposition of the theory in Meyer and Rowan's (1977) seminal article, focusing on the way in which it challenged then-dominant theoretical and empirical traditions in organizational research. We point up an apparent logical ambiguity in this formulation, one which involves the phenomenological status of structural arrangements that are the objects of institutionalization processes. In the remainder of the chapter, we offer a general model of institutionalization processes, as a means both of clarifying this ambiguity and of elaborating the logical and empirical implications of a phenomenologically based version of institutional theory, first developed by Zucker. Finally, on the basis of this analysis, we consider a range of issues that require further theoretical development and empirical study.

Our primary aims in this effort are twofold: to clarify the independent theoretical contributions of institutional theory to analyses of organizations, and to develop this theoretical perspective further in order to enhance its use in empirical research.[1] There is also a more general, more ambitious objective here, and that is to build a bridge between two distinct models of social actor that underlie most organizational analyses, which we refer to as a rational actor model and an institutional model. The former is premised on the assumption that individuals are constantly engaged in calculations of the costs and benefits of different action choices, and that behavior reflects such utility-maximizing calculations (Coleman 1990; Hechter 1990). In the latter model, by contrast, 'oversocialized' individuals are assumed to accept and follow social norms unquestioningly, without any real reflection or behavioral resistance based on their own particular, personal interests (see Wrong 1961). We suggest that these two general models should be treated not as oppositional but rather as representing two ends of a continuum of decision-making processes and behaviors. Thus, a key problem for theory and research is to specify the conditions under which behavior is more likely to resemble one end of this continuum or the other. In short, what is needed are theories of *when* rationality is likely to be more or less bounded. A developed conception of institutionalization processes provides a useful point of departure for exploring this issue.

SOCIOLOGICAL ANALYSES OF ORGANIZATIONS: THE ORIGINS OF INSTITUTIONAL THEORY

Functionalist Analyses of Organizations

The study of organizations has a relatively short history within sociology. Prior to the work of Robert Merton and his students in the late 1940s, organizations were not typically acknowledged as a distinctive social phenomenon, one worthy of study in its own right, by American sociologists. Although organizations had certainly been subjects of study by sociologists prior to the advent of functionalist analyses (see, for example, the work of American theorists associated with the Chicago School: Park 1922;

Thomas and Znaniecki 1927), such studies typically treated organizations as aspects of general social problems, such as social inequality, intercommunity relations, social deviance, and so forth; the focus of analysis was not on organizations *qua* organizations. Despite the key role assigned to formal organizations by Weber's (1946) and Michels's (1962) analyses of industrial orders, the notion that organizations represent independent social actors in modern societal processes was not widely recognized until after the pioneering work of Merton and colleagues (see Coleman 1980; 1990). As we shall explore later in our review, we conceive of both organizational and individual actors as potential creators of new institutional structure (Zucker 1988). (See also DiMaggio's 1988 discussion of 'institutional entrepreneurs'.)

Merton's (1948) initial interest in studying organizations appears to have been driven primarily by a concern with empirically testing and developing the general logic of functionalist social theory. Organizations, viewed as societies in microcosm, offered the opportunity to conduct the kind of comparative research required for empirical examination of functionalist tenets (see Selznick 1949; Gouldner 1950; Blau 1955). Thus, one of the major hallmarks of analyses of organizations produced by Merton and his students was a focus on the dynamics of social change, an issue functionalist theory had often been accused by its critics of neglecting (Turner 1974).

Concern with change was reflected in two main objectives that were characteristic of organizational studies in the functionalist tradition: examining the nature of covariation among different elements of structure, and assessing the dynamic balance between dysfunctional and beneficial outcomes of given structural arrangements. These foci directly address two key assumptions embedded in functionalist theory about survival requirements of social collectivities.

The first assumption is that the structural components of a system must be integrated in order for the system to survive, since the components are interrelated parts of the whole. A corollary derived from this main assumption is that change in one structural component necessitates adaptive changes in other components. Thus, given this general theoretical framework, empirical examination of the relationships among elements of organizational structure was a natural focus of study.

The second assumption is that existing structures contribute to a social system's functioning, at least on the balance; otherwise, the system could not survive. An implication of this assumption, adduced by Merton (1948), is that change is likely to occur when the functional contributions of a given structural arrangement are exceeded by dysfunctions associated with that arrangement. This reasoning led to an explicit concern with identifying both the dysfunctional and functional consequences of given structural arrangements.[2]

Quantitative Analyses of Structural Covariation

Pursuit of the first problem, examination of interrelations among structural elements, laid the foundation for one general line of research that came to dominate and define sociological studies of organizations for the next two decades. This line of research increasingly came to be typified by quantitative analyses of covariance among the elements of formal organizational structure and by essentially economic explanations of such covariation. The rapid ascendance of this approach to organizational analysis most likely reflects its affinity with established traditions of organizational research in the field of management science, well established in most business schools by the time sociologists turned their attention to the study of bureaucracy (Follett 1942; Fayol 1949; Gulick and Urwick 1937; Woodward 1965). Formal structure was assumed to reflect organizational decision-makers' rational efforts to maximize efficiency by securing coordination and control of work activities. Thus, the finding of a positive relationship between size and complexity was explained in terms of the needs and capacity of larger organizations for efficiency-enhancing specialization, the relation between complexity and size of the administrative component in terms of the increased needs for supervision to manage coordination problems accompanying specialization, and so forth.[3]

Organizational research shifted focus in the late 1960s to include consideration of the effects of environmental forces in determining structure, but the basic functionalist/economic explanatory framework was retained by most work (see for example, Thompson 1967; Lawrence and Lorsch 1967). Despite the dominance of this approach to analyzing and explaining formal organizational structure (or perhaps because of it), this paradigm came under increasing fire by the early 1970s. In part, increasing skepticism reflected the general lack of cumulative empirical findings from work in this tradition (Meyer 1979). The widespread revival and reassessment of the general applicability of arguments developed earlier by Barnard (1938), Simon (1947), and March and Simon (1957), emphasizing inherent limits on organizational decision-makers' ability to act with a high degree of rationality, may have also helped lay the groundwork for the acceptance of alternative paradigms (Weick 1969).

Reflecting the growing dissatisfaction with traditional explanations of formal structure, a new approach to organization–environment relations, labeled resource dependence (Pfeffer and Salancik 1978), became increasingly prominent during the 1970s. This perspective focused attention on decision-makers' concerns for maintaining organizational autonomy and power over other organizations. By emphasizing the determining role of power considerations in explaining organizations' structure (see Thompson and McEwen 1958), it challenged dominant theoretical approaches that focused largely or exclusively on production efficiency concerns. However, like earlier work, a resource dependence approach also was predicated implicitly on a rational actor model of decision-making in organizations, albeit one in which actors' behavior was based on calculation aimed at maximizing power and autonomy rather than pure efficiency. The operation of social influence processes, such as imitation or normatively based conformity, which might mitigate or limit autonomous decision-making, was largely ignored.

FORMAL STRUCTURE AS MYTH AND CEREMONY

Symbolic Properties of Structure

The analysis laid out in the now-classic paper by Meyer and Rowan (1977) thus offered a radical departure from conventional ways of thinking about formal structure and about the nature of organizational decision-making through which structure was produced. Their analysis was guided by a key insight, namely: formal structures have symbolic as well as action-generating properties. In other words, structures can become invested with socially shared meanings, and thus, in addition to their 'objective' functions, can serve to communicate information about the organization to both internal and external audiences (Kamens 1977). Explaining formal structure from this vantage point offered organizational researchers the opportunity to explore an array of new insights into the causes and consequences of structure.

The notion that organizations have symbolic aspects was not entirely novel: a variety of authors had previously underscored key symbolic functions served by mission statements, structural arrangements, and top-level members of organizations (Clark 1956; Selznick 1957; Zald and Denton 1963). In the functionalist tradition, such elements were argued to be critical to securing environmental support through demonstration of the consistency between core values of the organization and those in the larger society (Parsons 1956; 1960). Meyer and Rowan's contribution to this earlier, related work lay in their systematic development of the implications of the use of formal structure for symbolic purposes, particularly in terms of highlighting limitations of more rationalistic explanations of structure.

Implications

Based on the notion that formal structure can signal organizations' commitment to rational, efficient standards of organizing, and thus provide general social 'accounts' (Scott and Lyman 1968), Meyer and Rowan's analysis specified three major implications of this notion. The first is that the adoption of formal structure can occur regardless of the existence of specific, immediate problems of coordination and control of members' activities that an organization may face.

> Organizations are driven to incorporate the practices and procedures defined by prevailing rationalized concepts of organizational work and institutionalized in society. Organizations that do so increase their legitimacy and their survival prospects, independent of the immediate efficacy of the acquired practices and procedures. (1977: 340)

This argument challenged then-dominant causal models of structure in several respects. First, in terms of the determinants of structure, it directed attention to external influences not linked to actual production processes, such as the passage of legislation and the development of strong social norms within an organizational network. In so doing, the relative importance of internal organizational characteristics traditionally investigated as sources of formal structure, such as size and technology, was called into question. It also indirectly suggested alternative ways of interpreting such characteristics (e.g. as indicators both of organizations' visibility to the general public and of network linkages).

Moreover, in terms of consequences or outcomes, it led to a focus on the adoption of specific structural arrangements that had acquired social meanings, such as formal employment policies, accounting and budgeting practices, and offices and positions associated with employment equity. This indirectly challenged the utility of existing theoretical and empirical efforts to conceptualize and measure structure in terms of general, abstract dimensions, such as formalization, complexity, and centralization.

A second major implication pointed up in Meyer and Rowan's analysis is that the social evaluation of organizations, and hence organizational survival, can rest on observation of formal structures (that may or may not actually function), rather than on observed outcomes related to actual task performance.

> Thus, organizational success depends on factors other than efficient coordination and control of production activities. Independent of their productive efficiency, organizations which exist in highly elaborated institutional environments and succeed in becoming isomorphic with these environments gain the legitimacy and resources needed to survive. (1977: 352)

This claim sharply contradicted underlying market-oriented, or at least performance-oriented, assumptions about the functions of formal structure that dominated previous work: (1) that inefficient organizations – in production terms – would be selected out through a process of interorganizational competition; and (2) that correlations between measures of formal structure and such characteristics as size and technology thus resulted from the survival of organizations whose form matched the demands of their production environments. Although these assumptions underpinned the majority of quantitative analyses of determinants of structure, they were often made explicit only in studies directly examining organizational effectiveness (Goodman and Pennings 1977). The notion that organizations could survive despite very low objective performance implied the possibility of 'permanently failing' organizations (Meyer and Zucker 1989), that is organizations that survive despite evident inefficiencies that logically should cause them to fail.

Finally, the third major implication derived by Meyer and Rowan was that the relationship between actual, everyday activities and behaviors of organizational members and formal structures may be negligible.

> . . . (F)ormal organizations are often loosely coupled . . . structural elements are only loosely linked to each other and to activities, rules are often violated, decisions are often unimplemented, or if implemented have uncertain consequences, technologies are of problematic efficiency, and evaluation and inspection systems are subverted or rendered so vague as to provide little coordination. (1977: 342)

This implication also represented a direct challenge to traditional explanations of structure which, by treating formal structures as means for coordinating and controlling activities, necessarily assumed a tight connection between structures and actual behaviors of organizational members.

AMBIGUITIES IN INSTITUTIONAL THEORY

In drawing this last implication, Meyer and Rowan decouple formal structure from action, implicitly defining institutional structures as those that are subject to decoupling. However, earlier in their argument they use the concept of institutional structures much as Berger and Luckmann (1967) and as Zucker (1977): a structure that has become institutionalized is one that has become taken for granted by members of a social group as efficacious and necessary; thus it serves as an important causal source of stable patterns of behavior.

This creates an inherent ambiguity in their underlying phenomenological argument, because the definition of 'institutionalized' itself contradicts the claim that institutional structures are apt to be decoupled from behavior. To *be* institutional, structure must generate action. As Giddens (1979) argues, structure that is not translated into action is in some fundamental sense not 'social' structure. Geertz sounds a similar note: 'We gain access to symbol systems only through the flow of behavior – or, more precisely, social action' (1973: 17).

The discussion of the decoupling of structure and action implies a Goffmanesque 'backstage/frontstage' definition of institutionalized structures (Goffman 1959), where the belief in the efficacy and need for such structures is subject to dispute but the structures are nonetheless viewed as serving a useful presentational purpose. This implies that such structures fundamentally lack normative and cognitive legitimacy (Della Fave 1986; Walker et al. 1986; Stryker 1994; Aldrich and Fiol 1994), and that they are not at any time real signals of underlying intention. Whether such structures are appropriately described as institutionalized, given standard definitions of the term, is dubious.

Resource Dependence versus Institutional Processes

Moreover, the ambiguity that inheres in this view of structural change in organizations leads to a fundamental confounding of institutional and resource dependence theory (Zucker 1991: 104). Scott (1987: 497) has argued that a shift in institutional theory towards explaining 'the sources or loci of "rationalized and impersonal prescriptions"' and away from explaining the 'properties of generalized belief systems' has the advantage of enlarging the framework for explaining formal structures to include organizations' compliance with external actors' demands in order to obtain resources needed for survival. More recently, he elaborated: 'Much of the theoretical and empirical research on institutions correctly focuses on regulative agencies . . . which exercise legitimate powers to formulate and enforce rule systems . . . [which leads to an emphasis on] the flow of rewards and sanctions' (1994: 98). In this formulation, however, there is a blurring of the boundary between resource dependence and institutional theory, thereby obscuring the unique theoretical contributions of the latter, in particular, to organizational analysis.

Comparison of recent studies based on institutional theory with earlier studies cast within the framework of resource dependence serves to illustrate problems of distinguishing these theoretical perspectives. For example, using an institutional perspective to examine the effects of government laws and policies on employment structures, Sutton et al. argue: 'Faced with an apparently hostile legal environment, employers adopt due-process governance to cool out potentially litigious employees and demonstrate good-faith compliance with government mandates' (1994: 946). Likewise, Edelman suggests that organizations that construct formal structures as symbolic gestures of compliance with government policy 'are less likely to provoke protest by protected classes of employees within the firm or community members who seek jobs . . . are more likely to secure government resources (contracts, grants, etc.), and . . . are less likely to trigger audits by regulatory agencies' (1992: 1542). Thus, the adoption of structure is treated as a strategic, but apparently largely superficial change; it is the organizational counterpart of the manipulative actions of narcissistic persons who consciously use 'false fronts' as a means of gaining their own ends with other persons.[4]

Other studies described in Pfeffer and Salancik's (1978) development of resource dependence theory reflect a very similar explanatory logic. For example, they report (1978: 197–200) a case study by Pfeffer of an organization that intentionally created two separate structural units, one of which was non-profit, in order to conform to extant social definitions of appropriate form for educational organizations and to thereby secure necessary support from external constituents. Similarly, they describe (1978: 56–9) research conducted by Salancik which examined the relationship between indicators of firms' visibility and relative dependence on federal government contracts, and the presence of organizational arrangements showing commitment to equal employment opportunity. The results indicated that greater dependence was associated with more intensive signaling of compliance with affirmative action law via creation of formal positions and written documentation of programs and policies. The overlap between these arguments and those from more recent work cast within the framework of institutional theory is striking.

The lack of theoretical distinctiveness in these studies results in part from the de-emphasis on a distinguishing feature of institutional theory, a focus on the role of cultural understandings as determinants of behavior (Strang 1994) and on the normative bounds of rational decision-making. By shifting toward an emphasis on changes in 'appearance' and downplaying the internal consequences of institutionalized structure, treating structure as *merely* symbol and signal, we end up with the implicit argument that a structure can maintain its symbolic value in the face of widespread knowledge that its effect on individuals' behavior is negligible. How such a contradiction in cultural understandings (i.e. that structures signify commitment to some action, and that structures may be unrelated to action) can endure poses an unanswered riddle in this approach.

There is a related, general problem with work that emphasizes purely symbolic, resource-securing functions of structure, one which lies in the implicit assumption that the costs of creating such structural elements are relatively low compared to the potential gains in increased resources from the environment. This assumption presumably follows from the notion that changes in formal structures often do not alter action. Although there are often-cited theoretical claims, there is no supporting empirical evidence that social activity is as ubiquitous as air and just as costless (Granovetter 1985). From the research to date, we do not know in fact whether structure is regularly decoupled from the internal functioning of the organization, nor do we know the cost of creating such structure compared to any increase in resource flows to the organization (a review of the evidence can be found in Scott and Meyer 1994).

The recasting of institutional theory to be more derivative of a resource dependence approach probably reflects, in part, general discomfort with the lack of voluntarism implied by more phenomenologically oriented versions of institutional theory, or what Oliver calls an 'overly passive and conforming depiction of organizations' (1991: 146). It may also stem from the apparent bias toward *stasis* in a phenomenological approach (DiMaggio 1988):

as currently developed in organizational analyses, the focus of an institutional approach traditionally has been on the way in which actors follow extant institutional 'scripts', and questions of how these scripts are produced, maintained and changed have been largely neglected (Barley and Tolbert 1988). It is these questions to which we turn next, using theoretical analyses by Berger and Luckmann (1967) and Zucker (1977) as our point of departure.

In addressing these issues, we make the key assumption that creating new structure takes more resources than maintaining the old: alteration and creation of organizational structures *do* constitute costs for the organization. Social structure is not simply a by-product of human activity; rather, human agency is required to produce it (Zucker et al. 1995; Zucker and Kreft 1994). Thus, structures that are altered or created must be believed to have some positive value for the organization, or decision-makers typically would not allocate resources to altering or creating new formal structure. Organizational decision-makers, of course, may have more or less discretion: sometimes decision-making power is very broad, sometimes it is very circumscribed. The analysis developed here is most applicable to instances in which decision-makers have relatively high levels of discretion concerning the adoption of structures.[5]

PROCESSES OF INSTITUTIONALIZATION

Drawing on work identified with the philosophical tradition of phenomenology, Berger and Luckmann (1967) identified institutionalization as a core process in the creation and perpetuation of enduring social groups. An institution, the outcome or end state of an institutionalization process, was defined as 'a reciprocal typification of habitualized action by types of actors' (1967: 54; following Schutz 1962; 1967).

In this definition, habitualized action refers to behaviors that have been developed empirically and adopted by an actor or set of actors in order to solve recurring problems. Such behaviors are habitualized to the degree that they are evoked with minimal decision-making effort by actors in response to particular stimuli. Reciprocal typification, in their use, involves the development of shared definitions or meanings that are linked to these habitualized behaviors (see Schutz 1962; 1967). Since typifications entail classifications or categorizations of actors with whom the actions are associated, this concept implies that the meanings attributed to habitualized action have come to be generalized, that is, to be independent of the specific individuals who carry out the action. Zucker (1977) referred to this process of generalizing the meaning of an action as 'objectification', and identified it as one of the key component processes of institutionalization.

Earlier phenomenological analyses of institutions, then, suggest at least two sequential processes involved in the initial formation of institutions and in their spread: *habitualization*, the development of patterned problem-solving behaviors and the association of such behaviors with particular stimuli; and *objectification*, the development of general, shared social meanings attached to these behaviors, a development that is necessary for the transplantation of actions to contexts beyond their point of origination.

At a later point in their analysis, Berger and Luckmann (1967) suggest an additional aspect of institutionalization, one also identified by Zucker and termed 'exteriority'. Exteriority refers to the degree to which typifications are 'experienced as possessing a reality of their own, a reality that confronts the individual as an external and coercive fact' (1967: 58). It is related to the historical continuity of typifications (Zucker 1977), and in particular, to the transmission of typifications to new members who, lacking knowledge of their origins, are apt to treat them as 'social givens' (Berger and Luckmann 1967; Tolbert 1988). We refer to the processes through which actions acquire the quality of exteriority as *sedimentation*.

In an early experimental study, Zucker (1977) demonstrated that as the degree of objectification and exteriority of an action increased, so did the degree of institutionalization (indicated by individuals' conformity to others' behavior), and that when institutionalization is high, then transmission of the action, maintenance of that action over time, and resistance of that action to change are all also high. Nelson and Winter (1982) find a similar process operating in the creation of task routines within organizations: more institutionalized routines are more readily transmitted to new employees. Thus, transmission is both causally and consequentially related to institutionalization. By enhancing the exteriority of a set of behaviors, transmission increases the degree to which those behaviors are institutionalized; institutionalization, in turn, affects the ease of subsequent transmission (Tolbert 1988).

This set of sequential processes – habitualization, objectification and sedimentation – suggests variability in levels of institutionalization, thus implying that some patterns of social behavior are more subject to critical evaluation, modification, and even elimination than others. In short, such patterned behaviors can vary in terms of the degree to which they are deeply embedded in a social system (more objective, more exterior), and thus vary in terms of their stability and their power to determine behavior.

Berger and Luckmann's analysis was focused on the occurrence of institutionalization processes among individual actors, not organizational actors. Zucker's experimental research extended the analysis to organizations, but still at the micro-level. Organizational actors are distinguished by a number of properties – hierarchical authority, potentially unlimited life-span, unique legal responsibilities, and so forth (see Coleman 1980) – likely to affect the way in which institutionalization processes are played out. These processes are often played out *between* organizations as well as within them.[6] Thus, we consider the extension of this analysis specifically to *institutional flows* between formal organizations. Figure 1 presents a summary of our analysis of the process of institutionalization, and the causal forces that are key at different points in the process.[7]

Habitualization

In an organizational context, the process of habitualization involves the generation of new structural arrangements in response to a specific organizational problem or set of problems, and the formalization of such arrangements in the policies and procedures of a given organization, or a set of organizations that confront the same or similar problems. These processes result in structures that can be classified as being at the pre-institutionalization stage.

There are voluminous literatures on organizational innovation and on organizational change that are relevant to understanding these processes (e.g. Quinn and Cameron 1988; Huber and Glick 1993). What is key for the purposes of our analysis, however, is that in this stage the creation of new structures in organizations is largely an independent activity. Since organizational decision-makers may share a common core of knowledge and ideas that make an innovation feasible and attractive, the adoption of a given innovation may and often does occur in close association with adoption processes in other organizations (i.e. simultaneous invention). Organizations experiencing a problem may, as part of their search for solutions, also consider solutions developed by others (DiMaggio and Powell 1983). Imitation *may* follow, but there is little sense of the necessity of this among organizational decision-makers, since there is no consensus on the general utility of the innovation. Hence, adoption can be predicted largely by characteristics that make a change technically and economically viable for a given organization (Anderson and Tushman 1990;

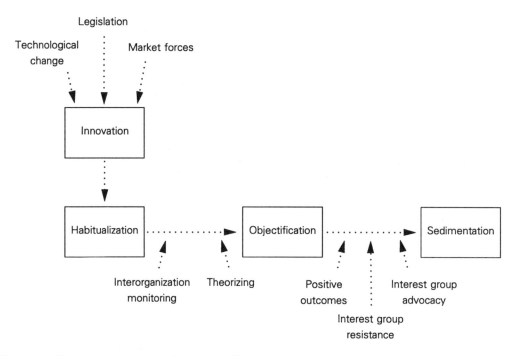

Figure 1   *Component processes of institutionalization*

Leblebici et al. 1991) and by internal political arrangements that make organizations more or less receptive to change processes (see March and Simon 1957).[8]

At the pre-institutionalization stage, then, there may be multiple adopters of a given structure, but these are likely to be comparatively few in number, limited to a circumscribed set of similar, possibly interconnected organizations facing similar circumstances, and to vary considerably in terms of the form of implementation. Such structures will not be the object of any sort of formal theorizing (Strang and Meyer 1993), and knowledge of the structures among non-adopters – especially those that are not in direct, frequent interaction with adopters – will be extremely limited, in terms of both operations and purpose (Nelson and Winter 1982).

Examples of structures at this stage of institutionalization can be readily found by comparing the organizational charts of any set of similar organizations. Such comparisons will almost certainly reveal an array of offices and policies that are idiosyncratic to one or a limited subset of the organizations – directors of electronic communications, departments of poultry science, marketing/manufacturing liaisons, etc. These sorts of structures tend to be relatively impermanent, sometimes enduring only for the length of the incumbent's tenure (see Miner 1987; 1991).

Objectification

The movement toward a more permanent and widespread status rests heavily on the next process, *objectification*, which accompanies the diffusion of structure. Objectification involves the development of some degree of social consensus among organizational decision-makers concerning the value of a structure, and the increasing adoption by organizations on the basis of that consensus. Such consensus can emerge through two different though not necessarily unrelated mechanisms.

On one hand, organizations may use evidence gathered directly from a variety of sources (the news media, first-hand observation, stock prices, and so on) to assess the risk parameters of adopting a new structure. To the extent that the results of structural change are expected to generalize, the apparent outcomes for prior organizations will be a significant determinant of the next adoption decision. Thus, objectification of structure is partially a consequence of organizations' monitoring of competitors, and efforts to enhance relative competitiveness. Recycling 'old social inventions' is a low-cost strategy, involving investment of fewer 'social resources' than creating new organizational structure.

By implication, diffusion of new structures to a given organization will have a lower hurdle than will creation *de novo* of comparable structures in that same organization, because other organizations will have 'pre-tested' the structure, and decision-makers' perception of relative costs and benefits of adopting will be influenced by observations of other organizations' behavior. Thus, the more organizations that have adopted the structure, the more likely will decision-makers perceive the relative balance of costs and benefits to be favorable.

Our arguments here are consistent with models of sequential decision-making recently developed by economists (Banerjee 1992; Bikchandani et al. 1992; see also David 1985). These models are premised on the assumptions that there is some degree of uncertainty in the outcomes of different choices, and that decision-makers will use information gained from observing the choices of others, as well as their own subjective assessments, in determining the 'best' choice. Under these conditions, the more widespread a given choice becomes, the more likely are individuals to view it as an optimal choice, and the less influential will be decision-makers' independent judgments of the value of the choice (see also Tolbert 1985; Abrahamson and Rosenkopf 1993).[9]

Objectification and diffusion of structure can also be spearheaded by what is sometimes referred to in the organizational change literature as a 'champion' – often, in this case, a set of individuals with a material stake in the promotion of the structure (DiMaggio 1988). Thus, for example, advocates of government civil service rules were often drawn from elite families whose traditional access to local political office had been broken by the development of immigrant-dominated machines (Tolbert and Zucker 1983); the spread of formalized selection procedures and performance evaluation procedures in businesses during the period following World War II was influenced by the promotional efforts of members of the emerging occupation of personnel management (Baron et al. 1986); and the role currently played by consultants in the adoption of practices identified with total quality management is widely acknowledged (Reeves and Bednar 1994; Sitkin et al. 1994). DiMaggio (1991), Rowan (1982), Covaleski and Dirsmith (1988), Chaves (forthcoming) and Ritti and Silver (1986) also offer examples of the role of interest groups in promoting structural changes in organizations.

Champions are most likely to emerge when there is a large potential 'market' for the innovation (e.g. when environmental changes have adversely affected the competitive positions of a number of established organizations). To be successful, champions must accomplish two major tasks of theorization (Strang and Meyer 1993): creation of a definition of a generic organizational problem, a definition that includes specification of the set or category of organizational actors characterized by the problem; and justification of a particular formal structural arrangement as a solution to the problem on logical or empirical grounds (see also Galaskiewicz 1985). The first task involves generating public recognition of a consistent pattern of dissatisfaction or organizational failing that is characteristic of some array of organizations; the second task involves developing theories that provide a diagnosis of the sources of dissatisfaction or failings, theories that are compatible with a particular structure as a solution or treatment.

By identifying the set of organizations that face a defined problem and providing a positive evaluation of a structure as an appropriate solution, theorizing invests the structure with both general cognitive and normative legitimacy. To be persuasive and effective, theorizing efforts must also provide evidence that the change is actually successful in at least some cases that can be examined by others considering the adoption of new structure. On the basis of such theorizing, and the accompanying evidence, champions encourage the diffusion of structures throughout a set of organizations that are not otherwise directly connected.

Structures that have been subject to objectification and have become fairly widely diffused can be described as being at the stage of semi-institutionalization. At this stage, adopters have typically become quite heterogeneous; consequently, specific characteristics of organizations that were previously identified with adoption will have relatively limited predictive power (Tolbert and Zucker 1983). The impetus for diffusion shifts from simple imitation to a more normative base, reflecting implicit or explicit theorization of structures. As theorization develops and becomes more explicit, variance in the form that the structures take in different organizations should decline.

Examples of structures that could be classified as being at this stage include team-based production, quality circles, gain-sharing compensation plans, internal consultants, sensitivity training programs for management, managers of work/family policy, and employee assistance programs, among others. While such structures generally have a longer rate of survival in organizations compared to those in the pre-institutionalized stage, clearly not all persist indefinitely. In fact, the ultimate fate of most such structures often invests them with a fad or fashion-like quality (Abrahamson 1991). This is because structures at the stage of semi-institutionalization typically have a relatively short history. Thus, while they have acquired some degree of normative acceptance, adopters nonetheless are apt to remain cognizant of their relatively untested quality, and consciously to monitor the accumulation of evidence (from their own organization as well as others) on the effectiveness of the structures. It is not until a structure has reached the stage of full institutionalization that actors' propensity to engage in independent evaluation of the structures significantly declines.

Sedimentation

Full institutionalization involves *sedimentation*, a process that fundamentally rests on the historical continuity of structure, and especially on its survival across generations of organizational members. Sedimentation is characterized both by the virtually complete spread of structures across the group of actors theorized as appropriate adopters, and by the perpetuation of structures over a lengthy period of time. Thus, it implies both 'width' and 'depth' dimensions of structures (Eisenhardt 1988).

Identification of factors that affect the extent of diffusion and the long-term retention of a structure is thus key to understanding the process of sedimentation. One such factor that has been pointed up in a variety of studies is the existence of a set of actors who are somehow adversely affected by the structures and who are able to collectively mobilize against them. Covaleski and Dirsmith's (1988) analysis of legislative resistance to a new budgeting arrangement in a university provides a within-organizational example of this sort of force. At an interorganizational level of analysis, Leblebici et al.'s (1991) depiction of changes in the radio broadcast industry highlights the crucial role of small competitor organizations that, disadvantaged by established practices, actively promote alternative practices in the industry. Likewise, Rowan (1982), analyzing the spread of three different structures across school districts in California, underscored the role of conflicting interests in stemming institutionalization processes.

Even in the absence of direct opposition, sedimentation may be truncated gradually because of a lack of demonstrable results associated with a structure. A weak positive relation between a given structure and desired outcomes may be sufficient to affect the spread and maintenance of structures, particularly if advocates continue to be actively involved in theorization and promotion. However, in many cases, the link between the structure and the intended outcomes is quite distant, and demonstration of impact exceedingly difficult. Given the development and promotion of alternative structures purported to achieve the same ends, organizations are likely to abandon older arrangements in favor of newer, promising structures (Abrahamson 1991; see analogous arguments by Abbott 1988 concerning changes in occupational jurisdictions), at least if costs associated with the change are relatively low.

Hence, full institutionalization of a structure is likely to depend on the conjoint effects of relatively low resistance by opposing groups, continued cultural support and promotion by advocacy groups, and positive correlation with desired outcomes. Resistance is likely to limit the spread of a structure among organizations identified by theorizing as relevant adopters, and continued promotion and/or demonstrable benefits are necessary to counteract entropic tendencies, and to thus ensure perpetuation of the structure over time (Zucker 1988). Examples of structures that could be characterized as fully institutionalized in the US range from tenure policies among higher education organizations, to beverage service on airplane flights, to the use of memos as a form of interoffice communication (Yates and Orlikowski 1992).

The reversal of this process, or deinstitutionalization, is likely to require a major shift in the environment (e.g. long-lasting alterations in markets, radical change in technologies) which may then allow a set of social actors whose interests are in opposition to the structure to self-consciously oppose it or to exploit its liabilities (see Rowan's 1982 description of the decline of health officers in schools following the advent of various vaccines; see also Aldrich 1979: 167; Davis et al. 1994).

Table 1 summarizes our arguments about the characteristics and consequences of the component processes of institutionalization.

IMPLICATIONS FOR RESEARCH

There are a number of implications of our analysis for empirical studies of organizations that draw upon institutional theory. Probably the most important implication, from our perspective, is the need to develop more direct measures and better documentation of claims of the institutionalization of structures, since outcomes associated with a given structure are likely to depend on the stage or level of institutionalization. Depending on the scope and form of data collection, different procedures could be used for this.

For example, analyses examining the level of institutionalization of contemporary structures could use survey research in which respondents were asked directly about the degree to which they perceived a given structure to be necessary

Table 1   *Stages of institutionalization and comparative dimensions*

Dimension	Pre-institutionalization stage	Semi-institutionalization stage	Full institutionalization stage
Processes	Habitualization	Objectification	Sedimentation
Characteristics of adopters	Homogeneous	Heterogeneous	Heterogeneous
Impetus for diffusion	Imitation	Imitative/normative	Normative
Theorization activity	None	High	Low
Variance in implementation	High	Moderate	Low
Structure failure rate	High	Moderate	Low

for efficient organizational functioning (e.g. Rura and Miner 1994), or use questionnaires that ask about attributes correlated with degree of institutionalization, such as the degree of subjective certainty about judgments made (Zucker 1977). While the development of items used to create adequate measures would undoubtedly be a contentious task, this is hardly a problem peculiar to the construct of institutionalization (we think of such standard concepts as productivity, effectiveness, uncertainty, for example). As with other difficult constructs, this problem could be grappled with in part through standard psychometric techniques.

Historical research utilizing archival data, on the other hand, could deal with the problem through more careful attention to and documentation of historical context and cultural changes surrounding the purported institutionalization of structures (Zucker 1988). Content analysis of written materials can, in some instances, provide a useful indicator of the cultural status of structures (Tolbert and Zucker 1983). Whatever methodology is used to collect data, however, plausible claims about the level of institutionalization of structures are likely to rest on a strategy involving triangulation of both sources and methods.

In addition, our analysis suggests that identification of the determinants of changes in the level of institutionalization of structures represents an important and promising avenue for both theoretical and empirical work. Extant studies have already suggested a number of potential determinants of how taken for granted a specific structure becomes, and thus how institutionalized. For example, a number of studies have shown that when large and more centrally linked organizations are innovators and early adopters of a given structure, that structure is more likely to become fully institutionalized than other structures (DiMaggio and Powell 1983; Fligstein 1985; 1990; Baron et al. 1986; Davis 1991; Palmer et al. 1993). Further, work by Mezias (1990) and his colleagues (Mezias and Scarselletta 1994) suggests that the social status of forces opposing the adoption of a structure

may operate in the opposite direction: as the status of those opposed increases, the degree of institutionalization decreases.

There are other factors that, intuitively, we would also expect to have an impact on institutionalization, including: the scope or range of organizations for which a given structure is theorized to be relevant (the broader the range of organizations, the more difficult it should be to provide convincing evidence of a structure's effectiveness, and hence the lower the level of institutionalization); the number of 'champions' or size of champion groups (the greater the number of champions, the less likely are entropic processes to become operative, and thus the higher the level of institutionalization); the degree to which adoption of a structure is linked to costly changes in adopting organizations (higher investment costs should also mitigate entropic tendencies, thus resulting in a higher degree of institutionalization); the strength of the correlation between adoption and desired outcomes (creating strong incentives to maintain the structure, thus resulting in a higher degree of institutionalization); and so forth.

Studying the determinants of institutionalization processes is likely to require comparative work on the development and spread of different structures. This might involve, for example, the construction and comparison of several natural histories of structures that have been recently made the object of theorizing – quality circles, employee assistance programs, telecommuting policies, and so forth. Comparative case studies of this sort could provide important insights into whether (or not) there are any similarities in the processes through which adoption and diffusion of different types of structures occur.

Alternatively, useful insights could also be provided by comparisons of the diffusion and fate of a given structure across several industries or across several countries (see Strang and Tuma 1993). Such research has the potential to address a number of puzzles about institutionalization processes that are suggested by various empirical observations. Why do some structures (e.g. team-based production) leap industries and not others (e.g. tenure systems)? Are institutionalization processes always less likely to affect structures in small organizations (Han 1994) and, if so, why? Why are biotechnological innovations located primarily in new small firms in the US, but primarily in large incumbent firms in Japan (Zucker and Darby 1994)?

A final major implication that we would draw from our analysis is the need to consider the contexts or conditions under which institutional, resource dependence and efficiency-oriented contingency theories are each more likely to provide useful insights for organizational scholars. Unfortunately, different theories often lead to the same predicted organizational outcomes – although the mechanisms that are postulated to produce the outcomes are quite different. Hence, it is often extremely difficult, if not impossible, to determine whether the factors highlighted by a given theoretical perspective are actually at work in determining organizational actions.

Because of this, it may be useful to confine empirical 'tests' of institutional theory to studies that are set in contexts where there are no major actors that are attempting to compel organizations to adopt a given structure, either through law or through the withholding of critical resources. Or it may be useful to compare directly unconstrained adoption processes to those that have some coercive elements, as in our examination of the adoption of civil service reform in states where it was not required by law and in states where it was legally required (Tolbert and Zucker 1983).

Likewise, it may also be useful to focus empirical application of institutional theory on analyses where the material benefits associated with a structure are not readily calculable (which is the case for many administrative innovations, as well as some technical innovations) – i.e. where efficiency-oriented contingency approaches are less obviously relevant. Or, again, it may be useful to assess how social institutions are used to increase material benefits, as for example when scientific collaborators tend to be selected from the same organization, effectively using the organizational boundaries as information envelopes to protect new discoveries from early exploitation by others (Zucker et al. 1995).

CONCLUSIONS

By highlighting the role of normative influences in organizational decision-making processes, institutional theory offers an important and distinctive extension to our repertoire of perspectives and approaches to explaining organizational structure. While the notion that decision-makers are characterized by bounded rationality has become a staple component of the catechism of organizational research, the implications of this are not explored in any depth in most contemporary theories.[10] *How* rationality is bounded and under what conditions it will be more or less bounded are questions that have rarely been addressed. Institutional theory offers a framework that can be useful in addressing these questions, but its utility in this respect requires further development of the theory to clarify the conditions and processes that lead structures to become institutionalized. A clearer understanding of institutionalization as a process would allow us to specify the impact of more social aspects of decision-making, such as the effects of social position of those providing information on choices made, and the conditions under which prediction of a particular choice is possible only if the social aspects are directly included in the analysis.

Addressing this general issue of conditions of applicability requires consideration of a number of problems: how and when choices or alternative lines of action become socially defined; who acts to cause change and to diffuse that change to multiple organizations, and why; and what are the potential benefits of creating similar structures, or converging to the same structures, that lead to the institutional isomorphism we so often observe. For institutional theory to develop as a coherent paradigm and thus to make an enduring contribution to organizational analyses, such questions about institutionalization processes require both conceptual and empirical answers. In this analysis, we have outlined some initial answers to these problems, answers whose extension and modification must await further theoretical development and empirical test.

NOTES

We would like to thank, without implication, Howard Aldrich, Michael Darby, Shin-Kap Han, John Meyer, Linda Pike and Peter Sherer for taking the time and effort to read and offer very useful comments on earlier drafts of this chapter. Lynne Zucker acknowledges support for this research by grants from the Sloan Foundation through the NBER Program on Industrial Technology, and from the University of California Systemwide Biotechnology Research Education Program. Opinions expressed here are those of the authors and not those of NBER.

1 Here we concentrate our analysis on institutionalization processes at the interorganizational level. Similar processes are likely to operate at the intraorganizational level as well, though the exact mechanisms as well as the consequences may differ.

See Tolbert (1988), Rura and Miner (1994) and Barley and Tolbert (1988) for discussions of the relation between intraorganizational and interorganizational processes. See Zucker (1977) for a discussion and experimental test of intraorganizational processes and consequences.

2 The evolution of this line of research includes work focusing on the relation between formal structure and the 'informal organization' and particularly on power relations among organizational members (e.g. Blau 1955; Zald and Berger 1978; Perrow 1984). Perhaps because such work was less compatible with extant management science literature, it did not achieve prominence as rapidly in the sociological literature on organizations as did work focusing on covariation among structural elements.

3 See, for example, Stinchcombe (1959), Thompson (1967), Pugh et al. (1969), Blau (1970). Hall (1987) provides a thorough review and summary of the findings of this literature.

4 Another individual-level analog is ingratiation, in which flattery and exaggerated compliance are used to meet personal needs by altering the response of someone with power or authority (Jones 1964; Jones and Wortman 1973). See also Elsbach and Sutton (1992) for a discussion of impression management by organizations.

5 D'Aunno et al. (1991) describe the way in which conflicting demands placed on community mental health organizations by different constituencies result in the adoption of incompatible and contradictory practices. We suggest that such contradictions in structure are most likely to occur when managers have little discretion over the adoption of structural changes.

6 We leave for later development change processes that operate inside a given organization. Inertia within organizations is often assumed to block internal change or at least to make it extremely difficult (Kanter 1983; 1989). Yet institutionalization processes are likely to be very important in internal organizational functioning (Zucker 1977; Pfeffer 1982).

7 As John Meyer pointed out to us, this model may be most applicable to societies that are characterized by relatively weak national states.

8 Leblebici et al. (1991) point out that when the advantages of an innovation are unclear, it is often smaller, less competitively advantaged firms who are most likely to adopt first, because the relative risks of making an error by adopting are lower for such firms.

9 This process of theorization has already been explicitly developed and empirically tested on the individual level as diffuse status characteristics (key references include Berger et al. 1972; Webster and Driskell 1978; Zelditch et al. 1980; Ridgeway and Berger 1986). It is easier to see errors in the generalization process when personal attributes such as gender or ethnicity are analyzed. But we expect similar errors at the organizational level.

10 A good example is provided by transactions costs theory (Williamson 1975), which is explicitly premised on the assumption of bounded rationality. However, work in this tradition appears to be predicated *implicitly* on the assumption that decision-makers are capable of carrying out extremely complex calculations required to estimate the relative transaction costs associated with different relational forms, and selecting an appropriate course of action based on those calculations (i.e. of relatively *un*bounded rationality).

REFERENCES

Abbott, Andrew (1988) *The System of Professions.* Chicago: University of Chicago Press.

Abrahamson, Eric (1991) 'Managerial fads and fashions: the diffusion and rejection of innovations', *Academy of Management Review*, 16: 586–612.

Abrahamson, Eric and Rosenkopf, Lori (1993) 'Institutional and competitive bandwagons: using mathematical modeling as a tool to explore innovation diffusion', *Academy of Management Review*, 18: 487–517.

Aldrich, Howard (1979) *Organizations and Environments.* Englewood Cliffs, NJ: Prentice-Hall.

Aldrich, Howard and Fiol, Marlene (1994) 'Fools rush in? The institutional context of industry creation', *Academy of Management Review*, 19: 645–70.

Anderson, Philip and Tushman, Michael (1990) 'Technological discontinuities and dominant design: a cyclical model of technological change', *Administrative Science Quarterly*, 35: 604–33.

Banerjee, Abhijit (1992) 'A simple model of herd behavior', *Quarterly Journal of Economics*, 107: 797–817.

Barley, Stephen and Tolbert, Pamela (1988) 'Institutionalization as structuration: Methods and analytic strategies for studying links between action and structure'. Paper presented at the Conference on Longitudinal Field Research Methods, University of Texas, Austin, TX.

Barnard, Chester (1938) *Functions of the Executive.* Cambridge, MA: Harvard University Press.

Baron, James, Dobbin, Frank and Jennings, P. Devereaux (1986) 'War and peace: the evolution of modern personnel administration in U.S. industry', *American Journal of Sociology*, 92: 384–411.

Berger, Joseph, Cohen, Bernard P. and Zelditch, Morris Jr (1972) 'Status characteristics and social interaction', *American Sociological Review*, 37: 241–55.

Berger, Peter and Luckmann, Thomas (1967) *Social Construction of Reality.* New York: Anchor Books.

Bikchandani, Sushil, Hirshleifer, David and Welch, Ivo (1992) 'A theory of fads, fashion, custom and cultural change as informational cascades', *Journal of Political Economy*, 100: 992–1026.

Blau, Peter (1955) *The Dynamics of Bureaucracy.* Chicago: University of Chicago Press.

Blau, Peter (1970) 'A formal theory of differentiation in

organizations', *American Sociological Review*, 35: 201–18.

Chaves, Mark (1996) 'Ordaining women: the diffusion of an organizational innovation', *American Journal of Sociology*, 101: 840–73.

Clark, Burton (1956) 'Organizational adaptation and precarious values', *American Sociological Review*, 21–7.

Coleman, James (1980) *Power and the Structure of Society*. New York: Norton.

Coleman, James (1990) *Foundations of Social Theory*. Cambridge, MA: Harvard University Press.

Covaleski, Mark and Dirsmith, Mark (1988) 'An institutional perspective on the rise, social transformation and fall of a university budget category', *Administrative Science Quarterly*, 33: 562–87.

D'Aunno, Thomas, Sutton, Robert and Price, Richard (1991) 'Isomorphism and external support in conflicting institutional environments: A study of drug abuse treatment units', *Academy of Management Journal*, 34: 636–61.

David, Paul (1985) 'Clio and the economics of QWERTY', *American Economic Review*, 75: 332–7.

Davis, Gerald (1991) 'Agents without principles? The spread of the poison pill through the intercorporate network', *Administrative Science Quarterly*, 36: 583–613.

Davis, Gerald and Powell, Walter (1992) 'Organization–environment relations', in M. Dunnette and L. Hough (eds), *Handbook of Industrial and Organizational Psychology*, vol. 3. Palo Alto, CA: Consulting Psychologists Press. pp. 317–75.

Davis, Gerald, Diekmann, Kristina and Tinsley, Catherine (1994) 'The deinstitutionalization of conglomerate firms in the 1980s', *American Sociological Review*, 59: 547–70.

Della Fave, L. Richard (1986) 'Toward an explication of the legitimation process', *Social Forces*, 65: 476–500.

DiMaggio, Paul (1988) 'Interest and agency in institutional theory', in Lynne G. Zucker (ed.), *Institutional Patterns and Organizations: Culture and Environment*. Cambridge, MA: Ballinger. pp. 3–22.

DiMaggio, Paul (1991) 'Constructing an organizational field as a professional project: U.S. art museums, 1920–1940', in W. Powell and P. DiMaggio (eds), *The New Institutionalism in Organizational Analysis*. Chicago: University of Chicago Press. pp. 267–92.

DiMaggio, Paul and Powell, Walter (1983) 'The iron cage revisited: institutional isomorphism and collective rationality in organizational fields', *American Sociological Review*, 48: 147–60.

Edelman, Lauren (1992) 'Legal ambiguity and symbolic structures: organizational mediation of civil rights law', *American Journal of Sociology*, 97: 1531–76.

Eisenhardt, Kathleen (1988) 'Agency and institutional theory explanations: the case of retail sales competition', *Academy of Management Journal*, 30: 488–511.

Elsbach, Kimberly and Sutton, Robert (1992) 'Acquir-
ing organizational legitimation through illegitimate actions: a marriage of institutional and impression management theories', *Academy of Management Journal*, 35: 699–736.

Fayol, Henri (1949) *General and Industrial Management*. London: Pitman.

Fligstein, Neil (1985) 'The spread of the multidivisional form among large firms, 1919–1979', *American Sociological Review*, 50: 377–91.

Fligstein, Neil (1990) *The Transformation of Corporate Control*. Cambridge, MA: Harvard University Press.

Follett, Mary (1942) *Dynamic Administration*. New York: Harper.

Galaskiewicz, Joseph (1985) 'Professional networks and the institutionalization of a single mind-set', *American Sociological Review*, 50: 639–58.

Geertz, Clifford (1973) *The Interpretation of Cultures*. New York: Basic Books.

Giddens, Anthony (1979) *Central Problems in Social Theory: Action, Structure, and Contradiction in Social Analysis*. Berkeley, CA: University of California Press.

Goffman, Irving (1959) *Presentation of Self in Everyday Life*. New York: Doubleday.

Goodman, Paul and Pennings, Johann (1977) *New Perspectives on Organizational Effectiveness*. San Francisco: Jossey-Bass.

Gouldner, Alvin (1950) *Patterns of Industrial Bureaucracy*. Glencoe, IL: Free Press.

Granovetter, Mark (1985) 'Economic action and social structure: the problem of embeddedness', *American Journal of Sociology*, 91: 481–510.

Gulick, Luther and Urwick, L. (eds) (1937) *Papers on the Science of Administration*. New York: Institute of Public Administration, Columbia University.

Hall, Richard (1987) *Organizations*. Englewood Cliffs, NJ: Prentice-Hall.

Han, Shin-Kap (1994) 'Mimetic isomorphism and its effect on the audit services market', *Social Forces*, 73: 637–64.

Hechter, Michael (1990) *Social Institutions: their Emergence, Maintenance, and Effects*. New York: Aldine de Gruyter.

Huber, George and Glick, William (1993) *Organizational Change and Redesign: Ideas and Onsights for Improving Performance*. New York: Oxford University Press.

Jones, E.E. (1964) *Ingratiation*. New York: Appleton-Century-Crofts.

Jones, E.E. and Wortman, C.B. (1973) *Ingratiation: an Attributional Approach*. Morristown, NJ: General Learning Press.

Kamens, David (1977) 'Legitimating myths and educational organization: the relationship between organizational ideology and formal structure', *American Sociological Review*, 42: 208–19.

Kanter, Rosabeth Moss (1983) *The Change Masters: Innovation for Productivity in the American Corporation*. New York: Simon and Schuster.

Kanter, Rosabeth Moss (1989) *When Giants Learn to*

Dance: Mastering the Challenge of Strategy, Management, and Careers in the 1990s. New York: Simon and Schuster.

Lawrence, Paul and Lorsch, Jay (1967) *Organization and Environment.* Boston: Graduate School of Business Administration, Harvard University.

Leblebici, Hussein, Salancik, Gerald, Copay, Anne and King, Tom (1991) 'Institutional change and the transformation of interorganizational fields: an organizational history of U.S. radio broadcasting industry', *Administrative Science Quarterly*, 36: 333–63.

March, James and Simon, Herbert (1957) *Organizations.* New York: Wiley.

Merton, Robert (1948) 'Manifest and latent functions', in R. Merton (ed.), *Social Theory and Social Structure.* Glencoe, IL: Free Press. pp. 37–59.

Meyer, John and Rowan, Brian (1977) 'Institutionalized organizations: formal structure as myth and ceremony', *American Journal of Sociology*, 83: 340–63.

Meyer, Marshall (1979) 'Organizational structure as signaling', *Pacific Sociological Review*, 22: 481–500.

Meyer, Marshall and Zucker, Lynne (1989) *Permanently Failing Organizations.* Newbury Park, CA: Sage.

Mezias, Stephen (1990) 'An institutional model of organizational practice: financial reporting at the Fortune 200', *Administrative Science Quarterly*, 35: 431–51.

Mezias, Stephen and Scarselletta, Mario (1994) 'Resolving financial reporting problems: an institutional analysis of the process', *Administrative Science Quarterly*, 30: 654–78.

Michels, Robert (1962) *Political Parties.* New York: Free Press.

Miner, Anne (1987) 'Idiosyncratic jobs in formal organizations', *Administrative Science Quarterly*, 32: 327–51.

Miner, Anne (1991) 'Organizational evolution and the social ecology of jobs', *American Sociological Review*, 56: 772–85.

Nelson, Richard and Winter, Sidney (1982) *An Evolutionary Theory of Economic Change.* Cambridge, MA: Harvard University Press.

Oliver, Christine (1991) 'Strategic responses to institutional processes', *Academy of Management Review*, 16: 145–79.

Palmer, Donald, Jennings, P. Devereaux and Zhou, Xueguang (1993) 'Late adoption of the multidivisional form by large U.S. corporations: institutional, political and economic accounts', *Administrative Science Quarterly*, 38: 100–31.

Park, Robert E. (1922) *The Immigrant Press and its Control.* New York: Harper and Row.

Parsons, Talcott (1956) 'Suggestions for a sociological approach to the theory of organizations', *Administrative Science Quarterly*, 1: 63–85.

Parsons, Talcott (1960) *Structure and Process in Modern Societies.* New York: Free Press.

Perrow, Charles (1984) *Normal Accidents.* New York: Basic Books.

Pfeffer, Jeffrey (1982) *Organizations and Organization Theory.* Boston: Pitman.

Pfeffer, Jeffrey and Salancik, Gerald (1978) *External Control of Organizations.* New York: Harper and Row.

Pugh, D.S., Hickson, D.J. and Hinings, C.R. (1969) 'An empirical taxonomy of structures of work organizations', *Administrative Science Quarterly*, 14: 115–26.

Quinn, Robert and Cameron, Kim (1988) *Paradox and Transformation: Toward a Theory of Change in Organization and Management.* Cambridge, MA: Ballinger.

Reeves, Carol and Bednar, David (1994) 'Defining quality: alternatives and implications', *Academy of Management Review*, 19: 419–45.

Ridgeway, Cecilia L. and Berger, Joseph (1986) 'Expectations, legitimation and dominance behavior in task groups', *American Sociological Review*, 51: 603–17.

Ritti, Richard and Silver, Jonathan (1986) 'Early processes of institutionalization: the dramaturgy of exchange in interorganizational relations', *Administrative Science Quarterly*, 31: 25–42.

Rowan, Brian (1982) 'Organizational structure and the institutional environment: the case of public schools', *Administrative Science Quarterly*, 27: 259–79.

Rura, Thekla and Miner, Anne (1994) 'Degrees of institutionalization in organizational routines'. Working paper 9–94–16, University of Wisconsin, Madison, School of Business.

Schutz, Alfred (1962) *Collected Papers: the Problem of Social Reality*, edited by M. Natanson. The Hague: Martinus Nijhoff.

Schutz, Alfred (1967) *The Phenomenology of the Social World.* Evanston, IL: Northwestern Press.

Scott, Marvin and Lyman, Stanford (1968) 'Accounts', *American Sociological Review*, 33: 46–62.

Scott, Richard (1987) 'The adolescence of institutional theory', *Administrative Science Quarterly*, 32: 493–511.

Scott, Richard (1994) 'Institutional analysis: variance and process theory approaches', in W.R. Scott and J.W. Meyer (eds), *Institutional Environments and Organizations: Structural Complexity and Individualism.* Thousand Oaks, CA: Sage. pp. 81–99.

Scott, Richard and Meyer, John (1994) *Institutional Environments and Organizations: Structural Complexity and Individualism.* Thousand Oaks, CA: Sage.

Selznick, Philip (1949) *TVA and the Grassroots.* Berkeley, CA: University of California Press.

Selznick, Philip (1957) *Leadership in Administration.* New York: Harper and Row.

Simon, Herbert (1947) *Administrative Behavior.* New York: Free Press.

Sitkin, Sim, Sutcliffe, Kathleen and Schroeder, Roger (1994) 'Distinguishing control from learning in total quality management: a contingency perspective', *Academy of Management Review*, 19: 537–64.

Stinchcombe, Arthur (1959) 'Bureaucratic and craft administration of production: a comparative study', *Administrative Science Quarterly*, 4: 168–87.

Strang, David (1990) 'From dependency to sovereignty: an event history analysis of decolonization 1870–1987', *American Sociological Review*, 55: 846–60.

Strang, David (1994) 'Institutional accounts of organizations as a form of structural analysis', *Current Perspectives in Social Theory*, 1: 151–74. Greenwich, CT: JAI Press.

Strang, David and Meyer, John (1993) 'Institutional conditions for diffusion', *Theory and Society*, 22: 487–511.

Strang, David and Tuma, Nancy (1994) 'Spatial and temporal heterogeneity in diffusion', *American Journal of Sociology*, 99: 614–39.

Stryker, Robin (1994) 'Rules, resources and legitimacy processes: some implications for social conflict, order and change', *American Journal of Sociology*, 99: 847–910.

Sutton, John, Dobbin, Frank, Meyer, John and Scott, W.R. (1994) 'The legalization of the workplace', *American Journal of Sociology*, 99: 944–71.

Thomas, W.I. and Znaniecki, Florian (1927) *The Polish Peasant in Europe and America*. New York: Dover.

Thompson, James (1967) *Organizations in Action*. New York: McGraw-Hill.

Thompson, James and McEwen, William (1958) 'Organizational goals and environment: goal-setting as an interaction process', *American Sociological Review*, 23: 23–31.

Tolbert, Pamela S. (1985) 'Institutional environments and resource dependence: sources of administrative structure in institutions of higher education', *Administrative Science Quarterly*, 30: 1–13.

Tolbert, Pamela S. (1988) 'Institutional sources of culture in major law firms', in L. Zucker (ed.), *Institutional Patterns in Organizations: Culture and Environment*. Cambridge, MA: Ballinger. pp. 101–13.

Tolbert, Pamela S. and Zucker, Lynne (1983) 'Institutional sources of change in the formal structure of organizations: the diffusion of civil service reform, 1880–1935', *Administrative Science Quarterly*, 28: 22–39.

Turner, Jonathan (1974) *The Structure of Sociological Theory*. New York: Dorsey.

Walker, Henry, Thomas, George and Zelditch, Morris (1986) 'Legitimation, endorsement and stability', *Social Forces*, 64: 620–43.

Weber, Max (1946) *The Theory of Social and Economic Organization* (1924 in German), edited by A.M. Henderson and Talcott Parsons. Glencoe, IL: Free Press.

Webster, Murray Jr. and Driskell, James E. (1978) 'Status generalization: a review and some new data', *American Sociological Review*, 43: 220–36.

Weick, Karl (1969) *Social Psychology of Organizations*. Reading, MA: Addison-Wesley.

Williamson, Oliver (1975) *Markets and Hierarchies*. New York: Free Press.

Woodward, Joan (1965) *Industrial Organization: Theory and Practice*. New York: Oxford University Press.

Wrong, Dennis (1961) 'The over-socialized conception of man in modern sociology', *American Sociological Review*, 26: 183–93.

Yates, Joanne and Orlikowski, Wanda (1992) 'Genres of organizational communication: a structurational approach to studying communication and media', *Academy of Management Review*, 17: 299–326.

Zald, Mayer and Berger, Michael (1978) 'Social movements in organizations: *coup d'état*, insurgency and mass movements', *American Journal of Sociology*, 83: 823–61.

Zald, Mayer and Denton, Patricia (1963) 'From evangelism to general service: the transformation of the YMCA', *Administrative Science Quarterly*, 8: 214–34.

Zelditch, Morris Jr, Lauderdale, Patrick and Stublarec, Stephen (1980) 'How are inconsistencies between status and ability resolved?', *Social Forces*, 58: 1025–43.

Zhou, Xueguang (1993) 'Occupational power, state capacities, and the diffusion of licensing in the American states: 1890–1950', *American Sociological Review*, 58: 536–52.

Zucker, Lynne G. (1977) 'The role of institutionalization in cultural persistence', *American Sociological Review*, 42: 726–43.

Zucker, Lynne G. (1988) 'Where do institutional patterns come from? Organizations as actors in social systems', in Lynne G. Zucker (ed.), *Institutional patterns and organizations: Culture and environment*. Cambridge, MA: Ballinger. pp. 23–49.

Zucker, Lynne G. (1991) 'Postscript: microfoundations of institutional thought', in Walter W. Powell and Paul J. DiMaggio (eds), *The New Institutionalism in Organizational Analysis*. Chicago, IL: University of Chicago Press. pp. 103–7.

Zucker, Lynne G. and Darby, Michael R. (1994) 'The organization of biotechnology science and its commercialization in Japan', UCLA Institute for Social Science Research Working Papers in the Social Sciences, Volume 6, Number 1, August.

Zucker, Lynne G. and Kreft, Ita G.G. (1994) 'The evolution of socially contingent rational actions: effects of labor strikes on change in union founding in the 1880s', in J. Baum and J.V. Singh (eds), *Evolutionary Dynamics of Organizations*. New York: Oxford University Press. pp. 294–313.

Zucker, Lynne G., Darby, Michael R., Brewer, Marilynn B. and Peng, Yusheng (1995) 'Collaboration structure and information dilemmas in biotechnology: organizational boundaries as trust production', in R. Kramer and T. Tyler (eds), *Trust in Organizations*. Thousand Oaks, CA: Sage.

1.7

Critical Theory and Postmodernism Approaches to Organizational Studies

MATS ALVESSON AND STANLEY DEETZ

Anyone who has followed the writings in critical theory and postmodernism during the last decade or so understands the difficulties we face in trying to provide a short, understandable and useful overview of this work. The two labels refer to massive bodies of literature, most of which are difficult to read. Compared to most other research perspectives treated in this *Handbook*, most of the various critical theory and postmodernist positions are still relatively new to management studies. Texts in the field cross many traditional disciplinary divisions. Many researchers draw on both traditions; others argue for irreconcilable differences between them. The differences and conflicts both within and between these two general headings have filled many pages both within and outside of organization studies. It might well be argued that nothing at once fair, coherent and brief can be written on this topic. But striving to understand these literatures is important.

The general projects of critical theory and postmodernism do not represent fad or simple fascination. Certainly some popular accounts on postmodernism invite such a critique, and we do not believe that this label is necessarily the best or will last. We believe that postmodernism – and critical theory for that matter – should be studied not because they are new and different, but because they provide unique and important ways to understand organizations and their management. Initially we will consider the social and historical context giving rise to these approaches and why the themes they address are becoming increasingly important to organization studies. We will then demonstrate ways postmodern and critical theories of organizations are different

from other approaches to organization studies as well as different from (and within) each other. As the chapter develops, we will consider different ways of doing postmodern and critical work. In addition to reviewing and discussing existing work, we will sketch some fruitful lines of development between and within these two approaches. Despite their importance, in the treatment of neither critical theory nor postmodernism will we cover gender issues in any specific or detailed way since this volume has a chapter devoted to feminist approaches (see Calás and Smircich in Chapter 1.8).

Researchers in organization and management studies came to critical theory and postmodern writings relatively late, with critical theory emerging in the late 1970s and early 1980s (for example, Benson 1977; Burrell and Morgan 1979; Frost 1980; Deetz and Kersten 1983; Fischer and Sirianni 1984) and the postmodernism writings in the late 1980s (for example, Smircich and Calás 1987; Cooper and Burrell 1988). This is no surprise given the 'modernist' assumptions embedded in organizations and the rather dogmatic and exclusionary character of dominant research traditions of either a positivist or a Marxist bent. Part of the reason both critical theory and postmodern writings have now found fertile ground in management studies is the decline and disillusionment of what is broadly referred to as modernist assumptions by both organizational theorists and practitioners. As will be developed, the attack on the modernist tradition is central to both critical and postmodern studies.

The increased size of organizations, rapid implementation of communication/information technologies, globalization, changing nature of work, reduction of the working class, less salient class conflicts, professionalization of the work force, stagnant economies, widespread ecological problems and turbulent markets are all part of the contemporary context demanding a research response. Some of these lines of development have weakened the soil for Marxism and other critiques of domination but improved it for the alternative orientations discussed here. Many of these developments provided a growing crisis in the heart of the modernist discourse with its instrumental rationality and connection to state democracies. Management in a modernist discourse works on the basis of control, the progressive rationalization and colonization of nature and people, whether workers, potential consumers, or society as a whole. But there are structural limits to control. The costs of integration and control systems often exceed the value added by management within the corporation. The shift from manufacturing to service industries as the most typical economic form in the Western world also has implications for control forms (Alvesson 1987). As the cost of control grows and the means/end chains grow longer, strategy and instrumental reasoning are strained. Themes like corporate culture, identity, quality management, service management and the renewed call for leadership, soul, and charisma during the late 1980s and early 1990s, illustrate this. Objects for management control are decreasingly labour power and behavior and increasingly the mindpower and subjectivities of employees. These new social conditions provide a new urgency and new areas of application for postmodern and critical theory work in organization studies – consider the amount of critical theory work on organizational culture (see Alvesson 1993a and Willmott 1993 for overviews) – but have little to do with their formation. These rather indicate the new social conditions to which critical theory and postmodern writing have provided innovative and instructive analyses.

While these new conditions have provided opportunity for organizational changes, we think little is gained by proclaiming a new postmodern period, or talking about postmodern organizations (Alvesson 1995). Empirical indications are highly selective and weak (Thompson 1993). The portrayal of one's own time as unique and a time of great transition is an unfortunate tendency of many periods in Western thought (Foucault 1983). Theoretically, this enterprise is equally unconvincing. The talk about postmodern organizations often means a relabeling of what is also called organic, adhocratic or post-Fordist organizations, with little or no conceptual gains and quite a lot of

confusion (Parker 1993, Thompson 1993). For example, Peters (1987) or even Clegg (1990) talk about significant changes in organizations that we think can be usefully explored using postmodern and critical theory discourses, but they do not. We are only interested in these theoretical approaches and what they offer to organization studies, not in claims of organizations as postmodern.

What is then included under the umbrella concepts of critical theory and postmodernism? Sometimes critical theory is given a broad meaning and includes all works taking a basically critical or radical stance on contemporary society with an orientation towards investigating exploitation, repression, unfairness, asymmetrical power relations (generated from class, gender, or position), distorted communication, and false consciousness. We, however, use the term here with a more restricted meaning, referring to organization studies drawing concepts primarily, though not exclusively, from the Frankfurt School (Adorno, Horkheimer, Marcuse and Habermas). Much of the foundation for this work is summarized, though not without some conceptual confusions, in Burrell and Morgan's (1979) radical humanism paradigm and in Morgan's (1986) images of domination and neuroses.

Postmodernism is in many ways much harder to delimit. In the social sciences, the term has been used to describe a social mood, a historical period filled with major social and organizational changes, and a set of philosophical approaches to organizational and other studies (Featherstone 1988; Kellner 1988; Parker 1992; Hassard and Parker 1993). We will focus on this last designation, emphasizing the more socially and politically relevant writings and the use of conceptions of fragmentation, textuality, and resistance in organization studies. These philosophically based approaches to organization studies have emerged out of works of Derrida and Foucault in particular, and to a lesser degree Baudrillard, Deleuze and Guattari, and Laclau and Mouffe. Much more so than with critical theory this is a wide group of writers and positions with quite different research agendas. Still their work shares features and moves that can be highlighted in treating them together.[1]

Their themes include focusing on the constructed nature of people and reality, emphasizing language as a system of distinctions which are central to the construction process, arguing against grand narratives and large-scale theoretical systems such as Marxism or functionalism, emphasizing the power/knowledge connection and the role of claims of expertise in systems of domination, emphasizing the fluid and hyperreal nature of the contemporary world and role of mass media and information technologies, and stressing narrative/fiction/rhetoric as central to the research process.

We emphasize the critical edge of post-modernism. We see it as part of a broader critical tradition which challenges the status quo and supports silenced or marginalized voices. This is a common emphasis, but by no means the only one. Many postmodernist ideas have been utilized for different political purposes. The critique of foundations and utopian ideals has been understood by some as leaving a distinctly apolitical, socially irrelevant, or even neo-conservative stance (Habermas 1983; Margolis 1989; Sarup 1988). The absence of a political stance grounded in a systematic philosophy has been a source of complaint, but this does not mean that a different, more 'local' and 'respon-sive', political stance is absent (see Walzer 1986). Sometimes people distinguish between 'reaction-ary postmodernism' and a 'postmodernism of resistance' (Foster 1983; Smircich and Calás 1987). Like the majority of authors in social science and organization theory, we choose the latter route in our account. Most applications in social science have taken postmodern concep-tions in a radical/critical direction – although an unconventional one.

THE DEVELOPMENT OF CRITICAL THEORY AND POSTMODERNISM

Every historical period has probably had its particular equivalences of traditionalists, mod-ernists, critical theorists, and postmodernists – those who lament the passing of a purer time, those instrumentally building a future, those concerned with disadvantaged segments and the direction of the future, and those seeing fragmentation and decay mixed with radical potential. In faster transitional periods as compared to relatively stable periods the mix of these figures is probably different. Remember-ing this more situates the historical account of critical theory and postmodernism than denies it as being interesting. Here we wish first to situate them in the history of ideas. Let us be clear at the start: all such social histories are types of fiction. They often serve present social purposes more than record the past. They are reconstruc-tions which give us a particular way to think about the present. The history is interesting because of its productive capacities. The devel-opmental accounts of critical theory and post-modernism are no exceptions.[2] These accounts emphasizing unity and distinction, while purpo-sive fictions, highlight central features of these bodies of work.

Theoretical Sources of Inspiration and Distinction

Both critical theory and postmodern writers position their work in regards to four specific developments in Western thought. The way they respond to and partly use mixes of these developments accounts for many of the differ-ences between and within postmodernism and critical theory. These are (1) the power/knowl-edge relation arising with Nietzsche's perspectiv-alism, (2) a nondualistic constructionist account of experience and language arising with phe-nomenological hermeneutics and structural lin-guistics, (3) a historically based social conflict theory arising from Marx, and (4) a complex human subject arising from Freud. The first posed a challenge to any possible foundations for knowledge: all knowledge claims primarily reference social communities filled with specific power relations rather than an essential world or knowing subjects. The second situated all perspectives within specific social/historical/lin-guistic contexts: the intersubjectivity preceding any subjectivity or objectivity is structured in specifiable ways. The third removed the inno-cence of social/historical/linguistic perspectives by positioning them within materially produced social divisions and denied any smooth unitary historical development. And the fourth provided for a complex, conflict ridden, and often mistaken *subject* in place of a knowing, unitary, autonomous *person*, thereby challenging any claim to simple rationality and a clear and fixed identity. Together people, realities, and social relations become nonessential constructions, constructed under specific conditions of power and contestation, and filled with opacities, contradictions, and conflict suppression. These different concepts provide the historically spe-cific tools for encountering the dominant discourses of the time.

These shared intellectual heritages should not prevent us from emphasizing the differences in how critical theory and postmodernism draw upon them. Postmodernism typically, for exam-ple, uses Freud much more unconventionally than critical theory, and merges psychoanalytic ideas with language philosophy in efforts to deconstruct and show the fragmentation of the subject. Important sources of inspiration that are clearly different from critical theory and post-modernism include structuralist language theory (Saussure), which postmodernism draws heavily upon, and Weberian notions of the rationaliza-tion process of modern society, which is central for critical theory. In addition, critical theory is inspired by German moral philosophy and its faith in autonomy and reason (Hegel, Kant).

Embedded in these choices are long term oppositions between French and German cultural contexts. If it were not for this historical context some of the differences would not be as clear. For example, Horkheimer and Adorno's (1979) cultural criticism of administratively induced control contingent upon the conception of progress in the Enlightenment can be read as sounding as close to Foucault as to Habermas's recent writings. But few would think of them in that way. It is interesting to note that Foucault, when towards the end of his life became acquainted with the Frankfurt School, expressed himself very positively, almost over generously, about it:

> if I had been familiar with the Frankfurt School . . . I would not have said a number of stupid things that I did say and I would have avoided many of the detours which I made while trying to pursue my own humble path – when, meanwhile, avenues had been opened up by the Frankfurt School. (1983: 200)

Critical Theory and Postmodernism Responses to Modernism

Since both postmodernism and critical theory writings are filled with attempts to distinguish themselves in comparison to the modernist project, a brief rendition of the latter may be helpful – though since it is familiar we will not be long. Kant described the Enlightenment as the escape from self-inflicted tutelage. In pre-Enlightenment communities, personal identities, knowledge, social order, and dominant historical narratives were carried and legitimized by tradition, though individuals actively 'inflicted' the tradition upon themselves. The Enlightenment promised an autonomous subject progressively emancipated by knowledge acquired through scientific methods. It noted the rise of reason over authority and traditional values. Its science developed and in time proclaimed a transparent language (freed from the baggage of traditional ideology) and representational truth, a positivity and optimism in acquisition of cumulative understanding which would lead to the progressive enhancement of the quality of life. The Enlightenment enemy was darkness, tradition, ideology, irrationality, ignorance, and positional authority. Each of these themes of the Enlightenment are deeply embedded in modernist management theory.

In the organizational context, we use the term 'modernist' to draw attention to the instrumentalization of people and nature through the use of scientific-technical knowledge (modeled after positivism and other 'rational' ways of develop-

ing safe, robust knowledge) to accomplish predictable results measured by productivity and technical problem-solving leading to the 'good' economic and social life, primarily defined by accumulation of wealth by production investors and consumption by consumers. Modernism initially represented emancipation over myth, authority, and traditional values through knowledge, reason, and opportunities based on heightened capacity. Early twentieth century organization studies were organized around development of modernist over traditional discourses. Taylor's and Weber's treatment of rationalization and bureaucratization showed from the start the corporation as a site of the development of modernist logic and instrumental reasoning. The traditional was marginalized and placed off in the private realm. While writings in human relations, quality of work life, and later cultural studies would continue to claim a place for traditional values and norms with their particular logics, each would be 'strategized' and brought to aid further rationalization of work for the sake of convenience, efficiency, and direction of the work effort. 'Performativity' would come to be valued over any earlier Enlightenment narrative of emancipation or human values (Lyotard 1984). In fact in the new age embellishment one could even be emancipated from the body's emotions and bring the body's spirit and faith under rational control. Foucault's (1977; 1980; 1988) demonstrations, and critical treatment, of the rise of self-surveillance and bio-power as control systems described the furthest development of self-rationalization in modernity. Critical theory and postmodernism open new discussions. In particular critical theory showed how modernism itself was based on myths, had acquired an arbitrary authority, subordinated social life to technological rationality and protected a new dominant group's interests (Horkheimer and Adorno 1979). The old conflict between a modern and a traditional discourse where the modern laid claim to all the positive terms is suddenly displaced by a new set of conflicts, those arising from the problems of modernity itself.

Both critical theory and postmodernism see their work as responses to specific social conditions. Contemporary society as a result of science, industrialization, and communication/information technologies has developed positive capacities but also dangerous forms of domination. Both critical theory and postmodernism describe Western development as one where a progressive, instrumental modernism gradually eclipsed traditional society with fairly clear payoffs but also great costs. They agree that something fundamental has gone awry and that more technical, instrumental 'solutions' will not fix it. While their diagnoses are similar (to use a less than totally adequate medical metaphor), they differ in their pronouncement and response. Critical theorists see the modernists' project as sick and see hope for reconstruction in recovery of good parts and redirecting the future. Postmodernists pronounce its death and proclaim the absence of a thinkable future.[3]

The critical theorists, especially Habermas (1984; 1987), focus on the incompletion of the positive potentialities of enlightenment. Different forces have utilized their power and advantages to force new forms of tutelage, often *consentful* in character. As we will discuss in regards to organizational studies, critical theorists have focused on the skewing and closure of the historical discourse through reification, universalization of sectional interests, domination of instrumental reasoning, and hegemony. In different ways they hope to recover a rational process through understanding social/historical/political constructionism, a broader conception of rationality, inclusion of more groups in social determination, and overcoming systematically distorted communication. Central to this is the critique of domination and the ways those subjugated actively participate in their own subjugation. The politically astute intellectual is given an active role in the production of an enlightened understanding. The hope is to provide forums so that different segments of the society and different human interests can be part of a better, more moral, historical dialogue, so that each may equally contribute to the choices in producing a future for all.

The postmodernists also focus on the dark side of the Enlightenment, its destruction of the environment and native peoples, its exclusions, and the concealed effects of reason and progress, but postmodernists see the entire project as wrong. The problem is not who or what participates in it. The project is inherently problematic. They seek to find the 'nonenlightened' voices, the human possibilities that the Enlightenment itself suppresses. This discourse is filled with the pronouncement of the end of the historical discourse of progress and emancipation and its endless deferral of social promise, that more technology, more knowledge and increased rationality will somehow accomplish the promise. Man (the humanist subject as a coherent entity with natural rights and potential autonomy) is pronounced dead and in *his* place appears the decentred, fragmented, gendered, classed subject; the grand narratives of theory and history are replaced by disjoined and fragmented local narratives potentially articulated and sutured; and metaphysics with its philosophies of presence and essence has lost

terrain to the celebration of multiple perspectives and a carnival of positions and structurings. The future is endlessly deferred and without positive direction, but life can be made more interesting through deconstruction and the recovery of suppressed conflicts and marginalized groups. The intellectual has no privileged position or special knowledge, but can only act in situational, local ways like all others. Since there can be no theory of history or projection into the future, resistance and alternative readings rather than reform or revolution become the primary political posture.

OPENING THE TENSIONS AND PROVIDING TEMPORARY UNITIES

In this section we will show a way of thinking about research positions that makes critical theory and postmodernism similar in contrast to other approaches to organizations and different from each other. To do this we will use a grid similar to the popular one by Burrell and Morgan (1979) but with changes that highlight similarities and differences more usefully (see Deetz 1994a; in press a; for development).[4] See Figure 1.

The consensus–dissensus dimension focuses on the relation of research practices to the dominant social discourses. Research perspectives can be contrasted based on the extent to which they work within a dominant set of structurings of knowledge, social relations, and identities, called here a 'consensus' discourse, and the extent to which they work to disrupt these structurings, called here 'dissensus' discourse. This dimension is used to show a significant way that we can think about what makes postmodernism and critical theory different from other current research programs. The second dimension focuses on the origin of concepts and problem statements as part of the constitutive process in research. Differences among research perspectives can be shown by contrasting 'local/emergent' conceptions with 'elite/*a priori*' ones. This dimension will be used to show one way to interestingly think about the difference between the postmodernism and critical theory discourses.

The two dimensions together attempt to show what is negotiable and not in research practice, how research reports are organized, and the anticipated political outcome of the research activity (the direction in which it points, whether or not it has a practical effect). Unlike Burrell and Morgan we do not wish to suggest that the grid identifies paradigms but rather we propose that it shows particular discourses which develop

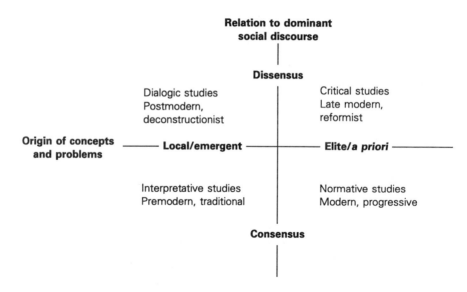

Relation to dominant social discourse

Dissensus

Dialogic studies
Postmodern,
deconstructionist

Critical studies
Late modern,
reformist

Origin of concepts and problems ——— **Local/emergent** ———|——— **Elite/*a priori*** ———

Interpretative studies
Premodern, traditional

Normative studies
Modern, progressive

Consensus

Figure 1   *Contrasting dimensions from the metatheory of representational practices*
Source: adapted from Deetz 1994c.

mobile but specifiable relations to each other and position particular types of conflicts and contradictions internal to them. Each of these issues will be taken up briefly below. We recognize that in naming these positions and the bodies of work exemplifying them, some things are pulled together that are still different in many now hidden ways and bipolar contrasts are created that change a continuous world to a discontinuous one. We hope the reader will work with us to see the various conceptualizations as interesting ways to call attention to similarities and differences that matter rather than as devices for division and classification. The differences between critical theory and postmodernism are often contested and many researchers draw on both traditions. Still it is useful to give some account of what makes these *different* traditions that do not easily collapse into each other.

The Consensus–Dissensus Dimension

Consensus or dissensus should be understood not primarily as agreement and disagreement but rather as presentation of unity or of difference, the continuation or disruption of a coherent dominant discourse, trust or doubt as basic anticipation. Key to this dimension is the argument from the dissensus end that people, orders, and objects are constructed in work, social interaction, and the process of research, and hence the perceived world is based on political processes of determination which often

demonstrate domination and could/should be contestable; while the consensus discourse provides the identities of people, social orders, and objects as natural, or if constructed, legitimate and given awaiting discovery by the researcher. When a construction view is advocated by certain consensus researchers, it tends to emphasize the natural, organic and spontaneous nature of the constructions, rather than, as in the version of dissensus seekers, its arbitrary and political character. To save space, see Table 1 for conceptualization of this dimension.

Local/Emergent–Elite/*A Priori* Dimension

The local/emergent–elite/*a priori* dimension will be used here primarily to call attention to a central difference between postmodern and critical theory positions but it also contrasts normative and interpretative studies. Table 2 presents an array of these contrasts. On the elite side, the discourse produces the researcher as a stronger agent with privileged insights – at least having the ability to produce reliable knowledge – and makes clear the commitment to political agendas.

The *a priori* set of conceptions demonstrates implicit or explicit alliances with different groups in society. For example, to the extent that normative researchers' concepts align with managerial conceptions and problem statements and are applied *a priori* in studies, the knowledge claims are intrinsically biased toward certain interests as they are applied within the site

Table 1   *Characterizations of the consensus–dissensus dimension*

Consensus	Dissensus
Trust	Suspicion
Hegemonic order as natural state	Conflicts over order as natural state
Naturalization of present	Present order is historicized and politicized
Integration and harmony are possible	Order indicates domination and suppressed conflicts
Research focuses on representation	Research focused on challenge and reconsideration (re-presentation)
Mirror (reflecting) dominant metaphor	Lens (seeing/reading as) dominant metaphor
Validity central concern	Insight and praxis central concern
Theory as abstraction	Theory as opening
Unified science and triangulation	Positional complementarity
Science is neutral	Science is political
Life is discovery	Life is struggle and creation
Researcher anonymous and out of time and space	Researcher named and positioned
Autonomous/free agent	Historically/socially situated agent

Source: adapted from Deetz in press a

Table 2   *Characterizations of the local/emergent–elite/a priori dimension*

Local/emergent	Elite/*a priori*
Comparative communities	Privileged community
Multiple language games	Fixed language game
Particularistic	Universalistic
Systematic philosophy as ethnocentric	Grounded in hoped-for systematic philosophy
Atheoretical	Theory driven
Situational or structural determinism	Methodological determinism
Nonfoundational	Foundational
Local narratives	Grand narrative of progress and emancipation
Sensuality and meaning as central concerns	Rationality and truth as central concerns
Situated, practical knowledge	Generalizable, theoretical knowledge
Tends to be feminine in attitude	Tends to be masculine in attitude
Sees the strange	Sees the familiar
Proceeds from the other	Proceeds from the self
Ontology of 'otherness' over method	Epistemological and procedural issues rule over substantive assumptions

Source: adapted from Deetz in press a

community. The knowledge claims become part of the same processes that are being studied, reproducing world views and personal identities, and fostering particular interests within the organization (see Knights 1992). Feminists and those primarily concerned with class analysis, while usually in sympathy with most aspects of postmodernism, often turn to critical theory (or a similar position) to acquire a political agenda based on preconceptions of social divisions and forms of domination that are considered general (see Fraser and Nicholson 1988; Flax 1990). While such conceptions from critical theory are critical of elite groups in the move to create a more equitable society, they tend to privilege the conceptions of disadvantaged groups or intellectual ideals, and hence produce their own, usually temporary, elitism. The local/emergent conceptions see social groupings themselves as constructions, power and domination as dispersed, and the research agenda as itself dominating. Words like 'women', 'worker', 'poor', 'owners', and so forth are accepted not as representations of 'reality', but as power-laden distinctions. An ordinary conception of political action as end-directed is thus difficult to sustain in either interpretative or postmodern (dialogic) work.

A Sketch of Alternative Research Approaches

The relation of postmodern and critical theory to each other and to normative and interpretative work can be shown by comparing the

Table 3 *Prototypical discursive features*

| Issue | Discourse | | | |
	Normative	Interpretative	Critical	Dialogic
Basic goal	Law-like relations among objects	Display unified culture	Unmask domination	Reclaim conflict
Method	Nomothetic science	Hermeneutics, ethnography	Cultural criticism, ideology critique	Deconstruction, geneology
Hope	Progressive emancipation	Recovery of integrative values	Reformation of social order	Claim a space for lost voices
Metaphor of social relations	Economic	Social	Political	Mass
Organization metaphor	Marketplace	Community	Polity	Carnival
Problems addressed	Inefficiency, disorder	Meaninglessness, illegitimacy	Domination, consent	Marginalization, conflict suppression
Concern with communication	Fidelity, influence, information needs	Social acculturation, group affirmation	Misrecognition, systematic distortion	Discursive closure
Narrative style	Scientific/technical, strategic	Romantic, embracing	Therapeutic, directive	Ironic, ambivalent
Time identity	Modern	Premodern	Late modern	Postmodern
Organizational benefits	Control, expertise	Commitment, quality of work life	Participation, expanded knowledge	Diversity, creativity
Mood	Optimistic	Friendly	Suspicious	Playful
Social fear	Disorder	Depersonalization	Authority	Totalization, normalization

Source: adapted from Deetz in press a

discourse they generate in regard to issues in organization studies. See Table 3. Since we will use these characterizations to build our discussion of studies in critical theory and postmodernism, we will not discuss them here.

CRITICAL THEORY AND ORGANIZATIONAL RESEARCH

The central goal of critical theory in organizational studies has been to create societies and workplaces which are free from domination, where all members have an equal opportunity to contribute to the production of systems which meet human needs and lead to the progressive development of all. Studies have focused externally on the relation of organizations to the wider society by emphasizing the possible social effects of colonization of other institutions and the domination or destruction of the public sphere, and internally on the domination by instrumental reasoning, discursive closures, and consent processes within the workplace. As indicated, critical researchers tend to enter their studies with a full set of theoretical commitments which aid them analytically to ferret out situations of domination and distortion. Organizations are largely seen as political sites, and thus

general social theories and especially theories of decision-making in the public sphere are seen as appropriate (see Deetz 1992; 1995).

Critical theorists sometimes have a clear political agenda focused on the interests of specific identifiable groups such as women, workers, or people of color, but usually address general issues of goals, values, forms of consciousness and communicative distortions within corporations. Increasingly important to critical studies is the enrichment of the knowledge base, improvement of decision process, and increases in 'learning' and adaptation. Their interest in ideologies considers the difficulties of disadvantaged groups in understanding their own political interest, but is more often addressed to limitations on people in general, challenging technocracy, consumerism, careerism, and exclusive concern with economic growth. Most of the work has focused on ideology critique which shows how specific interests fail to be realized owing partly to the inability of people to understand or act on these interests. In the context of management and organization studies, it should be emphasized that critical theory, compared to Marxism, is not anti-management *per se*, even though one tends to treat management as institutionalized and ideologies and practices of management as expressions of contemporary forms of domination. Critical theory can offer much to management and managers. Contributions include input to reflection on career choices, intellectual resources for counteracting totalitarian tendencies in managerially controlled corporate socialization, and stimulation for incorporating a broader set of criteria and consideration in decision-making – especially in cases where profit and growth do not clearly compete with other ends or where uncertainty exists regarding the profit outcomes of various alternative means and strategies (Alvesson and Willmott 1996: Chapter 8; Deetz 1995: Chapter 4). Two principal types of critical studies can be identified in organization studies: ideological critique and communicative action.

Ideology Critique

The earliest ideological critiques of the workplace were offered by Marx. In his analysis of work processes he focused primarily on practices of economic exploitation through direct coercion and structural differences in work relations between the owners of capital and the owners of their own labor. However, Marx also describes the manner in which the exploitative relation is disguised and made to appear legitimate. This is the origin of ideology critique. Economic conditions and class structure still were central to the analysis whether this misrecognition of interests was a result of the domination of the ruling class's ideas (Marx 1844) or of the dull compulsions of economic relations (Marx 1867).

The themes of domination and exploitation by owners and later by managers have been central to ideology critique of the workplace in this century by Marxist inspired organization theorists (for example, Braverman 1974; Clegg and Dunkerley 1980; Edwards 1979; Salaman 1981). Attention by analysts from the left focused on ideology since workers often seemed to fail to recognize this exploitation and their class-based revolutionary potential in the industrial countries. Gradually these later analyses became less concerned with coercion and class and economic explanations as their focus changed to why coercion was so rarely necessary and to systemic processes that produced active consent. Issues of 'workers' self-understanding of experience' become more central (for example, Gramsci 1929–35; Burawoy 1979; Willmott 1990). To an increasing degree, ideology critiques do not only or even strongly address class issues, but broaden the picture and study how cultural-ideological control operates in relationship to all employees, including levels of management (Hodge et al. 1979; Czarniawska-Joerges 1988; Deetz and

Mumby 1990; Kunda 1992). Ideology produced in the workplace would stand alongside that present in the media and the growth of the consumer culture and welfare state as accounting for workers' failure to act on their own interests. Ideology would also account for professionals' and managers' failure to achieve autonomy in relationship to needs and wants and the conformist pressure to standardize paths for satisfying these (conspicuous consumption, careerism, and self-commodification: see Heckscher 1995). This would fill out the tradition of ideology critique.

A considerable amount of critical work has addressed management and organization theory as expressions, as well as producers, of ideologies which legitimize and strengthen specific societal and organizational social relations and objectives (Burrell and Morgan 1979; Alvesson 1987; Alvesson and Willmott 1996; Steffy and Grimes 1992). Academics, particularly those in management studies, are often viewed as ideologists. They serve dominant groups through socialization in business schools, support managers with ideas and vocabularies for cultural-ideological control at the workplace level, and provide the aura of science to support the introduction and use of managerial domination techniques.

Four themes recur in the numerous and varied writings about organizations working from the perspective of ideology critique: (1) the naturalization of social order, or the way a socially/historically constructed world would be treated as necessary, natural, rational and self-evident; (2) the universalization of managerial interests and suppression of conflicting interests; (3) the domination by instrumental, and eclipse of competitive, reasoning processes; and (4) hegemony, the way consent becomes orchestrated.

Naturalization

In naturalization a social formation is abstracted from the historical conflictual site of its origin and treated as a concrete, relatively fixed, entity. As such the reification becomes the reality rather than life processes. Through obscuring the construction process, institutional arrangements are no longer seen as choices but as natural and self-evident. The illusion that organizations and their processes are 'natural' objects and functional responses to 'needs' protects them from examination as produced under specific historical conditions (which are potentially passing) and out of specific power relations. In organization studies, organismic and mechanistic metaphors dominate, thereby leading research away from considering the legitimacy of control and political relations in organizations (Morgan

1986). Examining the naturalization of the present and the reifications of social processes helps display the structural interrelation of institutional forces, the processes by which they are sustained and changed, and the processes by which their arbitrary nature is concealed and hence closed to discussion. Ideology critique reclaims organizations as social-historical constructions and investigates how they are formed, sustained, and transformed by processes both internal and external to them (see Lukács 1971; Benson 1977; Giddens 1979; Frost 1980; 1987; Thompson 1984; Deetz 1985; 1994d). The self-evident nature of an organizational society, the basic distinctions and division of labor between management and workers, men and women, and so forth are called into question by ideology critique which demonstrates the arbitrary nature of these phenomena and the power relations that result and sustain these forms for the sake of discovering the remaining places of possible choice.

Universalization of Managerial Interests

Lukács (1971) among many others (see Giddens 1979) has shown that particular sectional interests are often universalized and treated as if they were everyone's interests. In contemporary corporate practices, managerial groups are privileged in decision-making and research. Management is ascribed a superior position in terms of defining the interests and interest realizations of the corporation and thereby of wide segments of the population. The interests of the corporation are frequently equated with specific managerial self-interests. For example, worker, supplier, or host community interests can be interpreted in terms of their effect on corporate – i.e. universalized managerial – interests. As such they are exercised only occasionally and usually reactively and are often represented as simply economic commodities or 'costs' – for example, the price the 'corporation' must pay for labor, supplies, or environmental clean-up (Deetz 1995). Central to the universalization of managerial interest is the reduction of the multiple claims of ownership to financial ownership. The investments made by other stakeholders are minimized while capital investment is made central. Management by virtue of its fiduciary responsibility (limited to monetary investors) speaks for (and is often conceptually equated with) the corporation (Storey 1983). In such a move, since the *general* well-being of each group is conceptually and materially tied to the *financial* well-being of the corporation as understood by management, self-interest by nonmanagerial stakeholders is often ironically reinterpreted as accomplished by mini-

mizing the accomplishment of their own self-interests. In ideological critique managerial advantages can be seen as produced historically and actively reproduced through ideological practices in society and in corporations themselves (see Tompkins and Cheney 1985; Knights and Willmott 1985; Lazega 1992; Deetz 1992). Critical studies explore how interest articulation is distorted through the dominating role of money as a simple and powerful medium (Offe and Wiesenthal 1980) and confront productivity and consumption with suppressed values such as autonomy, creativity and pleasure as objectives for the organization of work (Burrell and Morgan 1979; Willmott and Knights 1982; Alvesson 1987).

The Primacy of Instrumental Reasoning

Habermas (1971; 1975; 1984; 1987) has traced the social/historical emergence of technical rationality over competing forms of reason. Habermas described *technical reasoning* as instrumental, tending to be governed by the theoretical and hypothetical, and focusing on control through the development of means–ends chains. The natural opposite to this Habermas conceptualizes as a *practical interest*. Practical reasoning focuses on the process of understanding and mutual determination of the ends to be sought rather than control and development of means of goal accomplishment (Apel 1979). As Habermas described the practical interest: 'a constitutive interest in the preservation and expansion of the intersubjectivity of possible action-oriented mutual understandings. The understanding of meaning is directed in its very structure toward the attainment of possible consensus among actors in the framework of a self-understanding derived from tradition' (1971: 310). In a balanced system these two forms of reasoning become natural complements. But, in the contemporary social situation, the form and content of modern social science and the social constitution of expertise align with organizational structures to produce the domination of technical reasoning (see Stablein and Nord 1985; Alvesson 1987; Alvesson and Willmott 1992; 1996; Mumby 1988; Fischer 1990). To the extent that technical reasoning dominates, it lays claim to the entire concept of rationality and alternative forms of reason appear irrational. To a large extent studies of the 'human' side of organizations (climate, job enrichment, quality of work life, worker participation programs, and culture) have each been transformed from alternative ends into new means to be brought under technical control for extending the dominant group interests of the corporation (Alvesson 1987). Sievers, for example, suggests that 'motivation only became an issue – for management and organization theorists as well as for the organization of work itself – when meaning either disappeared or was lost from work; that the loss of meaning is immediately connected with the way work has been, and still is organized in the majority of our Western enterprises' (1986: 338). The productive tension between technical control and humanistic aspects becomes submerged to the efficient accomplishment of often unknown but surely 'rational' and 'legitimate' corporate goals.

Hegemony

Although Gramsci's (1929–35) analysis and development of the concept of 'hegemony' aimed at a general theory of society and social change with the workplace as one component, his conceptions have been widely used as a foundation for an examination of the workplace itself (for example, Burawoy 1979; Clegg 1989). Gramsci conceives of hegemony as a complex web of conceptual and material arrangements producing the very fabric of everyday life. Hegemony in the workplace is supported by economic arrangements enforced by contracts and reward systems, cultural arrangements enforced by advocacy of specific values and visions, and command arrangements enforced by rules and policies. These are situated within the larger society with its supporting economic arrangements, civil society (including education/ intellectuals/media), and governmental laws.

The conception of hegemony suggests the presence of multiple dominant groups with different interests and the presence of power and activity even in dominated groups. The integration of these arrangements, however, favors dominant groups and the activity of both dominant and dominated groups is best characterized as a type of produced 'consent'. The hegemonic system works through pervading common sense and becoming part of the ordinary way of seeing the world, understanding one's self, and experiencing needs (see Angus 1992). Such a situation always makes possible a gap between that inscribed by the dominant order and that which a dominated group would have preferred. As Lukes argued, 'Man's wants themselves may be a product of a system which works against their interests, and in such cases, relates the latter to what they would want and prefer, were they able to make the choice' (1974: 34). A number of studies have investigated a variety of 'consent' processes (for example, Burawoy 1979; Kunda 1992; Vallas 1993). Several studies have shown how employees 'strategize their own subordination', achieving marginal gains for themselves through subordi-

nation but also perpetuating dominant systems which preclude their autonomy and ability to act on their own wider interests (see Burawoy 1985; Deetz 1995; in press b; Willmott 1993).

Organization studies in the 1980s and 1990s have exhibited a rather wide body of critical theory addressing corporate culture or proceeding from cultural perspectives on organizations, where culture and cultural engineering are defined as pointing towards hegemony (for example, Alvesson 1993a; Alvesson and Willmott 1996; Deetz 1985; Jermier 1985; Knights and Willmott 1987; Mumby 1988; Rosen 1985). Willmott, for example, has explored how 'corporate culture programmes are designed to deny or frustrate the development of conditions in which critical reflection is fostered. They commend the homogenization of norms and values within organizations . . . Cultural diversity is dissolved in the acid bath of the core corporate values' (1993: 534). In practice, as Willmott and other critical theorists point out, management control strategies are seldom fully successful. Resistance and some level of cultural diversity normally prevail. The role of critical theory, but even more so postmodernism, can be seen as trying to preserve and reinforce this diversity.

A Critique of Ideology Critique

Each of these four concerns raised in various ideological critiques has value. Yet, limitations of ideology critique have been demonstrated by many. Three criticisms appear most common. First, ideology critique often appears *ad hoc* and reactive. Most studies explain after the fact why something didn't happen rather than making predictive and testable statements about the future. Second, it appears elitist. Concepts like false needs and false consciousness which were central to early studies presume a basic weakness in insight and reasoning processes in the very same people it hopes to empower. The irony of an advocate of greater equality pronouncing what others should want or how they should perceive the world 'better' is not lost on either dominant or dominated groups. And, third, the accounts from early studies of ideology critique appear far too simplistic. According to Abercrombie et al.'s (1980) critique of the 'dominant ideology thesis', the conception of the dominant group remains singular and intentional, as if an identifiable group worked out a system whereby domination through control of ideas could occur and its interest could be secured.

A more sophisticated critique, coming from postmodernism, points out that the idea of the centred agent-subject is as central to ideology critique as it is to dominant groups and the systems that advantage them. The hope for a rational and reflective agent who is capable of acting autonomously and coherently may in itself be a worthy target of ideology critique. The modern corporation's legitimacy is based on both the assumption of the existence of such an individual and its ability to foster that individual's development. Ideology critique does not, on the whole, question this basic notion of the individual, even though authors are quick to point to the discrepancy between actual production of people and a potential development.

Clearly the power of ideology critique can be maintained without falling to these criticisms and many critical theorists have accomplished this as they have pulled the concept of ideology away from traditional Marxism. They have responded to the critics by (a) advocating research that empirically investigates expressions of dominating systems of thought in particular communicative situations rather than explains outcomes (for example, Alvesson 1996; Knights and Willmott 1987; Rosen 1985); (b) refraining from directive statements regarding what people should do (revolt, liberate) but emphasizing the problematization of dominating beliefs and values (Deetz 1992); (c) recognizing pluralistic qualities, but still insisting that there are strong asymmetries between various interests and perspectives; and (d) treating ideologies as dominating without seeing them as a simple instrument or in the interest of an elite group, thus showing that elites may have internalized and may suffer from the effects of dominating sets of ideas (such as pollution or through work processes: Heckscher 1995).

Another response to the problems of ideology critique is the development of a communicative perspective within critical theory. It represents a development from a focus on socially repressive ideas and institutions to the explorations of the communicative processes through which ideas are produced, reproduced and critically examined, especially in decision-making contexts.

Communicative Action

Unlike earlier advocates of critical theory, Habermas's work since the late 1970s has reduced the significance of traditional ideology critique and has concentrated instead on building a systematic philosophy in which theory and communicative action are of pivotal importance (Habermas 1984; 1987). This project retains many of the features of ideology critique, including the ideal of sorting out constraining social ideas from those grounded in reason, but it envisages procedural ideas rather than substantive critique and thus becomes quite different from traditional ideology critique. It

also introduces an affirmative agenda, not based on a utopia, but still a hope of how we might reform institutions along the lines of morally driven discourse in situations approximating an ideal speech situation.

Habermas separates two historical learning processes and forms of rationality, the technological-scientific-strategic, associated with the system world, and the communicative-political-ethical, associated with the lifeworld, and tries to contribute to the latter. He argues for the systematic improvement of the lifeworld through an expanded conception of rationality focusing on the creation and re-creation of patterns of meaning. The lifeworld can be regarded as fully rational – rather than instrumentalized or strategized – to the extent that it permits interactions that are guided by communicatively achieved understanding rather than by imperatives from the system world – such as those contingent upon the money code or formal power – or by the unreflective reproduction of traditional cultural values (Habermas 1984).

Communicatively achieved understanding is dependent on undistorted communication, the presence of free discussion based on goodwill, argumentation and dialogue. On the basis of undistorted, rational discussion he assumes that consensus can be reached regarding both present and desirable states. He maintains that in language itself and the way it is used there are certain conditions for achieving this ideal: the expectation and the wish to be understood and believed, and the hope that others will accept our arguments and other statements (see Thompson 1984; Deetz 1992: Chapters 6 and 7). Without such expectations and ambitions there is little point in either statements or discussions. Undistorted communication provides the basis for the 'highest' (or perhaps the widest, most reflective) form of rationality, namely communicative rationality. Here it is not power, status, prestige, ideology, manipulation, the rule of experts, fear, insecurity, misunderstanding or any other form of mischief that furnishes a base for the evolving ideas. Decision-making becomes based on the strength of the good, well-grounded argument provided in an open forum rather than authority, tradition, ideology, or exclusion of participants.

> This concept of communicative rationality carries with it connotations based ultimately on the central experience of the unconstrained, unifying, consensus-bringing force of argumentative speech, in which different participants overcome their merely subjective views and, owing to the mutuality of rationally motivated conviction, assure themselves of both the unity of the objective world and the intersubjectivity of their lifeworld. (Habermas 1984: 10)

Communicative rationality thus denotes a way of responding to (questioning, testing and, possibly, accepting) the validity of different claims. Communicative action thus allows for the exploration of every statement on a basis of the following (universal) validity criteria: comprehensibility, sincerity, truthfulness and legitimacy. Communicative action is therefore an important aspect of social interaction in society, in social institutions and in daily life. The ideal speech situation, which enables communicative rationality and is in turn pervaded by it, exists under the following conditions: 'the structure of communication itself produces no constraints if and only if, for all possible participants, there is a symmetrical distribution of chances to choose and to apply speech-acts' (Habermas, cited by Thompson and Held 1982: 123). Of course, the ideal speech situation is not a quality of ordinary communication, but a counterfactual anticipation we make when we seek mutual understanding, trying to accomplish the form of argumentation we presuppose we are able to step into when we seek to step aside from the flow of everyday action and check a problematic claim. As we will suggest in looking at critical theory's contribution, such an ideal when used as an analytic frame in organization studies can provide much guidance to restructuring discussions and decision-making in organizations (for example, Lyytinen and Hirschheim 1988; Power and Laughlin 1992).

We will not here repeat the critique of Habermas's theory (see Thompson and Held 1982; Fraser 1987; Burrell 1994), but just mention that it over stresses the possibility of rationality as well as value of consensus (Deetz 1992) and puts too much weight on the clarity and rationality potential of language and human interaction. To some extent, it relies on a model of the individual as potentially autonomous and clarified, but this assumption plays a less central role compared to earlier critical theory, as the focus is not on consciousness, but on the structure of communicative interaction as the carrier of rationality. But still Habermas can be criticized for his 'benign and benevolent view of human kind' (Vattimo 1992) which counts on knowledge and argumentation to change thought and action, a position about which postmodernists are highly skeptical.

The Contribution of Critical Organization Studies

Critical studies in organization theory have utilized the ideas sketched above, developed these and illustrated their relevance for the understanding of modern organizations, in particular corporations. Alvesson and Willmott (1996) have pointed at some metaphors for organizations and management from critical theory: organization as technocracy, mystification, cultural doping and colonizing power. These draw attention to how management expertise leads to passivity on the part of other organizational participants, how ambiguity and contradictions are masked, how the engineering of values and definitions of reality tend to weaken low-level and other marginal groups in the negotiation of workplace reality and, respectively, how the codes of money and formal power exercise a close to hegemonic position over workplace experiences and articulated values and priorities. As indicated above, two basic foci can here be pointed at: one content oriented emphasizing sources of constraints, one process oriented emphasizing variation in communicative action in organizations.

Critical theory draws attention, for example, to the narrow thinking associated with the domination of instrumental reason and the money code. Potentially, when wisely applied, instrumental reason is a productive form of thinking and acting. However, in the absence of practical reason (aiming at politically and ethically informed judgment), its highly specialized, means-fixated and unreflective character makes it strongly inclined to also contribute to the objectification of people and nature and thus to various forms of destruction. Most salient are (1) constrained work conditions where intrinsic work qualities (creativity, variation, development, meaningfulness) are ignored or subordinated to instrumental values (Alvesson 1987; Sievers 1986); (2) the development and reinforcement of asymmetrical social relations between experts (including management elites) and nonexperts (Alvesson and Willmott 1996; Fischer 1990; Hollway 1984); (3) gender bias in terms of styles of reasoning, asymmetrical social relations and political priorities (Calás and Smircich 1992a; 1992b; Mumby and Putnam 1992; Ferguson 1984; Hearn and Parkin 1987); (4) extensive control of employees' mindsets and a freezing of their social reality (Deetz and Kersten 1983; Frost 1987; Mumby 1987); (5) far-reaching control of employees, consumers and the general political-ethical agenda in society, though mass media and lobbying advocating consumerism and the priority of the money code as a yardstick for values and individual and collective political decision-making (Alvesson and Willmott 1996; Deetz 1992); and (6) destruction of the natural environment through waste and pollution (Shrivastava 1995; Stead and Stead 1992).

In the guise of technocracy, instrumental rationality has pretenses to neutrality and freedom from the value-laden realms of self-interest and politics. It celebrates and 'hides' behind techniques and the false appearance of objectivity and impartiality of institutionalized sets of knowledge, bureaucracy and formal mandates. Not surprisingly, technocracy is promoted by each of the management 'specialisms' as they claim a monopoly of expertise in their respective domains. Human resource specialists, for example, advance and defend their position by elaborating a battery of 'objective' techniques for managing the selection and promotion of employees (Hollway 1984; Steffy and Grimes 1992). Strategic management institutionalizes a particular way of exercising domination through legitimizing and privileging the 'management' of the organization–environment interface, producing some actors as 'strategists' and reducing others to troops whose role is to subordinate themselves and to implement corporate strategies (Shrivastava 1986; Alvesson and Willmott 1995). The concept of technocracy draws attention to some of the darker and more disturbing aspects of so-called 'professional management'. It points to a restricted understanding of human and organizational goals: those that are identified and validated by experts. By associating management with technocracy and its instrumentalization of reason, the domination of a narrow conception of reason is at once exposed and questioned.

The domination of groups, ideas and institutions producing and drawing upon the idea of technocracy leads to a technocratic consciousness (Habermas 1970; Alvesson 1987). Here basic conflicts between different ideals and principles are seen as dissolving as a consequence of the development of more and more rational methods. In work organizations, conflicts between practical reason (emphasizing the removal of repression) and instrumental reason (focused on the maximization of output) are portrayed as avoidable through the use of optimal management methods such as job enrichment, QWL, TQM, corporate culture and so forth, which simultaneously produce human well-being and development as well as high quality and productivity. Basic political issues are then transformed into technical problem-solving.

Habermas's ideas may also be used in a pragmatic way, more suitable for social science and organization studies than the original philosophical-theoretical version. With the communicative turn in Habermas's work, there follow possibilities for a more applied and empirical development in the use of critical theory. This means, as Forester argued, 'putting *ideal* speech aside' and expanding the exploration of 'the *actual* social and political conditions of

"checking", of political voice, and thus too of possible autonomy' (1993: 3, italics added). Forester (1985; 1989; 1992; 1993) has developed a 'critical pragmatism' based on an independent and creative reading of Habermas. Forester's work is particularly interesting as it combines theoretical sophistication with an empirical and applied orientation and can serve as an example here of what critical can look like in practice. To Forester, an empirically oriented critical theory should be '(1) empirically sound and descriptively meaningful; (2) interpretatively plausible and phenomenologically meaningful; and yet (3) critically pitched, ethically insightful, as well' (1993: 2).

In following this through, Forester (1989) distinguishes between unavoidable and socially unnecessary disturbances, between socially *ad hoc* problems and more socially systematic, structure-related sources of distortions. Organizations may be understood as structures of systematically (nonaccidentally and possibly avoidable) distorted communications or as social/communicative infrastructures mediating between structural relations and social actions in economic and working life contexts. Irrespective of the extent to which distortions can be avoided in practice, knowledge and insight of these distorted communications are certainly of value. From a communication perspective, organizations can be assessed and evaluated according to whether they approximate dogma (closed communication) or dialogue (open communication) (see Deetz 1992: Chapter 7). As Forester argued:

> When organizations or polities are structured so that their members have no protected recourse to checking the truth, legitimacy, sincerity, or clarity claims made on them by established structures of authority and production, we may find conditions of dogmatism rather than of social learning, tyranny rather than authority, manipulation rather than cooperation, and distraction rather than sensitivity. In this way critical theory points to the importance of understanding practically and normatively how access to, and participation in, discourses, both theoretical and practical, are systematically structured. (1983: 239–40)

Forester views the organizing of attention as a crucial feature of administrative and organizational processes of social reproduction. He draws upon Habermas's (1984) model of reproduction, which includes (1) cultural reproduction of world views (ideas, knowledge, beliefs), (2) social integration, in which norms, obligations and patterns of social membership are reproduced, and (3) socialization, in which social identities, motives and expressions of the self are altered and developed. At stake in specific communicative/organizational acts (and struggles) are thus the reproduction/challenging/ reformulation of beliefs, consent and identity. Crucial research as well as practical questions include 'what makes possible or impedes a worker's finding out information at the work-place, challenging rules or norms, or expressing needs, feelings, his or her identity, way of being?' (1993: 131). The problem here, Forester notes, is to link control structures to daily experience, voice and action. Such an account becomes a structural phenomenology: it is structural because it maps 'the systematic staging and framing of social action; it is phenomenology because it explores the concrete social interac-tions (promises, threats, agreements, deals, conflicts) that are so staged' (1993: 140). Forester (1992) illustrates his approach through a sensitive reading of a mundane, seemingly trivial empirical situation, a city staff planning meeting. He explores his data – twelve lines of transcript from the meeting – and shows how Habermas's pragmatic validity claims are pro-ductive in exploring how social and political relations are established, reordered, and repro-duced as the staff talk and listen.

POSTMODERNISM AND ORGANIZATIONAL RESEARCH

Much has been made of the multiple uses of the term 'postmodern' and the different versions of it (Alvesson 1995; Thompson 1993). We will not here deny the variation within the stream. Nevertheless, in contexts such as the present one it can be helpful to produce common themes in which variations in key authors' agendas are downplayed and commonalities highlighted. In postmodernism as a philosophically based research perspective, which is our major concern in this chapter, the following, on the whole interrelated, set of ideas is often emphasized: (a) the centrality of discourse – textuality – where the constitutive powers of language are empha-sized and 'natural' objects are viewed as discursively produced; (b) fragmented identities, emphasizing subjectivity as a process and the death of the individual, autonomous, meaning-creating subject where the discursive production of the individual replaces the conventional 'essentialistic' understanding of people; (c) the critique of the philosophy of presence and representation where the indecidabilities of language take precedence over language as a mirror of reality and a means for the transport of meaning; (d) the loss of foundations and the power of grand narratives where an emphasis on multiple voices and local politics is favored over

theoretical frameworks and large-scale political projects; (e) the power/knowledge connection where the impossibilities in separating power from knowledge are assumed and knowledge loses a sense of innocence and neutrality; (f) hyperreality – simulacra – replace the 'real world' where simulations take precedence in contemporary social order; and (g) research aims at resistance and indeterminacy where irony and play are preferred to rationality, predictability and order. Let us consider each briefly.

The Centrality of Discourse

Postmodernism grew out of French structural-ism by taking seriously the linguistic turn in philosophy. In this sense postmodernists in the French tradition made a move on structuralist thought similar to the one Habermas made on ideological critique in the German tradition. As systematically distorted communication replaces false consciousness in critical theory, textual/ discursive fields replaced the structure of the unconscious in postmodern thought. Both used these to fight a two front war, the objectivists on the one hand with their science aimed at predicting/controlling nature and people, and humanists on the other privileging the indivi-dual's reported experience and unique human rights, and advancing a naive version of human freedom. Focusing on language allowed a constructionism which denied the objectivist claim of certainty and objective truth and the humanists' reliance on essential claims which lead them to miss the social/linguistic politics of experience. As discussed later, the linguistic turn enabled a postmodern rejection of humanism through a critique of autonomy and unitary identities and a rejection of objectivism through a critique of the philosophy of presence and representation.

To note the primacy of discourse is to suggest that each person is born into ongoing discourses that have a material and continuing presence. The experience of the world is structured through the ways discourses lead one to attend to the world and provide particular unities and divisions. As a person learns to speak these discourses, they more properly speak to him or her in that available discourses position the person in the world in a particular way prior to the individual having any sense of choice. As discourses structure the world they at the same time structure the person's subjectivity, provid-ing him/her with a particular social identity and way of being in the world. The person, *contra* humanism, is always social first and only mis-takenly claims the personal self as the origin of experience.

There are two major versions of this theme. One emphasizes discourses in a special linguistic sense, where language in use is intrinsically related to meaning and perception. All perception and meaning entails a 'seeing as' and this 'seeing as' is described as a fundamental 'signifying' or 'language' relation. The distinctions historically carried in language enable a reproduction of specific 'seeing as' relations. Different discourses are always possible – although they may be more or less powerful or marginal. As a linguistic phenomenon, discourse is weakly coupled to material practices in this version (Weedon 1987). Another, Foucauldian version views discourses as systems of thought which are contingent upon as well as inform material practices which not only linguistically, but also practically through particular power techniques (clearly visible in prisons, psychiatric hospitals, schools, factories, and so forth), produce particular forms of subjectivity (Foucault 1977; 1980). In both versions, human subjectivity can be relatively open or closed. Discursive closure according to the first version is temporary, though often continually reproduced, while Foucault tends to emphasize a more systematic fixation of subjectivity as a result of the network of power relations in operation.

Many organizational researchers have used this insight productively. Most, but not all, have followed Foucault in their development. For example, Knights and Morgan used Foucault's discursive practices to show the construction of person and world in the discourse of corporate strategy. They argue that 'strategic discourse engages individuals in practices through which they discover the very "truth" of what they are – viz. "a strategic actor"' (1991: 260). They point at a number of power effects of corporate strategy discourse, including the sustaining and enhancement of the prerogatives of management, the generation of a sense of personal security for managers, the expression of a gendered masculinity for (male) management, and the facilitation and legitimization of the exercise of power.

Fragmented Identities

The position on the 'person' follows directly from the conception of discourse. Postmodernism rejects the notion of the autonomous, self-determining individual with a secure unitary identity as the centre of the social universe. Even though many other traditions have done so also (for example, behaviourists, structuralists), postmodernists have pushed this point strongly and in a sophisticated manner.

There are two versions of this critique of a secure unitary identity. The first suggests that the Western conception of *man* has always been a myth. It represents a rather ethnocentric idea. Freud's work on tensions and conflicts as central for the human psyche is used to show the growing awareness in Western thought of the fundamental inner fragmentation and inconsistency, but postmodernists go further in their deconstruction of the Western self-image. The conception of a unitary self is considered a fiction used to suppress those conflicts and privilege masculinity, rationality, vision, and control. To the extent that dominant discourses spoke the person (and produced the person as the origin of thought), the person gained a secure identity but participated in the reproduction of domination, thus marginalizing the other parts of the self and other groups. The sense of autonomy served to cover this subservience and give conflict a negative connotation.

The other version suggests that the view of the individual as coherent, integrated and (potentially) autonomous has become false in the contemporary historical and cultural situation. If identity is a social production, identity will be relatively stable in homogeneous and stable societies with few dominant discourses. In contemporary, heterogeneous, global, teleconnected societies the available discourses expand greatly. They also change rapidly. The individual comes to be spoken by so many discourses that fragmentation is virtually inevitable (Gergen 1991). As society becomes more fragmented and hyperreal or virtual (discourse is disconnected from any world reference, images reference images) the identity-stabilizing forces are lost.[5] Such a position suggests the possibility of tremendous freedom and opportunity for marginalized groups and aspects of each person to enter the discourse, but also insecurities which lead to normalization strategies in which people 'voluntarily' cling themselves to consumer identities offered by commercial forces or organizational selves through the orchestration of corporate cultures (Deetz 1995; Willmott 1994). This loose self is also very susceptible to manipulation and can be jerked about in the system, leading to ecstasy but domination without any dominant group as in Baudrillard's (1983; 1988) conception of simulation. These two versions – emphasizing human nature *per se* or only the contemporary, Western variant as discursively produced and fragmentary – are often a matter of emphasis (see Gergen 1991; 1992).

This view of the human subject however creates difficulties in developing political action. Flax (1990) for example shows the awkward position it leaves women in. If gender is treated as a social construction and dominant discourses have produced marginality and a sense of women being 'others' – taking all the negative terms in the linguistic system and discourse – then ridding society of strong gender ascriptions, making gender irrelevant in many situations, is a good idea. One should simply stop talking about 'men' and 'women', and stop reproducing this pervasive and powerful distinction (except in specific situations where it makes practical sense, i.e. in relationship to childbirth and a few diseases). But to accomplish such a move in the contemporary situation requires women to organize and show that gender is an issue across nearly all social situations. And similarly with the issue of experience: if women's experience arises out of an essential difference (bodily and/or socially produced), it cannot be denied as important and needing to be taken into account, but to make the essentialist argument denies social constructionism and can easily be used in a society where men have resources to further stigmatize women. Theoretical tensions are not easily escaped (see Fraser and Nicholson 1988). Ironically, however, this type of deep tension and inability to develop a single coherent position appears at the same time to weaken postmodern work and give it its reason for being. Such tensions have led some researchers to borrow from critical theory conceptions to add a clearer political program (see Martin 1990) and others to focus on more local forms of resistance (see Smircich and Calás 1987).

Important implications for organizational analyses follow from the destabilization of human actors and their organizing processes. Linstead suggests that 'organization then is continuously emergent, constituted and constituting, produced and consumed by subjects' and argues for investigations that move 'towards those processes which *shape* subjectivity rather than the process by which individual subjects act upon the word' (1993: 60). Knights and Willmott (1989) have provided such work, demonstrating the way being subjected leads to particular forms of subjugation. Pringle (1988) has shown how the identity of a 'secretary' becomes constructed and reproduced. Deetz (1994c; in press b; in press c) has shown how the nature of 'knowledge-intensive' work situates the production of specific work identities. In a similar way, Townley (1993) applied Foucault's analysis to the discourse of human resource management. In this work, Townley argued that the basic unit of analysis in understanding human resources management was 'the nature of exchange embodied in the employment relation'. Since this relation in itself is indeterminant, the exchange relation is

organized through imposing order on the inherently undecidable. The construction of knowledge in human resource management 'operates through rules of classification, ordering, and distribution; definition of activities; fixing of scales; and rules of procedure, which lead to the emergence of a distinct HRM discourse' (1993: 541). This body of knowledge operates to objectify (determine) the person, thus both constraining and subordinating the person's fuller social and personal character.

The Critique of the Philosophy of Presence

Normative social science as well as most of us in everyday life treat the presence of objects as unproblematic and believe that the primary function of language is to re-present them. When asked what something is we try to define it and list its essential attributes. Postmodernists find such a position to be illusionary in the same way as the conception of identity. The *stuff* of the world only becomes an *object* in a specific relation to a being for whom it can be such an object. Linguistic and nonlinguistic practices thus are central to object production. Such a position has been familiar for some time in works as varied as Mead, Wittgenstein, and Heidegger, but continues to lead to misunderstandings, the most common being the claim of relativism. The position is not, however, relativistic in any loose or subjective way. Those making the charge misunderstand the conception of objects or the strength of the conception of discourse. Most postmodernists are not concerned with the chance of being called relativistic, they are more concerned with the apparent stability of objects and the difficulty of unpacking the full range of activities that produce particular objects and sustain them.

As mentioned in the section of fragmented identities, postmodernists differ in the extent to which they describe discourse in textual versus a more extended form. On the whole, however, they start with Saussure's demonstration that the point of view creates the object. He meant this to attend to the importance of the value-laden nature of the system of distinctions in language, but the linguistic and nonlinguistic practices quickly interrelate. Let us use a brief example. A 'worker' is an object (as well as a subject) in the world, but neither God nor nature made a 'worker'. Two things are required for a 'worker' to exist: a language and set of practices which makes possible unities and divisions among people, and something to which such unities and divisions can be applied. The questions 'What is a worker really?', 'What is the essence of a worker?', 'What makes one a worker?' are not answerable by looking at the something that can be described as a worker, but are products of the linguistic and nonlinguistic practices that make this something into an object. In this sense, a worker is not an isolated thing. To have a worker already implies a division of labor, the presence of management ('nonworkers'). The 'essence' of worker is not the properties the 'object' contains but sets of relational systems including the division of labor. The focus on the object and object properties is the mistake; the attention should be to the relational systems which are not simply in the world but are a human understanding of the world, are discursive or textual. The meaning of 'worker' is not evident and present (contained there) but deferred to the sets of oppositions and junctures, the relations that make it like and unlike other things.

Since any something in the world may be constructed/expressed as many different objects, limited only by human creativity and readers of traces of past understandings, meaning can never be final but is always incomplete and indeterminate. The appearance of completeness and closure leads us to overlook both the politics in and of construction and the possibilities for understanding that are hidden behind the obvious. Language is thus central to the production of objects in that it provides the social/historical distinctions that provide unity and difference. Language cannot mirror the reality 'out there', or people's mental states (Shotter and Gergen 1989; 1994). Language is figural, metaphorical, full of contradictions and inconsistencies (Brown 1990; Cooper and Burrell 1988). Meaning is not universal and fixed, but precarious, fragmented and local (Linstead and Grafton-Small 1992). Organizational researchers have used these conceptions to deconstruct objects of organizational life including the bounded concept of an organization itself. Perhaps among the most productive have been those studying accounting practices. The bottom line, profit and loss, expenses, and so forth have no reality without specific practices creating them (Hopwood 1987; Power and Laughlin 1992; Montagna 1986). Others have looked at knowledge and information (Boland 1987). And yet others have examined reporting practices (Sless 1988) and categories of people (Epstein 1988). Each of these shows the conditions necessary for objects to exist in organizational life. Any attempt at representation is thus always partial (one-sided and favoring a side). The making of distinction through language use is both a necessary condition of life with others, and yet inevitably limiting in · that it hides important alternative distinctions (see Bourdieu 1984; 1991).

The Loss of Foundations and Master Narratives

The power of any position has been traditionally gathered from its grounding. This grounding could be to either a metaphysical foundation – such as an external world in empiricism, mental structures in rationalism or human nature in humanism – or a narrative, a story of history, such as Marxism's class struggle, social Darwinism's survival of the fittest, or market economy's invisible hand. With such groundings, positions are made to seem secure and inevitable and not opportunistic or driven by advantage. Certainly much organizational theory has been based on such appeals as has critical theory in its morally guided communicative action.

Again, as in the case of identity, postmodernists take two different but not incompatible stances, one categorical (valid throughout history and social context) and one interested in recent historical trends (thus overlapping the philosophy/periodization distinctions). Following the first position, foundations and legitimating narratives have always been a hoax. They have been used (usually unknowingly) to support a dominant view of the world and its order. Feminists, for example, have argued that the historical narrative has always been *his*tory. Empiricists' appeal to the nature of the external world covered the force of their own concepts (and those borrowed from elite groups), methods, instruments, activities, and reports in constructing that world.

Following the second position, other postmodernists note the growing social incredulity toward narratives and foundational moves. Lyotard (1984) showed the decline of grand narratives of 'spirit' and 'emancipation'. The proliferation of options and the growing political cynicism (or astuteness) of the public lead to a suspicion of legitimating moves. This conception is not far from Habermas's idea of legitimation crises in late capitalistic society (Habermas 1975). In Lyotard's sense perhaps all that is left is local narratives. Such a position has led to sensitive treatments of how stories in organizations connect to grand narratives and how different ones have a more local, situational character (see Martin 1990; Deetz in press c). Others have used this opening to display the false certainty in the master narratives in management (Jehenson 1984; Ingersoll and Adams 1986; Carter and Jackson 1987; Calás and Smircich 1991).

Not all postmodernists see this as necessarily positive. Certainly the decline of foundations and grand narratives takes away a primary prop of dominant groups' offer of security and certainty as a trade for subordination. But the replacement is not necessarily freedom and political possibility on the part of marginalized groups. Lyotard demonstrated the rise of 'performativity' where measures of means toward social ends become ends in themselves (see also Power 1994). Access to computers and information – contingent less upon knowledge integrated in the person ('scholarship') than upon financial resources – has become a significant source of knowledge and power. Along with this comes new forms of control directed not by a vision of society and social good but simply by more production and consumption.

Certainly the loss of grand integrative narratives has not been missed by management groups. One could perhaps say that corporate 'visions' and 'cultures' are strategic local narrative constructions to provide the integration and motivation in a pluralistic society formerly provided by wider social narratives. On the other hand one could say that these forms of management control represent large-scale systematic efforts which resemble grand narratives, though at a corporate level. Perhaps the development of management control can be seen as corporate grand narratives taking over some of the functions of political programs. The decline of vision, hope and community in politics has paved the way for management ideologies and practices that may fill parts of the vacuum (Deetz 1992). Postmodernists point to the precarious nature of this kind of project. Corporate cultures, for example, are seen as text and corporate members then become readers who 'bring awareness of other texts, other cultural forms, other evocations and explosions of meaning to their reading of any text, and enter into the text, changing its nature and reproducing it as they consume it' (Linstead and Grafton-Small 1992: 344).

The difficulty in postmodernism with this, as in the concept of fragmented identities, is how to generate a political stance in regard to these developments. If one rejects an essentialist foundation and believes that more than local resistance is needed, some kind of combination between postmodernism and critical theory may well provide the best remaining option. We will come back to this.

The Knowledge/Power Connection

Within postmodern writings power is treated far different from most writings on organizations. Foucault has been the most explicit (Foucault 1977; 1980; see Clegg 1994). The power that is of interest is not that one possesses or acquires. Such appearances of power are the outcome of more fundamental power relations. Power resides in the discursive formation itself – the combination of a set of linguistic distinctions, ways of reasoning and material practices that together organize social institutions and produce particular forms of subjects. As mentioned before, language is here less strictly focused than in many other variants of postmodernism. Following the earlier example, the discourse that produces a 'manager' both empowers and disempowers the group of individuals formed as that object. It simultaneously provides a solidarity and interests and sets into play conflicts, material and symbolic resources, self-understandings, and the same for others such as professionals and workers. Power thus resides in the demarcations and the systems of discourse that sustain them, including material arrangements, for example, recruitment and selection procedures, office arrangements, reward and control structures, inclusion/exclusion in significant meetings, and so forth. One of the most useful terms entering into organizational studies from this has been Foucault's (1977) concept of discipline. The demarcations provide forms of normative behavior supported by claims of knowledge. Training, work routines, self-surveillance, and experts comprise discipline in that they provide resources for normalization. Normative experts in particular and the knowledge they create provide a cover for the arbitrary and advantaging discursive practices and facilitate normalization (Hollway 1984; 1991). Townley's (1993) work, already discussed, carefully showed how the development of the human resource expert and human resource knowledge was used as a way to 'determine' and subordinate employees. Such knowledge can also be utilized by employees to engage in self-surveillance and self-correction of attitudes and behaviors toward norms and expectations established by others (Deetz 1995: Chapter 10; in press b).

Hyperreality

Postmodern writings vary in terms of how they handle the relation of language to the nonlinguistic realm of people and world. A strict linguistic focus and a strict critique of the philosophy of presence leave little interest in references to a pre-formed and relatively constant extra-textual reality. Most postmodernists treat the external as a kind of excess or 'otherness' which serves as a resource for formations and also prevents language systems from becoming closed and purely imaginary. While the referent has no specific character it always exceeds the objects made of it, and thus reminds one of the limited nature of all systems of representation and their fundamental indeterminacy (Cooper 1989). The presence of 'otherness' in the indeterminacy provides a moment to show the domination present in any system, to open it up, and to break the sealed self-referentiality of some textual systems.

Many existing linguistic or representational systems are shown to be self-referential by postmodernists. Such systems are not anchored in a socially produced as objective world, nor do they respect the excess of an outside. They produce the very same world that they appear to accurately represent. For example, contemporary media and information systems have the capacity to rapidly construct images which replace, more than represent, an outside world. Such systems can dominate the scene with an array of reproduced imaginary worlds. The referent disappears as anything more than another sign; thus signs only reference other signs; images are images of images. Such systems can become purely self-referential, or what Baudrillard calls *simulations* (see Deetz 1994b). In such a world, in Baudrillard's analysis, signs are disconnected from opening a relation to the world and the 'model' response to a 'model' world replaces responsive action in an actual changing one. Signs reach the structural limit of representation by referencing only themselves with little relation to any exterior or interior. Baudrillard expresses this relation as follows:

> The form-sign [present in a monopolistic code] describes an entirely different organization: the signified and the referent are now abolished to the sole profit of the play of signifiers, of a generalized formalization in which the code no longer refers back to any subjective or objective 'reality', but to its own logic . . . The sign no longer designates anything at all. It approaches its true structural limit which is to refer back only to other signs. All reality then becomes the place of semi-urgical manipulation, of a structural simulation. (1975: 127–8)

The world as understood is not really a fiction in this situation since there is no 'real' outside which it portrays falsely or which can be used to correct it. It is properly imaginary; it has no opposite, no outside. Baudrillard used the example of the difference between feigning and simulating an illness to show the character of this postmodern representation: 'feigning or dissimulation leaves the reality principle intact; the difference is always clear, it is only masked; whereas simulation threatens the difference between "true" and "false", between "real" and "imaginary". Since the simulator produces "true" symptoms, is he ill or not? He cannot be treated objectively either as ill, or not ill' (1983: 5). These ideas have inspired some organization studies emphasizing the imaginary

character of modern organizations (Berg 1989; Alvesson 1990; Deetz 1994c; 1995). As is common with postmodern ideas in organization theory, these studies do not follow the source of inspiration to its full (extreme) consequences.

Research as Resistance and Indeterminacy

The role of postmodern research is very different from more traditional roles assigned to social science. It primarily serves to attempt to open up the indeterminacy that modern social science, everyday conceptions, routines, and practices have closed off. The result is a kind of anti-positive knowledge (Knights 1992). The primary methods are deconstruction and resistance readings and genealogy. These terms have been used in many different ways and in the short space here we can do little beyond a sketch. Deconstruction works primarily to critique the philosophy of presence by recalling the suppressed terms (the deferred term) which provides the system and thus which allows the positive terms to appear to stand for an existing object. When the suppressed term is given value both the dependency of the positive term on the negative is shown and a third term is recovered which shows a way of world making that is not dependent on the opposition of the first two (see Cooper 1989; Martin 1990; Calás and Smircich 1991; Mumby and Putnam 1992). The resistance reading is less narrowly focused on terms. It both demonstrates the construction activity and provides indeterminacy based in the excess of the outside. The positive and the polar construction are both displayed as acts of domination, subjectivity doing violence to the world and limiting itself in the process. In this move, conflicts that were suppressed by the positive are brought back to redecision and the conflictual field out of which objects are formed is recovered for creative redetermination – constant dedifferentiation and redifferentiation. Given the power of closure and the way it enters common sense and routines, especially in simulations, such rereadings require a particular form of rigor and imagination. The rereadings are formed out of a keen sense of irony, a serious playfulness, and often guided by the pleasure one has in being freed from the dull compulsions of a world made too easy and too violent. A good example of such readings is Calás and Smircich's (1988) account of a mainstream positivist journal article – where they start with the question 'Why should we believe in this author?' and then point at the rhetorical tricks involved in order to persuade the reader. Another interesting example is Sangren's (1992) critical review of Clifford and Marcus's *Writing Culture* (1986). Sangren, drawing upon

Bourdieu (1979), uses their points about the politics of representation – intended to indicate the problems of ethnographies in mirroring cultures and exemplified through important anthropological works – against themselves, showing how representations of Clifford, Marcus and co-authors of earlier work can be seen in terms of politics. Particular kinds of representations are used that create the impression that earlier works are flawed and that there is a large and open space for novel contributions (and the career options) of the new heterodoxy (Clifford, Marcus et al.) and their more informed view on the politics of representation.

The point of social science is not to get it right but to challenge guiding assumptions, fixed meanings and relations, and to reopen the formative capacity of human beings in relation to others and the world, qualities that Gergen (1978) and Astley (1985) displayed as essential to any important theory. As Sangren (1992) illustrates, the challenge of dogma, fixed ideas and reopenings easily implies new dogmas, fixations and closures. Postmodernism is in no way immune to such implications (Alvesson and Sköldberg 1996).

One outcome of the themes reviewed above – in particular the critique of the philosophy of presence and the loss of master narratives, but also hyperreality and the focus on resistance – is a strong current interest in experimenting with different styles. This is prominent in anthropology (Clifford and Marcus 1986; Geertz 1988; Marcus and Fisher 1986; Rose 1990) but also in organization theory (for example, Calás and Smircich 1991; Jeffcutt 1993; Linstead and Grafton-Small 1990). Typically, 'realist' ways of writing are superseded or complemented by other styles, for example, ironic, self-ironic or impressionistic ones. In an investigation of texts in organizational culture and symbolism, Jeffcutt shows how it is 'distinguished by heroic quests for closure; being dominated by authors adopting representational styles that privilege epic and romantic narratives over tragic and ironic forms. These representational strategies expose an overriding search for unity and harmony that suppresses division and conflict' (1993: 32). Perhaps the inspiration to develop new ways of writing will turn out to be one of the most powerful and interesting contributions of postmodernism.

RELATING CRITICAL THEORY AND POSTMODERNISM

Critical theory and postmodernism, as has been shown, are both alike and different. Each has much to contribute to organizational studies, and we believe that they have a contribution to make together. Without considering postmodern themes, critical theory easily becomes unreflective in regard to cultural elitism and modern conditions of power; and without incorporating some measure of critical theory thought – or something similar that provides direction and social relevance – postmodernism simply becomes esoteric. Both draw attention to the social/historical/political construction of knowledge, people, and social relations, including how each of these appears in contemporary organizations. And they share a view that domination is aided, and both people and organizations lose much, if we overlook these construction activities by treating the existing world as natural, rational and neutral. In critical theory's language, the concern is reification; in postmodernism, the philosophy of presence. Based on this naturalization and freezing of contemporary social reality, important conflicts – options for reconsiderations and questioning – are lost and different groups of people as well as vital values are marginalized and disadvantaged. Both see organizations and the social sciences that support them as relying increasingly on a form of instrumental reasoning privileging the means over ends and aiding dominant groups' ability to invisibly accomplish their ends. Habermas describes this in terms of 'instrumental technical reasoning', Lyotard in terms of 'performativity'.

The differences are also important. Critical theory sees the response in terms of an expanded form of morally guided communicative reasoning leading to individual autonomy and better social choices. Through reflections on the ways ideology – taken for granted cultural ideas as well as specific messages engineered by powerful agencies – enters into person/world/knowledge construction and by providing more open forums of expression and a type of discourse aimed at mutual understanding, there is hope for the production of social consensus and social agreements that better fulfill human needs. The grand narrative of enlightenment might, according to critical theory, yet be advanced. But postmodernism rejects such reflection and consensus, suspecting the replacement of old illusions with new ones, and the creation of new elites and new forms of marginalizations. Critical theory replies: without reflection, consensus and rationality, there is no politics, no agenda for a constructive alternative. Postmodernism counters: politics are by necessity local and situational; responsiveness is more important than systematic planning. Critical theory responds: local politics is too weak to confront system-wide gender and class dominations as well as global poverty and environmental problems. Postmodernism maintains:

organizing against domination both props up and solidifies dominant groups; it creates its own forms of domination. The difference is in a sense the same as between a push and pull theory. Critical theory wants us to act and provides direction and orchestration; postmodernism believes that such a move will be limited by the force of our own subjective domination and encourages us to get out of the way and allow the world to pull us to feelings and thought heretofore unknown; but critical theory does not have enough faith to let go. And so on.

But there are ways to think them both at once, though not necessarily through some new synthesis. We have a need for both conflict and consensus, for resistance and plans. The issue is not which but the balance, choosing the right moments (Deetz 1992). To say that consensus implies domination means not that we should not make the best decisions we can together, but that we need to continue to look for domination and be ready to move on. To say that resistance lacks a clear politics does not mean that it is not doing something important and ultimately may be the only way we can see through dominations that we like or that benefit *and* limit us.

One option is thus to work with unresolved tensions within a text where one follows different themes of postmodernism and critical theory without attempting synthesis, working with the tensions and contrastive images. Examples of this include work by Martin (1990; 1995), Knights and Willmott (1989) and Deetz (1994c; in press b). Another version is to allow space for various discrete voices in texts through organizing these around conversations between various theoretical perspectives or interest groups (Alvesson and Willmott 1996: Chapter 7) or to conduct multiple interpretations of the same phenomenon (Alvesson 1996; Morgan 1986), such as interpreting a phenomenon from both critical theory and postmodernist (and perhaps other) positions. Another way of combining insights from critical theory and postmodernism is to see both as metatheories useful as inspiration for reflexivity rather than as theories directly relevant for guiding and interpreting studies of substantive matters (Alvesson and Sköldberg 1996). Still another option is to restrict the approach to the careful study of language use and communicative practices in 'real' social settings, which is done by discourse and conversation analysis (I. Parker 1992; Potter and Wetherell 1987) and constructivists (Shotter and Gergen 1994; Steier 1991). Such studies can be used to sensitize us to the power effects of language and ground Habermasian and postmodernist ideas in portions of organizational reality (Forester 1992). Such a language focus avoids the philosophy of presence but maintains an empirical context.

Perhaps the greatest criticism of critical theory and even more so postmodernism is the lack of clear empirical studies. Part of the criticism arises from a narrow view of the notion of 'empirical', but researchers can still be faulted for doing many conceptual essays without extended field experience and reports. Critical theory's and postmodernism's strong critique of empiricism, and their emphasis on data as constructions open to a multitude of interpretations, do not mean that reflective empirical work is not worth doing. Many texts have limited feelings for organizational contexts and the lives of real people. Much can be gained by allowing organizational participants to 'say something' that is not immediately domesticated by theories locating the material in an all too predictable 'bureaucracy', 'patriarchy', 'capitalism', 'managerialism' pejorative discourse, an all-embracing Foucauldian power concept, or a pacification and fragmentation of subjects as mere appendices of discourses. An empirical turn may also reduce the tendency of negativity in much of critical theory and some postmodernism. Having said this, we must acknowledge that recently more empirical work has been done, particularly with a critical theory orientation (for example, Rosen 1985; 1988; Knights and Willmott 1987; 1992; Alvesson 1996) but also using postmodern themes (Martin 1990; 1995; Deetz in press b; in press c). What is lacking, in particular, is serious efforts to ground ideas of local resistance in specific empirical contexts. There is a lot of talk of resistance in the postmodernist industry, but it is highly theoretical and generalized and remains quite esoteric. We need to go further than repeat programmatic slogans and use and refine the idea in close contact with the lives of subjects in organizational settings.

We will for space reasons not indulge in further treatment of these responses to various critiques of traditional ways of doing research brought forward by postmodern authors in particular, but in many cases also by authors not waving the postmodern flag. Suffice to say that there are various paths that address the middle ground between more traditional realist and hermeneutic epistemologies – where there is space for empirical studies of organizational phenomena – on the one hand and a postmodern philosophy threatening to turn all social science into a quite esoteric literary criticism on the other hand.

NOTES

1 Quite often when people talk about postmodernism and its shadow modernism, the former position is a

kind of synthesis and social science adaptation of what has been expressed by the gurus referred to. This means that there is not necessarily a one-to-one relationship between what one can find clear support for in key texts of Derrida, Foucault, etc. and what is summarized as a postmodernist position. We will here follow this practice and hold back doubts regarding the reasons for summarizing partly quite different authors and intellectual themes (cf. Alvesson 1995) – a move these people would probably have little sympathy for.

2 We should note before going on that one of the functions of histories is to produce a number of scholars/texts (a) as a school of thought, and (b) as new or different both for the professional advantages of its practitioners and as a way of demarking a community. It is interesting to note that this history production is important not for forerunners or gurus – who often resist labels such as postmodernism – but for followers and supporters. The political and identity-confirming advantages are clearest for these people.

3 As on many issues, there are variations here amongst postmodernists. Derrida does not directly address the issue. Foucault comes closest in supporting a critical theory view against social engineering as a solution, although he is not without ambiguity on this point. Lyotard appears to have mixed feelings about this matter. The majority of social science authors advocating postmodernism share the skepticism of critical theory on this point.

4 The discussion in this section is adapted from Deetz's (in press a) discussion of the problems of Burrell and Morgan's (1979) paradigm divisions. Several revisions of Burrell and Morgan are crucial. The term 'normative' is used to describe most of the same research positions that Burrell and Morgan called 'functionalist'. This frees the description from a particular school of sociological thought and draws attention to both their search for the normal, the regularity, and the value-laden nature of their use in 'normalizing' people, and the existing social conditions. 'Dialogic' draws attention to the relational aspect of 'postmodernism' and avoids the periodicity issue. Note too that critical work is shown with more affinity to 'normative' work (rather than the total opposition in Burrell and Morgan's 'functionalist/ radical-humanist' configuration) because of their directive qualities in contrast to the strong 'otherness' guidance in interpretive and dialogic work. The *a priori*/elite–local/emergent dimension replaces the subjective–objective dimension in Burrell and Morgan. The subject/object dualism on which their dimension was based is severely flawed. First it tends to reproduce the subject/object dualism that is present in the philosophies underlying 'normative' research but not the other positions. Second, it misplaces normative research, overlooking its subjectivity in domination of nature and in defining people's experience for them. And third, it fails to highlight the constructionist quality of all research programs.

5 This is then basically a sociological or period-ization type of postmodern psychology, and is also to some extent used by authors who do not see themselves as postmodernist or talk about postmodernism, for example, Berger et al. (1973) or Lasch (1978; 1984).

REFERENCES

Abercrombie, N., Hill, S. and Turner, B.S. (1980) *The Dominant Ideology Thesis*. London: Allen and Unwin.

Alvesson, M. (1987) *Organization Theory and Techno- cratic Consciousness: Rationality, Ideology, and Quality of Work*. Berlin, New York: de Gruyter.

Alvesson, M. (1990) 'Organization: from substance to image?', *Organization Studies*, 11: 373–94.

Alvesson, M. (1993a) *Cultural Perspectives on Organiz- ations*. Cambridge: Cambridge University Press.

Alvesson, M. (1993b) 'The play of metaphors', in J. Hassard and M. Parker (eds), *Postmodernism and Organizations*. London: Sage.

Alvesson, M. (1995) 'The meaning and meaningless- ness of postmodernism: some ironic remarks', *Organization Studies*, 15.

Alvesson, M. (1996) *Communication, Power and Organization*. Berlin/New York: de Gruyter.

Alvesson, M. and Sköldberg, K. (1996) *Towards a Reflexive Methodology*. London: Sage.

Alvesson, M. and Willmott, H. (eds) (1992) *Critical Management Studies*. London: Sage.

Alvesson, M. and Willmott, H. (1995) 'Strategic management as domination and emancipation: from planning and process to communication and praxis', in C. Stubbart and P. Shrivastava (eds), *Advances in Strategic Management*, vol. 11. Green- wich, CT: JAI Press.

Alvesson, M. and Willmott, H. (1996) *Making Sense of Management: a Critical Analysis*. London: Sage.

Angus, I. (1992) 'The politics of common sense: articulation theory and critical communication studies', in S. Deetz (ed.), *Communication Yearbook 15*. Newbury Park, CA: Sage. pp. 535–70.

Apel, K.-O. (1979) *Toward a Transformation of Philosophy*, translated by G. Adey and D. Frisby. London: Routledge & Kegan Paul.

Astley, G. (1985) 'Administrative science as socially constructed truth', *Administrative Science Quarterly*, 30: 497–513.

Baudrillard, J. (1975) *The Mirror of Production*, translated by M. Poster. St Louis: Telos Press.

Baudrillard, J. (1983) *Simulations*. New York: Semiotext(e).

Baudrillard, J. (1988) 'Simulacra and simulations', in M. Poster (ed.), *Jean Baudrillard: Selected Writings*. Stanford: Stanford University Press. pp. 166–84.

Benson, J.K. (1977) 'Organizations: a dialectical view', *Administrative Science Quarterly*, 22: 1–21.

Berg, P.O. (1989) 'Postmodern management? From facts to fiction in theory and practice', *Scandinavian Journal of Management*, 5: 201–17.

Berger, P., Berger, B. and Kellner, H. (1973) *The Homeless Mind: Modernization and Consciousness*. New York: Random House.

Boland, R. (1987) 'The in-formation of information systems', in R. Boland and R. Hirschheim (eds), *Critical Issues in Information Systems Research*. New York: Wiley. pp. 363–79.

Bourdieu, P. (1979) *Outline of a Theory of Practice*. Cambridge: Cambridge University Press.

Bourdieu, P. (1984) *Distinctions: a Social Critique of the Judgement of Taste*. Cambridge: Cambridge University Press.

Bourdieu, P. (1991) *Language and Symbolic Power*. Cambridge, MA: Harvard University Press.

Braverman, H. (1974) *Labor and Monopoly Capital*. New York: Monthly Review Press.

Brown, R.H. (1990) 'Rhetoric, textuality, and the postmodern turn in sociological theory', *Sociological Theory*, 8: 188–97.

Burawoy, M. (1979) *Manufacturing Consent*. Chicago: University of Chicago Press.

Burawoy, M. (1985) *The Politics of Production: Factory Regimes under Capitalism and Socialism*. London: Verso.

Burrell, G. (1994) 'Modernism, postmodernism and organizational analysis 4: the contribution of Jürgen Habermas', *Organization Studies*, 15: 1–19.

Burrell, G. and Morgan, G. (1979) *Sociological Paradigms and Organizational Analysis*. Aldershot: Gower.

Calás, M. and Smircich, L. (1988) 'Reading leadership as a form of cultural analysis', in J.G. Hunt et al. (eds), *Emerging Leadership Vistas*. Lexington, MA: Lexington Books.

Calás, M. and Smircich, L. (1991) 'Voicing seduction to silence leadership', *Organization Studies*, 12: 567–602.

Calás, M. and Smircich, L. (1992a) 'Feminist theories and the social consequences of organizational research', in A. Mills and P. Tancred (eds), *Gendering Organizational Analysis*. London: Sage.

Calás, M. and Smircich, L. (1992b) 'Rewriting gender into organizational theorizing: directions from feminist perspectives', in M. Reed and M. Hughes (eds), *Rethinking Organization: New Directions in Organizational Theory and Analysis*. London: Sage.

Carter, P. and Jackson, N. (1987) 'Management, myth, and metatheory – from scarcity to postscarcity', *International Studies of Management and Organization*, 17(3): 64–89.

Clegg, S. (1989) *Frameworks of Power*. London: Sage.

Clegg, S. (1990) *Modern Organization: Organization Studies in the Postmodern World*. London: Sage.

Clegg, S. (1994) 'Weber and Foucault: social theory for the study of organizations', *Organization*, 1: 149–78.

Clegg, S. and Dunkerley, D. (1980) *Organization, Class and Control*. London: Routledge & Kegan Paul.

Clifford, J. and Marcus, G.E. (eds) (1986) *Writing Culture*. Berkeley, CA: University of California Press.

Cooper, R. (1989) 'Modernism, postmodernism and organizational analysis 3: the contribution of Jacques Derrida', *Organization Studies*, 10: 479–502.

Cooper, R. and Burrell, G. (1988) 'Modernism, postmodernism and organizational analysis: an introduction', *Organization Studies*, 9: 91–112.

Czarniawska-Joerges, B. (1988) *Ideological Control in Nonideological Organizations*. New York: Praeger.

Deetz, S. (1985) 'Critical-cultural research: new sensibilities and old realities', *Journal of Management*, 11(2): 121–36.

Deetz, S. (1992) *Democracy in the Age of Corporate Colonization: Developments in Communication and the Politics of Everyday Life*. Albany, NY: State University of New York Press.

Deetz, S. (1994a) 'The future of the discipline: the challenges, the research, and the social contribution', in S. Deetz (ed.), *Communication Yearbook 17*. Newbury Park, CA: Sage. pp. 565–600.

Deetz, S. (1994b) 'Representative practices and the political analysis of corporations', in B. Kovacic (ed.), *Organizational Communication: New Perspectives*. Albany, NY: State University of New York Press. pp. 209–42.

Deetz, S. (1994c) 'The micro-politics of identity formation in the workplace: the case of a knowledge intensive firm', *Human Studies*, 17: 23–44.

Deetz, S. (1994d) 'The new politics of the workplace: ideology and other unobtrusive controls', in H. Simons and M. Billig (eds), *After Postmodernism: Reconstructing Ideology Critique*. Newbury Park, CA: Sage. pp. 172–99.

Deetz, S. (1995) *Transforming Communication, Transforming Business: Building Responsible and Responsive Workplaces*. Cresskill, NJ: Hampton Press.

Deetz, S. (in press a) 'Describing differences in approaches to organizational science: rethinking Burrell and Morgan and their legacy', *Organization Science*.

Deetz, S. (in press b) 'Discursive formations, strategized subordination, and self-surveillance: an empirical case', in A. McKinlay and K. Starkey (eds), *Managing Foucault: a Reader*. London: Sage.

Deetz, S. (in press c) 'The business concept, discursive power, and managerial control in a knowledge-intensive company: a case study', in B. Sypher (ed.), *Case Studies in Organizational Communication*, 2nd edn. New York: Guilford Press.

Deetz, S. and Kersten, A. (1983) 'Critical models of interpretative research', in L. Putnam and M. Pacanowsky (eds), *Communication and Organizations*. Beverly Hills, CA: Sage.

Deetz, S. and Mumby, D. (1990) 'Power, discourse, and the workplace: reclaiming the critical tradition in communication studies in organizations', in J.

Anderson (ed.), *Communication Yearbook 13*. Newbury Park, CA: Sage. pp. 18–47.

Edwards, R. (1979) *Contested Terrain: the Transformation of the Workplace in the Twentieth Century*. New York: Basic Books.

Epstein, C. (1988) *Deceptive Distinctions*. New Haven: Yale University Press.

Featherstone, M. (ed.) (1988) *Postmodernism*. Newbury Park, CA: Sage.

Ferguson, K. (1984) *The Feminist Case against Bureaucracy*. Philadelphia: Temple University Press.

Fischer, F. (1990) *Technocracy and the Politics of Expertise*. Newbury Park, CA: Sage.

Fischer, F. and Sirianni, C. (eds) (1984) *Critical Studies in Organization and Bureaucracy*. Philadelphia: Temple University Press.

Flax, J. (1990) *Thinking Fragments: Psychoanalysis, Feminism and Postmodernism in the Contemporary West*. Berkeley, CA: University of California Press.

Forester, J. (1983) 'Critical theory and organizational analysis', in G. Morgan (ed.), *Beyond Method*. Beverly Hills, CA: Sage.

Forester, J. (ed.) (1985) *Critical Theory and Public Life*. Cambridge, MA: MIT Press.

Forester, J. (1989) *Planning in the Face of Power*. Berkeley, CA: University of California Press.

Forester, J. (1992) Critical ethnography: on fieldwork in a Habermasian way', in M. Alvesson and H. Willmott (eds), *Critical Management Studies*. London: Sage.

Forester, J. (1993) *Critical Theory, Public Policy, and Planning Practice*. Albany: State University of New York Press.

Foster, H. (1983) *Postmodern Culture*. London: Pluto Press.

Foucault, M. (1977) *Discipline and Punish: the Birth of the Prison*, translated by A.S. Smith. New York: Random House.

Foucault, M. (1980) *Power/Knowledge*. New York: Pantheon.

Foucault, M. (1983) 'Structuralism and post-structuralism: an interview with Michel Foucault, by G. Raulet', *Telos*, 55: 195–211.

Foucault, M. (1988) 'Technologies of the self', in L. Martin, H. Gutman and P. Hutton (eds), *Technologies of the Self*. Amherst, MA: University of Massachusetts Press. pp. 16–49.

Fraser, N. (1987) 'What's critical about critical theory? The case of Habermas and gender', in S. Benhabib and D. Cornell (eds), *Feminism as Critique*. Cambridge: Polity Press.

Fraser, N. and Nicholson, L. (1988) 'Social criticism without philosophy: an encounter between feminism and postmodernism', *Theory, Culture & Society*, 5: 373–94.

Frost, P.J. (1980) 'Toward a radical framework for practicing organizational science', *Academy of Management Review*, 5: 501–7.

Frost, P.J. (1987) 'Power, politics, and influence', in F. Jablin, L. Putnam, K. Roberts and L. Porter (eds), *Handbook of Organizational Communication*. Newbury Park, CA: Sage.

Geertz, C. (1988) *Work and Lives: the Anthropologist as Author*. Cambridge: Polity Press.

Gergen, K. (1978) 'Toward generative theory', *Journal of Personality and Social Psychology*, 31: 1344–60.

Gergen, K. (1991) *The Saturated Self: Dilemmas of Identity in Contemporary Life*. New York: Basic Books.

Gergen, K. (1992) 'Organization theory in the postmodern era', in M. Reed and M. Hughes (eds), *Rethinking Organizations*. London: Sage.

Giddens, A. (1979) *Central Problems in Social Theory*. London: Macmillan.

Gramsci, A. (1929–35) *Selections from the Prison Notebooks*, translated by Q. Hoare and G.N. Smith. New York: International, 1971.

Habermas, J. (1970) *Toward a Rational Society*. London: Heinemann.

Habermas, J. (1971) *Knowledge and Human Interests*, translated by J. Shapiro. London: Heinemann.

Habermas, J. (1975) *Legitimation Crisis*, translated by T. McCarthy. Boston: Beacon Press.

Habermas, J. (1983) 'Modernity – an incomplete project', in H. Foster (ed.), *Postmodern Culture*. London: Pluto Press.

Habermas, J. (1984) *The Theory of Communicative Action. Vol. 1: Reason and the Rationalization of Society*, translated by T. McCarthy. Boston: Beacon.

Habermas, J. (1987) *The Theory of Communicative Action. Vol. 2: Lifeworld and System*, translated by T. McCarthy. Boston: Beacon Press.

Hassard, J. and Parker, M. (eds) (1993) *Postmodernism and Organizations*. London: Sage.

Hearn, J. and Parkin, W. (1987) *'Sex' at 'Work': the Power and Paradox of Organisation Sexuality*. Brighton: Wheatsheaf.

Heckscher, C. (1995) *White-collar Blues: Management Loyalties in an Age of Corporate Restructuring*. New York: Basic Books.

Hodge, H., Kress, G. and Jones, G. (1979) 'The ideology of middle management', in R. Fowler, H. Hodge, G. Kress and T. Trew (eds), *Language and Control*. London: Routledge & Kegan Paul.

Hollway, W. (1984) 'Fitting work: psychological assessment in organizations', in J. Henriques, W. Hollway, C. Urwin, C. Venn and V. Walkerdine (eds), *Changing the Subject*. New York: Methuen. pp. 26–59.

Hollway, W. (1991) *Work Psychology and Organizational Behavior*. London: Sage.

Hopwood, A. (1987) 'The archaeology of accounting systems', *Accounting, Organizations and Society*, 12: 207–34.

Horkheimer, M. and Adorno, T. (1979) *The Dialectics of Enlightenment* (1947). London: Verso.

Ingersoll, V. and Adams, G. (1986) 'Beyond organizational boundaries: exploring the managerial myth', *Administration and Society*, 18: 360–81.

Jeffcutt, P. (1993) 'From interpretation to representation', in J. Hassard and M. Parker (eds), *Postmodernism and Organizations*. London: Sage.

Jehenson, R. (1984) 'Effectiveness, expertise and excellence as ideological fictions: a contribution to a critical phenomenology of the formal organization', *Human Studies*, 7: 3–21.

Jermier, J. (1985) '"When the sleeper wakes": a short story extending themes in radical organization theory', *Journal of Management*, 11(2): 67–80.

Kellner, D. (1988) 'Postmodernism as social theory: some challenges and problems', *Theory, Culture and Society*, 5(2–3): 239–69.

Knights, D. (1992) 'Changing spaces: the disruptive impact of a new epistemological location for the study of management', *Academy of Management Review*, 17: 514–36.

Knights, D. and Morgan, G. (1991) 'Corporate strategy, organizations, and subjectivity: a critique', *Organization Studies*, 12: 251–73.

Knights, D. and Willmott, H. (1985) 'Power and identity in theory and practice', *Sociological Review*, 33: 22–46.

Knights, D. and Willmott, H. (1987) 'Organizational culture as management strategy', *International Studies of Management and Organization*, 17(3): 40–63.

Knights, D. and Willmott, H. (1989) 'Power and subjectivity at work: from degradation to subjugation in social relations', *Sociology*, 23: 535–58.

Knights, D. and Willmott, H. (1992) 'Conceptualizing leadership processes: a study of senior managers in a financial services company', *Journal of Management Studies*, 29: 761–82.

Kunda, G. (1992) *Engineering Culture: Control and Commitment in a High-Tech Corporation*. Philadelphia: Temple University Press.

Lasch, C. (1978) *The Culture of Narcissism*. New York: Norton.

Lasch, C. (1984) *The Minimal Self*. London: Picador.

Lazega, E. (1992) *Micropolitics of Knowledge: Communication and Indirect Control in Workgroups*. New York: Aldine de Gruyter.

Linstead, S. (1993) 'Deconstruction in the study of organizations', in J. Hassard and M. Parker (eds), *Postmodernism and Organizations*. London: Sage.

Linstead, S. and Grafton-Small, R. (1990) 'Theory as artefact: artefact as theory', in P. Gagliardi (ed.), *Symbols and Artefacts: Views of the Corporate Landscape*. Berlin/New York: de Gruyter.

Linstead, S. and Grafton-Small, R. (1992) 'On reading organizational culture', *Organization Studies*, 13: 331–55.

Lukes, S. (1974) *Power: a Radical View*. London: Macmillan.

Lukács, G. (1971) *History and Class Consciousness*, translated by R. Livingstone. Cambridge, MA: MIT Press.

Lyotard, J.-F. (1984) *The Postmodern Condition: a Report on Knowledge*, translated by G. Bennington and B. Massumi. Minneapolis: University of Minnesota Press.

Lyytinen, K. and Hirschheim, R. (1988) 'Information systems as rational discourse: an application of Habermas's theory of communicative action', *Scandinavian Journal of Management*, 4: 19–30.

Marcus, G. and Fischer, M. (1986) *Anthropology as Cultural Critique*. Chicago: University of Chicago Press.

Margolis, S. (1989) 'Postscript on modernism and postmodernism: both', *Theory, Culture & Society*, 6: 5–30.

Martin, J. (1990) 'Deconstructing organizational taboos: the suppression of gender conflict in organizations', *Organization Science*, 11: 339–59.

Martin, J. (1995) 'The organization of exclusion: the institutionalization of sex inequality, gendered faculty jobs, and gendered knowledge in organizational theory and research', *Organization*, 1: 401–31.

Marx, K. (1844) *Economic and Political Manuscripts of 1844*, translated by M. Miligan. New York: International, 1964.

Marx, K. (1867) *Das Kapital*, Bd 1. Berlin: Dietz, 1967.

Montagna, P. (1986) 'Accounting rationality and financial legitimation', *Theory and Society*, 15: 103–38.

Morgan, G. (1986) *Images of Organization*. Newbury Park, CA: Sage.

Mumby, D.K. (1987) 'The political function of narrative in organizations', *Communication Monographs*, 54: 113–27.

Mumby, D.K. (1988) *Communication and Power in Organizations: Discourse, Ideology, and Domination*. Norwood, NJ: Ablex.

Mumby, D.K. and Putnam, L. (1992) 'The politics of emotion: a feminist reading of bounded rationality', *Academy of Management Review*, 17: 465–86.

Offe, C. and Wiesenthal, H. (1980) 'Two logics of collective action: theoretical notes on social class and organizational form', in M. Zeitlin (ed.), *Political Power and Social Theory*, vol. 1. Greenwich, CT: JAI Press.

Parker, I. (1992) *Discourse Dynamics*. London: Routledge.

Parker, M. (1992) 'Post-modern organizations or postmodern organization theory?', *Organization Studies*, 13: 1–17.

Parker, M. (1993) 'Life after Jean-François', in J. Hassard and M. Parker (eds), *Postmodernism and Organizations*. London: Sage.

Peters, T. (1987) *Thriving on Chaos*. New York: Alfred A. Knopf.

Potter, J. and Wetherell, M. (1987) *Discourse and Social Psychology: Beyond Attitudes and Behaviour*. London: Sage.

Power, M. (1994) 'The audit society', in A. Hopwood and P. Miller (eds), *Accounting as Social and*

Institutional Practice. Cambridge: Cambridge University Press. pp. 299–316.

Power, M. and Laughlin, R. (1992) 'Critical theory and accounting', in M. Alvesson and H. Willmott (eds), *Critical Management Studies.* London: Sage. pp. 113–35.

Pringle, R. (1988) *Secretaries Talk: Sexuality, Power and Work.* London: Verso.

Rose, D. (1990) *Living the Ethnographic Life.* Newbury Park, CA: Sage.

Rosen, M. (1985) 'Breakfirst at Spiro's: dramaturgy and dominance', *Journal of Management,* 11(2): 31–48.

Rosen, M. (1988) 'You asked for it: Christmas at the Bosses' expense', *Journal of Management Studies,* 25(5): 463–80.

Salaman, G. (1981) *Class and the Corporation.* Glasgow: Fontana.

Sangren, S. (1992) 'Rhetoric and the authority of ethnography', *Current Anthropology,* 33(Supplement): 277–96.

Sarup, M. (1988) *An Introductory Guide to Post-Structuralism and Post-Modernism.* Hemel Hempstead: Harvester Wheatsheaf.

Shotter, J. and Gergen, K. (eds) (1989) *Texts of Identity.* London: Sage.

Shotter, J. and Gergen, K. (1994) 'Social construction: knowledge, self, others, and continuing the conversation', in S. Deetz (ed.), *Communication Yearbook 17.* Newbury Park, CA: Sage.

Shrivastava, P. (1986) 'Is strategic management ideological?', *Journal of Management,* 12.

Shrivastava, P. (1995) 'Ecocentric management for a risk society', *Academy of Management Review,* 20: 118–37.

Sievers, B. (1986) 'Beyond the surrogate of motivation', *Organization Studies,* 7: 335–52.

Sless, D. (1988) 'Forms of control', *Australian Journal of Communication,* 14: 57–69.

Smircich, L. and Calás, M. (1987) 'Organizational culture: a critical assessment', in F. Jablin, L. Putnam, K. Roberts and L. Porter (eds), *Handbook of Organizational Communication.* Newbury Park, CA: Sage. pp. 228–63.

Stablein, R. and Nord, W. (1985) 'Practical and emancipatory interests in organizational symbolism', *Journal of Management,* 11(2): 13–28.

Stead, W.E. and Stead, J.G. (1992) *Management for a Small Planet.* Newbury Park, CA: Sage.

Steffy, B. and Grimes, A. (1992) 'Personnel/organizational psychology: a critique of the discipline', in M. Alvesson and H. Willmott (eds), *Critical Management Studies.* London: Sage.

Steier, F. (1991) 'Reflexivity and methodology: an ecological constructionism', in F. Steier (ed.), *Research and Reflexivity.* London: Sage.

Storey, J. (1983) *Managerial Prerogative and the Question of Control.* London: Routledge & Kegan Paul.

Thompson, J. (1984) *Studies in the Theory of Ideology.* Berkeley, CA: University of California Press.

Thompson, J.B. and Held, D. (eds) (1982) *Habermas: Critical Debates.* London: Macmillan.

Thompson, P. (1993) 'Post-modernism: fatal distraction', in J. Hassard and M. Parker (eds), *Postmodernism and Organizations.* London: Sage.

Tompkins, P. and Cheney, G. (1985) 'Communication and unobtrusive control in contemporary organizations', in R. McPhee and P. Tompkins (eds), *Organizational Communication: Traditional Themes and New Directions.* Newbury Park, CA: Sage. pp. 179–210.

Townley, B. (1993) 'Foucault, power/knowledge, and its relevance for human resource management', *Academy of Management Review,* 18: 518–45.

Vallas, S. (1993) *Power in the Workplace: the Politics of Production at AT&T.* Albany, NY: State University of New York Press.

Vattimo, G. (1992) *The Transparent Society.* Baltimore: John Hopkins University Press.

Walzer, M. (1986) 'The politics of Foucault', in D. Hoy (ed.), *Foucault: a Reader.* Oxford: Basil Blackwell. pp. 151–68.

Weedon, C. (1987) *Feminist Practice and Poststructuralist Theory.* Oxford: Basil Blackwell.

Willmott, H. (1990) 'Subjectivity and the dialectic of praxis: opening up the core of labour process analysis', in D. Knights and H. Willmott (eds), *Labour Process Theory.* London: Macmillan.

Willmott, H. (1993) 'Strength is ignorance; slavery is freedom: managing culture in modern organizations', *Journal of Management Studies,* 30(4): 515–52.

Willmott, H. (1994) 'Bringing agency (back) into organizational analysis: responding to the crises of (post)modernity', in J. Hassard and M. Parker (eds), *Towards a New Theory of Organizations.* London: Routledge.

Willmott, H. and Knights, D. (1982) 'The problem of freedom: Fromm's contribution to a critical theory of work organization', *Praxis International,* 2: 204–25.

1.8

From 'The Woman's' Point of View: Feminist Approaches to Organization Studies

MARTA B. CALÁS AND LINDA SMIRCICH

During the last thirty years, the 'women's liberation' movement achieved profound social, political, and economic gains, improving the situation of many women. At the same time, feminist movements have contributed strongly to contemporary cultural analyses and, in universities all over the world, women's studies programs have helped foster energetic cross-disciplinary scholarship and a plurality of feminist 'theories' aimed at rethinking the grounds of knowledge. Despite these gains, however, the sex segregation of occupations and organizations persists world-wide, as does pay inequity between women and men (Adler and Izraeli 1988; Berthoin-Antal and Izraeli 1993; Brown and Pechman 1987; Davidson and Cooper 1984; Game and Pringle 1984; Kovalainen 1993; R. Morgan 1984; Reskin and Roos 1990; Strober 1984; Strober and Arnold 1987; United Nations 1995). The 'feminization of poverty' shows that lower income households are more likely to be headed by a female single parent, often out of work and on welfare (Pearce 1978). Meanwhile, women professionals experience the 'tipping' phenomenon, where traditionally male high paying occupations lose earning power once women dominate them (Strober 1984) while 'unequal opportunities' for husbands of working women keep them at lower pay scales and slow their move up the career ladder compared to men whose wives do not work outside the home (Stroh and Brett 1994). In transnational organizations in industrializing countries, women, who once occupied the lowest paying and more exploitative jobs, are now becoming unemployed as men,

earning the same low wages, take over these jobs (e.g. Fernández-Kelly 1994; Mies et al. 1988).

This and other evidence notwithstanding, some consider that feminism has gone *too far* toward benefiting women as charges of reverse discrimination and claims of sexual harassment of male workers give rise to what Faludi (1991) labels 'a backlash'. Others, however, complain that many feminisms have not gone *far enough*, because they are white, Western, and middle class, excluding many women (and men) in the world, their interests and their needs (e.g. Lugones and Spelman 1983; Mohanty 1991b).

In our view the task of feminism is not finished. Feminist concerns continue to intersect with organizational issues. Equally important, as we will suggest, 'feminist' theories are *not* only about 'women's' issues: by using feminist theories as conceptual lenses, we believe a more inclusive organization studies can be created, one that brings in the concerns of others, not just women, who are directly affected by organizational processes and discourses. Thus, feminist theories articulate problems in both the theory and practice of organizations which otherwise might go unnoticed (see also, Billing and Alvesson 1993; Cockburn 1983; 1985; 1991; K. Ferguson 1984; Ferree and Martin 1995; Jacobson and Jacques 1989a; Marshall 1984; 1995).

WHAT ARE FEMINIST THEORIES?

In this chapter, we will review liberal, radical, psychoanalytic, Marxist, socialist, poststructuralist, and Third World/(post)colonial feminist approaches, and discuss their contributions to organizational studies (see Table 1). Despite their diversity, most feminist theories share some assumptions, notably the recognition of male dominance in social arrangements, and a desire for changes from this form of domination (e.g. Flax 1987; 1990; A. Ferguson 1989). More generally, feminist theoretical perspectives are *critical* discourses in that feminist theory is a critique of the status quo, and therefore *always political*. Yet, the degree of critique and the nature of the politics vary, leading to agendas that range from 'reforming' organizations; to 'transforming' organizations *and* society; to transforming our prior understandings of what constitutes knowledge/theory/practice.

Sex, Gender or Gender Relations?

For example, one key conceptual distinction among feminist theories is the way *gender* is understood. Earliest theories of liberal feminism were concerned with inequality between 'the sexes', i.e. between two categories of persons ('males' and 'females') denoted by biological characteristics. Later, theorizing made a distinction between biologically based 'sex' and socially constructed 'gender', a product of socialization and experience. Even here, though, feminist theorizing differs over what aspects of experience are most important in constituting gender and gender relations: for instance, socialization into sex/gender roles according to liberal feminism; or cultural practices that value men's experiences over women's according to radical feminism; or early developmental relations with parents according to psychoanalytic feminism? Further, socialist feminists consider gender(ing) a process embedded in power relations and particular historical material conditions, while the black 'womanist' perspective addresses the question of which 'women's experiences' are constitutive of 'gender'. Both poststructuralists and Third World/(post)colonial approaches problematize the whole notion of 'experience'. They critique investing 'sex' and 'gender' with a certain stability as analytical categories, noting that subjectivity is constructed linguistically, historically, and politically, and is therefore flexible and multiple. Thus *gender* is a term 'in the making' that both reflects and constitutes the variety of feminist theorizing (Scott 1986).

FEMINIST APPROACHES AND ORGANIZATIONAL STUDIES

In this chapter we describe how various approaches in feminist thought intersect with theories of organization and organizational practices, and how each feminist theoretical strand highlights particular organizational issues while ignoring others. As we discuss these various approaches, the issues they address and the questions they raise shift, as does the vocabulary, from concerns about women (their access to organizations and their performance in organizations), to concerns about gender and organization (the notion of gendered organizational practices), to concerns about the very stability of such categories as 'gender', 'masculinity', 'femininity', and 'organization'. Each school of thought gives alternative accounts for gender inequality, frames the 'problem' differently and proposes different courses of action as 'solutions'.

Several key works shape our presentation of the history of feminist thought (Jaggar 1983; Tuana and Tong 1995; Tong 1989) and the discussion of gender conceptions and research (Harding and Hintikka 1983; Harding 1986; 1991; Lorber 1994; Reinharz 1992). Presenting each school of thought in sequence is somewhat misleading, however, for they developed and changed in response to one another: although they may look discrete and unified, their boundaries are blurry and blurring. Our goal is not to judge which approach is 'best', but to recognize that each has an important contribution to make, even if together they enact a somewhat uneasy conversation. Further, we acknowledge that the need for brevity in writing a chapter means a less detailed and nuanced exposition.

We do not claim to write as 'detached' observers: as authors we have our favored positions in between the 'post' discourses; as a Latina and a white US woman who write together and share their professional and personal lives, mostly within US contemporary institutions but also in other places in the world, we recognize that our writings come from particularly (dis)located positions. This, however, can be an advantage: the charge of relativism often leveled toward 'post' positions allows us to consider seriously the assertions made by each and all feminist theoretical claims even if we are similarly skeptical about the finality of any solution.

LIBERAL FEMINIST THEORY

This perspective has its roots in the liberal political tradition developed in the seventeenth and eighteenth centuries, when feudalistic, church dominated rule was giving way to capitalistic, civil society, and when aspirations for equality, liberty and fraternity were supplanting the

Table 1 *A summary of feminist approaches*

School of thought	Liberal	Radical	Psychoanalytic	Marxist	Socialist	Poststructuralist/ Postmodern	Third World/ (Post)Colonial
Intellectual roots	Evolved from 18th and 19th century political theory.	Generated in the contemporary women's liberation movements of the late 1960s.	Evolved from Freudian and other psychoanalytic theories, in particular object-relations theories.	Based on and a 'correction' of Marxist critique of capitalist society since the mid 19th century.	Emerged in the 1970s as part of women's liberation movements' attempts to synthesize Marxist, psycho-analytic and radical feminisms.	Located in contemporary French poststructuralist critiques of 'knowledge' and 'identity'.	Emerging from intersections of gendered critiques of western feminisms and postcolonial critiques of Western epistemologies.
Conception of human nature	Individuals are autonomous beings capable of rationality (mind/body dualism and abstract individualism).	Human beings are fundamentally embodied sexed beings.	Human nature develops biologically and psychosexually.	Human nature reflects historical, material conditions. The human essence is the ensemble of social relations.	Human nature is created historically and culturally through dialectical interrelations among human biology, society and human labor.	Decentering of the rational, self-present subject of humanism. 'Subjectivity' and 'consciousness' are discursive effects.	Analyzed as a Western construct that emerged by making its 'other' invisible or 'almost' human. Also 'strategic essentialism'.
Conception of sex/gender	Sex is part of essential biological endowment, a binary variable. Gender is socialized onto sexed human beings for appropriate behavior.	'Sex class' is the condition of women as an oppressed class. Gender is a social construction that ensures women's subordination to men.	Individuals become sexually-identified as part of their psychosexual development. Gender structures a social system of male domination which influences psychosexual development.	Gender is part of historical class relations which constitute systems of oppression under capitalism.	Gender is processual and socially constituted through several intersections of sex, race, ideology, and experiences of oppression under patriarchy and capitalism (that are distinct systems).	Sex/Gender are discursive practices that constitute specific subjectivities through power and resistance in the materiality of human bodies.	Considers the constitution of complex subjectivities beyond Western conceptions of sex/gender focusing on gendered aspects of globalization processes.

Conception of 'the good society'	The 'good society' is a just society that allows individuals to exercise autonomy and to fulfill themselves through a system of individual rights.	The 'good society' is a gender/sex-free society (or maybe a matriarchy).	The 'good society' has no gender structuring because both parents share children's upbringing.	The 'good society' is a classless society that allows for the full development of human nature.	The 'good society' has eliminated all systems of private/public oppression based on sex, gender, race, class, etc. and thus transformed social relations.	The 'good society' requires ongoing deconstruction and denaturalization of discourses and practices that constitute it.	The 'good society' is a Western ideology produced through colonial relationships that favor Westernization. Other social formations are possible.
Epistemological positions	Positivist, gender-neutral objectivity.	Holistic female-centered knowledge is possible outside of patriarchal structures.	Women's way of knowledge is different from men's because of different psychosexual development.	Feminism must take the standpoint of an oppressed class under capitalism for their knowledge interests to represent those of the social totality.	Feminist standpoints represent a particular historical condition of oppression that is more adequate for understanding contemporary society.	'Epistemology' is problematized by the heterogeneity of subject positions and social identities – i.e. there is no 'subject of knowledge' to sustain it.	'Knowledge' is a system of power relations deployed by the 'West' on 'the rest'. Other's knowledges/subjectivities are possible.
Some favored methodologies	Positivist social science; laboratory experiments; correlational analyses; mostly quantitative.	Consciousness-raising groups and case studies.	Clinical case studies, focus on context-specific social relations and developmental processes; life histories.	Econometrics, historical analyses of macro-social data.	Case studies, institutional ethnographies, ethnomethodology focus on micro-social activities as they connect to macro-social processes.	Textual analyses, deconstruction, Foucauldian genealogies.	Textual analyses, postcolonial deconstructions/reconstructions, testimonial writings, hybrid representations.

Sources: Jagger (1983); Mohanty, Russo and Torres (1991); Tong (1989); Tuana and Tong (1995); Weedon (1987).

monarchical order (Cockburn 1991). A new
vision of persons and society was emerging,
based on two key assumptions about human
nature: *normative dualism* (mind/body dualism)
where rationality is conceived as mental capacity,
separated from embodiment, and *abstract individualism*, where human action is conceived of in
abstraction from any social circumstances
(Jaggar 1983). Further, individuals were assumed
to inhabit a world of scarcity, and to be motivated
by the desire to secure as large an individual share
as possible of the available resources. Thus, for
liberal political theorists, a 'good' or 'just' society
allowed individuals to exercise autonomy and to
fulfill themselves through a system of individual
rights.

Where did women stand in this society?
Women were unable to vote, own property in
their own names, and, with the transition from a
home-centered form of economic production to
an industrial economy, increasingly economically dependent and isolated. Early liberal
political theorists, Mary Wollstonecraft (1792),
John Stuart Mill (1869), and Harriet Taylor Mill
(1851), said that women's true potential went
unfulfilled because of their exclusion from the
academy, the forum and the marketplace: they
were 'non-persons' in the public world (Tong
1989). Women needed the same access to
opportunities in all spheres of life as men, but
without radical transformation of the present
social and political system. Thus the early liberal
theorists were reformists rather than revolution-
aries: male was the paradigm of human nature;
their concern was to demonstrate that women
were as fully human as men (Jaggar 1983).

One hundred years later Betty Friedan (1963)
echoed Wollstonecraft and the Mills, as she
questioned the idea that women could find
satisfaction exclusively in the roles of wife and
mother. In the 1960s, the second wave women's
movement was aiming for equal access and
equal representation in public life for women;
any stressing of sex differences or acknowledgement of differences was seen to be
reactionary and harmful to the 'cause'. But by
the 1980s, Friedan (1981), among others, began
to question this reasoning, arguing it treated
women as 'male clones', when 'there has to be a
concept of equality that takes into account that
women are the ones who have the babies'
(Friedan, in Tong 1989: 27). Thus liberal
feminists made a transition from themes of
equality in the 1960s and 1970s to themes of
difference in the 1980s and 1990s, noting that
sex, a matter of chromosomes and anatomy, has
been conflated with gender, cultural constructs
about what are appropriately 'masculine' or
'feminine' traits and behavior. They charged that
women (and men) are handicapped by inap-

propriate judgments about the appropriate
behavior and work for persons of a particular
sex. Therefore, an overriding goal has been
sexual equity or 'gender justice'.

For some liberal feminists, gender stereotyping must be eliminated if the goals of equality
for both sexes are to be realized (e.g. Tong
1989). Others propose the notion of the
androgynous person as a solution to sex
discrimination: since the cultural overlay of
'sex roles' or 'gender traits' is culturally reinforced, along with sanctions and norms
concerning what is a 'real' man or woman,
androgynous personalities could liberate men
and women from their culturally constraining
roles (Tong 1989). Thus, the first view considers
that women have been held back because of
inappropriate sex stereotypes, questions the truth
of such stereotypes, and asks for individual
women to be judged on their merits. The second
view considers there to be sufficient overlap
between males and females, because structural
conditions imprison both men and women, that
the remedy is to erode the effects of gender.
Regardless of view, liberal feminist research
favors positivist epistemologies, which they
assume are gender-neutral (Jaggar 1983). Both
views adhere to an ideal, ahistorical, universal
humanity toward which both men and women
should aspire (Parvikko 1990). How close
individuals approximate that ideal humanity
determines their level of benefit and reward; yet,
this research seldom acknowledges that the 'ideal
humanity' and the 'ideal society' are modeled
after Eurocentric, elite, masculinist ideals.

Some black feminists are more critical,
contending that liberal feminism, as manifested
in the contemporary American women's movement, represented only the interests of white,
middle class, heterosexual women under the
guise of representing all women. They point to
the irony that both the first and second wave
American women's liberation movements
emerged out of the strength of race liberation
movements: the anti-slavery and civil rights
movements. At a minimum, they specify, it is
impossible to address issues of 'gender justice'
without taking race into account, for together
they constitute particular forms of oppression
and discrimination (e.g. Bambara 1970; Dill
1983; hooks 1981; Giddings 1984; Hull et al.
1982; Lewis 1977; Joseph and Lewis 1981).

Liberal Feminist Theory and the
Women-in-Management Literature

Organizational scholarship has been, primarily,
a literature written by men, for men and about
men: how to gain the cooperation of men to

achieve organizational ends through rationality: how to *man/age*. Despite the fact that women occupied organizational jobs from early industrialization (as documented in Taylor 1911), and women were organizational researchers soon after the turn of the century (e.g. Mary Parker Follett 1951; Lillian Gilbreth 1967), most writers addressed women in organizations as *anomalies* if in managerial positions (e.g. Alpern 1993; *Fortune* August 1935; September 1935) or *normalized* them in subordinate roles (e.g. Barnard 1938; Roethlisberger and Dickson 1939).

Most of the 'gendered' organizational literature since the 1960s falls under the category of women-in-management, and is consistent with liberal political theory's assumptions about human nature: abstract individualism; mind/body dualism; the separation of the private and the public spheres in social life; the right to ownership of private property; and a notion of rationality whereby self-interested individuals would see to it that scarce resources are distributed according to universal rules of fairness and moral judgment. For example, in 1965, a *Harvard Business Review* article, based on a survey of business people, asked 'Are women executives people?' It concluded:

> When women act like people, ask no special privileges, and display no undue temperament, they are more likely to be treated like people. Conversely, when women are treated like people on a case-by-case basis rather than as a category, they are more likely to think of themselves as managers, not women, and to behave naturally in a work situation. (Bowman et al. 1965: 174)

Male respondents 'overwhelmingly' agreed that *'only the exceptional*, indeed the overqualified, *woman can hope to succeed in management.* They see little, if any, chance for the woman of only average ability' (1965: 176, original emphasis).

In general, not much has changed in this literature since the 1960s. The majority of the women-in-management literature is still trying to demonstrate that women are people too. Consistent with the tenets of liberal political theory, it conceives of organizations as made up of rational, autonomous actors, whose ultimate goal is to make organizations efficient, effective, and fair (see Table 2). Thus the pursuit of sexual *equity* (gender justice), rather than the elimination of sexual *inequality*, is a central theme.

Thirty Years of Researching that Women are People Too

Below, we briefly discuss some representative themes in this literature, which is the most

extensive of the gendered organizational literatures that we review (also see Adler and Izraeli 1994; Fagenson 1993; Gutek and Larwood 1987; Moore 1986; Pilotta 1983; Powell 1988; 1993; Sekaran and Leong 1991; Terborg 1977). A substantial portion of this research has been devoted to documenting inequities in the workplace in terms of segregated occupations, salary inequalities and short career ladders (Larwood and Gutek 1984; Blau and Ferber 1986; Freedman and Phillips 1988). In general, research shows that attitudes, traditions, and cultural norms still represented barriers to women's access to higher status and higher paying positions in the workplace despite legal sanctions against sex discrimination (Nieva and Gutek 1981; Larwood and Gutek 1984). Given what is judged to be discriminatory patterns, researchers then try to determine factors that maintain such patterns.

The literature addresses these problems in different ways. Early women-in-management research placed strong emphasis on *psychological* variables that accounted for discrimination. More recently, there has been an increasing interest in structural explanations as the emphasis shifted to *sociological*-based research. A third approach goes beyond legal remedies to address the intersections of the *organization* and the *broader social system*.

Psychological and Individual-Level Research

This stream of research is strongly influenced by experimental and behaviorist psychology; thus the topics and research approaches tend to follow that disciplinary line as part of organizational behavior and human resources scholarship. 'Methods and theories applied previously to other topics have been transferred to this subject without modification or inspiration' (Brown 1979: 267), while the topics of investigation remain almost identical to those in 'nongendered' organizational research (Calás and Jacques 1988). Said differently, it is difficult to find any gender-specific theoretical development among these works. The questions that are asked, and the research approaches that are followed, mimic those developed and utilized in research that does not emphasize gender.

An overriding concern in this literature is to determine if there are sex/gender differences within traditional organizational concepts such as *leadership* (e.g. Adams et al. 1984; Butterfield and Powell 1981; Chapman 1975; Dobbins and Platz 1986; Eagly et al. 1992; Jago and Vroom 1982; Schneier and Bartol 1980); *uses of power* (e.g. Ayers-Nachamkin et al. 1982; Mainiero 1986; Wiley and Eskilson 1982) ; *job stress* (e.g. Jick and Mitz 1985; Nelson and Quick 1985); *job satisfaction* (e.g. Brockner and Adsit 1986; Smith

Table 2 *Liberal feminism and women-in-management: a comparison*

Liberal feminism	Represented in the women-in-management literature
Roots	**Roots**
Evolved from liberal political theory (18th, 19th centuries)	Evolved from the civil rights and second wave feminist movements of the 1960s
Basic assumptions	**Representative issues under these assumptions**
Human nature	*Human nature*
● Conceives of persons as autonomous individuals, capable of rationality (mind/body dualism)	● Are women executives people?
● Individuals have desires/interests that can be fulfilled apart from the interests/desires of others (abstract individualism)	● The women-in-management literature's general focus on 'women's issues', i.e. separate from 'men's issues'
● Sex is part of essential biological endowment	● Research conceives of 'sex' as a discrete demographic variable, 'women' as a homogeneous category
● Sex/gender roles are socialized on to the essential person 'underneath'	● Research on 'gender roles' and 'sex-typed' occupations
Nature of society	*Nature of organizations*
● Individuals inhabit a world of scarcity; each tries to secure as large an individual share as possible of the available resources	● Individuals aspire to occupy as high an (scarce) organizational position as possible; women may have been limited in attaining these positions
● The 'just society' is one that allows individuals to exercise autonomy and to fulfill themselves through a system of individual rights	● The 'just organization' is one that allows both men and women to exercise their capabilities and fulfill themselves through a merit system
Cause(s) of oppression of women	*Cause(s) of women's lack of organizational opportunities*
● Female subordination rooted in attitudes, customs, legal constraints that block women's entrance and/or success in the public world	● Glass ceiling, 'second shift', missing 'opportunity structure', non-sex-blind performance appraisals, sexual harassment, lack of mentoring and networks
Goals/agenda for change	*Goals/agenda for organizational change*
● Gender justice/sexual equity	● Sexual equity as instrument of improved organizational performance; equal pay for equal work
● Treat men and women differently, but equally	● Avoid sex discrimination litigation
● Humanistic personhood for all: full membership in the human community	● Cross-gendering jobs and occupations for full attainment of human potential
● Free women (and men) from oppressive gender roles	● Possibility of androgyny
Obstacles to achieving goals	*Obstacles to achieving goals*
● Lack of access to good jobs, unequal and/or inequitable pay	● Same
● Gender stereotypes	● Same
Path toward goal achievement/remedies sought	*Path toward goal achievement/remedies sought*
● Even the playing field	● Equal access; sex-blind performance appraisals
● Remove discriminatory laws	● Analyses of gender effects of organizational rules and regulations
● Reform oppressive structures; fight for affirmative action plans, equal pay, childcare	● Effects of affirmative action; work/family issues
● Education/training to eliminate stereotypes	● Assertiveness training for women; diversity trainings; supervisory appraisal trainings
● Stay within the system to make a fair society	● 'Numbers' argument, i.e. increased number of women will even out the situation; dual-career families

and Plant 1982; Varca et al. 1983; Waters and Waters 1969; Weaver 1978) and *organizational commitment* (e.g. Bruning and Snyder 1983; Chusmir 1982; Zammuto et al. 1979). Further, in this research sex/gender-specific concepts such as *sex stereotypes* (e.g. Brenner 1982; Cleveland and Landy 1983; Gordon 1974; Ilgen and Terborg 1975; Osborn and Vicars 1976) and *androgyny* (e.g. Bem 1976; Powell and Butterfield 1979; Sargent 1981; Spence and Helmreich 1981) seem to be of interest mostly for corrective purposes: the possibility of eliminating sex/gender differences from traditional organizational issues.

There is also a considerable amount of work focusing on traditional *human resource management* topics such as biases that could be attributed to sex/gender differences in *recruitment* (Forsythe et al. 1985; Powell 1987; Sterrett 1978); *selection* (Heilman and Martell 1986; Mai-Dalton and Sullivan 1981; Rosen and Mericle 1979); *performance appraisal* (Grams and Schwab 1985; Hall and Hall 1976; Heilman and Stopeck 1985; Nieva and Gutek 1980; Pulakos and Wexley 1983; Rose 1978); and *pay* (Cooper and Barrett 1984; Martin and Peterson 1987; Sigelman et al. 1982).

Sociological and Structural Research

Because of its more macro-structural focus, this literature can be considered organizational sociology or organization theory, but some research tries to integrate both structural and behavioral issues. The majority of this work appeared after the mid 1980s, and much of it is inspired by Kanter (1977) and Bartol (1978). Central to these writings is a concern around the sex structuring of organizations and its consequences for traditional organizational activities and expectations. Among representative topics are the *glass ceiling* (Morrison and Von Glinow 1990; Morrison et al. 1987); *organizational demography* (Bielby and Baron 1987; Ely 1995; Jacobs 1992; Perry et al. 1994; Pfeffer and Davis-Blake 1987; Tsui et al. 1992); and *careers and social networks* (Auster 1989; Bowen and Hisrich 1986; Hunt and Michael 1983; Ibarra 1992; Kram 1985; Gallos 1989; Ragins and Cotton 1991; Smith 1979; Tharenou et al. 1994).

The Organization and the Broader Social System

Within this strand is research that addresses topics of general social and legal concerns and their relationship to organizational issues. Among these are *equal opportunity*, *affirmative action* and *discrimination* (Barclay 1982; Bergmann 1995; Chacko 1982; *Gender, Work and*

Story 1: Ellen Randall as Liberal Feminist

Ellen Randall is a very impressive figure. She has worked her way up the ranks to become president of a business unit with full bottom-line responsibility, taken over in tough situations and worked things out, and added executive stripes to her sleeve. She is obviously the one in charge, but she is also warm and open. She makes you think that she's going places, that you'll be reading about her future promotions in the *Wall Street Journal*. She's going to the top, you think. But Ellen's future doesn't look so bright to her. When she looks ahead, she senses no realistic possibility for further advancement in her corporation. Instead, she senses a wall, a barrier between her – a woman – and a top job in her corporation. . . . Ellen sees a limit on how high she can go as an executive woman. Realistically, she said, she will probably have one or two more promotions in her company, but she will probably not reach the top executive level. . . . Why don't executive women move higher? What can be done about the barriers they believe are holding them back?

Source: Morrison et al. 1987: 4–5

Organization July 1995; Heilman and Herlihy 1984; Taylor and Ilgen 1981); *sexual harassment* (Gutek and Morasch 1982; Konrad and Gutek 1986; Paetzold and O'Leary-Kelly 1994) and *work/family* issues (Barling and Rosenbaum 1986; Beutell and Greenhaus 1983; Jones and Causer 1995; Norton 1994; Parasuraman et al. 1989).

In general, women-in-management research documents the persistence of sex segregation in organizations as it tries to elucidate its causes through measurable constructs. Its epistemological premises show a marked functionalist/positivist orientation, favoring quantitative methodologies but sometimes also using qualitative research (e.g. Ely 1995). In the majority of these studies, sex/gender is a *variable*, not an analytical framework (Balsamo 1985; Smircich 1985).

Yet, despite the voluminous literature and apparent variety, most of this research fails to recognize liberal feminism's political implications. Attaining the liberal goals might imply very fundamental organizational changes, not small corrections in what is taken to be, ultimately, a rational and just system and a desired state of affairs (i.e. the organizational rationality, its goals and values). No surprise then that this literature has been cautious in forwarding policy oriented remedies, often taking refuge in the scientistic dictum that 'more research is needed'. Among the exceptions, however, are writings that address intersections of race and gender in organization, and which tend to be more critical of both traditional organizational goals and conditions, and traditional organizational research (Bell 1990; Bell et al. 1993; Betters-Reed and Moore 1991; Cox and Blake 1991; Cox and Nkomo 1990; Jackson and Holvino 1986; Pettigrew and Martin 1987).

Nonetheless, we can conceive almost all of women-in-management research as *glass ceiling* research, since assuring women fair access to managerial positions has been its overriding objective. The type of problems addressed by this research and the way in which they are conceptualized is summed up by the situation facing Ellen Randall in Story 1 (Morrison et al. 1987). As we go on to discuss other feminist theories, Ellen Randall will become our guide: as her feminist 'consciousness' changes, so does the concept of the glass ceiling, its meaning, and its importance.

RADICAL FEMINIST THEORY

Radical feminism grew out of women's dissatisfaction with the sexism of the supposedly liberatory movements of new left politics, civil rights and opposition to the Vietnam War (Deckard 1979). It takes the subordination of women as its fundamental problematic: gender is a system of male domination, a fundamental organizing principle of patriarchal society, which is at the root of all other systems of oppression (Jaggar 1983). What are seen by liberal feminists as essentially personal and individual problems, such as failing to get a promotion, being sexually harassed, or being unable to achieve orgasm, are seen here more systemically, as the consequence of male gender privilege in a society where the male and the masculine define the norm (Jaggar 1983).

From its 1960s roots, radical feminism developed into a wide ranging and fluid perspective, calling for the transformation not only of the legal and political structures of patriarchy, but of social and cultural institutions, such as the family, the church, the academy, and even language (Tong 1989; Daly 1978). Radical feminism's stance marked an epistemological position in which there is no distinction between 'political' and 'personal' realms: every area of life is the sphere of 'sexual politics' (Jaggar 1983: 101) and worthy of political analysis. 'Consciousness raising' developed as a method located in practice, whereby women could interrogate their experiences in light of systemic male domination. Research, from this perspective, is always 'interested'. It is a political activity which locates the origins of women's oppression in patriarchy, and which tries to find ways to overcome it.

For example, Firestone (1970) argued that while women's subordination rests in human biological reproductive processes, biological imperatives are overlaid by social institutions, particularly sexual and child-rearing practices, that reinforce male dominance. New and developing technologies make it possible to free women from their historical reproductive roles, permitting development of a society no longer dependent upon the sexual division of labor and its biological base. Some radical feminists proposed androgyny as an answer, suggesting that the dualism of masculinity/femininity could be eradicated (A. Ferguson 1977). A biological male or female would be culturally 'androgynous', both masculine and feminine. While liberal feminists pursued the androgynous ideal as a strategy for deficient women, radical feminists sought, instead, a new ideal of human nature: one that mixes historical notions of masculinity and femininity and challenges norms of heterosexuality (e.g. Daly 1978; Rich 1980; see also Jacobson and Jacques 1989b). Other radical feminists rejected this image, however, arguing that although the intent may be to transcend gender, the notion of androgyny was more likely to perpetuate gender stereotypes.

Radical feminism is 'radical' because it is 'women centered'. It envisions a new social order where women are not subordinated to men. For this purpose, it focuses on the intersections of sexuality and power relations. It proposes alternative, often separatist, social, political, economic and cultural arrangements that challenge the values of male dominated culture (Koedt et al. 1973). Radical feminists have taken the traditional association of woman with nature (in contrast to man with culture) and found within it a source of strength and power. They emphasize the positive value of qualities identified with women: sensitivity, emotional expressiveness, nurturance. Because of their closer connection to nature, women have a different way of knowing the world: emotional, non-verbal, spiritual; in contrast to patriarchal ways of knowing, relying on reason and logic (Jaggar 1983). Radical feminism suggests that it is possible for women to regain a sense of wholeness and connectedness to the 'authentic feminine' outside of patriarchy through a female counter culture: a cultural feminism (Echols 1983; Eisenstein 1983). Generally then, radical feminists favor separatist politics at least until women and men become equals.

By stressing all women's values, radical

feminism has also provided a space for women of color as well as lesbians to articulate, not unproblematically, their differences, personal and political, from white heterosexual women (e.g. Frye 1983; Lorde 1983; Moraga and Anzaldúa 1983). Yet, the radical views of women of color tend to emphasize more fluid and flexible subjectivities than the strong essentialist positions of other radical perspectives (e.g. Alcoff 1988).

Radical Feminist Theory and Alternative Organizations

Starting in the late 1960s, radical feminists discovered and put into practice organizational forms that were reflective of feminist values, such as equality, community, participation, and an integration of form and content (Brown 1992; Ferree and Martin 1995; Koen 1984). In the early days of the women's liberation movement, this implied negation of leadership and negation of structure (Joreen 1973). They were thus reactive in nature, seeking to reject elements associated with male forms of power. Radical feminism focused on creating a 'womanspace' through alternative institutions and organizations to fulfill women's needs: putting medical care back into women's own hands; giving women skills they traditionally lacked, such as auto mechanics and carpentry; creating battered women's shelters and rape crisis centers, as well as cultural organizations such as bookstores, art galleries, film and music festivals, to nurture women's cultural expression. Such space is needed to nurture, and revalue, what is devalued in 'malestream' culture. As Ellen Randall illustrates in Story 2, the glass ceiling exists only because so much value is put into climbing the corporate ladder, a competitive approach to jobs and occupations that emphasizes scarcity.

Consciousness-raising groups, as forums for the collective analysis of women's oppression, were referred to as 'leaderless' and 'structureless'. For example, one group practice, 'the lot and disc system', attempted to institutionalize equality, participation, and skill development of the members (Koen 1984). Specific roles for each meeting, e.g. chair, secretary, were determined by lot, while other roles such as treasurer might be determined by lot to serve one month. At meetings an equal number of discs was distributed to all members and each time a member spoke, she had to turn in a disc. When her discs were spent, the member was expected to remain silent, letting others continue the discussion. This practice was intended to balance participation and prevent any individual from monopolizing discussions. While such organiz-

Story 2: Ellen Randall as Radical Feminist

Ellen Randall is a very impressive figure. She has worked her way up the ranks to become president of a business unit with full bottom-line responsibility, taken over in tough situations and worked things out, and added executive stripes to her sleeve. She is obviously the one in charge, but she is also warm and open. She makes you think that she's going places, that you'll be reading about her future promotions in the *Wall Street Journal*. She's going to the top, you think. But Ellen's future doesn't look so bright to her. Since she started participating in a women's consciousness-raising group she has become more aware of her oppression. She notices now the foolishness of her expectations. Not only is she not going to be promoted 'to the top', but she is actually contributing to the patriarchal existence of the organization. For there to be 'a top' there has to be 'a bottom', and this bottom seems to be overly populated by women. She recognizes that with her warm and open preferred mode of behavior she would feel more comfortable in a place with no hierarchy, surrounded by other women like herself. She decides to resign and start her own business with other 'sisters' from her consciousness-raising group.

ational forms proved excellent for creating communities for learning, they were less effective at sustaining political action: as their energy dissipated and fragmented, groups began to dissolve. Consequently, groups began to experiment with organizational forms that were egalitarian and non-oppressive, but that also acknowledged a role for forms of 'structure' and 'leadership' (Koen 1984; Brown 1992).

From the 1970s numerous case studies have detailed feminist organizational practices (e.g. Baker 1982; Brown 1992; Cholmeley 1991; Epstein et al. 1988; Farrell 1994; Ferree and Martin 1995; Hyde 1989; Koen 1984; Iannello 1992; Leidner 1991a; Morgen 1994; Reinelt 1994; Riger 1984; Rothschild 1992 (her six-point model reprinted in Robbins 1996: 568); Schwartz et al. 1988; Sealander and Smith 1986). Many of these organizations embrace the goals and values of radical feminism combined with attention to issues of hierarchy and organization structure similar to that found in theories of anarchy and in collectivist organizations (Iannello 1992; Rothschild-Whitt 1979). For example, Koen's (1984) ethnographic research on three explicitly 'feminist' businesses suggests that finding an organizational structure that facilitates rather than hinders member participation and empowerment

Table 3   *A comparison of four 'feminist organizational practices'*

Key features and design principles of feminist workplaces (Koen 1984)	Modified consensus organization (Iannello 1992)	Six characteristics of the feminine model of organization (Rothschild 1992)	Feminist management (P.Y. Martin 1993)
Participatory decision-making	A distinction between critical and routine decisions: critical reserved for the many, routine delegated horizontally to the few	Value members as individual human beings	Asking the woman question
System of rotating leadership	Recognition of ability or expertise rather than rank or position	Non-opportunistic relationships are valued	Using feminist practical reasoning
Flexible interactive job designs	Empowerment as a basis of consensual process	Careers are defined in terms of service to others	Doing consciousness raising
Equitable system of income distribution	Clear goals arrived at through consensual process	Commitment to employee growth	Promoting community and cooperation
Interpersonal and political accountability		Creation of a caring community	Promoting democracy and participation
		Power sharing	Promoting subordinate empowerment, power as obligation
			Promoting nurturing and caring
			Striving for transformational outcomes

is key to feminist practice. She identifies five organizational elements reflective of feminist values in organizing: a participatory decision-making system, a system of rotating leadership, flexible and interactive job designs, an equitable distribution of income, and interpersonal and political accountability. Of these she believes that structure and processes for decision-making, rather than leadership, are central to an organization's adherence to feminist values. Table 3 compares Koen's model with those of Rothschild, Iannello, and P.Y. Martin.

Are Feminist Organizations Really Possible?

Studies of feminist organizations, however, have seldom appeared in the mainstream organization studies literature (K. Ferguson 1994; Ferree and Martin 1995). One reason, perhaps, is that many of these organizations have an explicit agenda to invert the values of capitalist masculinist organization (P.Y. Martin 1990; 1993; Woodul 1978).

The nature of business will be changed by feminist operation of it. There should be structures for worker input, working toward meaningful worker control. Salaries should be set within a narrow range, with consideration of each woman's particular needs as well as her role in the company. Structures should be clear to all and determined on concrete bases. Decisionmaking methods should be set out, with the understanding that decisionmaking must presume responsibility. There must be a consciousness of accountability to the women's community. There must be a commitment to channel money back into the community or movement. Finally, there must be a commitment to radical change – to the goals of economic and political power for women. (Woodul 1978: 197–8)

In attempting to invent feminist business and organizational practices, women confront the practical dilemma of trying to actualize equality in concrete activities. For instance, Cholmeley describes her feminist business in a capitalist world as a 'living case study of a major theoretical problem of the women's liberation movement' (1991: 228). How can equality be enacted in the face of differences of class, race, sexuality, education, skills, dependants, financial resources? The identification of a shared set of core values informing organizing activity in the women's movement does not mean that their enactment is unproblematic or uncontentious (Brown 1992).

Further, feminist values in action challenge the impersonality of bureaucracies by blurring the distinction between the personal and the organizational. Many case studies report on situations that are emotionally charged. Struggles are documented where 'the rhetoric of equality, the collective decisionmaking structure, and the explicit goals of women's and community empowerment' confront differences in work styles and class, race and ethnicity conflicts (Morgen 1994: 681).

Under the inspiration of radical feminism, some scholars are revising not only organizational forms and practices, but forms and practices of organizational theorizing. They start from 'women-centered theorizing', theorizing from the lives and experiences of women, to create feminist revisions of basic organizational concepts such as work, career, and management (e.g. Freeman 1990; Marshall 1984; 1989; 1995; P.Y. Martin 1993; Shrivastava 1994; Tancred 1995). So, while liberal women-in-management research is uncritical of organization in taking a 'how to succeed' perspective (e.g. Brenner 1987; K. Ferguson 1994), organization studies from a radical feminist perspective puts the perspectives and practices of women at the center of analyses. As observed by Ferguson, it privileges 'the world as seen from this set of vantage-points, thus problematizing the conventional equation of men with humanity' (1994: 90). Yet, there is irony in 'using capitalist strategies as a road to liberation' (Woodul 1978: 203).

PSYCHOANALYTIC FEMINIST THEORY

Consistent with its intellectual roots, psychoanalytic feminist research favors clinical approaches that connect the mind-world of individuals with their developmental experiences. While a variety of methods are used, all share an emphasis in understanding the whole person and her mode of relating to her world. Most psychoanalytic feminist theorizing originated with Freudian psychoanalysis but as critique and correction of its misogynist biases, or as a basis for a female-centered psychoanalytic interpretation (Tong 1989).

Freud proposed that to develop as normal adults, children must pass through several stages of psychosexual development. Originally, children, regardless of biological sex, are 'poly-morphously perverse', deriving sexual pleasure from several forms of bodily stimulation. Children move out of this multiple and perverse sexuality toward normal heterosexual genital sexuality when they pass, successfully, through specific developmental stages. The most critical passage children must overcome resides in the resolution of the Oedipus complex, the mother as object of love and desire, which appears when they are about three or four years old. The fact that boys have penises and girls do not affects the ways they overcome this stage. For boys, the resolution of the Oedipus complex resides in their ability to transfer their love for mother into fear of father, which occurs when boys become aware that women do not have penises and assume that they have been castrated by the father. The fear of castration by the father makes them renounce their desire for the mother and submit to the father's authority, thus developing a strong superego and eventually becoming one of the fathers. Girls resolve their Oedipal drama differently. When girls realize they don't have a penis but boys do, they assume they have been castrated and start envying the superiority of the boy's (non-castrated) anatomy. Because of this, girls start rejecting their mothers and transfer their love to the (superior) father. Eventually the desire for the father's penis is transcended by their desire to have a baby, which becomes the most important penis substitute.

According to Freud's theory, females have more difficulties than males in attaining the mature, balanced post-Oedipal stage and in developing a normal adult sexuality. His writings are explicit about different neuroses and limitations in the psychosexual development of women, including references to their inferior ethical sense (Tong 1989). Women never attain men's same strong superegos: they lack men's strong sense of justice, are less likely to obey authority, are more influenced by feelings rather than reason. Feminist writers criticize Freudian theory as an insensitive and inaccurate view of women's psychological make-up (e.g. Firestone 1970; Millet 1970; Friedan 1963); or reject Freudian biological determinism and reinterpret psychoanalytic theory in terms of cultural influences which affect women's gender identity (e.g. Thompson 1964; Horney 1974).

In general, psychoanalytic feminisms deny the biological determinism embedded in traditional psychoanalytic interpretations of gender and sexuality. Rather, they consider specific social arrangements (e.g. the patriarchal family) as leading to distinctions in male and female psychological development, which can be changed by changing the structural conditions that produce unequal gender development (Flax

1990; Tong 1989). In this regard, an influential strand of contemporary psychoanalytic feminism, inspired by object-relations theory (e.g. Winnicott 1975), focuses on the pre-Oedipal rather than the Oedipal stage, and the relations between mother and child. For example, Dinnerstein (1977) argues that, as a result of their encounter with their mother as the basic source of both pain and pleasure, children learn to blame the woman/mother for all that goes wrong in life which, in turn, leads to a set of gender arrangements that produces the subordination of women to men. Chodorow (1978) emphasizes the reproduction of mothering. Boys see their mothers as different from themselves, as 'other', and eventually, during the Oedipal stage, cease to identify with them. Girls, however, never really break the connection to their mothers, whom they see as an extension of self. While girls do distance themselves from their mothers during the Oedipal stage, mostly a test of the possibility of a separate identity symbolized by the father, the separation is never complete. For this reason, women find their most solid emotional relations with other women, despite the fact that most girls develop into heterosexual women. Girls tend to have an overdeveloped capacity for relatedness in contrast to boys, but a balance is attained when girls and boys are brought up experiencing both their parents as loving and autonomous beings. Thus, changes in parenting arrangements are a way toward a less male dominated society.

Other theorists consider psychosexual development and the emergence of different notions of gendered self and identity not just as a problem to be resolved by socialization, but also as an epistemological problem regarding whose self-knowledge is valued and whose is devalued (e.g. Flax 1983; Braidotti 1989). Gilligan's (1982) work challenges the masculinist epistemological bases of traditional psychological research as, for instance, in Freud's contention that women did not develop a strong sense of justice. In her studies of solutions to moral dilemmas, Gilligan argues that women and men have *different* concepts of justice and morality, both reasonable and well developed. She describes 'male' morality as an *ethics of justice*, while 'female' morality supports an *ethics of care*.

Psychoanalytic feminism has, then, demonstrated the patriarchal orientation of most developmental personality theories, and the limitations (what has been valued/devalued) in what is considered a 'normal humanity'. Yet, even with these 'corrections', psychoanalytic feminism has been criticized by other feminists who hold, for example, that Chodorow's analysis represents the same white, middle class, heterosexual nuclear family in capitalist

societies that was the center of Freud's psychoanalysis (e.g. Brennan 1989; Spelman 1989). Although some see Chodorow's object-relations approach as a good starting point for articulating alternative identities that develop within differential conditions of race and class (e.g. Abel 1990; Flax 1990), critics note that other possible family arrangements, and the subjectivities that develop within them, have seldom been of interest in these theories.

Psychoanalytic Feminist Theory and Women's Ways of Managing

Psychoanalytic feminism, as applied to organization studies, considers the consequences of women's different psychosexual development for their roles in organization and management. Early 'applications' focused on feminine character traits to explain women's subordinate economic status (Blum and Smith 1988). For instance, Horner (1972) posited that women's 'fear of success' stemmed from a 'basic inconsistency' between femininity and achievement that derived from their sex-role socialization. Hennig and Jardim's (1977) research for *The Managerial Woman* examined how early socialization experiences of males and females, and their differing resolutions of the Oedipal complex, carried over into their managerial behavior. Most women are socialized to be passive, to see themselves as victims rather than agents; they are ambivalent toward career, and lack the drive for mastery that men have. Successful women managers, it was argued, have atypical relationships with their fathers. Thus, most women fall short in the corporate culture, because the rules, norms, ethos of modern business reflect the male developmental experience (Blum and Smith 1988: 531). For women to succeed they must change themselves but, unlike the liberal feminist literature which emphasizes an 'instant remaking' of women such as 'dressing for success' or assertiveness training, this literature sees psychosexual development as *both* a personal *and* a societal issue, with cultural and historical roots.

As Ellen Randall illustrates in Story 3, the persistence of the glass ceiling is traced back to historical and cultural forms of social relations; yet this approach still shares basic liberal assumptions about the 'goodness' of moving to the top.

The Woman's Advantage?

More recent research has treated these women's differences, not as a problem, but as an advantage. The influence of feminist psychologists

Story 3: Ellen Randall as Psychoanalytic Feminist

Ellen Randall is a very impressive figure. She has worked her way up the ranks to become president of a business unit with full bottom-line responsibility, taken over in tough situations and worked things out, and added executive stripes to her sleeve. She is obviously the one in charge, but she is also warm and open. She makes you think that she's going places, that you'll be reading about her future promotions in the *Wall Street Journal*. She's going to the top, you think. But Ellen's future doesn't look so bright to her. When she looks ahead, she senses no realistic possibility for further advancement in her corporation. Instead, she senses a wall, a barrier between her – a woman – and a top job in her corporation. . . . Ellen understands how her situation and that of those around her has been produced by childrearing practices, parenting patterns and childhood socialization in earlier decades. She, as well as her co-workers and superiors, are trapped into a mode of thinking and behaving that favors a 'male' mode of being in the world. She doesn't think that much will change for her: she is 'too warm and open' but she and her husband are making sure that their children grow up valuing and practicing both feminine and masculine forms of relating. As a dual-career family of the 1990s they are also dual parenting their children as a way to eventually break up patriarchal domination in organizations and society. Yet, in the back of her mind, Ellen still hopes that now that organizations are looking for alternative approaches to traditional management, she might be able to use her 'feminine values' as her trump card that will move her to the top.

and psychoanalysts, including Dinnerstein, Chorodow, Gilligan and others (e.g. Miller 1976; Belenky et al. 1986), as well as influences from radical/cultural feminisms, led to work that pointed out that women's different sex-role socialization and different character traits were not deficiencies to be overcome, but *advantages* for corporate effectiveness (Grant 1986; Jelinek and Adler 1988; Helgesen 1990; Loden 1985; Rosener 1990; 1995). Women's ways of knowing and leading were studied and advocated (e.g. S. Freeman 1990; Haring-Hidore et al. 1990; Valentine and McIntosh 1990; Rosener 1990; 1995). Women's relational skills, capacity for empathy and interpersonal sensitivity became critical human resources skills that could 'stop the tide of alienation, apathy, cynicism, and low morale in organizations' (Grant 1986: 62). Women's 'interactive leadership' was cited as 'the management style of choice for many organizations . . . as the work force increasingly demands participation and the economic environment increasingly requires rapid change' (Rosener 1990: 125). Women's approach to organizational structuring, favoring images of circle and web over those of pyramid and chain, suited the demands of the information economy and the team approach (Helgesen 1990). A feminine approach to conflict and interpersonal relations enabled women to accomplish previously male dominated jobs, such as prison guarding, in different and perhaps even better ways (Zimmer 1987). Women became a nontraditional but increasingly valuable and skillful resource for global competition (Jelinek and Adler 1988; Peters 1990; Rosener 1995).

Still, some question whether 'the focus on the female advantage actually "advantages" females' (Fletcher 1994a: 74), or further entrenches gender stereotypes. In many cases the women's ways perspective has been positioned as an 'enlightened' correction to liberal-inspired research, but also criticized as one in service of the usual instrumental ends of organizations that objectify women (Calás et al. 1990; Calás and Smircich 1993; Fletcher 1994a). Several feminist organizational scholars, nonetheless, find within this perspective a way to challenge the status quo by emphasizing the power of relational activities (Calvert and Ramsey 1992; Fletcher 1994a; 1994b; Kolb 1992; Kolb and Putnam (in press); Marshall 1984; 1995; Ramsey and Calvert 1994). Such work resists incorporation by the mainstream management discourse and, through women-centered approaches, seeks more fundamental organizational transformations.

MARXIST FEMINIST THEORY

Marxist theory was a reaction to, and a critique of, capitalism and the liberal political theory that served to justify it. In contrast to liberal political theory which conceptualizes humans as universally autonomous and rational beings, according to Marxist views, human nature reflects historical material conditions. In Marx's famous phrase: 'It is not the consciousness of men that determines their existence, but their social existence that determines their consciousness' (in Tong 1989: 40). Thus, the organization of economic life conditions social, political and intellectual life; and, for that reason, the capitalist mode of production, a class struggle between labor and capital, moves to the center of analysis in this perspective.

Consistent with their views on human nature, feminist perspectives inspired by Marxist thinking conceptualize gender and gender identity as structural, historical and material. From this perspective, 'gender' is similar to 'class', a social category, characterized by relations of domination and oppression, functioning as a determinant of structural patterns in society. Masculinity and femininity are not understood as psychological states, or as attributes of sex roles, amenable to 'role reversal'; they are much deeper, because our fundamental identities are as sexed beings, as men or women (Game and Pringle 1984: 16). Marxist feminist thought analyzes how identities are constructed through social practices such as work, observing that power and sexuality are interwoven in work relations.

Marxist feminism is not only critical of liberal feminism for its erroneous conception of human nature and its inadequate understanding of the labor process; it is also critical of traditional Marxism for its blindness to patriarchy (Hartmann 1976; Game and Pringle 1984). Thus, Marxist feminism *adds* gender to the analytical concerns of the Marxist perspective, to 'correct for' its inattention to gender dynamics. Even though a hierarchy exists among men through a system of class, men as a group dominate and control women as a group, through a system of gender (Jaggar 1983; Lorber 1994). Marxist feminism is thus concerned with women's double oppression of both class and sex.

From this perspective, liberal feminism is totally inadequate for explaining the situation of women in the economy. Its uncritical approach to women in organizations and overemphasis on women in management is ultimately inconsistent with women's interests. That is, to Marxist feminists the capitalist economy is *not* best described through such concepts as market forces, exchange patterns, supply and demand as liberal/classic economic theory posits; rather, capitalist economy should be analyzed by focusing on relations of inequality and power. In this sense, then, work organizations are important sites for analyzing the ongoing reproduction of sex/gender inequality as they expose the intersections of patriarchy *and* capitalism.

In summary, Marxist feminism analyzes the ongoing productive and reproductive gender dynamics of patriarchal, capitalist organization of economy and society, pointing out that gender inequality persists and will not change without major structural changes. Further, while seldom represented in organization studies, traditional Marxist feminist perspectives have given way to socialist feminist approaches, elaborated below, which are of special importance for organizational studies. Yet, some recent neo-Marxist works also promise significant analytical insights in the area of workplace–household relations (e.g. Gibson 1992; Fraad et al. 1989).

SOCIALIST FEMINIST THEORY

Socialist feminism is a confluence of Marxist, radical and psychoanalytic feminism (e.g. Jaggar 1983; A. Ferguson 1989), which resulted from Marxist feminists' dissatisfaction with the gender-blind character of Marxist thought and the tendency of traditional Marxisms to dismiss women's oppression as not nearly as important as workers' oppression (Tong 1989). Socialist feminists also critique radical and psychoanalytic feminism because they both exhibit universalizing tendencies, assuming (Western) patriarchal conditions as a normative phenomenon, with little regard for culture or historical circumstances. In particular, radical feminism is criticized as naive for pretending that there could be a separate 'women's culture' under patriarchy *and* capitalism. Socialist feminist theories thus claim to incorporate several positive insights of Marxist, psychoanalytic and radical feminist theories while overcoming most of their limitations. In particular, this view theorizes gender dynamically, in both processual and material ways. Here gender means more than a socially constructed, binary identity: 'Gender is a constitutive element of social relationships based on perceived differences between the sexes, and gender is a primary way of signifying relationships of power' (Scott 1986: 1067).

To analyze these relationships, socialist feminists employ two main approaches: dual-systems theory and unified-systems theory. Dual-systems theory considers capitalism and patriarchy as separate phenomena which intersect and dialectically relate to each other. Here, capitalism is always a material, historically rooted mode of production, but patriarchy is considered as either a material or an ideological structure. For example, Mitchell (1974) observes that a woman's status and function are jointly determined by her role in production, reproduction, the socialization of children and sexuality. Women's oppression will persist unless *their psyches* experience a revolution equivalent to the economic one that effects the transition from capitalism to socialism. In her view, capitalism is material but patriarchy is ideologically based and thus closer to the psychoanalytic view.

Other dual-systems approaches, similar to radical feminism, consider patriarchy as a material structure. For instance, Hartmann (1976; 1981a; 1981b) argues that Marxist feminism, by subsuming women's relation to men under workers' relation to capital, is slighting the real object of feminist analysis: male–female relations. A Marxist analysis of capitalism needs to be complemented with a feminist analysis of patriarchy: the different forms of men's interest in the domination of women. Thus the 'family wage' is negotiated by men to maintain wives' servitude and subordination at home; the 'dual income family' has not really changed the patriarchal situation: women in the workforce remain underpaid and overworked since they bear the major responsibilities for housework and family nurturance. From Hartmann's viewpoint, then, women have to fight against their material exploitation under patriarchy at the same time as they fight their material exploitation under capitalism. However, each of these wars has to be fought with different and very specific weapons, according to site of struggle: in the household or in the workplace.

Dual-systems theories have not been without their critics (e.g. Ferguson and Folbre 1981; Folbre 1985; 1987; Young 1980). Young's unified-systems approach considers materialist accounts of patriarchy as promoting a separate-spheres model of family and economy which does not question when and how the public/private split came about and is maintained. She also argues that patriarchy as a psychological construct could be falsely regarded as being less oppressive to women than capitalist economic oppression. Thus through the concept of *gendered division of labor*, Young highlights the individuals who do the producing in society and how they are differently exploited: for example, how women functioning as a secondary labor force became a fundamental characteristic of capitalism.

In summary, socialist feminists have emphasized the analytical integration of social structure and human agency in explaining the persistence of gender segregation and gender oppression (e.g. Wharton 1991). Further, through theoretical developments that address social location and relations, such as women's *standpoints* (Hartsock 1983; Harding 1986), they have been particularly concerned with epistemological issues: not only what is to be known, but how knowledge is constituted and for what purposes. For these reasons, socialist feminism has addressed intersections of gender, race, class, and sexuality more effectively than other feminist approaches already discussed (e.g. Collins 1990; Anzaldúa 1990; Lugones and Spelman 1983).

Socialist Feminist Theory and The Gendering of Organizing

From the standpoint of socialist feminism an organization studies that focuses on 'the organization' as a unit of analysis is a mistake. The

---

Story 4: Ellen Randall as Socialist Feminist

Ellen Randall is a very impressive figure. She has worked her way up the ranks to become president of a business unit with full bottom-line responsibility, taken over in tough situations and worked things out, and added executive stripes to her sleeve. She is obviously the one in charge, but she is also warm and open. She makes you think that she's going places, that you'll be reading about her future promotions in the *Wall Street Journal*. She's going to the top, you think. But Ellen's future doesn't look so bright to her. When she looks ahead, she senses no realistic possibility for further advancement in her corporation, but that is not the worst of it. In fact Ellen, a women's studies graduate from an elite liberal arts college, knows very well what her situation is all about. Her upper class location has contributed to her coming up the ranks, but patriarchy is still at work here. So, even though she is 'luckier' than her black secretary, who holds an MBA degree, and 'luckier' than her 'less connected' peers, she is still a woman under capitalism and under patriarchy. Every minute of her life she is involved in re-creating the structures that exploit her and most other women, even though to different degrees and apparently in different forms. She cannot stop thinking how she herself might contribute even more directly to this state of affairs by keeping the Nicaraguan maid who cooks and cleans her house, and takes care of her children, making it possible for her to have this job, working the long hours that she does. Her husband is also working hard to make it to the top, or maybe to make it at all now that his corporation is talking about downsizing. Ellen may be more secure in her job than he, since she is, after all, 'cheaper labor'.

---

private sphere cannot be separated from the public one, since organizations, families and societies are mutually constituted through gender relations, as Ellen Randall's heightened socialist feminist consciousness reveals in Story 4.

Historically, the transition from agrarian to industrial modes of production created the separation of workplace and home, and produced a gendered structure where women and men work at different jobs, in different industries and at different organization levels (Alpern 1993; Crompton and Sanderson 1990). The unequal, and persistent, sex-based patterns in employment, observable across multiple industries and situations, are referred to variously as the *sexual division of labor*, the *sex structuring* of organizations, and *occupational sex segregation* (Acker and Van Houten 1974; Game and Pringle 1984; Reskin and Roos 1990; Strober 1984). In general, research inspired by this approach favors case study methods that make visible the informal and invisible processes of segregation which remain inaccessible to those who favor survey research (e.g. Collinson et al. 1990). Empirical work by sociologists, labor process theorists, ethnomethodologists and organizational culture researchers shows how gender assumptions are embedded in societal expectations and how they interact with organizational rules and practices. It reveals the micro-processes and micro-practices that are 'underneath' and constitutive of macro-social structural arrangements (Acker 1990; 1994).

As conceptualized by Acker, persistent structuring along gender lines is reproduced in a number of ways. One is through ordinary, daily procedures and decisions that segregate, manage, control and construct hierarchies in which gender, class and race are involved (Acker 1990). The 'vicious circles of job segregation' are played out in recruiting and promoting practices (Collinson et al. 1990). When firms hire part-time workers, they tend to be women, thereby increasing the proportion of women at the lowest levels of the organization (Cockburn 1991). Gender structuring persists through wage setting practices and job evaluation schemes with embedded gender assumptions, resulting in the undervaluing of the interpersonal dimensions of work, such as nurturing, listening, empathizing. 'Caring work' is 'women's work' and caring work pays less (see Acker 1989; Fletcher 1994b). Gendering, and racializing, of organizations also occurs through symbols, images, ideologies that legitimate gender inequalities and differences (Acker 1990; 1994; Benschop and Doorewaard 1995; Billing and Alvesson 1993; Gherardi 1994; 1995; Mills 1988; 1995; Mills and Tancred 1992). Images of the ideal organization member, the top manager, and the organizational hero tend to be those of forceful masculinity (e.g. Kanter 1977; Aaltio-Marjosola 1994; Stivers 1993). Symbolic processes are also associated with work activities leading to gendered jobs. They constitute the gendered 'opportunity structures' through which sexed bodies get allocated, for example in academia (e.g. Morley 1994; J. Martin 1994) and insurance sales (Collinson and Knights 1986; Leidner 1991b).

Gender structuring is also sustained through social interactions that enact dominance and submission (Acker 1990; 1994; Cockburn 1991; Game and Pringle 1984; Hall 1993; Rantalaiho and Heiskanen forthcoming; P.Y. Martin 1996; D. Smith 1987; 1990a; 1990b; West and Fenstermaker 1995). Analysis of conversations shows how gender differences in interruptions, turn-taking, and setting the topic of discussion re-create gender inequality in the flow of ordinary talk (West and Zimmerman 1987) and joking (Collinson 1988), so that organization itself is shown to be a gendered communication act (Buzzanell forthcoming; Mills and Chiaramonte 1991). Through organizational conversations and interpersonal interactions, an individual's choices are limited (Nes and Iadicola 1989) and personality attributes are created and maintained ('too emotional', 'too sensitive', 'not sufficiently context independent for making the tough decisions') which can block human fulfillment. Identity-making processes – for example, the choice of appropriate work, use of language, style of clothing, and the presentation of self as a gendered member of an organization – also contribute to structuring along gendered lines (Acker 1990; 1994; Benschop and Doorewaard 1995; Hearn et al. 1989; Hearn and Parkin 1987; Rantalaiho and Heiskanen forthcoming; Reskin and Roos 1990). For example, Sheppard (1989) and Piller (1996) analyze the 'body work' necessary for women managers. Leidner (1991b) examines how gender segregated service jobs reinforce the conception of gender differences as natural, while Sahlin-Andersson's (1994) study of nurses shows how 'female identity' is reflected in the interactions among nurses and between nurses and doctors. Recently, researchers' attention is being drawn to 'men' as a social category with examination of the intersections of masculinities and management and organization (e.g. Collinson and Hearn 1994; 1996; Connell 1995; Kerfoot and Knights 1993; Kvande and Rasmussen 1994; and P.Y. Martin 1996). In Acker's view:

> Individual men and particular groups of men do not always win in these processes, but masculinity always seems to symbolize self-respect for men at the bottom and power for men at the top, while confirming for both their gender's superiority. Theories that posit organization and bureaucracy as gender neutral cannot adequately account for this continual gendered structuring. We need different theoretical strategies that examine organizations as gendered processes in which sexuality also plays a part. (1990: 145)

Finally, the persistent structuring of organizations along gender lines is supported and sustained by the gendered substructure of organizations, for example, the practices related to the 'extra-organizational reproduction of members' (Acker 1994: 118). Women are the 'hidden providers' in the economy (Stoller 1993:

153). The physical and social reproduction of employees happens outside the workplace and is done primarily by women, most of it as unpaid work (Acker 1994; Folbre 1994; Stoller 1993; Stromquist 1990). According to this view the sexual division of labour is a basic characteristic of capitalist society (Jaggar 1983) which affects men as well as women. Thus, in many ways, 'doing organization' implies 'doing gender' (West and Zimmerman 1987).

Socialist feminist analyses promote 'a society in which maleness and femaleness are socially *irrelevant*, in which men and women, as we know them, will no longer exist' (Jaggar 1983: 330). Yet, goals of gender equity and equality are too limited goals; they '[do] not challenge the concept of sex differences that leads to separate spheres in the family and marketplace division of labor, which in turn results in women's lesser access to control of valued resources and positions of power' (Lorber 1986: 577).

WHAT CAN BE DONE? THEORIZING A DIFFERENT SOCIAL ORDER

The creation of socially interchangeable 'women' and 'men' requires transformational change in social systems: the restructuring of our most intimate relations, kinship, sexuality, parenting, friendship, as well as relations in the workplace (Lorber 1986); the development of a gender-neutral wage structure where all work would be equally valued, and all wage workers would receive equal compensation for their labor; the disappearance of sexual division of labor in the marketplace and the family; the equal compensation of all work, including dependant care (e.g. Folbre 1994; Phillips and Taylor 1980); the enactment of non-gendered taxation and legal policies, non-gendered families and non-gendered sexuality (hooks 1984; Lorber 1986; 1994; Paige and Paige 1981). These solutions are much more 'radical' than those that attempt to place women and men workers on equal footing within an already organizationally established framework of job categories and relations (Brenner 1987; Feldberg 1984; Lorber 1986; Treiman and Hartmann 1981).

POSTSTRUCTURALIST / POSTMODERN FEMINIST 'THEORIES'

There are at least three different feminist strands in this literature. First, 'French' feminism includes the contributions of women authors such as Hélène Cixous and Catherine Clément

(1986), Luce Irigaray (1985a; 1985b) and Julia Kristeva (1980), who have engaged directly with the works of well known (male) figures in French poststructuralism, such as Jacques Lacan (1977) and Jacques Derrida (1976), and also with traditional Freudian psychoanalysis (Jardine 1985; Moi 1985; Tong 1989). The second strand, represented in Anglo-American theory, draws primarily from Michel Foucault's power/knowledge arguments regarding intersections of the body, discourses, and practices (Diamond and Quinby 1988; Sawicki 1991; Weedon 1987). Third, 'postmodern feminism' comprises a collection of eclectic approaches, drawing from diverse but sharing certain similar concerns, in particular, Lyotard's (1984) postmodern incredulity concerning metanarratives, a suspicion of the constitution of the 'feminine' within modernity, and the negative consequences of deconstructing this image for a 'politics of feminism' (e.g. Alcoff 1988; Butler and Scott 1992; K. Ferguson 1993; Nicholson 1990).

Unlike liberal and Marxist theories, which provide positive groundings for feminism, poststructuralist approaches question 'positive knowledge', as we know it, in a move toward periodizing the Enlightenment's (i.e. modern) philosophical and scientific traditions such as the existence of transcendental reason, and the possibility of objective knowledge. These approaches constantly interrogate the ontological and epistemological claims of modern theories: their foundationalism, essentialism, and universalism, including the claims of many feminist theories in so far as they articulate a 'privileged knowing subject' (e.g. women's experience; women's standpoint), an 'essential feminine', and a general representation of 'woman'. These approaches thus interrogate 'knowledge' and its constitution as such.

Poststructuralist approaches draw from Ferdinand de Saussure's (1966) structural linguistics, where language is a system of differences rather than a representation of essences, to demonstrate the instability of language as a representational form.[1] Language (broadly understood as a *system of signification*, beyond the ordinary written and spoken form) is not only malleable over time, but also ambiguous and excessive: any term is able to signify a multiplicity of things and ideas at any particular point in time. In so far as 'knowledge' depends on the possibility of representing a reality that exists outside its representation, outside of language, the correspondence between one and the other can be easily questioned. On the one hand, 'knowledge' is given to us only as a representation: for example, we learn as we read about something that is assumed to exist outside of the text we are reading, but we have immediate knowledge only about the textual representation. On the other hand, that which is represented in language has never been outside of language: it is through language that researchers constitute the subject of their investigations (what is to be researched, paid attention to, ignored) and their own subjectivities. That is, it is through language that we can 'tell' who we are. In this argument, 'knowledge' ends up being nothing but the difference from that which is 'not knowledge' – a representation that depends on an often devalued, invisible 'other' for legitimation.

The focus on the relationship between language and knowledge is extended in various directions by different theorists. Derrida's deconstructions emphasize the multiplicity of 'the other' as a condition that always defers the meaning of the primary term (what is claimed as 'knowledge'). Traditional logocentric notions about 'knowledge', deconstructed by Derrida in their immediate textuality, are analyzed by Foucault through historical genealogies. Foucault (1977; 1980) emphasizes the emerging power/knowledge relations constantly constituted in discourses and practices, through which we constitute our 'selves' and define our subjectivity. Thus, the human body becomes a locus that legitimates and normalizes certain discourses and practices as 'truth' and 'knowledge'. Lacan's (1977) arguments reinterpret Freudian theories about the Oedipal/pre-Oedipal stages in children's development by emphasizing the importance of children's entrance into the domain of language. He argues that splitting occurs as the child enters the symbolic (linguistic) stage and loses the sense of wholeness and completion of the imaginary (pre-linguistic) stage. Thus, the self that is possible within the symbolic order is always a lacking, desiring self, wanting to be whole again.

This brief excursion into some basic poststructuralist ideas sets the stage for the arguments of different strands of poststructuralist feminist 'theories'. French feminists focus their arguments around the relationship between language and 'being woman'. They extend Derridian and Lacanian insights to consider the particular space that the linguistic figure of 'woman' occupies as that which is 'other' to the dominant (phallogocentric) language, system of rules, and concepts of knowledge in modernity. For these authors, tenuously inspired by Simone de Beauvoir (1972), 'women's otherness' is a space to be both reclaimed and problematized. For example, Cixous and Clément (1986) articulate the possibility of *écriture féminine*, as a space where 'the other' would represent herself. The marginality and elusiveness of this idea makes it both a positive representation and

a constant reminder for the 'masters' about the equally precarious position of their claims to 'knowledge'. Irigaray uses images about the heterogeneity and multiplicity of 'woman', the multiple points of sexual pleasure in women's bodies, to counter philosophical and psycho-analytic arguments (e.g. Irigaray 1985a; 1985b). Kristeva (1980) dislodges the relationship between feminine/masculine language and the sexed bodies of men and women. The human search for a return of the repressed feminine language in the symbolic order renders human subjectivity unstable and always in process, thus allowing for more fluid and flexible gender identities and subject positions.

The influence of Michel Foucault has produced another line of poststructuralist feminism. While acknowledging the problems of adopting an uncritical stance toward his work (e.g. Sawicki 1991), Foucault's influence is not surprising if one considers the more immediate political appeal of his arguments around power, and his departure from traditional theories of the subject that privilege dominant (patriarchal) views about knowledge and knowing. Diamond and Quinby identify four intersections between Foucault and feminism:

> Both identify the body as the site of power, that is, as the locus of domination through which docility is accomplished and subjectivity constituted. Both point to the local and intimate operations of power, rather than focusing exclusively on the supreme power of the state. Both bring to the fore the crucial role of discourse in its capacity to produce and sustain hegemonic power and emphasize the challenges contained within marginalized and/or unrecognized discourses. And both criticize the ways in which Western humanism has privileged the experience of the Western masculine elite as it proclaims universals about truth, freedom, and human nature. (1988: x)

In addition, these authors argue that feminist and Foucaldian analyses offer distinctive insights that the other has ignored or missed.

However, several feminist theorists have expressed ambivalence toward postmodern/poststructuralist approaches, considering, for example, that it might be risky for women to abandon the Enlightenment projects concerning the 'good', the 'true', and the 'beautiful' since women never had the opportunity to offer their own understandings to these projects. Others claim that postmodern relativism denies core values that would otherwise legitimate theories of knowledge (e.g. Harding 1990) and morality (e.g. Benhabib 1984) based on women's standpoints and needs. Some of these critiques also argue that feminist politics is not yet strong enough to be able to withstand a decentered politics which prevents groups speaking from a unified subject position (di Stefano 1988); and that postmodernism's abandoning of universal categories would imply abandoning the category 'gender' in favor of endless difference attached to human bodies, rendering a coherent theory and politics impossible for those not privileged (e.g. Bordo 1990).

Advocates, on the other hand, assert that 'postmodern-feminist theory would replace unitary notions of woman and feminine gender identity with plural and complexly constructed conceptions of social identity, treating gender as one relevant strand among others, attending also to class, race, ethnicity, age' (Fraser and Nicholson 1988: 393). By recognizing the heterogeneity within the apparently unitary category 'gender', political engagement is possible in so far as women are willing to make up 'a patchwork of overlapping alliances, not one circumscribable by an essential definition' (1988: 394). Flax (1987) also articulates a politics of heterogeneity, reminding us that partiality and difference are the reality of everyday social relations. Any view that posits the world to be otherwise, such as Enlightenment views, mystifies and disempowers alternative political engagements.

Feminist theories should then engage directly in demonstrating the unstable, complex, and ambiguous 'nature' of social reality (e.g. de Lauretis 1984; 1987). For example, Alcoff (1988) proposes the notion of positionality as a political argument for locating 'woman' as a relative identity, both flexible and agential, while K. Ferguson (1993) considers the possibility of mobile subjectivities which, like Haraway (1985: 73) offer 'affinity, not identity': 'Already aware of themselves as incorporating contestation, mobile subjectivities could be prepared to accept the partiality of any set of solutions to public problems and the necessity of continued political struggle' (K. Ferguson 1993: 183).

In general, then, postmodern feminist views emphasize the complexity of social relations, requiring more than 'gender' as a category for effective critique. Feminist theories that insist on keeping 'gender' and 'women' as privileged universal and ahistorical analytical categories are rendered suspect, i.e., if they mean that otherwise feminism couldn't provide a coherent notion of social and political agency:

To what extent do words like 'poststructuralism' and 'postmodernism' . . . become the site for all sorts of fears about the diffusion of power and the loss of cognitive 'mastery'? To what extent do the terms used to defend the universal subject encode fears about those cultural minorities excluded in and by the construction of that subject; to what extent is the outcry against the 'postmodern' a defense of culturally privileged epistemic positions that leave unexamined the excluded domains of homosexuality, race, and class? (Butler and Scott 1992: xv)

Thus, postmodern/poststructuralist feminisms allow for more complex intersections of gender and other social categories that both deconstruct taken-for-granted analytical subject positions (e.g. women, and women's oppression as unitary categories) and open the space for different political engagements which recognize asymmetrical power relations among those who purport to be 'the same'.

Poststructuralist/Postmodern Feminist 'Theories' and Postmodern Feminist Organizational Analysis

Encounters between poststructuralist feminist literature and organization studies, while growing, are still quite limited, particularly in the USA. Most of the impact comes through organization studies' traditional relationship with other social sciences. For example, Dorinne Kondo's (1990) exemplar account draws on cultural anthropology. On telling the story of everyday life on the shop floor of a Japanese small, family-owned factory, this postmodern 'feminist' ethnography subverts many images about what it is to be a gendered self belonging to particular ethnic groups within particular life circumstances; as well as what counts as theory, and where the boundary is between the empirical and the theoretical. Kondo describes her project as making the following points:

[F]irst, that any account, mine included, is partial and located, screened through the narrator's eye/I; second, to emphasize the processual and emergent nature of ethnographic inquiry and the embeddedness of what we call theory in that process; and third, to argue that the liveliness and complexity of everyday life cannot be encompassed by theoretical models which rely on organizational structures, 'typical' individuals, referential meanings, or invocations of collective nouns like 'the Japanese'. Rather, my strategy will be to emphasize, through shifting, multiple voices and the invocation of the 'I', the shifting, complex, individual identities of the people with whom I lived and worked, and the processes by which I became acquainted with them. (1990: 8–9)

Another example of a feminist analysis inspired by poststructuralism is Rosemary Pringle's (1988) study of secretaries as a social group and their discursive constructions in the day-to-day relationships of power. She explores the connection between domination, sexuality and pleasure, using a Foucaldian approach.

Other contributions by writers in organization studies who have taken up these themes include Calás's (1993a) deconstruction of charismatic leadership from 'the other' viewpoint; Calás and Smircich's (1991) feminist deconstructions of traditional leadership writings as well as their feminist rewritings of organization studies (1992), organizational globalization (1993), and business ethics (forthcoming); Cullen's (1994) re-analysis of Maslow on self-actualization; Gray's (1994) feminist analysis of her own work on collaboration; R. Jacques's (1992) graftings of an 'ethics of care' around arguments of theory building; J. Martin's (1990) deconstruction of organizational taboos that allows for the reappearance of submerged gender conflict; and Mumby and Putnam's (1992) feminist analysis of 'bounded rationality'. Further, Holvino (1994) and Nkomo (1992) are exemplar works which question both the 'racializing' and 'gendering' of organizational discourse. However, there are no 'boundaries' around a single subdiscipline when considering postmodern organizational analysis. Representative research exists in accounting (e.g. Shearer and Arrington 1993), marketing (e.g. Bristor and Fischer 1993; Fischer and Bristor 1994) and educational administration (Capper 1992), among others.

All these works not only focus on the construction and precarious nature of gender in organization, but also reveal the involvement of 'organization studies' in the constitution of gendered arrangements. Thus, Ellen Randall portrays in Story 5 how the glass ceiling might look from a feminist poststructuralist perspective. The separation between the organizational practices that create the glass ceiling and research practices that produce knowledge about it dissolves: both are intertwined as 'the politics of knowledge' and 'the politics of identity' constitute each other.

THIRD WORLD/(POST)COLONIAL THEORIZATIONS

During the past ten years or so, several critical strands have challenged Western feminist theorizations of gender and gender relations for being based on images and social experiences of mostly privileged women (and men) in the 'First World'. While not monolithic, and in fact often contested, these arguments go beyond those already raised by black and other women who have questioned white, middle class, heterosexist, representations of gender in liberal, radical, psychoanalytic, and even socialist feminist theories. Otherwise different Third World/(post)colonial analyses hold in common a

---

Story 5: Ellen Randall as Poststructuralist Feminist

Ellen Randall is a very impressive figure. She has worked her way up the ranks to become president of a business unit with full bottom-line responsibility, taken over in tough situations and worked things out, and added executive stripes to her sleeve. She is obviously the one in charge, but she is also warm and open. She makes you think that she's going places, that you'll be reading about her future promotions in the *Wall Street Journal*. She's going to the top, you think. But Ellen's future doesn't look so bright to her. When she looks ahead, she senses no realistic possibility for further advancement in her corporation; but that is not what worries her the most. Ellen is actually a doctoral student doing a postmodern ethnography of 'The glass ceiling in US corporations'. She is concerned that after so many years in the field, she might be found out – now that she is almost at the end of her work. Her main dilemma at this point is how to represent the configuration of her identity as 'a woman encountering the glass ceiling'. She realizes that the discursive practices that give way to this contemporary organizational issue have a history: 'the glass ceiling' is the opposite of a discourse that assumes the possibility of an absence of barriers, a 'truth' that never was but that continues to be sustained by those who use liberal discourses to research 'the glass ceiling'. She observes her position as a node in a power/knowledge network, where her activities, normalized in apparent conformity to the corporate requirements, are also moments of resistance and transgression as she performs 'as a woman in the corporation'. She also knows that there is no way out. Once she leaves 'the corporation' she will constitute and will be constituted as an/other subject in power/knowledge networks within 'the ivory tower'.

---

fundamental suspicion of 'gender' as a stable and sufficient analytical lens that can be applied unproblematically across cultures and histories. They have extended the insights of postmodern and poststructuralist theorizations to their logical consequences: if Western knowledge has been constituted in difference from 'others', by rendering them invisible, what would happen if those 'others' were to speak back? What if they were to show how they are constituted as others? What if these others were to reclaim their own specificities, away from the dualisms (e.g. male/female) embedded in Western discourses of knowledge?

Chandra Mohanty (1991a) argues that 'third world women' have often been constituted as 'others' of 'first world women' by highlighting their underdevelopment, oppression, illiteracy, poverty, overpopulated conditions, etc. These representations reaffirm Western knowledges of 'indicators' such as life expectancy, sex ratio, nutrition, fertility, education and income-generating activities, which homogenize and freeze non-Western women, denying the fluid, historical and dynamic nature of their lives. They show 'third world peoples' (not just women) as backward, ignorant and passive recipients of Western 'knowledges', obliterating other representations which articulate their agency, capabilities, involvement in struggles, and strategies for survival. Mohanty calls for the rewriting of history based on the specific locations and histories of struggle of (post)colonial peoples to articulate 'other knowledges' which would illuminate '(1) the idea of the simultaneity of oppressions as fundamental to the experience of social and political marginality and the grounding of feminist politics in the histories of racism and imperialism; (2) the crucial role of a hegemonic state in circumscribing their/our daily lives and survival struggles; (3) the significance of memory and writing in the creation of oppositional agency; (4) and the differences, conflicts and contradictions internal to third world women's organizations and communities' (Mohanty 1991b: 10).

(Post)colonial analyses thus go beyond the deconstruction of Western texts. They show the production of knowledge at the (Western) center to be a form of self-fashioning, widely implicated in the constitution of the legitimation of imperialism and colonialism (e.g. Minh-ha 1989; Prakash 1995; Said 1978; 1989). These analyses often focus on the complex subjectivities produced by intersections of gender, race, class, ethnicity, etc. in the context of specific First World/Third World relationships. They theorize heterogeneous subject positions and relations different from the gendered and racialized images produced by Western categorizations (e.g. 'women', 'black').

The question remains, however, whose language and theories are being used by the 'rest' to deconstruct the 'West'? Some argue that the theoretical tools used in (post)colonial analyses are those of the oppressors; others try to demonstrate how the colonized always reappropriate the masters' tools (Lorde 1983) and redeploy them toward their own interests. Thus the deconstructive move is perfectly consistent with historical practices: a way to re-create them in the present. There is, however, still the nagging problem of the representational identity of the colonized: who is this 'other' who deconstructs the West? A dilemma exists in how to portray (post)colonial subjectivities without depicting them either as a romanticized 'native other' or only in their relationship with their oppressors. How can writers articulate a Third World/(post)colonial subject without reclaiming a pristine original space from which to represent her agency either historically or experientially? How can writers provide a space for representation outside the power engagements with the colonizer?

Parry (1995) identifies two different approaches in (post)colonial deconstructions, one exemplified by Gayatri Spivak's work (e.g. 1987; 1988), and the other by Homi Bhabha's (e.g. 1985; 1990). Spivak's deconstructions are produced through a double move. First, she considers the silence and muteness of the colonized (subaltern), who by intersecting his own patriarchal tradition with the interests of the colonizer, colluded in his own subjectification, and thus cannot speak as himself. The subaltern woman is even further silenced. Spivak's second move requires that the contemporary (post)colonial woman intellectual develop a specific strategy for reading the history of the colonized, plotting a story that gives the (female) subaltern a voice in history. It means a rereading of old colonial stories about, for example, Sati (widow sacrifice), disposing of the fixed (gender) categories on which they depended for their intelligibility by the West (also see Mani 1989). Bhabha follows a different approach. In his readings of colonial stories, he reveals that the colonized had already interrogated the colonialist text in their own ways: the shifting and contradictory subject positions that the colonized show in these texts are indicative of the representational difficulties that they posed for the colonizer.[2]

Concerns remain, however, about the political power of a discourse that relies on a decentered, unfixed, multiple, constituted-in-difference subject as a position for representing 'knowledge', when the 'politics of knowledge', as we know it, has relied on a universal, centered, essential subject for its legitimation. Is there a positive subjectivity from which the colonized could represent herself after the deconstructive gesture? Several responses to these concerns have been offered. The notion of strategic essentialism (e.g. Spivak 1988; Said 1989) describes 'a strategic use of positivist essentialism in a scrupulously visible political interest' (Spivak 1988: 13), and demonstrates the possibility for engaging in seemingly contradictory political struggles, while mobilizing support for and from groups that might otherwise appear to stand on different agendas. Yet, some (post)colonial theorists (e.g. Radhakrishnan 1994) consider strategic essentialism as another instance of redeploying the 'master's tools' through a reversal of its metropolitan tactics. Another notion, hybridization (e.g. Bhabha 1988; García-Canclini 1990), can be read as both resisting the forces of assimilation into a dominant culture, and representing new forms that simultaneously integrate and disintegrate modernity and tradition. Escobar (1995: 218) explores hybridization with particular reference to Latin America, in terms of 'continuous attempts at renovation, by a multiplicity of groups taking charge of the multitemporal heterogeneity peculiar to each sector and country'. Latin American testimonial writings offer another possibility for unique Third World representations of strong political force by portraying very different gender configurations through women 'from below' who speak up, initiate action, fight in all kinds of struggles, while resisting any easy classification within First World images of 'woman' or 'feminism' (e.g. Franco 1992; Marin 1991; Sternbach 1991; Sommer 1988; 1995).

These arguments are of pragmatic importance for the contemporary articulation of knowledges beyond those considered legitimate in conventional disciplinary discourses. How to speak (knowledge) as 'other' is perhaps the central

problematic in the current scramble for signification, for not all discourses enter the (post)colonial signifying space on the same footing. Thus, Third-World/(post)colonial arguments offer a much needed discursive space for engaging with the 'new colonialisms' of globalization and the market.

Third World/(Post)Colonial Theorizations and the Women-in-Development Literature

While Ellen Randall muses over her glass ceiling dilemma in Story 6, we must acknowledge that there is not much organizational literature to help her: she will be better off consulting her anthropologist friend. There is, however, considerable potential in the women-in-development literature if it were to focus on the intersections of gender with contemporary organizational issues, especially those that pertain to globalization and transnationalization (e.g. Acosta-Belén and Bose 1990).

Women-in-development research emerged in the early 1970s through intersections of economic development, feminist theories, and cultural anthropology. It offers 'feminist corrections' to development studies and to economic modernization interventions, especially industrialization,

---

Story 6: Ellen Randall as (Post)Colonial Feninist

Ellen Randall is a very impressive figure. She has worked her way up the ranks to become president of a business unit with full bottom-line responsibility, taken over in tough situations and worked things out, and added executive stripes to her sleeve. She is obviously the one in charge, but she is also warm and open. She makes you think that she's going places, that you'll be reading about her future promotions in the *Wall Street Journal*. She's going to the top, you think. But Ellen's future doesn't look so bright to her. When she looks ahead, she senses no realistic possibility for further advancement in her corporation. Instead, she senses a wall, a barrier between her as a woman and a top job in her corporation. . . . A possible way to the top, she reasons, is to literally continue to go places; that is, to continue traveling on foreign assignments often. Or at least that's what she was thinking until her recent trip to Sri Lanka, to visit the newest company factory. There, while having lunch with several of the women workers, she realized how little she really understood how other women in the world dealt with their work situation, and how little information about this is available. These were, after all, poor factory workers doing unskilled work, so she should have known better. In fact, the reason that she went there was to assess whether the company was providing fair working conditions to these women, so that the company would avoid any scandal regarding Third World sweatshops. Now she is quite confused. These women have little respect for the company. They have created their own community-based groups that determine what and how they work and how they get paid. Their struggles and resistances are difficult to explain. It is not a unionized situation, but rather a sort of community action group, including men and women, of whom some work in the factory and some don't. And they seem to be quite powerful. Upon reflection, she senses that when she talked to the women about having some opportunities for advancement in the corporation, through some more education, they pretty much laughed at her. Somehow she feels that she might have it all wrong, and that her own notion and strategies for 'corporate advancement' are the wrong notion and the wrong strategies. Maybe this whole idea of combating 'the glass ceiling' is a way to become disempowered if she buys into it. Well, live and learn! She has to talk to her postcolonial feminist anthropologist friend, when she gets back home. Maybe Ellen Randall is a very oppressed figure!

in the Third World by First World development agencies. This literature focused initially on liberal feminists' concerns around women's access to development resources and technology (Warren and Bourque 1987; 1991). Recently, these original theoretical frameworks have changed upon recognition that the configurations of 'women' they deployed had more to do with images and issues of First World women than with other women's interests in the context of development around the world (e.g. Mohanty 1991a).

One such change is the feminization-of-technology approach based on radical feminism. Here the focus has been on instilling feminine values into development strategies that, according to Western theorists, were the strength of traditional cultures and traditional women before they were tainted by modern Western values (e.g. Bergom-Larsson 1982; Boulding 1981). But this approach articulates a universal 'natural woman(ness)' that exists mainly as a product of the Western (romantic) imagination – egalitarian, non-violent, and nurturing:

> This perspective dangerously romanticizes women's values, the family, the separation of 'domestic' and 'public' spheres, and the nature of Third World societies. One has only to look at the complex and various constructions of gender in contemporary societies, the negotiation of gender identities as they are realized in practice, and the interplay of family dynamics and legal systems to challenge these images of male and female. (Warren and Bourque 1991: 287)

A structural-dynamics approach to these issues is the global economy perspective, which produced a large amount of women-in-development literature during the 1980s (e.g. Benería and Sen 1986; Etienne and Leacock 1980; Fernández-Kelly 1983; 1987; 1989; Nash 1983; Nash and Safa 1985). Closer to socialist feminist analytical critiques, this literature links capitalism, colonialism, and gender stratification, and produces more complex explanations of their intersections. It reveals not just the effects of modernization but the changes and diverse social configurations that modernization produces. For instance, Benería and Roldán (1987) analyzed decentralized production in households in Mexico City as an effect of multinational industrialization. They noticed how this new relationship between the private (household) and public (workplace) spheres was not a panacea for women as, perhaps, the feminization-of-technology would have it. The work created in the households for women otherwise assumed to be 'unemployed' also produced a fragmented and cheaper labor force for the multinationals.

Other approaches, closer to postmodern theorizations, consider 'gender' not as a property but as a relationship which brings about redefinitions of subjectivities and subject positions over time, both as products and as producers of the social context (e.g. Mies 1982). For instance, in a recent reanalysis of the maquiladora industry during the 1980s, Fernández-Kelly (1994: 270) shows how changes in this industry (more men employed in maquiladoras now than in the past) are related to 'the atomization of the labor force on the basis of new gender definitions [which] has brought about the promise of personal and economic independence for women as well as greater equality between the sexes. But, as the example of workers in Mexico's maquiladora industry suggests, greater equality between men and women may be the result of deteriorating conditions for the former, not solely the effects of gains by the latter'.

More poststructuralist analyses have concentrated on how textualizations of women-in-development 'discursively colonize the material and historical heterogeneities of the lives of women in the third world, thereby producing/representing a composite, singular, 'third world woman'– an image . . . which carries with it the authorizing signature of Western humanist discourse' (Mohanty 1991a: 53). Thus 'Third World women' are constituted in representations that are 'a way of knowing and a way of not knowing, a way of talking about women and a way of silencing women from speaking about the experiences of their own lives' (Mueller, quoted in Escobar 1995: 180). Such deconstructions reveal the fictive character of development narratives that fashion and/or obliterate an/other world (see Mueller 1987a; 1987b; also Dorothy Smith 1987; 1990a; 1990b).

Such work demonstrates that the first step toward (post)colonial theorizations is a deconstructive move that emphasizes the problems of Western representations. The next step belongs to (post)colonial writings, which face the challenge of representing 'the other' through 'unknown' subjectivities. An important work in this case is Aihwa Ong's (1987) ethnography of women workers in Japanese factories in Malaysia. Inspired by Michel Foucault's work on resistance, Ong focuses on the production of new subjectivities as peasant women become transformed into 'docile bodies' who can adapt to factory life. She genealogizes the conditions that give way to these contemporary 'female factory workers', and notices how traditional social relations and the new disciplinary standards of the factory create a series of power relations which are not always on the side of the 'colonizer'. A form of resistance by women workers, for instance, was to become possessed by spirits and disrupt the work situation. This possession, based on local traditions, was one of many forms in which agency and representation intersected, fashioning very specific contemporary gender configurations outside First World understandings.

As already mentioned, other than women-in-development literature there is little organizational literature located in the nexus between gender and (post)colonial analyses (see also the NGO literature). Yet , more might appear in the near future as scholars from various parts of the world make their voices heard in Western publications in response to issues of globalization and transnationalization. For instance, in a symposium on women and (post)coloniality at the US Academy of Management, Chio (1993) fashioned a hybrid text to problematize the representation of women in international management scholarship in terms of how the researcher tries to represent 'the other'. In her heteroglossic writing, she portrays the refractive and multivocal subjectivities that appear as she tries to include herself in the very act of representation. At the same symposium, Holvino (1993) focused on the other side of the (post)colonial dilemma: when the colonized is 'home'. Inspired by Zavella's (1991) work, her deconstructive writings interrogated the discourse of organizational development with the voices of 'Chicana factory workers' in California. Also in that symposium, Calás (1993b) discussed the possibilities for organizational research offered by testimonial writings, warning about (mis)appropriations of these critical theorizations when 'translated' into (First World) organizational scholarship.

More recently, Mir et al. (1995) have problematized the representational space available for Third World women's subjectivities when the forces of Westernization and transnationalization coalesce with traditional patriarchal practices, such as female feticide and infanticide; while Calás (1992) analyzed the rhetorical strategies used in organizational research when representing 'Hispanic woman', and the silences that such representations produced.

CONCLUSIONS: IT'S NOT ONLY ABOUT 'GENDER' ANYMORE

As the Third World/(post)colonial arguments make obvious, what we have written so far in this chapter comes from a very specific time period and place in the world. As such, we don't believe anything we write today will 'withstand the test of time' or perhaps even endure until the next handbook of organization studies. After all, we don't believe in ahistorical, acultural, universals. But from *where we do stand today* we want to underscore that we consider feminist approaches to organization studies one of the few spaces left for reflecting upon and criticizing the excesses and violence of contemporary global capitalism, as it impacts many people all over the world.

One only needs to read recent popular business publications (e.g. *Business Week*, 1994, special issue on '21st century capitalism'; *Business Week* 15 August 1994, cover story on 'Inequality: how the gap between rich and poor hurts the economy'; *Business Week* 17 July 1995, cover story on 'Wages stagnant while profits are soaring'; *Newsweek* 1995) to notice not only that social inequities are growing, but that they have become naturalized by a discourse that reemphasizes inequality as a normal condition for societies the world over. Under these tenets even gender-justice approaches in liberal feminism might seem radical. Our interest, therefore, is to maintain a location from which to denaturalize these conditions and to continue questioning the discrimination and oppression caused by contemporary forms of capitalisms, often widely implicated in organization studies.

And so, as we attempt to produce in Table 4 an evaluative summary of the contributions of the various perspectives, we do so with a concern for their capacity to examine taken-for-granted organizational conditions which more and more seem to advantage the few at the expense of the many. As this summary shows, it's not only about 'gender' any more, as both women and men, from both First and Third Worlds, employed and unemployed, with and without families, struggle with inequality, injustice, inequity and intolerance.

Finally, we are writing these last lines at the time of the UN World Conference on Women in Beijing, as they address many of the concerns already voiced in this chapter. From this location, then, it seems only fitting that we echo Betty Friedan's words on the occasion of the Conference:

> The problems in our fast-changing social world require a new paradigm of social policy, transcending all 'identity politics'. . . . Pursuing the separate interests of women isn't adequate and is even diversionary. Instead, there has to be some new vision of community. We need to reframe the concept of success. . . . 'Women's issues' are symptoms of problems that affect everyone. . . . Our job now is to move beyond polarization to a notion of community that can unite us as decent

Table 4 *Contributions to contemporary organization studies from feminist theories*

Feminist approaches to organization studies	Contributions	Shortcomings
Liberal feminism/WIM	• Provides evidence of inequities, particularly economic inequities, using a symbol (statistics) that carries strong social and academic credibility. Forms basis for other perspectives • Counts what can be counted, e.g. distribution of bodies, incomes, positions • Needed to counter the claims that feminism has gone too far and to counter the thesis that 'more women will make it better', e.g. documents discrimination in pay and allocation of positions	• Liberal thought accepts hierarchical division of labor and inequality as givens. Overriding aim is 'getting women to the top' • Individualistic in orientation; sees the status of women as an issue of individual accomplishment; doesn't acknowledge power relations within capitalist economic and social systems • Presumes the existence of sex (and gender) as discrete and definable dichotomous variable with universal characteristics
Radical-cultural feminism/ alternative organizations	• Portrays possibilities and visions of alternative worlds outside of patriarchy • Offers 'consciousness raising' as a unique form of organizational research and practice, developing political power for all participants • Documents alternative practices and alternative organizations; provides specific examples of successful non-bureaucratic organizations	• Separatist strategy is utopian in so far as social reality does not foster the required conditions for ongoing 'womanspaces' • The radical/cultural politics it portrays might represent only white and middle class women's interests • Alternative organizations do not overcome the contradictions of being radical(izing) forms engaged in (more or less) capitalist practices • Essentializes 'gender' and 'woman', celebrating 'the feminine' over 'the masculine'. Reifies these characteristics and heightens their stereotypical aspects, obscuring many important differences arising from, for example, culture and history
Psychoanalytic feminism/women's ways of managing	• Highlights the importance of psychosexual development in the formation of patriarchal social structures, including research structures • Fosters changes in gender relations and child-rearing practices as a step toward reducing gendered social inequality • In intersection with cultural feminism, documents the possibility of positive organizational practices (and organizational research) located in women's unique psychosexual orientations and experiences, particularly those associated with caring, nurturing and relating to others	• The focus on psychosexual development reduces power dynamics to psychodynamics; it distracts from paying attention to material structural conditions that perpetuate gender inequality • The family relations it portrays might only apply to certain Western and privileged gender-race-class family relations • Its potential critical impact on the work/family organizational literature has been so far nil • In the organizational literature, the 'female advantage' approach reiterates,

continued overleaf

Table 4   *(continued)*

Feminist approaches to organization studies	Contributions	Shortcomings
		uncritically, conditions that seem to be the source of women's oppression; it objectifies 'women's ways' into instrumental organizational benefits – i.e. competitive advantage – depriving these approaches of their potential for changing organizational and social ethics and values
Socialist feminism/ gendering of organizations and organizing	• Incorporates central insights from Marxist, radical and psychoanalytic feminism and alleviates some of their limitations • Focuses on gender relations and sex-gender *system* (rather than sex or gender) as dynamic and processual power relations that produce/reproduce gendered social inequality • Addresses the private/public divide as a false dichotomy historically produced by interactions of patriarchy and capitalism • Strong theoretical and epistemological concerns are articulated through analytical concepts such as *standpoints*, located in power relations. Analyses are expanded beyond gender relations to address other social formations emerging from intersections of – for example – gender, race, and class • The focus on the intersections of production/reproduction under patriarchy and capitalism has provided several important theoretical frames for organizational analysis. These are particularly helpful in documenting the perpetuation of oppression through conventional organizational practices and social interactions	• Internal debates over the nature and origin of gender and social oppression (i.e. dual versus unified system) have often made theorists appear too focused on their ideological differences and academic arguments, to the detriment of the practical application of their theories, e.g. the importance of different analytical insights in uncovering causes of oppression • Its proposed remedies to social inequalities may appear naive and utopic, unless they are accompanied by major – and unlikely at this point in time – revolutionary social changes • In organization studies, these theories have not crossed over well from their sociological and European locations into the USA mainstream organizational gender literature. The incisive, complex and critical analyses do not mesh at all with the latter's liberal, positivist, behaviorist, and instrumental orientations
Poststructuralist feminism/postmodern feminist organizational analysis	• Focuses on the discursive nature of 'social reality' and 'subjectivity', and its inessential nature. Emphasis on language as a system of differences permits questioning the limits imposed upon 'knowledge' by certain privileged discourses • Allows for articulating the 'politics of knowledge' as a form of power relations that attempts to naturalize a system of exclusion for certain *subject positions* (e.g. gendered)	• The focus on language and discourse has often been criticized as untenable for feminist politics. The deconstructive emphasis questions the possibility of a positive ground for knowledge and a knowing subject • Pluralistic politics are not always considered strong enough for eliminating systems of exclusion and oppression historically and culturally located in patriarchal and capitalist arrangements

Table 4   *(continued)*

Feminist approaches to organization studies	Contributions	Shortcomings
	● Offers a more pluralistic view of political engagements, where 'gender' becomes only one argument among others. Provides more complex views of social location and structures of oppression ● Deconstructive and genealogical analyses provide an important strategy for demonstrating the limits of organizational discourse and the often gendered structures of those limits	● Critiques of deconstruction and other poststructuralist analyses include the charges that they are elitist, inaccessible and full of jargon, making it difficult to utilize by most analysts, despite the democratizing impetus that is among the aims of these analyses
Third World/ (post)colonial feminism/WID	● Problematizes the concept of 'gender' as constituted in the West and opens the possibility of other gendered configurations and more complex relations between women and men, in the context of multiple oppressions produced by global capitalism ● Extends the critique of Western knowledge beyond deconstruction by articulating other possible conceptualizations and subjectivities. Produces positive images of 'Third World subjects' capable of agency and representation. Strongly located in specific cultures and histories, and gender/race/class/ethnicity intersections ● Demonstrates the possibilities of political action and political pluralism within the micro-political confines of everyday (organizational) life ● Illustrates additional approaches for organizing residing outside Western views of 'organization'. These approaches are often exemplified in new social movements and new manifestations of popular culture emerging in several (post)colonial countries	● In some cases it is subject to the same critiques of elitism and lack of accessibility leveled at poststructuralist approaches ● Traditional West/rest 'politics of knowledge' might be played out in the context of 'Western feminism', i.e. rendering 'the other' voiceless and invisible ● Its 'beyond gender' arguments need to be carefully positioned within critiques of neo-colonialisms and global exploitation, otherwise they might lead to cooptation and trivialization of gendered issues and concerns ● In organizational studies it seems to be particularly troublesome even for those who acknowledge their sympathies for postmodern feminism. There are concerns about accepting the existence of 'other knowledges' outside the bounds of 'Western(ized) knowledge'

people. Are women strong enough to join and even lead men in finding that new vision? (Friedan 1995: 31–2)

To which we respond: only if we are strong enough to challenge conventional notions of organization, their ethics and values; that is, if we are strong enough to challenge and change the dominant and colonizing organizational *discourse,* over and over again. That is the aim of this chapter.

NOTES

We are grateful to Jill Woodilla and Deborah Litvin for their assistance with research for this chapter. We also want to thank Deb Meyerson, Patricia Y. Martin, and Joyce Rothschild for sharing research materials with us. Many of the ideas we develop here had their beginnings in the course of our collaborations with Sarah Williams Jacobson and Roy Jacques. Finally, we acknowledge the extreme patience and helpfulness of the *Handbook* editors, in particular Cynthia Hardy and Sage's Sue Jones.

1 A core insight in Saussurean linguistics is the contingent relationship between signifier and signified. That is, from this perspective the sign that we use to signify anything is only meaningful because we are able to *differentiate* it from another sign rather than because it *names* any essential object or concept. Once this is accepted, the priority of language over thought is established, for language is thus *constitutive* of the things we can think/know rather than *representative* of that which we know.

2 Tom Stoppard's contemporary play, *Indian Ink*, provides a wonderful portrayal of the problems that representing the colonized causes/caused to the colonizer.

REFERENCES

Aaltio-Marjosola, Iiris (1994) 'Gender stereotypes as cultural products of the organization', *Scandinavian Journal of Management*, 10(2): 147–62.

Abel, Elizabeth (1990) 'Race, class, and psychoanalysis? Opening questions', in Marianne Hirsch and Evelyn Fox Keller (eds), *Conflicts in Feminism*. New York: Routledge. pp. 184–204.

Acker, Joan (1989) *Doing Comparable Worth*. Philadelphia: Temple University Press.

Acker, Joan (1990) 'Hierarchies, jobs, bodies: a theory of gendered organizations', *Gender & Society*, 4(2): 139–58.

Acker, Joan (1994) 'The gender regime of Swedish banks', *Scandinavian Journal of Management*, 10(2): 117–30.

Acker, Joan and Van Houten, Donald R. (1974) 'Differential recruitment and control: the sex structuring of organizations', *Administrative Science Quarterly*, 152–63.

Acosta-Belén, Edna and Bose, Christine E. (1990) 'From structural subordination to empowerment: women and development in Third World contexts', *Gender & Society*, 4(3): 299–320.

Adams, Jerome, Rice, Robert W. and Instone, Debra (1984) 'Follower attitudes toward women and judgements concerning performance by female and male leaders', *Academy of Management Journal*, 27(3): 636–43.

Adler, Nancy and Izraeli, Dafna (eds) (1988) *Woman in Management Worldwide*. Armonk, NY: M.E. Sharpe.

Adler, Nancy and Izraeli, Dafna (eds) (1994) *Competitive Frontiers: Women Managers in a Global-Economy*. Cambridge, MA: Blackwell.

Alcoff, Linda (1988) 'Cultural feminism versus post structuralism: the identity crisis in feminist theory', *Signs*, 13(3): 405–36.

Alpern, Sara (1993) 'In the beginning: a history of women in management', in Ellen A. Fagenson (ed.), *Women in Management: Trends, Issues, and Challenges in Managerial Diversity*. Newbury Park, CA: Sage. pp. 19–51.

Anzaldúa, Gloria (ed.) (1990) *Making Face, Making Soul: Haciendo Caras*. San Francisco: Aunt Lute.

Auster, E. (1989) 'Task characteristics as a bridge between macro- and microlevel research on salary inequality between men and women', *Academy of Management Review*, 14: 173–93.

Ayers-Nachamkin, Beverly, Cann, Carlton H. and Reed, Rosemary (1982) 'Sex and ethnic differences in the use of power', *Journal of Applied Psychology*, 67(4): 454–71.

Baker, Andrea J. (1982) 'The problem of authority in radical movement groups: a case study of lesbian-feminist organization', *Journal of Applied Behavioral Science*, 18(2): 323–41.

Balsamo, Anne (1985) 'Beyond female as variable: constructing a feminist perspective on organizational analysis'. Paper presented at the Critical Perspectives in Organizational Analysis Conference, Baruch College, SUNY, 5–7 September.

Bambara, Toni Cade (ed.) (1970) *The Black Woman: an Anthology*. New York: New American Library.

Barclay, Lizabeth (1982) 'Social learning theory: a framework for discrimination research', *Academy of Management Review*, 7(4): 587–94.

Barling, Julian and Rosenbaum, Alan (1986) 'Work stressors and wife abuse', *Journal of Applied Psychology*, 71(2): 346–8.

Barnard, Chester I. (1938) *The Functions of the Executive*. Cambridge, MA: Harvard University Press.

Bartol, Kathryn M. (1978) 'The sex structuring of organizations: a search for possible causes', *Academy of Management Review*, 3(4): 805–15.

Belenky, M.F., Clincy, B.M., Goldberger, N.R. and Tarule, J.M. (1986) *Women's Ways of Knowing*. New York: Basic Books.

Bell, Ella L. (1990) 'The bicultural life experience of career-oriented black women', *Journal of Organizational Behavior*, 11: 459–77.

Bell, Ella L., Denton, Toni C. and Nkomo, Stella (1993) 'Women of color: toward an inclusive analysis', in Ellen A. Fagenson (ed.), *Women in Management: Trends, Issues and Challenges in Managerial Diversity*. Newbury Park, CA: Sage. pp. 105–30.

Bem, S.L. (1976) 'Probing the promise of androgyny', in A.G. Kaplan and J.P. Bean (eds), *Beyond Sex-Role Stereotypes: Readings Toward a Psychology of Androgyny*. Boston: Little Brown.

Benería, Lourdes and Roldán, Martha (1987) *The Crossroads of Class and Gender: Industrial Homework, Subcontracting, and Household Dynamics in Mexico City*. Chicago: University of Chicago Press.

Benería, Lourdes and Sen, Gita (1986) 'Accumulation, reproduction, and women's role in economic development: Boserup revisited', in Eleanor

Leacock and Helen I. Safa (eds), *Women's Work: Development and the Division of Labor Gender.* South Hadley, MA: Bergin and Garvey. pp. 141–57.

Benhabib, S. (1984) 'Epistemologies of postmodernism: a rejoinder to Jean-Francois Lyotard', *New German Critique*, 33: 103–26.

Benschop, Yvonne and Doorewaard, Hans (1995) 'Covered by equality: the gendered subtext of organizations'. Unpublished manuscript, University of Nijmegen, The Netherlands.

Bergmann, Barbara R. (1995) 'Probing the opposition to affirmative action', *Gender, Work and Organization*, 2(2): 88–94.

Bergom-Larsson, Maria (1982) 'Women and technology in the industrialized countries', in Pamela M. D'Onofrio-Flores and Sheila M. Pfafflin (eds), *Scientific Technological Change and the Role of Women in Development.* Boulder, CO: Westview Press. pp. 29–75.

Berthoin-Antal, Ariane and Izraeli, Dafna N. (1993) 'A global comparison of women in management: women managers in their homelands and as expatriates', in Ellen A. Fagenson (ed.), *Women in Management: Trends, Issues, and Challenges in Managerial Diversity.* Newbury Park, CA: Sage. pp. 52–96.

Betters-Reed, Bonnie and Moore, Lynda L. (1991) 'Managing diversity: focusing on women and the whitewash dilemma', in Uma Sekaran and Frederick Leong (eds), *Womanpower: Managing in Times of Demographic Turbulence.* Newbury Park, CA: Sage.

Beutell, Nicholas J. and Greenhaus, Jeffrey H. (1983) 'Integration of home and nonhome roles: women's conflict and coping behavior', *Journal of Applied Psychology*, 68(1): 43–8.

Bhabha, Homi (1985) 'Signs taken for wonders: questions of ambivalence and authority under a tree outside Delhi, May 1817', *Critical Inquiry*, 12(1): 144–65.

Bhabha, Homi (1988) 'The commitment to theory', *New Formations*, 5: 5–23.

Bhabha, Homi (ed.) (1990) *Nation and Narration.* London: Routledge.

Bielby, William T. and Baron, James N. (1987) 'Undoing discrimination: job integrations and comparable worth', in Christine Bose and Glenna Spitze (eds), *Ingredients for Women's Employment Policy.* Albany, NY: State University of New York Press. pp. 211–29.

Billing, Yvonne Due and Alvesson, Mats (1993) *Gender, Managers and Organizations.* Berlin: Walter de Gruyter.

Blau, Francine and Ferber, Marianne A. (1986) *The Economics of Women, Men, and Work.* New York: Prentice-Hall.

Blum, Linda and Smith, Vicki (1988) 'Women's mobility in the corporation: a critique of the politics of optimism', *Signs*, 13(3): 528–45.

Bordo, Susan (1990) 'Feminism, postmodernism, and gender-scepticism', in L.J. Nicholson (ed.), *Feminism/Postmodernism.* London: Routledge. pp. 133–56.

Boulding, Elise (1981) 'Integration into what? Reflections on development planning for women', in Roslyn Dauber and Melinda L. Cain (eds), *Women and Technological Change in Developing Countries.* Boulder, CO: Westview Press. pp. 9–30.

Bowen, Donald D. and Hisrich, Robert D. (1986) 'The female entrepreneur: a career development perspective', *Academy of Management Review*, 11(2): 393–407.

Bowman, G.W., Worthy, N.B. and Greyser, S.A. (1965) 'Are women executives people?', *Harvard Business Review*, 43 (July–August): 14–178 (not continuous).

Braidotti, Rosi (1989) 'The politics of ontological difference', in Teresa Brennan (ed.), *Between Feminism and Psychoanalysis.* London: Routledge. pp. 97–8.

Brennan, Teresa (ed.) (1989) *Between Feminism and Psychoanalysis.* London: Routledge.

Brenner, Johanna (1987) 'Feminist political discourses: radical vs. liberal approaches to the feminization of poverty and comparable worth', *Gender & Society*, 1(4): 447–65.

Brenner, O.C. (1982) 'Relationship of education to sex, managerial status, and the managerial stereotype', *Journal of Applied Psychology*, 67(3): 380–3.

Bristor, Julia M. and Fischer, Eileen (1993) 'Feminist thought: implications for consumer research', *Journal of Consumer Research*, 19(March): 518–36.

Brockner, Joel and Adsit, Laury (1986) 'The moderating impact of sex on the equity-satisfaction relationship: a field study', *Journal of Applied Psychology*, 71(4): 585–90.

Brown, Clair and Pechman, Joseph A. (eds) (1987) *Gender in the Workplace.* Washington, DC: Brookings Institution.

Brown, Helen (1992) *Women Organizing.* London: Routledge.

Brown, Linda Keller (1979) 'Woman and business management', *Signs*, 5(2): 266–88.

Bruning, Nealia S. and Snyder, Robert A. (1983) 'Sex and position as predictors of organizational commitment', *Academy of Management Journal*, 26(3): 485–91.

Business Week (1994) (Special issue) '21st century capitalism'.

Business Week 'Inequity and the growing gap between rich and poor in America', 15 August 1994.

Business Week 'Wages Stagnant while Profits are Soaring' 17 July 1995.

Butler, J. and Scott, J.W. (eds) (1992) *Feminists Theorize the Political.* New York: Routledge.

Butterfield, D. Anthony and Powell, Gary N. (1981) 'Effect of group performance, leader sex, and rater sex on ratings of leader behavior', *Organizational Behavior and Human Performance*, 28(1): 129–41.

Buzzanell, Patrice M. (forthcoming) 'The social construction of the glass ceiling', *Communication Monographs*, 62(4).

Calás, Marta B. (1992) 'An/other silent voice? Representing "Hispanic woman" in organizational texts', in Albert J. Mills and Peta Tancred (eds), *Gendering Organizational Analysis*. Newbury Park, CA: Sage. pp. 201–21.

Calás, Marta B. (1993a) 'Deconstructing charismatic leadership: re-reading Weber from the darker side', *Leadership Quarterly*, 4(3/4): 305–28.

Calás, Marta B. (1993b) 'Testimonios de mis hermanas: research approaches from the Third World'. Paper presented at the National Meeting of the Academy of Management, Atlanta, August.

Calás, Marta B. and Jacques, Roy (1988) 'Diversity or conformity? Research by women on women or organizations'. Paper presented at the Seventh Annual Conference on Women and Organizations, Long Beach, CA, August.

Calás, Marta B. and Smircich, L. (1991) 'Voicing seduction to silence leadership', *Organization Studies*, 12(4): 567–602.

Calás, Marta B. and Smircich, L. (1992) 'Rewriting gender in organization theory', in M. Read and M. Hughes (eds), *Rethinking Organizations*. London: Sage.

Calás, Marta B. and Smircich, Linda (1993) 'Dangerous liaisons: the "feminine-in-management" meets globalization', *Business Horizons*, March/April: 71–81.

Calás, Marta B. and Smircich, Linda (forthcoming) 'Predicando la moral en calzoncillos? Feminist inquiries into business ethics', in R. Edward Freeman and Andrea Larson (eds), *Business Ethics and Women's Studies*. Oxford: Oxford University Press.

Calás, Marta B., Jacobson, S., Jacques, R. and Smircich, L. (1990) 'Is a woman centered theory of management dangerous?' Paper presented at the Annual Meetings of the Academy of Management, Miami, August.

Calvert, Linda McGee and Ramsey, V. Jean (1992) 'Bringing women's voice to research on women in management: a feminist perspective', *Journal of Management-Inquiry*, 1(1): 79–88.

Capper, Colleen A. (1992) 'A feminist poststructural analysis of non-traditional approaches in education administration', *Educational Administration Quarterly*, 28(1): 103–24.

Chacko, Thomas I. (1982) Women and equal employment opportunity: some unintended effects', *Journal of Applied Psychology*, 67(1): 119–23.

Chapman, J. Brad (1975) 'Comparison of male and female leadership styles', *Academy of Management Journal*, 18(3): 645–50.

Chio, Vanessa (1993) 'In search of a bridge to a bare wooden-floored stilthouse in Penampang'. Paper presented at the National Meeting of the Academy of Management, Atlanta, August.

Chodorow, Nancy (1978) *The Reproduction of Mothering*. Berkeley, CA: University of California Press.

Cholmeley, Jane (1991) 'A feminist business in a capitalist world', in N. Redclift and M.T. Sinclair (eds), *Working Women: International Perspectives on Labour and Gender Ideology*. London: Routledge. pp. 213–32.

Chusmir, Leonard H. (1982) 'Job commitment and the organizational woman', *Academy of Management Review*, 7(4): 595–602.

Cixous, Hélène and Clément, Catherine (1986) *The Newly Born Woman*. Minneapolis: University of Minnesota Press.

Cleveland, Jeanette N. and Landy, Frank J. (1983) 'The effects of person and job stereotypes on two personnel decisions', *Journal of Applied Psychology*, 68(4): 609–19.

Cockburn, Cynthia (1983) *Brothers: Male Domination and Change*. London: Pluto.

Cockburn, Cynthia (1985) *Machinery of Dominance*. London: Pluto.

Cockburn, Cynthia (1991) *In the Way of Women: Men's Resistance to Sex Equality in Organizations*. London: Macmillan.

Collins, Patricia Hill (1990) *Black Feminist Thought*. New York: Routledge.

Collinson, David (1988) '"Engineering humour": masculinity, joking, and conflict in shop-floor relations', *Organization Studies*, 9(2): 181–99.

Collinson, David and Hearn, Jeff (1994) 'Naming men as men: implications for work, organization and management', *Gender, Work and Organization*, 1(1): 2–22.

Collinson, David and Hearn, J. (eds) (1996) *Men as Managers, Managers as Men: Critical Perspectives on Men, Masculinities and Managements*. London: Sage.

Collinson, David and Knights, D. (1986) '"Men only": theories and practices of job segregation in insurance', in D. Knights and H. Willmott (eds), *Gender and the Labour Process*. Aldershot: Gower. pp. 140–78.

Collinson, David, Knights, D. and Collinson, M. (1990) *Managing to Discriminate*. London: Routledge.

Connell, R.W. (1995) *Masculinities*. Berkeley: University of California Press.

Cooper, E.A. and Barrett, G.V. (1984) 'Equal pay and gender: implications of court cases for personnel practices', *Academy of Management Review*, 9(1).

Cox, Taylor and Blake, Stacey (1991) 'Managing cultural diversity: implications for organizational effectiveness', *Academy of Management Executive*, 5(3): 45–56.

Cox, Taylor Jr and Nkomo, Stella (1990) 'Invisible men and women: a status report on race as a variable in organization behavior', *Journal of Organizational Behavior*, 11: 419–31.

Crompton, Rosemary and Sanderson, Kay (1990)

Gendered Jobs and Social Change. London: Unwin Hyman.

Cullen, Dallas (1994) 'Feminism, management and self-actualization', *Gender, Work and Organization*, 1(5): 127–37.

Daly, Mary (1978) *Gyn/Ecology*. Boston: Beacon.

Davidson, M.J. and Cooper, C.L. (eds) (1984) *Working Women: an International Survey*. Chichester: Wiley.

De Beauvoir, Simone (1972) *The Second Sex* (1949). Harmondsworth, Middlesex: Penguin.

Deckard, Barbara S. (1979) *The Women's Movement*. New York: Harper and Row.

De Lauretis, Teresa (1984) *Alice Doesn't: Feminism, Semiotics and Cinema*. Bloomington, IN: University of Indiana Press.

De Lauretis, Teresa (1987) *Technologies of Gender*. Bloomington, IN: Indiana University Press.

Derrida, Jacques (1976) *Of Grammatology*. Baltimore: Johns Hopkins University Press.

De Saussure, Ferdinand (1966) *Course in General Linguistics*. New York: McGraw-Hill.

Diamond, I. and Quinby, L. (eds) (1988) *Feminism and Foucault*. Boston: Northeastern University Press.

Dill, Bonnie Thornton (1983) 'Race, class, and gender: prospects for all-inclusive sisterhood', *Feminist Studies*, 9: 131–50.

Dinnerstein, Dorothy (1977) *The Mermaid and the Minotaur: Sexual Arrangements and Human Malaise*. New York: Harper.

Di Stefano, Christine (1988) 'Dilemmas of difference: feminism, modernity, and postmodernism', *Women and Politics*, 8(3/4): 1–24.

Dobbins, Gregory H. and Platz, Stephanie J. (1986) 'Sex differences in leadership: how real are they?', *Academy of Management Review*, 11(1): 118–27.

Eagly, Alice H., Makhijani, Mona G. and Klonsky, Bruce G. (1992) 'Gender and the evaluation of leaders: a meta-analysis', *Psychological Bulletin*, 111(1): 3–22.

Echols, Alice (1983) 'The new feminism of yin and yang', in Ann Snitow, Christine Stansell and Sharon Thompson (eds), *Powers of Desire: the Politics of Sexuality*. New York: Monthly Review Press. pp. 430–59.

Eisenstein, Hester (1983) *Contemporary Feminist Thought*. Boston: G.K. Hall.

Ely, Robin J. (1995) 'The power in demography: women's social constructions of gender identity at work', *Academy of Management Journal*, 38(3): 589–634.

Epstein, Sara, Russell, Glenda, and Silvern, Louise (1988) 'Structure and ideology of shelters for battered women', *American Journal of Community Psychology*, 16(3): 345–67.

Escobar, Arturo (1995) *Encountering Development*. Princeton: Princeton University Press.

Etienne, M. and Leacock, E. (eds) (1980) *Women and Colonialization*. New York: Praeger.

Fagenson, E. (ed.) (1993) *Women in Management: Trends, Issues and Challenges in Managerial Diversity*. Newbury Park, CA: Sage.

Faludi, Susan (1991) *Backlash*. New York: Anchor Books.

Farrell, Amy Erdman (1994) 'A social experiment in publishing: *Ms* magazine, 1972–1989', *Human Relations*, 47(6): 707–30.

Feldberg, Roslyn (1984) 'Comparable worth: toward theory and practice in the United States', *Signs*, 10: 311–28.

Ferguson, Ann (1977) 'Androgyny as an ideal for human development', in Mary Vetterling-Braggin, Frederick Elliston and Jane English (eds), *Feminism and Philosophy*. Totowa, NJ: Littlefield, Adams. pp. 45–69.

Ferguson, Ann (1989) *Blood at the Root*. London: Pandora.

Ferguson, Ann and Folbre, Nancy (1981) 'The unhappy marriage of capitalism and patriarchy', in Lydia Sargent (ed.), *Women and Revolution*. Boston: South End. pp. 313–38.

Ferguson, Kathy E. (1984) *The Feminist Case against Bureaucracy*. Philadelphia: Temple University Press.

Ferguson, Kathy E. (1993) *The Man Question: Visions of Subjectivity in Feminist Theory*. Berkeley, CA: University of California Press.

Ferguson, Kathy E. (1994) 'On bringing more theory, more voices and more politics to the study of organization', *Organization*, 1(1): 81–99.

Fernández-Kelly, Maria Patricia (1983) *For We Are Sold, I and My People: Women and Industry in Mexico's Frontier*. Albany, NY: State University of New York Press.

Fernández-Kelly, Maria Patricia (1987) 'Technology and employment along the US–Mexico border', in Cathryn L. Thorup (ed.), *The United States of Mexico: Face to Face with New Technology*. New Brunswick, NJ: Transaction Press.

Fernández-Kelly, Maria Patricia (1989) 'Broadening the scope: gender and international economic development', *Sociological Forum*, 4(4): 611–35.

Fernández-Kelly, Maria Patricia (1994) 'Making sense of gender in the world economy', *Organization*, 1(2): 249–75.

Ferree, Myra M. and Martin, Patricia Y. (eds) (1995) *Feminist Organizations: Harvest of the New Women's Movement*. Philadelphia: Temple University Press.

Firestone, Shulamith (1970) *The Dialectic of Sex*. New York: Morrow.

Fischer, Eileen and Bristor, Julia (1994) 'A feminist post-structural analysis of the rhetoric of marketing relationships', *International Journal of Research in Marketing*, 11: 317–31.

Flax, Jane (1983) 'Political philosophy and the patriarched unconscious: a psychoanalytic perspective on epistemology and metaphysics', in Sandra Harding and Merrill B. Hintikka (eds), *Discovering Reality*. Dordrecht, Holland: D. Reidel. pp. 245–81.

Flax, Jane (1987) 'Postmodern and gender relations in feminist theory', *Signs*, 16(2): 621–43.

Flax, Jane (1990) *Thinking Fragments: Psychoanalysis, Feminism, and Postmodernism in the Contemporary West*. Berkeley, CA: University of California Press.

Fletcher, Joyce (1994a) 'Castrating the female advantage: feminist standpoint research and management science', *Journal of Management Inquiry*, 3(1): 74–82.

Fletcher, Joyce (1994b) 'Toward a theory of relational practice in organizations: a feminist reconstruction of "real" work'. Doctoral dissertation, Boston University.

Folbre, Nancy (1985) 'The pauperization of motherhood: patriarchy and public policy in the US', *Review of Radical Political Economics*, 16(4): 72–88.

Folbre, Nancy (1987) 'Patriarchy as a mode of production', in Randy Albelda, Christopher Gunn and William Walker (eds), *Alternatives to Economic Orthodoxy*. New York: M.E. Sharpe. pp. 323–38.

Folbre, Nancy (1994) *Who Pays for the Kids?* London: Routledge.

Follett, Mary Parker (1951) *Creative Experience*. New York: Peter Smith. (Reprint of 1924 edition.)

Forsythe, Sandra, Drake, Mary Frances and Cox, Charles E. (1985) 'Influence of applicant's dress on interviewer's selection decisions', *Journal of Applied Psychology*, 70(2): 374–8.

Fortune (August, 1935) 'Women in business: II being a commentary upon the great American office and the distinction between the girl who works to marry and the girl who marries to work', pp. 50–86.

Fortune (September, 1935) 'Women in business: III sixteen exceptions to prove the rule that woman's place is not in the executive's chair', pp. 81–91.

Foucault, Michel (1977) *Discipline and Punish*.

Foucault, Michel (1980) *The History of Sexuality*. New York: Vintage.

Fraad, H., Resnick, S. and Wolff, R. (1989) 'For every knight in shining armor, there's a castle waiting to be cleaned: a Marxist-feminist analysis of the household', *Rethinking Marxism*, 2(4): 9–69.

Franco, Jean (1992) 'Going public: reinhabiting the private', in George Yudice, Jean Franco and Juan Flores (eds), *On Edge: The Crisis of Contemporary Latin American Culture*. Minneapolis: University of Minnesota Press. pp. 65–83.

Fraser, Nancy and Nicholson, Linda J. (1988) 'Social criticism without philosophy: an encounter between feminism and postmodernism', *Theory, Culture, and Society*, 5(2/3): 373–94.

Freedman, Sara M. and Phillips, James S. (1988) 'The changing nature of research on women at work', *Journal of Management*, 14(2): 231–51.

Freeman, Sue J.M. (1990) *Managing Lives: Corporate Women and Social Change*. Amherst, MA: University of Massachusetts Press.

Friedan, Betty (1963) *The Feminine Mystique*. New York: Dell.

Friedan, Betty (1981) *The Second Stage*. New York: Summit.

Friedan, Betty (1995) 'Beyond gender', *Newsweek*, 4 September: 30–2.

Frye, Marilyn (1983) *The Politics of Reality*. Freedom, CA: Crossing Press.

Gallos, J.V. (1989) 'Exploring women's development: implications for career theory, practice and research', in M.B. Arthur, D.T. Hall and B.S. Lawrence (eds), *Handbook of Career Theory*. Boston: Cambridge University Press. pp. 110–32.

Game, Ann and Pringle, Rosemary (1984) *Gender at Work*. London: Pluto.

García-Canclini, Nestor (1990) *Culturas Hibridas: Estradegias para Entrar y Salir de las Modernidad*. Mexico: Grijalbo.

Gender, Work and Organization (July 1995) 'Special Issue: The Economics of Equal Opportunities', 2(3): 99–156.

Gherardi, Silvia (1994) 'The gender we think, the gender we do in our everyday organizational lives', *Human Relations*, 47(6): 591–610.

Gherardi, Silvia (1995) *Gender, Symbolism and Organizational Culture*. London: Sage.

Gibson, Katherine (1992) 'Hewers of cake and drawers of tea: women, industrial restructuring, and class processes on the coalfields of Central Queensland', *Rethinking Marxism*, Winter, 5(4): 29–56.

Giddings, Paula (1984) *When and Where I Enter: the Impact of Black Women on Race and Sex in America*. New York: Bantam.

Gilbreth, Lillian (1967/1926) *What's Ahead for Management?* New York: Kraus Reprint of New York: American.

Gilligan, Carol (1982) *In a Different Voice*. Cambridge, MA: Harvard University Press.

Gordon, Francine E. (1974) 'Self-image and stereotypes of femininity – their relation to women's role conflicts and coping', *Journal of Applied Psychology*, 59(2): 241–3.

Grams, R. and Schwab, D.P. (1985) 'An investigation of systematic gender-related error in job evaluation', *Academy of Management Journal*, 28(2).

Grant, Jan (1986) 'Women as managers: what they can offer to organizations', *Organizational Dynamics*, 56–63.

Gray, Barbara (1994) 'A feminist critique of Collaborating', *Journal of Management Inquiry*, 3(3): 286–93.

Gutek, B.A. and Larwood, L. (eds) (1987) *Women's Career Development*. Newbury Park, CA: Sage.

Gutek, B.A. and Morasch, B. (1982) 'Sex-ratios, sex role spillover, and sexual harassment of women at work', *Journal of Social Issues*, 38: 55–74.

Hall, Elaine J. (1993) 'Smiling, deferring, and flirting: doing gender by giving "good service"', *Work and Occupations*, 20(4): 452–71.

Hall, Francine S. and Hall, Douglas T. (1976) 'Effects of job incumbent's race and sex on evaluations of managerial performance', *Academy of Management Journal*, 19(3): 476–81.

Haraway, Donna (1985) 'A manifesto for cyborgs: science, technology, and socialist feminism in the 1980s', *Socialist Review*, 80: 65–107.

Harding, Sandra (1986) *The Science Question in Feminism*. Ithaca, NY: Cornell University Press.

Harding, Sandra (1990) 'Feminism, science, and the anti-Enlightenment critiques', in L.J. Nicholson (ed.), *Feminism/Postmodernism*. London: Routledge. pp. 83–106.

Harding, Sandra (1991) *Whose Science? Whose Knowledge?* Ithaca, NY: Cornell University Press.

Harding, S. and Hintikka, M. (eds) (1983) *Discovering Reality: Feminist Perspectives on Epistemology, Metaphysics, Methodology, and Philosophy of Science*. Dordrecht, Holland: D. Reidel.

Haring-Hidore, M., Freeman, S.C. Phelps, S., Spann, N. and Wooten, R. (1990) 'Women administrators' ways of knowing', *Education and Urban Society*, 22(2): 170–81.

Hartmann, Heidi (1976) 'Capitalism, patriarchy, and job segregation by sex', *Signs*, 1(3), part 2: 773–6.

Hartmann, Heidi (1981a) 'The family as the locus of gender, class, and political struggle: the example of housework', *Signs*, 6(3): 366–94.

Hartmann, Heidi (1981b) 'The unhappy marriage of Marxism and feminism: towards a more progressive union', in Lydia Sargent (ed.), *Women and Revolution*. Boston: South End Press. pp. 1–41.

Hartsock, Nancy (1983) 'The feminist standpoint: developing the ground for a specifically feminist historical materialism', in Sandra Harding and Merrill B. Hintikka (eds), *Discovering Reality*. Dordrecht: D. Reidel. pp. 283–310.

Hearn, J. and Parkin, P.W. (1987) *'Sex' at 'Work'*. New York: St. Martin's Press.

Hearn, J., Sheppard, D., Tancred-Sheriff, P. and Burrell, G. (eds) (1989) *The Sexuality of Organization*. London: Sage.

Heilman, Madeline E. and Herlihy, Joyce Mardenfeld (1984) 'Affirmative action, negative reaction? Some moderating conditions', *Organizational Behavior and Human Performance*, 33(2): 204–13.

Heilman, Madeline E. and Martell, R.F. (1986) 'Exposure to successful women: antidote to sex discrimination in applicant screening decisions', *Organizational Behavior and Human Decision Processes*, 37: 376–90.

Heilman, Madeline E. and Stopeck, M.H. (1985) 'Being attractive, advantage or disadvantage? Performance based evaluations and recommended personnel actions as a function of appearance, sex, and job type', *Organizational Behavior and Decision Processes*, 35: 202–15.

Helgesen, Sally (1990) *The Female Advantage: Women's Ways of Leadership*. New York: Doubleday.

Hennig, M. and Jardim, A. (1977) *The Managerial Woman*. New York: Pocket Books.

Holvino, Evangelina (1993) 'The Chicana worker meets OD: a deconstructive reading of *Productive Workplaces*'. Paper presented at the National Meeting of the Academy of Management, Atlanta, August.

Holvino, Evangelina (1994) 'Women of color in organizations: revising our models of gender at work', in Elsie Y. Cross, Judith H. Katz, Frederick A. Miller and Edith W. Seashore (eds), *The Promise of Diversity*. New York: Irwin. pp. 52–9.

hooks, b. (1981) *Ain't I a Woman*. Boston: South End Press.

hooks, B. (1984) *Feminist Theory: from Margin to Center*. Boston: South End Press.

Horner, Matina (1972) 'Toward an understanding of achievement-related conflicts in women', *Journal of Social Issues*, 28(2): 157–76.

Horney, Karen (1974) *Feminine Psychology*. New York: W.W. Norton.

Hull, Gloria T., Scott, Patricia Dell and Smith, Barbara (eds) (1982) *But Some of Us Are Brave*. Old Westbury, NY: Feminist Press.

Hunt, David Marshall and Michael, Carol (1983) 'Mentorship: a career training and development tool', *Academy of Management Review*, 8(3): 475–85.

Hyde, Cheryl (1989) 'A feminist model for macro-practice: promises and problems', *Administration in Social Work*, 13(3/4): 145–81.

Iannello, Kathleen (1992) *Decisions without Hierarchy: Feminist Interventions in Organization Theory and Practice*. London: Routledge.

Ibarra, Herminia (1992) 'Homophily and differential returns: sex differences in network structure and access in an advertising firm', *Administrative Science Quarterly*, 37: 422–47.

Ilgen, Daniel R. and Terborg, James R. (1975) 'Sex discrimination and sex-role stereotypes – are they synonymous – no', *Organizational Behavior and Human Performance*, 14(1): 154–7.

Irigaray, Luce (1985a) *Speculum of the Other Woman* (1974), translated by Gillian C. Gill. Ithaca, NY: Cornell University Press.

Irigaray, Luce (1985b) *This Sex Which Is Not One* (1985), translated by Catherine Porter. Ithaca, NY: Cornell University Press.

Jackson, B.W. and Holvino, Evangelina (1986) 'Working with multicultural organizations: matching theory and practice', in *Proceedings of the OD Network Conference*. New York: OD Network. pp. 84–96.

Jacobs, Jerry A. (1992) 'Women's entry into management: trends in earnings, authority, and values among salaried managers', *Administrative Science Quarterly*, 37: 282–301.

Jacobson, Sarah Williams and Jacques, Roy (1989a) 'Feminism(s) and organization studies: possible contributions to theory from women's experiences'. Unpublished manuscript, University of Massachusetts, Amherst.

Jacobson, Sarah Williams and Jacques, Roy (1989b) 'Beyond androgyny: future direction for gender research'. Paper presented at the National Meeting of the Academy of Management, Washington, DC, August.

Jacques, Roy (1992) 'Critique and theory building: producing knowledge "from the kitchen"', *Academy of Management Review*, 17(3): 582–606.

Jaggar, Allison M. (1983) *Feminist Politics and Human Nature*. Totowa, NJ: Rowman and Allanheld.

Jago, Arthur G. and Vroom, Victor H. (1982) 'Sex differences in the incidence and evaluation of participative leader behavior', *Journal of Applied Psychology*, 67(6): 776–83.

Jardine, A.A. (1985) *Gynesis*. Ithaca, NY: Cornell University Press.

Jelinek, Mariann and Adler, Nancy J. (1988) 'Women: world class managers for global competition', *Academy of Management Executive*, 2(1): 11–19.

Jick, Todd D. and Mitz, Linda F. (1985) 'Sex differences in work stress', *Academy of Management Review*, 10(3): 408–20.

Jones, Carol and Causer, Gordon (1995) '"Men don't have families": equality and motherhood in technical employment', *Gender, Work and Organization*, 2(2): 51–62.

Joreen (1973) 'The tyranny of structurelessness', in A. Koedt, E. Levine and A. Rapone (eds), *Radical Feminism*. New York: Quadrangle Books. pp. 285–99.

Joseph, Gloria and Lewis, Jill (1981) *Common Differences: Conflicts in Black and White Feminist Perspectives*. New York: Anchor.

Kanter, Rosabeth Moss (1977) *Men and Women of the Corporation*. New York: Basic Books.

Kerfoot, Deborah and Knights, David (1993) 'Management, masculinity and manipulation: from paternalism to corporate strategy in financial services in Britain', *Journal of Management Studies*, 30(4): 659–77.

Klein, Melanie (1965) *Contributions to Psycho Analysis: 1921–1945*. London: Hogarth Press.

Koedt, A., Levine, E. and Rapone, A. (eds) (1973) *Radical Feminism*. New York: Quadrangle Books.

Koen, Susan (1984) *Feminist Workplaces: Alternative Models for the Organization of Work*. PhD dissertation, Union for Experimenting Colleges, University of Michigan Dissertation Information Service.

Kolb, Deborah M. (1992) 'Women's work: peacemaking behind the scenes', in D.M. Kolb and J. Bartunek (eds), *Hidden Conflict in Organizations*. Newbury Park, CA: Sage.

Kolb, D.M. and L.L. Putnam (in press) 'Through the looking glass: negotiation theory refracted through the lens of gender', in S. Geason (ed.), *Frontiers in Dispute Resolution in Labor Relations and Human Resources*. East Lansing, MI: Michigan State University Press.

Kondo, Dorinne K. (1990) *Crafting Selves*. Chicago: University of Chicago Press.

Konrad, Alison M. and Gutek, Barbara A. (1986) 'Impact of work experiences on attitudes toward sexual harassment', *Administrative Science Quarterly*, 31(3): 422–38.

Kovalainen, Anne (1993) 'At the margins of the economy: women's self employment in Finland 1960–1990'. Publications of the Turku School of Economics and Business Administration, Turku, Finland.

Kram, K.E. (1985) *Mentoring at Work*. Glenview, IL: Scott, Foresman.

Kristeva, Julia (1980) *Desire in Language* (1977). New York: Columbia University Press.

Kvande, Elin and Rasmussen, Bente (1994) 'Men in male-dominated organizations and their encounter with women intruders', *Scandinavian Journal of Management*, 10(2): 163–74.

Lacan, Jacques (1977) *Ecrits*. New York: W.W. Norton & Co.

Larwood, L. and Gutek, B. (1984) 'Women at work in the USA', in M.J. Davidson and C.L. Cooper (eds), *Working Women: An International Survey*. Chichester: Wiley. pp. 237–67.

Leidner, Robin (1991a) 'Stretching the boundaries of liberalism: democratic innovation in a feminist organization', *Signs*, 16(2): 263–89.

Leidner, Robin (1991b) 'Serving hamburgers and selling insurance: gender, work, and identity in interactive service jobs', *Gender and Society*, 5(2): 154–77.

Lewis, Diane (1977) 'A response to inequality: black women, racism, sexism', *Signs*, 3: 339–61.

Loden, Marilyn (1985) *Feminine Leadership, or How to Succeed in Business without Being one of the Boys*. New York: Times Books.

Lorber, Judith (1986) 'Dismantling Noah's Ark', *Sex Roles*, 14(11/12): 567–80.

Lorber, Judith (1994) *Paradoxes of Gender*. New Haven, CT: Yale University Press.

Lorde, Audre (1983) 'The master's tools will never dismantle the master's house', in Cherrie Moraga and Gloria Anzaldúa (eds), *This Bridge Called My Back*. New York: Kitchen Table Press. pp. 98–101.

Lugones, Maria C. and Spelman, Elizabeth V. (1983) 'Have we got a theory for you! Feminist theory, cultural imperialism and the demand for "the woman's voice"', *Women's Studies International Forum*, 6(6): 573–81.

Lyotard, J.F. (1984) *The Postmodern Condition: a Report on Knowledge*. Minneapolis: University of Minnesota Press.

Mai-Dalton, Renate R. and Sullivan, Jeremiah J. (1981) 'The effects of manager's sex on the assignment to a challenging or a dull task and reasons for the choice', *Academy of Management Journal*, 24(3): 603–12.

Mainiero, Lisa A. (1986) 'Coping with powerlessness: the relationship of gender and job dependency to empowerment-strategy usage', *Administrative Science Quarterly*, 31(4): 633–53.

Mani, Lata (1989) 'Multiple mediations: feminist scholarship in the age of multinational reception', *Inscriptions*, 5: 1–24.

Marin, L. (1991) 'Speaking out together: testimonials of Latin American women', *Latin American Perspectives*, 18(3): 51–68.

Marshall, Judi (1984) *Women Managers: Travelers in a Male World*. London: Wiley.

Marshall, Judi (1989) 'Revisioning career concepts: a feminist invitation', in M.B. Arthur, D.T. Hall and B.S. Lawrence (eds), *Handbook of Career Theory*. Boston: Cambridge University Press. pp. 275–91.

Marshall, Judi (1995) *Women Managers Moving On*. London: Routledge.

Martin, J.E. and Peterson, M.M. (1987) 'Two-tier wage structures: implications for equity theory', *Academy of Management Journal*, 30(2).

Martin, Joanne (1990) 'Deconstructing organizational taboos: the suppression of gender conflict in organizations', *Organization Science*, 1(4): 339–59.

Martin, Joanne (1994) 'The organization of exclusion: institutionalization of sex inequality, gendered faculty jobs and gendered knowledge in organizational theory research', *Organization*, 1(2): 401–31.

Martin, Patricia Yancey (1990) 'Rethinking feminist organization', *Gender and Society*, 4(2): 182–206.

Martin, Patricia Yancey (1993) 'Feminism and management', in Ellen Fagenson (ed.), *Women in Management: Trends, Perspectives and Challenges*. Newbury Park, CA: Sage.

Martin, Patricia Yancey (1996) 'Men, masculinities and managements: gendering and evaluating dynamics', in David Collinson and Jeff Hearn (eds), *Men as Managers, Managers as Men*. London: Sage.

Mies, Maria (1982) *The Lace Makers of Narsapur: Indian Housewives Produce for the World Market*. London: Zed Books.

Mies, Maria, Bennholdt-Thomsen, Vernika and von Werlhof, Claudia (1988) *Women: The Last Colony*. London: Zed.

Mill, Harriet Taylor (1851) 'Enfranchisement of women', in John Stuart Mill and Harriet Taylor Mill, *Essays on Sex Equality*, edited by Alice S. Rossi. Chicago: University of Chicago Press, 1970. pp. 89–122.

Mill, John Stuart (1869) 'The subjection of women', in John Stuart Mill and Harriet Taylor Mill, *Essays on Sex Equality*, edited by Alice S. Rossi. Chicago: University of Chicago Press, 1970. pp. 123–242.

Miller, Jean Baker (1976) *Toward a New Psychology of Women*. Boston: Beacon.

Millet, Kate (1970) *Sexual Politics*. Garden City, NY: Doubleday.

Mills, Albert J. (1988) 'Organization, gender and culture', *Organization Studies*, 9: 351–69.

Mills, Albert J. (1995) 'Managing subjectivity, silencing diversity: organizational imagery in the airline industry: the case of British Airways', *Organization*, 2(2): 243–69.

Mills, Albert. J. and Chiaramonte, S. (1991) 'Organization as gendered communication act', *Canadian Journal of Communication*, 16: 381–98.

Mills, Albert J. and Tancred, Peta (eds) (1992) *Gendering Organizational Analysis*. Newbury Park, CA: Sage.

Minh-ha, Trinh T. (1989) *Woman, Native, Other: Writing Postcoloniality and Feminism*. Bloomington, IN: Indiana University Press.

Mir, Raza, Calás, Marta and Smircich, Linda (1995) 'Global technoscapes and unborn voices: challenges to theorizing global cooperation'. Paper presented at the Conference on organizational dimensions of global change, Case Western Reserve University, Cleveland, Ohio.

Mitchell, Juliet (1974) *Psychoanalysis and Feminism*. New York: Vintage.

Mohanty, C.T. (1991a) 'Under western eyes: feminist scholarship and colonial discourses', in C.T. Mohanty, A. Russo and L. Torres (eds), *Third World Women and the Politics of Feminism*. Bloomington, IN: Indiana University Press. pp. 51–80.

Mohanty, C.T. (1991b) 'Introduction. Cartographies of struggle: Third World women and the politics of feminism', in C.T. Mohanty, A. Russo and L. Torres (eds), *Third World Women and the Politics of Feminism*. Bloomington, IN: Indiana University Press. pp. 1–47.

Mohanty, C.T., Russo, A. and Torres, L. (eds) (1991) *Third World Women and the Politics of Feminism*. Bloomington, IN: Indiana University Press.

Moi, Toril (1985) *Sexual/Textual Politics*. London: Methuen.

Moore, Lynda (1986) *Not as Far as You Think*. Lexington, MA: Lexington Books.

Moraga, Cherrie and Anzaldúa, Gloria (1983) *This Bridge Called My Back*. New York: Kitchen Table Press.

Morgan, Robin (1984) *Sisterhood is Global: the International Women's Movement Anthology*. Garden City, NY: Anchor Books.

Morgen, Sandra (1994) 'Personalizing personnel decisions in feminist organizational theory and practice', *Human Relations*, 47(6): 665–83.

Morley, Louise (1994) 'Glass ceiling or iron cage: women in UK academia', *Gender, Work and Organization*, 1(4): 194–204.

Morrison, Ann M., White, Randall P. and Van Velsor, Ellen (1987) *Breaking the Glass Ceiling*. Reading, MA: Addison-Wesley.

Morrison, Ann M. and Von Glinow, Mary Ann (1990) 'Women and minorities in management', *American Psychologist*, 45(2): 200.

Mueller, Adele (1987a) 'Peasants and professionals: the social organization of women in development knowledge'. PhD dissertation, Ontario Institute for Studies in Education, University of Toronto.

Mueller, Adele (1987b) 'Power and naming in the development institution: the "discovery" of "women in Peru"'. Paper presented at the Fourteenth Annual Third World Conference, Chicago.

Mumby, D.K. and Putnam, L.L. (1992) 'The politics of emotion: a feminist reading of bounded rationality', *Academy of Management Review*, 17: 465–86.

Nash, June (1983) 'The impact of the changing international division of labor on different sectors of the labor force', in June Nash and Maria Patricia Fernández-Kelly (eds), *Women, Men, and the International Division of Labor*. Albany, NY: State University of New York Press.

Nash, June and Safa, Helen (eds) (1985) *Women and Change in Latin America*. South Hadley, MA: Bergin and Garvey.

Nelson, Debra L. and Quick, James C. (1985) 'Professional women: are distress and disease inevitable?', *Academy of Management Review*, 10(2): 206–18.

Nes, Janet A. and Iadicola, Peter (1989) 'Toward a definition of feminist social work: a comparison of liberal, radical, and socialist models', *Social Work*, January: 12–21.

Newsweek (1995) 'The rise of the overclass', 31 July: 33–46.

Nicholson, L.J. (ed.) (1990) *Feminism/Postmodernism*. New York: Routledge.

Nieva, Veronica F. and Gutek, Barbara A. (1980) 'Sex effects on evaluation', *Academy of Management Review*, 5(2): 267–76.

Nieva, Veronica F. and Gutek, Barbara A. (1981) *Women and Work: a Psychological Perspective*. New York: Praeger.

Nkomo, Stella (1992) 'The emperor has no clothes: rewriting "race in organizations"', *Academy of Management Review*, 17(3): 133–50.

Norton, Sue M. (1994) 'Pregnancy, the family, and work: an historical review and update of legal regulations and organizational policies and practices in the United States', *Gender, Work and Organization*, 1(4): 217–26.

Ong, Aihwa (1987) *Spirits of Resistance and Capitalist Discipline: Factory Women in Malaysia*. Albany, NY: State University of New York Press.

Osborn, Richard N. and Vicars, William M. (1976) 'Sex stereotypes – an artifact in leader behavior and subordinate satisfaction analysis', *Academy of Management Journal*, 19(3): 439–49.

Paetzold, R.L. and O'Leary-Kelly, A.M. (1994) 'Hostile environment sexual harassment in the United States: post-*Meritor* developments and implications', *Gender, Work and Organization*, 1: 50–7.

Paige, K.E. and Paige, J.M. (1981) *The Politics of Reproductive Ritual*. Berkeley, CA: University of California Press.

Parasuraman, Saroj, Greenhaus, Jeffrey, Rabinowitz, Samual, Bedeian, Arthur G. and Mossholder, Kevin (1989) 'Work and family variables as mediators of the relationship between wives' employment and husbands' well-being', *Academy of Management Journal*, 32(1).

Parry, Benita (1995) 'Problems in current theories of colonial discourse', in Bill Ashcroft, Gareth Griffiths and Helen Tiffin (eds), *The Post-Colonial Studies Reader*. London: Routledge. pp. 36–44.

Parvikko, Tuija (1990) 'Conceptions of gender equality: similarity and difference', in Marja Keranen (ed.), *Finnish 'Undemocracy': Essays on Gender and Politics*. Jyväskylä: Finnish Political Science Association, Gummerus Printing. pp. 89–111.

Pearce, D. (1978) 'The feminization of poverty: women, work, and welfare', *Urban and Social Change Review*, 11(1/2): 28–36.

Perry, Elissa L., Davis-Blake, Alison and Kulik, Carol T. (1994) 'Explaining gender-based selection decisions: a synthesis of contextual and cognitive approaches', *Academy of Management Review*, 19(4): 786–820.

Peters, Tom (1990) 'The best new managers will listen, motivate, support: isn't that just like a woman?', *Working Woman*, September: 216–17.

Pettigrew, Thomas F. and Martin, Joanne (1987) 'Shaping the organizational context for black American inclusion', *Journal of Social Issues*, 43(1): 41–78.

Pfeffer, Jeffrey, and Davis-Blake, Alison (1987) 'The effect of the proportion of women on salaries: the case of college administrators', *Administrative Science Quarterly*, 32(1): 1–24.

Phillips, A. and Taylor, B. (1980) 'Sex and skill: notes towards a feminist economics', *Feminist Review*, 6: 79–88.

Piller, Patricia (1996) 'Women's bodies at work: the development of a typology of the female body in the workplace from a transnational (Canada and New Zealand) study of women's experiences'. Unpublished doctoral dissertation, The Fielding Institute, Santa Barbara, CA.

Pilotta, Joseph (ed.) (1983) *Women in Organizations*. Prospect Heights, IL: Waveland Press.

Powell, Gary N. (1987) 'The effects of sex and gender on recruitment', *Academy of Management Review*, 12(4): 731–43.

Powell, Gary N. (1988) *Women and Men in Management*. Newbury Park, CA: Sage.

Powell, Gary N. (1993) *Women and Men in Management*, 2nd edn. Newbury Park, CA: Sage.

Powell, Gary N. and Butterfield, D. Anthony (1979) 'The "good manager": masculine or androgynous?', *Academy of Management Journal*, 22(2): 395–403.

Prakash, Gyan (1995) *After Colonialism: Imperial Histories and Postcolonial Displacements*. Princeton: Princeton University Press.

Pringle, Rosemary (1988) *Secretaries Talk*. London: Verso.

Pulakos, E.D. and Wexley, K.N. (1983) 'The relationship among perceptual similarity, sex, and performance ratings in manager–subordinate dyads', *Academy of Management Journal*, 26(1).

Radhakrishnan, R. (1994) 'Postmodernism and the rest of the world', *Organization*, 1(2): 305–40.

Ragins, B.R. and Cotton, J. (1991) 'Easier said than done: gender differences in perceived barriers to gaining a mentor', *Academy of Management Journal*, 34: 939–51.

Ramsey, V. Jean and Calvert, Linda McGee (1994) 'A feminist critique of organizational humanism', *Journal of Applied Behavioral Science*, 30(1): 83–97.

Rantalaiho, Liisa and Heiskanen, Tuula (eds) (forthcoming) *Gendered Practices in Working Life.* Macmillan: London.

Reinelt, Claire (1994) 'Fostering empowerment, building community: the challenge for state-funded feminist organizations', *Human Relations*, 47(6): 685–705.

Reinharz, Shulamit (1992) *Feminist Methods in Social Research.* New York: Oxford University Press.

Reskin, Barbara F. and Roos, Patricia A. (1990) *Job Queues, Gender Queues.* Philadelphia: Temple University Press.

Rich, Adrienne (1980) 'Compulsory heterosexuality and lesbian existence', *Signs*, 5(4): 631–90.

Riger, Stephanie (1984) 'Vehicles for empowerment: the case of feminist movement organizations', *Prevention in Human Services*, 3(2–3): 99–117.

Robbins, Stephen P. (1996) *Organizational Behavior.* Englewood Cliffs, NJ: Prentice-Hall.

Roethlisberger, F.J. and Dickson, W. (1939) *Management and the Worker.* Belknap Press.

Rose, Gerald L. (1978) 'Sex effects on effort attributions in managerial performance evaluation', *Organizational Behavior and Human Performance*, 21(3): 367–78.

Rosen, Benson and Mericle, Mary F. (1979) 'Influence of strong versus weak fair employment policies and applicant's sex on selection decisions and salary recommendations in a management simulation', *Journal of Applied Psychology*, 64(4): 435–9.

Rosener, Judy B. (1990) 'Ways women lead', *Harvard Business Review*, November–December: 119–25.

Rosener, Judy B. (1995) *America's Competitive Secret: Utilizing Women as a Management Strategy.* New York: Oxford University Press.

Rothschild, Joyce (1992) 'Principles of feminist trade union organizations'. Paper presented at the Workshop on Feminist Organizations, Washington, DC.

Rothschild-Whitt, Joyce (1979) 'The collectivist organization: an alternative to rational-bureaucratic models', *American Sociological Review*, 44(August): 509–27.

Sahlin-Andersson, Kerstin (1994) 'Group identities as the building blocks of organizations: a story about nurses' daily work', *Scandinavian Journal of Management*, 10(2): 131–46.

Said, Edward (1978) *Orientalism.* Harmondsworth: Penguin.

Said, Edward (1989) 'Representing the colonized: anthropology's interlocutors', *Critical Inquiry*, 15: 205–25.

Sargent, A. (1981) *The Androgynous Manager.* New York: AMACOM.

Sawicki, Jana (1991) *Disciplining Foucault.* London: Routledge.

Schneier, Craig and Bartol, Kathryn M. (1980) 'Sex effects in emergent leadership', *Journal of Applied Psychology*, 65(3): 341–5.

Schwartz, A.Y., Gottesman, E.W. and Perlmutter, F.D. (1988) 'Blackwell: a case study in feminist administration', *Administration in Social Work*, 12(2): 5–15.

Scott, J.W. (1986) 'Gender: a useful category of historical analysis', *American Historical Review*, 91: 1053–75.

Sealander, J. and Smith, D. (1986) 'The rise and fall of feminist organizations in the 1970s – Dayton as a case-study', *Feminist Studies*, 12(2): 320–41.

Sekaran, U. and Leong, F. (eds) (1991) *Womanpower: Managing in Times of Demographic Turbulence.* Newbury Park, CA: Sage.

Shearer, Teri L. and Arrington, C. Edward (1993) 'Accounting in other wor(l)ds: a feminism without reserve', *Accounting, Organizations and Society*, 18(2/3): 253–72.

Sheppard, Deborah L. (1989) 'Organizations, power and sexuality: the image and self-image of women managers', in Jeff Hearn, Deborah L. Sheppard, Peta Tancred-Sheriff and Gibson Burrell (eds), *The Sexuality of Organization.* Newbury Park, CA: Sage. pp. 139–57.

Shrivastava, Paul (1994) 'Rereading *Bhopal: Anatomy of a Crisis* through a feminist lens', *Journal of Management Inquiry*, 3(3): 278–85.

Sigelman, Lee, Milward, H. Brinton and Shepard, Jon M. (1982) 'The salary differential between male and female administrators: equal pay for equal work?', *Academy of Management Journal*, 25(3): 664–71.

Smircich, Linda (1985) 'Toward a woman centered organization theory'. Paper presented at the Annual Meeting of the Academy of Management, San Diego, CA, August.

Smith, Catherine Begnoche (1979) 'Influence of internal opportunity structure and sex of worker on turnover patterns', *Administrative Science Quarterly*, 24(3): 362–81.

Smith, Dianne B. and Plant, Walter T. (1982) 'Sex differences in the job satisfaction of university professors', *Journal of Applied Psychology*, 67(2): 249–51.

Smith, Dorothy (1987) *The Everyday World as Problematic: a Feminist Sociology.* Toronto: University of Toronto Press.

Smith, Dorothy (1990a) *Texts, Facts, and Femininity: Exploring the Relations of Ruling.* London: Routledge and Kegan Paul.

Smith, Dorothy (1990b) *The Conceptual Practices of Power.* Boston: Northeastern University Press.

Sommer, Doris (1995) 'Taking a life: hot pursuit and cold rewards in a Mexican testimonial novel', *Signs*, 20(4): 913–40.

Sommer, Doris (1988) 'Not just a personal story: women's testimonials and the plural self', in B. Brodzki and C. Schenck (eds), *Life/Lines: Theorizing Women's Auto-Biography*. Ithaca, NY: Cornell University Press. pp. 107–30.

Spelman, Elizabeth V. (1989) *Inessential Woman: Problems of Exclusion in Feminist Thought*. Boston: Beacon Press.

Spence, J.T. and Helmreich, R.L. (1981) 'Androgyny versus gender schema: a comment on Bem's gender schema theory', *Psychological Review*, 88(4): 365–8.

Spivak, G.C. (1987) *In Other Worlds*. New York: Methuen.

Spivak, G.C. (1988) 'Can the subaltern speak?', in C. Nelson and L. Grossberg (eds), *Marxism and the Interpretation of Culture*. Chicago: University of Illinois Press. pp. 271–313.

Sternbach, N.S. (1991) 'Re-membering the dead: Latin-American women's "testimonial" discourse', *Latin American Perspectives*, 18(3): 91–102.

Sterrett, John H. (1978) 'The job interview: body language and perceptions of potential effectiveness', *Journal of Applied Psychology*, 63(3): 388–90.

Stivers, Camilla (1993) *Gender Images in Public Administration*. Newbury Park, CA: Sage.

Stoller, Eleanor Palo (1993) 'Gender and the organization of lay health care: a socialist-feminist perspective', *Journal of Aging Studies*, 7(2): 151–70.

Strober, Myra (1984) 'Toward a general theory of occupational sex segregation: the case of public school teaching', in Barbara F. Reskin (ed.), *Sex Segregation in the Workplace*. Washington, DC: National Academy Press. pp. 144–56.

Strober, Myra and Arnold, Carolyn L. (1987) 'The dynamics of occupational segregation among bank tellers', in Clair Brown and Joseph A. Pechman (eds), *Gender in the Workplace*. Washington, DC: Brookings Institution. pp. 107–57.

Stroh, Linda K. and Brett, Jeanne M. (1994) 'Dual-earner dads versus traditional dads: can we account for differences in salary progression?' Paper presented at the National Meeting of the Academy of Management, August.

Stromquist, Nelly P. (1990) 'Gender inequality in education: accounting for women's subordination', *British Journal of Sociology of Education*, 11(2): 137–53.

Tancred, Peta (1995) 'Women's work: a challenge to the sociology of work', *Gender, Work and Organization*, 2(1): 11–20.

Taylor, F.W. (1911) *The Principles of Scientific Management*. New York: Norton.

Taylor, M. Susan and Ilgen, Daniel R. (1981) 'Sex discrimination against women in initial placement decisions: a laboratory investigation', *Academy of Management Journal*, 24(4): 859–65.

Terborg, J.R. (1977) 'Women in management: a research review', *Journal of Applied Psychology*, 62: 647–64.

Tharenou, Phyllis, Latimer, Shane and Conroy, Denise (1994) 'How do you make it to the top: an examination of influences on women's and men's managerial advancement', *Academy of Management Journal*, 37(4): 899–931.

Thompson, Clara (1964) *Interpersonal Psychoanalysis: the Selected Papers of Clara Thompson*, edited by M.P. Green. New York: Basic Books.

Tong, Rosemarie (1989) *Feminist Theory: a Comprehensive Introduction*. Boulder, CO: Westview Press.

Treiman, Donald J. and Hartmann, Heidi (eds) (1981) *Women, Work, and Wages: Equal Pay for Jobs of Equal Value*. Washington, DC: National Academy Press

Tsui, Anne S., Egan, Terri D. and O'Reilly, Charles A. III (1992) 'Being different: relational demography and organizational attachment', *Administrative Science Quarterly*, 37: 549–79.

Tuana, Nancy and Tong, Rosemarie (eds) (1995) *Feminism and Philosophy*. Boulder, CO: Westview.

United Nations (1995) *Human Development Report*. Geneva: United Nations.

Valentine, Patricia and McIntosh, Gordon (1990) 'Food for thought: realities of a women-dominated organization', *Alberta Journal of Educational Research*, XXXVI(4): 353–69.

Varca, Philip E., Shaffer, Garnett Stokes and McCauley, Cynthia D. (1983) 'Sex differences in job satisfaction revisited', *Academy of Management Journal*, 26(2): 348–53.

Warren, Kay B. and Bourque, Susan C. (1987) 'Gatekeepers and resources: gender and change in Latin American countries'. Report for the Gender, Technology, and International Development Project, co-sponsored by the Rockefeller Foundation and the International Development Research Center.

Warren, Kay B. and Bourque, Susan C. (1991) 'Women, technology, and development ideologies: analyzing feminist voices', in Micaela di Leonardo (ed.), *Gender at the Crossroads of Knowledge: Feminist Anthropology in the Postmodern Era*. Berkeley, CA: University of California Press. pp. 278–311.

Waters, L.K. and Waters, Carrie Wherry (1969) 'Correlates of job satisfaction and job dissatisfaction among female clerical workers', *Journal of Applied Psychology*, 53(5): 388–91.

Weaver, Charles N. (1978) 'Sex differences in the determinants of job satisfaction', *Academy of Management Journal*, 21(2): 265–74.

Weedon, Chris (1987) *Feminist Practice and Post-structuralist Theory*. Cambridge: Basil Blackwell.

West, Candace and Fenstermaker, Sarah (1995) 'Doing difference', *Gender and Society*, 9: 8–37.

West, Candace and Zimmerman, Don H. (1987) 'Doing gender', *Gender and Society*, 1(2): 125–51.

Wharton, Amy S. (1991) 'Structure and agency in socialist-feminist theory', *Gender and Society*, 5(3): 373–89.

Wiley, Mary Glenn and Eskilson, Arlene (1982) 'Interaction of sex and power base on perceptions of managerial effectiveness', *Academy of Management Journal*, 25(3): 671–7.

Winnicott, D.W. (1975) *Through Paediatrics to Psycho-analysis*. New York: Basic Books.

Wollstonecraft, M. (1792) *A Vindication of the Rights of Woman*, edited by Carol Poston. New York: W.W. Norton, 1975.

Woodul, Jennifer (1978) 'What's this about feminist businesses?', in Alison Jagger and Paula S. Rothenberg (eds), *Feminist Frameworks*. New York: McGraw-Hill. pp. 196–204.

Young, Iris (1980) 'Socialist feminism and the limits of dual systems theory', *Socialist Review*, 10(2–3).

Zammuto, Raymond F., London, Manuel and Rowland, Kendrith M. (1979) 'Effects of sex on commitment and conflict resolution', *Journal of Applied Psychology*, 64(2): 227–31.

Zavella, Patricia (1991) 'Mujeres in factories: race and class perspectives on women, work, and family', in Micaela di Leonardo (ed.), *Gender at the Crossroads of Knowledge*. Berkeley, CA: University of California Press. pp. 312–36.

Zimmer, Lynn (1987) 'How women reshape the prison guard role', *Gender and Society*, 1(4): 415–31.

Part Two
CURRENT ISSUES IN ORGANIZATION STUDIES

2.1

Creative Deconstruction: Strategy and Organizations

RICHARD WHIPP

At a recent conference a sociologist was complaining of the pervasive use of the word 'strategy' during the proceedings. His remarks came close to a paraphrase of Goering's irritation with culture: 'when someone mentions strategy, I reach for my gun'. The episode illustrates the centrality of strategy to the field of organizational studies as well as its latent controversial power. The time is ripe therefore to take stock of the developments around what has become a core subject for social science in general. That the use of the word 'strategy', and its adjective 'strategic', has extended beyond managers and policy-makers to enter common parlance, makes the task all the more urgent.

This essay will explore the problem through four main stages. The first concerns the social construction of the term 'strategy' and its derivatives. The second and main stage examines the way in which the study of strategy has been pursued and its consequent intellectual evolution. The account will highlight the tensions between the economic and the social dimensions which have bedevilled those writing in the strategy and organization area. Stage three gives separate attention to some of the issues which seldom receive treatment in print, such as the differences between US and European approaches. The fourth stage sets out the challenges which the strategy domain faces in the form of major empirical research objects and their attendant problems. Each stage covers an important aspect of the strategy and organization area in the following way.

The first section has twin purposes. The primary task is to provide an account of the genesis and mutation of the term 'strategy'. The intention is not to provide a definitive etymology. Rather, in the spirit of *Keywords* (1976) by Raymond Williams, the section will dissect the layers of meaning which the word and its uses have carried. This will involve a discussion of the possibilities raised by the recent application of discourse analysis in the deconstruction of the language of strategy. The section sets out to demonstrate that these multiple constructions are a vital means of deciphering the varieties of academic use which have arisen. Above all, the section provides telling clues as to the intellectual contests which have ensued.

In the light of these issues, the job of the second section is to offer an overview of the treatment of the strategy and organization subject and its strengths and inherent tension. The distinctive feature of this tension has arisen from the way those involved have dealt with the economic and social aspects of strategy and organizations. An outline of the way the subject's treatment has unfolded will clarify the point. In its first incarnation the study of strategy leaned heavily on its neo-classical supports. The path-breaking work of Chandler (1962) and Ansoff (1965) was notable for its rationalism and driving economic determinism. In providing many of the basic building blocks of strategy studies these early authors held an essentially mechanistic appreciation of the operation of organizations. The 1970s saw sociologists and political scientists enter the domain. Their concerns swung towards the internal social character of organizations as a means of understanding strategy. Their preoccupations stemmed from the political and cognitive aspects of decision-making theory and an awareness of the combined political, cultural and educational processes which shape strategy at organizational level.

The late 1970s and the early 1980s constitute a separate period with two main strands of progress. The first arose directly from the work of Caves and Porter as they brought the techniques of neo-classical industry analysis to bear on 'business policy' (Barney 1986). The economic context of the strategic choices of the firm became the focal point, giving rise to models of 'extended competition' (Porter 1980), 'structure, conduct and performance' (Bourgeois 1984), and 'strategic groups' (Rumelt 1988). The interior processes of the firm remained largely unexplored. Followers subsequently reinforced the neglect by concentrating on the precise 'fit' of organizational form and action with industry and market type (Miles and Snow 1984) – a parallel line of thinking to the population ecologists. The second strand of this era was shaped by the so-called 'new competition' of the 1980s and the corporate trauma expressed in Ford's 'after Japan' project. An attempt was made to combine the economic and the social as a way of unravelling strategy as a means of organizational transformation. The result has been a mingling of those who had been extending the methods of the earlier decision-making approach, the work of institutional economists and the findings of second-generation business policy experts. The hallmark of strategy as a business tool has become its impermanence and fragility in the face of the technological and economic upheavals of the era.

The history of strategy and organization studies has produced a rich cacophony of intellectual and practical themes. However, there appears to have been a number of apparent silences, at least in the formal discussions of the strategy field. Such points are made in corridor and post-seminar exchanges rather than in print. The objective of the third section is to fill some of the silences. This will be attempted by addressing the issue of levels of analysis, the role of time, the non-reflexive character of strategy experts and thereby the relationship between the academic and the practitioner.

The challenge facing this diverse body of writers forms the centre-piece of the fourth and last section of the essay. Broadly speaking, the threat comes from new empirical research objects, all of which are wrapped in theoretical barbed wire. The major query has arisen from the received notion of 'global industries' (Bartlett and Ghoshal 1989) generated by business policy specialists on the one hand and yet the apparently enduring relevance of national business systems (Whitley 1992) asserted by organizational sociologists on the other. For some, inter-

organizational forms or the transition from public to private sector in both West and East are set to rewrite our comprehension of strategy. The purpose of this fourth section is also to perform some intellectual brokering through the identification of the common problems facing strategy and organization scholars. In particular, the deepening of the interpretative perspective (in alliance with institutional economists) has had precious little impact on those conducting specialist research on strategy and organizations with respect to new technology, manufacturing, or employee relations. It is ironic, for example, how critical studies of post-Fordism and flexibility employ the same rational assumptions of the Porterians.

The overall aim of the piece is to problematize the strategy concept: in other words, to confront the construction of the term, to unravel the epistemological assumptions which have informed the growth of the field, to break the public silences which have overlain key issues, and then, by laying out the problems facing strategy scholars, to suggest future research directions. Put in terms of the need for a map of the area, the chapter will supply a linguistic scale, a conceptual key with which to chart the intellectual topography of the subject; it will also supply the theoretical contours with the main debates acting as grid points. The nature of the field of enquiry means that the cartography will be one which is international and yet, paradoxically, revealing of previously uncharted terrains.

STRATEGY: BUZZWORD AND KEYWORD

The 1980s witnessed the entry of the word 'strategy' into popular parlance. Given the rise of neo-liberal economics and its political expression in 'Thatcherism' and 'Reganomics' the *zeitgeist* of the age was acutely commercial. It is virtually unremarked in the mid 1990s therefore when trade unionists, public sector workers or journalists litter their everyday speech with the words 'strategy' or 'strategic'. The use is often straightforward and its connotations positive. The intention is to convey the importance of the project in question and the elevated status of the aims, and to suggest the sense of coherent thinking and planning which is associated with the label 'strategic'. In July 1994, in a piece of introspection the *Financial Times* (St George 1994: 11) discovered that its pages contained a wide variety of applications. These embraced not only a defensive strategy in US politics, and myriad business uses such as Schroders' investment strategy, but also the adoption of strategy versus technique, used to report the activities of the Soccer World Cup held in the USA that month.

Is this popular use of the word merely a generalized confirmation of the relevance of the term found among managers? Had it become so well rooted in managerial discourse that the new competitive and political conditions of the last decade led to its wider dispersal? Certainly the term promised much, as was shown by Marjorie Lyles's (1990: 363) comment to academics that: '"strategic" has became a buzzword for all disciplines trying to stress the importance of their work.' Schendel and Cool (1988) point out that there was little use of the word in a management context before 1979. In fact, the apparently commonplace use of the word 'strategy' and its derivatives masks the varieties of construction and the layers of meaning which have been generated historically.

Using the approach suggested by Raymond Williams (1976), 'strategy' can emerge as a keyword of modernity rather than just a buzzword. The word 'strategy' derives from the Greek *strategia*, meaning generalship, and was first used in English in 1688. According to *James's Military Dictionary* of 1810, 'strategy' concerns something done out of sight of the enemy whereas 'tactics' were immediate measures taken in front of an adversary. The words 'strategist' and 'stratagem' appear in 1825 and 1838 respectively and are more closely related to the medieval notion of stratagem as an artifice or trick (St George 1994: 11). The translation of strategy into commerce occurred largely through the common theme of competition. Indeed one of the most frequently used reference points for the strategy field has been Andrews's formulation of strategy as 'rivalry amongst peers, for prizes in a defined and shared game' (Andrews 1971).

The dominant figures in the practitioner and academic worlds which employ the term have drawn heavily on the military and competitive sources of the word. Hence Schendel and Hofer (1979: 11) summarized the landmark University of Pittsburgh conference on strategic management by defining the subject as one which 'deals with the entrepreneurial work of the organization, with organizational renewal and growth, and more particularly, with developing and utilizing the strategy which is to guide the organization's operations'. In 1993, Howard Thomas reflected on the subsequent University of Texas 'Strategic Management Frontiers' conference of 1988 and the recent annual meetings of the Strategic Management Society. He concluded that it was possible to identify a shared view of strategy as 'something an organization needs or uses in order to win, or

establish its legitimacy in a world of competitive rivalry . . . strategy is what makes a firm unique, a winner, or a survivor' (1993: 3). As the two quotations confirm, the historic notions of generalship and competitive behaviour appear to have been sustained in the academic domain over the past three decades. For many practitioners the assumptions are often stronger. The consultants' newsletter *Strategic Directions* felt able therefore in 1991 to categorize the strategies being used in preceding years according to their principal aim. These included the conglomeration aims of the 1960s, the consolidation objectives in the following decade, through to the 'demassing' of the 1980s and the restructuring strategies of the 1990s (1991: 3). The efficiency of strategy was never in doubt.

Clearly, the leading authorities in the subject have constructed a meaning for the word 'strategy' which both exploits its purposive military origins and invests heavily in the rational expectations of those wishing to direct and manage an organization. However, whilst this representation of strategy, or the strategic management area, has gained widespread acceptance (notably in the USA) it does not reflect the true richness of the domain. In order to uncover the full character and potential of this keyword, it is necessary to go beyond its received usage and explore how it has been studied and researched. In this way, the contribution of organization writers becomes of vital significance.

Perhaps one of the most instructive attempts to link the fields of organization studies and strategy comes in the recent work of Knights and Morgan (1991). They argue that strategy is not simply a technique or body of knowledge. Instead, they apply linguistic theory to suggest that strategy is essentially a discourse. In other words, the very language, symbols and exchanges around the subject of strategy have important outcomes. Strategy is a mechanism of power. People within organizations may be identified according to their participation within the discourse around strategy and its related practices. Those who accept the constructs of strategy (such as market and industry analysis, for example) are able to enjoy the credentials of expertise and position within corporate hierarchies (1991: 251–3). The potency of the discourse around strategy is high because of the promise of complete knowledge. Those who subscribe to the rational, purposive notion of corporate strategy which dominates business schools and Western contemporary management rely on the belief that all is potentially knowable in commercial environments.

Clearly, the attraction of the rational model of strategy is considerable. Indeed, it is possible to point to those professional groups within organizations who have failed in their status and influence because of their inability to embrace the discourse of strategy. UK engineers and designers are cases in point. However, the use of linguistic theory by Knights and Morgan helps one to understand the cleavage among academics over strategy. Broadly speaking, in North America the strength of business schools and, of course, corporate power in society has enhanced the power effects of strategy as a subject. The result has been a market dominance of the rational model of strategy based firmly on neo-classical economics.

Organization writers have sought to enhance their status (and tenure) through clear identification with such orientations to strategy (see Burrell et al. 1994). In Europe, the converse has been true: organization analysts have not been confronted with such power effects. Strategy has been less central and more fragmented as a subject. The result has been therefore a deepening of the critical stance in organization studies. Credentials and preferment have simply not been given for competence in the strategy field until very recently. How this divergence has come about requires investigation in its own right.

THE DEVELOPMENT OF
THE STRATEGY FIELD

The fields of strategy and organization present very different profiles in contemporary university departments. As one might expect having read the previous section, strategy writers display an imposing conviction in both the certainty of their analytical frameworks and the relevance of their results to managers and policy-makers. Success, measured in sales and citation indexes, has been remarkable for leading authors such as Porter, fuelled by the management education boom of the 1980s. The keynote for the field's development has been a progressive extension of existing central areas of interest (such as industry analysis or acquisitions) to include new areas (such as alliances and cooperation). The vast majority of work has remained within the paradigm which gives purpose to strategy studies: neo-classical economics.

While the strategy area has its minority quota of renegades searching for alternative perspectives drawing on separate paradigms (see, for example, Bourgeois 1984; Weick 1987), organization studies has them in abundance. The core characteristic of organization scholars (especially in Europe) is the divergent strands of theoretical approaches, analytical frameworks and empiri-

cal targets. Lex Donaldson (1985) described the collection of academics as anarchic. More recently, groups have not only celebrated such diversity but explicitly rejected the paradigm consensus of disciplines such as economics. Moreover, they celebrate the theoretical openness and pluralism of their subject (Burrell et al. 1994: 7–8).

At first sight the two fields of strategy and organization would appear to have conflicting aspirations and value systems. Yet as the successful migrants have shown (see for example Van de Ven et al. 1989) it is possible to apply techniques from one domain to another, to import novel conceptions of central problems and adopt fresh methodologies. Before explaining how such exchanges have been attempted and the prospect for future joint endeavours there is a need to rehearse the unfolding of the strategy specialism and the opportunities produced.

In his recent book on business strategy, the economist John Kay (1993) is damning of the achievements of the field. In his words, 'the inability to distinguish sufficiently clearly between taxonomy, deductive logic, and empirical observations is responsible for the limited progress which is being made in the development of an organised framework for the study of business behaviour' (1993: 337–8). Casting his eye over the past thirty years, he is clear that the subject of strategy has suffered from the neglect of sociological, legal and alternative economic theory (1993: 362). Is Kay's conclusion appropriate (1993: 337–63)? If so, how can it be accounted for and what are the implications for organization analysts and others?

In many ways the appearance of Kay's challenge has unsettled the strategy field. It is certainly unusual in its attack on the certainties which characterize much strategy writing. The assault may appear to set up a contradiction. Why should a strategy writer and economist seek to undermine the edifice which his discipline had helped to create? The solution lies in the undifferentiated nature of his criticism. As the following pages will show, at various moments in the unfolding of the strategy literature leading works have differed greatly in their level of scholarship. Peters and Waterman (1982) made little use of formal methodologies or theoretical exploration. The same cannot be said of Chandler (1962) or Mintzberg (1978). Kay's assertions are useful though, since they alert us to the wide variations of technical accomplishment which are often concealed by the apparent relevance and potency of strategy texts.

Any reconstruction of the unfolding of strategic management thought is obliged to begin in the 1960s with the rise of strategic planning. It is important to note that the growth of the strategy area did not move through distinct and successive phases. Rather, approaches from the 1960s continued alongside new models which were established subsequently. In its first incarnation the study of strategy was inherently rational and unashamed of its economic determinism. Strategy and planning were synonymous. The essential aim was to assess the environment of the firm, forecast the future of the business and adjust internal structures and resources accordingly (Anthony 1965). Increasingly, high expectations were held of the application of computer technology and the reinforcing examples of planning apparatus erected by national governments. The portfolio matrix and product life-cycle were the most popular devices designed to aid the planning process (Levitt 1965). In many ways, the points made by Knights and Morgan in the previous section on the seductive power of such rational instruments of management are reinforced here. If the dominant, North American understanding of strategy is predicated on a 'knowable environment' then the planning techniques which emerged from the 1960s and 1970s illustrate the point admirably. It has been the simplicity of their core frameworks which has appealed to managers. The growth, maturity and decline of product demand over time in the 'product life-cycle' is one example. The apparently straightforward categorization of products or business areas according to a 2×2 matrix based on market share and market growth (the 'Boston Box') had enormous appeal to executives in multi-divisional firms.

Although planning approaches have continued through the use of information technology, both managers and commentators became impatient with the aridity of the financially driven frameworks and their disturbingly low level of use in practice. The 1970s saw a reaction against the mechanistic appreciation of strategy. Lindblom had offered his 'science of muddling through' in 1959. Yet his contention that planning and execution were seldom orderly and sequential but the victims of chance and the internal working of the firm, was only extensively taken up much later by, for example, March and Olsen (1976) or Mintzberg (1978). The debt to organizational decision-making theory was clear and it was in this era that the notions of strategy as a product of incremental, adaptive, emergent processes began (cf. Pettigrew 1973; Quinn 1980; Frederickson 1983).

The strengths of the processual tradition have been manifold. Taken together, it is the richness of the possibilities for development of the strategy idea which stand out. Mintzberg, for example, not only highlighted the inconsistent and often contradictory process of emergence but also drew attention to the way failed and aborted strategies litter the corporate world. Moreover, the processual writers opened up the opportunity for other organization writers to engage in the exploration of strategy. By exploding the assumption that strategic decisions evolve neatly from analysis through choice to implementation, writers such as Quinn and Pettigrew offered the chance for analysts of organizational power or culture to intervene.

The late 1970s and the 1980s constitute a readily identifiable phase in the evolution of the strategy domain. The diversification and corporate decentralization of the 1960s and 1970s failed to meet the demands of new international forms of competition (Best 1990). The emphasis shifted to a concentration on 'core businesses' (Peters and Waterman 1982) and the clarification of the objectives of the firm in the face of competitive pressures. It was here that Porter's (1980) 'generic strategies' of cost leadership and differentiation gained widespread acceptance. The preoccupations of the decade centred around the concepts of 'strategic intent' – the linking of narrow commercial actions with the broad aspirations of the firm (Prahalad and Hamel 1985) – and the problems involved in creating global strategies to meet world-wide competition (Bartlett and Ghoshal 1989).

The developments of the 1980s have an important contextual ingredient which conditioned the acceptance of the conclusions of Porter, Peters and Waterman and others. Given the epoch-making impact of Japanese manufacturers in Western markets, business people were virtually desperate for texts which offered hope of commercial salvation and, if possible, the restoration of self-belief. Porter's analysis of the extended competitive relations within industries and the resulting stark choices over cost or differentiation emphasis offered the first steps. His constructs took over from the earlier Boston Box frameworks in terms of appeal. Peters and Waterman's eight rules of excellence spoke most directly to the heartfelt need for Western businesses to discover what were the appropriate standards required to compete with the Japanese. Although fundamentally rationalist, Peters and Waterman skilfully combined an appreciation of superficial understandings of culture and structure with key features of the content of strategic choices. It is worth noticing that their work relied in part on the established techniques of the consulting firm McKinsey – a linkage which would repay further academic research more generally in Europe and North America.

In answering the questions posed at the start of this section, Kay's acerbic summary of the strategy field has validity. He is correct that the subject is a long way from exhibiting the characteristics of a discipline, that is, a broad organizing structure around key theories related to a corpus of empirical knowledge. There are many social scientists who pour scorn on the predominance of list-building, the rush to prescription and the statements of the obvious found in key strategy texts. Notwithstanding these doubts, it is possible to take a more generous position, one which recognizes the need to extract the implicit conceptual and analytical features of strategy writing. At the same time, it is necessary to admit the contribution (often indirect) made to the strategy field by earlier students of organization and sociology.

Zan has produced, in this spirit, a typology of the conceptions of strategy which is more helpful than blanket condemnation. The typology (Zan 1990: 96–7) relies on a set of distinctions between various orientations to strategy. These include a 'descriptive' tone concentrating on the reconstruction of events; an 'evaluative' aspect relying on the appraisal of management actions; the policy-making approach, concerned with how firms aspire to develop; and the interpretative perspective, aimed at examining how strategies come into being. Zan argues that it is possible to uncover four main meanings contained within the field over the last thirty years. The first is the 'evaluative policy-making' understanding of strategy which regards managerial volition as absolute; a core activity of strategic management therefore becomes evaluation of the internal and external conditions for the success of given policies. The second is 'descriptive policy-making' which concentrates on the intentions and choices of management from within the firm with a view to completing given projects but not necessarily as means to market dominance (Chandler 1962). The third version is labelled the 'evaluative/interpretative' approach. Here, as was suggested for the 1980s, strategy is seen as the means of achieving 'fit' between firm and environment and is judged according to how sustainable that conduct by management might be (cf. Miles and Snow 1984). The last category, the 'descriptive/interpretative', emerges from the writers we identified in the 1970s in the more processual orientation to strategy. In this category strategy is equated with the logic of the firm's behaviour within a 'stream of actions' (Mintzberg 1978). The logic is established by reference to the dialectical relationship between the firm, its internal systems and its environment.

As with all typologies the fourfold categorization says nothing of the scope of work completed under each type. Its main service though is to point to the wider range of constructions of meaning of the term 'strategy' in existence than most people in the organization studies and related areas assume. It is instructive that critical studies of post-Fordism and the flexible organization (Gilbert et al. 1992), for example, employ broadly similar rationalist notions of strategy as say Porter or Chandler. To take a current example, the debaters around the issue of 'flexible specialization' treat the statements and actions of managers in a very literal way. Seldom does one encounter an appreciation of the accidental emergent quality of a given production policy or the inherent contradictions of market understandings. More pointedly, the typology of Zan alerts one to the existence of more sophisticated conceptions of management and the firm in the strategy world than is commonly recognized. Moreover, these emergent understandings cry out for assistance from the organization camp. Some examples from strategy writers will illustrate the claims.

As far back as 1984 Bourgeois bemoaned the restrictive influence of industrial organization economics, contingency theory and population ecology models of organisation on the development of the strategic management field. As he put it, informed by these frameworks, management 'may as well resign itself to succumbing to the matrix of deterministic forces presented by the environmental, technical, and human forces that impinge upon its freedom of choice. At best, management becomes a computational exercise.' The reductionism of such models eliminated much of the richness that characterizes the strategic management process, and constrained the 'advancement of the strategic management discipline' (1984: 586). Above all, Bourgeois was arguing for basic recognition of the way organizational actors make strategic choices which in turn determine how a firm discovers itself within a given context. He went on to plead for the adoption of a dialectical view and the recognition of reciprocal causality. It is tantalizing that such strategy writers had made no use of Giddens or his concepts of structuration (Giddens 1981). The potential is almost breathtaking to contemplate. Rather than seeing structures within the organization or its environment as separate, 'out there', or distant from a social actor, it is possible to link the two intimately. In other words, managers do not only operate within corporate structures (such as divisions or business units): they are part of their creation. If this is accepted, then organizational sociologists have much to offer the strategy field in their techniques of researching action, perception and social construction.

Other students of strategy in the 1980s made equally telling *cris de coeur* which remained unanswered by organization scholars. Chaffee (1985) concluded that the strategy concept had emerged with three distinct 'mental models' – the linear, the adaptive and the interpretative – and that conflicting views abounded. In particular, she maintained that such differences were rarely analysed, and that the strategy construct was multi-faceted and evolving 'to a level of complexity almost matching that of organizations themselves' (1985: 89). Yet instead of seeking support from the emerging innovations in organizational analysis (outlined in the introduction) to pursue the potential in her questions, Chaffee stopped. Her rather tame conclusion was that the three models represented stages through which organizations pass (1985: 96).

In 1988, another strategy professional encapsulated the huge benefit of linking organization and strategy research. Wensley (1988: 21) considered that 'a concept of organisation is inevitably bound with most of what is written and researched in the field of strategic management.' Given the attempts to reveal the implicit richness of the strategy theme, together with the latent possibilities of bringing more recent organizational frameworks to the area, it would be unfortunate if the opportunity were missed again. An illustration of those possibilities is supplied by brief examination of the related empirical areas of markets and competition.

Strategy and Organizations: Markets and Competition

From the vantage point of the UK especially, it would seem that hardly an aspect of the public or private sector has escaped the impact of the forces of market relations and competition. The two words 'market' and 'competition' became the hallmarks of one of the most powerful political imperatives to drive a series of government administrations over the past fourteen years. The core belief of the new right rested on the assumed superiority of market relations to deliver competitive efficiency. The effects have been widespread. Simultaneously, market mechanisms have been introduced within organizations (for example, through profit centres), across professions and 'knowledge workers', and throughout the public sector in the form of tendering or the 'internal market' of the British National Health Service (NHS) (McNulty et al. 1994). In spite of the profound economic and social implications of these programmes, in the UK and elsewhere, the strategy and organization scholars have mounted separate investigations of the phenomena. The contention of this section is that market relations and competition offer one of the most promising sites for cooperation between the two fields.

Much of the reason for the mutual antipathy of the work of strategy and organization analysts stems from the contribution of economic theory to the former. Those who constructed the world of *Homo economicus*, and supplied the basic concepts of monopoly, oligopoly and perfect competition, came predominantly from the micro-economics tradition (Jain 1985). Students of organizational behaviour have been virtually allergic to such work given the micro-economics training of many strategy specialists. The result has been strategists writing on competition with the reliance on: rational, profit-maximizing behaviour by all economic agents, the absence of chronic information problems, little time for the ignorance shown routinely by firms and consumers, and the preoccupation with equilibrium states (Hodgson 1988: 4–21).

Many of the conceptions of competition and markets displayed by the leading strategy writers of the 1980s (commonly referred to as the industrial organization or IO school) exemplify the economic rationalism of their trade and would try the patience of the most forbearing organization scholar (cf. Barney 1986). The emphasis among the strategy specialists of the last decade has been therefore on explaining the creation of strategies which exploit a firm's uniqueness (Lenz 1980), heed the rivalry among competing firms and suppliers/buyers (Porter 1980) and take account of the classification of the industry involved (Gilbert and Strebel 1988).

It is understandable that many social scientists have been repelled by the assumptions of the IO writers and expended no further effort on penetrating the field. However, if they had battled through the undergrowth of this part of the strategy territory they might have encountered more useful inhabitants: the 'new competition' school. These academics are interesting for their heretical attitudes to strategy and their deployment of not just alternative forms of economic theory but a range of disciplinary models and techniques. The arch-heretics were Hayes and Abernathy (1980) who accused corporate USA of 'managing our way to industrial decline' in a now celebrated *Harvard Business Review* article. The pair attacked the dominant logic of the strategy experts head-on. Their argument centred on the way return on investment-based financial controls and portfolio management techniques (supplied by the authors mentioned in the first section) had stifled innovation. They challenged the accepted notions of life-cycle models of the IO school and rejected the 'static optimization' paradigm. Above all, they mobilized the Schumpeterian theory of competition (Schumpeter 1950: 82–3) to argue that technological innovation within the firm could create new sources of demand which in turn might provoke wholesale restructuring of existing markets and industries (Abernathy et al. 1983).

Subsequently, their followers have gone further into the role of management and the problems of innovation. Sadly the intellectual demands which their heresies created have not been heard by organizational scholars. In spite of the opportunity to link strategic management, technological innovation and aspects of the social organization of production (in Bill Abernathy's shorthand, 'bringing together technological hardware and human software') few organization specialists picked up the gauntlet (Whipp and Clark 1986); most seemed unaware of it ever having been thrown down. What has the organization literature been missing?

In brief, the new competition writers were drawing on the institutional economists (Langlois 1986; Hodgson 1988), a group who rejected the deterministic and static models of neoclassical micro-economics. Institutional economists see market relations and competition as the product of human experience. Market relations are seen as informed by a variety of 'social institutions', that is, agreed forms of behaviour which specify conduct in recurrent situations (Schotter 1981: 11); examples include property rights or employment contracts. Moreover, institutionalists have sought to explain competition as a sequence of events taking place in real time, involving people who have highly imperfect information and for whom specific benefits are often transitory. Investigations of UK industry have been mounted by institutional economists using such a perspective. The results have been telling but isolated. Elbaum and Lazonick (1986) argued that social institutions in Britain restrained the growth of mass production techniques and the forms of corporate coordination found in the USA, Germany and Japan. The interlocking constraints included the retention of family-controlled firms, the absence of bank involvement within industry and the inability of education systems to provide managers and applied scientists (1986: 6). Lewchuk (1987), in the same vein, explained the differences in the technological base of the US and British motor industries by reference to the social institutions surrounding the effort bargain at shopfloor level (cf. Whipp 1990).

In truth, strategy experts and organization analysts have remained apart, to the detriment of all concerned. It is frustrating that the wealth of analytical tools and empirical material generated by organizational scholars has been so seldom engaged with the institutional and new competition work. Both groups would be beneficiaries of collaboration via, minimally,

simple exchange. In broad terms, the organization specialist could supply much sharper tools for exploring the subjective dimension of economic agents, most notably management. Conversely, institutional economists would offer organization analysts an expanded set of frameworks for comprehending a market. Taken together the promise of unlocking the motors which drive the dynamic of competitive relations is considerable.

It is not the intention to suggest such crossdisciplinary endeavour is unknown; the point is its rarity. Gospel's (1993) work on British labour and management or Scott and Lodge's (1985) study of competition in the USA are worthy examples of the synthesis of institutional economics, organization theory and industrial sociology. Some of the commentators on strategy grouped under the interpretative label in the first section, have made sporadic connections between their adaptive view of management and the social institutions which shape the market (for example, Teece 1987). The sceptic may well comment, 'does it matter?' The apparent dominance of market structures and the espousal of competition by the previous opponents of liberal capitalism led Fukuyama (1989) to proclaim 'the end of history'. The implications are non-trivial, to say the least. Given the commitment of resources in the name of market efficiency it smacks of negligence for academics to remain locked within their disciplinary stockades.

Perhaps some indication of the intellectual benefits and an example of the research involved will help support the need for more collaboration and exchange. In conceptual terms, bringing together institutional economics, an interpretative perspective on strategy and organizational theories, points to a more demanding appreciation of management and competition. Organizations may aspire to Chandler's (1962) original definition of strategy as the 'determination of the basic long term goals of an enterprise, and the adoption of courses of action and the allocation of resources necessary for carrying out those goals'. In practice, strategy is far more complicated. Allegedly objective decisions relating to finance or products are conditioned by the social character of an organization. Business strategy is by no means rational. Managerial action is notable for the limits of its impact and the way it is victim to chance. Organization specialists are well equipped to examine the intricacies of the interior life of the firm. Who better to deconstruct strategic management than the academics for whom structure, culture and politics are their stock-in-trade? Such forces transform given strategic intentions and account for the ambiguity of much managerial activity. The institutional economists have highlighted the impermanence of market relations. Organizational researchers should find it intriguing to supply complementary explanations of the instability and interdeterminacy of the behaviour of those responsible within organizations for activity in the market (Whittington and Whipp 1992). Studying the attempted creation of the internal market in the UK NHS reinforces the point. Our conclusion was that the market supplies no more unambivalent sources of managerial control than the earlier Fordist hierarchical variant. The strategy of employing market relations is characterized by compromise, contradiction and unintended consequences.

Research which draws on the range of conceptual and analytical devices offered by the specific types of organization, economics and strategy scholars outlined here, promises much. Put simply, the result would be an account of strategic management and market forms which reveals how they are socially constructed, their inherent irrationality and, not least, their conspicuous instability. Empirical targets for those willing to operate this intellectual equipment are growing apace. Nonetheless, if market relations and competition offer a strong example of a productive combined assault then the lost opportunities are equally apparent. In many ways the silences among strategy scholars over certain issues are almost deafening. Three examples of such silences may be instructive for both illustrating the essential character of the area and yet indicating possible lines of future development.

RESOUNDING SILENCES

The silences or absences which stand out in the corpus of strategy and organization writing are threefold: they include the issues of levels of analysis, the problem of change and time, and the non-reflexive nature of most strategy authors.

Levels of Analysis

The levels problem is ironic. The earlier strategy experts of the industrial organization literature (Barney 1986) were at pains to emphasize the goal of strategic management as the maximization of the unique strengths of a firm within its markets and industry settings. The general acceptance of Porter's (1985) form of industry analysis or the popularity of strategic intent (Prahalad and Hamel 1985) shaped by the industry context has been readily visible. Yet,

very few strategy or organization experts have sought to link systematically and investigate the multiple linkages which connect firm-level behaviour and the operation of markets *and* industries. Perhaps the silence is partly explained by the vested interests of specialists who have excavated the area along distinct channels such as industry groups or value chains. What is required to fill the silence is a more inclusive orientation which uses economic and social modes of analysis to open up the array of intersecting relationships.

Constructive steps in this direction are suggested by Boons and Roberts (1994) who align a resource-based view of the firm with industry-level understandings. As their recent work shows, making such linkages obliges them to combine economic laws with the subjective determinants of exchange relationships. In addition, such combinations require the study of an array of organization and external features. The result is a joining of: the technical resources of the firm and their means of conversion into final products or services; the highly indeterminate organization processes which mobilize the firm's tangible and intangible assets; the way resources and capabilities face often incomplete markets; and how each may fall victim to unpredictable outcomes arising from the contradictory perceptions of suppliers, new entrants, intermediaries and regulators.

Change and Time

The second absence concerns the subject of change and time. To many the assertion that anything like silence exists around the words 'change', 'strategic change' or 'change management' would seem perverse. Such phrases appear almost universally in the subtitles of academic papers, while the cliché of managing change is applied to almost every management area from IT to supply chain development. Of course, strategic change has been researched by academics anxious to synthesize analytical perspectives from the economics, strategy and organization traditions (see, for example, Kanter 1990; Pettigrew and Whipp 1991).

Nevertheless, even allowing for the work of the process scholars outlined earlier in this chapter the central problem of time is at once generally acknowledged but not the subject of searching examination. The work of Miller and Friesen (1980) or more recently Greenwood and Hinings (1988) has made great strides in developing the conceptual framework necessary to describe the momentum of change, transition and adaptation in organizations. The problem has been that very few writers on strategic change have ever challenged their mathematically based, linear and Newtonian conceptions of time, either in their theory-building or in their empirical investigations (Whipp 1994; Wilson 1992). The resulting lacuna is disturbing for two main reasons. First, strategy analysts are missing the opportunity to mobilize the abundant richness of time ordering systems found with organizations (for example, subjective industry maps versus rational planning manuals). It is this diversity of understandings of time which goes a long way to explaining the uneven rhythms of the process of corporate change and its indeterminacy. Second, in the practical sphere, the claims that business processes are amenable to 're-engineering' along a single time dimension, for example, are in danger of reducing our appreciation of the multiple sources of time ordering by people in contemporary organizations.

Reflexivity

The third major silence is perhaps the most serious and potentially debilitating for the strategy territory. It is no surprise that strategy scholars who predominantly regard their subject as applied and resting on neo-classical economic assumptions show little evidence of reflexivity. As the previous sections have shown, the aim of the majority of such writers is highly positivist: to understand the problem of renewal and growth in order to provide better guidance for the strategic direction of an organization (Lyles 1990: 363). Critical self-appraisal of motivations or core beliefs by those in the strategy literature is not widespread. *Pace* Kay's (1993) criticisms, the conviction of most North American strategy academics is that the industrial organization framework (see earlier) provides a common foundation for their work. The variety of their research objects, from 'intrapreneurship' to international strategic alliances, is made possible, they argue, precisely because of this common platform. It is telling that attempts to question the paradigmatic and theoretical starting-points of the strategy areas have come from those whose training lay outside (see, for example, Zan 1990; Johnson 1987). In a similar way, the questioning of the motives and assumptions which underpin the actions of those responsible for strategy within organizations has received correspondingly scant attention. Whilst process analysts take seriously the cultural and political diversity within an organization (see, for example, Kunda 1992) few of their number have addressed the wider social and political conditioning of the senior management. As Willmott (1993b) points out, the spread of corporate culture programmes, for example, has seen little attempt to scrutinize

the assumptions and prescriptions of the 'excellence' movement and its ideological base. The only exception currently to be found is in volume 9 of the 'Advances in Strategic Management' series (Shrivastava et al. forthcoming) – *Critical Perspectives on Strategic Management* – which observes that 'one source of progress in a scientific field is its ability to engage in critical self-reflection.'

The reason for emphasizing the seriousness of the need for greater reflexivity is partly due to the intellectual and practical opportunities which beckon. As will be apparent from the earlier pages of this chapter, the strategy specialists founded their work on the conviction that it was possible to capture the workings of markets and competition and to advise practitioners accordingly. The pervasive take-up of 'Boston Box' or 'product life-cycle' devices is testimony to the relevance of such work (Kay 1993: 340–9). However, it is arguably research which has questioned the fundamental nature of strategy (cf. Knights and Morgan 1991) which offers the most exciting practical insights. In short, reflexiveness could lead to more profound research and equally challenging applied projects.

Mintzberg's work provides an instructive example in the way he criticizes the narrowness of much strategy writing. His central argument is that organizations should engage in strategic thinking rather than the planning espoused by many experts. Strategic thinking is about synthesis, involving intuition and creativity; it is not constrained by established categories. To paraphrase Mintzberg, strategy-making should occur outside the 'boxes' or conventional perspectives. His iconoclastic approach attacks the fallacious assumptions that prediction is possible, that strategists can be detached from the subjects of their strategies and that the strategy-making process can be formalized (Mintzberg 1994). Others have offered practical advice by adopting a similar questioning of the taken-for-granted truths of strategic management (for a review of competing theories and multiple diagnoses see Edmondson 1994). Extending such interrogation to include the highly active critical literature within organization studies would be invigorating in academic terms. Given the current experience of the disenchantment of managers with 'fad theories', a more reflexive mode of strategy and organization research could well appeal to practitioners for its candour.

FUTURE POSSIBILITIES

Many of the silences in the strategy area are so resounding because of the needs which are not being met and the opportunities which risk being missed. In this sense, much of the foregoing argument about the dominant tendencies amongst strategy writers points to the future direction which the field may take. The potential avenues of study are vast, as surveys of academics and practitioners have found (Lyles 1990: 369). However, four areas give a strong indication of such future possibilities, namely: the nature of industries, new technology, global operations and the public sector.

Although micro-economists have been to the fore in the study of industries, alternative understandings have arisen from collaboration between strategy and organization specialists. Sometimes writers from either area have usefully employed one another's concepts and frameworks.

Management writers such as Huff (1982) and Spender (1989) argue that industries are informed by 'dominant logics' or 'recipes' that limit decision-making at firm level. Industry studies from within the broad strategy area have shed light on the collective mindset of an industry as a key influence on competition. Porac and Thomas (1992) maintain that managerial cognitive structures contain the consensually held beliefs within an industrial community. If they stabilize, the structures become interpretative frames which shape the way managers make sense of actions and circumstances outside the firm. The authors contend that industrial belief systems mature through 'strategic paradigms' as managers make resource allocation decisions and 'reputational orderings' as all involved evaluate the relative strength of firms. Meanwhile, others from outside the North American strategy stable have extended the coverage of the non-material features of an industry. Melin and Hellgren (1993) claimed that a specific 'industrial wisdom' has conditioned the strategic choices of firms in the Swedish paper industry over time. Durand (1993) has explored the dynamics of cognitive technological maps and how firms draw on them to adapt to market demands. Shearman and Burrell (1987: 330) point to the social structures which support such cognitive processes. The 'community' and 'formal and informal networks' and the 'club' forms represent the specific formations of power, status and negotiated order found at different stages of the industry life-cycle.

The outcome of these authors' work is that the meso-level phenomenon of the industry is a worthy object of enquiry for two main reasons: (1) it is a vital arena for understanding the interior life of organizations; and (2) it contains rich potential within its non-material aspects for comprehending the collective and inter-organizational aspects of economies. The sector concept

has provided one means of releasing these possibilities (cf. Whipp and Clark 1986: Chapter 1; Child 1988; Rasanen and Whipp 1992). Furthermore, it might prove a useful meeting point where various organizational sociologists might apply their expertise to the issues of strategic management and competition.

The term 'sector' refers to a historical formation of complementary, co-evolving business activities. It is often, though not invariably, attached to specific locations, such as a region or country. A sector includes organizations which provide similar goods or services together with those who regularly transact with them in supplying, servicing, regulatory or customer roles (Rasanen and Whipp 1992: 47). Mature sectors may exhibit formal social networks but their capacity to coordinate the whole may be limited. Sectors cannot be taken as governance structures in a strong sense; rather they are arenas of cooperation and competition. Given this community of diverse actors, conventional IO economics is ill equipped to capture the social and political processes concerned.

The forest sector is a useful example (see Lilja et al. 1992). Forestry has certain economic features, such as vertical integration, capital intensity, and low and cyclically dominated returns, which shape the forms of business organization. In reality, the pattern of organization cannot be explained by reference to these economic aspects alone. National forest sectors (notably in Finland, Sweden, Canada and the USA) can be distinguished by the respective combination of social networks, ownership and control relationships and their relation to government. In many senses, the sector is an accomplishment of multiple actors with often diverse logics of action. The sector is never a completed project but is a contradictory whole in a state of relative impermanence and tension, with constantly emerging alternative organizational solutions.

Even in this brief rendition of the sector concept, one hopes the opportunities for intervention by organizational/industrial sociologists, historians and certain breeds of strategy scholars begin to appear. The linkage of cognitive, economic and socio-political perspectives raises the prospect of much fuller accounts than are currently available of not only nationally based sectors but their international operation (Porter 1990). In turn, these broader analyses of sectors could help clarify the character and emergence of national business systems (Whitley 1992: Chapter 1). This might take the form, for example, of testing the extent to which national institutions are able to shape the evolution of individual sectors, or conversely, how far the changes in national business systems or national systems of innovation are accounted for by the shifts in sector patterns of development.

The potential for collaborative research which blends the theories and techniques of strategy and organization studies is considerable. As the example of the sector shows, the research canvas is extensive. Allying analytical frameworks around such fundamental problems (as with industry form and operation) can be used with other major segments of economic life. New technology is a strong example. The strategy field has clearly identified information technology as a critical feature to be managed, given the aspiration of strategists to supply appropriate direction to the growth and renewal of the firm. Equally, organization scholars have been drawn to the rise of 'new organizational forms' which challenge many of the precepts behind previous notions of rational bureaucracy. It is interesting that both sets of writers have arrived at similar positions. Two parallel projects make the point. Rockhart and Short, in their 'management in the 1990s' programme at MIT, conclude that 'organizations today are disintegrating – their borders punctured by the steadily decreasing costs of electronic interconnection among firms, suppliers, and customers' (1989: 7). Meanwhile Lash and Urry (1987) are able to supply highly appropriate frameworks for the social and economic 'disorganization' of capitalist systems in the late twentieth century. The problem of technology is so quintessentially a defining feature of the postmodern age that the need for synthesis of strategic and organizational research has reached screaming point (for examples of bold attempts in this spirit, see Scott-Poole and Van de Ven 1989).

A similar pressure is building in the area of international business. The advent of 'globalization' has been trumpeted for some years. A rich vein of research from strategy academics has produced a mature appreciation of the international operations of business. A distinction is drawn now between the fragmented multinational strategies pursued by Western firms and the globally integrated approach of the Japanese. The technical debate over the optimum strategies has been pursued around the issues of global marketing, world-scale efficiencies and the use of cross-subsidization between markets. Put in a summary way, the current consensus emphasizes the study of 'corporate capabilities'. The aim is to generate global efficiency, national responsiveness and an ability to exploit knowledge on a world-wide basis simultaneously (Bartlett and Ghoshal 1989). The conclusions of the international business specialists are dripping with questions that could be explored by organization analysts. The core concept of organizational capabilities (Prahalad

and Hamel 1985), to take one instance, could be developed by such analysts applying their understanding of the processes of innovation, learning and adaptation – pressures which have been assumed rather than researched by their strategy colleagues. The critical excavation of the interior life of the transnational organization beckons as one of the overwhelming collaborative projects for the next decade.

The third example of the type of area where the strategy and organization fields may develop is in the public, or not-for-profit, sector. Here the work of organization experts had led the way but could well benefit from adopting the tools of strategic management. The attraction of the public sector as a laboratory of managerial experiment is well known. Public services have been reorganized through privatization, decentralization and the use of contractual and 'quasi-market' apparatus. The changes have occurred against a backcloth of government financial crises and have been legitimated by reference to the language of the sovereign consumer (McNulty et al. 1994). While organization departments have offered subtle interpretations of the combination of restructuring, improved efficiency and highly imperfect markets, their work is stunted by their crude appreciation of strategy. Quite apart from the pressing need for thorough empirical investigation of such a shift within Western economies, the chance to stretch and test strategy concepts established within the private sector offers a substantial prize.

Certainly, these three areas of future development in no way exhaust the schedule of research objects which have assembled in recent years. Others include the market and diffusion of managerial knowledge, the establishment of commercial and industrial entities *de nouveau* in former communist states, and the elevation of ethical and environmental dimensions of business life. All are amenable to the synthetic approaches described here.

CONCLUSION

This chapter began with an acknowledgement of the sensitivities which bedevil the relationships across the academic division of labour. The hope of this review is that it might, at least, persuade some of our colleagues in the organization studies sphere to put away their metaphorical guns. Such tensions, however, are indicative of the vibrant character of the strategy debate.

The approach taken in this treatment of the area has been unambiguously positive. As the first part of the piece tried to show, military and one-dimensional views of 'strategy' have dominated its use. Yet it is the diversity of constructions of the term which give rise to contention and the hope of fruitful exchanges. The dialectic has not been well represented in the past. Instead, narrow conceptions of strategy have been allowed to dominate, almost by default. The time for a corrective therefore was overdue. The core of the chapter has been at pains to draw attention to the varieties of perspective and use of the strategy concept. The evolutionary path from mechanistic strategic planning, through cognitive decision-making formats, to the resurgence of business policy and processual orientations has been as fragmented as it has been divergent. It is unsurprising that reductionist versions of the subject of strategy are retailed across the business studies field.

The contention of this essay is that the term 'strategy' is usefully problematic. There is no denying the ideological turbulence which surrounds it and the difficulties which new entrants face in coming to terms with such cleavage. Yet if the past thirty years show anything, then it is that where specialists have combined or attempted to mix organization and strategy frameworks, genuinely searching progress has occurred. In short, strategy is too important to be annexed by a single discipline.

The signs for synthetic and boundary-crossing projects are currently good. The 'death of certainty' (Appleby et al. 1994) has been marked by the outbreak of epistemological doubt across many disciplines in North America. The challenges of multi-culturalism, a new world economic order and demographic turmoil have made certain academics receptive to alternative orientations. It is instructive that in the results of a recent questionnaire of strategic management, 'organization theory' was identified as the third main subject which will have 'the most impact on strategic research in the next ten years' (Lyles 1990: 370). In the previous pages, the examples of industry form, new technology, globalization and new public management provide an indication of the possible sites for stretching the joint endeavours of strategy and organization scholars.

The central assertion of the exchange or reshaping of the instruments of strategy and organization academics is uncomfortable for many. Ideology, epistemology and methodology separate and divide. Moreover, the calls for the strengthening of field boundaries in order to ward off 'hostile takeover' by leading figures such as Pfeffer (Burrell et al. 1994: 7) highlight the problems involved. Yet, rather than seeing openness and pluralism as weaknesses in these respective subject areas, the converse could be true. The defining character of organizations at

the close of the twentieth century is the fragility of their shapes and the turbulence born of the co-existence of order and disorder (Sminia 1994: 53) in their strategic processes. Such ferment would be best approached by academics if they were to take seriously their own intellectual turmoil. Reference to Kuhn's model of the dynamics of scientific knowledge development may be of help. Those attempting to research such order and disorder should be prepared to work at the process of struggle which is impelled by an accumulation of anomalies in existing theories and which stimulates alternative theorizing (Willmott 1993a: 683). Such creative deconstruction is to be welcomed.

REFERENCES

Abernathy, W., Clark, K. and Kantrow, A. (1983) *Industrial Renaissance: Producing a Competitive Future for America*. New York: Basic Books.

Andrews, K. (1971) *The Concept of Corporate Strategy*. Homewood, IL: Irwin.

Ansoff, H. (1965) 'The firm of the future', *Harvard Business Review*, 43(5): 162–78.

Anthony, T. (1965) *Planning and Control Systems: a Framework for Analysis*. Boston: Harvard University Press.

Appleby, J., Hunt, L. and Jacob, M. (1994) *Telling the Truth about History*. New York: Norton.

Barney, J.B. (1986) 'Types of competition and the theory of strategy: towards an integrative framework', *Academy of Management Review*, 11(4): 791–800.

Bartlett, C. and Ghoshal, S. (1989) *Managing across Borders*. Boston: Harvard Business Review.

Best, M. (1990) *The New Competition: Institutions of Industrial Restructuring*. Cambridge: Polity Press.

Boons, A. and Roberts, H. (1994) 'The resource-based view of the firm'. Paper presented to the 2nd Workshop on Accounting, Strategy and Control, EIASM, Brussels, September.

Bourgeois, L.J. (1984) 'Strategic management and determinism', *Academy of Management Review*, 9(4): 586–96.

Burrell, G., Reed, M., Alvesson, M., Calás, M. and Smircich, L. (1994) 'Why organization? Why now?', *Organization*, 1(1): 5–18.

Chaffee, E. (1985) 'Three models of strategy', *Academy of Management Review*, 10(1): 89–98.

Chandler, A. (1962) *Strategy and Structure*. Boston: MIT Press.

Child, J. (1988) 'On organizations and their sectors,' *Organizational Studies*, 9: 13–19.

Donaldson, L. (1985) *In Defence of Organisation Theory*. Cambridge: Cambridge University Press.

Durand, T. (1993) 'The dynamics of cognitive technological maps' in P. Lorange, B. Chakravarthy, J.

Roos and A. Van de Ven (eds), *Implementing Strategic Processes: Change, Learning and Co-operation*. Oxford: Blackwell. pp. 394–410.

Edmondson, A. (1994) 'Three faces of Eden: the persistence of competing theories and multiple diagnoses in organization intervention research'. Unpublished paper, Harvard Graduate School of Business Administration.

Elbaum, B. and Lazonick, W. (1986) *The Decline of the British Economy*. Oxford: Clarendon Press.

Frederickson, J. (1983) 'Strategic process research: questions and recommendations', *Academy of Management Review*, 8(4): 565–75.

Fukuyama, F. (1989) 'The end of history?', *Financial Times*, 19 October: 2.

Giddens, A. (1981) *A Contemporary Critique of Historical Materialism*. London: Macmillan.

Gilbert, N., Burrows, R. and Pollert, A. (eds) (1992) *Fordism and Flexibility: Divisions and Change*. London: Macmillan.

Gilbert, X. and Strebel, P. (1988) 'Developing competitive advantage', in J. Quinn, H. Mintzberg and R. James (eds), *The Strategy Process: Concepts, Contexts and Cases*. Engelwood Cliffs, NJ: Prentice-Hall. pp. 70–9.

Gospel, H. (1993) *Markets, Firms and the Management of Labour: the British Experience in Historical Perspective*. Cambridge: Cambridge University Press.

Greenwood, R. and Hinings, C. (1988) 'Organizational design types, tracks and the dynamics of strategic change', *Organization Studies*, 9(3): 293–316.

Hayes, R. and Abernathy, W. (1980) 'Managing our way to industrial decline', *Harvard Business Review*, July/ August, 69–77.

Hodgson, G. (1988) *Economics and Institutions*. Cambridge: Polity Press.

Huff, A. (1982) 'Industry influences on strategy-formulation', *Strategic Management Journal*, 3: 119–30.

Jain, S. (1985) *Marketing, Planning and Strategy*. Cincinnati: South Western.

Johnson, G. (1987) *Strategic Change and the Management Process*. Oxford: Basil Blackwell.

Kanter, R. (1990) *The Change Masters*. London: Unwin.

Kay, J. (1993) *Foundations of Corporate Success*. Oxford: Oxford University Press.

Knights, D. and Morgan, G. (1991) 'Strategic discourse and subjectivity: towards a critical analysis of corporate strategy in organizations', *Organization Studies*, 12(2): 251–73.

Kunda, G. (1992) *Engineering Culture: Control and Commitment in a High-Tech Corporation*. Philadelphia: Temple University Press.

Langlois, R.N. (ed.) (1986) *Economics as a Process: Essays in the New Institutional Economics*. Cambridge: Cambridge University Press.

Lash, S. and Urry, J. (1987) *The End of Organised Capitalism*. Oxford: Polity Press.

Lenz, R. (1980) 'Strategic capability: a concept and framework for analysis', *Academy of Management Review*, 5(2): 225–34.

Levitt, T. (1965) 'Exploit the product life-cycle', *Harvard Business Review*, November–December: 81–94.

Lewchuk, W. (1987) *American Technology and the British Vehicle Industry*. Cambridge: Cambridge University Press.

Lilja, K., Rasanen, K. and Tainio, R. (1992) 'A dominant business recipe: the forest sector in Finland', in R. Whitley (ed.), *European Business Systems*. London: Sage. pp. 137–54.

Lindblom, L. (1959) 'The science of muddling through', *Public Administration Review*, 19 (Spring): 78–88.

Lyles, M. (1990) 'A research agenda for strategic management in the 1990s', *Journal of Management Studies*, 27(4): 363–75.

March, J. and Olsen, J. (1976) *Ambiguity and Choice in Organisations*. Bergen: Universitetsforlaget.

McNulty, T., Whittington, R., Whipp, R. and Kitchener, M. (1994) 'Implementing marketing in NHS hospitals', *Public Money and Management*, April–June.

Melin, L. and Hellgren, B. (1993) 'Industrial wisdom: the case of the Swedish paper industry', Mimeo, University of Linköping.

Miles, R. and Snow, C. (1984) 'Fit, failure and the hall of fame', *California Management Review*, 3: 10–28.

Miller, D. and Friesen, A. (1980) 'Momentum and revolution in organization adaptation', *Academy of Management Journal*, 23: 591–614.

Mintzberg, H. (1978) 'Patterns in strategy formation', *Management Science*, 24(9): 934–48.

Mintzberg, H. (1994) *The Rise and Fall of Strategic Planning*. Hemel Hempstead: Prentice-Hall.

Peters, T.J. and Waterman, R.H. (1982) *In Search of Excellence: Lessons from America's Best Run Companies*. New York: Harper & Row.

Pettigrew, A. (1973) *The Politics of Organisational Decision Making*. London: Tavistock.

Pettigrew, A. and Whipp, R. (1991) *Managing Change for Competitive Success*. Oxford: Blackwell.

Porac, J. and Thomas, H. (1992) 'The cognitive construction of industries'. Unpublished paper, Department of Management, New York University.

Porter, M. (1980) *Competitive Strategy*. New York: Free Press.

Porter, M. (1985) *Competitive Advantage: Creating and Sustaining Superior Performance*. New York: Free Press.

Porter, M. (1990) *The Competitive Advantage of Nations*. New York: Free Press.

Prahalad, C. and Hamel, G. (1985) 'Strategic intent', *Harvard Business Review*, May–June: 63–76.

Quinn, J (1980) *Strategies for Change: Logical Incrementalism*. Homewood, IL: Irwin.

Rasanen, K. and Whipp, R. (1992) 'National business recipes: a sector perspective', in R. Whitley (ed.),

European Business Systems. London: Sage. pp. 46–60.

Rockhart, J. and Short, J. (1989) 'IT in the 1990s: managing organizational interdependence', *Sloan Management Review*, 30: 7–17.

Rumelt, R. (1988) 'The evaluation of business strategy', in J.B. Quinn, H. Mintzberg and R.M. James (eds), *The Strategy Process: Concepts, Contexts and Cases*. Engelwood Cliffs, NJ: Prentice-Hall. pp. 50–6.

Schendel, D. and Cool, K. (1988) 'Development of the strategic management field', in J. Grant (ed.), *Strategic Management Frontiers*. Greenwich, CT: JAI Press. p. 7032.

Schendel, D. and Hofer, C. (1979) *Strategic Management: a New View of Business Policy and Planning*. Boston: Little Brown.

Schotter, A. (1981) *The Economic Theory of Social Institutions*. Cambridge: Cambridge University Press.

Schumpeter, J.A. (1950) *Capitalism, Socialism, and Democracy*, 3rd edn. New York: Harper.

Scott, R. and Lodge, G. (1985) *US Competitiveness in the World Economy*. Boston, MA: Harvard Business School Press.

Scott-Poole, M. and Van de Ven, A. (1989) 'Toward a general theory of innovation processes', in A. Van de Ven, H. Angle and M. Scott-Poole (eds), *Research on the Management of Innovation*. New York: Harper & Row. pp. 637–62.

Shearman, C. and Burrell, G. (1987) 'The structures of industrial development', *Journal of Management Studies*, 24(4): 326–45.

Shrivastava, P., Stubbart, C., Huff, A. and Dutton, J. (forthcoming) *Critical Perspectives on Strategic Management. Vol 9. Advances in Strategic Management*. New York: JAI Press.

Sminia, H. (1994) *Turning the Wheels of Change*. Groningen: Wolters-Noordhoff.

Spender, J. (1989) *Industry Recipes*. Oxford: Blackwell.

St George, A. (1994) 'Strategy', *Financial Times*, 11 July: 11.

Strategic Directions (1991) April, 2–5.

Teece, D. (ed.) (1987) *The Competitive Challenge: Strategies for Industrial Innovation and Renewal*. Cambridge, MA: Ballinger.

Thomas, H. (1993) 'Perspectives on theory building in strategic management', *Journal of Management Studies*, 30(1): 3–10.

Van de Ven, A., Angle, H. and Scott-Poole, M. (eds) (1989) *Research on the Management of Innovation*. New York: Harper & Row.

Weick, K.E. (1987) 'Substitutes for corporate strategy', in D.J. Teece (ed.), *The Competitive Challenge: Strategies for Industrial Innovation and Renewal*. Cambridge, MA: Ballinger.

Wensley, R. (1988) 'Strategic management: avoiding economic errors and managerial myths', *University of Wales Review of Business and Economics*, 2.

Whipp, R. (1990) *Patterns of Labour: Work and Social Change in the Pottery Industry*. London: Routledge.

Whipp, R. (1994) 'A time to be concerned', *Time and Society*, 3(1): 99–116.

Whipp, R. and Clark, C. (1986) *Innovation and the Auto Industry: Product, Process and Work Organisation*. London: Frances Pinter.

Whitley, R. (ed.) (1992) *European Business Systems*. London: Sage.

Whittington, R. and Whipp, R. (1992) 'Professional ideology and marketing implementation', *European Journal of Marketing*, 26, 31(1): 52–63.

Williams, R. (1976) *Keywords: a Vocabulary of Culture and Society*. London: Fontana.

Willmott, H. (1993a) 'Breaking the paradigm mentality', *Organization Studies*, 14(5): 681–719.

Willmott, H. (1993b) 'Strength is ignorance; slavery is freedom: managing culture in modern organizations', *Journal of Management Studies*, 30(4): 515–52.

Wilson, D. (1992) *A Strategy of Change*. London: Routledge.

Zan, L. (1990) 'Looking for theories in strategy studies', *Scandinavian Journal of Management*, 6(2): 89–108.

2.2

Leadership in Organizations

ALAN BRYMAN

Leadership has long been a major area of interest among social scientists and in particular psychologists. However, the field of leadership in organizations seemed to be in a trough in the early 1980s. For some time there had been a feeling that the field lacked an agreed-upon framework (a paradigm) within which research took place and that the findings of a century of research were trivial or contradictory. New approaches continued to surface (e.g. Hunt et al. 1982) but the field seemed to lack coherence and there was a sense of despondency about its future direction. There was even a call for the temporary abandonment of the concept (Miner 1982), but such extreme views did not find many adherents, because, for all the undoubted problems with the area in those years (some of which have not gone away), the notion of leadership is one that continues to attract generations of writers, in large part because we tend to view leadership as an important feature of everyday and organizational affairs.

Leadership, as one might anticipate, is not an easy concept to define. Its widespread currency and use in everyday life as an explanation affects the way it is defined and indeed probably makes it more difficult to define than a concept that is invented as an abstraction *ab initio*. Most definitions of leadership have tended to coalesce around a number of elements which can be discerned in the following definition by a researcher whose work had a profound impact on one of the stages of theory and research to be encountered below:

> Leadership may be considered as the process (act) of influencing the activities of an organized group in its efforts toward goal setting and goal achievement. (Stogdill 1950: 3)

Three elements can be discerned in this definition that are common to many definitions: influence, group and goal. First, leadership is viewed as a process of influence whereby the leader has an impact on others by inducing them to behave in a certain way. Second, that influence process is conceptualized as taking place in a group context. Group members are invariably taken to be the leader's subordinates and hence the persons for whom the leader has some responsibility. This focus on the leader in relation to a definable group is invariably translated into research in which sergeants and their combat units or supervisors and their work groups constitute the focus of analysis. Third, the leader influences the behaviour of group members in the direction of goals with which the group is faced. Effective leadership – the holy grail of leadership theory and research – will be that which accomplishes the group's goal(s).

This definition applies best to theory and research which was conducted up to the mid 1980s. While it by no means fell into disuse, later definitions, in so far as they were specifically articulated, tended to dwell on the leader as a *manager of meaning* – a term employed by Smircich and Morgan (1982). In a similar fashion, Pfeffer (1981) writes about leadership as symbolic action, by which he means that leaders engage in 'sense-making' on behalf of others and develop a social consensus around the resulting meanings. In both cases, leadership is seen as a process whereby the leader identifies for subordinates a sense of what is important – defining organizational reality for others. The leader gives a sense of direction and of purpose through the articulation of a compelling worldview. There is an irony in the use of the phrase 'manager of meaning', because one of the most intractable problems is that of distinguishing *leadership* from *management*. Many of the types of leader behaviour examined by leadership researchers, which are explored below, were underpinned by the previous definition of leadership as an influence process of moving a group to achieve its goal. These conceptions of leader behaviour might just as appropriately have been called 'managerial behaviour'. For writers like Zaleznik (1977) and Kotter (1990), the key to the difference between leadership and management lies in the orientation to change. Management is concerned with the here-and-now and does not ask broader questions about purpose and organizational identity; leaders by contrast 'change the way people think about what is desirable, possible and necessary' (Zaleznik 1977: 71). Thus, the phrase 'manager of meaning' (and the congruent notion of 'symbolic leadership') is meant to draw attention to the defining characteristic of true leadership as the active promotion of values which provide shared meanings about the nature of the organization. This emphasis has the further potential to differ from the earlier definition of leadership in that the focus on meaning might be taken to imply that a wider constituency of organizational members are implicated in leadership, in that meanings will tend to be the product of the interpretation by others of the messages intended by the leader. Influence, by contrast, implies a much more one-way leadership process. However, the definition of leadership in terms of influence, group and goal tended to hold sway, albeit in various guises, in much of the history of leadership theory and research. This history can be broken down into four main stages, which are the focus of the next section, and the influence-group-goal definition predominated in the first three of these stages.

FOUR STAGES OF LEADERSHIP THEORY AND RESEARCH

Each of the four approaches to the study of leadership covered in this section is associated with a particular time period. The *trait approach* dominated the scene up to the late 1940s; the *style approach* held sway from then until the late 1960s; the heyday of the *contingency approach* was from the late 1960s to the early 1980s; and the *New Leadership approach* has been the major influence on leadership research since the early 1980s. Each of these stages signals a change of emphasis rather than the demise of the previous approach(es). Trait research, for example, is still very much alive in the 1990s: the point is that each of the time periods is associated with a change of prominence.

The Trait Approach

The trait approach seeks to determine the personal qualities and characteristics of leaders. This orientation implies a belief that leaders are born rather than made – nature is more important than nurture. Research tended to be concerned with the qualities that distinguished leaders from non-leaders or followers. For many writers concerned with leadership in organizations the findings of such research had implications for their area of interest because of a belief that the traits of leaders would distinguish effective from less effective leaders, although relatively few trait studies examined this specific issue.

A host of different traits were examined by researchers. The bulk fall into three main groups: physical traits, such as physique, height, and appearance; abilities, such as intelligence and fluency of speech; and personality characteristics, such as conservatism, introversion–extroversion, and self-confidence. A key event in the history of the trait approach was the publication of an influential review of relevant findings by Stogdill (1948), who, along with a review by Gibb (1947), questioned the fruits of years of trait research. Both Stogdill and Gibb found the consistency of trait research to be questionable; this received confirmation in a later review by Mann (1959). While studies might find a certain trait to be significant, there always seemed to be considerable evidence that failed to confirm that trait's importance. Although it was not Stogdill's intention to bring trait research to a halt, writing in the *Handbook of Leadership* in 1974 he recognized that his review along with that of others 'sounded the seeming deathknell' of the approach (Bass 1990: 78). In fact, trait research did not grind to a halt and, in his 1974 review of the evidence, Stogdill appeared more sanguine about what had been accomplished within its purview (1990: 87).

Indeed, trait research enjoyed something of a renaissance in the late 1980s. A number of instances of this can be cited. Lord et al. (1986) reanalysed the studies on which Mann (1959) had drawn his pessimistic conclusions. They employed a technique called 'meta-analysis' which pools the findings of research in an area to generate an overall assessment of the impact of independent variables. Lord et al. found that the evidence for the importance of three of the six traits (intelligence, masculinity and dominance) was much stronger than Mann had recognized. However, the theoretical perspective taken by Lord et al. is different from that of the early trait researchers in that they argue that traits are important as 'perceiver constructs' (Lord and Maher 1991), that is, traits influence how people are perceived so that being a leader or a follower is inferred by people from evidence about traits that they exhibit. A further indication of the resurgence of trait thinking is an examination of evidence on real-life successful leaders which found that such leaders 'are strongly driven, have a strong desire to lead and exercise power, exhibit honesty and integrity, and are highly self-confident' (Locke et al. 1991: 34). Finally, a study of US presidents found a number of personality factors to be related to presidential performance; for example, need for power and activity inhibition both affected performance in a positive direction (House et al. 1991).

However, the key point is to recognize that the reviews by writers like Stogdill led to a disillusionment with trait investigations and from the late 1940s the trend shifted to the examination of leadership *style*.

The Style Approach

The emphasis on leadership style from the late 1940s signalled a change of focus from the personal characteristics of leaders to their behaviour as leaders. As much as a change in what was to be studied, this shift denoted an alteration in the practical implications of leadership research. The trait approach drew attention to the kinds of people who become leaders and in the process had great potential for supplying organizations with information about what should be looked for when *selecting* individuals for present or future positions of leadership. By contrast, since leader behaviour is capable of being changed, the focus on the behaviour of leaders carried with it an emphasis on *training* rather than selecting leaders.

There are a number of possible exemplars of the style approach but arguably the best known is the stream of investigations associated with an approach generated by a group of researchers at the Ohio State University, one of whose main figures was Stogdill. Not only did the Ohio State researchers generate a large number of studies, but the concepts and methods that they employed were widely used well beyond the confines of the Ohio group, an influence that can still be felt in the 1990s. The chief approach taken by the Ohio researchers was to administer questionnaires to the subordinates of leaders in one or a number of organizations, which in the early years tended to be military organizations. The questionnaire comprised a battery of items each of which was a statement about a leader's behaviour. Each subordinate was asked to indicate how well each statement reflected the behaviour of his or her leader. Subordinates' replies were aggregated to provide an overall score for each leader on each of a number of aspects of leader behaviour. The two main components of leader behaviour that Ohio State researchers tended to focus upon were dubbed *consideration* and *initiating structure*. The former denotes a leadership style in which leaders are concerned about their subordinates as people, are trusted by subordinates, are responsive to them, and promote camaraderie. Initiating structure refers to a style in which the leader defines closely and clearly what subordinates are supposed to do and how, and actively schedules work for them. Leaders' scores on these two styles were then related to various measures of outcome like group performance and subordinate job satisfaction. Early findings tended to be that consideration was associated with better morale and job satisfaction among subordinates but lower levels of performance. Initiating structure tended to be associated with poorer morale but better group performance. Later research often suggested that high levels of both consideration and initiating structure were the best leadership style.

At quite an early stage in the development of the Ohio Studies, it was noted by Korman (1966) that they were plagued by inconsistent results. He noted also that insufficient attention was paid to the possibility that the effectiveness of the two types of leader behaviour is situationally contingent; in other words, what works well in some situations may not work well in others. Later research in the Ohio tradition reflected a greater sensitivity to this possibility (for example, Kerr et al. 1974), a trend that was consistent with the growing adherence to a contingency approach that marked the 1970s (see below). Other problems contributed to the gradual drift away from the Ohio State approach. The kind of research design typically used in Ohio research allows relationships between leadership style and various outcomes to be determined, but could not sustain the causal interpretations that were invariably inferred from findings, for example, that consideration influenced job satisfaction. Indeed, studies using experimental and longitudinal research designs often found the leader-causes-outcome inference to be highly questionable (e.g. Lowin and Craig 1968; Greene 1975). Second, the tendency for research to be conducted on formally designated leaders meant that informal leadership processes were rarely investigated, though such processes have rarely been the focus of researchers in later years either. Third, the aggregation of subordinates' ratings of their leaders tended to neglect the significance of intra-group differences in the perception of leaders. Finally, there was growing recognition of measurement problems with the Ohio scales to measure leadership. In particular, the recognition of the impact of people's 'implicit leadership theories' on how they rated the behaviour of leaders was very damaging to the Ohio researchers. Rush et al. (1977), for example, showed that when rating the behaviour of an imaginary leader, people generated ratings that were very similar to those pertaining to real leaders in Ohio investigations. In other words, Ohio research might merely be tapping people's generalized perceptions of the behaviour of leaders. The theoretical implications of such research have become an area of interest in their own right (Lord and Maher 1991).

The significance of the Ohio State approach is as much methodological as it is substantive. While the terms 'consideration' and 'initiating structure' were still being employed in studies many years after the approach had lost favour (for example, Fry et al. 1986), the general methodological strategy that was signalled continues to be used in a variety of guises. Ironically, research on one aspect of leader behaviour – leaders' reward and punishment behaviour – proved to be very robust in terms of both consistency of findings and the imputation of causal interpretations (for example, Sims and Manz 1984; Podsakoff et al. 1984; 1990). However, the main drift from the late 1960s was toward contingency models of leadership.

Contingency Approach

Proponents of contingency approaches place situational factors towards the centre of any understanding of leadership. Typically, they seek to specify the situational variables which will moderate the effectiveness of different leadership approaches. This development parallels the drift away from universalistic theories of organization in the 1960s and the gradual adoption of a more particularistic framework which reflected an 'it all depends' style of thinking (e.g. Lawrence and Lorsch 1967).

Arguably, one of the best known exemplars of contingency thinking is Fiedler's contingency model of leadership effectiveness (Fiedler 1967; 1993; Fiedler and Garcia 1987). Fiedler's approach has undergone a number of revisions and changes of emphasis over the years. At its heart is a measurement instrument known as the least preferred coworker (LPC) scale which purports to measure the leadership orientation of the person completing it. It comprises a number of pairs of adjectives – the number varies from eighteen to twenty-five – with each pair being separated by an eight-point scale. The respondent is asked to think about the person with whom he or she has least liked working, either currently or in the past, and then to describe that

person in terms of each of the pairs of adjectives. Examples of the pairs of adjectives are: pleasant–unpleasant; friendly–unfriendly; rejecting–accepting; and distant–close. Each respondent's reply to each pair is scored one to eight, with a score of eight indicating a positive view of the least preferred coworker (pleasant, friendly, accepting, close, etc.) and a score of one indicating a negative view (unpleasant, unfriendly, rejecting, distant, etc.). Fiedler argues that the higher are people's LPC scores, the more relationship-motivated they are as leaders. This means that they are primarily concerned to foster good relationships with subordinates and are considerate. Leaders with low LPC scores are deemed to be task-motivated, that is, they are preoccupied with task accomplishment. In spite of an apparent similarity with the Ohio consideration and initiating structure pairing, it should be appreciated that for Fiedler there is a key difference between his and other conceptualizations like that of the Ohio researchers. Whereas for the latter there was a focus on consideration and initiating structure as contrasting styles of leadership, for Fiedler relationship and task motivation are *personality* attributes, a conceptualization which ties his work much more with earlier trait approaches.

From results relating to numerous studies conducted in a variety of work and non-work settings, Fiedler found that the effectiveness of relationship- and task-motivated leaders varied according to how favourable the situation was to the leader. More recently, this notion of situational favourableness has been dubbed 'situational control'. This idea has three components: leader–member relations; task structure; and position power. Fiedler's accumulated evidence led him to propose that task-oriented leaders are most effective in high control and low control situations; relationship-oriented leaders perform best in moderate control situations. The practical implication of Fiedler's work was that since a person's personality is not readily subject to change, it is necessary to change the work situation to fit the leader rather than the other way around.

Fiedler's model has been the subject of a great deal of controversy and debate. Much of this has centred upon the LPC scale, with many writers and researchers unconvinced by the link that is made between people's LPC scores and their approach to leadership. There has also been considerable unease over the conceptualization of situational control or favourableness. Many students of leadership asked why situational control was the only situational factor that was the object of attention and why the three components previously mentioned were the only crucial elements in situational control.

Fiedler has responded to some extent to this kind of criticism by including stress within the model's purview in more recent years (Fiedler and Garcia 1987; Fiedler 1993). But probably most damaging of all is that there has been widespread disagreement over the model's validity, that is, whether results really are consistent with the model. The three dimensions of situational control are usually presented as dichotomies, which, when differentially weighted, yield eight 'octants' of situational control. The results relating to two of these octants tend to yield reasonably consistent results, but for the other six the degree of variability of findings is often great (Bryman 1986: 129). Thus, for octant 2 (good leader–member relations, presence of task structure, and weak position power), LPC–performance correlations varied between 0.60 and -0.55. However, a meta-analysis by Strube and Garcia (1981) concluded that there was strong support for the model, although Vecchio (1983) noted some technical problems with the analysis. A later meta-analysis by Peters et al. (1985), using a different set of techniques, generated a more mixed set of findings. For example, it was found that results were more likely to be consistent with the theory in laboratory studies than in field studies, where other non-specific variables seemed to moderate LPC–performance relationships. Fiedler's contingency approach shares with the Ohio Studies a tendency to emphasize formally designated leaders to the virtual exclusion of informal leadership processes.

In the end, contingency approaches like Fiedler's probably became less popular because of inconsistent results that were often generated by research conducted within their frameworks and problems with the measurement of key variables. The idea of a contingency approach still has considerable support, although research sometimes suggests that situational factors are not always as important as might be expected. A study by Kennedy (1982) of leaders with LPC scores in the middle of the range found them to perform better than low and high LPC leaders regardless of levels of situational control. Podsakoff et al. (1984) found that the reward and punishment behaviour of leaders related to various measures of outcome irrespective of a wide range of situational factors that were examined. Nonetheless, by the early 1980s, there was considerable disillusionment with contingency theories.

The New Leadership Approach

The term 'New Leadership' has been used to describe and categorize a number of approaches to leadership which emerged in the 1980s which seemed to exhibit common or at least similar themes, although there were undoubtedly differences between them (Bryman 1992a). Together these different approaches seemed to signal a new way of conceptualizing and researching leadership. Writers employed a variety of terms to describe the new kinds of leadership with which they were concerned: transformational leadership (Bass 1985; Tichy and Devanna 1986), charismatic leadership (House 1977; Conger 1989), visionary leadership (Sashkin 1988; Westley and Mintzberg 1989); and, simply, leadership (Bennis and Nanus 1985; Kotter 1990). Together these labels revealed a conception of the leader as someone who defines organizational reality through the articulation of a vision which is a reflection of how he or she defines an organization's mission and the values which will support it. Thus, the New Leadership approach is underpinned by a depiction of leaders as managers of meaning rather than in terms of an influence process.

While many of the ideas associated with the New Leadership approach were presaged by some earlier writers like Selznick (1957) and Zaleznik (1977), its intellectual impetus derives in large part from the publication of Burns's study of political leadership in 1978. In this work, Burns proposed that political leaders could be distinguished in terms of a dichotomy of transactional and transforming leadership. Transactional leadership comprises an exchange between leader and follower in which the former offers rewards, perhaps in the form of prestige or money, for compliance with his or her wishes. In Burns's view, such leadership is not ineffective but its effectiveness is limited to the implicit contract between leaders and their followers. They are not bound together 'in a mutual and continuing pursuit of a higher purpose' (1978: 20). The transforming leader raises the aspirations of his or her followers such that the leader's and the followers' aspirations are fused. Burns's distinction was popularized by Peters and Waterman's (1982) hugely successful book *In Search of Excellence*, where they asserted that almost all of the highly successful companies that they studied had been influenced by a transforming leader at some stage in their development. The link between transforming leadership and vision was forged by a number of writers at around the same time and can be seen in the work of Bass (1985), Bennis and Nanus (1985), and Tichy and Devanna (1986). In the process, the nomenclature changed and transfor*ming* became transform*ational* leadership.

Bennis and Nanus and Tichy and Devanna adopted a similar approach of interviewing successful chief executives to determine the nature of their approaches to leadership. Bennis and Nanus are somewhat different in that they also tracked a number of their subjects. They also viewed their chief executives as leaders rather than as managers, suggesting a parallel between transactional/transforming and manager/leader. In both cases, the importance of articulating a vision was found to be a central element of their leadership which invariably involved the transformation of followers and often of organizations in correspondence with their vision. Both pairs of writers recognized that the vision must be communicated and made intelligible and relevant to the leader's followers. Roberts (1985) provided an interesting case study of a single transformational leader, a school superintendent in the USA, who, shortly after taking office, found herself in the midst of a budgetary crisis which she overcame; indeed, she helped the school district to prosper through the articulation and promotion of a vision about the aims of schooling. Peters and Austin also formulated a view of leadership which saw the formulation of a vision as central to leadership:

> You have got to know where you are going, to be able to state it clearly and concisely – and you have got to care about it passionately. That all adds up to vision, the concise statement/picture of where the company and its people are heading and why they should be proud of it. (1985: 284)

Writers on charismatic leadership also depicted vision as central to such leadership in organizational settings. This emphasis is not surprising since a vision or mission is almost a defining characteristic of charismatic leadership. As Weber, whose writings are central to an understanding of charisma, wrote: 'The bearer of charisma enjoys loyalty and authority by virtue of a mission believed to be embodied in him' (1968: 1117). In his study of charismatic leaders in business, Conger (1989) broke down charismatic leadership into four stages. First, the leader recognizes opportunities and the need for change and formulates a vision in relation to those needs. Second, the leader communicates that vision, a process which entails depicting the status quo as unacceptable and generating a rhetoric which aids the understanding of the vision. Third, the leader builds trust in the vision. Last, the leader helps others to achieve the vision through leading by example (role modelling) and by empowering followers.

These various writings on the New Leadership can, then, be viewed as signalling a change of orientation towards the leader as a manager of meaning and the pivotal role of vision in that process. However, two other ingredients stand out. First, in the New Leadership most research is conducted on very senior leaders, often chief executive officers, rather than low- to middle-level leaders such as supervisors, sergeants, middle managers, foremen, and sports coaches, as in the Ohio and Fiedler research. For example, in their article on different types of visionary leader, Westley and Mintzberg (1989) base their distinctions on case studies of two founders of organizations (Jobs of Apple and Land of Polaroid), two chief executives (Carlzon of SAS and Iacocca of Chrysler), and one leader of a political party (René Lévesque of the Parti Québecois). Second, unlike the three earlier stages of leadership research, substantial use is made of qualitative case studies. Some writers, like Bennis and Nanus and Tichy and Devanna, employed informal, semi-structured interviews as their chief source of data; others, like Westley and Mintzberg, employed documentary evidence. The use of such methods represents a substantial methodological shift from the quantitative studies that were typical of earlier phases of leadership research. However, a stream of highly influential research inaugurated by Bass includes leaders at lower levels and uses a quantitative approach in the manner of much leadership style and contingency research.

Bass's Research on Transactional and Transformational Leadership

Bass's approach (Bass 1985; Bass and Avolio 1990) draws heavily on Burns's (1978) work for its basic ideas, but goes much further in two respects. First, rather than as opposite ends of a continuum, Bass views transactional and transformational leadership as separate dimensions. Indeed, for Bass, the ideal approach exhibits both forms of leadership (Bass and Avolio 1993: 72). Second, in contrast to Burns's broad-brush style of discussing the two types of leadership, Bass has specified their basic components and has developed a battery of quantitative indicators for each component. His specification of these components has varied somewhat as his model has undergone development. Transformational leadership is made up of four components:

- *charisma* – developing a vision, engendering pride, respect and trust
- *inspiration* – motivating by creating high expectations, modelling appropriate behaviour, and using symbols to focus efforts
- *individualized consideration* – giving personal attention to followers, giving them respect and responsibility
- *intellectual stimulation* – continually challenging followers with new ideas and approaches.

Transactional leadership is conceptualized in terms of two components:

- *contingent rewards* – rewarding followers for conformity with performance targets
- *management by exception* – taking action mainly when task-related activity is not going to plan.

Each of these components is measured in a manner similar to the Ohio approach, in that followers complete questionnaires which specify types of leader behaviour each of which relates to one of these components. Leaders are then scored in terms of each component and their scores are correlated with various outcomes, which are usually a measure of performance and/ or a measure of 'extra effort', which refers to the respondent's preparedness to expend extra effort on behalf of the leader and the organization. Much of the research up to 1991 is summarized in Bryman (1992a: 121–8), while Bass and Avolio's (1993: 67) summary includes the results of some of the more recent research. The research, which has been conducted on a host of different levels of leader in a variety of settings, typically shows charisma and inspiration to be the components of leader behaviour that are most strongly associated with desirable outcomes such as performance of subordinates. Individualized consideration and intellectual stimulation typically come next, while contingent reward usually exhibits quite a strong correlation. Management by exception produces inconsistent results in that in some studies it is positively and in others negatively related to desirable outcomes. Programmes for the selection and training of leaders which draw on this conceptualization and measurement of transactional and transformational leadership have been developed (Bass and Avolio 1990).

Bass's framework has generated an impressive set of findings and has made a great impact on the study of leadership. Some reflections about the approach can be found in the following overview.

Overview of the New Leadership Approach

The New Leadership offers a distinctive approach which ties in with the great appetite for stories about heroic chief executives which was referred to above and with the growing self-awareness of many organizations about their missions. The New Leadership is at once cause, symptom and consequence of this self-reflection that can be seen in the widespread reference to visions and missions in newspaper advertisements and company reports. The approach has been critically examined in Bryman (1992a) from which the following selection of points has been gleaned.

With the exception of the research stemming directly or indirectly from Bass's work, the New Leadership approach can be accused of concentrating excessively on top leaders. While a switch toward the examination of the leadership *of*, rather than *in*, organizations is an antidote to the small-scale, group-level studies of earlier eras, it could legitimately be argued that the change in focus has gone too far and risks having little to say to the majority of leaders. Second, as with earlier phases of research, the New Leadership has little to say about informal leadership processes, though the qualitative case studies that have grown in popularity have great potential in this regard. On the other hand, quantitative approaches like Bass's work are likely to replicate the tendency to focus on formally designated leaders. Third, there has been little situational analysis. The tendency to extol the virtues of transformational leadership and other forms of New Leadership risks creating a return to universalistic thinking. Avolio and Bass (1987) depict situational factors as largely unimportant because transformational leaders are able to change the situation in their quest for the enhancement of subordinate performance. The problem with this position is that it comes perilously close to presenting a view which makes success an essential ingredient of transformational leadership. The neglect of situational factors seems to be changing. Keller (1992) reports the results of a study of R&D groups which uses Bass's measures and which shows that transformational leadership was a stronger predictor of project quality for research than for development projects. Bryman et al. (1996) show from a multiple case study of specialized transportation organizations in England how such factors as pre-existing levels of trust and resource constraint can have a pronounced impact on the prospects of transformational leadership. Similarly, Leavy and Wilson conclude from their investigation of four private and public sector Irish organizations that their leaders were 'tenants of time and context' (1994: 113). In so doing they draw attention to a wide range of contextual factors that can limit the room for manoeuvre of prospective transformational leaders. The contextual factors that they identified were: technology; industry structure; the international trading environment; national public policy; and social and cultural transformation. Therefore, there is growing evidence that situational constraints may be much more important in restricting the transformational leader's room for manoeuvre than is generally appreciated. Fourth, Bass's research approach probably suffers from some of the technical problems identified in relation to the Ohio research, such as problems of direction of causality and of implicit leadership theories (for a discussion of such issues, see Bass and Avolio 1989; Bryman 1992a). Fifth, there is a tendency for New Leadership writers to emphasize the exploits of successful leaders. This can generate a distorted impression since there may be important lessons to be learned from failed transformational leaders.

In spite of such problems, the New Leadership approach provided a 'shot in the arm' for leadership researchers. It enjoyed a broad swathe of support among both leadership researchers and writers of popular works on management, and broke with many aspects of earlier phases of the field. It is possible to exaggerate the differences. Like its predecessors, much if not most New Leadership writing is wedded to a rational model of organizational behaviour, while the growing popularity of a quantitative research approach within the New Leadership tradition (in particular the stream of research associated with Bass) seems to herald a return to a style of research associated with an earlier era.

Dispersed Leadership

The New Leadership approach has not completely superseded previous approaches but more significantly other perspectives have emerged during the 1980s and 1990s that cannot be encapsulated by it. Indeed, at the time of writing a reaction seems to be developing to three tendencies exhibited by New Leadership writers (though these points do not apply to the bulk of the work inaugurated by Bass): a focus on heroic leaders; a preoccupation with leadership at the highest echelons; and a focus on individuals rather than teams. A separate tradition which focuses on 'dispersed leadership' seems to be emerging to offset these tendencies. Four strands in recent writing illustrate this development. First, Manz and Sims (1991) and Sims and Lorenzi (1992) have developed an approach which specifies the advantages of a type of leadership that is expected to supersede the 'visionary hero' image which is a feature of the perception of leaders in the New Leadership tradition. They develop the idea of SuperLeadership, which is 'the leadership culture of the future, the new leadership paradigm' (Sims and Lorenzi 1992: 296). A keynote feature of Super-Leadership is the emphasis that is placed on 'leading others to lead themselves' (1992: 295), so that followers are stimulated to become leaders themselves, a theme that was in fact a feature of Burns's (1978) perspective on transforming leadership. SuperLeadership is to do with both developing leadership capacity in others and nurturing them so that they are not dependent on formal leaders to stimulate their talents and motivation. A second example is Katzenbach and Smith's (1993) book in which they extol the virtues of 'real teams', that is teams with 'a small number of people with complementary skills who are committed to a common performance purpose, performance goals, and approach for which they hold themselves mutually accountable' (1993: 45). Katzenbach and Smith view the role of leaders of such teams in terms of developing leadership in others by building commitment and confidence, removing obstacles, creating opportunities and being part of the team. Thus, in a manner similar to the SuperLeader, the leader of real teams is a facilitator who cultivates the group and its members. As a result, leadership is dispersed throughout the team. Third, Kouzes and Posner (1993) argue that credible leaders develop capacity in others. They 'turn their constituents into leaders' (1993: 156). For Kouzes and Posner, the issue is not one of handing down leadership to others, but one of liberating them so that they can use their abilities to lead themselves and others. These three strands signal a change of focus away from heroic leaders, from the upper echelons, and towards a focus on teams as sites of leadership (see also Reich 1987).

The fourth expression of an emergent dispersed leadership tradition can be seen in the suggestion that there should be much greater attention paid to leadership processes and skills, which may or may not reside in formally designated leaders. Hosking (1988; 1991) conceptualizes leadership in terms of an 'organizing' activity and spells out some of the distinctive features of leadership in terms of such a perspective. For example, she identifies 'networking' as a particularly notable organizing skill among leaders, in which the cultivation and exercise of wider social influence is a key ingredient. But such skill is not the exclusive preserve of formally appointed leaders; it is the activity and its effects that are critical to understanding the distinctiveness of leadership. In like fashion, Knights and Willmott (1992) advocate greater attention to what they call the 'practices' of leadership. This emphasis means looking at how leadership is constituted in organizations, so that in their study of a series of verbal exchanges at a meeting in a British financial services company, they show how the chief executive's definition of the situation is made to predominate. Unfortunately, the distinctiveness of this research and Hosking's (1991) investigation of Australian chief executives is marred somewhat by a focus on designated leaders. As a result, it is difficult to disentangle leadership as skill or activity from leadership as position. However, the potential implication of these ideas is to project an image of leadership as much more diffuse and dispersed within organizations than would be evident from the tendency for leadership to be viewed as the preserve of very few leaders, as in many versions of the New Leadership approach. However, Vanderslice's (1988) investigation of the Mousewood restaurant collective in New York State shows that the functions of leadership can exist without formal leaders since they are dispersed throughout the collective. For example, authority and responsibility exist but are rotated and hence are dependent on the task at hand rather than on a formal leader. As Vanderslice observes, Mousewood is not leaderless but 'leaderful' since the functions of leadership are dispersed throughout the collective.

In these four sets of writings, we can see an alternative perspective which emphasizes the importance of recognizing the need for leadership to be viewed as a widely dispersed activity which is not necessarily lodged in formally designated leaders, especially the heroic leader who is a feature of much New Leadership writing.

LEADERSHIP AND ORGANIZATIONAL CULTURE

There is an affinity in many discussions between the concentration on vision in the New Leadership approach and organizational culture. This tendency can be seen in the advantages which were seen as stemming from an organization's possession of a 'strong culture' (for example, Peters and Waterman 1982). Strong cultures were seen as providing organizational members with a sense of their distinctiveness, a sense of purpose and the 'glue' which binds people together. Companies became increasingly self-conscious and forthcoming about their values and traditions. Moreover, the visions of leaders were seen by many writers as making a distinctive contribution to cultures. The notion of leadership as having culture creation as a core (if not *the* core) element can be discerned in a number of writings, other than that of Peters and Waterman. Schein, for example, wrote that 'the unique and essential function of leadership is the manipulation of culture' (1985: 317). In Bass's model, changing organizational culture is an outcome of transformational leadership which in turn has an impact on the follower's level of effort and performance.

The connection between leadership and organizational culture is especially noticeable in the case of the founders of new organizations whose values and preoccupations often leave a distinctive imprint on their creations (Schein 1985). Leaders who follow in the founder's footsteps often see their role as that of maintaining and reinforcing the early culture. At a later stage in their development the distinctive cultures that were created might come to be seen as liabilities, as environmental realities change. Trice and Beyer (1990; 1993) helpfully distinguish between the maintenance and innovation aspects of 'cultural leadership'. Innovation takes place as the founder creates a new culture or when a new leader replaces an existing culture. Much of the New Leadership writing tended to concentrate on situations in which the leader is confronted with a culture that is in need of change because it is out of tune with current realities or because the culture is a barrier to a change of strategic direction. Such a view is exemplified by an investigation of Jaguar and Hill Samuel in the UK, which concluded that a transformation of the organization's culture was a prerequisite for radical strategic change (Whipp et al. 1989). Similarly, Kotter and Heskett's (1992) quantitative study of the links between organizational culture and firms' performance led them to conclude that the really critical factor is that a culture is adaptive, that is, it seeks to anticipate and adapt to environmental change. Leadership becomes a particular consideration for Kotter and Heskett in that it is needed to change cultures so that they are more adaptive. Here too, then, is a depiction of leaders as having a responsibility for culture creation.

It is striking that this perspective on leadership as culture management ties the study of leadership to 'value engineering': the leader comes to be seen as someone who moulds how members are to think about the organization and their roles within it. In this way, leadership theory and research become implicated in the drift in the study of organizational culture from essentially academic discussions towards more normative, managerial approaches (Barley et al. 1988). Willmott (1993) argues that in these managerial discussions, culture is little more than an extension of management control in which the aim is to colonize the minds of members of the organization. Therefore, the wider political and ethical ramifications of cultural manipulation tend to be marginalized. Equally, the predominant paradigm for examining leadership in relation to culture is imbued with what Martin (1992) refers to as an 'integration' perspective. Martin distinguishes this approach from two others – a differentiation and a fragmentation perspective. Each represents a unique way in which an organizational culture can be 'read'. None of the three perspectives can be absolutely valid and all of them should be employed to draw out the full complexity of images and themes. Martin's elaboration of different approaches to reading cultures provides a helpful framework for further exploring the link between leadership and culture.

In the integration perspective, there is consistency between the various components of culture and there is fairly widespread agreement and understanding of the culture's precepts. Leadership is about creating, maintaining or changing cultures along the lines that have just been encountered in the writings of Schein, Kotter and Heskett, Peters and Waterman, and Trice and Beyer. Alvesson (1992) provides an alternative position within an integration perspective which views leaders as transmitters of culture within organizations. He shows how subsidiary managers in a Swedish computer consultancy firm have a social integrative function in that they transmit the organization's culture to combat the potential for the firm to splinter due to the highly decentralized and heterogeneous nature of the work of consultants. In this case, leaders transmit rather than mould culture.

In the differentiation perspective, leadership occupies a quite different position. Culture is seen as pervaded by lack of consensus across the organization. The perspective particularly draws attention to subcultural diversity and the resulting enclaves of consensus that form within the wider organization. Martin suggests that when investigators have explored leadership within a differentiation perspective, they have typically examined leadership exercised by groups. Such a perspective brings into play informal leadership processes which have invariably been absent in organizational research. However, it is difficult to believe that individual leaders, albeit informal ones, do not exercise leadership to promote or express subcultural positions. The notion of a collective arrogation of leadership by a group is feasible, but it is hard to believe that individual leaders are not instrumental in the process. Indeed, Martin cites the illustration from her own research (Martin and Siehl 1983) of the way in which John DeLorean formed a contraculture in his division at General Motors. He employed alternative dress codes, physical arrangements, and formal practices to promote an oppositional culture within the company. It may be that leadership by individuals has a greater role to play in the fostering of contracultures than of subcultures, but studies of informal organization have frequently pointed to the important role played by leaders in the context of subcultures (Homans 1950). The issue of how senior organizational leaders deal with subcultural variety within organizations also needs greater attention than it has been given so far, but the

main contribution of the differentiation perspective is that it departs from the naive view of consensus within organizations and of leaders as sources of that integration.

Martin distinguishes a third approach to reading organizational cultures – the fragmentation perspective. This approach seems almost to decentre if not eliminate the role of leadership in organizational cultures. The fragmentation perspective characterizes organizational cultures as suffused with ambiguity and confusion. The meaning of cultural artefacts and their relationships to each other are unclear and confusing to members of the organization. The sheer complexity and heterogeneity of modern organizations tends to engender cultures whose elements lack the capacity to provide 'sense-making' that was often attributed to them by earlier generations of culture researchers in the early 1980s and by the exponents of the integration perspective in particular. The decentring of leadership in the fragmentation perspective can be discerned through a number of themes in Martin's (1992) writing, though it is not confronted in a direct way. She argues that the perspective offers very few guidelines to those individuals (presumably mainly senior executives) who might wish to implement cultural change. Indeed, from the fragmentation perspective the attempt to impose a coherent culture by dint of one's organizational vision is futile and dishonest because it fails to acknowledge the diversity, ambiguity and fluidity of modern cultures. However, the fragmentation perspective need not marginalize leadership as much as Martin's analysis implies.

An important feature of leadership within the fragmentation perspective is that leaders, far from being the sources of a coherent world-view as in the integration perspective, may come to be sources of ambiguity themselves. Tierney (1989) notes how the presidents of thirty-two higher education establishments in which he conducted his research frequently sent out symbols which were inconsistent with other cultural elements or with other symbols in which they dealt. In another investigation, an ethnographic study of a Catholic liberal arts college in crisis, Tierney (1987) shows how the new leader's symbols and messages were consistently misunderstood by others. The new president, Sister Vera, attempted to change the organization's culture from a family orientation to a more professional one. She introduced an executive committee, a forum for the discussion of important decisions and for broadening the constituency of staff involved in decision-making. For Sister Vera, the executive committee was meant to symbolize a shift away from autocracy and towards a team approach to decision-making, but instead of signifying 'open communication and more team involvement' it actually signified the opposite (1987: 242). When she decided that the committee's agenda should be published as a further sign of her commitment to openness, this too was widely interpreted as the opposite of what was intended. Even her 'open door' policy was interpreted, not as a symbol of openness, but as indicative of a failure of communication. In large part, this misinterpretation (though within a fragmentation perspective it is questionable whether the notion of misinterpretation has any meaning) arose because of the clash between the open door and other signs and symbols that she emitted that indicated otherwise, such as her practice of not going into staff members' rooms to chat to them. Perhaps at one level, and from the frame of reference of the integration perspective, Sister Vera was simply a poor leader who was not able to influence the organization's culture. However, this case and the fragmentation perspective more generally may provide the lesson that leaders' signs and symbols may be inherently more tenuous and equivocal than has typically been appreciated. Equally, the case demonstrates how matters of leadership can have a significant role within the purview of the fragmentation perspective, but perhaps their chief frame of reference is not so much leadership through the management of meaning as the transmission of equivocality. The former is intentional and is indicated by attempts to impose clear-cut meanings on others; the second is often an unintended consequence of the management of meaning in that the resulting messages may be more ambiguous to the listener than is typically appreciated by writers within the integration perspective and leaders themselves.

Imaginative Consumption of Culture

One of the implications of the fragmentation perspective is that the visions of leaders and their strategies for enshrining these visions in their organizations' cultures is problematized. Even though it has been suggested in the previous paragraph that leadership maintains its significance within a perspective on culture in which ambiguity is a central ingredient, the impact of the kinds of leader-inspired actions that were the focus of attention among New Leadership writers (and among those who emphasized leaders as creators and managers of cultures) are viewed within the fragmentation approach as less central and indeed as less effective than within an integration framework.

This tendency receives reinforcement from an emerging emphasis within organizational culture research on how culture is received. It is ironic

that writers who view the role of leaders as culture manipulators in largely positive terms (e.g. Peters and Waterman 1982; Schein 1985) share with critics of cultural manipulation like Willmott (1993) a belief that culture control is largely successful, that is values, beliefs and symbols are imbibed by those at whom these cultural artefacts are projected. In contrast, Linstead and Grafton-Small argue for greater understanding 'through the examination of users' meanings and the practice of *bricolage*' of the creativity that is involved in culture *consumption* (1992: 332). This orientation shifts attention away from examinations of culture production, which is the main interest of New Leadership, culture management and integration perspective writers, towards the investigation of the imaginative consumption of cultural messages. In the process the role of leadership in culture production shifts from the centre to the periphery of the empirical agenda. This kind of position can be discerned in Hatch's (1993) reworking of an ethnographic investigation of strategic change by the new president at a large US university who employed a 'symbolic vision' to propel the change (Gioia and Chittipeddi 1991). Hatch notes that the president's actions underwent modifications and were even resisted by many organizational members. She argues that

> although the president was a major player in the initiation of strategic change, his influence depended heavily on the ways in which others symbolized and interpreted his efforts. The outcome of the president's influence ultimately rested with others' interpretations and the effect these interpretations had on cultural assumptions and expectations. In this light, it is worthwhile questioning whether the president was as central to the initiation effort, or the organizational culture, as he first appeared to be. (1993: 681–2)

The implication which can be derived from Linstead and Grafton-Small and Hatch, as well as from the foregoing discussion of leadership within a fragmentation perspective, is that organizational members are not passive receptacles, but *imaginative consumers*, of leaders' visions and of manipulated cultural artefacts.

There is much that is attractive about this view of organizational members as imaginative consumers of culture. There is a kind of optimism in the view that people are able to carve out spheres of interpretative autonomy which distance them from the mind-games of leaders who attempt to control what others think and feel. It countervails the tendency for studies of organizational culture to adopt the managerialist, normative stance with an emphasis on the control which was identified by Barley et al. (1988). It also has affinities with the interpretative stance with which much culture research is imbued (for example, Louis 1991), but as Linstead and Grafton-Small (1992) recognize, it is inconsistent with the emphasis on shared meanings which is a feature of much interpretative thinking. Also, it is congruent with and probably requires the kind of in-depth ethnographic approach to which many culture researchers are drawn.

However, the implicit optimism of the imaginative consumer account of organizational culture and of the roles of leaders in relation to it requires an element of caution. It must not be forgotten that visions and the cultures which may spring from them are attempts to frame people's ways of thinking. This is to suggest not that organizational members passively absorb cultural messages, but that these messages set limits and boundaries on how people are supposed to think and respond. The very language within which visions and cultures are couched and the intentional privileging of some themes and issues over others frame how people think about organizational issues, even if it means that some people reject the message or react with cynicism. The rejection of the messages takes place within the frame of those messages. Organizational members can only respond to the messages that are transmitted. They cannot be imaginative consumers of cultural messages which are absent. Those messages which are transmitted will have been designed with certain effects (such as control, performance enhancement, or reorientation) at their core. They may have a greater impact on how members think about organizational issues than the emphasis on imaginative consumption implies, since senior leaders' control over the cultural agenda means that many potential themes do not surface. Organizational members cannot be imaginative consumers of wilfully omitted messages and symbols, and therefore the impact of cultural manipulation and of the part played by leaders in moulding organizational members' thinking should not be under-estimated. Instead, there should be direct examination of the extent to which leaders' attempts to manage culture are subverted in the act of consumption by others. This would involve attention being paid to the significance of leaders' control over the cultural agenda as well as to how the messages and symbols are consumed. A balance is needed in empirical investigation which assumes neither that people are cultural dopes who passively imbibe cultural messages emanating from leaders, nor that the manipulation of organizational culture is constantly being undermined through imaginative consumption on the part of organizational members. The former position also invites us to question the seeming omnipotence with which leaders are

often imbued by New Leadership writers, whereby the capacity of leaders to effect fundamental change is barely questioned.

The examination of leadership in relation to organizational culture has been a fertile area for theory and research. After an initially rather naive view in which leaders were viewed as builders of cultures, which in turn had an impact on the thinking and behaviour of members of the organization, the role of leaders and the implications of culture were problematized. Leadership seemed to be marginalized as a focus for analysis. It is being suggested here that the processes whereby leaders frame the ways in which members conceptualize organizational concerns and how the ensuing culture closes down alternative discourses and modes of thinking should be major issues in their own right. When issues such as these have been touched on, it has been shown that even when a culture and the vision that maintains it is treated with considerable scepticism, the culture nonetheless has considerable implications for how people apprehend organizational matters (for example, Smircich and Morgan 1982; Smircich 1983). Interestingly, there is an affinity between the fragmentation perspective and the emerging focus on dispersed leadership in that both emphasize the diffusion of power. Also culture can be instrumental (or not) in conditioning people's responsiveness to such things as self-leadership. However, a fragmentation analysis invites us to question whether the symbols of a cultural emphasis on dispersed leadership will be unambiguously understood and whether it might sometimes be viewed as a political manoeuvre for securing greater effort from employees under the guise of handing over greater responsibility and empowerment.

METHODOLOGICAL AND EPISTEMOLOGICAL ISSUES IN THE STUDY OF LEADERSHIP

There can be little doubt that the bulk of leadership research has been conducted within the tradition of quantitative research in which leadership variables are related to various outcomes. Qualitative research has had little influence on the field, in spite of its impact on the social sciences more generally where its strengths relative to quantitative research have been a subject of considerable discussion (Bryman 1988). The drift towards the New Leadership approach in the 1980s and the growing interest in organizational culture resulted in greater use of qualitative research. The emphasis within the New Leadership approach on the leader as a manager of meaning has led to an awareness that the ways in which this process occurs requires in-depth understanding of particular cases and detailed probing among both leaders and subordinates of aims and impacts. To such ends, a methodological strategy seems required which involves observation, in-depth interviewing and the detailed examination of documents, all of which are closely associated with qualitative research. However, there are two forms of qualitative research in the New Leadership. One is to produce essentially hagiographic pen pictures of successful leaders from whom 'lessons' can be learned. Leaders' exploits serve as illustrations of the leadership or culture change principles that the writer endorses (for example, Tichy and Devanna 1986; Kotter 1990). The second type of qualitative research is more 'academic' and involves either detailed explorations of one or a small number of cases (for example, Alvesson 1992; Smircich and Morgan 1982; Roberts 1985; Gioia and Chittipeddi 1991; Tierney 1987) or semi-structured interviews with a number of leaders (for example, Bennis and Nanus 1985; Bensimon 1989; Tierney 1989).

The role that is typically given to qualitative research by quantitative researchers is as preparation; in other words, if it has a role at all, qualitative research has often been reduced to a source of hypotheses to be taken up by quantitative researchers for subsequent verification. Such a division of labour keeps quantitative research very much in the methodological driving seat. However, in the social sciences at large there is a growing recognition of the contribution that qualitative studies can make. In the process of generating such a recognition, it has been necessary to discard some of the baggage of epistemological debate that has sometimes held back discussions of quantitative and qualitative research. For some writers, quantitative research is ineluctably tied to the label of positivism, while qualitative research is similarly enjoined with phenomenology. As a result of such associations, quantitative and qualitative research are deemed to be irreconcilable paradigms because of their incompatible epistemological underpinnings (e.g. Smith and Heshusius 1986). An alternative view is to recognize that quantitative and qualitative research are simply different approaches to the research process, and as such can be mutually informative and illuminating about an area like leadership, and can even be combined (Bryman 1988; 1992b). In fact, as awareness of the strengths of qualitative research for the study of leadership becomes better known, future researchers may be drawn to the wider range of issues concerning leadership raised by qualitative investigations.

There can be little doubt that quantitative research on leadership offers huge advantages to the researcher who wants clear-cut specification of causal connections between different types of leader behaviour and various outcomes (like subordinate job satisfaction and performance) under specific conditions. The very fact that the New Leadership seems to be drifting towards a more quantitative research approach is a testament to these strengths, which can be seen in the stream of research deriving from Bass's work, as well as that of alternative quantitative research approaches such as those of Leithwood and Steinbach (1993) and Podsakoff et al. (1990). On the other hand, qualitative research brings to the study of leadership an approach which sees leadership through the eyes of leaders and followers. In the process, the very notion of leadership is problematized by depicting the variety of meanings associated with 'leadership' or 'good leadership' among leaders and followers (for example, Tierney 1989).

Qualitative research is also acutely sensitive to the contexts of leadership. Through the use of a single case over time or the judicious comparison of cases, the qualitative researcher is able to highlight specific features of context and how they impinge on leaders. Roberts and Bradley (1988) show that the charismatic school superintendent who had been the focus of Roberts's (1985) study lost the aura of charisma when she moved to a state-level post and that a number of specific situational factors can account for that change (such as her more limited authority). In the multiple case study by Bryman et al. (1988) of three construction projects in England, the specific circumstances of such projects and the variations in those circumstances proved to be important factors which influenced the styles of construction project leaders. For example, projects are of limited duration and vary considerably in the degree to which there is a sense of urgency. Some projects seem to have more leeway in this regard than others, while it is often found that there are variations within a project's life in terms of this sense of urgency. This was one of three contextual factors which are fairly specific to the construction industry which had a considerable impact on leaders' styles. Also, qualitative research can be especially instructive when it comes to the examination of processes of leadership. By 'process' is here meant how leadership is accomplished and how leadership impacts occur over time. In detailed case studies, both features of a processual investigation may be in evidence. An illustration is Roberts's (1985) account of how a school superintendent actually had an impact and how that impact was gradually fostered.

Equally, as in the social sciences generally, quantitative and qualitative studies can usefully be combined (Bryman 1988: 127–56). The use of quantitative and qualitative research in tandem is still quite unusual in leadership studies. Kirby et al. (1992) employed a combined approach in the context of an investigation of school leaders and found a slight difference between the two sets of findings. When they employed Bass's framework and measures, their findings were extremely similar to those typically found by researchers using this approach. By contrast, their analysis of narrative descriptions of 'extraordinary leaders' found that the capacity of leaders to provide opportunities for professional development was more prominent than the kinds of leadership orientation identified by Bass. It is easy to view these differences within a framework of 'triangulation' (Webb et al. 1966) and to ask which is right. However, a much more promising avenue is to ask why the different contexts of questioning produce contrasting results and to see them as having gained access to different levels of cognition about leadership – general behaviours in the case of the quantitative study and more specific behaviours in the qualitative one – and to recognize that the research question needs to be linked to the appropriate kind of research design and instruments.

The injection of qualitative research into the study of leadership has great potential for the field. It can allow a different set of questions to be addressed and can address issues that are not readily accessible to a quantitative approach. For example, informal leadership has typically been neglected by quantitative researchers but may be more accessible to qualitative research. In this connection, it is interesting to speculate that the ideas associated with the idea of 'dispersed leadership', in which leaders as such are decentred and the focus turns to leadership in terms of acts and processes, may require a qualitative approach if it is to turn into a major framework for systematic research. One of the reasons why quantitative researchers concentrate on leaders is that they provide a ready-made focus for the administration of questionnaires. If acts of leadership are indeed dispersed, an important issue for researchers is that of identifying leadership and the acts and skills associated with it. Qualitative research is much more likely to provide the open-endedness that such a stance requires.

OVERVIEW

There is clearly much greater optimism about the field of leadership in organizations than in the early 1980s. In shifting towards a view of leadership as the management of meaning and in recognizing the potential of a greater range of research styles, the subject is well placed as a major area within the field of organization studies. Here I want to suggest two issues that may need to be particularly high on the agenda of leadership researchers in the coming years. Each relates in different ways to wider issues and perspectives within organization studies. Leadership theory and research have been remarkably and surprisingly uncoupled from the more general field in which they are located, so that the raising of these issues is meant to point to possible ways of offsetting that tendency. First, one of the more influential theories in the field since the late 1970s has been the population ecology perspective (Hannan and Freeman 1984). This approach represents something of a critique of leadership theory and research, but has hardly been acknowledged as such by those working within the leadership field. Population ecology proposes that the environments within which populations of organizations operate have a limited carrying capacity and that as a result some organizations are 'selected out' and die. This perspective suggests that human agency is of limited help in effecting the survival of organizations. The implications for the study of leadership are considerable because population ecology seems to reduce the importance of leadership greatly. The specific issue of whether leadership can make a difference to organizational survival is an important one for students of leadership and cannot be ignored.

Secondly, much of the field is still imbued with the rational model of organizational thinking which is a product of the modernist stance within much of the field of organization studies and of leadership studies in particular (Bryman 1992a: 162–4; Reed 1993). The fragmentation perspective within organizational culture research may counteract this tendency to a degree, since its emphasis on ambiguity is clearly at odds with the means–end theorizing that is a feature of rational model thinking. The institutional perspective may offer some interesting insights which are less wedded to rational model assumptions (DiMaggio and Powell 1983; Meyer and Rowan 1977). This perspective draws attention to the ways in which organizations take on forms that serve to enhance their legitimacy in the eyes of important constituencies within their environments. As a result, organizational forms are deemed often to arise not purely as a result of a quest for efficiency, at least not in the later stages in the diffusion of a form, but for reasons of appearance and image. It is not inconceivable that leadership processes are susceptible to the same kinds of impulse. Alvesson (1990), for example, has drawn attention to the ways in which organizational images are managed. Accordingly, we might wonder whether the widespread predilection for superficial tokens of New Leadership ideas proliferated in the 1980s and 1990s for this kind of reason. During this period, many senior executives were keen to propound their 'visions', announce 'cultural change', explicate 'mission statements', induce staff to 'lead rather than manage', and implant 'new values'. Doubtless organizational functioning undergoes change in the process, but it is conceivable from an institutional viewpoint that in many cases their role has been as much about being seen to be doing the right things as out of a conviction of their effectiveness. Accordingly, the diffusion of leadership themes and practices through mimetic processes and their ramifications for organizations are a worthy area of research which would loosen the bonds of the rational model on leadership research.

The aim of this final section is to suggest a need for leadership researchers to engage more with broader ideas and controversies within organization studies as part of their enterprise. Leadership theorists and researchers must not let the study of leadership in organizations become a hermetically sealed sub-discipline and exponents of organization studies must not let it happen.

REFERENCES

Alvesson, M. (1990) 'Organization: from substance to image?', *Organization Studies*, 11: 373–94.

Alvesson, M. (1992) 'Leadership as social integrative action: a study of a computer consultancy company', *Organization Studies*, 13: 185–209.

Avolio, B.J. and Bass, B.M. (1987) 'Transformational leadership, charisma and beyond', in J.G. Hunt, H.R. Baliga, H.P. Dachler, and C.A. Schriesheim (eds), *Emerging Leadership Vistas*. Lexington, MA: Heath.

Barley, S.R., Meyer, G.W. and Gash, D.C. (1988) 'Cultures of culture: academics, practitioners and the pragmatics of normative control', *Administrative Science Quarterly*, 33: 24–60.

Bass, B.M. (1985) *Leadership and Performance beyond Expectations*. New York: Free Press.

Bass, B.M. (1990) *Bass and Stogdill's Handbook of Leadership: Theory, Research and Managerial Applications*, 3rd edn. New York: Free Press.

Bass, B.M. and Avolio, B.J. (1989) 'Potential biases in leadership measures: how prototypes, leniency, and general satisfaction relate to ratings and rankings of transformational and transactional leadership constructs', *Educational and Psychological Measurement*, 49: 509–27.

Bass, B.M. and Avolio, B.J. (1990) 'The implications of transactional and transformational leadership for individual, team, and organizational development', *Research in Organizational Change and Development*, 4: 231–72.

Bass, B.M. and Avolio, B.J. (1993) 'Transformational leadership: a response to critiques', in M.M. Chemers and R. Ayman (eds), *Leadership Theory and Research: Perspectives and Directions*. New York: Academic Press.

Bennis, W.G. and Nanus, B. (1985) *Leaders: the Strategies for Taking Charge*. New York: Harper & Row.

Bensimon, E.M. (1989) 'The meaning of "good presidential leadership": a frame analysis', *The Review of Higher Education*, 12: 107–24.

Bryman, A. (1986) *Leadership ad Organizations*. London: Routledge & Kegan Paul.

Bryman, A. (1988) *Quantity and Quality in Social Research*. London: Routledge.

Bryman, A. (1992a) *Charisma and Leadership of Organizations*. London: Sage.

Bryman, A. (1992b) 'Quantitative and qualitative research: further reflections on their integration', in J. Brannen (ed.), *Mixing Methods: Qualitative and Quantitative Research*. Aldershot, Hants: Avebury.

Bryman, A., Bresnen, M., Beardsworth, A and Keil, T. (1988) 'Qualitative research and the study of leadership', *Human Relations*, 41: 13–30.

Bryman, A., Gillingwater, D and McGuinness, I. (1996) 'Leadership and organizational transformation', *International Journal of Public Administration*, 19: 849–72.

Burns, J.M. (1978) *Leadership*. New York: Harper & Row.

Conger, J.A. (1989) *The Charismatic Leader: Behind the Mystique of Exceptional Leadership*. San Francisco: Jossey-Bass.

DiMaggio, P.J. and Powell, W.W. (1983) 'The iron cage revisited: institutional isomorphism and collective rationality in organizational fields', *American Sociological Review*, 35: 147–60.

Fiedler, F.E. (1967) *A Theory of Leadership Effectiveness*. New York: McGraw-Hill.

Fiedler, F.E. (1993) 'The leadership situation and the black box in contingency theories', in M.M. Chemers and R. Ayman (eds), *Leadership Theory and Research: Perspectives and Directions*. New York: Academic Press.

Fiedler, F.E. and Garcia, J.E. (1987) *Improving Leadership Effectiveness: Cognitive Resources and Organizational Performance*. New York: Wiley.

Fry, L.W., Kerr, S. and Lee, C. (1986) 'Effects of different leader behaviors under different levels of task interdependence', *Human Relations*, 39: 1067–82.

Gibb, C.A. (1947) 'The principles and traits of leadership', *Journal of Abnormal and Social Psychology*, 42: 267–84.

Gioia, D.A. and Chittipeddi, K. (1991) 'Sensemaking

and sensegiving in strategic change initiation', *Strategic Management Journal*, 12: 433–48.

Greene, C.N. (1975) 'The reciprocal nature of influence between leader and subordinate', *Journal of Applied Psychology*, 60: 187–93.

Hannan, M.T. and Freeman, J.H. (1984) 'Structural inertia and organizational change', *American Sociological Review*, 49: 149–64.

Hatch, M.J. (1993) 'The dynamics of organizational culture', *Academy of Management Review*, 18: 657–93.

Homans, G.C. (1950) *The Human Group*, New York: Harcourt, Brace.

Hosking, D.M. (1988) 'Organizing, leadership and skilful process', *Journal of Management Studies*, 25: 147–66.

Hosking, D.M. (1991) 'Chief executives, organising processes, and skill', *European Journal of Applied Psychology*, 41: 95–103.

House, R.J. (1977) 'A 1976 theory of charismatic leadership', in J.G. Hunt and L.L. Larson (eds), *Leadership: the Cutting Edge*. Carbondale, IL: Southern Illinois University Press.

House, R.J., Spangler, W.D. and Woycke, J. (1991) 'Personality and charisma in the U.S. presidency: a psychological theory of leader effectiveness', *Administrative Science Quarterly*, 36: 364–96.

Hunt, J.G., Sekaran, U. and Schriesheim, C.A. (eds) (1982) *Leadership: Beyond Establishment Views*. Carbondale, IL: Southern Illinois University Press.

Katzenbach, J.R. and Smith, D.K. (1993) *The Wisdom of Teams: Creating the High-Performance Organization*. Boston, MA: Harvard Business School.

Keller, R.T. (1992) 'Transformational leadership and the performance of research and development project groups', *Journal of Management*, 18: 489–501.

Kennedy, J.K. (1982) 'Middle LPC leaders and the contingency model of leadership effectiveness', *Organizational Behavior and Human Performance*, 31: 1–14.

Kerr, S., Schriesheim, C.A., Murphy, C.J. and Stogdill, R.M. (1974) 'Toward a contingency theory of leadership based upon the consideration and initiating structure literature', *Organizational Behaviour and Human Performance*, 12: 62–82.

Kirby, P.C., King, M.I. and Paradise, L.V. (1992) 'Extraordinary leaders in education: understanding transformational leadership', *Journal of Educational Research*, 85: 303–11.

Knights, D. and Willmott, H. (1992) 'Conceptualizing leadership processes: a study of senior managers in a financial services company', *Journal of Management Studies*, 29: 761–82.

Korman, A.K. (1966) '"Consideration", "initiating structure", and organizational criteria – a review', *Personal Psychology*, 19: 349–61.

Kotter, J.P. (1990) *A Force for Change: How Leadership Differs from Management*. New York: Free Press.

Kotter, J.P. and Heskett, J.L. (1992) *Corporate Culture and Performance*. New York: Free Press.

Kouzes, J.M. and Posner, B.Z. (1993) *Credibility: How Leaders Gain and Lose It, Why People Demand It*. San Francisco: Jossey-Bass.

Lawrence, P.R. and Lorsch, J. (1967) *Organization and Environment*. Cambridge, MA: Harvard University Press.

Leavy, B. and Wilson, D. (1994) *Strategy and Leadership*. London: Routledge.

Leithwood, K. and Steinbach, R. (1993) 'Total quality leadership: expert thinking plus transformational practice'. Paper presented at the annual meeting of the American Educational Research Association, Atlanta, Georgia.

Linstead, S. and Grafton-Small, R. (1992) 'On reading organizational culture', *Organization Studies*, 13: 331–55.

Locke, E.A. and associates (1991) *The Essence of Leadership: the Four Keys to Leading Successfully*. New York: Lexington.

Lord, R.G., DeVader, C.L. and Alliger, G.M. (1986) 'A meta-analysis of the relation between personality traits and leadership perceptions: an application of validity generalization procedures', *Journal of Applied Psychology*, 71: 402–10.

Lord, R.G. and Maher, K.J. (1991) *Leadership and Information Processing: Linking Perceptions and Performance*. Cambridge, MA: Unwin Hyman.

Louis, M.R. (1991) 'Reflections on an interpretative way of life', in P.J. Frost, L.F. Moore, M.R. Louis, C.C. Lundberg and J. Martin (eds), *Reframing Organizational Culture*. Newbury Park: Sage.

Lowin, A. and Craig, C.R. (1968) 'The influence of performance on managerial style: an experimental object lesson in the ambiguity of correlational data', *Organizational Behavior and Human Performance*, 3: 440–58.

Mann, R.D. (1959) 'A review of the relationship between personality and performance in small groups', *Psychological Bulletin*, 56: 241–70.

Manz, C.C. and Sims, H.P. (1991) 'SuperLeadership: beyond the myth of heroic leadership', *Organizational Dynamics*, 19: 18–35.

Martin, J. (1992) *Cultures in Organizations: Three Perspectives*. New York: Oxford University Press.

Martin, J. and Siehl, C. (1983) 'Organizational culture and counterculture: an uneasy symbiosis', *Organizational Dynamics*, 12: 52–64.

Meyer, J.W. and Rowan, B. (1977) 'Institutionalized organisations: formal structure as myth and ceremony', *American Journal of Sociology*, 83: 340–63.

Miner, J.B. (1982) 'The uncertain future of the leadership concept: revisions and clarifications', *Journal of Applied Behavioral Science*, 18: 293–307.

Peters, L.H., Hartke, D.D. and Pohlmann, J.T. (1985) 'Fiedler's contingency theory of leadership: an application of the meta-analysis procedures of Schmidt and Hunter', *Psychological Bulletin*, 97: 274–85.

Peters, T. and Austin, N. (1985) *A Passion for Excellence*. New York: Random House.

Peters, T. and Waterman, R.H. (1982) *In Search of Excellence: Lessons from America's Best-Run Companies*. New York: Harper & Row.

Pfeffer, J. (1981) 'Management as symbolic action: the creation and maintenance of organizational paradigms', *Research in Organizational Behavior*, 3: 1–52.

Podsakoff, P.M., MacKenzie, S.B., Moorman, R.H. and Fetter, R. (1990) 'Transformational leader behaviors and their effects on followers' trust in leader, satisfaction, and organizational citizenship behaviors', *Leadership Quarterly*, 1: 107–42.

Podsakoff, P.M., Todor, W.D., Grover, R.A. and Huber, V.L. (1984) 'Situational moderators of leader reward and punishment behaviors: fact or fiction?', *Organizational Behavior and Human Performance*, 34: 21–63.

Reed, M.I. (1993) 'Organizations and modernity: continuity and discontinuity in organization theory', in J. Hassard and M. Parker (eds), *Postmodernism and Organizations*. London: Sage.

Reich, R.B. (1987) 'Entrepreneurship reconsidered: the team as hero', *Harvard Business Review*, 65: 77–83.

Roberts, N.C. (1985) 'Transforming leadership: a process of collective action', *Human Relations*, 38: 1023–46.

Roberts, N.C. and Bradley, R.T. (1988) 'Limits of charisma', in J.A. Conger and R.N. Kanungo (eds), *Charismatic Leadership: the Elusive Factor in Organizational Effectiveness*. San Francisco: Jossey-Bass.

Rush, M.C., Thomas, J.C. and Lord, R.G. (1977) 'Implicit leadership theory: a potential threat to the internal validity of leader behavior questionnaires', *Organizational Behavior and Human Performance*, 20: 93–110.

Sashkin, M. (1988) 'The visionary leader', in J.A. Conger and R.N. Kanungo (eds), *Charismatic Leadership: the Elusive Factor in Organizational Effectiveness*. San Francisco: Jossey-Bass.

Schein, E.H. (1985) *Organizational Culture and Leadership*. San Francisco, CA: Jossey-Bass.

Selznick, P. (1957) *Leadership in Administration*. New York: Harper & Row.

Sims, H.P. and Lorenzi, P. (1992) *The New Leadership Paradigm*. Newbury Park: Sage.

Sims, H.P. and Manz, C.C. (1984) 'Observing leader behavior: toward reciprocal determinism in leadership theory', *Journal of Applied Psychology*, 69: 222–32.

Smircich, L. (1983) 'Leadership as shared meanings', in L. Pondy, P. Frost, G. Morgan and T. Dandridge (eds), *Organizational Symbolism*. Greenwich, CT: JAI Press.

Smircich, L. and Morgan, G. (1982) 'Leadership: the management of meaning', *Journal of Applied Behavioral Science*, 18: 257–73.

Smith, J.K. and Heshusius, L. (1986) 'Closing down the conversation: the end of the quantitative–qualitative debate among educational inquirers', *Educational Researcher*, 15: 4–12.

Stogdill, R.M. (1948) 'Personal factors associated with leadership: a survey of the literature', *Journal of Psychology*, 25: 35–71.

Stogdill, R.M. (1950) 'Leadership, membership and organization', *Psychological Bulletin*, 47: 1–14.

Stogdill, R.M. (1974) *Handbook of Leadership: a Survey of Theory and Research*. New York: Free Press.

Strube, M.J. and Garcia, J.E. (1981) 'A meta-analytic investigation of Fiedler's contingency model of leadership effectiveness', *Psychological Bulletin*, 90: 307–21.

Tichy, N.M. and Devanna, M.A. (1986) *The Transformational Leader*. New York: Wiley.

Tierney, W.G. (1987) 'The semiotic aspects of leadership: an ethnographic perspective', *American Journal of Semiotics*, 5: 233–50.

Tierney, W.G. (1989) 'Symbolism and presidential perceptions of leadership', *Review of Higher Education*, 12: 153–66.

Trice, H.M. and Beyer, J.M. (1990) 'Cultural leadership in organizations', *Organizational Science*, 2: 149–69.

Trice, H.M. and Beyer, J.M. (1993) *The Cultures of Work Organizations*. Englewood Cliffs, NJ: Prentice-Hall.

Vanderslice, V.J. (1988) 'Separating leadership from leaders: an assessment of the effect of leader and follower roles in organizations', *Human Relations*, 41: 677–96.

Vecchio, R.P. (1983) 'Assessing the validity of Fiedler's contingency model of leadership effectiveness', *Psychological Bulletin*, 93: 404–8.

Webb, E.J., Campbell, D.T., Schwartz, R.D. and Sechrest, L. (1966) *Unobtrusive Measures*. Chicago: Rand McNally.

Weber, M. (1968) *Economy and Society* (1925), 3 vols, edited by G. Roth and C. Wittich. New York: Bedminster.

Westley, F.R. and Mintzberg, H. (1989) 'Visionary leadership and strategic management', *Strategic Management Journal*, 10: 17–32.

Whipp, R., Rosenfeld, R. and Pettigrew, A. (1989) 'Culture and competitiveness: evidence from two mature UK industries', *Journal of Management Studies*, 26: 561–85.

Willmott, H. (1993) 'Strength is ignorance; slavery is freedom; managing culture in modern organizations', *Journal of Management Studies*, 30: 515–52.

Zaleznik, A. (1977) 'Managers and leaders: are they different?', *Harvard Business Review*, 55: 67–78.

2.3

Decision-Making in Organizations

SUSAN J. MILLER, DAVID J. HICKSON
AND DAVID C. WILSON

The area of organizational decision-making is part of the broader field of organization studies and organization theory. It has therefore followed a similar pattern of evolution, drawing on a variety of paradigms and perspectives and being characterized by a multiplicity of theories, models and methodologies.

This chapter charts its development as a subject of study. The chapter attempts to show how competing views and alternative theoretical frameworks of the way in which decisions are made have shaped both the methods of enquiry and subsequent explanations. The central concepts of rationality and power in decision-making are discussed. Further, the understanding of decision-making as an organizational *process* is explored in detail, as is the relatively neglected area of implementation. Decision-making overlaps other areas, notably strategic management, so the ways in which strategic decisions and strategies may be related are addressed.

Finally, the chapter recognizes that most work on decision-making implicitly assumes culturally bounded Western views of the world and its management processes.

Why Decision-Making?

Why should decision-making be studied at all? Although its popularity has waxed and waned over time it has continually stayed on the stage of organizational debate, though not always in the spotlight. Why should this be so?

There are a number of reasons. Certainly the increasing complexity of 'modern organizations'

which needed both differentiation and integration (Lawrence and Lorsch 1967) meant that key decisions about the organization of central operational and transformational processes were required. The overarching paradigm of structural functionalism (which continues to be a dominant perspective) viewed management as being fundamentally concerned with rational decision-making in order to facilitate the smooth running and goal attainment of the modern, complex, structurally and functionally differentiated organization. Rational-legal authority (Weber 1947) appeared to both empower and compel managers to take rational decisions. This emphasis upon unemotional, impersonal, objective logic has persuasively shaped managerial beliefs and action, and will be discussed further in this chapter.

If the dynamics of organizing created a need for decision-making, studies of managerial work confirmed that this was indeed how managers spent a large proportion of their time. Mintzberg's (1973) early work and Stewart's (1967; 1976; 1983) ongoing studies have both placed decision-making high on the managerial agenda, while Simon (1945) has suggested that 'managing' and 'decision-making' are practically synonymous.

A further reason concerns the intrinsic nature of the decision-making process itself. Decisions can be viewed as being fundamentally concerned with the allocation and exercise of power in organizations. The making of decisions, especially the larger, consequential ones which govern what things are done and shape the future direction of the organization and the lives of people within it, are of vital significance to organizational stakeholders. The issues of who is involved in the making of decisions; who is left out or kept out; who is in a position to exercise influence; who is able to introduce items on to the decision-making agenda or keep them off; are all central to an understanding of the politics of organizational behaviour. The study of decision-making is crucial to the comprehension of how and why organizations come to be what they are and to control whom they do.

To summarize, there are a number of reasons why this topic is of interest to both practitioners and theorists. Modern organizations need decisions to be made in order that they can function effectively; managers spend much of their time in making decisions at both the operational and the strategic level; and decision-making can be seen to focus political activity in organizations and so provide a window on to a less observable but nonetheless influential 'underworld'. There is clearly a contrast here between seeing decision-making as a functional prerequisite of effective organization and seeing it as a maelstrom of political activity and sectional conflict, where power games are played out in an arena which is only partially open to view, and this accounts in part for the differences in approaches to research and discussion.

The variety of contrasting assumptions and preconceptions is compounded because the subject crosses several academic disciplines. Choice behaviour under optimum and sub-optimum conditions is examined using rational choice models from economics and modelling techniques from mathematics and statistics; the behavioural aspects of making decisions in organizations are discussed by organization theorists, sociologists and social psychologists; while psychologists concentrate on individual cognitive behaviour. This chapter will not and could not address all these perspectives. What it will do is focus on the way in which decisions are made and implemented in an organizational setting. It will therefore draw mainly on material from organization theory which takes the organization with its members as the subject of analysis. Drawing the boundary in this way does not mean that what is inside it is a discrete area of understanding; the influence of the other disciplines mentioned above still permeates the discourse.

The next section will begin our scrutiny in earnest, by looking at the beginnings of decision theory. The approach first taken, with its central notion of rational behaviour, still retains a pivotal position in the field: an orthodox, normative model of decision-making within a paradigm which many other approaches still need to acknowledge before they attempt to dismantle its arguments.

MANAGERIAL RATIONALITY IN DECISION-MAKING

Neo-classical economic assumptions lie at the heart of rational choice models of decision-making. Predicated on the supposition that individuals normally act as maximizing entrepreneurs, decisions are thought to be arrived at by a step-by-step process which is both logical and linear. Essentially, the decision-makers identify the problem or issue about which a decision has to be made, collect and sort information about alternative potential solutions, compare each solution against predetermined criteria to assess degree of fit, arrange solutions in order of preference and make an optimizing choice. Often such models leave out, or assume, the implementation stage which in principle follows the formal decision itself. Throughout the thrust is to maximize rewards and minimize costs for those involved.

As Zey (1992: 9) has shown, this kind of logic, although by no means new, has increasingly dominated many areas of government and business over the last twenty years, especially in the United States and Western Europe. The implicit assumption is that if individuals behave in accordance with rationality then little or no interference is required by any superordinate bodies.

At the level of the organization, or firm, this view aggregates the behaviour of individuals and groups without compunction. Since individual managers make rational decisions, the decisions made by groups within organizations will be equally rational. At the macro level, a competitive economic environment is both efficient and equitable because of its inherent dynamic logic.

Such a view of organizations and decision-making represents a mainstay of functionalist thinking and has been elaborated by other writers, notably Williamson (1975) with his account of what he terms 'markets and hierarchies', hierarchies here meaning organizations. However, the limitations of the approach have long been recognized by theorists from inside and outside the neo-classical paradigm.

Simon (1945) was one of the earliest authors to provide a comprehensive critique of the limitations of 'rational economic man' or the 'rational actor' model. Simon asserted that, constrained as they were by the complexity of modern organizations and by their own limited cognitive capacities, decision-makers were unable to operate under conditions of perfect rationality. The issue for decision is likely to be unclear or open to varying interpretation; information about alternatives may be unavailable, incomplete or misrepresented; and criteria by which potential solutions are to be evaluated are often uncertain or not agreed. In addition, the time and energy available to decision-makers to pursue a maximizing outcome is both limited and finite. Searching for better choices can simply take too long. The net result of these constraints is that the outcome is likely to be a 'satisficing' rather than an optimizing choice: one which both satisfies and suffices in the circumstances, for the time being. The absolutely rational model is beyond reach. Decision-making does not work that way.

Simon accepts that managers have to operate within a 'bounded rationality'. They intend to be rational, and indeed their behaviour is *reasoned* – it is not *irrational*, which is an important distinction – but it is unrealistic to expect them to meet the stringent requirements of wholly rational behaviour. Human frailties and demands from both within and outside the organization limit the degree of rationality which can be employed.

Even so, Simon makes the important observation that different types of decisions can be processed in different ways. Some decision processes may approximate to rational prescriptions, others may not. Decisions which occur more frequently, which are familiar, almost routine, may be made in a relatively straightforward fashion. These decisions are comprehensible to managers and usually there exist tried and tested protocols, formulae or procedures for making them. They are 'programmed' (Simon 1960), in the sense that they can be made by reference to existing rubrics. Programmed decisions are often made lower down in the organizational hierarchy; they are the operational decisions which can be safely left to subordinates. It is likely that they can be made in a way which closely parallels the prescripts of rational choice models. In fact there may be little in the way of formal deciding to be done.

In contrast, 'non-programmed' decisions are those which are unfamiliar: they have not been encountered in quite the same way before, they are to some extent novel, unusual. They therefore present a challenge to managers, for there are no obvious well-trodden paths to follow. To make matters even more challenging, these decisions are usually about the more significant areas of organizational activities. They will have consequential repercussions and will set precedents for other decisions which follow. Since decisions are intended to shape actions for the future and since the future is inherently uncertain, the potential consequences of non-programmed, or *strategic*, decisions have worrying implications for managers. Because of their consequentiality, these decisions are usually

sanctioned or authorized by the most senior executives in the elite. Since there is less likely to be an existing template to shape the process by which they are made, what happens may differ considerably from what might be fully rational. The topic for decision may be complex, making definition problematic; information may be needed which is difficult both to collect and to categorize; potential solutions may be hard to recognize and may in turn create new problems. It is not easy to follow a step-by-step, smoothly escalating, sequential process under such conditions. 'Problemistic search' may occur, where activity is spurred by the immediate problem, rather than being an orderly collection of information prompted by foresight (Cyert and March 1963).

This continuum of decisions along a programmed/non-programmed dimension represents an early but significant step in distinguishing the characteristics of decisions and associating them with types of process. It is a field of enquiry that has been explored in greater detail since Simon, and we will return to this later in the chapter.

The issue of rationality in decision-making is therefore a vexed one. Decisions in organizations are subject to constraints endemic to the context in which they are made. The lone decision-maker making choices about his or her own interests might be thought to act rationally (although psychologists may argue the evidence here) but the complexities of managerial decision-making in concert with others have been well documented (for example, see Asch 1955; Janis 1972).

So rational choice models have been the target of sustained criticism for over four decades. Although there are those who continue to call for attempts at synthesis and reconciliation of contradictions (Schoemaker 1993), it has been suggested (Eisenhardt and Zbaracki 1992) that it is time for theorists concerned with organizational behaviour to drop such models in favour of a more realistic approach to decision-making, particularly one which recognizes how it is imbued with power.

DECISION-MAKING AS THE ENACTMENT OF POWER

In Simon's definition of the term, 'bounded rationality' is the result of human and organizational constraints. It can be argued that this view underplays the role of power and political behaviour in setting those constraints. Many writers have pointed out that decision-making may be seen more accurately as a game of power in which competing interest groups vie with each other for the control of scarce resources.

Power is an ever-present feature of organizational life. Legitimate power is allocated to positions of authority in the hierarchy. This 'rational-legal' power (Weber 1947) is given according to status and regularizes access to the decision-making process. Those with the requisite authority can participate in what occurs. Some can both discuss decisions and authorize them. The contribution of others is relegated to just the providing or cataloguing of data, or the recording of outcomes. Still others do not take part at all, and in the majority of organizations they are the great majority.

However the use of power legitimately is not the only way in which influence is exercised. Power-holders may choose to behave in ways which further their own, or others', interests. They may frame the matter for decision in a way which suits their own ends or blocks the objectives of others. They push for preferred alternatives, whether or not these will lead to decisions which are of organizational benefit. They manipulate information, withhold it, ignore some or all of it. They negotiate for support and suppress opposition. This applies not only to those who are directly engaged in the process, but also to those who, although only indirectly involved, still have the power to influence the process in some way – such as by having access to those who are more closely involved, or by providing information for the process. Since all interest groups may be engaging in similar behaviour the process may be characterized by various forms of bargaining, negotiation and compromise that may lead to outcomes which are less than optimum for all parties. So although it might seem rational for each to pursue their own sectional interests in this way, from the perspective of neo-classical theory this can lead to outcomes which for the whole are less than rational. Thus the *means* by which decisions are made may be separably rational while the *ends* may not be.

Some writers have long considered power to be the key factor in explaining how decisions are made. Pettigrew's (1973) longitudinal analysis of a British retail business reached that conclusion. A similarly vivid example of politics at work has been described by Wilson (1982) in his account of a chemical manufacturer where a decision about electricity generation turned into an intense and sometimes bitter career struggle between two senior executives.

One way of explaining this kind of power play is to see it as the inevitable outcome of the way we organize. The intrinsic nature of organizations as entities which are driven by the imperatives of division of authority and division of labour leads inexorably to fragmentation. Differentiation, which is required to maintain efficiency and cope with turbulent, unpredictable environments, also creates sectional interests, each with their own needs and priorities. A functionalist paradigm has difficulty with the notion of goal dissensus, but the reality of organizations appears to be that once organizational groups are given different tasks they also begin to formulate their own sets of norms and goals. They either reinterpret objectives or construct personal goals which serve their own interests.

This notion of differentiation is at the heart of the resource dependence perspective (Pfeffer and Salancik 1978). This explores how some parts of the organization gain power as a result of their ability to control access to resources. In this view, an organization, being an 'open system' which interacts with its environment in order to survive, is crucially dependent on obtaining resources from suppliers. Power accrues to those parts of the organization that can control the flow of resources, especially if these are scarce and critical for organizational functioning.

In this vein Crozier's (1964) seminal study of a French tobacco company showed how the exclusive possession of expert knowledge allowed maintenance workers to gain and maintain control over production processes (although gender was also crucial since they were male and production workers female). The idea of expertise being a potential source of influence germinated even earlier with March and Simon (1958), and it is expertise rather than resources which underlies the strategic contingencies theory enunciated by Hickson et al. (1971) in their explanation of why some 'subunits' (departments and the like) within organizations exert more influence than others. They showed (Hinings et al. 1974) that if the differential allocation of tasks confronts a subunit in its specialist area with an uncertainty that is critical for its organization, and it copes in such a way as to buffer other subunits from any resulting instability, then it can widely influence decisions even beyond its own competence. This influence is conditional upon it being sufficiently central and non-substitutable for the others to be dependent upon it. So, for example, a marketing department which can iron out fluctuations in demand by shrewd pricing and advertising gains influence. It is this *coping with uncertainty* which confers power. Since organizations are beset by uncertainty arising from suppliers, customers, competitors, outside agencies, government and so on, as well as from internal difficulties, the ability to manage uncertainty on behalf of others provides a vital power base.

Hence organizations can be seen as *ensembles des jeux* (Crozier and Friedberg 1980) where individuals and groups jockey for position in a hierarchy which is mediated by ongoing negotiation and bargaining. There are shifting, multiple coalitions of interests and thus only 'quasi-resolution of conflict' as interests seek to impose their own 'local rationalities' on any given decision (Cyert and March 1963). The existing structural framework undergoes subtle (or even radical) change as a result of the day-to-day interactions of organizational members. It functions as a 'negotiated order' (Strauss et al. 1982). Particular decisions will enfold particular subsections, drawn into the game by the nature of what is being decided. The topics on hand will attract those who have something to protect: they will want to be involved because they are affected by what is being decided or they see a chance to influence matters in their favour. The matter for decision therefore shapes the interests which become involved and the way the game is played. In this way power positions are formed and transformed depending on what is on the agenda.

This acknowledges the increased political complexity of decisions made in organizational settings. The rational model of decision-making begins to break down when faced with this pluralist vision of multiple, competing interest groups vying for supremacy. Allison (1971) explores this by showing how both organizational interests and government influence can shape events. He also shows how different assumptions and ways of viewing the world provide different interpretations of, and explanations for, these events. Using as an example the Cuban missile crisis (when the USA and the Soviet Union, as it was then, teetered on the brink of war) Allison offers three alternative models for viewing what happened: the rational actor model (which views the situation as an outcome of logical and rational decisions), the organizational process model (which takes into account the complicating effects of the organizational context from which the events arose), and the governmental politics model (which focuses on the various bargaining games played out on the larger scale between actors at the level of government). The model produces alternative views of reality which sometimes complement one another, but often conflict. So ways of seeing produce ways of understanding, which has penetrating implications for the ways in which research is done.

Pluralist positions are predicated upon the notion of unequal but shifting power relations among elites, under the auspices of a largely neutral set of institutional arrangements. Here Schattsneider's statement begins to have reso-nance: 'All forms of political organisation have a bias in favour of some kinds of conflict and the suppression of others because organisation is the mobilisation of bias. Some issues are organised into politics while others are organised out' (1960: 71). This suggests that something else is happening 'behind the scenes' of even the pluralists' complex scenario – that the action is not all that it might seem at first glance. This in turn implies that to gain an even deeper understanding of power in organizations we need to look beyond what is readily observable. So attending solely to manifest conflict reveals only the most easily discernible 'face' of power. Ideally, what is going on beneath the surface also needs to be fully understood: the less explicit, more covert, subtle and insidious exercise of power which is used to suppress conflict in the first place. Conflict can be kept quiet; it is not allowed to surface into open debate and so does not become an item for discussion. This means that some decisions do not get onto the agenda. This is the 'second face' of power which Bachrach and Baratz (1962) argue has such import for organizational decision-making. This is the sphere of 'non-decisions'.

What then are non-decisions and do they have a place in the study of decision-making? Bachrach and Baratz maintain that non-decisions are equally if not more important than the decisions which are overtly made. Non-decisions are the covert issues about which a decision has effectively been taken that they will not be decided. They are the controversial topics which go against the interests of powerful stakeholders: they do not engender support, they do not fit with the prevailing culture, they are not considered acceptable for discussion, so they are quietly side-stepped or suppressed or dropped. A knowledge of what these issues are is likely to be as revealing, or more so, as knowledge of what is overtly being discussed. They are what is really going on, not just on the surface but underneath it. The decisions which are being discussed in the board room, in meetings, by executives and management represent the tip of the iceberg, according to this view. As the complete shape of the iceberg can only be revealed by going under the water, so the really key issues and problems are only partially apparent from studies of topics which are being decided. Each topic needs to be embedded in a wider picture which gives it a context – and future decisions may come from under the surface.

Bachrach and Baratz's ideas have been the spur to a broadening of debate about power and decisions. But they have come under criticism from those who ask questions about how the existence of non-decisions can be investigated. If even decision-making itself is a fairly ephemeral, intangible activity (how do you spot a decision, where are decisions made?) then the epistemological and methodological problems associated with the discovery and analysis of non-decisions are yet far more difficult. Bachrach and Baratz maintain that non-decisions are rooted in observable behaviour, that is in pre-existing conflict which leads to action to close off areas of decision-making, but those attempting to carry out empirical research in organizations have so far found this a difficult lead to follow.

Going beyond this position, Lukes (1974) developed a third dimension, or 'face', of power. He maintains that the weakness of Bachrach and Baratz's approach is that the second face of power is still primarily concerned with what should be intrinsically observable behaviour and conflict, even though it be so difficult to detect. Surely a more sinister, insidious and yet ultimately more effective way of exercising power would be to prevent any awareness of conflict in the first place? One way of achieving this would be to shape views and beliefs in such a way that one's own interests are not recognized by others. If all interests are perceived to be shared then conflict does not occur. This Orwellian view of the world echoes Marx's concept of 'false consciousness' whereby the hearts and minds of the proletariat are so manipulated by dominant institutions of state (abetted by the hegemony of religious institutions) that they only see things as others wish them to be seen. It also echoes Giddens's (1990) and Beck's (1992) view of society overall as 'unreflexive'. That is, the current state of affairs is left unquestioned. Firms can implement decisions which are hazardous, risky and detrimental to the environment. Yet, such corporate actions are, according to Giddens, largely taken for granted and left unquestioned. Awareness that such action might be in conflict with large sections of society is suppressed and rarely open to question.

Such non-reflexivity takes us a long way from the ideas of rational economic behaviour. Decision-making is far removed from the coolly logical appraisal and selection of alternatives. Rather it is at the centre of political machinations and intrigue, the true nature of which is not always fully recognized, even by those involved.

So although some may see conflict as an endemic, but controllable, part of organizational life, created by the dysfunctions of a functional drive for efficiency, others explain conflict as arising from inherently inequitable power relationships in wider society. In the former view, the context for decision-making is the ongoing power play between interest groups, in which situations of disharmony are an expected but usually reconcilable by-product of organiz-

ational structure. In the latter view, decisions are shaped in ways which are not always obvious, by unseen influential power-holders playing within a larger arena.

This has spurred some writers to press for a more radical organization theory (Burrell and Morgan 1993) which would show greater awareness of the macro factors beyond the organization. Radical organization theory recognizes that the nature of economic relations in any economic system must breed inter-class conflict since such relations are essentially exploitative. Under capitalism management serves the interests of capital and therefore subordinates enter into a relationship in which they exchange their labour power for subsistence. Radical theorists criticize conventional organizational analysis for neglecting the power of the state and of those who control capital in shaping wider social relations, maintaining that orthodox theories are 'locked into an acceptance of managerially defined problems' (1993: 366). Conventional theory acknowledges that conflict may occur, but both seeks and expects equilibrium in organizations, and looks for ways to reduce conflict to arrive at a sustainable balance. In contrast, radical theory expects conflict because it is the result of the incongruent objectives of management and labour. Decision-making theory should therefore take cognizance of this radical standpoint which throws a different light on how decisions arise and come to be taken 'at the top'.

Whilst the power perspective opens up the heart of organizational decision-making, it brings with it difficult methodological questions of its own, as mentioned earlier. How is power to be conceptualized and how is it to be studied? If much of power is employed covertly, how can it be reached? The fact that it is all-pervading does not help to make it any more tangible. Recognizing that political behaviour does shape decisional processes, what other factors besides power might be important?

For empirical researchers these are some of the issues with which they have to grapple and some of the questions they have attempted to answer. The following section looks at studies which try to understand the way power is enacted in the making of decisions.

PROCESSES, PRESCRIPTIONS AND EXPLANATIONS

Empirical studies of decision-making have added weight to the criticisms of rational choice models as being idealized prescriptions, depicting an unreality.

Lindblom's early work in the American public sector (Lindblom 1959; Braybrooke and Lindblom 1963) quickly dispelled the myth that decision-making, in public institutions at least, was a linear, sequential process. Decisions here were made in a halting 'incremental' way with periods of recycling, iteration and reformulation. The process was a non-linear one.

So instead of final choices being arrived at after the full rational process of search and evaluation is completed, small adjustments are made to ongoing strategies. The full range of alternative solutions is not considered, only ones which do not differ markedly from the status quo. Decisions proceed by a series of small steps, rather than attaining and implementing the complete solution in one large step. For Lindblom the advantages of this approach are clear. Because each step, in itself, is not too dissimilar from what is already being done, it does not upset too many stakeholders. They do not feel threatened by radical change so it is possible to gain commitment for what is being done. The repercussions from changes which, initially at least, are relatively minor, are likely to be less serious and more predictable. Most importantly, the decision has more chance of being 'undone' if necessary; it is more reversible. Once each small step has been taken it gives a clearer picture of what has to be done and the future becomes more focused. If the chosen path now seems unlikely to lead to the desired destination, or if changing circumstances make the destination less appropriate, the step can be retraced with less difficulty than a larger one.

Lindblom argues that this is not only a description of what is done in organizations but also what ought to be done, given the inherent unpredictability of the context in which most decision-makers work. The incrementalist model is therefore in the interesting position of being both normative and descriptive as Smith and May (1980) have commented.

Some have suggested that incrementalism, or 'muddling through' as Lindblom has referred to it, is less a recipe for change, more likely a formula for inertia. It has been argued that small decisions which are only marginally different from the status quo are fine – if the current position is acceptable. But if change needs to be immediate and substantial, for example if the organization is in crisis, then incrementalism is not enough. Lindblom has countered that radical change can be equally swift whether it is effected by a series of small frequent steps or one large stride. In fact, smaller steps may be quicker since they may encounter less delaying opposition. Although Lindblom's work began in public administration, further work in private sector organizations has come to similar conclusions.

Quinn's (1978; 1980) development of the concept into 'logical incrementalism' comes from the very similar processes which can be found in private sector organizations. It appears that all kinds of decision-makers operate in an incremental fashion.

When Mintzberg and his colleagues (1976) studied 25 strategic decisions in a variety of Canadian organizations they found even clearer evidence of cycling and recycling of information and alternatives, again showing that the making of this level of decision is likely to require constant adjustment and reappraisal. Their study distinguished seven kinds of process: simple impasse, political design, basic search, modified search, basic design, blocked design, and dynamic design processes. Most of these experience delays and interruptions, and repeated reconsideration. Nutt's (1984) work analysed 73 decisions in health-related organizations in the USA and noticed some similar patterns occurring in search processes.

On the other hand, Heller et al. (1988) were prepared to assume common sequential phases across decision processes in British, Dutch and (former) Yugoslav organizations. They examined 217 cases of medium- and long-term decisions in each of these three countries: 80 cases in the UK, 55 in the Netherlands and 82 in former Yugoslavia (in addition to lower-level operational decision-making, which is not relevant for our purposes here). Four distinct phases were identified, namely: start-up; development (which includes the search for alternatives); finalization; and implementation. Not everything may be circuitous. Indeed, it is claimed that in periods of crisis decisions can be made in a relatively speedy and straightforward way (Dutton 1986; Rosenthal 1986). When organizations are in trouble and urgent action is required, those in authority can be given great freedom to act, even by subordinates whose jobs may be affected, particularly if they are perceived to have the necessary grasp of the situation and are likely to be able to do something to help.

So whilst it has become a truism that decision-making by the elite takes place in a state of political excitation and is not at all straightforward, this is a view that can be taken too far. All decision-making need not be so. Not all decisions are made the same way. Why is this? Why are decision processes the way that they are? What factors influence process?

The Bradford Studies: Finding Explanations for Process

The Bradford Studies (Hickson et al. 1986; also Cray et al. 1988; 1991) set out to try and answer these questions. The Bradford team investigated the making of 150 decisions in 30 organizations in England (5 decisions in each), covering manufacturing and service industries in both public and private sectors. Examples include glass and engineering manufacturers, brewers, electricity and water utilities, insurance companies and financial institutions, universities and polytechnics, and local government. Using face-to-face interviews with senior executives as well as a number of in-depth case studies with a range of informants, the research built up a picture of decision-making from initiation to authorization. That is, from 'the first recalled deliberate action which begins movement towards a decision (when, for example, the matter is discussed in a meeting, or a report is called for)', to a point 'when the decision and its implementation are authorized'. A further development of the research, discussed later in this chapter, focuses on the implementation and outcomes of a subset of 55 of these decisions.

As the researchers recognize, decision start and end points are not easy to identify. The beginnings and endings of organizational processes commingle and it is no simple matter to carve out a slice of time for detailed investigation. Nevertheless, the limits of time and attention which hamper all research necessitate selection. Given this caution, an interesting statistic emerges from the Bradford work. The mean time that it takes to make a strategic decision is just over twelve months. An unexpectedly short time perhaps? The range, however, is from one month to four years. Immediately then, a wide variation along this dimension – duration – emerges. How else did decision-making differ and why?

Three kinds of processes were found, labelled *sporadic*, *fluid* and *constricted*. The sample of cases divided almost evenly between each cluster, so about a third of all the decisions studied were made in sporadic ways, a third were made in a fluid manner, while a third followed a constricted path.

Sporadic processes are subject to more disrupting delays than either fluid or constricted processes. The information used will be uneven in quality, some good, some bad, and will come from a wide range of sources, and there will be scope for negotiation. This kind of process is 'informally spasmodic and protracted' (Hickson et al. 1986: 118). The tale of electricity generation already referred to in this chapter (Wilson 1982) is a colourful example.

Fluid processes are almost the opposite of sporadic ones. There is much less informal interaction and the process flows more through formal meetings with fewer impediments and delays. These processes are rather faster and the decision is likely to be made in months, rather than years. In short, a fluid process is 'steadily paced, formally channelled and speedy' (Hickson et al. 1986: 120).

Lastly, constricted processes share some of the characteristics of each of the other two but have features distinctive from both. They are less fluid than the fluids and less sporadic than the sporadics, but constrained in a way that neither of the others is. They tend to revolve around a central figure such as a finance or production director who draws on a wide range of expertise in other departments before arriving at a decision. In short, they are 'narrowly channelled' (1986: 122).

Although public sector organizations and manufacturing firms each show some bias towards sporadic processes, each process is found in every type of organization. So the managements of organizations in any sector or type of business, making strategic decisions about any aspect of their products or services, may go through any of the three kinds of process, sporadic, fluid or constricted. The type of organization is not the strongest determinant of process. So what is? The Bradford team found that the primary and 'dual' explanation is the degree of *politicality* and *complexity* inherent in the matter for decision itself.

In other words, it is the political and complex nature of what is being decided which is all-important. With regard to politicality, all decisions draw in a specific 'decision set' of interests: those who have a stake in the outcome. These are drawn from inside and outside the organization: individuals, departments, divisions, owners, suppliers, government agencies and so on. But not all interests are equally influential and not every decision draws in the same number or configuration of them. Some decisions attract less attention: they are less controversial, perhaps, or require work to be done by relatively fewer people. Others are a whirl of interested activity. So every decision is shaped to some degree by the influence of the decision set. Politicality refers to the degree of influence which is brought to bear on a decision and how this influence is distributed within and without the organization.

Complexity refers to the problems which making the decision encompasses. The reasons for complexity are varied. Some decisions are more unusual than others: they may require information to be garnered from more diverse sources, they may have more serious or widespread consequences, or set more fundamental precedents for the future. Since each decision process is made up of various problems – some of which are more complex than others – decisions will vary in terms of how comprehensible they are. Some will be relatively straightforward while others will be more problematic, depending on the nature of the issues involved.

Together, these concepts of politicality and complexity are the primary explanation of why strategic decisions follow the processes they do. The strength and distribution of influence, coupled with the complexity of what is being decided, shape the process which ensues. As the authors put it, in accounting for what happens 'the matter for decision matters most' (1986: 248).

By their comprehensive mapping of decision processes the Bradford team demonstrate that not all decision-making is politically tumultuous. Far from it. Sporadic processes are most inclined that way, perhaps a third of all decisions at most. The greater proportion of decisions are more deliberative and less contentious.

Yet below what was reached empirically must have lain the concealed second and third faces of power. Were there no signs of what lay beneath? The research did show that in at least a third of all decisions the outcome was a foregone conclusion. The results were known before the process of deciding was completed, indeed often before it began. The Bradford team call this 'quasi-decision-making' (1986: 52). Sometimes this occurred because there was only one realistic alternative, but on other occasions quasi-decision-making must have been the result of prior manoeuvres by powerful parties involved. This strongly suggests that overt, aware decision-making frequently does 'go through the motions' within limits set by pre-existent positions.

A great deal of influence is exercised overtly, of course, and this research also has much to say about who has it and who does not. Generally, trade unions do not influence decisions, neither does the personnel function nor the purchasing department, nor government in most cases. The most influential interests (apart from the CEO) come from production (or the equivalent), sales and marketing, and accounting. This core triad of 'heavyweight' functions is involved more often and exerts most influence whatever the type of organization. Although external power-holders do take part in the game the balance of power is held internally. And this remains true throughout the process, for these same interests hold sway over implementation.

Building on the Bradford Studies, Butler et al. (1993) studied seventeen cases of a specific decision topic – strategic investment decisions. Reflecting Thompson and Tuden (1959), they argued that four elements were important in realizing effective investment decisions, namely, computation, judgement, negotiation and inspiration. They found that inspiration alone was not a recipe for effectiveness, since decision-making not only had to have accurately analysed the complexity of the situation (judgement and computation) but also had to steer a course through the political reality of persuading others of the inspirational idea (negotiation).

But does what happens in the process leading to the formal decision have any effect on the subsequent outcomes? What factors lead to success during implementation and beyond?

IMPLEMENTATION AND OUTCOMES

Getting things done in an organizational setting is not always easy, and many writers have drawn attention to the problems of 'collective action' (for example, Pressman and Wildavsky 1973). The act of deciding may not be trouble-free, but implementing the decision can be worse![1]

Several authors have looked at the way in which implementation is carried out. It has been suggested (Nutt 1986; 1987; 1989) that managers choose from a repertoire of implementation tactics. These are the ways managers get others to action decisions. According to Nutt, they comprise *intervention*, where key executives justify the need for change by introducing new norms to identify performance inadequacies; *participation*, where task forces are set up to develop implementation and identify stake-holders; *persuasion*, when implementation strategies are delegated to technical staff or experts who then 'sell' their ideas back to the decision-makers; and finally, *edict*, where decision-makers use control and personal power while avoiding any form of participation (1986: 249). In Nutt's American sample, persuasion has been shown to be the most popular form of implementation tactic (it was used in 42 per cent of the cases), followed by edict (23 per cent), then intervention (19 per cent), and least of all participation (17 per cent). But if the measure of success is taken as being whether decisions are fully 'adopted' (that is, implemented) at the end of this process, then intervention with a 100 per cent success rate is clearly the most successful tactic. Persuasion and participation were moderately successful and edict was the least successful with a success rate of 43 per cent. One conclusion from this work is that managers only rarely hit on implementation strategies which are likely to lead to complete success.

But since there are so many dicta as to what managers need for strategic success it is unsurprising if they are perhaps rather non-plussed at how to act for the best . Some have argued that 'ownership' of the original strategy is crucial (Giles 1991), but so too is the need to gain acceptance (Piercy 1989). Setting clear objectives and 'milestones' is thought to be helpful (Owen 1993), while the 'excellence' literature (Peters and Waterman 1982) stresses the importance of a cohesive corporate culture.

Bourgeois and Brodwin (1984) have made a useful assessment of some of the literature and have distinguished five approaches to implementation. Each approach has its own view of the challenges of strategic action and thus the priorities to be tackled to implement successfully. Each therefore suggests a different way to put strategies into effect.

The first of these schemata is entitled the commander model. In this form of implementation the reliance is on centralized direction. The decision is made and others implement in accordance with instructions. The change model emphasizes the role of structure and of control and rewards systems in effecting change. The third approach sees strategy as a negotiated outcome at a senior level and is called the collaborative model. The cultural model relies on a strong culture which infuses the whole organization. The fifth and final model, the crescive model, advocates '"growing" strategy from within the firm' (1984: 242) and encourages managers to champion good strategies.

Bourgeois and Brodwin suggest when each of these approaches may be more or less appropriate. For example the commander model may work best when the change is unthreatening, when senior management already has a great deal of power and when existing systems and behaviours do not get in the way of what is required for implementation. In addition, objective planners and good information systems are called for. In contrast, the cultural model needs decentralized power and shared goals. This model may work best when the organization is stable and growing (1984: 252).

These several approaches lead to the conclusion that it is still not clear what factors influence successful implementation. With this in mind the Bradford Studies work has been extended by the authors of this chapter to cover what happened when the decisions were put into effect during the years following the original fieldwork. As already mentioned, a subset of 55 of the original 150 decisions has been chosen to search for any identifiable factors which might have affected the success of what was done. Success in implementing is assessed primarily by performance in terms of what was intended by the decision-makers, that is 'achievement'.

It has been found that decisions, once taken, are carried out. Very rarely are decisions left undone once they have been authorized. Suspicions that senior executives are preoccupied by

taking decisions and then overlook whether anything is done about them are not borne out, at any rate in these British organizations. So once a formal decision is made, something happens. Many also achieve more or less what was intended. But not all; things do go wrong, there are unforeseen happenings, and decision-makers can get surprises.

The example of a regional brewer in the UK shows this. Seeking to expand capacity the company (a small owner-managed firm) discovered another brewery far larger than itself was for sale and bought it. An opportunistic decision which appeared to be a fortuitous answer to the firm's needs initially worked out well. The purchase price was very favourable, there were few production problems and the demand for the product was clear and sustainable. Yet over time, and with hindsight, it was evident that the buying and running of such a disproportionately larger second brewery had put insupportable strain on the whole operation. Cash flow problems ensued, were met by an injection of funds from outside, arose again when these funds proved insufficient, eventually leading to the take-over of the company and its disappearance as an entity. This was not at all what its owner-managers had intended when they set out to expand it as an independent firm. This shows how unexpected outcomes can result from decisions which at first seem to be wholly successful, and that a long time frame is needed to evaluate what transpires.

This study may be able to shed some light on some of the prescripts for success discussed earlier. As we have seen, a prime tenet of the 'excellence' debate, and one which has been greatly enlarged upon elsewhere in the literature, is the need to have a strong corporate culture. It is also felt to be particularly helpful to have a *champion* – someone in a powerful position who can foster support and drive implementation through the organization. The idea of the 'powerful leader' is one which is mythologized in management literature; witness the wealth and popularity of material written by impassioned entrepreneurs and sundry captains of industry in recent years. Indeed, the 'edict' mode of implementation and the 'commander model' both recognize the attraction of dynamic, charismatic centralized control – both in theory and in actuality. Several of our cases tell a different story. A champion can lead an organization to a series of failures, pushing on to realize his own vision but taking no heed of uncomfortable facts or doubting colleagues. This we call the 'blinkered' champion. How much worse the potential consequences if the culture is so cohesive, or the champion so powerful, that no one else sees the danger ahead, or dares to speak out.

In manufacturing firms we have found a tendency to 'over-reach' (Wilson et al. 1994) whereby firms stretch themselves beyond the limits of what they can manage and are forced to retract, if they can. The example of the regional brewer cited above provides an apt illustration here. Over-reach can easily lead to failure, depending on the degree to which decisions can be 'undone' once the danger is recognized. If the decision is largely irreversible, and if the scale or scope of the decision is too disproportional to the size of the company, then the likelihood of failure increases.

There is another body of thought, to which this chapter now turns, that stands distinct from both rational models and politicized views. Both of these are attempts to elucidate causal relationships between events and outcomes. From this other more challenging perspective, both are misunderstandings of the world in general and organizations in particular.

STRATEGIES AND GARBAGE-CANS: CHAOS AND DISORGANIZED ORDER

The most imaginative, coherent and penetrating perspective is that of the evocatively named 'garbage-can' model (Cohen et al. 1972). This is a depiction of decision-making which turns much of what we have previously discussed on its head. Garbage-cans are found predominantly in 'organized anarchies', complex organizations whose internal processes are not really understood, even by people working in them. In these situations the means and ends of decisions become 'uncoupled' (Weick 1976) so that actions do not lead to expected outcomes, but are hijacked along the way by other decisions and other actions. The main components of decisions – problems, solutions, participants and choice situations – pour into the organizational garbage-can in a seemingly haphazard way, a stream of demands for the fluid attention and energy of decision-makers. If problem, solution, participant and choice situation happen to collide appropriately, then a decision occurs. It may not be foreseen. It may not be one which actually solves the problem to which it has been attached. For not only are the means and ends of decisional processes disconnected, but solutions to problems are in existence before the problems themselves are recognized.

All the while participants move in and out of decision-making processes since 'every entrance is an exit somewhere else' (March and Olsen 1976), which creates discontinuity. Perversely, actors jostle for the right to get involved and then appear uninterested either in exercising it, or in whether decisions are carried out. The conventionally accepted order of things is transformed, put back to front, jumbled beyond recognition. The picture is one of seeming chaos, of disorder. And yet there are some patterns under the confusion and these can be modelled once the parameters are known. The process is not truly random and can be predicted to some extent, although it can feel like chaos to participants. Decisions do get made, although the process is about as far removed from rational choice prescriptions as it is possible to get.

Outside direct research into decision-making in organizations, chaos theories have received increasing attention in recent years. Beginning with iconoclastic revelations in the natural and physical sciences, their provocative and rather disturbing conclusions have thrown many orthodox assumptions into turmoil. With the basic postulate that small changes can, by means of complex feedback cycles, result in ever more complex, dynamic changes of unpredictable and epic proportions, it asks fundamental questions about the nature of cause-and-effect mechanisms. As yet, these ideas are feeding slowly into theories about organizations and management. 'Normal', positivistic, and functional orthodoxies still have a central place in organization theorizing, although other positions are generating increasing interest. The garbage-can model, together with the work of authors such as Weick (1976) and Brunsson (1985), can be seen as forerunners of this growing interest in chaos and complexity.

MAPPING THE TERRAIN OF DECISION PROCESS RESEARCH

The range of work on decision-making covered in this chapter may be contrasted along two key dimensions. One is concerned with the nature of the decision process itself over time, the other with the involvement of various interests in the process. They may be termed the dimension of process *action* and the dimension of political *interest*. The principal researchers are 'mapped' on them in Figure 1 to present an overview of research and researchers. This is as we see it, of course, and others, especially the researchers and theorists themselves, may have differing views on where particular work should be positioned. Such a diagram is illustrative rather than precise.

The Action Dimension

On the action dimension, decision-making processes may be viewed as running from the

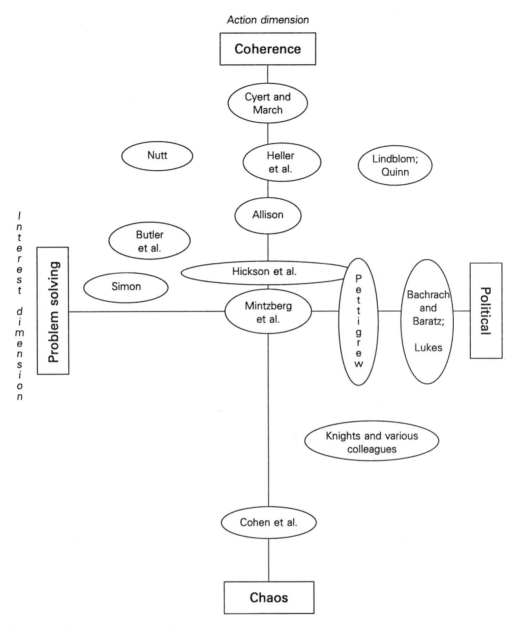

Figure 1   *Mapping decision studies*

more *coherent* to the more *chaotic*. Authors who take a predominantly coherent view of process subscribe to the notion that decision process trajectories can be relatively sequenced and linear, and reflect attempts by decision-makers to achieve step-by-step progress toward stated goals or objectives. Lindblom's (1959) incrementalism and Quinn's (1980) description of progressive change through step-by-step actions are examples of the coherent approach, as are Heller et al.'s (1988) linear phases. Coherence

implies 'intended rationality' (Cyert and March 1963). Individuals strive to achieve rational decision-making, but are prevented from achieving this through lack of perfect knowledge, through cognitive limits and so on. Nevertheless, the intention is coherence. Butler et al. (1993) show how coherence can be better achieved by attention to specific factors (inspiration, judgement and computation). Hickson et al. (1986) claim to have uncovered a spectrum of process characteristics, so logically they also tend toward the coherent view, since their characterizations presuppose some degree of detectable order in the process.

A diametrically opposite perspective on process is adopted by those who argue that coherence is a myth derived from rational economics. Neat and precise its descriptions may be, but they do not describe the reality of decision processes which are not necessarily linear, sequenced or intendedly rational. At the extreme of this chaotic view of decision process lie the garbage cans of Cohen et al. (1972). Here, solutions are generated prior to processes and are attached to problems in a seemingly random fashion. Cohen et al. (1972) stand alone to define the chaos end of the action dimension. Processes are part of the embeddedness of the organization and are not always under control (e.g. Knights and Morgan 1991; Knights and Murray 1992). Chaotic action can also be seen in less extreme form in Mintzberg et al.'s (1976) recycling and discontinuous processes. Here, decisions stop, start again, and revisit their point of origin. They are still processes occurring over time, yet they lack the apparent linear sequential characteristics of their more coherent counterparts. It is very visible that this lower half of Figure 1 is least filled (or most empty). The intellectual boldness and empirical ingenuity to follow where Cohen et al. (1972) led does not come easily.

The Interest Dimension

The more political interest dimension runs from a purely *problem-solving* view to a negotiated order view in which diverse interests give a *political* colour to decision-making.

The problem-solving view is perhaps best typified by Simon's (1960) description of decision-making as a 'new science'. It is 'new', because Simon rejected the prevailing orthodoxy of his coeval economists, who believed economic models of individual choice behaviour could be applied directly to organizational decision processes. It is 'scientific', however, since Simon still held centrally the notion of problem-oriented behaviour from those involved. Goals were specified, targets were set and the overall problem was held in view, whilst decision participants sought solutions which were satisfactory and which were sufficient to address the problem. This 'satisficing' behaviour is firmly rooted in the problem-solving perspective. Radical though Simon's ideas may have been to economists at the time, his relative orthodoxy is revealed when reflected against the more political perspectives which gained momentum in the 1970s. At the other extreme are the analyses of Bachrach and Baratz (1962; 1970),

who completely eschew problem-solving approaches. All activity is politically driven, they argue, to the extent that certain items are deliberately kept off decision agenda. Whoever defines the agenda or the problem holds the key to decision-making. Bachrach and Baratz are clear about emphasizing politics over problem-solving perspectives, yet reveal far less detail about the action dimension of the decision process. Presumably to them this could be either chaotic or coherent. To them the most important dimension is the extent to which decisions are either made in advance, or kept off the agenda altogether by powerful interests. Pettigrew (1973; 1985; 1987) is less extreme, taking problems as given and overt, but agreeing that the predominant focus is political, as gatekeepers screen information or as interests negotiate in the decision arena. This places Pettigrew's work firmly on the political end of the interest dimension, but there is a similar lack of attention in his work to the relative degrees of coherence and chaos in the process. Hence his location on Figure 1 spans only a small range on the action dimension.

Since the explanation of differences in process advanced by Hickson et al. (1986) includes both the nature of the problem and its politics, their work is shown as extending in both directions along the interest dimension.

All the authors in Figure 1 have focused on decision-making *per se*. They have started from the decision as the unit of analysis around which other factors might vary. Decisions may vary in content (what they are about) and in process (how the decision moves through the organization) and they may vary in importance (operational or strategic). The common feature, however, is that the concept of decision is the primary unit of analysis. Suppose that the decision itself cannot be taken for granted? Suppose that the very idea of 'a decision' is misleading?

THE CONCEPT OF 'A DECISION'

The realism of much of the decision-making research has been called into question by those who feel that the very concept of decision has outlived its usefulness. According to writers such as Mintzberg and Waters (1990) it 'gets in the way' of understanding organizational processes. They argue that there are inherent problems with the concept, one of these being that while decisions imply a commitment to action there are situations where actions are taken without decisions having been made. They argue that to see organizational shifts in terms of the deliberate making of decisions over-concretizes the rather ambiguous, uncertain processes of change and underplays the continual redefinition, reshaping and reformulation which commitments to action constantly undergo. It is possible that the 'quasi-decisions' about foregone conclusions mentioned earlier (Hickson et al. 1986) are an empirical verification of this.

Mintzberg and Waters (1990) claim the notion of decision is particularly unhelpful when thinking about strategies which organizations pursue. This opens up a large area which has not yet received full attention. For although the literature on strategic decisions often discusses corporate strategy (and vice versa) the links between the two are implicit rather than defined. Do strategic decisions implement some overarching strategy, are they made within the context of pre-existing strategies, and what is the interactive effect of decisions and strategies? Are decisions more successful if they are part of a 'global' strategy, or do they exist separately, and does this matter?

Mintzberg and Water's (1982) earlier work on strategy formulation prompted their subsequent musings. In this earlier work they defined strategy as a 'pattern in a stream of decisions'. Yet further ruminations along the lines discussed above refined the description to a 'pattern in a stream of actions' (Mintzberg and Waters 1985). Thus strategies may *emerge* rather than be deliberately decided in advance. Organizations may find themselves going in a particular strategic direction without anyone explicitly having decided that they should do so. The way this happens is that a strategy materializes from the combined effects of various actions which may or may not be directly connected. Over time, and with hindsight, these may be sufficiently consistent to be viewed as forming some kind of pattern. In this case it is possible to talk of the organization having a strategy, although it may not have been intentional.

For students of decision-making, this casts fresh doubt on the validity of the idea of decisions being deliberate, purposeful and planned, even on their 'happening' at all in an explicit way at particular points in time. Some authors in the area of strategic management have linked this with chaos theories (for example, see Stacey 1993a; 1993b). Yet this view may go too far. Others have countered (Butler 1990; Pettigrew 1990) that to discard the concept of a decision altogether 'throws the baby out with the bath water'. They maintain that the usefulness of the concept outweighs its limitations.

Subsuming the analysis of individual decisions into the patterns made by planned or emergent strategies is one example of the different levels of analysis in decision theory. Another in sharp contrast rests on the premise that decision-making is best studied by looking at interactions, interpretations of meaning and the significance of symbols, given by common-sense accounts by individuals of how and why they acted in certain ways. Such accounts produce a richness of data, largely consisting of definitions of the situation and interpretations by individuals (see Silverman 1970; Clegg 1975; Goffman 1982). What would such an analysis do to some of the research we have described earlier? It would have radically changed our own account of the expansion decision in the regional UK brewer, for example. Instead of giving a single picture of this decision process composed from managers' recollections, at the level of political balance and financial capacity, as we did, an interactionist perspective would have described in detail each manager's own account of the situation. In this way, the overarching constructs of 'decision' are removed. The account of what happened (and why) is expressed and contained only in the eyes and language of participants.

Although these perspectives draw heavily from earlier works concerned with existentialism (e.g. Sudnow 1965), concerns with postmodernity have also prompted decision theory to re-examine its basic assumptions. As Jeffcutt (1994: 241) says, 'the understanding of organization is inseparable from the organization of understanding.' Understanding decisions, therefore, is a process of analysing narratives, interpreting actions and identifying meaning in symbols as articulated by individuals. Such a perspective questions the constructs of late modernity (such as organizational size, technology, subunit power and characterizations of decision processes as incremental or sporadic) and argues that trying to draw conclusions about the relative contribution of such constructs to comprehending decision-making is fruitless. How different, then, would be our understanding (and data base) for decision theory had this perspective gained dominance whilst Simon, Cyert and March and Lindblom were first uncovering the details of decision process in the 1960s? Characterizations and aggregations of organizational and process data would be replaced by tales, folklore, dreams, symbols and myths. Case studies of decisions would not exist in their current form since they are argued to be imposed narrative, corresponding more to the logical constructs of an author rather than reflecting the 'reality' of the situation. It remains to be seen whether decision theory will look like this in the future, or whether it could even exist, then, as a separate focus of research since a decision is a false construct itself through postmodern eyes.

At a macro level, organizations can be seen to be imitative whereby their managements follow leads taken by other organizations in the sector and sometimes outside it (see Grinyer and Spender 1979; Hinings and Greenwood 1988; Fombrun and Shanley 1990). This follow-my-leader approach has some appeal, since competing firms within the same business sector will be likely to adapt and react to each other's strategies and may be seen to be following one another. For example, in our case of the regional brewer, it would be plausible to argue that growth in scale of operations was a 'recipe' prevalent in the brewing sector at the time (Grinyer and Spender 1979). The directors were merely following the trend. Similarly, Cyert and March's (1963) characterizations of 'satisficing' or 'sequential attention to goals' could be interpreted as cautious corporate action taken with an eye on the competition in the sector (rather than as managerial limitations). The electricity generation undertaken by a chemical company (Wilson 1982) could equally be seen as an example of a diversification strategy, prevalent in the chemical industry at the time, as much as an example of political careerism which is how it was presented.

Keat and Abercrombie (1990) go further and imply that the study of individual decisions in an organization is inappropriate since they fit into a pattern determined largely by socio-political factors. They cite the emergence of the 'enterprise culture' in Britain (1979 onwards) whereby particular strategic decisions in firms are framed by interventionist government policies such as privatization (for public sector organizations), reduction of dependencies (on suppliers and government agencies) and an increased emphasis on the customer as a major influence in product and service decisions. They argue that although

individual strategic decisions may vary in topic content they will fit into this overall pattern if a wide enough frame of reference is adopted.

Yet even at this level of analysis, Child (1972) argues that managers do have a choice. They are not, he argues, deterministically led by the actions of other organizations. The regional brewer described above could have chosen to stay small and on a single site, and the chemical company could have chosen not to diversify into unrelated activity.

Voluntarist–determinist debates are provoked here. Do managers have the content and process of decision imposed upon them, or do they exercise a degree of strategic choice?

One final challenge to the contentious but stimulating area of research that this chapter has described arises from the differences in socio-economic context around the world. Yet the knowledge base from which virtually all decision theory emanates is socio-culturally North American or Western European. The implications of this partiality are examined next.

NORTH, SOUTH, EAST AND WEST: THE CULTURE SHOCK FOR RESEARCHERS ON DECISION-MAKING PROCESSES

Take another look from a different angle at the main empirical research into the overt, empirically traced, processes of decision-making, *and* at the researchers who did it. Working around Figure 1 (in a clockwise direction) is revealing. What it reveals is shown in Table 1. It is startling when listed in this way.

The researchers are almost all Westerners,

Table 1 *Researcher nationality and research location*

Researchers	Research nationality	Research location
Cyert and March	American	American firms
Lindblom	American	American public administration
Quinn	American	American and European firms
Pettigrew	British	British firms
Knights and colleagues	British	British firms
Cohen et al.	American, Norwegian (Olsen)	Scandinavian and American organizations
Simon	American	American, mainly business
Butler et al.	British	British firms
Nutt	American	American health services organizations
Heller et al.	British (Heller), Dutch, Yugoslavian (Rus)	British, Dutch, and Yugoslavian organizations
Allison	American	American government
Hickson et al.	British, American (Cray), Swedish (Axelsson)	Diverse organizations in England
Mintzberg et al.	Canadian, Indian (Raisinghani)	Diverse Anglo-Canadian organizations

from the United States, Canada, Britain, and Scandinavia. They are almost all Northerners, from North America and Northern Europe. The data themselves are drawn almost exclusively from managers of the same genre. So here are researchers and research subjects all from the distinctively individualistic, most coolly impersonal cultures of what is loosely called 'the West'. The only exceptions are Rus, who contributed data from two organizations in the former Yugoslavia to the work by Heller et al., and Raisinghani, an Indian in Canada with Mintzberg.

Of course, even among these Westerners and Northerners there are societal differences. There are cultural variations within 'the West'. It is tempting to think that some part of the differences in ideas about decision-making is traceable to this.

For example, Anglo-Canadian society is held to be more considerate and less urgently impelled to action than its giant American neighbour (e.g. Hofstede 1980; 1991; Carroll 1990; Lipset 1986). Could this be why recycling features in Mintzberg et al.'s (1976) findings? Are Canadian managers more willing than Americans to cautiously refer to matters so that they can be reconsidered over and over again?

How then, it might be asked, could Lindblom (1959) have discerned step-by-step incrementalism in American practice? It does not fit the bold decisiveness of the 'Yankee' stereotype. Speculatively, this could be because the politicality which Pettigrew (1973) and Hickson et al. (1986) found pronounced in processes in organizations in England was at an extreme in the government administration observed by Lindblom (1959), so that in this kind of organization the need to manoeuvre issues along thwarted the underlying American desire for quick decisions. Societal culture is not the only explanation for what happens.

Yet it can hardly be surprising that self-assertive political activity is a feature of the managerial echelons of the individualistic Anglo nations (especially the English?). Nor that the only work influenced by the careful, thorough, Dutch (Lawrence 1991), that by Heller et al. (1988), should have divided processes into conspicuously orderly phases.

Quite the opposite is the most radical notion of all, 'the garbage-can model' put forward by Cohen et al. (1972). As described earlier in the chapter, this is imaginative, even fanciful, in supposing that decisions can occur by the chance coinciding of their ingredients. Could its conception have been influenced by one author being Norwegian and all the authors being in continual contact with other Scandinavian researchers (as in March and Olsen 1976), who

bring from that part of the world the vivid if not outlandish imagery of its traditional literature?

Further, research emanating from that by Hickson et al. (1986) has shown specific differences in the handling of time between Western decision-making processes. The British take more time over a decision than the Americans do (Mallory et al. 1983), and the Swedes are even slower than the British (Axelsson et al. 1991). Or, to put it the other way around, the Americans are faster than either (which does fit their stereotype).

In so far as these differences among the Westerners could be due in some measure to differences in societal cultures, attention is alerted. For if this is so, then how very different again must be processes in the wider world. Do the typological concepts and the models which have been examined in this chapter apply only to the organizations of 'Northern/Western' societies? Although that is probably too pessimistic a suggestion since there will be commonalities across societies, yet differences of degree, and inadequacies of concept, must surely be anticipated in other societies with other cultures. Indeed, it is possible that some completely fresh ideas might be needed.

This is no criticism of the researchers concerned. For decades they have had their hands full – or, rather, their heads full – of trying to make sense of something as elusive empirically and theoretically as powerful elite decision-making, just using organizations in the nearest available society. It would have been too much to take on the subtleties of cultural variation in addition. Moreover, only now are the beginnings of a truly world view of organizations and the organized taking shape (e.g. Hickson and Pugh 1995).

Since it is predominantly Western researchers who have had a rare tradition of fundamental research, some money for it, and some accessible organizations, the main ideas about decision-making have come from within their pluralistic, bluntly competitive, impersonal cultures. So there is nothing in this chapter that emphasizes, say, personal loyalties or the very personal wielding of supreme authority, or harmony-preserving devices, which are more pronounced in the wider world. The prevalence of the impersonal bureaucratic norms and forms whose early stages Weber (1947) analysed so insightfully is taken for granted, together with cultures that in their work-related aspects are comparatively individualistic and of low power distance, as Hofstede (1980; 1991) has termed them.

Yet most of the world struggles to reconcile this Western view of organization and management, carried by its expatriate managers and its exported teaching, with ways of managing more appropriate to Easterners and Southerners in Asia, Africa, Arabia, and South America. In their more person-centred approach it is people to whom loyalty is owed, often overriding any loyalty to the abstract fictions of organizational roles and departments. Harmony and consideration for others on the job moderate the drive for self-assertive achievement. Respect for higher authority is inconsistent with the idea that an ultimately uncontrollable chaos could be at the core of organizational behaviour (even where organizational practice may malfunction chaotically). For these are the relatively personalistic, collectivistic, higher power distance cultures (e.g. Hofstede 1980; 1991; Alston 1986; Lincoln and McBride 1987; Redding 1990; Child 1994; Jaeger and Kanungo 1990; Muna 1980) whose managerial decision-making processes might well not be adequately encompassed by concepts of satisficing search, incrementalism, rationality and politicality, recycling, sporadic or fluid or constricted movement, or coinciding garbage.

Although there is very little direct evidence to go on for that, what there is does signal the significance of non-Western, non-Northern cultures for decision-making, as the broad theoretical framework for cultures postulated by Lachman et al. (1994) predicts it should.

Management in the Arabian Middle East, for example, share the higher regard for status-based authority, especially when it goes with seniority and family position, which is general outside the West (e.g. Muna 1980; El-Ashker 1987; Attiyah 1992). So decision-making tends to be more centralized. Yet this hold on power can be felt to carry an obligation to personally consult underlings, even if this be what Westerners call 'pseudo-participation' in which no real power is shared. The well-known Japanese *ringi* system of confirming concurrence with a decision can also be 'pseudo' in that sense, but it does affirm at worst that those concerned will go along with a decision, at best that they fully support it. This is the practice of circulating among appropriate managers a document to which they may (or may not) affix an assenting personal signature stamp, *after* a prolonged period of largely informal discussion or *nema-washi* (Alston 1986; Lincoln and McBride 1987).

The Latin world has something of both the centralization and the personal touch, and more. Brazil, for instance, adds the immediatism of a 'New World' culture which has no time to wait for the future. Compared to English decision-making processes, those of Brazil are inclined to be far shorter, even hasty, yet despite that they are much more personal and sociable with management meetings inclined to meander and decisions not infrequently taking shape at weekend barbecues (Oliveira 1992; Amado and Brasil 1991).

By contrast, decision-making in sub-Saharan Africa, where government involvement is closer and instability usually greater, is widely authoritarian and politicized (e.g. Kiggundu 1989; Jaeger and Kanungo 1990; Blunt and Jones 1992). Indeed, planned or controlled economies of a kind not found in the Western nations always reduce the scope for decisions to be taken by the managers of operating organizations, and centralize those decisions that are allowed to them, as for instance in countries as different as Egypt (Badran and Hinings 1981) and China (Child 1994).

Is it then really conceivable that where there is an authoritative hand holding down the lid, there could be Anglo-Scandinavian chancy garbage-can processes? How could there be as many politically imbued sporadic processes as were found in England when there is not the same underlying individualistic pluralism? As yet, who knows?

The trite conclusion to this chapter therefore can only be that more research is needed. Trite it may be, but specifically it means more research beyond the confines of the (Northern) Western world. Of course, work should continue within that world on patterns of process, their conclusions, implementations, and consequences, and hopefully researchers doing this will become more cognizant than hitherto of the cultures they are working within. But research on decision-making at the managerial apex should extend to organizations in other societies. In this it is lagging behind the rest of organization theory. More has been done in more societies on the use of authority, on bureaucratization, on commitment and loyalties, on the use of time, and so on. Perhaps this is because of the empirical obstacles. Even Western managers accustomed to talking impersonally to all comers in comparatively open societies are cautious enough when asked to reveal to strangers something as sensitive as how a major decision is arrived at. Many managers elsewhere in the world would see no reason for doing anything so peculiar. Researchers in this difficult area will have to find means to break its culture bounds, nonetheless. Unless they can, Western models of decision-making will remain bounded by Western thinking and by Western constituted organizations. Although these organizations do make up a large proportion of the world's most developed economies, they are managed by and employ only a small proportion of humankind. Those who research their decision-making have come from an even smaller minority of human societies. Conceptual progress needs the stimulus of both non-Western data and non-Western researchers.

NOTE

1 Away from studies which specifically focus on the implementation of strategic decisions there is a range of work in other areas, including the broad area of change management, which can be considered to be related to this subject. This is not the place to deal with this material in any depth and readers are advised to refer to Chapter 2.9 in this *Handbook*.

REFERENCES

Allison, G.T. (1971) *Essence of Decision: Explaining the Cuban Missile Crisis*. Boston: Little Brown.

Alston, Jon P. (1986) *The American Samurai: Blending American and Japanese Managerial Practices*. De Gruyter.

Amado, Gilles and Brasil, Haroldo Vinagre (1991) 'Organizational behaviour and cultural context: the Brazilian "Jeitinho"', *International Studies of Management and Organization*, 21(3): 38–61.

Asch, S.E. (1955) 'Studies in independence and conformity: a minority of one against unanimous majority', *Psychological Monographs*, 20 (whole no. 416).

Attiyah, Hamid S. (1992) 'Research in Arab countries, published in Arabic', *Organization Studies*, 13(9): 105–10.

Axelsson, Runo, Cray, D., Mallory, G.R. and Wilson, D.C. (1991) 'Decision style in British and Swedish organizations: a comparative examination of strategic decision making', *British Journal of Management*, 2(2): 67–79.

Bachrach, P. and Baratz, M.S. (1962) 'The two faces of power', *American Political Science Review*, 56: 947–52.

Bachrach, P. and Baratz, M.S. (1970) *Power and Poverty: Theory and Practice*. London: Oxford University Press.

Badran, Mohamed and Hinings, Bob (1981) 'Strategies of administrative control and contextual constraints in a less developed country: the case of Egyptian public enterprise', *Organization Studies*, 2(1): 3–21. Reprinted in D.J. Hickson and C.J. McMillan (eds) (1981), *Organization and Nation: the Aston Programme IV*. Gower.

Beck, V. (1992) *The Risk Society*. London: Sage.

Blunt, Peter and Jones, Merrick L. (1992) *Managing Organizations in Africa*. De Gruyter.

Bourgeois, L.J. and Brodwin, D.R. (1984) 'Strategic implementation: five approaches to an elusive phenomenon', *Strategic Management Journal*, 5: 241–64.

Braybrooke, D. and Lindblom, C.E. (1963) *A Strategy of Decision*. New York: Free Press.

Brunsson, N. (1985) *The Irrational Organization*. New York: Wiley.

Burrell, Gibson and Morgan, Gareth (1993) *Sociological Paradigms and Organisational Analysis: Elements of the Sociology of Corporate Life*. Hants, UK: Ashgate.

Butler, R.J. (1990) 'Studying deciding: an exchange of views between Mintzberg and Waters, Pettigrew, and Butler', *Organization Studies*, 11(1): 2–16.

Butler, R.J., Davies, L., Pike, R. and Sharp, J. (1993) *Strategic Investment Decisions*. London: Routledge.

Carroll, Barbara W. (1990) 'Systemic conservation in North American organizations', *Organization Studies*, 11(3): 413–34.

Child, J. (1972) 'Organizational structure, environment and performance: the role of strategic choice', *Sociology*, 6: 1–22.

Child, J. (1994) *Management in China during the Age of Reform*. Cambridge University Press.

Clegg, S. (1975) *Power, Rule and Domination*. London: Routledge and Kegan Paul.

Cohen, M.D., March, J.G. and Olsen, J.P. (1972) 'The garbage can model of organizational choice', *Administrative Science Quarterly*, 17 (March): 1–25.

Cray, David, Mallory, Geoffrey R., Butler, Richard J., Hickson, David J. and Wilson, David C. (1988) 'Sporadic, fluid and constricted processes: three types of strategic decision-making in organizations', *Journal of Management Studies*, 25(1): 13–39.

Cray, David, Mallory, Geoffrey R., Butler, Richard J., Hickson, David J. and Wilson, David C. (1991) 'Explaining decision processes', *Journal of Management Studies*, 28(3): 227–51.

Crozier, Michel (1964) *The Bureaucratic Phenomenon*. London: Tavistock.

Crozier, Michel and Friedberg, Erhard (1980) *Actors and Systems*. Chicago: University of Chicago Press (published in French in 1977 by Editions du Seuil).

Cyert, R. and March, J.G. (1963) *A Behavioural Theory of the Firm*. Englewood Cliffs, NJ: Prentice-Hall.

Dutton, Jane E. (1986) 'The processing of crisis and non-crisis strategic issues', *Journal of Management Studies*, 23(5): 501–17.

Eisenhardt, K. and Zbaracki, M.J. (1992) 'Strategic decision making', *Strategic Management Journal*, 13: 17–37.

El-Ashker, Ahmed Abdel-Fattah (1987) *The Islamic Business Enterprise*. Beckenham: Croom Helm.

Fombrun, C. and Shanley, M. (1990) 'What's in a name? Reputation building and corporate strategy', *Academy of Management Journal*, 33(2): 233–58.

Giddens, A. (1990) *The Consequences of Modernity*. Cambridge: Polity Press.

Giles, William D. (1991) 'Making strategy work', *Long Range Planning*, 24(5): 75–91.

Goffman, E. (1982) *The Presentation of Self in Everyday Life*. Harmondsworth: Penguin.

Grinyer, P.H. and Spender, J.C. (1979) 'Recipes, crises and adaptation in mature businesses', *International Studies of Management and Organization*, IX(3): 113–33.

Heller, F., Drenth, P., Koopman, P. and Rus, V.

(1988) *Decisions in Organizations – a Three Country Comparative Study*. London: Sage.

Hickson, D.J., Butler, R.J., Cray, D., Mallory, G.R. and Wilson, D.C. (1986) *Top Decisions: Strategic Decision-Making in Organizations*. Oxford: Basil Blackwell. San Francisco: Jossey-Bass.

Hickson, D.J., Hinings, C.R., Lee, C.A., Schneck, R.C. and Pennings, J.M. (1971) 'A strategic contingencies theory of intra-organizational power', *Administrative Science Quarterly*, 16(2): 216–29.

Hickson, D.J. and Pugh, D.S. (1995) *Management Worldwide: the Impact of Societal Culture on Organizations Around the Globe*. Harmondsworth: Penguin.

Hinings, C.R. and Greenwood, R. (1988) 'The normative prescriptions of organizations', in L.G. Zucker (ed.), *Institutional Patterns and Organizations: Culture and Environment*. Cambridge, MA: Ballinger.

Hinings C.R., Hickson, D.J., Pennings, J.M. and Schneck, R.E. (1974) 'Structural conditions of intraorganizational power', *Administrative Science Quarterly*, 19(2): 21–44.

Hofstede, Geert (1980) *Culture's Consequences: International Differences in Work Related Values*. London: Sage.

Hofstede, Geert (1991) *Cultures and Organizations: Software of the Mind*. McGraw-Hill.

Jaeger, Alfred M. and Kanungo, Rabindra N. (1990) *Management in Developing Countries*. London: Routledge.

Janis, I.L. (1972) *Victims of Groupthink: a Psychological Study of Foreign Policy Decisions and Fiascos*. Boston: Houghton Mifflin.

Jeffcutt, P. (1994) 'From interpretation to representation in organizational analysis: postmodernism, ethnography and symbolism', *Organization Studies*, 15(2): 241–74.

Keat, R. and Abercrombie, N. (eds) (1990) *Enterprise Culture*. London: Routledge.

Kiggundu, M.N. (1989) *Managing Organizations in Developing Countries*. Kumarian Press.

Knights, D. and Morgan, G. (1991) 'Corporate strategy, organizations and subjectivity', *Organization Studies*, 12(2): 251–73.

Knights, D. and Murray, F. (1992) 'Politics and pain in managing information technology: a case study from insurance', *Organization Studies*, 13(2): 211–28.

Lachman, Ran, Nedd, Albert and Hinings, Bob (1994) 'Analyzing cross-national management and organizations: a theoretical framework', *Management Science*, 40(1): 40–55.

Lawrence, Peter (1991) *Management in the Netherlands*. Oxford: Clarendon Press.

Lawrence, P.R. and Lorsch, J.W. (1967) *Organization and Environment*. Cambridge, MA: Harvard Graduate School of Business Administration.

Lincoln, James R. and McBride, Kerry (1987) 'Japanese industrial organization in comparative perspective', *Annual Review of Sociology*, 13: 289–312.

Lindblom, C.E. (1959) 'The science of "muddling through"', *Public Administrative Review*, 19(2): 79–88.

Lipset, Seymour Martin (1986) 'Historical traditions and national characteristics: a comparative anlaysis of Canada and the United States', *Canadian Journal of Sociology*, 11: 113–55.

Lukes, S. (1974) *Power: a Radical View*. London: Macmillan.

Mallory, G.R., Butler, R.J., Cray, D., Hickson, D.J. and Wilson, D.C. (1983) 'Implanted decision-making: American owned firms in Britain', *Journal of Management Studies*, 20(2): 191–211.

March, J.G. and Olsen, J.P. (1976) *Ambiguity and Choice in Organizations*. Bergen, Oslo, and Tromsø: Universitetsforlaget.

March, J.G. and Simon, H.A. (1958) *Organizations*. New York: Wiley.

Mintzberg, H. (1973) *The Nature of Managerial Work*. New York: Harper and Row.

Mintzberg, H., Raisinghani, D. and Theoret, A. (1976) 'The structure of "unstructured" decision processes', *Administrative Science Quarterly*, 21: 246–75.

Mintzberg, H. and Waters, J.A. (1982) 'Tracking strategy in an entrepreneurial firm', *Academy of Management Journal*, 25(3): 465–99.

Mintzberg, H. and Waters, J.A. (1985) 'Of strategies, deliberate and emergent', *Strategic Management Journal*, 6: 257–72.

Mintzberg, H. and Waters, J.A. (1990) 'Studying deciding: an exchange of views between Mintzberg and Waters, Pettigrew, and Butler', *Organization Studies*, 11(1): 2–16.

Muna, Farid A. (1980) *The Arab Executive*. London: Macmillan.

Nutt, Paul C. (1984) 'Types of organizational decision processes', *Administrative Science Quarterly*, 29(3): 414–50.

Nutt, Paul C. (1986) 'Tactics of implementation', *Academy of Management Journal*, 29(2): 230–61.

Nutt, Paul C. (1987) 'Identifying and appraising how managers install strategy', *Strategic Management Journal*, 8: 1–14.

Nutt, Paul C. (1989) 'Selecting tactics to implement strategic plans', *Strategic Managment Journal*, 10: 145–61.

Oliveira, Beto (1992) 'Societal culture and managerial decision-making: the Brazilians and the English'. PhD thesis, University of Bradford Management Centre, England.

Owen, Arthur A. (1993) 'How to implement strategy', in C. Mabey and B. Mayon-White (eds), *Managing Change*. London: Paul Chapman.

Peters, T. and Waterman, R. Jr (1982) *In Search of Excellence: Lessons from America's Best-Run Companies*. New York: Harper and Row.

Pettigrew, A.M. (1973) *The Politics of Organizational Decision-Making*. London: Tavistock.

Pettigrew, A.M. (1985) 'Examining change in the long term context of culture and politics', in J.M. Pennings (ed.), *Organizational Strategy and Change*. San Francisco: Jossey-Bass.

Pettigrew, A.M. (1987) 'Context and action in the transformation of the firm', *Journal of Management Studies*, 24(6): 649–99.

Pettigrew, A.M. (1990) 'Studying deciding: an exchange of views between Mintzberg and Waters, Pettigrew, and Butler', *Organization Studies*, 11(1): 2–16.

Pfeffer, J. and Salancik, G.R. (1978) *The External Control of Organizations: a Resource Dependence Perspective*. London: Harper and Row.

Piercy, Nigel (1989) 'Diagnosing and solving implementation problems in strategic planning', *Journal of General Management*, 15(1): 19–38.

Pressman, J.L. and Wildavsky, A. (1973) *Implementation*. Berkeley, CA: University of California.

Quinn, James B. (1978) 'Strategic change: logical incrementalism', *Sloan Management Review*, Fall: 7–21.

Quinn, James B. (1980) *Strategies for Change: Logical Incrementalism*. Homewood, IL: Irwin.

Redding, S. Gordon (1990) *The Spirit of Chinese Capitalism*. De Gruyter.

Rosenthal, U. (1986) 'Crisis decision-making in the Netherlands', *The Netherlands Journal of Sociology*, 22(2): 103–29.

Schattsneider, E. (1960) *Semi-Sovereign People: a Realist's View of Democracy in America*. Holt, Rinehart and Winston. Quoted in Anthony G. McGrew and M.J. Wilson (eds) (1982), *Decision-Making: Approaches and Analysis*. Manchester University Press.

Schoemaker, Paul J.H. (1993) 'Strategic decisions in organizations: rational and behavioural views', *Journal of Management Studies*, 30(1): 107–29.

Silverman, David (1970) *The Theory of Organizations*. London: Heinemann.

Simon, Herbert A. (1945) *Administrative Behaviour*, 2nd edn. New York: Free Press.

Simon, Herbert A. (1960) *The New Science of Management Decision*. New York: Harper & Row.

Smith, G. and May, D. (1980) 'The artificial debate between rationalist and incrementalist models of decision-making', in Anthony G. McGrew and M.J. Wilson (eds) (1982), *Decision Making: Approaches and Analysis*. Manchester University Press.

Stacey, Ralph (1993a) *Strategic Management and Organizational Dynamics*. London: Pitman.

Stacey, Ralph (1993b) 'Strategy as order emerging from chaos', *Long Range Planning*, 26(1): 10–17.

Stewart, R. (1967) *Managers and their Jobs*. Maidenhead: McGraw-Hill.

Stewart, R. (1976) *The Reality of Management*. London: Pan.

Stewart, R. (1983) 'Managerial behaviour: how research has changed the traditional picture', in M. Earl (ed.), *Perspectives on Management: a Multidisciplinary Analysis*. Oxford: Oxford University Press. pp. 82–98.

Strauss, A., Schatzman, L., Ehrlich D., Bucher R. and Sabshin, M. (1982) 'The hospital and its negotiated order', in *People and Organisations*. Essex, UK: Longman.

Sudnow, D. (1965) 'Normal crimes: sociological features of the penal code in a public defender office'. *Social Problems*, 12(3): 255–76.

Thompson, J.D. and Tuden, A. (1959) 'Strategies, structures and processes of organizational decision', in J.D. Thompson et al. (eds), *Comparative Studies in Administration*. Pittsburgh, PA: University of Pittsburgh Press.

Weber, Max (1947) *The Theory of Social and Economic Organization*, translated by A. Henderson and T. Parsons. Glencoe, IL: Free Press.

Weick, Karl E. (1976) 'Educational organizations as loosely coupled systems', *Administrative Science Quarterly*, 21(1): 1–19.

Williamson, O.E. (1975) *Markets and Hierarchies*. New York: Free Press.

Wilson, D.C. (1982) 'Electricity and resistance: a case study of innovation and politics', *Organization Studies*, 3(2): 119–40.

Wilson, D.C., Hickson, D.J. and Miller, S.J. (1995) 'Decision overreach as a reason for failure: how organizations can overbalance', *American Behavioral Scientist* (in press).

Zey, Mary (1992) *Decision Making: Alternatives to Rational Choice Models*. London: Sage.

2.4

Cognitions in Organizations

ANN E. TENBRUNSEL, TIFFANY L. GALVIN,
MARGARET A. NEALE AND MAX H. BAZERMAN

Over the last decade, the study of organizational behavior has witnessed a dramatic shift toward a more cognitive perspective. This change in perspective has influenced both research and application in the field, and, more recently, has redefined topics typically viewed under the heading of organizational behavior (OB). Through the years, organizational behavior, particularly that segment of OB that is based on the study of the individual, has been chastised for lacking a central set of theories, for offering limited theoretical development of the theories it imports from psychology, and for covering topics that are over-researched and lacking connection to issues of interest to practitioners (O'Reilly 1991). We believe that these criticisms are the result of a traditional definition of the field that consists of a narrow set of topics that is more reflective of the table of contents of textbooks than the actual activity and interest of organizational scholars and practitioners. To remedy this problem a broader definition of organizational behavior is needed that includes the study of psychological issues that are relevant to understanding behavior in organizations. We see the cognitive perspectives and theories of psychology as central to this definition. By expanding the topics that the field encompasses, barriers that limit inquiry will be reduced and researchers in the field will be allowed to use and develop the very best psychological and cognitive ideas available to facilitate our knowledge about individual behavior in organizations.

In the 1988 *Annual Review of Psychology*, Ilgen and Klein wrote about what Markus and Zajonc (1985) term 'a shift of near revolutionary proportions in the behavior sciences: the cogni-

tive perspective'. Ilgen and Klein documented the ways in which many traditional topics in organizational behavior were being influenced by this cognitive revolution. While their review is important, we believe that the cognitive revolution has created even more dramatic changes by altering the perception of what constitutes an OB topic to incorporate decision-making processes. The journal *Organizational Behavior and Human Performance* reflected this transition with a name change to *Organizational Behavior and Human Decision Processes*, clarifying the increasing importance of decision behavior to the study of OB. Indicative of the change taking place in the field, decision processes emerged as a mainstream topic within OB, with researchers focusing on how decisions influence managerial behavior (Bazerman 1994; Gioia and Sims 1986). In addition, negotiation has emerged as a new, central topic of OB, and has been dominated by a cognitive orientation (Neale and Bazerman 1991). As evidence of these changes, negotiation has become the most commonly published topic in *Organizational Behavior and Human Decision Processes*, and both decision processes and negotiation have been institutionalized as part of the field by the creation of new divisions within the Academy of Management that specifically address these topics.

We believe that these developments are not random. Rather, the tension between research and practice in business and management schools has resulted in a demand for research in OB that provides managers with more levers for change. This requires that researchers provide practitioners with new skills, and there is no skill more central to managerial behavior than decision-making. As a result, decision-making, and the broader topic of cognition, have gained centrality in OB in the 1990s, fueled by the demands of both researchers and practitioners.

The purpose of this chapter is to provide the background for researchers to appreciate the cognitive revolution in OB, to see its advantages, and to provide direction for future research. First, we discuss our underlying research values which bias the material that is reviewed and the conclusions that we reach. Next, we examine the psychological foundations for a cognitive perspective to organizations; specifically, we overview the development of the areas of social cognition and behavioral decision theory (BDT). We then examine and evaluate the contributions of the cognitive perspective to micro and macro OB topics. Finally, we conclude with an overall evaluation of the application of the cognitive perspective to organizations and discuss an agenda for future research possibilities.

Values and Assumptions behind our Cognitive Perspective

Much of our own research, and that of other cognitive researchers in OB, is affected by a series of underlying values and assumptions (Bazerman 1993). We choose to be explicit about these goals since we believe that these underlying values distinguish cognitive from noncognitive work in OB and motivate much of the cognitively based research in OB (Bazerman 1993).

Research should attempt to understand the world as it is, not as we would like it to be or think that it should be. The assumption of rationality or utility maximization on the part of human actors is a hallmark of economics, but also is ubiquitous among organizational theories and researchers. The rationality assumption characterizes many micro-level OB theories, including virtually all of expectancy theory research (Lawler 1971) and the path-goal theory of leadership (House 1971). This assumption is also extended to the more macro-level rationality of organizational selection in population ecology (Hannan and Freeman 1989). Further, many behavioral researchers offer advice that is based on their assumptions rather than on the empirical realities of the organizations. For example, the field of OB has long conveyed the importance of participation, cooperation, collectivism, and empowerment before sufficient empirical support for these notions exists. Indeed, much of OB has been based on the way we think the world should be. In contrast, we believe that the field should be

based on a more accurate understanding of human behavior as it is observed.

Descriptive research is strengthened by comparisons to normative benchmarks The descriptive nature (the study of what we actually do) of the OB literature is a natural extension of the descriptive orientation of the disciplines, social psychology and sociology, from which such literature is traditionally drawn. This predisposition toward a descriptive orientation is exacerbated by organization scholars who view prescription/application as being of lesser value, often associated with instrumental pursuits rather than scientific values. Yet, many of these same scholars will offer prescriptions when they change from the role of researcher to that of teacher or consultant. Rather than foster such dualistic thinking or sacrifice one component for another, we believe there should be a more direct connection between the empirical and theoretical literature of OB and the prescriptive base we offer. We will return to this value in the behavioral decision research section, and outline what this interaction would look like. For now, we simply note that the tension between these two perspectives may increase our ability to communicate with other disciplines (e.g. economics), improve the theoretical base of organizational research, and help create a defensible, empirically based position from which to inform practitioners.

Descriptive research can provide important adaptations to normative prescriptions. Just as normative benchmarks serve to direct improvements in descriptive models, descriptive research can enhance the quality of normative models. If one assumes that actors are not typically rational utility maximizers, then the predictive quality of the normative models is enhanced by knowledge of the way in which individuals deviate from rationality. This argument is central to Raiffa's (1982) argument that prescriptive models need to better incorporate descriptive models of human behavior.

Decisions are a core unit of activity for both understanding and changing individual behavior in organizations. Historically, behavioral researchers have debated whether the person or the situation is more influential in the particular behavioral responses of individuals. This debate has led to the proposal that the way in which the individual perceives, filters, and conceptualizes information is critical to how he or she responds to situations; these responses in turn change the nature of their interaction and enact their perceptions of the environment (Weick 1992). This view emphasizes the importance of developing better models of decision making and cognition to understand behavior in organizations.

The values described above underlie many of the judgments that we will make throughout the chapter. We will return to these values when we evaluate the cognitive perspective of OB near the end of the chapter.

PSYCHOLOGICAL FOUNDATIONS OF COGNITIVE RESEARCH IN ORGANIZATIONS

Two primary research areas of psychology – social cognition and behavioral decision theory – have served to inform organizational researchers in their attempts to understand the influence of human cognitions on OB. While there may be overlap between these two perspectives, there are also some sharp differences in orientation. Social cognition research is a purely descriptive field which tries to explain how people make sense of the world. Behavioral decision research, while also being a descriptive field, uses normative models as 'straw men' to explain imperfections in human decision processes. Where the broader interpretative process is the focus of the social cognition area, the decision is the key unit of action in BDT. Our review of these two areas will highlight some of the key differences between BDT and social cognition in terms of their influence on OB. As our goal is to provide a sufficient appreciation of the backgrounds of these basic literatures to evaluate the developments that have occurred within OB, we will not provide comprehensive reviews of these two fields. However, we will suggest where such reviews can be found.

Social Cognition

Social cognition has been defined as the study of how people make sense of other people and themselves, and how cognitive processes influence social behavior (Fiske and Taylor 1991). The social cognition approach attempts to understand the storage of social behavior in our cognition, the aspects or dimensions of stored social knowledge that affect our information processing, inferences, judgments, decisions, and actions, and the factors that influence changes in stored social information or knowledge (Sherman et al. 1989). Traditionally, this line of study has been associated with the proposition that people perceive and think about the social world differently than what would be expected based solely on stimulus information and principles of formal logic (Higgins and Bargh 1987).

Over the last decade, social cognition has become the dominant perspective in social psychology (Schneider 1991). Within this domain, social cognition has been applied to several phenomena including oneself, others, imaginary persons, interpersonal relationships, groups, and memory of social information (see Leyens and Codol 1988). Despite the breadth of applicability that the field offers, several limitations to its approach should be noted. As Schneider (1991) points out, the research is often driven more by model testing than by traditional social psychological efforts to explain social phenomena. In addition, there is often the argument that the 'social' aspect of social cognition is missing. Many critics share Schneider's complaint that 'at less than its best, however, social cognition research can be more concerned with the latest fashions from cognitive psychology than with social phenomena' (1991: 553). The implication is that social cognition researchers borrow cognitive psychology models originally developed for nonsocial objects and test their generalizability to social objects (Levine et al. 1993). In defense of these limitations and weaknesses, Higgins (1992) argues that there have been several cognitive models originated by social psychologists, such as the study of attribution processes, which have in turn been imparted into the field of cognition.

Research in the field of social cognition can be categorized into the following areas: (1) attribution theories, (2) memory, (3) knowledge structures (schemata, person perception, categorization, and stereotyping), (4) self-concepts, (5) attitudes and attitude changes, and (6) mental control (Schneider 1991; Sherman et al. 1989). While a complete review of each area would be impossible within the context of this chapter, we will provide definitions and examples of research to overview each of the areas of social cognition.

Attribution Theories

Many scholars categorize attribution theory as the core of social cognitive psychology. Attribution theory is concerned with the way that people associate behavior with discrete causes, and thus focuses on the everyday, common-sense explanations that individuals construct for social events or actions of others. Theories in this field examine how the social perceiver gathers, combines and uses information to arrive at causal explanations for events (Fiske and Taylor 1991). While work in this area dates back to the mid 1940s, current research continues to be undertaken in quantity. There are three main theories which are considered to be the defining contributions to attribution theory. These theories stem from the works of Heider (1944), Jones and Davis (1965), and Kelley (1967). Combined, their work and resulting theories share a concern with common-sense explanations and answers to the question 'why,' while attempting to formalize the rules people might be using to make causal attributions.

Heider's (1944) work on naive psychology treated the lay person as a naive scientist who linked observable behavior to unobservable causes. Naive psychology maintained that the natural language people use to characterize causal action can form the basis for a theory of causal inference. Heider's major contribution to attribution theory was the division of potential sources of action into internal (personal) and external (environmental) types. Heider asserts that social perception research must consider attributes of the target person and the perceiver as well as the context and manner in which the perception occurs. The perceiver is proposed to decide whether an action results from something within the person who is performing the action or from some external source.

A second main contribution to attribution theory involves Jones and Davis's (1965) correspondent inference theory. This theory maintains that the goal of the causal attribution process is to infer that the observed behavior and the intention that produced it correspond to stable, underlying attributes of individuals, and thus to explain their behavior across situations. There are two major stages in the process of inferring personal dispositions: the attribution of intention and the attribution of dispositions. A noncommon effects principle is also at work, which maintains that a perceiver makes a correspondent inference by identifying the distinctive (noncommon) consequences of an actor's chosen course of action. The fewer the distinctive consequences, the more confident the inference about the causal attribution. According to the theory, the perceiver processes information backwards from effects, through action, to inferences about knowledge and ability. Behaviors/actions that are believed (by the perceiver) to be unconstrained, freely chosen, out of character/role, socially undesirable, violating prior expectations, and producing distinctive consequences are all believed to reveal underlying attributes.

The third main cornerstone of attribution theory involves Kelley's (1967) theories about the process of ascribing causes. His covariation model explores how individuals form causal inferences when they have access to multiple instances of similar events. In order to attribute the outcome to a stable cause or pattern of causes, individuals employ a covariation principle to determine how the outcome in question varies across entities, time, and people. However, if the perceiver is faced with only a single

observation, then he/she must take account of the plausible causes of the observed effect, employing what are known as causal schemata. These schemata are ready-made beliefs, preconceptions, and theories, formed by experience, that help an individual ascertain how certain kinds of causes interact to produce a specific effect. Thus, for a given attribution, the perceiver may have to interpret information and events by comparison and integration of schemata.

Outside of the three theories mentioned, there have been other lines of work that influenced early attribution formulations. For example, Weiner's (1986) work on attribution theory develops dimensions of attributional experience, integrates attributions with emotional processes, and enlightens the attributional and affective experience that underlies concrete domains of experience (see Fiske and Taylor 1991 for a more detailed discussion of other perspectives in attribution theory).

Attribution research has been extensive and varied and represents one of social cognition's most popular exports to other fields (see Harvey et al. 1976; 1978; 1981; Kelley and Michela 1980; Ross and Fletcher 1985; and Fiske and Taylor 1991 for more extensive reviews of the attribution field). Hundreds of empirical studies were prompted by the theories previously discussed and various other social phenomena have been analyzed within a causal attribution framework. Tests of attribution theory have uncovered various biases that people employ during the attribution process (e.g. fundamental attribution error, use of consensus information, and the self-serving attributional bias: see Ross 1977; Marks and Miller 1987; Zuckerman 1979; cf. Harvey, et al. 1976; 1978; 1981 for further discussion). The empirical research that has been conducted has been used as a basis for many attributional theories that analyze a variety of social and personal issues.

Memory

Memory extends itself as both a theoretical and a methodological orientation throughout various areas within the realm of social cognition research. Issues surrounding memory have been examined in conjunction with other cognitive areas such as schemata, knowledge structures, categories, and encoding processes, and have been used as an approach to understanding other more social psychological concerns such as attitudes, person perception, stereotypes, judgment and decision making, and the self (see Sherman et al. 1989). The study of memory extends itself across various other topics and, as such, is seen as representing a central totem of modern social cognition (Schneider 1991) as well as ranking as a top cognitive export from the field. The importance of memory is seen in the several books and reviews that thoroughly cover the research in this area (see Martin and Clark 1990; Ostrom 1989; and Wyer and Srull 1988, for example).

The area of memory can be thought of as the examination of the manner in which people remember other individuals and complex social events (Fiske and Taylor 1991). Over the years, there have been several models proposed and tested which hold importance for different types of memory (or memory as viewed in different situations or contexts). More recently, research has drawn away from testing these models and has extended to explaining other social phenomena. Specifically, research on the accuracy, efficiency and representation of affect, mood, and emotion in memory has been increasing (Sherman et al. 1989).

Knowledge Structures: Schemata, Person Perception, Categories and Stereotyping

Social objects, when they are targets of perception and cognition, are distinct from natural objects in a number of ways that influence the processing of information about them (Markus and Zajonc 1985). A major assumption of classic social cognition is that because our information-processing apparatus is resource-limited, we develop highly abstract knowledge structures (Schneider 1991). One such knowledge structure is a schema, which may be defined as a cognitive structure that represents knowledge about a concept or type of stimulus, including its attributes and the relations among those attributes (Fiske and Taylor 1991). Categories and schemata refer to people's expectations about themselves, other people, the situations they encounter, and the effects of these expectations. People have available to them a repertoire of schemata representing situations as well as a catalog of actors or personality types (person schemata) which encompass our organized knowledge (or knowledge structures) of other people (Bazerman and Carroll 1987). The basic premise of schema research has been that individuals simplify reality by storing knowledge at a broader, inclusive level rather than acquiring specific experiences and incorporating these on an individual basis.

The schema concept originated in person perception research with Asch's (1946) configural model of impression formation and Heider's (1958) balance theory of relationship. Their work focused on people's tendency to form unified overall impressions from discrete social elements (Fiske and Taylor 1991). Person schemata were proposed to constitute a knowledge structure which, when evoked, influences social judgments, behavior, and responses to that individual (as dictated in part by the characteristics of the person schema). Person schemata are believed to represent classifications that contain a great deal of information about traits, preferences, and goals that enable the perceiver to understand exhibited behavior, predict future behavior, and develop appropriate responses (Bazerman and Carroll 1987). The field of person perception has been built around the assumption that information about others includes both instances and abstractions, and that these abstract judgments in impression formation can be an overall evaluation of the target derived either from trait attributes or from behaviors performed by the target (Sherman et al. 1989). Research in this area continues to explore the role of information processing and the storage of information during schema formation and person perception.

Before schematic prior knowledge can be applied to social perception, the person or situation has to be classified into a category (Fiske and Taylor 1991). Categories are useful in distinguishing among people, interpreting information, and evaluating others and thus play an important role in providing meaning for social perceivers (Fiske 1993). While schema research is more concerned with the application of organized, generic prior knowledge to the understanding of new information, the domain of categorization research is more concerned with the classification of instances (Fiske and Taylor 1991). Categorization does not merely serve cognitive purposes; it also operates within a social and motivational context and can have important evaluative implications (Fiske 1993). Categorization research is abundant (see Hamilton and Sherman 1993), and has focused on a variety of areas, including an exploration of the information basis of knowledge structures, the cognitive representation of categories, the processing of category relevant information, the choice of categories, an understanding of the categorization process and how it can be controlled, and the relation of categorization to other processes such as attributions (see Schneider 1991). The resulting research has explored models of social categorization, identified core categories used by people to portray other people, and, in contrast, identified the use of concrete representation, exemplars, and target cases instead of person schemata (or stereotypes) (see Fiske 1993).

Significant advances have also been made in the area of stereotyping and prejudice (Markus and Zajonc 1985). Tajfel (1969), one of the first to bring more of a cognitive focus to the social phenomenon of stereotyping, proposed that stereotypes can be viewed as special cases of categorization which accentuate similarities within groups and differences between groups. Categorization models of stereotyping focus on the pragmatic implications for perceivers who use the stereotypes as a rich resource for making sense of their world (Fiske 1993). People use stereotypes when they seem to have explanatory value, give information, provide motivation, or comply with social norms. The effects of categorization on stereotyping have been a major concern, particularly with the attribution of characteristics to in-groups/out-groups, inter-individual and inter-group relationships and conflict, and work on illusory correlation (see reviews, e.g. Messick and Mackie 1989; Hamilton and Sherman 1989; Mullen and Johnson 1990). As social categorization and stereotyping extend to other areas and topics, the cognitive antecedents of these areas can also be explored from the basis of knowledge structures and schemata research.

Self-Concepts

Understanding the concept of the self has been one of the oldest and most pursued goals in psychology. Social psychologists did much of the work in this area during the 1950s. For the next twenty years, however, it appeared that self-concept declined while other issues took center stage with experimental social psychologists. By the late 1970s, the concept of the self 'leaped back into the limelight' (Higgins and Bargh 1987). In the past decade or so, social cognition researchers have taken up the challenge of understanding the self-concept, and have thus added to our fundamental understanding of its structure and functioning (Fiske and Taylor 1991).

Much theory and empirical evidence have been offered in support of the self-concept as a multifaceted, diverse, and complex concept (see Cantor et al. 1986; Greenwald and Pratkanis 1984; and Markus and Wurf 1987 for reviews). Encompassing roles and attributes as key elements, self-concept has been viewed and explained as a collection of schemata, conceptions, and/or images arranged in a system or space. The self-concept has been defined and redefined structurally, thought of in its relation to ego, and considered in terms of its temporal qualities (Sherman et al. 1989). Though much of the early work concerning the self-concept was devoted to specifying its contents, more recent attention has turned to its structure and how it is cognitively represented (Sherman et al. 1989). Through a cognitive analysis of the self-concept and an emphasis on the nature of the knowledge

structures relevant to the self-concept, researchers have been able to empirically validate many of the assumptions of the early self theorists about the referencing, channeling and distorting functions of the self-concept (see Markus and Zajonc 1985).

The dominant position in the literature has been that the self is an unusually rich and highly organized structure (Higgins and Bargh 1987). Researchers have debated, however, whether the self is actually a unique cognitive structure (particularly in terms of its effects) or if it is even a cognitive structure at all. Much of the argument about the special quality of the self has been based on experimental evidence of the information-processing effects of the self and has centered around the research done on Rogers' (1977) self-referent effects (Higgins and Bargh 1987). At present, however, there is still insufficient information available to determine whether the self has unique cognitive properties. There is, however, a recognition that the self-concept is one of the most highly articulated and differentiated constructs that any individual has. Thus the self-concept is clearly important in producing reliable effects on processing (Fiske and Taylor 1991).

Attitudes and Attitude Change

Attitudes are believed to be an intervening variable or a nonobservable link between an observable stimulus and an observable response. Attitudes are defined as an evaluation of the attitude object that often includes cognitive and behavioral tendencies (Fiske and Taylor 1991). Traditional attitude research focused on first defining attitude as a construct and then developing descriptive models and acceptable indicators or measurements of the construct (as discussed in Stahlberg and Frey 1988). Historically, attitude has mainly been defined as a set of overt responses to a questionnaire; consequently, several acceptable scales have been developed in accordance with this approach (e.g. the Likert and equal appearing scales), and other measurement techniques have also been explored. It is believed that most attitude theorists would agree that evaluation constitutes a central aspect of attitudes, that attitudes are represented in memory, and that affective, cognitive, and behavioral antecedents and consequences of attitudes can be distinguished (Olson and Zanna 1993).

The structure, measurement, and functions of attitude and the relationship between attitudes and behavior have become a renewed research interest in recent years (after a decline in interest in the late 1960s and 1970s). The level of activity in the attitude literature is visible in the number of books that have appeared recently (numerous texts, specific books on attitude measures, social judgment, propaganda, and prejudice: see Olson and Zanna 1993) and the comprehensive reviews of attitude literature (e.g., Eagly and Chaiken 1992). Recent research has focused on exploring the formation of attitudes and how such attitudes (as cognitive representations in long-term memory) can be evaluated, altered, or changed (Sherman et al. 1989). As the interest in attitude attributes has grown, more integrative models of the attitude–behavior relationship, as well as the relation of attitude to other topics such as persuasion, prejudice, and stereotyping, are being explored (Olson and Zanna 1993). There has also been a recent trend toward exploring attitude change as a strategy which influences behavior (Stroebe and Jonas 1988).

Various cognitive approaches have also been taken toward attitudes. From traditional theories to those exploring new processes, those emphasizing attitudes as a thoughtful, conscious process versus a more automatic process, and those debating the role of cognition versus motivation in attitude formation, the field of attitude research continues to thrive.

Mental Control

The extent to which our cognitive processes are automatic continues to be a major focus of social cognition research (Schneider 1991). Outside of a level of consciousness, various tasks tend to be encoded without intention or effort. In this sense, the associated actions occur in a relatively automatic fashion. Bargh (1984; 1990) has done extended reviews of automatic processes and its dimensions. Research on proceduralized inference suggests that practice seems to be the crucial foundation for developing automatic responses (Fiske and Taylor 1991).

At a basic level, automaticity can be considered a form of behavior in which people attempt to gain control over their thoughts. Exploration about the varying kinds and degrees of mental control continues to spark research, and extends itself to studies on thought suppression and will-power in social and personality psychology (Schneider 1991).

Social cognition is a rich and broad perspective represented in various fields and disciplines, particularly within social and cognitive psychology. As Schneider (1991) points out, 'social cognition is alive and well and feeling strong.' Because of the blend of various issues and methodologies used throughout research in the field, many of the concepts and developments are easily applicable to understanding the cognitions and behavior of people in structured

social contexts such as organizations. We will return to the relevance of these theories when we consider their application to OB later in the chapter.

Behavioral Decision Theory

The standard of economic rationality has long been the cornerstone of the formal study of decision making. Individuals were assumed to act in accordance with their self-interest and make choices that were consistent with the predictions of maximizing this self-interest. The tenets of rational action, however, have not proved particularly useful in describing the actual choice or decision behavior of individuals, nor were they particularly useful in prescribing or predicting actual choice behavior. Real decision makers typically behaved in ways that deviated from the predictions of economic models, made decisions that were not Pareto efficient, and were inconsistent in their choices or made decisions based on normatively irrelevant factors (Bazerman 1994). From the perspective of economic rationality, these errors were assumed to be the result of ignorance, lack of correct incentives, or unrevealed preferences.

What was presumed to be a result of inattention, ignorance, or error by those subscribing to the notion of rational decision-making was viewed by another group of researchers as systematic variations that were, in their own right, deserving of attention. The systematic study of choice, especially in the behavioral sciences, had as its roots the publication, almost forty years ago, of two seminal pieces. First, Edwards (1954) introduced behavioral scientists to the work on decision behavior conducted by economists, statisticians, and philosophers. Second, Simon's (1957; March and Simon 1958) work on bounded rationality suggested that if economists wanted to understand real decision behavior, they had to focus on the perceptual, psychological, and cognitive factors that caused human beings to make decisions that deviated from the predictions of the 'rational man'.

The discrepancies between the formal prescriptions of economists and the descriptive observations of Simon's bounded rationality result, according to Simon, from our inability to evaluate decision alternatives simultaneously (rather than sequentially), from failing to choose the optimal alternative (preferring, instead, to select an alternative that is 'good enough' – to satisfice), and from using simplifying rules or heuristics to reduce the cognitive demand of decision making. Thus, Simon's (1957) concept of bounded rationality highlighted the differences between what normative models predict and what people actually do. As suggested by Bell et al. (1988), behavior decision theory's primary focus encompasses the normative, descriptive and prescriptive perspectives of decision making, with a somewhat greater emphasis on the latter two. That is, BDT research seems more concerned with the empirical validity of descriptive models and the pragmatic value of prescriptive models than with the development of normative models.

A central question in the area of behavioral decision research, then, is how decision makers actually go about making decisions, using as a comparison the benchmark of optimal (i.e. rational) performance. Juxtaposing the standard of rationality against actual behavior, several researchers in the decision arena began mapping the systematic deviations from rationality that they observed. Behavioral decision researchers focus on these systematic inconsistencies in the decision-making process that prevent humans from making fully rational decisions. Kahneman and Tversky (1979; Tversky and Kahneman 1974) have provided critical information about specific systematic biases that influence judgment. This work has elucidated our modern understanding of judgment.

When making decisions, people rely on a number of simplifying strategies, or rules of thumb, called heuristics. Although heuristics often prevent us from finding the optimal decision by eliminating the best choice, they do have some benefits: the expected time saved by using them could outweigh any potential loss resulting from a full search strategy. By providing people with a simple way of dealing with a complex world, heuristics produce correct or partially correct judgments more often than not. In addition, it may be inevitable that humans will adopt some way of simplifying decisions. The only drawback is that individuals frequently adopt these heuristics without being aware of them. The misapplication of heuristics to inappropriate situations, unfortunately, often leads people astray.

The three most important heuristics are the availability heuristic, the representativeness heuristic, and anchoring and adjustment. Decision makers assess the frequency, probability or likely causes of an event by the degree to which instances or occurrences of that event are readily 'available' in memory (Tversky and Kahneman 1973). To the extent that an event evokes emotions and is vivid, easily imagined, and specific, it will be more 'available' from memory than equally occurring events which are unemotional in nature, bland, difficult to imagine, or vague. For example, the subordinate in close proximity to the manager's office will receive a more critical performance evaluation at year-end,

since the manager is more aware of this subordinate's errors (Bazerman 1994).

People also assess the likelihood of an event's occurrence by the similarity of that occurrence to their stereotypes of similar occurrences. As Nisbett and Ross note, 'A botanist assigns a plant to one species rather than another by using this judgment strategy. The plant is categorized as belonging to the species that its principal features most clearly resemble' (1980: 7). In this case, the degree to which the unknown plant is representative of a known species of plant is the best information available to the botanist.

People also make assessments by 'anchoring' on an initial value and adjusting to yield a final decision. The initial value, or starting point, may be suggested from historical precedent, the way in which a problem is presented, or random information. For example, managers make salary decisions by adjusting from an employee's past year's salary. In ambiguous situations, a trivial factor can have a profound effect on our decision if it serves as a starting point from which we make adjustments (Dawes 1988). Frequently, people will realize the unreasonableness of the anchor (e.g. 'the other firm was *only* paying her $22,000 a year'), yet their adjustment will often remain irrationally close to this anchor.

Unfortunately, heuristics lead to predictable biases. A number of the predominant biases described in this literature are reviewed below (this summary is based on Bazerman [1994]):

Ease of recall Individuals judge events which are more easily recalled from memory, based upon vividness or recency, to be more numerous than events of equal frequency whose instances are less easily recalled (Tversky and Kahneman 1974).

Retrievability Individuals are biased in their assessments of the frequency of events based upon how their memory structures affect the search process (Tversky and Kahneman 1983).

Presumed associations Individuals tend to overestimate the probability of two events co-occurring based upon the number of similar associations which are easily recalled, whether from experience or social influence (Chapman and Chapman 1967).

Insensitivity to base rates Individuals tend to ignore base rates in assessing the likelihood of events when any other descriptive information is provided – even if the information is irrelevant (Kahneman and Tversky 1972).

Insensitivity to sample size Individuals frequently fail to appreciate the role of sample size in assessing the reliability of sample information (Tversky and Kahneman 1974).

Misconceptions of chance Individuals expect a

sequence of data generated by a random process to look 'random', even when the sequence is too short for those expectations to be statistically valid (Kahneman and Tversky 1972).

Regression to the mean Individuals often ignore the fact that extreme events tend to regress to the mean on subsequent trials (Kahneman and Tversky 1973).

The conjunction fallacy Individuals falsely judge that conjunctions, i.e., two events co-occurring, are more probable than a more global set of occurrences of which the conjunction is a subset (Tversky and Kahneman 1983).

Anchoring Individuals make estimates for values based upon an initial value (derived from past events, random assignment, or whatever information is available) and typically make insufficient adjustments from that anchor when establishing a final value (Slovic and Lichtenstein 1971).

Conjunctive and disjunctive events bias Individuals exhibit a bias toward overestimating the probability of conjunctive events and underestimating the probability of disjunctive events (Bar-Hillel 1973).

Overconfidence Individuals tend to be overconfident of the infallibility of their judgments when answering moderately to extremely difficult questions (Alpert and Raiffa 1969).

The confirmation trap Individuals tend to seek confirmatory information for what they think is true and neglect the search for disconfirmatory evidence (Wason 1960).

Hindsight After finding out whether or not an event occurred, individuals tend to overestimate the degree to which they would have predicted the correct outcome (Fischhoff 1975).

Framing Individuals are influenced by irrelevant information concerning how questions are framed (Kahneman and Tversky 1979).

During the 1980s and 1990s, these biases have had a profound influence on the field of OB. They have been used to help organizational members better understand their limitations, and have been extended to the organizational level of analysis to help account for the systematic errors of organizations.

However, it should be noted that BDT is not without its critics. Garb (1989) and Kagel and Levine (1986) suggest that experience may eliminate or at least attenuate decision bias as performance feedback can correct the inappropriate use of information and decision heuristics. These researchers see these well-replicated effects as the artificial creation of one-shot experiments. While much of the seminal work in the area of BDT was conducted in the relatively context-free environment of the laboratory, it is not so clear that real-world experience would provide

decision makers with superior information or useful feedback. As Tversky and Kahneman (1986) suggest, responsive learning requires accurate and immediate feedback which is rarely available because:

1 Outcomes are commonly delayed and not easily attributable to a particular action.
2 Variability in the environment degrades the reliability of the feedback.
3 There is often no information about what the outcome would have been if another decision had been made.
4 Most important decisions are unique and therefore provide little opportunity for learning: 'any claim that a particular error will be eliminated by experience must be supported by demonstrating that the conditions for effective learning are satisfied' (see Einhorn and Hogarth 1978: 274–5).

In fact, recent research has shown that most of the effects described above occur with real managers, with multiple trials available for learning, and with rewards for successful performance. In virtually all cases, these biases are robust to the tests that critics have provided (Bazerman 1994).

The research in social cognition and BDT is theoretically and empirically rich. The two fields have both unique and overlapping topic areas. Together, these two literatures will provide the basic structure for reviewing and evaluating the development of a cognitive perspective within OB.

COGNITIVE PERSPECTIVES IN MICRO ORGANIZATIONAL BEHAVIOR

Social Cognition in Micro Organizational Behavior

Social cognition can be characterized as the application of cognitive research methods to social contexts, with the organization being one of these contexts (Brewer and Kramer 1985). Micro organizational research, a central component of organizational research, has been criticized in the past for the relatively passive role it affords to individuals (Brief and Aldag 1981). In response to this charge, it has been argued that this research could be enhanced by addressing the interaction among employee behavior, cognitions and the environment (Brief and Aldag 1981). Indeed, Cummings (1982) goes as far as stating that 'the work on cognitive processing of stimuli comes as close as organizational behavior has come to date in understanding the processes which underlie so many of the functional relationships central to the discipline.'

Our literature search for social cognitive research in micro OB found this research most commonly connected to three central domains of research: leadership, motivation, and performance appraisals. Each of these topics will be addressed by investigating the impact that social cognition has had in these areas.

Leadership

Leadership is an old topic in OB, yet our review shows the area to be alive in producing new empirical research, with social cognition playing an active role. Social cognition has been applied to the study of leadership in a number of ways. An attributional perspective on leadership has been hailed as one of the most important cognitive applications (Cummings 1982). In addition, the simultaneous study of attitudes and leadership has been the focus of numerous studies. Finally, memory, self-concepts and stereotyping have also been linked, albeit to a lesser degree, to the study of leadership.

Attributional studies of leadership have incorporated leadership attributions, subordinate attributions, or some combination of these two. Heneman et al. (1989) found that internal, but not external, attributions were significantly related to critical performance incidents and leader–member exchange. An effort (versus ability) attribution has been shown to influence the variance in performance evaluations (Knowlton and Mitchell 1980).

In addition to influencing evaluations, attributions made by the leader also influence actions taken by that leader. Green and Mitchell (1979) proposed an attributional model of leader behavior that suggested that a leader's attributions influenced their subsequent actions. Evidence suggests that the belief about the cause of a subordinate's performance affects the choice of supervisory actions (Tjosvold 1985) and the extent to which organizational policy is implemented (Green and Liden 1980). This relationship has been shown to be impacted by the type of situation (James and White 1983), the gender compatibility between the leader and the subordinate (Dobbins et al. 1983), and the nature of the relationship (Heneman et al. 1989).

An attributional perspective has also been used to address attributions made by subordinates about their leader. Meindl et al. (1985) propose that leadership is a romantic concept that individuals utilize to make causal attributions about organizational outcomes. Meindl and Ehrlich (1987) provide support for this proposition in their findings that performance evaluations of leaders were better when the cause

was attributed to leadership rather than non-leadership factors.

There has been a recognition that both leader and member attributions may have important implications for organizational research. Integrating these two concepts, Martinko and Gardner (1987) proposed a model that combines the attributions of members and leaders. The simultaneous study of self-serving biases in both leader and member decision-making processes suggested that leaders attributed poor performance to internal subordinate factors while subordinates attributed poor performance to internal leader factors (Dobbins and Russell 1986).

Attitudinal research has also enhanced leadership research. Wexley and Pulakos (1983) found that the more aware a subordinate was of their manager's work-related attitudes, the more favorable they were in evaluating the leader. In addition, attitudes, such as intrinsic job satisfaction, have been proposed as substitutes for leadership behavior, thus negating the leader's ability to influence the subordinate (Kerr and Jermier 1978). Leadership styles and employee attitudes have also been used together as independent variables. For example, work group effectiveness has been found to be positively associated with the match between leadership style and the members' attitude toward the leader's style (White and Bassford 1978).

Memory and self-concept have also been integrated with leadership research. Specifically, the attitudes ascribed to leader behavior have been studied from a memory perspective. Phillips (1984) found that leader behavior that was consistent with the initial leadership labels of subordinates influenced the frequency with which subordinates assigned a particular behavior to a leader. Memory (selective encoding specifically) has also been proposed as a mediator of the performance/leader-ratings relationship (Larson et al. 1984). Finally, the idea of self-concept has been used to separate leaders from nonleaders (Peppers and Ryan 1986).

Motivation

Motivation has paralleled leadership as a topic rich in history in OB and yet disappointing to many. Again, we found many contemporary research efforts centering on this topic, with social cognition playing a critical role. Attributions of behavior in organizations have been shown to have important implications for explaining employee motivation (Knowlton and Mitchell 1980). Addressing this assertion, frameworks that integrate models of motivation and attributional processes have been proposed (for example, see Teas and McElroy 1986). One such framework examines the impact of attributions on affective, cognitive and behavior reactions to goals and feedback (Klein 1989). Within these models, there is some debate as to whether attributions are antecedent to cognitions and behavior or are in fact determined by them (Lord and Smith 1983).

The effect of attributions on motivation has also been empirically tested. Arnold (1985) found that the level of task performance was related to perceived competence and attributions, which in turn were related to intrinsic motivation. Attributions for failure have also been shown to influence the direction of motivation, in that salespeople worked harder if they attributed failure to lack of effort and worked smarter (changed the direction and focus of their work) if they attributed failure to the use of poor strategies (Sujan 1986). Supervisors and subordinates were found to have similar causal schemata; both attributed success to intrinsic motivation and ability while attributing failure primarily to low motivation (Huber et al. 1986). Performance trends also have attribution consequences, with descending or ascending performance attributed more to motivation than to consistently average performance (Karl and Wexley 1989).

In certain situations, memory has been proposed as an alternative to the role of attributions. Cellar and Barrett (1987) found that the use of a play script affected intrinsic motivation. As a result, they asserted that people may not make attributions in situations where automatic processes such as scripts serve as behavioral guides. Staw (1984) concurs with the notion that scripts are a valuable means for studying motivation.

Attitudes have also been linked up with motivation in OB research. Some of this research investigates causal relationships between these two constructs, such as the impact of motivation on attitudes and/or the impact of attitudes on motivation (Feldman and Weitz 1988). Bagozzi et al. (1992) investigated the attitude–motivation relationship, and posited that changing people's attitude toward the process of learning may improve their motivation to learn. Job satisfaction is one attitude that is often studied in conjunction with motivation, with respect to job enrichment (Katerberg et al. 1979), union strength (Hammer 1978), job characteristics (Hackman et al. 1978), and corporate savings (Mirvis and Lawler 1977). Attitudes and motivation have also been compared against each other, as seen in a study by Drake and Mitchell (1977) which found that differences in power between members and leaders affected attitudes rather than motivation.

Self-concept research has been proposed as an important addition to the study of motivation. Sullivan (1989) states that theories about the self as a source of motivation may have implications for employee motivation. Shamir (1991) also agrees that motivation theories could be enhanced by incorporating a theory of self-concept. Implications of this inclusion are that job motivation could be enhanced if (1) job-related identities are salient in an employee's self-concept, (2) the job offers opportunities for the enhancement of self-esteem and self-worth, (3) actions required on the job are consistent with the employee's self-concept, and (4) career opportunities are congruent with a person's possible selves.

Performance Appraisals

The topic of performance appraisal has a long history of research in OB and in industrial/organizational psychology. Through the 1970s, this research largely ignored the role of the appraiser, focusing instead on instrument development. In the 1980s, the focus changed, and the cognitions of the appraiser came to dominate performance appraisal research (Feldman 1981). A summary of this type of research is provided by Ilgen et al. (1993). Their review is focused around a three-stage process model emphasizing the gathering, storing and retrieving of performance information.

Research has investigated the underlying cognitive structures involved in the performance appraisal process. For example, Jolly et al. (1988) proposed and tested a model designed to uncover a summary cognitive map of performance appraisals. Results of this type of research have revealed consistent cognitive structures with regard to appraisals. Gioia et al. (1989) discovered that there were shared cognitive structures, or scripts, used in appraisal interviews. Similarly, Borman (1987) found that there was a core set of categories or schemata used in the formation of personal work constructs, although different people may emphasize different combinations of this core set.

A significant portion of the study of attributions in performance appraisals has examined the differences in causal attributions of success and failure between subordinates and superiors. Disagreement within dyads between the subordinate and superior may lead to disagreements over performance evaluations (Huber et al. 1986). In recognition of this, Bannister and Balkin's (1990) performance evaluation and compensation model identifies causal attributions made by the superior and recipient as a central component of these processes. One common attribution studied involves the judgment of a cause as either internal (i.e. personality, lack of motivation) or external (i.e. job environment) to the actor. These studies have emphasized that actors (typically the subordinates) and observers (the superiors) make different attributions with regard to the internal/external distinction (Huber et al. 1986; Bannister and Balkin 1990). Bernardin (1989) found that actors attributed performance failures to external factors beyond their control while observers attributed failures to internal factors. Similarly, Harrison et al. (1988) found that superiors' initial attributions were internal relative to the subordinate and that they were more inclined to seek out information on internal factors. The feedback provided to the subordinate has been shown to be distorted by these types of attributions. Knowlton and Ilgen (1980) found that the nature of feedback varied as a function of the performance attributions; more positive feedback was provided to low performers when ability was diagnosed as the cause.

Factors influencing the relationship between attributions and performance appraisal have also been studied. James and White (1983) found that managers' attributions of the cause of performance varied according to the situation. Knowledge of the outcome of the behavior has also been shown to influence the attribution process, with knowledge of a negative outcome resulting in more internal attributions than behaviors not associated with an outcome (Mitchell and Kalb 1981). Similarly, Gioia and Sims (1986) found that managers showed different patterns of attribution toward subordinates in a failure condition as opposed to a success condition. Managers in the failure condition tended to seek reasons for the failure by asking attribution-seeking questions.

Attributions have also been studied from a subordinate perspective. Larson (1989) posits that employee feedback-seeking behavior can influence the nature of feedback given, particularly when the feedback is sought to mitigate attributions of personal responsibility and blame. Rose (1978) found that sex moderated effort attributions made by subordinates, with greater effort attributed to managers whose subordinates were of the opposite sex than to those of the same sex.

Obstacles to accurate performance are attributed in part to limitations in human processing capacity (Bernardin and Cardy 1982). Consequently, the study of memory has been incorporated into performance appraisal research. DeNisi et al. (1984) proposed a model that described the performance appraisal process as a set of social cognitive operations that include the acquisition of information, the organization and storage of that information in memory, the retrieval of the information from memory and the integration of the information to formation of a judgment. Performance appraisal researchers who incorporate memory in their studies often examine the organization of performance information in memory. DeNisi et al. (1989) found that raters stored unorganized performance information in memory patterns consistent with organizational diaries. Support has also been found for the systematic distortion hypothesis which asserts that raters' semantic conceptual similarity schemata serve to guide and constrain the rating judgment process (Kozlowski and Kirsch 1987). In their examination of appraisal salience on information processing, Williams et al. (1990) discovered that high appraisal salience was related to online information processing while low appraisal salience was related to memory-based processing.

Memory structures have also been used as an independent variable in examining performance rating accuracy. Raters are seen to be more accurate if they have high memory capacity (Heneman et al. 1987) and high selectivity (Cardy and Kehoe 1984). Williams et al. (1990) found that certain organizational strategies used during the encoding process were able to improve rating accuracy. Performance observation with delays between observations has been found to affect the accuracy of behavioral ratings and recognition memory (Murphy et al. 1989). Memory biases, such as recall of behavior that is consistent with impression of the ratee (Murphy et al. 1986), the halo effect, the leniency/stringency effect, and racial, sexual, ethnic and personalistic influences, have also been found to affect assignment and recall (Feldman 1981).

Performance appraisal research has also joined forces with attitudinal research. The effect of performance appraisals and feedback on attitudes has been one of the results of this union, including studies on the effects on organizational commitment (Pearce and Porter 1986), job satisfaction (Daley 1985), the development of professional attitudes (Yeager et al. 1985) and perceptions of unfairness (Dailey and Kirk 1992). Similarities between rater and ratee job attitudes have been found to increase rating accuracy (Zalesny and Highhouse 1992). Attitudes toward the appraisal system have also been studied. Worker involvement in the appraisal system has been shown to positively impact perceptions of the appraisal system (Cummings 1973; Daley 1988) as well as the manner in which feedback is received (Harris 1988).

Research on stereotyping and person perception has also enhanced performance appraisal research. Evaluations have been shown to be influenced by age and sex stereotpying (Schwab and Heneman 1978; Pazy 1986; Ferris et al. 1985) while person perception and performance appraisals were found to be significantly affected by nonverbal cues (De Meuse 1987).

Behavioral Decision Theory in Micro Organizational Behavior

Behavioral decision theory has developed into a recognized topic of the field of organizational behavior. This can be seen in the existence of OB textbook chapters on the topic (Northcraft and Neale 1994), a mainstream OB journal that focuses much attention on the topic (*Organizational Behavior and Human Decision Processes*), and faculty courses in organizational behavior departments devoted to BDT at many leading management schools (e.g. MIT, Cornell, Duke, Northwestern, and Chicago). From a theoretical and empirical standpoint, BDT has been used as a basic component in the development of the literatures on negotiation, group decision making, and human resource management. A review of each of these application areas is provided below.

Negotiation

The last decade has seen a proliferation of interest in the topic of negotiation by OB researchers. Many scholars outside the BDT area have argued that the central negotiation perspective by OB researchers has been Neale and Bazerman's (1991) BDT perspective which focuses on the decisions made by negotiators (Greenhalgh 1993).

The development of this descriptive literature, which accounts for the limitations in negotiator decision making, is closely connected to the leading prescriptive work on negotiation (Raiffa 1982). Raiffa argues for an asymmetrically prescriptive/descriptive approach. This approach suggests that the decision analyst should asymmetrically (to only one of the actors) provide prescriptions to the negotiator based on the best possible description of the likely behavior of the opponent. In contrast to mainstream economic and game theoretic approaches, Raiffa explicitly acknowledges that the actual behavior of the opponent may fall far short of rationality.

Raiffa's work was a key turning point in negotiation research for a number of reasons. First, in the context of developing a prescriptive model, he explicitly realizes the importance of forming accurate descriptions of the opponent rather than assuming them to be fully rational. Second, his realization that negotiators need

advice implicitly acknowledges that negotiators do not intuitively follow purely rational strategies. Most importantly, he initiated the ground for dialogue between prescriptive and descriptive researchers. His work utilizes descriptive models which allow the focal negotiator to anticipate the likely behavior of the opponent. In addition, we argue that a central focus of the decision analyst should be to realize that the focal negotiator may have decision biases that limit his/her ability to follow such advice.

Our research has addressed some of the questions that Raiffa left behind. For example, if the negotiator and his or her opponents do not act rationally, what systematic departures from rationality can be predicted? Initial research has addressed some of the questions and has provided a set of empirical studies that integrate the value of existing descriptive and prescriptive research in creating a decision perspective of negotiation.

Building on BDT, a number of deviations from rationality that can be expected in negotiations have been identified. Specifically, research on two-party negotiations suggests that negotiators tend to: (1) be inappropriately affected by the frame in which risks are viewed (Huber et al. 1987a; Neale and Bazerman 1985; Bazerman et al. 1985), (2) anchor their judgments in negotiation based on rationally irrelevant information (Tversky and Kahneman 1974; Huber and Neale 1986; Northcraft and Neale 1987), (3) overweight readily available information (Neale 1984), (4) be overconfident (Neale and Bazerman 1985; Bazerman and Neale 1982), (5) nonrationally assume that negotiation tasks are fixed-sum, and thus miss opportunities for mutually beneficial trade-offs (Bazerman et al. 1985), (6) nonrationally escalate commitment to a previously selected course of action (Northcraft and Neale 1986; Bazerman and Neale 1983), (7) ignore the valuable information that is available by considering the cognitions of others (Bazerman and Carroll 1987), (8) devalue any concession that is made by the other side, i.e. reactive devaluation (Stillinger et al. in press), (9) erroneously assume that opponents' interests are completely opposed to their own, when in fact negotiators' interests are perfectly compatible with those of the other party (Thompson and Hastie 1990), and (10) egocentrically interpret what would be fair in a negotiated agreement (Thompson and Loewenstein 1992; Loewenstein et al. 1993).

These results have had a strong influence on research and teaching in negotiation; BDT-influenced negotiation research is now commonly seen in organizational behavior journals and negotiation has been the fastest new topic in organizational behavior courses during the 1980s and 1990s. Many of these courses try to provide students with useful prescriptions based on descriptive models rooted in BDT.

Group Decision Making

As characterized in the description of BDT, individuals often use heuristics to make decisions. Often, these heuristics are incorrectly used, resulting in biased decision making. Several researchers have extended the concept of biases in individual decision making to a group context. Specifically, group decision making research has influenced BDT research in two ways: (1) the application of 'individual' biases to a group context, and (2) the identification of group-specific heuristics and biases.

One of the individual biases that has been applied to group research is the framing bias. In an attempt to explain Stoner's (1961) finding that groups are more risk-seeking, Bazerman (1984) offered framing as an alternative interpretation which focused on group discussion as a mechanism for mitigating any one individual's frame. Following this line of reasoning, Bazerman predicted that a positive frame would mitigate risk-averse behavior displayed by individuals, thus creating an apparent risk-seeking tendency on the part of groups. Likewise, a negative frame in a group context would appear to create risk-averse behavior for groups when they were compared to individuals. Neale et al. (1986) find support for this prediction.

The tendency to adhere to the representativeness heuristic has also been studied in groups. Argote et al. (1986) found that this heuristic is used by both individuals and groups, with groups exhibiting an even greater biasing effect than individuals. This result was later clarified in a paper by Argote et al. (1990), who tested subjects' ability to judge the probabilities that an individual belonged to a certain category. They found that groups tend to judge primarily by representativeness when individuating information is informative, but were less affected by this heuristic when descriptions were not representative of categories. Overconfidence is also characteristic of both groups and individuals. Specifically, Sniezek and Henry (1989) found that groups, while perhaps more accurate in their judgments regarding uncertain ends, fell prey to the overconfidence bias just as often as individuals. Egocentrism appears to occur at both the individual and the group level, with group-serving biases having an even greater effect than self-serving biases (Taylor and Doria 1981).

Bazerman et al. (1984) discovered that groups exhibited a similar tendency to nonrationally escalate to a course of action as individuals. Whyte (1991), however, found that when responsibility was varied, groups in a group-responsibility condition actually exhibited a decrease in the escalation of commitment as compared to individuals in a responsibility condition. The explanation for this effect centers around the ability of members of a group to diffuse responsibility for a decision which is not a possibility in individual decision making.

The formation, maintenance and interaction of coalitions has also been informed by BDT research. Mannix and White (1992) found that the anchoring and adjustment heuristic characterized the distribution of resources within a coalition. In particular, in the absence of a distribution rule, past performance information served as an anchor for distributive outcomes. Bazerman (1994) suggests that coalitions may also be influenced by other biases. For example, Bazerman asserts that the reemergence of successful coalitions may be because of a reliance on the availability heuristic. In addition, the escalation of commitment bias and the positive framing effect imply that individuals may stay in a coalition longer than they should. Furthermore, individuals may be overconfident in their ability to form a new coalition.

Janis's (1972) work on groupthink suggests that groups may also exhibit biases unique to a group context. The eight symptoms of groupthink (illusion of invulnerability, collective rationalization, a belief in the group's inherent morality, stereotypes of outgroups, direct pressure on dissenters, self-censorship, illusion of unanimity and the use of self-appointed mind guards) are believed to lead to deficiencies in the decision-making process of groups, including an incomplete survey of alternatives and objectives, a failure to examine the risks of choices and reappraise initially rejected alternatives, poor information search, biased processing of information, and a failure to work out contingency plans (Janis and Mann 1977). Thus, groupthink can be thought of as a heuristic within highly cohesive groups that interferes with rational decision making (Bazerman 1994).

Human Resource Management

Another important area to which BDT has contributed is human resource management (HRM). Decision-making research is considered to be a fruitful source of knowledge for HRM (Northcraft et al. 1988). Part of the reasoning behind this claim focuses on the inadequacy of human decision makers who face two impediments: cognitive limitations and biases from social influence (Northcraft et al. 1988). The review of BDT's influence in human resources thus involves an understanding of how biases can influence decisions made in this domain.

One bias that is particularly relevant in personnel decisions is the anchoring and adjustment bias (Slovic and Lichtenstein 1971). This bias reflects the tendency to insufficiently adjust away from a chosen reference point. The anchoring and adjustment bias is particularly prevalent in performance appraisals, which can be influenced by a halo effect (favorable performance in one area leads to favorable ratings in all job performance categories) and a pitchfork effect (behavior related to a trait that the rater doesn't like leads to negative performance rating) (Kelley 1950; Lowe 1986). Past performance can also be an anchor that influences judgments about current performance (Huber et al. 1987b). Furthermore, the order of the performance appraisal format can serve as an anchor, such that information presented early in the job description has a disproportionate influence on the entire evaluation (McArthur 1983).

In addition to the influence of anchors on raters, it has also been shown that ratees are subject to the anchoring and adjustment bias. People believe initial impressions of their performance and ignore or discount future evaluations (Ross et al. 1975). Similarly, Cervone and Peake (1986) discovered that self-efficacy, subsequent performance and persistence in solving novel problems were influenced by a random anchor of a performance rating. Salespeople's call selection decisions were found to be influenced by their position in relation to established quotas (Ross 1991). Locke et al. (1983) found that subjects adjusted goals in the direction shown by performance, suggesting that assigned goals may serve as an anchor by influencing perceptions of what is possible (Northcraft et al. 1988).

Anchoring also influences applicant selection and compensation. Huber et al. (1990) presented evidence that the number of openings in a firm anchored subjects' judgments of the number of suitable candidates. Similarly, the salary level of one's supervisor can also serve as an anchor in decisions regarding employee compensation (Goodman 1974).

The representative heuristic has also had an impact in HRM research. This heuristic involves the process through which people assess the likelihood of an event's occurrence by the similarity of that occurrence to their stereotypes of similar occurrences (Bazerman 1994). Common in selection and evaluation decisions, this heuristic can lead an organization to select their 'type' of employee (Dipboye and Macan 1987), resulting in a homogeneous workforce. Indeed, job classifications have been shown to influence stereotypes (Jackson et al. 1982). Huber (1986) provides further evidence that

people are in fact insensitive to base rates in their judgments of qualified applicants.

One negative implication of the representativeness heuristic is discrimination (Bazerman 1994). Use of this heuristic can lead to inappropriate hiring decisions based on sex and attractiveness of the candidate, with male and attractive applicants preferred (Cann et al. 1981). Job evaluations can also be biased, with more points given to job criteria drawn from male job evaluation plans than those drawn from female job evaluation plans (Cascio and O'Reilly 1982). Conversely, females are found to be awarded more in grievance settlements than men (Dalton and Todor 1985). The representativeness heuristic may also result in biases in instances where physical disabilities (Rose and Brief 1979; Czajka and DeNisi 1988), age (Haefner 1977), and race (Wendelken and Inn 1981) are considered in HRM decisions.

An Evaluation of Cognition Perspectives in Micro Organizational Behavior

We concur with Ilgen and Klein's (1988) conclusion about the important and growing role of cognitive perspectives in OB. In general, we consider our review of the social cognition area to be extremely consistent with the perspectives of Ilgen and Klein. Both regard social cognitive research as critical to the continued development of traditional micro OB topics (e.g. leadership, motivation, and performance appraisal). Our review of BDT research in the micro OB literature suggests that in addition to helping with the advancement of traditional OB areas (e.g. group decision making and human resource management), BDT has also been instrumental in creating new topics in the field of OB, namely, decision making and negotiation. Both are now common topics of leading OB journals, textbooks, and courses. This was not true two decades ago.

We believe that the success of BDT in creating new topics is tied to the values and assumptions that we offered at the beginning of this chapter. We argued that research should understand the world as it is, not as we would like it to be. Both the social cognition and BDT literatures achieve this objective by avoiding the limitations of making obviously false assumptions about humans. We also argued that descriptive research is strengthened by comparison to a normative benchmark. We believe that this is an important lever of the BDT approach which highlights areas in which we can see limitations in behavior in organizations. We further argued that descriptive research can inform prescriptive frameworks. We believe that this aspect of BDT has been critical to its level of influence in the negotiation area. People want to know how to negotiate better, and BDT provides useful insights. Finally, we argued that decisions are a core activity in organizations. This obvious yet ignored perspective is critical to the emergence of decision making as a topic of inquiry by OB scholars.

Collectively, we see both social cognition and BDT playing a crucial role in contemporary micro OB. We believe that BDT has been particularly important in helping to identify the topics that define OB as we head into the next decade.

COGNITIVE PERSPECTIVES IN MACRO ORGANIZATIONAL RESEARCH

The last decade has also witnessed the influence of cognitive perspectives on macro research. Efforts to apply psychological theories and cognitive perspectives to organization-level behavior began with the work of Katz and Kahn (1966; 1978), Weick (1969; 1979a; 1979b), Pondy and Mitroff (1979) and Daft and Weick (1984). This perspective describes organizations as 'enacting bodies' or 'interpretation systems', emphasizing the importance of language and symbols in the social construction of reality in organizations (Pfeffer 1981) and drawing parallels between schema concepts and strategy (Weick 1979a; Schwenk 1986; 1988). This work established the groundwork for general cognitive concepts to be adapted to the descriptions of organizations and their actions and to the diagnosis of organizational properties and problems.

Subsequent research has examined how the organizational context can be influenced by individual behaviors. Autonomous individuals are seen as posing as organizations (Staw and Sutton 1992), taking actions that reflect their own preferences, and yet disguising them as actions reflecting organizational policies and/or procedures (Staw 1991). As such, psychological and social cognitive theories are useful for explaining the behavior of organizations. As of yet, however, such concepts have not been explicitly studied (Mowday and Sutton 1993).

Related research focusing on the role of leaders suggests that, while leaders of organizations are not completely powerful in scope, they have at least a modest influence on organizations, particularly on small and young firms (Bass 1990; Pfeffer and Davis-Blake 1986; Thomas 1988). There are numerous ways that leaders and other key individuals can influence organizations, including shaping thoughts, feel-

ings, perceptions, and actions of people inside and outside the organization and making decisions that affect the organization (Mowday and Sutton 1993). In addition to shaping the set of members who make up the organization, leaders also create conditions that influence members' emotion, behaviors, and cognitions (Staw and Sutton 1992).

Closely related to our cognitive focus is the stream of literature that focuses on the leader's role of providing explanations, legitimization, and rationales for organizational activities (symbolic management as proposed by Pfeffer 1981). Several studies have related concepts of attribution theories to leadership, including an examination of explanations provided by CEOs in regard to corporate performance (Staw et al. 1983; Salancik and Meindl 1984; Bettman and Weitz 1983). They suggest that CEOs use self-serving attributions to explain their own behavior by attributing good performance to internal organizational actions and factors and unsuccessful performance to events external to the organization. Staw et al. (1983) found that these self-serving attributions affected shareholders' perceptions, resulting in improved stock prices. Similarly, Salancik and Meindl (1984) found that management, particularly in unstable firms, strategically manipulated causal attributions to manage impressions of their control.

Another way in which powerful people influence organizations is through the decisions that they make. Strategy formulation is often treated as a process in which decisions are incremental, interdependent, and shaped by a variety of contextual and psychological influences (see Bateman and Zeithaml 1989). The study of strategists' cognition provides information about the workings of these informed minds and, therefore, the factors which contribute to the successes and failures of organizations (Schwenk 1988). This stream of research tends to focus more on cognitive structures and processes which may be shared by multiple strategists than on individuals and their differences in cognition. It calls for more detailed descriptions of the ways that individual-level cognitions contribute to organization-level strategies.

Drawing from the literature on social cognitive influences, there has been a stream of articles relating organizational decision making to cognitive structures and processes. This research addresses such topics as a decision maker's frame of reference (e.g. Mason and Mitroff 1981; Shrivastava and Mitroff 1983; 1984), strategic assumptions (e.g. Schwenk 1988), knowledge structures (Prahalad and Bettis 1986; Lyles and Schwenk 1992), categorization (Dutton and Jackson 1987), and the concepts of scripts, cognitive maps, schemata, organizational learning, and interpretative systems (see Lyles and Schwenk 1992). Specific examples of the application of social cognitive concepts include Dutton and Jackson's (1987) model which integrates interpretative views of organizational decision making with categorization theory. It attempts to explain why organizations in the same industry respond differently to the same environmental trends and events. Prahalad and Bettis (1986) and Lyles and Schwenk (1992) suggest that the shared perspectives of organization members create knowledge structures for environmental events and organization capabilities. These structures can store a shared dominant general management logic which influences strategic actions and organization learning within the firm. Analysis of executives' strategic schemata is thought to help explain strategic choices in response to environmental and industry forces (Schwenk 1988).

Other research concentrates on the cognitive shortcomings that can affect the decisions made by top managers, which in turn affect the organization. This research stems directly from BDT literature and the notion that decision heuristics – including representativeness, framing, availability, anchoring, the hindsight bias, and overconfidence – influence managerial behavior (Bazerman 1994). As Schwenk (1988) supports, decisional biases found in many laboratory contexts can also affect strategic decision making. He lists applicable biases, such as those previously mentioned, along with selective perception bias, illusory correlation, conservatism, the law of small numbers, regression bias, illusion of control, logical reconstruction and wishful thinking. It is argued that such heuristics allow organizational experts to make sense of strategic issues quickly and respond in an efficient and effective manner (Day and Lord 1992).

Zajac and Bazerman (1991) integrated theory concerning cognitive shortcomings with insights from the strategy literature to develop hypotheses about why and how decision makers in competitive situations make nonrational judgments. They provided explanations for the persistence of poor strategic decisions that result in industry overcapacity, new business failures, and acquisition premiums. Their perspective illustrates how leaders' and key decision makers' cognitive limitations can lead to decisions or actions that affect organizational attributes such as size, mission, and performance. Duhaime and Schwenk (1985) support this notion with their theory that business decision makers may use cognitive simplifying processes in defining ill-structured problems such

as acquisition and divestment decisions. Other examples include Staw et al.'s (1981) work on the threat-rigidity model which suggests that distress can hinder the cognitive processes of leaders and cause them to make poor decisions.

Next steps in strategic decision-making agendas include more integration of psychological and cognitive research through the exploration of which heuristics are most relevant to strategic decision makers, how they work, why they work, and when they are most appropriate (Eisenhardt and Zbaracki 1992). In addition, researchers are attempting to describe the ways that individual biases interact to affect strategic decisions (Schwenk 1986).

In addition to the influence of individual members, there also exists the argument that organizations are influenced by the aggregation of individual attributes, thoughts, feelings, and behaviors (Mowday and Sutton 1993; Staw and Sutton 1992). Using a cognitive perspective to understand more about the sum of individual beliefs is seen as a way to provide better explanations for organizational-level actions. Work on organizational learning and memory, for example, draws parallels between individual processes and organizational processes. As Staw and Sutton (1992) note, the classic work of March and Simon (1958) illustrates this analogy through its treatment of organizational information processing as synonymous with individual information processing. Another example is present in Walsh and Ungson's (1991) review and integration of the literature on organizational memory. They suggest that an organization's memory is an individual-level phenomenon since it is determined partly by the aggregation of individuals' remembered information and records.

In summary, the topic of cognition has reached the agendas of several macro organization behavior researchers, from the field of strategic management to more interdisciplinary areas, focusing on the states and traits of individuals as explanations of collective behavior. The extension of applicable findings within the areas of BDT and social cognition provides more than alternative explanations; in many contexts, it is possible that it brings a more realistic interpretation of organizational action than traditional sociological approaches. Cognitive-based theories can add theoretical substance to existing macro models by supplying missing mechanisms to explain the behavior of organizations (Staw and Sutton 1992). More importantly, the integration of nontraditional disciplines in the development of theoretical ideas in macro organizational behavior also helps to make the existing lines between micro and macro organization behavior a little less obvious. This represents a realm for future research as well as a renewal of ideas within the field of organization behavior.

THE FUTURE OF COGNITION IN ORGANIZATIONS

As is evident in our review, social cognition and BDT have had a significant influence on micro and macro organizational research. We do not view this as a fad but rather strongly believe that these two theoretical frameworks will continue to impact the field of OB. We see this influence as coming from several directions, including additional theoretical and empirical research in topic areas previously mentioned in this chapter, in the identification of additional topics that are important to the field, and in the integration of concepts from social cognition and BDT.

As previously discussed, memory and self-concept have been identified as important factors in the topics of leadership, motivation, and performance appraisal. This research is still in the recognition phase, with many propositions offered but little empirical evidence presented. Further theoretical clarification and additional empirical research will enhance our understanding of these areas and in turn present useful recommendations to organizations. For example, additional research on the role of memory in the evaluation of leaders and in performance appraisals of employees promises to identify sources of errors in these processes which in turn may indicate potential areas for improvement. Similarly, an understanding of self-concept differences in leaders versus nonleaders and motivated employees versus unmotivated employees will result in the development of propositions and suggestions aimed at self-concept improvement, which will in turn enhance leadership and productivity in organizations.

One of the primary contributions of BDT research has been the identification of biases that lead to a decrement in decision performance. The identification of new biases is expected to continue, albeit at a diminishing rate. Increased attention is expected to be directed at how this information can be used to increase decision-making ability. Heuristics are helpful shortcuts only when they are appropriately applied; identification of the factors that result in misapplication will enhance the usefulness of this research. Furthermore, inquiry into the process of 'unbiasing' decision-makers promises to increase individual and organizational performance. The increased popularity of the use of groups in organizations suggests that the

identification of unique group biases will also be a focus of BDT research in the future.

A consideration of the integration of BDT and social cognition theories raises several questions, the answers to which could further augment micro organizational research. For example, a relatively untouched but nonetheless important question centers around the influence of attitudes on the prevalence of biases. Are some attitudes influential in promoting the inappropriate use of heuristics? What role do anchoring and adjustment play in the attribution process? What is the connection between memory and the representativeness heuristic?

From a macro standpoint, both BDT and social cognition will be influential in the development of new research paradigms. Theories from memory and attribution research may open up new avenues for research in the organizational learning area. Similarly, the identification of biases (i.e. anchoring and adjustment) instrumental in retarding organizational change is certain to expand our knowledge of this organizational phenomenon.

In conclusion, a new definition of OB that encompasses both social cognition and BDT addresses many of the criticisms aimed at this field. As evident in both past research and potential future research, these perspectives give new light to old issues and open up new doors to additional topics. Incorporating the theories of social cognition and BDT into the OB domain will ensure that OB remains a field that is alive and here to stay.

REFERENCES

Alpert, M. and Raiffa, H. (1969) 'A progress report on the training of probability assessors'. Unpublished manuscript, Harvard University.

Argote, L., Devadas, R. and Melone, N. (1990) 'The base-rate fallacy: contrasting processes and outcomes of group and individual judgment', *Organizational Behavior and Human Decision Processes*, 46: 296–310.

Argote, L., Seabright, M.A. and Dyer, L. (1986) 'Individual versus group: use of base-rate and individuating information', *Organizational Behavior and Human Decision Processes*, 38: 65–75.

Arnold, H.J. (1985) 'Task performance, perceived competence, and attributed causes of performance as determinants of intrinsic motivation', *Academy of Management Journal*, 28: 876–88.

Asch, S.E. (1946) 'Forming impressions of personality', *Journal of Abnormal and Social Psychology*, 41: 1230–40.

Bagozzi, R.P., Davis, F.D. and Warshaw, P.R. (1992)

'Development and test of a theory of technological learning and usage', *Human Relations*, 45: 659–86.

Bannister, B.D. and Balkin, D.B. (1990) 'Performance evaluation and compensation feedback messages: an integrated model', *Journal of Occupational Psychology*, 63: 97–111.

Bargh, J.A. (1984) 'Automatic and conscious processing of social information', in R.S. Wyer Jr and T.K. Srull (eds), *Handbook of Social Cognition*, vol. 3. Hillsdale, NJ: Erlbaum.

Bargh, J.A. (1990) 'Auto-motives: preconscious determinants of social interaction', in E.T. Higgins and R.M. Sorrentino (eds), *Handbook of Motivation and Cognition: Foundations of Social Behavior*, vol. 2. New York: Guilford Press.

Bar-Hillel, M. (1973) 'On the subjective probability of compound events', *Organizational Behavior and Human Performance*, 9: 396–406.

Bass, B.M. (1990) *Bass and Stogdill's Handbook of Leadership*. New York: Free Press.

Bateman, T.S. and Zeithaml, C.P. (1989) 'The psychological context of strategic decisions: a test of relevance to practitioners', *Strategic Management Journal*, 10: 587–92.

Bazerman, M.H. (1984) 'The relevance of Kahneman and Tversky's concept of framing to organization behavior', *Journal of Management*, 10: 333–43.

Bazerman, M.H. (1993) 'Fairness, social comparison, and irrationality', in J.K. Murnighan (ed.), *Social Psychology in Organizations: Advances in Theory and Research*. Prentice-Hall.

Bazerman, M.H. (1994) *Judgment in Managerial Decision Making*. New York: Wiley.

Bazerman, M.H. and Carroll, J.S. (1987) 'Negotiator cognition', *Research in Organizational Behavior*, 9: 247–88.

Bazerman, M.H. and Neale, M.A. (1982) 'Improving negotiation effectiveness under final offer arbitration: the role of selection and training', *Journal of Applied Psychology*, 67: 543–8.

Bazerman, M.H. and Neale, M.A. (1983) 'Heuristics in negotiation: limitations to dispute resolution effectiveness', in M.H. Bazerman and R.J. Lewicki (eds), *Negotiating in Organizations*. Beverly Hills: Sage.

Bazerman, M.H., Giuliano, T. and Appelman, A. (1984) 'Escalation in individual and group decision making', *Organizational Behavior and Human Performance*, 33: 141–52.

Bazerman, M.H., Magliozzi, T. and Neale, M.A. (1985) 'The acquisition of an integrative response in a competitive market', *Organizational Behavior and Human Performance*, 34: 294–313.

Bell, D.E., Raiffa, H. and Tversky, A. (1988) *Decision Making: Descriptive, Normative, and Prescriptive Interactions*. Cambridge: Cambridge University Press.

Bernardin, H.J. (1989) 'Increasing the accuracy of performance measurement: a proposed solution to erroneous attributions', *Human Resource Planning*, 12: 239–50.

Bernardin, H.J. and Cardy, R.L. (1982) 'Appraisal accuracy: the ability and motivation to remember the past', *Public Personnel Management*, 11: 352–7.

Bettman, J.R. and Weitz, B.A. (1983) 'Attributions in the board room: causal reasoning in corporate annual reports', *Administrative Science Quarterly*, 28: 165–83.

Borman, W.C. (1987) 'Personal constructs, performance schemata, and "folk theories" of subordinate effectiveness: explorations in an Army officer sample', *Organizational Behavior and Human Decision Processes*, 40: 307–22.

Brewer, M.B. and Kramer, R.D. (1985) 'The psychology of intergroup attitudes and behavior', *Annual Review of Psychology*, 36: 219–43.

Brief, A.P. and Aldag, R.J. (1981) 'The "self" in work organizations: a conceptual review', *Academy of Management Review*, 6: 75–88.

Cann, A., Siegfried, W.D. and Pearce, L. (1981) 'Forced attention to specific applicant qualifications: impact on physical attractiveness and sex of applicant biases', *Personnel Psychology*, 34: 65–75.

Cantor, N., Markus, H., Niedenthal, P. and Nurius, P. (1986) 'On motivation and the self-concept', in R.M. Sorrentino and E.T. Higgins (eds), *Handbook of Motivation and Cognition: Foundations of Social Behavior*. New York: Guilford Press.

Cardy, R.L. and Kehoe, J.F. (1984) 'Rater selective attention ability and appraisal effectiveness: the effect of a cognitive style on the accuracy of differentiation among ratees', *Journal of Applied Psychology*, 69: 589–94.

Cascio, W.F. and O'Reilly, C.A. (1982) 'Comparable worth and job evaluation: the biasing effect of subfactors and contextual cues'. Paper presented at the 89th Annual Meeting of the American Psychological Association.

Cellar, D.F. and Barrett, G.V. (1987) 'Scripts processing and intrinsic motivation: the cognitive sets underlying cognitive labels', *Organizational Behavior and Human Decision Processes*, 40: 115–35.

Cervone, B. and Peake, P.K. (1986) 'Anchoring, efficacy, and action: the influence of judgmental heuristics on self-efficacy judgments and behaviors', *Journal of Personality and Social Psychology*, 50: 492–501.

Chapman, L.J. and Chapman, J.P. (1967) 'Genesis of popular but erroneous diagnostic observations', *Journal of Abnormal Psychology*, 72: 193–204.

Cummings, L.L. (1973) 'A field experimental study of the effect of two performance appraisal systems', *Personnel Psychology*, 26: 489–502.

Cummings, L.L. (1982) 'Organizational behavior', *Annual Review of Psychology*, 33: 541–79.

Czajka, J.M. and DeNisi, A.S. (1988) 'Effects of emotional disability and clear performance standards on performance ratings', *Academy of Management Journal*, 31: 394–404.

Daft, R.L. and Weick, K.E. (1984) 'Toward a model

of organizations as interpretation systems', *Academy of Management Review*, 9: 284–95.

Dailey, R.C. and Kirk, D.J. (1992) 'Distributive and procedural justice as antecedents of job dissatisfaction and intent to turnover', *Human Relations*, 45: 305–17.

Daley, D. (1985) 'An examination of the MBO/ performance standards approach to employee evaluation: attitudes toward performance appraisal in Iowa', *Review of Public Personnel Administration*, 6: 11–28.

Daley, D. (1988) 'Profile of the uninvolved worker: an examination of employee attitudes toward management practices', *International Journal of Public Administration*, 11: 65–90.

Dalton, D.R. and Todor, W.D. (1985) 'Gender and workplace justice: a field assessment', *Personnel Psychology*, 38: 133–51.

Dawes, R.M. (1988) *Rational Choice in an Uncertain World*. New York: Harcourt Brace Jovanovich.

Day, D.V. and Lord, R.G. (1992) 'Expertise and problem categorization: the role of expert processing in organizational sense-making', *Journal of Management Studies*, 29: 35–47.

De Meuse, K.P. (1987) 'A review of the effects of nonverbal cues on the performance appraisal process', *Journal of Occupational Psychology*, 60: 207–26.

DeNisi, A.S., Cafferty, T.P. and Meglino, B.M. (1984) 'A cognitive view of the performance appraisal process: a model and research propositions', *Organizational Behavior and Human Performance*, 33: 360–96.

DeNisi, A.S., Robbins, T. and Cafferty, T.P. (1989) 'Organization of information used for performance appraisals: role of diary-keeping', *Journal of Applied Psychology*, 74: 124–9.

Dipboye, R.L. and Macan, T.M. (1987) 'A process view of the selection/recruitment interview', in R. Schuler, S. Youngblood and V. Huber (eds), *Readings in Personnel and Human Resources Management*. St Paul: West Publishing.

Dobbins, G.H., Pence, E.C., Orban, J.A. and Sgro, J.A. (1983) 'The effects of sex on the leader and sex of the subordinate on the use of organizational control policy', *Organizational Behavior and Human Performance*, 32: 325–43.

Dobbins, G.H. and Russell, J.M. (1986) 'Self-serving biases in leadership: a laboratory experiment', *Journal of Management*, 12: 475–83.

Drake, B. and Mitchell, T. (1977) 'The effects of vertical and horizontal power on individual motivation and satisfaction', *Academy of Management Journal*, 20: 573–91.

Duhaime, I.D. and Schwenk, C.R. (1985) 'Conjectures on cognitive simplification in acquisition and divestment decision making', *Academy of Management Review*, 10: 287–95.

Dutton, J.E. and Jackson, S.E. (1987) 'Categorizing strategic issues: links to organizational action', *Academy of Management Review*, 12: 76–90.

Eagly, A.H. and Chaiken, S. (1992) *The Psychology of Attitudes*. California: Harcourt Brace Janovich.

Edwards, W. (1954) 'The theory of decision making', *Psychological Bulletin*, 51: 380–417.

Einhorn, H.J. and Hogarth, R.M. (1978) 'Confidence in judgment: persistent illusion of validity', *Psychological Review*, 85: 395–416.

Eisenhardt, K.M. and Zbaracki, M.J. (1992) 'Strategic decision making', *Strategic Management Journal*, 13: 17–37.

Feldman, D.C. and Weitz, B.A. (1988) 'Career plateaus reconsidered', *Journal of Management*, 14: 69–80.

Feldman, J.M. (1981) 'Beyond attribution theory: cognitive processes in performance appraisal', *Journal of Applied Psychology*, 66: 127–48.

Ferris, G.R., Yates, V.L., Gilmore, D.C and Rowland, K.M. (1985) 'The influence of subordinate age on performance ratings and causal attributions', *Personnel Psychology*, 38: 545–57.

Fischhoff, B. (1975) 'Hindsight foresight: the effect of outcome knowledge on judgment under uncertainty', *Journal of Experimental Psychology: Human Perception and Performance*, 1: 288–99.

Fiske, S.T. (1993) 'Social cognition and social perception', *Annual Review of Psychology*, 44: 155–94.

Fiske, S.T. and Taylor, S.F. (1991) *Social Cognition*, 2nd edn. New York: McGraw-Hill.

Garb, H.N. (1989) 'Clinical judgment, clinical training, and professional experience', *Psychological Bulletin*, 105: 387–96.

Gioia, D.A., Donnellon, A. and Sims, H.P. (1989) 'Communication and cognition in appraisal: a tale of two paradigms', *Organization Studies*, 10: 503–29.

Gioia, D.A. and Sims, H.P. (1986) 'Cognition–behavior connections: attribution and verbal behavior in leader–subordinate interactions', *Organizational Behavior and Human Decision Processes*, 37: 197–229.

Goodman, P. (1974) 'Effect of perceived inequity on salary allocation decisions', *Journal of Applied Psychology*, 21: 372–5.

Green, S.G. and Liden, R.C. (1980) 'Contextual and attributional influences on control decisions', *Journal of Applied Psychology*, 65: 453–8.

Green, S.G. and Mitchell, T.R. (1979) 'Attributional processes of leaders in leader–member interactions', *Organizational Behavior and Human Performance*, 23: 429–58.

Greenhalgh, L. (1993) 'Discussant remarks'. Negotiating in Organizations Conference, Georgetown University, Washington, DC.

Greenwald, A.G. and Pratkanis, A.R. (1984) 'The self', in R.S. Wyer Jr and T.K. Srull (eds), *Handbook of Social Cognition*, vol. 3. Hillsdale, NJ: Erlbaum.

Hackman, J.R., Pearce, J.L. and Wolfe, J.C. (1978) 'Effects of changes in job characteristics on work attitudes and behaviors: a naturally occurring quasi-experiment', *Organizational Behavior and Human Performance*, 21: 289–304.

Haefner, J.E. (1977) 'Race, age, sex and competence as factors in employer selection of the disadvantaged', *Journal of Applied Psychology*, 62: 199–202.

Hamilton, D.L. and Sherman, J.W. (1993) 'Stereotypes', to appear in R.S. Wyer Jr and T.K. Srull (eds), *Handbook of Social Cognition*, 2nd edn. Hillsdale, NJ: Erlbaum.

Hamilton, D.L. and Sherman, S.J. (1989) 'Illusory correlations: implications for stereotype theory and research', in D. Bar-Tal, C.F. Graumann, A.W. Kruglanski and W. Stroebe (eds), *Stereotypes and Prejudice: Changing Conceptions*. New York: Springer-Verlag.

Hammer, T.H. (1978) 'Relationships between local union characteristics and worker behavior and attitudes', *Academy of Management Journal*, 21: 560–77.

Hannan, M.T. and Freeman, J. (1989) *Organizational Ecology*. Cambridge, MA: Harvard University Press.

Harris, C. (1988) 'A comparison of employee attitudes toward two performance appraisal systems', *Public Personnel Management*, 17: 443–56.

Harrison, P.D., West, S.G. and Reneau, J.H. (1988) 'Initial attributions and information-seeking by superiors and subordinates in production variance investigations', *Accounting Review*, 63: 307–20.

Harvey, J.H., Ickes, W.J. and Kidd, R.F. (eds) (1976) *New Directions in Attribution Research*, vol. 1. Hillsdale, NJ: Erlbaum.

Harvey, J.H., Ickes, W.J. and Kidd, R.F. (eds) (1978) *New Directions in Attribution Research*, vol. 2. Hillsdale, NJ: Erlbaum.

Harvey, J.H., Ickes, W.J. and Kidd, R.F. (eds) (1981) *New Directions in Attribution Research*, vol. 3. Hillsdale, NJ: Erlbaum.

Heider, F. (1944) 'Social perception and phenomenal causality', *Psychological Review*, 51: 358–74.

Heider, F. (1958) *The Psychology of Interpersonal Relations*. New York: Wiley.

Heneman, R.L., Greenberger, D.B. and Anonyuo, C. (1989) 'Attributions and exchanges: the effects of interpersonal factors on the diagnosis of employee performance', *Academy of Management Journal*, 32: 466–76.

Heneman, R.L., Wexley, K.N. and Moore, M.L. (1987) 'Performance-rating accuracy: a critical review', *Journal of Business Research*, 15: 431–48.

Higgins, E.T. (1992) 'Social cognition as a social science: how social action creates meaning', in D.N. Ruble, P.R. Costanzo and M.E. Oliveri (eds), *The Social Psychology of Mental Health*. New York: Guilford Press.

Higgins, E.T. and Bargh, J.A. (1987) 'Social cognition and social perception', *Annual Review of Psychology*, 38: 369–425.

House, R.J. (1971) 'A path-goal theory of leadership', *Administrative Science Quarterly*, 16: 321–38.

Huber, V.L. (1986) 'Managerial applications of judgmental biases and heuristics', *Organizational Behavior Teaching Review*, 10: 1–24.

Huber, V.L. and Neale, M.A. (1986) 'Effects of cognitive heuristics and goals on negotiator performance and subsequent goal setting', *Organizational Behavior and Human Decision Processes*, 38: 342–65.

Huber, V.L., Neale, M.A. and Northcraft, G.B. (1987a) 'Decision bias in personnel selection decisions', *Organizational Behavior and Human Decision Processes*, 40: 136–47.

Huber, V.L., Neale, M.A. and Northcraft, G.B. (1987b) 'Judgment by heuristics: effects of rater and ratee characteristics and performance standards on performance-related judgments', *Organizational Behavior and Human Decision Processes*, 40: 149–69.

Huber, V.L., Northcraft, G.B. and Neale, M.A. (1990) 'Effects of decision contexts and anchoring bias on employment screening decisions', *Organizational Behavior and Human Decision Processes*, 45: 276–84.

Huber, V.L., Podsakoff, P.M. and Todor, W.D. (1986) 'An investigation of biasing factors in the attributions of subordinates and their supervisors', *Journal of Business Research*, 14: 83–98.

Ilgen, D.R., Barnes-Farrell, J.L. and McKellin, D.B. (1993) 'Performance appraisal process research in the 1980s: what has it contributed to appraisals in use?', *Organizational Behavior and Human Decision Processes*, 54: 321–68.

Ilgen, D.R. and Klein, H.J. (1988) 'Organization behavior', *Annual Review of Psychology*, 40: 327–51.

Jackson, D.N., Peacock, A.C. and Holden, R.R. (1982) 'Professional interviewers' trait inferential structures for diverse occupational groups', *Organizational Behavior and Human Performance*, 29: 1–20.

James, L.R. and White, J.F. (1983) 'Cross-situational specificity in managers' perceptions of subordinate performance, attributions, and leader behaviors', *Personnel Psychology*, 36: 809–56.

Janis, I.L. (1972) *Victims of Groupthink*. Boston: Houghton Mifflin.

Janis, I.L. and Mann, L. (1977) *Decision Making*. New York: Free Press.

Jolly, J.P., Reynolds, T.J. and Slocum, J.W. (1988) 'Application of the means-end theoretic for understanding the cognitive bases of performance appraisal', *Organizational Behavior and Human Decision Processes*, 41: 153–79.

Jones, E.E. and Davis, K.E. (1965) 'From acts to dispositions: the attribution process in person perception', in L. Berkowitz (ed.), *Advances in Experimental Social Psychology*, vol. 2. New York: Academic Press.

Kagel, J.H. and Levine, D. (1986) 'The winner's curse

and public information in common value auctions', *American Economic Review*, 76: 894–920.

Kahneman, D. and Tversky, A. (1972) 'Subjective probability: a judgment of representativeness', *Cognitive Psychology*, 3: 430–54.

Kahneman, D. and Tverksy, A. (1973) 'On the psychology of prediction', *Psychological Review*, 80: 237–51.

Kahneman, D. and Tversky, A. (1979) 'Prospect theory: an analysis of decision under risk', *Econometrica*, 47: 263–91.

Karl, K.A. and Wexley, K.N. (1989) 'Patterns of performance and rating frequency: influence on the assessment of performance', *Journal of Management*, 15: 5–20.

Katerberg, R., Hom, P.W. and Hulin, C.L. (1979) 'Effects of job complexity on the reactions of part-time employees', *Organizational Behavior and Human Performance*, 24: 317–32.

Katz, D. and Kahn, R.L. (1966) *The Social Psychology of Organizations*. New York: Wiley.

Katz, D. and Kahn, R.L. (1978) *The Social Psychology of Organizations*, 2nd edn. New York: Wiley.

Kelley, H.H. (1950) 'The warm–cold variable in first impressions of persons', *Journal of Personality*, 18: 431–9.

Kelley, H.H. (1967) 'Attribution theory in social psychology', in D. Levine (ed.), *Nebraska Symposium on Motivation*, vol. 15. Nebraska: University of Nebraska Press. pp. 192–240.

Kelley, H.H. and Michela, J.L. (1980) 'Attribution theory and research', *Annual Review of Psychology*, 31: 457–501.

Kerr, S. and Jermier, J.M. (1978) 'Substitutes for leadership: their meaning and measurement', *Organizational Behavior and Human Performance*, 22: 375–403.

Klein, H.J. (1989) 'An integrated control theory model of work motivation', *Academy of Management Review*, 14: 150–72.

Knowlton, W.A. and Ilgen, D.R. (1980) 'Performance attributional effects on feedback from superiors', *Organizational Behavior and Human Performance*, 25: 441–56.

Knowlton, W.A. and Mitchell, T.R. (1980) 'Effects of causal attributions on a supervisor's evaluation of subordinate performance', *Journal of Applied Psychology*, 65: 459–66.

Kozlowski, S.W. and Kirsch, M.P. (1987) 'The systematic distortion hypothesis, halo, and accuracy: an individual-level analysis', *Journal of Applied Psychology*, 72: 252–61.

Larson, J.R. (1989) 'The dynamic interplay between employees' feedback-seeking strategies and supervisors' delivery of performance feedback', *Academy of Management Review*, 14: 408–22.

Larson, J.R., Lingle, J.H. and Scerbo, M.M. (1984) 'The impact of performance cues on leader-behavior ratings: the role of selective information availability

and probabilistic response bias', *Organizational Behavior and Human Performance*, 33: 323–49.

Lawler, E.E. (1971) *Pay and Organizational Effectiveness: a Psychological View*. New York: McGraw-Hill.

Lawrence, P.R. and Lorsch, J.W. (1967) *Organization and Environment: Managing Differentiation and Integration*. Boston: Graduate School of Business Administration, Harvard University.

Levine, J.M., Resnick, L.B. and Higgins, E.T. (1993) 'Social foundations of cognition', *Annual Review of Psychology*, 44: 585–612.

Leyens, J.P. and Codol, J.P. (1988) 'Social cognition', in M. Hewstone, W. Stroebe, J.P. Codol, and G. Stephenson (eds), *Introduction to Social Psychology: A European Perspective*. Oxford: Basil Blackwell.

Locke, E.A., Frederick, E., Buckner, E. and Bobko, P. (1983) 'Effects of previously assigned goals on self-set goals and performance', *Journal of Applied Psychology*, 69: 694–9.

Loewenstein, G., Issacharoff, S., Camerer, C. and Babcock, L. (1993) 'Self-serving assessments of fairness and pretrial bargaining', *Journal of Legal Studies*, 23: 135–59.

Lord, R.G. and Smith, J.E. (1983) 'Theoretical, information processing and situational factors affecting attribution theory models of organizational behavior', *Academy of Management Review*, 8: 50–60.

Lowe, T.R. (1986) 'Eight ways to ruin a performance review', *Personnel Journal*, 65: 60–2.

Lyles, M. and Schwenk, C. (1992) 'Top management, strategy, and organization knowledge structures', *Journal of Management Studies*, 29: 155–74.

Mannix, E.A. and White, S.B. (1992) 'The impact of distributive uncertainty on coalition formation in organizations', *Organizational Behavior and Human Decision Processes*, 51: 198–219.

March, J.G. and Simon, H.A. (1958) *Organizations*. New York: Wiley.

Marks, G. and Miller, N. (1987) 'Ten years of research on the false-consensus effect: an empirical and theoretical review', *Psychological Bulletin*, 102: 72–90.

Markus, H. and Wurf, E. (1987) 'The dynamic self-concept: a social psychological perspective', *Annual Review of Psychology*, 38: 299–337.

Markus, H. and Zajonc, R.B. (1985) 'The cognitive perspective in social psychology', in G. Lindzey and E. Aronson (eds), *The Handbook of Social Psychology*. New York: Random House.

Martin, L.L. and Clark, L.F. (1990) 'Social cognition: exploring the mental processes involved in human social interaction', in M. Eysenck (ed.), *Cognitive Psychology: An International Review*, vol. 1. Chichester: Wiley.

Martinko, M.J. and Gardner, W.L. (1987) 'The leader/member attribution process', *Academy of Management Review*, 12: 235–49.

Mason, R.O and Mitroff, I.I. (1981) *Challenging Strategic Planning Assumptions*. New York: Wiley.

McArthur, L.Z. (1983) 'Social judgment biases in comparable worth analyses'. Paper presented at the Committee on Women's Employment and Related Social Issues Seminar on Comparable Worth Research.

Meindl, J.R. and Ehrlich, S.B. (1987) 'The romance of leadership and the evaluation of organizational performance', *Academy of Management Journal*, 30: 91–109.

Meindl, J.R., Ehrlich, S.B. and Dukerich, J.M. (1985) 'The romance of leadership', *Administrative Science Quarterly*, 30: 78–102.

Messick, D.M. and Mackie, D.M. (1989) 'Intergroup relations', *Annual Review of Psychology*, 40: 45–81.

Mirvis, P.H. and Lawler, E.E. (1977) 'Measuring the financial impact of employee attitudes', *Journal of Applied Psychology*, 62: 1–8.

Mitchell, T.R. and Kalb, L.S. (1981) 'Effects of outcome knowledge and outcome valence on supervisors' evaluations', *Journal of Applied Psychology*, 66: 604–12.

Mowday, R.T. and Sutton, R.I. (1993) 'Organizational behavior: linking individuals and groups to organizational contexts', *Annual Review of Psychology*, 44: 195–229.

Mullen, B. and Johnson, C. (1990) 'Distinctiveness-based illusory correlations and stereotyping: a meta-analytical integration', *British Journal of Social Psychology*, 29: 11–28.

Murphy, K.R., Gannett, B.A., Herr, B.M. and Chen, J.A. (1986) 'Effects of subsequent performance on evaluations of previous performance', *Journal of Applied Psychology*, 71: 427–31.

Murphy, K.R., Philbin, T.A. and Adams, S.R. (1989) 'Effect of purpose of observation on accuracy of immediate and delayed performance ratings', *Organizational Behavior and Human Decision Processes*, 43: 336–54.

Neale, M.A. (1984) 'The effect of negotiation and arbitration cost salience on bargainer behavior: the role of arbitrator and constituency in negotiator judgment', *Organizational Behavior and Human Performance*, 34: 97–111.

Neale, M.A. and Bazerman, M.H. (1985) 'The effects of framing and negotiator overconfidence on bargainer behavior', *Academy of Management Journal*, 28: 34–49.

Neale, M.A. and Bazerman, M.H. (1991) *Cognition and Rationality in Negotiation*. Free Press.

Neale, M.A., Bazerman, M.H., Northcraft, B.G. and Alperson, C.A. (1986) '"Choice shift" effects in group decisions: a decision bias perspective', *International Journal of Small Group Research*, 2: 33–42.

Nisbett, R. and Ross, L. (1980) *Human Inference: Strategies and Shortcomings of Social Judgment*. Englewood Cliffs, NJ: Prentice-Hall.

Northcraft, G.B. and Neale, M.A. (1986) 'Opportunity costs and the framing of resource allocation decisions', *Organizational Behavior and Human Decision Processes*, 37: 348–56.

Northcraft, G.B. and Neale, M.A. (1987) 'Expert, amateurs, and real estate: an anchoring-and-adjustment perspective on property pricing decisions', *Organizational Behavior and Human Decision Processes*, 39: 228–41.

Northcraft, G.B. and Neale, M.A. (1994) *Organizational Behavior: a Management Challenge*. Fort Worth, TX: Dryden Press.

Northcraft, G.B., Neale, M.A. and Huber, V.L. (1988) 'The effects of cognitive bias and social influence on human resources management decisions', *Research in Personnel and Human Resources Management*, 6: 157–89.

Olson, J.M. and Zanna, M.P. (1993) 'Attitudes and attitude change', *Annual Review of Psychology*, 44: 117–54.

O'Reilly, C.A. (1991) 'Organizational behavior: where we have been, where we're going', in *Annual Review of Psychology*. Palo Alto, CA: Annual Reviews.

Ostrom, T.M. (1989) 'Three catechisms for social memory', in P.R. Solomon, G.R. Goethals, C.M. Kelley, and B.R. Stephans (eds), *Memory: Interdisciplinary Approaches*. New York: Springer-Verlag.

Pazy, A. (1986) 'The persistence of pro-male bias despite identical information regarding causes of success', *Organizational Behavior and Human Decision Processes*, 38: 366–77.

Pearce, J.L. and Porter, L.W. (1986) 'Employee responses to formal performance appraisal feedback', *Journal of Applied Psychology*, 71: 211–18.

Peppers, L. and Ryan, J. (1986) 'Discrepancies between actual and aspired self: a comparison of leaders and nonleaders', *Group and Organization Studies*, 11: 220–8.

Pfeffer, J. (1981) 'Management as symbolic action: the creation and maintenance of organizational paradigms', *Research in Organizational Behavior*, 3: 1–52.

Pfeffer, J. and Davis-Blake, A. (1986) 'Administrative succession and organizational performance: how administrator experience mediates the succession effect', *Academy of Management Journal*, 29: 72–83.

Phillips, J.S. (1984) 'The accuracy of leadership ratings: a cognitive categorization perspective', *Organizational Behavior and Human Performance*, 33: 125–38.

Pondy, L.R. and Mitroff, I.I. (1979) 'Beyond open system models of organizations', *Research in Organizational Behavior*, 1: 3–39.

Prahalad, C.K. and Bettis, R.A. (1986) 'The dominant logic: a new linkage between diversity and performance', *Strategic Management Journal*, 7: 485–501.

Raiffa, H. (1982) *The Art and Science of Negotiation*. Cambridge, MA: Belknap.

Rogers, T.B. (1977) 'Self-reference in memory:

recognition of personality items', *Journal of Research in Personality*, 11: 295–305.

Rose, G.L. (1978) 'Sex effects on effort attributions in managerial performance evaluation', *Organizational Behavior and Human Performance*, 21: 367–78.

Rose, G.L. and Brief, A.P. (1979) 'Effects of handicap and job characteristics on selection evaluation', *Personnel Psychology*, 32: 385–92.

Ross, L. (1977) 'The intuitive psychologist and his shortcomings: distortions in the attribution process', in L. Berkowitz (ed.), *Advances in Experimental Social Psychology*, 35: 485–94.

Ross, L., Lepper, M. and Hubbard, M. (1975) 'Perseverance on self perception and social perception: biased attributional processes in the debriefing paradigm', *Journal of Personality and Social Psychology*, 32: 880–92.

Ross, M. and Fletcher, G.J.O. (1985) 'Attribution and social perception', in G. Lindzey and A. Aronson (eds), *The Handbook of Social Psychology*, 3rd edn, vol. 2. Reading, MA: Addison-Wesley.

Ross, W.T. (1991) 'Performance against quota and call selection decision', *Journal of Marketing Research*, 28: 296–306.

Salancik, G.R. and Meindl, J.R. (1984) 'Corporate attributions as strategic illusions of management control', *Administrative Science Quarterly*, 29: 238–54.

Samuelson, W.F. and Bazerman, M.H. (1985) 'The winner's curse in bilateral negotiations', in V. Smith (ed.), *Research in Experimental Economics*, vol. 3. Greenwich, CT: JAI Press. pp. 105–37.

Schneider, D.J. (1991) 'Social cognition', *Annual Review of Psychology*, 42: 527–61.

Schwab, D.P. and Heneman, H.G. (1978) 'Age stereotyping in performance appraisal', *Journal of Applied Psychology*, 63: 573–8.

Schwenk, C. (1986) 'Information, cognitive biases, and commitment to a course of action', *Academy of Management Review*, 11: 298–310.

Schwenk, C. (1988) 'The cognitive perspective on strategic decision-making', *Journal of Management Studies*, 25: 41–55.

Shamir, B. (1991) 'Meaning, self and motivation in organizations', *Organizational Studies*, 12: 405–24.

Sherman, S.J., Judd, C.M. and Park, B. (1989) 'Social cognition', *Annual Review of Psychology*, 40: 281–326.

Shrivastava, P. and Mitroff, I.I. (1983) 'Frames of reference managers use: a study in applied sociology of knowledge', in R. Lamb (ed.), *Advances in Strategic Management*, vol. 1. Greenwich, CT: JAI Press.

Shrivastava, P. and Mitroff, I.I. (1984) 'Enhancing organizational research utilization: the role of decision makers' assumptions', *Academy of Management Review*, 9: 18–26.

Simon, H.A. (1957) *Models of Man*. New York: Wiley.

Slovic, P. and Lichtenstein, S. (1971) 'Comparison of Bayesian and regression approaches to the study of

information processing in judgment', *Organizational Behavior and Human Performance*, 6: 649–764.

Sniezek, J.A. and Henry, R.A. (1989) 'Accuracy and confidences in group judgment', *Organizational Behavior and Human Decision Processes*, 43: 1–28.

Stahlberg, D. and Frey, D. (1988) 'Attitudes I: structure, measurement and functions', in M. Hewstone, W. Stroebe, J.P. Codol and G. Stephenson (eds), *Introduction to Social Psychology: A European Perspective*. Oxford: Basil Blackwell.

Staw, B.M. (1984) 'Organizational behavior: a review and reformulation of the field's outcome variables', *Annual Review of Psychology*, 35: 627–66.

Staw, B.M. (1991) 'Dressing up like an organization: when psychological theories can explain organizational action', *Journal of Management*, 17: 805–19.

Staw, B.M., McKechnie, P.I., and Puffer, S.M. (1983) 'The justification of organizational performance', *Administrative Science Quarterly*, 28: 582–600.

Staw, B.M., Sandelands, L.E., and Dutton, J.E. (1981) 'Threat-rigidity effects in organizational behavior: a multilevel analysis', *Administrative Science Quarterly*, 26: 501–24.

Staw, B.M. and Sutton, R.I. (1992) 'Macro organizational psychology', in J.K. Murnighan (ed.), *Social Psychology in Organizations: Advances in Theory and Research*. Englewood Cliffs, NJ: Prentice-Hall.

Stillinger, C., Epelbaum, M., Keltner, D. and Ross, L. (in press) 'The "reactive devaluation" barrier to conflict resolution'. Working Paper.

Stoner, J.A.F. (1961) 'A comparison of individual and group decisions involving risk'. Unpublished master's thesis, Massachusetts Institute of Technology, School of Industrial Management.

Stroebe, W. and Jonas, K. (1988) 'Attitudes II: strategies of attitude change', in M. Hewstone, W. Stroebe, J.P. Codol and G. Stephenson (eds), *Introduction to Social Psychology: a European Perspective*. Oxford: Basil Blackwell.

Sujan, H. (1986) 'Smarter versus harder: an exploratory attributional analysis of salespeople's motivation', *Journal of Marketing Research*, 23: 41–9.

Sullivan, J.J. (1989) 'Self theories and employee motivation', *Journal of Management*, 15: 345–63.

Tajfel, H. (1969) 'Cognitive aspects of prejudice', *Journal of Social Issues*, 25: 79–97.

Taylor, D.M. and Doria, J.R. (1981) 'Self-serving and group-serving bias in attribution', *Journal of Social Psychology*, 113: 201–11.

Teas, R. and McElroy, J.C. (1986) 'Causal attributions and expectancy estimates: a framework for understanding the dynamics of salesforce motivation', *Journal of Marketing*, 50: 75–86.

Thomas, A.B. (1988) 'Does leadership make a difference to organizational performance?', *Administrative Science Quarterly*, 33: 338–400.

Thompson, L.L. and Hastie, R. (1990) 'Negotiator's perceptions of the negotiation process', in B.H. Sheppard, M.H. Bazerman and R.J. Lewicki (eds),

Research in Negotiation in Organizations, vol. 2. Greenwich, CT: JAI Press.

Thompson, L.L. and Loewenstein, G.F. (1992) 'Egocentric interpretations of fairness and interpersonal conflict', *Organizational Behavior and Human Decision Processes*, 51: 176–97.

Tjosvold, D. (1985) 'The effects of attribution and social context on superiors' influence and interaction with low performing subordinates', *Personnel Psychology*, 38: 361–76.

Tversky, A. and Kahneman, D. (1973) 'Availability: a heuristic for judging frequency and probability', *Cognitive Psychology*, 5: 207–32.

Tversky, A. and Kahneman, D. (1974) 'Judgment under uncertainty: heuristics and biases', *Science*, 185: 1124–31.

Tversky, A. and Kahneman, D. (1983) 'Extensional versus intuitive reasoning: the conjunction fallacy in probability judgement', *Psychological Review*, 90: 293–315.

Tversky, A. and Kahneman, D. (1986) 'Rational choice and the framing of decisions', *Journal of Business*, 59: 251–84.

Walsh, J.P. and Ungson, G.R. (1991) 'Organizational memory', *Academy of Management Review*, 16: 57–91.

Wason, P.C. (1960) 'On the failure to eliminate hypotheses in a conceptual task', *Quarterly Journal of Experimental Psychology*, 12: 129–40.

Weick, K.E. (1969) *The Social Psychology of Organizing*. Reading, MA: Addison-Wesley.

Weick, K.E. (1979a) 'Cognitive processes in organizations', *Research in Organizational Behavior*, 1: 41–74.

Weick, K.E. (1979b) *The Social Psychology of Organizing*. Reading, MA: Addison-Wesley.

Weick, K.E. (1992) 'Sensemaking in organizations: small structures with large consequences', in J.K. Murnighan (ed.), *Social Psychology in Organizations: Advances in Theory and Research*. Englewood Cliffs, NJ: Prentice-Hall.

Weiner, B. (1986) *An Attributional Theory of Motivation and Emotion*. New York: Springer-Verlag.

Wendelken, D.J. and Inn, A. (1981) 'Nonperformance influences on performance evaluation: a laboratory phenomenon?', *Journal of Applied Psychology*, 66: 150–8.

Wexley, K.N. and Pulakos, E.D. (1983) 'The effects of perceptual congruence and sex on subordinates' performance appraisals of their managers', *Academy of Management Journal*, 26: 666–76.

White, H.C. and Bassford, G. (1978) 'Industrial effectiveness: leadership style and small groups', *Industrial Management*, 63: 277–88.

Whyte, G. (1991) 'Diffusion of responsibility: effects on the escalation tendency', *Journal of Applied Psychology*, 76: 408–15.

Williams, K.J., Cafferty, T.P. and DeNisi, A.S. (1990) 'The effect of performance appraisal salience on recall and ratings', *Organizational Behavior and Human Decision Processes*, 46: 217–39.

Wyer, R.S. and Srull, T.K. (1988) 'Understanding social knowledge: if only the data could speak for themselves', in D. Bar-Tal and A.W. Kruglanski (eds), *The Social Psychology of Knowledge*. Cambridge: Cambridge University Press.

Yeager, S.J., Rabin, J. and Vocino, T. (1985) 'Feedback and administrative behavior in the public sector', *Public Administration Review*, 45: 570–5.

Zajac, E.J. and Bazerman, M.H. (1991) 'Blind spots in industry and competitor analysis: implications of interfirm (mis)perceptions for strategic decisions', *Academy of Management Review*, 16: 37–56.

Zalesny, M.D. and Highhouse, S. (1992) 'Accuracy in performance evaluations', *Organizational Behavior and Human Decision Processes*, 51: 22–50.

Zuckerman, M. (1979) 'Attribution of success and failure revisited, or: the motivational bias is alive and well in attribution theory', *Journal of Personality*, 47: 245–87.

2.5

Diverse Identities in Organizations

STELLA M. NKOMO AND TAYLOR COX JR

In the last few years with the release of the Workforce 2000 Report and other publications predicting a more diverse workforce in the United States and throughout the world (Fullerton 1991; Johnston and Packer 1987; Johnston 1991), diversity has gained currency as a topic in the study of organizations. The most attention has come from practitioners interested in how to 'manage diversity' in light of these predictions (Cross et al. 1994; Morrison 1992; Loden and Rosener 1991; Thomas 1991). Organizational researchers have only recently turned their attention to the topic (Cox 1993; Cox and Blake 1991; Ferdman 1992; Jackson and associates 1992; Watson et al. 1993). For the most part the concept of diversity lacks rigor, theoretical development, and historical specificity.

The current state of theoretical knowledge and research on diversity in organizations might be likened to the situation of discovering the many tributary streams to a larger body of water but being uncertain about the very nature of the larger body of water. There are a number of theoretical and research areas which influence current understandings of diverse identities in organizations. The vastness of what might be assumed under the rubric of diversity reflects one of its major theoretical dilemmas – the lack of specificity of the concept. Diversity is underdeveloped as a scientific construct and has largely drawn its present meaning from the work of organizational practitioners. It is also very much a contested term. Current definitions of diversity range from narrow to very broad, expansive conceptualizations.

Narrow definitions emphasize race, ethnicity, and gender. For instance, Cross et al. (1994:

xxii) view diversity as 'focusing on issues of racism, sexism, heterosexism, classism, ableism, and other forms of discrimination at the individual, identity group, and system levels'. Cox (1993: 5–6) focuses on cultural diversity, which he defines as 'the representation, in one social system, of people with distinctly different group affiliations of *cultural* significance'. Examples of very broad definitions include Thomas (1991: 10) who states: 'Diversity includes everyone, it is not something that is defined by race or gender. It extends to age, personal and corporate background, education, function, and personality. It includes lifestyle, sexual preference, geographic origin, tenure with the organization, exempt or nonexempt status, and management or nonmanagement.' In a like fashion, Jamieson and O'Mara (1991: xvi) argue for a 'broadened view of diversity, adding values, age, disabilities, education to the more common interpretation that focuses exclusively on women and people of color'. Even more generally, Jackson et al. (1993: 53) use diversity 'to refer to situations in which the actors of interest are not alike with respect to some attribute'. Loden and Rosener (1991) also take a broad view but distinguish between primary dimensions consisting of immutable human differences like age, ethnicity, gender, race, sexual orientation, and physical abilities; and secondary mutable differences like educational background, geographic location, and work experience.

Broad definitions imply that the term refers to *all* individual differences among people – that is, everyone is different. This conceptualization mirrors the individualism that structures much of our thinking about organizations. On the other hand, narrow approaches which constrict diversity to race, ethnicity, and gender, tend to be interpreted as referring only to people who are in a particular gender or racioethnic[1] minority group in a social system (i.e. diversity refers to white women and racial minorities).

To achieve conceptual clarity in the language and meaning of diversity we have to begin with framing the concept itself. The specifics of how the term is defined and treated will go a long way toward establishing the ideology that will shape thinking about the topic in important ways. Indeed the very term is incomplete because it immediately raises the question: diversity in what? Despite the confusion over what constitutes diversity, it is somewhat clear that scholars are referring to 'diversity in identities' based on membership in social and demographic groups and how differences in identities affect social relations in organizations. We define diversity as a mixture of people with different group identities within the same social system. The concept of identity appears to be at the core of understanding diversity in organizations. Thus, our discussion of diversity in this chapter is centered around the very meaning of *identity* and its treatment in the study of organizations.

Because diversity is perceived to be such a new issue, an implicit assumption appears to be that there is little available knowledge relevant to its development as a topic. However, a close review of the organizational literature indicates a number of bodies of work relevant to diversity in identities. Our belief is that in order for theory and research on diversity to advance, it is important to critically review in one chapter theories and research which currently qualify as major orientations. The work reviewed includes social identity theory, embedded intergroup theory, racioethnicity and gender research, organizational demography, and ethnology. We do not undertake an exhaustive review of the empirical research each has generated. Our main concern is how identity has been conceptualized in each body of work. For each theory/body of work reviewed, we focus on six dimensions of the treatment of identity: (1) explicitly versus implicitly defined; (2) physically versus culturally defined; (3) proposed measurement; (4) self versus other defined; (5) levels of analysis; and (6) effects of diversity (see Table 1). Additionally, we review three recently proposed metatheoretical diversity frameworks (Cox 1993; Jackson et al. 1995; Triandis et al. 1994). We end our review with prescriptions for how identity might be reframed and expanded. Finally, we explore the methodological and research implications of these prescriptions. We begin first, however, with a review of the relevant literature.

LITERATURE REVIEW

Social Identity Theory

We have defined diversity as a mixture of people with different group identities within the same social system. Intergroup perspectives have been one of the major frameworks for understanding human interactions involving individuals perceiving themselves as a member of a social category or being perceived by others as belonging to a social category (Taylor and Moghaddam 1987). These perspectives cover a range of concerns from intergroup conflict to prejudice (Brewer and Kramer 1985; Hewstone and Brown 1986; Kramer 1991; Messick and Mackie 1989; Sherif and Sherif 1953; Tajfel 1982). One of the most prominent intergroup theories informing us about group identity effects on human behavior has been social identity theory (SIT). SIT is a cognitive theory which holds that individuals tend to classify themselves and others into social categories and that these classifications have a significant effect on human interactions. The foundational work on social identification was done in the field of social psychology principally by Henry Tajfel and John Turner (Tajfel 1972; Turner 1975; Tajfel and Turner 1979). The treatment of group identity in social identity theory is somewhat inconsistent. For example, major contributors to the development of the theory differ on how much members must share in common in order to constitute a social identity group (Rabbie and Horwitz 1988). Thus, it is not entirely clear whether social identity categories are assumed to have cultural implications or simply represent different phenotypes or social categories. However, most SIT writers seem to lean toward the latter interpretation. It should be emphasized however that SIT does not treat group identity as a nominal scale measure. On the contrary, one of the most important contributions of SIT to the field of diversity research is the notion that people within social groups differ in the relative importance that any particular social identity has in their self-concept (Jackson 1981). Hence, one of the implications of SIT is that group identity should ideally be operationalized for research as a continuous scale measure.

There is also some ambiguity as to the extent to which how one is defined by others is relevant to one's social identity. For example Turner defined social identification as 'the process of locating oneself *or another person* within a system of social categorizations' but simultaneously defined 'social identity' as the 'sum total of the social identifications used by a person to define him or herself' (1982: 18). We believe that the categorical 'locations' attributed to one

Table 1 *Summary of approaches to identity in organizations*

Treatment of identity	Embedded group theory	Social identity theory	Race/gender research	Organization demography	Ethnology	Suggested
Explicitly addressed vs implied	Explicit	Explicit	Implied	Explicit	Explicit	Explicit
Physical vs cultural	Physical	Physical	Physical	Physical	Cultural	Cultural/historical/political
Nominal vs interval/ratio	Nominal	Both	Nominal	Nominal	Interval/ratio	Both
Self-definition vs defined by others	Self	Self	Others	Self	Self	Both
Levels of analysis (individual, group, organization)	Group/organization	Individual/group/organization	Individual/group	Organization	Group	Individual/group/organizational/societal
Effect of diversity	Depends on congruency with subsystem and suprasystem	Conflict; competition; in-group favoritism; stereotyping	Exclusion of minorities and women; discrimination	Adverse effects on cohesiveness, turnover, commitment, communication; enhances creativity, innovation and decision quality	Misunderstanding; conflict; stress; ethnocentrism	All potential effects should be understood; focus on understanding cirumstances under which positive effects can be increased; dysfunctions decreased

person by other people are crucial to understanding the full implications of social identity. On balance, however, the clear emphasis of SIT is on self-definition, a fact that we find poses limitations for the usefulness of the concept as the focal point in diversity research. We believe that how one is defined by others both influences one's self-identity to some degree and has group affiliation effects in its own right (i.e. independent of one's self-definition). For example, the fact that a person does not identify strongly with being male or female does not mean that her/his gender will not be important in how other people relate to him/her, and thus gender identity can affect life experiences whether one self-identifies by gender or not. In light of this, to the extent that social identity is to be understood as limited to a person's self-conception (Abrams and Hogg 1990), some other concept is needed to capture the role that others play in defining the relevant group identities of a person.

Although well developed in the social psychology literature, social identification theory has only recently been applied to the organizational setting. Ashforth and Mael (1989) and Wharton (1992) present theoretical work which addresses the interaction of social identity with one or more aspects of the social context. Ashforth and Mael (1989) note that a combination of factors prevalent in organizations work to intensify the effects of group identification. These factors include the presence of numerous formal and informal groups and the distinctiveness of traits of the various groups (e.g. differences in goals and processes between work units).

Wharton (1992) and Ridgeway (1991) take a social construction approach to show how social identity is specifically applicable to the topic of workforce diversity in organizations. Wharton (1992) argues that gender and race should be viewed as socially constructed categories in organizational research. For her, one implication of this approach is that identification with gender and race groups should be understood as evoked by contextual stimuli rather than as fixed components of an individual's self-concept. This view follows closely previous work on situational ethnicity and emergent ethnicity (e.g. Yancey et al. 1976; Okamura 1981; McGuire et al. 1978; Stayman and Deshpande 1989). A central contribution of this body of work is to illuminate the contextual forces that determine identity salience such as the type of task to be performed and the demographic make-up of work groups.

Ridgeway's (1991) work focuses on the status value of nominal characteristics. Using the structural theory of Blau (1977) and the

expectation-states theory of Berger and Zelditch (1985), she explains why group identities like gender and race impact levels of social interaction with persons who have access to resources and thereby become independent status indicators (i.e. independent of possession of resources or other status relevant traits). The core of her argument is that when group identifications become highly correlated with a difference in exchangeable resources, the group identification becomes an indicator of status which is then used to determine inclusion or exclusion from important social networks and ultimately is taken as a proxy for general competency. Using equations developed by Skvoretz (1983) she predicts that gender is a group identity which is especially vulnerable to the cycle because men and women are about equally represented in the population.

One noteworthy contribution of these social construction theorists to the work on diversity is that they discuss the applicability of social identity on multiple levels of analysis. Traditionally, SIT has focused on the individual level, but by emphasizing the social context, these writers make clear the importance of group- and organization-level social identity phenomena.

We now come to the central question of what SIT has to say about the effects of diversity on work group and organizational processes and outcomes. For the most part, this body of work seems to suggest that social identification and related processes produce mainly detrimental effects on the group-level outcomes of diverse groups. The following comment by Brewer is illustrative:

> The common goals and cooperative interdependence characteristic of work teams should provide a context for breaking down barriers to communication and exploiting the benefits of diverse skills and perspectives. However, various aspects of intergroup relations (in-group loyalties, implicit intergroup rivalries, negative stereotypes and distrust of outgroups) often conspire to impede coordination among members of diverse work teams and reduce effective performance. (1995: 10)

On a similar note, Ashforth and Mael (1989) identify three general consequences of group identification which are especially relevant to organizational behavior/outcomes as follows: (1) individuals tend to choose activities and institutions which are congruent with their salient identities; (2) identification affects outcomes such as intragroup cohesion and cooperation; and (3) identification reinforces attachment to the group and its values and increases competition with out-groups. The second and third consequences suggest that the existence of diversity in group identifications may lead to some difficulty in relations between people of different salient group identities. To the extent that identities with sub-groups (micro-identities in the organization context) take precedence over the common organizational identity (macro-identity), the ability of people to work together in teams composed of members from different group identities may be hampered by the consequences of group identification.

Embedded Intergroup Relations Theory

Like SIT, embedded intergroup relations theory also falls under the general rubric of intergroup perspectives. However, Alderfer and Smith (1982) have developed a theory of embedded intergroup relations specifically for organizations which explicitly integrates identity group membership and group membership resulting from organizational categorization. Their theory posits that two types of groups exist within organizations: identity groups and organization groups.

An identity group is a group whose members share some common biological characteristic such as sex, have participated in equivalent historical experiences, are currently subjected to similar social forces, and as a result have consonant world views (Alderfer 1987). The most commonly recognized identity groups are those based on gender, family, ethnicity, and age (Alderfer and Smith 1982). While there is little choice about physical membership in identity groups, there is some degree of choice about psychological membership. Like SIT, embedded intergroup theory argues that individuals may feel more or less identified with their identity group. The focus is on self-identification.

An organization group is one in which members share common organization positions, participate in equivalent work experiences and as a consequence have consonant world views. Identity group membership precedes organization group membership. Thus, the identity of people in organizations is a function of their identity group membership and their organization group membership.

The theory contains a rather complex set of interactions for understanding the effects of diversity in identities in organizations. Identity group and organization group membership are seen as highly related in their effects on social relations in organizations. Certain organization groups tend to be populated by members of particular identity groups. For example, positions in upper management in organizations in the United States and other industrialized countries tend to be concentrated with older white males. According to embedded intergroup theory, individuals and organizations are constantly attempting to manage potential conflicts arising from the interface between identity groups and organization group membership. How tensions are managed depends on several factors, the most important of which is how the groups are embedded in the larger 'suprasystem' (Alderfer and Smith 1982). Alderfer and Smith (1982) use the term 'embedded intergroup relations' to capture the dynamics among identity groups, organization groups, and the suprasystem in which they are embedded. Embeddedness can be either congruent or incongruent. Congruent embeddedness exists when power relations among groups at one level are reinforced by power relations at the suprasystem and subsystem level (Alderfer 1987). Incongruent embeddedness exists when power relations are not consistent with suprasystem dynamics. Understanding diverse identities in organizations therefore requires an understanding of the group affiliation profile of the parties as well as the larger context within which the parties interact.

Embedded intergroup theory has been used to study women and minorities in predominantly white male organizations (Alderfer et al. 1980; Thomas 1990). Exemplary of research using the theory is the work of Alderfer et al. (1980). Alderfer and his colleagues studied race relationships among managers of a large business corporation. Their research demonstrated how racial group identity influenced cognitions of race relations within the organization. One significant finding was the existence of both parallel and nonparallel perceptions between black and white racial groups. Each racial group reported that members of the other group socialized more with each other than with members of the other race. Each racial group tended to see this pattern as weaker in its own group than in the other group. Identity group membership was the most powerful predicator even when there were objective facts about an issue.

The significance of embedded intergroup theory for understanding identity is its attention to the effects of diverse identities within a larger organizational context. The identity of individuals in organizations is said to be determined not only by organizational categorization but also by identity group membership. It recognizes that individuals don't leave their racial, gender, or ethnic identities at the door when they enter an organization. Embedded intergroup theory also suggests that identity group categorization will always be relevant in an organization context.

Organizational Demography

Organizational demography research refers to the study of 'the causes and consequences of the composition or distribution of specific demographic attributes of employees in an organization' (Tsui et al. 1995: 4). The origin of organizational demography as a field of study is often attributed to Pfeffer (1983). The review of organizational demography research by Tsui et al. (1995) identifies fifteen empirical studies and one edited volume published since Pfeffer's seminal article. Their review indicates that organizational demographers have focused primarily on the group identities of age, tenure, education and functional background. Of the fifteen empirical studies located by their review, tenure was addressed in thirteen, age in nine, and education and functional background in six each. By contrast, gender and race were included in only three studies each (Tsui et al. 1995).

Our study of this work suggests that group identity is generally treated as a nominal scale variable which signifies social categories based on physical or work history characteristics. In addition, it relies largely on self-definitions of group identity most commonly taken from surveys or company background data files. As implied by the name 'organizational demography', this work focuses on the macro level of analysis more so than the group or individual level. A notable exception is the work of Tsui and O'Reilly (1989) on relational demography which focuses attention on the demographics of superior–subordinate dyads.

One limitation of organizational demography research which is suggested by the early theory on diversity in organizations (and the work presented earlier on social identity theory) has to do with how the dimensions of difference are operationalized. Writers on workforce diversity have emphasized the cultural significance of demographic categories such as gender, race and work function and the notion of differential levels of identification with the group within categories. For example, Cox (1993) notes that many identity groups represent both physical distinctiveness (phenotypes) and cultural distinctiveness (cultural identity). He also argues that members of identity groups vary in the extent to which they display both the cultural and, for certain types of diversity, even the physical characteristics which are prototypical of the group. One implication of this treatment is that identity should be measured as a continuous variable rather than as a nominal variable. Alternatively, organizational demography writers have typically treated the dimensions of difference as simply physical categories.

Tsui et al. (1992) argue that a distinction

between diversity research and organizational demography research is that the former limits attention to the effect of group identity differences on members of minority groups while the latter is interested in effects on all workers. However, we believe that research which addresses the impact of identity on minority group members simultaneously reveals effects for majority group members. For example, research which reveals that being female has a negative effect on promotion prospects or on compensation also reveals that being male (the majority group) has a positive effect. In this regard, even research which focuses on a single dimension of diversity (e.g. gender) provides information that is relevant to all workers rather than only to members of minority groups. Also theory and research on diversity are increasingly addressing multiple dimensions of group identity, a trend that we expect to continue.

Of all the research areas discussed here, the work on organizational demography offers the most direct and extensive research on specific effects of diversity on work outcomes and performance. Indeed, the central thrust of empirical work on organizational demography has been to determine the impact of the demographic composition of organizations or work groups on work outcomes (Tsui et al. 1995). A review of the empirical research suggests that demographic heterogeneity potentially has both positive and negative effects on work outcomes of interest to practitioners. On the one hand, heterogeneity (compared to homogeneity in groups) reduces intragroup cohesiveness, lowers member satisfaction (at least for members of the majority group) and increases turnover (Jackson et al. 1991; Tsui et al. 1992; Wharton and Baron 1987). On the other hand, heterogeneity, at least under certain conditions, increases creativity, decision-making quality and innovation (Jackson and associates 1992; Ancona and Caldwell 1992; Bantel and Jackson 1989).

It is significant to note that this body of research addresses what we call 'unmanaged diversity', that is, no apparent efforts were made to reduce the potential negative effects of difference in work groups or to accentuate the potential positive effects. The question which therefore arises is: can steps such as education about cultural differences, allowing more time to reach decisions, and other interventions be used to reduce the negative effects of heterogeneity and increase the positive effects? We believe the answer is yes. There is some empirical research which seems to support this conclusion. Adler (1986) reports on an experimental study in which culturally diverse teams were compared to culturally homogeneous teams on productivity. Results indicated that conscious attention to the dynamics of diversity may be the difference between positive and negative overall effects on group performance outcomes. In another study, the creativity scores of heterogeneous dyads (defined as different in attitudes) were compared to those of homogeneous dyads. Findings indicated that when there was no intervention to address the attitude differences, the heterogeneous dyads were less creative than the homogeneous dyads, but when there was some training given to increase understanding and communication among the members, the results were reversed (Triandis et al. 1965).

Research on Racioethnicity and Gender

Prior to the late 1960s, little attention was paid to issues of race and gender in the study of organizations (Cox and Nkomo 1990) suggesting that employees were void of these identities. Large-scale attention to issues of race and gender in organizations began after the passage of equal employment opportunity and anti-discrimination legislation in the late 1960s and early 1970s in the United States and to a lesser degree in countries of Western Europe, especially Britain (Cox and Nkomo 1990; Nkomo 1992; Sivanandan 1985). The literature that sprung up revolved around those categories covered by the legislation: sex, race, national origin, religion, and age. Since the greatest amount of research has been accumulated on racioethnicity and gender, we focus our attention on those two areas. Much less attention has been given to sexual orientation and physical ability (Hall 1989; Harris 1994; Munyard 1988; Stone et al. 1992; Woods 1993).

The goal of much of this research has been to document differential treatment in organizations based on racioethnicity and gender. The early research on racioethnicity and gender was heavily influenced by assimilation theories found in the work of scholars like Allport (1954), Myrdal (1944), and Park (1950). The emphasis was on psychological expressions of racism, sexism, and other forms of discrimination. The major issue was assumed to be assimilating white women,[2] racial minorities and those who were 'different' into organizations.

For the most part identity has not been explicit in the treatment of race and gender in organizations. Indeed the concepts of *racial identity*, *ethnic identity*, and/or *gender identity* are rarely found in the work. Yet, implicitly the literature suggests the notion of identity embedded in research on racioethnicity and gender is one of identity as a variable. Race and gender have largely been studied as objective, fixed properties of individuals that can be operationalized into measurable levels (e.g. 1 = white and 2 = black; 1 = male and 2 = female). Researchers have largely relied on nominal measures in carrying out their research. The bulk of the research on racioethnicity in organizations in the US has compared blacks and whites. This narrow focus is problematic in itself. Other racioethnic groups have received much less attention (Knouse et al. 1992).

Two major strands of research can be identified. One strand focuses on uncovering objective, quantifiable evidence of race and gender discrimination in organizational practices. Although results of these studies are mixed, taken as a whole they suggests that blacks and women face both access and treatment discrimination in organizations (Collins 1989; Kraiger and Ford 1985; Greenhaus et al. 1990). The literature is replete with studies documenting negative effects on the careers of racial minorities and white women, including tokenism, differential access to mentoring, exclusion from informal networks, glass ceilings, and other forms of restricted career mobility (Antal and Izraeli 1993; Bell 1990; Collins 1989; Cox and Nkomo 1991; Fernandez 1981; Greenhaus et al. 1990; Ibarra 1993; Iles et al. 1991; Morrison et al. 1987; Pettigrew and Martin 1987; Thomas 1990; Cahoon and Rowney 1993; Freedman and Phillips 1988; Stroh et al. 1992; Raggins and Cotton 1991).

A second strand of research focuses on race and gender differences in a host of traditional organizational behavior topics. The types of studies done reflect an assumption that racioethnicity and gender are objective, essentialist properties of individuals. That is, differences in identity reflect innate differences between racioethnic groups and men and women. For example, researchers have tested for racial differences in job satisfaction and job attitudes (e.g. O'Reilly and Roberts 1973; Weaver 1978), leadership styles (e.g. Bartol et al. 1978) and motivation (e.g. Brenner and Tomkiewcz 1982; McClelland 1974). Despite a sizable quantity of work, the results are largely inconsistent, with little evidence of systematic differences between blacks and whites in job attitudes and motivation. In the case of gender differences, a number of studies have raised the question of whether women managers have different leadership styles compared to men (Eagly and Johnson 1990; Powell 1990; Rosener 1990). Some researchers suggest that women do not use hierarchical styles of leadership but have more democratic, participative styles (Rosener 1990). Still other researchers have found that successful women managers do not differ in style from successful male managers (Powell 1990). Despite a proliferation of studies focusing on gender differences, cumulatively it is difficult to make blanket statements about what systematically differentiates female managers from male managers in attitudes toward work, personality, and behavior.

Explanations for the negative consequences for racial minorities and white women in organizations range from prejudice and discrimination stemming from stereotyping to structural explanations centering on their proportional representation in organizational hierarchies (Kanter 1977). The influence of assimilation theory is evident in the kinds of questions studied and solutions proposed. Much of the work suggests that the solution to the negative effects of diversity lies in the successful integration of racial minorities and white women into organizations. Implicitly, for the minority group, successful assimilation means a loss of identity – adapting to the norms and behaviors of the dominant group.

Ethnology

Another part of the foundation of research on diversity is ethnology. Ethnology is the branch of anthropology which deals with the social and cultural characteristics of different 'tribal' groupings of people. We prefer the term 'ethnology' rather than 'ethnography' because it includes the comparison and analysis of cultures rather than merely their description. Although historically the term has referred to cultural characteristics of different race or ethnic groups, we intend a somewhat broader application here to refer to any group identity to which distinctive cultural traits may be identified by systematic research. Therefore, in this context, ethnology represents work which identifies cultural similarities and differences between identity groups, as well as analysis of cultural phenomena such as cultural distance and culture clash. In our view this work is central to understanding the effect of diversity in organizations.

In applying ethnology to organizational settings and organizational issues, researchers have mainly concentrated on the group identity of nationality. Among the most influential work is that of Hofstede (1980; 1984), Hall (1976; 1982), Laurent (1983), and Tung (1988a; 1988b).

Hofstede's studies of value differences among people of more than forty countries of the world identified four core values which differentiated people of different nationality groups and which he argues hold implications for work behavior in organizations. The values were power distance, uncertainty avoidance, individualism–collectivism and masculinity–femininity.

Using measures adjusted for language and other cultural differences in the countries involved, Hofstede determined that the populations of different nations of the world differ significantly on these four values and that these differences have important implications for application of management theories and concepts in cross-national work groups. A significant amount of empirical research has been done using one or more of these cultural dimensions (e.g. Yu and Murphy 1993; Farh et al. 1991; Davidson 1993; Cox et al. 1991).

Edward T. Hall (1976; 1982) has written extensively about the impact of culture and cultural differences on human behavior. His work is noteworthy for providing concrete examples of how specific, especially nonverbalized, cultural differences can become barriers to communication and understanding between people. For example his concept of action chains helps us to understand how behavioral choices are constrained by rituals and norms which are seldom made explicit. An example is the expectation that the existing members of a community are expected to initiate acquaintanceship with newcomers rather than the other way around. This norm makes it possible for those already in the in-group to exclude newcomers without overtly rejecting them. This insight may be applicable to the often cited problem of unequal accessibility across identity groups to informal networks in organizations.

Other writers have made extensions and applications of Hall's work to the work setting, especially in the areas of marketing research (e.g. Graham 1981; Cote and Tansuhaj 1989), and preferred work styles (e.g. Cox 1993).

André Laurent (1983) is among a growing number of European scholars who have contributed to work on diversity (others include Stamp 1989; De Vries 1992; Essed 1991). Laurent's work has focused on identifying cultural differences in expectations of managers. His research is helpful in identifying specific ways in which cultural misunderstanding can lead to ineffective relationships in organizations especially in dyadic relationships between a supervisor and his/her direct reports. For example, according to his survey data of 1,762 respondents from ten countries, only 13 per cent of United States' workers expect that a manager should have precise answers to questions that subordinates may raise about their work, compared to 59 per cent in France, 67 per cent in Indonesia and 77 per cent in Japan. This suggests that the definition of competence to manage will vary greatly among persons of these different nationalities and that management theories and practices cannot be universalized. Similarly, Tung (1988a; 1988b) found in her study of motivation patterns among Chinese workers that the Chinese are much more tolerant and accepting of rule enforcement. She relates this to the existence of a rigidly planned socialist economy, and notes that Chinese employees (both managers and nonmanagers) are accustomed to receiving very detailed prescriptions of their work roles (Tung 1988a).

It is important to note that in view of high rates of immigration in the United States (and increasing rates in many other parts of the world), and because individuals with roots in micro-culture groups (groups within a particular national culture such as Chinese-Americans) are influenced by cultural norms and values of their root cultures, the work on nationality differences is relevant to domestic workforces in many parts of the world as well as to organizations with multinational operations. In addition, the basic principle behind this research, that differences in culture are central to understanding intergroup dynamics, is applicable to group identities beyond nationality.

Another area of theory and research in ethnology which is highly relevant to work on diversity in organizations is that on acculturation. This work focuses on the processes for resolving cultural differences among members of a nation at the societal level (e.g. Berry 1987; Padilla 1980), between organizations with different cultures (e.g. Nahavandhi and Malekzadeh 1988; Sales and Mirvis 1984), between organizations and their members (e.g. Cox and Finley-Nickelson 1991), and within individuals (e.g. Hazuda et al. 1988; Wong-Reiger and Quintana 1987). By resolving cultural differences 'within individuals' we mean the process by which individuals establish a cultural identity that responds to the differences between norm and value systems of the different cultural groups of which she/he is a part. For example, Cox (1993) reviews nine empirical studies addressing the extent to which members of racioethnic minority groups in the United States identify with their racioethnic group versus the Anglo majority group. This body of work links ethnology to social identity theory, a combination which offers a rich and substantial base of knowledge for understanding the cultural dynamics of diversity in organizations.

In general, ethnology researchers have focused less attention than organizational demographers on specifying the effects of diversity on work processes and outcomes. However it is fair to say that their work is more revealing of the potential difficulties, such as miscommunication, intergroup conflict, loss of effectiveness, and stress, than the potential benefits of cultural diversity. For example Hall (1976) points out that many instances of ineffective management, even among people of the same nationality and working for the same organization, are due to

failure to recognize intercultural differences, and both Hofstede (1984) and Laurent (1983) make the point that ignorance of cultural differences has led to the misapplication of management theories of motivation and leadership.

In summary, the concept of group identity is explicitly addressed in the ethnology literature. Cultural aspects of identity are emphasized and identity is treated as a continuous measure recognizing the intragroup differences in how strongly one identifies with the group. The focus is on self-identification with the group rather than how others define one. The work on ethnology gives greatest attention to the group level of analysis through intergroup comparisons of cultural traditions. However, in the work on acculturation, individual identity structures and the interplay between individual identity and organizational identity as well as inter-organizational cultural differences are beginning to receive attention. Thus, ethnology is making a contribution on all three levels of analysis in organization behavior. Finally, because of the possibility of culture clash, ethnology research suggests that mixing people of different group identities in one social system may lead to a variety of dysfunctional outcomes unless steps are taken to overcome this problem.

Theoretical Models of Diversity

Taken in isolation, none of the research streams reviewed here are sufficiently complex to do justice to the topic of diversity. Several scholars have recently published conceptual models of diversity which specifically combine and translate the information from these older streams of research. We were able to identify three such models. They are those of Cox (1993), Jackson et al. (1995), and Triandis et al. (1994). Each of these will be briefly reviewed next. We chose these models because they each make an attempt to utilize the information from the relevant contributing disciplines, they are comprehensive in scope, acknowledging the complexity of the topic, and they were specifically designed to explicate the impact of diversity in identities for organizational behavior and organizational outcomes.

The interactional model of cultural diversity (IMCD) developed by Cox (1993) holds that differences in group identities among individuals (both physical and cultural identities) interact with a complex set of individual, intergroup, and organizational factors (the diversity climate) to determine the impact of diversity on both individual and organizational outcomes. The individual outcomes which are predicted by the model are divided into affective response variables (satisfaction, organizational identification, and job involvement) and achievement variables (performance, job mobility, and compensation). Organizational outcomes are divided on the basis of the expected directness of impact into first level (e.g. attendance, turnover, and work quality) and second level (e.g. profits). Central to this model is the notion that the presence of diversity in organizations will impact measures of effectiveness at both the individual and the organizational levels, and that the organizational context for diversity is pivotal in determining whether the overall impact of group identity differences on effectiveness will be positive or negative. Other salient features of the model are that it is structured around social psychological phenomena which have clear applicability across many dimensions of group identity (i.e. not only gender and race but nationality, work function, religion, class and so on), and it has application to the experience of both majority and minority group members of organizations. For example, the tendency for unmanaged diversity to lead to heightened intergroup conflict between majority and minority group members will potentially lower the affective outcomes of work for members of both groups.

A second comprehensive theoretical model is that of Triandis et al. (1994). The model (labeled simply 'A theoretical model for the study of diversity') defines and specifies interrelationships among nineteen variables. A full list of the variables and their definitions will not be attempted here. However, some of the major linkages will be specified. Core concepts in the model include perceived similarity, degree of interaction and rewards. The primary outcome variable is positive intergroup attitudes. Following a Skinnerian line of reasoning (Skinner 1981), positive intergroup attitudes are posited to occur when transactions between people of different groups are experienced as rewarding. A sense of obtaining rewards, in turn, will occur when the parties perceive one another as similar, when they have opportunity to have positive contact, when they have a shared sense of goals, and when the society or recognized authorities in the social setting are encouraging of contact. The specifications of the model indicate that all of these factors have independent (main) effects on rewards.

A pivotal concept in the Triandis et al. (1994) framework is perceived similarity. Although this point of emphasis suggests that increasing diversity will tend to hinder work group and organization performance, the authors are careful to point out types of interventions which may avoid this.

The final theoretical model to be discussed here is Jackson et al.'s 'framework for understanding the dynamics of diversity in work teams' (Jackson et al. 1995). The model explicitly names more than thirty variables and some of these have multiple components. In recognition of this complexity, the authors do not attempt to specify the interrelationships among the numerous variables but rather present a collection of relevant concepts organized into a conceptual framework. The three main parts to the framework are aspects of diversity, mediating states and processes, and behavioral manifestations/consequences. All three are analyzed on three levels of analysis – individual, interpersonal and team – and within a broader context of organizational and societal forces. According to their framework, one can analyze 'diversity' as a characteristic: of individuals, of the difference between an individual and his/her work group, and as a characteristic of the work group itself. Also, dimensions of diversity are listed as either task-related (tenure, education, etc.) or relations-oriented (sex, race, etc.). The combination of individual attributes, interpersonal similarity and team composition is posited to affect outcomes like personal performance, power balance and team creativity. However, this relationship is mediated by a multitude of task and relational variables like attention, recall, stage of socialization, and cognitive and affective responses.

In summary, all three of these models have similar architectures in that they are collections of learnings about what is important and not parsimonious theoretical statements which are easily adapted to mathematical equations for testing with linear statistics. Also, as might be expected, there is considerable overlap in the concepts included although the definitions and positioning of the concepts within the frameworks differ considerably. The level of complexity of the models, while appropriate to the phenomena, will likely preclude empirical testing of the full models. Instead, it seems that they are best used as heuristic models which can guide empirical research designed to test various sub-configurations. To facilitate such utilization, Cox (1993) offers more than forty testable theoretical propositions which are derived from the IMCD framework.

REFRAMING DIVERSE IDENTITIES IN ORGANIZATIONS

Having now reviewed some of the theory and research which largely forms the foundation for diversity research, in the last column of Table 1 we offer our suggested treatment of the concept of identity. To advance the theoretical development of diversity in organizations, we must begin with reframing the concept of identity. Specifically, the understanding of diversity identities will be advanced by theoretical perspectives which: (1) explicitly define and measure the group identity of individuals; (2) attend to the cultural, historical, and social meaning of identity; (3) treat identity as a continuous scale measure rather than merely as discrete categories, thereby allowing for members of groups to differ in the extent to which a specific identity is salient for them; (4) address the relevance of the social categorization by others to one's group identity; (5) address affects of identity on multiple levels of analysis (individual, group, organizational, and societal); and (6) address explicitly the effects of diversity without assuming the inevitability of negative consequences. Our alternative framing requires elaboration.

The main implication of this set of prescriptions is that identity should be understood as a complex, multifaceted, and transient construct (Bhavnani and Phoenix 1994). The fact that individuals have multiple identities and not a single identity contributes to the complexity of identity in organizations. Individuals are not just African, European, Korean, white, black, women, men, marketing managers, or operations managers. Identities intersect to create an amalgamated identity. The ways in which identities interact or become salient are important in an organizational context. Thus, the study of one identity necessarily involves attending to its interaction with other identities.

Distinctions should be made, however, between identities based on social categories like race, gender, ethnicity, and class, and identities based on categories like organization function or tenure. Social identity theory may appear to be a general model for examining the consequences of all types of group identities. However, its original empirical grounding in minimal group experiments limits its application to the understanding of group identities based upon socially marked categories like racioethnicity, gender, and class (Henriques 1984; Lloyd 1989; Michael 1990). According to Michael (1990) intergroup theories and social identity theory, in particular, have systematically neglected content, preferring to illuminate the processes or mechanisms underlying intergroup behavior. Consequently, exclusion of content tends to elevate process suggesting that the processes are universal regardless of the basis for identity. However, identity based on organization function or tenure may be donned or shed or lost when an individual exits an organization. When sociohistorical identity categories are equated with less socially marked categories like organization function, the significance of racism, sexism, and other forms of domination in organizations and the broader society is overlooked.

Accordingly, the study of diverse identities in organizations should be situated in their cultural context and the specific content of different social categories should be explicated (Duveen and Lloyd 1986). Specifically, to establish the dialectic between intergroup content and process, there is a need for some theory of the relation that exists between particular groups, and for the sociohistorical circumstances that have given rise to relevant identities. In other words, this means identifying and describing the content of racial identity, gender identity, ethnic identity, cultural identity, etc. versus a generic social identity, or at a minimum to think in terms of the social identity of a particular group (e.g. the social identity of women). There is some research in other disciplines on racial identity (e.g. Helms 1990; Cross 1991; Tinsley 1994); the meaning of race (e.g. Omni and Winant 1986); the meaning of gender (e.g. Acker 1990; Calás and Smircich 1992; Mills and Tancred 1992); the social identity of women (e.g. Skevington and Baker 1989); and homosexual identity (e.g. Cass 1979) which has relevance for research on diverse identities in organizational settings. For example, there is an emerging body of work exploring the meaning of white racial identity and the social construction of whiteness (e.g. Carter et al. 1994; Frankenberg 1993; Helms 1990; Roediger 1991).

At the same time, we must avoid essentialism in our treatment of identity, recognizing its variability. Identity is socially constructed and not innate. It cannot be measured nominally as an objective property of an individual. As Stuart Hall (1992) has emphasized, identity is not stable or fixed but socially and historically constructed and subject to contradictions, revisions, and change. A social construction view emphasizes understanding the processes through which identity distinctions emerge and become salient to individuals and groups in organizations (Wharton 1992).

Identity needs to be understood at four levels of analysis: individual, group/intergroup, organizational, and societal. This is particularly important in order to avoid the tendency for research on diverse identities to imply that the burden of change rests solely on individual members of the organization. And to avoid the assumption that the negative effects of diverse identities are rooted in the faulty cognition processes of individuals. If we confine our analysis to the individual level, then the more systemic intergroup, organizational, and societal dynamics will be left underexplored and consequently the possibility of real organizational change is diminished. Important aspects of identity as a group position can also be overlooked if researchers confine their analysis to the individual level. On the other hand, sole reliance upon group-level analysis fails to recognize there may be individual differences in group identity. Identity is also not homogeneous within social groups. That is, attention must be paid to within-group differences in identities. Many individuals may not share the norms, values, and language of a group despite similarity in a demographic or cultural sense. At the organizational level, attention must be given to the broader contextual factors that affect and shape identity. Societal meanings and constructions of identity and identity formation also permeate organizational boundaries. For example, new legislation, political developments, and demographic changes have all affected how identity is perceived and understood.

Finally, much of the work on diversity in identities has been dominated by the negative effects of differences. There has been a tendency to universalize the conditions for intergroup conflict and to view diversity in identities as a 'problem' that cannot be avoided. This suggests that the negative consequences of categorization are a default condition of human nature and that little can be done to change group phenomena. However, we argue that all potential effects should be understood, and the focus must be on understanding categorization as a discursive practice (see Marshall and Wetherell 1989).

METHODOLOGICAL ISSUES AND DILEMMAS

Dichotomous Thinking

The aforementioned prescriptions give rise to a number of practical methodological issues and dilemmas. Understanding these is important to moving beyond the research paradigms that have dominated organizational research on diversity and identity. For the most part, the research that has grown out of the theories and bodies of literature reviewed in this chapter reflect dichotomous thinking about identity (e.g. black versus white; Anglo versus Latino, male versus female, etc.). Oppositional thinking is problematic for several reasons. Fixed oppositions conceal the extent to which things presented as oppositional are, in fact, interdependent and relational.[3] Hall points out that 'For example, there are differences between the ways in which genders are socially and

psychically constructed. But there is no fixity to those oppositions. It is a relational opposition; *it is a relation of difference*' (1991: 16, emphasis ours). Oppositional thinking implies not only difference but hierarchy where one group is usually superior and the other inferior (Derrida 1976). The dominant group in fact derives its privilege from the curtailment or suppression of its opposite. Martin (1992: 136) further notes that oppositional thinking cannot value diversity in all of its complexity because it cannot account for mixed attributes which may fall between polar opposites.

Related to the above discussion is the whole question of representation. It raises two related issues. First, who is the 'diverse' in organizations? Who indeed is being studied? Current research and theoretical approaches imply traditional employee populations – white, male, Western, heterosexual, middle/upper class, abled – are the norms against which some become 'diverse' or 'others'. Second, to the extent our understanding of 'others' is embedded in notions of a dominant identity, it sets limits on the possibility of the representation of 'others' outside of this knowledge (Calás 1992). Research and theoretical frames are needed that allow scholars to 'notice the diverse under their own representational logic' (1992: 205).

This project is particularly pressing given that much of current rhetoric is framed within the notion of 'managing diversity' as a problem. Underlying the discourse are assumptions like 'minority workers are less likely to have had satisfactory schooling and training. They may have language, attitude, and cultural problems that prevent them from taking advantage of the jobs that will exist' (Johnston and Packer 1987: xxvi) or that it is important to have 'productive diversity and turn it to the advantage of the organisation' (Office of Multicultural Affairs, 1994). By implication such descriptions suggest that unmanaged diversity is unproductive and disadvantageous to organizations. Such constructions can end up serving particular purposes, often maintaining the existing pattern of social relations. Research emphasis should also be placed on examining how organizations produce and reproduce differences between social groups. This requires researchers to understand the social construction of diversity in organizations rather than viewing it as a reflection of natural category differences. In much of the research on diversity in organizations, the legitimacy and basic values of the organization are not in question. Organizations are regarded *a priori* as fundamentally sound and neutral sites. Inevitably, attention must be paid to what sustains and maintains the pattern of power relations in organizations.

The Measurement of Identity

Much of the work on the effects of diversity and heterogeneity in identity (particularly those premised upon intergroup theory) has been done as laboratory studies. More work is needed in field settings. Among the questions needing attention are the following: How do group identities operate in practice? What factors determine the salience given to different group identities? How do people think about their group identities in organizations? How do people make sense of themselves in relation to their jobs and their identity(ies)? How do organizational practices and policies produce and reproduce diverse identities, valuing some and devaluing others? An example of an effort to address the last question can be found in the work of Collinson et al. (1990). In their study of forty-five companies in five industries in the United Kingdom, they show how sex discrimination can be reproduced, rationalized, and resisted by those in positions of both domination and subordination within the recruitment and selection processes (see also Cockburn 1991).

The study of identity is especially difficult because identity does not lend itself to discrete measurement. Quantitative survey methods may fail to capture the complex meaning and construction of identity. Scales can only measure quantity (or strength) of identity, answering the question: how much identification (Condor 1989)? They cannot measure the quality: in what way is identity manifested? To understand the cultural meaning and the variability in the meaning of identity among social groups within organizations, researchers need to expand their methodologies to include ethnographic approaches. In traditional research approaches, categorization of groups is seen as a natural phenomenon rather like breathing (Potter and Wetherell 1987). In more linguistically oriented approaches like ethnomethodology and discourse analysis, the interest is in how categories are constituted in everyday discourse and the various functions they satisfy (Potter and Wetherell 1987). Categorization is regarded as a complex and subtle social accomplishment. Discourse theory and analysis cover the study of all types of written texts and spoken interaction (formal and informal), with particular attention to the functions served by language and the implications of particular linguistic constructions. It asks how categories are flexibly articulated in the course of certain sorts of talk and writing to accomplish particular goals such as exclusions, blamings or justifications (Parker 1992; Potter and Wetherell 1987). Studying the language we use to talk about diversity in identities is so important because, as Parker (1992: xi) points out, 'Language is so structured to mirror power relations that often we can see no other ways of being, and it structures ideology so that it is difficult to speak both in and against it.'

There are ready examples of the application of discourse analysis in the study of identity. Open-ended interviews have been used by some scholars to focus on the content of identity categories and their construction from social experience (e.g. see Condor 1986). Discourse analysis has been used as a way of understanding how gender identity is constituted in discourse (Skevington and Baker 1989; Marshall and Wetherell 1989). The emphasis is upon examining how people talk about a particular identity. In a 1989 article, Marshall and Wetherell examined how a group of women and men students, just embarking on their careers as lawyers, construct their identity and their image of themselves in relation to their gender. They found many inconsistencies and contradictions across their sample of interviewees. Most respondents developed an essentialist model of gender and many also argued that men and women were the same in outlook and abilities. This kind of variability, argued Marshall and Wetherell (1989), is commonplace in natural discourse. Such analyses help capture the fluid and contradictory nature of identity.

Wetherell and Potter (1992) used discourse analysis to map the language of racism in New Zealand. Their case-study of white New Zealanders' accounts of relations with Maori New Zealanders revealed the heterogeneous and layered texture of practices, arguments and representations which make up the taken for granted in a particular society. They concluded that racism is a manifestation of the pattern of uneven power relations in New Zealand and not the result of one ethnic group having irrational delusions in relation to another ethnic group.

Related to the measurement of identity is how to account for intragroup differences. We cannot assume sameness in identity within a group. Not all members of a group may construct or respond to their group identity in the same way. Instead of assuming homogeneity in identity, research designs must explicitly test for within-group differences in identity. The question of how to treat multiple identities remains relatively underexplored. Although scholars have echoed the need to examine the interactions between different social categories, there are few empirical studies which demonstrate how this might be achieved. Measurement is problematic because the interactions are synergistic rather than additive. Additionally, little attention has been paid to the relationship between group identities based on socially marked categories like race and gender and other bases of identity like work style or career. However, Marshall and Wetherell's (1989) study does shed light on the interaction between women's and men's construction of their professional/occupational identity and their gender identity. In their study, the relation between women and occupational identity became problematized, whereas the relation between men and occupational identity became normalized. Women *and* lawyers were portrayed as dissonant, the identity relationship became a site of struggle; but, in contrast, the masculine *and* the law became synonymous, with the masculine personality portrayed as identical with the legal personality. There is some research suggesting members of subordinated groups have a more limited range of acceptable behavior than majority group members. Eagly et al. (1992: 16), in a review of data from sixty-one research studies on gender and leadership concluded that 'men have greater freedom than women to lead in a range of styles without encountering negative reactions.'

Terminology

Finally, a word must be said about the very use of the term 'diversity'.[4] It should be recognized that diversity is a description of the total workforce, not a name for members of minority groups. Additionally, diversity should be distinguished from related concepts such as affirmative action, gender research, and racioethnicity research while at the same time preserving the legitimacy of these areas. Researchers must be careful to make clear how diversity relates to such topics as equal opportunity, discrimination, research on racioethnicity and gender, and affirmative action. Perhaps the greatest difficulty so far has occurred around affirmative action. While affirmative action is within the umbrella of diversity, the two concepts are clearly not equivalent. Those doing work on diversity in organizations are more comprehensive in the types of human group identities addressed, and affirmative action applies specifically to a remedial tool legislated to achieve equal opportunity. Diversity represents a much more expansive concept aimed at understanding the multidimensional structure and effects of differences in organizations. To avoid conflation of diversity with more traditional topics, researchers might use the label of 'diversity research' when addressing multiple dimensions of difference and phenomena which are common across dimensions. For instance, it seems appropriate to label a paper which addresses gender, race,

and nationality as 'diversity research'. On the other hand a paper which examines the decision styles of Latinos and Anglos seems to fall with the domain of 'racioethnicity research' or, at the very least, should be specified as 'racioethnic diversity'.

Conclusion

We have attempted to map the terrain for examining diverse identities in organizations. We reviewed several bodies of literature that have been the dominant bases for research on diversity in organizations. Our review suggests the need to move beyond traditional modes of thinking about the concept of identity which lies at the heart of this research. The breadth of our review reflects the complexity of the topic and the challenges that lie ahead.

Notes

1 There are contradictions in how people use race and ethnicity. For example, African-Americans in the United States are said to be a 'racial group', while Latinos and Asians are sometimes viewed as ethnic groups. Ethnicity has been traditionally used for immigrants who came to the United States from Europe. However, in Britain and some other European countries, immigrants from Africa, the Caribbean, India and Pakistan are often viewed as 'blacks'. Taylor Cox Jr (1990) notes that 'classifications are often inappropriate because they imply a group is either biologically or culturally distinct from another, whereas it generally is both'. He has suggested the use of the term 'racioethnic' to refer to biologically (we personally prefer 'phenotypical' instead of 'biological') and/or culturally distinct groups. Further, scholars of race and ethnic relations often wind up espousing a theory of racial and ethnic relations.'

2 We explicitly use the terms 'white women' and 'racial minorities' to avoid the tendency of writers to refer to 'women and minorities'. The latter terminology does not acknowledge that women have both race and gender. It also omits the category of racial minority women.

3 A quote from Stuart Hall (1991) elegantly captures the relational nature of identity: 'Only when there is an other, can one know their identity'.

4 Much of this discussion is drawn from Taylor Cox Jr (1994) and Stella M. Nkomo (1993). The title of the latter paper, 'Much to do about diversity', is used not to suggest that the topic of diversity is frivolous, but to stress that researchers have much work to do towards understanding diversity in organizations. If this challenge is not met, then perhaps diversity will join the archives of other short-lived management fads.

REFERENCES

Abrams, D. and Hogg, M. (1990) *Social Identity Theory: Constructive and Critical Advances*. New York: Harvester Wheatsheaf.

Acker, J. (1990) 'Hierarchies, jobs, bodies: a theory of gendered organizations', *Gender and Society*, 4: 139–58.

Adler, N. (1986) *International Dimensions of Organizational Behavior*. Boston: P.W.S. Kent.

Alderfer, C.P. (1987) 'An intergroup perspective on group dynamics', in Jay W. Lorsch (ed.), *Handbook of Organizational Behavior*. Englewood Cliffs, NJ: Prentice-Hall. pp. 190–222.

Alderfer, C.P. and Smith, K.K. (1982) 'Studying intergroup relations embedded in organizations', *Administrative Science Quarterly*, 27: 35–65.

Alderfer, C.P., Alderfer, C.J., Tucker, L. and Tucker, R. (1980) 'Diagnosing race relations in management', *Journal of Applied Psychology*, 16: 135–66.

Allport, G. (1954) *The Nature of Prejudice*. New York: Doubleday.

Ancona, D.G. and Caldwell, D.F. (1992) 'Demography and design: predictors of new product team performance', *Organization Science*, 3(3): 321–41.

Antal, A.B. and Izraeli, D. (1993) 'A global comparison of women in management: women managers in their homelands and as expatriates', in Ellen Fagenson (ed.), *Women in Management: Trends, Issues, and Challenges in Managerial Diversity*. Newbury Park, CA: Sage. pp. 52–96.

Ashforth, B.E. and Mael, F. (1989) 'Social identity theory and the organization', *Academy of Management Review*, 14: 20–39.

Bantel, K.A. and Jackson, S.E. (1989) 'Top management and innovations in banking: does the composition of the top team make a difference?', *Strategic Management Journal*, 10: 107–24.

Bartol, K.M., Evans, C.L. and Stith, M. (1978) 'Black versus white leaders: a comparative review of the literature', *Academy of Management Review*, 3: 294–304.

Bell, E. (1990) 'The bi-cultural life experience of career-oriented black women', *Journal of Organizational Behavior*, 11: 459–77.

Berger, J and Zelditch, M. Jr (eds) (1985) *Status, Rewards, and Influence*. San Francisco: Jossey-Bass.

Berry, J.W. (1987) 'Acculturation and psychological adaptation: a conceptual view', in J.W. Berry and W. Annis (eds), *Ethnic Psychology: Research and Practice with Immigrants, Refugees, Native Peoples, Ethnic Groups and Sojourners*. Lisse, Netherlands: Swets and Zeitlinger. Berwin, PA: Swets North American.

Bhavnani, K.K. and Phoenix, A. (eds) (1994) *Shifting Identities; Shifting Racisms: a Feminism and Psychology Reader*. London: Sage.

Blau, Peter (1977) *Inequality and Heterogeneity*. New York: Free Press.

Brenner, O.C. and Tomkiewcz, J. (1982) 'Job orientation of black and white college graduates in business', *Personnel Psychology*, 35: 89–103.

Brewer, M.B. (1995) 'Managing diversity: the role of social identities', in S. Jackson and M. Ruderman (eds), *Diversity in Work Teams: Research Paradigms for a Changing Workplace*. New York: American Psychological Association. pp. 47–68.

Brewer, M.B. and Kramer, R.M. (1985) 'The pyschology of intergroup attitudes and behavior', *Annual Review of Psychology*, 36: 219–43.

Cahoon, A.R. and Rowney, J. (1993) 'Valuing differences: organization and gender', in R.T. Golembiewski (ed.), *Handbook of Organizational Behavior*. New York: Marcel Dekker. pp. 339–54.

Calás, M. (1992) 'An/other silent voice? Representing "Hispanic woman" in organizational texts', in A. Mills and P. Tancred (eds), *Gendering Organizational Analysis*. Newbury Park, CA: Sage. pp. 201–21.

Calás, M. and Smircich, L. (1992) 'Using the "F" word: feminist theories and the social consequences of organizations', in A. Mills and P. Tancred (eds), *Gendering Organizational Analysis*. Newbury Park, CA: Sage. pp. 222–34.

Carter, R.T., Gushue, G.V. and Weitzman, L.M. (1994) 'White racial identity development and work values', *Journal of Vocational Behavior*, 44(2): 185–97.

Cass, V.C. (1979) 'Homosexual identity formation: a theoretical model', *Journal of Homosexuality*, 4(3): 219–35.

Cockburn, Cynthia (1991) *In the Way of Women: Men's Resistance to Sex Equality in Organizations*. Ithaca, NY: ILR Press.

Collins, S. (1989) 'The marginalization of black executives', *Social Problems*, 36(4): 317–31.

Collinson, D.L., Knights, D. and Collinson, M. (1990) *Managing to Discriminate*. London: Routledge.

Condor, S. (1986) 'From sex categories to gender boundaries: reconsidering sex as a stimulus variable in social psychological research', *BPS Social Psychology Section Newsletter*, Spring.

Condor, S. (1989) '"Biting into the future": social change and the social identity of women', in S. Skevington and D. Baker (eds), *The Social Identity of Women*. London: Sage. pp. 15–19.

Cote, J.A. and Tansuhaj, P.S. (1989) 'Culture bound assumptions in behavior intention models', *Advances in Consumer Research*, 16: 105–9.

Cox, T. Jr (1993) *Cultural Diversity in Organizations: Theory, Research, and Practice*. San Francisco: Berrett-Koehler.

Cox, T. Jr (1990) 'Problems with doing research on race and ethnicity', *Journal of Applied Behavioral Science*, 26(1): 5–24.

Cox, T. Jr. (1994) 'A comment on the language of diversity', *Organization*, 1(1): 51–8.

Cox, T. Jr. and Finley-Nickelson, J. (1991) 'Models of acculturation for intraorganizational cultural diversity. *Canadian Journal of Administrative Sciences*, 8(2): 90–100.

Cox, T. Jr and Nkomo, S.M. (1990) 'Invisible men and women: a status report on race as a variable in organizational behavior and research', *Journal of Organizational Behavior*, 11: 419–31.

Cox T.H. and Nkomo, S.M. (1991) 'A race and gender group analysis of the early career experience of MBAs', *Work and Occupations*, 18(4): 431–46.

Cox, T. Jr, Lobel, S. and P. McLeod (1991) 'Effects of ethnic group cultural differences on cooperative and competitive behavior of a task group', *Academy of Management Journal*, 34(4): 827–47.

Cross, E.Y., Katz, J.H., Miller, F. and Seashore, E.W. (1994) *The Promise of Diversity*. Burr Ridge, IL: Irwin.

Cross, W.E. (1991) *Shades of Black: Diversity in African-American Identity*. Philadelphia: Temple University Press.

Davidson, M.N. (1993) 'The effect of racioethnicity on beliefs about coping with interpersonal conflict: a comparison of African-American and European Americans'. Working paper 298, Amos Tuck School of Business, Darmouth College.

Derrida, J. (1976) *Speech and Phenomenon*. Evanston IL: Northwestern University Press.

De Vries, S. (1992) *Working in Multi-Ethnic Groups: The Performance and Well Being of Minority and Majority Workers*. Amsterdam: Gouda Quint bu-Arnhem.

Duveen, G. and Lloyd, B. (1986) 'The significance of social identities', *British Journal of Social Psychology*, 25: 219–30.

Eagly, A.H. and Johnson, B.T. (1990) 'Gender and social influence: a social psychological analysis', *American Psychologist*, 38(9): 971–81.

Eagly, A.H., Makhijani, M.G. and Klonsky, B.G. (1992) 'Gender and the evaluation of leaders: a meta-analysis', *Psychological Bulletin*, 111(1): 3–22.

Essed, P. (1991) *Understanding Everyday Racism: an Interdisciplinary Theory*. Newbury Park, CA: Sage.

Farh, J.L., Dobbins, G.H. and Cheng, B. (1991) 'Cultural relativity in action: a comparison of self-ratings made by Chinese and U.S. workers', *Personnel Psychology*, 44: 129–47.

Ferdman, B. (1992) 'The dynamics of ethnic diversity in organizations: toward integrative models', in K. Kelley (ed.), *Issues, Theory and Research in Industrial/Organizational Psychology*. Amsterdam: North Holland. pp. 339–84.

Fernandez, John (1981) *Racism and Sexism in Corporate Life*. Lexington, MA: Lexington Books.

Frankenberg, R. (1993) *White Women, Race Matters: the Social Construction of Whiteness*. Minneapolis: University of Minnesota Press.

Freedman, S.M. and Phillips, J.S. (1988) 'The changing nature of research on women at work', *Journal of Management*, 14(2): 251.

Fullerton, H.N. (1991) 'Labor force projections: the

baby boom moves on', *Monthly Labor Review*, 114(11): 31–44.

Graham, R.J. (1981) 'The role of perception of time in consumer behavior', *Journal of Consumer Research*, 7(March): 335–42.

Greenhaus, J., Parasuraman, S. and Wormley, W. (1990) 'Effects of race on organizational experiences, job performance evaluation, and career outcomes', *Academy of Management Journal*, 33: 64–86.

Hall, E.T. (1976) *Beyond Culture*. New York: Doubleday.

Hall, E.T. (1982) *The Hidden Dimension*. New York: Doubleday.

Hall, M. (1989) 'Private experiences in public domains: lesbians in organizations', in A. Mills and P. Tancred (eds), *Gendering Organizational Analysis*. Newbury Park, CA: Sage. pp. 125–38.

Hall, S. (1991) 'Ethnicity: identity and difference', *Radical America*, 23(4): 9–20.

Hall, S. (1992) 'The question of cultural identity', in S. Hall, D. Held and T. McGrew (eds), *Modernity and its Futures*. Cambridge: Polity. pp. 273–316.

Harris, C. (1994) 'Acknowledging lesbians in the workplace: confronting the heterosexuality of organizations'. Paper presented at the 1994 Academy of Management Meeting, Dallas.

Hazuda, H., Stern, M. and Haffner, S.M. (1988) 'Acculturation and assimilation among Mexican-Americans: scales and population-based data', *Social Science Quarterly*, 69(3): 687–706.

Helms, J.E. (ed.) (1990) *Black and White Racial Identity*. New York: Greenwood Press.

Henriques, J. (1984) 'Social psychology and the politics of racism', in J. Henriques, W. Hollway, C. Urwin, C. Venn and V. Walkerdine (eds), *Changing the Subject: Psychology, Social Regulation and Subjectivity*. London: Methuen. pp. 60–90.

Hewstone, M. and Brown, R. (eds) (1986) *Contact and Conflict in Intergroup Encounters*. Oxford, New York: Basil Blackwell.

Hofstede, G. (1980) 'Motivation, leadership and organization: do American theories apply abroad?', *Organizational Dynamics*, 9 (Summer): 43–62.

Hofstede, G. (1984) 'The cultural relativity of the quality of life concept', *Academy of Management Review*, 9: 389–98.

Ibarra, H. (1993) 'Personal networks of women and minorities in management: a conceptual framework', *Academy of Management Review*, 18(1): 56–87.

Iles, P., Keynes, M. and Auluck, R. (1991) 'The experience of black workers', in M. Davidson and J. Earnshaw (eds), *Vulnerable Workers: Psychosocial and Legal Issues*. London: Wiley.

Jackson, S.E. (1981) 'Measurement of commitment to role identities', *Journal of Personality and Social Psychology*, 40: 138–46.

Jackson, S.E. and associates (1992) *Diversity in the*

Workplace: Human Resource Initiatives. New York: Guilford Press.

Jackson, S.E., Brett, J.F., Sessa, V.I., Cooper, D.M., Julin, J.A. and Peyronnin, K. (1991) 'Some differences do make a difference: individual dissimilarity and group homogeneity as correlates of recruitment, promotion, and turnover', *Journal of Applied Psychology*, 75(5): 675–89.

Jackson, S.E., Stone, V. and Alvarez, E.B. (1993) 'Socialization amidst diversity: the impact of demographics on work team oldtimers and newcomers', in L.L. Cummings and B. Staw (eds), *Research in Organizational Behavior*, vol. 15. Greenwich, CT: JAI Press.

Jackson, S.E., May, K. and Whitney, K. (1995) 'Diversity in decision-making teams', in R.A. Guzzo and E. Salas (eds), *Team Decision Making Effectiveness in Organizations*. San Francisco: Jossey-Bass. pp. 204–61.

Jamieson, D. and O'Mara, J. (1991) *Managing Workforce 2000*. San Francisco: Jossey-Bass.

Johnston, W. (1991) 'Global workforce 2000: the new world labor market', *Harvard Business Review*, 69: 115–27.

Johnston, W. and Packer, A. (1987) *Workforce 2000: Work and Workers for the 21st Century*. Indianapolis: Hudson Institute.

Kanter, R.M. (1977) 'Some effects of proportions on group life: skewed sex ratios and responses to token women', *American Journal of Sociology*, 82: 965–91.

Knouse, S.B., Rosenfeld, P. and Culbertson, A.L. (eds) (1992) *Hispanics in the Workplace*. Newbury Park, CA: Sage.

Kraiger, K. and Ford, J. (1985) 'A meta-analysis of ratee race effects in performance ratings', *Journal of Applied Psychology*, 70: 56–65.

Kramer, R. (1991) 'Intergroup relations and organizational dilemmas: the role of categorization processes', in L.L. Cummings and B.M. Staw (eds), *Research in Organizational Behavior*, vol. 13. Greenwich, CT: JAI Press. pp. 191–228.

Laurent, A. (1983) 'The cultural diversity of western conceptions of management', *International Studies of Mananagement and Organization*, 13(1–2): 75–96.

Lloyd, Barbara (1989) 'Foreword', in Suzanna Skevington and Deborah Baker (eds), *The Social Identity of Women*. London: Sage. pp. vii–x.

Loden, M. and Rosener, J. (1991) *Workforce America*. Homewood, IL: Business One Irwin.

Marshall, H. and Wetherell, M. (1989) 'Talking about career and gender identities: A discourse analysis perspective', in S. Skevington and D. Baker (eds), *The Social Identity of Women*. London: Sage. pp. 106–29.

Martin, J. (1992) *Culture in Organizations: Three Perspectives*. New York: Oxford University Press.

McClelland, D.A. (1974) 'Effects of interviewer–respondent race interactions on household interview measures of motivation and intelligence', *Journal of Personality and Social Psychology*, 29: 392–7.

McGuire, W.J., McGuire, C.V., Child, P. and Fujioka, T. (1978) 'Salience of ethnicity in the spontaneous self-concept as a function of one's ethnic distinctiveness in the social environment', *Journal of Personality and Social Psychology*, 36(5): 511–20.

Messick, D.M. and Mackie, D.M. (1989) 'Intergroup relations', *Annual Review of Psychology*, 40: 45–81.

Michael, M. (1990) 'Intergroup theory and deconstruction', in Ian Parker and John Shotter (eds), *Deconstructing Social Psychology*. London: Routledge.

Mills, Albert J. and Tancred, Peta (eds) (1992) *Gendering Organizational Analysis*. Newbury Park, CA: Sage.

Morrison, A.M. (1992) *The New Leaders: Guidelines on Leadership Diversity in America*. San Francisco: Jossey-Bass.

Morrison, A.M., White, R.P., Van Velsor, E. and the Center for Creative Leadership (1987) *Can Women Reach the Top of America's Largest Corporations?* Reading, MA: Addison-Wesley.

Munyard, T. (1988) 'Homophobia at work and how to manage it', *Personnel Management*, June: 46–50.

Myrdal, G. (1944) *An American Dilemma*. New York: Harper & Row.

Nahavandi, A. and Malekzadeh, A. (1988) 'Acculturation in mergers and acquisitions', *Academy of Management Review*, 13(1): 79–90.

Nkomo, S.M. (1992) 'The emperor has no clothes: rewriting "race" in the study of organizations', *Academy of Management Review*, 17(3): 487–513.

Nkomo, S.M. (1993) 'Much to do about diversity'. Paper presented at the Society for Industrial Psychology Conference, San Francisco.

Nkomo, S.M. and Cox, T. Jr (1989) 'Gender differences in the upward mobility of black managers: double whammy or double advantage', *Sex Roles*, 21: 825–39.

Okamura, J.Y. (1981) 'Situational ethnicity', *Ethnic and Racial Studies*, 4(4): 452–65.

Omni, M. and Winant, H. (1986) *Racial Formation in the United States: from the 1960s to the 1980s*. New York: Routledge and Kegan Paul.

O'Reilly, C.A. and Roberts, K.M. (1973) 'Job satisfaction among whites and nonwhites: a cross-cultural approach', *Journal of Applied Psychology*, 57: 295–9.

Padilla, A.M. (1980) *Acculturation: Theory, Models, and Some New Findings*. Boulder, CO: Westview.

Park, R.E. (1950) *Race and Culture*. Glencoe, IL: Free Press.

Parker, I. (1992) *Discourse Dynamics*. London: Routledge.

Pettigrew, T.F. and Martin, J. (1987) 'Shaping the organizational context for black American inclusion', *Journal of Social Issues*, 43(1): 41–78.

Pfeffer, J. (1983) 'Organizational demography', in L.L. Cummings and B. Staw (eds), *Research in Organiz-*

ational Behavior, vol. 5. Greenwich, CT: JAI Press. pp. 299–357.

Potter, J. and M. Wetherell (1987) Discourse and Social Psychology: Beyond Attitudes and Behavior. London: Sage.

Powell, G. (1990) 'One more time: do female and male managers differ?', The Academy of Management Executive, 4: 68–75.

Rabbie, J.M. and Horwitz, M. (1988) 'Categories versus groups as explanatory concepts in intergroup relations', Journal of Social Psychology, 18: 117–23.

Raggins, B.R. and Cotton, J.L. (1991) 'Easier said than done: gender differences in perceived barriers to gaining a mentor', Academy of Management Journal, 34(4): 939–51.

Ridgeway, C. (1991) 'The social construction of status value: gender and other nominal characteristics', Social Forces, 70(2): 367–86.

Roediger, D. (1991) The Wages of Whiteness: Race and the Making of the American Working Class. London: Verso.

Rosener, J.B. (1990) 'Ways women lead', Harvard Business Review, November–December: 119–25.

Sales, A.L. and Mirvis, P.H. (1984) 'When cultures collide: issues of acquisition', in J.R. Kimberly and R.E. Quinn (eds), Managing Organizational Transition. Homewood, IL: Irwin. pp. 107–33.

Sherif, M. and Sherif, C. (1953) Groups in Harmony and Tension. New York: Harper & Row.

Sivanandan, A. (1985) 'RAT and the degradation of black struggle', Race and Class, 26: 1–34.

Skevington, S. and Baker, D. (eds) (1989) The Social Identity of Women. London: Sage.

Skinner, B.F. (1981) 'Selection by consequences', Science, 213: 501–4.

Skvoretz, J. (1983) 'Salience, heterogeneity and consolidation of parameters: civilizing Blau's primitive theory', American Sociological Review, 48: 360–75.

Stamp, G. (1989) 'Tokens and glass ceilings: the real issues of "minorities" in organisations', International Journal of Career Management, 1(2): 1–9.

Stayman, M.H. and Deshpande, R. (1989) 'Situational ethnicity and consumer behavior', Journal of Consumer Research, 16: 361–71.

Stone, E.F., Stone, D.L. and Dipboye, R.L. (1992) 'Stigmas in organizations: race, handicaps, and physical attractiveness', in E. Kelley (ed.), Issues, Theory and Research in Industrial/Organizational Psychology. Amsterdam: North Holland.

Stroh, L.K., Brett, J.M. and Reilly, A.H. (1992) 'All the right stuff: a comparison of female and male managers' careers' progression', Journal of Applied Psychology, 77: 251–60.

Tajfel, H. (1972) 'Social categorization', English version of 'La catégorisation sociale', in S. Moscovici (ed.), Introduction à la psychologie sociale, vol. I. Paris: Larousse.

Tajfel, H. (ed.) (1982) Social Identity and Intergroup Relations. Cambridge: Cambridge University Press.

Tajfel, H. and Turner, J.C. (1979) 'An integrative theory of intergroup conflict', in W.G. Austin and S. Worchel (eds), The Social Psychology of Intergroup Relations. Monterey, CA: Brooks/Cole.

Taylor, D.M. and Moghaddam, M. (eds) (1987) Theories of Intergroup Relations: International Social Psychological Perspectives. New York: Praeger.

Thomas, D.A. (1990) 'The impact of race on managers' experiences of developmental relationships: an intraorganizational study', Journal of Organizational Behavior, 11(6): 479–92.

Thomas, R.R. Jr (1991) Beyond Race and Gender: Unleashing the Power of your Total Work Force by Managing Diversity. New York: AMACOM.

Tinsley, E.A. (1994) 'Racial identity and vocational behavior', Journal of Vocational Behavior, 44(2): 115–17.

Triandis, H.C., Hall, E.R. and Ewen, R.B. (1965) 'Member heterogeneity and dyadic creativity', Human Relations, 18: 33–55.

Triandis, H.C., Kurowski, L.L. and Gelfand, M.J. (1994) 'Workplace diversity', in H.C. Triandis, M.D. Dunnette and L.M. Hough (eds), Handbook of Industrial and Organizational Psychology. Palo Alto, CA: Consulting Psychologists Press.

Tsui, A.S. and O'Reilly, C.A. (1989) 'Beyond simple demographic effects: the importance of relational demography in superior–subordinate dyads', Academy of Management Journal, 32: 402–23.

Tsui, A.S., Egan, T.D. and O'Reilly, C. (1992) 'Being different: relational demography and organizational attachment', Administrative Science Quarterly, 37: 549–79.

Tsui, A.S., Egan, T. and Xin, K. (1995) 'Diversity in organizations: lessons from demography research', in M. Chemers, S. Oskamp and M. Costanzo (eds), Diversity in the Workplace. Thousand Oaks, CA: Sage. pp. 37–61.

Tung, R.L. (1988a) 'People's Republic of China', in R. Nath (ed.), Comparative Management: A Regional View. Cambridge, MA: Ballinger. pp. 139–68.

Tung, R.L. (1988b) 'Toward a conceptual paradigm of international business negotiations', Advances in International Comparative Management, 3: 203–19.

Turner, J.C. (1975) 'Social comparison and social identity: some prospects for intergroup behaviour', European Journal of Social Psychology, 5: 5–34.

Turner, J.C. (1982) 'Towards a cognitive redefinition of social group', in H. Tajfel (ed.), Social Identity and Intergroup Relations. New York: Cambridge University Press.

Watson, E.E., Kumar, K. and Michaelson, L.K. (1993) 'Cultural diversity's impact on interaction processes and performance: comparing homogeneous and diverse task groups', Academy of Management Journal, 36: 590–602.

Weaver, C.N. (1978) 'Black–white correlates of job satisfaction', *Journal of Applied Psychology*, 63: 255–8.

Wetherell, M. and Potter, J. (1992) *Mapping the Language of Racism: Discourse and the Legitimation of Exploitation*. New York: Columbia University Press.

Wharton, A.S. (1992) 'The social construction of gender and race in organizations: a social identity and group mobilization perspective', *Research in the Sociology of Organizations*, 10: 55–84.

Wharton, A.S. and Baron, J.N. (1987) 'So happy together? The impact of gender segregation on men at work', *American Sociological Review*, 52(5): 574–87.

Wong-Reiger, D. and Quintana, D. (1987) 'Comparative acculturation of Southeast Asian and Hispanic immigrants and sojourners', *Journal of Cross-Cultural Psychology*, 18(3): 345–62.

Woods, J.D. (1993) *The Corporate Closet: The Professional Lives of Gay Men in America*. New York: Free Press.

Yancey, W.L., Ericksen, E.P. and Juliani, R.N. (1976) 'Emergent ethnicity: a review and reformulation', *American Sociological Review*, 41: 391–403.

Yu, J. and Murphy, K.R. (1993) 'Modesty bias in self-ratings of performance: a test of the cultural relativity hypothesis', *Personnel Psychology*, 46: 357–63.

2.6

Putting Group Information Technology in its Place: Communication and Good Work Group Performance

ARTHUR D. SHULMAN

This chapter examines the relationships between good work group performance and information technologies in the light of current work group theory and research. I focus on information technologies for two reasons: firstly, their roles in effecting group performance are claimed to be of increasing importance, yet they are little understood; and secondly, by focusing on the question of what are the relationships between good work group performance and information technology, it becomes apparent that the answers rely on our underlying assumptions about communication within the organizations in which these work groups are partially embedded. By reflecting upon these assumptions, a more informed view of work group performance emerges.

My approach builds upon prior arguments that focused on the interface of information technology systems with human systems at the individual level by Shulman et al. (1990) and at the organizational level by Orlikowski (1992), but does it with regard to recent work group theory and communication theory. In common with these past reviews, I take the position that how researchers conceptualize the interface between technology and the work groups that use them has major implications for our understandings. The chapter argues that these implications are related to a misunderstanding not so much of group performance or of technology, but of the differences between information and communication. It is through the human communication infrastructure that

we negotiate the meanings of the technological infrastructure. These negotiations are not neutral but morally based. It is within these moral frames that our understandings of good work group performance can be advanced. This argument is philosophically constructionist in the sense of reducing indeterminacy of possible meanings and directions and in the constitutive sense of creating possibilities (Philp 1985).

The examination is presented in four sections. In the first section, I consolidate the major themes that consistently occur in reviews of work group theory and research. In the second section, these themes are used as a background for examining research efforts that have attempted to address the relationships between work group performance and information technologies. The third section addresses the assumptions about communication processes that underlie these research programs. The last section focuses on future pathways.

MAJOR THEMES IN WORK GROUP PERFORMANCE RESEARCH

Since the late 1980s there has been an upsurge of reviews of work group research. These reviews include Ancona and Caldwell (1988), Campion et al. (1993), Guzzo and Dickson (1996), Guzzo and Shea (1992), Hackman (1986; 1987), Levine and Moreland (1990) and Sundstrom et al. (1990).

With regard to work group performance, all the reviews have at least the following seven explicit themes in common.

Reviewers Recognize that Good Work Group Performance is Important, but Assume that What is Good Performance is Self-Evident

The first theme is that understanding what fosters good work group performance is of increasing importance to organizations, at least within the industrialized countries where work groups or work teams are increasingly being used. (Consistent with the above reviews, I combine the terms 'work groups' and 'work teams' – because they are often used interchangeably.) For instance, one often quoted survey suggests that 47 per cent of the *Fortune* 1000 firms are using self-managing work teams with at least some employers and that they have been increasingly doing so for some time (Lawler et al. 1992). Rationales for this growth range from it being a response to increased pressures and complexities that can no longer be adequately handled by individuals, to a form of organizational structuring that fosters empowered and motivated workers at a time when changes such as automation and downsizing are also occurring. However, the reviews also point out that forming and using work groups do not always lead to better performance; it depends upon the coexistence of an enabling context, group design, and resource factors. At the same time these reviews give scant attention to the more fundamental issue of what are the standards for good work group performance. Hackman's proposition that a good outcome of the interaction of enabling conditions would be 'full exploitation of favourable performance conditions' (1987: 332), and Guzzo and Shea's adoption of the socio-technical school's definition of good performance as 'the joint optimization of social and task goals' (1992: 279), are examples of the current understandings of what is good performance. But how are groups to know when such optimization has occurred? They probably don't. What groups often have access to are judgments from their constituents as to whether the group outputs are adequate. The importance of managing this access with external constituents is highlighted in such studies as Ancona and Caldwell (1990) and reviews by Sundstrom et al. (1990). However, throughout the literature, it is almost as if there is a shared understanding of what is good performance.

There is a Lack of Consistency of Findings across Studies of Work Group Performance

Results across studies are inconsistent. The field 'though quite vigorous, is badly fragmented' (Levine and Moreland 1990: 586). The reviewers claim that this has occurred because work group behaviors are complex, dynamic and context dependent. The inconsistencies also are associated with how and what researchers attend to. These inconsistencies are summarized in the next five themes.

Work Groups are Multi-Functional Open Systems, but are Often Defined by Researchers as Single Purpose and Closed

There is a lack of consistency across research in what is a work group or work team. How researchers construe work groups is quite variable, reflecting what they choose to study. These vary from normative definitions such as

a team is a small number of people with complementary skills who are committed to a common purpose, set of performance goals, and approach for which they hold themselves mutually accountable. (Katzenbach and Smith 1993: 112)

to more descriptive definitions such as

Groups are assumed to be complex, intact social systems that engage in multiple, interdependent functions [production, member support, and group well being] on multiple concurrent projects, while partially nested within and loosely coupled to surrounding systems. (McGrath 1991: 151)

McGrath's definition provides further insight into the lack of consistency of findings across work group performance studies. For McGrath, groups are engaged in a messy array of projects, tasks and steps operating simultaneously. And as McGrath (1990: 28), points out, a group is playing several games at once, with different agendas for different audiences and different functions. These functions include: to support its members; to maximize its well-being; and to contribute to the organization it is embedded in. With regard to the last, there is a distinct shift to emphasize the difference between outputs and outcomes. Good group performance requires that the outputs are acceptable to those who receive or review them. These three functions are highlighted to different degrees in the above reviews. In comparison to McGrath (1991) and Hackman (1987), most investigators have assumed that groups are engaged in (almost) independent functions with group members being solely engaged in a single project with a single agenda. The lack of consistency across studies may be because different investigators are choosing to focus on different functions, at different levels, at different times, and to be more output oriented than outcome oriented. An implication of this is that if researchers were able and willing to specify a more complex 'contingency' model of context, that presumably matches the underlying complexity of work groups, then progress in understanding work group performance would occur. Hackman (1987), however, suggests that more complex models are not likely to be useful if they are deterministic. Groups are messy because they are open systems that possess human agency – a human quality that, by definition, cannot be completely predicted. Because of this quality, reviewers such as Hackman (1987) are recognizing that studies which employ deterministic methodologies based on logical positivism are likely to have limited value in advancing our understandings of ways of improving work group practices.

Work Group Performances are Dependent upon Social and Organizational Contexts

What is meant by context differs from study to study, hence, overall generalizations are problematic. Recognizing that work groups operate within layers of socially constructed aggregates of organizations and communities, researchers are now attempting to develop understandings of the ways in which sets of actions within meetings are related to activities that are associated with the completion of projects (see Hackman 1987 and McGrath 1991 for an expansion of this theme).

An important implication of this is that much of the past research on groups that has focused on single meetings, and/or studies that failed to address the group's contribution and costs to its embedding system, may have added little to our understanding of how work groups go about achieving their objectives. All reviews point out the implication of this for the researcher's choice of methods. Groups in organizations are not like the *ad hoc* aggregates of individuals brought together in a laboratory for the occasion of research. As pointed out by McGrath (1991), group members have a history together, and they expect to have futures, but their memberships change from one occasion to another. If we want to understand work group performance we are going to have to use non-laboratory methods and build in ways of examining the group's contribution and costs to its embedding system.

Temporal Contexts Shape Work Group Performance

All reviews except one have emphasized that what work groups do, and how they do it, changes over time. (The one review where temporal context is not an explicit theme is Campion et al. 1993, who do address change over time in a follow-up study: see Campion and McClelland 1993.) Such changes over time appear to be related to the task requirements and the time constraints under which groups operate. An illustrative study of this is Gersick's (1988) study of eight groups, each of which had a single mission and a predetermined life span, throughout their life course. The eight project groups varied in lifespan from a few days to fourteen weeks, but each had, from its beginning, a definite time deadline and an expected product. She provides evidence that every one of the groups made a major shift in what they did and how they did it at a point almost halfway through its lifespan. Regardless of the progress a given group made during the first half of the group life, each group had a more or less dramatic meeting at about the midpoint of its projected life, and as a consequence changed the course and pattern of its activity. After this mid-life crisis, each group moved in a fairly direct way to complete their task. This study, perhaps more than others, has led group researchers such as Hackman (1987; 1990) and McGrath (1991) to further question and explore developmental and time-based theories of functional groups. However, as classification schemes for organizational contexts, tasks and time constraints are often not comparable across studies, further generalizations are problematic. This is amply demonstrated in studies such as Ginnett (1990), which reports where a new work group (in her case a flight crew) become effective immediately, largely due to organizational context. But most reviewers do acknowledge that what a group does has a beginning, an execution and an end stage. Depending upon the group studies, these stages are sometimes interspersed with stages that focus on technical issues and other stages that focus on political choices. There are also acknowledgements that these temporal sequencings are somehow related to the development of perceived capacity of the group to work together in the future (see, in particular, Levine and Moreland 1990).

Other insights into non-linear processes can be gleaned from research which focuses on bad work group practices which can lead to escalation of commitment to an inappropriate course of action. In the most relevant work of Ross and Staw (1986; 1993) the investigators describe an array of forces (project, organizational, social, psychological) that interact dynamically to lead to escalation problems. Ross and Staw (1986) used a case analysis of the top team managing Expo 86 to lay out the temporal unfolding of the determinants of escalation of commitment to paths which subsequently were judged as too costly. Their major thesis is that project variables (e.g. cost/benefit analyses) are most important at early stages of the escalation episode. Psychological variables (e.g. individual motivations and biases) and social variables (e.g. cultural norms favoring consistent, strong leadership) are dominant at the middle stages, while both project variables and organizational variables (e.g. level of political support, or showcasing of a project as a symbol of the firm's values) become most important at the late or ending stage of the typical escalation episode. Recognizing the weaknesses of their data, and the *post hoc* interpretation of these data, Ross and Staw (1993) engaged in another case study to provide an *a priori* test of their temporal model of escalation and to extend the model to account for the exit of organizations from escalation. The case they selected was the building of the Shoreham nuclear power plant on Long Island, New York. This plant eventually incurred expenditures of over US$5.5 billion before it was abandoned in 1989. Like the Expo 86 case, it involved large expenditures of resources for construction. Using a mixture of archival material and interviews with top team members, they were able to test whether their hypothesized sets of determinants were present before, and during, the escalation of commitment, and if these sets of determinants were indeed ordered as predicted. An iterative theory–data checking approach was used to extend their model to capture some of the determinants of exiting from escalation. In general, their analyses confirmed their temporal model. However unpredictively, organizational determinants appeared as an early influence of escalating commitment. That is, nuclear power became an important part of the firm's long term strategy at a relatively early phase. Moreover, they found that a fifth set of determinants, which they labeled contextual forces – which included the role of government and alliances with other utilities – seemed to account for much of the continuing escalation. An important implication of all of these longitudinal studies is that much of the past research, which has assumed that group processes are linear or consist of a fixed sequence of phases, may have added little to our understanding of how work groups go about achieving their objectives. These studies concerned with temporal context also reinforce the previous theme that studies which failed to address the group's contribution and costs to its embedding system may have added little to our understanding of how work groups go about achieving their objectives and how they may do it better.

Groups Derive their Competitive Advantage from Better Sharing and Coordination

'Sharing' is a key to good work group performance. The authors all stress the importance of shared norms, with differential emphasis on shared visions, shared meanings, a sense of shared responsibility for group outcomes and coordination amongst group members. Though what they emphasize differs, they state that these sharings can be facilitated by 'shared' experiences, with a canvassing of options that lead to a shared understanding amongst group members of the ways each will need to behave. However, these reviewers also acknowledge that sharing of ideas is not always productive. For instance the sharing of low productivity norms can lead to poor performance, and too much sharing of views can lead to premature closure and group think. That is, well performing groups are proposed to manage their communication so that a canvassing of views is encouraged as well as sharing a view for going forward. The questioning of whether there is a universal temporal ordering of seeking diversity versus sharing of views was raised under the preceding theme.

Sharing is also presented as a means of facilitating the coordination of actions. Along this line, most of the reviewers point to McGrath's (1984; 1991) work in which problem solving and conflict resolution are hypothesized to occur through the coordination, synchronization (or 'entertainment') of behaviors. The exception is Campion and McClelland (1993: 830) who do not mention coordination. Instead they point out that the related concepts of cooperation/communication (which Beer et al. 1990; Smith et al. 1995 have proposed as prerequisites of coordination) have not been extensively field tested.

Unfortunately, though some studies (for example Fulk 1993) operationalize sharing of views in terms of statistical analysis of central tendencies of five-point rating scales, none of the studies reviewed question the basic assumption of whether the sharing of views is possible. This is an assumption which I will question seriously in the third section of this chapter.

Group Performances are not due Solely to the Group Processes that its Members Jointly Engage in

Many studies are now focusing on antecedent factors which directly impact upon performance and/or act in combination with group processes to affect performance. The vast majority of these follow a contingency hypothesis in which performance is seen as contingent on the match between the 'requisite variety' of characteristics of group members and task demands. Such member characteristics include the homogeneity of values, experience and skills that members have, or that others assume they possess. The models taking these alternative paths to group effectiveness are summarized in Guzzo and Dickson (1996), Guzzo and Shea (1992) and Hackman (1987). While studies are now showing that homogeneity of values and skills is related to various performances of top management teams (for instance, Daboub et al.'s 1995 examination of top management team characteristics and corporate illegal activity), an assumption underlying most of these studies is that these demographic combinations affect performance by first changing the engagement processes employed by the teams. Unfortunately there are few studies that have employed methodologies that allow an examination of the validity of this assumption. That is, they use archival records of top team makeup and then correlate differences in the degree of homogeneity across team members with differences of organizational performance. One implication of these models and studies of work group performance is that non-process factors can affect performance; however how such antecedent factors lead to the choice of paths members use in engaging in group tasks and projects is unknown.

In summary, these seven themes suggest that research has yet to address the fundamental issue of what constitutes good work group performance, except it requires that the outputs are acceptable to those who receive or review them. There is consensus that work group performance is dependent upon social, organizational and temporal contexts, though there is a lack of agreement on specific contexts. Furthermore, researchers are increasingly viewing work groups as open systems, that operate episodically, within multiple levels addressing multiple functions. There is also a growing consensus on the methodological implications of these understandings of work group performance: work group performance cannot be understood from studies of single meetings, or from studies which do not focus on the nexus between the work group and the organization in which it is embedded. There are also paradoxical implications for improving group performance: leaders of work groups need to encourage diversity of possible ways of achieving objectives, and at the same time foster 'shared' views on how to proceed. Changing the available mix of non-process skill bases can be used to influence group performance. These thematic generalizations form the basis for examining the impacts of electronic information technologies on work group performance.

IMPACTS OF ELECTRONIC INFORMATION TECHNOLOGIES ON WORK GROUP PERFORMANCE

With few exceptions, the above reviews do not link work group performance with the use of electronic information technologies. Levine and Moreland (1990: 588) briefly review this area and conclude that there is little evidence that electronic communication improves productivity. The review by Guzzo and Shea suggests (in passing) that one of the topics that will appear as a center of attention in the future is the capacity of group computerization and software to change 'how information is communicated, stored and combined in the service of effective decision making' (1992: 307). Likewise, Guzzo and Dickson call (in passing) for future research to focus on 'team effectiveness under different ways of utilizing available technologies' (1996: 333). This theme about the potential impacts of electronic information technologies on work group performance is not mentioned in any of the other above reviews. The absence or relegation of technology to a minor category has recently been commented on by Polley and Van Dyne (1994) in their review of the limits and liabilities of self-managing work teams. They point out that given the central position that technology has in job design models (Hackman and Oldham 1980) and socio-technological systems models of work groups (Emery and Trist 1965), it is surprising that the impact of technologies on team performance has received relatively little attention. Their interpretation of this is that many of the followers of these models appear to concentrate on motivation, training and leadership with 'the assumption that work reorganization and change in technology will be considered by the work team after the team has been given training and autonomy' (Polley and Van Dyne 1994: 5).

While these recent reviews of work group performance do not place emphasis on the role of information technology at the work group

362 HANDBOOK OF ORGANIZATION STUDIES

level, there are models and studies of work groups that do. This section focuses on these studies. I limit this review to studies that concentrate on the nexus of work group performance with information technologies that are commonly called interactive, whether asynchronous as computer networking, or synchronous as teleconferencing, video conferencing, mobile telephone, etc. I also include hardware, software, and the programmed procedures as components of these technologies.

This review is also limited because most researchers who focus on the nexus have not addressed the major themes that emerged in the previous section. That is, they have tended to study a single meeting of a group without any attention to its social, organizational and temporal contexts, and without attention to multiple functions, and without attention to how changes in process are related to group performance. Furthermore, the researchers who do focus on the impact of information technologies on group performance also tend to focus on prototypes of a new technology and not on technologies that appear to be variants of commonly used existing systems. Hence, much more attention has been given to e-mail (for a review of e-mail research see Garton and Wellman 1995) than to mobile telephones – though the impact of mobile telephones on work group practices and performance is probably much more substantial than that of e-mail. This tendency of work-group/ information-technology researchers to avoid the obvious has also been raised by Kiesler and Sproull (1992). It took fifty to seventy-five years for researchers to acknowledge the ways in which the ordinary telephone allowed the creation of the city landscape and different physical layout of organizations. For instance, without the telephone, buildings would have had wider stairways and fewer floors in order to accommodate the large number of runners needed to convey messages between departments. It also is obvious that the presence of the telephone had major impacts on the ways of doing business. For example, the telephone created new possibilities for centralized control in organizations with physically separate operations (Brooks 1976).

Within these limiting contexts, the majority of studies that have focused on the nexus of work group performance and information technology can be categorized as those that portray the nexus as if the link was a mostly closed system, a mostly open system or a mixture of both.

Mostly Closed System Approaches

Researchers that appear to follow a closed system approach tend to focus on the ways in which various external factors affect the internal dynamics of the work groups and how these dynamics affect the groups' output. All the research that has followed Steiner's (1972) model of group process loss, and most of the research that falls into the input–process–output model of group effectiveness, is grouped within this approach (see Guzzo and Shea 1992 for an excellent review of these models). There are at least two variations of this approach. One focuses on electronic information systems as substitutes for face to face processes in which the underlying assumption is that modes do not matter. The other focuses on the ways electronic information systems can act as a substitute for the content of what a group does, such as controlling, developing, and monitoring expertise, and therefore change what the work group does and the output it produces.

For those following a process substitution approach, the emphasis is often on identifying those input factors that lead to better cooperation, often subsequently leading to better coordination, and eventually better performance. When information technology use is included within these studies, most assume that information technology acts as a substitute for face to face communication, or at least part of it. (See Shulman et al. 1990 and Nohria and Eccles 1992 for a review of limits of the substitution hypothesis when applied to the use of electronic networks when other modes of communicating are possible.) For substitution process researchers, context is often something that resides in the group as shared knowledge of the tasks, roles, habits and group norms, or comprises psychological motivational factors such as trust that are hypothesized as antecedents to cooperation and coordination (Beer et al. 1990; Smith et al. 1995: 11). In this sense, information technologies are a means of coordination, and coordination is taken to be equivalent to communication (McGrath 1990). For researchers such as Rice (1992), it is only when these contextual elements are certain and unambiguous that electronically mediated exchanges are chosen or preferred over face to face exchanges. Like the majority of studies of group processes, as summarized above, almost all of the electronic communication studies which have been guided by the process substitution hypothesis have tended to focus on single meetings and avoided examining the group's contribution and costs to its embedding system. There are notable exceptions. An example of a study that examined the context of use and functions of electronically mediated exchanges in ongoing work groups is McKenny et al.'s (1992) study of e-mail use by a systems design team. They followed Daft et al.'s (1987) elaboration of an information processing perspective. In this perspective the work group was construed as 'a set of actors exchanging information to accomplish tasks and build knowledge' (McKenny et al. 1992: 263). Their analyses were based on the pattern of interactions and on the content of those interactions in situations where the problem could be defined versus situations where the problem itself defied interpretation – that is, where equivocality existed. For these researchers, a building of shared understanding of a situation was necessary before group members can act. They hypothesized that managers exchanging information with their staff would be more likely to use e-mail for situations where problems did not exist or were well defined, than for situations where problem solving was necessary. The logic for this choice of mode follows the view that face to face interaction is a richer mode, allowing more flexibility of format, the use of simultaneous non-verbal channels, and more back and forth exchanges in which ambiguities can be resolved. However, face to face modes can be more costly in coordination and travel, and because of a bias to 'appropriately match' tasks with communication mode, people will choose to use a less costly mode, as e-mail, when the richness of face to face is not really needed. (See Rice 1992 for a summary of the history and status of media richness theory.) McKenny et al. (1992) also predicted that a pattern or program of combined use of these modes would occur that reflected the work routines of the group. As predicted, e-mail was primarily used to monitor status, send alerts, broadcast information and invoke action. These uses were often followed by face to face meetings by subgroups of staff who then discussed problems and maintained context under shifting priorities. Weekly face to face meetings also served as a routine context building process.

Not all substitution studies have found such patterning in the use of e-mail. In fact a recent review of studies of e-mail (Garton and Wellman 1995) concludes that there is no clear pattern concerning process or function substitution of face to face by e-mail across studies. Nor are there clear patterns of substitution associated with other electronic means of communication (Shulman et al. 1990). And some researchers are suggesting that one possible reason why no clear pattern has emerged is that other more established electronic modes, such as video and audio conferencing and fax, are now creating 'conditions more like face to face conversation' (Kiesler and Sproull 1992: 97). That is, the mixed results are in part due to the ability to use the modes to achieve the same purposes that can be achieved in ongoing face to face communication, but to do it in different ways. Such explanations of equifinality are consistent with McGrath's (1991) time, interaction and performance (TIP) theory of groups. Unfortunately, the problematic 'social and temporal context' themes that were summarized in the first section of this chapter are compounded when we further limit the literature to incidences where the potential evolution of patterns of mode use across meetings and episodes has been studied. There are, however, models and anecdotal evidence that when group members recognize that they have a future, that there will be other encounters, they modify their behaviors, depending upon the urgency of task demands and the modes that are anticipated to be available (Shulman and Steinman 1978). Further support for the view that people's anticipation of future encounters on different modes matters at least in terms of group processes is reviewed in Walther (1994); however, almost all of the work has concentrated on well-being or satisfaction and not on task performance outcomes.

For other researchers who appear to follow a substitution of group activity as opposed to the previous process substitution approach, information technologies are often regarded as input tools for structurally determining and eliminating/adding to functions of group processes either positively or negatively, and therefore indirectly affecting work group outputs. These researchers regard the technologies as exerting unidirectional influence over the group. There are those, described variously as optimists (Hirschheim 1985) or utopians (Bryant 1988), who view information technology as the solution to all, or almost all, group coordination problems. An example of this can be found in work on group decision support systems (GDSSs) by DeSanctis and Gallupe, who state: 'A GDSS aims to improve the process of group decision making by removing communication barriers, providing techniques for structuring decision analysis, and systematically directing the pattern, timing and content of discussion' (1987: 589). Here, we have an example that not only perpetuates the belief in substitutability, but introduces the added element that technology will improve the organizational communication process. At no point in their argument do DeSanctis and Gallupe question the tenability of their optimistic assumption.

At the other extreme are those described as pessimists (Hirschheim 1985). From this doom laden position, the electronic information technologies are seen as the source or exacerbation of control of the workers by management. For example, Duran (1990) describes a case where the implementation of information systems removed problem solving activities from task execution, leading to the disintegration of work teams. Allen (1994) suggests that increased mutual access to electronically conveyed information about others' performance can lead to excessive pressure for tighter monitoring and control. Although this belief predicts the opposite of the first, it is in fact based on a similar technocratic faith. In both instances, the technology is assumed to take on an existence independent of group users, but one that still determines group behavior.

Others take a more circumspect view. Some suggest that the technology does determine outcomes but the effects are likely to be of a second order. Some question it on grounds that studies of the cost/benefit of such systems have yielded marginal results on return on investment, at best (*The Economist*, 1991). In fact, at least one information technology vendor, WANG, has acknowledged this lack of productivity gain as a selling point to encourage businesses to use their expertise to get it right (Wilde 1991). Others suggest a second order determinism that the availability and use of electronic systems in work groups leads people to shift attention to different things, have contact with different people, and do things differently (Kiesler and Sproull 1992: 99). Likewise group researchers such as McGrath (1990) put forward some interesting conjectures of how asynchronous systems, in particular, may expand possible participation from physically distant nodes and at different stages of group activity, to increase performance on well learned tasks, but at the same time suggest that they may also restrict participation and reduce the attention that the group pays to the well-being and member support functions. In contrast, Bikson et al. (1989) acknowledge that the interactive information technologies are overcoming space/time constraints, but seem to be supplementing and not replacing existing preferences, opportunities, and methods for interaction.

The above positions have not provided the manager or researcher with a pathway to bring about the innovative potential or minimize negative consequences. In other words there is no unequivocal set of conjectures or results (Kraemer and Danziger 1990; Robey 1987). As suggested by Bikson et al.: 'Successful new modes of work group collaboration will require more social and managerial innovation than has been evidenced to date' (1989: 112).

All the above models rest on certain implicit beliefs about the nature of information technologies and their use in work groups. Specifically, it has been assumed that information technologies will lead to increased efficiencies and effectiveness and that the use of information technology would be consistent with formal theories of rational choice. Neither of these implicit assumptions about the nature and use of information technology has received convincing empirical support (Orlikowski 1992; Shulman et al. 1990).

Mostly Open System Approaches

There are at least two open system approaches. In one the emphasis is on the group becoming more self-directed through the availability of empowering information exchanges within the group, whereas in the second the emphasis is on the empowerment coming about through electronically mediated exchanges with others outside of the group. In both open system approaches, the effects of the information technologies are not limited to their actual use, but also include the effects associated with their symbolic presence or absence. Thus some of these researchers are likely to focus on the ways people's concepts of the technology affect their behaviors and relationships with others inside and outside of the work group. Like the determinists, some of these researchers act as if the concepts of technology can be used as an excuse for bringing about other changes, but for these researchers such changes are not determined by the technology, but enable occasions for different configurations to be explored.

In the first, 'groupware' information technologies are seen as providing opportunities for group members to increase their capacity to be more self-directed and actively create and change themselves within the group. An example of this is the use of an Internet bulletin board to search for a new editor of a journal as a means of providing more equal access to the views of other members within the membership (Zuboff 1988: 371).

Followers of the second open system approach see 'collaborativeware' information systems as flexible means of creating new relationships within a dynamic context which they are both affecting and being affected by, particularly with persons outside of the work group. (Examples of this view are provided in Kiesler and Sproull 1992: 98.) Thus researchers following this second approach focus on how the electronic technology provides an opportunity for new interest groups to form over the electronic highway or how increased stakeholder access to the electronic modes changed the makeup and nature of the ways the group performed. What much of the research suggests is that enlarged groups will behave in unexpected ways. Whether such differences lead to better performance is an open question.

Mixture of Open and Closed Systems

Many of the researchers cited above appear at times to take a mixture of open and closed system approaches, focusing on the group as an open system with persons creating enabling constructs of information technology, but also acknowledging the deterministic impacts of the hard wiring of the information system on its users. That is, what occurs within the group is somewhat determined by the technology, but the persons within the group have some agency of choice within the constraints that are imposed by the technology. Other proponents of this view often build upon the socio-technical systems school of Emery and Trist (1965) or upon Giddens's (1979) structuration theory.

Taylor and Felten (1993) provide a historical account of the development of current variations of socio-technical systems. Followers of this approach place an emphasis on the necessity of attending to the social structuring of work groups to maximize the fit between technology and human systems. Most of the humanistic oriented models on group task design (Hackman 1987; Campion et al. 1993) are consistent with this perspective. Yet as pointed out in the introduction to this section, most work group researchers following the socio-technical systems school have not focused on technology. Those that have included Gutek et al. (1986), who studied the implementation of computer-based office information technologies in fifty-five offices and their relation to organizational structure defined in terms of the primary occupational function of the unit (clerical, managerial) and the nature of the technology. The latter was defined in terms of its physical attributes (age, micro/mini). They found some support for covariation of structure and technology, but little support for a relationship between organizational outcome (in this study, productivity and satisfaction) and this covariation.

In fact, the current state of our knowledge about possible ways of maximizing technology and work group design fit is quite limited. The contingency hypothesis and related context fit hypothesis have had little empirical support. (See Markus and Robey 1988 for a review of related organizational imperative studies.) Furthermore, researchers ignore the processes by which congruence can be achieved (Gutek et al. 1986). Suffice to say that the contingency hypothesis will probably remain attractive to researchers hopeful of eventually finding the elusive key element that will make heterogeneous findings homogeneous. However, the real limitations of the contingency hypothesis become apparent when it is realized that information and the relevant technologies are not just about rational control of the organizational environment.

In structuration theory, and consistent with the more general constructionist perspective, more emphasis is placed on humans (as agents) being both enabled and constrained by technical structures, yet these very same structures are the result of previous actions (Giddens 1979). Within an agency view, human interaction is concerned with the communication of meaning. To accomplish this, interpretative schemes must be used by the actors to interact in a sense-making manner with the world. Through the use of one's interpretative scheme and communication, the structures of signification are created which represent the rules that inform and define interaction (Orlikowski 1992). The rules however are not 'fixed'. Having been created by actors who are both knowledgeable and reflexive, the rules can be challenged or reaffirmed. That is, through the use of their knowledge base, actors are able to observe and understand what they are doing whilst they are doing it. Thus actors can potentially change the existing structure, but the extent or type of change cannot be predicted with complete accuracy, in part because of attention to the notion of 'unintended consequences of action'. The usefulness of applying structuration theory to the study of information technology derives from the fundamental premise of the 'duality of structure'. Unlike closed system substitution approaches that may overemphasize the importance of technical constraints on action, and their humanist open system counterparts that may overemphasize the importance of the capability of human actors, the structural approach provides a means by which researchers (such as Fulk 1993; Robey and Azevedo 1991: 11; Orlikowski 1992) can acknowledge the tangible constraints that technology may impose as well as accounting for the phenomena of 'interpretative flexibility' and adaptation of information technology for evolving purposes.

For these researchers, because information technology is highly susceptible to reinterpretation and social construction, the impact of information technology on work groups cannot be produced independently of human action and interpretation (Robey and Azevedo 1991: 13). This is because interactive electronic information systems, more so than other technologies, can be put to varied uses and are therefore more open to reinterpretation. The studies of Kraut et al. (1989) and Nelson (1990) provide good examples of technology being put to a variety of uses that were not initially intended by the original designers. Interpretative flexibility has important consequences for group processes, as technology can be seen to be a product of human action, while it simultaneously presents a constraint on that action.

However, the concept of interpretative flexibility is not infinite. While there may be a degree of flexibility in the design, use and interpretation of technology, the level of flexibility is constrained by the physical characteristics of the technology. Apart from information technology's obvious physical constraints, it is also constrained by the organizational as well as the social and temporal structures that it is embedded in. (These latter constraints also were raised in the first section. Consistent with the 'duality of structure' approach, Kohut (1994) has illustrated, using key informants and participants of a work group of system designers involved in the introduction and use of a new computer system, that the level of interpretative flexibility tends to taper off once the electronic information system has been in place for a while. That is, the degree to which group members take advantage of the possibilities decreases as the technology becomes institutionalized. Why this pattern of decreased exploration over time occurred isn't clear. Perhaps it is related to the tendency of groups using interactive computer technology over a period of time to decrease their use of the technology for group maintenance purposes unless they are instructed (to provide feedback) to increase it (Losada et al. 1990). Or it may be related to the group going through the mid-life transition referred to above (Gersick 1988) in which the declining use for experimentation is associated with the team members just getting on a direct path to project completion.

While the interpretations afforded through structuration theory and the assumptions of duality of infrastructures are much richer than those offered by the previous schools, we are left with little guidance as to what is good work group performance or how its occurrence is facilitated by the symbolic or actual use of information technology.

In this section, I have presented closed system, open system and a combination of open and closed system stances that have been taken on the role and impact of information technology on group performance. It appears that the same seven themes raised in the previous section, that characterized current research of good work group performance, are also applicable to researchers who have been examining the nexus between work groups and electronic information technology. The impact of information technologies varies from study to study. For every research study that shows a particular impact of information technology, there is either another study that shows the reverse or a study that concludes that the impacts are more complex

than had been previously assumed. This is a pattern of results that occurred with the information technologies of the 1980s, and still holds today (see Markus and Robey 1988; Robey 1986; 1987; Siegel et al. 1986). Put another way, the impacts of information technology on work group performance are organizationally, socially and temporally dependent.

One can also conclude from this review, that work group research has neither significantly helped nor hindered the introduction of information technology into groups. Although there are numerous reasons why this came about (see Rice 1984), an obvious practical reason is that by the time researchers produced results, the users were already onto the next generation of technology. For the researchers, the technologies themselves ·became moving targets (Tomarzky 1986). For work group members, the ongoing updating of information technology has become a fact of life. For most researchers, these technology changes are yet to be seen as part of the dynamic ongoing episodes of work groups.

There are suggestions in the above reviews that the failure of researchers to focus on this dynamic can be traced to the inappropriateness of the models and methods of study used – models and methods based on an empiricist tradition. As pointed out in the first section, the inappropriateness of this tradition has been well argued by Hackman (1987) for work group research. Others, such as Shulman et al. (1990) and Orlikowski (1992), have raised parallel concerns for information technology research. For these researchers, the models and methods commonly employed within the empiricist tradition do not distinguish methodologically between the work group and technological infrastructure. As such, researchers operating in that tradition are inadvertently led to adopt some kind of technological determinism. The empiricist tradition does have its place as a symbolic way of acting as if people were technology.

But there are important lessons that emerge from the information-technology/work-group research that can lead to a better understanding of good work group performance. This is because those interested in the impacts of the information technologies have articulated their assumptions about the roles of information and communication much more sharply than those directing their research efforts at work group performance in general. In the next section, these insights build upon categorizations of how researchers of information technology have portrayed information and communication (Shulman et al. 1990) and recent advances in communication theory by Penman (1995a; 1995b). These give rise to a different conception of communication that in turn leads us to ask new questions about information technologies and good group performance. These new questions also allow us to put information technology in its place – as a potential aid to the real business of work groups, not as a substitute for it. The next section concludes with a different view of the duality of infrastructures that can address the moral question of what is good work group performance.

RECONSIDERING INFORMATION TECHNOLOGY, COMMUNICATION AND WORK GROUP PERFORMANCE

Perhaps the most striking feature of all the literature reviewed here is its faith that work group members understand and share the same view (symbolic or otherwise) of information and communication. With the exception of the dualistic position taken by constructionists, researchers of information technology took the communication process for granted. (See Shulman et al. 1990 for a review of definitions of information and communication used by information technology researchers.) Most seem to follow Shannon and Weaver's (1949) definition of communication, that is, information is the signal sent or received, with communication being a process of sending and receiving information or messages. This definition was originally developed to deal with electronic systems but is commonly applied to human systems. The key elements still remain in contemporary work group researchers' definitions of communication (McGrath 1990; Kiesler and Sproull 1992).

With the new information technologies we are presumably able to speed up the transmission and to increase the storage of ideas much more than we could if we were relying on simple human 'connections' and the fallible human mind (Guzzo and Shea 1992: 307). But as the research demonstrates, there is little evidence that information technology can act as a substitute for human communication, let alone do it better. As described elsewhere (Shulman and Penman 1992; Sless 1986b), the major consequence of the introduction of new information technologies within organizations has not been better communication, only faster misunderstandings.

The belief that communication and therefore the information technology is a tool – an instrument for getting your message across – has led to false and exaggerated expectations about what information technology can do. And as such it has also led many practitioners and researchers alike along an unproductive pathway with substantial hidden costs. Ineffective and costly management decisions based on false expectations about information technology as a tool for getting a message across are shown in studies demonstrating that new computer systems can result in lower profitability and reduce production (Dougherty 1988).

In other words, how we think about information technology and communication is not simply a matter of scholarly indulgence; it determines the decisions and actions we all take in our practical communicative activities. As pointed out in the previous section, there is an emerging recognition that there is a need to use different models for the human versus mechanical-technological infrastructure. Researchers who adhere to the transmission view of work group communication treat the technological and human aspects of the infrastructure of communication as if they were part of the same phenomenon.

The key point so far, then, is that most contemporary research has failed to make the distinction between these two infrastructures and has applied a technical means of knowing to human problems. This is well illustrated by the assumptions of causality that underlie most research in this area (see the review by Markus and Robey 1988). Strictly speaking, causality is a concept that belongs only to the technical realm, where external events can directly cause or determine other events. When we enter the human realm and attribute humans with any agency or intention in their communicative actions, then we cannot assume simultaneously that those actions are caused by external events. From this constructionist position, causality has no place in the human infrastructure. When inappropriate technical concepts, such as causality, continue to be used to understand the human realm, the real problems will never be addressed, let alone resolved. And the real problems can never be addressed until we discard the technical, instrumental view of communication.

New Conceptions of Information and Communication

Communication is a messy and uncertain business. Communication is always partially ineffective, potentially wasteful, and to some degree beyond the control of any one individual or organization. Here, I am concerned with developing a description of communication that can account for these practical observations which reinforce the seven themes raised in the first section. Much of the confusion in the work group research literature, as well as in practice, rests on the failure to make a critical conceptual distinction between information and communication. Sless (1981) has developed an extensive argument regarding the differences and I draw heavily on this here as I have done elsewhere (Shulman et al. 1990).

Information

In the common sense view of information as an entity, all things that exist in the physical world are potential sources of information. As such, information has the properties of the physical world and exists regardless of our perception of it. In other words, information is something independent of humans. It is inanimate, incapable of acting or exhibiting agency. When the human agent enters the scene and reads the information a fundamental change takes place. In the relationship between human agent and information something new is created that we usually call meaning. Information does not contain meaning *per se*. Meaning is brought about in the relationship between the reader and the information being read.

The concept of information has some similarities with common sense views that also see information as an entity. But Sless's view does not falsely attribute the 'entity' with meaning independent of the human reader. Those views that equate information and meaning are making a category mistake in the same way that Ryle (1963) argued for the mind/body dualism. Similarly, those who expect meaning to be a property of information mistakenly believe meaning to be a part that can be separately identified, rather than the outcome of an interaction between information and human agent. The problem of a category mistake in the field of information technology is that meaning is taken as belonging to the category of the physical world, when it actually belongs in the human world (Shulman et al. 1990).

When meaning is assumed to exist independent of humans, it is easy (although false) to conceive of technical/mechanical means for storing, transferring, and transforming this meaning, as Guzzo and Shea (1992) have done. When meanings are seen as stored in words or other signals, then the more signals we can create and preserve, presumably the more ideas we transfer and store. This very mistaken view has, according to Reddy (1979), significant social consequences. If we do not cultivate our abilities to create and reconstruct meanings we will end up with a culture less sophisticated rather than more. On the other hand, if we take meaning to be a process in the human infrastructure, we are correctly placing the responsibility for meaning creation and manipulation in human hands, not mechanical ones.

Communication

For communication to occur, a further condition is necessary: a communicative intent must be inferred in the information being read. By this I mean that if we believe the information in our environment was generated by someone else in order to communicate then the necessary and sufficient conditions exist to describe the phenomenon as communication. It is important to note here that it is the inference of the 'other' and their intent that is critical, not the physical presence, nor that the 'other' really had a communicative intent.

Communication then is also a relational phenomenon, but one involving more than one person, whether assumed or real. Thus, the communication process incorporates the meaning generation process, but in a particular way. The communication process incorporates more than one 'reader' and this adds complexity to the meaning generation process. It is the way in which these people are in relation with each other that provides the basis for our conception of communication. Moreover, this process not only creates its own internal structure but also sets its own boundaries. Communication, as an autopoietic process (Maturana and Varela 1980), is self-generating, structure-creating, and boundary-setting. In acting in this process we find ourselves in a rather more difficult place than conventionally proposed. Communication activity is not only self-generating, it is also self-specifying. It is self-specifying in the sense that our past activities point to the directions of our present activities. 'Rather than acting "out of" an inner plan or schema, we can think of ourselves as acting "into" our own present situation' (Shotter 1986: 203).

The meanings generated in this process arise from unique patterns of interaction between the participants – patterns beyond the control or intention of any individual party. The meanings are also subject to continual modification with the evolving temporal context. As we act into our communicative situation we are at the same time changing it by that action. In continually bringing about a new state of affairs, joint communicative actions and the implicated meanings are always emergent and never finished.

The meanings generated in this process are also position specific. In this sense everyone is in a unique position, shaped by both history and the perceived future: hence the meanings generated in this process cannot be identical, and 'shared' understandings are at best transitory. David Sless has poignantly captured this momentary, changing nature of understanding: 'Understanding is the dead spot in our struggle for meaning: it is the momentary pause, the stillness before incomprehension continues. . . . Thus understanding is a temporary state of closure' (1986a: i).

A critical point in this argument, then, is that meaning is inherently indeterminate. We cannot guarantee, predict or fully control the direction of the process or the nature of the meaning inferred. Instead, the 'organized settings' we are led into by our past actions and implicated meanings act as constraints (in contrast to determinants) on the range of possible future meanings. These constraints provide temporary closure in an otherwise unstable and indeterminate social world. In this way, although there may be potential for an infinite range of meanings, in practice this is limited by the closure we impose. Thus, our key concern is one not of determining (or even believing in) the stability of meaning, but of understanding the points and procedures for closures. Meaning cannot be controlled or predicted, but it can be managed and constrained.

The essential indeterminacy of meaning logically leads us to challenge the metaphysics of foundationalism (see Rorty 1980) – a metaphysics that assumes there can be a stable foundation, a certain objective and unchangeable knowledge base. From our point of view, it is logically impossible to establish foundations for, and derive predictable long term generalizations from, anything as inherently unstable as human social life (see MacIntyre 1985). This, then, is the real key to the failure of past research on information technology reviewed in this chapter. The past research attempted to predict the impact of technology on work group activity, when that activity itself is inherently unstable.

From the point of view of the management of the work group information and technology nexus, our major concern is with generating and managing better expectations. Better expectations are those that are based on a realistic conception of the communication process and its inherently problematic nature. When we take misunderstandings to be the norm rather than the exception we are more alert for the problems and more able to manage them. In this sense, then, better expectations take the technology to be both an enabling and a constraining device, depending on how well it is designed, implemented and used.

When we are concerned with strictly information-based activities (cf. communication), information technology systems provide us with a range of opportunities for modeling and rehearsal of information activities. When we are concerned with communication activities *per se*, the technology once again provides us with certain opportunities. In particular, the various technologies offer people opportunity for greater access, different types of access – such as voice, data, and graphics – and facility for faster access. But technology only provides us with more and faster opportunities for communication. It does not provide us with communication *per se*, let alone better communication. The problems inherent in the communication process are not removed by that technology. In fact, given the state of user unfriendliness of many of these technologies, problems in the communication process are more likely to be exacerbated than minimized. (See Shulman et al. 1990 for a review of information technology design faults.)

Given this indeterminacy and instability, the management of meaning can be construed as one of autopoietic deviation, amplification, and counteraction. As Nord (1985) has pointed out, managing involves understanding both the conditions where small deliberate changes – as in bringing in a new information technology in a complex system – can produce a self-sustaining (deviation amplifying) change in the complex system, and the conditions where the change will be overwhelmed by the system (deviation counteracting) (Nord 1985: 188–9). When new technology is managed as if it were an innovation, then deviation amplification occurs. When new technology is managed as if it were a substitution, then deviation counteraction occurs. Either style of management depends on managing meanings.

When we are concerned with the role of information technology in work groups we need to be concerned with questions of how the meanings attributed to information technologies are maintained and amplified by organizational members. We need also to be concerned with how these meanings change with the physical characteristics and distribution of the technology from different positions and with how these meanings are related to changing patterns of technology use. Thus, in our account gathering we are not gathering the truth in any objective or absolute sense. Instead, our accounts indicate a range of possible interpretations, including our own.

I have suggested that some of the problematics of work group performance research that were highlighted in the first section can be associated with the proclivity of researchers to examine human work groups as if they were technology. In the second section I pointed towards the advances made by researchers who are using dualistic approaches that recognize both the human and the technology aspects of work group performance. In the third section I developed the theme that many of these research efforts are still limited, in part because they still hold onto a transmission view of information and communication. This transmission view has constrained the recognition that the performance of groups can never be completely determined. Once recognized, new possibilities for management of the nexus of information technologies and work groups emerge. However, recognition of this has not provided a direct insight into what is good work group performance. In order to make that connection, in the next section I draw on recent work by Penman (1995; in press) where in the very process of acting into our communicative practices we are acting into some moral order.

INFORMATION TECHNOLOGY AND GOOD WORK GROUP PERFORMANCE: FUTURE DIRECTIONS

Any question of what is 'good' – including what is good work group performance – is a moral one. As social scientists, we have tended to treat 'morality' as ideas that exist independent of the participants involved. However, in the previous section I have argued that ideas do not exist independently of the participants involved, nor can the meanings be completely determined. In this section I draw on Penman's (1995; in press) development of the implications of the constructionist view for addressing the question of what is good.

Penman (in press) uses the arguments of two twentieth-century authors drawing on different, but compatible, traditions: Hans-Georg Gadamer and John Shotter. Gadamer's (1992) major philosophical concern was with elucidating the hermeneutical nature of the human sciences and human experience generally. As pointed out by Penman, Gadamer's argument relies on Aristotle's major distinction between technical or theoretical knowledge and moral knowledge. 'For moral knowledge, as Aristotle describes it, is clearly not objective knowledge. The knower is not standing over against a situation that he merely observes; he is directly confronted with what he sees. It is something that he has to do' (Gadamer 1992: 314). For Gadamer, moral knowledge is in the domain of the full human experience; moral knowledge is always incipient in practice.

John Shotter (1990; 1993) uses three distinctions to arrive at a similar understanding. Taking Ryle's distinction between 'knowing that' (facts or theoretical principles) and 'knowing how' (technique), he adds a third, moral, kind that he calls 'knowing from' (Shotter 1990: 12). This knowing of the moral kind is a form of practical knowledge, as Aristotle and later Gadamer would characterize it. But Shotter, drawing on Vico, Vygotsky and Mead, emphasizes the social realm of this moral knowing; it is knowing that comes from our relations with others.

Shotter makes the same point as does Gadamer – that moral knowledge is about doing. But Shotter expands on this by arguing that it is something that is about doing with other people. Moral knowing does not exist independently of a social situation, it is brought about within it. You cannot reiterate a long list of professional ethics for this form of 'knowing from'; it emerges from what you do. The point that these authors make that is relevant to the argument here is that moral knowing is immanent in our practice of communicating within work groups.

Penman (1995) points out that most studies do not incorporate 'knowing from', but reflect the conventional wisdom of the past three centuries: that communication is immaterial; it is merely a trivial vehicle for something far more important. This 'wisdom' is reflected in arguments about the need to investigate how the electronic information system can be best 'shaped' and manipulated in order to best 'transmit' the ideas it 'contains' and to bring about desired effects on others.

This approach to communication, that treats the very process as immaterial, has been directly linked to the moral order of the twentieth century by Alasdair MacIntyre (1985) in his important book, *After Virtue*. His conclusion is that the prevalent moral order in our Western world is an amoral one. It is an amoral order in which the distinction between manipulative and non-manipulative relations between people has been obliterated in such a way that it seems impossible for people to conceive of communication as anything but a manipulative tool, as a means of predictability and control (Penman 1995).

For Penman, once the limitations of the conventional, Enlightenment wisdom and its amoral consequences are recognized we have three choices: to accept, to reject or to deny. To accept the conventional wisdom is to do what much of what is called communication or cultural studies has done, however unknowingly. To reject the conventional wisdom we also have to reject the basic division between material and immaterial. This approach is exemplified by Rorty's (1980) anti-foundational arguments. For Rorty, the profound error of the Enlightenment scholars was to base all their arguments on the belief that there was a true, immutable foundation to knowledge, and the scientific task was to seek this foundation. In arguing against this belief, however, Rorty chose to reject all foundations and thus all materiality, and to embrace everything as immaterial. With his choice, communication is everything and nothing. There are serious problems associated with this choice, particularly moral ones. Accepting a view of communication, along with everything else, as immaterial is to celebrate the insignificance of Being itself (Shepherd 1993). In such a celebration notions of good or right are replaced with an amoral stance of anything goes (e.g. Feyerabend 1975).

The third choice is to deny the conventional wisdom and to assert that communication is material. It is only this choice that offers the possibility of a communication view (as distinct from any other disciplinary view). It is a view that says communication is foundational to our being, it is material and it does matter (Sless 1991). While this goes against the last three centuries of mainstream philosophical tradition, it is a view that nevertheless has had its own advocates for centuries (e.g. Vico in the 1700s: Vico 1986). And these advocates for the materiality of communication are now coming to the fore again. As many recent authors who have made this last choice argue, there is a general transformation under way in the humanities and social sciences based on the recognition of the role communication plays in constructing our lives (e.g. Craig 1993; Gergen 1982; Penman 1988; 1992). And it is only in working within this transformation that questions of the broad moral dimension are possible.

Communicating in a Moral Frame

Penman (1992; 1995) suggests that in reconstruing communication as material, because our knowing is not independent of ourselves and our communicative actions, all of our knowing and our actions have a valuational base. As such we have incorporated, by implication, what we believe is good and desirable. Following Penman's argument, then, all communicative practices, by virtue of their being communicative, have a moral dimension. 'In the very process of acting into our communicative practices we are acting into some moral order or another' (Penman 1995).

As work group researchers we could well ask in what ways are moral orders indicated and acted out in communicative action. The work of Harré (1983), Pearce and Cronen (1987; Cronen 1986) and Penman (1991) provide recent examples of approaches to this question, by specifying characteristics of moral orders in action. But even these approaches operating within the new paradigm are not exempt from having to come to terms with the second aspect of the moral issue: the moral dimension to research and theory. If all theory and research is invention and not neutral discovery, then all research is also value based. If all research is intervention, then it is in some way or another intervention into a moral order.

The above argument has major implications for future research about good work group performance and the role of information technology. It strongly suggests that a researcher's understandings of the possibilities and constraints of electronic information technologies can best be advanced by actively engaging in the communicative activity of work groups and not just studying them at a distance. Penman (in press) has construed this as the primary research position: one where the researchers are directly participating in conversations with others as the generative source of their consequent understandings. For Penman this does not mean researchers can or should avoid retrospective analysis. She extends Dewey's (1981) argument that both participation and reflection are necessary – but that one precludes the other. 'You cannot be looking back – to study antecedents – while looking forward – to understand the possibilities – within the same communication process' (Penman in press). For understanding the possibilities of information technology to foster good work group performance, we need to look forward. In looking forward we are presented with the unfolding of options and the closing off of others. The episodic nature of work groups, documented through participant observation by McGrath and O'Connor (1996), provides an opportunity for researchers to sequentially act in, and reflect on, work group processes.

Throughout this chapter, I have provided a snap-shot of the contributions and limitations of current research into work group performance and its relationship with information technologies. The review relied heavily on the writings of researchers that took a neutral – 'passive' – role. I suggest that recent advances have been made where researchers have taken at least a slightly active participatory role in their engagement with groups (for instance, Hackman 1990). The argument developed here has attempted to provide a conceptual base for extending this participation. What possibilities will emerge by engaging more directly into the conversations of work groups are dependent, in part, on the tools we use to move the conversations forward. Given the increasing avalanche of the use of work groups and their access to others through information technologies, it is likely that new understandings will emerge – not because the information technologies are a substitute for the conversations, but because they provide an opportunity for engaging within the conversations.

NOTES

The themes that are presented within this chapter emerged within conversations with my colleagues at the Communication Research Institute. The insights constructed within these interactions with Robyn Penman, David Rogers and David Sless guided the arguments. Other insights emerged from my participation in the R&D work teams led by Jenny Bellamy, Peter Cox and Neil MacLeod of CSIRO. I thank them for allowing me to engage with them in exploring these themes in practice, and the LWRRDC, GRDC and RIRDC Australia for partially funding these activities.

REFERENCES

Allen, J.P. (1994) 'Mutual control in newly integrated work environments', *Information Society*, 10(2): 129–38.

Ancona, Deborah G. and Caldwell, David F. (1988) 'Beyond task and maintenance: defining external functions in groups', *Group and Organization Studies*, 13(4): 468–94.

Ancona, Deborah G. and Caldwell, David F. (1990) 'Beyond boundary spanning: managing external dependence in product development teams', *The Journal of High Technology Management Research*, 1(2): 119–35.

Beer, M., Eisenstat, R.A. and Spector, B. (1990) *The Critical Path to Corporate Renewal*. Boston: Harvard Business School Press.

Bikson, Thomas K., Eveland, J.D. and Gutek, Barbara A. (1989) 'Flexible interactive technology for multi-person tasks: current problems and future prospects', in Margrethe H. Olson (ed.), *Technological Support for Work Group Collaboration*. Hillsdale, NJ: Lawrence Erlbaum. pp. 89–112.

Brooks, John (1976) *Telephone*. New York: Harper & Row.

Bryant, A. (1988) 'The information society: computopia, dystopia, myopia', *Prometheus*, 6: 61–77.

Campion, M.A. and McClelland, C.L. (1993) 'Follow-up and extension of the interdisciplinary costs and benefits of enlarged jobs', *Journal of Applied Psychology*, 78: 339–51.

Campion, M.A., Medsker, G.J. and Higgs, A.C. (1993) 'Relations between work group characteristics and effectiveness: implications for designing effective work groups', *Personnel Psychology*, 46: 823–50.

Craig, R. (1993) 'Why are there so many communication theories?', *Journal of Communication*, 43(3): 26–33.

Cronen, V. (1986) 'The individual in a systemic perspective'. Paper presented at the 15th Anniversary of Interaktie Akademie, Antwerp, 30 May.

Daboub, A.J., Rasheed, A.M., Priem, R.L. and Gray, D.A. (1995) 'Top management team characteristics and corporate illegal activity', *Academy of Management Review*, 20(1): 138–70.

Daft, R.L., Lengel, R.H. and Trevino, L.K. (1987) 'Message equivocality, media selection and manager performance', *MIS Quarterly*, 11(3): 355–66.

DeSanctis, G. and Gallupe, R.B. (1987) 'A foundation for the study of decision support systems', *Management Science*, 33: 589–609.

Dewey, J. (1981) *The Philosophy of John Dewey*, 2nd edn. New York: Crossroad.

Dougherty, B. (1988) 'DEC warns of hidden costs', *Financial Review*, 18 July: 63.

Duran, J.P. (1990) 'Information technology and the legacy of Taylorism in France', *Employment and Society*, 4(3): 407–27.

Emery, F. and Trist, E. (1965) 'The causal texture of organizational environments', *Human Relations*, 18: 21–31.

Feyerabend, P. (1975) *Against Method*. London: NLB.

Fulk, J. (1993) 'Social construction of communication technology', *Academy of Management Journal*, 36: 921–50.

Gadamer, H.G. (1992) *Truth and Method*, 2nd edn. New York: Crossroad.

Garton, Laura and Wellman, Barry (1995) 'Social impacts of electronic mail in organizations: a review of the research literature', in *Communication Yearbook 18*. pp. 434–53.

Gergen, K. (1982) *Toward Transformation in Social Knowledge*. New York: Springer-Verlag.

Gersick, C.J.G. (1988) 'Time and transition in work teams: toward a new model of group development', *Academy of Management Journal*, 31: 9–41.

Giddens, A. (1979) *Central Problems in Social Theory*. London: Macmillan.

Ginnett, R.C. (1990) 'The airline cockpit crew', in J.R. Hackman (ed.), *Groups that Work (and Those that Don't): Creating Conditions for Effective Teamwork*. San Francisco: Jossey-Bass.

Gutek, B.A., Sasse, S.H. and Bikson, T.K. (1986) 'The fit between technology and work group structure: the structural contingency approach and office automation'. Paper presented at Conference on Technology: its Meaning, Measurement and Impact in the Age of Computerized Work, Academy of Management, Chicago.

Guzzo, R.A. and Dickson, M.W. (1996) 'Teams in organizations: recent research on performance and effectiveness', *Annual Review of Psychology*, 47: 307–40.

Guzzo, R.A. and Shea, G.P. (1992) 'Group performance and intergroup relations in organizations', in M.D. Dunnette and L.M. Hough (eds), *Handbook of Industrial and Organizational Psychology*, vol. 3. Palo Alto: Consulting Psychologists Press. pp. 269–313.

Hackman, J.R. (1986) 'The psychology of self-management in organizations', in M.S. Pallack and R.O. Perloff (eds), *Psychology and Work: Productivity,*

Change and Employment. Washington, DC: American Psychological Association. pp. 86–136.

Hackman, J.R. (1987) 'The design of work teams', in J.W. Lorsch (ed.), *Handbook of Organizational Behavior.* Englewood Cliffs, NJ: Prentice-Hall. pp. 315–42.

Hackman, J.R. (ed.) (1990) *Groups that Work (and Those that Don't): Creating Conditions for Effective Teamwork.* San Francisco: Jossey-Bass.

Hackman, J.R. and Oldham, G.R. (1980) *Work Redesign.* Reading, MA: Addison-Wesley.

Harré, R. (1983) *Personal Being.* Oxford: Blackwell.

Hirschheim, R.A. (1985) *Office Automation: a Social and Organizational Perspective.* London: Wiley.

Katzenbach, Jon R. and Smith, Douglas K. (1993) 'The discipline of teams', *Harvard Business Review*, March–April: 111–20.

Kiesler, Sara and Sproull, Lee (1992) 'Group decision making and communication technology', *Organizational Behavior and Human Decision Processes*, 52: 96–123.

Kohut, Thomas, L. (1994) 'The mutuality of influence: using the theory of structuration to explore organisations and information technology'. Dissertation for Bachelor of Commerce with Honours, Griffith University.

Kraemer, K.L. and Danziger, J.N. (1990) 'The impacts of computer technology on the work life of information workers', *Social Science Computer Review*, 8(4): 592–613.

Kraut, R., Dumais, S. and Koch, S. (1989) 'Computerisation, productivity and quality of work-life', *Communications of the ACM*, 32: 220–38.

Lawler, E.E., Mohrman, S.A. and Ledford, G.E. Jr (1992) *Employee Involvement and Total Quality Management: Practices and Results in Fortune 1000 Companies.* San Francisco: Jossey-Bass.

Levine, J.M. and Moreland, R.L. (1990) 'Progress in small group research', *Annual Review of Psychology*, 41: 585–634.

Losada, Marcial, Sánchez, Pedro and Noble, Elizabeth E. (1990) 'Collaborative technology and group process feedback: their impact on interactive sequences in meetings', in *Proceedings of the Conference on Computer-Supported Cooperative Work*, 7–10 October, Los Angeles. New York: Association for Computing Machinery. pp. 53–64.

MacIntyre, A. (1985) *After Virtue.* London: Duckworth.

Markus, M.L. and Robey, D. (1988) 'Information technology and organizational change: causal structure in theory and research', *Management Science*, 34: 583–98.

Maturana, H. and Varela, F. (1980) *Autopoiesis and Cognition.* Dordrecht, Holland: D. Reidel.

McGrath, Joseph E. (1984) *Group: Interaction and Performance.* Englewood Cliffs, NJ: Prentice-Hall.

McGrath, Joseph E. (1990) 'Time matters in groups', in J. Galegher, R.E. Kraut and C. Egido (eds),

Intellectual Teamwork: Social and Technological Foundations of Cooperative Work. Hillsdale, NJ: Lawrence Erlbaum. pp. 23–62.

McGrath, Joseph E. (1991) 'Time, interaction, and performance (TIP): a theory of groups', *Small Group Research*, 22(2): 147–74.

McGrath, J.E. and O'Connor, K.M. (1996) 'Temporal issues in work groups', in M.A. West (ed.), *Handbook of Workgroup Psychology.* Chichester, UK: John Wiley. pp. 25–52.

McKenny, James L., Zack, Michael H. and Doherty, Victor S. (1992) 'Complementary communication media: a comparison of electronic mail and face-to-face communication in a programming team', in N. Hohria and R.G. Eccles (eds), *Networks and Organizations: Structure, Form, and Action.* Boston: Harvard Business School Press. pp. 262–87.

Nelson, D.L. (1990) 'Individual adjustment to information driven technologies: a critical review', *MIS Quarterly*, Special Issue, 79–98.

Nohria, Nitin and Eccles, Robert (1992) 'Face-to-face: making network organizations work', in N. Nohria and R.G. Eccles (eds), *Networks and Organizations: Structure, Form, and Action.* Boston: Harvard Business School Press. pp. 288–308.

Nord, W. (1985) 'Can organizational culture be managed? A synthesis', in P. Frost, L. Moore, M. Louis, L. Lundberg and I. Martin (eds), *Organizational Culture.* Beverley Hills, CA: Sage. pp. 187–96.

Orlikowski, W.J. (1992) 'The duality of technology: rethinking the concept of technology in organisations', *Organisation Science*, 3(3): 398–427.

Pearce, W.B. and Cronen, V. (1987) 'Intervention: technologies for changing social systems'. Paper presented at Conflict Intervention Conference, Temple University, 26–28 March.

Penman, Robyn (1988) 'Communication reconstructed', *Journal for the Theory of Social Behaviour*, 18: 301–10.

Penman, Robyn (1991) 'Goals, games and moral orders: a paradoxical case in court', in K. Tracy (ed.), *Goals and Discourse.* Hillsdale, NJ: Lawrence Erlbaum.

Penman, Robyn (1992) 'Good theory and good practice: an argument in progress', *Communication Theory*, 2(3): 234–50.

Penman, Robyn (1995) 'Communicating: a moral frame(up)', *Australian Journal of Communication*, 22(2): 48–58.

Penman, Robyn (in press) 'The researcher in communication: the primary position', in J. Owen (ed.), *Context and Communication.* Reno, NV: Context Press.

Philp, M. (1985) 'Michel Foucault', in Q. Skinner (ed.), *The Return of Grand Theory in the Human Sciences.* Cambridge: Cambridge University Press. pp. 65–82.

Polley, Douglas and Van Dyne, Linn (1994) 'The limits and liabilities of self-managing work teams',

Advances in Interdisciplinary Studies of Work Teams, 1: 1–38.

Reddy, M. (1979) 'The conduit metaphor', in A. Ortony (ed.), *Metaphor and Thought*. London: Cambridge University Press. pp. 301–22.

Rice, R.E. (1984) 'Development of new media research', in R.E. Rice (ed.), *The New Media*. Beverley Hills, CA: Sage. pp. 15–31.

Rice, R.E. (1992) 'Task analyzability, use of new media, and effectiveness: a multi-site exploration of media richness', *Organization Science*, 3(4): 475–98.

Robey, D. (1986) *Designing Organizations*, 2nd edn. Homewood, IL: Richard D. Irwin.

Robey, D. (1987) 'Implementation and the organizational impacts of information systems', *Interfaces*, 17: 72–84.

Robey, D. and Azevedo, A. (1991) 'Information technology and organisational culture'. Paper presented to the College of Business Administration, Florida International University, Miami, Florida.

Rorty, R. (1980) *Philosophy and the Mirror of Nature*. Oxford: Blackwell.

Ross, Jerry and Staw, Barry M. (1986) 'Expo 86: an escalation prototype', *Administrative Science Quarterly*, 131: 274–9.

Ross, Jerry and Staw, Barry M. (1993) 'Organizational escalation and exit: lessons from the Shoreham nuclear power plant', *Academy of Management Journal*, 36(4): 701–32.

Ryle, G. (1963) *The Concept of Mind*. Harmondsworth: Penguin.

Shannon, C.E. and Weaver, W. (1949) *Mathematical Theory of Communication*. Urbana, IL: University of Illinois Press.

Shepherd, G. (1993) 'Building a discipline of communication', *Journal of Communication*, 43(3): 83–91.

Shotter, J. (1986) 'A sense of place: Vico and the social production of social identities', *British Journal of Social Psychology*, 25: 199–211.

Shotter, J. (1990) *Knowing of the Third Kind*. Utrecht: ISOR.

Shotter, J. (1993) *Cultural Politics of Everyday Life*. Toronto: University of Toronto Press.

Shulman, A.D. and Steinman, J.I. (1978) 'Interpersonal teleconferencing in an organizational context', in M. Elton (ed.), *The Evaluation and Planning of Interpersonal Telecommunication Systems*. New York: Plenum. pp. 399–424.

Shulman, A.D., Penman, R. and Sless, D. (1990) 'Putting information technology in its place', in J. Carroll (ed.), *Applied Social Psychology and Organizational Settings*. Hillsdale, NJ: Lawrence Erlbaum. pp. 155–92.

Shulman, A.D. and Penman, R. (1992) 'Developing information infrastructures that work', in *Service Delivery Communications in the 1990s*. Canberra: Department of Transport and Communication. pp. 1–7.

Siegel, J., Dubrovsky, V., Kiesler, S. and McGuire, T.O. (1986) 'Group processes in computer mediated communication', *Organizational Behavior and Human Decision Processes*, 37: 157–87.

Sless, D. (1981) *Learning and Visual Communication*. London: Croom Helm.

Sless, D. (1986a) *In Search of Semiotics*. London: Croom Helm.

Sless, D. (1986b) 'Repairing messages: the hidden cost of inappropriate theory', *Australian Journal of Communication*, 9(10): 82–93.

Sless, D. (1991) 'Communication and certainty', *Australian Journal of Communication*, 18(3): 19–31.

Smith, Ken G., Carroll, Stephen J. and Ashford, Susan J. (1995) 'Intra- and interorganizational cooperation: toward a research agenda', *Academy of Management Journal*, 38(1): 7–23.

Steiner, I.D. (1972) *Group Process and Productivity*. New York: Academic Press.

Sundstrom, E., De Meuse, K.P. and Futrell, D. (1990) 'Work teams: applications and effectiveness', *American Psychologist*, 45: 120–33.

Taylor, James C. and Felten, David F. (1993) *Performance by Design: Sociotechnical Systems in North America*. Englewood Cliffs, NJ: Prentice-Hall.

Tomarzky, L.G. (1986) 'Technological change and the structure of work', in M.S. Pallak and R.O. Perloff (eds), *Psychology and Work: Productivity, Change and Employment*. Washington, DC: American Psychological Association. pp. 53–84.

Vico, G. (1986) *The New Science of Giambattista Vico*, translated and edited by T. Bergin and M. Fisch. Ithaca, NY: Cornell University Press.

Walther, Joseph B. (1994) 'Anticipated ongoing interaction versus channel effects on relational communication in computer-mediated interaction', *Human Communication Research*, 20(4): 473–501.

Wilde, W. (1991) *Office 2000: Business Process Management*. Waltham, MA: Wang Laboratories.

Zuboff, S. (1988) *In the Age of the Smart Machine*. New York: Basil Books.

2.7

Metaphors of Communication and Organization

LINDA L. PUTNAM, NELSON PHILLIPS AND PAMELA CHAPMAN

Perhaps no other construct pervades organizational studies more than the term *communication*. The ubiquitous nature of the term, however, contributes to its elusiveness and to the difficulty in distinguishing it from such related terms as *information, channel*, and *media* and from the myriad of organizational concepts that incorporate nuances of the term. Classical organizational theorists have equated communication with written documents and the authority to give commands (Weber 1947), the upward flow of messages and the persuasion of workers (Taylor 1947), the horizontal flow of information (Fayol 1949), listening and informal communication (Roethlisberger 1941), feedback and circular behavior (Follett 1941), decision premises (Simon 1957), and formal channels of communication (Barnard 1968). Contemporary organizational theorists treat communication as synonymous with such constructs as information processing (Galbraith 1973), social networks (Rogers and Kincaid 1981; Tichy and Fombrun 1979), coordination (Hage 1974), and participation (Likert 1967; Miller and Monge 1986). Communication, then, has become a catch-all term that infuses most topics in organization studies and crosses most chapters in this *Handbook*.

Confusion also exists, at both the theoretical and the practical level, concerning the relationship between organization and communication (Smith 1993; Taylor 1995; Taylor and Van Every 1993). Do organizations determine the type and flow of communication or does communication shape the nature of organizing? Does message flow follow organizational structure or do communication patterns develop structures and shape task-related coordination? In effect, how does the organizational context affect communication and how does communication shape the organizational context?

Smith (1993) sets forth three ways that organization and communication are related: containment, production, and equivalency. The *containment* relationship treats communication as located within a reified, materialistic organizational structure. Thus, the structural-functional elements of communication are critical to the maintenance of the organizational container. The second type of relationship, *production*, examines the way organizations produce communication, or communication produces organization, or the two co-produce each other. That is, organizations are not simply containers in which communication activities occur, but rather communication and organization may produce each other. For example, the sharing of rituals enacts organizational culture as it operates from the residual of past communication practices. The production relationship, then, wrestles with the dilemma of whether one has *a priori* existence over the other or do they develop concomitantly. The third approach, *equivalence*, posits an even more radical turn in this relationship. It treats communication and organization as a monastic unity or as the same phenomenon expressed in different ways. That is, communicating is organizing and organizing is communicating: the two processes are isomorphic (Smith 1993; Taylor 1995).

This dilemma on the relationship between organizing and communicating calls into question the metaphors that we use to depict organizations (Morgan 1986). In these metaphors, organization is placed in the role of *figure* or principal subject, and communication assumes the position of *ground* or secondary subject (Black 1962; Taylor 1995). Thus, traditional images of organizations are influenced by relationships in which communication plays a non-existent or tangential role. But, if we take communication theory as central and equivalent to organizing, new metaphors emerge that represent the organization–communication relationship in different ways.–Thus, for the purpose of exploring this relationship, the organizing scheme of this chapter positions communication as the producer of organizations. However, even though this chapter privileges communication, it examines metaphors that exemplify all three of Smith's (1993) orientations. These metaphors reveal alternative ways of thinking about the origin and nature of organizing, its processes, and the constructs that form its ontological roots.

Beginning with a brief overview of organizational communication, this chapter tracks the history and chronology of research domains within the field. Then it discusses how the study of metaphor has surfaced in the organizational literature. We then examine seven metaphor clusters that represent different threads of organizational communication research: conduit, lens, linkage, performance, symbol, voice, and discourse. Each of these metaphors introduces alternative ways of seeing organizations which emerge from the communication–organization relationship. The conclusion then unpacks the nuances of this relationship for these metaphors, discusses the contributions and omissions of each, and explores the implications of this analysis for developing organizational theories.

This chapter is not an exhaustive review of the organizational communication literature, as it appears in Jablin et al. (1987), Goldhaber and Barnett (1988), or Jablin and Putnam (in press). Readers searching for reviews of the extensive body of organizational communication research should consult these volumes. Instead, this chapter casts a broad stroke across the canvas of this literature to highlight studies that illustrate the various metaphors. Thus, the literature cited within each section serves primarily as exemplars of the field. Criteria for selecting exemplars include: relevance to the metaphor cluster, recency of the work, and representation of a wide array of research domains. This chapter, then, reviews and integrates a complex body of communication literature, not only to show its relevance to organization studies, but also to explain how different streams of this work can illuminate our understanding of what organizations *are*.

HISTORY AND DEVELOPMENT OF ORGANIZATIONAL COMMUNICATION RESEARCH

The early work in organizational communication was shaped by interests in business and industrial communication from the 1920s to the 1950s and the human relations movement from the 1950s to the mid 1970s. The writings of Dale Carnegie and texts on business rhetoric focused on the persuasive strategies of top management, the accuracy and readability of reports, and the effectiveness of different communication media (Putnam and Cheney 1985; Redding 1985). In the 1960s and 1970s, the dominant perspective shifted to the study of messages that flowed through organizations and the way communication climates influenced the adequacy and effectiveness of these transmissions. Throughout this work, communication was treated as a variable that influenced individual and organizational performance.

Two dominant interests, then, formed the foundation of the field: (1) the skills that made individuals more effective communicators on the job; and (2) the factors that characterized system-wide communication effectiveness (Redding and Tompkins 1988). This period, called the *modernist* orientation, depicted the majority of work conducted prior to the 1980s (Putnam and Cheney 1985; Redding and Tompkins 1988). It also subsumed psychological studies that focused on such topics as superior–subordinate interaction, communication climate, and information processing as well as sociological studies that centred on communication networks, work group coordination, and adoption and use of new communication technologies.

In the modernist tradition, organizations were rational, instrumental entities; thus, communication embodied a utilitarian or instrumental bias. Both organizations and communication were objective realities that could be measured and tested under controlled research conditions with methodological tools borrowed from the natural sciences. Modernists also embraced the idea of objective boundaries that separated hierarchical levels, departmental units, and organizational parameters (Redding and Tompkins 1988).

The early 1980s marked a radical shift in organizational communication scholarship, although not necessarily a complete break with the past. Concomitant with similar critiques in organizational studies, scholars challenged the research traditions in organizational communication, particularly the absence of theoretical frameworks and the nature of organizational reality embedded in modernist work (Putnam and Cheney 1983; Redding and Tompkins 1988). Nested within these critiques were challenges to the treatment of communication as a variable or a linear transmission (Putnam 1983). Organizational communication became defined as 'the study of messages, information, meaning, and symbolic activity' that constitutes organizations (Putnam and Cheney, 1985: 131). New research domains began to focus on the meanings of organizational events (Donnellon et al. 1986; Gray et al. 1985); strategic ambiguity (Eisenberg 1984); language, symbols, and organizational culture (Frost et al. 1985; Pacanowsky and O'Donnell-Trujillo 1983; Pondy et al. 1983; Rosen 1985; Smircich 1983); organizational identification and unobtrusive control (Tompkins and Cheney 1983; 1985); communication rules and scripts (Harris and Cronen 1979; Schall 1983); corporate public discourse (Cheney 1983; Cheney and Vibbert 1987; Grunig 1984); and the exercise of power and control through distorted communication (Conrad 1983; Deetz and Kersten 1983; Edwards 1979; Riley 1983).

One stream of research, *naturalistic*, centred on making interpretations grounded in context and situation. Naturalists adopted a stance that was pluralistic by viewing organizational life from multiple perspectives, not just managerial ones. Since organizational boundaries and structures were socially constituted, they were permeable and negotiable. Another orientation was that of the *critical* approach, which appeared in the mid to late 1980s. This orientation extended social constructivist views by centering on power and control. It purported that individuals and groups had differential control in constructing the meanings that mattered in organizations. Since dominant groups had more access to information and more opportunities to construct broad-ranged interpretations than did other groups, communicative processes in organizations were not neutral (Deetz 1985; Deetz and Kersten 1983). Discourse, symbolic actions, and meaning were the ways that ideology became natural and legitimate in organizations and the way subordinate groups participated in their own domination (Deetz and Kersten 1983; Mumby 1988).

This overview provides a framework for thinking about topics and research domains in organizational communication, but it fails to uncover the subtle and complex ways that communication and organization are interrelated.

Moreover, it does not account for new developments in discourse and language analysis that set forth what communication is and how it operates as organizing. One of the ways to unpack these complexities is to probe into the metaphors of organizational communication that represent research domains in the field. In particular, this chapter centers on the subtle features of metaphor clusters that reveal diverse representations of communication and organization.

METAPHORS AND IMAGES OF ORGANIZATIONS

Metaphor has become a common topic in organizational studies (Brink 1993; Deetz 1986; Deetz and Mumby 1985; Krefting and Frost 1985; Koch and Deetz 1981; Manning 1979; Morgan 1980; 1983; 1986; Pinder and Bourgeois 1982; Pepper 1995; Pondy 1983; Smith and Eisenberg 1988; Smith and Turner 1995; Stohl 1995; Trice and Beyer 1984). Although originally examined as a literary trope, metaphors are more than ornaments that decorate language. They operate at multiple levels of analysis to provide insights into how we understand organizational life.

A metaphor is a way of seeing a thing as if it were something else (Lakoff and Johnson 1980). It is a particular linguistic expression that provides a cognitive bridge between two dissimilar domains. For some theorists, metaphors link abstract constructs to concrete things (Ortony 1979), while for others, metaphors tie the familiar to the unknown (Hawkes 1972). Perhaps even more significantly, metaphors legitimate actions, set goals, and guide behaviors (Lakoff and Johnson 1980). Metaphors are also constitutive in that they facilitate the creation and interpretation of social reality. In effect, metaphors shape how we see and make sense of the world by orienting our perceptions, conceptualizations, and understanding of one thing in light of another.

Metaphor is probably best understood as a system of beliefs about figure and ground relationships which serve to highlight certain features while suppressing others. For example, to treat organizational mergers as 'ambushes and shootouts' highlights the surprise attack, hostile takeover, winners and losers, and hired guns who orchestrate the deal (Hirsch and Andrews 1983). This imagery, however, conceals the wooing, matchmaking, and compatibility issues that a courtship metaphor might reveal. In this chapter, different elements of communication surface as figure for some metaphors and ground for other ways of thinking. What becomes highlighted about organizational communication reveals the nature of the metaphor.

Functions of Metaphor Analysis

Metaphors facilitate theory building by examining images at multiple levels of analysis. In organizational theory, metaphor analysis contributes to theory construction through: (1) articulating the ontological assumptions of different views of organizations (Morgan 1980; 1986); (2) revealing the assumptive ground of key organizational constructs (Alvesson 1993a; Buzzanell and Goldzwig 1991; Smith and Turner 1995; Stutman and Putnam 1994); and (3) generating new constructs such as a garbage can model of decision-making (Cohen et al. 1972). Organizational members also use metaphors to depict their own organizations. Metaphors such as families, zoos, savage tribes, and sporting games are ways that members construct implicit theories of organizing (Deetz 1986; Koch and Deetz 1981). Of these approaches, the most cited study of metaphors is Morgan's (1986) *Images of Organizations*. By examining dominant theories and research domains in organizational studies, Morgan uncovers diverse images that depict different ways that individuals conceive of organizations. Each image is partial, highlights different features of organizations, finds roots in diverse organizational assumptions, and embodies different strengths and weaknesses. His analysis delineates dominant or root metaphors of organizations such as machines, organisms, cultures, psychic prisons, brains, political systems, and instruments of domination. These metaphors are referenced extensively in both the communication and the management literatures (May 1993; Miller 1995; Stohl 1995).

METAPHORS OF COMMUNICATION AND ORGANIZATION

This chapter calls into question the traditional metaphors used to depict organizations by exploring relationships between communication and organization represented in the research literature (Smith 1993; Taylor 1995). By taking communication as figure and organization as ground, we hope to unearth new ways of thinking about organizations, as well as alternative metaphors that lie in the spaces between figure and ground and within the schisms inherent in the field. In effect, this project moves away from such universal metaphors as

machines and organisms as cornerstones of organizational theory.

This chapter also departs from earlier work by developing metaphor clusters within the organizational communication literature. A cluster refers to groups of metaphors or submetaphors that can be arrayed as distinct but interrelated categories. Within each cluster, metaphors subsume other metaphors, including ones that embody different assumptive ground about organizations.

A major weakness of traditional metaphor analysis is a tendency to lock categories into fixed meanings and relationships. Smith and Turner (1995) overcome this problem by employing chains of figure–ground relationships in which the ground, once presented, becomes the figure for the next metaphor. Through continual reflexivity in their analysis, they uncover the assumptions that underlie relationships among metaphors. Even though this chapter relies on traditional metaphor analysis, it tries to avoid freezing metaphorical relationships by tracking chains of metaphors between the categories.

First, we identify seven metaphor clusters that direct or guide research programs in organizational communication. Next, we describe the central features of these metaphors; note streams and schools of metaphor clusters that stem from these images; illustrate how these metaphors are employed in recent organizational communication studies; and describe how they cast the communication–organization relationship in very different ways. In the conclusion, we track chains of metaphors between the categories and clusters. The seven metaphor clusters are conduit, lens, linkage, performance, symbol, voice, and discourse. This list of metaphors is neither exhaustive nor mutually exclusive. In many respects, metaphors represent 'blurred genres' (Geertz 1973) and mutations (Weick 1979). The conclusion of this chapter, then, explores the ways that these seven metaphors overlap and contradict.

The *conduit metaphor* encompasses orientations to communication that treat organizations as *containers* or channels for amount, type, direction, and structure of information flow. Research domains that embrace this perspective focus on communication as *transmission*, and include studies on information overload and adequacy; comparisons among communication media; communication technology as media choice; communication as a tool for accomplishing organizational goals; directionality of communication flow; and organizational units as communication hubs or nodes. Metaphor clusters subsumed in this category include tool, channel, and media.

The *metaphor of lens* provides a different slant on the conduit view of communication. This cluster centers on the literature that treats organizations as perceptual systems or *eyes* that scan the environment, filter data, distort and delay information, screen or gatekeep, route messages, and disseminate innovation and change. Thus communication is *filtered* and often distorted as it passes through the various 'membranes' between organization and environment, between departments, and between individuals. Metaphors subsumed within this category include gatekeeper, sensor, and shield. The *linkage metaphor* treats organizations as *networks* or systems of interconnected individuals in which communication acts to *connect* by forming relational bonds; patterns of contacts and interconnectedness; global integration; and ties among work, home, and community (Stohl 1995). Metaphors that appear in this cluster include web, bridge, bonds, and relationships.

The next cluster of metaphors shifts from the transmission roots of communication to highlight meaning, interpretation, and sensemaking as the nature of organizing. Drawn from social constructivist roots, the *metaphor of performance* casts communication as *social interaction*, as seen in the work on jamming and improvisation, performing managerial roles, shared meanings, and theatrical productions. In this metaphor, organizations emerge as *coordinated actions*. Metaphors subsumed in this category include enactments, co-production, drama, and storytelling. The *metaphor of symbol* draws from organizational culture to cast communication as interpretation of literary forms such as narratives, metaphors, rites and rituals, and paradoxes. These symbols are not simply artifacts of cultures; instead they operate as a means of public persuasion, as ways of knowing, as options for managing identities, and as political control. Thus, the organization emerges as a *novel* jointly authored by organizational members as they create and interpret a range of symbolic activities. Metaphors subsumed in this category are semiotics, sign, culture, and shared meanings.

Drawing from critical and postmodern views of organizations, the *metaphor of voice* encompasses a number of related clusters, including distorted voices; voices of domination through ideology and unobtrusive control; a different voice through feminist perspectives; and access to voice through participatory and democratic practices. Metaphor clusters that surface within the category of voice include communication distortion and conflict suppression (Redding and Tompkins 1988). Communication is *expression* and the organization becomes a *chorus* of stilled or singing voices. Finally, the *metaphor of*

discourse is equally diverse in its underpinnings and representations of communication. It highlights communication as *conversation*, in which organizations surface as *texts* that consist of genres and dialogues. Metaphor clusters subsumed within this category include language, talk, linguistics, speech acts, emotions, and discursive practices.

These metaphors serve as alternative frames for examining the organizational communication literature and the relationship between communication and organization. They are not paradigms or discrete categories; rather they serve as perspectives to facilitate understanding the diverse and multifaceted field of organizational communication. This chapter, then, is not trying to unify divergent research metaphors, nor to embrace pluralism for pluralism's sake. Nor do we advocate that researchers borrow from a pot-pourri of metaphors, unconscious of the assumptions and obligations embedded in each. Indeed, immersion in one or several closely related submetaphors typically provides the most coherent and logically congruent line of research. Instead, this chapter seeks to generate new ways of thinking about the origins and nature of organizations by exposing readers to a body of literature than can yield new insights about organizing.

The Conduit Metaphor

As developed from early studies on communication 'within' the organization, the most common view of communication is a conduit in which messages are transmitted throughout the organization (Axley 1984; Reddy 1979). A *conduit* is a channel through which something is conveyed, such as a tube, cable, or cylinder (Axley 1984). In this metaphor, communication is equated with *transmission* and organizations appear as *containers*, physical systems, or passageways for the conduit.

Words that signal the use of a conduit metaphor are 'send', 'exchange', 'relay', and 'convey' (Axley 1984). The conduit metaphor treats transmission as figure and message and sender/receiver as ground. Communication within this metaphor is primarily a one-way, linear flow (Shannon and Weaver 1949), even though amendments to this approach add feedback, two-way flow, and process (Rogers 1994). But the centrality of transmission remains constant, even with variations in directionality of information flow. According to this perspective, a manager who communicates 'effectively' is transferring ideas to his or her subordinates with minimal spillage (Eisenberg and Phillips 1991). Words contain information, language transfers thoughts and feelings, and listeners extract ideas from transmission (Axley 1984). The conduit metaphor evokes an image of communication as easy, effortless, and linear. Miscommunication occurs when no information is received or when the information received is not what the sender intended (Eisenberg and Phillips 1991). According to this view, receivers are typically passive and reactive.

Examples of organizational research that incorporates this metaphor include studies on: (1) the links between organizational structure and the amount of communication (Jablin 1987; Katz and Kahn 1966); (2) the uses of formal and informal communication channels (Downs 1967); (3) communication as task coordination (Allen and Hauptman 1990; Fulk et al. 1987; Tushman 1979); (4) comparisons among communication media (Rice 1993; Short et al. 1976); (5) the adoption of new communication technology (Rice and Shook 1988; 1990); (6) information overload and adequacy (Miller 1960; O'Reilly 1980); and (7) organizational units as hubs through which information passes (Zmud 1990; Rice and Aydin 1991; Zmud et al. 1990). Since the concept of communication as a conduit is so ubiquitous, other reviews cover the many domains subsumed under this metaphor (Allen et al. 1993; Fulk and Boyd 1991; Jablin 1987; Rice and Gattiker in press; Redding and Tompkins 1988; Wert-Gray et al. 1991).

An image of communication that falls within this category is the tool metaphor. A *tool* is an instrument, a device, a function, or a means of accomplishing an instrumental goal. Researchers who treat communication as a tool focus on how communication influences work effectiveness, improves performance feedback, diffuses organizational innovations, and fosters organizational change (Earley 1988; Rice and Gattiker in press). The tool metaphor includes research on communication technologies such as electronic mail, voice mail, audio and video conferencing, and computer conferencing. These technologies differ from face-to-face interactions in their speed, ability to span distance, asynchronous links between individuals at different points in time, and retrieval systems. It also incorporates studies of computer-assisted decision aids, such as group decision support systems (GDSS), expert systems, and management information systems (Miller 1995). Although GDSS studies on decision quality, satisfaction, and effectiveness are contradictory (Fulk and Boyd 1991), they demonstrate how scholars use communication technology as an instrument for organizational ends.

Some of the work under the tool metaphor overlaps with other metaphors. For example, work on communication technologies that emphasizes social network formation, connectedness, and task dependencies (Bikson and Eveland 1990) converges with the linkage metaphor. The work of authors like Poole and DeSanctis (1990), whose model of GDSS shows how group members interact about information technologies, and Yates and Orlikowski (1992), who examine communication media as genres, moves away from the tool metaphor toward a view of organizational communication as discourse.

The conduit and tool metaphors treat communication as an object that flows from a source to a receiver. Communication is a channel, a technology, or a task that organizational members have or must do. If information is adequate and accurate in transmission (message fidelity), communication is effective. Communication media are effective if the technologies aid in reaching organizational goals. The conduit metaphor depicts an organization as a *container* or a hollow physical object that houses communication and information systems. Containers have discrete boundaries, barriers that block information flow, and physical separation that may cause breakdowns and omissions. Thus, organizations function like telephone switchboards, computer memory banks, or television signal systems (Morgan 1986). Even research which aims to stretch the physical boundaries of organizations, for example, new communication technologies, unknowingly reifies the borders of both organization and communication.

The Lens Metaphor

A second metaphor that complements and overlaps with the conduit view of communication is a lens. A *lens* is a screen that *filters*, protects, shields, and guides transmission. Studies that center on 'distortion', 'gatekeeping', 'blocking', 'information search and acquisition', and 'accessibility' typically exemplify the lens metaphor. In this metaphor, communication is equated with a *filtering process*: searching, retrieving, and routing information. Thus the organization, as it appears in this metaphor, is an *eye* that scans, sifts, and relays.

The lens metaphor shares some assumptions of the conduit perspective. It relies on transmission and is rooted in the transfer of ideas, but, unlike the conduit metaphor, senders and receivers are active agents in the process. Distortion and filtering occur naturally, as in the game of 'telephone' in which messages change in content and form as they travel from individual to individual and unit to unit. Message simplification, the most general level of distortion, encompasses 'abbreviations, condensations, and loss of detail that occur through message flow' (Stohl and Redding 1987: 479). Reception plays a significant role in the lens metaphor whereas sending is the critical element in the conduit perspective.

Both the eye and lens metaphors are housed in containers. Just as the lens overlaps with the conduit metaphor of communication, the eye is encased in a socket. The socket or skull has physical structure, membranes, and eyelids that control access to light. Thus, organizational boundaries and structures aid in sensing and filtering stimuli. The lens metaphor also supports a containment relationship between communication and organization. The eye contains the lens that filters and screens information.

The research in organizational communication influenced by the lens metaphor ranges from studies of information flow and superior-subordinate communication to recent work on perceived environmental uncertainty, information acquisition and decision-making, media richness, and communication technology. Early studies include how employees: suppress unpleasant messages (Tesser and Rosen 1975); distort and withhold information that travels up the channel (O'Reilly and Roberts 1974); sharpen and assimilate messages through serial transmission (Davis and O'Conner 1977; Ackoff and Emery 1972); and provide access to information sources (O'Reilly 1978). These studies concentrate primarily on what senders believe that receivers want to hear.

Research on performance feedback that focuses on the timing and the delivery of messages exemplifies the lens metaphor (Cusella 1987). Studies on information sources, perceptions of ambiguity, accessibility and decision-making, and consequences of information seeking behaviors also employ themes drawn from the lens metaphor (Miller and Jablin 1991; O'Reilly et al. 1987; Stohl and Redding 1987). In these studies, the organization functions visually to open and close access to information and to route internal and external stimuli.

Two research domains that adopt a lens metaphor merit further consideration. Media richness, as one domain, purports that some communication channels which limit natural language use filter or screen out more verbal and nonverbal cues more than do others. The richest media convey the greatest amount of information (Daft and Lengel 1984; Trevino et al. 1987). Media richness theorists contend that managers will be more effective if they choose a communication medium that matches the ambiguity of their task. Although some research supports this hypothesis (Daft et al. 1987; Russ et al. 1990), other studies claim that managers are not rational in their media use and that the

characteristics of media are not necessarily objective or stable (Rice 1993; Rice et al. 1989).

The second domain guides the research on information environments, contributing not just to the ways that organizations process external cues, but also to conceptions of the environment itself. The lens metaphor underlies research on strategy formulation and implementation, image making and public relations, and stakeholder interaction. These studies examine how organizations process and interpret external information and how they influence stakeholders through external information flow.

When organizations act as sensors, top managers scan the environment and construct images or visual pictures of external stimuli (Daft et al. 1993; Huber 1991; Pfeffer and Salancik 1978). They attend to particular stimuli more closely if they are addressing broad-based, nonroutine problems than if they are just scanning (Glick et al. 1993). Organizations that engage in intense scanning and high levels of performance monitoring are more effective at handling environmental problems than are those that lack routine monitoring (Eisenhardt 1989; Huber 1991).

In addition to scanning environments, organizations manage external information flow to organizational publics (Grunig 1984; Grunig and Grunig 1992). Strategic public relations employs the lens metaphor to examine one-way (inside–outside) and two-way (inside–outside, outside–inside) dissemination between organizations and stakeholders. Two-way dissemination models preempt problems and ascertain risks by actively defining stakeholder relationships (Heath 1988). Two-way models, then, spill over into the performance metaphor of communication in which environments are enacted rather than perceived.

A basic assumption of the lens metaphor is that information is incomplete. In transmitting a message, different backgrounds and goals of senders and receivers increase the likelihood that information will be converted, simplified, reduced, or summarized (Smith 1973; Stohl and Redding 1987). The inevitability of misperception challenges traditional notions of accuracy, clarity, and communication effectiveness by introducing meaning and interpretation into message transmission.

Ambiguity and misunderstanding of messages are not necessarily breakdowns in communication as the conduit metaphor would suggest (Eisenberg and Phillips 1991; Eisenberg and Witten 1987). Rather they result from message modification and the need to balance relational and political goals. Ambiguity, defined as the failure to understand the link between a symbol and a referent, may be intentional. In this respect, the lens metaphor plays an important symbolic role in promoting surveillance, fostering legitimation, and providing evidence of rationality (Feldman and March 1981). The lens metaphor overlaps with the performance metaphor through using ambiguity strategically to unify diverse goals, protect confidentiality, build camaraderie, and facilitate organizational change (Eisenberg 1984). Misperception, then, is inevitable and information acquisition is slow. Consequently, the issue is no longer accuracy but plausibility (Sutcliffe in press). Thus, taking action provides a better test for plausibility and learning than does continual scanning and filtering (Weick 1990).

The image of organizations for the lens metaphor is the *eye*, or the visual organ of sight. The eye represents perception, point of view, the center of visual processing. Even though it is part of the brain's information processing system (Morgan 1986), the eye is the center or the core in which perception activities function, like the 'eye of the storm', or 'the eye of a flower'. Information processing in organizations, although linked to cognition, is a visual process in that the eye performs the critical perceptual functions. The lens metaphor, however, highlights the boundaries and structural properties of organizations; scanning and screening occur across static borders. Perception, the locus of organizing, alters the way that information is conceived.

The Linkage Metaphor

The conduit and lens metaphors of organizational communication share an interest in transmission and in treating organizations as containers. The linkage metaphor shifts the focus from transmission to *connection*. Thus, the communication is the connector that links people together and constitutes organizations as *networks* of relationships. In the linkage metaphor, organizations are not entities with fixed structures and boundaries. Interactants are intertwined through dyadic processes that reside within relationships rather than perceptual systems. Thus, the relationship between communication and organization moves from one of containment to one of production. Network studies, however, vary as to whether organizations produce communication or communication produces organizations. In research on network roles and structures, organizations produce linkages; while in the studies on emergent networks, communication produces organizations.

The metaphor of linkage, however, continues to rely on a conduit view of communication in that transmission and amount of communication are the key elements that connect individuals and units together. Recent work on semantic networks depart from this tradition (Stohl 1993). Linkages define network roles, create patterns and structures, determine the strength or weakness of ties, and shape interorganizational networks (Monge and Eisenberg 1987). The degree of participation or inclusion in networks stems from the presence or absence of a link, the amount of communication exchanged, the directionality of messages, and the kinds of content that flow through a link. Propensity to form communication links emanates from structural properties of networks, interpersonal attraction, proximity and contextual factors, and social activity patterns (McPhee and Corman 1995). A few studies explore linkages formed through vocabularies and interpretations rather than frequency of contacts (Monge and Eisenberg 1987). These studies move toward a symbol rather than a conduit metaphor.

The metaphor of linkage underlies research on *network roles*, the structural positions of individuals within a network. Isolates are individuals who have few communication links. Bridges, liaisons, and linking pins connect individuals and groups (Farace et al. 1977); while stars are individuals who have many linkages, both inside and outside the network (Tushman and Scanlan 1981). Stars may also be boundary spanners, ambassadors, or guards who survey, monitor, and exchange information with groups outside the network (Ancona and Caldwell 1988). Role configurations also emerge from interaction strategies and task activities. Barley's (1986; 1990) research demonstrates how communication links based on expertise, technology, and task activity shape informal roles that counter formal organizational positions of medical personnel. This positional approach to the study of networks differs from the relational or emergent perspective by treating organizational boundaries as *a priori* and by treating organizations as producing communication networks.

Network patterns and structures also vary in centrality, formality, content, and density (Monge and Eisenberg 1987). Centralized networks have a high degree of vertical differentiation, many isolates, and few liaisons, while decentralized networks involve more participation and information sharing (Pearce and David 1983). Centrality, however, is determined by arrangements of individuals in formal positions (Bavelas 1950; Leavitt 1951) and it is criticized for presuming that roles and structures are stable and for assuming that formal arrangements such as organizational charts determine information flow (Monge and Eisenberg 1987).

Studies of centralized/decentralized networks also examine discrepancies between the formal and the informal patterns. For example, Davis (1953) notes how the grapevine or rumor mill travels diagonally across the organizational hierarchy. Both the informality and the dynamic quality of the grapevine contribute to its speed and kernels of accuracy (Hellweg 1987). Studies that track who talks to whom, how often, and about what topics map configurations of cliques, groups, and isolates (Monge and Contractor 1988). The properties that aid in forming these configurations include numbers of contacts per week (frequency of communication), agreement on type of linkage shared (reciprocity), and one-way versus two-way communication (symmetry/asymmetry).

Network configurations also vary in content of communication, with organizational members developing different networks for task, innovation, and social support activities (Albrecht and Ropp 1984; Albrecht and Hall 1991). If individuals talk only about one function, they develop a uniplex network; if they deal with multiple topics in their interactions, they form multiplex linkages. Multiplex linkages provide richer information, are more enduring and stable, and are more influential and supportive than are relationships that share only one or two topics (Albrecht and Hall 1991; Stohl 1995).

Research on the function and content of communication casts linkages as producing organizations. Organizations move from uniplex to multiplex relationships by extending the function of work teams to innovation, social support, and occupational networks (Stohl 1995). As work teams develop complex networks among employees, they typically increase concertive control and reduce dependence on authority structures (Barker 1993). Linkages among church members also develop informally from the number, size, and type of communication activities of individuals (McPhee and Corman 1995).

Network patterns also vary in density, defined as the ratio of actual contacts to the total number of possible linkages in the system. Density of a network plays a key role in adopting new ideas. Close connections among employees make people feel more comfortable with an innovation (Albrecht and Hall 1991) and facilitate positive attitudes toward new communication technologies (Fulk 1993; Rice et al. 1990). In fact, having a critical mass of users in a dense network is vital for the adoption of e-mail and voice mail systems (Ehrlich 1987; Fulk et al. 1990; Rice and Danowski 1993). Drawing from a social influence theory, Schmitz and Fulk (1991) attribute this pattern to the support that coworkers provide, vicarious learning of the new media, and norms for how the new media should be used (Fulk and Boyd 1991).

Dense or tightly interconnected links form *strong ties* in which frequent communication links endure for long periods of time. Individuals joined through strong ties experience greater pressure to adopt norms, values, and expectations than do employees who are loosely coupled (Stohl 1995). Although dense networks are supportive, they become self-conforming and may inhibit opportunities for risk, change, and adaptability (Papa 1990). Thus, *weak ties* maintain an organization's stability and help it adapt to environmental changes. As a whole, organizational members acquire more information from multiple, loosely connected links than from dense, tightly coupled ones (Granovetter 1973).

Patterns of loose and tight couplings also affect *interorganizational networks*. Interorganizational networks are fields or systems of organizations; thus, an organization's environment can be viewed as a network (Perrow 1986). Jolts or rapid changes within this network can disrupt an entire industry of tightly coupled linkages (Eisenberg and Goodall 1993). Organizations communicate with each other through interlocking boards of directors, interaction among boundary spanners (Adams 1980), and exchanging personnel (Eisenberg et al. 1985). Organizations form interdependent and complementary services, for example providing parts for assembling an engine, or passing clients to each other. They develop linkages through joint ventures, agency-sponsored projects, and trade associations (Oliver 1990). These connections allow organizations to enhance their legitimacy and meet legal and regulatory requirements. Many linkages form through contacts outside of work, for example at professional and occupational meetings (Stohl 1995).

The study of interorganizational linkages treats communication as a connector or a contact system. In most studies, communication is implicit, defined as a tool for building the network. One type of research, however, departs from this approach by treating communication as sensemaking formed through relationships. Rather than focusing on information flow, a sensemaking perspective highlights the symbolic nature of communication, reinforcing the position that communication produces organizations. In particular, research on semantic networks examines the connections between people who hold similar interpretations of key organizational events (Monge and Eisenberg 1987). In a study of mission statements, dense semantic networks indicate that employees share perceptions of the organization's goals and its culture (Stohl 1993).

Rogers and Kincaid's (1981) convergence model of network analysis contends that individuals converge on shared meanings through network participation. Studies of memorable messages illustrate how particular phrases hold significance for network members. Individuals recall them readily, share them privately, and use them to determine the appropriateness of behaviors (Stohl 1986; 1993). For some postmodernists, who aim to move organizations beyond hierarchical and exploitative structures, the linkage metaphor offers opportunities for voice, democracy, and multiplicity (Rosenau 1992). Information networks focus on a plurality of voices and reduce dependence on instrumental rationality.

In the linkage metaphor, organizations consist of multiple, overlapping networks with permeable boundaries. Members are interlocked in a variety of relationships that 'transcend office walls' through community projects, child care concerns, informal friendships, neighbourhood activities, and company socials (Stohl 1995). Since communication serves as a building block that connects individuals, group, and interorganizational levels, organizations are clusters or constellations of task activities, social interactions, innovations, and a variety of organizational processes (McPhee and Corman 1995; Mintzberg 1979).

Connections among people imply collaboration and interdependence; linkages promote coordinated action and extend webs of social influence. Since communication alters network patterns, linkages shift with issues, topics, and context. Thus, network roles and patterns are fluid and dynamic. Treating organizations as networks challenges traditional notions of static boundaries, unidimensional functions, and immobile structures.

The Metaphor of Performance

A major factor that distinguishes the conduit, lens, and linkage metaphors from the next four perspectives is an emphasis on interaction and meaning. In the performance metaphor, *social interaction* becomes the focal point for organizational communication research. Performance refers to process and activity, rather than to an organization's productivity or output. Performance combines Turner's (1980) view of 'accomplishment' with Goffman's (1959) notion of 'presentation'. In this metaphor, 'organizational reality is brought to life in communicative performance' (Pacanowsky and O'Donnell-Trujillo 1983: 131). Communication consists of interconnected exchanges, for example, message–feedback–response, action–reaction–adjustment, symbolic action–interpretation–reflection, and action–sensemaking. Social interaction is rooted

in the sequences, patterns, and meanings that stem from exchanging verbal and nonverbal messages.

The key features that distinguish social interaction from the conduit and lens metaphors are dynamic processes, interlocking behaviors, reflexivity, sensemaking, and collaboration (Fisher 1978). Performances, then, are interactional, contextual, episodic, and improvisational (Pacanowsky and O'Donnell-Trujillo 1983). Communication becomes part of an ongoing series of cues, without a clear beginning and ending. Individuals bracket or punctuate streams of experience to make sense of their interactions (Watzlawick et al. 1967; Weick 1979). Communicative acts form patterns of contiguous acts, interlocked behaviors, episodes, and incidents. Rather than centering on task activities, organizational communication functions as passion developed through organizational storytelling, sociality through performing small talk, and politics through displaying personal strength (Pacanowsky and O'Donnell-Trujillo 1983). The flow of actions and interpretations reflects back on and constrains previous message activities.

In the performance metaphor, organizations emerge as *coordinated actions*, that is, organizations enact their own rules, structures, and environments through social interaction. Performance, however, serves as an umbrella for perspectives that stem from such diverse roots as cybernetic theory, self-referential systems, dramaturgy, symbolic interaction, phenomenology, and hermeneutics. These schools form different approaches to the metaphor of performance: those rooted in *enactment* (Weick 1979); in coconstructing or *co-production* (Boje 1991; Eisenberg 1990); and in *storytelling*, folklore, and symbolic convergence (Boje 1991; 1995; Bormann 1983; Jones et al. 1988). Social interaction is both behavioral and symbolic, with a simultaneous emphasis on action and sensemaking. Storytelling in this metaphor is not monologic but is interactionally achieved through discourse (Boje 1991). Storytellers and listeners serve as coauthors to simultaneously construct and make sense of their interactions. Researchers act as organizational detectives who engage in storytelling through constructing plots based on organizational talk (Goodall 1989) and through writing and staging organizations as theatrical productions (Mangham and Overington 1987).

Enactment, the first major school in the performance metaphor, emanates from Weick's (1979) model of organizing. Communication in this approach is a double interact, the basic building block of organizations. A double interact consists of an action–reaction–adjustment which forms interlocked behaviors or behavioral cycles. Individuals make sense of double interacts through retrospective analysis and causal maps. Enactment is the way individuals bracket or punctuate the streams of ongoing organizational experiences; selection is the process of interpreting these experiences through constructing causal maps or developing collective sensemaking; and retention is the storing of causal maps and routines for future action. Drawn from evolutionary theory, Weick's (1979) double interacts are triggered by organizational equivocality, which occurs when individuals interpret organizational events in multiple, plausible ways. Organizations reduce equivocality through coordinated action rather than through planning, goal-setting, or calculated decisions. People act and then reflect on their actions to make sense of organizing.

Weick's conception of organizing underlies empirical studies on the way message equivocality influences information processing (Bantz and Smith 1977; Daft and MacIntosh 1981; Kreps 1980; Putnam and Sorenson 1982); how meanings are enacted and changed as events unfold (Donnellon et al. 1986; Isabella 1990); and how media industries produce news through organizational sensemaking (Bantz 1990). Enactment also serves as a heuristic in which organizational scholars theorize about the role of communication in organizational culture (Bantz 1989; 1993); strategic management (Gioia 1986; Smircich and Stubbart, 1985); negotiation and conflict management (Putnam 1989); and public relations (Sproule 1989).

Weick's (1979) view of enactment liberates communication from its bondage as an object that is stored and transmitted. Enactment also liberates organizational environments from being objective events assessed through measures of turbulence, complexity, and load. In the enactment perspective, organizational environments are constructions. Organizations enact their environments which they, in turn, rediscover and use to constrain or to enable future actions.

In Weick's (1979) model, organizations surface as charades, improvisational theater, orchestras, and soliloquies. *Soliloquy* serves as the forerunner of self-organizing systems (Lotman 1977; Luhmann 1990). Organizations talk to themselves to clarify their surroundings and they act to discover what they are doing. The application of self-referential or auto-communication systems to organizations provides new insights into the ways that organizations develop identities and markets through interactions with stakeholders and publics (Cheney and Christensen in press; Steier and Smith 1992). Both the enactment and the soliloquy approaches treat communication as producing organizations.

In Weick's (1979) model, enactment continues to ground social interaction and sensemaking in

individuals rather than collaborative processes or cultural performances (Taylor and Robichaud 1992). A variation on this approach captures the *co-productive process* in which communication arises collectively rather than through an individual's cognitive experience. Co-productions are collaborative performances that stem from the way participants come together to produce social practices and coordinate local agreements. For example, improvisations of jazz performances are not simply in the minds of the musicians who created their environments; they are worked out through mutual responsiveness, complex verbal and nonverbal cues, shared focus and attention, and altercasting (Bastien and Hostager 1988; 1992). The dynamic and simultaneous flow of performance and the joint cueing of meanings of the event leads to co-constructing improvisations.

In like manner, *jamming* is a co-production in which participants experience a transcendence through suspending self-consciousness, co-orienting to each other, and surrendering to the experience (Eisenberg 1990). Jamming reflects those moments in which organizing magically comes together, as in the 'flow and zone' of street basketball or a serendipitous encounter of guitarists. As the metaphor of performance suggests, jamming and improvisation treat communication and organizations as co-constructing each other. Communication produces organizations while organizations produce communication.

Another way in which organizational members co-construct performances is through *storytelling*. Storytelling is how members dramatize organizational life and transform mundane events into passions and zeal (Pacanowsky and O'Donnell-Trujillo 1983). This approach focuses on the way organizational members introduce stories in conversations; how listeners co-produce them through prompting the teller; how stories unravel through subsequent performances of sharing them (Boje 1991). Stories, then, are not simply cultural artifacts or monologues; rather they emerge as performances that are never complete. Storytelling is often challenged by the listener who interrupts and adds elements to the narrative. Individuals often tell bits and pieces of stories with elaboration developed through pattern fitting. The chaining out of a story is adapted to different audiences through highlighting, eliminating, or modifying the narrative.

Symbolic convergence theory also emanates from storytelling, particularly through the way narratives chain out over time. Rooted in dramaturgical theory, this approach centers on how meanings, values, and motives converge through forming group narratives (Bormann

1983; 1985). As organizational members get caught up in a story, they participate in the drama and feel psychologically invested in its plot, motives, and characters. Research on teacher–administrator negotiations reveals that both sides converged on common enemies and contract issues through co-constructing stories of the accounts, past negotiators, and third-party mediators (Putnam et al. 1991). Convergence on the value of reaching a settlement was reinforced through chaining out stories on impasse and past failures to reach agreement. Symbolic convergence theory shows how organizational members come to stand on common ground through an emotional climate and an identity with the enacted drama (Bormann 1983).

At the macro level of analysis, organizations are also storytellers. Their images and identities emerge, in part, from the narratives that they construct with different publics (Alvesson 1990). In a postmodern world in which the presence of grand narratives is problematic (Lyotard, 1984), images become hyper-real: that is, many competing narratives surface, become disassociated from their signifiers, and vie for representational space (Baudrillard 1983). Images represent a world of flickering images that play upon other images, making it difficult to distinguish between the real and the pseudo-events (Boorstin 1961). Storytelling about organizations entails a plurality of narratives with multiple voices and interpretations (Boje 1995). An organization such as Disney Studios aims to write its own historical narrative, but in trying to tell its story it conflicts with and marginalizes some discourses while privileging others.

Enactment, co-constructing, and storytelling represent three diverse but related threads of the performance metaphor. This approach treats communication as an outgrowth of a collaborative process in which social and symbolic interaction is dynamic, interconnected, reflexive, and simultaneous. Meaning surfaces through retrospective sensemaking, co-constructing interpretations, and collaborative storytelling. Organizations emerge from *coordinated actions*: hence, social interaction is both the process and the product of organizing. Performance is not, however, a univocal metaphor. Multiple approaches surface through pluralistic constructions of enactments, improvisations, jamming, and storytelling. Performance, then, provides an interactive view of organizational communication, one that treats it as joint production.

The Symbol Metaphor

Storytelling in the performance metaphor has a direct tie to organizational symbols. In this metaphor, communication functions as the creation, maintenance, and transformation of meanings (Bantz 1993; Carey 1989). In effect, the symbolic aspect of communication becomes the figure while social interaction become the ground. A symbol is something that stands for or suggests something else through association or convention (Saussure 1983). Symbols are complex signs in that they suggest cultural, historical, or political interpretations; that is, they go beyond signaling a particular response, like a traffic light indicating stop. The meaning of a symbol is typically rooted in cultural significance, for example, an emblem that represents the values and history of a nation.

In this metaphor, communication is *interpretation* through the production of symbols that make the world meaningful. Communication becomes a process of representation. Organizational members use language, exhibit insight, produce and interpret ideas, vest meaning in events, and make sense of their lives: in short, they act symbolically (Morgan et al. 1983). The organization is a complex collection of representations that define a symbolic milieu; it is a *novel* or a *literary text* that organization members inscribe as they construct their reality (Calás and Smircich 1985; Czarniawska-Joerges 1995). Researchers who embrace this perspective emphasize the complex meanings that members construct rather than the formal and rational aspects of organization (Alvesson and Berg 1992; Czarniawska-Joerges 1992). Life in organizations becomes a literary activity in which members interpret the symbols that they inscribe on the organizational landscape.

Studies that focus on the construction and maintenance of organizational cultures (Alvesson and Berg 1992; Bantz 1993; Goodall 1989; Wuthnow and Witten 1988), organizational identification and commitment (Cheney 1991); organizational folklore (Bell and Forbes 1994; Jones et al. 1988); and shared meanings (Kelly 1985; Young 1989) rely on the symbol metaphor. Studies of organizational symbols encompass a broad range of forms, from institutional architecture to company logos to reports, charts, and documents (Berg and Kreiner 1990; Daft 1983; Johnson 1977). To illustrate the symbol metaphor, however, this chapter highlights the forms linked to literature, namely, narratives, metaphors, rites and rituals, and paradox and irony.

Narratives are ubiquitous symbols that are prevalent in all organizations (Martin 1982). Also referred to as stories, scripts, myths, legends, and sagas, narratives are accounts of events, usually developed chronologically and sequentially to indicate causality. Action, as revealed through intentions, deeds, and consequences, holds a central place in narratives (Czarniawska-Joerges 1995). Narratives are produced and reproduced in organizations as members make sense of a sequence of events, its causes, and its significance for the organization.

In an organizational context, narratives function to socialize newcomers (Brown 1985), to solve problems (Mitroff and Kilmann 1976), to legitimate power relationships (Mumby 1987; Clair 1993a; Witten 1993), to enhance bonding and organizational identification (Kreps 1989; Trujillo 1985), and to reduce uncertainty (Brown 1990). They are the vehicles through which organizational values and beliefs are produced, reproduced, and transformed (Smircich 1983). They shape organizational meanings through functioning as retrospective sensemaking (Wilkins 1983), serving as premises of arguments and persuasive appeals (Browning 1992; Weick and Browning 1986), acting as implicit mechanisms of cultural control (Clegg 1993; Kunda 1992), and constituting frames of reference for interpreting organizational actions (Shrivastava and Schneider 1984). Wilkins (1984), for example, argues that organizations high in performance have more concrete action stories than do their less successful counterparts. They also act as repositories of organizational intelligence for employees to update collective sensemaking (Kreps 1989).

Several empirical studies illustrate how narratives are enacted to manage organizational meanings. In a study of a hospital organization, narratives function as symbols of ideological positioning in a struggle to define quality medical care among administrators, nurses, and doctors. Through sharing stories of quality care, organizational members challenge the hospital's political structures and negotiate an alternative ideology (Geist and Hardesty 1990). Just as narratives construct ideology, stories also constitute individual and organizational identities. Czarniawska-Joerges's (1994) research in the Swedish public sector shows how identity construction is a process of narrative production between an actor and an audience.

A second important symbol for understanding *interpretation* in organizations is *metaphor*. Just as metaphors contribute to theory construction, as exemplified in this chapter, they also help organizational members structure their beliefs and behaviors. Metaphors enable individuals to express abstract ideas, convey vivid images, transfer information, and structure coherent systems (Ortony 1979). For example, the phrase that 'life is a game' provides a simple and well understood framework of rules, players, moves, winners, and losers to understand a complex phenomenon. Thus, metaphors are enacted and surface through everyday language

use. Phrases like 'waging campaigns', 'gathering intelligence', 'conferring with the brass' may symbolize a military metaphor in which bypassing the 'chain of command' becomes 'insubordination' (Deetz 1986; Weick 1979). Some metaphors become so sedimented in everyday use that their status as metaphors becomes obscured. These conventional or literal metaphors may become root metaphors that subsume other metaphors and provide rich summaries of worldviews (Smith and Eisenberg 1987).

Researchers also use metaphors as analytic tools to gather data about specific organizations. In particular, scholars use metaphor as 'a master detective' (Manning 1979) to infer norms, motives, and meaning in studying organizational cultures (Bantz 1993; Pondy 1983; Trice and Beyer 1984). Research on conflicting metaphors reveals the nature of struggles between competing ideologies (Hirsch and Andrews 1983; Smith and Eisenberg 1987) and covert practices that mask power relationships (Deetz and Mumby 1985). By isolating the predominant metaphors in organizations, researchers can describe organizational reality and the relation of power to metaphor structure. Through what metaphors hide, they support the status quo by treating routine practices as natural and immutable. For example, when organizational members treat human labor as a resource to be 'invested' and 'measured', the distinctions between meaningful and meaningless work become erased (Lakoff and Johnson 1980).

Practitioners often employ metaphor analysis to help organizational members diagnose problems, manage cultures, and enhance organizational effectiveness (Brink 1991; Broms and Gahmberg 1983; Coffman and Eblen 1987; Krefting and Frost 1985). Through the use of metaphors, practitioners can critique current understandings, note possibilities for organizational change, and introduce alternative metaphors. Metaphor, then, is a flexible analytical tool that can be used to understand an organization's culture and to evoke change in past practices.

Unlike metaphor, rites and rituals center on events and behavioral practices that enact organizational meaning. *Rites* are elaborate, dramatic activities that consolidate cultural expressions into one event, while *rituals* are the norms and behaviors that enact the rites (Trice and Beyer 1984). Rites and ceremonies are public events like retirement dinners, new member orientations, and award ceremonies, whereas rituals are less scripted behaviors like handshakes, coffee breaks, gift giving, and staff meetings. Although these symbols are commonplace in organizations (Siehl et al. 1992; Trice and Beyer 1984; 1985), they lack conceptual rigor and systematic distinction (Alvesson and Berg 1992; Knuf 1993). While their exact nature remains contested, researchers acknowledge that patterned and repeated social activities serve an important role in maintaining an organization's infrastructure.

In particular, rites and ceremonies make public the private values of a group. They perform both instrumental and expressive functions that confer status, evaluate performance, anoint membership, and recognize commitment. But in enacting routines and annual events, they reaffirm the status quo and the power relations of dominant groups. In his analysis of a corporate awards breakfast and an annual Christmas party, Rosen (1985; 1988) illustrates how these seemingly routine performances reaffirm patterns of dominance, reward performance, and admonish failure. Rites, rituals, and ceremonies are communicative acts performed as part of the accomplishment of organizing. As Knuf argues, this performance is tantamount to a single symbol or sign (1993: 85). Hence, rites and rituals overlap with enactment in the performance metaphor.

Paradoxes and ironies differ from other literary forms in focusing on relationships among messages rather than on the meanings of a particular symbol. *Paradoxes* are statements and actions that are self-contradictory but seemingly true (Putnam 1986), while *irony* arises when intended meanings contradict customary meanings (Brown 1977). Paradoxes are common features of organizations. Paradoxical goals can lead to enacting reward structures and operating procedures that violate the overall mission of the organization. For instance, orphanages that develop stringent rules to limit adoptions work against their goal of getting children placed in homes; seniority systems that reward longevity contradict the goal of meritorious performance (Kerr 1975). Paradoxes are evident in double-loop learning and organizational changes (Argyris 1988; Ford and Backoff 1988; O'Connor 1995); incongruities between individual and group goals (Smith and Berg 1987); dialectical tensions rooted in the 'deep structures' of organization life (Benson 1977; Putnam 1986); and double-bind messages in superior–subordinate communication (Putnam 1986; Tompkins and Cheney 1983). They appear in the interwoven but oppositional forces that evoke organizational change, namely through struggles between action and structure, internal and external, and stability and instability (Van de Ven and Poole 1988).

Paradoxical situations cause tensions and feelings of paralysis. Individuals can choose to live with a paradox and conform to one of the contradictory messages (Wood and Conrad 1983); or to step outside of the paradoxical frame and comment on it (Putnam 1986); or to abide by one aspect of the paradox at one time and the other at a different time (Van de Ven and Poole 1988); or to change levels of analysis to address the problem (Quinn and Cameron 1988). In another vein, individuals can introduce a new logic and transcend the contradictions through reframing the experience, transforming the situation, or integrating the oppositions (Bartunek 1988). This second type of response resembles a second-order change and involves a discontinuous shift in an organization's culture, ideology, or deep structure.

Another response to contradictions and paradoxical situations stems from research on irony (Filby and Willmott 1988; Hatch and Ehrlich 1993; Kunda 1992). Ironic remarks and ironic humor acknowledge the contradictory and paradoxical nature of organizing by disrupting historical frames through reversals in meanings. Irony transforms organizational experiences by providing members with an opportunity to confront new versions of social reality and grasp unthinkable propositions (Hatch and Ehrlich 1993).

Communication as organizational interpretation lies at the core of creating and responding to paradoxes. Irony as a play on actual versus expected meanings is a form of communication. In a postmodern world characterized by rapid changes and fragmentation, the management of ironies and paradoxes becomes particularly vital. Although individuals can reduce contradictions and understand the puzzles in organizational paradoxes, they cannot eliminate or escape from them (Handy 1994). The central dilemma that organizations face is learning to survive and flourish in a world defined by the paradoxical situations that they themselves have created (Smith and Berg 1987).

The metaphor of symbol provides a direct link between representation and interpretation. Symbols such as narratives, metaphors, rites and rituals, and paradoxes and ironies are literary tropes used to inscribe organizational texts. Symbols constitute the novel and novels reflect symbolic forms. Hence, the relationship between communication and organization is one of production, with symbols producing texts. Analyzing the elements of the novel is the way that organizational members interpret events, position themselves in the organizational scenario, and understand the motives and values in their everyday lives. Symbols provide ways for organizational members to negotiate scripts but they also serve as subtle means of preserving the status quo and re-create traditional modes of control. Symbols are more than manifestations of an organization's culture; they are the means through which organizing is accomplished.

The Metaphor of Voice

The metaphor of voice appears in different forms in the organizational literature, but each form shares an interest in the practices and structures that affect who can speak, when, and in what way. Understanding this metaphor entails focusing on communication as the *expression* or *suppression* of the voices of organizational members. To have a voice is to be able to speak in the context of the organization; organizations, then, exist as a *chorus* of member voices. But not all the members of an organization have an equal voice and not all members of the chorus sing the same tune. This metaphor focuses our attention on the ability of members to make their experiences heard and understood; on the existence of an appropriate language of expression; on the availability of occasions to speak; on the willingness of others to listen; and on the values, structures, and practices that suppress voice.

Each of these perspectives, however, emanates from different theoretical traditions, including rhetorical theory, critical theory, and feminist theory. The metaphor of voice clusters into the subcategories of distorted voices, voices of domination, different voices, and access to voice. In *distorted voices*, members are able to speak, but not in ways that represent their interests (Alvesson 1993b; Deetz 1992a; Haslett 1990; Thompson 1984; 1990). Such ideological aspects (Eagleton 1991; Therborn 1980; Thompson 1984) of communication draw attention to the role that meaning plays in the service of power (Fairclough 1992; Thompson 1990). Thus, the study of ideology generally focuses on the ways that powerful groups use communication for organizational control (Tompkins and Cheney 1985; also see Alvesson 1993b; Barker 1993). When particular understandings of the world become naturalized and taken-for-granted, other modes of knowing are excluded, resistance to authority is limited, and communication supports the status quo rather than each member's genuine interests (Clair 1993a; 1993b).

Communication distortion shapes members' ways of speaking, their understandings, and the structures and practices that constitute the organization (Mumby 1988). Power and meaning join together to distort voices so that even though voices may be heard, they echo the sentiments of the elite. However, since multiple coalitions often exist in complex organizations, theorists argue that resistance is typically present in some form and the ideological landscape reflects struggles between competing rather than univocal positions (Haslett 1990). Despite the limits to this perspective, distortion and suppression of voice

result in highly undemocratic organizations, in which resistance is problematic.

When meaning mystifies relations of power, the only voice left is the *voice of domination*. Speaking, then, becomes hegemonic in that patterns of activity and institutional arrangements culminate in common sense, thus concealing the choices and interests of the dominant group (Deetz 1992a; 1992b; Deetz and Mumby 1990; Fairclough 1992; Mumby forthcoming). Hegemony exists in everyday activities and influences the way dominant coalitions control organizations through political, cultural, and economic actions (Deetz 1992b).

Deetz's (1992a) study of the role of the corporation in modern society illustrates how the political ideology of managerialism has become hegemonic in that no other solution to organizational problems seems conceivable. As a result, the corporation as the primary institution in society continues to encroach on activities traditionally organized in other ways. Corporations control everything from personal identity to the use of natural resources to definitions of value and distribution of goods and services (Deetz 1992a: ix).

This concern with the ability to speak arises in other forms. The voice metaphor finds perhaps its most direct and common usage in feminist organizational studies (e.g. Bullis 1993; Buzzanell 1994; Fine 1993; Marshall 1993). This work highlights the fact that some people need to speak in a *different voice*. Because their voices are unique, they are often ignored, silenced, or misunderstood.

The idea of speaking in a different voice appears in two guises. First, researchers must speak differently (Mumby 1993) to uncover the bias inherent in the way we talk about gender and organizations (see Calás and Smircich, Chapter 1.8 in this volume). Feminist scholars are developing ways of speaking that challenge the unexamined assumptions about patriarchal organizations and that represent women's experiences in organizations. Since the voice that expresses women's experience is often silenced (Clair 1993a; Marshall 1993), researchers must work against the backdrop of patriarchy in trying to communicate authentically about women's organizational experiences. Dominant academic forms that shape writing styles and research methods limit efforts to undo the gendered pattern of theorizing (Marshall 1993: 140). Feminist literature, then, addresses issues of gaining a voice for academic writers and 'unlearning to not speak' (Piercy in Marshall 1993).

A second way in which the concept of a different voice guides organizational scholarship is concern about the patriarchal bias in organizations. Researchers center on the way this bias limits opportunities for women to participate as women in organizational activities (Bullis 1993; Marshall 1993; Rakow 1986). Organizational communication practices which range from conversational turn-taking to storytelling enact gendered organizations and re-create gender inequality (Bullis 1993). These studies question the role of communication in constructing gendered organizations and the need for research to move away from treating gender as a variable to conceive of it as a fundamental organizing principle (Marshall 1993).

This notion of a different voice extends to issues of race and ethnicity in organizations (see Nkomo and Cox, Chapter 2.5 in this volume, for a discussion of race and organizations; see Kim 1994 for a discussion of race and communication). Work in this area examines the communication practices through which race and ethnicity are accomplished (Frankenberg 1993; Kim 1994; Nakayama and Kriziek 1995) and the role of race and ethnicity in organizations (Nkomo 1992). In each case, a central concern is that minority groups are marginalized because they speak in a different voice.

Another metaphor in the cluster of voice is *access to voice*. In traditional, hierarchical organizations, voice typically increases as one moves up the organizational ladder. Organizational members near the bottom of the ladder have little or no access to voice. While most research that studies access to voice targets traditional bureaucratic organizations, other work focuses on alternative organizational forms such as democratic institutions (Cheney 1995; Deetz 1992a; Harrison 1994; Rothschild-Whitt 1986). These organizations take specific steps to provide members with access to voice. Alternative organizational forms demonstrate how communication develops interdependence and provides a balanced understanding of institutions (Harrison 1994: 249). Democratic organizations also provide a basis upon which to critique traditional bureaucratic forms.

Another alternative for investigating access to voice is through participative management programs that vary from ones aimed at improving organizational efficiency to ones driven by a belief in the collective good (Gordon 1994: 293). In each case, the success of the democratization program depends on the development of alternative patterns of communication (Eisenberg 1994; Harrison 1994). But the rationale behind them and the approach to studying them is quite different.

For some scholars the empowerment of individuals and the democratization of organizations is a way *to make a difference through voice*, which aims to improve both work experience and effectiveness. To be empowered means that a person believes that he or she can direct organizational events toward desired ends (Albrecht 1988: 380). Organizational members who are empowered feel that they are partners with others in influencing their organizations and being influenced by them (Pacanowsky 1988: 371). Empowerment depends on communication structures that give individuals voice and that provide broad frameworks for understanding sagas that interpret the organization and its goals (Bormann 1988).

Empowerment is the use of voice to provide active participation and commitment to organizational members. For example Pacanowsky's (1988) study of empowerment at W.L. Gore & Associates describes a lattice structure that embodies decentralized power structures and produces what Pacanowsky calls a 4,500 member improvisational jazz group. He outlines six characteristics of empowering firms: (1) power and opportunity are distributed widely; (2) a full, open and decentralized communication system is maintained; (3) integrative problem solving is used; (4) a climate of trust is maintained; (5) people are rewarded and recognized in ways that encourage high performance and self-responsibility; and (6) people learn from organizational ambiguity, inconsistency, contradiction, and paradox. These characteristics incorporate a full, open, and decentralized communication system that allows direct participation by organizational members and transmits a strong enabling culture (1988: 374). Empowerment is therefore inextricably linked to communication (Bormann 1988).

An alternative view of organizational democracy returns to the metaphor of distorted voices. In any movement towards democratization, employees face the asymmetry of power based on managerial possession of capital (Gordon 1994: 286). Consequently, workers find it difficult to develop ways of 'making a difference through voice'. For example, Barker (1993) provides an ethnographic account of 'self-regulated work teams' designed to free employees from bureaucratic control. But rather than freeing workers, the system of concertive control that was developed was more powerful, more invisible, and more difficult to resist than the former managerial control (Barker 1993: also see the concluding chapter of this *Handbook*). In this example, voice overlaps with the metaphor of symbol as managers use unobtrusive controls to distort communication (Tompkins and Cheney 1985). The metaphor of voice overlaps with the metaphor of discourse when ideological practices and discipline undermine efforts to make a difference through voice. These efforts stem from cultural-ideological control as Alvesson (1993b) sets forth in his fourfold theory: (1) *collective control*, based on a sense of community; (2) *performance-related control*, based on norms for collective performance; (3) *ideological control*, based on values, norms, and ideas about what is good or important; and (4) *perceptual control*, based on the management of beliefs about what exists and how things are (see also McPhee 1993; Kersten 1993). In each case, modes of control move away from focusing on the labor process itself toward the ideological frame in which work is accomplished.

The metaphor cluster of voice brings together different orientations to the issues of speaking, hearing, and making a difference in organizations. The voice metaphor centers on implicit factors that shape the role of communication, namely, ideology, hegemony, legitimation to speak, and unobtrusive control. It connects the issues of power and meaning with communication, although in very different ways. In this metaphor communication functions simultaneously to express and suppress voice; that is, voices may be heard but they are distorted or dominated; new voices may be added to change existing asymmetries, but they result in merely echoing them. The organization constitutes a chorus of diverse and often muted voices; the tune they sing is not always clear.

The Metaphor of Discourse

One major critique of the voice metaphor is its failure to account for the micro processes that contribute to the origin and development of organizational arrangements. The performance metaphor centers on these dynamic, ongoing processes, but fails to demonstrate how organizations emerge as institutional forms. The *discourse* metaphor provides alternatives that address the weaknesses in both the performance and the voice metaphors.

Discourse refers to language, grammars, and discursive acts that form the foundation of both performance and voice. In the discourse metaphors, communication is a *conversation* in that it focuses on both process and structure, on collective action as joint accomplishment, on dialogue among partners, on features of the context, and on micro and macro processes (Taylor 1993). Conversation, in this metaphor, is a simile for organizations as sequential interactions among people. Bergquist (1993) contends that conversations are both the essence and the product of organizations. In many ways, conversations lay the groundwork for community.

Conversation is immediate in its claim on attention, instantaneous in its moment to moment occurrence, and fleeting or ephemeral in its form, yet it relies on patterns that become culturally sanctioned, frames that presuppose prior knowledge, and macro processes in which individuals speak as representatives for others. Conversations embody many of the elements that characterize communication as symbols, performance, and voice; however, discourse foregrounds language as the nexus for untangling relationships among meaning, context, and praxis. Unlike the symbol metaphor, discourse centers less on cultural forms such as narratives and rituals and more on the co-production of language in situated practice. Thus, text and context are intertwined with action and meaning.

In the discourse metaphor, communication casts organizations as *texts* (Barthes 1981; Geertz 1983; Ricoeur 1979). Texts are sets of structured events or ritualized patterns of interaction that transcend immediate conversations (Taylor 1993). However, scholars differ in the various senses in which they use texts: (1) as the discursive acts inscribed in institutions, (2) as the interpretations of organizational life, and (3) as the ways that organizations are written or authored (Cheney and Tompkins 1988).

Research within the discourse metaphor, however, is very disparate and ranges from studies that treat language as a reflection of culture and society to ones that view language as ongoing conversations and discursive practices. These studies differ markedly in their orientation to language. Thus, the use of discourse as a metaphor serves as a category under which a number of separate and disparate perspectives reside. These perspectives fall into the arenas of (1) discourse as artifacts, (2) discourse as structure and process, and (3) discourse as discursive acts. In the artifact category, words represent 'fixed' objects; whereas in the discursive acts category, language is a 'fluid' negotiation of meanings through interplays among texts (actions performed at any given moment) and context (the circumstances in which those actions take place). In the first two categories, language is unidimensional and goal-oriented; while as a discursive act, language is multifaceted and situated in everyday interaction. Some perspectives of language locate meaning in relational, organizational, and socio-cultural context while others situate meaning at the intersection of conversation, text, and praxis.

The orientation that casts *discourse as an artifact* treats language as representing objects and as signaling particular meanings. Meanings reside in words, syntax, systems of codes, and social orders reflected in language use. Work on structural semiotics, general semantics, and sociolinguistics adopts these assumptions of language and meaning. Through analyzing surface and deep structures, studies of common codes uncover subtleties of organizational life, tacit understandings developed through complex systems of meaning, and the way social systems constrain language use (Barley 1983; Fiol 1989; Manning 1992). Discourse facilitates organizational processes by developing structural arrangements as in Barley's (1983) analysis of the themes of 'naturalness' and 'familiarity' in funeral parlors or Tway's (1976) study of code systems among factory workers. Labels function as control systems that enhance organizational understanding (Czarniawska-Joerges and Joerges 1988). Analysis of code systems reveals how rules, underlying orders, and language patterns work against each other, as in Manning's (1988) analysis of communication technology in two police departments and Fiol's (1989) study of oppositional tensions in CEO letters to stockholders about organizational boundaries. Code systems can reveal unstable images of firms and their internal relations.

In like manner, research on the way language classifies and reflects social structures falls into the category of discourse as artifact. In this perspective, language becomes a fixture of reified social systems such as occupations, departments, and administrative roles. Meaning, then, is embodied in social orders and represented through language use. Taylor's (1987) study of slang in a British financial institution shows how bank tellers avoid the use of words that refer to monetary denominations to distract attention from money. The use of technical terms adheres to geographic proximity, departmental boundaries, and common task operations (Tway 1975), while slang terms in hospitals provide emotional distance between patients and caretakers (Gordon 1983). In a merger and acquisition situation, changes in language codes and dress signal willingness to integrate employees, accommodation to the aggressive firm, and social differentiation of subgroups (Bastien 1992).

A second major orientation centers on the study of *discourse as structure and process*. In this perspective, language reflects the intent or functions of what is said and meaning resides in the structure of ongoing conversations. Meaning is located in discourse patterns rather than in semantics, semiotics, or word choice. This perspective includes the research on speech acts, conversational analysis, and interaction patterns in organizations. Speech act theory treats discourse as spoken or written utterances accomplished through being uttered. Such actions as promising, requesting, demanding, and apologizing occur through the form and rules of language use. In speech act research, language performs relational and organizational functions, such as exercising control, executing influence, reaching agreements, expressing politeness, and managing impressions (Donohue and Diez 1985; Gioia et al. 1989).

Speech act research also underlies studies on the ethnography of speaking and the appropriateness of language use in organizational settings. For example, Van Maanen's (1973; 1978) classic investigations on the language of policemen and Spradley and Mann's (1975) seminal work on the cocktail waitress examine norms and functions of interactions in particular organizations. Gregory (1983) identifies lexical and semantic fields of native views in subcultures among Silicon Valley employees. Investigations of humor and informal interactions in organizations illustrate how language relieves tensions, defines status relationships, sabotages work processes, and forms informal groups (Duncan 1983; Duncan and Feisal 1989; Ullian 1976).

Conversational analysts center on talk turns, interruptions, talkovers, topic switching, and questions/answers (McLaughlin 1984). When organizational members violate implicit rules, individuals engage in conversational repairs, accounts, and disclaimers. Organizational researchers use conversational analysis to study superior–subordinate communication, organizational control (Barley 1986), selection interviews (Morris 1988; Ragan 1983; Ragan and Hopper 1981), and group decision-making. Drawing from research on powerful and powerless speech, Fairhurst and Chandler (1989) show how topic control, disclaimers, and hedges distinguish conversational patterns of in-group from outgroup members. Fairhurst (1993) extends this work to female managers to reveal the way moves of alignment differ for pairs of high, medium, and low leader–member relationships. In like manner, Gronn (1983) describes how a school principal controls issues of staffing through everyday talk that tightens and loosens administrative reins. In a study of decision-making in a psychiatric health care facility, Geist and Chandler (1984) note that conversational accounts serve as arguments for and against group proposals and signal organizational identification. The decision to take a common organizational action may emerge from linguistic indirectness and dissimilar meanings among members of different departments (Donnellon et al. 1986).

Interactional analysis focuses on coding verbal messages in organizational settings. As such it derives meaning from the structures of messages that evolve in organizational contexts, such as performance behaviors (Komaki et al. 1986; Komaki 1986; Komaki and Citera 1990), leader behaviors and perceptions of power (Gioia and Sims 1983; Sims and Manz 1984), managerial control (Fairhurst et al. 1987; 1995; Watson-Dugan 1989), and labor–management negotiations (Putnam and Roloff 1992).

One particular type of interaction analysis that moves toward an interpretative model is adaptive structuration theory, drawn from Giddens's (1979) principles of structuration. This approach focuses on the way interactions among organizational group members appropriate technology and decision support systems (DeSanctis and Poole 1994). Basically, the effects of GDSS on decision-making and group process vary depending on how each group makes sense of the technology (DeSanctis et al. 1992; Poole and DeSanctis 1992). Structuration theory can move interaction analysis beyond micro levels of talk to global considerations of genres and institutional texts (DeSanctis and Poole 1994).

A third stream of research within the discourse metaphor centers on *discourse as discursive practices*. It subsumes research on language as social construction, as emotional expressions, as knowledge, as genres, and as dialogue. Discourse, in this orientation, is the way that organizational understanding is produced and reproduced. In the *social construction* perspective, discourse not only reflects language use, but also creates social meanings in organizations. Labels such as 'ideal patient' and 'health care provider' are not simply terms that classify occupational groups. Rather they define expectations, forms of knowledge, and task activities for organizational groups. Adjustments to new organizational experiences may stem from the way that discourse reconstitutes these institutional labels (Loseke 1989; Sigman 1986).

In like manner, *emotions* as discursive acts center on the way that members regulate, interpret, control, and resist organizational actions (Conrad and Witte 1994; Fineman 1993; Waldron 1994). Regulation occurs through display rules that translate emotions into acceptable organizational forms (Hochschild 1983; Rafaeli and Sutton 1987; Waldron and Krone 1991). Rules for expressing feelings may yield positive organizational outcomes while simultaneously creating estrangement and emotional numbness (Van Maanen and Kunda 1989). Emotional expression is intertwined with dichotomies that privilege a rational view of work and marginalize the private, feminine, and informal side of organizational life (Mumby and Putnam 1992; Putnam and Mumby 1993).

Most of these studies, however, treat emotional language as an artifact of organizational culture rather than as a social construction of reality. In effect, labeling an emotion as anger, fear, pride, or surprise is an ambiguous and complex process. Both the display and the interpretation of emotion hinge on the way that feelings are legitimated and on the social costs for displaying emotions (Conrad and Witte

1994). The control of emotional expression, even in strong cultures, acknowledges that affect rules are complex and malleable. Thus, the study of emotional expressions in organizations needs to consider how interactions shape the way feelings emerge, develop, and transform.

Emotional expression also functions as a discursive practice when it is treated as *knowledge*. That is, language is the depository of reconstructed discourses that legitimate particular practices (Deetz 1992a). Discourse in this orientation overlaps with the voice metaphor and centers on historically situated thoughts, expressions, and actions (Foucault 1980). Through embedding discursive practices in history, language functions as an institutional text. Genres or technologies such as interviews, therapeutic discourse, and legal discourse embody social and institutional conventions. Hence, the selection interview is not simply a language game of questions and answers; it is a genre that incorporates bureaucratic placement, market demands, and employee relationships into its discursive practice (Fairclough 1989).

The study of *communication genres* as discursive practices centers on the form, audience, and socio-historical situation (Yates and Orlikowski 1992). Developed from structuration theory, genres are recurring patterns of communicative practices that form types of interaction, for example, reports, memos, meetings, and e-mail. Organizational members enact genres for particular purposes; hence, they become institutional templates for social interaction (Orlikowski and Yates 1994). However, member actions can deviate from genre templates and change an organization's discourse (Yates 1993); thus, as people interact, they draw on rules developed through tradition to produce, reproduce, and change genres. Orlikowski and Yates (1994) show how the presence and the absence of genres such as memos, reference manuals, and dialogue establish an organization's identity as temporary, accountable to a professional community, and flexible in work processes.

Another type of communication genre, *dialogue*, merits separate attention as a discursive practice. Participants who engage in dialogue suspend defensive exchange, share and learn from experiences, foster deeper inquiry, and resist synthesis or compromise (Eisenberg and Goodall 1993). Drawn from Bakhtin (1981) and Buber (1985), dialogue strives for a balance between individual autonomy and organizational constraint through incorporating diverse voices. Dialogue can transform action and promote organizational learning through developing synergy, empathy, and authentic deliberation among individuals (Evered and Tannenbaum 1992; Isaacs 1993). Dialogue legitimates each person's experience from connecting with others to determine what counts as knowledge and how it is valued. Self-recognition and transformation arise from the additive nature in which each person's experience contributes to the whole (Eisenberg 1994).

Although dialogue places humanism at the forefront of organizing, it often misses the politics of experience by grounding discourse in individual identity. When dialogue incorporates postmodernism, it emphasizes how discourse decenters subjects and fragments identities, situates meanings, and locates power in systems that normalize discursive practices (Deetz forthcoming). By rejecting the notion of autonomous, self-determined individuals, theorists treat discourse as producing identity and as spoken by different selves; thus, the individual is fragmented. Fragmentation provides an opportunity for dialogue, as Townley (1993) illustrates in his essay on discourses of human resource management.

In this poststructuralist treatment of dialogue, meaning is fragmented and localized rather than being universal or fixed. Even phrases like 'the bottom line' and 'profit and loss', and particular accounting practices, have meaning only within the localized, situated discourses that create them (Miller and O'Leary 1987). A deconstruction of management theories demonstrates how organizational texts are localized meanings that often marginalize the voices of those who are absent in these works (Mumby and Putnam 1992). Finally, consistent with the metaphor of distorted voices, power resides in discourse, not through dominant coalitions, but through the way discursive practices like discipline and surveillance become normalized in social interactions (Foucault 1977; Knights 1992).

Treating organizational communication as a discursive practice clarifies the relationship between discourse and texts. A text is the structured sets of events that comprise the organization. These events, created and reconstituted through discourse, have symbolic meaning to participants. A text as symbolic meaning substitutes for treating organizations as objects or entities. Texts are the *Gestalt* meanings aligned with the underlying frames of discursive practices (Strine 1988; Taylor 1993).

The organizational text, however, should not be treated as a social fact or as a 'fixed' meaning. Rather texts are symbolic forms, open to multiple and unlimited readings, frequently ruptured displays, reflexivity between authors and texts, and concerns for transcendence and transformation (Strine 1988). Researchers serve as authors who produce both the texts and the readings of the texts as they engage in organizational studies (Cheney and Tompkins 1988).

DISCUSSION AND CONCLUSIONS

This chapter sets forth seven metaphor clusters drawn from the organizational communication literature. By reversing the figure–ground relationship between organization and communication, these metaphors recast our images of organizations to adhere to the linguistic turn in social sciences. In many ways this chapter responds to Pondy and Mitroff's (1979) appeal to embrace language-based conceptions of organizations. Boje echoes this appeal by claiming that 'it is time to heed Pondy and Mitroff's advice and move [organizational theory] to discursive metaphors, such as Lyotard's (1984) "conversation," Bakhtin's (1981) "novel," and Thachankary's (1992) "text"' (1995: 1000). This chapter, through its examination of metaphors of communication, takes a step in this direction.

The metaphor clusters included in this chapter present different alternatives for conceptualizing communication and organization. As perspectives, researchers can examine any organizational topic from one of these clusters. In particular, this review demonstrates how communication technology, typically treated as a *tool* in the conduit metaphor, can also be viewed as a *lens* in media richness research, as dense *networks* in the social influence model of media adoption and use, as a *symbol* in studying how social meanings are managed through media use, as the *voice* of domination that enables certain groups to control decision-making processes, as *discourse* or social interaction that structures communication technology, and as *genre* through the historical and habitual use of communication media. The criteria for choosing a particular metaphor are the researcher's goals, the ontological basis of both communication and organization, and the phenomenon that is most central to the organizing process.

Some metaphors include more aspects of the communication process than do others. For example, the discourse, performance, and voice metaphors draw their insights from examining the relationship among messages, meaning, and context, while the conduit, lens, and linkage metaphors, in their pure forms, typically exclude key elements of communication. In effect, some metaphors are more complete and complex than are others.

In this section, we explore the communication–organization relationship embedded in each metaphor, show how the metaphor clusters are interwoven through related chains, and review the contributions and omissions embedded in each metaphor. The end of this section explores the implications of this analysis for theory building in organizations.

In general, the relationship that surfaces from the conceptions of communication and organization within each metaphor is equivalency. That is, a closer examination of each metaphor shows how the two constructs are isomorphic. At first glance, the conduit and the lens metaphors point to a containment relationship between communication and organization. A deeper examination, however, reveals that the two constructs are similar in structure and function. In the conduit metaphor, both communication and organization are containers. Just as communication functions as a channel to contain messages, so organizations act as containers of tasks, technologies, and job functions. In this metaphor, both constructs are defined instrumentally: communication is the way to attain message fidelity; organization is the means of attaining productivity and efficiency. As containers, both processes appear as material objects that isolate form from substance through reliance on discrete boundaries.

In the lens metaphor, both communication and organization are forms of selective perception; that is, the lens and the eye define the boundaries of the system, control access to it, and open and close the system. The lens and the eye identify the parameters of an organization through selecting, screening, and routing information. In this metaphor, communication and organization become synonymous with information management.

In the linkage metaphor, communication contacts are the building blocks of organizational networks. Linkages, then, form the web or structural framework of the organization. Organizations, as networks of relationships, are communication systems defined through the presence or absence of interlocked activities. In contrast, the performance metaphor supports a production relationship between communication and organizations. Either communication produces organizations as in enactment, or the two co-produce each other as in storytelling and collaborative performance. Close examination, however, reveals an equivalency relationship in that organization as coordinated actions parallels communication through social interaction.

In the symbol metaphor, communication is sensemaking through the use of a set of literary tropes that inscribe a novel. Even though this process suggests a production relationship, a novel becomes isomorphic with its symbolic forms. The metaphors of voice and discourse are so multifaceted that it is difficult to isolate the relationship between communication and organization. Production seems paramount in developing the organizational chorus. However, close examination indicates that the presence or absence of voice is consistent with hegemony

and unobtrusive control. Speaking in a different voice and access to voice can alter the gendered practices of organizing and enhance democratization of organizational life; hence, the relationship between organizing and communicating is equivalence.

The discourse metaphor includes subgroups that support all three types of relationships between communication and organization. Language as artifact operates from the containment metaphor while language as structure and process emphasizes the co-productive relationship. Discourse as discursive practices, however, casts the relationship as equivalence. Conversations are texts and texts embody conversations (Taylor 1993). Discourse is organizing in that language shapes discursive practices that, in turn, constitute knowledge, genres, and dialogue. In effect, then, metaphors of communication suggest an equivalency relationship between communication and organization, even though assumptions of social reality may differ within and between metaphor clusters.

Each metaphor in this chapter subsumes clusters of related metaphors. These categories then are not locked into particular labels or modes of meaning. Threads from each cluster extend to metaphors in other categories and reveal interrelationships. The conduit, lens, and network metaphors chain together through their foci on transmission. Network research that centers on meanings and relationships overlaps with the symbol metaphor.

Performance chains into discourse metaphors through an emphasis on grammars and recipes for organizing. Speech acts and conversational analysis in the discourse metaphor are performative in nature. Discursive practices in the discourse metaphor are linked to improvisations through routines that form communicative structures and collective moves. Jamming and dialogue are interrelated, providing a chain between the performance and discourse metaphors. Many threads tie the voice to the discourse metaphors through discursive practices, knowledge, and language as ideology. Speaking in a different voice, although not logically tied to the linkage metaphor, treats relationships and connections as the fundamental processes of organizing. In effect, overlaps among these seven clusters suggest new metaphors that might emerge as research develops.

Studies that mix metaphors, however, run the risk of confounding the assumptive ground of both communication and organization. For instance, research on the way leaders transmit organizational narratives combines the conduit with symbol metaphors. However, in this type of research, symbols become transformed into signals sent to receivers. Hence, meanings are relayed and 'exchanged' through channels, rather than being socially constructed. Chaining across metaphors, then, can lead to converting one type of organizational communication research into another and confound the assumptions that underlie the nature of communication.

The concluding chapter of this *Handbook* illustrates how theories of organizations are really different representations. In like manner, metaphor clusters described in this chapter are different representations of communication and organizations. Being aware of what each metaphor captures – and what it neglects – adds insights to organizational studies and reflexiveness to research. The conduit and lens metaphors, with their concern for transmission, instrumentality, and message fidelity, highlight the container images of organizations and neglect meaning, context, and social interaction. The linkage metaphor captures elements that the conduit and lens metaphors miss, namely, the give and take of transactions, organizations as relationships, and the erosion of physical boundaries. Without a physical structure, communication becomes even more central to the essence of organizing.

Both the network and the performance metaphors emphasize patterns of organizing, but performance moves to the collective production of interlocked behaviors. Meaning and sensemaking become the basis for coordinated actions. The symbol metaphor adds representation to the process of organizing, but it often reproduces the meanings that service organizational elites. The voice metaphor introduces power and control as factors that influence who can speak and who can be heard in organizations. This metaphor, however, fails to capture the way resistance influences the micro processes that constitute organizing. The discourse metaphor incorporates these micro processes through research on language, but many of these studies neglect the critical role of nonverbal communication and silence in organizing and of authors who write and read organizational texts. Research on communication genres, discursive practices, and dialogue provides notable exceptions to some of these shortcomings. In effect, each image is partial and highlights different elements of organizational communication. Somewhere in the crevices within and schisms between these metaphors, other metaphors reside, ones that account for missing elements and synthesize critical factors in each perspective.

In concluding this chapter, three implications for organizational studies stem from this analysis. First, the conduit and the lens metaphors are the primary ways that organizational scholars treat communication. These metaphors limit not only the way communication is conceived, but also the way organizations are cast. To study language as an artifact of culture or communication technology as an organizational tool limits the complexity and completeness of both communication and organization. Hence, in selecting a particular metaphor, scholars should note the contributions and omissions that a perspective holds. For example, when a crisis like an oil spill occurs, it may seem appropriate to focus on effective transmission of information. However, sending information about an oil spill is a rhetorical process rooted in concerns for audience analysis, persuasive appeals, social and political context, and ethical considerations (Heath 1988). A discourse or symbol metaphor includes more of these factors and can still probe for issues of effectiveness in message transmission. Effectiveness, however, is no longer message fidelity; it is understanding the rhetorical circumstances that govern sending messages to particular audiences. Moreover, to force the study of language or symbols into a transmission metaphor alters the way that both communication and organizations are conceived.

Second, although organizational theorists like Barnard (1968) and Weick (1979) imply that communication and organization are equivalent, a close examination of the metaphors in this chapter provides even stronger support for this supposition. If, indeed, the two constructs are isomorphic, then all organizational theories contain implicit notions about communication and all communication theories, in turn, provide important insights about organizing. Weick (1987) illustrates this point though a deconstruction of the principles of communication embodied in Burns and Stalker's (1961) description of mechanistic and organic organizations. Perhaps, more importantly, theorists could embellish ways of thinking about organizations through applying metaphors of communication. This chapter takes a step in this direction.

Third, the field of organizational communication, like that of organizational studies, faces a crisis of representation. Communication no longer mirrors or reflects reality, rather it is formative in that it creates and represents the process of organizing. The range of metaphors reviewed in this chapter attests to the scope of this crisis. This crisis is also evident in recent challenges to orthodox views of organizations and in critiques of modernism in all its forms. This crisis is also apparent in the fluidity of new organizational forms such as chains, clusters, and strategic alliances (see the introduction to this volume) and in dynamic collaborative relationships between competitors, often developed through linkages in cyberspace.

Other signs of this crisis appear in postmodern approaches to organizations, often described as 'communication-intensive organizations' (Galbraith et al. 1993). These organizations are decentralized in activities, fluid in boundaries, hybrid in forms, cyclical in order and chaos, and integrative in embracing diversity (Bergquist 1993). Their images are fragmented and inconsistent, characterized by paradoxes and contradictions in a global world of shifting visions. Metaphors of organizations as conversations, texts, and voice become increasingly viable.

This chapter explores a body of literature that many writers in organizational studies have previously ignored. The nature of communication and the links between communication and organization suggest that these metaphors are viable alternatives for rethinking organizational theories. If organizational reality is determined, in part, by the perspectives that we take rather than the phenomena we observe (Bergquist 1993), then this chapter responds to the plea for new perspectives and alternative metaphors of organizing.

REFERENCES

Ackoff, R.L. and Emery, F.E. (1972) *On Purposeful Systems*. Chicago: Aldine/Atherton.

Adams, J. (1980) 'Interorganizational processes and organizational boundary activities', in Larry L. Cummings and Barry Staw (eds), *Research in Organizational Behavior*, vol. 2. Greenwich, CT: JAI Press. pp. 321–55.

Albrecht, Terrance L. (1988) 'Communication and personal control in empowering organizations', in James A. Anderson (ed.), *Communication Yearbook 11*. Newbury Park, CA: Sage. pp. 380–90.

Albrecht, Terrance L. and Hall, Bradford (1991) 'Facilitating talk about new ideas: the role of personal relationships in organizational innovation', *Communication Monographs*, 58: 273–88.

Albrecht, Terrance L. and Ropp, V.A. (1984) 'Communicating about innovation in networks of three U.S. organizations', *Journal of Communication*, 34: 78–91.

Allen, Myria Watkins, Gotcher, J. Michael and Seibert, Joy Hart (1993) 'A decade of organizational communication research: journal articles 1980–1991', in Stanley A. Deetz (ed.), *Communication Yearbook 16*. Newbury Park, CA: Sage. pp. 252–330.

Allen, Thomas J. and Hauptman, Oscar (1990) 'The substitution of communication technologies for organizational structure in research and development', in Janet Fulk and Charles W. Steinfield (eds), *Organizations and Communication Technology*. Newbury Park, CA: Sage. pp. 275–94.

Alvesson, Mats (1990) 'Organization: from substance to image'?, *Organization Studies*, 11(3): 373–94.

Alvesson, Mats (1993a) *Cultural Perspectives on Organizations*. Cambridge: Cambridge University Press.

Alvesson, Mats (1993b) 'Cultural-ideological modes of management control: a theory and a case study of a professional service company', in Stanley A. Deetz (ed.), *Communication Yearbook 16*. Newbury Park, CA: Sage. pp. 3–42.

Alvesson, Mats and Berg, Per Olof (1992) *Corporate Culture and Organizational Symbolism*. Berlin: Walter de Gruyter.

Ancona, Deborah and Caldwell, D.F. (1988) 'Beyond task and maintenance: defining external functions in groups', *Group and Organizational Studies*, 13: 468–94.

Argyris, Chris (1988) 'Crafting a theory of practice: the case of organizational paradoxes', in Robert E. Quinn and Kim S. Cameron (eds), *Paradox and Transformation: Toward a Theory of Change in Organization and Management*. Cambridge, MA: Ballinger. pp. 255–78.

Axley, Stephen (1984) 'Managerial and organizational communication in terms of the conduit metaphor', *Academy of Management Review*, 9: 428–37.

Bakhtin, M. (1981) *The Dialogic Imagination*, translated by Caryl Emerson and Michael Holquist. Austin, TX: University of Texas Press.

Bantz, Charles R. (1989) 'Organizing and the *Social Psychology of Organizing*', *Communication Studies*, 40(4): 231–40.

Bantz, Charles R. (1990) 'Organizational communication, media industries, and mass communication', in James A. Anderson (ed.), *Communication Yearbook 13*. Newbury Park, CA: Sage. pp. 503–10.

Bantz, Charles R. (1993) *Understanding Organizations: Interpreting Organizational Communication Cultures*. Columbia, SC: University of South Carolina Press.

Bantz, Charles R. and Smith, David H. (1977) 'A critique and experimental text of Weick's model of organizing', *Communication Monographs*, 44: 171–84.

Barker, James (1993) 'Tightening the iron cage: concertive control in self-managing teams', *Administrative Science Quarterly*, 38: 408–37.

Barley, Steve (1983) 'Semiotics and the study of occupational and organizational culture', *Administrative Science Quarterly*, 23: 393–413.

Barley, Steve (1986) 'Technology as an occasion for structuring: evidence from observations of CT scanners and the social order of radiology departments', *Administrative Science Quarterly*, 31: 78–108.

Barley, Steve (1990) 'The alignment of technology and structure through roles and networks', *Administrative Science Quarterly*, 35: 61–103.

Barnard, Chester (1968) *The Functions of the Executive* (1938). Cambridge MA: Harvard University Press.

Barthes, R. (1981) 'Theory of the text', in R. Young (ed.), *Untying the Text: a Post-Structuralist Reader*. Boston: Routledge & Kegan Paul. pp. 31–47.

Bartunek, Jean M. (1988) 'The dynamics of personal and organizational reframing', in Robert E. Quinn and Kim S. Cameron (eds), *Paradox and Transformation: Toward a Theory of Change in Organization and Management*. Cambridge, MA: Ballinger. pp. 137–62.

Bastien, David T. (1992) 'Change in organizational culture: the use of linguistic methods in corporate acquisition', *Management Communication Quarterly*, 5: 403–42.

Bastien, David T. and Hostager, Todd J. (1988) 'Jazz as a process of organizational innovation', *Communication Research*, 15: 582–602.

Bastien, David T. and Hostager, Todd J. (1992) 'Cooperation as communicative accomplishment: a symbolic interaction analysis of an improvised jazz concert', *Communication Studies*, 43: 92–104.

Baudrillard, J. (1983). *Simulations*. New York: Semiotext.

Bavelas, A. (1950) 'Communication patterns in task-oriented groups,' *Acoustical Society of America Journal*, 22: 727–30.

Bell, Elizabeth and Forbes, Linda C. (1994) 'Office folklore in the academic paperwork empire: the interstitial space of gendered (con)texts', *Text and Performance Quarterly*, 14(3): 181–96.

Benson, J. Kenneth (1977) 'Organizations: a dialectical view', *Administrative Science Quarterly*, 22: 1–26.

Berg, Per Olof and Kreiner, K. (1990) 'Corporate architecture: turning physical settings into symbolic resources', in P. Gagliardi (ed.), *Symbols and Artifacts: Views of the Corporate Landscape*. Berlin: Walter de Gruyter.

Bergquist, William (1993) *The Postmodern Organization: Mastering the Art of Irreversible Change*. San Francisco, CA: Jossey-Bass.

Bikson, T. and Eveland, J.D. (1990) 'The interplay of work group structures and computer support', in J. Galegher, R. Kraut and C. Egido (eds), *Intellectual Teamwork: Social and Technological Bases of Cooperative Work*. Hillsdale, NJ: Erlbaum. pp. 245–90.

Black, Max (1962) *Models and Metaphors*. New York: Cornell University Press.

Boje, David M. (1991) 'The storytelling organization: a study of story performance in an office-supply firm', *Administrative Science Quarterly*, 36: 106–26.

Boje, David M. (1995) 'Stories of the storytelling organization: a postmodern analysis of Disney as "Tamara-Land"', *Academy of Management Journal*, 38(4): 997–1035.

Boorstin, D. (1961) *The Image: a Guide to Pseudo-Events in America*. New York: Atheneum.

Bormann, Ernest G. (1983) 'Symbolic convergence: organizational communication and culture', in Linda L. Putnam and Michael E. Pacanowsky (eds), *Communication and Organization: an Interpretative Approach*. Beverly Hills, CA: Sage. pp. 99–122.

Bormann, Ernest G. (1985) 'Symbolic convergence theory: a communication formulation based on *homo narrans*', *Journal of Communication*, 35: 128–39.

Bormann, Ernest G. (1988) '"Empowering" as a heuristic concept in organizational communication', in James A. Anderson (ed.), *Communication Yearbook 11*. Newbury Park, CA: Sage. pp. 391–404.

Brink, T.L. (1991) 'Corporate cultures: a color coding metaphor', *Business Horizons*, September/October: 39–44.

Brink, T.L. (1993) 'Metaphor as data in the study of organizations', *Journal of Management Inquiry*, 2(4): 366–71.

Broms, H. and Gahmberg, H. (1983) 'Communication to self in organizations and cultures', *Administrative Science Quarterly*, 28: 11–21.

Brown, Mary Helen (1985) '"That reminds me of a story": speech action in organizational socialization', *Western Journal of Speech Communication*, 49: 27–42.

Brown, Mary Helen (1990) 'Defining stories in organizations: characteristics and functions', in James A. Anderson (ed.), *Communication Yearbook 13*. Newbury Park, CA: Sage. pp. 162–90.

Brown, Richard H. (1977) *A Poetic for Sociology*. Cambridge: Cambridge University Press.

Browning, Larry D. (1992) 'Lists and stories as organizational communication', *Communication Theory*, 4: 281–302.

Buber, M. (1985) *Between Man and Man*, 2nd edn. New York: Macmillan.

Bullis, Connie (1993) 'At least it is a start', in Stanley A. Deetz (ed.), *Communication Yearbook 16*. Newbury Park, CA: Sage. pp. 145–54.

Burns, T. and Stalker, G.M. (1961) *The Management of Innovation*. London: Tavistock.

Buzzanell, Patrice M. (1994) 'Gaining a voice: feminist organizational communication theorizing', *Management Communication Quarterly*, 7: 339–83.

Buzzanell, Patrice M. and Goldzwig, Steven R. (1991) 'Linear and nonlinear career models', *Management Communication Quarterly*, 4: 466–505.

Calás, Marta B. and Smircich, Linda (1985) 'The metaphor of the text/the paradigm of reading: interpretive organization', Paper presented at the Academy of Management Meeting.

Carey, James W. (ed.) (1989) *Communication as Culture: Essays on Media and Society*. New York: Routledge.

Cheney, George (1983) 'The rhetoric of identification and the study of organizational communication', *Quarterly Journal of Speech*, 69: 143–58.

Cheney, George (1991) *Rhetoric in Organizational Society: Managing Multiple Identities*. Columbia: University of South Carolina Press.

Cheney, George (1995) 'Democracy in the workplace: theory and practice from the communication perspective', *Journal of Applied Communication Research*, 23: 167–200.

Cheney, George and Christensen, Lars Thoger (forthcoming 1997) 'Identity at issue: linkages between "internal" and "external" organizational communication', in Fred M. Jablin and Linda L. Putnam (eds), *The New Handbook of Organizational Communication*. Thousand Oaks, CA: Sage.

Cheney, George and Tompkins, Phillip K. (1988) 'On the facts of the text as the basis of human communication research', in James A. Anderson (ed.), *Communication Yearbook 11*. Newbury Park, CA: Sage. pp. 455–81.

Cheney, George and Vibbert, Steven L. (1987) 'Corporate discourse: public relations and issue management', in Fredric M. Jablin, Linda L. Putnam, Karlene H. Roberts and Lyman W. Porter (eds), *Handbook of Organizational Communication: an Interdisciplinary Perspective*. Newbury Park, CA: Sage. pp. 165–94.

Clair, Robin (1993a) 'The use of framing devices to sequester organizational narratives: hegemony and harassment', *Communication Monographs*, 60: 113–36.

Clair, Robin (1993b) 'The bureaucratization, commodification, and privatization of sexual harassment through institutional discourse', *Management Communication Quarterly*, 7: 123–57.

Clegg, Stewart R. (1993) 'Narrative, power, and social theory', in Dennis K. Mumby (ed.), *Narrative and Social Control: Critical Perspectives*. Newbury Park, CA: Sage. pp. 15–45.

Coffman, S.L. and Eblen, A.L. (1987) 'Metaphor use and perceived managerial effectiveness', *Journal of Applied Communication Research*, 1–2: 53–66.

Cohen, M., March, J. and Olsen, J. (1972) 'A garbage can model of organizational choice', *Administrative Science Quarterly*, 17: 1–25.

Conrad, Charles (1983) 'Organizational power: faces and symbolic forms', in Linda L. Putnam and Michael E. Pacanowsky (eds), *Communication and Organizations: an Interpretive Approach*. Beverly Hills, CA: Sage. pp. 173–94.

Conrad, Charles and Witte, Kim (1994) 'Is emotional expression repression oppression? Myths of organizational affective regulation', in Stanley A. Deetz (ed.), *Communication Yearbook 17*. Thousand Oaks, CA: Sage. pp. 417–28.

Cusella, Louis P. (1987) 'Feedback, motivation, and performance', in Fredric M. Jablin, Linda L. Putnam, Karlene E. Roberts and Lyman W. Porter (eds), *Handbook of Organizational Communication: an Interdisciplinary Perspective*. Newbury Park, CA: Sage. pp. 624–78.

Czarniawska-Joerges, Barbara (1992) *Exploring Complex Organizations: a Cultural Perspective*. Newbury Park, CA: Sage.

Czarniawska-Joerges, Barbara (1994) 'Narratives of individual and organizational identities', in Stanley A. Deetz (ed.), *Communication Yearbook 17*. Thousand Oaks, CA: Sage. pp. 193–221.

Czarniawska-Joerges, Barbara (1995) 'Narration or science? Collapsing the division in organization studies', *Organization*, 2(1): 11–33.

Czarniawska-Joerges, Barbara and Joerges, B. (1988) 'How to control things with words: organizational talk and control', *Management Communication Quarterly*, 2(2): 170–93.

Daft, Richard L. (1983) 'Symbols in organizations: a dual-content framework of analysis', in Louis R. Pondy, Peter J. Frost, Gareth Morgan and Thomas C. Dandridge (eds), *Organizational Symbolism*. Greenwich, CT: JAI Press. pp. 199–206.

Daft, Richard L., Bettenhausen, K.R. and Tyler, B.B. (1993) 'Implications of top managers' communication choices for strategic decisions', in George P. Huber and William H. Glick (eds), *Organizational Change and Redesign: Ideas and Insights for Improving Performance*. New York: Oxford University Press. pp. 112–46.

Daft, Richard L. and Lengel, R.H. (1984) 'Information richness: a new approach to managerial information processing and organizational design', in Larry L. Cummings and Barry M. Staw (eds), *Research in Organizational Behavior*, vol. 6. Greenwich, CT: JAI Press. pp. 191–234.

Daft, Richard L., Lengel, R.H. and Trevino, Linda K. (1987) 'Message equivocality, media selection, and manager performance: implications for information systems', *MIS Quarterly*, 11: 355–66.

Daft, Richard L. and MacIntosh, N. (1981) 'A tentative exploration into the amount and equivocality of information processing in organizational work groups', *Administrative Science Quarterly*, 26: 207–24.

Davis, Keith (1953) 'A method of studying communication patterns in organizations', *Personnel Psychology*, 6: 301–12.

Davis, W.L. and O'Conner, J.R. (1977) 'Serial transmission of information: a study of the grapevine', *Journal of Applied Communication Research*, 5: 61–72.

Deetz, Stanley A. (1985) 'Ethical considerations in cultural research in organizations', in P. Frost, L. Moore, L. Louis, C. Lundberg and J. Martin (eds), *Organizational Culture*. Newbury Park, CA: Sage. pp. 251–69.

Deetz, Stanley A. (1986) 'Metaphors and the discursive production and reproduction of organizations', in Lee Thayer (ed.), *Organization–Communication: Emerging Perspectives I*. Norwood, NJ: Ablex. pp. 168–82.

Deetz, Stanley A. (1992a) *Democracy in an Age of Corporate Colonization*. Albany, NY: State University of New York Press.

Deetz, Stanley A. (1992b) 'Disciplinary power in the modern corporation', in Mats Alvesson and Hugh Wilmott (eds), *Critical Management Studies*. Newbury Park, CA: Sage. pp. 21–45.

Deetz, Stanley A. (forthcoming 1997) 'Conceptual foundations for organizational communication studies', in Fredric M. Jablin and Linda L. Putnam (eds), *The New Handbook of Organizational Communication*. Thousand Oaks, CA: Sage.

Deetz, Stanley A. and Kersten, Astrid (1983) 'Critical models of interpretive research', in Linda L. Putnam and Michael E. Pacanowsky (eds), *Communication and Organizations: an Interpretive Approach*. Beverly Hills, CA: Sage. pp. 147–71.

Deetz, Stanley, A. and Mumby, Dennis K. (1985) 'Metaphors, information and power', *Information and Behavior*, 1: 369–86.

Deetz, Stanley A. and Mumby, Dennis K. (1990) 'Power, discourse, and the workplace: reclaiming the critical tradition', in James A. Anderson (ed.), *Communication Yearbook 13*. Newbury Park, CA: Sage. pp. 18–47.

DeSanctis, G. and Poole, Marshall Scott (1994) 'Capturing the complexity in advanced technology use: adaptive structuration theory', *Organizational Science*, 5: 121–47.

DeSanctis, G., Poole, M.S., Lewis, H. and Desharnais, G. (1992) 'Using computing in quality team meetings: initial observations from the IRS–Minnesota Project', *Journal of Management and Information Systems*, 8: 7–26.

Donnellon, Anne, Gray, Barbara and Bougon, M. (1986) 'Communication, meaning, and organized action', *Administrative Science Quarterly*, 31: 43–55.

Donohue, William A. and Diez, Mary E. (1985) 'Directive use in negotiation interaction', *Communication Monographs*, 52: 305–18.

Downs, Anthony (1967) *Inside Bureaucracy*. Boston: Little Brown.

Duncan, W.J. (1983) 'The superiority theory of humor at work: joking relationships as indicators of formal and informal status patterns in small, task-oriented groups', *Small Group Behavior*, 16: 556–64.

Duncan, W.J. and Feisal, J.P. (1989) 'No laughing matter: patterns of humor in the work place', *Organizational Dynamics*, 17(4): 18–30.

Eagleton, Terry (1991) *Ideology: an Introduction*. London: Verso.

Earley, P.C. (1988) 'Computer-generated performance feedback in the magazine-subscription industry', *Organizational Behavior and Human Decision Processes*, 41: 50–64.

Edwards, Richard (1979) *Contested Terrain: the Transformation of the Workplace in the Twentieth Century*. New York: Basic Books.

Ehrlich, S. (1987) 'Strategies for encouraging successful adoption of office communication systems', *ACM Transactions on Office Information Systems*, 5: 340–57.

Eisenberg, Eric M. (1984) 'Ambiguity as strategy in organizational communication', *Communication Monographs*, 51: 227–42.

Eisenberg, Eric M. (1990) 'Jamming: transcendence through organizing', *Communication Research*, 17: 139–64.

Eisenberg, Eric M. (1994) 'Dialogue as democratic discourse: affirming Harrison', *Communication Yearbook 17*. Thousand Oaks, CA: Sage. pp. 275–84.

Eisenberg, Eric M., Farace, R., Monge, P., Bettinghaus, E., Kurchner-Hawkins, R., Miller, K. and Rothman, L. (1985) 'Communication linkages in interorganizational systems: review and synthesis', in Brenda Dervin and M. Voight (eds), *Progress in the Communication Sciences*, vol. 6. Norwood, NJ: Ablex. pp. 231–58.

Eisenberg, Eric M. and Goodall, H.L. Jr. (1993) *Organizational Communication: Balancing Creativity and Constraint*. New York: St Martin's Press.

Eisenberg, Eric M. and Phillips, Steven R. (1991) 'Miscommunication in organizations', in N. Coupland, H. Giles and J. Wiemann (eds), *'Miscommunication' and Problematic Talk*. Newbury Park, CA: Sage. pp. 244–58.

Eisenberg, Eric M. and Witten, M. (1987) 'Reconsidering openness in organizational communication', *Academy of Management Review*, 12: 418–26.

Eisenhardt, K.M. (1989) 'Making fast strategic decisions in high-velocity environments', *Academy of Management Journal*, 32: 543–76.

Evered, R. and Tannenbaum, R. (1992) 'A dialog on dialog', *Journal of Management Inquiry*, 1: 43–55.

Fairclough, Norman (1989) *Language and Power*. New York: Longman.

Fairclough, Norman (1992) *Discourse and Social Change*. Cambridge: Polity Press.

Fairclough, Norman (1993) 'Critical discourse analysis and the marketization of public discourse: the universities', *Discourse and Society*, 4: 133–68.

Fairhurst, Gail T. (1993) 'The leader–member exchange patterns of women leaders in industry: a discourse analysis', *Communication Monographs*, 60: 321–51.

Fairhurst, Gail T. and Chandler, Teresa A. (1989) 'Social structure in leader–member interaction', *Communication Monographs*, 56: 215–39.

Fairhurst, Gail T., Green, Stephen and Courtright, John (1995) 'Inertial forces and the implementation of a socio-technical systems approach: a communication study', *Organizational Science*, 6(2): 168–85.

Fairhurst, Gail T., Rogers, E. and Sarr, R. (1987) 'Manager–subordinate control patterns and judgments about the relationship', in Margaret McLaughlin (ed.), *Communication Yearbook 10*. Beverly Hills, CA: Sage. pp. 395–415.

Farace, R., Monge, P. and Russell, H. (1977) *Communicating and Organizing*. Reading, MA: Addison-Wesley.

Fayol, H. (1949) *General and Industrial Management* (1925). New York: Pitman.

Feldman, Martha and March, James (1981) 'Information in organizations as signal and symbol', *Administrative Science Quarterly*, 26: 171–86.

Filby, Ivan and Willmott, Hugh (1988) 'Ideologies and contradictions in a public relations department: the seduction and impotence of living myth', *Organization Studies*, 9(3): 335–49.

Fine, Marlene (1993) 'New voices in organizational communication: a feminist commentary and critique', in S.P. Bowen and Nancy Wyatt (eds), *Transforming Visions: Feminist Critiques in Communication Studies*. Cresskill, NJ: Hampton Press. pp. 125–66.

Fineman, Stephen (1993) 'Organizations as emotional arenas', in Stephen Fineman (ed.), *Emotion in Organizations*. London: Sage. pp. 9–35.

Fiol, C.M. (1989) 'A semiotic analysis of corporate language: organizational boundaries and joint venturing', *Administrative Science Quarterly*, 34: 277–303.

Fisher, B. Aubrey (1978) *Perspectives on Human Communication*. New York: Macmillan.

Follett, Mary Parker (1941) 'Constructive conflict', in H.C. Metcalf and L. Urwick (eds), *Dynamic Administration: the Collected Papers of Mary Parker Follett*. New York: Harper. pp. 30–49.

Ford, Jeffrey D. and Backoff, Robert H. (1988) 'Organizational change in and out of dualities and paradox', in Robert E. Quinn and Kim S. Cameron (eds), *Paradox and Transformation: Toward a Theory of Change in Organization and Management*. Cambridge, MA: Ballinger. pp. 81–121.

Foucault, Michel (1977) *Discipline and Punish: the Birth of the Prison*, translated by A. Sheridan Smith. New York: Random House.

Foucault, Michel (1980) *Power/Knowledge: Selected Interviews and Other Writings, 1972–1977*. New York: Pantheon.

Frankenberg, R. (1993) *White Women, Race Matters: the Social Construction of Whiteness*. Minneapolis, MN: University of Minnesota Press.

Frost, Peter J., Moore, Larry L., Louis, Meryl Reis, Lundberg, Craig C. and Martin, Joanne (eds) (1985) *Organizational Culture*. Beverly Hills, CA: Sage.

Fulk, Janet (1993) 'Social construction of communication technology', *Academy of Management Journal*, 36: 921–50.

Fulk, Janet and Boyd, Brian (1991) 'Emerging theories of communication in organizations', *Journal of Management*, 17(2): 407–46.

Fulk, Janet, Steinfield, Charles and Schmitz, Joseph (1990) 'The social influence model of technology use', in Janet Fulk and Charles Steinfield (eds), *Organizations and Communication Technology*. Newbury Park, CA: Sage. pp. 117–40.

Fulk, Janet, Steinfield, Charles, Schmitz, Joseph and Power, J.G. (1987) 'A social information processing model of media use in organizations', *Communication Research*, 14: 529–52.

Galbraith, J.R. (1973) *Designing Complex Organizations*. Reading MA: Addison-Wesley.

Galbraith, J.R., Lawler, E.E. and Associates (1993) *Organizing for the Future*. San Francisco: Jossey-Bass.

Geertz, Clifford (1973) *The Interpretation of Cultures*. New York: Basic Books.

Geertz, Clifford (1983) *Local Knowledge: Further Essays in Interpretive Anthropology*. New York: Basic Books.

Geist, Patricia and Chandler, Teresa (1984) 'Account analysis of influence in group decision making', *Communication Monographs*, 51: 67–78.

Geist, Patricia and Hardesty, Monica (1990) 'Ideological positioning in professionals' narratives of quality medical care', in Norman K. Denzin (ed.), *Studies in Symbolic Interaction*, vol. 2. Greenwich, CT: JAI Press. pp. 257–84.

Giddens, Anthony (1979) *Central Problems in Social Theory: Action, Structure and Contradiction in Social Analysis*. Berkeley: University of California Press.

Gioia, D.A. (1986) 'Symbols, scripts, and sensemaking: creating meaning in the organizational experience', in Hank P. Sims, Jr., Dennis A. Gioia, and Associates (eds), *The Thinking Organization*. San Francisco. Jossey-Bass. pp. 49–74.

Gioia, Dennis A. and Sims, Hank P. (1983) 'Perceptions of managerial power as a consequence of managerial behavior and reputation', *Journal of Management*, 9: 7–26.

Gioia, Dennis A., Donnellon, Anne and Sims, Hank P., Jr. (1989) 'Communication and cognition in appraisal: a tale of two paradigms', *Organization Studies*, 10(4): 503–30.

Glick, William H., Miller, C.C. and Huber, George P. (1993) 'Upper-echelon diversity in organizations: demographic, structural, and cognitive influences on organizational performance', in George W. Huber and William H. Glick (eds), *Organizational Change and Redesign: Ideas and Insights for Improving Performance*. New York: Oxford University Press. pp. 176–214.

Goffman, Erving (1959) *The Presentation of Self in Everyday Life*. New York: Doubleday Anchor.

Goldhaber, Gerald M. and Barnett, George A. (eds) (1988) *Handbook of Organizational Communication*. Norwood, NJ: Ablex Publishing.

Goodall, H.L., Jr. (1989) *Casing A Promised Land: The Autobiography of an Organizational Detective as Cultural Ethnographer*. Carbondale, Ill.: Southern Illinois University Press.

Gordon, David Paul (1983) 'Hospital slang for patients: crocks, gomers, gorks, and others', *Language in Society*, 12: 173–85.

Gordon, William I. (1994) '"Wego" comes in several varieties and is not simple', in Stanley A. Deetz (ed.), *Communication Yearbook 17*. Thousand Oaks, CA: Sage. pp. 285–97.

Granovetter, M. (1973) 'The strength of weak ties', *American Journal of Sociology*, 78: 1360–80.

Gray, Barbara, Bougon, M. and Donnellon, Anne (1985) 'Organizations as constructions and destructions of meaning', *Journal of Management*, 11: 83–98.

Gregory, K.L. (1983) 'Native-view paradigms: multiple cultures and culture conflicts in organizations', *Administrative Science Quarterly*, 28: 359–76.

Gronn, P.C. (1983) 'Talk as the work: the accomplishment of school administration', *Administrative Science Quarterly*, 28: 1–21.

Grunig, James E. (1984) 'Organizations, environments, and models of public relations', *Public Relations Research and Education*, 1: 6–29.

Grunig, James E. and Grunig, Laura A. (1992) 'Models of public relations and communication', in James E. Grunig (ed.), *Excellence in Public Relations and Communication Management*. Hillsdale, NJ: Erlbaum. pp. 285–325.

Hage, J. (1974) *Communication and Organizational Control: Cybernetics in Health and Welfare Agencies*. New York: Wiley.

Handy, C. (1994) *The Age of Paradox*. Boston: Harvard Business School Press.

Harris, Linda and Cronen, Vernon E. (1979) 'A rules-based model for the analysis and evaluation of organizational communication', *Communication Quarterly*, 27: 12–18.

Harrison, Teresa M. (1994) 'Communication and interdependence in democratic organizations', in Stanley A. Deetz (ed.), *Communication Yearbook 17*. Thousand Oaks, CA: Sage. pp. 246–74.

Haslett, Beth (1990) 'Discourse, ideology, and organizational control', in James A. Anderson (ed.), *Communication Yearbook 13*. Newbury Park, CA: Sage. pp. 48–58.

Hatch, M.J. and Ehrlich, S.B. (1993) 'Spontaneous humor as an indicator of paradox and ambiguity in organizations', *Organization Studies*, 14: 505–26.

Hawkes, D.F. (1972) *Metaphor*. London: Methuen.

Heath, R.L. (ed.) (1988) *Strategic Issues Management: How Organizations Influence and Respond to Public Interests and Policies*. San Francisco: Jossey-Bass.

Hellweg, Susan (1987) 'Organizational grapevines: a state of the art review', in Brenda Dervin and M. Voight (eds), *Progress in the Communication Sciences*, vol. 8. Norwood, NJ: Ablex.

Hirsch, Paul M. and Andrews, John A.Y. (1983) 'Ambushes, shootouts, and knights of the roundtable: the language of corporate takeovers', in Louis R. Pondy, Peter J. Frost, Gareth Morgan and Thomas C. Dandridge (eds), *Organizational Symbolism*. Greenwich, CT: JAI Press. pp. 145–55.

Hochschild, A. (1983) *The Managed Heart: Commercialization of Human Feeling*. Berkeley: University of California Press.

Huber, George A. (1991) 'Organizational learning: the contributing processes and literatures', *Organizational Science*, 2: 88–115.

Isaacs, William N. (1993) 'Taking flight: dialogue, collective thinking, and organizational learning', *Organizational Dynamics*, 22(2): 24–39.

Isabella, Lynn A. (1990) 'Evolving interpretations as a change unfolds: how managers construe key organizational events', *Academy of Management Journal*, 33: 7–41.

Jablin, Fredric M. (1987) 'Formal organizational structure', in Fredric M. Jablin, Linda L. Putnam, Karlene H. Roberts and Lyman W. Porter (eds), *Handbook of Organizational Communication: an Interdisciplinary Perspective*. Newbury Park, CA: Sage. pp. 389–419.

Jablin, Fredric M., Putnam, Linda L., Roberts, Karlene H. and Porter, Lyman W. (eds) (1987) *Handbook of Organizational Communication: an Interdisciplinary Perspective*. Newbury Park, CA: Sage.

Jablin, Fredric M. and Putnam, Linda L. (eds) (forthcoming 1997) *The New Handbook of Organizational Communication*. Thousand Oaks, CA: Sage.

Johnson, Bonnie (1977) *Communication: the Process of Organizing*. Boston: Allyn-Bacon.

Jones, Michael O., Moore, Michael D. and Snyder, Richard C. (eds) (1988) *Inside Organizations: Understanding the Human Dimension*. Newbury Park, CA: Sage.

Katz, D. and Kahn, Robert (1966) *The Social Psychology of Organizations*. New York: Wiley.

Kelly, Jan W. (1985) 'Storytelling in high tech organizations: a medium for sharing culture', *Journal of Applied Communication Research*. 13: 45–58.

Kerr, S. (1975) 'On the folly of rewarding A, while hoping for B', *Academy of Management Journal*, 47: 469–83.

Kersten, Astrid (1993) 'Culture, control, and the labor process', in Stanley A. Deetz (ed.), *Communication Yearbook 16*. Newbury Park, CA: Sage. pp. 54–60.

Kim, Young Yun (1994) 'Interethnic communication: the context and the behavior', in Stanley A. Deetz (ed.), *Communication Yearbook 17*. Thousand Oaks, CA: Sage. pp. 511–38.

Knights, D. (1992) 'Changing spaces: the disruptive impact of a new epistemological location for the study of management', *Academy of Management Review*, 17: 514–36.

Knuf, Joachim (1993) 'Ritual in organizational culture theory: some theoretical reflections and a plea for greater terminological rigor', in Stanley A. Deetz (ed.), *Communication Yearbook 16*. Newbury Park, CA: Sage. pp. 61–103.

Koch, Susan and Deetz, Stanley A. (1981) 'Metaphor analysis of social reality in organizations', *Journal of Applied Communication Research*, 9: 1–15.

Komaki, Judith L. (1986) 'Toward effective supervision: an operant analysis and comparison of managers at work', *Journal of Applied Psychology*, 71: 270–8.

Komaki, Judith L. and Citera, M. (1990) 'Beyond effective supervision: identifying key interactions between superior and subordinate', *Leadership Quarterly*, 1: 91–106.

Komaki, Judith L., Zlotnick, S. and Jensen, M. (1986) 'Development of an operant-based taxonomy and observational index of supervisory behavior', *Journal of Applied Psychology*, 71: 260–9.

Krefting, Linda A. and Frost, Peter J. (1985) 'Untangling webs, surfing waves, and wildcatting: a multiple-metaphor perspective on managing organizational cultures', in Peter J. Frost, Larry F. Moore, Meryl Reis Louis, Craig C. Lundberg and Joanne Martin (eds), *Organizational Culture*. Beverly Hills, CA: Sage. pp. 155–68.

Kreps, Gary L. (1980) 'A field experimental test and revaluation of Weick's model of organizing', in Dan Nimmo (ed.), *Communication Yearbook 4*. New Brunswick, NJ: Transaction Books. pp. 389–98.

Kreps, Gary L. (1989) 'Stories as repositories of organizational intelligence: implications for organizational development', in James A. Anderson (ed.), *Communication Yearbook 13*. Newbury Park, CA: Sage.

Kunda, Gideon (1992) *Engineering Culture: Control and Commitment in a High-tech Corporation*. Philadelphia: Temple University Press.

Lakoff, George and Johnson, Mark (1980) *Metaphors We Live By*. Chicago: University of Chicago Press.

Leavitt, Harold (1951) 'Some effects of certain communication patterns on group performance', *Journal of Abnormal and Social Psychology*, 46: 38–50.

Likert, R. (1967) *The Human Organization: Its Management and Value*. New York: McGraw-Hill.

Loseke, D.R. (1989) 'Creating clients: social problems work in a shelter for battered women', *Perspectives on Social Problems*, 1: 173–93.

Lotman, J.M. (1977) 'Two models of communication', in D.P. Lucid (ed.), *Soviet Semiotics: an Anthology*. London: Johns Hopkins. pp. 99–101.

Luhmann, N. (1990) *Essays on Self-Reference*. New York: Columbia University Press.

Lyotard, J.-F. (1984) *The Postmodern Condition: a Report on Knowledge*, translated by G. Bennington and B. Massumi. Minneapolis: University of Minnesota Press.

Mangham, I.L. and Overington, M.A. (1987) *Organizations as Theatre: a Social Psychology of Dramatic Appearances*. New York: Wiley.

Manning, Peter K. (1979) 'Metaphors of the field: varieties of organizational discourse', *Administrative Science Quarterly*, 24: 660–71.

Manning, Peter K. (1988) *Symbolic Communication: Signifying Calls and the Police Response*. Cambridge, MA: MIT Press.

Manning, Peter K. (1992) *Organizational Communication*. New York: Aldine De Gruyter.

Marshall, Judi (1993) 'Viewing organizational communication from a feminist perspective: a critique and some offerings', in Stanley A. Deetz (ed.), *Communication Yearbook 16*. Newbury Park, CA: Sage. pp. 122–43.

Martin, Joanne (1982) 'Stories and scripts in organizational settings', in A. Hastorf and A. Isen (eds), *Cognitive Social Psychology*. London: Routledge. pp. 255–305.

May, Steven K. (1993) 'A communication course in organizational paradigms and metaphors', *Communication Education*, 42: 234–54.

McLaughlin, Margaret (1984) *Conversation: How Talk Is Organized*. Beverly Hills, CA: Sage.

McPhee, Robert D. (1993) 'Cultural-ideological modes of control: an examination of concept formation', in Stanley A. Deetz (ed.), *Communication Yearbook 16*. Newbury Park, CA: Sage. pp. 43–53.

McPhee, Robert D. and Corman, Seven R. (1995) 'An activity-based theory of communication networks in organizations, applied to the case of a local church', *Communication Monographs*, 62: 132–51.

Miller, J.G. (1960) 'Information input, overload, and psychopathology', *American Journal of Psychiatry*, 116: 695–704.

Miller, Katherine I. (1995) *Organizational Communication: Approaches and Processes*. Belmont, CA: Wadsworth.

Miller, Katherine I. and Monge, Peter R. (1986) 'Participation, satisfaction, and productivity: a meta-analytic review', *Academy of Management Journal*, 29: 727–53.

Miller, P. and O'Leary, T. (1987) 'Accounting and the construction of the governable person', *Accounting, Organizations, and Society*, 12: 235–65.

Miller, Vernon D. and Jablin, Fredric M. (1991) 'Information seeking during organizational entry: influences, tactics, and a model of the process', *Academy of Management Review*, 16: 92–120.

Mintzberg, Henry (1979) *The Structuring of Organizations*. Englewood Cliffs, NJ: Prentice-Hall.

Mitroff, Ian I. and Kilmann, Ralph H. (1976) 'On organizational stories: an approach to the design and analysis of organizations through myths and stories', in Ralph H. Kilmann, Louis R. Pondy and D.P. Slevin (eds), *The Management of Organizational Design*, vol. 1. New York: Elsevier North-Holland. pp. 189–207.

Monge, Peter R. and Contractor, Noshir (1988) 'Communication networks: measuring techniques', in C.H. Tardy (ed.), *A Handbook for the Study of Human Communication*. Norwood, NJ: Ablex. pp. 107–38.

Monge, Peter R. and Eisenberg, Eric (1987) 'Emergent communication networks', in Fredric M. Jablin, Linda L. Putnam, Karlene H. Roberts and Lyman W. Porter (eds), *Handbook of Organizational Communication*. Newbury Park, CA: Sage. pp. 304–42.

Morgan, Gareth (1980) 'Paradigms, metaphors and puzzle solving in organizational theory', *Administrative Science Quarterly*, 25: 605–22.

Morgan, Gareth (1983) 'More on metaphor: why we cannot control tropes in administrative science', *Administrative Science Quarterly*, 28: 601–7.

Morgan, Gareth (1986) *Images of Organizations*. Beverly Hills, CA: Sage.

Morgan, Gareth, Frost, Peter J. and Pondy, Louis R. (1983) 'Organizational symbolism', in Louis R.

Pondy, Peter J. Frost, Gareth Morgan and Thomas C. Dandridge (eds), *Organizational Symbolism*. Greenwich, CT: JAI Press. pp. 3–35.

Morris, G.H. (1988) 'Accounts in selection interviews', *Journal of Applied Communication Research*, 15(2): 82–98.

Mumby, Dennis K. (1987) 'The political function of narrative in organizations', *Communication Monographs*, 54: 113–27.

Mumby, Dennis K. (1988) *Communication and Power in Organizations: Discourse, Ideology, and Domination*. Norwood, NJ: Ablex.

Mumby, Dennis K. (1993) 'Feminism and the critique of organizational communication studies', in Stanley A. Deetz (ed.), *Communication Yearbook 16*. Newbury Park, CA: Sage. pp. 155–66.

Mumby, Dennis K. (forthcoming 1997) 'Power, politics and organizational communication: theoretical perspectives', in Fredric M. Jablin and Linda L. Putnam (eds), *The New Handbook of Organizational Communication*. Thousand Oaks, CA: Sage.

Mumby, Dennis K. and Putnam, Linda L. (1992) 'The politics of emotion: a feminist reading of bounded rationality', *Academy of Management Review*, 17: 465–86.

Nakayama, T. and Kriziek, Robert (1995) 'Whiteness: a strategic rhetoric', *The Quarterly Journal of Speech*, 81: 291–309.

Nkomo, Stella (1992) 'The emperor has no clothes: rewriting "race in organizations"', *Academy of Management Review*, 17: 487–513.

O'Connor, Ellen S. (1995) 'Paradoxes of participation: a textual analysis of case studies on organizational change', *Organization Studies*, 16(5): 769–803.

Oliver, C. (1990) 'Determinants of interorganizational relationships: integration and future directions', *Academy of Management Review*, 15: 241–65.

O'Reilly, Charles A. (1978) 'The intentional distortion of information in organizational communication: a laboratory and field approach', *Human Relations*, 31: 173–93.

O'Reilly, Charles A. (1980) 'Individuals and information overload in organizations: is more necessarily better?', *Academy of Management Journal*, 23: 684–96.

O'Reilly, Charles A., Chatman, Jennifer A. and Anderson, John C. (1987) 'Message flow and decision making', in Fredric M. Jablin, Linda L. Putnam, Karlene H. Roberts and Lyman W. Porter (eds), *Handbook of Organizational Communication: an Interdisciplinary Perspective*. Newbury Park, CA: Sage. pp. 600–23.

O'Reilly, Charles A. and Roberts, Karlene H. (1974) 'Information infiltration in organizations: three experiments', *Organizational Behavior and Human Performance*, 11: 253–65.

Orlikowski, Wanda J. and Yates, JoAnne (1994) 'Genre repertoire: the structuring of communicative practices in organizations', *Administrative Science Quarterly*, 39: 541–74.

Ortony, A. (ed.) (1979) *Metaphor and Thought*. Cambridge: Cambridge University Press.

Pacanowsky, Michael E. (1988) 'Communication in the empowering organization', in James A. Anderson (ed.), *Communication Yearbook 11*. Newbury Park, CA: Sage. pp. 356–79.

Pacanowsky, Michael E. and O'Donnell-Trujillo, Nick (1983) 'Organizational communication as cultural performance', *Communication Monographs*, 50: 126–47.

Papa, Michael (1990) 'Communication network patterns and employee performance with new technology', *Communication Research*, 17: 344–68.

Pearce, M. and David, J. (1983) 'A social network approach to organizational design-performance', *Academy of Management Journal*, 26(3): 436–44.

Pepper, Gerald L. (1995) *Communicating in Organizations: a Cultural Approach*. New York: McGraw-Hill.

Perrow, Charles (1986) *Complex Organizations: a Critical Essay*, 3rd edn (1st edn 1972). New York: Random House.

Pfeffer, J. and Salancik, G.R. (1978) *The External Control of Organizations: a Resource Dependence Perspective*. New York: Harper & Row.

Pinder, C.C. and Bourgeois, V.W. (1982) 'Controlling tropes in administrative sciences', *Administrative Science Quarterly*, 27: 641–52.

Pondy, Louis R. (1983) 'The role of metaphors and myths in organizations and in the facilitation of change', in Louis R. Pondy, Peter J. Frost, Gareth Morgan and Thomas D. Dandridge (eds), *Organizational Symbolism*. Greenwich, CT: JAI Press. pp. 157–66.

Pondy, Louis R. and Mitroff, Ian (1979) 'Beyond open systems models of organization', in Barry M. Staw (ed.), *Research in Organizational Behavior*, vol. 1. Greenwich, CT: JAI Press. pp. 3–39.

Pondy, Louis R., Frost, Peter J., Morgan, Gareth and Dandridge, Thomas C. (eds) (1983) *Organizational Symbolism*. Greenwich, CT: JAI Press.

Poole, Marshall S. and DeSanctis, G. (1990) 'Understanding the use of group decision support systems: the theory of adaptive structuration', in Janet Fulk and Charles Steinfeld (eds), *Organizations and Communication Technology*. Newbury Park, CA: Sage. pp. 173–93.

Poole, Marshall S. and DeSanctis, G. (1992) 'Microlevel structuration in computer-supported group decision-making', *Human Communication Research*, 19: 5–49.

Putnam, Linda L. (1983) 'The interpretive perspective: an alternative to functionalism', in Linda L. Putnam and Michael E. Pacanowsky (eds), *Communication and Organizations: an Interpretive Approach*. Beverly Hills, CA: Sage. pp. 31–54.

Putnam, Linda L. (1986) 'Contradictions and paradoxes in organizations', in Lee Thayer (ed.), *Organization–Communication: Emerging Perspectives I*. Norwood, NJ: Ablex. pp. 151–67.

Putnam, Linda L. (1989) 'Negotiating as organizing: two levels within the Weickian model', *Communication Studies*, 40: 249–57.

Putnam, Linda L. and Cheney, George (1983) 'A critical review of the research traditions in organizational communication', in Mary S. Mander (ed.), *Communication in Transition*. New York: Praeger. pp. 206–24.

Putnam, Linda L. and Cheney, George (1985) 'Organizational communication: historical development and future directions', in Thomas W. Benson (ed.), *Speech Communication in the Twentieth Century*. Carbondale, IL: Southern University Press. pp. 130–56.

Putnam, Linda L. and Mumby, Dennis K. (1993) 'Organizations, emotion, and the myth of rationality', in Stephen Fineman (ed.), *Emotions in Organizations*. London: Sage. pp. 36–57.

Putnam, Linda L. and Roloff, Michael E. (eds) (1992) *Communication and Negotiation*. Newbury Park, CA: Sage.

Putnam, Linda L. and Sorenson, Ritch L. (1982) 'Equivocal messages in organizations', *Human Communication Research*, 8: 114–32.

Putnam, Linda L., Van Hoeven, Shirley A. and Bullis, Connie A. (1991) 'The role of rituals and fantasy themes in teachers' bargaining', *Western Journal of Speech Communication*, 55: 85–103.

Quinn, Robert E. and Cameron, Kim S. (eds) (1988) *Paradox and Transformation: Toward a Theory of Change in Organization and Management*. Cambridge, MA: Ballinger.

Rafaeli, A. and Sutton, Robert I. (1987) 'Expression of emotion as part of the work role', *Academy of Management Review*, 12: 23–37.

Ragan, Sandra L. (1983) 'A conversational analysis of alignment talk in job interviews', in Robert Bostrum (ed.), *Communication Yearbook 7*. Beverly Hills, CA: Sage. pp. 502–16.

Ragan, Sandra L. and Hopper, Robert (1981) 'Alignment talk in the job interview', *Journal of Applied Communication Research*, 9: 85–103.

Rakow, Lana F. (1986) 'Rethinking gender research in communication', *Journal of Communication*, 36: 11–26.

Redding, W. Charles (1985) 'Stumbling toward identity: the emergence of organizational communication as a field of study', in Robert D. McPhee and Phillip K. Tompkins (eds), *Organizational Communication: Traditional Themes and New Directions*. Beverly Hills, CA: Sage. pp. 15–54.

Redding, W. Charles and Tompkins, Phillip K. (1988) 'Organizational communication – past and present tenses', in Gerald M. Goldhaber and George A. Barnett (eds), *Handbook of Organizational Communication*. Norwood, NJ: Ablex. pp. 5–33.

Reddy, M. (1979) 'The conduit metaphor – a case of frame conflict in our language about language', in A. Ortony (ed.), *Metaphor and Thought*. Cambridge: Cambridge University Press. pp. 284–324.

Rice, Ron E. (1993) 'Media appropriateness: using social presence to compare traditional and new organizational media', *Human Communication Research*, 19: 451–84.

Rice, Ron E. and Aydin, C. (1991) 'Attitudes toward new organizational technology: network proximity as a mechanism for social information processing', *Administrative Science Quarterly*, 36: 219–44.

Rice, Ron E. and Danowski, James (1993) 'Is it really just like a fancy answering machine? Comparing semantic networks of different types of voice mail users', *Journal of Business Communication*, 30(4): 369–97.

Rice, Ron E. and Gattiker, Urs E. (forthcoming 1997) 'New media and organizational structuring: the sublimation of boundaries in meaning and relations', in Fredric M. Jablin and Linda L. Putnam (eds), *The New Handbook of Organizational Communication*. Thousand Oaks, CA: Sage.

Rice, Ron E., Grant, A., Schmitz, J. and Torobin, J. (1990) 'Individual and network influences on the adoption and perceived outcomes of electronic messaging', *Social Networks*, 12(1): 27–55.

Rice, Ron E., Hughes, D. and Love, G. (1989) 'Usage and outcomes of electronic messaging at an R&D organization: situational constraints, job level, and media awareness', *Office: Technology and People*, 5(2): 141–61.

Rice, Ron E. and Shook, D. (1988) 'Access to, usage of, and outcomes from an electronic message system', *ACM Transactions on Office Information Systems*, 6(3): 255–76.

Rice, Ron E. and Shook, D. (1990) 'Relationships of job categories and organizational levels to use of communication channels, including electronic mail: a meta-analysis and extension', *Journal of Management Studies*, 27: 195–229.

Ricoeur, P. (1979) 'The model of the text: meaningful action considered as a text', in P. Rabinow and W.M. Sullivan (eds), *Interpretive Social Science: a Reader*. Berkeley: University of California Press. pp. 73–102.

Riley, Patricia (1983) 'A structurationist account of political culture', *Administrative Science Quarterly*, 28: 414–37.

Roethlisberger, F.J. (1941) *Management and Morale*. Cambridge, MA: Harvard University Press.

Rogers, Everett M. (1994) *A History of Communication Study: a Biographical Approach*. New York: Free Press.

Rogers, Everett M. and Kincaid, D. (1981) *Communication Networks: Toward a New Paradigm for Research*. New York: Free Press.

Rosen, M. (1985) 'Breakfast at Spiro's: dramaturgy and dominance', *Journal of Management*, 11(2): 31–48.

Rosen, M. (1988) 'You asked for it: Christmas at the bosses' expense', *Journal of Management Studies*, 25: 463–80.

Rosenau, P. (1992) *Post-Modernism and the Social*

Sciences: Insights, Inroads, and Intrusions. Princeton, NJ: Princeton University Press.

Rothschild-Whitt, J. (1986) *The Cooperative Workplace: Potentials and Dilemmas of Organizational Democracy and Participation.* London: Cambridge University Press.

Russ, G.S., Daft, R.L. and Lengel, R.H. (1990) 'Media selection and managerial characteristics in organizational communications', *Management Communication Quarterly*, 4: 151–75.

Saussure, Ferdinand de (1983) *Course in General Linguistics.* La Salle, IL: Open Court.

Schall, M.S. (1983) 'A communication-rules approach to organizational culture', *Administrative Science Quarterly*, 28: 557–81.

Schmitz, Joseph and Fulk, Janet (1991) 'Organizational colleagues, media richness, and electronic mail: a test of the social influence model of technology', *Communication Research*, 18: 487–523.

Shannon, Claude E. and Weaver, Warren (1949) *The Mathematical Theory of Communication.* Urbana, IL: University of Illinois Press.

Short, J., Williams, E. and Christie, B. (1976) *The Social Psychology of Telecommunications.* London: Wiley.

Shrivastava, P. and Schneider, S. (1984) 'Organizational frames of reference', *Human Relations*, 37: 795–809.

Siehl, Caren, Bowen, David E. and Pearson, Critine M. (1992) 'Service encounters as rites of integration: an information processing model', *Organizational Science*, 3(4): 537–55.

Sigman, Stewart, J. (1986) 'Adjustment to the nursing home as a social interactional accomplishment', *Journal of Applied Communication Research*, 14: 37–58.

Simon, Herbert A. (1957) *Administrative Behavior.* New York: Free Press.

Sims, Hank P. and Manz, C.C. (1984) 'Observing leader verbal behavior: toward reciprocal determinism in leadership theory', *Journal of Applied Psychology*, 69: 222–32.

Smircich, Linda (1983) 'Concepts of culture and organizational analysis', *Administrative Science Quarterly*, 28: 339–58.

Smircich, Linda and Stubbart, Charles (1985) 'Strategic management in an enacted world', *Academy of Management Review*, 10: 724–36.

Smith, A.G. (1973) 'The ethic of the relay men', in Lee Thayer (ed.), *Communication: Ethical and Moral Issues.* London: Gordon & Breach. pp. 313–24.

Smith, Kenwyn K. and Berg, David N. (1987) *Paradoxes of Group Life.* San Francisco: Jossey-Bass.

Smith, Ruth C. (1993) 'Images of organizational communication: root-metaphors of the organization–communication relation'. Paper presented at the International Communication Association Conference, Washington, DC.

Smith, Ruth C. and Eisenberg, Eric M. (1987)

'Conflict at Disneyland: a root-metaphor analysis', *Communication Monographs*, 54: 367–80.

Smith, Ruth C. and Eisenberg, Eric M. (1988) 'Root metaphor analysis: a heuristic method for studying organizational change. Paper presented at the Academy of Management Meetings, Anaheim, California.

Smith, Ruth C. and Turner, Paaige (1995) 'A social constructionist reconfiguration of metaphor analysis: an application of "SCMA" to organizational socialization theorizing', *Communication Monographs*, 62: 152–81.

Spradley, J.P. and Mann, B.J. (1975) *The Cocktail Waitress.* New York: Wiley.

Sproule, J. Michael (1989) 'Organizational rhetoric and the public sphere', *Communication Studies*, 40: 258–65.

Steier, Fred and Smith, K. (1992) 'The cybernetics of cybernetics and the organization of organization', in Lee Thayer (ed.), *Organization–Communication: Emerging Perspectives III.* Norwood, NJ: Ablex.

Stohl, Cynthia (1986) 'The role of memorable messages in the process of organizational socialization', *Communication Quarterly*, 34: 231–49.

Stohl, Cynthia (1993) 'European managers' interpretations of participation: a semantic network analysis', *Human Communication Research*, 20: 97–117.

Stohl, Cynthia (1995) *Organizational Communication: Connectedness in Action.* Thousand Oaks, CA: Sage.

Stohl, Cynthia and Redding, W. Charles (1987) 'Messages and message exchange processes', in Fredric M. Jablin, Linda L. Putnam, Karlene H. Roberts and Lyman W. Porter (eds), *Handbook of Organizational Communication: an Interdisciplinary Perspective.* Beverly Hills, CA: Sage. pp. 451–502.

Strine, Mary S. (1988) 'Constructing "texts" and making inferences: some reflections on textual reality in human communication research', in James A. Anderson (ed.), *Communication Yearbook 11.* Newbury Park, CA: Sage. pp. 494–500.

Stutman, Randall K. and Putnam, Linda L. (1994) 'The consequences of language: a metaphorical look at the legalization of organizations', in Sim B. Sitkin and Robert J. Bies (eds), *The Legalistic Organization.* Thousand Oaks, CA: Sage. pp. 281–302.

Sutcliffe, Kathleen M. (forthcoming 1997) 'Organizational environments and organizational information processing', in Fredric M. Jablin and Linda L. Putnam (eds), *The New Handbook of Organizational Communication.* Thousand Oaks, CA: Sage.

Taylor, Frederic W. (1947) *Principles of Scientific Management* (1912). New York: Harper.

Taylor, James R. (1993) *Rethinking the Theory of Organizational Communication: How to Read an Organization.* Norwood, NJ: Ablex.

Taylor, James R. (1995) 'Shifting from a heteronomous to an autonomous worldview of organizational communication: communication theory on the cusp', *Communication Theory*, 5(1): 1–35.

Taylor, James R. and Robichaud, Daniel (1992) 'A new look at enactment'. Paper presented at the International Communication Association Conference, Miami, Florida.

Taylor, James R. and Van Every, Elizabeth J. (1993) *The Vulnerable Fortress: Bureaucratic Organization and Management in the Information Age.* Toronto: University of Toronto Press.

Taylor, M.E. (1987) 'Functions of in-house language: observations on data collected from some British financial institutions', *Language in Society*, 16: 1–7.

Tesser, A. and Rosen, S. (1975) 'The reluctance to transmit bad news', in Leonard Berkowitz (ed.), *Advances in Experimental Social Psychology*, vol. 8. New York: Academic Press. pp. 193–232.

Thachankary, T. (1992) 'Organizations as "texts": hermeneutics as a model for understanding organizational change', *Research in Organizational Change and Development*, 6: 197–233.

Therborn, G. (1980) *The Ideology of Power and the Power of Ideology.* London: Verso.

Thompson, John B. (1984) *Studies in the Theory of Ideology.* Berkeley, CA: University of California Press.

Thompson, John B. (1990) *Ideology and Modern Culture.* Stanford, CA: Stanford University Press.

Tichy, N. and Fombrun, C. (1979) 'Network analysis in organizational settings', *Human Relations*, 32: 923–65.

Tompkins, Phillip K. and Cheney, George (1983) 'Account analysis of organizations: decision making and identification', in Linda L. Putnam and Michael E. Pacanowsky (eds), *Communication and Organizations: an Interpretive Approach.* Beverly Hills, CA: Sage. pp. 123–46.

Tompkins, Phillip K. and Cheney, George (1985) 'Communication and unobtrusive control in contemporary organizations', in Robert D. McPhee and Phillip K. Tompkins (eds), *Organization Communication: Traditional Themes and New Directions.* Beverly Hills, CA: Sage. pp. 179–210.

Townley, B. (1993) 'Foucault, power/knowledge, and its relevance for human resource management', *Academy of Management Review*, 18: 518–45.

Trevino, Linda K., Lengel, R.H. and Daft, Richard L. (1987) 'Media symbolism, media richness, and media choice in organizations: a symbolic interactionist perspective', *Communication Research*, 14: 553–74.

Trice, Harrison M. and Beyer, Janice M. (1984) 'Studying organizational culture through rites and ceremonies', *Academy of Management Review*, 9: 653–69.

Trice, Harrison M. and Beyer, Janice M. (1985) *Using Six Organizational Rites to Change Culture.* San Francisco: Jossey-Bass.

Trujillo, Nick (1985) 'Organizational communication as cultural performance: some managerial considerations', *Southern Speech Communication Journal*, 50: 201–24.

Turner, Victor (1980) 'Social dramas and stories about them', *Critical Inquiry*, 7: 141–68.

Tushman, Michael L. (1979) 'Work characteristics and subunit communication structure: a contingency analysis', *Administrative Science Quarterly*, 24: 82–98.

Tushman, Michael L. and Scanlan, T.J. (1981) 'Boundary spanning individuals: their role in information transfer and their antecedents', *Academy of Management Journal*, 24: 289–305.

Tway, P. (1975) 'Workplace isoglosses: lexical variation and change in a factory setting', *Language in Society*, 4: 171–83.

Tway, P. (1976) 'Verbal and nonverbal communication of factory workers', *Semiotica*, 16: 29–44.

Ullian, J.A. (1976) 'Joking at work', *Journal of Communication*, 26: 479–86.

Van de Ven, Andrew H. and Poole, Marshall Scott (1988) 'Paradoxical requirements for a theory of organizational change', in Robert E. Quinn and Kim S. Cameron (eds), *Paradox and Transformation: Toward a Theory of Change in Organization and Management.* Cambridge, MA: Ballinger. pp. 19–64.

Van Maanen, John (1973) 'Observations on the making of policemen', *Human Organization*, 32: 407–18.

Van Maanen, John (1978) 'The asshole', in Peter K. Manning and John Van Maanen (eds), *Policing.* New York: Random House.

Van Maanen, John and Kunda, Gideon (1989) 'Real feelings: emotional expression and organizational culture', in Larry L. Cummings and Barry M. Staw (eds), *Research in Organizational Behavior*, vol. 6. Greenwich, CT: JAI Press. pp. 287–365.

Waldron, Vincent R. (1994) 'Once more, with feeling: reconsidering the role of emotion in work', in Stanley A. Deetz (ed.), *Communication Yearbook 17.* Thousand Oaks, CA: Sage. pp. 388–416.

Waldron, Vincent R. and Krone, Katherine (1991) 'The experience and expression of emotion in the workplace: a study of a corrections organization', *Management Communication Quarterly*, 4: 287–309.

Watson-Dugan, K.W. (1989) 'Ability and effort attributions: do they affect how managers communicate performance feedback information?', *Academy of Management Journal*, 32: 87–114.

Watzlawick, Paul, Beavin, Janet Helmick and Jackson, Don D. (1967) *Pragmatics of Human Communication: a Study of Interactional Patterns, Pathologies, and Paradoxes.* New York: W.W. Norton.

Weber, Max (1947) *The Theory of Social and Economic Organization.* New York: Free Press.

Weick, Karl E. (1979) *The Social Psychology of Organizing* (1969). Reading, MA: Addison-Wesley.

Weick, Karl E. (1987) 'Theorizing about organizational communication', in Fredric M. Jablin, Linda L. Putnam, Karlene H. Roberts and Lyman W. Porter (eds), *Handbook of Organizational Communication.* Newbury Park, CA: Sage. pp. 97–122.

Weick, Karl E. (1990) 'Cartographic myths in organizations', in Anne S. Huff (ed.), *Mapping Strategic Thought*. New York: Wiley. pp. 1–10.

Weick, Karl E. and Browning, Larry (1986) 'Arguments and narration in organizational communication', *Journal of Management*, 12: 243–59.

Wert-Gray, S., Center, C., Brashers, Dale and Meyers, Renee (1991) 'Research topics and methodological orientations in organizational communication. A decade in review', *Communication Studies*, 42: 141–54.

Wilkins, Alan L. (1983) 'Organizational stories as symbols which control the organization', in Louis R. Pondy, Peter J. Frost, Gareth Morgan and Thomas C. Dandridge (eds), *Organizational Symbolism*. Greenwich, CT: JAI Press. pp. 81–92.

Wilkins, Alan L. (1984) 'The creation of cultures: the role of stories and human resource systems', *Human Resource Management*, 23: 41–60.

Witten, Marsha (1993) 'Narrative and the culture of obedience at the workplace', in Dennis K. Mumby (ed.), *Narrative and Social Control: Critical Perspectives*. Newbury Park, CA: Sage. pp. 97–118.

Wood, Julia T. and Conrad, Charles (1983) 'Paradox in the experiences of professional women', *Western Journal of Speech Communication*, 47: 305–22.

Wuthnow, Robert and Witten, Marsha (1988) 'New directions in the study of culture', *Annual Review of Sociology*, 14: 49–67.

Yates, JoAnne (1993) 'Co-evolution of information processing technology and use: interaction between the life insurance and tabulating industries', *Business History Review*, 67: 1–51.

Yates, JoAnne and Orlikowski, Wanda (1992) 'Genres of organizational communication: an approach to studying communication media', *Academy of Management Review*, 17: 299–326.

Young, Ed (1989) 'On the naming of the rose: interests and multiple meanings as elements of organizational culture', *Organizational Studies*, 10(2): 187–206.

Zmud, Robert W. (1990) 'Opportunities for strategic information manipulation through new information technology', in Janet Fulk and Charles W. Steinfield (eds), *Organizations and Communication Technology*. Newbury Park, CA: Sage.

Zmud, Robert W., Lind, M. and Young, F. (1990) 'An attribute space for organizational communication channels', *Information Systems Research*, 1(4): 440–57.

2.8

Organizations, Technology and Structuring

KARLENE H. ROBERTS AND MARTHA GRABOWSKI

Everywhere one looks technology seems to rapidly advance. As just one example, when the University of Hawaii's eighty-eight inch telescope on Mauna Kea (on the state's 'big island' of Hawaii) was commissioned in 1970, it was the fourth largest telescope in the world. Today it isn't even the fourth largest telescope on Mauna Kea. In the organizational literature, there is a great deal of overlap in discussions of technology, technological systems, and environment. A whole raft of issues are conceptualized and studied under the rubric of technology.

Historically, discussions of technology have involved descriptions of technology and problems with technology. Little has been written about difficulties associated with measuring or assessing technology. Exploration of technology characteristics and challenges develops *descriptive* pictures of what technology is, how it grew, and its role in organizations. In contrast, *relational* approaches focus on relationships between technology and organizations, and incorporate problems of assessment because it is difficult to assess fluid concepts and relationships.

This chapter adopts the dual challenge of providing a descriptive view of technology and organizations followed by a relational examination of technology and organization structure. The descriptive picture is an important first step that sets the context for the rest of the chapter. The relational view develops for us the continuous, changing, and interactive nature of technology and organizations, a perspective both related to and distinct from the impacts technology has on organizations. These relational constructs between organizations and technology are particularly useful for managing

organizations in the post-industrial age (Huber 1984).

Organizational constructs give us important insights into the role of technology in organizations, and highlight the importance of considering technology as a process as well as a product in our examination. Given the development of such a descriptive and relational picture, it is worthwhile considering whether technology is still a useful construct in organizational studies. We answer in the affirmative, but caution that such an affirmative answer is contingent upon two important findings of this chapter:

- Technology's dual nature as a product and a process suggests that sociotechnical frameworks need to change significantly to accommodate longitudinal, temporal views of technology.
- Technology has increasingly become the *structuration process* by which tasks and people in an organization change in response to demands in the post-industrial age.

We consider each of these points in turn. In this chapter, we first examine definitions of technology, technological growth, and the role of technology in organizations as descriptive views of technology. We next note problems with those views, particularly in a changing world. We then focus on the technology organizational relationship most frequently studied, the relationship of technology and structure, and move from considering organizations taken one at a time to thinking about systems of organizations. We conclude with a discussion of the utility of technology as a construct and provide suggestions for further research.

DESCRIPTIVE APPROACHES
TO TECHNOLOGY

Definitions

Definitions of technology in the literature focus our attention on different issues. Some examples are:

1 In contemporary society, the most powerful engines of change are human invention, innovation, and the applications of scientific knowledge. Collectively, we call these functions 'technology'. (Wenk 1989: 6)
2 In defining my concept of technology I restrict its *scope* to material artifacts (various configurations of hardware and software). I wish to sustain a distinction – at least theoretically – between the material nature of technology and the human activities that design or use those artifacts. (Orlikowski 1992: 403)
3 To focus on the technology of an organization is to view the organization as a place where some type of work is done, as a location where energy is applied to the transformation of inputs into outputs. The concept is broadly defined by organization theorists and includes not only the hardware used in performing work but also the skills and knowledge of workers, and even the characteristics of the objects on which work is performed. (Scott 1992: 20, 227)
4 We define technology as the physical combined with the intellectual or knowledge processes by which materials in some form are transformed into outputs used by another organization or subsystem within the same organization. (Hulin and Roznowski 1985: 47)
5 Organizations have two other characteristics that might provide a basis for a typology: raw materials (things, symbols, or people), which are transformed into outputs through the application of energy; and tasks or techniques, or techniques of effecting the transformation . . . 'Technology' is not used here in its commonplace sense of machines or sophisticated devices for achieving high efficiency, as in the term, 'technologically advanced society', but in its generic sense of the study of techniques or tasks. (Perrow 1986: 141)
6 Technology refers to a body of knowledge about the means by which we work on the world, our arts and our methods. Essentially, it is knowledge about the cause and effect relations of our actions. . . . Technology is knowledge that can be studied, codified, and taught to others. (Berniker 1987: 10)
7 The central idea is captured by the phrase *technology as equivoque*. An *equivoque* is something that admits of several possible or plausible interpretations and therefore can be esoteric, subject to misunderstandings, uncertain, complex, and recondite. (Weick 1990: 2)

Definition 1 focuses attention on the knowledge and scientific aspects of innovation. The invention of the wheel added to mankind's knowledge base but certainly did not reflect applications of science as today's technological innovations frequently do. Definition 2 severely limits technology's focus. Definition 3 brings the organization into the picture, adding hardware and workers' skills and knowledge to definition 1's focus on knowledge. It includes the components discussed by most organizational researchers interested in technology.

Definition 4 is consistent with definition 3 but, according to Weick:

> in contrast to many other definitions, however, explicit mention is made of raw materials and a transformation process, items that are often implicit in other definitions. Also novel to this definition is the mention that output might also be used within the same organization. Inclusion of this contingency makes it possible to talk about multiple, diverse technologies within the same organization. Finally, this definition is noteworthy because of its emphasis on process rather than on static knowledge, skills, and equipment. By equating technology with process, the authors alert us to the importance of changes over time and sequence. (1990: 3)

Definition 5 introduces yet other components of the definitional space of technology. The notions of energy application and specific tasks or techniques are highlighted. Perrow also positions the conceptual definition of technology away from the layman's definition. Definition 6 focuses on the knowledge aspects of technology, and provides an important distinction when coupled with the author's definition of a technical system as 'a specific combination of machines, equipment, and methods used to produce some valued outcome. . . . Every technical system embodies a technology. It derives from a large body of knowledge which provides the basis for design decisions' (Berniker 1987: 10; cited in Weick 1990). As Weick notes:

> By differentiating between the opportunities provided by knowledge ('technology') and the choice of one combination from this larger set as 'the' technical system, Berniker makes the design of technology a more explicit, more public process that need not be left to engineers . . . the very complexity and incomprehensibility of new technologies may warrant a new reexamination of our knowledge of cause–effect relations in human actions and the choice of a different combination of machines, equipment, and methods to produce the outcomes for which new technologies are instrumental. (1990: 4)

Definition 7 puts a whole new twist on the notion of technology. It says that technology has multiple meanings. 'Complex systems . . . make limited sense because so little is visible and so much is transient, and they make many different kinds of sense because the dense interactions within them can be modelled in so many different ways' (1990: 2).

Integrating these distinct views of technology is difficult. For instance, several of them contradict one another (e.g. Orlikowski and everyone else), and one definition includes almost everything (Weick). In and of themselves, these factors make the development of common conceptual models and empirical studies of technology and organizations difficult. In one attempt to integrate such views, Collins et al. (1986) provide an overarching paradigm for technology, suggesting that such systems are 'the set of mechanical, knowledge, and human technologies used to convert inputs into outputs in the production sector' (1986: 82).

Mechanical technologies refer to the physical machines, tools and equipment used to produce goods and are featured in most approaches to technology. *Human technologies* consist of the skills and physical energy involved in producing goods and can be substituted for mechanical technologies. *Knowledge technologies* refer to the abstract meanings and concepts used in production. Because knowledge technologies may constrain or facilitate the development and utilization of the mechanical and human technologies, many writers consider them the most important technologies (e.g. Perrow 1967). Interestingly, each of these technologies is interdependent: they coexist and covary in systems and organizations, which has significant impact for current and future organizations.

Technological Growth

Current lay thinking about technological change often assumes that technological development is analogous to natural selection in the sense that the best technology survives. But we all know the story of the QWERTY typewriter keyboard and its competitor. In reality, the technological developer comes to his or her work with as many prejudices as anyone else, influenced by his or her culture, career considerations, intellectual enthusiasm, incentives, etc. The full range of technologies is never considered because these prejudices determine the range of real possibilities. Technological development may, in fact, have more to do with interaction of technical options with organization and interorganization dynamics (Tushman and Rosenkopf 1992), or with evolutionary 'technology cycles' of recipro-

cal interactions among 'researchers' beliefs, the artifacts they create, and the evaluation routines they foster' (Garud and Rappa 1994: 346).

The growth and consolidation of technology are often explained by two factors (Hughes 1987). One is the drive for high diversity and load factors, and a good economic mix. The load factor concept, now applied in many industries, was derived in the electric power industry. It refers to the ratio of average output to maximum output over a specified period. In an electric power system, the load factor is desirably diverse when customers make demands evenly across the twenty-four hour day. When this does not happen, managers try to expand the system to acquire a more desirable load or diversity. Thus, in northern California, when the demand factor exceeds the ability of the current mix of power plants (e.g. hydro, nuclear), managers might bring on power generated in a fossil fuel plant or buy power from another geographical area. The mix they choose depends on power availability and cost.

The other factor often cited as contributing to technological development is the effect of 'reverse salients' (Hughes 1987). 'A salient is a protrusion in a geometric figure, a line of battle, or an expanding weather front. As technological systems expand, reverse salients develop . . . components in the system that have fallen behind or are out of phase with the others' (Hughes 1987: 73). Attention is given to the reverse salient often through invention to bring it, once again, into line with other characteristics of the technological system. Other explanations of the shaping of technology focus on science's role in shaping technology, technology's role, the role of economics, political interests, and the social shaping of technology (MacKenzie and Wajcman 1985; Piore and Sabel 1984). The difficulty with each of these diagnoses of technological growth is that they are easy to describe, and challenging to assess: few metrics or standards exist, and little empirical or other work has been conducted that might develop such measures.

The Role of Technology in Organizations

Weick reminds us that technology in organizations is a source of stochastic events, continuous events, and abstract events, and each type of event presents difficulties. Technologies are a source of *stochastic events* in organizations. Because they are not deterministic, with clear cause and effect relationships between what is to be done, how it is to be done, and when it is to be done, organizations face a variety of problems:

- A large repertoire of skills must be maintained, even though the skills are infrequently used.
- Special attention must be paid to start-ups in systems, and to anticipating faults that may lead to downtime.
- Distinctions between operators and maintenance skills become blurred, and skills in monitoring and diagnosis become critical skill sets (Weick 1990: 4).

Stochastic events pose difficulties for organizations, as they provide moving targets for learning, because environmental changes occur more quickly than people in organizations can learn about them. Since recurrence is scarce, learning is scarce, and stochastic events become repetitive patterns and 'permanent fixtures' in organizations (1990: 6).

People in such organizations face further problems:

- Routine tasks become automated and non-routine tasks are left to human judgment, resulting in humans being faced with a complex task composed of an unbroken string of tough decisions.
- A reliability imperative develops, which places a premium on maintenance and integrity responsibilities, rather than responsibility.
- People must be committed to do what is necessary on their own, and be autonomously motivated to act on their own, at the same time that they assume the role of 'variance absorber', dealing with counteracting the unexpected (Davis and Taylor 1976: 388–9; Weick 1990: 4).

Continuous events precipitated by technology also cause difficulties. Whereas reliability is the hallmark of the industrial era (populated by stochastic events), efficiency is the hallmark of the post-industrial era, which is characterized by continuous events, especially over disparate geographical areas. New technologies knit people, transactions, and locations together in a continuous process, and they combine both craft and continuous processing in the same enterprise. The result of continuous events is that the required people skills are different from those required by discontinuous events: emphasis is given to work processes, rapid response to emergencies, the ability to stay calm in tense environments, and attempts to detect early malfunctions in such continuous systems. As a result, supervisors often pay more attention to processes and products than to people.

If individuals lose a sense of cause and effect with the advent of continuous process technology, the resulting systems can become much more interactively complex and more prone to failure. Since buffers may be eliminated (in the form of mental models in operators' heads of safe and unsafe operations), these continuous processes and events compound the difficulties associated with stochastic events and higher mental workloads (Weick 1990).

Technology is increasingly a source of *abstract events*, as more and more work associated with new technologies has disappeared into machines. The result is inadequate sampling of displayed information, inattention to information on the periphery, and distractions when building problem representations. New technologies have essentially dual characters: they involve self-contained, invisible unfolding *material processes*, and equally self-contained, invisible *imagined processes* that mentally unfold in the mind of the individual or team (Weick 1990). As noted before, these technologies exist as much in the head of the operator as on the plant floor. The result is that both managers and operators experience increasing cognitive demands for inference, imagination, integration, problem solving and mental mapping to understand what is going on out of sight. People thus need sufficient understandings of abstract events so they can intervene at any time, pick up the process, and assemble a recovery (1990: 8).

By 1992, there seemed to be three perspectives on the role of technology in organizations (Orlikowski 1992). The first body of work (to which comparative research belongs) is the *technological imperative* model. This model 'treats technology as an independent influence on human behavior or organizational properties, that exerts unidirectional, causal influences over humans and organizations similar to those operating in nature' (Giddens 1984; Orlikowski 1992: 400). This is a very mechanical view of technology and structure.

The second perspective is the *strategic choice* model. From this perspective, technology is not an external object but a product of ongoing human action. Three streams of research are within this perspective. One stream focuses on how a particular technology is constructed through social interactions. 'Particularly relevant here are socio-technical studies, which are premised on the belief that outcomes such as job satisfaction and productivity of workers can be manipulated by jointly "optimizing" the social and technical factors of jobs [Davis and Taylor 1986; Trist et al. 1963]' (Orlikowski 1992: 400). These analyses rely too heavily on the capability of humans, assuming that once managers are committed to the right strategy, good things will come for their organizations and the people in them. The second stream within this second perspective examines how shared interpretations around a certain technology arise and affect interaction with that technology (e.g. Bijker 1987; Wynne 1988). This research tends to downplay the material and structural aspects of interacting with technology, but implicitly recognizes structure as a social construction.

The third stream is represented in Marxist accounts of technology (e.g. Braverman 1974; Noble 1984). These studies focus on how technology is devised and deployed to serve the purposes of political and economic interests of powerful capitalists, but fail to consider the person in the workplace. It is characteristic of these writers 'to emphasize the unevenness and unexpectedness of change and the diversity of causes and connections' (Scott 1992: 245). Of concern to them is 'roads not taken'.

The third model views *technology as a trigger of structural change*. This model portrays technology as an intervention in the relationship between people and organizational structure (Barley 1986). However, this model makes no room for physical changes which may occur during technology use. This view may be appropriate to the technological subject of Barley's study, CT scanners, but may work less well for information technology.

Within each of these models there are many studies that describe the role of technology in organizations, but few measure or assess those roles. One difficulty in conducting such studies is the complete absence of metrics or standards by which to judge good or poor performance, appropriate or inappropriate roles. This was one goal of the 'Management in the 1990s' project at MIT; however, the project focused solely on the role and relationships of information technology to organizations, rather than undertaking a more broadly based examination of roles and relationships of technology in and to organizations (Morton 1991).

TECHNOLOGY AND A CHANGING WORLD

Organizations and the world in which they exist are undergoing profound changes; consequently, many of the conceptions of technology presented here are simply inadequate. In an organizational growth scenario that includes increased knowledge, complexity, and turbulence, the attributes of technologies are expanding and no longer bear much resemblance to the definitions above. Huber suggests that, as a result, 'post industrial organizations will adopt on a widespread basis three design features: (1) advanced communication and computer (C^2) technologies, (2) improved decision-group technologies and structures, and (3) "decision process management"' (1984: 934). In contrast, Barley (1988) indicates that technological attributes include semiotic properties, cybernetic controls, and radical versus incremental innovation. He suggests that work is an interpretative act and technology affects that act in three ways: by creating codes as outputs, by generating codes as a byproduct of functioning, and by circumventing existing codes. Some technologies produce codes, as in medical imaging; some may generate codes as byproducts, as in machines that emit sounds and smells that indicate their status; and some circumvent codes that have served as an occupation's source of influence, as when they alter power structures in organizations. These technological attributes seem much clearer and more precise descriptors of organizational realities in a changing world than do definitions that focus on mechanical, human, and knowledge aspects of transformation but which fail to specify transformation processes.

Much discussion in the technological literature is about the impact of the cultural milieu on technological development (e.g. Noble 1984; Barley 1988). One problem in understanding technological development is that the national political milieux in which some organizations are trying to develop and adopt technology are changing in ways that are difficult to understand. At the same time cultural aspects of organizations are also changing, through the move to diversity in some work forces. Thus, environments are turbulent and dynamic, and cause organizations in turn to be turbulent and dynamic.

What gets done in organizations is also changing. For example, American organizations are turning increasingly to creating information – information made out of nothing, and once made, difficult to destroy. Other societies are very good at taking this information and selling it back to Americans and others in the form of hard goods (Thurow 1992a; 1992b; Lucky 1991). Current discussions of technology often fail to take the invisible nature of information into account even though many of the technologies focused on are information processing technologies.

New Technologies that Strain Old Models

One of the difficulties with technology discussions and descriptions has to do with the ever-changing nature of technology. Current technologies in many cases strain and stretch old models of technology and organizations. These technologies include, among others, advances in biomedical engineering, virtual reality, genetic and chemical process engineering, and information technology (Teich 1993; Morton 1991).

Let us consider one of these examples. Information technology comprises mechanical (i.e. computer-based hardware), human, and knowledge technologies, coexisting to greater or lesser degrees in different systems and organizations, with greater or lesser performance impacts (National Research Council 1994). Integrating Anthony's (1965) management activities and organizational functions, Davis and Olson define information systems (IS) as:

a federation of functional subsystems, each of which is divided into four major information processing components: transaction processing, operational control information system support, managerial control information system support, and strategic planning information system support. (1985: 45)

The strategic importance of information technology (IT) has increased as computing power and communication facilities have been enhanced. Indeed, it is believed that 'more than being helped by computers, companies will live by them, shaping strategy and structure to fit new information technology' (*Fortune* 1988). Examples of strategic uses of information technology often cited in the literature include airline reservation systems (Copeland and McKenney 1988), automated teller machines (Gerstein 1987), and computer-aided design/manufacturing (CAD/CAM) (Ohara 1988; Liker et al. 1992). The resulting importance of the relationship between IT and organizational performance is evidenced by the considerable literature on the subject.

Information technology is not the only new technology to stretch and strain existing organizational models; a quick perusal of virtual reality, CAD/CAM, chemical and continuous process technologies, and the human genome project in biomedical engineering are other examples of new technologies which call for a reexamination of organizational and technological models. Each of these technologies contributes to the development of stochastic, continuous, and abstract events in organizations. Each increases and changes the nature of human mental work by reason of their introduction and adoption in organizations. Each incorporates powerful linking mechanisms that produce or facilitate the development of virtual organizations (Goldman et al. 1995), and the technologies themselves are increasingly intelligent and sophisticated, assimilating more and more 'human' processing into their domain.

Such technologies will proliferate, and be restructured and integrated as organizations mature in technology utilization. McKenney and McFarlan (1982) observe that organizations are experiencing multiple technology assimilation patterns associated with new technology.

They recommend managing these assimilations in phases, since assimilation patterns are different for each system, despite their coexistence.

The magnitude of investment in technology, and particularly information technology, in the past decade has prompted questions about payoff for both the nation and the individual enterprise. Because technology is often used to automate processes, and because automation is popularly associated with efficiency and cost reduction, questions about payoff usually center on productivity. In particular, some economic studies suggest that large investments in information technology by the service sector are not associated with substantial gains in productivity as measured by national macroeconomic statistics – the so-called IT paradox (Morton 1991; Thurow 1992b; National Research Council 1994). While some studies indicate that US productivity levels themselves compare quite favorably with those of international competitors in several important service industries, others suggest little correlation between investments in IT and productivity, profitability, or return on investment at the industry or enterprise level (National Research Council 1994). Each of these concerns and developments calls us to reexamine the paradigms we historically used to examine and assess technology, organizations and structures.

RELATIONAL VIEWS OF TECHNOLOGY AND ORGANIZATIONS

Relational views of technology focus away from snapshots of technology or its characteristics, and refocus on relationships between organizations and technology, primarily organizational structure. In this section we develop such a view and use that view to develop a research agenda.

Organization Structure and Technology

The concept of structure is usually understood to mean the configuration of activities in an organization that is enduring and persistent and provides the organization's patterned regularity (Ranson et al. 1980). Structure is a social construction of reality, a view sometimes called the positional view of structure (Monge and Eisenberg 1987). Research on the relationship of structure and technology has only been conducted since the 1960s (Gerwin 1981), though, as previously indicated, it has been frequently studied. By the 1980s, the structure-task-technology paradigm embraced 'two major perspectives: comparative analysis contributed by sociologists, and systems design developed by sociotechnical-systems advocates and administrative theorists' (1981: 3). Both were interested in the impact of task and technology on organization structure.

Comparative analysis studies treat systems as wholes, and the system is usually an organization. The studies by Blau and Shoenherr (1971), Child and Mansfield's (1972) research, Hage and Aiken (1967), the Aston Group (Pugh et al. 1969), and Woodward (1965) are all examples. Comparative analysis tries to draw general conclusions across many organizations and industries, but is 'short on conceptual insights, strong on empirical work, and explanation-oriented' (Gerwin 1981: 4).

A number of cross-national comparative analysis studies have been done in the last fifteen years, several of which show that structure differs across cultures regardless of technology. For example, Maurice et al. (1980) report relatively large differences in the organization of work in France, Britain and Germany: German firms exhibited higher levels of worker expertise, flexibility, and autonomy; British firms showed intermediate levels; and French firms concentrated expertise in decision-making in top managers and staff. Lincoln and his colleagues (Lincoln et al. 1986; Lincoln and Kalleberg 1990) compared American and Japanese manufacturing plants, and reported that the impact of technology on organizations was stronger in American than Japanese firms. Japanese firms were found to be less specialized and have taller hierarchies than American firms.

In contrast to comparative analyses, *systems design* studies differ in a number of ways. One premise of these studies is that organizations cannot be understood without specifying their components and the interrelationships among components. Research by Chapple and Sayles (1961), Lawrence and Lorsch (1967), Miller and Rice (1967), and Thompson (1967) represents this position. 'Systems research is rich on insights, weak on empirical work, and normatively oriented' (Gerwin 1981: 4) because it focuses on detailed observation of one organization at a time and, consequently, does not measure technology and structure and relate them.

A number of authors note that positionally structured organizations of the nineteenth and twentieth centuries, structured around traditional functions such as marketing, accounting, and finance, are obsolete. To replace them, Miles and Snow (1978) suggest that four strategic types of organizations have risen in response to different adaptations to technology, engineering, and administrative requirements:

defenders, prospectors, analyzers, and reactors. Three of the four strategic types are successful and one, reactors, is unsuccessful.

In this typology, defenders seek to create a stable entrepreneurial domain. They do this by developing a single core technology that is highly cost efficient, to corner a narrow segment of the potential market. Prospectors maintain a broad and continuously developing domain, monitoring a wide range of environmental conditions and events in search of new product and market opportunities. Analyzers are interested in locating and exploiting new product and market opportunities, while maintaining a firm base of traditional products and customers. The perpetual instability and resultant poor performance of reactors arises from their inability to respond appropriately to their environments.

Neither the comparative analysis nor the system design approach to the relationship of structure and technology represents the more variegated view of technology seen in the literature since the mid 1980s. To meet global challenges and uncertainties, a number of authors call for restructuring organizations using available technologies. Peters (1987) calls for flatter organizations that rely on information brought in by information technologies. Kanter (1989) and Senge (1990) also call for interesting structural modifications to meet global changes, with Senge focusing on appearing, changing, and disappearing boundaries in organizations. Mitroff et al. (1994) propose that to meet tomorrow's challenges, organizations must be structured around five new organizational entities: a knowledge/learning center, a recovery development center, a world service/spiritual center, a world class operations center, and a leadership institute. These organizational forms may be yet another approach to functional specialization.

If technology is sector-specific in organizations, greater structural differentiation, which we see much of in today's organizations, will result in weaker correlations between technology in one sector and the structure of another sector. Thus, studies that examine relationships among technology and structure at the organizational level fail to tell a very interesting or true story. The result is that studies of the relationships between organizational structure and technology are interesting, but not particularly helpful in managing processes in the post-industrial age.

Organizations as Technology

Two alternatives to the positional view of organizational structure and technology have been identified: the relational and cultural views of structure (Monge and Eisenberg 1987), which view organizations as networks of systems, people, and groups. Writers in the relational tradition focus on how humans forge and maintain communication linkages, thus enacting structure. Writers in the cultural tradition emphasize the roles of symbols, their meanings, and their transmission through the social system. Some writers attempt to integrate these two perspectives with the positional tradition. Structure is then seen as a complex medium of control which is continually produced and re-created in interaction and yet shapes that interaction; structures are constituted and constitutive.

> Formal and emergent networks coexist, and each can be best understood in the context of the other. . . . This implies that the constraints imposed by an existing structure limit and shape the interactions of people who work in various roles and fulfill various status sets. It also implies the converse, that the interaction of people helps to shape and define the social networks . . . the predominance of either type of structure is to some degree a function of where the organization is in its evolutionary life cycle. In most contemporary organizations both formal and emergent networks are in constant change. This change, however, is not simply the substitution of people in positions as characterized by the positional perspective. Rather, the positions themselves are somewhat altered and the structure significantly changed as a result. (1987: 309)

Network research, which positions organizations as technology, centers around describing characteristics of networks and their linkages, including their strength or intensity, symmetricality, reciprocity, and multiplexity. The strength or intensity of a linkage is a reflection of the amount of information, affect, or resources flowing through the system. Symmetricality refers to the degree to which both people enter into the same kind of relationship with one another. Reciprocity refers to the degree that two people supposedly in a relationship report the relationship. Multiplexity refers to the degree to which the same people are involved in different networks in an organization. Content of linkages is also frequently studied because it determines what flows through the network.

Environmental, organizational, and individual influences are often examined in network studies; for instance, environmental effects such as national character have been shown to influence organizational communication patterns. French employees, for example, avoid close ties at work while Japanese employees seek such ties (Crozier 1964; Yoshino 1968); French organizational network structure patterns would thus differ from Japanese patterns. Other environmental influences include local character, changes in the business environment, and characteristics of specific industries. The characteristics of jobs, tasks, technology, and the organization as a whole also influence emergent structures:

> In a recent review, Fulk, Power, and Schmitz (1986) presented support for four propositions linking electronic messaging to organizational communication networks. Specifically, they argue that electronic mail facilitates (1) more horizontal linkages across geographical distances thus linking a diversity of people who would otherwise not communicate; (2) more vertical linkages across status levels, leading to a flattening of the hierarchy by encouraging less social inhibition about such contacts; (3) less dense networks, in which a person's contacts are less likely to know each other; and (4) linkages that 'spill over' to the relational non-electronic communication network in the organization, this having implications for changes in friendship patterns and enduring organizational structures. (Monge and Eisenberg 1987: 320–1)

The emergence of informal structure as a result of organizations acting as technology is dependent on individual differences. People express their preferences for interacting or not interacting with others through their network behaviors. A well developed line of research at the individual level focuses on the roles people occupy: liaisons and isolates have different characteristics, with liaisons being better educated, of higher status, with higher rank and tenure (e.g. Schwartz and Jacobson 1977; Roberts and O'Reilly 1974).

Assessments of organizational networks focus on technical complexity, uncertainty, and interdependence. According to Scott (1992: 231):

- The greater the technical complexity, the greater the structural complexity.
- The greater the technical uncertainty, the less formalization and centralization.
- The greater the technical interdependence, the more resources must be devoted to coordination.

Galbraith (1973; 1977) argues that one way the varying demands of technologies on structure can be summarized is to ascertain how much information must be processed during the execution of a task sequence. Network approaches are ideally suited to this. Information requirements increase as a function of increasing diversity, uncertainty, and interdependence of work flow, and formal structures can be employed to manage work flow: rules and programs, schedules, departmentalization, hierarchy and delegation, and micro coordination.

Technology as Structuration

Positional views of structure focus on rigid and very narrow structural and technological constructs (i.e. complexity, task definition, work flow integration, etc.). Relational and cultural views of structure add the notion of a sense of process. They also introduce other technological constructs such as complexity, uncertainty, and interdependence. Because this research primarily emanates from the body of research concerned with organizational communication, this literature is often not considered by researchers concerned with technology.

A merger of the positional and relational or cultural views of structure is a step toward developing a more comprehensive view of technology and organizations in the post-industrial age. If this were done, a more fluid approach to structure would be required. Returning to the definitions first presented in this chapter, it seems one would want as variegated a conceptualization of technology as one would have developed of structure. Collins et al. (1986) and Barley (1988) offer beginnings of that task.

Orlikowski (1992) and later De Sanctis and Poole (1994) propose a reconceptualization of technology that takes into account both the older view of technology as an objective external force and the newer view of technology as the outcome of strategic choice and social action. This view is also quite consistent with a merger of positional and relational views of structure, since such a merger combined with the world changes described previously suggests the emergence of fluid organizational forms with appearing, disappearing, and changing boundaries within and between organizations. This structuration view is also adaptable to thinking about structure and technology at the systems level. Essentially, a *structurational model of technology* collapses previous thinking about structure and technology and their interrelationship into a single set of constructs from which it is difficult, if not impossible, to separate technology and structure. In contrast to structure, the emergent property of ongoing action (Weick 1969), *structuration* is the production and reproduction of a social system through members' use of rules and resources in interaction. Structuration suggests, then, that systems are built from rules and interactions; that resources, like actions, are tools people use to enact organizations; and that structures are the medium and outcome of the interaction (Weick 1990: 18). Structuration is a particularly useful construct for technology and organizational studies, as it 'sensitizes the observer to look for ongoing redefinition among structure, action, and technology', and it suggests that

technology is both a cause and a consequence of structure (1990: 18).

> The theory of structuration recognizes that human actions are enabled and constrained by structures, yet that these structures are the result of previous actions. In Giddens' framework, structure is understood paradigmatically, that is, as a generic concept that is only manifested in the structural properties of social systems (Giddens 1979, pp. 64–65). Structural properties consist of the rules and resources that human agents use in their everyday interaction. These rules and resources mediate human actions, while at the same time they are reaffirmed through being used by human actors.
>
> In this theory, the role of human actors in reaffirming structural properties is highlighted so as to avoid reification. The recognition that actors are knowledgeable and reflective is a central premise. (Orlikowski 1992: 404)

Orlikowski introduces a recursive notion of technology as created and changed by human action and also used to accomplish some action, which is consistent with our earlier definitions. She calls this the duality of technology. Technology is interpretatively flexible (consistent with definition 7), and the interaction of technology and organization is a function of the different actors and socio-historical contexts in which it develops.

Technological development and use are often done in different organizations. Thus, much work that constitutes technology is separate in time and space from actions constituted by technology. Recognizing this time–space discontinuity helps us understand how researchers came to view technology as a fixed object *or* as a *product* of human interaction (Tyre and Orlikowski 1994). It depended on when and where they looked:

> Technology is the product of human action, while it also assumes structural properties. That is, technology is physically constructed by actors working in a given social context, and technologies are socially constructed by actors through the different meanings they attach to it and the various features they emphasize and use. However, it is also the case that once developed and deployed, technology tends to become reified and institutionalized, losing its connection with the human agents that constructed it and gave it meaning, and it appears to be a part of the objective, structural properties of the organization. (Orlikowski 1992: 406)

These arguments about technology are consistent with those we might pose about structure. Structure is both changed and used by humans. Structure can be interpretatively flexible. Structure development and use are often viewed by researchers at different times. Thus, the constituents of structure are often perceived as separate from what it constitutes. Recognizing this time–space discontinuity helps us see how researchers came to see structure as fixed (the positional view) or as a product of human interaction (the relational view).

Extending the view of the duality of technology, it becomes increasingly clear that technology and structure are thus both a *process* and a *product* of human action and interaction. Understanding this should increase our impatience with sociotechnical frameworks that fail to account for the duality, or for the increasingly important longitudinal and temporal view of technology and organizations. This duality also highlights that technology is increasingly becoming the *structuration process* by which tasks and people in organizations change in response to the demands of post-industrial society.

Systems of Organizations

Defining technology as Wenk does in definition 1, or perhaps as Orlikowski does in definition 2, technology, and particularly information technology, is rapidly changing the nature of organizations, and the structuring of decision-making in them. Traditionally, most discussions of technology and organizations have focused on impacts of technology on an industry, an enterprise, or an organizational activity. However, the advent of several technologies also heralds the arrival of new organizational constructs:

- relatively affordable and widely distributed global telecommunications capabilities, which link together geographically dispersed parts of an organization
- decision support technologies which emulate or replicate human capabilities and allow for quick decisions based on much information
- technologies which allow decision-makers to participate in remote discussions through teleoperation, telepresence, and teleconferencing, thereby increasing interconnectedness and interdependence
- technologies which permit the development of virtual communities and participation by remote participants.

These technologies make possible the blurring of organizational boundaries and the creation of virtual organizations, tied together in pursuit of specific opportunities, or for mutually beneficial (symbiotic) relationships in a market. Many of these organizational constructs are now touted as being instrumental in defining and producing competitive advantage in a number of industries

(National Research Council 1994; Goldman et al. 1995). Vendors and suppliers, customers, and support organizations can be bound together in virtual temporary or permanent systems that can effectively defeat competitors in the marketplace, and which can provide significant added value to the host organization, as well as to the participating customers and suppliers. Thus, rather than technology and organizational constructs coexisting and covarying as in the past, organizations in the future can be expected to be much more fluid, with teaming arrangements and organizational partners defined on an opportunity, or market, basis.

New technologies and global economic development increasingly produce systems of organizations tied together through interdependencies. The notion of organization sets has been around for some time (e.g. Evan 1966). In 1979, and again in 1986, Perrow suggested using network methodology to study forces among organizations that contribute to their behavior. Such studies are non-existent in the organizational literature.

In one of the few pieces in the organizational literature that addresses issues of interorganizational linkages, Mitroff and Mohrman (1986) discuss what happened during a run on savings and loan institutions in Ohio. The fate of these organizations was tied to that of an obscure securities firm in Florida and the value of British oil stocks was linked to both. These authors point out that managers need to develop holistic or systems views of their organizations (as should researchers).

Another example of systems of organizations operating together is taken from Piers Paul Read's (1993) account of the meltdown at the Soviet power reactor at Chernobyl. This example is filled with technological overlays. In designing the Chernobyl power plant, the axiom, 'the bigger the better' was put to full use. The plant was to be the largest in the world with each of its six units having enormous generating capacity.

The framework for the development of reactor number four and nuclear power in the Soviet Union was based on deliberations by the Central Committee, the military high command, and the Ministry of Medium Machine Building. These debates were embedded in the Soviet history of nuclear development and focused on cost; safety was never an issue. In addition to this kind of interorganizational interaction, when construction of the power station was begun at Chernobyl, its manager had the awesome task of supervising the building of both the power station and the town of Pripyat. The parts specified by the plant's designer were frequently impossible to find and had to be manufactured on site. This encouraged a spirit of improvisation which can be dangerous in nuclear power generation.

In addition, many of the goods supplied by other organizations were shoddy, reflecting a spirit of low concern for quality by those organizations. The plant manager reported to both the Ministry of Medium Machine Building and the Communist Party, which acted as a shadow administration in every social, political, industrial, or cultural structure. A number of other interorganizational interactions and inter-dependencies characterized this situation. It is possible organizations can live without consider-ing these kinds of interdependencies if their technological cores are unsophisticated. But as these cores become more sophisticated and as various cores become more tightly tied to one another, designers and managers must manage the linkages among organizations. To date, organizational researchers have provided no conceptual tools to help manage these linkages.

Some systems theorists have dwelled at length on the conceptualization of interdependence (e.g. Thompson 1967), but have failed to develop good operational measures of the concept. Similarly, some comparative researchers have also developed concepts of interdependence: for instance, when the performance of one or more operations has consequences for others. This research shows that as one moves from the work level, through the department level, to the organizational level, the chances of a relation-ship between structure and interdependence decreases (Gerwin 1981).

Each of these concepts poses interesting and unique measurement difficulties. Requirements for new metrics are emerging at the same time that current metrics explaining burgeoning technological growth are showing their age. Neither natural selection, nor load factors, nor reverse salients are adequate constructs for understanding or measuring technology, or its relationship to an organization. What is needed is a different vantage point, and along with the vantage point, different constructs, to better understand relationships between organizations and technology.

A RESEARCH AGENDA

Before moving to specific discussion of future research, we consider the lingering and impor-tant question of whether technology is today a useful construct with which to gauge and measure organizations. With the plethora of organizational and technological changes occur-ring today, some of which have been catalogued in this chapter, organizations and researchers are increasingly questioning the utility of traditional paradigms and metrics. Thus, the notion of technology as a vulnerable construct is worth considering. Technology is rapidly changing, as are organizations, but neither is disappearing. Although we have difficulties in measuring and assessing technology, and although organiz-ational researchers are searching for useful constructs with which to assess the relationships between organizations and technology, neither of these developments suggests that the concept of technology is antiquated, or that technologi-cal impacts on organizations can be expected to disappear or dissipate in the years to come. A perspective is needed that incorporates new views of useful organizational constructs (i.e. duality of technology, structuration rather than structure, etc.) to understand relationships between technology and organizations.

We have not discussed at length in this chapter such a contingency framework of organizational and technological utility; yet, such a framework clearly makes sense. Uniform or generalized descriptions of technology and organizational applicability, adaptability, or utility are increas-ingly artifacts of simpler technological eras. Here we call for increasing attention to the nature of temporal and longitudinal studies of organiz-ations and technology.

The need to understand technology as a process intertwined with other processes under-scores the importance of research that consider the following:

- Measurement and assessment difficulties with technology produce systemic difficulties in managing organizations.
- Technology's and organizations' dual nat-ures as product and process suggest that sociotechnical frameworks need to change significantly to accommodate longitudinal, temporal views of technology.
- Technology has increasingly become the *structuration process* by which tasks and people in an organization change in response to demands in the post-industrial age.

Researchers need to address the immediate problem of measuring or assessing technology. Currently, technology is often measured in terms of inputs, processes, and outputs, a rather traditional systems-oriented paradigm that blurs distinctions between processes, and muddies cause and effect relationships so important to understanding technologies. Current measure-ments are also insensitive to sources or con-sequences of stochastic events, and to interactions between technology; the result is that it is difficult to envision how current approaches to measuring and assessing technology can assist in deciphering changing and complex roles of technology in

organizations, and relationships between organizations and technology.

Weick (1990) suggests that understanding the
importance of stochastic, continuous and
abstract events in technology and in organizations highlights additional difficulties with
measuring and assessing technology. For
instance, if organizational members using technology 'lose the bubble' with respect to cause
and effect, and the system becomes more
interactively complex and more prone to failure,
perhaps the concept of *operator error*, long used
as a measure of how 'safe' an organization or
system is, should be replaced. Since such a term
is now no longer reflective of unique and sizable
cognitive demands, and since operators are often
blamed for designer and system errors (Perrow
1984), perhaps the term might best be replaced
with the term *operator mistakes*, which emanate
from a misunderstanding, a misidentification, or
a misconception rather than from straying from
guided or prescribed paths (i.e. an error) (Weick
1990: 7).

In addition, the measurement of *formation of
intention* becomes increasingly important in
abstract systems, as does the measurement of
individual and organizational 'mental maps',
since the relational information contained in
such maps is most important. The measurement
dilemmas of *technology on the floor* and *technology in the head*, as well as the measurement of
the *role of emotion* in technology and in society,
with proliferating continuous, stochastic, and
abstract events, are equally challenging measurement difficulties (Weick 1990).

Several other research agendas are suggested
by this review. More refined typologies of technology, and further study of issues of our
changing world, as well as technological constructs, are traditional types of 'next steps'.

Decision settings in the future will be
characterized by more and increasing knowledge, complexity, and turbulence (Huber 1984).
As a result, technologies that increase the
efficiency and effectiveness of meetings and
interactions will be of particular significance.
Some types of these technologies have already
been developed for teleconferencing, video
conferencing, and electronic mail services for
aiding distributed groups (Hogan 1989; Johansen et al. 1979); integrating these technologies
into reasoning and decision systems is a natural
evolution.

Following our discussion of structure and
technology, we might merge the positional and
more fluid approaches to organizational structure and relate the derived structural constructs
to technology. It should be clear that examining
the technology–structure relationship at the level
of the organization probably does not make

much sense because different technologies and
different levels of technological development
are represented in different parts of any
organization. We do, however, need to develop
conceptual ways to think about *systems of
organizations*, and about *systems of advanced
technologies* which reside in and coexist with
organizations.

Following a structurational view of technology, we might well recognize that many notions
advanced by researchers interested in structure
are similar to, identical to, or subsumed under
notions discussed by technology researchers. It
may well be time to merge the two approaches
and work toward deriving one model of
structure/technology.

Thoughtful examinations of new technologies
and the nature of stochastic, continuous and
abstract events in organizations suggest that a
number of research studies are required:

- investigations into concepts intended to
  differentiate among the different forms that
  stochastic events can take, i.e. using measures of predictability, efficacy, equivocality,
  clarity and task complexity, among others
  (Campbell 1988; Dornbusch and Scott 1975;
  Daft and Lengel 1986)
- examinations of differences in diagnosis,
  analysis, and problem solving tasks in order
  to account for new mental demands consequent with new technologies
- investigations that utilize multiple measures
  in order to assess performance of complex
  tasks in actual and virtual organizations
- investigations of the nature and role of
  interruptions and arousal in simple and
  complex technological organizations
- examinations of the role that increased
  cognitive demands, increased electronic
  complexity, and dense organizational interdependence over large areas have on
  increases in incidences of unexpected outcomes that produce unexpected ramifications
- investigations of whether such unexpected
  outcomes and ramifications are occasions for
  failure or opportunities for innovation and
  learning
- explorations of the nature and importance of
  temporal and longitudinal views of technology and organizational relationships, as
  well as the importance of contingency
  frameworks which consider organizational
  types as constructs in organizational and
  technological studies.

In short, investigations of how best organizations can compensate for the energizing,
debilitating or systemic effects of technology
are well intentioned and important. In designing

such technologies and organizations, future researchers might do well to examine how best to make complex judgment tasks simpler, to distribute responsibility among team members, to reduce distractions and provide incentives for early reporting of error and problem solving, to reduce production pressures and heighten perceptions of control, and to add slack capacity to attention (Weick 1990: 33). These, of course, are hardly new organizational or technology challenges. However, in the wake of an environment characterized by stochastic events, continuous processing, and higher cognitive workload, increased attention to fundamental outstanding research issues such as these is ever more important.

REFERENCES

Anthony, R.N. (1965) *Planning and Control Systems: a Framework for Analysis*. Cambridge, MA: Harvard University Press.

Barley, S. (1986) 'Technology as an occasion for structuring: evidence from observation of CT scanners and the social order of radiology departments', *Administrative Science Quarterly*, 31: 78–108.

Barley, S. (1988) 'Technology, power, and the social organization of work: towards a pragmatic theory of skilling and deskilling', in P. Torbert and S. Barley (eds), *Research in the Sociology of Organizations*, vol. 6. Beverly Hills, CA: Sage. pp. 33–80.

Berniker, E. (1987) 'Understanding technical systems'. Paper presented at the Symposium on Management Training Programs: Implications of New Technologies, Geneva, Switzerland, November.

Bijker, W.E. (1987) 'The social construction of bakelite: toward a theory of invention', in W.E. Bijker, T.P. Hughes and T. Pinch (eds), *The Social Construction of Technological Systems*. Cambridge, MA: MIT Press. pp. 159–87.

Blau, P.M. and Schoenherr, R.A. (1971) *The Structure of Organizations*. New York: Basic Books.

Braverman, H. (1974) *Labor and Monopoly Capital: the Degradation of Work in the Twentieth Century*. New York: Monthly Review Press.

Campbell, D.J. (1988) 'Task complexity: a review and analysis', *Academy of Management Review*, 13: 40–52.

Chapple, E.D. and Sayles, L.R. (1961) *The Measure of Management*. New York: Macmillan.

Child, J. and Mansfield, R. (1972) 'Technology, size, and organization structure', *Sociology*, 6: 369–93.

Collins, P.D., Hage, J. and Hull, F. (1986) 'A framework for analyzing technical systems in complex organizations', in *Research in the Sociology of Organizations*, vol. 6. Greenwich, CT: JAI Press. pp. 81–100.

Copeland, D.G. and McKenney, J.L. (1988) 'Airline reservations systems: lessons from history', *MIS Quarterly*, 12(3): 353–69.

Crozier, M. (1964) *The Bureaucratic Phenomenon*. Chicago: University of Chicago Press.

Daft, R.L. and Lengel, R.H. (1986) 'Organizational information requirements, media richness and structural design', *Management Science*, 32: 554–71.

Davis, G.B. and Olson, M.H. (1985) *Management Information Systems*, 2nd edn. New York: McGraw-Hill.

Davis, L.E. and Taylor, J.C. (1976) 'Technology, organization and job structure', in R. Dubin (ed.), *Handbook of Work, Organization, and Society*. Chicago: Rand-McNally. pp. 379–419.

De Sanctis, G. and Poole, M.S. (1994) 'Capturing the complexity in advanced technology use: adaptive structuration theory', *Organization Science*, 5: 121–47.

Dornbusch, S M. and Scott, W.R. (1975) *Evaluation and the Exercise of Authority*. San Francisco: Jossey-Bass.

Evan, W.M. (1966) 'The organization set: toward a theory of interorganizational relations', in J.D. Thompson (ed.), *Approaches to Organizational Design*. Pittsburgh: University of Pittsburgh Press. pp. 175–91.

Fortune (1988) 'The winning organization', 26 September: 50–60.

Fulk, J., Power, J.G. and Schmitz, J. (1986) 'Communication in organizations via electronic mail: An analysis of behavioral and relational issues'. Paper presented at the Annual Meeting of the American Institute of Decision Sciences, Honolulu, HA.

Galbraith, J. (1973) *Designing Complex Organizations*. Reading, MA: Addison-Wesley.

Galbraith, J. (1977) *Organization Design*. Reading, MA: Addison-Wesley.

Garud, R. and Rappa, M.A. (1994) 'A socio-cognitive model of technology evolution: the case of cochlear implants', *Organization Science*, 5: 344–62.

Gerstein, M.S. (1987) *The Technology Connection*. Reading, MA: Addison-Wesley.

Gerwin, D. (1981) 'Relationships between structure and technology', in P.C. Nystrom and W.H. Starbuck (eds), *Handbook of Organizational Design*, vol. 2. New York: Oxford. pp. 3–38.

Giddens, A. (1979) *Central Problems in Social Theory: Action, Structure and Contradiction in Social Analysis*. Berkeley, CA: University of California Press.

Giddens, A. (1984) *The Constitution of Society: Outline of the Theory of Structure*. Berkeley, CA: University of California Press.

Goldman, S.L., Nagel, R.N. and Preiss, K. (1995) *Agile Competitors and Virtual Organizations: Strategies for Enriching the Customer*. New York: Van Nostrand Reinhold.

Hage, J. and Aiken, M. (1967) 'Program change and

organizational properties: a comparative analysis', *American Journal of Sociology*, 72: 503–19.

Hogan, N. (1989) 'Controlling impedance at the man–machine interface', in *Proceedings of the 1989 IEEE Conference on Robotics and Automation*, Scottsdale, Arizona, 14–19 May.

Huber, G.P. (1984) 'The nature and design of post-industrial organizations', *Management Science*, 30: 928–51.

Hughes, T.P. (1987) 'The evolution of large technological systems', in W.E. Bijker, T.P. Hughes, and T.J. Pinch (eds), *The Social Construction of Technological Systems*. Cambridge, MA: MIT Press.

Hulin, C.L. and Roznowski, M. (1985) 'Organizational technologies: effects on organizations' characteristics and individuals', in L.L. Cummings and B.M. Staw (eds), *Research in Organizational Behavior*, vol. 7. Greenwich, CT: JAI Press. pp. 39–86.

Johansen, R., Vallee, J. and Spangler, K. (1979) *Electronic Meetings*. Reading, MA: Addison-Wesley.

Kanter, R. (1989) *When Giants Learn to Dance: Mastering the Challenges of Strategy, Management, and Careers in the 1990s*. New York: Simon & Schuster.

Lawrence, P.R. and Lorsch, J.W. (1967) *Organization and Environment*. Boston: Graduate School of Business Administration, Harvard University.

Liker, J.K., Fleischer, M. and Arnsdorf, D. (1992) 'Fulfilling the promises of CAD', *Sloan Management Review*, Spring: 74–86.

Lincoln, J.R., Matsuo, H. and McBride, K. (1986) 'Organization structures in Japanese and U.S. manufacturing', *Administrative Science Quarterly*, 31: 338–64.

Lincoln, J.R. and Kalleberg, A. (1990) *Culture, Control, and Commitment: a Study of Work Organization and Work Attitudes in the United States and Japan*. New York: Cambridge University Press.

Lucky, R. (1991) *Silicon Dreams*. New York: Van Nostrand Reinhold.

McKenney, J.L. and McFarlan, F.W. (1982) 'The information archipelago – maps and bridges', *Harvard Business Review*, September–October: 100–17.

MacKenzie, D. and Wajcman, J. (1985) *Social Shaping of Technology*. Philadelphia, PA: Open University Press.

Maurice, M., Sorge, A. and Warner, M. (1980) 'Societal differences in organizing manufacturing units: a comparison of France, West Germany, and Great Britain', *Organization Studies*, 1: 59–86.

Miles, R.E. and Snow, C.C. (1978) *Organizational Strategy, Structure and Process*. New York: McGraw-Hill.

Miller, E.J. and Rice, A.K. (1967) *Systems of Organizations*. London: Tavistock.

Mitroff, I.I. and Mohrman, S. (1986) 'The whole system is broke and in desperate need of fixing: notes on the second industrial revolution', *International Journal of Technology Management*, 1: 65–75.

Mitroff, I.I., Mason, R.O. and Pearson, C.M. (1994) *Framebreak*. San Francisco: Jossey-Bass.

Monge, P.R. and Eisenberg, E.M. (1987) 'Emerging communication networks', in F. Jablin, L. Putnam, K.H. Roberts and L.W. Porter (eds), *Handbook of Organizational Communication*. Beverly Hills, CA: Sage. pp. 304–42.

Morton, M.S. (ed.) (1991) *The Corporation of the 1990s: Information Technology and Organizational Transformation*. New York: Oxford University Press.

National Research Council. (1994) *Information Technology in the Service Society: a Twenty-First Century Lever*. Washington, DC: National Academy Press.

Noble, D.F. (1984) *Forces of Production: a Social History of Industrial Automation*. New York: Oxford University Press.

Ohara, M. (1988) 'CAD/CAM at Toyota Motor Company', in T. Kitagawa (ed.), *Computer Science and Technologies*. New York: North Holland.

Orlikowski, W. (1992) 'The duality of technology: rethinking the concept of technology in organizations', *Organization Science*, 3: 398–426.

Perrow, C. (1967) 'A framework for the comparative analysis of organizations', *American Sociological Review*, 32: 194-208.

Perrow, C. (1979) *Complex Organizations: a Critical Essay*, 2nd edn. New York: Random House.

Perrow, C. (1984) *Normal Accidents: Living with High Risk Technologies*. New York: Basic Books.

Perrow, C. (1986) *Complex Organizations: a Critical Essay*, 3rd edn. New York: Random House.

Peters, T. (1987) *Thriving on Chaos*. New York: Knopf.

Piore, M.J. and Sabel, C.F. (1984) *The Second Industrial Divide: Possibilities for Prosperity*. New York: Basic Books.

Pugh, D.S., Hickson, D.J., Hinings, C.R. and Turner, C. (1969) 'The context of organization structure', *Administrative Science Quarterly*, 14: 91–114.

Ranson, S., Hinings, B. and Greenwood, R. (1980) 'The structuring of organizational structures', *Administrative Science Quarterly*, 25: 1–17.

Read, P.P. (1993) *Ablaze: the Story of the Heroes and Victims of Chernobyl*. New York: Random House.

Roberts, K.H. and O'Reilly, C.A. (1974) 'Some correlates of communication roles in organizations', *Academy of Management Journal*, 22: 42–57.

Schwartz, D. and Jacobson, E. (1977) 'Organizational communication network analysis: the liaison communication role', *Organization Behavior and Human Performance*, 18: 158–74.

Scott, W.R. (1992) *Organizations: Rational, Natural, and Open Systems*. Englewood Cliffs, NJ: Prentice-Hall.

Senge, P.M. (1990) *The Fifth Discipline: the Art and*

Practice of the Learning Organization. New York: Doubleday Currency.

Teich, A.H. (1993) *Technology and the Future.* New York: St Martin's Press.

Thompson, J.D. (1967) *Organizations in Action.* New York: McGraw-Hill.

Thurow, L.C. (1992a) 'Who will own the 21st century?', *Sloan Management Review*, Spring: 5–18.

Thurow, L.C. (1992b) *Head to Head: Coming Economic Battles among Japan, Europe, and America.* New York: William Morrow.

Trist, E.L., Higgin, G.W., Murray, H. and Pollock, A.B. (1963) *Organizational Choice.* London: Tavistock.

Tushman, M.L. and Rosenkopf, L. (1992) 'Organizational determinants of technological change: toward a sociology of technological evolution', in B.M. Staw and L.L. Cummings (eds), *Research in Organizational Behavior*, vol. 14. Greenwich, CT: JAI Press. pp. 311–47.

Tyre, M.J. and Orlikowski W.J. (1994) 'Windows of opportunity: temporal patterns of technological adaptation in organizations', *Organization Science*, 5(1): 98–118.

Weick, K.E. (1969) *The Social Psychology of Organizing.* Reading, MA: Addison-Wesley.

Weick, K.E. (1990) 'Technology as equivoque: sensemaking in new technologies', in P.S. Goodman and L. Sproull (eds), *Technology and Organizations.* San Francisco: Jossey-Bass.

Wenk, E. (1989) *Tradeoffs: Imperatives of Choice in a High Tech World.* Baltimore, MD: Johns Hopkins University Press.

Woodward, J. (1965) *Industrial Organization: Theory and Practice.* London: Oxford University Press.

Wynne, B. (1988) 'Unruly technology: practical rules, impractical discourses and public understanding', *Social Studies of Science*, 18: 147–67.

Yoshino, M. (1968) *Japan's Managerial System.* Cambridge, MA: MIT Press.

2.9

Organizing for Innovation

DEBORAH DOUGHERTY

The ability to develop viable new products and services is important to many organizations. Product innovation enables organizations to improve the quality of their output, revitalize mature businesses, enter new markets, react to competitive encroachment, try out new technologies, leverage investment in technologies that are so expensive that no single product can recoup them, and develop alternative applications for existing product categories, to name just a few outcomes. For organizations which must adapt to changing competition, markets, and technologies, product innovation is not simply a fad. It is a necessity (Hage 1988; Jelinek and Schoonhoven 1990; Zahra and Covin 1995).

Not surprisingly, the literature relevant to innovation includes thousands of books and articles. Just within the fields of management, many review articles have been written. See, for example, Cooper (1983), Crawford (1983), Gatignon and Robertson (1985), and Johne and Snelson (1988) in marketing; Burgelman (1983), Johnson (1988), and Day (1990) in strategy; Rothwell (1977), Roberts (1988), and Rothwell and Whiston (1990) in technology management; Downs and Mohr (1976), Kimberly (1981), Van de Ven (1986), Nord and Tucker (1987), Hage (1988), Kanter (1988), and Damanpour (1991) in organization theory.

Despite all this attention, organizations continue to have problems innovating effectively. They have difficulty shifting to new technologies (Tushman and Anderson 1986); moving away from familiar customers (Christensen and Bower 1993); changing their strategic paradigm (Johnson 1988); breaking out of prevailing patterns of decision-making (Starbuck and Milliken 1988); adjusting their product architecture (Henderson and Clark 1990); using marketing tools appro-

priately (Mahajan and Wind 1992); and learning from experience (Van de Ven and Polley 1992). According to Cooper and Kleinschmidt, 'What the literature prescribes and what most firms do are miles apart' (1986: 73).

The persistence of these problems suggests that more theory building is necessary. However, the existence of this large literature suggests that a fresh perspective is also necessary, since established conceptual views do not address all the problems. The purpose of this chapter is to build theory on organizing for innovation by changing the perspective on the topic in three ways.

The first change in perspective is to *build up from the activities of innovation*. Most organization views of innovation are not anchored on underlying activities, because 'innovation' is defined very broadly as the adoption of any device, system, process, problem, program, product, or service that is new to the organization (Downs and Mohr 1976; Kanter 1988; Damanpour et al. 1989). Within this 'anything goes' framework, research relies on broad constructs like administrative versus technical, development stage, and radical versus incremental. These constructs may correlate with various outcomes (albeit at a low level – Damanpour 1991), but researchers still find what Downs and Mohr (1976) called a 'troublesome instability' in their relationships (Takeuchi and Nonaka 1986; Nord and Tucker 1987; Day 1994). This chapter focuses on the activities of product innovation, and how to organize effectively for them. My central premise is straightforward: theories of organization should reflect the activities that are being organized. Focusing on the activities of product innovation limits the generalizability of the implications, but it allows a more thorough treatment of the particular processes, dynamics, and events underlying this kind of innovation.

My second change in perspective is to *shift the level of analysis*. Much of the innovation literature concerns either individual innovation projects (Brown and Eisenhardt 1995) or successful high technology organizations (Kanter 1983; Jelinek and Schoonhoven 1990). These theories address project management and 'best practices' for technology-centered, simple organizations, but they apply less well to organizations which have the most trouble with product innovation – the large, complex firm. In this setting, product innovation involves the re-innovation of the project and the simultaneous adaptation of the organization, not just the management of separate projects (Leonard-Barton 1988; Tyre and Orlikowski 1994). By concentrating on projects or simple organizations, theorists overlook the most problematic relationship between innovation and the organization. In addition, not all large, complex organizations are successful with innovation. By concentrating on successful practices, theorists overlook the question of how noninnovative organizations can *become* innovative (Hage 1988; Van de Ven 1986; Hedlund and Ridderstrale 1994).

The third change is to *deal with the fact that complex organizations have difficulty with innovation* (Hage 1988). Rather than simply present another normative model of 'the innovative organization', this chapter first examines why existing models are not adequate. The basic questions are how and why do large, complex organizations inhibit the activities necessary to effective product innovation? I use the metaphor 'tension' to frame the discussion. Both Pelz and Andrews (1966) and Jelinek and Schoonhoven (1990) characterize innovation as 'tensions', because the term captures very well the organizing challenges of iterating between diverse activities, working around barriers, combining insights, and resolving the conflicts of seemingly opposing forces, all of which can be found in the innovation process. Thinking of the organizing challenges of innovation as inherent tensions that must be accommodated emphasizes the dialectical nature of innovation, in which the organization and the new products are mutually constitutive (Barley 1986; Scarborough and Corbett 1992; Heller 1994).

In the following sections, findings from a number of fields of study are first synthesized into four sets of activities that are necessary for effective product innovation. Next, the organizing problems associated with each set of activities are summarized in terms of the inherent tensions which must be managed if the organization is to enable those activities.

Research suggests that people have developed ways to handle these tensions effectively at the project level, but still not at the organization level. I then go back to Burns and Stalker's (1966) classic discussion, because they provided initial insights into how these tensions might be managed across the organization. I flesh out their largely overlooked insights into possible solutions, and conclude with some new, or in fact *re*newed, directions for research.

PROBLEMS IN ORGANIZING FOR PRODUCT INNOVATION

'Product innovation' is defined as the conceptualization, development, operationalization, manufacture, launch, and ongoing management of a new product or service (Cooper 1983; Imai et al. 1985; Dougherty 1992a). 'New' means new to the organization, and can involve new customers, new uses, new manufacturing, new distribution and/or logistics, new product technology, and any combination of these. Product innovation is inherently interfunctional, and, according to Crawford (1983), is second only to corporate strategy in the way it involves all aspects of all functions of management. It is also inherently ambiguous, and therefore involves perception and social construction (Daft and Weick 1984).

To translate product innovation into organizational terms, it helps to focus on the underlying activities of the process. Four sets of activities are described in turn: (1) conceptualizing the product to integrate market needs and technological potential; (2) organizing the process to accommodate creative problem solving; (3) monitoring the process; and (4) developing commitment to the effort. Although discussed separately, these four activities interrelate in practice.

Market–Technology Linking

A new product is a package of features and benefits, each of which must be conceived, articulated, designed, and 'operationalized', or brought into existence. This set of activities is called market–technology linking (Burgelman 1983). To carry out market–technology linking effectively, innovators need to conceptualize the product as fully as possible as early as possible, so that its design reflects customer needs, market structure, technological capability, manufacturability, selling and distribution, and the firm's unique competencies (Bacon et al. 1994). Clark and Fujimoto use the term 'product integrity' to describe how these elements are integrated into a comprehensive package:

Product integrity has both internal and external dimensions. Internal integrity refers to consistency between the function and structure of the product – e.g., the parts fit well, components match and work well together, layout achieves maximum space efficiency. External integrity is a measure of how well a product's function, structure and semantics fit the customers' objectives, values, production system, lifestyle, use-pattern, and self-identity. (1991: 30)

Market–technology linking is multi-functional, because all functions have vital knowledge to contribute. Understanding customer needs is essential to product success (Myers and Marquis 1969; Rothwell et al. 1974), but, since these needs must be operationalized through technology, marketing must be complemented with input from other functions (Allen 1977; Cohen and Levinthal 1990). The product's design actually emerges from the development process, because both market and technological issues are ambiguous. On the market side, customers cannot articulate needs if the application is new, and needs may change in any case as the product is used (Rosenberg 1982). In addition, market information is 'sticky', or embedded in a context and not retrievable except by hands-on interaction within the context (von Hippel 1994). On the technical side, it is not always apparent to a scientist if she is working on a minor problem of adjustment or a major problem of principle (Schon 1967). Market–technology linking thus involves the creation of knowledge through hands-on learning, as innovators work with customers, experiment with new designs, and test different approaches (Freeman 1982; Kanter 1988; Nonaka 1994).

A number of techniques have been developed for market–technology linking in a specific project. One approach is to look for 'lead users', or people on the leading edge of a new market who already have experience with the problem the product will solve (von Hippel 1986). These users can provide some actual product design insights (Bailetti and Guild 1991). Another approach is 'empathetic design', through which multidisciplinary teams work in an anthropological mode with potential users to develop the product's design (Leonard-Barton 1991). Ideas on quality function deployment (Griffin and Hauser 1993) and team visits with customers also are useful (McQuarrie 1993).

Organization-Wide Tensions for Market–Technology Linking

To advance our understanding of organizing for innovation, however, research must also reckon with the fact that many organizations do not carry out market–technology linking very well, despite the wide availability of techniques (Cooper and Kleinschmidt 1986; Mahajan and Wind 1992; Dougherty and Corse 1995). In a study which included firms that are usually considered as exemplars of the 'innovative organization', Bacon et al. conclude: 'many of the firms in our study used surprisingly rudimentary procedures to bring together the requisite product definition information' (1994: 1). The pervasiveness and persistence of problems with market–technology linking suggests that these problems are not rooted only in poor project management.

Looking at market–technology linking from the perspective of 'tension', one can see that these activities embody a tension between outside (market) and inside (the firm's operations and technology). This inherent tension can be handled within a single project, if the multi-functional team members collaborate among themselves and with users and suppliers over the product's conceptualization and operationalization. The market–technology linking activities cannot be confined within a project, however, because the necessary technology may exist in another division, while vital elements of the specific design (e.g. a sales force for distribution) might be controlled by another unit. Innovators must simultaneously relate their product to these other resources and incorporate the organization's competencies into their product (Prahalad and Hamel 1990). To be innovative, therefore, the whole organization needs to be capable of balancing this outside–inside tension.

Unfortunately, many large, complex organizations focus inward on the efficiency of their operations, thus tilting inward the balance between inside and outside. Because of the pressures of day-to-day operations, people follow standard operating procedures to ensure that the work of the organization does not grind to a halt. These procedures, however, filter out extraneous (i.e. new) information, punish people for stepping out of 'normal' work roles, and focus attention on immediate issues (March and Simon 1958; Quelsh et al. 1987; see examples by Wheelwright and Clark 1992). One department may also have more power than the others because historically it has managed more of the uncertainties in the firm (Pfeffer and Salancik 1978; Nelson and Winter 1982). Workman (1993), for example, describes how the engineering department in a high technology firm dominated product development and kept manufacturing and marketing out of the market–technology linking process, despite official integrating structures. The outcome of this internally oriented operational pressure is that different bits of information about the outside and inside are fragmented into different 'thought worlds' (Dougherty 1992b), and become difficult to integrate.

In addition, new products by definition constitute a new understanding of the firm's market and technology, so managers must reconceptualize the business (however slightly in some cases) to incorporate them into the organization. However, operational pressures lead to a fixed understanding of 'our business' which inhibits reconceptualization (Johnson 1988; Henderson and Clark 1990). Senior managers concentrate on what has been successful in the past, fixating on 'current strategy' (Burgelman 1983; Bower 1970), while know-how becomes abstracted into 'core rigidities' or simplifications which no longer adapt with market and/or technology changes (Leonard-Barton 1992; Miller 1993).

To summarize, linking customer needs with the organization's technical capabilities is necessary to create a viable new product. The ability to manage this linkage and its inherent tension between outside and inside must permeate the entire organization, since a specific product must draw on resources around the organization, and all those resources must accommodate multiple sets of market–technology linkages. However, the pressures to make operations efficient focus attention inward on day-to-day procedures, and narrow the kinds of business that are considered appropriate. These inward pressures serve the important functions of focusing attention, reducing ambiguity, and 'getting the iron out the door', but they inhibit the organization-wide market–technology linking that is necessary for innovation. A theory of organizing for innovation in large, complex organizations must explain how to manage operations efficiently *and* overcome these inward pressures.

Organizing for Creative Problem Solving

The product's conceptualization and development require that innovators solve complex problems to overcome surprises, work around barriers, merge processes from different functions, and weave together resources from different locations. Innovators must push issues along within each function, such as setting up manufacturing processes, establishing the selling and distribution system, and working through the details of design. At the same time, they must jointly focus on problems that affect more than one function, and solve them by taking the constraints of

the other functions into account (Yang and Dougherty 1993).

Organizing for problem solving is multi-functional in that work must be coordinated, sometimes in a parallel fashion, and sometimes in a joint fashion. For example, to reduce time to market, the engineers must be designing the parts for the product at the same time that the manufacturing people are designing the production process. To coordinate such highly interdependent activities, innovators must understand the constraints in other functions, anticipate others' needs, and use dense, two-way communication to process fragmentary information (Clark and Fujimoto 1991). Relationships among the team emerge through mutual adaptation, in response to the needs of the task (Mintzberg and McHugh 1985; Leonard-Barton 1988). As well, innovators and their managers must make decisions quickly, or small problems will snowball into huge ones. This also requires hands-on experimenting both within and across functions, as people iterate across options and possibilities.

Structures have been developed to enable this complicated form of organizing at the project level. Souder (1987) found that when the technology and market are unfamiliar, the most successful structure is the 'task dominant' team approach, in which everyone focuses on the entire development process rather than one piece of it. People are functional specialists, but their interactions are continuous and frequent, and information flows freely along multiple channels. Coordination mechanisms are diffused among team members rather than clearly assigned, so there are no formal handoffs, transfer points, or transfers of personnel. Other structural elements include: (1) a variety of boundary spanning roles to handle inter-functional communication (Ancona and Caldwell 1990); (2) a 'heavyweight' project manager when it is necessary to work through conflicts with higher level functional managers (Clark and Fujimoto 1991); (3) coordination mechanisms which vary with the project's analyzability, the novelty of connection between units, and differences in development phases (Adler 1995); and (4) multi-team structures which leverage technologies across multiple products (Jelinek and Schoonhoven 1990; Cusumano and Nobeoka 1994).

Organization-Wide Tensions for Creative Problem Solving

Despite all the insights into project management, organizations still have difficulty especially with multiple projects. From the perspective of tension, we can see that organizing for creative problem solving embodies a tension between the old and the new. For example, a new product may require new supplier relationships, new parts handling, and new selling procedures, all of which can conflict with existing procedures designed for old products. The old–new tensions can be managed within the individual project through collaborative teaming, communication, and hands-on practice. Unfortunately, many problems do not fall within the control of a project team: innovations must tap into the firm-wide budgeting process, access resources in other divisions, and compete with existing businesses for time in the tool room, space on the shop floor, or inclusion in the sales people's kits. To be innovative, the whole organization must be capable of balancing the tension between the old and the new.

Unfortunately, the tension between the old and the new is easily disrupted and tilted toward the old in the large, complex organizations. A primary source of the disruption is 'segmentalism' (Kanter 1983), which emerges from the mechanistic system that predominates in many large organizations (Burns and Stalker 1966; Mintzberg 1979; Dougherty and Corse 1995). Segmentalism reduces complexity by breaking big problems down into smaller pieces, which are separated further into product lines that are managed by different people. In such compartmentalized systems, the conduits that are needed to coordinate the creative problem solving and to process the fragmentary information between the different units do not exist. Problem solving comes to a screeching halt when a boundary is reached; action stops, problems fester, and the development languishes. The power in the organization reinforces segmentalism because it is attached to existing boundaries and established routines (Nelson and Winter 1982). The power of resources that is embedded in funds, expertise, information, and credibility is in the hands of managers who are not part of the innovative initiative, so it sustains current activities rather than solves new problems. The power of process such as agenda-setting, budgeting, and decision-making also channel attention to established businesses, not to innovation (Hardy 1994; Dougherty and Hardy 1995).

To summarize, managing the tension between the new and the old to creatively solve problems on an organization-wide basis is necessary for effective new product development. However, the complexity of work in these large organizations reinforces a tendency to separate and compartmentalize work, locates power in the established businesses, not new ones, and hinders integrated problem solving. A theory of organizing for innovation must, then, grapple with the need to deal with complexity and also overcome the pressures to focus on established routines.

Monitoring and Evaluation

A third set of activities essential to effective product innovation concerns monitoring and evaluating the product innovation process. New product efforts need to be evaluated throughout their development, because they can absorb enormous amounts of resources with no sure payoff. Changes in markets, technologies, or competition also can quickly turn a good idea into a bad one, so the development effort needs to be monitored to see if design premises still hold. Despite the fanciful sense of unfettered freedom for innovation sometimes found in the organization literature, evaluation is necessary for innovation, since random 'variation' will not produce comprehensive design or thorough problem solving. Indeed, Van de Ven and Polley (1992) illustrate how easily an innovation can fall into disabled learning.

Monitoring and evaluation require multi-disciplinary team work, because innovators must rely on one another to assess progress. A multi-functional 'community of practice' jointly selects possible courses of action and judges progress (Brown and Duguid 1991). Requisite collaborative skills for this activity include the ability to accept the judgement of others, to integrate diverse views without compromising the project, and to take responsibility for the choice rather than to second-guess. Criteria for evaluation emerge during the development, because product innovations cannot be evaluated by formula or algorithm (Johne and Snelson 1988). Indeed, Brock and MacMillan (1993) argue that standard controls are not just obstacles to innovation, but the primary cause of cost overruns. Evaluation also depends on hands-on, experiential learning, because useful heuristics arise from experience.

The project management, technology, and marketing literatures offer a variety of techniques for evaluation and control (Cooper 1983; Urban and Hauser 1988; Wheelwright and Clark 1992). A phase review helps to assure that necessary activities occur at the right time – for example, doing market research to establish customer needs, not to 'confirm' presumptions at the end of the development (Deshpande and Zaltman 1982). Other criteria assure that necessary modifications are made before the project moves forward, that funding is adequate, and that design premises have been verified. Budget reviews held after key milestones such as concept testing, first process design and test, or prototype provide a more realistic sense of progress (Brock and MacMillan 1993).

Organization-Wide Tensions for Monitoring and Evaluation

Despite all the models, the monitoring and evaluation of product innovation are even more problematic than the first two activities (Griffin and Page 1993). This set of activities embodies a tension between strategic emergence and strategic determination. If new products are forced to conform to top-down plans they would not address new opportunities, but if the organization relied strictly on bottom-up emergence, its innovations would not build on one another (Day 1990). This tension between determination and emergence can be handled within a project if senior managers exert 'subtle control' by framing the domain for the innovation, and then allowing the innovators to work out the specifics (Takeuchi and Nonaka 1986; Quinn 1985). But evaluation cannot be limited to the project level, since the success of an innovation may depend on how well it embodies the firm's unique competencies (Crawford 1983; Cooper and Kleinschmidt 1987). Connecting innovations to a larger plan allows firms to leverage investments across several projects (Jelinek and Schoonhoven 1990), and to build innovations on one another in a 'rapid inch-up' process (Clark and Fujimoto 1991). To be innovative, the whole organization must balance the tension between determination and emergence.

Large, complex organizations tend to emphasize determination over emergence, however. To control the wide variety of activities under them, managers rely on abstracted and generalized criteria, but these obliterate the unique aspects of an innovation. Because senior managers are detached from the situated specifics of work, they may force a uniform development time on all innovations regardless of differences, intervene in day-to-day problem solving even though they are not familiar with the issues, and impose rigid controls when delays crop up (Rosenbloom and Abernathy 1982; Dougherty and Cohen 1995). Brown and Duguid (1991), Van de Ven and Polley (1992), and Dougherty and Heller (1994) illustrate how, by following routine procedure, the situated realities of a given innovation are ignored as team members with vital experience are transferred, new project goals are imposed midstream, and processes are formalized inappropriately. In addition, most organizations do not have the kind of forward-reaching, adaptive strategies that are described in the practitioner models (Wheelwright and Clark 1992). Strategic intent becomes the rule (Mintzberg 1994), so there is no 'umbrella

strategy' that encourages innovations to emerge and develop (Mintzberg and McHugh 1985).

To summarize, evaluating and monitoring are necessary to create a viable new product. The ability to manage the tension between determination and emergence that is inherent in these activities must permeate the entire organization, because most innovations need to be linked with the firm's resources and strategy. However, abstracted processes for control emphasize determination over emergence, and senior managers are too detached from the specifics of innovation to enable learning. A theory of organizing for product innovation must explain how large, complex organizations can control such a variety of activities and still enable emergence to co-exist with determination.

Commitment to the Innovation Process

The three sets of activities described above require enormous investment in time, and perhaps more importantly, in psychic energy and attention. Innovation requires a deeper commitment than regular work, according to Burns and Stalker (1966), because the boundaries of responsibility must be broader and more inclusive in the rapidly changing, ambiguous conditions of innovation. An individual needs to: 'see himself as fully implicated in the discharge of any task . . . and as committed to the success of the firm's undertaking' (1966: iv). A broader, more inclusive job can create serious problems, however:

> The organic form, by departing from the familiar clarity and fixity of the hierarchic structure, is often experienced by the individual manager as an uneasy, embarrassed, or chronically anxious quest for knowledge about what he should be doing, or what is expected of him, and a similar apprehensiveness about what others are doing. (1966: 122)

Multidisciplinary teams help innovators generate commitment by providing a sense of 'inclusion', or the feeling of centrality, regardless of their official status (Van Maanen and Schein 1979). An interdisciplinary team provides a comfortable sense of accountability and commitment for participants, because innovators share the work with others who can be trusted to do their part (Dougherty and Corse 1995). Collaborative skills for this set of activities include the ability to trust others to do their part even when it may seem that they will not, and the ability to fulfil one's own part in a reliable fashion. Responsibilities vary across team member and over time, so roles emerge as the development proceeds.

A number of techniques have been proposed to help broaden commitment. One approach focuses on personality factors: finding people with the requisite independence and creativity to work as champions and sponsors, and then training and encouraging them (Roberts 1988). In addition, work roles can be defined more broadly so people do not constrain the breadth of issues they attend to (Kanter 1988; 1989). People can be given greater autonomy over the operational aspects of their work, which expands their sense of inclusiveness without overwhelming them (Bailyn 1985; Katz 1988). Career paths can be designed to accommodate people's life trajectories, which enables them to take on more responsibility at work in sync with lessening responsibility at home (Bailyn 1993).

Organization-Wide Tensions for Commitment

Commitment is the most problematic activity of product innovation, even at the project level. It embodies the tension between freedom and responsibility, which is one of the most challenging trade-offs in theory as well as in practice (see Weber 1946; Barnard 1938; Kunda 1992). For innovation, it is desirable that people feel free to generate ideas, create possible solutions to problems, and experiment with various courses of action. It is also desirable that people feel responsible to work toward common goals, use organizational resources efficiently, and achieve budgets and milestones. Despite the difficulties, this tension can be managed within a project if managers create a high commitment 'skunkworks', and hand-pick people who are both committed to the innovation and professional enough to see it through (Peters 1983). But commitment to innovation cannot be separated from the organization as a whole. Over time, individuals will be on different teams, report to multiple supervisors, and work with people who are not willing to commit themselves totally to their job (i.e. normal people). To be innovative, therefore, the organization as a whole needs to embody the tension between freedom and responsibility.

Large, complex organizations emphasize responsibility over freedom, however, because accountability is defined in precise, legalistic ways. This impersonal governance focuses on 'doing things right', not 'doing the right things', and inhibits the sense of inclusion that is essential for commitment. Westley (1990) argues more generally that middle-level people are often excluded from strategic conversations, which demoralizes them and reduces their commitment. Such demoralization is unfortunately common for innovation, since surveys show that most innovators think their senior managers are not committed to innovation (Gupta and Wilemon 1990). Despite all the lip service paid to it, innovation is often not legitimate within the organization, which further reduces the probability that people will commit to it.

To summarize, people throughout the organization need to feel committed to product innovation if viable new products are to be developed more than occasionally. The ability to manage the tension between freedom and responsibility inherent in commitment to innovative action must permeate the entire organization. However, because accountability is difficult to determine, people rely on precise measures and legalistic job definitions, which make innovation illegitimate, and inhibit their ability to develop the sense of inclusion that innovation requires. A theory of organizing for product innovation must explain how large, complex organizations can govern work effectively and still balance freedom and responsibility.

A Summary of Organizational Problems

I have argued that four sets of activities underlie the development of commercially successful new products. Innovators must work with potential customers to identify needs and link those needs with technological possibilities. They must organize the flow of work to collaborate across boundaries over problems, and solve them within the context of the whole system of attributes that comprise the product. They must monitor and evaluate their progress. And they must develop a sense of commitment which enables participants to take more responsibility without feeling overwhelmed. I have also argued that one reason why the vast organization studies literature provides relatively little insight into the organizational problems of innovation is that it is not anchored in the basic activities which underlie product innovation.

Recasting the activities as tensions suggests a new perspective on the organizing problems of product innovation. Ideally: (1) market–technology linking balances outside and inside; (2) organizing for problem solving balances new with old; (3) evaluating the process balances determination with emergence; and (4) developing commitment to innovation balances freedom with responsibility. These tensions cannot be eliminated because they are inherent in the activities, and help to power the innovation process. These tensions must be balanced throughout the organization, because the activities of innovation extend beyond a project, and are inextricably bound up with the organization as a whole.

Table 1 *The tensions, what perpetuates imbalances, and how to restore balance*

Activity	Tension	Problem of normal functioning that disrupts tension	Particular practices which perpetuate disruption	Capacities to restore the balance in the tension
Market–technology linking	Outside vs inside	Keeping operations efficient	Inward emphasis on dept thought worlds and units; fixed sense of business	Generate and maintain an identity based on the value provided to customers
Organizing for creative problem solving	New vs old	Managing complexity	Segmentalist thinking and compartmentaliza-tion of work; power based on current work	See work of organization in terms of process, focusing on relationships among parts, and changes
Evaluating and monitoring innovation	Determined vs emergent	Controlling multiple activities	Abstracting work into generic standards; no strategy making	Situated judgement, collective ability to be engaged in details of work but also appreciate unstructured problems
Developing commitment to innovation	Freedom vs responsibility	Accounting for work, results	Illegitimacy of innovation; illegitimacy of inclusion	Collective accountability, accept and share responsibility, legitimize innovation and inclusion

Because theories focus either on the project level of analysis or on entirely innovative organizations, they do not address the fundamental organizing question identified in this chapter: how can large, complex organizations solve the problems of normal functioning (i.e. efficient operations, reduction of complexity, control, and governance), and still embody the tensions which power innovation? In other words, how can we organize *organizations* to be more effectively innovative? Continued research at the project level is important, of course, but it does not grapple with this central question of organizing for innovation. Moreover, organizations that are now trapped by the problems discussed above cannot simply snap their collective fingers to be innovative. Change theories remind us of how difficult managing change can be: current practices must be 'unfrozen'; new 'mindsets' must be developed along with new practices through which the mindsets can be fleshed out and put into practice; and the new system of action must be stabilized or refrozen, or practices will revert to the old system (Schein 1990; Mintzberg and Westley 1992). In the next section, I sketch out possible mindsets to restore the balance in the tensions, along with some behavioral repertoires through which organizations can implement the new approach to organizing.

RENEWED DIRECTIONS FOR RESEARCH

Table 1 summarizes the four tensions, the problems of normal functioning that disrupt them, and the particular practices which perpetuate the disruptions. These tensions are not new to organization theory, since the problems of responsiveness, complexity, control, commitment, and so forth have been central to organizational analysis since the inception of the field (Weber 1946; Barnard 1938; Gouldner 1954). Most classic discussions of these problems have not connected them directly to the practice of innovation, however, or to the question of how to change the organization. Work by Burns and Stalker (1966) is an exception, because their study combined the classic concerns with tensions such as the ones outlined above with managing innovation. Indeed, they argued that organizations need to be able to combine mechanistic and organic systems, but this aspect of their work has been largely overlooked. Starting with Burns and Stalker's forgotten insights is a way to *re*new theory on the innovative organization.

One of Burns and Stalker's forgotten insights is that many firms in their study did not become organic, even though their environment had become more complex (see preface and p. 4 of

1966 edition). Much of their book was devoted to exploring why the organic form was tenuous, and what managers could do about that. Burns and Stalker explained that few organizations became organic because people did not know how to organize, except for the bureaucracy:

> The ideology of formal bureaucracy seemed so deeply ingrained in industrial management that the common reaction to unfamiliar and novel conditions was to redefine, in the most precise and rigorous terms, the roles and working relationships obtaining within management along orthodox lines . . . and to reinforce the formal structure. In these concerns, the efforts to make the orthodox bureaucratic system work (because it was seen as the only possible way to organize . . .) produced dysfunctional forms of the mechanistic system. (1966: ix)

A second lost insight is that culture, not just structure, is central to organizing for innovation. Burns and Stalker argued that before an organization could become organic, it was necessary to develop 'codes of conduct' which would enable people to 'comprehend more eventualities and more information . . . and [in which] the limits of feasible action could be set more widely' (1966: 11). Codes of conduct were defined as an expression of a shared system of belief, or culture (1966: 119).

To build on Burns and Stalker, it is necessary to clarify the nature of 'code of conduct', and to describe the codes of conduct that would enable organizations to balance the tensions inherent in innovation. Swidler's (1986) discussion of cultural capacities addresses the nature of codes of conduct. She argues that culture affects behavior by providing people with a 'tool kit' of cultural material such as symbols, stories, habits, categories, and skills, which become a set of general 'capacities'. People draw on these cultural capacities to construct larger assemblages of action within which particular choices make sense, and for which certain culturally shaped skills and habits are useful. Established capacities persist because people come to value ends for which their cultural equipment is well suited (Geertz 1973). Established cultures also suppress alternative capacities. For example, Swidler suggests that people raised in impoverished urban ghettos fail to adopt a middle class life style, not because they lack the necessary values or have a bad attitude toward work, but because they lack the capacities for such a life style:

> One can hardly pursue success in a world where the accepted skills, style, and informal know-how are unfamiliar. . . . To adopt a line of conduct, one needs an image of the kind of world in which one is trying to act, a sense that one can read reasonably accurately (through one's own feelings and through the responses of others) how one is doing, and a capacity to choose among alternative lines of action. (1986: 275)

In the same fashion, organizations may not innovate well because the people lack the requisite codes of conduct, or capacities, that would enable them to carry out the four activities of innovation. Organizations therefore must develop capacities which provide an image of an organization which can manage the four tensions throughout. Otherwise, the existing capacities which concentrate attention inward on current, standardized operations will persist. In the next subsections, I outline some of the themes from theory on organizing for innovation, suggest that they do not quite provide a way to restore the balance in the four areas, and then suggest four capacities that fill in the gaps. These capacities are purely speculative, and my goal in suggesting them is to prompt others to develop ideas to replace, challenge, or elaborate them.

A Capacity for Organization-Wide Market–Technology Linking

Research in marketing and in technology development indicates that a capacity for market–technology linking will involve the development and exploitation of knowledge. First, the idea of being 'customer oriented', defined as having a set of norms that put customer interest first, has been around at least since Drucker (1954). Recent research in marketing confirms that a customer orientation relates to improved product innovation (Narver and Slater 1990; Deshpande et al. 1992; Moorman 1995). Second, the idea of having core competencies or resources has been around at least since Penrose (1959), and recent research confirms that developing technological knowledge also relates to improved performance (Cohen and Levinthal 1990; Henderson and Cockburn 1994). It seems clear that an organization must develop thorough knowledge of its markets and technologies, and be able to apply this knowledge, if it is to develop new products successfully.

While necessary to innovativeness, these two sets of knowledge are not sufficient, because in most theories the two sides remain separated, so the capacity for linking is still missing (Gatignon and Xeureb 1995). I propose that organizations must also develop a capacity to generate an organizational identity that combines internal and external issues. According to Fiol (1991), an organization identity describes what people define as central, distinctive, and enduring about their organization. If people understood their organization's identity in terms of *the value* it provides to customers, they could bridge inside technology and outside customers. To provide value, an organization must solve actual customer problems and fulfil needs, so value, by definition, is grounded in specific customer issues. Technologies can be seen as solutions to problems, so value is also grounded in specific technical possibilities.

An identity based on value would help organizations break out of the strong inward pull of internal operations and still meet efficiency needs. Bureaucratic efficiency is based on economies of scale, which are increasingly inefficient when markets are fragmenting (Hage 1988). Defining the collective organizational self in terms of providing value shifts attention to alternative kinds of efficiency based on economies of scope (the ability to produce an array of products), or economies of substitution (the ability to substitute modules of technology in an overall system, see Garud and Kumaraswamy 1995). The capacity to combine inside and outside in an identity enables the organization to become an 'enacting organization' (Daft and Weick 1984) rather than stay mired in a rigid view of 'our business'.

Generating and maintaining a value-based identity will be challenging, especially for organizations whose identity is now centered internally on technologies or products. However, a number of behavioral repertoires can be implemented concurrently with an emphasis on customer orientation and R&D competence, to unfreeze the day-to-day practices which reinforce the imbalance between inside and outside. First, value is a common language that can bridge the departmental thought worlds. If people in all departments interact with potential customers, they can learn the common language and begin to see how to apply their technical solutions to customer problems. People can extend this experience to the management of established businesses by learning how to track emerging trends in both markets and technologies, and then relating those changes to specific changes in businesses (Wheelwright and Clark 1992). Within the umbrella of organizational identity as value, a business unit can define itself in terms of how it contributes to the creation of the organization's value, strengthening the inside–outside thinking throughout the organization. Organizing business units into product families reinforces the combined thinking by embodying market–technology linking into the management processes.

A Capacity For Organization-Wide Creative Problem Solving

The organization studies literature suggests that a capacity for organization-wide problem solving will involve teams and networks. The innovative organization is usually described as comprising small, autonomous work units, which proliferate as the variety of products proliferates (Galbraith 1982; Peters 1983; Van de Ven 1986; Kanter 1988). To connect all these teams, communication in the innovative organization is based on consultation rather than command, and its content consists of information and advice rather than instructions and decisions (Burns and Stalker 1966). Different networks exist to handle: (1) the production process, extending both backward to suppliers and forward to customers; (2) joint ventures with other firms; (3) venture capital with former employees; and (4) various research consortia (Hage 1988).

Replacing the hierarchy with networked teams seems necessary for continual problem solving, but not sufficient. As noted in Table 1, the pressures of complexity have pushed many large, complex organizations to break down tasks and compartmentalize action. If anything, multiple teams would heighten complexity and segmentalism. I suggest that a capacity to see the organization as process – thus focusing on *organizing* – is also a necessary ingredient that is missing from our understanding of organizing for innovation. The capacity to see the organization as a process would enable people to shift the boundaries of their work over time more comfortably, and to accommodate the multi-paced, emergent processes of innovation. Seeing the organization as a process manages complexity without eliminating the ability to solve cross-boundary problems, so this capacity can restore the balance between the old and the new.

With the capacity to understand work as process, people still consider sets of work, but, rather than bracketing a particular set of work out of the whole, people would emphasize relationships among the sets. Effective management of complexity comes not from sticking to the tried and true, but from changing different aggregates of action at different times. For example, managers can shift smaller sets of work such as job definitions or pilot production processes, while holding larger sets constant, such as the strategy or manufacturing regime, and then reverse the focus (Leonard-Barton 1988). Time itself can also segment work without separating it. Tyre and Orlikowski (1994) argue that the implementation of new technologies is best managed by iterating bursts of innovative activity with stable periods during which people focus on normal operations. They recommend that managers deliberately punctuate adaptation with routine rather than focus only on one or the other, because problems are more likely to be surfaced and solved effectively. Gersick (1994) also shows how the manager of a new venture used temporal pacing to set the speed of development, and event planning to regulate attention.

'Process' is not new, since it underlies emergent strategy, total quality management, and process re-engineering. The idea of process as a shared image of organizing can be difficult to implement, however, since it violates the established image of organization as boxes or states of being (Pettigrew 1992). Shifting to the process-based image of organizing may be possible if teams and networking are coupled with day-to-day practices which reinforce thinking in terms of processes and relationships over time. For example, Jelinek and Schoonhoven (1990) describe organizing around development of technology. In this context, individuals can see their work in terms of how it flows into other people's work. Business unit managers can see product lines in terms of how they flow into generations or product revolutions. In manufacturing, planning and thinking concerns *changing* the manufacturing processes to fit with shifts in products and customer trends. In technology, planning and thinking concerns *developing* competencies. With the process as central, power can be aligned to orient the flows of resources, decision-making, reporting, and communication around integrating innovation into the organization, not around protecting turf (Hardy 1994).

A Capacity for Organization-Wide Monitoring and Evaluation

The organization studies literature indicates that organization-wide monitoring and evaluation for innovation involves senior management leadership and a risk-taking culture. In innovative organizations, senior managers must translate market needs for organization members, work closely with customers in order to stay on top of shifting needs, and channel innovation by setting goals, selecting key people, and establishing a few critical limits (Burns and Stalker 1966; Jelinek and Schoonhoven 1990; Quinn 1985; Imai et al. 1985). A cultural context which values change, risk-taking, and learning reinforces the need to take innovative action (Peters 1983; Quinn and Pacquette 1990).

The insights of senior managers must be grounded in the everyday business of the organization and must frame and guide the actions of others in order to achieve effective monitoring and evaluation. However, leadership and culture *per se* do not address the problems of control in large, complex organizations, where managers come to rely on predetermined standards. I suggest that a capacity for situated judgement is a necessary ingredient that must be added to effective leadership and culture if organization-wide monitoring and evaluation are to enable innovation. Relying on situated judgement fills the need for control, but still enables innovation.

'Situated' refers to being engaged in the details of the innovation and its relationship to the organization's value, because these are complex, often tacit issues that must be 'visceralized' to be understood (Brown and Duguid 1991; Dougherty 1992a; Eisenhardt and Zbaracki 1992). 'Judgement' refers to the capability to use insights and heuristics developed from know-how and experience, and to 'appreciation', which Vickers (1965) uses to refer to sizing up unstructured situations and making judgements about the significance of various facts (see also Schon 1983). The capacity for situated judgement gives people throughout the organization the skills for and orientation to evaluating complex, fuzzy problems, making difficult choices, quickly reassessing choices and adjusting as necessary. This capacity restores the balance between determination and emergence, because it enables people to decide how and when to use rules, not to apply them unthinkingly.

Implementing the capacity for situated judgement would also be difficult, because it violates the premises of optimization and precision which underlie many views of management. However, if strong strategic leadership can be combined with several behavioral repertoires, perhaps this capacity can be developed. First, situated judgement is a collective version of Eisenhardt's (1990) high velocity decision-making. She found that to make high velocity decisions, managers used lots of real-time information on the firm's operations and competitive environment, and built on multiple alternatives simultaneously. Eisenhardt also found considerable collaboration, as managers relied on counsellors, continually sought advice, and made decisions using 'consensus with qualification'. Jelinek and Schoonhoven's (1990) description of the 'operations reviews' used in electronics organizations to evaluate multiple innovations also illustrates situated judgement. These organizations have a strong norm that employees will both develop and exercise their ability to judge the viability of innovations. During the actual review process, managers work closely with teams, and everyone studies detailed operational data, focuses relentlessly on problem solving, and uses the reviews as a forum in which to discuss problems and consider alternatives. Situated judgement can be further developed through the recognition of 'communities of practice' with the firm, which emphasize learning in working, and the circulation of knowledge across various boundaries (see Brown and Duguid 1991).

A Capacity for Organization-Wide Commitment to Innovation

The organization studies literature suggests that different understandings of work and of governance are important to commitment to innovation. To paraphrase Burns and Stalker (1966: 121–2), innovative work roles emphasize the contributive nature of special knowledge and expertise, not its differentiation into separate tasks; tasks are understood realistically as part of the business as a whole rather than abstracted out; tasks are adjusted through interaction with others rather than through reconciliation by the next level up; and 'the sanctions which apply to the individual's conduct in his working role derive more from presumed community of interest . . . and less from a contractual relationship between himself and a non-personal corporation' (1966: 121). In addition, decision-making is no longer part of the hierarchy but is shared among autonomous units (Hage 1988). Organizations must learn how to cooperate, even with competitors, because as networks proliferate 'they are not part of the same hierarchy, [so] many of the standard control mechanisms of central headquarters no longer apply' (1988: 58). Negotiation skills will become more important than accounting, loyalty more important than price, and, according to Powell (1990), trust more important than contracts.

While new understandings of work and governance are important, they do not address the underlying problem so clearly articulated by Burns and Stalker – the chronic anxiety induced in employees by the organic organization over what they should be doing. Both managers and employees may gladly settle for a precise, legalistic job definition which fully accounts for people's responsibilities. To break out of the noninnovative mindset and generate the broader sense of commitment required by innovation, I suggest that the capacity for collective accountability needs to permeate the organization as a whole. Collective accountability is similar to the accountability developed in a well-functioning innovation team: since all participants take on some responsibility, the work is not overwhelming for anyone. Collective accountability requires that innovation become legitimate. That

is, instead of following the authority of the boss, relying on rules, and sticking to one's own area of expertise, which are legitimate activities in bureaucratic organizations, the four sets of innovative activities need to be understood as proper and appropriate activities for all employees. Collective accountability also requires that inclusion becomes legitimate, because the sense of inclusion seems essential to people's ability to become more broadly committed.

I find the capacity for collective accountability the most challenging to articulate, because theory does not seem to relate this complex issue to actual practice very well. However, some suggestions for implementation can be made, at least to point to areas for research. First, people must be trained to take on broader roles, by providing them with expertise as well as experience. As well, the organization must be free of harassment and other debilitating power ploys (Kanter 1988). Second, asking people to accept more accountability takes control away from them, so they must be given more control in return or they will slip back into mechanistic roles. Allowing employees operational control over how day-to-day work is done is one element (see Bailyn 1985). Broadening people's participation in the rules of work is another – see Adler's (1993) development of Gouldner's (1954) ideas of the representational bureaucracy, for example. Perhaps more importantly, senior managers need to learn how to include middle and operating managers in their ongoing 'strategic conversations'. As Westley (1990) illustrates, when lower-level managers could participate in setting framing rules for decisions, contribute their own framing rules, and at least participate in dominating some of the conversation, they felt included, energized, and committed.

CONCLUSION

In this chapter, I have argued that we have not adequately addressed the question of how to organize *an organization* for innovation – at least not a large, complex organization. Most of the theories concern projects or simple organizations, while most of the problems now concern the practice of innovation in large organizations that cannot be entirely innovative. By focusing on how to carry out the essential activities of product innovation throughout the organization, I highlighted four tensions that must be balanced. The key problem for the theory of the innovative organization suggested by this analysis is how can complex organizations solve the problems of normal functioning (i.e. efficient operations, reduction of complexity, control, and governance), and still embody the tensions which power innovation?

Many organizations emphasize one side of the balance – the inside, the old, the determined, and the responsible. Interestingly, many organization theories emphasize the other side of the balance – the outside, the new, the emergent, and the free. To fill in this gap and restore balance between the sides, I recommend going back to Burns and Stalker's ideas regarding cultural codes of conduct, or capacities for action (Swidler 1986). From this framework, it seems that fundamentally new capacities for organizational action are necessary if large organizations are to actually become adept with ongoing product innovation. The innovative organization is indeed a new form, a new kind of social system. However, the new capacities suggested above are not alien, because aspects of them have already been widely discussed in the literature.

The primary insight of this chapter is that the many bits of behavior and culture which comprise the innovation literature need to be crystallized into skill sets or systematic patterns of thinking and acting – called capacities – that enable the activities of innovation throughout the organization. I do not argue that the vast literatures on tools and techniques for measuring, managing, strategizing, evaluating, organizing, and so forth are not important, since they are (see Wheelwright and Clark 1992; Griffin and Page 1993). I do argue that organizations cannot simply adopt all these tools and techniques. Rather, they must *also* develop underlying capacities for action which enable people to use these tools effectively for innovation. The capacities sketched out here would enable people throughout complex organizations to work with customers, form teams, solve problems creatively, apply technical potential to market needs, appreciate the relationships among functions and businesses well enough to shift them as necessary, and develop an ongoing sense of how well they are doing.

Much more research is necessary, of course. These proposed capacities may not be fully or correctly articulated, or they may not exist at all. These ideas are 'testable', however, since I predict that organizations that are more adept with product innovation have these capacities. How the capacities relate to different structures, processes, tools, and techniques has been discussed only in passing, and also needs more study. Perhaps most important, how established organizations can develop these capacities needs to be examined. The alternative approach to the 'innovative organization' in this chapter challenges researchers to address the organization as a whole, and the problem of changing non-innovative organizations. These issues shape the theoretical frontier for theory on organizing for innovation.

REFERENCES

Adler, P. (1993) 'The learning bureaucracy: new United Motor Manufacturing, Inc', *Research In Organization Behaviour*, 111–94.

Adler, P. (1995) 'Interdepartmental interdependence and coordination: the case of the design/manufacturing interface', *Organization Science*, 6: 147–67.

Allen, T. (1977) *Managing the Flow of Technology*. Cambridge, MA: MIT Press.

Ancona, D. and Caldwell, D. (1990) 'Beyond boundary spanning: managing external development in product development teams', *High Technology Management Research*, 1: 119–36.

Bacon, G., Beckman, S., Mowery, D. and Wilson, E. (1994) 'Managing product definition in high-technology industries: a pilot study', *California Management Review*, 36: 32–56.

Bailetti, A. and Guild, P. (1991) 'A method for projects seeking to merge technical advancements with potential markets', *R&D Management*, 21: 291–300.

Bailyn, L. (1985) 'Autonomy in the R&D lab', *Human Resource Management*, 24: 129–46.

Bailyn, L. (1993) *Breaking the Mold: Women, Men, and Time in the New Corporate World*. New York: Free Press.

Barley, S. (1986) 'Technology as an occasion for structuring: evidence from observations of CT scanners and the social order of radiology departments', *Administrative Science Quarterly*, 31: 78–109.

Barnard, C. (1938) *The Functions of the Executive*. Cambridge, MA: Harvard University Press.

Bower, J. (1970) *Managing the Resource Allocation Process: a Study of Corporate Planning and Investment*. Boston: Graduate School of Business Administration.

Brock, Z. and MacMillan, I. (1993) *Corporate Venturing: Creating New Businesses within the Firm*. Boston: Harvard Business School Press.

Brown, J. and Duguid, P. (1991) 'Organizational learning and communities of practice', *Organization Science*, 2: 40–57.

Brown, S. and Eisenhardt, K. (1995) 'Product development: past research, present findings, and future directions', *Academy of Management Review*, 20: 343–78.

Burgelman, R. (1983) 'A process model of internal corporate venturing in the diversified major firm', *Administrative Sciences Quarterly*, 28: 223–44.

Burns, T. and Stalker, G.M. (1966) *The Management of Innovation*, 2nd edn. London: Tavistock.

Christensen, C. and Bower, J. (1993) 'Catching the next wave: why good customers make it hard'. Working paper, Harvard Business School.

Clark, K. and Fujimoto, T. (1991) *Product Development Performance*. Boston: Harvard Business School Press.

Cohen, W.M. and Levinthal, D. (1990) 'Absorptive capacity: a new perspective on learning and innovation', *Administrative Science Quarterly*, 35: 128–52.

Cooper, R. (1983) 'A process model for industrial new product development', *IEEE Transactions on Engineering Management*, 30: 2–11.

Cooper, R. and Kleinschmidt, E. (1986) 'An investigation into the new product process: steps, deficiencies, and impact', *Journal of Product Innovation Management*, 3: 71–85.

Cooper, R. and Kleinschmidt, E. (1987) 'Success factors in product innovation', *Industrial Marketing Management*, 16: 215–33.

Crawford, C.M. (1983) *New Products Management*. Homewood, IL: Richard D. Irwin.

Cusumano, M. and Nobeoka, K. (1994) 'Multi-project management: strategy and organization in automobile product development'. Paper presented at ORSA-TIMS, Boston, April.

Daft, R. and Weick, K. (1984) 'Toward a model of organizations as interpretive systems', *Academy of Management Review*, 9: 43–66.

Damanpour, F. (1991) 'Organizational innovation: a meta-analysis of effects of determinants and moderators', *Academy of Management Journal*, 34: 555–90.

Damanpour, F., Szabat, K. and Evan, W. (1989) 'The relationship between types of innovation and organizational performance', *Journal of Management Studies*, 26: 587–602.

Day, D. (1994) 'Raising radicals: different processes for championing innovative corporate ventures', *Organization Science*, 5: 148–72.

Day, G. (1990) *Market Driven Strategy: Processes for Creating Value*. New York: Free Press.

Deshpande, R., Farley, J. and Webster, F. (1992) 'Corporate culture, customer orientation, and innovativeness in Japanese firms: a quadrad analysis'. Report 92-100, Marketing Science Institute.

Deshpande, R. and Zaltman, G. (1982) 'Factors affecting the use of market research information: a path analysis', *Journal of Marketing Research*, 19: 14–31.

Dougherty, D. (1992a) 'A practice-centered model of organizational renewal through product innovation', *Strategic Management Journal*, 13: 77–92.

Dougherty, D. (1992b) 'Interpretative barriers to successful product innovation in large firms', *Organization Science*, 3: 179–202.

Dougherty, D. and Cohen, M. (1995) 'Product innovation in mature firms', in E. Bowman and B. Kogut (eds), *Resdesigning the Firm*. New York: Oxford University Press.

Dougherty D. and Corse, S. (1995) 'When it comes to product innovation, what is so bad about bureaucracy?', *Journal of High Technology Management Research*, 6: 55–76.

Dougherty, D. and Hardy, C. (1995) 'Powering innovation: problems and prospects in large bureaucracies'. Working paper, McGill University Faculty of Management, Montreal.

Dougherty, D. and Heller, T. (1994) 'The illegitimacy of successful product innovation in established firms', *Organization Science*, 5: 200–18.

Downs, G. and Mohr, L. (1976) 'Conceptual issues in the study of innovation', *Administrative Science Quarterly*, 21: 700–14.

Drucker, P. (1954) *The Practice of Management*. New York: Harper and Row.

Eisenhardt, K. (1990) 'Speed and strategic choice: how managers accelerate decision making', *California Management Review*, 32: 1–16.

Eisenhardt, K. and Zbaracki, M. (1992) 'Strategic decision making', *Strategic Management Journal*, 17–38.

Fiol, M. (1991) 'Managing culture as a competitive resource: an identity-based view of sustainable competitive advantage', *Journal of Management*, 17, 191–211.

Freeman, C. (1982) *The Economics of Industrial Innovation*. Cambridge, MA: MIT Press.

Galbraith, J. (1982) 'Designing the innovative organization', *Organizational Dynamics*, Winter: 5–25.

Garud, R. and Kumaraswamy, A. (1995) 'Technological and organizational designs for realizing economies of substitution', *Strategic Management Journal*, 16: 93–111.

Gatignon, H. and Robertson, T. (1985) 'A propositional inventory for new diffusion research', *Journal of Consumer Research*, 11: 849–67.

Gatignon, H. and Xeureb, J.M. (1995) 'Strategic orientation of the firm and new product performance'. Working paper, INSEAD and ESSEC, France.

Geertz, C. (1973) *The Interpretation of Cultures*. New York: Basic Books.

Gersick, C. (1994) 'Pacing strategic change: the case of a new venture', *The Academy of Management Journal*, 37: 9–45.

Gouldner, A. (1954) *Patterns of Industrial Bureaucracy*. New York: Free Press.

Griffin, A. and Hauser, J. (1993) 'The voice of the customer', *Management Science*, 12: 1–27.

Griffin, A. and Page, A. (1993) 'An interim report on measuring product development success and failure', *Journal of Product Innovation Management*, 10: 291–309.

Gupta, A. and Wilemon, D. (1990) 'Accelerating the development of technologically based new products', *California Management Review*, 24–44.

Hage, J. (ed.) (1988) *Futures of Organizations.* Lexington, MA: Lexington Books.

Hardy, C. (1994) *Managing Strategic Action: Mobilizing Change.* London: Sage.

Hedlund, G. and Ridderstrale, J. (1994) 'International development projects – key to competitiveness, impossible, or mismanaged?'. Working paper, Stockholm School of Economics.

Heller, T. (1994) 'Organizing for innovation: optimizing the project–organization relationship and the matter of context'. Paper presented at the Academy of Management Meetings.

Henderson, R. and Clark, K. (1990) 'Architectural innovation: the reconfiguration of existing product technologies and the failure of established firms', *Administrative Science Quarterly,* 35 (March): 9–31.

Henderson, R. and Cockburn, I. (1994) 'Measuring core competence? Evidence from the pharmaceutical industry', *Strategic Management Journal,* 15: 63–84.

Imai, K., Nonaka, I. and Takeuchi, H. (1985) 'Managing product development: how Japanese companies learn and unlearn', in K. Clark, R. Hayes and C. Lorenz (eds), *The Uneasy Alliance: Managing the Productivity–Technology Dilemma.* Boston: Harvard Business School Press. pp. 337–76.

Jelinek, M. and Schoonhoven, C. (1990) *The Innovation Marathon: Lessons from High Technology Firms.* Oxford: Basil Blackwell.

Johne, F.A. and Snelson, P. (1988) 'Success factors in product innovation: a selective review of the literature', *Journal of Product Innovation Management,* 114–128.

Johnson, G. (1988) 'Rethinking incrementalism', *Strategic Management Journal,* 9: 75–91.

Kanter, R.M. (1983) *The Changemasters.* New York: Simon and Schuster.

Kanter, R.M. (1988) 'When a thousand flowers bloom', in *Research in Organization Behaviour.* Greenwich, CT: JAI Press. pp. 169–211.

Kanter, R.M. (1989) 'The new managerial work', *Harvard Business Review,* November–December.

Katz, R. (ed.) (1988) *Managing Professionals in Innovative Organizations: a Collection of Readings.* Cambridge, MA: Ballinger.

Kimberly, J. (1981) 'Managerial innovation', in P. Nystrom and W. Starbuck (eds), *Handbook of Organizational Design,* vol 1. New York: Oxford University Press. pp. 84–104.

Kunda, G. (1992) *Engineering Culture: Control and Commitment in a High-Tech Corporation.* Philadelphia: Temple University Press.

Leonard-Barton, D. (1988) 'Implementation as mutual adaptation of technology and organization', *Research Policy,* 17: 251–67.

Leonard-Barton, D. (1991) 'Inanimate integrators: a block of wood speaks', *Design Management Journal,* 2: 61–7.

Leonard-Barton, D. (1992) 'Core capabilities and core rigidities: a paradox in managing new product

development', *Strategic Management Journal,* 13: 111–26.

Majahan, V. and Wind, J. (1992) 'New product models: practice, shortcomings and desired improvements', *Journal of Product Innovation Management,* 128–39.

March, J. and Simon, H. (1958) *Organizations.* New York: Wiley.

McQuarrie, E. (1993) *Customer Visits: Building a Better Market Focus.* Newbury Park, CA: Sage.

Miller D. (1993) 'The architecture of simplicity', *Academy of Management Review,* 18: 116–39.

Mintzberg, H. (1979) *The Structuring of Organizations.* Englewood Cliffs, NJ: Prentice-Hall.

Mintzberg, H. (1994) *The Rise and Fall of Strategic Planning.* New York: Free Press.

Mintzberg, H. and McHugh, A. (1985) 'Strategy formation in an adhocracy', *Administrative Science Quarterly,* 30: 160–97.

Mintzberg, H. and Westley, F. (1992) 'Cycles of organizational change', *Strategic Management Journal,* 13: 39–60.

Moorman, C. (1995) 'Organizational market information processes: cultural antecedents and new product outcomes', *Journal of Marketing Research,* 22: 318–35.

Myers, S. and Marquis, D. (1969) *Successful Industrial Innovations.* NSF report 69-17.

Narver, J. and Slater, S. (1990) 'The effect of a market orientation on business profitability', *Journal of Marketing,* 54: 20–35.

Nelson, R. and Winter, S. (1982) *An Evolutionary Theory of Economic Change,* Boston: Belkamp Press.

Nonaka, I. (1994) 'A dynamic theory of organizational knowledge creation', *Organization Science,* 5: 14–37.

Nord, W. and Tucker, S. (1987) *Implementing Routine and Radical Innovations.* Lexington, MA: Lexington Books.

Pelz, D. and Andrews, F. (1966) *Scientists in Organizations.* New York: Wiley.

Penrose, E. (1959) *The Theory of Growth of the Firm.* New York: Wiley.

Peters, T. (1983) 'The mythology of innovation, or a skunkworks tale, Part II', *The Stanford Magazine.*

Pettigrew, A. (1992) 'The character and significance of strategy process research', *Strategic Management Journal,* 13: 39–60.

Pfeffer, J. and Salancik, G. (1978) *The External Control of Organizations: A Resource Dependence Perspective.* New York: Harper and Row.

Powell, W. (1990) 'Neither market nor hierarchy: network forms of organization', *Research in Organization Behaviour,* 12: 295–336.

Prahalad, C.K. and Hamel, G. (1990) 'The core competence of the corporation', *Harvard Business Review,* May–June.

Quelsh, J., Farris, P. and Olver, J. (1987) 'The product

management audit: design and survey findings', *The Journal of Consumer Marketing*, 3: 45–58.

Quinn, J.B. (1985) 'Managing innovation: controlled chaos', *Harvard Business Review*, 3: 78–84.

Quinn, J.B. and Pacquette, P. (1990) 'Technology in services: creating organizational revolutions', *Sloan Management Review*, Winter.

Roberts, E. (1988) 'What we've learned: managing invention and innovation', *Research Technology Management*, January–February, 11–29.

Rosenberg, N. (1982) *Inside the Black Box: Technology and Economics*. Cambridge: Cambridge University Press.

Rosenbloom, R. and Abernathy, W. (1982) 'The climate for innovation in industry', *Research Policy*, 11: 209–25.

Rothwell, R. (1977) 'The characteristics of successful innovators and technically progressive firms', *R&D Management*, 7: 191–206.

Rothwell, R., Freeman, C., Horsley, A., Jervis, V.T.P., Robertson, A. and Townsend, J. (1974) 'SAPPHO Updated – Project SAPPHO Phase II', *Research Policy*, 3: 258–91.

Rothwell, R. and Whiston, T. (1990) 'Design, innovation and corporate integration', *R&D Management*, 20: 193–201.

Scarborough, H. and Corbett, J.M (1992) *Technology and Organization*. London: Routledge.

Schein, E. (1990) *Organizational Culture and Leadership*. San Francisco: Jossey-Bass.

Schon, D. (1967) *Technology and Change*. Oxford: Pergamon.

Schon, D. (1983) *The Reflective Practitioner: How Professionals Think in Action*. New York: Basic Books.

Souder, W. (1987) *Managing New Product Innovations*. Lexington, MA: Lexington Press.

Starbuck, W. and Milliken, F. (1988) 'Challenger: finetuning the odds until something breaks', *Journal of Management Studies*, 25: 319–40.

Swidler, A. (1986) 'Culture in action: symbols and strategies', *American Sociological Review*, 51: 273–86.

Takeuchi, H. and Nonaka, I. (1986) 'The new product development game', *Harvard Business Review*, 64: 137–46.

Tushman M. and Anderson, P. (1986) 'Technological discontinuities and organizational environments', *Administrative Science Quarterly*, 31: 439–65.

Tyre, M. and Orlikowski, W. (1994) 'Windows of opportunity: temporal patterns of technological adaptation in organizations', *Organization Science*, 5: 98–118.

Urban, G. and Hauser, J. (1988) *The Design and Marketing of New Products*, 2nd edn. Englewood Cliffs, NJ: Prentice Hall.

Van de Ven, A. (1986) 'Central problems in the management of innovation', *Management Science*, 32: 590–608.

Van de Ven, A. and Polley, D. (1992) 'Learning while innovating', *Organization Science*, 3: 92–116.

Van Maanen, J. and Schein, E. (1979) 'Toward a theory of organizational socialization', *Research in Organizational Behaviour*, 1: 209–64.

Vickers, G. (1965) *The Art of Judgement*. New York: Basic Books.

von Hippel, E. (1986) 'Lead users: a source of novel product concepts', *Management Science*, 32: 791–805.

von Hippel, E. (1994) 'Sticky information and the locus of problem solving: implications for innovation', *Management Science*, 40: 429–39.

Weber, M. (1946) *From Max Weber: Essays in Sociology*, translated, edited, and introduced by H.H. Gerth and C. Wright Mills. New York: Oxford University Press.

Westley, F. (1990) 'Middle managers and strategy: microdynamics of inclusion', *Strategic Management Journal*, 11: 337–51.

Wheelwright, S. and Clark, K. (1992) *Revolutionizing Product Development*. New York: Free Press.

Workman, J. (1993) 'Marketing's limited role in new product development in one computer systems firm', *Journal of Marketing Research*, 30: 405–21.

Yang, E. and Dougherty, D. (1993) 'Product innovation: more than just making a new product', *Creativity and Innovation Management*, 2.

Zahra, S. and Covin, J. (1995) 'Contextual influences on the corporate entrepreneurship–performance relationship: a longitudinal analysis', *Journal of Business Venturing*, 10: 43–58.

2.10

Organizational Learning: Affirming an Oxymoron

KARL E. WEICK AND FRANCES WESTLEY

Organizing and learning are essentially antithetical processes, which means the phrase 'organizational learning' qualifies as an oxymoron. To learn is to disorganize and increase variety. To organize is to forget and reduce variety. In the rush to embrace learning, organizational theorists often overlook this tension, which explains why they are never sure whether learning is something new or simply warmed-over organizational change. Either way, the reluctance to grapple with the antithesis has led to derivative ideas and unrealized potential.

As if this were not enough trouble, there appear to be more reviews of organizational learning than there is substance to review. Most reviews now available are competent summaries of a common body of work (e.g. Dodgson 1993; Levitt and March 1988) and we see no purpose in duplicating once more what they say. Instead, this chapter extends and complements those reviews by taking seriously the hope Cohen and Sproull (1991) voiced for the concept of learning. They described the problem and the hope this way:

> better theories of learning will provide a positive alternative to rational choice assumptions. Much empirical work on both individual behaviour and organizational processes rests on a negative theme of counterevidence to rational actor assumptions (e.g. Kahneman, Slovic, and Tversky 1982; Allison 1971). This produces a peculiar intellectual schizophrenia, with rigorous theories built on rationality assumptions and substantial empirical work denying those assumptions, but not proposing a positive theoretical alternative. . . . It is essential to develop a coherent large scale alternative view, one that

satisfactorily accounts for phenomena such as culture and institutionalization. Learning is the most attractive alternative engine for such theoretical development.

The word 'affirming' in our title is tied directly to Cohen and Sproull's agenda. Existing discussions of organizational learning, especially those linked directly to information processing and indirectly to rational choice assumptions (e.g. Huber 1991), threaten to create once more an idealized sequence which is then shown to be something organizations don't follow. The potential is ripe for more 'negative themes of counterevidence'. And if the basic phenomenon is oxymoronic, then the temptation to unmask should be even stronger. If we're not careful, all we'll have to show for our efforts to grasp learning will be the assertion that, not only are organizations non-rational, they are also non-learners as well.

To consolidate an infrastructure for organizational learning in the face of an inherent oxymoron and temptations to highlight the affinity between learning and rational choice, we do several things in this chapter. First, we explore the need to ground the idea of organizational learning in concepts which connect the theoretical to the experiential. Secondly, we deal with the problem of how to distinguish between individual and organizational learning and why this is necessary. In response to both these issues we argue that theories which focus on cultural aspects of organizations can perhaps provide us with images at once social and experiential with which we can explore and ground a discussion of organizational learning.

Once having determined the context of exploration, we resume our examination of the oxymoron inherent in the concept of organizational learning in three subsystems of culture: language, artifacts and action routines. Lastly, we seek to enlarge our understanding of the set of conditions under which organizational learning is most likely to occur in these cultural subsystems. Consistent with the notion that organizational learning is oxymoronic, we treat occasions which juxtapose order and disorder as social spaces where learning is possible. These juxtapositions include moments of humour, improvisation, and small wins. The juxtaposition of order–disorder found in a joke, for example, provides no less a window to learning than a false alarm of imminent nuclear attack. A concept that is capable of spanning that range of phenomena surely does deserve attention.

In summary, our intent in this chapter is to articulate and affirm the conditions under which moments of learning occur in organizations, while remaining attentive to the many ways in which efforts to preserve the organization undermine such moments.

IMAGES OF ORGANIZATION CONDUCIVE TO LEARNING ANALYSIS

As we hinted in the introduction, the experiential referent for the term 'organizational learning' is elusive. This is so for at least three reasons: imprecise referents for the word 'organization', misinterpretations of the achievement verb (Ryle 1949) 'learning'; and debate about whether learning is an individual or organizational phenomenon. After discussing each of these three issues, we review attempts to describe organizations as cultures, at once repositories and self-designing systems. We do so because such an approach represents a solution to the basic invisibility of organization, and carries with it a tacit theory of learning that suggests the importance of juxtaposing order and disorder.

The lack of an experiential referent for the word 'organization' is discussed by Sandelands and Srivatsan (1993). They argue that organizations cannot be perceived, which means that it is difficult to theorize about them. Organizational scientists have too often resorted therefore to theories based on metaphors, as opposed to experience, hence abandoning the healthy tension between experience and conceptualization which drives the natural sciences.

Sandelands and Srivatsan suggest that there are three ways to deal with the fact that we cannot experience organizations directly. Each of these solutions has a different set of implications for the conceptualization of learning, as it does for the conceptualization of organizations. The experience of organizations can be made a clearer object for theorizing if people use such artifacts as models or cause maps (e.g. Barr et al. 1992; Voyer and Faulkner 1989) that 'condense large tracts of organized activity into a single surveyable region' (1993: 16), or computer simulations (Lant and Mezias 1990) that reproduce the capacities or tendencies of organizations. The experience of organizations can also be made clearer if middle-range concepts are identified which can 'stand in' for the concept of organization, and which more closely correspond to experience, such as those concepts developed through grounded theory (Glaser and Strauss 1967). Finally, the experience of organizations can also be made clearer if non-traditional sensitivities are used to capture qualities of experience that are usually neglected. Thus, 'even though organizations cannot be seen, [perhaps] they can be felt' (1993: 17). Attention to feeling, emotion and affect, and methodologies which employ empathy and artistic apprehension of experience can perhaps allow us to grasp the experience of organization in ways which maintain the healthy tension between theory and experience.

Clearly, if we are not able to conceptualize organizations while maintaining a hold on experience, developing a theory of organizational learning becomes even more difficult. 'Learning', as Sandelands and Drazin (1989) point out, is an achievement verb. This means that the same word 'learning' refers to both an outcome and a process, giving it a circular, tautological sense, and concealing rather than revealing the dynamics of the process and the exact nature of the outcome. Coupled with the lack of empirical referents for organization described above it is not surprising that, indeed, there seems very little of organization in the existing literature on organizational learning. Perhaps in response to the frustrations of grasping the nature of organization, many students of organizational learning such as March and Olsen, Argyris and Schon, and Simon simply sidestep the issue by treating organizational learning as individual learning in an organizational context. And they have no trouble pointing to individuals in a context. Others such as Hedberg, Weick, and Cyert and March argue that organizations learn the same way individuals learn, which means they too can point to individual action as the datum to be explained. When either group feels more emboldened to claim an organizational referent, they are likely to be caught reifying, confusing the map with the territory, or committing the error of hypostatization (treating that which cannot be denoted as if it could).

But such sidestepping of the issues leaves us again with the depressing lack of a truly social science of organization or of learning. Surely, if we in the organizational sciences are going to adopt the concept of learning just as the psychologists seem on the verge of abandoning it, we must proceed with the faith that social learning processes have something to teach us about individual learning, as well as vice versa. So in our effort to contribute to a greater understanding of organizational learning we now focus on 'getting the organization right', by which we mean selecting those images of organizing which are most conducive to grasping the nature of the learning experience. We then turn to vocabularies of learning which seem best designed to grasp the fundamentally 'organized' nature of that experience. Finally we reach the heart of our own argument, the oxymoron inherent in coupling learning with organizing, and its pertinence to understanding the phenomena at hand.

IMAGES OF ORGANIZATION CONDUCIVE TO LEARNING

Those who embed knowledge in culture and its artifacts seem to be in an unusually good position to draw inferences about learning. This is illustrated in Cook and Yanow's (1993) work. They define culture as 'a set of values, beliefs, and feelings, together with the artifacts of their expression and transmission (such as myths, symbols, metaphors, rituals), that are created, inherited, shared, and transmitted within one group of people and that, in part, distinguish that group from others' (1993: 379). Hence learning is inherent in culture. Normann emphasizes this intriguing connection further:

> I would interpret the increasing interest in the concept of culture as really an increasing interest in organizational learning – in understanding and making conscious and effective as much as possible all the learning that has taken place in an organization. To be aware of culture is to increase the likelihood of learning. Only when the basic assumptions, beliefs, and success formulas are made conscious and visible, do they become testable and open to reinforcement or modification. (1985: 231)

The existing literature on organizational learning as cultural process is slim, but instructive. When researchers focus on organizations as cultures, they focus less on cognition and what goes on in individual heads, and more on what goes on in the practices of groups. This is a key shift for students of organizational as opposed to individual learning. For example Argote and

McGrath (1993: 53) observe that organizational learning 'focuses on how organizations acquire knowledge as they gain experience, how this knowledge is embedded in organizations, and what the effect of such changes in knowledge is on later performance'. The key point turns on the word 'embedded'. For Argote and McGrath, it makes a big difference whether knowledge is embedded in work group structures, roles, and procedures, or in individual workers. The difference is that turnover is less disruptive when knowledge is embedded in structures rather than people (see also Corbett and Van Wassenhove 1993). The way investigators handle the question of where and how knowledge is embedded in organizations affects how they will then handle learning.

What all of this comes down to is the conclusion that conceptualizing organizations as cultures makes it easier to talk about learning. It is less of a conceptual leap to treat an organization as a tribe, than to treat it as a brain or a person or computer (Cook and Yanow 1993: 383). Attention to culture as an organizational system helps us to grasp more not only about the nature of organizing, but also about the nature of learning.

Culture is a complex and much debated concept. However, culture has the great advantage over such concepts as organization or even structure in that it is embodied in specific, visible, tangible products of social systems. First and foremost it is embodied in the language, the words, phrases, vocabularies, and expressions which individual groups develop. Secondly, it is embodied in artifacts, the material objects a group produces, from machines to decorative objects, from buildings to paintings. Lastly, and most ephemerally, it is embodied in coordinated action routines, predictable social exchanges from highly stylized rituals to the informal (but socially structured) convention of greetings with acquaintances. Thus culture as theoretical construct meets all three of Sandelands and Srivatsan's criteria for social science of organizations: the invisible (social relations) made manifest in the tangible (artifacts as models); the middle-range concepts which offer experiential reference points; and an option of approaching the phenomena with methodologies which build on empathy and empathize feeling (such as literary analysis, ethnographic analysis and ethnomethodology).

Having underlined the value of an approach to learning which involves treating organizations as cultures, we now look at a body of literature related to a cultural approach: that of treating organizations as repositories and as self-designing systems. We note that, as with culture, these images of organizations are highly conducive to illuminating learning.

Organizations as Repositories

The image of organizations as repositories, as found in Schon's (1983b) work, is conducive to descriptions of learning. A static rendering of the idea of repository is found in the following:

A manager's reflection-in-action also has special features of its own. A manager's professional life is wholly concerned with an organization which is both the stage for his activity and the object of his inquiry. Hence, the phenomena on which he reflects-in-action are the phenomena of organizational life. Organizations, furthermore, are repositories of cumulatively built-up knowledge: principles and maxims of practice, images of mission and identity, facts about the task environment, techniques of operation, stories of past experience which serve as exemplars for future action. When a manager reflects-in-action, he draws on this stock of organizational knowledge, adapting it to some present instance. And he also functions as an agent of organizational learning, extending or restructuring, in his present inquiry, the stock of knowledge which will be available for future inquiry. (1983b: 242)

Schon's image of the learning organization as a stage is also found in Hedberg (1981: 6) who describes the organization as a repertory company, and in Czarniawska-Joerges (1992: 223) who feels that the theatre helps us understand the practical, the symbolic, and the political complexities of organization. Schon's description of the content in the repository (principles, maxims, images, etc.) anticipates those who discuss artifacts as the locus of learning in organizational culture. And Schon's observation that managers who draw on the repository also extend and restructure it, is reminiscent of people like March (1991) who emphasize that organizations not only socialize their members but also learn from them.

Schon portrays the organization in more dynamic images in the following description:

Finally, managers live in an organizational system which may promote or inhibit reflection-in-action. Organizational structures are more or less adaptable to new findings, more or less resistant to new tasks. The behavioral world of the organization, the characteristic pattern of interpersonal relations, is more or less open to reciprocal reflection-in-action – to the surfacing of negative information, the working out of conflicting views, and the public airing of organizational dilemmas. Insofar as organizational structure and behavioral world condition organizational inquiry, they make up what I will call the 'learning system' of the organization. (1983b: 242)

Here we get a clearer sense of the dimensions along which organizational structures can vary in ways that affect individual learning.

Organizations as Self-Designing Systems

The image of organizations as self-designing systems blends the image of repository with that of culture, as is seen in this description:

Self-designing knowledge work systems are thinking and learning organizations that have well-developed self-diagnostic capacities, allowing them to question their governing assumptions and reassess their relationship to changing environmental demands. . . . Knowledge work organizations 'learn how to learn' by maintaining processes that critically examine key assumptions, beliefs, tasks, decisions, and structural issues. (Purser and Pasmore 1992: 55)

Further discussion of these systems is found in Eccles and Crane (1988), Hedberg et al. (1976), Weick (1977), and Weick and Berlinger (1989). The suitability of self-designing systems for learning is evident in Metcalfe's observation that, in a self-designing organization, 'routine interaction with the task environment should generate information about ways to improve performance' (1981: 503). Notice that, up to now, routines have been treated as collective activities that encode rather than generate improvements. Self-designing organizations use routines consisting of small continuous changes in the interest of frequent, adaptive updating rather than less frequent convulsing and crisis.

Continuous updating results from a combination of continuous redesign, underspecified structures, reduced information filtering, intentional imbalance, and cultivation of doubt. Continuous redesign consists of discarding 'even adequate old methods in order to try new ones, looking upon each development as an experiment that suggests new experiments' (Hedberg et al. 1976: 45). As Torbert (1987) suggests, self-designing systems gain their identity from their capacity to restructure. Underspecification of structure encourages both heightened sensitivity to local conditions and continuous mutual adjustment as local learnings keep changing among interdependent individuals. Self-designing systems intentionally try to undermine the seduction of Miller's (1993) architecture of simplicity by creating structures that do less filtering and less uncertainty absorption, by replacing specialists with generalists so that specialist labels do not dominate perception, and by flattening hierarchies to put more people closer to the action. Intentional imbalances, instituted in the belief that low contentment sharpens perception, are a signature of such systems: 'Ambiguous authority structures, unclear objectives, and contradictory assignments of responsibility can legitimize controversies and challenge traditions. . . . Incoherence and indecision can foster exploration, self-evaluation, and learning. Redundant task allocation can provide experimental replications and partial incongruities can diversify portfolios of activities' (Hedberg et al. 1976: 45).

Self-designing systems are also characterized by the institutionalization of doubt (Weick 1979). If organizations are repositories, they are flawed sources of guidance, both because storage is imperfect and because retrieval is an act of reconstruction. Memory is imperfect twice over, which is bad enough. Even worse, organizations face a chronically 'novel present'. To rely on a repository of built-up knowledge is to rely on approximations rather than certainties. To underscore the approximate character of prior learning, self-designing systems apply lessons of the past while simultaneously questioning their relevance.

As culture is explicated, people see more clearly the learning that has already taken place. Once they see past learning more clearly, they are in a better position to retest, modify, and/or reaffirm it. A good example of this sequence of culture explication and learning occurred when the Strategic Air Command under General Chain abandoned its motto 'peace is our profession' and replaced it with the motto 'war is our profession: peace is our product'. This culture shift away from a culture of guardians to a culture of warriors emphasized the greater necessity to maximize military power as a deterrent, and also the likelihood that safety might be traded off for readiness and risk (Sagan 1993: 271–2). Both shifts alarmed key stakeholders. The moment General Chain was replaced by a new commander (General Butler), the old motto was reinstated, peace once more became SAC's profession, the warriors became a bit less conspicuous, and the stakeholders became a bit less anxious.

Thus, we come full circle back to culture. And we complete the circle with a final description of organizing from Schon that incorporates repositories, self-design, culture, and the collective. To conceptualize an organization so that its manner of learning is more apparent, one can begin by asserting that the organization

> *acts* when individual members, functioning as agents of the collectivity, carry out their parts of the larger task system. Like the individual craftsman, the collective has a theory-in-use implicit in the norms, strategies, and assumptions that govern its regular patterns of task performance. As in his case, their theory-in-use may be inferred from the evidence of intelligent action, especially from the detection and correction of errors. But in their case, intelligent action depends on a continuing mutual adjustment of individual behaviours, one to another. Their organizing depends, in turn, on each person's image of the

larger system. In this sense, the organization exists in its members' heads. But the members also have access to external maps, memories, and programs, which they must continually complete through mutually adjusted actions. (Schon 1983a: 118)

Schon's description lends itself to an analysis of learning. His theory-in-use equates with cultural know-how; theories implicit in norms equate with beliefs embedded in artifacts; intelligent action equates with heedful conduct; correction and detection of error equate with feedback; mutual adjustment equates with interaction that is both artifactual and face to face; images of the larger system equate with culture; the organization in the head equates with individual learning in an organizational context; and external maps, memories and programs equate with routines, repositories, and institutions. The investigator whose thinking about organization is primed with these images is then likely to frame learning not only in ways that are truly organizational, but also in ways that recognize the tension between learning and organizing. For in both the notions of organizations as repositories and of organizations as self-designing systems there is the explicit notion of juxtaposition, the individual against the organization, the present against the past, the new against the routine. And so, in our images of organization conducive to learning, we find that learning appears to be about repunctuating the continuous experience of the organization. To make this repunctuation even a possibility, organization must be reduced and doubt and curiosity must be cultivated. In the section which follows we continue our exploration of organizational learning, viewed in the context of culture, i.e. in the context of language, artifacts and action routines. Here our emphasis shifts, however, to the oxymoron inherent in the concept.

LEARNING AND ORGANIZING: THE OXYMORON WRIT LARGE

The relationship between learning and organizing is inherently uncomfortable, a tension rather than a compatibility. This tension has been represented in the literature as a choice between structural forms. Certain forms, such as self-designing organizations or adhocracies, are, as we have noted, particularly good at adapting to changing environments and at innovating in response to environmental demands. In terms of creativity or original thinking, this seems to be a recommended form, associated with high creativity.

Other forms, such as bureaucracies, are dedicated to efficiencies, reaping the benefits of learning curves. Bureaucracy is associated with more mechanical division of labour, more rigid chain of command, clearcut distinctions and technical rationality, qualities which are designed to repress or forget confusing or contradictory qualities.

This dichotomy suggests that self-designing organizations learn, while bureaucracies organize. However, on closer examination, the picture seems more complex. March (1991) suggests that each form learns, but the learning is of a different order. Self-designing organizations have a tendency to explore, bureaucracies to exploit. Both are a form of learning and the most resilient organizations of either form do both. The challenge is not to choose between these structures, but rather to strike a balance:

> In studies of organizational learning, the problem of balancing exploration and exploitation is exhibited in distinctions made between refinement of an existing technology and invention of a new one. . . . It is clear that exploration of new alternatives reduces the speed with which skills at existing ones are improved. It is also clear that improvements in competence at existing procedures make experimentation with others less attractive. . . . Finding an appropriate balance is made particularly difficult by the fact that the same issues occur at levels of a nested system – at the individual level, the organizational level, and the social level.

Balance is important because it is evident that either form, taken to its extreme, results in a paralysed organization, unable either to learn or to act. For example, while organizations seem to learn when they exploit routines and develop functioning 'communities of practice' (Brown and Duguid 1991), after a certain point such specialization results in a simplicity which renders the organization so rigid, and so incapable of new response, that it is prone to failure and even death (March 1991; Miller 1993), even in slowly changing environments. On the other hand, while looser, more chaotic forms seem good designs in creating alignment, clearly an important part of organizational learning (Fiol and Lyles 1985), too much alignment can also result in a loss of integrity and hence of an organization's capacity to learn. This would appear to be associated with the system theorists' conception of the totally open system, one in which the boundaries become so permeable as to lose all definition.

So it would appear that learning is associated with both exploitation and exploration, with both establishing routines and accepting disruptive, non-routine behaviour in the interests of alignment. Too much of either ultimately results in the destruction of the system. This suggests that the problem of learning should be viewed not as a choice between exploitation at the expense of exploration, or exploration at the expense of exploitation, but rather as an optimal juxtaposition of the two. Another way of looking at the problem which ties learning back to organizing is that the optimal learning point, whether for the individual or the organization, is in circumstances when order and disorder are juxtaposed, or exist simultaneously. Such moments represent the intersection of double-loop learning (discovery, exploration, proactive learning, revolutionary learning, frame breaking) and single-loop learning (exploitation, adaptation, habit formation, deviation reduction, reactive learning, evolutionary learning). The optimal juxtaposition between order and disorder is created not through alternation between the two but through the intimate and continuing connection between the two.

Exploitation and Exploration in Cultural Systems

Existing definitions of organizational learning tend to focus either on learning as exploitative (Simon 1991: 125) or on learning as exploration (Buckley 1968). For a definitional option that begins to combine themes of exploration and exploitation we are brought again to culture and the related concepts of repository and self-designing systems. Recall Normann's (1985) earlier observation that, as culture is explicated, people see more clearly the learning that has already taken place. Normann (1985: 230) defines culture as 'the institutionalized language and values of an organization, together with their symbolic and structural manifestations'. Culture is important to learning because it acts 'as a symbol and storage of past learning', and it works as an instrument to communicate this learning throughout the organization.

If we combine these images of culture with images of exploration and exploitation, we begin to get a definition that sounds like this: organizational learning is 'the acquiring, sustaining, and changing, through collective actions, of the meanings embedded in the organization's cultural artifacts' (Cook and Yanow 1993: 384). Cook and Yanow avoid the blind spots of 'learning' as an achievement verb when they insist that observers pay attention to the acquiring, sustaining, and changing of intersubjective meanings. And they also avoid the non-experiential references to whole organizations when they use artifactual vehicles that embody collective know-how as their referent.

Cook and Yanow's definition focuses on intersubjective meanings rather than knowledge or information or behaviour as the outcome of interest. Notice, however, that the meanings that are learned are not free-standing, existential, philosophical profundities. Far from it. They are embedded in cultural artifacts, which means the meanings likely represent a tacit synthesis of knowledge, information, and behaviour. Furthermore, the definition lends itself to conceptualization of organizational learning as a capacity possessed not only by individual members, but by the aggregate itself. Language, action routines and material artifacts are both the means to produce and share meanings and the resource from which further cultural artifacts are created.

With these fundamentals and definitions in hand, we can now afford to look more closely at three cultural subsystems mentioned earlier – those of language, material artifacts and action routines – in search of a more experientially based understanding of the oxymoron of organizational learning. In each case, we discover that learning seems to be as much about reaffirmation, conservation, complication, efficacy, appreciation, community, and sometimes even self-destruction, as it is about change and improvement. Learning is not a synonym for change, and here we get our first glimpse of why that is so.

Language and Learning

When we approach the task of examining the tension between learning and organizing, we cannot avoid looking at the role of language. As the central cultural system of any social organizing, language is vital to both learning and organizing. To learn is to use language, to communicate, both at the interpersonal and at the intrapersonal level. At the intrapersonal level, language allows for the reflection which, along with action or behaviour, is a critical part of learning as described by most organizational theorists (Fiol and Lyles 1985). Children, given the opportunity to move, will develop motor skills without the benefit of human interaction (as in the case of 'feral' children), but their ability to learn is fundamentally inhibited by failure to acquire language. Skilled athletes exhibit what Gardner (1983) has called 'physical intelligence'; it would appear that their bodies 'learn' without conscious, analytic reflection. However, the universal phenomenon of the coach is evidence that there are limits to the purely physical action-based learning, even among gifted athletes. At a certain point the coach assumes the role of reflection *vis-à-vis* the action of the athlete. So even among athletes, where much learning is physical, communication at the interpersonal and intrapersonal levels has an important place.

This becomes even more critical in team sports. Here the coach must provide the structure through which the actions of individual actors become the game of the team, and this is done through language. It is true that this metastructure becomes embedded in 'plays' which technically can be carried out wordlessly. The coach, however, is still critical to learning, as it is the coach who orchestrates how the plays are sequenced in each game and from one game to the next.

At the primary level then, all learning occurs through social interaction. Language is both the tool and the repository of learning. It is the critical tool for reflection at both the interpersonal and intrapersonal levels. And language is a social phenomenon. Stated differently, learning is embedded in relationships or relating. By this we mean that learning is not an inherent property of an individual or of an organization, but rather resides in the quality and the nature of the relationship between levels of consciousness within the individual, between individuals, and between the organization and the environment. Thus learning at the individual level (intrapersonal) and at the organizational level (interpersonal or interorganizational) evolves through a continual process of mutual adjustment.

Language has the interesting property that it is as closely linked to forgetting as it is to learning. Koestler (1964), Freud (1905), Levi-Strauss (1963), and Leach (1972) all note that the human ability to create and use language allows finer distinctions to be made in the overall pattern of experience. Through the naming of things, however, we are not only seeing, we are suppressing awareness in order to distinguish one thing from another. The best example of this is perhaps the colour spectrum. In reality the colour spectrum represents a continuum. In order to differentiate red from orange from yellow, however, it is necessary 'not to see' the part of the spectrum which joins red to orange (Leach 1970). As a given culture places greater importance on certain parts of experience than others, words proliferate to distinguish ever greater nuances. The multiple words which Eskimos use to describe snow is often cited as an example. The irony is however that while the Eskimos seem to have a richer experience of snow than the average non-Eskimo, and a perception of greater variety, they must also work harder at not seeing, at ignoring the anomalies that threaten to blend one category with another. While they therefore see more, they must simultaneously ignore more as well. For the average non-Eskimo snow is a bland continuum, which may be sensed or felt, but is rarely explored or exploited.

And here we get our first intimation of how in language as a cultural system we may see the manifestations of exploitative or explorative learning. When we speak of articulating ideas in an organizational context, we refer to this movement from vague, unspecified sensing to increasing precision of language (highly technical, scientific or logical language being the most precise). Paradoxically we lose some awareness as we increase variety and specificity but such loss is necessary to carry on the partitioning and labelling that we conceive of as rational or logical thinking. As Bateson (1972) points out, we can deal with only a fragment of the mind's totality at any given moment. In fact, to think rationally it is necessary to isolate a figure and then ignore the background. This is in no way automatic and often requires great 'concentration'.

> All thought involves a certain mental tension. In controlled and rational thought this takes on the form of attention which serves two distinct functions. On the one hand the mind takes on a certain imperviousness, a 'hide' which protects it from irrelevant stimuli. This is called the surface tension. On the other hand, the act of attending also serves to direct the mind along certain definite channels. When a thinking process continues organized and controlled in this manner and progresses towards an end, it is termed rational. (Munro 1951: 176)

So rational, logical thinking involves a closing, a protecting of the figure from disruption by irrelevant material, be it thoughts or stimuli, through the forging and selection of words which increase variety and precision at the expense of experience. This, of course, is the linguistic equivalent of exploitative learning. We progress through rational thought processes to logical conclusions, which one assumes are different and technically superior to the vague, unformed hunches which may have triggered the process of articulation. We think of Weber's (1978) notion of the momentum of processes of technical rationality and the 'disenchantment' of the world which accompanies this movement.

However, this kind of learning might be seen as 'normal science' or single-loop learning. Creativity or original thinking seems to involve exactly opposite processes. Instead of protecting the figure from disruption, 'insight' involves the disruption of these same controlled thinking processes. According to Koestler, in the 'flash of insight' which characterizes the creative act (and which he terms bi-association), the mind 'connects previously unconnected matrices [contexts] of experience, shows a familiar situation or even in a new light and elicits a new response to it' (1964: 659). Just as conscious thought involves a

movement from generalization to specificity, creative thought 'regresses' to find its source in the 'phylogenetically and ontologically older underground layers of the mind. He (the creator) can only reach them through a regression to earlier, more primitive, less specialized levels of mentation, through a *reculer pour mieux sauter*' (1964: 659). Here we retreat from language itself, to a realm of experience beyond words.

Learning is intimately connected to the dynamics of communication and to the tension between levels of consciousness. To 'see' we must 'not see', but to learn, i.e. to see more, we must retrieve what we deliberately forgot. To communicate what we have seen anew, we must again resort to words, to logics of communication, to semantics, and so 'forget' again in the interest of precision. If we forget too much or fail to allow the unseen to disrupt the order, Koestler argues, we become trapped in habit, repetitiveness, eventually dogmatism. Learning requires the ability both to see and not to see, to name and not to name, to organize our thinking and to disorganize it.

Learning and Artifacts

Organizational identity is what members perceive as central, enduring, and unique or distinctive about their organization and believe others share as well (Dutton and Penner 1993: 95; Albert and Whetten 1985). It 'is a subset of the collective beliefs that comprise an organization's culture' (Dutton and Penner 1993: 95), and identity is created and distributed by the cultural system. Identity is described by Ring and Van de Ven (1994: 100) as an image that aids sensemaking: 'By projecting itself onto its environment, organization develops a self-referential appreciation of its own identity, which in turn, permits the organization to act in relation to its environment.' Organizations learn something about their core attributes when they see what they can and cannot enact. And more often than not, for an organization, that identity is embodied by a tangible symbol, be it logo or product. To understand the oxymoron of organizational learning we may look at efforts to juxtapose innovation and preservation at the level of the material artifacts themselves.

Cook and Yanow (1993) have provided us with an excellent example of such a juxtaposition in their study of the Powell flutemaking workshop. At Powell, people make an effort to maintain unique core patterns of activity while socializing new craftsmen and marketing to customers who have changing needs. These conflicting pulls toward innovation and preservation converged in 1974 when Albert Cooper, an independent English flutemaker, developed a new scale (a new configuration of tone holes in a flute) that flute players strongly preferred. This created a dilemma at Powell because their identity as maker of 'the best flutes in the world' was tied in part to the fact that the 'best' flute had a Powell scale that 'had been developed by Mr Powell himself and was felt to be an intimate part of the Powell flute' (1993: 382). To adopt the Cooper scale would amount to changing the identity of the company. The dilemma, recast as a learning issue, was: can Powell build a Powell flute based on a Cooper scale and still have it be a Powell flute?

To see if they could make something different without becoming a different company, the Powell craftsmen made a prototype Powell flute with a Cooper scale. Cook and Yanow catch several subtleties in this prototyping. In building the prototype, craftsmen did *not* test the Cooper scale, because that had already been done. Instead,

> making the prototype enabled Powell, almost cere-monially, to go through the motions of making a Cooper-scale Powell flute and in doing so, to assure itself that the flute and the company's style would be preserved through the Cooper innovation. Powell was not so much learning a new technology as learning – collectively, as an organization – how to maintain its identity in the face of a new undertaking. (1993: 383)

It was decided to offer the Cooper scale as an option. Unfortunately, Cook and Yanow do not unpack this decision so we are left to speculate about the exact process by which people were reassured that innovation would not erode identity. Virtually all customers chose the Cooper scale option once it was offered, yet the quality, feel, and style of Powell flutes was maintained. Cook and Yanow interpret that outcome this way: 'At root, Powell adopted a new technology to maintain and reaffirm its own self-image as makers of "the best" – that is, to sustain what the group felt, believed, and valued' (1993: 383). Learning did not change the organization and that is the measure of its success. People underwent a change, yet were able to 'maintain', 'reaffirm', and 'sustain' their feelings, beliefs, and values. If they had any doubts about whether there really was a distinctive Powell flute, this incident laid them to rest.

The larger point regarding moments of learning in organizations is that they may involve the basic oxymoron writ small. In moments of organizational learning, people may want to take on a new situation but not a new identity (1993: 385). Learning may be most likely to occur when situations are explored but

identities are exploited. People learn how to innovate, but they also learn how to reaccomplish their identity amidst a new set of threats.

When organizations fail to innovate, this may signify an inability to decouple innovation from identity. This could take one of two forms. First, an inability to decouple identity from innovation could lead to no innovation at all. The firm is unwilling to become something else. Second, the same inability could be resolved in favour of innovation rather than identity, meaning that a firm has as many identities as it has innovations: in other words, no identity at all. The Powell flutemakers show that there is a third option, namely, 'ambivalence as the optimal com-promise'. They juxtapose order and disorder, exploration and exploitation, first- and second-order learning, and incremental and transforma-tional change. In doing so, they affirm an oxymoron and grow.

Learning and Action Routines

The image of 'a moment in a process' is Mary Parker Follett's (1924). It appears in the context of her discussion of the ways in which stimulus–response (SR) language can mislead:

> The activity of the individual is only in a certain sense caused by the stimulus of the situation because that activity is itself helping to produce the situation which causes the activity of the individual. In other words behaviour is a relating not of 'subject' and 'object' as such, but of two activities. . . . Stimulus is not cause and response the effect. Some writers, while speaking otherwise accurately of the behav-iour process, yet use the word result – the result of the process – whereas there is no result *of* process but only a moment *in* process. . . . On the social level, cause and effect are ways of describing certain moments in the situation when we look at those moments apart from the total process. (1924: 60–1)

Since most ideas about learning, at least in their earliest form, contained some variant of SR language, more recent extensions may still understate the degree to which learning occurs amidst flows and cycles where responding co-defines the conditions for its own unfolding.

Efforts to capture patterns, cycles, and flows of organizational life more richly are found in the work of people like Gersick (1988), Cowan (1993), and Cohen et al. (1972). Learning in this context involves a different vocabulary. Learn-ing amidst flows and cycles is a matter of alignment, timing, opportunities that open and then close, patterns that form and dissolve, entrainment, synchronicity, coincidence, luck, chance, rhythms of variation (Cowan), unfold-ing, passages, and recapitulation. Learning is not about the artificial beginnings of stimulation that end in a response. Instead, it is about punctuation, forgetting, and not-seeing portions of the flow in order to justify naming, categorizing, and protecting the remaining portions that are seen. Learning as a moment in a process draws our attention to learning as it may be seen in action routines.

If we view learning as a mindful moment in action routines when order and disorder are juxtaposed, then we look for occasions when this might occur and we count the frequency of such occasions. For example, a survivable error from which a system gets information is a learning moment. A near-miss between two aircraft flying on the same course (Tamuz 1988) mixes the order of a safe separation with the disorder of a non-fatal loss of this separation. Literally, a moment is created when the air traffic system can see what it has forgotten. But the moment is fleeting. The opportunity opens and then closes swiftly as those involved get their accounts in order. As Cohen and Gooch put it,

in the chaos of the battlefield there is the tendency of all ranks to combine and recast the story of their achievements into a shape which shall satisfy the susceptibilities of national and regimental vainglory. . . . On the actual day of battle naked truths may be picked up for the asking; by the following morning they have already begun to get into their uniforms. (1990: 44)

It is not just efforts to deflect blame that make learning moments fleeting. The very fact that there is evidence of both order and disorder thwarts conclusion drawing.

Every time a pilot avoids a collision, the event provides evidence both for the threat and for its irrelevance. It is not clear whether the learning should emphasize how close the organization came to disaster, thus the reality of danger in the guise of safety, or the fact that disaster was avoided, thus the reality of safety in the guise of danger. (March et al. 1991: 10)

If the moment is interpreted as safety in the guise of danger, then learning should be diminished because 'more thorough investigations, more accurate reporting, deeper imagination, and greater sharing of information' are all discouraged (Sagan 1993: 247). Even if it is decided later, during more formal inquiry, to reverse the interpretation, qualities of the original moment such as the preconditions that led up to it will be underdeveloped. Close inspection of the last twenty minutes before a near-miss overlooks the possibility that this is simply the last distraction set in motion much earlier, much farther away (e.g. an unresolved quarrel).

Survivable errors are prototypes of moments which juxtapose order and disorder, moments which partially disorganize the organized, and partially dismantle routines. The errors testify to the entropy that gnaws constantly at organization. The survival testifies that the entropy can be controlled. The fact that errors broke through previous controls, however, signifies the need to rework them. This is the opportunity that opens and closes abruptly. How organizations respond to such moments affects their learning.

So far we have talked most about flows and their effects on learning. More needs to be said about cycles. Adler and Cole's (1993) comparison of learning at NUMMI and Volvo-Uddevalla automobile manufacturing plants provides insight into cycles and learning. Although both plants involve labour-intensive production of relatively standardized products, the cycles are radically different. At NUMMI, teams of four or five workers perform a work cycle that is well documented in which each member has a cycle lasting about sixty seconds. The system 'is based on specialized work tasks supplemented by modest doses of job rotation and great discipline in the definition and implementation of detailed work procedures' (1993: 85). At Uddevalla, teams of ten workers perform a work cycle that is less well documented and that lasts about two hours. These greatly lengthened work cycles represent 'a return to craftlike work forms that give teams substantial latitude in how they perform their tasks and authority over what have traditionally been higher-level management decisions' (1993: 85).

Adler and Cole argue that these differences in documentation and cycle length create a distinct learning advantage for NUMMI. NUMMI is better able to identify problems in detail, define improvements, implement improvements, share improvement opportunities, and continue to improve. These learning advantages are seen to occur because NUMMI workers have a more explicit idea of what they think they already know, which facilitates re-examination. And with shorter cycles, it is easier to spot changes that may correct unwanted deviations.

It is much more difficult to learn collectively at Volvo. Individuals improve their individual skills, but not mutual adjustment. There are few shared views of what interdependencies are in place. And, when deviations occur, there are two hours' worth of activities that potentially may be their source. Learning at Volvo is a textbook case of individual learning in an organizational context, whereas NUMMI exemplifies organizational learning (1993: 92).

These seemingly straightforward findings are not as simple as they appear. We see in them echoes of several earlier themes. For example, the shorter, more precise learning cycles at NUMMI are a good example of exploitative learning. Learning which depends upon having 'a more explicit idea of what they think they already know, which facilitates reexamination . . . [and corrects] unwanted deviations' would seem to be learning highly dependent on precise articulation and exploitation of the underlying system. In contrast, the longer cycles in Volvo could allow for greater exploration. The shorter cycles at NUMMI and the more rigid procedures make it less likely that workers will 'explore' alternatives together. We should ask not only how the length of cycles impacts on learning, but perhaps when those fleeting learning opportunities occur in short cycles? in long cycles?

Furthermore, if we re-examine the Powell flutemakers in this context, they appear to have the best of both worlds. Their work has longer cycles and more craftwork than NUMMI and more group learning and more structure than Uddevalla. The level of documentation at Powell is less than at NUMMI and greater than at Uddevalla since it is carried indirectly by artifacts rather than directly by detailed methods and standards. As a result, workers at Powell have more flexibility and more personal learning opportunities than those at NUMMI, more structure and more cross-individual learning opportunities than those at Uddevalla. Powell flutemakers have broader knowledge than workers at NUMMI, deeper knowledge than those of Uddevalla. In short, Powell has more moments of juxtaposition.

Alder and Cole's findings allow us to make a point about culture and learning. The NUMMI edge could disappear if more attention were paid to the culture at Uddevalla. Recall that there was no detailed documentation available to workers at Uddevalla that 'described how to perform each work task and [specified] how long it should take' (1993: 89). But neither was such documentation available at Powell. A representative worker at Uddevalla said, 'You don't really need all that detail because you feel it when the task isn't going right; you can feel the sticking points yourself' (1993: 89). That too is no different from Powell. Then what's different? Either the culture at Volvo was not coincident with know-how as it was at Powell, or it was, but Adler and Cole missed it because of their prior assumption that 'without a well documented, standardized process, it is hard to imagine how these people could have spotted improvement opportunities or shared them across teams. You cannot sustain continual improvement in the production of products as standardized as automobiles without clear and detailed methods and standards' (1993: 89).

It may be hard for Adler and Cole to imagine how opportunities can be spotted and shared without formal documentation, but not for Cook and Yanow who argue that opportunities can be felt. The difference is that Cook and Yanow look for more artifacts of culture and therefore spot more vehicles for learning than simply those of a well-documented process. Furthermore, Cook and Yanow are attentive to identity. If workers at Uddevalla truly are slow learners, which is not proven simply by the existence of inferior documentation, they may fear that too much will change too fast if they learn too well. Such may be the Achilles heel in a self-managed team where intense interactions create vivid identities that threaten to vanish with any change whatsoever.

In summary, what we wish to emphasize here is that in looking more closely at the workings of cultural systems such as language, material artifacts and action routines we can better apprehend learning and its tension with organizing. That all three cultural systems serve to reinforce each other in situations where exploitative learning is high (as in the case of NUMMI) should not surprise us. Neither should it surprise us that conflict between the three cultural systems (as was the case at Uddevalla, where action routines did not seem to be supported by a similarly patterned linguistic protocol) may produce the ideal context for exploration. For explorative learning feeds on the idiosyncratic, the unexpected, the serendipitous and atrophies in the face of tight and centralized control.

FACILITATORS OF ORGANIZATIONAL LEARNING

Improbable though learning may be in the context of imperatives towards order associated with organizing, there are moments when order is juxtaposed with disorder and people get a glimpse of the forgotten and the unseen. These are moments when learning is possible. But these are also moments that are fleeting and short-lived. Recall the 'naked truths of battle' that swiftly get back into their uniforms the next day. If moments of balance between exploration and exploitation are transient, then researchers need to look at uncommon, often inconspicuous events to spot learning. And practitioners need to be less enamoured with large-scale training programs and campaigns of transformation and more alert to places and moments where canons and dogma become suspect.

Learning moments and spaces tend not to be obvious precisely because they retain vestiges of order, routine, and expected exploitation. They are *almost* business as usual. What keeps them from being nothing but business as usual is some quirk of language embodied in a joke, or an improvised routine, or a misunderstood instruction leading to a near-miss, or a speculation that serves as an irreverent gloss on institutionalized practice. The irreverent gloss uncovers forgotten meanings, hints at flaws or limits in current practice, redirects thought toward new channels, or detects pervious areas in the impervious 'hide' of controlled thinking (recall Bateson's image of rational thought). This is not simply quantum change or brute exploration or sudden second-order learning. Those are possible, of course – but relatively rare. More common and more crucial in the determination of learning over the long haul are *approximations* to quantum change, approximations in the sense that their disorder is nested in and balanced by orderly ongoing organized practice. The limits of that ongoing practice become visible precisely because that very same ongoing practice reveals some of its own flaws. Flawed practices that generate self-criticism can't be all that flawed . . . and yet they are. That is the complex message implicit in the juxtaposition of order and disorder that precedes learning. That is the complex message conveyed by humour, improvisation, and small wins, all of which represent small moments of learning with large consequences. We conclude this chapter with brief discussions of all three.

Humour as a Moment of Learning

Both Salman Rushdie (1992) and Michael Cole (1990) have recently discussed the relation between power and memory in the context of Milan Kundera's (1981) book *The Book of Laughter and Forgetting*. Cole (1990: vii), citing efforts by the Chinese government to deny that anyone was killed in Tienanmen Square, argues that the increasing incidence of socially organized forgetting seems to illustrate George Orwell's assertion that 'He who controls the past controls the future. He who controls the present controls the past.' Rushdie argues, therefore, that 'Redescribing a world is the necessary first step to changing it' (1992: 14).

This perspective implies that power, particularly absolute power, presents a major impediment to learning, linked as it is to rigid taboos, autocracy, impression management, sycophancy, and hubris. What the title of Kundera's book suggests is that in this 'struggle against forgetting', humour is an invaluable tool.

But how does humour provide learning or, as we have elaborated the concept above, how does humour provide identity maintenance, moments in a process, and in what way does it provide the juxtaposition of action and reflection, emotion and rationality, order and disorder in the kind of release of energy which we have categorized as 'learning as coincident with action'?

A sense of humour, according to Robertson Davies (1958), is 'a sense of anarchy, a sense of chaos'. On a purely linguistic level, studies of the joke form have indicated that it is precisely designed to name the unnamed, confuse sense with non-sense, and create disorder of our ordered thought systems.

Bateson (1972) lumps humour with art and madness under the general heading of creativity. Specifically, he describes the use of humour as a completed circuit involving a dissolution and re-establishment of the figure–ground relationship:

> in the first phase of telling a joke, the information content is on the surface, the other content types in various forms are implicit in the background. When the point of the joke is reached, suddenly this background material is brought into attention and a paradox or something like it is touched off. A circuit of contradictory notions is completed.

Koestler uses humour as the example *par excellence* of the creative act on which he based his description of other areas of creativity. The entire spectrum of creativity he divides into three: humour, discovery, and art. All three are based on the bisociation of two matrices and result in either 'a collision ending in laughter, a fusion in a new intellectual experience, or a confrontation in an aesthetic experience' (1964: 45). But, unlike art or discovery, humour is not constructive–destructive. Rather, it is a tolerated and permitted expression of the unconscious, neither a true merging, nor a suspension of consciousness. In this sense, it meets our criteria for juxtaposition.

Freud (1905) noted that jokes involve taking mental shortcuts with words or ideas: condensing, unifying, modifying to create 'double meanings'. In the process we name the unnamed and connect things previously kept separate. As Freud put it, 'Joking is the disguised priest who weds every couple . . . he likes best to wed couples whose union their relatives frown upon' (1905: 11). Freud concluded that this 'play with words' was in fact a regression to a preverbal state and that herein lay the source of our pleasure in humour. Children are not restrained by the rules of grammar. The child is permitted to talk 'non-sense.' Nevertheless, the nonsense of the joke is not the nonsense of the child. In order for the joke to be appreciated, in order for it to be intelligible, it must take a specific form. A joke, as every child must learn, is culturally defined, following a definite pattern (Sils 1972).

It is this pattern which protects and permits the regression, the release of unconscious sense to the conscious mind. The laugh, then, is one of combined relief and pleasure. The experience is that of a child who escapes unpunished with forbidden behaviour. The joke form simultaneously plays with order and maintains it. We momentarily escape 'this strict, untiring, troublesome governess, the reason', but we must, in order to feel this pleasure, acknowledge her continued authority.

Sociological and anthropological studies of humour and its function in social situations would seem to support this view; in interpersonal relations, as well as intrapersonally, humour acts to simultaneously blur and support social distinctions. Conditions most conducive to humour in groups were 'anxiety about self, submission to rigid authority structure, and adjustment to a rigid routine (Coser 1959: 175). Jokes provide an 'institutionalized means for the expression of social tensions', particularly in very structured, authoritarian situations (Daniels and Daniels 1964). In a study of joking relationships in a hospital setting, Emerson (1969) suggests that joking functions among patients and staff as a covert way of dealing with taboo subjects, in this case, death. Again, the joking form is key as 'the joking form is in itself a negation.' By choosing a joking mode, patients at once break and support a taboo.

Studies of the social role of joker or fool provide additional support. Clown or joker roles are almost universal (Charles 1945; Welsford 1935). In most situations, the clown acts as a mediator, to bring the forgotten or repressed material of the collective unconscious to the public eye in order that it may be put to use for 'further social progress' (Charles 1945: 25). However, the anarchy and disruption which the clown is allowed to create are, like the joking relationship, carefully controlled by ritual form and often restricted to certain time periods (carnival is a notable example).

So jokes, joking, and humour act both to confirm identity and to allow it to evolve our first context for learning. Dying patients can admit they are dying without negating the healing situation; friends can incorporate hostility into close relationships. Anxiety and competence can co-exist, enmity and solidarity can be juxtaposed (Coombs and Goldman 1973; Stebbins 1979; Bradney 1957).

In addition, jokes provide moments in a process in which alternative realities, 'forgotten' truths, anomalous information can, in a transitory and non-disruptive way, be introduced into the flow of events. Humour is the enemy of hubris, while being the friend of authority. In classical literature, the king needs his fool as much as his sage, as it is the fool who dares (under the cloak of foolery) to criticize authority or its rigid assumptions of omnipotence (Kets de Vries 1990). Studies of humour in organizations suggests that it is a vehicle for expressing criticism and contradiction of existing policies and procedures, of unmasking ambiguities, of making hitherto unrecognized connections (Linstead 1985; Weick and Browning 1986; Hatch and Ehrlich 1993). Organizational foolery provides a counterpoint to canonical practice (Locke 1992), and hence offers the same potential for learning as other forms of non-canonical practice described by Seeley Brown.

And humour has the fleeting, ephemeral quality that we have recognized in other learning moments. It has nothing to do with stimulus–response and everything to do with timing, synchronicity, coincidence, and luck. It is also a visceral more than rational activity, inimitably connected to the release of energy. Humour is the only form of creative activity which produces a massive physical response (laughter) which is simultaneously physical and social. The pleasure in the joke comes not from creating it but from sharing it. In this sense, humour is like jazz, 'the spontaneous joke organizes the total situation in its joke patterns' (Douglas 1975: 97). It becomes part of action, producing energy and subtly redirecting the flow of events it responds to (Hatch 1992). And when others enter into playfulness of this kind, we move from joking to improvisation.

In sum, humour provides flexibility, adjustment, insight without the loss of order. We may conclude from our discussion that learning organizations differ from highly explorative organizations, in that they retain greater integrity of structure; they differ from highly exploitative organizations in that they retain an element of slack, redundancy, disorder, and hence, flexibility. Humour is a good example of the creation of disorder within order. Starting from the other viewpoint, we must consider improvisation as a means of creating order while simultaneously maintaining disorder.

Improvisation as a Learning Place

The joker provides one set of clues about conditions that facilitate learning, and the improvisation of the jazz musician provides another set. What is distinctive about jazz improvisation is that it requires learning co-incident with action. There is 'on-the-spot surfacing, criticizing, restructuring, and testing of intuitive understandings of experienced phenomena' while the ongoing action can still make a difference (Schon 1987: 26–7). In the case of jazz, what is surfaced on the spot is an activity rather than an object. Like cinema and dance, jazz is a performance art that cannot be grasped in an instant. The hallmark of jazz is improvisation, 'playing extemporaneously, i.e., without the benefit of written music . . . composing on the spur of the moment' (Schuller 1968: 378). Thus, the traditional distinction between composition and performance, which mirrors the rational distinction between planning and doing, disappears in jazz when the creator becomes the interpreter. Unlike an architect who works from plans and looks ahead, a jazz musician cannot 'look ahead at what he is going to play, but he can look behind at what he has just played; thus each new musical phrase can be shaped with relation to what has gone before. He creates his form retrospectively' (Gioia 1988: 61). Since intention is loosely coupled to execution, the jazz musician essentially wades in, guided by the minimal structure of a melody, and makes sensible, after the fact, whatever becomes visible in hindsight.

Improvisation is not confined to jazz. It occurs in other places such as psychotherapy and combat. First, we sample psychotherapy:

> Given the unpredictable nature of a client's communication, the therapist's participation in the theatrics of a session becomes an invitation to improvise. In other words, since the therapist never knows exactly what the client will say at any given moment, he or she cannot rely exclusively upon previously designed lines, patter, or scripts. Although some orientations to therapy attempt to shape both the client and therapist into a predetermined form of conversation and story, every particular utterance in a session offers a unique opportunity for improvisation, invention, innovation, or more simply, change. (Keeney 1990: 1)

If therapy is viewed as improvisation, then therapies are viewed as songs. The song can be played exactly as scored or with improvisation, but one would not expect an improvisational therapist to play only one song over and over, any more than one would expect a jazz musician to play only one song throughout a lifetime.

Second, we sample the combat soldier. Contrary to stereotypes, this seeming ideal model of a rule-following bureaucrat 'is not detached, routinized, and self-contained; rather his role is one of constant improvisation . . . The impact of battle destroys men, equipment, and organization, which need constantly and continually to be brought back into some form of unity through on-the-spot improvisation' (Janowitz 1959: 481).

None of these extensions portray some kind of second-class rationality practised by people who read about rational choice and missed the point. Instead, this is the activity of people who are thrown into the middle of things and play their way out by thinking while doing. In other words, this is everyday organizational life. To borrow Thayer's (1988: 254) Spanish proverb, 'No es lo mismo hablar de toros, que estar en el redondel', which translates, 'It is not the same thing to talk of bulls as to be in the bullring.' To talk of intelligent action, to talk of leadership, to prepare for war (Cohen and Gooch 1990: 236) are not the same things as acting, leading, and fighting. The trick is to learn *in* the bullring and *during* wartime conditions. Once the bull enters and the war starts, surprise is inevitable. Failure to learn how to learn, faster, can be fatal. This is why learning coincident with action is crucial.

Good jazz, like good conversation, is collective improvisation. Both mix together listening to others with listening to self, mutual elaboration, on-line invention, all within an underlying structure. 'Improvisation consists in varying, combining, and recombining a set of figures within a schema that gives coherence to the whole piece. As the musicians feel the directions in which the music is developing, they make new sense of it. They reflect-in-action on the music they are collectively making' (Schon 1987: 30).

The interesting thing about such moments and spaces is that when they truly involve learning, they are remembered as organizational 'peak experiences', when the coordinated action seemed particularly fluid and effortless, when language seemed to invent rather than merely to describe experiences, when the old was suddenly seen anew, in a blend of discovery and nostalgia. Individuals recognize the experience as social, not individual, and as a 'place' which might possibly be recaptured with the right combination of people, resources and circumstances. But such moments or places are hard to plan or design; rather they perpetually have an improvisational quality. Here we are reminded again about methodologies which emphasize feeling. When learning occurs, it may be 'felt' rather than programmed or monitored. To apprehend and duplicate an organizational learning experience may be to search for a remembered place which feels both old and new, stimulating and reassuring. Learning moments, like surprises, may only be known after they are felt.

To understand how learning is facilitated by improvisation, one needs to appreciate the role of feeling, but one also needs to appreciate the role of songs as minimal structures and the role of imperfections as aesthetic structures.

Songs provide the minimal order that is partially disordered in the interest of learning. Sudnow describes songs this way:

song is a social organizational device *par excellence*, a format of two or more individuals. Its metrical structure, with a beginning and an end and a definite number of grouped pulses, furnishes a planful means for coordinating simultaneous movement and allocating little batches of talk among various players over the course of on-going play. (1979: 105)

Songs coordinate diversity, impose order across time, provide cues for elaboration, encourage mutual adjustment, afford a continuing sense of common place and, because of their simplicity, do not get in the way of imagination. The key issue for organizational learning becomes: what is the equivalent of a song in a organization? Candidates include a vision statement, a credo (e.g. General Electric's 'speed, simplicity and self-confidence'), milestones, a role, developmental sequences, routines, past history, traditions, and rituals. Whatever the source, learning is more likely to occur when there are songs and a songbook, rather than endless variations on the same old melody. 'The energy and creativity it would take to keep one's imagination alive under the constraint of playing the same song time and time again is unimaginable' (Keeney 1990: 8).

Improvisation requires minimal structure but it also requires a capacity to tolerate and elaborate errors. This is especially true with jazz. Jazz is an imperfect art. As Gioia puts it, 'errors will creep in, not only in form but also in execution; the improviser, if he seriously attempts to be creative, will push himself into areas of expression which his technique may be unable to handle. Too often the finished product will show moments of rare beauty intermixed with technical mistakes and aimless passages' (1988: 66). The 'errors' attendant on the juxtaposition of order and disorder in jazz can be recast as opportunities rather than threats to performance. Expressions that seem not to fit with what is now under way can be seen as experiments from which people learn, oddities to be incorporated and made normal, outcomes to be isolated and localized, evidence of reaching, testing of one's limits, transient dissonance that will soon be resolved, lyrical moments for a different context, avoidance of traps and clichés, or clever solutions of an even bigger problem glimpsed after the fact. A more nuanced interpretation of what error means in improvisation heightens the chance for threats to be recast as opportunities, and for the balance between order and disorder to be sustained. With a deep appreciation of the aesthetics of imperfection, people can sustain the balance of order and disorder for a longer period and increase the chance that learning moments will materialize some time during that extended interval.

Small Wins as Learning Moments

The organizational context within which learning occurs often works against that occurrence.

In a complex environment, major changes are hard to accomplish and even harder to control; they typically entail the manipulation of so many variables simultaneously that one must strain to learn anything from the experience. Moreover, major change is likely to be a day late and a dollar short. That is, the environment in many instances is changing faster than major planned change attempts. An alternative, then, is small change attempts started in many locations.

The moderate size, implemented outcome is a special form of change: it is manageable; its impact is not disruptive; it is designed to improve learning about the system. Moreover, it acts as part of a pattern and as such the necessary prelude to further adjustments and, finally, possibly larger changes. (Peters 1977: 358, 4)

This 'special form of change' is called a small win, and is defined as controllable opportunities of modest size that produce visible and tangible outcomes (Weick 1984). Small wins, despite their seeming embodiment of nothing but order and incremental exploitation, in fact often produce a more complex mixture of exploitation, exploration, and learning. Although there is a tangible outcome, the meaning and significance of that outcome are not fixed. Instead, it becomes an occasion that attracts unexpected allies, deters opponents for reasons that had not been foreseen, uncovers new opportunities, breaches old assumptions, and juxtaposes new symbols with old artifacts to produce new forgetting. Small wins can churn old routines into new learning.

To illustrate, consider the relative success feminists have had with the smaller win of making people more conscious of gender bias in language (e.g. chair*man*) compared to their relative failure in removing gender bias through legislation (e.g. equal rights amendments). Attempts to induce self-consciousness about gender references in speech revealed that language was more susceptible to change than people had realized; that the opponents to language change were more dispersed and less formidable than anticipated; that gender-biased language was more pervasive and therefore a stronger leverage point than people realized; and that language reform could be incorporated into a wide variety of agendas (e.g. various revisions of style manuals could feature gender-fair speech). These small language experiments uncovered entrenched sexism that had been invisible. These discoveries created disorder in taken-for-granted, orderly speech patterns and opened the possibility for learning. This disorder was relatively short-lived because the old categories of 'male' and 'female' were forgotten and the flow of experience was repunctuated into new, equally arbitrary distinctions involving 'people' and 'persons'. This reshuffling of language and routines, done in response to the co-presence of order and disorder, is a fundamental episode of learning that results in people giving a new response to an old stimulus.

To take a different example, when Greyhound of Canada was faced with a steady decline of riders there was no shortage of theories about what the problem was. Senior Vice President John Munro decided to do something, so he started with Greyhound's unclean restrooms. To launch his cleanup campaign Munro began holding candlelight dinners for management, complete with white tablecloths – in depot restrooms. Passengers were diverted to employee restrooms. The result?

Half the [staff] thought I was crazy and half thought, 'He's serious about this,' says Munro. 'Since then we had some black tie [dinners] – with caterers. Now managers do it in their own locations.' [As a result] more than 70 percent of the 570 restrooms have been kept immaculate. Munro hired janitorial services to guide depot staff in scrubbing the offending 30 percent – and sent the depot managers the bills. . . . Female ridership has increased by 10 percent. . . . Total ridership grew in 1989 for the first time since '82, and 1990 saw further growth. (*Tom Peters on Achieving Excellence* 1991: 12)

Munro juxtaposed the order of a banquet with the disorder of an unclean place designed for other purposes. As a result he learned about the willingness and capability for change at depots and about the distribution of zest for innovation among the management team. The depot managers themselves learned about Munro's intentions and his level of seriousness as well as about their own depots. Old meanings and labels were forgotten and replaced by new ones. Much like Follett's neighbours who treated their trees as apple-bearing trees and produced apples, Munro treated his system restrooms as locales for delight and produced renewal. Both sets of actions juxtaposed order with chaos and produced new structures. Juxtaposition created the conditions for learning, and the realignment of forgetting produced the learning itself. Social construction of a restroom as a place to dine forces people to suppress a wide variety of other constructions.

A small win is not simply a large task broken down into a series of smaller, logically related subtasks as people like Kouzes and Posner (1987: 218) argue. Decomposing a large task into a series of incremental steps is itself a precarious venture since it assumes that the steps will be carried out in a stable environment. Small wins are opportunistic as well as logical. They are local, stand-alone, completed actions that may bear little relation to one another. Each change may be an improvement, may move towards something or away from something, may demonstrate efficacy or controllability, may suggest the feasibility of a larger goal or the availability of an unexpected set of allies or affirm a key value. Small wins are experiments, as well as logically derived subtasks. Because they are opportunistic, and because opportunities are widely distributed, small wins resemble uncorrelated probes in an evolutionary system. Since they are diverse rather than homogeneous explorations, they are more likely to uncover unanticipated properties of the environment and promote learning.

Small wins are criticized by those who argue that resistance to change is countered only by changes that are dramatic, revolutionary, transformational. Small wins, as exemplified in Bateson's fable of 'the boiled frog' (Tichy and Sherman 1993: 73), encourage people to learn too little, too slowly. That fate is possible, but it overlooks three dynamics. First, small wins in large systems can occur in parallel as well as serially, which means that several small changes in the aggregate can approximate those of a radical transformation. Second, a series of small wins often precedes and paves the way for a revolution. Small wins provide the momentum and basic learnings that make revolution possible. And third, many so-called revolutions consist in part of a retrospective packaging of a series of prior small wins, all of which are interpreted as moving in a similar new direction.

Small wins embed the disorder of a nonroutine event in the order of an action routine and the two are balanced in a specific setting for a relatively short period of time. A small win is *almost* business as usual in the same sense that a near-miss is *almost* business as usual. The juxtaposition is brief, local, and transient, as is the chance to learn. The chances for learning increase as more small wins are initiated by more people in more places.

SUMMARY AND CONCLUSIONS

One reviewer of an early version of this chapter described an oxymoron as a 'language's learning'. What this reviewer meant was that paradoxes reveal the limitations of conventional grammar based on conventional logic. When these paradoxes are expressed in contradictions, ironies, and oxymorons, the resulting juxtapositions both reveal the limits of the conventions and supply the pretext for the language to renew itself. Hence, the language learns.

The language that learns is a microcosm of the organization that learns. We have argued that learning is an ongoing and implicit feature of the organizing process. By this we mean that as organizing unfolds, it does so in ways that intermittently create a set of conditions where learning is possible. We call these 'learning moments'. As organizing becomes disorganized, the forgotten is remembered, the invisible becomes visible, the silenced becomes heard. These changes create an opportunity for learning. Learning can be said to occur when forgetting, concealing, and silencing hide a *new* set of continuities and in their place create new categories, different meaning, and more organization.

These learning moments, which vary in their frequency, value, and duration, are occasions when people can renegotiate which portions of their continuing collective experience they will next forget, render invisible, and silence, and which discontinuous residuals they will treat as current meaningful artifacts of culture.

The act of repunctuating continuous experience is what we mean by learning. What people learn are intersubjective meanings embedded in culture. To make repunctuation even a possibility, organization must be reduced and doubt and curiosity must be cultivated. These changes, which mix together order and disorder, juxtapose sufficient order to sustain a learning entity and sufficient disorder to mobilize forgotten material and new alternatives. This juxtaposition is dynamic and represents a transient window of opportunity. Examples of occasions which juxtapose order and disorder are humour (an instance of culture as language), improvisation on a routine (an instance of culture as action routine), and a pocket of order in a setting of chaos which takes the form of a small win (an instance of culture as artifact).

The likelihood of learning drops quickly when invention and disorder overwhelm capacities for retention and identity, or when systems, routines, and order overwhelm capacities for unjustified variation. These tendencies towards overwhelming are a constant threat because each one represents a simpler way of dealing with the world. To learn is to dwell in the oxymoron of 'organizational learning', to be pulled simultaneously in multiple directions, and to have no assurance of success when engaged in fresh forgetting. To 'affirm the oxymoron of organizational learning' is to keep organizing and learning connected despite the fact that they pull in opposite directions.

Different forms of organizing create different problems for learning. Adhocracies explore, create, and align with changes but, in embracing disorder with disorderly forms, they risk integrity, a loss of identity, and a loss of lessons learned from the past that undergird current efficiencies. Bureaucracies exploit lessons from the past as well as past identities. Adhocracies trade away retention for variation, bureaucracies trade away variation for retention. Adhocracies embody disorder, bureaucracies embody order. Only as each form adopts some of the other, or imitates the other, is it possible to achieve repunctuation that persists.

Finally, if organization is conceptualized in terms of culture, it is easier to talk about organizational learning. It is easier because cultural artifacts and practices preserve past learning; cultural awareness and criticism may provide occasion for cultural change; organizations have multiple cultures which allows for ongoing comparison and review of what any one culture fails to see; and culture underscores that the object of most learning is intersubjective meaning.

In the final analysis all organizations are the authors and readers of their own near-miss narratives. What distinguishes the *learning* organization is its capability to confront the possibility that the story being told is simultaneously a tale of disorder in which the reality of danger masquerades as safety, and a tale of order in which the reality of safety masquerades as danger. To hold onto both possibilities long enough to restir the forgotten is to affirm the oxymoron of organizational learning.

References

Adler, P.S. and Cole, R.E. (1993) 'Designed for learning: a tale of two plants', *Sloan Management Review*, 34(3): 85–94.

Albert, S. and Whetten, D. (1985) 'Organizational identity', in L.L. Cummings and B.M. Staw (eds), *Research in Organizational Behavior*, vol. 7. Greenwich, CT: JAI Press. pp. 263–95.

Allison, G. (1971) *Essence of Decision*. Boston: Little Brown.

Argote, L. and McGrath, J.E. (1993) 'Group processes in organizations: continuity and change', in C.L. Cooper and I.T. Robertson (eds), *International Review of Industrial and Organizational Psychology*. New York: Wiley.

Barr, P.S., Stimpert, J.L. and Huff, A.S. (1992) 'Cognitive change, strategic action, and organizational renewal', *Strategic Management Journal*, 13: 15–36.

Bateson, G. (1972) *Steps to an Ecology of Mind*. New York: Ballentine.

Bradney, P. (1957) 'The joking relationship in industry', *Human Relations*, 10: 179–87.

Brown, J.S. and Duguid, P. (1991) 'Organizational learning and communities-of-practice: toward a unified view of working, learning, and innovation', *Organization Science*, 2: 40–57.

Buckley, W. (1968) 'Society as a complex adaptive system', in W. Buckley (ed.), *Modern Systems Research for the Behavioral Scientist*. Chicago: Aldine. pp. 490–513.

Charles, L.H. (1945) 'The clown's functions', *Journal of American Folklore*, 58: 25–35.

Cohen, M.D., March, J.G. and Olsen, J.P. (1972) 'A garbage can model of organizational choice', *Administrative Science Quarterly*, 17: 1–25.

Cohen, M.D. and Sproull, L.S. (1991) 'Editors' introduction', *Organization Science*, 2(1): i–iii.

Cole, M. (1990) 'Preface', in D. Middleton and D. Edwards (eds), *Collective Remembering*. Newbury Park, CA: Sage. pp. vii–ix.

Cook, S.D.N. and Yanow, D. (1993) 'Culture and organizational learning', *Journal of Management Inquiry*, 2: 373–90.

Coombs, R.H. and Goldman, (1973) 'Maintenance and discontinuity of coping mechanisms in an intensive care unit', *Social Problems*, 20: 342–55.

Corbett, C. and Van Wassenhove, C. (1993) 'Trade-offs? What trade-offs? Competence and competitiveness in manufacturing strategy', *California Management Review*, 35(4): 107–20.

Coser, R.L. (1959) 'Some social functions of laughter', *Human Relations*, 12: 171–8.

Cowan, D.A. (1993) 'Rhythms of variation: patterns that integrate individual and organizational learning'. Paper presented at the International Workshop on Managerial and Organizational Cognition, Brussels, Belgium.

Czarniawska-Joerges, B. (1992) *Exploring Complex Organizations: a Cultural Perspective*. Newbury Park, CA: Sage.

Daniels, A. and Daniels, R. (1964) 'The social function of the career fool', *Psychiatry*, 27: 219–30.

Davies, R. (1958) *A Mixture of Frailties*. London: Macmillan.

Dodgson, M. (1993) 'Organizational learning: a review of some literatures', *Organization Studies*, 14(3): 375–94.

Douglas, M. (1975) *Implicit Meanings*. London: Routledge and Kegan Paul.

Dutton, J.E. and Penner, W.J. (1993) 'The importance of organizational identity for strategic agenda building', in J. Hendry and G. Johnson (eds), *Strategic Thinking: Leadership and the Management of Change*. pp. 89–113.

Eccles, R.G. and Crane, D.B. (1988) *Doing Deals*. Boston: Harvard Business School.

Emerson, J. (1969) Negotiating the serious import of humour', *Sociometry*, 32: 169–81.

Fiol, C.M. and Lyles, M.A. (1985) 'Organizational learning', *Academy of Management Review*, 10: 803–13.

Follett, M.P. (1924) *Creative Experience*. New York: Longmans, Green.

Freud, S. (1905) *Jokes and their Relation to the Unconscious*. London: Hogarth.

Gardner, H. (1983) *Frames of Mind: an Outline of Interpretative Sociology*. New York: Basic Books.

Gersick, C.J.G. (1988) 'Time and transition in work teams: toward a new model of group development', *Academy of Management Journal*, 31: 9–41.

Gioia, T. (1988) *The Imperfect Art*. New York: Oxford University Press.

Glaser, B.G. and Strauss, A.L. (1967) *The Discovery of Grounded Theory*. Hawthorne, NY: Aldine.

Hatch, M.J. and Ehrlich, S.B. (1993) 'Spontaneous humour as an indicator of paradox and ambiguity in organizations', *Organization Studies*, 14: 505–26.

Hedberg, B.L.T. (1981) 'How organizations learn and unlearn', in P.C. Nystrom and W.H. Starbuck (eds), *Handbook of Organizational Design*, vol. 1. New York: Oxford University Press. pp. 3–27.

Hedberg, B.L.T., Nystrom, P.C. and Starbuck, W.H. (1976) 'Camping on seesaws: prescriptions for a self-designing organization', *Administrative Science Quarterly*, 21: 41–65.

Huber, G.P. (1991) 'Organizational learning: the contributing processes and the literatures', *Organization Science*, 2(1): 88–115.

Janowitz, M. (1959) 'Changing patterns of organizational authority: the military establishment', *Administrative Science Quarterly*, 3(4): 473–93.

Kahneman, D.P. Slovic, P. and Tversky, A. (eds) (1982) *Judgment under Uncertainty*. Cambridge: Cambridge University Press.

Keeney, B.P. (1990) *Improvisational Therapy*. New York: Guilford Press.

Kets de Vries, M. (1990) 'The organizational fool: balancing a leader's hubris', *Human Relations*, 43(8): 751–70.

Koestler, A. (1964) *The Act of Creation*. London: Hutchinson.

Kouzes, J.M. and Posner, B.Z. (1991) *The Leadership Challenge*. San Francisco: Jossey-Bass.

Kundera, M. (1981) *The Book of Laughter and Forgetting*. New York: Penguin.

Lant, T.K. and Mezias, S.J. (1990) 'Managing discontinuous change: a simulation study of organizational learning and entrepreneurship', *Strategic Management Journal*, 11: 147–79.

Leach, E. (1970) *Levi-Strauss*. London: Fontana/Collins.

Leach, E. (1972) 'Anthropological aspects of language: animal categories and verbal abuse', in P. Maranda (ed.), *Mythology*. London: Penguin.

Levi-Strauss, C. (1963) *Structural Anthropology*. New York: Harper and Row.

Levitt, B. and March, J.G. (1988) 'Organizational learning', *Annual Review of Sociology*, 14: 319–40.

Linstead, S. (1985) 'Jokers wild: the importance of humour in the maintenance of organizational culture', *Sociological Review*, 33(4): 741–67.

Locke, K. (1992) 'Organizational foolery: mixing canonical and carnivalesque cultures in the delivery of medicine'. Paper presented at the SCOS conference.

March, J.G. (1991) 'Exploration and exploitation in organizational learning', *Organization Science*, 2: 71–87.

March, J.G., Sproull, L.S. and Tamuz, M. (1991) 'Learning from samples of one or fewer', *Organization Science*, 2: 1–13.

Metcalfe, L. (1981) 'Designing precarious partnerships', in P.C. Nystrom and W.H. Starbuck (eds), *Handbook of Organizational Design*, vol. 1. New York: Oxford University Press. pp. 503–30.

Miller, D. (1993) 'The architecture of simplicity', *Academy of Management Review*, 18: 116–38.

Munro, D.H. (1951) *Argument of Laughter*. Melbourne: Melbourne University Press.

Normann, R. (1985) 'Developing capabilities for organizational learning', in J.M. Pennings (ed.), *Organizational Strategy and Change*. San Francisco: Jossey-Bass. pp. 217–48.

Peters, T.J. (1977) 'Patterns of winning and losing: effects on approach and avoidance by friends and enemies'. Unpublished dissertation, Stanford University, Stanford, California.

Purser, R.E. and Pasmore, W.A. (1992) 'Organizing for learning', in W.A. Pasmore and R.W. Woodman (eds), *Research in Organizational Change and Development*, vol. 6. Greenwich, CT: JAI Press. pp. 37–114.

Ring, P.S. and Van de Ven, A.H. (1994) 'Developmental processes of cooperative interorganizational relationships', *Academy of Management Review*, 19: 90–118.

Rushdie, S. (1992) *Imaginary Homelands*. New York: Penguin.

Ryle, G. (1949) *The Concept of Mind*. Chicago: University of Chicago Press.

Sagan, S.D. (1993) *The Limits of Safety*. Princeton: Princeton University Press.

Sandelands, L. and Drazin, R. (1989) 'On the language of organizational theory', *Organization Studies*, 10: 457–78.

Sandelands, L. and Srivatsan, V. (1993) 'The problem of experience in the study of organizations', *Organization Studies*.

Schon, D.A. (1983a) 'Organizational learning', in G. Morgan (ed.), *Beyond Method*. Beverly Hills, CA: Sage. pp. 114–28.

Schon, D.A. (1983b) *The Reflective Practitioner*. New York: Basic Books.

Schon, D.A. (1987) *Educating the Reflective Practitioner*. San Francisco: Jossey-Bass.

Schuller, G. (1968) *Early Jazz*. New York: Oxford University Press.

Sils, J.M. (1972) 'Two stage models for the appreciation of jokes', in J. Goldstein (ed.), *The Psychology of Humour*. New York: Academic Press.

Simon, H.A. (1991) 'Bounded rationality and organizational learning', *Organization Science*, 2(1): 125–34.

Stebbins, R.A. (1979) 'Comic relief in everyday life: dramaturgic observations on the functions of humour', *Symbolic Interaction*, 2(1): 95–104.

Sudnow, D. (1979) *Talk's Body*. New York: Knopf.

Tamuz, M. (1988) 'Monitoring dangers in the air: studies in ambiguity and information'. Unpublished doctoral dissertation, Stanford University.

Thayer, L. (1988) 'Leadership/communication: a critical review and a modest proposal', in G.M. Goldhaber and G.A. Barnett (eds), *Handbook of Organizational Communication*. Norwood, NJ: Ablex. pp. 231–63.

Tichy, N.M. and Sherman, S. (1993) *Control your Destiny or Someone Else Will*. New York: Doubleday.

Tom Peters on Achieving Excellence (1991), 'Terminal cleanliness leads to a new lease on life', 6(2): 12.

Torbert, W.R. (1987) *Managing the Corporate Dream*. Homewood, IL: Dow-Jones-Irwin.

Voyer, J.J. and Faulkner, R.R. (1989) 'Organizational cognition in a jazz ensemble', *Empirical Studies of the Arts*, 7(1): 57–77.

Weber, M. (1978) *Economy and Society*. Berkeley, CA: University of California Press.

Weick, K.E. (1977) 'Organizations as self-designing systems', *Organizational Dynamics*, 6(2): 30–46.

Weick, K.E. (1979) *The Social Psychology of Organizing*, 2nd edn. Reading, MA: Addison-Wesley.

Weick, K.E. and Berlinger, L. (1989) 'Career improvisation in self-designing organizations', in M.B. Arthur, D. Hall and B.S. Lawrence (eds), *Handbook of Career Theory*. New York: Cambridge University Press. pp. 313–28.

Weick, K.E. and Browning, L.D. (1986) 'Argument and narration in organizational communication', in J.G. Hunt and J.D. Blair (eds), *1986 Yearly Review of Management of the Journal of Management*, 12(2): 243–59.

Welsford, E. (1935) *The Fool*. Gloucester, MA: Faber and Faber.

2.11

Organizations and the Biosphere: Ecologies and Environments

CAROLYN P. EGRI AND LAWRENCE T. PINFIELD

Theories about nature and theories about society have a history of interconnections. A view of nature can be seen as a projection of human perception of self and society onto the cosmos. Conversely, theories about nature have historically been interpreted as containing implications about the way individuals or social groups behave or ought to behave. (Merchant 1980: 69)

A significant feature of contemporary society is the increasing concern expressed for the current and emerging quality of the natural environment. This concern has taken many forms, from the establishment of global forums on environmental issues (e.g. World Commission on Environment and Development 1987; the 1992 United Nations Conference on the Environment and Development), to formal assessments of the environmental records of large US manufacturing firms (Rice 1993), to reports of 'ecotage' by radical environmentalists determined to limit business activities which are claimed to be degrading the natural environment (Day 1989; Egri and Frost 1994). This brief sample of indicators suffusing the public media represents a significant challenge to traditional ways of thinking about societal and industrial activities, including the conceptual models of organizations which inform and direct those activities.

What are these concerns and challenges? While we have some difficulty in prioritizing or even grouping all the issues associated with the environmentalist movement, they are manifest in expressed anxieties regarding current and future life-styles, quality of life, economic prosperity, and more generally the future of *Homo sapiens* on planet earth. A number of both specific and general considerations trigger these anxieties: population growth and its consequences for the carrying capacity of planet earth; increasing aspirations for a more urban and materialistic life-style on the part of the growing number of citizens of less developed nations; the nature of industrialization which results in high levels of waste and pollution while depleting nonrenewable resources. Associated with these concerns are others such as the loss of biodiversity and the irretrievable change of bioregions and natural environments into areas forever hostile to human habitation (Brown 1991; Buchholz 1993; Commoner 1990; Daly and Cobb 1994; Paehlke 1989).

These issues are symptomatic of the deep structure of beliefs regarding the consequences of an industrialized society. Governmental and business organizations are judged not to take the interests, aspirations, and needs of their citizenry into account in their pursuit of organizational goals and objectives. From the perspective of those wishing to act on beliefs such as these, the situation is even more difficult because direct action is unlikely to be successful. The 'environmental problem' is a consequence of how society is structured, for as multiple organizations pursue their self-interests, the interstices of society become an increasingly degraded residual. The institutionalized and taken-for-granted assumptions of an organizationally based, contemporary society produce consequences that are barely discernible and actionable within the logics of that frame of reference.

Exploration of the topic of organizations and the biosphere requires a holistic approach that is multi-faceted, cross-disciplinary and controversial. Multi-faceted because one investigates phenomena at different levels (individual, group, organizational, societal and global) from alternative perspectives (physical, technical, economic, social and ethical). Cross-disciplinary because one delves into both the natural sciences (ecology, biology, chemistry, physics) and the social sciences (philosophy, sociology, organization theory) in a search for areas of intersections and divergence. Controversial because it is an evolving arena replete with political conflict between and among societal actors proposing alternative courses of action. As identified in the opening quote by Merchant, there are those who contend that our theories of nature and of societies are inextricably intertwined and cannot (or should not) be regarded as separate. Alternatively, there are others such as Schnaiberg and Gould (1994) who argue that there is an 'enduring conflict' between the logic and dynamics of natural ecosystems and those of industrialized society which prevent any meaningful synthesis at either theoretical or practical levels. It is the latter view that appears to have been adopted by traditional organizational theorists and practitioners for both conceptual and practical convenience. However, those who challenge this traditional worldview argue that there is an urgent need to incorporate ecological principles and the natural environment into both organization theory and practice. Who are these champions of change? What is their vision and agenda for change in modern organizations and societies? What are the implications for our theories of organization? These are only a few of the questions which can be explored to develop an understanding of the theoretical and practical intersections between organizations and the biosphere.

Our exploration will start with the historical origins and current state of ecological theory and modern environmentalist perspectives. Three perspectives on eco-environments are presented to demonstrate how ecological values are intertwined with human values concerning desired social, political and economic realities. These vary from the very strong anthropocentric values of the *dominant social paradigm* which sees unlimited progress resulting from the exploitation of infinite natural resources (Catton and Dunlap 1978; Daly 1977) to the biocentric values of the *radical environmentalism* philosophy of deep ecology which advocates 'biospecies egalitarianism' in which economic advancement is forgone for harmony with nature (Devall and Sessions 1985; Naess 1973). Other radical environmentalism philosophies such as spiritual ecology (Fox 1990), social ecology (Bookchin 1990a), and ecofeminism

(Merchant 1980; 1992; Salleh 1984; Warren 1990) advocate social and biological arrangements in which there is a balance between the interests of humanity and nature. In this idealized conceptualization of ecocentric values, the ecological relationships among people and nature within communities are integrated with others sharing ecoregions which, in turn, cooperate to sustain the shared ecosphere of the plant (Tokar 1988). More intermediate perspectives are termed *reform environmentalism* which represents degrees of modification of anthropocentric values to include the natural environment in human endeavours. In sustainable development proposals, all types of capital and environmental resources are considered in local and national policy development (Colby 1990; World Commission on Environment and Development 1987) and risk management emerges as a critical task (Kleindorfer and Kunreuther 1986). In addition, environmental protection policies maintain the strongly anthropocentric posture of the dominant social paradigm within a system of tradeoffs between economic growth and environmental degradation (Berkes 1989; Colby 1990). Each perspective is described and then critically analysed to identify contradictions between proposals and enactment. To facilitate conceptual clarity, perspectives at the endpoints of the environmentalist perspective continuum (i.e. the dominant social paradigm and radical environmentalism) are presented before focusing on the middle ground of reform environmentalism.

The next section of the chapter explicates how the concept of 'environment' has been treated in orthodox and more recent organization theories. How different conceptualizations of organizations are either compatible with or in conflict with environmentalist points of view is discussed. Current and potential areas for a confluence of theories concerning eco-environments and organizations are identified. In addition, the concepts of self-interest and systems theory are used to illustrate the conceptual and practical challenges of integrating environmentalist views of biophysical environments into organizational views of environments. Finally, the chapter closes with summary conclusions and thoughts regarding future directions in both theory and research.

ECOLOGY AND ENVIRONMENTALIST PERSPECTIVES

The historical origin of the term *ecology* can be traced back to 1866 when German zoologist Ernst Haeckel combined the two Greek words *logos* (meaning 'the study of') and *oikos* (meaning 'house' or 'place to live') (Buchholz 1993). As elaborated by Haeckel in 1870, 'ecology' was originally defined as:

> the body of knowledge concerning the economy of nature – the investigation of the total relations of the animal both to its inorganic and to its organic environment; including above all, its friendly and inimical relations with those animals and plants with which it comes directly and indirectly into contact – in a word, ecology is the study of all those complex interrelations referred to by Darwin as the conditions of the struggle for existence. (translated in Allee et al. 1949: frontispiece; as cited by McIntosh 1985: 7–8)

From its nineteenth century conceptualization as a branch of biology, ecology has become a 'polymorphic science' accessed and extended to encompass various aspects of natural and social phenomena (McIntosh 1985). Fundamental to theoretical conceptualizations of ecology and ecosystems[1] are the principles of: holism (interconnections within and amongst systems and environments); the balance of nature (self-regulating equilibria of biological and nonbiological systems); diversity (tendency towards greater biodiversity in natural systems); finite limits of planetary life-support systems (carrying capacity to support populations and communities of organisms); and dynamic change of natural processes and cycles (Daly and Cobb 1994; Buchholz 1993; Lovelock 1979; Sarkar 1986; Serafin 1988; Wilson 1992). At its core, ecology represents the body of knowledge which is concerned with the relations between organisms and their organic and inorganic environments.

Within ecology, the term *environment* 'refers to all of the external physical and biological factors that directly influence the survival, growth, development, and reproduction of organisms' (Colby 1990: 10). *Environmentalism* is primarily concerned with the interactions between the biosphere and the technosphere and sociosphere.[2] At one level, environmentalism is the application of ecological theory to understanding the development and operation of social systems within the biosphere. At another level, environmentalism is the study of human sociopolitical values which inform the conceptualization and enactment of human relations with the natural environment (Bird 1987; Hays 1987; Paehlke 1989).

It was only after World War II that environmentalism gained sufficient grass-roots support to become the nascent social movement which presently manifests itself as a dominant social concern (Hays 1987: 3). Different origins have moulded different national movements. In Britain and other parts of Europe, most environmentalist groups originated from established nature groups which had a long tradition of access to decision-making (Rudig and Lowe 1986), whereas movements in North America and Australasia had little or no connection with previous social groups (Fox 1981; Hay and Haward 1988). In North America, environmentalism began with a focus on conservation and protection of natural environments for the purposes of outdoor recreation and preservation of wilderness. Natural resources were increasingly valued for their existential qualities in a natural state as well as their amenity for other aesthetic pursuits. Environmental concerns, especially among the younger generation, therefore became associated with deeply rooted human aspirations for a better life, and hopes for personal and social achievement. In other arenas, notably Western Europe, anti-nuclear sentiments had both a radical and an integrating impact on the green movement. In all countries, additional attention and support flowed to environmentalist causes as a consequence of increased scientific capacity to detect, measure and link environmental contaminants to human health and ecological degradation (Carson 1962; Sarkar 1986). Reports from the Club of Rome in the early 1970s also focused public attention on the insidious dangers of uncontrolled industrial growth for natural and social environments. Increasingly, the prevalent notions of the supremacy of science, technology and industrialization have come under challenge (Sarkar 1986). Although the dominant political ideology of the 1970s and 1980s, as well as the oil-cartel-induced economic crisis of the 1970s, could have restrained the growth of environmentalist movements during those decades, environmental activism has proved to be a persistent, deeply rooted, organized feature of contemporary society (Dunlap 1989; Sale 1993).

While there are commonalities in the evolution of environmentalist movements, there also exist fundamental differences. Green movements in general have been fragmented and under-organized with various subgroups independently representing more specialized interests such as preservation of wilderness, environmental policy development, toxic waste management, resource protection and conservation, animal rights, and so forth (Sale 1993; Snow 1992a). Presently, there is no clear focus to these different sub-movements other than their general association with some aspect of environmentalism which challenges in various ways the traditional conceptualizations and practices of a predominantly urban, industrial, developed and organizationally based society.

Three frameworks of environmental philosophy and concepts represent the primary schools of thoughts concerning the human–nature relationship. The dominant social paradigm is not an 'environmentalist' perspective *per se*, but rather represents the traditional worldview of industrialized society – the status quo against which other environmentalist perspectives are compared. The radical environmentalism perspective represents the worldview of those who advocate transformational change. The reform environmentalism perspective represents those occupying the middle ground in both environmental philosophy and practice. The historical origins, beliefs and assumptions of each perspective are presented and then critically discussed.

Dominant Social Paradigm

We are the absolute masters of what the earth produces. We enjoy the mountains and the plains. The rivers are ours, we sow the seed and plant the trees. We fertilize the earth. . . . We stop, direct, and turn the rivers. In short, by our hands we endeavour, by our various operations on this world, to make, as it were, another nature. (Cicero, 106–43 BC, as quoted by Hughes 1975: 30)

The advent of ancient urban civilizations marked the emergence of anthropocentrism in spiritual and philosophical thought on humankind's relationship with nature. For ancient Mesopotamians, humans possessed a divine right to tame the 'monstrous chaos' of nature; for classical Greek humanists (Aristotle, Plato) and the early Stoics, humans claimed the resources of nature for their own exclusive use (Hughes 1975; Sessions 1987; Wall 1994). Early evidence of the ecological price of human order and domination would become apparent in the destruction of the ancient cedar forests of Lebanon, the desertification of the once Fertile Crescent of Mesopotamia, and the erosion, pollution and extinction of numerous species under imperial Rome (Hughes 1975). Judaeo-Christian teachings are also identified as promoting an anthropocentric worldview in which humanity's role was to 'be fruitful and multiply' as well as to 'have dominion over every living thing that moveth upon the earth' (Merchant 1980; White 1967).

One critical aspect of the anthropocentric worldview is the notion of dualisms such as the ideological separation of the human mind and spirit from the physical reality of existence and the division into higher and lower entities. The dualism of mind and matter was fundamental to the advocacy by seventeenth century Age of Enlightenment philosophers (in particular, Bacon, Descartes, Newton, Hobbes) of mastery over nature as essential for scientific and social progress (Daly and Cobb 1994; Ehrenfeld 1978; Merchant 1980). Mechanistic materialism, rationality and scientific reductionism became the ideological cornerstones of the Scientific and Industrial Revolutions of Western societies and are now regarded as core elements of the dominant social paradigm (Bramwell 1989; Fox 1990).

As represented in modern industrialized society, the dominant social paradigm (DSP) represents an adherence to neoclassical economic principles and goals (economic growth and profits) with natural factors treated as either externalities or infinitely exploitable resources. If there are observable environmental problems, these can easily (or eventually) be solved through scientific and technological progress (Daly and Cobb 1994; Hawken 1993; Milbrath 1989). The DSP is most closely associated with Western capitalist societies in which the principles of 'free markets' and private property ownership reign. However, closed economic systems informed by Marxist philosophy are also included in this perspective. This apparently paradoxical ideological marriage is justified by virtue of Marxism's strong anthropocentric bias which supports the capital intensive production goals of modern industrialism (Daly and Cobb 1994; Jacobs 1993; Jung 1991; Lee 1980; Porritt 1984).[3] Additional justification is offered by the evidence of environmental degradation in modern socialist states which many assert exceeds that of unfettered capitalism (Clow 1986; Davies 1991; Feshbach and Friendly 1992; Jancar-Webster 1993).

Other facets of the dominant social paradigm concern the notion of individual self-determinism and the centralized control of societies by social, political and economic elites. In societies premised on hierarchical structures and relationships, both persons and nonhuman nature are objectified and valued only in instrumental terms (as inputs or consumers of production) rather than for their intrinsic or spiritual value (Cotgrove and Duff 1981; Devall and Sessions 1985; Drengson 1980).

Radical Environmentalism Perspective

The politics of the Industrial Age, left, right and centre, is like a three-lane motorway, with different vehicles in different lanes, but *all* heading in the same direction. Greens feel it is the very direction that is wrong, rather than the choice of any one lane in preference to the others. It is our perception that the motorway of industrialism inevitably leads to the abyss – hence our decision to get off it, and seek an entirely different direction. (Porritt 1984: 43)

The radical environmentalism perspective promotes a vision of the biosphere and human society based on the ecological principles of holism, the balance of nature, diversity, finite limits and dynamic change (Catton and Dunlap 1978; Cotgrove and Duff 1981; Drengson 1980; Devall and Sessions 1985; among others). As identified by Donald Worster (1977), the 'idea of ecology is much older than the name.' Aspects of the radical environmentalism perspective have been shown to predate as well as to have developed in opposition to anthropocentric ideologies. Archaeological evidence of the early hunter-gatherer societies and ancient civilizations offers a picture of nature and its forces personified as deities to be worshipped and obeyed (Eisler 1987; Merchant 1980). Vestiges of nature deities were/are present in the spiritual traditions of shamanism, Egyptian, Greek and Roman pantheism (with Gaia as the Earth Mother), Eastern mysticism (Taoism, Sufism, Zen, Buddhism), Islam, and paganism (Earth Mother goddess) (Wall 1994). Underlying these conceptualizations of an all-powerful nature is the belief that human survival depends on a holistic synthesis and integration of humanity with the natural environment. The philosophical holism of the early Greek philosopher Heraclitus (c. 535–475 BC) is echoed in the work of seventeenth and eighteenth century natural philosophers and theologians (von Linné, Emerson, Malthus, Thoreau) who wrote of the interconnectedness of humans and nature in the 'web of life' (Wall 1994). The concept of organismic holism would be developed further in the early twentieth century by Jan Smuts (1926: 86) as a synthesis or 'a unity of parts which is so close and intense as to be more than the sum of its parts . . . and the whole and the parts therefore reciprocally influence and determine each other'.

The biocentric respect for other life forms can be traced back to the vegetarianism of Eastern religions, classical Greek philosophers, St Francis of Assisi of the thirteenth century, and the late eighteenth century English Romantics (e.g. Blake, Shelley, Wollstonecraft) who equated animal rights with human rights (Wall 1994). Critiques of scientific industrial society are found in the writings of the seventeenth to eighteenth century European Romantic movement as well as in the works of transcendentalist philosophers in the United States (Sessions 1987). One of the central tenets of the radical environmentalism perspective is the recapturing of a pre-Enlightenment organismic worldview in which the universe is seen as organic, living and spiritual (Cotgrove and Duff 1981; Devall and Sessions 1985; Drengson 1980; Sale 1985).

The modern radical environmentalism perspective is positioned in direct opposition to the dominant social paradigm's support of modern industrialism as the revolutionary alternative required for long-term ecological survival. The radical environmentalism perspective advocates the massive redesign of industrial and agricultural systems of production and transportation (Commoner 1990). Instead of developing large-scale capital intensive technologies for the industrial-military complex, science needs to be redirected to developing technologies which reduce human interference with the nonhuman world. This is to be accomplished through the development and use of intermediate (appropriate) technologies which reduce the depletion and pollution of natural resources as well as provide for craftsmanship in human labour (Commoner 1990; Schumacher 1973). In contrast to the DSP belief in unlimited material and economic growth, the radical perspective asserts that the limits and delicate balance of the biosphere require the preservation and conservation of natural resources through anti-consumptionist and anti-materialism ethics.

One important facet of the radical environmentalism perspective is bioregionalism as the organizing principle for decentralized social, economic and political systems (Irvine and Ponton 1988; Leopold 1949; Mumford 1938; Sale 1985). A bioregion is 'a place defined by its life forms, its topography and its biota, rather than by human dictates; a region governed by nature, not legislature' (Sale 1985: 43). While natural criteria for a bioregion's boundaries are neither mutually exclusive nor devoid of human criteria of use and perception (Alexander 1990), communities within bioregions would regain local decision-making authority to engender environmental and economic self-sufficiency of production and use.

Within the radical environmentalism perspective there are four prominent philosophies – deep ecology, spiritual ecology, social ecology, ecofeminism – which differ primarily in terms of emphasis and means rather than ends of the radical agenda for transformational change in the human–nature relationship.

Deep Ecology

Deep ecology is a holistic perspective which integrates biological-psychological-spiritual-metaphysical dimensions of interdependent and interacting ecosystems (Devall and Sessions 1985; Naess 1973; 1984). As proposed by Norwegian philosopher Arne Naess, deep ecology questions the normative and descriptive premises (why? how?) at a more fundamental level than the everyday technical and scientific levels of ecosystems. Drawing from the philosophies of Spinoza, Gandhi and Thoreau, and various spiritual traditions (Buddhist, Christian, Native American), deep ecology proposes the moral goal of 'self-realization' which is attained through an identification with 'the interest or interests of another being [which] are reacted to as our own interest or interests' (Naess 1988: 261). The deep ecology platform posits 'biospherical egalitarianism', that is, humans have no rights to interfere with the richness and diversity of all life forms (human and non-human) which have intrinsic or inherent value. Deep ecologists identify as epistemologically problematic, but practically necessary, the application of human cultural concepts such as rights, values and ethics to the natural environment (Manes 1990; Sessions 1987). Nature is to be viewed not as an extension of humans but rather as the basic element on which human civilizations are based. The moral and ethical imperative of deep ecology is that humans have an obligation to implement (by example and by direct action) these changes in society.

Spiritual Ecology

Spiritual ecology or transpersonal ecology (Berry 1988; Fox 1990; Hull 1993; Reason 1993) shares deep ecology's emphasis on the need for transformational changes in human consciousness as a prerequisite to changes at physical levels of existence. The alienation caused by the mechanistic and dualistic worldview of industrialized society can only be healed through a recapturing of humanity's sacred connections with all aspects of creation.

Social Ecology

Social ecologist Murray Bookchin (1980; 1982; 1990a; 1990b) advances a more secular approach to understanding the relationship between society and nature.

> The ways in which we interact with each other as social beings profoundly influence attitudes we are likely to have toward the natural world. Any sound ecological perspective rests in great part on our social perspectives and interrelationships; hence, to draw up an ecological agenda that has no room for social concerns is as obtuse as to draw up a social agenda that has no room for ecological concerns. (Bookchin 1990b: 24–5)

As a result of both social evolution and natural evolution, human society has developed patterns of hierarchical domination which are socially and environmentally destructive. Unlike non-human species, humanity is unique in its capacity for creative and self-conscious thought to alter the course of social evolution. Bookchin (1980; 1990b) offers a vision of a reconstructed sociopolitical order premised on 'libertarian

municipalism' which involves decentralized grass-roots bioregionally based planning and governance in human settlements which mirror local ecosystems. Only through ecological community and participatory democracy can a new society free of ecological and cultural oppression be created.

Ecofeminism

The integration of social and political change as part of ecological change is also echoed in definitions of ecofeminism:

> Ecofeminism is a term that some use to describe both the diverse range of women's efforts to save the Earth and the transformations of feminism in the West that have resulted from the new view of women and nature ... ecofeminism is not a monolithic, homogeneous ideology ... Indeed, it is precisely the diversity of thought and action that makes this new politics so promising as a catalyst for change in these troubled times. (Diamond and Forenstein 1990: ix, xii)

Ecofeminists (King 1989; Merchant 1980; Plant 1989; Warren 1990) also posit that while humans are members of the ecological community, they are different from (but not equivalent to) other life forms. The domination of nature is viewed as being interconnected with hierarchical domination of humans based on gender, race, ethnicity and social class. The central concern of ecofeminism is 'to end all forms of oppression' (Warren 1990), especially that of women within patriarchical cultures. The ecofeminist antidote to exploitative societal structures and processes is social justice based on the principles of egalitarianism, inclusiveness, communitarianism, consensual decision-making, mutual care and responsibility (Cheney 1987).

Reform Environmentalism Perspective

> Man has too long forgotten that the earth was given to him for usufruct alone, not for consumption, still less for profligate waste. ... The earth is fast becoming an unfit home for its noblest inhabitant, and another era of equal human crime and human improvidence ... would reduce it to such a condition of impoverished productiveness, of shattered surface, of climatic excess, as to threaten the depravation, barbarism, and perhaps even extinction of the species. (George Perkins Marsh, *Man and Nature*, 1863, as cited by Strong 1988: 35)

The origins of the reform environmentalism perspective can be traced to early critics of nineteenth century industrialism who alerted the public and reformers to its side effects on human health and environmental degradation (Devall

1988). George Perkins Marsh, a nineteenth century geographer, is viewed as instrumental in the transition of earlier romantic views of nature to advocacy for the stewardship of nature for long-term human survival. From the 1880s to the 1920s, the conservation and preservation of natural resources and habitats would become the mission of the newly founded ecological and natural history societies throughout North America, the United Kingdom and Europe (Jancar-Webster 1993; McIntosh 1985; Strong 1988). The work of the founders of the American conservation movement (John Muir, Aldo Leopold, Gifford Pinchot) continues to inform the operating philosophy of the mainstream organizations in the environmental movement to this day (McIntosh 1985; Snow 1992a; Strong 1988).

The reform environmentalism perspective represents a modification of anthropocentric values to include biocentric values to the extent that there is sustainable development, which is defined as meeting 'the needs of the present without compromising the ability of future generations to meet their own needs' (World Commission on Environment and Development 1987: 43). In this perspective, technology is the vehicle for scientific and economic progress as well as the means for detecting and managing environmental risks which threaten human survival and well-being. The operation of the mechanistic metaphor is evident in reform environmentalism's focus on the efficient use of natural resources and the minimization of negative economic effects of pollution (Dorfman and Dorfman 1977). However, unlike the dominant social paradigm perspective, the reform environmentalism perspective attempts to incorporate a systems approach and the thermodynamic laws of conservation and entropy into the calculations of environmental sustainability (Georgescu-Rogen 1971; Stead and Stead 1992).[4] The physical limits of living and economic systems necessitate the development of renewable energy resources and the conservation of nonrenewable resources.

Ecological economics and industrial ecology represent two means by which the natural environment is incorporated into industrial decision-making processes. Ecological economics may be utilized for the quantification of tradeoffs between economic and environmental benefits and costs, and for environmental risk management (the determination of optimum pollution levels and economic compensation for the depletion and/or degradation of natural resources) (Dorfman and Dorfman 1977). The methodological challenges of measuring the ecological impact of industries are demonstrated in recent studies by Schaltegger (1993) and

Ilinitch and Schaltegger (1993). For example, when there are questions regarding the validity of proposed pollution measures such as the toxicity levels of different chemical pollutants, how does one accurately compare the ecological impact of lead versus ammonia versus dioxins? More generally, how does one calculate the synergy effects of combinations of pollutants in different ecosystems?

Industrial ecology is concerned with the means for achieving environmentally sustainable systems of production (Allenby 1992; Hawken 1993; Stead and Stead 1992). Industrial ecology proposes that the impact of industrial systems on the natural environment can be minimized by adopting total environmental quality management (TEQM) principles for product and process design (Callenbach et al. 1993; Cairncross 1991; Baram and Dillon 1993; Flannery and May 1994; Hawken 1993; Sharfman and Ellington 1993; Shrivastava 1994). In industrial closed systems, the use of nonrenewable natural resources is minimized and/or supplanted by renewable sources of energy and natural resources. Industrial wastes and pollutants are reduced, recycled, and/or disposed of in an ecologically safe manner. Whereas technological systems are closed, industrial environmental policy and strategy processes are open to include collaborative decision-making with multiple stakeholders (community and interest groups, government agencies, employees). Ecological auditing procedures are used to measure environmental performance and industrial activities are disclosed to employees and interested publics.

One important feature of the reform environmentalism perspective is the concept of stakeholders and stakeholder rights (McGowan and Mahon 1991; Shrivastava 1994; Stead and Stead 1992; Steger 1993; Throop 1991; Westley and Vredenburg 1991). Whilst not extending to include the natural environment and nonhuman entities as formal stakeholders, public interests in ensuring long-term environmental sustainability are recognized. Thus from the reform environmentalism perspective, the relevant question is not *whether* non-industrial stakeholders (e.g. governments, environmentalist organizations, the general public) are included in organizational decision-making but rather *how* and *to what degree* they are included in decisions concerning the natural environment (Bennett 1991; Berle 1990; Elkington and Burke 1989; Schmidheiny 1992; Scott and Rothman 1992; Steger 1993; and others). Generally, it is the large mainstream reform environmentalist organizations that have developed collaborative arrangements with industry and government (McCloskey 1991; Sale 1993; Snow 1992a).

Managing the Environmental Commons

Reform environmentalism's goal of sustainable development represents 'an accommodation between economic growth and environmental protection' (Cairncross 1991: 26) at local, national and global levels. Proponents of sustainable development identify one major cause of environmental degradation as being the inequitable distribution of economic wealth between industrialized nations and 'Third World' countries. Economically impoverished Third World countries are unable to develop or purchase the scientific technologies to conserve and protect their natural environment. Nor can they afford to prevent the exploitation and export of their natural resources required to maintain the higher standard of living in industrialized nations (e.g. with only one-fifth of the world's population, industrialized nations consume four-fifths of fossil fuel and metal mineral resources produced). While recognizing that consumption patterns of industrialized nations are environmentally unsustainable and need to be curtailed, the eradication of poverty in Third World countries is viewed as an integral part of economic, social and political self-sustainability. In addition, alternative styles and modes of economic development appropriate to local cultures and biophysical environments need to be developed. Thus one of the concerns of sustainable development is management of the bioregional and local commons but not in isolation from the global commons – a more inclusive vision than the radical environmentalist closed bioregional concept (Keating 1993; Sitarz 1993; World Commission on Environment and Development 1987).

In that the biosphere represents a global commons, the potential for a 'tragedy of the unmanaged commons' necessitates that formal government involvement and regulation be instituted to develop and manage natural resources (Hardin 1968; 1991; *The Ecologist* 1993; Throop 1991). As proposed by Hardin (1991), informal pressures to prevent the ruination of the commons are only workable with small groups involving 50 to 150 actors. If the global commons is left unmanaged and unregulated, the motivation of individual parties to play the 'commonize the costs while privatizing the profits' (CC-PP) game inevitably leads to the degradation of the commons. Within the reform environmentalism perspective there are variations in regards to the desired nature of governments' responsibility and involvement in managing the global and local commons. Towards the anthropocentric end of the anthropocentric–ecocentric continuum, government assumes limited responsibility for the conservation and management of public natural resources (e.g. in national parks), levying taxes for the use of public resources, and regulating pollution levels. In the mid-range, government assumes a more active role by developing and administering environmental regulations, taxes and marketable permits for industrial pollution (Cairncross 1991; Hahn and Hester 1989). While there is a general preference for voluntary informal pressures to encourage environmental responsibility, policy strategists acknowledge that the potential for environmental free-ridership necessitates active government intervention. However, the record to date of such interventions has not been very encouraging as environmental regulations have proved to be expensive, unwieldy and often, ineffective (Baram and Dillon 1993; Nemetz 1986; Paehlke 1990; Schweitzer 1977; Simmons and Wynne 1993).

Another approach to management of the global commons is one based on the principle of collaboration rather than competition between public and private institutions at local, national and international levels (Colby 1990). As identified in the United Nations Conference on Environment and Development (UNCED) Agenda 21 (Keating 1993; Sitarz 1993), the global liberalization of trade and cultures necessitates a redefinition of public and private institutional roles for the protection of global and local commons. Efforts to develop international environmental regulations and enforcement mechanisms include the Montreal Protocol (signed by eighty-one nations by 1992) in which signatories have pledged to end the use of CFCs (chlorofluorocarbons, which threaten the planet's ozone layer) by the year 2000 (Cairncross 1991). Less successful have been international efforts to remedy the environmental degradation of the Canada–US Great Lakes ecosystem (Colburn et al. 1990; MacLarkey 1991). Initiated in 1972 and expanded in 1978, the International Joint Commission for the Great Lakes Water Quality Agreement was bold in its goal of involving government agencies (at federal, provincial/state and local levels), industry, academia and environmental groups to develop and implement an action plan. Despite the best of intentions, after ten years of efforts the participants agree that

> In many respects, it has been a frustrating period: new discoveries often seem to have served to extend the tangle of environmental relationships, making action more difficult and solutions seemingly ever more complex, difficult, time consuming, and perhaps ultimately impossible. (Colburn et al. 1990: 11)

As revealed in studies of other multi-stakeholder initiatives to develop environmental public policy, interorganizational collaboration to establish new sociopolitical systems of governance is much easier said than done (Crowfoot and Wondolleck 1990; Egri and Frost 1992; Feyerherm 1994; Gray 1989; Pasquero 1991). One critical issue revolves around the degree to which true collaboration is practised or even possible when the parties at the table are unequal and/or different in terms of philosophical values, resources, power and influence.

A CRITICAL ANALYSIS OF ENVIRONMENTALIST PERSPECTIVES

In his critique of alternative ecological paradigms, Routley (1983) cautions that contemporary paradigms often contain overlapping or contradictory elements, thus failing to offer unified systems of beliefs. As identified by Colby (1990), this lack of conceptual clarity counterindicates a linear interpretation of perspectives which are still in their evolutionary stages of development. Whereas the dominant social paradigm and radical environmentalism perspectives offer a greater degree of contrasts, within the intermediate reform environmentalism perspective there is considerable variability in the degree of inclusiveness of ecological assumptions and prescribed ends and means for environmental sustainability. See Table 1 for a summary of the salient features of each perspective.

The reform environmentalism perspective is the least clear conceptually because it represents the current state of flux and change in human society in regards to the natural environment. It is also the site of political and social contests regarding the ends, forms and means of resolving ecological concerns. From the radical environmentalism perspective, reform environmentalism is an incremental (and some would assert superficial or shallow) response to ecological issues (Devall 1988), whereas from the dominant social paradigm perspective, reform environmentalism is a progressive response (Cairncross 1991; Schmidheiny 1992). The merits of each position in this debate concerning environmental philosophy and practice are examined next.

Critiques of the Dominant Social Paradigm

In many respects, the DSP perspective has been positioned as the 'straw man' in the ecological debate (Fox 1990; Routley 1983; Wexler 1990). In its pure form, the DSP exists primarily in the abstract principles of neoclassical and Marxist economic theories or as an incomplete historical representation of industrialized society. In reality, rational free market principles are continuously compromised and adjusted to accommodate the subjective 'irrationality' of governments, organizations and individuals in society. As identified by economic theorists and environmentalist critics alike (Cairncross 1991; Daly and Cobb 1994; Dorfman and Dorfman 1977; Friend 1992; Hawken 1993; Jacobs 1993), neoclassical economic assumptions and techniques are ill equipped to accurately reflect environmental externalities, qualitative costs and benefits, public goods and resources, limits to substitutions, resource depletion costs, long-term projected costs and benefits, complex systems, and so forth. One oft-cited example used to illustrate the inadequacies of neoclassical economics is the paradox that the cleanup of environmental disasters is accounted for as growth in a country's GNP while the preservation and conservation of environmental resources are regarded as costs (Cairncross 1991; Daly and Cobb 1994). Given these contradictions in practice, the dominant social paradigm can be most accurately regarded as an ideological perspective which serves as a conceptual endpoint against which other environmentalist perspectives and actions can be measured.

Critiques of the Radical Environmentalism Perspective

As the most extreme set of these alternative perspectives, radical environmentalism proposes a complete philosophical reformation of society based on DSP principles. However, it is the utopian political, social and economic agenda of deep ecology which has evoked the strongest reactions from philosophers within and outside of the environmentalist movement (Fox 1990; Jacobs 1991). Both radical and reform environmentalist critics of deep ecology highlight its disassociation of ecological issues from social problems (Bookchin 1994; Bradford 1987); its advocacy of interference with individual freedom of humans but not that of wildlife or nature (Fox 1990); and its parallel to ancient neostoicism (Cheney 1989). In addition, deep ecology is criticized for its lack of a theory of transition to a biocentric world (Fox 1990; Luke 1988) and its logically inconsistent and simplistic position (Wexler 1990). Bookchin (1994: 6) provides the most condemning critique of what he regards as the 'intellectual, cultural, and spiritual poverty' of the deep ecology approach which he says verges on 'ecofascist propaganda'. Deep ecologists who advocate that there is only 'one way', that is, 'their way' of reconstructing the human–nature relationship may be more like

Table 1   *Typology of environmentalist perspectives*

	Dominant social paradigm	Reform environmentalism	Radical environmentalism
Human–nature relationship	Domination over nature (very strong anthropocentrism)	Stewardship of nature (modified anthropocentrism)	Cooperation and harmony with nature (ecocentrism → biocentrism)
Approach to natural environment	Dominionistic (mastery) Utilitarian (material) Negativistic (avoidance)	Naturalistic (conservation) Utilitarian (modified) Scientific	Moralistic (spiritual) Aesthetic (preservation) Symbolic Humanistic (affection/emotion)
Nature of social order	Hierarchical Centralized authority Competitive Individualistic	Hierarchical Centralized with stakeholder consultation Competitive/collaborative Individualism/collectivist	Egalitarian Decentralized participatory (minority tradition on bioregional basis) Communalism Collectivist
Assumptions: Knowledge	Reductionism Rationality of means Dualism	Reductionism-systems Rational-political means/ends	Holism Rationality of ends Integrative/dialectic
Economic	Neoclassical economics (unlimited economic and material growth essential for human progress)	Ecological economics (neoclassical plus natural capital for optimal decision-making)	Steady state economics (homeostasis)
Natural resources	Infinite natural resources (unlimited substitutes available)	Nonrenewable and renewable natural resources (limits to substitutes)	Very limited natural resources ('spaceship earth')
Scientific technology	Technological optimism	Technological optimism	Technological scepticism
Dominant goals	Unlimited economic and material growth essential for human progress Scientific and technological progress	Sustainable development of natural environment Economic and industrial development to reduce local/global societal inequities	Holistic balance with a fragile nature (symbiosis) Environmental and social justice
Environmental management Technologies and strategies	Modern industrialism Unrestricted consumerism Pollution dispersion Large-scale capital intensive technologies Unregulated free markets	Green industrialism Green consumerism Pollution reduction Eco-technologies to develop and conserve natural resources (technical and environmental efficiency) Utilitarian biodiversity Monitoring and regulation of environmental risks in local and global commons (calculate tradeoffs)	Bioregional planning and control Post-consumption ethic Pollution elimination Intermediate (appropriate) technologies Cultural and biological diversity Government regulation for preservation/conservation of natural environment
Operating metaphor	Machine	Machine-systems	Organism

Sources: Catton and Dunlap 1978; Colby 1990; Cotgrove and Duff 1981; Devall and Sessions 1985; Drengson 1980; Kellert 1993; Routley 1983

their DSP opponents than they would realize or wish to acknowledge. It could be argued that deep ecologists are falling into the positivist trap of taking as natural and uncontestable sets of assumptions which are the result of political and social interaction rather than a unitary version of reality or 'truth'. Despite these criticisms, deep ecology has proved to be significantly influential in ecophilosophy discourse (Fox 1990) as well as becoming the operating philosophy of many radical environmentalists (Devall 1988; Manes 1990).

The utopian, abstract radical nature of the social and biological objectives subsumed under the label of radical environmentalism has limited the degree to which this philosophy has influenced the day-to-day affairs of modern society. Nevertheless, radical environmentalism serves as a useful philosophical umbrella for several special interest groups whose own objectives overlap only partially with other radical environmentalists. The composition of particular groups which combine to undertake action depends therefore on the specific action being contemplated. Radical environmentalism has achieved a formal political voice in the election of green party candidates in the EEC Parliament and various European governments (Fisher 1993; Jancar-Webster 1993; Spretnak and Capra 1986). Within North America, green parties have been less able to garner the support of the voting public (McCloskey 1991; Slaton 1992). Instead, radical environmentalism has been more often adopted by grass-roots advocacy organizations (Sale 1993; Snow 1992a; 1992b). For radical environmentalist organizations such as Earth First!, the Sea Shepherd Society, Friends of the Earth, Rainforest Action Network and others, deep ecology principles provide a rationale for direct action campaigns of ecotage (ecological sabotage) and civil disobedience against those they view as enemies of nature. Not all radical environmentalists condone the use of violence in the struggle for transformational change in the human–nature relationship. More numerous have been campaigns of passive resistance against governments and industrial interests such as the Chipko movement of women in northern India to prevent logging in the Himalayan foothills (Shiva 1988) and environmentalist blockades to prevent logging in the Clayoquot Sound old-growth forests of coastal British Columbia. In pre-democratic Eastern Europe, there are numerous examples of effective large-scale grass-roots protests against environmental degradation, nuclear power projects, polluting industrial projects and the damming of the Danube River (Jancar-Webster 1993). On a smaller scale, grass-roots organizations have focused on local and regional environmental crises such as the Love Canal toxic waste dump (Wallace 1993).

Nevertheless, radical environmentalists have had limited influence on social change because they clearly oppose the most powerful arrangements and institutions in modern society. Rather than working less visibly from within, and running the risk of cooptation, proponents of radical environmentalism have attempted to effect social change from outside. While they may have had some marginal effect on selected local issues such as the reduction of clear-cutting in old-growth forests (Egri and Frost 1994), they have not yet produced either a coherent social movement or a set of proposed social reforms likely to be accepted or adopted by organizational members in mainstream society.

Critiques of the Reform Environmentalism Perspective

While the reform environmentalism perspective is not a 'pure' paradigm, it does represent a diversity of means by which industrialized society has sought to integrate the natural environment into decision-making. As observed by Gladwin (1993) the concept of 'greening' in society and its organizations is replete with ambiguity and contradictions more indicative of the garbage-can model of decision-making (March 1978) than any rational choice or planning.

Reform environmentalism has been criticized more by radical environmentalists than by the mainstream agencies it has sought to reform. While reform environmentalism proponents claim to be environmentally responsible, one critique by radical environmentalists is that the anthropocentric bias of reform environmentalists proposes only minor incremental adjustments to economic and technological systems rather than transformational changes in human society (Colby 1990).

The concept of sustainable development is perhaps the most contentious aspect of the reform environmentalism perspective for both reform and radical environmentalists (Hawken 1993; Jacobs 1993; McRobert and Muldoon 1992; Schnaiberg and Gould 1994; *The Ecologist* 1993). Intended to encompass a wide variety of approaches and initiatives, the imprecision of the term 'sustainable development' allows for a wide variety of interpretations and enactments. One position is that sustainable development is not possible given the fundamental contradictions between the principles and goals of environmental sustainability and those of economic development (Schnaiberg and Gould 1994).

Critics argue that the concept of sustainable development enables governments and industry to 'embrace environmentalism without commitment' (Jacobs 1993: 59). It is also charged that participants in high-profile public events such as the UNCED are engaging in symbolic politics – projecting the illusion of substantive environmental change while simultaneously protecting and promoting their economic self-interests and power bases. For example, the UNCED endorsement of the global liberalization of capital and trade is regarded as antithetical to the environmentalist principle of bioregionalism (Hawken 1993; McRobert and Muldoon 1992). Hawken is especially wary about the potential efficacy of international standards for environmental regulations and trade given the environmental records of multinational corporations as well as the nature of existing free trade governing bodies (such as GATT) which exclude small businesses, farms, churches, environmentalist organizations and trade unions. There is also little confidence in the ability of international bodies (such as the World Bank) to effectively institute environmentally sustainable economic policies in the face of contradictory pressures from member governments (Hawken 1993; Rich 1990).

Radical environmentalist critics also identify the Brundtland Report's and UNCED's Agenda 21 support of development of nuclear energy and biogenetic engineering technology as being environmentally destructive, not sustainable (Rifkin 1983; Shiva 1993; Women's Environment and Development Organization (WEDO) 1992). Ecofeminists find the identification of women's fertility rates as one of the major causes of environmental degradation to be particularly objectionable (WEDO 1992). Population control policies which violate the reproductive rights of women are seen as symptomatic of the continued marginalization of women and overall neglect of gender issues in the reform environmentalist agenda for change.

In regards to industrial organizations, environmental responsibility is seen as one facet of a wider range of corporate social responsibilities encompassing economic, legal, ethical and philanthropic concerns (Carroll et al. 1988). Whilst some argue that social and environmental performance objectives conflict with economic performance objectives (Buchholz 1993; Hawken 1993; Jacobs 1993), others assert that what is morally and ethically right is also economically beneficial for industrial organizations (Elkington and Burke 1989; Rice 1993; Russo and Fouts 1993; Schmidheiny 1992). However, empirical research indicates that corporate environmental responsibility is rarely voluntary and more often in response to strong regulatory and consumer pressures (Ilinitch and Schaltegger 1993; Schnaiberg and Gould 1994; Schot 1991; Steger 1993). This would tend to support mainstream (DSP) criticisms that the reform environmentalism agenda is both economically impractical (increased costs, fewer jobs) and procedurally undesirable (increased bureaucracy, less democracy). Both radical and reform environmentalists are sceptical about the promotion of the reformist vision of a 'green consumerism' and 'green capitalism' which can be regarded as oxymorons that permit a state of false ecological consciousness (Ekins 1991; Hawken 1993; Jacobs 1993).

Within the 'hydra-headed' environmental movement (Sale 1993; Snow 1992a), radical environmentalist and grass-roots advocacy groups often charge that large institutionalized bureaucratic reform environmentalist organizations have been coopted by the industrial and government status quo. Despite growth in memberships, a wide range of activities and public support, the record of mainstream reform environmentalist organizations has been less than exemplary in terms of the enactment of environmental statutes and mobilization of support for issues other than nature protection (McCloskey 1991).

In its defence, the reform environmentalism agenda of incremental change offers several positive features. Compared to the radical environmentalism position, the reform approach is more inclusive of diverse constituencies within government, industry and the general public in both the negotiation and implementation of environmentally informed action. Transformational potential can thereby be realized by the multiple incremental initiatives of wide breadth which in total may result in a fundamental shift in the human–nature relationship. However, one essential problem in regards to the 'sustainable development' concept as currently envisioned and enacted is that it represents a reluctance to totally abandon the DSP assumptions of infinite growth, consumerism, belief in technological fixes, and hierarchical social relations. There is the fundamental risk that an incremental approach may be concerned with only solving superficial symptoms rather than addressing the root causes of environmental degradation. It may be illusory that the environmental crisis is manageable and soluble through human ingenuity.

Summary Comments

As revealed by this review of environmentalist perspectives, there is no 'perfect' approach to envisioning and enacting the human–nature relationship. One theme for the three perspectives on eco-environments described here is their common focus on the physical environment as the lens through which each views the consequences of social, political and economic activities. At one end of the continuum, the dominant social paradigm represents an approach wherein the economic interests and needs of human society are pre-eminent over all other concerns. While it can be argued that this is a caricature of reality (both present and past), the DSP offers a useful conceptual point of departure for other perspectives which advocate changes to existing human–nature relationships. The primary strength of the radical environmentalism perspective resides in its (relative) philosophical coherence whilst its prescriptions for enactment remain largely untested. Although based on a less cohesive (and often contradictory) set of philosophical assumptions, the reform environmentalism perspective engenders a more optimistic pragmatic approach to resolving immediate environmental problems.

However, both reform and radical environmentalism challenge established conceptions we have of the purposes and consequences of modern industrial organizations. As a means of developing a further appreciation of the tensions between these perspectives, we now consider environments as seen through the lens of organization theory.

THE ENVIRONMENT IN ORGANIZATION THEORY

Not unlike environmentalists, organization theorists claim a centrality of their worldview. 'Organizations . . . are the fundamental building blocks of modern societies' (Aldrich and Marsden 1988: 361). Even a Nobel laureate in economics has argued that when viewing earth, a mythical visitor from space would discover that 'organizations would be the dominant feature of the landscape' (Simon 1991: 27). More recently, sociologists Schnaiberg and Gould (1994) have typified the dominant worldview as being a 'treadmill of production' in which the industrial logic of firms and other economic organizations maintains '*society-wide* social and political institutions which . . . expand both production . . . and ecological extraction' (Schnaiberg and Gould 1994: 45). Alternative theories or competing modes of thought, such as those of eco-environmentalism, will have to be particularly robust if they are to modify or displace established models of organizations based on an orgocentric perspective.

Traditional orthodoxy in organization theory has been dominated by functionalist perspectives in which organizations have been viewed as either machines or organisms or some combination of each metaphor (Morgan 1980). In the machine metaphor, organizations are viewed primarily as rational instruments for the accomplishment of pre-formed and internally generated objectives. Contextual or environmental constraints which limit the attainment of goals and objectives are given scant attention as the environment is taken as immutable and given by organizational actors. Such perspectives are consistent with the economic institutions of capitalism and the social ethos of individual competition. Market environments are considered to be self-regulating. Individual and collective welfare are maximized through the pursuit of individual self-interest and social and economic competition.

When organizations are viewed as organisms, the continued survival of an organization is seen as being dependent on an appropriate interactive and interdependent relationship between the organization and its environment. Thus, environments are attended to in so far as they constrain or risk organizational survival. In the short and not necessarily glorious history of organization theory (Perrow 1973), perspectives which emphasize ideas of environmental dependence are relatively new. While there were previous scatterings of ideas regarding the consequences of this environmental dependence (Dill 1958; Burns and Stalker 1961), sustained research on the nature of organizational environments did not begin to develop fully until the latter part of the 1960s and the early 1970s (Duncan 1972; Emery and Trist 1965; Evan 1966; Jurkovich 1974; Lawrence and Lorsch 1967; Osborne and Hunt 1974; Thompson 1967). Since then, there have been scattered assessments of organizational environments which have not radically changed traditional orgocentric perspectives (Aldrich 1979; Aldrich and Marsden 1988; Aldrich and Pfeffer 1976; Carroll et al. 1988; Meyer and Scott 1983; Starbuck 1976).

Current conceptualizations of organizational environments can be traced to the seminal work of Emery and Trist (1965). Their development of the 'causal texture' of organizational environments envisaged a set of transactional dependencies among a set of organizations viewed from the perspective of a single focal organization. The first-order environment of any focal organization consists of the relationships between that organization and others with which it has direct transactions – such as suppliers and customers. The second-order environment of the focal organization consists of all other relationships, or transactional dependencies, between organizations in the first-order environment and all other organizations. The causal texture of the environment of the focal organization therefore is a conceptual map of the causal linkages in which a change in the behaviour of any organization in that environment would influence the functioning of the focal organization. In this conceptualization, the second-order rather than the first-order environment is potentially more problematic for the functioning of a focal organization. First, changes in environmental elements are less visible in second-order environments. Second, the nature of the causal interdependencies in second-order environments is rarely known or understood by representatives of the focal organization.

Emery and Trist extended this framework to develop an initial classification of organizational environments. Organizational environments are problematic as a function of the degree of uncertainty they pose for organizational decision-makers. Such uncertainty is indicated by the strength of interorganizational linkages and the rates of change of the organizational elements in an environment. Environmental conditions are most problematic and produce greatest uncertainty when interorganizational linkages are dense and rates of change are high. Such environments are characterized as being 'turbulent'. In a potentially prophetic extension of the Emery and Trist model, Terryberry (1967) examined the trends in modern society and predicted that the environments of most organizations would evolve into turbulence – a condition not unfamiliar to students of the contemporary business press or chaos theory (Gleick 1987).

In developing these conceptualizations of environments, organization and management theorists extended traditional functionalist ways of thinking beyond organizational boundaries. For example, organizations need to spend more time and energy aligning collective actions under conditions of uncertainty than when conditions are stable and known (Thompson 1967). Thus, uncertainty detracts from organizational efficiency (a machine attribute) as less energy is available to pursue agreed-upon objectives. Moreover, because environments could potentially mean everything outside the organizational boundary, attention is focused on only those environmental attributes which make the pursuit of organizational objectives problematic. Organizational decision-makers are indifferent to events having consequences for other 'environmental' stakeholders but which have little consequence for the focal organization.

There have been relatively few attempts to define environments independently of a specific single or group of focal organizations. Scott (1981: 170) identified different levels of analysis

for the study of organizational environments. His review included concepts of the organization set (Blau and Scott 1962; Evan 1966) and the related term of organizational domain (Levine and White 1961; Thompson 1967) which were both similar to Emery and Trist's (1965) ideas of first-order environments. At broader and more encompassing levels of analysis, environments can also be considered as all organizations constituting either the ecological community (Hawley 1950) or the interorganizational field (Warren 1967; Trist 1983). For example, a more recent development regarding the nature of organizational environments originated with Hannan and Freeman's (1977) population ecology theory of organizations. Although these theories apply models, theories and methods from the biological sciences to populations of organizations, environments are again defined in relational terms. Organizational environments have no definition independent of those attributes, primarily their carrying capacity, which influences the survival characteristics of a population of organizations. In fact, population ecology models of organizations and their environments are extensions of the functionalist perspectives which have dominated organization theorizing. It is both ironic and misleading that the models derived from biology, applied to the analysis of organizations and their environments, and provided with an ecological label, should have so little to do with the biosphere (Young 1988). Other attempts to arrive at independent definitions of organizational environments have been used to define attributes of organizations themselves. Thus, Scott (1992) uses economists' definitions of markets such as pure competition or oligopoly to illustrate and summarize the consequences of attributes of a firm's environment for organizational design.

In all of these instances, conceptualizations of organizational environments fail to explicitly include considerations of the natural environment. Even attempts to define environments at environmental levels of analysis rely on relational constructs. That is, environments are defined as having no character to define other than their organizationally relevant attributes. Within the dominant paradigms of organizationally defined environments, we have few, if any, means of assessing the consequences of organizational actions for the qualities of the environment(s) which contain them.

Traditional perspectives on organizations and their environments have gained acceptance because of their utility for the initiation and engagement of collective action (Starbuck 1983), especially by powerful organizational decision-makers whose personal interests were assumed to be aligned with those of the organizations they represent. In the burgeoning market of professional business education during the post World War II period, at least two generations of managers in training have been exposed to limited rationales such as these. However, other open systems views of organizations and their environments have been developed from more institutional and critical perspectives.

In open systems perspectives, the boundary between organizations and their environments is viewed as permeable. Organizations cannot be easily separated from the environments in which they are embedded. They not only adapt to their environments but also strongly influence the nature of those environments. Derived from Selznick's (1948; 1957) seminal work in organizational sociology, numerous studies have examined the processes of organizational adaptation. Perrow (1972) outlines two generic options. Less powerful organizations are 'captured' by powerful environmental elements and modify their goals and objectives to ensure both the survival of the organization and presumably a continuation of the entitlements of organizationally dependent actors. Alternatively, more powerful organizations are able to impose their worldview on other organizations and agencies. In this latter scenario, powerful organizational leaders shape the ideology and resources under their control to produce environmental exigencies that are advantageous for the members of the dominant coalition which controls that organization (Aldrich and Pfeffer 1976). It is in the latter conceptualization that the fears of some environmentalists can be found. Organizations adapt to their task-defined environments, but individual, societal and (biophysical) environmental interests are not necessarily factored into the priorities of organizational decision-makers. This view assigns large degrees of relative influence to organizations over their environments. While such characterizations are undoubtedly true of a small number of large, powerful organizations, this perspective ignores the larger proportion of organizations which are more environmentally dependent. In addition, this perspective also fails to take into account the potential for environmental beliefs, norms and values to be incorporated into the axioms, assumptions, and values of powerful organizational members (Beyer 1981).

Organizational activities are not independent of the larger social, economic, cultural, political and technical systems of which they are a part. All have outside interests and commitments which inform their behaviours inside the organization as well as their intended objectives for organizational activities. Organizations import knowledge and technologies into their internal domains. They also take in resources and supplies which are combined and transformed to provide outputs to the larger social environment. In the long run, organizations need to continue to provide valued functions to the larger society if they are to continue to survive (Fellmeth 1970; Maniha and Perrow 1965).

The net consequence of these pressures is for organizations to become more or less isomorphic with their environments as this 'fit' is required if they are to acquire the resources and legitimacy needed to operate in those environments. Conventionally, environmentally dependent organizations will have to adjust to strong environmental demands whereas more powerful organizations can shape environmental exigencies to better suit their requirements. In either case, social values will be carried by organizational participants into the direction and guidance of organizational activities. Thus organizations can be considered to adapt to their environments in at least two ways. First, within the limited perspective of a rational, mechanistic model, organizations change when it is within the limited self-interests of the organization to do so. Second, from an institutional point of view, organizations will accommodate changing social values as these are imported into the decision premises of members of the organization's dominant coalition (Meyer and Rowan 1983; Powell and DiMaggio 1991). It is quite clear, though rarely examined explicitly, that orgocentric conceptions of organizational environments have little apparent overlap with the concerns of environmentalists. None has a complete view of any other, and misconceptions are actively encouraged. The 'straw man' environmentalist perspective of the dominant social paradigm, as well as that of radical environmentalists, fails to acknowledge open systems characteristics of organizations. Advocates of the bounded rationality embedded in DSP perspectives fear the indeterminacy associated with the inclusion of humanistic values into organizational considerations. Radical environmentalists have so far only proposed romantic ideals with little thought being given to the practical manner in which their nirvana may be attained. Reform environmentalists have proposed various modifications to DSP values – but relatively few of these have been translated into orgocentric action frames.

From the perspective of organization theory, environmental degradation becomes relevant only when the performance of a focal organization and the welfare of organizational participants are affected by such concerns. Organizational actions which degrade the local environment become pertinent when future organizational survival or profitability is threatened by legislated restrictions or scarcity of natural resources. In contrast, a clear theme of many environmentalists is that the limited and shortsighted actions of organizational actors inevitably degrade the natural environment. From their perspective, there is a clear link between organizational actions and their conception of what constitutes the environment. However, the exhortations of environmentalists for organizations to modify their behaviours without framing such persuasion in terms of organizational self-interests is to misunderstand the logics of organizational action.

Despite these confusions, we believe there is a nexus for these different perspectives. We argue that functionalist abstractions of organizational environments understate the potential for aspects of the natural environment to be included in the decision premises of organizational actors. As persons who hope to continue to exist in the bounded biosphere of spaceship earth, we believe that self-interested environmental actions will be informed by the values, knowledge and experiences of organizational actors.

INTEGRATING PERSPECTIVES ON ECO-ENVIRONMENTS AND ORGANIZATIONS

Essentially, the environmentalist debate is concerned with fundamental and transformational changes in the deep structure of society (see Elliott 1988; Egri and Frost 1994; and others). A compelling question therefore concerns the extent to which, both conceptually and practically, the present state of affairs should remain or whether there are advantages to greater overlap and synthesis of these disparate ideas. That is, to what extent can and should environmentalist views of biophysical environments be incorporated into organizational views of their environments? In this section of the chapter, we focus on two issues – self-interest and systems theory – which illustrate the challenges of integrating these disparate approaches to eco-environments.

Self-Interest and Environmental Change

The dominant features of contemporary society are deeply embedded. Challenges to the status quo need to be based on powerful motives if they are to modify existing arrangements which may contain strong tendencies for global self-destruction. Thus, our discussion of self-interest is presented as a device for merging concerns for the environment with the possibility of organizational action.

In contemporary society, organizations are the primary means for accomplishing collective action. However, collective actions are usually framed within a hierarchy of nested systems. Individual actors confront the reality of conflicting objectives in their individual experiences of ambivalence. Individuals also experience tension between their personal objectives and the immediate social systems such as families and work groups which frame individual action. At larger and broader levels of analysis, the salience of individual perspectives diminishes as organizational, regional and possibly national interests provide the frames through which prospective collective actions are assessed. A common thread throughout the cognitions and rationalizations associated with the intentionality of action is self-interest.

Self-interests can be viewed through a number of different lenses. At its most primitive and selfish level, self-interest is short term and totally preoccupied with the physical survival of the individual. At one level removed from this primitive conceptualization is a concept of self-interest based on immediate family and progeny (cf. Simon 1993; Samuelson 1993; Wilson 1975). Individuals could consider sacrificing their well-being (their lives??) for an improved change for the survival of progeny which carry their genes. Thus parents forgo leisure and consumption to invest in the education of their children and provide them with resources which improve their life chances. At a small remove from this would be self-interest based on a loose family collectivity such as a clan or a tribe. The widest conceptualization of self-interest is one based on the species (*Homo sapiens*). Individuals and collectives forgo returns from immediately beneficial activities, such as the development of nuclear energy or the usage of fossil fuels, to improve the chances that both current and future citizens of the whole planet would be exposed to less environmental risk from increased solar radiation, proliferation of nuclear weapons, global warming or elevated sea levels.

Two aspects of competing perceptions of reality complicate assessments of self-interest which frame action perspectives. On the one hand, we can consider the immediacy or distance of environmental threat. On the other hand, environmental threats can be considered as being experienced (and therefore motivated) by individuals, genetically similar groups, or whole societies. When self-interest can be shown to be immediately at risk as a consequence of actions over which they have control, those actions will be changed. But when the consequences of current actions are problematic, unclear and not necessarily experienced until several decades or longer into the future, self-interests of those benefiting from current arrangements will lead to resistance of environmentalist advocates. In contested situations such as these, claims for legitimacy based on partial scientific evidence, normative ideology, and political contests become the currency of public debate (Pinfield and Berner 1992; Samuel and Spencer 1993; Schelling 1992).

Nevertheless, a shared appreciation of environmental issues is critical as resolution of environmental threats invariably requires interdependent collective action. Without substantial agreement regarding the nature of collaborative actions, individual actions are unlikely to serve the interests of any higher-level collectivity. Similarly, local actions taken by collectives will have little effect on global consequences unless other collectives, which also contribute to environmental degradation, modify their behaviours as well. Moreover, we should recognize that not all persons and collectivities are similarly situated either to see or to experience scarce or degraded resources.

Expression of special interests and the working through of collective actions require the agency of organizations. Attainment of the outcomes desired by any environmentalist group requires an appreciation of how special interest and collective objectives may be obtained. We live in an organizational world in which organizations are the means through which interests are realized. No matter which environmental perspective is accepted, orgocentric tradition, philosophy, and knowledge are required if goals are to be attained. Organizations are special purpose social collectivities whose activities are informed by the interests of organizational participants. These interests are circumscribed by those of other actors who operate both within and outside of organizational boundaries, and are considered to be essential to organizational functioning. Organizationally defined environments are functionally useful constructs for the accomplishment of collective actions. The environmental perspective described as the dominant social paradigm is a crude and limited interpretation of action perspectives on organizations as it ignores the relationally defined construct of organizational environments. Nevertheless, open systems models of organizations, while still problematic, permit the introduction of environmentalist concerns into organizational decision criteria. The attributions (caricatures) by environmentalists of hermetically sealed boundaries between organizations and their eco-environments as characterizations of the DSP are inaccurate representations of contemporary organizations. Moreover, contemporary organizational parallels of the DSP do encourage action perspectives

which eventually could include amelioration of environmental abuses.

In contrast, the radical environmentalism perspective presents a transformational view of desired outcomes. Organizational actions required 'to get there from here' are not considered. Organizational and radical environmentalist perspectives are presently incompatible and the possibility for a synthesis of the two is minimal. In the short term, proponents of the radical environmentalist perspective need to use and master mass media if their message is to be received and accepted by mainstream members of society. We speculate that the requirements for collective action would likely produce conflict between orgocentric ideas and the coherence of the radical environmentalist position. Proponents of radical environmentalism may find their accomplishments limited by their inherent denial of self-interest in organizational actions. As have others who have argued for larger social concerns to be factored into organizational objectives, advocates of radical environmentalism may find their emotional energies sapped by lack of progress and their attention claimed by other issues (Downs 1972). The ideological pull of radical environmentalism will remain, but in a muted form that will help ground further elaborations of the reform environmentalist viewpoint.

Reform environmentalism offers a viable long-term perspective on bio-environments because it is this perspective alone which more or less accepts the collective action utilitarianism of relational definitions of organizational environments. Evaluations of environments defined in biophysical terms are relevant to organizational decision-makers when translated into terms of their self-interest. These self-interests can be defined in increasingly broad terms of societal values, informed by new information regarding the consequences of individual and collective organizational actions. While we have incomplete information regarding these consequences (Hawken 1993; Shrivastava 1994; Stead and Stead 1992), this clearly represents an opportunity for further truly interdisciplinary organizational research.

Once such information becomes available, what are the chances it will be used to inform and redirect the activities of organizational participants? For those persons whose interests are not served, or are possibly even harmed, by the activities of a focal organization, two sets of tactics are available to them to change that situation. The first is to find avenues for influence through the existing institutional superstructure (Astley and Fombrun 1987) of the community of which the focal organization is a member. If the existing institutional superstructure provides little or no recourse, then citizens (at least those in democratic societies) have opportunities to elaborate that superstructure in the form of new legislation and regulations. Such developments are not likely to occur quickly. We recognize it is possible that the long-term harm from the activities of focal organizations could be well established before any meaningful restrictions could be developed and applied. Moreover, the development of new legislation is likely to be contested by those who benefit from the absence of such legislation and those whose interests would be harmed by the passage of such legislation. Nevertheless, the formal and informal 'rules' governing the conduct and consequences of organizational activities would be subject to both scientific and political scrutiny.

Political scrutiny and evaluation occur within an existing normative ideology. As part of the process of attempting to change or elaborate existing legislation, political action necessarily involves attempts to change existing ideologies. Proponents of new legislation can attempt to apply moral suasion to the activities of a focal organization. They can attempt to change the values of the members of the dominant coalition or work to change the larger social values so that the activities of targeted firms are perceived as being less and less legitimate. In either case, the legitimacy of existing organizational arrangements becomes the trigger for change of organizational activities in which the self-interests of the dominant coalition are judged to run counter to those of other members of society. There will be continuing political conflict between social and organizational objectives and the quality of the natural environment (Schnaiberg and Gould 1994).

The Promise of Systems Theory

Systems theory appears to be a common conceptual framework for both environmentalist and organizational domains. Indeed, one common prescription amongst environmentalist writers is for the wholesale adoption of ecological systems principles in societies and organizations as the 'only path' towards environmental sustainability (Milbrath 1989; Shrivastava 1992; 1994; Stead and Stead 1992). What is less discussed within each perspective is that reality is socially constructed with the consequence being that the temporal and spatial boundaries which both focus and limit attention are problematic. Paradoxically, these problematic features of both domains permit an optimistic, adaptive future confluence of two historically separate conceptual schemata. As information on the consequences of collective

human and organizational actions on the biosphere becomes available, it will gradually be enacted into the beliefs of social actors (Gamson et al. 1992). Individuals, whether through self-interest or through a cultivation of ecological consciousness, will modify collective conceptualizations of organizations and their environments.

There are a number of theoretical issues which remain largely unresolved in the sociological and organization theory literatures about social systems, and within ecological theory about ecological systems. Open systems theory directs us to view organizations and the biosphere as dynamic phenomena which are constantly adjusting to changing environments. Systems comprise subsystems and individual units which are also in states of dynamic change in relation to each other. However, the linkages between individual action and system-level consequences (the micro–macro relationship) and linkages between system-level changes and individual consequences (the macro-micro relationship) remain largely unexplored by social scientists (Ashmos and Huber 1987; Coleman 1986; Namboodiri 1988). One important exception is the exploration of the nature of connections between social and ecological systems in terms of tight and loose coupling (Weick 1979).

In general, loosely coupled systems have often been regarded as a positive feature of organizations, with tightly coupled systems being regarded as less desirable in modern organizations. As determined by Perrow (1984), tightly coupled technological systems are prone to 'normal accidents'. More recently, Weick and Roberts (1993) have proposed that tightly coupled *social* systems can mediate or neutralize the dangers inherent in tightly coupled *technological* systems. Conceptualizing the collective mind as 'the pattern of heedful interrelations of actions in a social system', Weick and Roberts (1993: 357), propose that individual actions in high reliability (dangerous) systems need to be both representative of, and subordinate to, mutually shared meanings and communities of practice. Cooperation, rather than individualism, is essential for heedful (careful) action in systems of interactive complexity. This introduces more complexity to developing an appreciation of the dynamics of tight and loose coupling between organizational and ecological systems.

Within the reform environmentalism perspective, industrial ecology proposes that environmental safety is enhanced through the development of closed tightly coupled industrial systems of production. The underlying assumption is that industrial activity is inherently dangerous to ecological systems, therefore industrial systems need to be heedful but disengaged from wider eco-environments. Consistent with Weick and Roberts's observations regarding tightly coupled social systems under such conditions, individual actions are informed and subordinate to that of the collective value of environmental sustainability.

More problematic for concerted environmental action are what Weick and Roberts identify as conditions where there is an undeveloped collective mind. As learned in the analysis of the reform environmentalism perspective, there remain significant contradictions between espoused environmentalist values and visible actions concerning the natural environment. While part of this can be attributed to the early stage of the sustainable development concept, much can be traced to the lack of willingness to totally abandon the values of individualism and competitive free market principles of Western industrialized societies. These values inform loose coupling within and between social, technological and ecological systems. As identified by Weick and Roberts (1993: 378): 'A culture that encourages individualism, survival of the fittest, macho heroics, and can-do reactions will often neglect heedful practice of representation and subordination.' To the degree that these cultural values remain within the reform environmentalism perspective, heedful environmental action will continue to be compromised and incremental changes may remain isolated or absorbed into the status quo. Systems theory also offers an alternative hypothesis concerning the outcome of incremental actions. Consistent with the underlying premise of the environmentalist credo 'Think globally, act locally', what may appear to be incremental change in one small part of a system may, over time, amplify to effect a large-scale transformation in macro-level systems. Irrespective, traditional research methodologies which limit the spatial and temporal scope of inquiry appear to be ill suited to addressing questions concerning multi-faceted systems phenomena. Organizational research needs to further develop a diversity of approaches to studying organizations and their eco-environments.

CONCLUDING THOUGHTS

The more we get out of the world the less we leave, and in the long run we shall have to pay our debts at a time that may be inconvenient for our own survival. (Wiener 1954: 2)

The 'issue–attention cycle' of social issues would suggest that current concern with environmental issues is only temporary and will fade away as problems are resolved and a bored public turns its attention to other issues (Downs 1972). However, historical and empirical evidence is proving otherwise (Dunlap 1989). Concern with the natural environment has a long history and has proved to be remarkably resilient despite temporary detours and lulls in activity. One reason why the environmental challenge to society and its organizations promises to remain and become more prominent is that humans are witnessing and experiencing the deleterious effects of the degradation of the natural environment on a scale and scope unprecedented in human history.

Another reason can be found in the concept of biophilia, which is defined as the 'innately emotional affiliation of human beings to other living organisms' (Wilson 1984: 31). The biophilia hypothesis proposes that humans' relations with the natural environment are simultaneously concerned with the material, emotional, cognitive, aesthetic and spiritual dimensions of human existence (Kellert 1993). The three alternative perspectives on eco-environments identified in this chapter represent degrees of emphasis on each interconnected dimension. While the dominant social paradigm emphasizes humans' dominionistic and utilitarian relations with nature, the radical environmentalism perspective emphasizes humans' emotional, aesthetic and spiritual connections with the natural environment. The mid-range reform environmentalism perspective represents a more cognitive (or scientific) approach to integrating and balancing these sometimes contradictory dimensions. The central tenet of the biophilia hypothesis is that each approach has a place and role to play in the evolutionary history of humanity. Overemphasis on one or a few to the exclusion of other facets can have destructive consequences for both humans and the natural environment. For example, focusing solely on the material value and benefits to be derived from the natural environment (as per the dominant social paradigm) informs environmentally unsustainable actions and will ultimately threaten humans' long-term needs for sustenance, protection and security. Similarly, preserving the natural environmental purely for its aesthetic value (as per deep ecology) to the exclusion of other relations with the natural environment denies the development of material relations necessary for human physical existence. In the end, there is a need for a balance among these disparate and sometimes conflicting relationships with the natural environment – not a static final balance, but a dynamic balancing between evolving human and natural systems of existence.

A similar argument can be made concerning the introduction of the natural environment into the discourse of organization theory and practice. As learned in our discussion of organization theory, orthodox conceptualizations of organizational interests and actions have been largely devoid of considerations of the human–nature connection. And yet, there is increasing evidence that changes in the biophysical environment will clearly bring societal change. From environmentalist perspectives, biophysical and social change is imminent and inevitable. Thus adhering to the status quo in both organizational theory and action is not a safe avenue but a destructive one for the biosphere and the human species. That change is inevitable is not at issue. It is the direction and nature of change which are the focus of the environmentalist challenge to organization science. As Lovelock (1988) proposes in his Gaia principle, the biosphere of the planet will continue to adapt and change as a result of human and nonhuman phenomena: the essential question is whether the future biosphere will be one which includes the human species.

NOTES

1 In 1935, British plant ecologist Tansley would introduce the concept of *ecosystems* as being: 'the whole *system* (in the sense of physics) including not only the organism-complex, but also the whole complex of physical factors forming what we call the environment of the biome – the habitat factors in the widest sense' (as cited by McIntosh 1985: 193).

2 As proposed by Kassas and Polunin (1989), ecosystems comprise of three systems: the *biosphere*, which encompasses the planet's lower atmosphere, lithosphere (land), hydrosphere (aquatic) and life systems; the *technosphere*, which is composed of the systems of human structures within the biosphere; and the *sociosphere*, which is composed of the sociopolitical, socioeconomic and sociocultural institutions created by humans. The biosphere performs three interrelated functions in maintaining living systems, that is, it provides resources, it provides environmental services (such as life support and amenities) and it accumulates waste products (Jacobs 1993).

3 However, defenders of Marxist theory assert that the original Marxist teachings were not antagonistic to the natural environment but rather that the centralized practices of modern socialist states were based on a Stalinist interpretation of communism (Grundmann 1991; McLaughlin 1990; Raskin and Bernow 1991). As Pepper (1993: 109) contends, Marx's 'society–nature dialectic appears to be, in reality, deeply organic (seeing them both as making up one organic body) and monist (physical and mental phenomena can be analyzed in terms of a common underlying reality)'.

4 The first law of thermodynamics is the conservation law, which states that the total amount of energy is constant, is not destroyed or created but is transformed from one state to another (Stead and Stead 1992). The second is the entropy law, which posits that when energy changes state, a portion of available useful energy is lost. In respect to living systems, there is the potential for negative entropy in that the import of additional energy can forestall decline and death (Georgescu-Rogen 1971).

REFERENCES

Aldrich, H.E. (1979) *Organizations and Environments*. Englewood Cliffs, NJ: Prentice-Hall.
Aldrich, H.E. and Marsden, P.V. (1988) 'Environments and organizations', in N.J. Smelser (ed.), *The Handbook of Sociology*. Newbury Park, CA: Sage.
Aldrich, H.E. and Pfeffer, J. (1976) 'Environments of organizations', *Annual Review of Psychology*, 27: 79–105.
Alexander, D. (1990) 'Bioregionalism: science or sensibility?', *Environmental Ethics*, 12(2): 161–73.
Allenby, B.R. (1992) 'Achieving sustainable development through industrial ecology', *International Environmental Affairs*, 4(1): 56–68.
Ashmos, D.P. and Huber, G.P. (1987) 'The systems paradigm in organization theory: correcting the record and suggesting the future', *Academy of Management Review*, 12(4): 607–21.
Astley, W.G. and Fombrun, C.J. (1987) 'Organizational communities: an ecological perspective', *Research in the Sociology of Organizations*, 5: 163–85.
Baram, M. and Dillon, P. (1993) 'Corporate management of chemical accident risks', in K. Fischer and J. Schot (eds), *Environmental Strategies for Industry: International Perspectives on Research Needs and Policy Implications*. Washington, DC: Island Press. pp. 227–41.
Bennett, S.J. (1991) *Ecopreneuring: the Complete Guide to Small Business Opportunities from the Environmental Revolution*. New York: Wiley.
Berkes, F. (ed.) (1989) *Common Property Resources: Ecology and Community-Based Sustainable Development*. London: Belhaven.
Berle, G. (1990) *The Green Entrepreneur: Business Opportunities that can Save the Earth and Make You Money*. Liberty Hall Press.
Berry, T. (1988) *The Dream of the Earth*. San Francisco: Sierra Club Books.
Beyer, J.M. (1981) 'Ideologies, values, and decision making in organizations', in P.C. Nystrom and W.H. Starbuck (eds), *Handbook of Organizational Design*, vol. 2. New York: Oxford University Press.
Bird, E.A.R. (1987) 'The social construction of nature: theoretical approaches to the history of environmental problems', *Environmental Review*, 11(4): 255–64.

Blau, P.M. and Scott, W.R. (1962) *Formal Organizations*. San Francisco: Chandler.

Bookchin, M. (1980) *Toward an Ecological Society*. Montreal: Black Rose Books.

Bookchin, M. (1982) *The Ecology of Freedom: the Emergence and Dissolution of Hierarchy*. Palo Alto, CA: Cheshire Books.

Bookchin, M. (1990a) *Philosophy of Social Ecology: Essays on Dialectical Naturalism*. Montreal: Black Rose Books.

Bookchin, M. (1990b) *Remaking Society: Pathways to a Green Future*. Boston: South End Press.

Bookchin, M. (1994) *Which Way for the Ecology Movement?* San Francisco: Ak Press.

Bradford, G. (1987) 'How deep is deep ecology? A challenge to radical environmentalism', *Fifth Estate*, 22(Fall).

Bramwell, A. (1989) *Ecology in the 20th Century*. New Haven, CT: Yale University Press.

Brown, L.R. (ed.) (1991) *The WorldWatch Reader on Global Environmental Issues*. New York: W.W. Norton.

Buchholz, R.A. (1993) *Principles of Environmental Management: the Greening of Business*. Englewood Cliffs, NJ: Prentice-Hall.

Burns, T. and Stalker, G.M. (1961) *The Management of Innovation*. London: Tavistock.

Cairncross, F. (1991) *Costing the Earth: the Challenge for Governments, the Opportunities for Business*. Boston: Harvard Business School Press.

Callenbach, E., Capra, F., Goldman, L., Lutz, R. and Marburg, S. (1993) *EcoManagement: the Elmwood Guide to Ecological Auditing and Sustainable Business*. San Francisco: Berrett-Koehler.

Carroll, G.R., Delacroix, J. and Goodstein, J. (1988) 'The political environments of organizations: an ecological view', *Research in Organizational Behaviour*, 10: 359–92.

Carson, R. (1962) *Silent Spring*. Boston: Houghton Mifflin.

Catton, W.R. Jr and Dunlap, R.E. (1978) 'Environmental sociology: a new paradigm', *The American Sociologist*, 13(February): 41–9.

Cheney, J. (1987) 'Eco-feminism and deep ecology', *Environmental Ethics*, 9(2): 115–45.

Cheney, J. (1989) 'The neo-stoicism of radical environmentalism', *Environmental Ethics*, 11(4): 293–325.

Clow, M. (1986) 'Marxism and the "environmental question": an assessment of Bahro', *Studies in Political Economy*, 20(Summer): 171–86.

Colburn, T.E., Davidson, A., Green, S.N., Hodge, R.A., Jackson, C.I. and Liroff, R.A. (1990) *Great Lakes Great Legacy?* Washington, DC: Conservation Foundation. Ottawa: Institute for Research for Public Policy.

Colby, M.E. (1990) 'Ecology, economics, and social systems: the evolution of the relationship between environmental management and development'. PhD dissertation, University of Pennsylvania.

Coleman, J.S. (1986) 'Social theory, social research, and a theory of action', *American Journal of Sociology*, 91(6): 1309–35.

Commoner, B. (1990) *Making Peace with the Planet* (1975). New York: Pantheon Books.

Cotgrove, S. and Duff, A. (1981) 'Environmentalism, values and social change', *British Journal of Sociology*, 32(1): 92–110.

Crowfoot, J.E. and Wondolleck, J.M. (1990) *Environmental Disputes: Community Involvement in Conflict Resolution*. Washington, DC: Island Press.

Daly, H.E. (1977) *Steady-State Economics*. New York: Freeman.

Daly, H.E. and Cobb, J.B. Jr (1994) *For the Common Good: Redirecting the Economy toward Community, the Environment, and a Sustainable Future*, 2nd edn. Boston: Beacon Press.

Davies, C. (1991) 'The need for ecological cooperation in Europe', *International Journal on the Unity of the Sciences*, 4(2): 201–16.

Day, D. (1989) *The Environmental Wars: Reports from the Front Lines*. New York: St Martin's Press.

Devall, B. (1988) *Simple in Means, Rich in Ends: Practicing Deep Ecology*. Salt Lake City: Peregrine Smith Books.

Devall, B. and Sessions, G. (1985) *Deep Ecology*. Salt Lake City: Peregrine Smith Books.

Diamond, I. and Forenstein, G. (eds) (1990) *Reweaving the World: The Emergence of Ecofeminism*. San Francisco: Sierra Club Books.

Dill, W.R. (1958) 'Environment as an influence on managerial autonomy', *Administrative Science Quarterly*, 2: 409–43.

Dorfman, R. and Dorfman, N.S. (eds) (1977) *Economics of the Environment: Selected Readings*, 2nd edn. New York: W.W. Norton.

Downs, A. (1972) 'Up and down with ecology: the "issue-attention cycle"', *The Public Interest*, 28(Spring): 38–50.

Drengson, A. (1980) 'Shifting paradigms: from the technocratic to the person-planetary', *Environmental Ethics*, 2(3): 221–40.

Duncan, R.B. (1972) 'Characteristics of organizational environments and perceived environmental uncertainty', *Administrative Science Quarterly*, 17: 313–27.

Dunlap, R.E. (1989) 'Public opinion and environmental policy', in J.P. Lester (ed.), *Environmental Politics and Policy: Theories and Evidence*. London: Duke University Press. pp. 87–134.

Egri, C.P. and Frost, P.J. (1992) 'The power and politics of interorganizational collaboration to engender environmental sustainability in agriculture'. Paper presented at the 1992 Academy of Management Meeting, Las Vegas.

Egri, C.P. and Frost, P.J. (1994) 'The organizational politics of sustainable development', in H. Thomas, D. O'Neal, R. White and D. Hurst (eds), *Building the Strategically-Responsive Organization*. Chichester: Wiley. pp. 215–30.

Ehrenfeld, D. (1978) *The Arrogance of Humanism*. New York: Oxford University Press.

Eisler, R. (1987) *The Chalice and the Blade: Our History, Our Future*. San Francisco: Harper & Row.

Ekins, P. (1991) 'A strategy for global development', *Development*, 2: 64–73.

Elkington, J. and Burke, T. (1989) *The Green Capitalists: How to Make Money and Protect the Environment*. London: Victor Gollancz.

Elliott, B. (ed.) (1988) *Technology and Social Process*. Edinburgh: Edinburgh University Press.

Emery, F. and Trist, E.L. (1965) 'The causal texture of organizational environments', *Human Relations*, 18(1): 21–32.

Evan, W.M. (1966) 'The organization set: toward a theory of interorganizational relations', in J. Thompson (ed.), *Approaches to Organizational Design*. Pittsburgh: University of Pittsburgh Press.

Fellmeth, R.C. (1970) *The Interstate Commerce Commission*. New York: Grossman.

Feshbach, M. and Friendly, A. Jr (1992) *Ecocide in the USSR: Health and Nature under Siege*. New York: Basic Books.

Feyerherm, A.E. (1994) 'Leadership in collaboration: a longitudinal study of two interorganizational rule-making groups', *Leadership Quarterly*, 5(3/4).

Fisher, D. (1993) 'The emergence of the environmental movement in Eastern Europe and its role in the revolutions of 1989', in B. Jancar-Webster (ed.), *Environmental Action in Eastern Europe: Responses to Crisis*. Armonck, NY: M.E. Sharpe. pp. 89–113.

Flannery, B.L. and May, D.R. (1994) 'Prominent factors influencing environmental leadership: application of a theoretical model in the waste management industry', *Leadership Quarterly*, 5(3/4).

Fox, S. (1981) *John Muir and his Legacy*. Boston: Little, Brown.

Fox, W. (1990) *Toward a Transpersonal Ecology: Developing New Foundations for Environmentalism*. Boston: Shambhala.

Friend, A.M. (1992) 'Economics, ecology and sustainable development: are they compatible?', *Environmental Values*, 1(2): 157–70.

Gamson, W.A., Croteau, D., Hoynes, W. and Sasson, T. (1992) 'Media images and the social construction of reality', *Annual Review of Sociology*, 18: 373–93.

Georgescu-Rogen, N. (1971) *The Entropy Law and the Economic Process*. Cambridge, MA: Harvard University Press.

Gladwin, T.N. (1993) 'The meaning of greening: a plea for organizational theory', in K. Fischer and J. Schot (eds), *Environmental Strategies for Industry: International Perspectives on Research Needs and Policy Implications*. Washington, DC: Island Press. pp. 37–61.

Gleick, J. (1987) *Chaos: Making a New Science*. New York: Penguin.

Gray, B. (1989) *Collaborating: Finding Common Ground for Multiparty Problems*. San Francisco: Jossey-Bass.

Grundmann, R. (1991) *Marxism and Ecology*. Oxford: Clarendon Press.

Hahn, R.W. and Hester, G.L. (1989) 'Marketable permits: lessons for theory and practice', *Ecology Law Quarterly*, 16(2): 361–406.

Hannan, M.T. and Freeman, J. (1977) 'The population ecology of organizations', *American Journal of Sociology*, 82: 929–64.

Hardin, G. (1968) 'The tragedy of the commons', *Science*, 162(13 December): 1243–8.

Hardin, G. (1991) 'The tragedy of the unmanaged commons: population and the disguises of providence', in R.V. Andelson (ed.), *Commons without Tragedy: Protecting the Environment from Overpopulation – a New Approach*. London: Shepheard-Walwyn. pp. 162–85.

Hawken, P. (1993) *The Ecology of Commerce: A Declaration of Sustainability*. New York: Harper Business.

Hawley, A.H. (1950) *Human Ecology*. New York: Ronald.

Hay, P.R. and Haward, M.G. (1988) 'Comparative green politics: beyond the European context?', *Political Studies*, 36: 433–48.

Hays, S.P. (1987) *Beauty, Health, and Permanence: Environmental Politics in the United States 1955–1985*. New York: Cambridge University Press.

Hughes, J.D. (1975) *Ecology in Ancient Civilizations*. Albuquerque: University of New Mexico Press.

Hull, F. (ed.) (1993) *Earth and Spirit: the Spiritual Dimension of the Environmental Crisis*. New York: Continuum.

Ilinitch, A.Y. and Schaltegger, S.C. (1993) 'Eco-integrated-portfolio analysis: a strategic tool for managing sustainably'. Paper presented at the 1993 Academy of Management Meeting, Atlanta.

Irvine, S. and Ponton, A. (1988) *A Green Manifesto*. London: Macdonald Optima.

Jacobs, M. (1993) *The Green Economy: Environment, Sustainable Development and the Politics of the Future*. Vancouver, BC: UBC Press.

Jacobs, R. (1991) 'Deep ecology: a philosophy for the twenty-first century?', *Tijdschrift voor Sociale Wetenschappen*, 36(4): 364–99.

Jancar-Webster, B. (ed.) (1993) *Environmental Action in Eastern Europe: Responses to Crisis*. Armonck, NY: M.E. Sharpe.

Jung, H.Y. (1991) 'Marxism and deep ecology in postmodernity: from *Homo oeconomicus* to *Homo ecologicus*', *Thesis Eleven*, 28: 86–99.

Jurkovich, R. (1974) 'A core typology of organizational environments', *Administrative Science Quarterly* 19(3): 380–90.

Kassas, M. and Polunin, N. (1989) 'The three systems of man', *Environmental Conservation*, 16(1): 7–11.

Keating, M. (1993) *The Earth Summit's Agenda for Change: a Plain Language Version of Agenda 21 and the Other Rio Agreements*. Geneva: Centre for Our Common Future.

Kellert, S.R. (1993) 'The biological basis for human

values of nature', in S.R. Kellert and E.O. Wilson (eds), *The Biophilia Hypothesis*. Washington, DC: Island Press. pp. 42–69.

King, Y. (1989) 'The ecology of feminism and the feminism of ecology', in J. Plant (ed.), *Healing the Wounds: The Promise of Ecofeminism*. Santa Cruz, CA: New Society. pp. 18–28.

Kleindorfer, P.K. and Kunreuther, H.C. (eds) (1986) *Insuring and Managing Hazardous Risks: from Seveso to Bhopal and Beyond*. Berlin/New York: IIASA and Springer-Verlag.

Lawrence, P.R. and Lorsch, J.W. (1967) *Organization and Environment*. Boston: Harvard University Press.

Lee, D.C. (1980) 'On the Marxian view of the relationship between man and nature', *Environmental Ethics*, 2(1): 3–16.

Leopold, A. (1949) *A Sand County Almanac with Essays on Conservation from Round River*. New York: Ballantine Books, 1966.

Levine, S. and White, P.E. (1961) 'Exchange as a conceptual framework for the study of interorganizational relationships', *Administrative Science Quarterly*, 5: 583–601.

Lovelock, J.E. (1979) *Gaia: a New Look at Life on Earth*. Oxford: Oxford University Press.

Lovelock, J.E. (1988) *The Ages of Gaia: a Biography of Our Living Earth*. Oxford: Oxford University Press.

Luke, T. (1988) 'The dreams of deep ecology', *Telos*, 76(Summer): 65–92.

MacLarkey, R.L. (1991) 'The emergence of environmental legislation and policy in the Great Lakes ecosystem', *International Review of Modern Sociology*, 21(2): 93–111.

Manes, C. (1990) *Green Rage: Radical Environmentalism and the Unmaking of Civilization*. Boston: Little, Brown.

Maniha, J.K. and Perrow, C. (1965) 'The reluctant organization and the aggressive environment', *Administrative Science Quarterly*, 10: 238–57.

March, J.G. (1978) 'Bounded rationality, ambiguity, and the engineering of choice', *Bell Journal of Economics*, 9: 587–608.

McCloskey, M. (1991) 'Twenty years of change in the environmental movement: an insider's view', *Society and Natural Resources*, 4(3): 273–84.

McGowan, R.A. and Mahon, J.F. (1991) 'Multiple games multiple levels: the greening of strategy on environmental issues'. Paper presented at the Strategic Management Society Annual Conference, Toronto.

McIntosh, R.P. (1985) *The Background of Ecology: Concept and Theory*. Cambridge: Cambridge University Press.

McLaughlin, A. (1990) 'Ecology, capitalism and socialism', *Socialism and Democracy*, 10 (Spring–Summer): 69–102.

McRobert, D. and Muldoon, P. (1992) 'Towards a bioregional perspective on international resource-use conflicts: lessons for the future', in M. Ross and J.O. Saunders (eds), *Growing Demands on a*

Shrinking Heritage: Managing Resource-Use Conflicts: Essays from the Fifth Institute Conference on Natural Resources Law. Calgary: Canadian Institute of Resources Law. pp. 187–215.

Merchant, C. (1980) *The Death of Nature: Women, Ecology, and the Scientific Revolution*. New York: Harper & Row.

Merchant, C. (1992) *Radical Ecology: the Search for a Livable World*. New York: Routledge.

Meyer, J.W. and Rowan, B. (1983) *Organizational Environments: Ritual and Rationality*. Beverly Hills, CA: Sage.

Meyer, J.W. and Scott, W.R. (1983) *Organizational Environments: Ritual and Rationality*. Beverly Hills, CA: Sage.

Milbrath, L.W. (1989) *Envisioning a Sustainable Society: Learning Our Way Out*. Albany, NY: State University of New York Press.

Morgan, G. (1980) 'Paradigms, metaphors, and puzzle solving in organizational theory', *Administrative Science Quarterly*, 25: 605–22.

Mumford, L. (1938) *The Culture of Cities*. New York: Harcourt Brace Jovanovich.

Naess, A. (1973) 'The shallow and the deep, long-range ecology movements: a summary', *Inquiry*, 16: 95–100.

Naess, A. (1984) 'A defense of the deep ecology movement', *Environmental Ethics*, 6(3): 265–70.

Naess, A. (1988) 'Identification as a source of deep ecological attitudes', in M. Tobias (ed.), *Deep Ecology*. San Marcos, CA: Avant Books. pp. 256–70.

Namboodiri, K. (1988) 'Ecological demography: its place in sociology', *American Sociological Review*, 53(August): 619–33.

Nemetz, P.N. (1986) 'Federal environmental regulation in Canada', *Natural Resources Journal*, 26(Summer): 551–608.

Osborne, R.N. and Hunt, J.G. (1974) 'Environment and organizational effectiveness', *Administrative Science Quarterly* 19(2): 231–46.

Paehlke, R.C. (1989) *Environmentalism and the Future of Progressive Politics*. New Haven, CT: Yale University Press.

Paehlke, R.C. (1990) 'Regulatory and non-regulatory approaches to environmental protection', *Canadian Public Administration*, 33(1): 17–36.

Pasquero, J. (1991) 'Supraorganizational collaboration: the Canadian environmental experiment', *Journal of Applied Behavioral Science*, 27(1): 38–64.

Pepper, D. (1993) *Eco-socialism: from Deep Ecology to Social Justice*. London: Routledge.

Perrow, C. (1972) *Complex Organizations: a Critical Essay*. Glenview, IL: Scott, Foresman.

Perrow, C. (1973) 'The short and glorious history of organization theory', *Organizational Dynamics*, 2(1): 2–15.

Perrow, C. (1984) *Normal Accidents: Living with High-Risk Technologies*. New York: Basic Books.

Pinfield, L. and Berner, M. (1992) 'The greening of the

press: a case study of stakeholder accountability and the corporate management of environmentalist publics', *Business Strategy and the Environment*, 1(3): 23–33.

Plant, J. (ed.) (1989) *Healing the Wounds: the Promise of Ecofeminism*. Santa Cruz, CA: New Society Press.

Porritt, J. (1984) *Seeing Green: The Politics of Ecology Explained*. Oxford: Blackwell.

Powell, W.W. and DiMaggio, P.J. (eds) (1991) *The New Institutionalism in Organizational Analysis*. Chicago: University of Chicago Press.

Raskin, P.D. and Bernow, S.S. (1991) 'Ecology and Marxism: are green and red complementary?', *Rethinking Marxism*, 4(10): 87–103.

Reason, P. (1993) 'Reflections on sacred experience and sacred science', *Journal of Management Inquiry*, 2(3): 273–83.

Rice, F. (1993) 'Who scores best on the environment', *Fortune*, 128(2): 114–22.

Rich, B. (1990) 'The emperor's new clothes: the World Bank and environmental reform', *World Policy Journal*, 7(2): 305–29.

Rifkin, J. (1983) *Algeny: a New Word – a New World*. New York: Penguin.

Routley, R. (1983) 'Roles and limits of paradigms in environmental thought and action', in R. Elliot and A. Gare (eds), *Environmental Philosophy*. St Lucia, Queensland, Australia: University of Queensland Press. pp. 260–93.

Rudig, W. and Lowe, P.D. (1986) 'The withered "greening" of British politics: a study of the Ecology Party', *Political Studies*, 34: 262–84.

Russo, M.V. and Fouts, P.A. (1993) 'The green carrot: Do markets reward corporate environmentalism?'. Paper presented at the Academy of Management Annual Meeting, Atlanta.

Sale, K. (1985) *Dwellers of the Land: the Bioregional Vision*. San Francisco: Sierra Club.

Sale, K. (1993) *The Green Revolution: the American Environmental Movement 1962–1992*. New York: Hill and Wang.

Salleh, A.K. (1984) 'Deeper than deep ecology: the eco-feminist connection', *Environmental Ethics*, 6: 339–45.

Samuel, P. and Spencer, P. (1993) 'Facts catch up with "political" science', *Consumer's Research*, May: 1–14.

Samuelson, P.A. (1993) 'Altruism as a problem involving group versus individual selection in economics and biology', *AEA Papers and Proceedings*, 83(2): 143–8.

Sarkar, S. (1986) 'The green movement' in West Germany', *Alternatives*, 11: 219–54.

Schaltegger, S.C. (1993) 'Strategic management and measurement of corporate pollution. Ecological accounting: a strategic approach for environmental assessment'. Discussion paper 183, Strategic Management Research Center, University of Minnesota.

Schelling, T.C. (1992) 'Some economies of global warming', *American Economic Review*, 82(1): 1–14.

Schmidheiny, S. (1992) *Changing Course: a Global Business Perspective on Development and the Environment*. Cambridge, MA: MIT Press.

Schnaiberg, A. and Gould, K.A. (1994) *Environment and Society: the Enduring Conflict*. New York: St Martin's Press.

Schot, J. (1991) 'Credibility and markets as greening forces for the chemical industry'. Paper presented at the Strategic Management Society Annual Conference, Toronto.

Schumacher, E.F. (1973) *Small is Beautiful: a Study of Economics As If People Mattered*. London: Sphere.

Schweitzer, G.E. (1977) 'Regulations, technological progress, and societal interests', *Research Management*, 20(1): 13–17.

Scott, M. and Rothman, H. (1992) *Companies with a Conscience: Intimate Portraits of Twelve Firms that Make a Difference*. New York: Birch Land Press.

Scott, W.R. (1981) *Organizations: Rational, Natural and Open Systems*. Englewood Cliffs, NJ: Prentice Hall.

Scott, W.R. (1992) *Organiztions: Rational, Natural and Open Systems*, 3rd edn. Englewood, NJ: Prentice Hall.

Selznick, P. (1948) 'Foundations of a theory of organizations', *American Sociological Review*, 13: 25–35.

Selznick, P. (1957) *Leadership in Administration*. Evanston, IL: Row, Peterson.

Serafin, R. (1988) 'Noosphere, Gaia, and the science of the biosphere', *Environmental Ethics*, 10(2): 121–37.

Sessions, G. (1987) 'The deep ecology movement: a review', *Environmental Review*, 11(2): 105–25.

Sharfman, M. and Ellington, R.T. (1993) 'Management for total environmental quality: antecedents and organizational implications'. Paper presented at the 1993 Academy of Management Annual Meeting, Atlanta.

Shiva, V. (1988) *Staying Alive*. London: Zed Books.

Shiva, V. (1993) *Monocultures of the Mind: Perspectives on Biodiversity and Biotechnology*. London: Zed Books.

Shrivastava, P. (1992) 'Corporate self-greenewal: strategic responses to environmentalism', *Business Strategy and the Environment*, 1(3): 9–22.

Shrivastava, P. (1994) *Greening Business: towards Sustainable Corporations*. Cincinnati: Thompson Executive Press.

Simmons, P. and Wynne, B. (1993) 'Responsible care: credibility, trust and environmental management in the British chemical industry', in K. Fischer and J. Schot (eds), *Environmental Strategies for Industry: International Perspectives on Research Needs and Policy Implications*. Washington, DC: Island Press. pp. 201–26.

Simon, H.A. (1991) 'Organizations and markets', *Journal of Economic Perspectives*, 5(2): 25–44.

Simon, H.A. (1993) 'Altruism and economics', *AEA Papers and Proceedings*, 83(2): 156–61.

Sitarz, D. (ed.) (1993) *Agenda 21: the Earth Summit Strategy to Save Our Planet*. Boulder, CO: Earth-Press.

Slaton, C.D. (1992) 'The failure of the United States greens to root in fertile soil', *Research in Social Movements, Conflicts and Change*, Supplement 2: 83–117.

Smuts, J. (1926) *Holism and Evolution*. London: Macmillan.

Snow, D. (1992a) *Inside the Environmental Movement: Meeting the Leadership Challenge*. Washington, DC: Island Press.

Snow, D. (ed.) (1992b) *Voices from the Environmental Movement: Perspectives for a New Era*. Washington, DC: Island Press.

Spretnak, C. and Capra, F. (1986) *Green Politics*. Santa Fe, NM: Bear.

Starbuck, W.H. (1976) 'Organizations and their environments', in M.D. Dunnette (ed.), *Handbook of Industrial and Organizational Psychology*. Chicago: Rand McNally.

Starbuck, W.H. (1983) 'Organizations as action generators', *American Sociological Review*, 48: 91–102.

Stead, W.E. and Stead, J.G. (1992) *Management for a Small Planet: Strategic Decision Making and the Environment*. Newbury Park, CA: Sage.

Steger, U. (1993) 'The greening of the board room: how European companies are dealing with environmental issues', in K. Fischer and J. Schot (eds), *Environmental Strategies for Industry: International Perspectives on Research Needs and Policy Implications*. Washington, DC: Island Press. pp. 147–66.

Strong, D.H. (1988) *Dreamers and Defenders: American Conservationists*. Lincoln, NE: University of Nebraska Press.

Terryberry, S. (1967) 'The evolution of organizational environments', *Administrative Science Quarterly*, 12(4): 590–613.

The Ecologist (1993) *Whose Common Future? Reclaiming the Commons*. Philadelphia: New Society Publishers.

Thompson, J.D. (1967) *Organizations in Action*. New York: McGraw-Hill.

Throop, G.M. (1991) 'Strategy in a greening environment: supply and demand matching in U.S. and Canadian electricity generation'. Paper presented at the Strategic Management Society Annual Conference, Toronto.

Tokar, B. (1988) 'Social ecology, deep ecology, and the future of green political thought', *The Ecologist*, 18(4/5): 132–45.

Trist, E.L. (1983) 'Referent organizations and the development of interorganizational domains', *Human Relations*, 36: 247–68.

Wall, D. (1994) *Green History: a Reader in Environmental Literature, Philosophy and Politics*. New York: Routledge.

Wallace, A. (1993) *Eco-Heroes: Twelve Tales of Environmental Victory*. San Francisco: Mercury House.

Warren, K.J. (1990) 'The power and the promise of ecological feminism', *Environmental Ethics*, 12(2): 125–46.

Warren, R.L. (1967) 'The interorganizational field as a focus for investigation', *Administrative Science Quarterly*, 12: 396–419.

Weick, K.E. (1979) *The Social Psychology of Organizing*, 2nd edn. Reading, MA: Addison-Wesley.

Weick, K.E. and Roberts, K.H. (1993) 'Collective mind in organizations: heedful interrelating on flight decks', *Administrative Science Quarterly*, 38: 357–81.

Westley, F. and Vredenburg, H. (1991) 'Strategic bridging: the collaboration between environmentalists and business in the marketing of green products', *Journal of Applied Behavioral Science*, 27(1): 65–90.

Wexler, M. (1990) 'Deep ecology: grounding a contemporary argument field', *International Journal of Sociology and Social Policy*, 10(1): 47–70.

White, L. Jr (1967) 'Historical roots of our ecologic crisis', *Science*, 155: 1203–7.

Wiener, N. (1954) *The Human Use of Human Beings: Cybernetics and Society*. Boston: Houghton Mifflin.

Wilson, E.O. (1975) *Sociobiology: the New Synthesis*. Cambridge, MA: Harvard University Press.

Wilson, E.O. (1984) *Biophilia: the Human Bond with Other Species*. Cambridge, MA: Harvard University Press.

Wilson, E.O. (1992) *The Diversity of Life*. Cambridge, MA: Belknap Press of Harvard University Press.

Women's Environment and Development Organization (WEDO) (1992) *Official Report: World Women's Congress for a Healthy Planet*. New York: Women's Environment and Development Organization.

World Commission on Environment and Development (1987) *Our Common Future*. New York: Oxford University Press.

Worster, D. (1977) *Nature's Economy: the Roots of Ecology*. San Francisco: Sierra Club Books.

Young, R.C. (1988) 'Is population ecology a useful paradigm for the study of organizations?', *American Journal of Sociology*, 94(1): 1–24.

2.12

Evolution and Revolution: from International Business to Globalization

BARBARA PARKER

There is a growing sense that events occurring throughout the world are converging rapidly to shape a single, integrated world where economic, social, cultural, technological, business, and other influences cross traditional borders and boundaries such as nations, national cultures, time, space, and industries with increasing ease. The resulting dissolution of traditional boundaries of every kind has blurred distinctions that once seemed clear. Business activities, for example, are conducted or shaped by enterprises outside the business sector such as nongovernmental organizations. Activities such as these blur the borders between sectors that once were more clearly defined: it is no longer so easy as it once was to call on visual or verbal cues to distinguish between advertisements and content; between men and women; between what is real and what is virtual; between what organizations can do and what they should do. The implications of such changes are potentially *revolutionary*, leading to significant and wide-ranging changes in every sphere of life and creating new challenges and responsibilities for organizations of all types.

The conceptual and practical demands for interpreting any single aspect of global change are enormous, and these demands multiply when rapid and simultaneous change occurs in many sectors, interacts, and changes again. Global economic shifts, for example, motivated political sponsorship of the World Trade Organization and common commercial rules worldwide. Simple enough. But because trade barriers are embedded in each nation's traditions, dismantling them forces us to breach still other boundaries. Traditional practices are recast as

human rights violations; cultural traditions add up to an affront to immigration policies; diseases that afflict humans, animals and crops are exported along with consumer durables. This example illustrates that political and economic events of global scope also have cultural, political, technological and human implications; and as the economic fortunes of individuals, organizations, and nations are linked to one another, new interdependencies of many kinds also are created. Organizations are not simply affected by globalization: the combined activities of all kinds of organizations stimulate, facilitate, sustain, and extend globalization. In the search for new products and markets, business enterprises spread not only consumer goods but ideas concerning wealth creation; ideals concerning how people should live and work; ideologies concerning political and business governance. Nor are the parameters of business in the global world easily controlled: a telephone link to the Internet yields tips on guerrilla tactics or access to kiddie porn as readily as it provides the latest Dow-Jones index; mafia organizations and drug cartels operate in a worldwide arena with as much expertise as Shell, Imperial Chemical Industries or Exxon. Global business is not, then, just about business: it has cultural, legal, political and social effects as much as economic ones.

Current knowledge of such global phenomena might, however, be described as *evolutionary*. As academics and practitioners, we still know so little about globalization. Reports from business people confirm that organizational life, as well as life apart from organizations, occurs in the context of an increasingly global world. Most would doubtless agree that this global world is having a revolutionary effect on life and work; that the dissolution and permeation of boundaries of every type create both opportunities and challenges for organizations and their people. Those who manage organizations under conditions of globalization also recognize the multiplicity, variety and complexity of issues associated with it, but many are too busy coping with change either to document or to explain it. Consequently, descriptions of the practices associated with these revolutionary changes are more anecdotal than organized.

Writers disagree about the impact of globalization: some contest that globalization is a phenomenon deserving of notice (Farnham 1994); others believe globalization began some time ago (Ohmae 1985) and so now the challenge is simply to face up to it (Henzler and Rall 1986). There is a lack of consensus about what globalization is and means. In the social sciences alone, Pieterse (1995) points out there are almost as many conceptualizations of globalization as there are disciplines. Some writers have focused on globalization as the crossing of national borders; others have emphasized its effect on other boundaries as traditional concepts of time, space, scope, geography, functions, thought, cultural assumptions, and the understanding of the self in relation to others are redefined and reduced (Rhinesmith 1993). Some writers have emphasized the permeation of boundaries between organizations as new alliances are formed; others have pointed to changes with organizations as vertical boundaries of level and rank are razed, and horizontal boundaries of function and discipline are merged (Ashkenas et al. 1995).

These definitional differences are more than semantic; each shapes assumptions about what the other is saying or should be allowed to say, and directs and limits the further exploration of globalization. For example, a sociological approach to globalization represents this phenomenon as 'the compression of the world and the intensification of consciousness of the world as a whole' (Robertson 1992: 8). Globalization is more usually described in the business literature as shifts in traditional patterns of international production, investment, and trade (Dicken 1992); or as interconnections between overlapping interests of business and society (Brown 1992; Renesch 1992). A popular view of globalization is as the absence of borders and barriers to trade between nations (Sera 1992; Ohmae 1995).

This conceptualization of globalization as national 'borderlessness' might lead some to conclude that globalization is producing a worldwide trend towards homogeneity and uniformity. Others, however, have pointed out that as boundaries dissolve, as barriers are permeated, as the world compresses, as we become interdependent, we become more aware of cultural *difference* and diversity (Kahn 1995; Robertson 1995):

> one paradoxical consequence of the process of globalization, the awareness of the finitude and boundedness of the planet and humanity, is not to produce homogeneity but to familiarize us with greater diversity, the extensive range of local cultures. (Robertson 1995: 86)

Thus the call to 'act global, think local' and become part of the 'global village' worldwide is hindered by the tendency to define, describe and envision globalization in quite different ways.

If we are confused about what globalization means now, we are also perplexed about what it will mean for the future. Some observers argue that the domestic and international diversity promoted by globalization will be 'the engine that drives the creative energy of the corporation of the 21st century' (Rhinesmith 1993: 4). According to this view, globalization will create worldwide opportunities for growth and development by expanding options for both organizations and people across the world; create employment opportunities for thousands of impoverished people; help forge entrepreneurial infrastructure for developing countries; contribute to the process of democratization; and address global social problems (e.g. Pieterse 1995; Cooperrider and Passmore 1991; see Gergen 1995). Others believe that the same activities will lead to the exploitation of foreign workers; limit choices to unappealing options like 'McWorld' and 'Jihad'; and destroy natural resources and local cultures (e.g. Lavipour and Sauvant 1976; Barber 1992).

So, despite the magnitude of the global 'revolution'; despite the complexities, uncertainties, and rapid rates of change that it has brought about; despite the degree to which business is implicated in and affected by globalization, it remains difficult, from an academic perspective, to say what is occurring and why. And it is even more difficult to say which tools and techniques are appropriate when managing the global enterprise, particularly since globalization makes it possible for organizations of every size and type and from any geographic location to participate in business activities. These changes suggest that current theories of markets and organizations bear reexamination and possible revision in the light of globalization. For example, while some writers proclaim that bureaucracy in its various forms is, or ought to be, dead, there is evidence to show that principles of bureaucracy may have as much currency today as ever. But in a new form: coexisting alongside newer organizational forms, some of which are distinctly counter-bureaucratic. The expanding choices for organizations involve more complex, hybrid structures and processes capable of surviving and thriving in the global marketplace. This, in turn, requires more sophisticated research 'which combines a comprehensive overview of the systems in which firms operate with examination of specific inner workings of the systems themselves' (Earley and Singh 1995: 337), research that can deal with the complexity of the global enterprise (see Melin 1992).

There is, then, a need for a comprehensive, interdisciplinary look at globalization and its effects on late twentieth century life. This chapter structures this task by looking at the nature of globalization in the business context: what causes it; what it looks like; how business drives it; how business is affected by it; and what it might mean, not just for business, but for those of us, all of us, who make up the global world. The first section describes how international business research has changed over the last fifty years. The second discusses the characteristics of the global enterprise, showing how it engages in a different set of activities than the international or multinational business. The third section shows how globalization is a phenomenon which embraces far more than just the global enterprise: it involves far more fundamental and broadly based changes. It explores how five particular contexts are affected by these changes: economy; politics; culture; technology; and natural resources. Finally, some of the implications of globalization for business and other organizations are discussed.

In the end, this chapter asks more questions than it answers. Rather than document what we know about the comparatively evident field of international business, it points out what we do not know about globalization. It tries to clarify some of the profound implications that globalization has for all societies. In pointing out these implications and the tensions they involve, we may be better prepared to consider how a new research agenda might evolve.

THE PATH FROM INTERNATIONAL TO GLOBAL BUSINESS

There is not yet a clear answer to the question: what is globalization? Global challenges traditionally have been those that impact the planet and its people as a whole, because 'virtually all human activity is confined to the biological and physical boundaries of the Earth' (Stead and

Stead 1994: 369). Air and water, for example, have long been identified as a global common because the earth's population equally depends on these resources for survival, and all are affected by activities that degrade or alter availability for these commonly held resources. Today, concern for use of natural resources is joined by other global concerns, concerns not nearly so visible but just as important to the future. This section starts the examination of what globalization is, making particular reference to the business world by showing how business research has evolved. In the following section, a closer look is given to the global enterprise, and it is argued that the global firm engages in a different set of activities and creates additional responsibilities for organizations than does international business. In particular, we stress that business enterprises operate in a world with more permeable borders along national, spatial, and cultural divides as interconnections between business and other activities increase, but that organizational borders are themselves more permeable than they once were.

The academic study of international business (IB) is a fairly recent phenomenon, beginning with formal IB studies that appeared after World War II as US exports and foreign direct investment (FDI) came to play an important role in world reconstruction and development. Until the 1960s, the bulk of IB research focused on economic explanations for trade flows between countries, reflecting its roots in macro-economic theory and a heavy emphasis on the theory of comparative advantage (Bartlett and Ghoshal 1991; also see Grosse and Behrman 1992; Dunning 1993).

From the 1960s on, the field grew and diversified (Melin 1992). An impetus was Hymer's (1976) thesis, originally published in 1960, on patterns of FDI triggered by the post-war expansion of multinational enterprises (MNEs), which led to the development of different, complementary streams of research: on the link between FDI and oligopolistic competition (e.g. Caves 1971); on the relationship between the product life cycle and internationalization (e.g. Vernon 1966); and, by the late 1970s, on the existence and behavior of MNEs using Williamson's (1975) work on transaction costs (e.g. Buckley and Casson 1976; Rugman 1980; Hennart 1982; see Bartlett and Ghoshal 1991). Another stream of research stemmed from the Uppsala School, which studied how firms gradually increase their international involvement (e.g. Johanson and Vahlne 1977; also see Melin 1992).

By the 1970s, a field of IB, separate from economics, had been established. First, it concentrated on:

firm-level business activity that crosses national boundaries or is conducted in a location other than the firm's home country. (This activity may be the movement of goods, capital, people, and know-how, or it may be manufacturing, extraction, construction, banking, shipping, advertising, and the like.) Second, it [was] concerned in some way with the interrelationships between the operations of the business firm and international or foreign environments in which the firm operates. (Nehrt et al. 1970)

During this time, the focus shifted from the international economy to include the firm and internal processes within the firm, as synthesized by Dunning's (1988) 'eclectic paradigm' of FDI, which included ownership-specific, localization and internationalization explanatory variables of an MNE's pattern of FDI. Work in this growing field was published in newly founded journals: nineteen journals publishing IB research were introduced in the 1970s, a 50 per cent increase in the number of outlets previously available for IB research, and another eighteen were added in the 1980s (Pierce and Garven 1995). The growing importance of trade and investments to firms and the increased complexity of their operating environments also made it possible to publish IB research in non-IB journals, although its impact was still limited: Adler's (1983) review of publishing trends in cross-cultural management throughout the 1970s showed that less than 5 per cent of articles appearing in the top management journals looked at organizational behavior issues from a cross-cultural or international perspective. Consistent with the definition provided by Nehrt et al. (1970), this IB research did *not* include studies of economic development, foreign trade, or the international monetary system (because they 'belonged' to academic fields in development and international economics); or foreign legal, political, economic and social environments (because they fell under the purview of academic disciplines like law, political science, economics and behavioral science).

At the same time as formal studies of IB were emerging, international management (IM) research also developed with an emphasis on a stronger administrative focus following the work of writers like Aharoni (1966), who explored the process of FDI from a managerial perspective; Fayerweather (1969) who discussed MNE responsiveness to the cultural, political and economic characteristics of individual countries; and Perlmutter (1969) who described the evolution of the structures of MNEs. Stopford and Wells (1972), Franko (1976) and Dyas and Thanheiser (1976) extended Chandler's (1962) strategy/structure work to the international organization. Over time, other writers such as Prahalad, Doz, Bartlett and Hedlund started to

examine management actions and strategic processes in MNEs (see Bartlett and Ghoshal 1991; Melin 1992).

The 1970s also marked a change in the types of issues tackled by researchers, as host countries started to question MNEs' ethnocentric stances and, in some cases, reject the role multinationals played (Robinson 1981). Growing nationalism and concerns about the political roles of MNEs led to nationalization of some industries and firms, and increased regulations for others. At the same time, competition was increasingly coming from Europe and from Japan. Accordingly, research started to examine links between the firm and its political environment; political risk analysis and bargaining represented two approaches to understanding the political environment of international business (e.g. Moran 1973; 1974; Rummel and Heenan 1978). Competitive strategy analyses focused on the relationship between industry conditions and organizations (e.g. Porter 1980; 1985). The growing importance of cultural sensitivity to international business success was demonstrated by Hofstede's (1980; 1983) comparative studies of national culture traits, and Ronen and Shenkar's (1985) clustering of countries on the basis of work values and attitudes. In as much as many of the new powerhouse competitors were Japanese firms, interest also developed in studies of Japanese firms and business techniques unique to Japan, particularly total quality concepts and their implications for non-Japanese firms (Reitsperger and Daniel 1990). The structures first suggested by Stopford and Wells (1972) were further explored to identify structural forms appropriate to a variety of multinational strategies (Daniels et al. 1984) or to include contingencies as a factor in explaining MNE choices (Lemak and Bracker 1988). The interest in structural forms and formal control mechanisms in the 1970s shifted towards less formal forms of coordination (Melin 1992; see Martinez and Jarillo 1989). A more sophisticated and process-oriented view of international strategy replaced the work on strategy/structure 'fit' (e.g. Beamish et al. 1991; Melin 1992), focusing attention on the need to achieve a broader congruence between strategy, structure, and systems (Ghoshal and Bartlett 1995). Other researchers focused on network approaches to understanding international business (e.g. Hedlund 1986); designing global strategies (e.g. Kogut 1989); global alliances (Hamel 1991; Hedlund and Rolander 1990); and learning (Bartlett and Ghoshal 1989; Hamel 1991).

Much of the early research in IB had exhibited a belief in US superiority expressed by Henry Luce when he called this time period 'the American century'. Research had been characterized by 'American researchers focused on American firms, American perspectives, and those questions most salient to American managers' (Boyacigiller and Adler 1991: 264). Economic success and both public and academic reinforcement doubtless confirmed an impression that bureaucratic management practices as developed by US firms were superior, an impression Robinson (1971) referred to in his presidential address to the Association for Education in International Business. Despite some changes, IB research continues to be produced primarily by scholars in the US (Pierce and Garven 1995) focusing on a small group of countries and explicitly or implicitly reinforcing Western business practices as a norm (Boyacigiller and Adler 1991). For example, a twenty-five year review of the *Journal of International Business Studies* revealed that published studies primarily examined G-7 nations with fully 40 per cent featuring the US (Thomas et al. 1994).

IB research has also developed, primarily, along disciplinary lines. Originally, many distinguished international scholars were lodged in existing departments. Today, although many departments of international business exist, IB research continues to be functionally oriented (Inkpen and Beamish 1994). Melin (1992) identifies seven fairly distinct areas of IB built on relatively narrow disciplinary lines, including finance, cross-cultural management, human resource management, and foreign direct investment. In addition, international business research has often been viewed as peripheral and less important than 'mainstream' disciplinary research (Thomas et al. 1994).

The disciplinary basis and the Western orientation that continue to characterize much of the research in the field of IB hamper comprehensive international research and teaching. In addition, the experience of globalization presents further challenges, to which IB research also must respond. One concerns the complexity of the global enterprise: a weakness in the understanding of *processes* has made it difficult for researchers to explain and document the new and different practices that are emerging in these organizations (Melin 1992). As individual, autonomous organizations are evolving into complex global networks, the organization as a unit of analysis is no longer the most useful way to study them. As the intricacies of diffusing learning across a spatially dispersed, culturally diverse enterprise become apparent, the focus on formal structure and coordination seems misplaced. As the complexity of sustaining a global strategy becomes more difficult, the need for a more sophisticated examination of the link between structure, strategy, systems and processes within an environment becomes apparent

(see Bartlett and Ghoshal 1991; Melin 1992). The next section examines the complexity and confusion concerning the global enterprise in more detail.

THE GLOBAL ENTERPRISE

The global enterprise is not well defined. There has been a strong research emphasis on large organizations, and large organizations have been important actors in internationalization as well as globalization. Either of these facts might lead some to conclude that globalization affects only large organizations from economically developed countries. This section will demonstrate how inconsistent use of the term 'global' has led to this misconception; it will define the global enterprise and identify those core competencies that appear to be most important to success and survival in a globalizing world. In so doing, it will demonstrate that the potential to engage in global activities is not confined to large organizations, but that many different types of organizations are 'going global' and they face similar challenges as a result.

The global enterprise is associated with both different activities and a different attitude from its more circumscribed, international predecessor.

> internationalization connotes expanding interfaces between nations sometimes implying political invasion or domination. Internationalization of business, therefore, is a concept of an action in which nationality is strongly in people's consciousness. It means the flow of business, goods or capital from one country into another. Globalization, by contrast, looks at the whole world as being nationless and borderless. Goods, capital, and people have to be moving freely. (Sera 1992: 89)

The international firm is one whose business activities cross national boundaries (Ball and McCullough 1990), or that is involved in business in two or more countries (Daniels and Radebaugh 1992). According to Hordes et al. (1995) its headquarters are almost always based in a single country, although it might establish partial or complete operations in others. Its culture and organizational structure are consistent with the practices and norms of the home or headquarters country. It adopts standardized technologies and business processes throughout its operations, regardless of where they are located, and it relies on similar policies, especially regarding human resources, worldwide.

Despite what is likely to be a consensus that the global enterprise differs from the international enterprise, the exact nature of the former and its distinction from, say, the multi-national enterprise is far less clear and particularly less clear to practitioners (Leong and Tan 1993). Research has tended to produce different and often confusing definitions. For example, Bartlett and Ghoshal (1989) differentiate between the international organization, which is a coordinated federation in which the parent company transfers knowledge and expertise to foreign markets; the multinational organization, which is a 'decentralized federation of assets and responsibilities' (1989: 49) that allows foreign operations to respond to local differences; and the global organization, which is a centralized hub where most assets and decisions are centralized. Bartlett and Ghoshal (1989) found empirical evidence for all three types but maintained that each encountered problems in dealing with globalization. They proposed an ideal form called the transnational organization, an integrated network where efficiency is balanced with local responsiveness to obtain both global competitiveness and flexibility in an organization dedicated to organizational learning and innovation. Thus, according to these and other authors (Adler and Bartholomew 1992) it is the transnational organization, which was not derived from empirical evidence, that offers the solution to the complex problems of globalization. In other quarters, however, transnational corporations are viewed as 'synonymous with multinational enterprises' (Daniels and Radebaugh 1992: G-21) or simply as those that see the world as a single market (Ohmae 1989).

Global companies have also been defined as those with global strategies where economies of scale are realized from worldwide integration and standardization (Hout et al. 1982; Levitt 1983; Bartlett and Ghoshal 1989). For example, worldwide integration of design groups as well as other restructuring at Ford Motor Company led to production of a 'world car' able to enjoy scale economies and earning Ford the sobriquet of a global company (Kerwin 1995). However, as Yip (1995) notes, a global strategy is not necessarily synonymous with a global firm since the latter can sustain an integrated standard for one business line and be locally responsive in other business lines. This suggests that the global enterprise might be more or less global depending on the amount of its business that has a worldwide presence. Efforts to balance worldwide standards with demands for the localization of products and services have also been called a global strategy (Hamel and Prahalad 1985), although Yip describes this approach as *multilocal* (1995: 8), and Phatak (1992) and Ashkenas et al. (1995) call it *glocal*.

In summary, different uses of the word 'global' may be diluting any specific meaning it

has in describing a strategy (Yip 1995: 8). Such definitional differences are one legacy of growing awareness of complex, and often intractable, changes occurring in the world that put new emphasis on internal coordination among firm functions and also generate greater awareness of the need to analyze events occurring throughout the world. Paradoxically, while definitions vary, the focus on the world's largest firms in the research is consistent. Public ownership and size make the world's largest 37,000 MNEs identifiable, and their control over 206,000 affiliates worldwide and combined assets in the trillions of dollars underscore their contributions to economic growth and development around the world. The world's largest 100 MNEs (not including those in banking and finance) held over US$3 trillion in global assets in 1992 (United Nations 1994a: 5). They include firms like Daimler Benz, Hanson, Glaxo, McDonald's, Siemens, Saint Gobain, Sony, Itochu, Amoco, Michelin, and Grand Met; all are from economically developed countries. It is these types of organizations that usually are thought of as 'global'.

Firms of many other types also may be considered global. Many small and medium-sized firms are breaking with existing business traditions within nations to go global, spearheading what it means to be global (Bannon 1994; *Business Week* 1995a; Shrivastava 1995). Firms of small and medium size play a growing role in global exports, and in 1995 small US businesses are for the first time expected to have sent more exports abroad than big business (Barrett 1995). Small and medium-sized firms also play a role in foreign direct investment (FDI). Examples from the developed world show that FDI on the part of small and medium-sized firms in 1992 contributed $43 billion or about 7.5 per cent of total direct investments by developed European nations, $40 billion (15 per cent) of total Japanese foreign direct investment abroad, and $15 billion in FDI (3 per cent) of total US FDI abroad. Looked at another way, about 28 per cent of small to medium-sized US firms have some direct investment abroad, but as many as 60 per cent of similarly sized Japanese firms participate in some way in equity investments abroad (Bleakley 1993). Family-owned businesses from South and Central America, Portugal, Spain, Asia, and India also are focused on global growth. Kim Woo-choong, founder of Daewoo, asserts that the firm's goal 'is to become a company without borders' (*Forbes* 1995). The growing influence of 'overseas' Chinese and Indians demonstrates that there is more than one model for family-owned enterprise. As a group, the overseas Chinese generate an estimated annual economic output equivalent to $500 billion, comparable to mainland China's 1993 gross national product; as individuals, most of the billionaires in South East Asia are ethnic Chinese living outside of China. And these ethnic Chinese business people are believed to command only a portion of the growing wealth of the overseas Chinese worldwide, and especially in South East Asia (Drucker 1994). Whether they are independently owned or run by a close-knit or far-flung 'family', enterprises like these contribute to the diversity of management practices and business objectives in the global sphere, but as yet little is known about them.

Government/business ventures as well as businesses established by global start-ups (Oviatt and McDougall 1995) are a part of global business growth, and many disenfranchised by modern business tradition now are finding it possible to become part of the global business scene (Hymowitz 1995). Nonprofit organizations increasingly contribute to economic activities (Salamon and Anheier 1994) as do nongovernmental organizations (Commission on Global Governance 1995). Finally, global gangs, pirates, warlords and others of their ilk also populate the landscape for global business. To the extent that global markets are characterized by these multiple competitors of varying size and shapes operating with differing competitive motives, global management may be said to be both more complex and less certain than when market competitors share similarities of size and motives.

This chapter argues that globalization is not confined to large organizations: it lies in 'virtually every industry' (Yip 1995), making it difficult for any firm to remain totally unaffected by global conditions. But, while virtually all organizations may be affected by globalization of business and all firms increasingly operate in a global business sphere, this is not to say that every firm is a global one. Global enterprises might more generally be described as those that establish or maintain a *worldwide presence* in one or more businesses. Firms like Pepsi Cola, CNN ('the global news network') and Benetton can be readily identified as global enterprises because they establish a global presence in virtually all their businesses. Although smaller, firms like Britain's R. Griggs (maker of Doc Martens boots), Israel's VocalTech (developer of software facilitating long-distance telephone calls over the Internet), or the Netherlands' Digicash (developer of the digital equivalent of cash for electronic purchases) also can be described as global enterprises because they are committed to establishing a worldwide presence in most or all of their product lines. Whether large or small, these firms face the same managerial challenge:

creating organization-wide processes and structures in support of their global commitment. Large firms like Nestlé and Unilever also have a significant global presence, although not in every business line – just as independent Washington State fruit growers often sell one but not all fruit lines worldwide. These firms also face managerial challenges in creating organization-wide processes and structures capable of achieving balance between what could become competing interests.

These examples demonstrate that organizations of any size can establish a global presence and can be thought of as global enterprises, and also show that establishing global presence in one, many, or all businesses creates unique challenges for organizational leaders. We can, then, think of 'global' as a worldwide view of business markets, using descriptors such as 'multilocal' to refer to strategies that firms employ when they combine worldwide standards with local responsiveness, or 'worldwide standardization' when referring to integration and standardization of products and services on a worldwide basis. For firms with a global presence, either of these strategies could be one measure of the degree to which a firm is global.

The global enterprise may also be described according to its abilities to transcend existing boundaries of three kinds. First, global enterprises cross external boundaries of nations (Ohmae 1995), space and time, or responsibilities (Brown 1992) that are in some sense measurable. Second, less tangible boundaries like culture, thought, or the relationship between self (organization) and others (Rhinesmith 1993) must also be crossed if global opportunities are to be reached. Third, some boundaries internal to the global organization have to be bridged, including vertical and horizontal barriers (Ashkenas et al. 1995), those pertaining to task or rank (Ghoshal and Bartlett 1995), and even more amorphous barriers like attitude. The importance of breaking down boundaries between departments, shifting hierarchical to contractual management, and sharing values to successful global activity was noted long ago by Stopford and Wells (1972) and Franko (1976) although, as Melin (1992) notes, these observations were not taken up by researchers at the time. More recently, they have been explored in the context of global networks, global alliances and global learning (e.g. Hedlund 1986; Hedlund and Rolander 1990; Hamel 1991).

To this point, the global enterprise has been defined as one that establishes a worldwide presence in one or more businesses, one that adopts a worldwide strategy, and one that is able to cross external and internal boundaries. We have shown that firms of any size can be defined as global enterprises, and suggested that all face significant and distinct challenges. Hordes et al. (1995) describe one form that a global firm might take: it is organized around a few core values; although it has a headquarters, it is most often managed by a team operating in diverse locations; it adopts an organizational culture that values diversity; except for a few standardized policies, its processes, policies, and technologies are diverse. A combination of mission, vision, education and training is combined with an emphasis on processes of global corporate culture (Evans et al. 1990). Knowledge (D'Aveni 1995; Senge 1990) and diversity of people, processes, or structures (Hoecklin 1995; Rhinesmith 1993; Trompenaars 1994) are essential to sustain flexibility and adapt quickly to opportunities and threats in a rapidly globalizing world. 'The ability to link and leverage knowledge is increasingly the factor that differentiates the winners and the losers and the survivors' (Bartlett and Ghoshal 1989: 12). Global firms often take unconventional approaches, developing 'a strategic innovation to change the rules of the competitive game in its particular industry' (Hout et al. 1982: 100).

The global enterprise thus organizes itself along lines different from the internally focused international firm of the 1960s and 1970s and even from the multinational enterprise that responded to a limited number of political, competitive or cultural challenges in the 1970s and early 1980s. The global firm develops a worldwide presence; it does not hesitate to cross traditional boundaries, whether these are attempts to break through national borders and nationalistic thinking more deliberately as it reconceptualizes its activities to integrate worldwide perspectives and capitalize on both global and local advantages, or internal barriers that impede its ability to leverage knowledge and diversity to sustain a global position. The importance of these internal and external boundaries may vary according to size, industry or other factors and individual firms might prioritize them in different ways. For example, a start-up in an Internet-dependent industry might place highest priority on leveraging knowledge technology; whereas an established firm might see a greater need to break down internal barriers to diversity in order to leverage knowledge. In this context, it is important to note that diversity is represented not only by visible differences like gender or ethnicity, but also by differences in rank, functional assignments, or role. While there is considerable debate and differences in opinion concerning the global organization, it seems clear that such activity is not confined simply to large organizations with a physical presence in different countries, but also includes more flexible arrangements that allow smaller organizations to benefit from global opportunities.

GLOBALIZATION: A PERVASIVE PHENOMENON

While globalization may be driven and shaped by the activities of business, it extends well beyond the individual and collective boundaries of global organizations, regardless of how broadly they are defined. Globalization is a pervasive phenomenon, and interest should not be confined to business activities alone. In this section, interest expands to five arenas that extend beyond business organizations and a business focus. They include: the economy; politics; culture; technology; natural resources. Separating them is somewhat artificial since they interact naturally and synergistically, but doing so clarifies the content of each and provides a way to illustrate national and organizational tensions that result from globalization.

Global Economy

The world economy is growing, with the world gross domestic product likely to increase from $26 trillion in 1994 to $48 trillion in 2010 (Richman 1995). Funds can be transferred worldwide electronically and instantly via computer technology; in 1995 Citibank alone moved over $500 billion per day through electronic transfers. Trade in equities need never stop since trading bourses now span the world. In the last decade trading has expanded from the established financial centers of New York, Tokyo, and London to include Egypt, Namibia, China, Kenya, Hungary, and Bermuda, to name a few.

While this global economy offers opportunities, it also produces increased challenges. For example, the central banks now face the force of the independent traders who manage over $1 trillion per day. Efforts by the US, Japanese and German central banks to shore up the dollar poured $30 billion into global markets between January and May of 1995. Nevertheless, the dollar fell 17 per cent against the yen and 11 per cent against the mark (Sesit 1995), proving that it may be currency speculators who increasingly play the dominant role in determining the values of currency (Millman 1995). While Millman (1995) believes these traders provide discipline for global financial markets, others suggest they undermine world economic order by making it difficult for government officials to maintain the public's interest (Solomon 1995). As a senior Canadian official attending a 1994 G-7 meeting reportedly said, 'with one trillion dollars flowing through the markets daily, there's little governments can do except stop the momentum for one day, one hour – or more like 10 minutes' (Gumbel and Davis 1994).

Where once the banks managed capital assets, today's capital markets are increasingly dominated by mutual and hedge-fund investors from the US who control about $3 trillion in assets. The global search for increasing returns on these investments creates 'hot' money that funds rapid economic growth, job creation and political stabilization, but just as easily can be withdrawn from these investments in the pursuit of higher returns elsewhere (Kwan 1991). Private capital also is displacing the need for capital from institutions like the World Bank and the IMF, and leading to questions about the continuing viability of these kinds of financial institutions in the current global milieu (Bello and Cunningham 1994; Owen 1994).

Increased globalization of economic activity is also drawing more organizations into the marketplace, stimulating trade and dispersing production facilities throughout the world (Dicken 1992). Whereas once industrialized countries were the major sources of world economic growth, today it also comes from 'reverse linkages' with the developing world, as foreign direct investment is transferred from the developing to the developed world. Whereas North America, Europe, and Japan accounted for about 65 per cent of world GDP in 1993, the figure will have dropped to 55 per cent by 2010 as China and countries in Asia and South America develop (World Bank 1995). In the last decade, firms from newly industrialized countries like South Korea, Taiwan, Thailand, and Singapore have increased their roles in the global economy from 4 per cent in the 1960s to 25 per cent in the 1990s (Farrell 1994). Moreover, the speed of development is quickening. Britain doubled its per capita income in fifty-eight years following the Industrial Revolution in 1789; then, starting in 1839, America took forty-seven years; Japan took thirty-four years from 1885; South Korea managed it in the eleven years after 1966; and more recently still, China has done it in less than ten years (*The Economist* 1994). Thus, while a global economy has the capacity to correct current economic imbalances between the developed and the developing world, this development does not come without a price. Newly industrialized countries have had to learn in a relatively short time what countries like Britain and the US took one hundred or more years to master. So economic growth incurs penalties such as child labor, dangerous workplaces, and degraded environments.

It is important to note that it is not only the legal, the legitimate and the respectable who participate in this global arena. For example, freer access to the global arena is also enjoyed by scam artists and others who live outside the law of both domestic and global business activities, as hackers prowl throughout the Internet looking for the electronic equivalent of an unlocked door or an unguarded vault. Mafia-type organizations, gangs, pirates, and drug cartels also have emerged to carve out territory in the fertile economic realm for world trade, responding to opportunities in what Interpol estimates is a $400 billion illegal drug market; providing illegal papers to smuggle human beings willing to work; or responding to growing global demand for all manner of illicit goods and services.

The increased economic activity associated with globalization focuses attention on previously unquestioned economic assumptions. It becomes more difficult to ignore economic activities outside the paid sector, since unpaid labor worldwide has an uncounted value of $16 trillion, $11 trillion of which is generated by women (United Nations 1995). Self-interest assumptions of free market capitalism also bear re-examination in light of evidence showing that in the US the individual person or organization is expected to be the self-interested actor, while in Japan national economic interests motivate and, in Western Europe, quality of life is important (Hampden-Turner and Trompenaars 1993; Sharp 1992). While measures like gross domestic product (GDP) once were considered almost universal standards of a nation's economic development, the applicability of this measure is increasingly suspect in a global world. GDP does not adjust for varying costs of living, for differences between rich and poor within the same nation, or for those intangibles that also contribute to quality of life (Ibbotson and Brinson 1993).

Thus a globalizing economy requires a re-examination of many of our assumptions concerning wealth, in particular: whether the world economy must be played according to a zero-sum game; how resources can be allocated fairly within market systems that differ; whose and what labor 'counts' as a productive factor; even how economic criteria should be evaluated. While economic globalization can create convergence between self-interest and collective or community interests (Naisbitt 1994), self-interested economies do not operate in a vacuum, but are instead shaped by global politics (Sorenson 1995) and other national, regional, and global factors.

Global Politics

The political sphere encompasses a tension between autonomy and dependency in so far as national governments attempt to dismantle trade barriers. Economist Robert Reich (1991) emphasizes that globalization will not only cause businesses leaders to think of themselves less as autonomous actors and more as participants inextricably linked to one another in global industries, but also reduce national autonomy. As the dismantling of boundaries opens up opportunities, it also creates dependencies that curtail autonomy. Seeking an economic payoff, few recognize that bilateral, multilateral and unilateral trade agreements necessarily reduce national autonomy through special arrangements like foreign economic zones and city-states within nations; industry alliances such as OPEC; regional alliances such as the EU, ASEAN, MEROCUR and NAFTA; or world-wide alliances such as GATT and its successor the World Trade Organization (WTO) and APEC.

These groups reduce not only barriers to trade, but also national autonomy. For example the WTO promises to phase in a common set of worldwide commercial rules. Unlike GATT, which tended to favor larger countries, the WTO promises a more level playing field, benefiting smaller countries more than in the past (*Wall Street Journal* 1995d) and encouraging more countries to join (Becker 1994) which will, in turn, place additional restraints on countries previously accustomed to more latitude. The leveling process does not come without costs. After the ten year phase-in for the WTO, sub-Sarahan Africa will suffer a net trade loss of $2.6 billion per year due mainly to increases in costs of food imports to Africa as subsidies are erased for the developed world. While the costs of the WTO incurred by countries in Africa could be met with increased aid, and while debt relief measures generate benefits to the developed world, such an occurrence is by no means a certainty. Countries in the developed world also face challenges in the form of job losses to cheaper labor elsewhere, and a possible decline in living standards if worldwide wages fall to meet global supply rather than rise to meet current standards (*World Bank Policy Research Bulletin* 1995).

Another global theme affecting the political arena concerns a change in government responsibilities: privatization all over the world has brought business into industries such as prisons, transportation, and infrastructure projects previously managed or controlled by governments. In North America, eroding confidence in the welfare state and a heightened awareness of the inefficiencies of nationalized firms have been important triggers for privatization. In Western Europe, government policies have emphasized extensive privatization, particularly in Britain. In parts of the developing world, privatization has resulted from government inability to address perceived gaps in needed products and services. The volume of privatization has been greatest in Western Europe followed by the Asian/Pacific region, Eastern Europe, and Latin America, and sales of previously state-owned enterprises climbed dramatically from just under $20 billion in 1989 to just under $70 billion in 1994 (*Wall Street Journal* 1995c). In Eastern Europe, the end of communism and the Cold War led to a reduction of government influence on many business activities, as private enterprises have attempted to respond to and profit from new entrepreneurial initiatives.

Globalization has thus moved influence from the hands of national political leaders and concentrated it in the business domain, weakening the ability of policy-makers to control key economic processes (Simai 1994). Accordingly there are growing expectations for businesses to adapt roles previously played by government entities (Brown 1992; Drucker 1989; Renesch 1992). While some global firms like The Body Shop, Levi Strauss, and Canon embrace, and even lead, new demands for social stewardship, others resist, obstruct, and willfully exploit both natural and human resources. There is now a global market for child prostitution, both male and female, fuelled by tourists and a tour industry to exploit others sexually (Shoup 1994). These activities raise concerns about the role business can, should or will play on the world's political stage: whether the authority of governments is eroding (Korten 1995), making it more difficult to regulate activities of firms (MacEwen 1994); whether, as the economic and social power of business increases, a few hundred corporations will become world empires in the twenty-first century, amassing sufficient resources to become powerful shadow governments (Barnet and Cavanagh 1994); and whether, as businesses exercise their power, a new form of imperialism will emerge as stronger economic entities use their strength to exact concessions from weaker ones (Wanniski 1995).

At the same time that global trade agreements reduce the role of national governments in global affairs, they may free up resources which governments can use to develop the nation. So, there is evidence to suggest that globalization will not phase out the role of national government completely but create a reason for its transformation. The national resources saved by the diminishing need to monitor and enforce global commercial regulations may provide opportunities for politicians to redeploy resources in education, training, or other modes of knowledge creation (Marshall and Tucker 1992). In so far as the latter leads to creativity, it may be a source of the national innovativeness needed for economic success (McRae 1995; Porter 1990).

Global Culture

As globalization calls into question the concept of nation-state, it also focuses attention on culture. Business organizations operating solely in a domestic environment traditionally derive their cultural habits and values from the nation of origin. Although regional or ethnic variations might arise, for the most part such organizations subscribed to the values of the dominant culture. Even as firms became international, they continued to derive their cultural habits and values from their nation of origin, as Hofstede's (1980) work illustrates. But when organizations increasingly operate across borders, their members are exposed to additional cultures and adopt some measure of norms, habits, and even values from them. As sales and profits increasingly depend on foreign markets, it makes sense to hire employees who have knowledge of those markets, and managers may decide it is no longer possible or desirable to remain entirely congruent with the home culture.

Such changes in organizational practices create other changes in organizational culture, which, in the world of global business, are fed back to the parent culture as it too changes. In this way business enterprises construct and are constructed by business activities in which they and others engage. For example, organizational changes among giant conglomerates or *chaebol* like Samsung, Sunkyong, and Daewoo focus on quality improvement initiatives, all of which call for some individual initiative and accountability instead of the deference to authority more traditional to Korean culture. Changes like this then presage national change as business enterprises become conduits for a 'global' culture as well as recipients of multiple national cultures. This suggests that in a globalizing world, the nation-state is not necessarily the main source of culturally acceptable behaviors or beliefs as behaviors, norms, assumptions, and values emerge from outside national boundaries. In this sense, culture becomes 'boundaryless' as business activities transcend national borders.

Through global information and communication technologies, people throughout the world witness cultural norms, values, and behaviors reflective of many nations, and many now think and behave in ways that are increasingly global.

Business promotes, across the world, both a global language that is English, and a proliferation of consumer goods that range from cola beverages to blue jeans, from television entertainment to rock stars. Some argue that such cultural invasion provides teens and young adults with global habits that include similar modes of dress, jargon, music, entertainment preferences, and even converging values from environmental stewardship (Tully 1994) to individualism (Rohwedder 1994). Television reached 800 million homes in 1995, conveying fantasy images like 'Mighty Morphin Power Rangers' and 'Dynasty' as readily as CNN reports. Images of real and imagined violence, from a martial arts tradition filtered through the Hong Kong film industry (Dannen 1995) as well as from Hollywood, foster a culture for violence around the world that is particularly attractive to young men (Appadurai 1990).

Some writers view these influences as potential sources of cultural corruption (Finel-Honigman 1993). They see cultural convergence as a form of neo-imperialism capable of eliminating cultural variety (Tomlinson 1991), and producing cultural pressures that lead to destructive forms of conflict (Barber 1992; Huntington 1993). Others challenge these assumptions, arguing that the cultural borrowing associated with 'creolization', 'mestizaje', 'orientalization' and the like enhance, but do not redefine, culture (Pieterse 1995). 'Glocalization' or loose connections between what is local and what is global are forged (Robertson 1995), leading to the multiplication of cultural differences rather than their reduction (Kahn 1995). Instead of globalization leading to a predominantly Westernized culture, where business language, values and behaviors are standardized and homogenized on a worldwide basis, Robertson (1995) argues that cultural influences *from* East *to* West have been seriously underestimated, as, for example, values concerning religion, home and community, have become more rather than less important (Abu-Lughod 1994).

Those who categorize culture as either a global phenomenon or a series of diverse national cultures may be taking a limited view. Rather than this either/or approach we see instead a tension between homogeneity and heterogeneity played out by nations, organizations, and individuals, as demonstrated by armed conflict based on ethnicity, by public dialogue over immigration, and in private debates over religious fundamentals. While estimates suggest that the number of nations could grow from 300 to 1,000 in the twenty-first century (*Outlook* 1994), partly because of cultural differences (Davis 1994), heterogeneous countries are also coming together to form homogeneous trading blocs. The signals are mixed: as ethnic conflict has broken out in the former Yugoslavia, religious violence subsides in Northern Ireland; as political, religious and ethnic divisions fragment the Middle East, racial differences are put aside in South Africa; as Czechoslovakia, reacquainted with the democratic process, votes to separate, Quebec narrowly votes to stay part of Canada.

Global Technologies

Digital electronics, miniaturization, telecommunications, computers, robotics, artificial intelligence, genetic engineering, low-flying satellites, and laser conductors are only a few of many technologies revolutionizing relationships between people, organizations, and nations worldwide. Medical breakthroughs from birth control to disease control bring more people to the workplace; product and process breakthroughs constantly alter the nature of their work; and information-based technologies have made people and information critical resources for organizations. Unlike the land, labor, and capital so important to economic growth during the Industrial Revolution, the driving force behind the Information Revolution is an intangible: knowledge. Because individuals own knowledge, it becomes an organizational asset only when people share it (Handy 1994), and this characteristic of knowledge creates a potential for greater equality and for worse inequality.

Telecommunication technology, capable of transmitting information almost instantaneously throughout the world, has made it possible for people and businesses to communicate and operate twenty-four hours a day, seven days a week. Moreover, the unit cost of computing power has declined rapidly in recent years. As the cost comes down, proliferation of digital technologies may encompass the globe, providing computing power, far advanced of what is available today, to users of every income level. The low cost and worldwide availability of this technology offer extraordinary potential for opportunity and equity (Negroponte 1995), but only to those with access to education and the occasion to use it. Otherwise technology may present threats rather than opportunities, by deskilling work (Rifkin 1995), and creating a greater divide between people and the activities that enrich their lives (Stoll 1995).

The digital revolution has distributed powerful tools across a huge sweep of humanity, and relocated sources of technical innovation from developed to developing world as Indian, Bulgarian, or Israeli scientists participate in technological development. Since mathematics is the foundation of all digital advances, nations well versed in that discipline, including nations like China, India, and those of South East Asia, could turn their homelands into formidable technological powers. Individual entrepreneurs and small businesses now have access to technologies previously available only to larger firms. Almost any firm can gain access to technical expertise and to knowledge workers throughout the world. Yet there are fears of what this redistribution of knowledge may mean for developed countries if companies withdraw resources there to invest them in lower-cost wages elsewhere (Rifkin 1995).

The potential for new opportunities created by these technologies is balanced by fears that those without access to the Internet will become the 'road kill' of the information highway as new categories of 'haves' and 'have-nots' emerge. The advantages of easy access to information may be offset by the loss of privacy (Gandy 1995), and information thus gained can be used to harm rather than help. Problems with 'peepers' reading one's private mail, or 'hackers' obtaining banking and credit information are now obvious. Less obvious to the general public are rising threats to intellectual property as digitalization makes it easier to pirate software, to photocopy or plagiarize copyrighted works, to reverse engineer. The Software Publishers Association estimated that software pirates illegally copied over $8 billion in software in 1994; while the London-based Business Software Alliance claimed the costs of software piracy in Europe alone totalled $6 billion in 1994 (Pope 1995).

Information associated with video and entertainment industries also offers advantages and disadvantages to equitable globalization. Video conferencing with built-in language translation across national borders may become as common as today's word-processing programs and spreadsheets; this technology would make it possible for people to 'meet' without the added costs of spatial travel. By 1997, low earth orbiting satellites will make it possible to communicate with underserved areas of Africa, Latin America, Asia and elsewhere (Boyd 1995), but those without telephones and other equipment will find this technology to be of little use. In publishing and entertainment, readers and viewers will pull news, movies, or documents directly from the 'bitstream', but these vast galaxies of digitized video, sound, and data swirling in cyberspace remain far from the reach of those who cannot read or do not have electricity. Moreover, as in other fields, technology development reflects the interests of the developer. Thus, ASCII characters are English-language characters; many computer games have greater appeal for boys than for girls (Bulkeley 1994); computer icons represent Western, and more particularly, US cultural experiences; and the format of computer games and programs reflects a Western bias for action, linear thinking, and self-determination (Goulet 1977; Magnet 1994).

Globalization of Natural Resources

The natural environment is another arena of globalization. It intertwines people with the natural environment of which they are a part (also see Chapter 2.11 by Egri and Pinfield). Existing inequities between North and South, and along ethnic and gender lines, are often increased by globalization practices that exploit both natural and human resources.

Oil spills, nuclear disasters and similar accidents destroy natural resources, while industrialization consumes or depletes them. For example, water consumed during industrial production can pollute water worldwide just as airborne emissions reduce air quality or reduce the ozone layer. According to scientific testimony at the 1995 UN Climate Conference, by 2000 anticipated ozone reductions and global warming are expected to displace 95 million people who live at sea level, cause ecosystems to disappear, deserts to expand, and storms to become more violent and frequent. While industrialization creates jobs and a standard of living that individuals as well as nations seek, it also gathers people into densely populated areas where urban problems of garbage, water treatment, and noise pollution further affect the environment. Industrialization is a mixed blessing in improving world prosperity at the same time that it increases the potential for ecological disruption.

Ecological disruption increases as business activities transport plants and animals greater distances. For example, brown tree snakes introduced to Guam thirty years ago have killed off virtually all species of birds and many other animals; zebra mussels travelling on Russian ships clog intake pipes in the Great Lakes; rainbow jellyfish that entered Black Sea waters in 1982 are destroying plankton, fish eggs, and the larvae of flora and fauna. Diseases that afflict both people and plants also are going global. For example, the A2 strain of potato virus recently migrated from central Mexico to US potato fields, devastating crops and costing farmers millions of dollars (Winslow 1995). WTO reduction in agricultural trade barriers is likely to increase similar opportunities for agricultural diseases to spread.

The AIDS virus has been perhaps the first to earn the epithet of a 'global' disease, even though African adults have borne its brunt as entire generations have been wiped out, leaving grandparents to raise children, and no one to provide financial support to either. Lethal epidemics like tuberculosis, Ebola fever and dengue are expected to increase worldwide along with global interconnections among people (Garrett 1994; Preston 1994). Even natural disasters confined to one part of the world have worldwide implications because of global connections. For example, floods in Europe and an earthquake in Japan in early 1995 disrupted world trade flows throughout the world because so many goods flow through Rotterdam and Kobe.

Some argue that economic development along free market lines must be replaced with principles of sustainable development that ensure a viable future for succeeding generations (Gore 1992; Hawken 1993). Proposals for sustainable development call for fundamental changes. For example, while markets often create divisions between rich and poor, sustainable development calls for a greater degree of world economic equity. This is not to say that the world's wealth will be redistributed, but that long-standing inequities between richer and poorer nations must be overcome, providing poorer nations with better economic opportunities than in the past. According to authors of the United Nations (1994b) *Human Development Report*, 'the concept of one world and one planet simply cannot emerge from an unequal world. . . . Global sustainability without global justice will always remain an elusive goal.'

Ironically, even as some argue that lifestyles in the rich nations must be altered to consume less, many in developing countries advocate the opposite change to adopt the habits of materialism consistent with a consumption-based society. Some are willing to trade their land or raw materials for consumer goods, while others find it impossible to survive unless they exploit resources available to them. As these resources disappear, forests and water disappear and desertification grows. Given a competitive business environment, and a world population anxious or forced to join the world economy, business organizations unwilling to compromise the natural environment may lose opportunities; while those that take active steps to preserve the environment may be accused of imposing their own values on host countries anxious to develop economically. Thus, one of the challenges of sustainable development is to manage the paradox of exploiting current economic growth against protection of the natural environment and the people who live in it.

Individuals throughout the world, because of globalization, have changed their expectations concerning wealth. Labor has begun to move more freely in response to employment needs throughout the world, and because people's expectations cannot be met in emerging countries, they look elsewhere for work. Labor shortages in industrializing countries like Japan and South Korea, and limited opportunities in other parts of Asia, have led over 2 million men and women from East and South East Asia to leave home for work in nearby nations (Pura 1992). China's rural poor migrate to cities or pay large sums for illegal exit to countries where jobs are to be found. Worldwide immigration, both legal and illegal, is increasing. In the US, immigration accounted for 39 per cent of US growth in the last decade, and large population increases in Europe have occurred in the last twenty years due to economic integration and to immigration. At the same time as immigration occurs and, in some cases, is actively encouraged, barriers such as the Schengen agreement are erected to prevent some migration flows, individuals are returned to their countries of origin, and immigrants have been subjected to violent attacks against them, their property and their rights in Europe, the US, Japan (Fernandez 1991) and throughout the world.

The tradeoff between human and economic investment is greatest for those who have least. Often the people who lose the most from an emphasis on growth and development are women. The UN *Human Development Report* finds that among those countries providing gender-based statistics, no country treats women as well as it treats men. In many countries, differential treatment for women includes poor access to basic safety, security, nutrition, educational opportunities or health care resources. Women from emerging countries increasingly are sent abroad to work in menial jobs that provide opportunities for abuse. Some are sold into slavery or prostitution to become the lure for global sex tours. Accordingly, economic development is often built upon only half of the population, robbing future generations of opportunities to reach a full potential. Without education, women tend to remain net recipients of national goods rather than contributors in the form of labor or taxes paid, and less attractive to global companies seeking workers.

In industrialized nations, differential treatment toward women often is reflected in unequal pay and status inequities between women and men. The female-to-male weekly wage ratio ranged from 80 to 90 per cent in Australia, Denmark, France, New Zealand, Norway, and Sweden, while other countries in Western Europe also had ratios of roughly 65–75 per cent. Women in the US earn about 76 per cent of what men earn, while Japanese women earn about 61 per cent of what a Japanese man would earn in a similar job (*Wall Street Journal* 1995a). However, there is some evidence that women are making progress in achieving managerial positions. For example, between 1985 and 1991, the percentage of women managers increased in 39 of the 41 countries that report comparative labor statistics (*World of Work – US*, 1993). As these inequities reach resolution, they simultaneously raise awareness of other forms of inequity. For example, educational improvements for women in the developing as well as the developed world go first to those with economic resources. The poor remain poor.

Globalization often results in inequities, whether they occur between richer Northern countries and poorer Southern countries, between men and women, or within and between ethnic groups. Organizations and especially business organizations are often expected to address these inequities but, in so doing, they face a tension between capitalizing on the potential for growth and protecting and redressing such inequities.

In summarizing this section, we can say that globalization involves revolutionary changes in economic, political, cultural, technological, and natural spheres. A global pursuit of the benefits of wealth creation has altered traditional relationships among and between business, government, and society (Hawken 1993). Political responsibilities are increasingly met by consumer advocacy groups and business enterprises; while some business responsibilities have been taken on by government and nongovernmental organizations. Organizations in all sectors are under increased pressure to be more efficient, to measure the relationship between input and outcome, to be more 'business-like'. At the same time, business enterprises are implored to be more socially responsible in the way they globalize, to accommodate homogeneity and heterogeneity, to reduce inequities while maintaining internal profitability, to sustain as well as exploit. Thus globalization, in permeating far beyond the confines of business, creates significant new challenges for all parts of society.

IMPLICATIONS FOR ORGANIZATIONS

The strategy/structure/systems approach to managing multinationals yielded efficiencies realized through hierarchical structures supported by complex and sophisticated management systems (Ghoshal and Bartlett 1995). The value of hierarchical structures and the strategy/structure/systems approach to practice is eroding in a world populated with firms of every size, and a global environment characterized by rapid change, but the need to generate efficiencies remains great. This managerial challenge is but one of many paradoxes challenging organizations as they face increasing demands to be many things to many people all at the same time (Handy 1994). Within the firm, the paradox may be managed by increased focus on organizational processes like entrepreneurship, competence building, and renewal (Ghoshal and Bartlett 1995), and by change champions with two capabilities: anticipating the future and willingness to swim up-stream against internal tides of resistance (Handy 1994). Champions of change thoughout the world can be found in every type of organization, in business, government, and academic circles. The many questions they raise about the role of business and other types of organizations in the world today give rise to still other questions about the strategy, structures and processes appropriate to organizations in a global world. The nature of globalization raises a number of important implications concerning the social responsibility of the global organization, whether business or otherwise. It also creates new demands for organizational strategy and structure. These implications are discussed in this section.

Social Responsibility

As they assume roles previously played by government entities, e.g. via privatization (Drucker 1989), business organizations are expected to behave more as a community member than a corporate entity alone (Brown 1992); as they globalize, the costs of large, powerful worldwide organizations *not* acting responsibly increase. On the other hand, some writers believe that business may be the only mechanism strong enough to reverse many of the social problems that currently exist (Hawken 1993). In view of slowing economic growth in the industrialized world and rapid growth in the developing world, organizations have greater motivation to participate in activities that result in economic development (Handy 1994).

Regulations are one means of forcing socially responsible behavior from organizations, although the difficulties of regulating on a worldwide scale are tremendous. The Parliament of World's Religions produced a *Global Ethic,* calling for the reduction of environmental and human abuses throughout the world; the UN has produced many statements on individual and organizational rights; and in 1995 the US

government introduced a voluntary code of corporate behavior. The global business community itself produced the Caux Round Table *Principles for Business* by combining basic Eastern ideals of *kyosei* (living and working for the common good) and human dignity (referring to the sacredness or value of each person) into a set of common ethical principles. Developed in 1994 through collaboration among business leaders in Japan, Europe, and the US, these principles suggest that some business leaders have the will to assume greater social responsibility. Also in 1995, forty-one major nations founded Transparency International, a group patterned after Amnesty International, and funded by European aid agencies and some multinationals, to combat large-scale corruption involving corporations and holders of public offices around the world.

Any attempt to develop global ethical codes has to address at least two key problems. The first concerns the problems inherent in policing activities that can easily cross boundaries and disappear from view. These difficulties are compounded when governments of developing countries, anxious for hard currency and economic development, are willing to tolerate, and in some cases encourage, business practices that are illegal elsewhere and which may involve dangers for a population either ignorant of them or unable to resist them. A second difficulty concerns the fact that ethical standards vary widely throughout the world: what is bribery in one country might be viewed as standard business practice in another. Values vary tremendously across the world (Hofstede 1980; Hampden-Turner and Trompenaars 1993; Kanter 1991; Schwartz 1992), leading to differences in work behaviors and attitudes (Hofstede 1983). Even Kanter's (1991) survey of 12,000 managers, which showed commonly held views on world problems, did not indicate common solutions.

Other means to encourage socially responsible behavior do exist. For example, consumer groups have assumed a new role in encouraging social responsibility from firms. According to *The Economist* (1995b), consumer pressure motivated firms like IKEA, Levi, and Nike to tackle human rights issues. Supra-national organizations like the United Nations and the International Labor Organization attempt to transcend national politics to promote a democratic society organized around values such as justice, equality, and mutual respect (Commission on Global Governance 1995) in the face of growing gaps between rich and poor, armed conflict around the world, minimal legal protection in some parts of the world, and corrupt regimes (Kennedy 1993). While business and government can be expected to assume responsibility for filling some of these gaps, partnerships among groups of business people, governmental officials, and nongovernmental representatives are most likely to lead to results that achieve some degree of balance or equity. Politicians anxious to realize advantages of something like the WTO for their countries or regions may overlook the transitional costs borne by others; markets are unlikely to pay the full or long-term costs of unanticipated change; consumers may be underinformed; or businesses may be unable to foresee the outcome of decisions they are pressured to make. For example, legitimate efforts to alleviate labor abuses of children could result in change for the worse if children suspended from factory work are forced into worse jobs or families starve. Partnerships of interest play an important role in seeing that one correction does not lead to another higher cost.

Nongovernment organizations (NGOs) have also taken on a global mandate, dubbed a global 'associational revolution' (Salamon 1994) because of the size and effect NGO activities have had on business practices worldwide. For example, consumer boycotts in Germany led by Greenpeace resulted in worldwide protest, and led to a reversal by Royal Dutch Shell of its earlier decision to bury the oil rig *Brent Spar* at sea. Less successfully, Greenpeace has played a key role in the global protest against French nuclear testing in the Pacific. NGOs also conduct global business activities such as providing seed money to the informal work sector (*World of Work* 1994); organizing workers (Frenkel 1993); or underwriting economic development (Hymowitz 1995). These activities question traditional assumptions about where business interests are served. For example, Grameen Bank loans to 3 million women in thousands of small Bangladeshi villages not only lifted half the recipients from poverty, but provided Grameen with resources to expand globally. The resulting surge in micro banks (*Wall Street Journal* 1995b) challenges traditional assumptions about the ability of the poor to repay loans and, since many of these loans go to women, they also shift traditional assumptions about the economic roles women can play.

As NGOs play business roles, expectations increase for them to be more business-like in managing money and even people. Just as business organizations face calls for social responsibility, nonprofit organizations are urged to think of people as 'customers' and to adopt accounting practices mirroring those used in business (Greenberger 1995). These demands for accountability blur the distinction between human need and business practice; between the

economic and the social; between business and politics.

There are, then, many questions concerning the social role of global organizations of all types. Many observers have expressed concern about the potential for social irresponsibility on the part of these organizations and the inability of governments and other actors to regulate them. Gergen (1995), on the other hand, argues that the postmodern attributes of the global organization: the dispersion of intelligibilities; disruptions in chains of authority; the erosion of rationality; a reduction in centralized knowledge; and undermined autonomy, provide the potential for 'ethically generative practices'. Clearly, then, this is one area where more research has much to offer.

Organizational Strategy

Globalization calls for new approaches to strategy-making compared to traditional models. Global strategies must, for example, be informed by political, legal and social, as well as economic, considerations (Buckley 1990; Boddewyn and Brewer 1994; Earley and Singh 1995). In a global world, where it is difficult to sustain competitive advantage (D'Aveni 1995), being competitive involves rethinking many of the basic strategy concepts (Hamel and Prahalad 1989). Unanticipated opportunities arise only when traditional assumptions are challenged: organizational survival depends on seeing the future first and in a different way (Hamel and Prahalad 1994). Consequently, planning techniques must rely less on historical data to aid scenario planning or competitive analysis, and more on those that yield industry foresight and leverage global knowledge (Ghoshal and Bartlett 1995). The global organization represents a major departure from the more traditional strategy-making practices of both East and West, as organizations from different nations participate in international business activities and contribute to changes concerning how and why business is conducted. For example, in contrast to 'bigger is better' philosophies of Westernized firms, Taiwan's Acer Inc. has established itself as a global power in the personal computer market by becoming more compact. The company reorganized from a centralized structure into small business units whose managers have autonomy to make business decisions in their own markets. So, while the family-based nature of many Chinese enterprises encourages family hiring, Acer has taken an opposite tack by keeping family members out of management and giving workers a financial stake in the company (*Wall Street Journal* 1994).

The global organization also depends upon organizational learning (Bartlett and Ghoshal 1989), which has been described as the ability to develop insight and knowledge of the relationships between past actions, their effectiveness, and future actions (Lyles 1988). This learning is expected to come not just from personal mastery but from shared vision and team work (Senge 1990). As knowledge is unleashed through team as well as individual efforts, a tenuous balance is generated between flexibility and efficiency; between collaboration and autonomy; between consensus and risk. Individuals trained in the context of a collectivistic culture face a challenge in becoming individually competitive; while people from individualistic societies may find it difficult to operate as a member of a team. Organizational challenges come from nurturing and rewarding the type of learning sought, and coping with anger when learning needs change more rapidly than people.

Unlike more tangible factors of production like equipment or capital, the knowledge that stems from organizational learning is more difficult to monopolize and measure (Handy 1994). Because knowledge need not be concentrated in one place, business activities can be redistributed throughout the world to take advantage of highly skilled and educated workforces. International Data Solutions, for example, scans case and client files for US law firms and transmits them in digital form via satellite to the Philippines. There, workers organize and index the documents so they can be readily retrieved by a computer network in the US. An emphasis on everyone being both a learner and a teacher represents a profound change from traditional management principles which more clearly allocated the job of thinking and teaching to top managers alone.

Thus global strategies have profound implications for human resource strategies (e.g. Adler and Bartholomew 1992; Schuler et al. 1993). The successful global manager is less likely to be the international specialist than a generalist who can cope with complex cross-border strategies, develop appropriate personnel, and integrate across and between people and functions (Bartlett and Ghoshal 1992). According to Adler and Bartholomew (1992) these skills transcend those traditionally required from expatriate managers but are nonetheless crucial to managing an increasingly diverse workforce within and between countries whose skills, interests, and work motivations vary on the basis of gender, nationality, work role, and background (Gibson 1995; Laurent 1986; Parker 1991; Welsh et al. 1993).

There is, then, scope for further study of the different strategies that are evolving in the global marketplace: not only those adopted by Western enterprises, but also those of other countries; not only those spearheaded by business organizations, but also those in other sectors; and not only those of large, well-known multinationals, but also those of smaller and different types of global organizations.

Organizational Structure

Bureaucracy creates organizations in the form of tall pyramids; it removes managerial expertise from the shop floor; and it emphasizes the importance of a clearly defined, autonomous entity. Although organizations from the West tend to prefer operating autonomously (Janger 1980) globalization makes different demands: there is evidence of a growing need for various forms of partnership between organizations such as spider webs (Harrigan 1985), global webs (Reich 1991), networks (Ghoshal and Bartlett 1990), or joint ventures (Kanter 1991). In international joint ventures, greater diversity between partners' societal and corporate cultures or managerial practices requires learning to bridge those gaps (Parkhe 1991). Internally, organizations may be structured less as pyramids or hierarchies, directed from the top, and more as networks guided by the shared purpose of interdependent and diverse teams (Brown 1992); by common values (Hordes et al. 1995); or by core organizational processes (Ghoshal and Bartlett 1995). The shift from hierarchical organizations to flatter or 'horizontal' structures and the move from functional to cross-functional thinking may require new structures instead of the pure form of bureaucracy. Often these new structures involve some form of hybrid that enables the global firm to be price competitive, efficient and able to compete with other global firms as well as local and regional firms.

The knowledge revolution associated with globalization has a potential to restructure not only existing organizations but also how work is organized. It is possible for some people to 'telecommute', on a long-distance, international basis, and accomplish work from home or other locales. More localized, flexible working arrangements in different countries may offer community-based groups the means to combine business opportunities with local social needs. Business activities transacted between countries and at arm's length via fax, e-mail, and computers may hide color, gender, nationality or similar factors, freeing groups from some of the discriminating effects that they might encounter inside more traditional organizational arrangements. These opportunities may be leading increasing numbers of women in Europe to leave traditional organizations to establish companies that better suit their interests and needs (Conference Board Europe 1991). A similar pattern in the US has led to an increase in female-controlled businesses: 9.1 per cent of all businesses in 1994, with recent gains found in traditionally male industries such as finance, transportation, construction and manufacturing (*Business Week* 1995b). A third to a half of small entrepreneurs in Latin America are believed to be women (Santiago 1994); and micro bank loans throughout Asia stimulate business growth, particularly for women (*Wall Street Journal* 1995b).

This is not to say that the global organization represents a transformation in the organization of work (Whitaker 1992). We should not forget that in a global world competition is high, and old principles still apply: the new core may cluster around providing service, but the old imperatives continue to emphasize the need to deliver that service at the least cost; notions of efficiency are not dead; financial pressures continue to curtail innovation and experimentation; new organizational forms as well as other 'take charge' initiatives meet needs for creating 'illusions of managerial control' (Salancik and Meindl 1984) even as they undermine morale or lead to dead-ends; the interest in cooperative links does not signal an end to competition since alliance partners may collaborate on one product line but compete on another; and, while some multinational organizations have incorporated diversity into top management, most have few women or foreign nationals in top managerial positions or on boards (*The Economist* 1995a).

In summary, the global organization often represents a hybrid of the old and the new, of the modern and the postmodern organization. It certainly is a demanding and difficult organization to manage (Melin 1992). Without profound changes in thinking throughout the organization, the changes associated with globalization may be perceived as little more than fads. The process of adapting organizational structure to globalization requires not only incremental changes in how organizations function, but a fundamental rethinking of how organizational participants think about their relationship with the organization and the organization's role in a global world.

CONCLUSION

The challenge for research on globalization is not whether progress is being made, but whether it is being made quickly enough (Dunning 1989; Inkpen and Beamish 1994). For example, Ricks et al. (1990: 219) noted that while 'virtually every area of management has an international dimension . . . many of these areas are [only] just beginning to be investigated.' Adler and Bartholomew's (1992) data base search of publications in seventy-three academic and professional management journals from 1985 to 1990 revealed growing interest and focus on cross-cultural interactions of many kinds, but also found publications on international organizational behavior and human resource management had not increased in two decades. One particular demand is for more interdisciplinary research (Dunning 1989; Inkpen and Beamish 1994), and Dunning (1993) warns that future scholars will reach their full potential only by combining the knowledge of disciplinary scholarship with insights provided by other disciplines. Multinational organizations are believed to have developed beyond the relevance and legitimacy of single academic disciplines to explain them (Sundaram and Black 1992). Others underscore an apparent need to move away from emphasis on quantitative research to incorporate more qualitative research (Wright and Ricks 1994) and engage in more flexible forms of theorizing that can accommodate the diversity and scope of global practices.

Such a research agenda is not without problems, as the efforts of one multinational, multicultural, interdisciplinary research consortium to generate multiple perspectives and levels of analysis bear witness (Teagarden et al. 1995). Such research requires considerable collaboration and time if scholars are to understand multiple academic fields; is difficult to carry out unless resources are made available; and journals are not always geared to such multidisciplinary, qualitative work. Since few scholars have infinite resources of time or money, and many operate in systems that reward frequent annual productivity in top disciplinary journals, the academic system may discourage interdisciplinary research even as the business world needs it more.

An interdisciplinary approach invites academicians to take on additional complexity, to learn new skills, and to question assumptions. It also invites individuals to step outside comfort zones and blur customary distinctions: between disciplines; between those who theorize and those who practice; between many of the other traditional boundaries observed in knowledge generation. By developing global practices in academia, however, we may be in a better position to study them: business organizations may provide some of the resources to fund this research; global technologies undoubtedly help build worldwide academic networks; collaboration between schools and scholars that span the globe will help provide a more supportive, sensitive global culture that both facilitates and improves research. If students of organizations do not rise to the study of globalization in this way, an important chapter in business history will not be written and the lessons that could have been learned will be lost.

NOTE

The author would like to acknowlege the help of Cynthia Hardy, McGill University and Sue Jones, Sage Publications, in writing this chapter, and to thank Anne Smith, McGill University for contributing several valuable ideas.

REFERENCES

Abu-Lughod, J. (1994) 'Diversity, democracy, and self-determination in an urban neighorhood: the East Village of Manhattan', *Social Research*, 61(1): 181–204.

Adler, N.J. (1983) 'Cross cultural management research: the ostrich and the trend', *Academy of Management Review*, 8(2): 226–32.

Adler, N.J. and Bartholomew, S. (1992) 'Academic and professional communities of discourse: generating knowledge on transnational human resource management', *Journal of International Business Studies*, 23(3): 551–69.

Aharoni, Y. (1966) *The Foreign Investment Decision Process*. Boston: Division of Research, Harvard University.

Appadurai, A. (1990) 'Disjunctures and difference in the global cultural economy', in M. Featherstone (ed.), *Global Culture*. Newbury Park, CA: Sage. pp. 295–310.

Ashkenas, R., Ulrich, D., Jick, T. and Kerr, S. (1995) *The Boundaryless Organization*. San Francisco: Jossey-Bass.

Ball, D.A. and McCullough, W.J. Jr (1990) *International Business*, 4th edn. Homewood, IL: Irwin.

Bannon, L. (1994) 'Natuzzi's huge selection of leather furniture pays off', *Wall Street Journal*, 17 November: B4.

Barber, Benjamin. (1992) 'Jihad vs. McWorld', *Atlantic Monthly*, 269(3): 53–61.

Barnet, R.J. and Cavanagh, J. (1994) *Global Dreams: Imperial Corporations and the New World Order*. New York: Simon & Schuster.

Barrett, A. (1995) 'It's a small (business) world', *Business Week*, 17 April: 96–101.

Bartlett, C.A. and Ghoshal, S. (1989) *Managing Across Borders: the Transnational Solution*. Boston: Harvard Business School Press.

Bartlett, C.A. and Ghoshal, S. (1991) 'Global strategic management: impact on the new frontiers of strategy research', *Strategic Management Journal*, 12: 5–16.

Bartlett, C.A. and Ghoshal, S. (1992) 'What is a global manager?', *Harvard Business Review*, September/October: 124–32.

Beamish, P., Killing, J.P., Lecraw, D.J. and Crookell, H. (1991) *International Management*. Burr Ridge, IL: Irwin.

Becker, G. (1994) 'Why so many mice are roaring', *Business Week*, 7 November: 20.

Bello, W. and Cunningham, S. (1994) 'Reign of error: the World Bank's wrongs', in *Real World International*, 2nd edn. pp. 26–30.

Bleakley, F.R. (1993) 'Smaller US firms lag counterparts overseas in setting up business abroad', *Wall Street Journal*, 8 August: A2.

Bleakley, F.R. (1995) 'Foreign investment in the US surged in 1994', *The Wall Street Journal*, 15 March: A2, A10.

Boddewyn, J.J. and Brewer, T.L. (1994) 'International-business political behavior: new theoretical directions', *Academy of Management Review*, 19(1): 119–43.

Boyacigiller, N. and Adler, N.J. (1991) 'The parochial dinosaur: organizational science in a global context', *Academy of Management Review*, 16(2): 262–90.

Boyd, R.S. (1995) 'Satellites spur new space race', *Seattle Times*, 1 February: A3.

Brown, J. (1992) 'Corporation as community: a new image for a new era', in J. Rensch (ed.), *New Traditions in Business*. San Francisco: Berrett-Koehler. pp. 123–39.

Buckley, P. (1990) 'Problems and developments in the core theory of international business', *Journal of International Business Studies*, 21(1): 657–65.

Buckley, P. and Casson, M. (1976) *The Future of the Multinational Enterprise*. London: Macmillan.

Bulkeley, W.M. (1994) 'A tool for women, a toy for men', *Wall Street Journal*, 16 March: B1, B3.

Business Week (1995a) 'The *Mittlestand* takes a stand', 10 April: 54–5.

Business Week (1995b) 'The big picture: where women are making great strides', May: 8.

Caves, R. (1971) 'International corporations: the industrial economics of foreign investment', *Economica*.

Chandler, A. (1962) *Strategy and Structure*. Cambridge, MA: MIT Press.

Commission on Global Governance (1995) *Our Global Neighbourhood*. Oxford: Oxford University Press.

Conference Board Europe (1991) 'Europe's glass ceiling'. RM5, Conference Board Europe, Brussels.

Cooperrider, D. and Passmore, W. (1991) 'The organizational dimension of global change', *Human Relations*, 44: 763–87.

Daniels, J.D., Pitts, R.A. and Tretter, M.J. (1984)

'Strategy and structure of U.S. multinationals: an exploratory study', *Academy of Management Journal*, 6(3): 223–7.

Daniels, J.D. and Radebaugh, L.H. (1992) *International Business*, 6th edn. Reading, MA: Addison-Wesley.

Dannen, F. (1995) 'Hong Kong Babylon', *New Yorker*, 7 August: 30–8.

D'Aveni, R.A. (1995) *Hypercompetitive Rivalries*. New York: Free Press.

Davis, B. (1994) 'Growth of trade binds nations, but it also can spur separatism', *Wall Street Journal*, 20 June: A1, A6.

Dicken, P. (1992) *Global Shift*, 2nd edn. London: Guilford Press.

Drucker, P. (1989) *The New Realities*. New York: Harper & Row.

Drucker, P. (1994) 'The new superpower: the overseas Chinese', *Wall Street Journal*, 20 December: A16.

Dunning, J. (1988) 'The eclectic paradigm of international production: a restatement and some possible extensions', *Journal of International Business Studies*, 1–31.

Dunning, J. (1989) 'The study of international business: a plea for a more interdisciplinary approach', *Journal of International Business Studies*, 20(3): 411–36.

Dunning, J. (1993) *The Globalization of Business*. London: Routledge.

Dyas, G. and Thanheiser, H. (1976) *The Emerging European Enterprise*. London: Macmillan.

Earley, P.C. and Singh, H. (1995) 'International and intercultural management research: what's next?', *Academy of Management Journal*, 38(2): 327–40.

Economist, The (1994) 'A game of international leapfrog', in 'Survey: the global economy', 1 October: 6–9.

Economist, The (1995a) 'Who wants to be a giant?', in 'Multinationals survey', 24 June: 4.

Economist, The (1995b) 'Human rights', 3 June: 58–9.

Evans, P., Doz, Y. and Laurent, A. (eds) (1990) *Human Resource Management in International Firms: Change, Globalization, Innovation*. New York: St Martin's Press.

Farnham, A. (1994) 'Global – or just globaloney?', *Fortune*, 27 June: 97–100.

Farrell, C. (1994) 'The triple revolution', *Business Week*, bonus issue: 16–25.

Fayerweather, J. (1969) *International Business Management*. New York: McGraw-Hill.

Fernandez, J.P. (1991) *Managing a Diverse Work Force: Regaining the Competitive Edge*. Lexington, MA: Lexington Books.

Finel-Honigman, I. (1993) 'Popular culture in the global economy: antithesis or reconcilation?', in R.R. Sims and R.F. Dennehy (eds), *Diversity and Differences in Organizations*. Westport, CT: Quorum. pp. 123–33.

Forbes (1995) 'Index to foreign billionaires', 17 July.

Franko, L.G. (1976) *The European Multinationals: a Renewed Challenge to American and British Big Business*. Stamfort, CT: Greylock.

Frenkel, S. (1993) 'Organized labor in the Asia-Pacific region'. Cornell International Industrial and Labor Relations Report 24, Cornell University, Ithaca, NY.

Gandy, O.H. Jr (1995) 'It's discrimination, stupid', in J. Brook and I.A. Boal (eds), *Resisting the Virtual Life*. San Francisco: City Lights Books. pp. 35–48.

Garrett, L. (1994) *The Coming Plague: Newly Emerging Diseases in a World out of Balance*. Farrar Straus Giroux.

Gergen, K.J. (1995) 'Global organization: from imperialism to ethical vision', *Organization*, 2(3/4): 519–32.

Ghoshal, S. and Barlett, C. (1990) 'The multinational corporation as an interorganizational network', *Academy of Management Review*, 15(4): 603–25.

Ghoshal, S. and Barlett, C. (1995) 'Changing the role of top management: beyond structure to processes', *Harvard Business Review*, January/February: 86–96.

Gibson, C.B. (1995) 'An investigation of gender differences in leadership across four countries', *Journal of International Business Studies*, 26(2): 255–79.

Gore, A. (1992) *Earth in the Balance: Ecology and the Human Spirit*. Boston: Houghton Mifflin.

Goulet, D. (1977) *The Uncertain Promise: Value Conflicts in Technology Transfer*. New York: North America.

Greenberger, R.S. (1995) 'Developing countries pass off tedious job of assisting the poor', *Wall Street Journal*, 6 June: A1, A9.

Grosse, R. and Behrman, J.N. (1992) 'Theory in international business', *Transnational Corporations*, 1(1): 93–126.

Gumbel, P. and Davis, B. (1994) 'G-7 countries show limits of their powers', *Wall Street Journal*, 11 July: A3, A4.

Hamel, G. (1991) 'Competition for competence and inter-partner learning within international strategic alliances', *Journal of Strategic Management*, 12: 83–104.

Hamel, G. and Prahalad, C.K. (1985) 'Do you really have a global strategy?', *Harvard Business Review*, July/August: 139–48.

Hamel, G. and Prahalad, C.K. (1989) 'Strategic intent', *Harvard Business Review*, May/June: 63–75.

Hamel, G. and Prahalad, C.K. (1994) *Competing for the Future*. Cambridge, MA: Harvard Business School Press.

Hampden-Turner, C. and Trompenaars, F. (1993) *The Seven Cultures of Capitalism*. New York: Doubleday.

Handy, C. (1994) *The Age of Paradox*. Cambridge, MA: Harvard Business School Press.

Harrigan, K. (1985) *Strategies for Joint Ventures*. Lexington, MA: Lexington Books.

Hawken, Paul (1993) *The Ecology of Commerce*. New York: Harper Business.

Hedlund, G. (1986) 'The hypermodern MNC: a

heterarchy?', *Human Resource Management*, 25: 9–35.

Hedlund, G. and Rolander, D. (1990) 'Action in heterarchies: new approaches to managing the MNC', in C. Bartlett, Y. Doz and G. Hedlund (eds), *Managing the Global Firm*. London: Routledge. pp. 15–46.

Hennart, J.F. (1982) *A Theory of Multinational Enterprise*. Ann Arbor: University of Michigan Press.

Henzler, H. and Rall, W. (1986) 'Facing up to the globalization challenge', *McKinsey Quarterly*, Winter: 52–68.

Hoecklin, L. (1995) *Managing Cultural Differences: Strategies for Competitive Advantage*. Wokingham: Addison-Wesley.

Hofstede, G. (1980) *Culture's Consequences*. Beverly Hills, CA: Sage.

Hofstede, G. (1983) 'The cultural relativity of organization practices and theories', *Journal of International Business Studies*, 14(2): 75–90.

Hordes, M.W., Clancy, J.A. and Baddeley, J. (1995) 'A primer for global start-ups', *Academy of Management Executive*, 9(2): 7–11.

Hout, T., Porter, M. and Rudden, E. (1982) 'How global companies win out', *Harvard Business Review*, 60(2): 98–108.

Huntington, S. (1993) 'The clash of civilizations', *Foreign Affairs*, Summer: 22–49.

Hymer, S.H. (1976) *The International Operations of National Firms*. Cambridge, MA: MIT Press.

Hymowitz, C. (1995) 'World's poorest women advance by entrepreneurship', *Wall Street Journal*, 5 September: B1, B2.

Ibbotson, R.G. and Brinson, G.P. (1993) *Global Investing*. New York: McGraw-Hill.

Inkpen, A. and Beamish, P. (1994) 'An analysis of twenty-five years of research', *Journal of International Business Studies*, 25(4): 703–13.

Janger, A.R. (1980) *Organization of International Joint Ventures*. New York: Conference Board.

Johanson, J. and Vahlne, J. (1977) 'The internationalisation process of the firm: a model of knowledge development on increasing foreign commitments', *Journal of International Business Studies*, 8: 23–32.

Kahn, J.S. (1995) *Culture, Multiculture, and Postculture*. Beverly Hills, CA: Sage.

Kanter, R.M. (1991) 'Transcending business boundaries: 12,000 world managers view change', *Harvard Business Review*, May/June: 151–64.

Kennedy, P. (1993) *Preparing for the Twenty-First Century*. New York: Vintage Books.

Kerwin, K. (1995) 'Getting "two big elephants to dance"', *Business Week*, special issue: '21st century capitalism': 83.

Kogut, B. (1989) 'A note on global strategies', *Strategic Management Journal*, 10(4): 383–9.

Korten, David C. (1995) *When Corporations Rule the World*. San Francisco: Berrett-Koehler.

Kwan, R. (1991) 'Foot loose and country free', in *Real World International*, 2nd edn. Somerville, MA: Dollars and Sense.

Laurent, A. (1986) 'The cross-cultural puzzle of international human resource management', *Human Resource Management*, 25(1): 91–102.

Lavipour, F.G. and Sauvant, K. (1976) *Controlling Multinational Enterprises: Problems, Strategies, Counterstrategies*. Boulder, CO: Westview.

Lemak, D. and Bracker, J. (1988) 'A strategic contingency model of multinational corporate structure', *Strategic Management Journal*, 9(5): 521–6.

Leong, S.M. and Tan, C.T. (1993) 'Managing across borders: an empirical test of the Bartlett and Ghoshal [1989] organizational typology', *Journal of International Business Studies*, 24(3): 449–64.

Levitt, T. (1983) 'The globalization of markets', *Harvard Business Review*, May/June: 92–102.

Lyles, M.A. (1988) 'Learning among joint venture-sophisticated firms', in F.J. Contractor and P. Lorange (eds), *Cooperative Strategies in International Business*. Lexington, MA: Lexington Books. pp. 301–16.

MacEwen, A. (1994) 'Markets unbound: the heavy price of globalization', in *Real World International*, 2nd edn. Somerville, MA: Dollars and Sense.

McRae, H. (1995) *The World in 2020*. Cambridge, MA: Harvard Business School Press.

Magnet, M. (1994) 'The productivity payoff arrives', *Fortune*, 27 June: 79–84.

Marshall, R. and Tucker, M. (1992) *Thinking for a Living: Education and the Wealth of Nations*. New York: Basic Books.

Martinez, J.I. and Jarillo, J.C. (1989) 'The evolution of research on coordination mechanisms in multinational corporations', *Journal of International Business Studies*, 20(3): 489–514.

Melin, L. (1992) 'Internationalization as a strategy process', *Strategic Management Journal*, 13: 99–118.

Millman, G. (1995) *The Vandal's Crown: How Rebel Currency Traders Overthrew the World's Central Banks*. Cambridge, MA: Free Press.

Moran, T.H. (1973) 'Transnational strategies of protection and defense by multinational corporations: spreading the risk and raising the cost for nationalization in natural resources', *International Organization*, 27: 273–89.

Moran, T.H. (1974) *Multinational Corporations and the Politics of Dependence*. Princeton, NJ: Princeton University Press.

Naisbitt, John (1994) *Global Paradox*. New York: William Morrow.

Negroponte, N. (1995) *Being Digital*. New York: Alfred A. Knopf.

Nehrt, L.C., Truitt, J.F. and Wright, R.W. (1970) *International Business Research: Past, Present, and Future*. Bloomington, IN: Indiana University Bureau of Business Research.

Ohmae, Kenichi (1985) *Triad Power: the Coming Shape of Global Competition*. New York: Free Press.

Ohmae, Kenichi (1989) 'The global logic of strategic alliances', *Harvard Business Review*, March/April: 143–54.

Ohmae, Kenichi (1995) *The End of the Nation State*. Cambridge, MA: Free Press.

Outlook (1994) 'World affairs', September/October: 42.

Oviatt, B. and Phillips McDougall, P. (1995) 'Global start-ups: entrepreneurs on a worldwide stage', *Academy of Management Executive*, 9(2): 30–43.

Owen, H. (1994) 'The World Bank: is 50 years enough?', *Foreign Affairs*, 73(5): 97–108.

Parker, B. (1991) 'Employment globalization', *Journal of Global Business*, 39–46.

Parkhe, A. (1991) 'Interfirm diversity, organizational learning, and longevity in global strategic alliances', *Journal of International Business Studies*, 22(4): 579–601.

Perlmutter, H.V. (1969) 'The tortuous evolution of the multinational corporation', *Columbia Journal of World Business*, 9–18.

Phatak, A.V. (1992) *International Dimensions of Management*, 3rd edn. Boston: PWS-Kent.

Pierce, B. and Garven, G. (1995) 'Publishing international business research: a survey of leading journals', *Journal of International Business Studies*, 26(1): 69–89.

Pieterse, J.N. (1995) 'Globalization as hybridization', in M. Featherstone, S. Lash and R. Robertson (eds), *Global Modernities*. London: Sage. pp. 45–68.

Pope, K. (1995) 'Software piracy is big business in East Europe', *Wall Street Journal*, 4 April: A10.

Porter, M.E. (1980) *Competitive Strategy*. New York: Free Press.

Porter, M.E. (1985) *Competitive Advantage*. New York: Free Press.

Porter, M.E. (1990) *The Competitive Advantage of Nations*. New York: Free Press.

Preston, R. (1994) *The Hot Zone*. New York: Random House.

Pura, R. (1992) 'Many of Asia's workers are on the move', *Wall Street Journal*, 5 March: A10.

Reich, R. (1991) *The Work of Nations: Preparing Ourselves for 21st Century Capitalism*. New York: Alfred A. Knopf.

Reitsperger, W.D. and Daniel, S.J. (1990) 'Japan vs Silicon Valley: quality–cost tradeoff philosophies', *Journal of International Business Studies*, 21(2): 289–300.

Renesch, J. (ed.) (1992) *New Traditions in Business*. San Francisco: Berrett-Koehler.

Rhinesmith, S.H. (1993) *A Manager's Guide to Globalization*. Homewood, IL: Business One Irwin.

Richman, L.S. (1995) 'Global growth is on a tear', *Fortune*, 20 March: 108–14.

Ricks, D., Toyne, B. and Martinez, Z. (1990) 'Recent developments in international management research', *Journal of Management*, 16(2): 219–53.

Rifkin, J. (1995) *The End of Work*. New York: G.P. Putnam's Sons.

Robertson, R. (1992) *Globalization: Social Theory and Global Culture*. London: Sage.

Robertson, R. (1995) 'Glocalization: time–space and homogeneity–heterogeneity', in M. Featherstone, S. Lash and R. Robertson (eds.), *Global Modernities*. London: Sage. pp. 25–44.

Robinson, R. (1971) 'The future of international management', *Journal of International Business Studies*, 2(1): 60–70.

Robinson, R. (1981) 'Background concepts and philosophy of international business from World War II to the present', *Journal of International Business Studies*, Spring/Summer: 13–21.

Rohwedder, C. (1994) 'Youths in Germany put individualism ahead of politics', *Wall Street Journal*, 18 Oct: A12.

Ronen, S. and Shenkar, O. (1985) 'Clustering countries on attitudinal dimensions: a review and synethesis', *Academy of Management Review*, 10(3): 435–54.

Rugman, A. (1980) 'A new theory of the multinational enterprise: internationalization versus internationalization', *Columbia Journal of World Business*, 15: 23–9.

Rummel, R.J. and Heenan, D.A. (1978) 'How multinationals analyze political risk', *Harvard Business Review*, January/February: 67–76.

Salamon, L.M. (1994) 'The rise of the nonprofit sector', *Foreign Affairs*, July/August: 109–22.

Salamon, L.M. and Anheier, H.K. (1994) *The Emerging Sector*. Baltimore: Johns Hopkins University Institute for Policy Studies.

Salancik, G.R. and Meindl, J.R. (1984) 'Corporate attributions as strategic illusions of management control', *Administrative Science Quarterly*, 29(2): 238–54.

Santiago, F. (1994) 'Latin American women to forge agenda for change', *Seattle Times*, 4 April: A11.

Schuler, R.S., Dowling, P.J. and De Cieri, H. (1993) 'An integrative framework of strategic international human resource management', *Journal of Management*, 19(2): 419–59.

Schwartz, S.H. (1992) 'Universals in the content and structure of values: theoretical advances and empirical tests in 20 countries', *Advances in Experimental Social Psychology*, 25: 1–62.

Senge, P. (1990) *The Fifth Discipline: the Art and Practice of the Learning Organization*. New York: Doubleday.

Sera, Koh (1992) 'Corporate globalization: a new trend', *Academy of Management Executive*, 6(1): 89–96.

Sesit, M.R. (1995) 'Central banks' efforts to bolster the dollar spur mostly decline', *Wall Street Journal*, 25 April: C1.

Sharp, Margaret (1992) 'Tides of change: the world economy and Europe in the 1990s', *International Affairs*, 17–35.

Shoup, Mike (1994) 'Tourism's ugly side: child prostitution', *Seattle Times*, 18 September: K10–11.

Shrivastava, A. (1995) 'Smaller firms lead German push to East', *Wall Street Journal*, 14 June: A10.

Simai, Mikaly (1994) *The Future of Global Governance*. New York: US Institute of Peace Press.

Solomon, S. (1995) *The Confidence Game*. New York: Simon & Schuster.

Sorenson, G. (1995) 'Four futures', *Bulletin of the Atomic Scientists*, July/August: 69–72.

Stead, W.E. and Stead, J.G. (1994) 'Strategic decisions and not-so-natural disasters: understanding the way in and the way out', *Organization*, 1(2): 369–73.

Stoll, C. (1995) *Silicon Snake Oil: Second Thoughts on the Information Highway*. New York: Doubleday.

Stopford, J.M. and Wells, L.T. (1972) *Managing the Multinational Enterprise*. New York: Basic Books.

Sundaram, A.K. and Black, J.S. (1992) 'The environment and internal organization of multinational enterprises', *Academy of Management Journal*, 17(4): 729–57.

Teagarden, M.B. and 13 others (1995) 'Toward a theory of comparative management research: an idiographic case study of the best international human resources management project', *Academy of Management Journal*, 38(5): 1261–87.

Thomas, A.S., Shenkar, O. and Clarke, L. (1994) 'The globalization of our mental maps: evaluating the geographic scope of JIBS coverage', *Journal of International Business Studies*, 25(4): 675–86.

Tomlinson, J. (1991) *Cultural Imperialism*. Baltimore: Johns Hopkins University Press.

Trompenaars, F. (1994) *Riding the Waves of Culture*. Burr Ridge, IL: Irwin.

Tully, S. (1994) 'Teens, the most global market of all', *Fortune*, 16 May: 90–6.

United Nations (1994a) *World Investment Report*. New York and Geneva: United Nations, UNCTC.

United Nations (1994b) *Human Development Report*. New York and Geneva: United Nations.

United Nations (1995) *Human Development Report*. New York and Geneva: United Nations.

Vernon, R. (1966) 'International trade and inter-national investment in the product cycle', *Quarterly Journal of Economics*, June: 190–207.

Wall Street Journal (1994) 'Acer emerges as global PC power and Asian pacesetter', 1 December: B4.

Wall Street Journal (1995a) 'Comparing women around the world', 26 July: B1.

Wall Street Journal (1995b) 'Women's banks stage global expansion', 30 September: A10.

Wall Street Journal (1995c) 'What is privatization, anyway?', 2 October: R4.

Wall Street Journal (1995d) 'US may be losing its trade-bully status', 13 October: A7.

Wanniski, J. (1995) 'The new American imperialism', *Wall Street Journal*, 6 July: A8.

Welsh, D.H.B., Luthans, F. and Sommer, S.M. (1993) 'Managing Russian factory workers: the impact of US-based behavioral and participative techniques', *Academy of Management Journal*, 36(1): 58–79.

Whitaker, A. (1992) 'The transformation in work: post-Fordism revisited', in M. Reed and M. Hughes (eds), *Rethinking Organization*. London: Sage. pp. 182–206.

Williamson, O. (1975) *Markets and Hierarchies*. New York: Free Press.

Winslow, Ron (1995) '"Fungus fatale" poses a threat to potato crop', *Wall Street Journal*, 1 January: B1, B5.

World Bank (1995) 'Reverse linkages – everybody wins', Development brief, May. Additional information is available in *Global Economic Prospects and the Developing Economies 1995*. Washington, DC: World Bank.

World Bank Policy Research Bulletin (1995) 'Targeting the impact', 6(1): 4.

World of Work (1994) 'Women shoulder the burden of Cambodia's economy', 9: 24–5.

World of Work – US (1993) 'Unequal race to the top', 2: 6–7.

Wright, R.W. and Ricks, D.A. (1994) 'Trends in international business research: twenty-five years later', *Journal of International Business Studies*, 25(4): 687–701.

Yip, G.S. (1995) *Total Global Strategy*. Englewood Cliffs, NJ: Prentice-Hall.

Part Three
REFLECTIONS ON RESEARCH, THEORY AND PRACTICE

3.1

Data in Organization Studies

RALPH STABLEIN

Organization studies (OS) is about understanding the social world we organization students inhabit. It is not a closed system of study like logic or mathematics. OS is necessarily an empirical study, exploring attitudes, behaviours, experiences, artefacts, symbols, documents, texts, feelings, beliefs, meanings, measures, facts and figures. Even the armchair/conceptual theorists must muse on empirical data.

But what is to count as data of organizational life? There is no clear consensus on an answer among the community (or is it communities?) of scholars who study organizations. Some organizational students (OSers) run well-controlled experiments to produce data which others claim 'have little or nothing to say about the realities of organizational behavior' (Lawler 1985: 4). Some spend months 'in the field' reporting their data as ethnographic tales that others dismiss as mere anecdotes (Martin 1990). Some ask hundreds and thousands of people to answer carefully chosen questions producing data which others disparage as simplistic, distorted reflections of the respondents' organizational reality, unrelated to their organizational behaviour.

Can we reconcile these paradigm-laden positions and arrive at an acceptable definition of data for OS? The advantages of a common position are clear. If the field can establish a common paradigm, resources will flow more freely, and research will accumulate more 'successfully' (Pffefer 1993). We could all use the money! However, will the accumulation of knowledge reflect the variety and complexity of organizational reality? Many argue that accumulation is an illusion (see Canella and Paetzold 1994 and Jaros 1994 for specific responses to Pfeffer). These critics rely on contemporary philosophy of science (Kuhn 1970) and the sociology of scientific knowledge (Ashmore 1989) to support their position. The arguments applied to OS are well developed (Burrell and Morgan 1979; Morgan 1983; Hartman 1988).

A more recent challenge comes from postmodern and poststructural theorizing in the humanities (Zald 1994). Cooper (Cooper and Burrell 1988; Cooper 1989) and Burrell (1988) have written extensively on the implications of postmodernism for organizational studies. Hassard and Parker (1993) provide a sampler of views on the utility and significance of postmodernism for organization studies. Postmodern theorizing challenges the very notion of a common ground. In particular, postmodernists warn against any totalizing narrative (e.g. Jeffcut 1994a), i.e. an attempt to provide an all-encompassing explanation. They would argue that any attempt to develop a universal definition of data for OS is doomed.

Yet, my strategy in this review will be to offer such a definition of data in organization studies. However, I make no claim to absolute truth in doing so. Instead, I offer this grand narrative, bracketed as a heuristic for OS. I believe we can self-consciously use modernist writing techniques to forge temporary consensus, to create the shared tacit knowledge and assumptions required to do OS. Thus I do not write in opposition to the postmodern. As Deetz has noted in discussing competing research programs, they can be seen not as 'alternative routes to truth, but as specific discourses which, if freed from their claims of universality and/or completeness, could provide important moments in a larger dialogue about organizational life' (1995: 5). Though I cannot promise the beauty of *Kubla Khan*, I join Coleridge in asking you, the reader, for the suspension of your disbelief.

THE UNIVERSAL NARRATIVE

When one abstracts highly enough, the differences between entrenched research practices blur, revealing the contours of the research landscape. From this height, we can describe the universal characteristics of all OS research. Three features stand out: researcher purpose, audience, and data.

Purpose

Organizational research is a purposeful human activity. These purposes can be described broadly by Habermas's (1971) typology of human interests. OSers may work for a technical interest in control and prediction, for a practical interest in achieving mutual action-oriented understanding or for an emancipatory interest in extending human autonomy and responsibility (Stablein and Nord 1985; Rao and Passmore 1989). More local descriptions of purpose might be 'resolving a debate in the literature', 'being concerned for the welfare of the group', 'solving a morale problem', 'developing an understanding of . . .', 'legitimating resistance in a workplace'. The purpose of a research project or program is often called the research question. This expression is too suggestive of traditional hypothesis testing to cover the varieties of contemporary organization studies.

Note that purpose is research-specific. More basic human motivations such as 'to get tenure' or 'to help humankind' must be funnelled through a particular research endeavour. Each research project or research stream has a purpose or purposes.

Like all people, OSers are complex. They are limitedly rational, and more than rational. Their purposes may be multiple, changing, emergent, even conflicting. Their purposes may be conscious or not. But all OS is 'on purpose'.

Audience

The second feature of all OS is audience. Organization studies, like all knowledge production, is a social business (Frost and Stablein 1992: 253). Though we may toil individually, we always work on common problems. Kuhn (1970) described most natural science as 'puzzle-solving' with paradigm-defined problems and boundaries. The description holds for OS. The very structure of OS journal articles, opening with introduction and literature review, illustrates the social nature of our activity. The ritualistic, even cynical, nature of these 'paeans'

in no way reduces their function of linking individual projects to a larger community of understanding. Even paradigm-making research defines itself in relation to existing puzzles and solutions (Gersick 1992).

Of course, an individual may have a personal understanding of organization that he or she does not or cannot share. While it remains an idiosyncratic insight, OS is not enriched or changed. Our studies are incomplete until we communicate our results to others who study organization.

Usually this communication is written: working paper, journal article, consulting report, book chapter. The postmodernists emphasize the role of the audience. They remind us that these papers are not just written, they are read as well (Cooper 1989; Smircich 1992). The failure of authors to acknowledge diverse audiences and the expectation of readers that all reports are written for them has created unnecessary and unresolvable debates, such as that over the relevance of OS (Cartner and Stablein 1994). When we acknowledge the audience, it is no surprise that the elegant technical jargon intended for other initiates of the researcher cult is nearly indecipherable for the novice student or stressed-out employee.

Four key audiences can be identified for OS. Smallest in number, but most important to the organizational scholar, is the audience of his or her peers, other organizational researchers. If we limit our count to active researchers, i.e. those who publish in English language researcher-oriented journals, the total would not exceed a few thousand world-wide. Academic book authors and contributors would add a few more. The audience for a particular manuscript in a sub-field is a good deal smaller. If we limit the circle of active researchers to those whose work is cited, the estimate of their numbers falls to the hundreds. The majority of publishing organizational scholars received their PhDs from, and are employed in, a relatively small number of 'elite' North American universities.

Those who primarily teach organizational studies comprise the next largest group, numbering in the tens of thousands. Most have earned research degrees. They read the research literature. It is the teachers who pay the bills for research publications by maintaining professional association memberships and seeing that their libraries order the books and journals. In the USA, some of these teachers will be employed in tertiary institutions with an explicit teaching mission. Many in the USA and elsewhere work in institutions which espouse research values. However, the empirical reality is that many employed in these institutions will publish infrequently over their career.

For students, we write textbooks, in which we try to provide uncomplicated summaries of research. Most texts also include attempts to create proxy organizational experiences. We may even try to make OS 'interesting'.

Participants in organizations, in their millions, include almost everyone in the world, but organizational researchers show interest in reaching but a few. As critical scholars are fond of reminding us (Alvesson and Willmott 1992), managers benefit most from the vast bulk of participant-oriented writing efforts. Their dollars for practice-oriented journals, executive education and consultancy provide welcome additions to the researcher's personal bank balance and the university's drooping bottom line.

Data

The third universal feature of organization studies, data, links the researcher's purpose and the audience. More specifically, all organization students select and interpret data for their audience in the attempt to achieve their purposes. I choose the phrase 'interpret data' quite carefully over alternatives such as 'present data' or 'summarize data'. These phrases suggest a mechanical process of recording and playing back, i.e. that the data speak for themselves. This does not do justice to the effort and creativity required of researchers in data collection, analysis and reporting (Frost and Stablein 1992; Hackman 1992; Meyer et al. 1992). This language also hides the researcher in a haze of 'objectivity' that is unwarranted in reports of quantitative (Gephart 1988) or qualitative studies (Van Maanen 1988).

In another modernist move, I will draw a boundary around my aims for this text. I will attempt to focus my attention on the data of OS, i.e. data collection as opposed to data analysis. I leave discussion of the various data analytic techniques to others (see e.g. Bryman 1989; Pedhazur and Schmelkin 1991; Miles and Huberman 1994).

So, What Are Data?

All data are representations. Respondents' questionnaire answers, experimental subjects' behaviours, employee records, financial records, boardroom conversations, production records, shopfloor humour, corporate balance sheets, informants' expressions, participant or non-participant observations and emotional reactions, annual reports, acetycoline blood levels and pulse rates, photos, videos, corporate architecture and the products of earlier research may all be used by organization students to represent aspects of organizational reality.

However, not all representations are data. For example, one might estimate the morale of assembly line workers by speaking to the firm's public relations officer. The polished response is a representation, but it is unlikely to be data, that is, it will do little to inform our understanding of shopfloor attitudes. At the extreme, one could use a random number generator to represent respondents' ages. Not very smart, not data, but it is a representation. We need to identify what kinds of representations are to count as data.

As representations, data imply things that are represented, and a process of representing. Both characteristics must be examined to separate data from other sorts of representations.

The 'Thing' Represented

Traditionally, scientists understood the empirical world, the thing measured, as the 'real thing', 'out there' waiting to be discovered (Lakatos 1965). That view of science has been thoroughly revised. Philosophers of science have undermined the logical foundations of deduction, induction and falsification (see Chalmers 1982 for an accessible account). Historians of science (e.g. Kuhn 1970) and sociologists of scientific knowledge (see Ashmore 1989 for a review) have studied historical and contemporary scientific practice. They have discovered that the traditional account bears little resemblance to the practices of working scientists. Mitroff and Kilmann (1978), Burrell and Morgan (1979), Astley (1985), Hartman (1988), and others have applied and extended these views to OS.

Today most scholars would conclude that we invent rather than discover the empirical world. Any appeal to scientific evidence regarding the 'true' nature of the world is suspect and subject to revision as science evolves and changes (Kuhn 1970; Tibbetts 1990). The 'thing' that our data represent is not a concrete object or experience. Instead it is a human conception, constituted by the sensemaking of scientists.

The impact of this conclusion for OS is sometimes misunderstood. Some would conclude that 'anything goes', that each individual scientist is free to proceed as they prefer. However, it is strikingly clear that this is *not* the case. Science is never an isolated individual activity. It is a social practice. In the words of Vidich and Lyman:

> Although it is true that at some level all research is a uniquely individual enterprise — not part of a sacrosanct body of accumulating knowledge — it is

also true that it is always guided by values that are not unique to the investigator: we are all creatures of our own social and cultural pasts. However, in order to be meaningful to others, the uniqueness of our own research experience gains significance when it is related to the theories of our predecessors and the research of our contemporaries. (1994: 42)

For a study to be *personally* meaningful (Sandelands 1993), an organizational scholar may hold a realist metaphysical belief, e.g. how can I accept that there is no underlying structure to the world? Doing organization studies does not require revision of such a belief. Similarly, the ontological commitment of an individual postmodernist to language as the only reality is acceptable, but irrelevant to organization studies.

The empirical world that we represent is what we, as a human scholarly community, understand it to be. It amounts to the ideas and conceptions we use to understand: the constructs and relations of our theories. The 'we' is important. Individuals may claim anything they like about organizations but a claim does not become organizational reality until it is socially accepted. Dissertation advisers, editors, reviewers, readers and conference participants must 'see' the reality, too.

As a social practice, OS is not only an intellectual enterprise. It is an economic, political and moral enterprise as well.

As the title of this *Handbook* suggests, there is no *one* study of organization. There is not a single community of organizational scholars. This opens the possibility of multiple organizational realities. Some aspects of organizational reality are universally perceived by organization studiers, e.g. workers and managers. Other aspects are contested, e.g. whether the organization is a reification or a legitimate social actor (Hartman 1988). Still other organizational phenomena are perceived by some groups of organization students but not others, e.g. class (Burrell and Morgan 1979).

Discussions of this issue in OS are often framed as discussions of paradigm incommensurability. Groups holding diverse paradigms 'see' different worlds and set different questions. My position is in line with Weaver and Gioia (1994), Martin (1990), Hassard (1990) and others who argue that complete incommensurability is rare, if not impossible. Studying different organizational realities will yield different questions and answers which are more, or less, insightful for the various paradigms represented with OS. (See the dialogue between Stewart Clegg and John Jermier for a thoughtful discussion of the relationship between empirical research and theory: Jermier 1994.)

The relationship between critical organizational researchers and managerialist researchers provides an example. The critical research community sees organizational reality as a structure of exploitation and power. One aspect of modern organizational society is self-exploitation (Gramsci 1971). The notion of false consciousness is sometimes employed to help explain this self-exploitation. Many researchers find this concept absurd, yet they can accept some of the data produced by critical researchers as relevant to constructs they employ, such as socialization and organizational culture, even while they differ on its interpretation.

In summary, if data are representations, they must represent empirical things. The 'things' are our ideas about empirical 'reality'. Organizational students attempt to represent aspects of empirical, organizational reality. Different groups of scholars will have different ideas about different empirical realities. Thus, each will try to represent a different organizational reality. Successful data require that other scholars understand the reality a researcher's data are trying to represent. The starting point of any data-producing effort must be participation in a shared understanding of the empirical organizational phenomena to be represented.

The Process of Representing

Representing a shared organizational reality requires systematic activity undertaken by the researcher. Often, this activity goes unnoticed, or unreported, in OS. It is part of the background, taken-for-granted assumptions that lie behind our organizational explorations. A successful representation process provides data that organizational scholars can interpret and analyse in ways that increase their shared understanding of an empirical reality. Such data are characterized by a *two-way correspondence* between the data and the organizational reality the data represent.

The term comes from a well-established tradition in mathematical psychology that approaches the measurement of psychological attitudes as a representational problem (Coombs et al. 1970). I will develop their ideas in defining data for organization studies. Remembering that the empirical world is a shared system of concepts, representation is achieved when one maps the 'thing' that we have conceptualized into a symbol system, what Dawes (1972) would call a 'one-way correspondence' between the empirical world and the symbolic system. But for the representations to produce data, there is a stronger requirement, a two-way correspondence. The mapping must be into a symbolic system which allows one to map back from the symbolic system to the original empirical system of interest. An example should help make sense of this rather awkward criterion.

I use a ruler to independently measure the height of Jena in one room, then Sal in another room. I am using the ruler to map a one-way correspondence between an empirical quality (our concept of height) and a symbolic system (the real numbers – a ratio scale). Relying solely on the relations of this symbolic system, I am able to determine that Jena is taller than Sal. If this conclusion holds when I bring Jena and Sal together and see them standing side-by-side, then two-way correspondence has been achieved. I have used properties of the symbolic system to make true inferences about the empirical world. In this example, the real number system property of magnitude or order allows me to determine who is taller without reference to the empirical world. Six is bigger than five, therefore Jena is taller than Sal. If I apply my ruler to lots of people, I might use additional properties of the real number system (addition and division to calculate a *t*-test) to confirm that, for example, basketball players are generally taller than football players. In both cases, the mapping from the empirical world, via symbolic manipulation, mapped back on to the empirical world, providing insight. The data are successful in representing an empirical world in a way that produces shared understandings.

By way of counterexample, a Maori activist in New Zealand recently adopted the name 'Te Ureturoa' which means 'mighty warrior'. A newspaper (*The Press* 6 November 1994) reported his name to mean 'the long penis'. This embarrassing mistake occurred when a newspaper reporter used a Maori–English dictionary (the 'ruler' which the journalist used to map the world of Maori words into the symbol system of the English language) to map a one-way correspondence between the activist's name and an English language representation. The reporter presumed that the literal translation would provide English speaking readers with data on the reality of Maoridom. But the one-way representation did not provide data about the Maori world. Two-way correspondence, i.e. a meaningful understanding of the activist's name, is not achieved. The literal translation, in this case, is *not* data. As is often the case, literal translation was not an effective representational strategy. A more sophisticated strategy, taking into account context and utilizing back-translation, would be required to produce successful data.

The representational measurement theorists are especially interested in representing psychological attributes using the properties of various formal number systems to produce measuring scales (e.g. nominal, ordinal, interval and ratio). They warn us that just because one assigns numerals to an empirical phenomenon (one-way correspondence), it does not follow that these numerals are from the real number system. The manner of assigning the numerals must reflect the relations of the empirical world and match the real number system relations (i.e. equal intervals relative to an absolute zero). As parametric statistics are derived from the properties of the real number system, representational measurement theorists are wary of the extensive use of statistics in empirical research. (For reviews of the issues and subsequent controversies, see Michell 1986.)

If one measures several persons' preferences for participation in two groups on a Likert scale where 1 equals strong agreement to the statement, 'I like to work in a participative group', one-way correspondence is achieved. But the numerals 1, 2, 3, 4 and 5 represent real numbers only if the psychological distances represented by these reports are equal relative to an absolute zero point of no preference for participation. Can one calculate a *t*-test using real number properties to determine if the two groups are equivalent in their preferences? Lord (1953) suggests that the numbers don't know where they come from. Indeed the computer will churn out a *t*-ratio. However, as MacRae (1988) and others have correctly observed, the researcher does know where the numbers come from!

Therefore representational measurement theorists insist on a representation theorem. For a particular measuring strategy, the representational theorem is an explicit statement of the assumptions required to justify the claim that data, i.e. two-way correspondence, have been produced. In the case of measurement of preferences on a ratio scale, the representational theorem is that transitivity (i.e. if *a* is preferred to *b*, and *b* is preferred to *c*, then *a* is preferred to *c*) applies to the preferences (Coombs et al. 1970: 13). Because of their exclusive interest in numerical symbol systems, the representation theorem consists of a mathematical proof. This requirement limits the representational theorist to a small number of alternative symbol systems. Even within the scope of numerical systems, only a few types are considered, usually counting, ratio, interval, ordinal, or nominal. OS scholars tend to be less orthodox. In the participation item above, most OSers would agree that the measuring strategy fails to map into a ratio or even an interval scale. In terms of an ordinal scale, the representational measurement theorist would argue that any monotonic transformation (i.e. order preserving) of the respondents' answers would yield the same information about the respondents' attitudes. However, I suspect most OSers would be very surprised if people gave the same responses when the alternatives offered were 1, 2, 3, 4, and 500.

Thus most psychologically oriented scholars implicitly consider Likert scale responses to roughly map the empirical world of respondent opinion onto a mixed ordinal/interval numerical system which can be manipulated statistically to produce roughly valid inferences about the respondents' psychological states.

The representational assumptions for Likert-style research might include:

- Respondents are willing to respond truthfully, e.g. no socially desirable responding (Zerbe and Paulus 1987). If this assumption is untenable, then we might consider unobtrusive, non-reactive measures (Webb et al. 1966).
- Respondents understand the item as the researchers intended it to be understood, including such issues as respondent literacy, shared dialect, and framing (Clark and Schrober 1992).
- Respondents can make the judgement the item requires, e.g. memory retrieval and information processing capacities are adequate (Ericsson and Simon 1980; Arkes and Hammond 1986).
- Respondents can report the judgement, e.g. translate it into the metric of the response format.

However, in OS, we are not limited to numerical symbol systems. Much of our data utilize natural language or various technical languages as the symbol systems which represent the empirical world. Then, we manipulate these symbols to make inferences about the organizational world. John Van Maanen's (1979) elegant title to his preface of the landmark *Administrative Science Quarterly* special issue on qualitative methodology expresses my sentiment: 'The map is not the territory'. The tape recordings and field notes of the fieldworker are not the culture of the group. They are the symbols which are analysed to present, we hope, an insightful description of the culture.

For a non-quantitative example of representational assumptions consider Spradley (1979a), which provides an introduction to semantic ethnography. The researcher and the researched speak different languages or dialects. As an ethnographer, I must map the meaning of the native speaker into my language, such that a two-way correspondence is achieved. The inferred meanings must allow me to use the phrase correctly in new situations and settings to establish that two-way correspondence has been achieved. If I am able to operate successfully in novel situations then true measurement or understanding has occurred. A researcher who can demonstrate this level of cultural understanding will be taken seriously by other ethnosemanticists.

Data in OS should be representations which maintain a two-way correspondence between the empirical world and the symbol system. The rule for evaluating the criterion is the adequacy of the representational process. The representational process is essentially a theory of data production. Like all theories, measurement theories cannot be proven correct. However, if we make our representational process explicit, we can examine the representational assumptions and actively consider evidence relevant to them. Consider again the introductory example of the ruler and height. As an everyday practice, we measure away with no concern for the validity of the ruler. But, if we consciously attend to the rationale for ruler use, we can develop demonstrations that are socially accepted evidence in favour of this representational process. The same is true for representational processes in OS. We can, for example, develop scales to detect socially desirable responding or compare the reports of various informants to increase our confidence that we have achieved two-way correspondence.

A Definition of Data

Data in OS are representations which maintain a two-way correspondence between an empirical reality and a symbol system.

An empirical reality is the set of ideas constituted, developed and sustained by a subcommunity of organizational scholars. Data are produced by a representing process that is documented by the representational assumptions. Data are then manipulated within the symbol system, yielding results which increase our understanding of an organizational reality.

Applying an explicit and defensible representational process to a well-known portion of empirical reality yields good organizational data. Poor data result from an inadequate representational process and/or an inadequate understanding of the organizational phenomenon represented. If the phenomenon is understood and the representational strategy is flawed, the data are usually found wanting, the article rejected (Schwab 1985). If the underlying empirical phenomenon is not well understood, messier data are acceptable. As our understanding increases, we generally insist on better data.

KINDS OF DATA

We have arrived at a general definition of data in organizational studies. Now it is time to return from the heights of generalization to the diversity of data produced in organizational researches. The heart of the postmodern and poststructural challenge is the challenge to *one* answer, *one* empirical reality, *one* representational strategy. At the local sites of organizational studies, differences in culture, moral ethic, intellectual history, academic discipline, etc. have yielded different subcommunities of organizational scholars who produce different sorts of data. Thus, for example, we observe differences between North American and European scholarship, between organizational psychology, organizational sociology, organizational economics, and organizational anthropology, between managerial studies, critical studies, and feminist studies.

Different kinds of data result from the intersection of the nature of the empirical reality each subcommunity is attempting to understand, and the representational processes each uses to represent aspects of that organizational world. Each combination is institutionalized as the research practice that each subcommunity develops, teaches and enforces. It would be neat if these various data could be logically connected in a two-dimensional space of shared organizational reality and representational practice. Alas, my perception of the organizational studies landscape is not so simple. In descending from the conceptual heights of a data definition to represent the data-using reality of OS, I do not find consistent groupings. Rather than attempt to force the variety of organizational data into a clean typology, I will try to do justice to the diversity of OS research. In most instances, I adopt conventional terms: survey data, experimental data, case data, secondary data.

One conventional category of organizational data, interviewing, receives no mention because interviewing does not constitute data in the framework proposed here. The term is used so loosely that the only commonality across uses is simply talking. The term is too broad. It does not stand as a symbol system oriented to the representation of an organizational reality. To become a distinct sort of data it requires an adjective, such as in ethnographic interviewing (Spradley 1979a) or behaviour description interviewing (Janz et al. 1986).

Abandoning the Quantitative/Qualitative Divide

I do not use the distinction between quantitative and qualitative data in categorizing OS data, despite the fact that this is the most frequently used typology. Instead, I attempt to reposition this key distinction in the organizational sciences. The quantitative/qualitative distinction is a binary opposition that hides a more complex, non-dichotomous, and non-hierarchical distinction.

The popular quant/qual distinction is rooted in the separation of numerical representations from non-numerical representations. As we have seen above, numerical representations are not members of a single class. The Arabic numerals 1, 2, 3, etc. may represent counting, positions on the real number line, equally spaced intervals, ordered magnitudes on an ordinal scale, labels in a nominal classification system, or some hybrid of these systems. In many cases these numerals represent non-numbers, e.g. the sentence: 'I agree strongly with the statement.' Thus, I find the distinction hazy and not very informative on the numerical side of the divide.

The quant/qual distinction condemns 'everything else' to the non-numerical, subordinate side of the divide. The 'everything else' includes a diverse set of target organizational realities and representational practices (Van Maanen et al. 1982: 15). Thus, attempts to define 'qualitative' data are hopeless. Instead, I develop the notion of ethno-data. Ethno-data are the extraction, from the qualitative morass, of those data which researchers claim represent the native experience. Ethno-data emerge from a variety of representational strategies, but are united in their commitment to representing the empirical reality as it is experienced by the organizational participants.

In the following sections, I will briefly characterize the natures of the empirical realities and the types of representational processes utilized in the production of various kinds of organizational data. Together these provide an overview of data used in contemporary organization studies.

Survey Data

The paper-and-pencil questionnaire is probably the most frequently used method of data production in organization studies. Podsakoff and Dalton (1987) have provided one estimate of usage. They surveyed the 193 empirical research articles published in the 1985 volumes of *Academy of Management Journal, Administrative Science Quarterly, Journal of Applied Psychology, Journal of Management and Organizational Behaviour* and *Human Decision Processes*. The authors of over a third (36 per cent) of the articles primarily employed the questionnaire.

The organizational reality of the questionnaire user is a nomological net of causal relationships between constructs. The nomological relations hypothesized by the researcher constitute middle range theories intended to explain a portion of organizational reality (Pinder and Moore 1980), e.g. employee turnover. The terminology of middle range theory is Merton's (1962). He developed the term to contrast his 'modest' approach with that of comprehensive (i.e. 'grand') social theories such as those of Parsons and Marxist scholars. Middle range theory is an analytic approach to understanding organization. The researcher simplifies the complexity of organizational life by specifying a subset of relations that can be extracted and explored with relative independence from the rest.

The basic organizational phenomenon is the *construct*. For organization studies, an annual chapter by Donald Schwab (1980) has emerged as a foundational statement for this approach to data. Schwab defines the construct as 'a conceptual variable', i.e. an 'entity capable of assuming two or more values which is of a mental nature' (1980: 5). Thus a construct is an idea, a researcher's idea, related to other ideas in a theory of organizational behaviour, belief, etc. As the construct only exists in the head of the individual researcher and the collective head of the community as revealed by the 'literature', only indirect assessment of organizational reality is possible. To study organizational life, the construct must be represented by a concrete operation.

The first step in the representational process for survey data is careful definition of the construct, its psychometric properties, and the relationship between the construct and other constructs in the researcher's theory. Next, questions which are intended to represent (measure) the construct are developed. Individual respondents are asked to answer the questions. These answers are data.

The method for demonstrating the two-way correspondence of the data is called *construct validation*. The construct validity of the data is defined as 'the correspondence between a construct and the operational procedure to measure or manipulate that construct' (Schwab 1980: 6). The correspondence can never be directly demonstrated. However, several procedures can provide falsifying or confirming evidence regarding the degree of construct validity of a data-producing operation.

Description of the representational process is the most important way to demonstrate the correspondence of construct and measure. The ability to do so relies on clear definition of the construct. Ironson et al. (1989) provide an example in the measurement of job satisfaction.

They carefully distinguish between the constructs of overall (general) job satisfaction, job facet satisfactions (e.g. with pay, co-workers, etc.) and facet composites (e.g. averaging pay and coworker satisfaction). Only in the light of these distinctions does the fancy number crunching that follows make sense as evidence of validity.

Having achieved clear definition of the construct, current practice requires developing multiple questions to represent all but the most straightforward of constructs (e.g. self-reported sex, age, etc.). This representational strategy allows estimation of internal consistency reliability, i.e. the degree to which the multiple items which are intended to measure the same construct actually are interrelated. Other types of reliability may also be estimated, in particular, reliability over time (stability or test–retest reliability).

Again, note the importance of defining the construct when conducting reliability analyses. Some constructs, such as personality states, are expected to be stable over time. Thus, high test–retest reliability estimates for the measure would provide evidence of construct validity. Other constructs, e.g. mood, are not expected to be stable: thus high reliability could provide evidence of construct invalidity.

It is a truism among questionnaire data users that appropriate demonstration of reliability is a necessary but not a sufficient condition for judging the data to be construct valid. Reliability evidence establishes that respondents view the multiple items (a *scale*) in a common way, but it does not establish that the respondents view the items in the way that the researcher intended. The appropriate evidence would show that the scale is related to other scales which are construct valid measures of the same construct (convergent validity) and relate less strongly to construct valid measures of related, but not identical, constructs (differential or discriminant validity). For example, a questionnaire measure of global work satisfaction should relate more closely to other general work satisfaction scales than to measures of specific facets of job satisfaction (Ironson et al. 1989). Schwab (1980) is especially keen to encourage the demonstration of differential construct validity.

Research practice does not always live up to prescription. Relying, again, on the Podsakoff and Dalton (1987) survey, about two-thirds of published articles reported reliability evidence. A paltry 4.48 per cent of authors provided validity evidence. The failure to provide validity data is extremely important if one accepts the definition of data proposed here. The failure to provide validity evidence is a failure to document two-way correspondence. The representational assumptions underlying survey data require construct validation evidence. Substantive findings from surveys assume that the inferences are from construct valid measures. Schwab argues that our failure to provide for adequate construct validation of our measures means that 'our knowledge of substantive relationships is not as great as is often believed, and (more speculatively) not as great as would be true if the idea of construct validity received greater attention' (1980: 4).

Should researchers choose to demonstrate reliability and validity, a variety of methods are available. Primarily, correlation and factor analytic techniques are used. Increasingly, the measurement model is estimated by treating the latent variables calculated by LISREL as estimates of the constructs. This approach is becoming available to a wider set of researchers as recent releases of the program are increasingly user-friendly.

Sometimes experimental data are produced to support the construct validity of a measure. For example, Breaugh and Becker (1987) report three studies as part of a larger research program to provide construct validity evidence for the three facets of the work autonomy scale (Breaugh 1985). One of these studies is an experiment in which the authors created high and low autonomy working conditions for experimental subjects. The subjects were then asked to complete the questionnaire. The answers varied from high to low, as predicted. The authors interpret these data as evidence of construct validity.

This tradition of data production is associated with researchers in the areas of industrial/ organizational (I/O) psychology and organization behaviour (OB). It has its roots in psychological testing (Cronbach and Meehl 1955). I/O psychologists and mainstream OB researchers will find the language of this section familiar. Other OSers who use questionnaires may find the language alien but the essential view of organizational reality and the survey representational process should still hold. For example, Schwab (1980) points out the similarity of his construct validation position and Blalock's (1968) discussions of questionnaires in sociological research.

Experimental Data

In an earlier handbook review, Weick (1965) observed that the experiment was an infrequent, but useful, way to generate organizational data. Today, experimental data are a frequent base for organizational studies. One indicator, the Podsakoff and Dalton (1987) data, is a bit ambiguous, but it would appear that about 30 per cent of the articles reviewed used experimental procedures in either the laboratory or the field.

The empirical reality of the organizational experimentalist is essentially the same as that of the survey user. Both test middle range theories which posit causal relations among constructs. They differ on one important point. The experimentalists are far less optimistic about the ability to isolate the set of causal relations of interest from the rest of organizational reality. Experimentalists are convinced that the world is a densely interrelated net of constructs with subtle, complex and powerful effects on each other. They have shown that seemingly minor factors can destroy the two-way correspondence of a representational process (Rosenthal and Rosnow 1969). For example, if the experimenter is aware of the hypotheses under study, his or her expectations can influence the responses of experimental subjects.

Two-way correspondence for experimental data is achieved by demonstrating *internal validity*. To do so, the experimental representational strategy follows the traditional natural scientific method (Boring 1969). A hypothesized cause (independent variable) is varied by the experimenter. The effect or dependent variable is observed. If the dependent variable varies more than could be expected by chance alone, a causal relation is inferred. Because the world is causally dense, other possible causes (*alternative explanations*) of any effect must be discounted to produce experimental data. This sort of experimental design is said to possess internal validity. It yields 'interpretable' data.

There are three strategies for eliminating alternative explanations (Caporaso 1973). First, the experimenter can control other possible causes, seeing to it that they do not vary. Second, potential causes that cannot be held stable may be measured and accounted for in the statistical analysis of the effect. Third, protection against the effects of causes that can be neither controlled nor measured is gained through random assignment of subjects to the different states of the hypothesized cause. This strategy is the least desirable because it increases the total variation of the dependent variable, making it harder to detect the covariation of the hypothesized cause and effect. However, randomization has the strength of protecting against unanticipated causes. Taken together, these strategies can produce an experimental situation which generates two-way correspondence. When there is adequate control for the effects of alternative explanations, experimental data can be informative.

The organizational experimentalists appear to rely on the behaviourist tradition in psychology for their version of this model of data production. Individual subjects (rats, people) are placed in simplified environments to control other causes. The researcher manipulates an aspect of the environment, the hypothesized cause (reinforcement schedule, pay plan), called the stimulus, operation, manipulation, condition or treatment. The effect, the subjects' 'behaviour' (bar pressing, widgets produced), is recorded. This is called the response.

The cognitive revolution in psychology has left the behaviourists behind (Bruner 1990), but their influence on representational strategy remains (see Landy 1986 for a discussion of this point with respect to testing). For example, the behaviourist assumptions are betrayed in the experimentalist's treatment of behavioural versus verbal data. Behavioural data are counted and treated as unproblematic. Verbal data are treated with suspicion (Nisbet and Wilson 1977) and require elaborate defences (Ericsson and Simon 1980). In contrast, other subcommunities within OS, e.g. ethnographers, tend to privilege the verbal and worry about the meaning of the behavioural.

Field experiments play an important role in organization studies. Just how important is an issue of perennial debate (Bryman 1989; Locke 1986). The foundational guidance for organizational field experimentation is provided by Campbell and Stanley (1966) in their discussions of how to design experiments that produce valid data. The Cook and Campbell (1979) update expands their discussion of threats to validity. Limiting the threats to validity increases the likelihood that the experiment will produce good data, i.e. that two-way correspondence is achieved.

Where the surveyor measures constructs, the experimentalist manipulates constructs. Where the surveyor emphasizes the measurement of each construct, the experimentalist is more concerned about representing the relationships between constructs.

Ethno-data

Many terms could be used to describe this sort of data. Evered and Louis (1981) describe ethno-research as 'inquiry from the inside' as opposed to 'from the outside'. Their catalogue of synonyms includes: antipositivistic, phenomenological, ethnomethodological, experiential, existential, ideographic, participative, anthropological, qualitative, dialectic, pragmatic, subjective, intensive, soft, and high context. Morey and Luthans (1984) draw on the emic–etic distinction from anthropology for a label. Burrell and Morgan (1979) popularized the term 'interpretative'.

The defining characteristic of this sort of organizational data is the nature of the empirical reality that the researcher is attempting to represent. Ethno-researchers are intent on discovering and communicating an organizational reality as it is experienced by the inhabitants of that reality. The 'ethno-' prefix has come to be associated specifically with this view. The phrase 'ethno-data' is intended to be broad enough to encompass a variety of research practices and traditions that aim to produce data that represent insiders' lived experiences.

The organizational reality studied by the ethno-researcher is different from that of the experimenter or survey researcher. In contrast to their researcher-designed organizational reality of constructs to be measured or manipulated, the ethno-researcher's organizational world is full of constructs to be discovered. The participants of this world make their own meanings and weave their own patterns. The ethno-researcher is a visitor, a voyeur, a stranger on a journey of discovery.

The quality of ethno-data, i.e. the degree to which two-way correspondence has been achieved, is equivalent to the *fidelity* with which representation matches the native viewpoint. There is strong agreement on the organizational reality to be represented, but much less consensus on the representational strategies which yield two-way correspondence. Some ethno-researchers discuss this in terms of reliability and validity, as defined above (Becker 1970). Kunkel and McGrath (1972) argue that there is a necessary trade-off between the two. Others explicitly deny the applicability of these criteria. As substitutes, Lincoln and Guba (1985) propose the criteria of credibility, transferability, dependability and confirmability. Golden-Biddle and Locke (1993) identify authenticity, plausibility and criticality in their analysis of three exemplary ethno-research reports. The Denzin and Lincoln (1994) handbook devotes several chapters to the discussion of criteria (Guba and Lincoln 1994; Altheide and Johnson 1994; Denzin 1994).

Achieving two-way correspondence for the ethno-researcher usually involves 'firsthand involvement in the social world' (Filstead 1970: title) as a participant observer. Participant observers listen, learn, take notes, converse, interview, ask questions, test preliminary understandings, watch, read, count, and anything else that seems to 'help' them understand the meanings of the world they are exploring. Participant observation is best characterized as immersion in the field setting. Participant observation is a multi-method representational enterprise. Participant observation in organizations almost always includes: casual and systematic interviewing, casual and systematic observation, and collection of substantial documentary materials.

There has been an emphasis on learning how to do 'fieldwork' (a synonym for participant observation) by actually going out and doing it. The 'do-it-yourself' tradition is giving way to more regularized specifications of representational practice. Methodological appendices (Whyte 1955; Mills 1959) and collections of war stories (Hammond 1964) are being replaced or complemented by textbooks. Some ethno-data representational processes are very systematic, for example ethnosemantics. Spradley's (1979a; 1979b) manuals lay out step-by-step protocols for ethnosemantic investigations.

Note that ethno-data need not be produced by participant observation techniques. Gersick (1988) provides an example of non-participant observation of work groups. In other cases, the ethno-researcher may interpret artefacts from the field. For example, Barley et al. (1988) develop a sophisticated content analysis technique to represent the insider's understanding of organizational culture. They argue that the symbolic and conceptual view of organizational culture held by academic and practitioner subcultures can be derived from analyses of the pragmatics of written communications in each subculture's journals. The paper provides an excellent exposition of their theoretical rationale, and of the representational process they designed. The recently published *Handbook of Qualitative Research* describes a variety of representational processes, many of which could be used to produce ethno-data for organization studies (Denzin and Lincoln 1994).

Ethno-data were brought into the consciousness of OS in a big way by the explosion of organizational culture research in the early 1980s (e.g. Pondy et al. 1983; documented by Barley et al. 1988) and the discussion of alternative paradigms (Van Maanen 1979; Burrell and Morgan 1979; Morgan 1983; Lincoln and Guba 1985). Corners of OS have been long aware of this sort of data, e.g. occupations' and professions' folks could not avoid the Chicago School sociology of the 1920s onward (e.g. Becker et al. 1961; Roy 1952).

Conferences and subsequent publications have served to support the use of ethno-data in the study of organizations. Key conferences have included those held in Illinois (Pondy et al. 1983); Vancouver (Frost et al. 1985), and a series of small conferences on interpretative approaches held at Alta. Of particular note is the biennial meeting sponsored by the mainly European Standing Conference on Organizational Symbolism (SCOS). European OS has shown a greater affinity for ethno-data. Until recently, research using ethno-data has had limited access to the mainstream journals of OS, with the exception of special issues (*Administrative Science Quarterly*, Van Maanen 1979; *Journal of Management*, Frost 1981; *Administrative Science Quarterly*, Jelinek et al. 1983). In their survey of 1985 journals, Podsakoff and Dalton (1987) classified only two studies that may have been based on ethno-data. In part, this may be due to the tradition of reporting in books. The amount of data produced, the 'wordiness' of the symbolic system and the subsequent analyses often require more pages than the journals allow. Another explanation offered is the failure of positivitically oriented editorial boards to recognize ethno-data as anything more than anecdote (Morgan 1985).

Case Data

In the early days of OS, case studies were an important type of data. Daft (1980) documents the dominance of case reports in the *Administrative Science Quarterly* in 1959. The foundational works in organizational sociology are cases (Blau 1955; Gouldner 1954a; 1954b). Cases undergirded the theory and practice of the Tavistock Institute (e.g. Trist and Bamforth 1951; Rice 1958). By the late 1960s there is evidence of a decline in the reliance on cases in *Administrative Science Quarterly* (Daft 1980) and in sociology (Hamel 1993). However, there is evidence of increased interest in case studies in the 1980s and 1990s in the US and Europe (Hamel 1993; Ragin and Becker 1992; Bartunek et al. 1993).

The 'case study method' is a well-used term that has many meanings. Ragin (1992) discusses these at length. Gummesson (1991) offers an interesting discussion of case varieties from a Scandinavian point of view. For organization studies, I argue there are three main types of case data. The various types of cases share the focus on one, complex organizational unit. The various types of cases share a common representational process of multi-method immersion. However, they differ in important aspects of the organizational reality that is studied. The three types of case studies are: ethno-cases, usually known as ethnographies; 'theory-generating' cases; and 'exemplar' cases.

The ethno-case or ethnography produces ethno-data. It is oriented to representing the native participants' reality, as described in the previous section. The classic cases in this tradition include Whyte's (1955) *Street Corner Society*, Dalton's (1959) *Men Who Manage*, and Becker et al.'s (1961) *Boys in White*. The tradition continues with recent organizational ethnographies such as Kunda's (1992) *Engineering Culture*,

Collinson's (1992) *Managing the Shopfloor* and Jackall's (1988) *Moral Mazes*.

The second sort of case data is oriented to generalizable theoretical propositions. Thus the organizational reality of this sort of case writer is the world of researcher-defined constructs. Unlike the world of the questionnaire researcher, the organizational world is a complex and tangled world where cutting the Gordian knot is not as simple as asking the right questions. Experimentation is not an available strategy because the case researcher's issues are more sociological and there are insufficient independent units for a field experiment. Case research in this tradition generally involves the same multiple method immersion of the ethno-researcher, but researcher views are the starting point. The classic cases of industrial sociology fit this mould. For example, in *Patterns of Industry Bureaucracy*, Gouldner (1954a) attempts to discover and describe the ways Weber's ideal bureaucracy is found in an American factory and mine. In *The Dynamics of Bureaucracy*, Blau (1955) tackles a similar project in two government agencies.

Kanter's (1977) case study of *Men and Women of the Corporation* is frequently cited as a masterpiece of this genre of case research. In her methodological appendix, she clearly states: 'This study represents primarily a search for explanation and theory rather than just a report of an empirical research' (1977: 291). In justifying the representational strategy of case immersion, she quotes another pioneer of organizational studies:

> Crozier, who framed the methodological problems inherent in studies of large-scale organizations well: 'Comprehensive studies of human relations problems at the management level are usually hampered by two sets of difficulties. First, the complexity of the role structure in modern organisations causes much ambiguity and overlapping, making it impossible to match really comparable cases and to use rigorous methods meaningfully. Second, the general emphasis on status and promotions gives a crucial importance to the human relations game, thus preventing the researcher from obtaining reliable data on the central problem of power relationships' (Crozier, 1964, p. 112).
>
> Thus, a combination of methods such as used in the classical sociological field studies emerges as the most valid and reliable way to develop understanding of such a complex social reality as the corporation. (1977: 297)

The exemplar case is the third sort of case data. It is amongst the most influential data in OS. Exemplary case data are influential because they are often presented to organizational participants and students in OS classrooms. Often, such presentations are oriented to action. The audience comprises powerful organizational participants who can follow the template provided by an exemplar to intervene in their own organizations. For students, these vivid cases provide ersatz organizational experiences against which they test other data and ideas.

The organizational reality of the exemplar-based researcher consists of nearly universal problems, processes or solutions relevant to most organizations. The lessons drawn from studying individual leaders, events or organizations are taken to be informative for most organizational behaviour. Sometimes, this understanding of organizational reality is explicitly acknowledged (Frost and Stablein 1992; Schon 1987). Often, it is implicit.

The representational strategy for the exemplary case varies on an important dimension from that of other cases. For the types of data that we have discussed, the representational strategies are sensitive to issues of bias, authenticity, and validity using a variety of techniques such as reliability, experimental control, triangulation, multiple informants, etc. The researcher, as data generator, has taken a critical stance in their work. The exemplary case researcher tends to be less concerned about this aspect of the representational process. Sometimes, the reporter is a key organizational participant and clear partisan, e.g. the CEO of Johnsonville Sausage. Sometimes, the researcher is ideologically committed, e.g. Walton (1977) at Topeka Pet Food, or may be acting as a paid consultant.

Exemplary case data make a bigger break with the traditional views of 'scientific' that linger in OS approaches. Thus, other OS researchers have tended to ignore or attack exemplary case data. I argue that this reflects an outdated view of science. The impetus of the approach suggested in this chapter is to be more open-minded in considering OS data. In identifying the organizational reality and representational strategy of the exemplary case researcher, other researchers can more carefully develop their views regarding a particular exemplar.

Yes, the lack of criticality may be taken as a disadvantage for OS purposes and audiences. However, there may be offsetting advantages, beginning with the availability of the data. The access and resources of top consultants and powerful organizational participants are beyond the reach of most OS researchers. The particular bias of exemplary data is not *a priori* worse than the bias of a critical or cynical view.

Secondary Data

Data interpreted by an organizational scholar that were originally collected for another purpose are called secondary data. Secondary data could be employment records, annual reports, government censuses, production figures, regulatory reports, meeting minutes, etc. Secondary data could have been collected for another research project, but, usually, have been collected for non-research purposes, such as regulatory compliance or management control.

It is difficult to meet the criteria of good data using secondary data. The secondary data user has the task of demonstrating that the data represent the organizational reality of interest in the second research project. This reality may be the same as that of the original data collector, or it may not be. The researcher cannot assume that the original collector was trying to represent the same organizational reality. The burden of proof is on the secondary data user to demonstrate that the data work for the new use. Stewart and Kamins (1993) provide many colourful examples of the misuse of secondary data and an introduction to their proper use.

Difficulty is often encountered when organizational researchers use performance data in studies of employee behaviour. Sometimes explicitly, sometimes implicitly, organizational indices collected for technical or management reasons are used as measures of employee-controlled outcomes. When these numbers, which may be excellent data for production planning, are used in models of employee behaviour, two-way correspondence can break down.

Sutton and Rafaeli (1988; 1992) discovered the problem in their attempt to use a convenience store's sales figures to represent the effectiveness of employee friendliness. When they found a negative relationship between friendliness and sales, they did not advise store owners to hire gruff sales clerks. Instead they accepted that two-way correspondence had broken down. The data did not inform them about organizational reality. Next, they generated ethno-data in a variety of field settings. With a richer understanding of organizational reality in this particular retail setting, they realized that sales represented how busy a store was, i.e. store pace. Sales did not represent the original dependent variable (clerk performance) that the authors thought clerk friendliness would influence. A slow pace, reflected in low sales, provides both the opportunity and the motivation for otherwise bored sales clerks to be friendly.

The secondary data user cannot design a representational process that will yield the desired two-way correspondence. Nor can the researcher assume that the original data collector did. Thus, the researcher must demonstrate that the existing data do represent the empirical reality of interest.

Text as Data

The texts authored by organizational scholars are the data for postmodernist scholars. Postmodern organizational scholars are not interested in the organizational reality that the authors try to expose, understand, predict, etc. They deny the existence of any organizational reality other than the text itself. The original writer presents the text as a report of his or her interpretation of the data, yielding greater understanding of organizational reality. In contrast, the postmodernist treats the text as the empirical reality to be studied. As presented by the original author the text constitutes *a* reality. For the postmodern researcher the text is data which represent and constitute multiple realities. However, the representational process of *deconstruction* is required to reveal these realities. The deconstructive process involves overturning and displacing the intended meanings of the text (Linstead 1993; Cooper 1990). It is not simply a dialectical process of antithesis and synthesis. Deconstruction has been associated with revealing patriarchal, capitalist and racial oppression but, much to the dismay of some feminists, critical theorists, and colonial theorists, it does not privilege the cause of the previously oppressed or hidden. Nor does it deny the validity of the intended meanings of the powerful. It does not simply reverse the ordering or priority of meaning. A good deconstruction represents and constitutes multiple realities without freezing the potential meanings of the text. Two-way correspondence for textual data means unsettling, discomforting and disturbing our taken-for-granted knowledge of reality.

Therefore, not every text provides data for the deconstructionist. Texts which are considered significant and influential in forming our knowledge of organization are the appropriate raw data. It is 'foundational' texts that constitute our well-accepted, comfortable empirical reality. Thus, Kilduff (1993) chose March and Simon's *Organizations*, and Calás and Smircich (1991) chose Mintzberg's *oeuvre*, as organizational texts to deconstruct.

A related interest of the postmodernist is in the ways that authors construct texts which readers accept as authentic and credible accounts. For example, Jeffcut (1994b) treats organizational ethnographies as data. In his analysis, he identifies the epic structure of the ethnographic account as crucial to the effectiveness of ethnographic accounts. In this sense, postmodern analyses are meta-analyses: analyses of the products of other organizational scholars.

DISCUSSION AND FUTURE DIRECTIONS

In my attempt to survey the breadth and depth of OS data, much has been lost. I have violated the integrity of the organizational research I describe. I have torn data from their analyses. I have largely ignored the content that the symbols have represented and the insight that subsequent analyses have generated. Fortunately, other chapters in this volume do summarize and review the substantive gains of various data users in their endeavours to understand organization.

What do I offer in defence of this exercise? First, I present a definition of data in OS that takes account of contemporary views on the nature of organizational studies as a human enterprise. A subcommunity of organizational studies shares a view of an empirical, organizational reality. Members of that community attempt to represent that empirical reality in ways that allow the development of that view and the generation of deeper understanding. Two-way correspondence between the reality and the symbol system used to represent it will yield success in the attempt. By thinking about data in this way, we can be clearer about what we are doing. This will benefit the development of research within subcommunities, and communication across subcommunity boundaries.

Second, I present a survey of the kinds of data in use in OS. The definition offers a different perspective on what we do, and invites different sorts of comparisons. It is not a comprehensive, a complete, or a final survey. I hope the definition offered here invites new categories and comparisons. My closing hope is that this chapter (1) contributes to the understanding and development of our research practices and thus to our insights, and (2) reduces the forces of fragmentation, while denying the need for unification in OS.

NOTE

I thank Stewart Clegg, Cynthia Hardy, and the reviewers for their feedback on this chapter.

REFERENCES

Altheide, D.L. and Johnson, J.M. (1994) 'Criteria for assessing interpretive validity in qualitative research', in N.K. Denzin and Y.S. Lincoln (eds), *Handbook of Qualitative Research*. Thousand Oaks, CA: Sage. pp. 485–99.

Alvesson, Mats and Willmott, Hugh (1992) *Critical Management Studies*. Newbury Park, London: McGraw-Hill.

Arkes, Hal R. and Hammond, Kenneth R. (1986) *Judgement and Decision Making: an Interdisciplinary Reader*. Cambridge: Cambridge University Press.

Ashmore, Malcolm (1989) *The Reflexive Thesis*. Chicago: University of Chicago Press.

Astley, W.G. (1985) 'Administrative science as socially constructed truth', *Administrative Science Quarterly*, 30: 497–513.

Barley, Stephen, Meyer, Gordon and Gash, Debra (1988) 'Cultures of culture: academics, practitioners and the pragmatics of normative control', *Administrative Science Quarterly*, 33: 24–60.

Bartunek, Jean M., Bobko, Phillip and Venkatraman, N. (1993) 'Toward innovation and diversity in management research methods', *Academy of Management Journal*, 36: 1362–73.

Becker, Howard S. (1970) 'Problems of inference and proof in participant observation', in W.J. Filstead (ed.), *Qualitative Methodology: Firsthand Involvement with the Social World*. Chicago: Markham.

Becker, Howard S., Greer, Blanche, Hughes, E.C. and Strauss, A.L. (1961) *Boys in White*. Chicago: University of Chicago Press.

Blalock Jr., H.M. (1968) 'The measurement problem: a gap between the languages of theory and research', in H.M. Blalock, Jr. and A.B. Blalock (eds), *Methodology in Social Research*. New York: McGraw-Hill. pp. 5–27.

Blau, Peter M. (1955) *The Dynamics of Bureaucracy: a Study of Interpersonal Relations in Two Government Agencies*. Chicago: University of Chicago Press.

Boring, Edwin G. (1969) 'Perspective: artifact and control', in R. Rosenthal and R. Rosnow (eds), *Artifact in Behavioural Research*. New York: Academic Press.

Breaugh, James A. (1985) 'The measurement of work autonomy', *Human Relations*, 38: 551–70.

Breaugh, James A. and Becker, Alene S. (1987) 'Further examination of the worker autonomy scales: three studies', *Human Relations*, 40: 381–400.

Bruner, Jerome (1990) *Acts of Meaning*. Cambridge, MA: Harvard University Press.

Bryman, A. (1989) *Research Methods and Organisations Studies*. London: Unwin Hyman.

Burrell, G. (1988) 'Modernism, postmodernism and organizational analysis 2: the contribution of Michel Foucault', *Organisation Studies*, 9: 221–35.

Burrell, G. and Morgan, G. (1979) *Sociological Paradigms and Organisational Analysis*. Portsmouth, NH: Heinemann.

Calás, M.B. and Smircich, L. (1991) 'Voicing seduction to silence leadership', *Organization Studies*, 12: 567–602.

Campbell, Donald T. and Stanley, Julian C. (1966)

Experimental and Quasi-Experimental Designs for Research. Chicago: Rand McNally.

Canella, Albert A. Jr and Paetzold, Ramona L. (1994) 'Pffefer's barriers to the advance of organisational science: a rejoinder', *Academy of Management Review*, 19: 331–41.

Caporaso, James E. (1973) 'Quasi-experimental approaches in social science', in James Caporaso and Leslie L. Roos Jr (eds), *Quasi-Experimental Approaches: Testing Theory and Evaluating Policy.* Evanston, IL: Northwestern University Press.

Cartner, Monica and Stablein, Ralph E. (1994) 'Dimensions of relevance: mediating barriers between the management sciences and management practice'. ANZAM Conference Presentation, Wellington.

Chalmers, A.F. (1982) *What Is This Thing Called Science?* 2nd edn. Brisbane: University of Queensland Press.

Clark, Herbert H. and Schrober, Michael F. (1992) 'Asking questions and influencing answers', in Judith M. Tanur (ed.), *Questions about Questions: Inquiries into the Cognitive Bases of Surveys.* New York: Russell Sage Foundation.

Collinson, David (1992) *Managing the Shopfloor: Subjectivity, Masculinity and Workplace Culture.* New York: Walter de Gruyter.

Cook, Thomas D. and Campbell, Donald T. (1979) *Quasi-Experimentation.* Chicago: Rand McNally.

Coombs, Clyde H., Dawes, Robyn M. and Tversky, Amos (1970) *Mathematical Psychology: an Elementary Introduction.* Englewood Cliffs, NJ: Prentice-Hall.

Cooper, Robert (1989) 'Modernism, post-modernism and organisational analysis 3: the contribution of Jacques Derrida', *Organization Studies*, 10: 479–502.

Cooper, Robert (1990) 'Organisation/disorganisation', in John Hassard and Denis Pym (eds), *The Theory and Philosophy of Organization: Critical Issues and New Perspectives.* London: Routledge.

Cooper, Robert and Burrell, Gibson (1988) 'Modernism, postmodernism and organisational analysis: an introduction', *Organisation Studies*, 9: 91–112.

Cronbach, J.L. and Meehl, P.E. (1955) 'Construct validity in psychological tests', *Psychological Bulletin*, 52: 281–302.

Crozier, M. (1964) *The Bureaucratic Phenomenon.* London: Tavistock.

Daft, Richard L. (1980) 'The evolution of organisational analysis in *ASQ*: 1959–1979', *Administrative Science Quarterly*, 25(4): 623–36.

Dalton, Melville (1959) *Men who Manage: Fusions and Theory in Administration.* New York: Wiley.

Dawes, Robyn M. (1972) *Fundamentals of Attitude Measurement.* New York: Wiley.

Deetz, S. (1996) 'Describing differences in approaches to organisation science: rethinking Burrell and Morgan and their legacy', *Organisation Science*.

Denzin, N.K. (1994) 'The art and politics of interpretation', in N.K. Denzin and Y.S. Lincoln (eds), *Handbook of Qualitative Research.* Thousand Oaks, CA: Sage. pp. 500–15.

Denzin, N.K. and Lincoln, Y.S. (eds) (1994) *Handbook of Qualitative Research.* Thousand Oaks, CA: Sage.

Ericsson, K. Anders and Simon, Herbert A. (1980) 'Verbal reports and data', *Psychological Review*, 87: 215–51.

Evered, R. and Louis, M.R. (1981) 'Alternative perspectives in the organisational sciences: "inquiry from the inside" and "enquiry from the outside"', *Academy of Management Review*, 5: 385–95.

Filstead, W.J. (1970) *Qualitative Methodology: First-hand Involvement with the Social World.* Chicago: Markham.

Frost, P.J. (ed.) (1981) 'Special issue on organizational symbolism', *Journal of Management*, 11(2).

Frost, Peter J. and Stablein, Ralph E. (1992) *Doing Exemplary Research.* Newbury Park, London: Sage.

Frost, P.J., Moore, L.F., Louis, M.R., Lundberg, C.C. and Martin, J. (eds) (1985) *Organizational Culture.* Beverly Hills, CA: Sage.

Gephart, R.P. (1988) *Ethnostatistics: Qualitative Foundations for Quantitative Research.* Newbury Park, CA: Sage.

Gersick, Connie C.J. (1988) 'Time and transition in work teams: toward a new model of group development', *Academy of Management Journal*, 31: 9–41.

Gersick, Connie C.J. (1992) 'Time and transition in my work on teams: looking back on a new model of group development', in Peter J. Frost and Ralph E. Stablein (eds), *Doing Exemplary Research.* Newbury Park, London: Sage.

Golden-Biddle, D. and Locke, K. (1993) 'Appealing work: an investigation of how ethnographic texts convince', *Organisation Science*, 4(4): 595–616.

Gouldner, A.W. (1954a) *Patterns of Industrial Bureaucracy.* New York: Free Press.

Gouldner, A.W. (1954b) *Wildcat Strike: a Study in Worker–Management Relationships.* New York: Harper and Row.

Gramsci, A. (1971) *Selections from the Prison Notebooks.* New York: International.

Guba, E.G. and Lincoln, Y.S. (1994) 'Competing paradigms in qualitative research', in N.K. Denzin and Y.S. Lincoln (eds), *Handbook of Qualitative Research.* Thousand Oaks, CA: Sage. pp. 105–17.

Gummesson, E. (1991) *Qualitative Methods in Management Research.* Newbury Park, CA: Sage.

Habermas, Jurgen (1971) *Knowledge and Human Interest.* Boston: Beacon Press.

Hackman, Richard J. (1992) 'Doing research that makes a difference', in Edward E. Lawler III, Allen M. Mohrman Jr, Susan A. Mohrman, Gerald E. Ledford Jr, Thomas G. Cummings and Associates (eds), *Doing Research that is Useful for Theory and Practice.* San Francisco: Jossey-Bass.

Hamel, Jacques (1993) *Case Study Methods. Qualitative Research Methods*, vol. 32. Newbury Part, CA: Sage.

Hammond, P.E. (ed.) (1964) *Sociologists at Work*. New York: Basic Books.

Hartman, E. (1988) *Conceptual Foundations of Organization Theory*. Cambridge, MA: Ballinger.

Hassard, John (1990) 'An alternative to paradigm incommensurability in organisation theory', in John Hassard and Denis Pym (eds), *The Theory and Philosophy of Organization: Critical Issues and New Perspectives*. London: Routledge.

Hassard, J. and Parker, M. (eds) (1993) *Postmodernism and Organizations*. London: Sage.

Ironson, G.H., Smith, P.C., Brannick, M.T., Gibson, W.M. and Paul, K.B. (1989) 'Construction of a job in general scale: a comparison of global, composite, and specific measures', *Journal of Applied Psychology*, 74: 193–200.

Jackall, Robert (1988) *Moral Mazes: the World of Corporate Managers*. New York: Oxford University Press.

Janz, T., Hellervik, L. and Gilmore, D.C. (1986) *Behavior Description Interviewing*. Boston: Allyn & Bacon.

Jaros, Stephen J. (1994) 'Reconciling knowledge accumulation and resource acquisition: issues in organisational science', *Academy of Management Review*, 19: 643–4.

Jeffcut, Paul (1994a) 'The interpretation of organization: a contemporary analysis and critique', *Journal of Management Studies*, 31: 225–50.

Jeffcut, Paul (1994b) 'From interpretation to representation in organisational analysis: postmodernism, ethnography and organisational symbolism', *Organisation Studies*, 15: 241–74.

Jelinek, M., Smircich, L. and Hirsch, P. (1983) 'Introduction: a code of many colours', *Administrative Science Quarterly*, 28: 331–8.

Jermier, John M. (1994) 'Critical issues in organization science', *Organizational Science*, 5: 1–13.

Kanter, Rosabeth M. (1977) *Men and Women of the Corporation*. New York: Basic Books.

Kilduff, M. (1993) 'Deconstructing organization', *Academy of Management Review*, 18(1): 13–31.

Kuhn, Thomas S. (1970) *The Structure of Scientific Revolutions*. Chicago: University of Chicago Press.

Kunda, Gideon (1992) *Engineering Culture: Control and Commitment in a High Tech Corporation*. Philadelphia: Temple University Press.

Kunkel, P.J. and McGrath, J.E. (1972) *Research in Human Behaviour*. New York: Holt, Rinehart and Winston.

Lakatos, Imre (1965) 'Falsification and the methodology of scientific research programmes', in Imre Lakatos and A. Musgrove (eds), *Criticism and the Growth of Knowledge*. Cambridge: Cambridge University Press.

Landy, F.J. (1986) 'Stamp collecting versus science validation as hypothesis testing', *American Psychologist*, 41(11): 1183–92.

Lawler, Edward E. III (1985) 'Challenging traditional research assumptions', in Edward E. Lawler III,

Allen M. Mohrman Jr, Susan A. Mohrman, Gerald E. Ledford Jr, Thomas G. Cummings and Associates (eds), *Doing Research that is Useful for Theory and Practice*. San Francisco: Jossey-Bass.

Lincoln, Yvonna S. and Guba, Egon G. (1985) *Naturalistic Inquiry*. Beverly Hills, CA: Sage.

Linstead, S. (1993) 'Deconstruction in the study of organizations', in J. Hassard and M. Parker (eds), *Postmodernism and Organizations*. London: Sage. pp. 49–70.

Locke, E.A. (ed.) (1986) *Generalizing from Laboratory to Field Settings: Research Findings from Industrial-Organizational Psychology, Organizational Behavior, and Human Resource Management*. Lexington, MA: Lexington Books.

Lord, F.M. (1953) 'On the statistical treatment of football numbers', *American Psychologist*, 8: 756–61.

MacRae, George (1988) 'Measurement scales and statistics: what can significance tests tell us about the world?', *British Journal of Psychology*, 79: 161–71.

March, J.G. and Simon, H.A. (1958) *Organizations*. New York: Wiley.

Martin, J. (1990) 'Breaking up the mono-method monopolies in organisational analysis', in John Hassard and Denis Pym (eds), *The Theory and Philosophy of Organization: Critical Issues and New Perspectives*. London: Routledge.

Merton, Robert K. (1962) *Social Theory and Social Structure*. Glencoe, IL: Free Press.

Meyer, Gordon W., Barley, Stephen R. and Gash, Debra C. (1992) 'Obsession and niavete in upstate New York', in Peter J. Frost and Ralph E. Stablein (eds), *Doing Exemplary Research*. Newbury Park, CA: Sage.

Michell, J. (1986) 'Measurement scales and statistics: a clash of paradigms', *Psychological Bulletin*, 100: 398–407.

Miles, Matthew and Huberman, A. Michael (1994) *Qualitative Data Analysis: An Expanded Sourcebook*, 2nd edn. Thousand Oaks, CA: Sage.

Mills, C.W. (1959) *The Sociological Imagination*. London: Oxford University Press.

Mitroff, I.I. and Kilmann, R.H. (1978) *Methodological Approaches to Social Science*. San Francisco: Jossey-Bass.

Morey, N.C. and Luthans, F. (1984) 'An emic perspective and ethnoscience methods for group research', *Academy of Management Review*, 9: 27–36.

Morgan, Gareth (ed.) (1983) *Beyond Method: Strategies for Social Research*. Beverly Hills, CA: Sage.

Morgan, Gareth (1985) 'Journals and the control of knowledge: a critical perspective', in L.L. Cummings and Peter J. Frost (eds), *Publishing in the Organisational Sciences*. Homewood, IL: Richard D. Irwin.

Nisbet, R.E. and Wilson, T.D. (1977) 'Telling more than we can know: verbal reports on mental processes', *Psychological Review*, 4: 231–59.

Pedhazur, E.J. and Schmelkin, L.P. (1991) *Measurement, Design and Analysis: An Integrated Approach*. Hillside, NJ: Lawrence Erlbaum Associates.

Pffefer, Jeffrey (1993) 'Barriers to the advance of organisational science: paradigm development as a dependent variable', *Academy of Management Review*, 18: 599–620.

Pinder, Craig C. and Moore, Larry F. (1980) *Middle Range Research and the Study of Organisations*. Boston: Nijhoff.

Podsakoff, Philip M. and Dalton, Dan R. (1987) 'Research methodology in organisational studies', *Journal of Management*, 13: 419–41.

Pondy, Louis R., Frost, Peter J., Morgan, Gareth and Dandridge, Thomas C. (1983) *Organisational Symbolism: Monographs in Organisational Behaviour and Industrial Relations*. Greenwich, CT: JAI Press.

Ragin, C.C. (1992) 'Introduction: cases of "What is a case?"', in C.C. Ragin and H.S. Becker (eds), *What is a Case?* Cambridge: Cambridge University Press.

Ragin, C.C. and Becker, H.S. (eds) (1992) *What is a Case? Exploring the Foundations of Social Enquiry*. Cambridge: Cambridge University Press.

Rao, M.V.H. and Passmore, W.A. (1989) 'Knowledge and interests in organisation studies: a conflict of interpretations', *Organization Studies*, 10(2): 225–39.

Rice, A.K. (1958) *Productivity and Social Organisation: the Ahmedabad Experiment*. London: Tavistock.

Rosenthal, R. and Rosnow, R.L. (eds) (1969) *Artifact in Behavioral Research*. New York: Academic Press.

Roy, D. (1952) 'Quota restriction and goldbricking in a machine shop', *American Journal of Sociology*, 57: 427–42.

Sandelands, L. (1993) 'A review of *Doing Exemplary Research*', *Academy of Management Review*, 18(2): 377–80.

Schon, Donald A. (1987) *Educating the Reflective Practitioner: Toward a New Design for Teaching and Learning in the Professions*. San Francisco: Jossey-Bass.

Schwab, Donald P. (1980) 'Construct validity in organizational behaviour', *Research in Organisational Behaviour*, 2: 3–43.

Schwab, Donald P. (1985) 'Reviewing empirically based manuscripts: perspectives on process', in L.L. Cummings and P.J. Frost (eds), *Publishing in the Organisational Sciences*. Homewood, IL: Irwin.

Smircich, Linda (1992) 'Stories of Mike Armstrong and the idea of exemplary research', in Peter J. Frost and Ralph E. Stablein (eds), *Doing Exemplary Research*. Newbury Park, CA: Sage.

Spradley, James P. (1979a) *The Ethnographic Interview*. New York: Holt, Rinehart and Winston.

Spradley, James P. (1979b) *Participant Observation*. New York: Holt, Rinehart and Winston.

Stablein, Ralph E. and Nord, W. (1985) 'Practical and emancipatory interests in organizational symbolism: a review and evaluation', *Journal of Management*, 11: 13–28.

Stewart, D.W. and Kamins, M.A. (1993) *Secondary Research: Information Sources and Methods*, 2nd edn. Newbury Park, CA: Sage.

Sutton, Robert I. and Rafaeli, Anat (1988) 'Untangling the relationship between displayed emotions and organisational sales: the case of convenience stores', *Academy of Management Journal*, 31(3): 416–87.

Sutton, Robert I. and Rafaeli, Anat (1992) 'Untangling the relationship between displayed emotions and organisational sales: the case of convenience stores', in Peter J. Frost and Ralph E. Stablein (eds), *Doing Exemplary Research*. Newbury Park, CA: Sage.

Tibbets, P. (1990) 'Representation and the realist–constructivist controversy', in M. Lynch and S. Woolgar (eds), *Representation in Scientific Practice*. Cambridge, MA: MIT Press.

Trist, E.A. and Bamforth, K.W. (1951) 'Some social and psychological consequences of the long wall method of coal getting', in D.S. Pugh (ed.), *Organisational Theory*. Harmondsworth: Penguin, 1971.

Van Maanen, John (ed.) (1979) 'Qualitative methodology', Special Edition of *Administrative Science Quarterly*, 24.

Van Maanen, John (1988) *Tales of the Field: On Writing Ethnography*. Chicago: University of Chicago Press.

Van Maanen, John, Dabb Jr, James M. and Faulkner, Robert, R. (1982) *Varieties of Qualitative Research*. Beverly Hills, CA: Sage.

Vidich, A.J. and Lyman, S.M. (1994) 'Qualitative methods: their history in sociology and anthropology', in N.K. Denzin and Y.S. Lincoln (eds), *Handbook of Qualitative Research*. Thousand Oaks, CA: Sage. pp. 23–59.

Walton, R.E. (1977) 'Work innovation at Topeka: after six years', *Journal of Applied Behavioural Science*, 13: 422–34.

Weaver, Gary R. and Gioia, Dennis A. (1994) 'Paradigms lost: incommensurability vs structurationist inquiry', *Organisation Studies*, 15: 565–89.

Webb, E.J., Campbell, D.T., Schwartz, R.D. and Sechrest, L. (1966) *Unobtrusive Measures: Nonreactive Research in the Social Sciences*. Chicago: Rand McNally.

Weick, Karl E. (1965) 'Laboratory experimentation with organisations', in James G. March (ed.), *Handbook of Organisations*. Chicago: Rand McNally.

Whyte, William F. (1955) *Street Corner Society*. Chicago, IL: The University of Chicago Press.

Zald, M.N. (1994) 'Organisation studies as a scientific and humanistic enterprise: towards a reconceptualisation of the foundations of the field', *Organizational Science*, 4: 513–28.

Zerbe, Wilfred J. and Paulus, Delroy L. (1987) 'Socially desirable responding in organizational behaviour: a reconception', *Academy of Management Review*, 12: 250–64.

3.2

Action Research for the Study of Organizations

COLIN EDEN AND CHRIS HUXHAM

In common with other forms of qualitative research (Miles and Huberman 1984; Strauss and Corbin 1990; Gummesson 1991; Denzin and Lincoln 1994), *action research* has become increasingly prominent among researchers involved in the study of organizations as an espoused paradigm used to justify the validity of a range of research outputs. The term is sometimes used rather loosely to cover a variety of approaches. In this chapter we shall use the term to embody research which, broadly, results from an involvement by the researcher with members of an organization over a matter which is of genuine concern to them and in which there is an intent by the organization members to take action based on the intervention.

Interventions of this kind will necessarily be 'one-offs', so action research has frequently been criticized for its lack of repeatability, and, hence, lack of rigour. These criticisms are countered by the argument that the involvement with practitioners over things which actually matter to them provides a richness of insight which could not be gained in other ways (Rowan and Reason 1981; Whyte 1991). This is a valid and important argument to which we shall return. However, in this chapter a major concern is to identify the range of approaches over which the argument may apply. For example, we would not consider any organizational intervention project to be necessarily action research, unless it satisfies characteristics which make it *rigorous research*. Similarly, we would not consider any piece of research within an organization to be necessarily action research, unless it satisfies characteristics which make it *action oriented*.

Aguinis (1993) argues that action research has much in common with traditional scientific method. Our own view, however, is that good action research will be good science though not in a way which depends necessarily upon meeting all the tenets of traditional scientific method. But this requires a clear understanding of what is needed to achieve 'good quality research' *in this type of setting*. Criticism of action research as poor social science is often made without understanding the (albeit often unrealized) *potential* for rigour. Nevertheless, the label 'action research' *is* unfortunately often used as an excuse for sloppy research.

The main thrust of this chapter is thus an exploration of the nature and boundaries of good action research in the context of the study of organizations. We are not attempting to argue, in general, for action research as against other types of research. We do not intend to formulate a definition of action research because we do not believe this would be helpful or productive. To do so is likely to narrow its application as well as encourage wasteful definitional debate. We believe that action research is better captured through an interlocking set of characteristics than a definition. Inevitably many of the characteristics of good action research apply to any good research, but we see those identified in this chapter as particularly pertinent for those undertaking action research. In relation to action research these characteristics are often ignored, because they are either seen as not relevant or taken to be not attainable.

We indicated, in the first paragraph of the chapter, our starting point for an exploration of the nature and boundaries of action research, where we asserted that:

Action research involves the researcher in working with members of an organization over a matter which is of genuine concern to them and in which there is an intent by the organization members to take action based on the intervention.

The underlying argument of the chapter will be that while the above attributes are clearly important to action research, they do not alone give sufficient guidance about its nature. The chapter will thus both narrow down this initial description and elaborate on the detail of it.

We shall begin this process by setting action research in context, both in relation to its history and in relation to similar approaches. Our exploration will continue with the development of characteristics which are required if action research is to satisfy the criterion of being *both* action oriented and research oriented. The characteristics, when taken together, will act as a summary of the important aspects of action research, and of the features which distinguish it both from pure consultancy-type interventions and from other forms of research for the study of organizations. The chapter concludes firstly with a discussion of some of the issues concerned with the reporting of action research, and finally with some commentary about the real world context of organizational action researchers.

A CONTEXTUAL PERSPECTIVE

Our concern in this chapter is with that particular form of action research which is *relevant in the context of the study of organizations*. In order to clarify how this relates to other forms of research, we shall review briefly a number of others which are closely related. Firstly, however, we will present a brief review of the history of these kinds of approaches.

Historical Context

The notion of action research is often considered to have been first identified by Lewin in the 1940s (Lewin 1946; 1947), although it is worth noting that Ketterer et al. (1980) mention Collier's (1945) research on 'American Indians' as an early example of action research. Lewin argued that research for social practice needs to take an integrated approach across social science disciplines and should be concerned with 'two rather different types of questions, namely the study of general laws . . . and the diagnosis of a specific situation' (1946: 36). His approach was to design hypothesis testing experiments into workshops which he had been asked to run for delegates who

were concerned, for example, to design ways of tackling race relations issues. He emphasized that the research data (in his case, concerned with understanding the kinds of change the workshops had produced) would be complex and difficult to keep hold of. The need to design methods for recording ill-structured data was therefore seen as important, as was a focus on the relationship between perception and action – an interpretativist approach to research.

Lewin's (1943) work on encouraging the use of meat entrails in everyday cooking is one of the first applications of social science knowledge which was to be labelled 'action research'. In some ways, this was more akin to the traditional controlled experimentation of the physical sciences (Clark 1972), but it did have the explicit aim of changing behaviour and recording the outcomes of the attempts to do so. The crucial difference between this work and others' was the recognition that the researcher was visible and was expected to have an impact on the experiment. Lewin's work produced a great deal of mistrust about the research conclusions because of the difficulties in measuring outcomes and controlling contextual variables.

The emphasis on hypothesis testing is still prevalent among some groups of action researchers (see, for example, the special issue of the *Journal of Applied Behavioural Science*: Alderfer 1993). However, as the approach has gained credence, the early notions have been used, extended or re-created by others. This process has led to a variety of action-oriented methods being developed.

Soon after the pioneering work in the US, the Tavistock Institute in the UK began a programme of research in the coal mining industry which gradually led to an exposition of the relationship between investigatory research and its implications for action (Trist and Bamforth 1951). This work was to lead to the development of the socio-technical systems approach to thinking about organizational interventions (Emery and Trist 1963). The work was strongly aimed at conducting research and undertaking associated theory development alongside attempting to make significant changes in organizations. Socio-technical thinking was to dominate action research across the globe, and the work of the Tavistock Institute continued to act as a reference point for others wishing to undertake action research (see Clark 1975). Collaboration between UK and Norwegian researchers led to Scandinavia enjoying a long association with the development of action research (Emery and Thorsrud 1969; Thorsrud 1970; and recently Elden 1979; Elden and Levin 1991). Notably, significant institutional support was provided for extensive work in Sweden on the democratization of the workplace. All of this early work focused upon understanding organizations and organizational change.

Alternative Interpretations and Related Concepts

In recent times it has become more difficult to identify the main thrust of action research; the literature has become confused in a variety of ways. On the one hand, there have been a number of different interpretations of the term *action research*, while on the other, an assortment of different (but similar) terms has sprung up. Action learning, action science, participatory action research, and action inquiry have each become important labels applied to research which aims to build 'theories within the practice context itself, and test them there through intervention experiments' (Argyris and Schon 1991: 86). A further confusion arises from the range of other qualitative research approaches which have many characteristics in common with action research. Collaborative and participatory research are possibly the most closely related (Rowan 1981; Torbert 1981) with many authors, in contrast to ourselves, arguing that action research is necessarily of this type (Peters and Robinson 1984). Having considered, in the previous section, the historical context, we will now review briefly a number of examples of these closely related, contemporary alternative interpretations and related concepts.

In the last fifteen years or so, a network of scholars has developed whose main concern is with the use of some of the principles of action research as a method for *developing effective professional practice*. The focus of this form of action research is the *individual* practitioner rather than the organization. Individuals thus undertake research on their own personal practice, in their own practical context, and seek to use the research for their own personal benefit. This kind of action research is thus a form of self-development.

This use of action research has sometimes arisen in the context of education research. Indeed the work of Corey (1953) on improving school practices is one early example of action research. It is used by those who are concerned with 'how to live one's values more fully in the workplace in a way which protects integrity, freedom, justice and democracy, [and] how to find new qualitative research forms of accounting for oneself within particular social contexts, [and] how to account for the processes of personal understanding' (this was the explicit aim of the 3rd World Congress on Action Learning, Action Research and Process Man-

agement, 1994). Thus, for example, 'academics research their own practice as teachers, managers and researchers . . . action research is a systematic form of enquiry undertaken by practitioners into their attempts to improve the quality of *their own* practice' (Whitehead 1994: 138, our emphasis).

This focus on the researcher as investigator, subject, and consumer can be seen as an extension of the work of Argyris and Schon (1974) related to 'double-loop' and 'deutero' learning and its role in developing a 'reflective practitioner' (Argyris and Schon 1978; Argyris 1982). Similarly, Torbert (1976; 1991), building on what Argyris and Schon prefer to call 'action science', talks of 'action inquiry' as consciousness in the midst of action. The term 'action learning' is perhaps the most common currency presently used to describe this kind of approach (Revans 1977; 1978; 1982). In a similar fashion, at the organizational rather than the individual level, some action researchers use the term 'action research' and 'organization development' as if they were synonymous and seem to imply that action research is *solely* about creating organizational change (Alderfer 1993).

Another extension of action research is an approach called 'participatory action research'. The key distinguishing feature of this approach is the combination of (i) the central principle of 'participatory' or 'collaborative' research, the notion that some members of the organization being studied should actively participate in the research process rather than just be subjects, with (ii) the central principle of action research, that there should be an intent to take action (Whyte 1991). This suggests a two-way relationship; the researcher becomes involved in and contributes to the practitioner's world, and the practitioner becomes involved in and contributes directly to the form of the research output.

In itself this is simply a refinement of the kind of action research with which we are concerned. However, participatory action research developed largely within the context of social research concerned with ideological issues such as worker participation in decision-making. Thus, as with the educationalists' version of action research above, participatory action research is often driven by concerns for the emancipation and empowering of groups and individuals. In this case, 'the values researchers hold and the ideological perspectives that guide them exert a powerful influence on choices they make in the course of inquiry' (Brown and Tandon 1983: 281). In practice this has often meant being interested in helping underprivileged groups and being concerned with the kind of social change which seriously questions the dominant values within society. This contrasts starkly with most action research aimed at the study of organization and organizations – the concern of this chapter – where it is likely that the researcher accepts the dominant managerial ideology.

While the focus on the underprivileged thus dominates some participatory action researchers, others are driven by a different form of ideology. For this group, 'one important difference between classical action research and participatory action research is that in addition to solving practical problems and contributing to general theory, contemporary forms of action research also aim at making change and learning a self-generating and self-maintaining process in the systems in which action researchers work' (Elden and Chisholm 1993a: 125).

Participatory action research is thus often inspired by considerations that are not necessary – or even appropriate – for the study of organizations. Interesting and contemporary explorations of a number of these are contained in Fals-Borda and Rahman (1991) and the special issue of *Human Relations* in February 1993 (Elden and Chisholm 1993b) on the subject.

The Congruence of Action-Oriented Approaches

Throughout the history of these action-oriented approaches to research and learning, whichever tradition has been followed, there has been a consistent defensiveness on the part of researchers attached to it. In 1972 Clark argued that the distinctive features tend to be neglected and slighted, albeit unintentionally, and that much academic commentary is little more than negative criticism. However in the late 1970s and early 1980s a number of attempts were made to argue positively not just that action research was valid, but that in a number of respects it was better than the alternatives. Notably a book by Reason and Rowan (1981) sought to bring together writers from all of the traditions mentioned above and argue for the legitimacy of a 'new paradigm' of research based upon cooperative and collaborative research.

In the US a paper by Susman and Evered (1978) had sought to legitimize action research within the context of a system of research accreditation in North American academia which has been – some would argue still is – driven by positivism. In North America and Europe all of these 'action'-oriented approaches to research are still finding difficulty in acceptance on the grounds that they are not science. Argyris and Schon argue that there is 'a fundamental *choice* that hinges on a dilemma of rigour or relevance' (1991: 85), as if the researcher chooses between scientific or action research. *In this chapter it is argued that good action research must, and can, meet both of these requirements.*

In defence of its scientific merits it is, perhaps, significant that it is now commonplace for those engrossed in all the related endeavours of action learning, action science, action research and participatory action research to be concerned, at least, with the validity of research data (Aguinis 1993). Thus there is a concern to collect more subtle and significant data than those which are easily accessed through traditional research methods. For example, in action science Argyris and Schon argue for placing emphasis on the 'spontaneous, tacit theories-in-use . . . especially whenever feelings of embarrassment or threat come into play' (1991: 86). They argue that without an awareness of the impact of these dimensions it is not possible to be certain of the status of data.

Most action researchers now pay a great deal of attention to the intricacies of research data and argue that traditional positivist research methods trivialize data collection. Although the above discussion has sought to distinguish action research aimed at the study of organizations from the other approaches, the latter do offer important comment on data collection which is highly relevant to action research as we define it. They also similarly have much of relevance to say about issues such as analysis or synthesis of data and about the presentation of results. Since many of these issues are of concern to all action-oriented researchers, this chapter will draw selectively from all of the traditions when to do so is consistent with its outlook.

ACTION RESEARCH CHARACTERIZED

The purpose of the last section was to begin to build up a picture of the kind of action research with which we are concerned, by placing it in the context of its historical development and of other contemporarily related approaches. With that as background, we now continue to enhance the picture by exploring its important characteristics in much greater depth.

We have divided our discussion of the characteristics of action research for the study of organizations into three groups. In this preliminary section we will discuss just one characteristic: the key feature which distinguishes action research from other forms of management research. The following sections focus firstly on action research *outcomes* and secondly on action research *processes*. The broad issues that we regard as particularly important are: the action focus of action research; generality; theory development; the type of theory development appropriate for action research; the pragmatic focus of action research; designing action research; and the validity of action research.

We are seeking to identify a set of characteristics which can inform practically the research process. Ultimately we shall commend the final list of fifteen characteristics as a check-list to guide thinking about the design and validity of action research. However, we wish to make clear that the discussion leading to the derivation of each characteristic is crucial to a proper understanding of its use in this way.

The Action Focus of Action Research

Our first characteristic is almost, but not, definitional:

1 Action research demands an integral involvement by the researcher in an intent to change the organization. This intent may not succeed – no change may take place as a result of the intervention – and the change may not be as intended.

This is saying that action research must be concerned with intervening in action; it is not enough for the researcher simply to study the action of others. While the latter can be a valid alternative form of management research it is not action research. Action research thus carries a particular set of concerns along with it which the remaining characteristics seek to encapsulate.

THE CHARACTERISTICS OF ACTION RESEARCH OUTCOMES

Generality

In common with Lewin, many authors on action research stress the importance of the work being useful to the client. For example, Reason (1988) quotes Torbert as arguing that action research must be 'useful to the practitioner *at the moment of action* rather than a reflective science about action' (our emphasis), and Elden and Levin (1991) argue that action research should be a way of *empowering* participants. Although these two outcomes are related – because empowering demands use at the moment of action – empowering goes significantly further by demanding a change in the power relationships within the organization. Other authors stress that the development of 'local theory' – theory which applies in the specific context of the

research – is a central feature of the approach (Elden 1979).

While these comments support the role of action research for enhancing action (characteristic 1) they tend to ignore the role of research for a wider audience. They also ignore the role of reflection to the practitioner as a part of changing their future behaviour (as with action learning). For the practitioner there will be benefits that go beyond the moment of action towards some generality which is related to their expectation of implications for future situations. This circumstance provides the opportunity for collaborative or participatory research. For other practitioners, and researchers, the generality will go even beyond this by having something to say about other contexts than that within which this specific practitioner operates.

Many critics of action research reasonably take from the above authors the view that results can only be bounded tightly by context. We, however, see action research as an approach which can build and extend theory of more general use than implied above. We are not, of course, arguing for a level of generality which is devoid of context. Rather, we are arguing that the general theory derived from action research must be applicable significantly beyond the specific situation.

Following from this, our second characteristic is that:

2 Action research must have some *implications beyond those required for action or generation of knowledge in the domain of the project*. It must be possible to envisage talking about the theories developed in relation to other situations. Thus it must be clear that the results *could* inform other contexts, at least in the sense of suggesting areas for consideration.

This means that the outcomes must be capable of being couched in other than situation-specific terms. Thus, 'the name you choose [for a category] . . . must be a more abstract concept than the one it denotes' (Strauss and Corbin 1990). It is important to be careful, of course, to avoid the danger that the abstractness is meaningless, generates more unnecessary jargon and obfuscates the power of the research. The ability of the researcher to characterize or conceptualize the particular experience in ways which make the research *meaningful to others* is crucial. This usually means that the reported research must be translated so that different circumstances can be envisaged by others. It is this that may promote interest from other practitioners in how to understand situations they expect to find themselves in, and from researchers by informing their own theory development.

Theory Development

It is the careful *characterization and conceptualization* of experiences which amount to the theory which is carefully drawn out of action research. This leads to our third characteristic, that:

3 As well as being usable in everyday life, action research demands *valuing theory*, with theory elaboration and development as an explicit concern of the research process.

This may appear to suggest a dichotomy between research aims and intervention aims (Friedlander and Brown 1974). There is, however, no reason why the two need to be seen as mutually exclusive. It is possible to fulfil the requirements of the client and at the same time consider the more theoretical implications, though it should be recognized that addressing these dual aims often means that more effort has to be put into achieving research results than would be the case with more conventional research paradigms. Research output can often be the direct converse of what is required for a client, where situation-specific terminology may be the key to gaining ownership of the results.

The research output will also tend to be different from the immediate concerns of professional interventionists (that is, consultants) even though the latter may have an interest in generally transferable aspects of their interventions in order to enhance their professional adequacy. Our fourth characteristic, below, relies on exploring this point further.

Professional interventionists are sometimes engaged by immediate and incremental development of practice: 'how will I do better, work more effectively and efficiently, on my next project?' Among other things, they will be interested in a transfer of tools, techniques, models and methods from one specific situation to another. This does demand the need to generalize from the specific, but this is most likely to be an incremental transfer from one specific context to another specific context. By contrast, observations about the specific situation will, *for the researcher*, raise broader questions that are of interest to a wider community who will work in a wider variety of contexts.

Researchers *qua* interventionists, as distinct from interventionists *qua* researchers, address themselves to a different primary audience. The 'interventionist as researcher' seeks to uncover general principles with implications for practice which can be shared between practitioners. The 'researcher as interventionist' seeks to talk to other researchers, and so, in addition, to other interventionists. Notably both reflect a practical orientation and both are focusing on the generality of the ideas expressed (that is, they are extending them beyond the setting in which they were designed) but they are meeting different needs and (in the first instance) satisfying different audiences. There is a distinction here between concern with direct practice and the concern of action research to *develop theory to inform a more reliable and robust development of practice.* Lewin's much quoted 'there's nothing so practical as a good theory' should perhaps become the action researcher's motto.

Despite this we emphasize the importance of the development of tools, techniques, models, or methods as possible expressions of the outcome of action research. These can be an excellent outcome of action research, providing they embody a clear expression of theory. Unfortunately, often the embodiment is implicit, if it exists at all. Action research demands that the research output explain the link between the specific experience of the intervention and the design of the tool or method; it is this *explanation which is a part of theory generation.* Thus:

4 If the generality drawn out of the action research is to be expressed through the design of tools, techniques, models and method then this, alone, is not enough. The basis for their design must be explicit and shown to be related to the theories which inform the design and which, in turn, are supported or developed through action research.

The Type of Theory Development Appropriate for Action Research

What kind of theory then is an appropriate output of action research? The notion of *drawing out* theory is important for action research and suggests an approach to theory development which recognizes that while the researcher always brings a pre-understanding (Gummesson 1991) – a starting theoretical position – to the situation, it is important to defer serious reflection on the role of this until the later stages of the project. This contrasts with other research approaches which are committed to setting out in advance the biases of the researcher.

In action research the researcher needs to be committed to *opening up the frame* within which the research situation and the data related to it are explored. To do so requires the researcher to have a commitment to the temporary suppression of pre-understanding. This decreases the likelihood of the researcher's theoretical stance closing off new and alternative ways of understanding the data and so extending theory. In addition, suppression of pre-understanding encourages generation of a holistic and complex body of theory, concepts, and experience. By contrast, being explicit about pre-understanding tends to result in a neatly bounded and 'chunked' list of biases which inevitably, even if unintentionally, take on the form of separable propositions.

Thus, for action research it is important to move towards reflecting upon the role of pre-understanding only as theories begin to emerge, rather than in advance of the research. This is a matter of emphasis and timing, not a question about whether the researcher's own theoretical stance is influential and needs to be made explicit. This *is* influential and it *must* be made explicit, but its influence will be less constraining if made explicit later rather than earlier. It is important to note that this is neither the position taken by Glaser (1992), who argues for the complete suppression of pre-understanding, nor, at the other extreme, the emphasis within the collection of papers in the *Journal of Applied Behavioural Science* (Alderfer 1993) which seem to assume a hypothesis testing approach for action research.

By its very nature, action research does not lend itself to repeatable experimentation; each intervention will be different from the last. Over time, it is possible to try out theories over and over again, but each context will be slightly different, so each time it will be necessary to adjust the interpretation of the theory to the circumstances. Action research is therefore not a good vehicle for rigorous and detailed theory *testing* (at least in the traditional sense where explicit awareness of a theoretical pre-understanding is crucial).

On the other hand, interventions in organizations provide ideal opportunities for experimentation in the sense that they provide opportunities to try out complex theoretical *frameworks* that cannot be pulled apart for controlled evaluation of individual theories. This is important in organization studies research where it is often the systemic nature of a uniquely interlocking set of theories from many disciplines that makes the body of theory powerful and useful. Action research is, at its best, therefore, importantly concerned with such *systemic relationships*, rather than with single theories: the aim is to understand conceptual and theoretical *frameworks* where each theory must be understood in the context of other related theories.

Intervention settings can also provide rich data about what people do and say – and what theories are used and usable – when faced with a genuine need to take action. These settings are thus likely to provide both new and often unexpected insights. They are settings that are much more amenable to theory generation and development than theory testing.

It would be unusual for action research to deliver fundamentally new theories. Rather, the research insights are likely to link with, and so elaborate, the work of others. The areas in which action researchers choose to work will often be influenced by their interest in the kinds of theory that already exist (or do not exist) in the area. So each intervention provides an opportunity to revisit theory and develop it further (Diesing 1972). The overall process of theory development is a *continuous cyclic process* in which the combination of the developing theory from the research and implicit pre-understanding informs action, and reflection upon the action informs the theory development. There will be a close interconnection between what may emerge from the data (and indeed what data are used) and what will emerge from the implicit, and explicit, use of theory for driving the intervention (Figure 1).

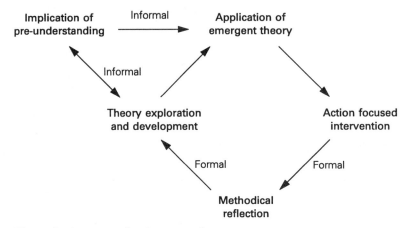

Figure 1   *The cyclical process of action research*

Thus:

5 Action research will be concerned with a system of *emergent theory*, in which the theory develops from a synthesis of that which emerges from the data and that which emerges from the use in practice of the body of theory which informed the intervention and research intent.

6 Theory building, as a result of action research, will be incremental, moving through a cycle of developing theory to action to reflection to developing theory, from the particular to the general in small steps.

This contrasts with Lewin's argument for hypotheses to be empirically testable. The very richness of the insights which action research should produce and the relative complexity of the theoretical frameworks suggest that it will usually be difficult – even logically impossible – to design experimental situations in which we could be clear about confirmation or disconfirmation (Sandford 1981; Eden 1994).

The value of action research can therefore be seen to be in *developing and elaborating theory from practice*. As an aside, developing 'grounded theory' (Glaser and Strauss 1967; Strauss and Corbin 1990; Glaser 1992) is a well recognized example, but only one of many, of emergent theory building.

The Pragmatic Focus of Action Research

Most of the often referred to writers on action research, including Lewin, demand that it be pragmatic. This is not a criterion which distinguishes action research from consultancy, but one which justifies the use and value of action research rather than other forms of research.

If the practicality criterion is taken seriously, this might be interpreted as suggesting that prescriptive theory is more appropriate than descriptive theory. This is a false dichotomy. Descriptive theory can, and does, seriously influence the actions of the consumer of the research because it does (not necessarily intentionally) highlight the important factors the consumer should be concerned about. For example descriptive insights about why things go wrong are suggestive of actions that might be taken to avoid problems in similar situations. By implication, descriptive theory also draws attention away from those aspects of the situation that are not included in the description. It is thus, by implication, prescribing one way of accounting for a situation rather than another (Allison 1971). But if descriptive theory is to be the output of action research it is important that

its practical implications be recognized even if these are presented implicitly. This means that the researcher must recognize that the language, metaphors, and value orientation used to present the theory will seriously influence the understanding of the theory in relation to the future thinking and actions of the consumer of the research.

Thus our seventh characteristic is that:

7 What is important for action research is not a (false) dichotomy between prescription and description, but a recognition that description will be prescription, even if implicitly so. Thus presenters of action research should be clear about what they expect the consumer to take from it and present it with a form and style appropriate to this aim.

The Characteristics of Action Research Processes

Designing Action Research

In order to be effective in the sort of action research we are concerned with, it is clearly important to be credible as an interventionist. A researcher thus needs to pay a great deal of attention to developing a competent intervention style and process. However, while consultancy skills are an important part of the action research toolkit, they do not, in themselves, justify the activity as *research*. Much more fundamental is *the need to be aware of what must be included in the process of consulting to achieve the research aims*. This, of course, implies being aware of the research aims themselves.

This is not intended to imply that the researcher should have a precise idea – or preunderstanding – of the nature of the research outcome of any intervention at the start; rather, the researcher should have a strategic intent for the research project. Indeed, since action research will almost always be inductive theory-building research, the really valuable insights are often those that emerge from the consultancy process in ways that cannot be foreseen. Whilst it is legitimate for an action researcher to enter a consultancy interaction with no expectation about what the specific research output will be, it is crucial that an *appropriate degree of reflection* by the researcher is built into the process. This process must include some means of recording both the reflection itself and the method for reflecting.

Action research therefore demands a high degree of *self-awareness* in knitting together the role of the consultant with that of researcher. In

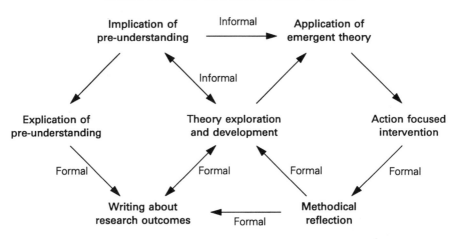

Figure 2 *The latter stages of an action research project*

addition, researchers must recognize that they not only have the roles of researcher and interventionist, but – because of their role as interventionists – are also a part of the situation which is being researched.

It is also important to consider the role that the client or other participants play in the generation of theory. There are many different levels at which they may be involved, ranging from 'pure subjects' whose aim is to get the benefits of the intervention but have no involvement with the research, to 'full collaborating partners' in the research (Rowan 1981). Exactly how the roles of the action researcher and the practitioners are played out at any level of involvement can vary, but they need to be thought about and understood.

Designed into any action research programme should thus be a consciousness of the roles to be played by the researcher and the participants and a process of reflection and data collection which is an activity separate from – though often connected to – the intervention itself (Figure 1). At the least, this demands that extensive amounts of time away from the intervention setting and the 'hands-on' problems be devoted to reflecting about process and data in relation to research issues. The exact nature of the reflection is relatively immaterial, though we may debate the validity of any particular one; what is crucial is that the process exists explicitly. Glaser and Strauss (1967) suggest an appropriate approach to this process of methodical reflection, and Richardson (1994: 526) builds on this approach by suggesting that the time away from the intervention setting is used to record observation notes, methodological notes, theoretical notes, and personal notes which are a journal recording of feelings about the research.

Thus our eighth characteristic is that:

8 For high quality action research a high degree of systematic method and orderliness is required in reflecting about, and holding on to, the research data and the emergent theoretical outcomes of each episode or cycle of involvement in the organization.

Furthermore, and our ninth characteristic:

9 For action research, the processes of exploration of the data – rather than collection of the data – in the detecting of emergent theories and development of existing theories must either be replicable or, at least, capable of being explained to others.

Thus the outcome of data exploration cannot be defended by the role of intuitive understanding alone: any intuition must be informed by a *method of exploration*. In essence this means that compared to 'everyman' as researcher, professional researchers need to be professional.

Towards the closing stages of a project, the design of action research must also acknowledge an important extension of the cycle depicted in Figure 1. This is concerned with the process of explication about pre-understanding and the role of writing about research outcomes in a formal manner for theory development (see Figure 2). Writing about research outcomes is a 'way of "knowing" – a method of discovery and analysis' (Richardson 1994: 516). It is a *formal process* of integrating the records of methodical reflection, prior theory development and the explication of pre-understanding. At this stage the use of pre-understanding is more formal than the reciprocal influence between – the deliberately suppressed – implicit pre-understanding and theory exploration and development which has been occurring throughout the project

(Figure 1). This writing process continues to inform theory exploration and implicit pre-understanding. Also, in this way, action researchers use this cycle to acknowledge to themselves and the consumers of the research that the research process and outcomes were influenced by the researcher's particular pre-understanding.

10 The full process of action research involves a series of interconnected cycles, where writing about research outcomes at the latter stages of an action research project is an important aspect of theory exploration and development, combining the processes of explicating pre-understanding and methodical reflection to explore and develop theory formally.

The Validity of Action Research

We have argued above that action research as intervention does not lend itself to repeatable experimentation; indeed its distinctive role is played when such experiments are inappropriate. The results of action research lie open to criticism if their validity is judged *solely* by the traditional criteria of positivist social science. Under these circumstances, we would agree with Susman and Evered (1978) that it is likely to fail.

Action researchers therefore need to be keenly aware of the key issues in the validity of action research and that a designed action research process must address these. In this section, we consider what we see as the most important of these.

The Validity of Action Research: Adhering to Action Research as a Coherent Paradigm

First and foremost, we consider:

11 Adhering to characteristics 1 to 10 is a necessary *but not sufficient* condition for the validity of action research.

Without attention to each of these characteristics, an intervention cannot be considered as research at all. These characteristics may thus be thought of as concerned with the *internal validity* of the research *as action research*. By contrast, the remaining topics that we discuss are concerned with *external validity*. That is, they are concerned with the degree to which the results may both be justified as representative of the situation in which they were generated and have claims to generality.

The Validity of Action Research: Theory in Use

Our second point then stresses the need to be aware that much of action research's validity comes from the theory developed not simply being 'grounded in the data' in Glaser and Struass's (1967) sense, but being *grounded in action* (cf. characteristic 1). One of the most persuasive reasons for using action research is that when subjects do not have to commit to real action and to creating a future which they will inhabit, any data gained from them are inherently unreliable (Eden 1994). This is because it is impossible to test whether what people say they would do is what they actually do if it 'came to the crunch'.

The role of the past, of history, and of the significance of established patterns of social relationships in determining organizational behaviour cannot be overestimated (Vickers 1983). Reliable data, and hence theories, about both past and future aspects that influence the way in which people change a situation are much more likely to emerge from a research process which is geared to action than from more traditional approaches. This is because it is possible to track what participants actually say and do *in circumstances that really matter to them*, as compared with what they might say hypothetically, or do in controlled circumstances (as for example in the use of students as research subjects acting as if participants in an organization). Using Argyris and Schon's (1974) terms, an action research setting increases the chances of getting at participants' 'theory in use' rather than their 'espoused theory'. It is in this way that action research can be regarded as action science. The change process provides a forum in which the articulation of complex or normally hidden factors is likely to emerge as well as an incentive to participants for spending time in articulating.

However, in the action research setting there will be forces pushing against, as well as in favour of, the articulation of theories in use. Most obviously, it is important to recognize that the intervention will result in organizational change and will challenge the *status quo*. Inevitably some people will anticipate being disadvantaged by the proposed changes and it is unlikely that the interventionist will gain full trust from all parties (Argyris and Schon 1991). *The politics of organizational change are thus a force acting against getting fully reliable data from all concerned.*

Yet there are other arguments, not directly linked to the reliability issue, in favour of the action orientation. One important one is the notion that the best way of learning about an organization is by attempting to change it. The very process of change is likely to reveal factors which would not have been unearthed in a stable environment. *The process of change forces a dialectic – a contrast – which helps articulation.* For example, Fineman's (1983) research on unemployed executives probably provided more useful data about the nature of *employment* than it did about unemployment. It was the dialectical experience of unemployment which enabled an understanding and so articulation about the role employment played in the lives of the research subjects.

In summary, we are arguing that while there may be some forces acting against easily getting reliable data through action research, *the method is likely to produce insights which cannot be gleaned in any other way.* This means – as with any kind of research – that it is important to consider explicitly where the kinds of weaknesses and strengths discussed above are likely to occur in any particular research situation. But it also means that:

12 It is difficult to justify the use of action research when the same aims can be satisfied using approaches (such as controlled experimentation or surveys) that can demonstrate the link between data and outcomes more transparently. Thus in action research, the reflection and data collection process – and hence the emergent theories – are most valuably focused on the aspects that cannot be captured by other approaches.

This, in turn, suggests that having knowledge about, and skills to apply, the method and analysis procedures for collecting and exploring rich data are essential. A detailed introduction to methods for the analysis of rich data is beyond the scope of this chapter, and has, in any case, been covered in a much more appropriate level of detail by others. The kinds of approaches suggested by Miles and Huberman (1984), Strauss and Corbin (1990), Glaser (1992) and Cassell and Symon (1994) fulfil most of the requirements for a systematic and methodical exploration of data. In addition a form of 'cognitive mapping' along with associated computer software (Graphics COPE) provides an extremely powerful method for 'playing' with the *structure*, as well as content, of qualitative research data (Cropper et al. 1990; Eden et al. 1992). The added advantage of using computer software of this sort is that it can provide a continuous record of the process of play and exploration and so of the emerging theory development.

None of these methods are easy to use; they all require a great deal of skill both in applying the analysis to the data and, more significantly, in moving from analysis of the data themselves to the more valuable insights and conceptualization that result from discussion of and reflection on the data. The analysis of action research data thus requires craft skills, which takes time for an individual researcher to develop, as well as knowledge about specific methods of data analysis.

The Validity of Action Research: Triangulation

In the course of the preceding discussion, we have highlighted some concerns about getting at particular 'truths' of situations, rather than 'the truth'. Argyris et al. (1985) also emphasize the difficulty of ensuring that the theories identified by the research process are thoroughly developed or the only theories that could have been developed. Our third topic therefore focuses on *triangulation*.

Triangulation of research data refers to the method of checking their validity by approaching the research question from as many different angles as possible and employing redundancy in data collection (Denzin 1989). The principle is that if different research approaches lead to the same conclusions our faith in the validity of those conclusions is increased. The analogy with the triangulation process surveyors use to check a sequence of measurements from one point to another is clear. Triangulation is always important in understanding uncertainty in interpretation or measurement.

In part, this is an argument for a multimethod approach to research. Denzin (1978a; 1978b) provides a comprehensive argument for the use of multiple studies where each study acts as a cross-check on others, and so the process of developing reliable conclusions is enhanced. Denzin also argues for triangulation to be applied in five aspects of the research: methodology, data, investigator, theoretical, and multiple triangulation.

Triangulation to check the validity of data is as important in action research as in other forms of research. However, action research provides *also* a uniquely different interpretation of the concept of triangulation. Exceptionally, action research provides an opportunity to seek out triangulation between (i) the *observation* of events and social processes, (ii) the *accounts* each participant offers, and (iii) the changes in these accounts and interpretation of events *as time passes* (Harré and Secord 1976). From *these* three perspectives *the data are not expected to triangulate* (agree). Indeed we may be more surprised if they do agree than if they do not, given the deliberate attempts at discovering multiple views. This procedure 'underlines the possibilities of multiple, competing perspectives on how organizations are and might be' (Jones 1987: 45). Importantly a lack of triangulation acts as an effective dialectic for the generation of new concepts. The focus is therefore on what could be rather than what is (Elden and Chisholm 1993a).

Thus triangulation has a different significance for action research compared with using triangulation only as a cross-checking method. Similarly, action research provides the opportunity for *cyclical* data collection through exploiting more continuous and varied opportunities than is occasioned by more controlled research. The chaos and the changing pace and focus of action research are used as a virtue. Thus:

13 In action research, the opportunities for triangulation that do not offer themselves with other methods should be exploited fully and reported. They should be used as a dialectical device which powerfully facilitates the incremental development of theory.

The Validity of Action Research: the Role of History and Context

The previous two topics have been largely about external validity in the specific project context. The fourth topic focuses on the problems of generalizing beyond that. It concerns the need to understand and project the role of history and context in deriving research outcomes (Pettigrew 1985; 1990). Given that action research generally deals with a one-off case study, and hence incurs all the issues inherent in case study research (Yin 1984):

14 The history and context for the intervention must be taken as critical to the interpretation of the likely range of validity and applicability of the results of action research.

Identification of the crucial variables that determine the particularity of the context is non-trivial and it is likely that individuals with different experiences and aims would focus in different areas. Discovering history and its relevance is, in any case, more problematic than Pettigrew implies. History, and context, are differently defined by different actors in the situation and by different observers: historians have always recognized the contribution of bias, selectivity and interpretation. Nevertheless, even given these difficulties, *a concern* to understand

the role of context, and the different interpretations of it, is a most important requirement of action research. Indeed working with *the selective nature of different accounts* of how a history of the organization, of the individuals and their relationships with one another, and of the wider context within which the research took place, is as important as paying attention to their role.

EXPOSING ACTION RESEARCH

So far we have addressed issues in doing action research. Disseminating to the world beyond where the research was undertaken, however, raises a number of additional issues. For example the seventh characteristic raises an issue about the style of presentation (recognizing the prescriptive aspects of action research). Also the fourteenth characteristic suggests that it is important to consider the possible interpretation of results in the light of history and context. Each of these has specific implications for the style of dissemination of action research. In this section we shall discuss some of the difficulties inherent in writing about action research. Our final characteristic is:

15 Action research requires that the theory development which is of general value is disseminated in such a way as to be of interest to an audience wider than those integrally involved with the action and/or with the research.

The demands we have set out, in the first fourteen characteristics, mean that it is unlikely that action research can be written about fully in anything shorter than a book-type format. Relative to 'straightforward' positivist research there will always be more to say about: the incremental nature of the theory development; research method in overall terms as well as the detail of data exploration method; history and context; and implications of theory for practice. This is more material than can be contained easily within the confines of a chapter. A chapter always leaves many important questions about the status of the research unanswered.

In writing this chapter we have been particularly interested in the difficulty we have had in finding written exemplars of action research which have been explicitly acknowledged by the author to be action research. Most action research sees the light of day through a variety of indirect methods. Clearly some explanation for this phenomenon can be derived from the circumstances discussed in the above paragraph. There is also some resistance from academic journals to publishing action research.

However we do find many written examples of the outcome of action research. In these instances, we believe – because we have had the opportunity to discuss, in depth, the research process with the authors – that the action research satisfies the majority of our first fourteen characteristics. These examples have in a sense cheated the action research paradigm by disseminating research outcomes in a way which hides the method in a variety of forms of presentation.

Thus one example is the promulgation of action research through the discussion of a methodology for organizational intervention. Here the theoretical framework is explicated as the *raison d'être* for the design of a method, technique, or tool for intervention. In most examples of this way of exposing the outcomes of action research, the authors make no explicit mention of action research as the research paradigm for theory exploration, but exemplify the relationship between theory and practice through technique and tool (our fourth characteristic). It is clear that their technique and tool have been developed in parallel with *theory development through its application* in long sequences of action settings which have been fully researched following an action research procedure. In the US, Nutt and Backoff (1992) and Bryson (1988) build theory and practice from undeclared action research. In the UK, Checkland (Checkland 1981; Checkland and Scholes 1991) and Eden (Eden et al. 1983; Eden 1993) follow the 'cycle of developing theory to action to reflection to developing theory, from the particular to the general in small steps' (our sixth characteristic).

A second example is where researchers use action research to provide a rich source of examples and *stories to illustrate theory*. For example, Mangham (1979; 1986) has used many projects where he was involved as an organization development consultant as the action research basis for his development and elaboration of 'symbolic interactionism' into a coherent dramaturgical theory. The theory has been more persuasive and more practical because of the rich examples within the text. But nowhere is there acknowledgement of the role action research, conducted in a manner which would meet most of the standards established here, played in the written outcome.

A further example for indirectly reporting the outcomes of action research is through the use of 'faction' (fiction which is a version of fact). An interesting example of this type of approach is the book called *The Carpetmakers* by Jones and Lakin (1978). Here one of the authors was an interventionist and the other author was one of the managers in the client organization – that

made carpets! The book is written and presented as if it were a novel, and the content makes no reference to the roles played by the authors. And yet the authors conducted a form of action research which enabled them to develop a theory of the 'four orders of administration' which is exposed in the middle section of the book. We have no indication of the nature of the method and nature of the research; indeed we are never sure that the story is of a real case, even though it is clear that the theory derives from the story. The use of journalism and 'faction' to report research is not necessarily misplaced: it provides an entertaining and engaging way of learning about research outcomes. However once again the use of action research is not made explicit.

Is it easier to promulgate research outcomes without reference to the messiness of the empirical research which provided the richness of experience and meaning to the theory presented? As Richardson notes, 'how we are expected to write affects what we can write about ... inductively accomplished research is to be reported deductively ... the conventions [of the journals] hold tremendous material and symbolic power over social scientists ... using them increases the probability of one's work being accepted into "core" social science journals, but it is not *prima facie* evidence of greater – or lesser – truth value or significance than social science writing using other conventions' (1994: 520). We do not agree with Richardson and others who subscribe to a postmodernist view of writing, that any form of writing about research is satisfactory. The conventions are of some significance, but they do seem to be forcing many action researchers to hide behind the conventions in a manner which does not give due credit to the research process.

COMMENT

The standards we have set for action research to be considered as *research* (pulled together in Table 1) are undoubtedly hard to achieve. Understanding the methodological issues involved in action research in practice is difficult and must be expected to take time and experience: action research is an imprecise, uncertain, and sometimes unstable activity compared to many other approaches to research. Enacting the standards in practice demands holistic attention to all the issues. Given the complexity and pressure of the real world action research setting, this provides a major challenge. Indeed, it is probably not an achievable challenge, though this should neither deter researchers from trying to achieve the standards nor, worse perhaps,

Table 1 *The fifteen characteristics of action research*

1 Action research demands an integral involvement by the researcher in an intent to change the organization. This intent may not succeed – no change may take place as a result of the intervention – and the change may not be as intended.

2 Action research must have some *implications beyond those required for action or generation of knowledge in the domain of the project.* It must be possible to envisage talking about the theories developed in relation to other situations. Thus it must be clear that the results *could* inform other contexts, at least in the sense of suggesting areas for consideration.

3 As well as being usable in everyday life, action research demands *valuing theory*, with theory elaboration and development as an explicit concern of the research process.

4 If the generality drawn out of the action research is to be expressed through the design of tools, techniques, models and method then this, alone, is not enough. The basis for their design must be explicit and shown to be related to the theories which inform the design and which, in turn, are supported or developed through action research.

5 Action research will be concerned with a system of *emergent theory*, in which the theory develops from a synthesis of that which emerges from the data and that which emerges from the use in practice of the body of theory which informed the intervention and research intent.

6 Theory building, as a result of action research, will be incremental, moving through a cycle of developing theory to action to reflection to developing theory, from the particular to the general in small steps.

7 What is important for action research is not a (false) dichotomy between prescription and description, but a recognition that description will be prescription, even if implicitly so. Thus presenters of action research should be clear about what they expect the consumer to take from it and present it with a form and style appropriate to this aim.

8 For high quality action research a high degree of systematic method and orderliness is required in reflecting about, and holding on to, the research data and the emergent theoretical outcomes of each episode or cycle of involvement in the organization.

9 For action research, the processes of exploration of the data – rather than collection of the data – in the detecting of emergent theories and development of existing theories must either be replicable or, at least, capable of being explained to others.

10 The full process of action research involves a series of interconnected cycles, where writing about research outcomes at the latter stages of an action research project is an important aspect of theory exploration and development, combining the processes of explicating pre-understanding and methodical reflection to explore and develop theory formally.

11 Adhering to characteristics 1 to 10 is a necessary *but not sufficient* condition for the validity of action research.

12 It is difficult to justify the use of action research when the same aims can be satisfied using approaches (such as controlled experimentation or surveys) that can demonstrate the link between data and outcomes more transparently. Thus in action research, the reflection and data collection process – and hence the emergent theories – are most valuably focused on the aspects that cannot be captured by other approaches.

13 In action research, the opportunities for triangulation that do not offer themselves with other methods should be exploited fully and reported. They should be used as a dialectical device which powerfully facilitates the incremental development of theory.

14 The history and context for the intervention must be taken as critical to the interpretation of the likely range of validity and applicability of the results of action research.

15 Action research requires that the theory development which is of general value is disseminated in such a way as to be of interest to an audience wider than those integrally involved with the action and/or with the research.

from using action research at all. For ourselves we are not convinced that our own research has fully satisfied the standards we have set. However what is important is having a sense of the standards that make for good action research and evaluating the research in relation to them.

Action research is also challenging for two further reasons: (i) the uncertainty and lack of control creates anxiety for anyone other than confident and experienced researchers; and (ii) doing *action* in action research demands experience and understanding of methods for consultancy and intervention. This second challenge suggests the need to face up to conceptual issues about the nature of problems in organizations and the concomitant demands for change, the nature of a client-centred activity, the issues involved in building and sustaining a consultant–client relationship, and so the nature of power and politics in the context of intervention.

We have set out a framework for undertaking research through fifteen characteristics. Each of these represents, in effect, a test against which action research may be judged. We have argued that each of them is an important aspect of good action research, and to that extent we suggest that the complete list (shown in Table 1) can be used as a 'check-list'. Because action research is difficult to undertake and to publish we believe that it is even more important than in other types of research for researchers to have a set of standards that can be used to guide and inform the process of undertaking the research.

The standards we have sought to establish in this chapter are not the only set that could be applied to action research; others might argue for an alternative check-list. Nevertheless, the fifteen characteristics serve a dialectical purpose for researchers. Individuals can then add further standards of their own as they attempt to evaluate their own action research against those established in this chapter.

We suspect that the current environment for research in business schools throughout the world is putting extraordinary demands on the delivery of research output. These demands can easily lead to a gradual reduction in standards. Alongside the increased competition for research funds and research publications is the demand made of business school academics to undertake consultancy and demonstrate the relevance of their research and teaching to practising managers. It is possible that consultancy and action research get confused at the expense of research standards.

Many business school academics value their consultancy both as a way of informing and legitimizing their teaching and as a source of extra cash. There is thus a danger that consultancy done for these reasons, rather than as part of a deliberate design for research, may become their major source of research output. While consultancy settings may be a valuable source of 'real' data, unless these are entered with a more sophisticated view of action research there is a danger that sloppy research will result. As we suggested earlier, the 'action research' label is often used as a way of excusing sloppy research.

Not all academics are necessarily driven by the consultancy motivation however. Many are involved in projects with outside organizations set up and funded by the organizations as *research* projects, but aiming to address specifically a problem or issue which is of concern to the organization. Under these circumstances it is questionable how many 'researchers' stop to ask whether the project has wider research implications and how the project should be tackled in order to ensure that these are addressed.

There is a great deal of pressure towards this behaviour. Firstly, in an era where research grants count so vitally on both the individual

and the institutional curricula vitae, it may not pay researchers to turn down opportunities of this kind. Secondly, the sponsoring organization cannot necessarily be expected to be concerned with general research and would often be concerned, quite naturally, with ensuring that it gets value for money for the specific project. Thirdly, in some management disciplines the preponderance of what are seen (rightly or wrongly) as over-theoretical (and hence non-practical) papers has led to a call – perhaps sparked by practitioners rather than academics – for publication of more case studies describing specific problem solving situations. Fourthly, in some disciplines there is a great deal of pressure on researchers to be directly involved in 'real world' situations in order to demonstrate the applicability of what they say. Finally, while methodological issues may be central concerns to those in the management disciplines most closely allied to mainstream social science, it seems reasonable to suppose that there are areas of management research where researchers are hardly aware of the existence of a methodological debate, let alone of the issues in it or of ways of addressing them in practice.

A further source of confusion may stem from outside the academic community: that is, from professional consultants and practising managers themselves. Though many of these just 'get on with the job', a small number take time to reflect upon and publish what they are doing. That these are often valuable contributions to the field of management is not in question. But given the everyday concerns of consultants and managers, it would be unreasonable to expect them to be motivated by the criteria which must be applied to judging high quality research outcomes. As Lake (1968), quoted in Clark (1972: 145), argued after reviewing papers published by the *Journal of Applied Behavioural Sciences*, 'it would seem that those most central to, and actively engaged in, the process of planned organizational change are not careful analytical researchers.'

This chapter is a 1990s attempt to reinforce the value of action research as a legitimate and rigorous research method, and to suggest standards which will encourage 'careful analytical researchers' who are also concerned with intervention and action.

REFERENCES

Aguinis, H. (1993) 'Action research and scientific method: presumed discrepancies and actual similarities', *Journal of Applied Behavioural Science*, 29: 416–31.

Alderfer, C.P. (1993) 'Emerging developments in action research', *Journal of Applied Behavioural Science, Special Issue*, 29(4).

Allison, G.T. (1971) *Essence of Decision: Explaining the Cuban Missile Crisis*. Boston: Little, Brown.

Argyris, C. (1982) *Reasoning, Learning, and Action*. San Francisco: Jossey-Bass.

Argyris, C. and Schon, D.A. (1974) *Theories in Practice*. San Francisco: Jossey-Bass.

Argyris, C. and Schon, D.A. (1978) *Organizational Learning: a Theory of Action Perspective*. Reading, MA: Addison-Wesley.

Argyris, C. and Schon, D.A. (1991) 'Participatory action research and action science compared: a commentary', in W.F. Whyte (ed.), *Participatory Action Research*. London: Sage. pp. 85–96.

Argyris, C., Putnam, R. and Smith, D.M. (1985) *Action Science*. San Francisco: Jossey-Bass.

Brown, D. and Tandon, R. (1983) 'Ideology and political economy in inquiry', *Journal of Applied Behavioural Science*, 19: 277–94.

Bryson, J. (1988) *Strategic Planning for Public and Nonprofit Organizations*. San Francisco: Jossey-Bass.

Cassell, C. and Symon, G. (1994) *Qualitative Methods in Organisational Research: a Practical Guide*. London: Sage.

Checkland, P. (1981) *Systems Thinking, Systems Practice*. London: Wiley.

Checkland, P. and Scholes, J. (1991) *Soft Systems Methodology in Action*. New York: Wiley.

Clark, A.W. (ed.) (1975) *Experimenting with Organizational Life*. New York: Plenum.

Clark, P.A. (1972) *Action Research and Organizational Change*. London: Harper & Row.

Collier, J. (1945) 'United States Indian administration as a laboratory of ethnic relations', *Social Research*, 12: 275–6.

Corey, S. (1953) *Action Research to Improve School Practices*. New York: Bureau of Publications, Columbia University.

Cropper, S., Eden, C. and Ackermann, F. (1990) 'Keeping sense of accounts using computer-based cognitive maps', *Social Science Computer Review*, 8: 345–66.

Denzin, N.K. (1978a) *The Research Act: a Theoretical Introduction to Sociological Methods*, 2nd edn. New York: McGraw-Hill.

Denzin, N.K. (1978b) *Sociological Methods: a Sourcebook*, 2nd edn. New York: McGraw-Hill.

Denzin, N.K. (1989) *The Research Act*, 3rd edn. Englewood Cliffs, NJ: Prentice-Hall.

Denzin, N.K. and Lincoln, Y.S. (eds) (1994) *Handbook of Qualitative Research*. Thousand Oaks, CA: Sage.

Diesing, P. (1972) *Patterns of Discovery in the Social Sciences*. London: Routledge & Kegan Paul.

Eden, C. (1993) 'Strategy development and implementation: cognitive mapping for group support', in J. Hendry and G. Johnson with J. Newton (eds), *Strategic Thinking: Leadership and the Management of Change*. Chichester: Wiley.

Eden, C. (1995) 'On the evaluation of 'wide-band' GDSS's', *European Journal of Operational Research*, 81: 302–11.

Eden, C., Ackermann, F. and Cropper, S. (1992) 'The analysis of cause maps', *Journal of Management Studies*, 29: 309–24.

Eden, C., Jones, S. and Sims, D. (1983) *Messing About in Problems*. Pergamon: Oxford.

Elden, M. (1979) 'Three generations of work democracy experiments in Norway', in C. Cooper and E. Mumford (eds), *The Quality of Work in Eastern and Western Europe*. London: Associated Business Press.

Elden, M. and Chisholm, R.F. (1993a) 'Emergent varieties of action research: introduction to the special issue', *Human Relations*, 46: 121–42.

Elden, M. and Chisholm, R.F. (1993b) *Action Research Special Issue. Human Relations*. 46.

Elden, M. and Levin, M. (1991) 'Cogenerative learning: bringing participation into action research', in W.F. Whyte (ed.), *Participatory Action Research*. London: Sage. pp. 127–42.

Emery, F.E. and Thorsrud, E. (1969) *Democracy at Work*. Leiden: Martinus Nijhoff.

Emery, F.E. and Trist, E.L. (1963) 'Sociotechnical systems', in C.W. Churchman (ed.), *Management Science: Models and Techniques*. London: Pergamon.

Fals-Borda, O. and Rahman, M.A. (1991) *Action and Knowledge*. New York: Apex Press.

Fineman, S. (1983) *White Collar Unemployment: Impact and Stress*. London: Wiley.

Friedlander, F. and Brown, D. (1974) 'Organization development', *Annual Review of Psychology*, 25: 313–41.

Glaser, B.G. (1992) *Basics of Grounded Theory*. Mill Valley, CA: Sociology Press.

Glaser, B.G. and Strauss, A.L. (1967) *The Discovery of Grounded Theory*. Chicago: Aldine.

Gummesson, E. (1991) *Qualitative Methods in Management Research*. London: Sage.

Harré, R. and Secord, P.F. (1976) *The Explanation of Social Behaviour*. Oxford: Blackwell.

Jones, R. and Lakin, C. (1978) *The Carpetmakers*. London: McGraw-Hill.

Jones, S. (1987) 'Choosing action research', in I.L. Mangham (ed.), *Organisation Analysis and Development: a Social Construction of Organisational Behaviour*. London: Wiley.

Ketterer, R., Price, R. and Politser, P. (1980) 'The action research paradigm', in R. Price and P. Politser (eds), *Evaluation and Action in the social Environment*. New York: Academic Press.

Lake, D. (1968) 'Concepts of change and innovation in 1966', *Journal of Applied Behavioural Science*, 4: 3–24.

Lewin, K. (1943) 'Forces behind food habits and methods of change', *Bulletin of the National Research Council*, CVIII: 35–65.

Lewin, K. (1946) 'Action research and minority problems', *Journal of Social Issues*, 2: 34–46.

Lewin, K. (1947) 'Frontiers in group dynamics: channel of group life: social planning and action research', *Human Relations*, 1: 143–53.

Mangham, I.L. (1979) *The Politics of Organizational Change*. London: Associated Business Press.

Mangham, I.L. (1986) *Power and Performance in Organizations*. Oxford: Basil Blackwell.

Miles, M.B. and Huberman, A.M. (1984) *Qualitative Data Analysis: a Sourcebook of New Methods*. London: Sage.

Nutt, P. and Backoff, R. (1992) *Strategic Management of Public and Third Sector Organizations*. San Francisco: Jossey-Bass.

Peters, M. and Robinson, V. (1984) 'The origins and status of action research', *The Journal of Applied Behavioural Science*, 20: 113–24.

Pettigrew, A.M. (1985) *The Awakening Giant*. Oxford: Blackwell.

Pettigrew, A.M. (1990) 'Longitudinal field research on change theory and practice', *Organisation Science*, 1: 267–92.

Reason, P. (ed.) (1988) *Human Inquiry in Action*. London: Sage.

Reason, P. and Rowan, J. (eds) (1981) *Human Inquiry: a Sourcebook of New Paradigm Research*. Chichester: Wiley.

Revans, R.W. (1977) 'Action learning and the nature of knowledge/learning', *Education and Training*, 19: 318–20.

Revans, R.W. (1978) 'Action learning and the nature of knowledge/learning', *Education and Training*, 20: 8–11.

Revans, R.W. (1982) *The Origins and Growth of Action Learning*. Bickley, Kent: Chartwell-Bratt.

Richardson, L. (1994) 'Writing: a method of inquiry', in N.K. Denzin and Y.S. Lincoln (eds), *Handbook of Qualitative Research*. Thousand Oaks, CA: Sage.

Rowan, J. (1981) 'A dialectical paradigm for research', in P. Reason and J. Rowan (eds), *Human Inquiry: a Sourcebook of New Paradigm Research*. Chichester: Wiley. pp. 93–112.

Rowan, J. and Reason, P. (1981) 'On making sense', in P. Reason and J. Rowan (eds), *Human Inquiry: a Sourcebook of New Paradigm Research*. Chichester: Wiley. pp. 113–40.

Sandford, N. (1981) 'A model for action research', in P. Reason and J. Rowan (eds), *Human Inquiry: a Sourcebook of New Paradigm Research*. Chichester: Wiley. pp. 173–82.

Strauss, A. and Corbin, J. (1990) *Basics of Qualitative Research*. London: Sage.

Susman, G.I. and Evered, R.D. (1978) 'An assessment of the scientific merits of action research', *Administrative Science Quarterly*, 23: 582–603.

Thorsrud, E. (1970) 'A strategy for research and social change in industry: a report on the industrial democracy project in Norway', *Social Science Information*, October: 65–90.

Torbert, W.R. (1976) *Creating a Community of Inquiry: Conflict, Collaboration, Transformation*. New York: Wiley.

Torbert, W.R. (1981) 'Why educational research has been so uneducational: the case for a new model of social science based on collaborative inquiry', in P. Reason and J. Rowan (eds), *Human Inquiry: a Sourcebook of New Paradigm Research*. Chichester: Wiley. pp. 141–51

Torbert, W.R. (1991) *The Power of Balance: Transforming Self, Society, And Scientific Inquiry*. Newbury Park, CA: Sage.

Trist, E. and Bamforth, K.W. (1951) 'Some social and psychological consequences of the longwall method of coal getting', *Human Relations*, 4: 3–38.

Vickers, G. (1983) *The Art of Judgement*. London: Harper and Row.

Whitehead, J. (1994) 'How do I improve the quality of my management?', *Management Learning*, 25: 137–53.

Whyte, W. (ed.) (1991) *Participatory Action Research*. London: Sage.

Yin, R. (1984) *Case Study Research: Design and Methods*. New York: Sage.

3.3

Emotion and Organizing

STEPHEN FINEMAN

Writers on organizations have been slow to incorporate emotions into their thinking. A scan of the indexes of mainstream textbooks on organizational behaviour and organizational theory reveals few, if any, entries under 'emotions' or 'feelings'. This itself is a clue to the historical status of emotion, and the framing of organizational studies. But the frame is now shifting to include emotion, offering exciting possibilities for interdisciplinary convergence and the theoretical and empirical insights that this brings. We can draw profitably from sociology, psychology, history, anthropology and philosophy.

The resonance of 'emotion' and 'feelings' in working is not hard to grasp. Literary accounts about work by writers such as Terkel (1975) and Wallraff (1985) are engaging for the precise sense of passion, distress, joy, or drudgery that they convey. For those who spend much of their time in organizations, emotion talk is often taken for granted: the gripes, the anger, the anxiety, the frustrations; the glee, the joys, the tedium; the embarrassments and the despair. These are part of the social creation and personal expression of work and organizational life. Specific work activities – making decisions, persuading, negotiating, counselling, selling, meeting, interpreting data, hiring, firing, fighting, resisting, surviving – are more than a set of robotic responses. They are felt, and shaped by feelings.

This chapter initially presents a historical context to the framing of emotion in organizations – where the main influences have been and how they have shaped our current conceptualizations. Ideas from academic psychology – both behavioural and clinical – are germane here; however, particular emphasis will be placed on the recent growth of sociologically inspired studies. With this backcloth in mind, specific areas are discussed where an emotion perspective illuminates current issues in organizational studies. These include the concept of the rational organizational actor, order and control in organizations, organizational culture, stress, and the 'marketing' of emotional performance. Finally, directions for the further study of organizational emotion are elaborated.

FINDING A PLACE FOR EMOTION

Academic psychology has been the traditional guardian of emotions. We can trace the first psychological theory of emotions in William James's paper, 'What is emotion'? published in 1884. James emphasized the importance of perception of an event, object or circumstance as a precursor to emotion. This process, he contended, activated changes to internal bodily activities. The feelings of these reactions are the emotional experience. James's formulation turned common sense on its head: we do not smile because we are happy, we are happy because we smile.

Since James's time the psychological conceptualization of emotion has developed in many different directions. Some still broadly favour a James-type rationale (e.g. Zajonc et al. 1989). Others emphasize the motivational properties of emotion (Leeper 1965), emotion as a specific personality trait (Spielberger 1966), or emotion as a sign of inadequate personal adaptation (Plutchik 1970). Furthermore, some theorists look to cognitive processes as sufficient explanations of things 'emotional', while others focus on the experiential or the unconscious (Strongman 1978).

Emotion as an individual or group construct has infiltrated the study of organizations in various ways, although it has only recently been taken as an important organizational topic in its own right (see Fineman 1993a). It is camouflaged somewhat by different terminologies – such as 'sentiment', 'mood', 'affect', 'valence' or 'morale'. For example, the social scientists studying Western Electric Company's Hawthorne plant in the 1930s spoke of workers' 'sentiments':

> the values residing in interhuman relations of the different groups within the organization. . . . Examples of what is meant here are the arguments employees give which center around the 'right to work', 'seniority', 'fairness', 'the living wage'. This logic, as its name implies, is deeply rooted in sentiment and feeling. (Roethlisberger and Dickson 1939: 564)

The effects of negative emotions on work behaviour were particularly stressed at this time (see review by Pekrun and Frese 1992). Only a few writers offered a different emotional tone – such as Munsterberg (1912) on joy at work and Hersey (1951) on zest. During the 1940s and 1950s the concept of morale began to be used by occupational and industrial psychologists, especially in military contexts. Morale has distinct emotional overtones: the feelings of attachment or belonging that a person has to a work group and his or her sense of commitment to the group task and spirit (Guba 1958).

In the 1950s, psychoanalytically inspired organizational researchers-cum-consultants were beginning to plough their own furrow from London's Tavistock Institute of Human Relations (Jaques 1951; Miller 1993). This work presented, and continues to present, a dramatic contrast to the consciously driven actor influenced by here-and-now emotions. Again, negative feelings predominate: organizational psychoanalysis posits a shifting sea of unconscious desires and anxieties which are expressed in the organization's processes of leadership, structuring and group functioning.

From the 1950s into the 1970s attention switched to the study of job attitudes. Attitudes are commonly presented as having an 'affective' component – a feeling, preference, or mood about a person, idea, event or object (Warr 1971; Fishbein and Ajzen 1975). Vroom (1964) and others have argued that such a predisposition, or valence, is a crucial feature of human motivation. One particular attitude – job satisfaction – absorbed much attention. Job satisfaction is a 'pleasurable or positive emotional state resulting from the appraisal of one's job or job experiences' (Locke 1976: 1300). Original job satisfaction research used questionnaires or interviews to measure overall reactions, such as how people felt about their job as a whole, using seven-point scales such as 'I love it' to 'I hate it' (Hoppock 1935). Later work tended to focus satisfaction on segments of the job, such as the physical working conditions, rewards, co-workers or job content (Brayfield and Rothe 1951; Smith et al. 1969). Job satisfaction, a fairly gross emotion concept, still occupies researchers. Recent work continues examining ways different work factors (e.g. goals, fringe benefits, work challenge) influence satisfaction and how work satisfaction levels may relate to performance on the job and satisfaction in the rest of life (Landy 1985; Iaffaldano and Muchinsky 1985; Judge and Watanabe 1993; O'Reilly 1991).

Since the 1970s the study of human behaviour has taken a strong swing to the cognitive. The positive, free-will aspects of human behaviour are emphasized, with cognition, the act of knowing, as the main unit of analysis. The focus on 'information', 'expectancies', 'demands', 'incentives', 'problem-solving', 'decision-making' and 'thinking' has tended to obscure emotion and feelings. In recent years cognitive theorists have tried to incorporate emotion into their models, most conservatively through the notion of 'hot' cognitions, or by adding the influence of specific emotions (such as fear, anxiety or anger) to models of the decision-making process (Donahue and Ramesh 1992). More radical perspectives reconceptualize cognition as inseparable from emotion (Stein and Trabasso 1992; Bloom and Beckwith 1989; Howard 1993; Ortony et al. 1988). The work of Park et al. (1986) is noteworthy in this respect. They explore the interplay of affect and cognition on performance appraisal in organizational settings, arguing that information-processing models ignore the influence of the mood of the rater (which can influence attention and recall) and specific feelings triggered by the ratee's appearance, such as dress, hairstyle, race, gender. For these authors affect and cognition interact in managerial action and judgement.

An additional facet of post 1970s psychological research has been greater attention to positive emotions. So Abramis (1987) speaks of fun at work, while Frese (1990) explores the mechanisms of pride. Isen and Baron (1991) and Argyle and Martin (1991) make a strong plea for organizations to engineer a specific sense of job enjoyment and happiness (which they distinguish from job satisfaction) by improving physical working conditions, remodelling organizational culture and enhancing communication. Mild shifts in positive affect or mood can, they contend, improve task perception and decision-making, face-to-face bargaining (Carnevale and Isen 1986), conflict resolution (Baron 1993), performance appraisal (Brief and Motowidlo 1986), absenteeism and labour turnover (George 1990; 1991). The benefits of the 'feel good' factor are echoed by Harrison (1987) and Peters and Austin (1985), who say that love, empathy, verve, zest and enthusiasm are the *sine qua non* of managerial success and organizational 'excellence'.

THE IDEOLOGICAL CONTEXTS OF EMOTION THEORY

The psychologizing of emotion, in its various guises, needs to be seen in its ideological contexts. The acceptability of emotion in the work setting is tied to the way work and labour are construed. For example, deeply rooted in Western (especially male) cultural beliefs about the expression of emotion is the belief that organizational order and manager/worker efficiency are matters of rational, that is non-emotional, activity (Lakoff and Johnson 1980; Putnam and Mumby 1993). Cool, clear strategic thinking is not to be sullied by messy feelings. Efficient thought and behaviour tame emotion. Accordingly, good organizations are places where feelings are managed, designed out, or removed. Or, put another way, behaviour control and cognitive processes should be the central substance of organizational theory.

Such a perspective fits comfortably with the machine-like organization where uniformity of behaviour is regarded as crucial to the profitable production of goods and services; a manifestation, of sorts, of Max Weber's early thinking on the 'ideal' bureaucracy, unsullied by 'love, hatred and all purely personal, irrational and emotional elements' (Gerth and Mills 1958: 216). Indeed, the tight control of work processes and emotions was manifest in the missions of turn-of-the-century management consultants and engineer/entrepreneurs (Kakar 1970; Jardin 1970; Morgan 1986). Human 'factors' were to serve, lubricate and extend the machineries of the factory, and no more. When open feelings threatened to disrupt the managerially desired flow of work, management would respond with even tighter controls – or bewilderment. For example, Frederick Winslow Taylor and Elton Mayo, influential in the design of industrial organizations in the 1920s and 1930s, were appalled at the strong hostility they witnessed amongst rank-and-file workers. And they were singularly unsuccessful in their initial attempts at curbing it (Stearns 1989). The continuing industrial disputes of the late twentieth century reveal that strong worker feelings – anger, disaffection, humiliation – can still breach organizational controls, although they are now channelled through more elaborate social conduits and transformations.

Stearns (1993) points out that the Victorian emotional culture saw intense feeling as a source of danger. The early male, middle class captains of industry, and the equally middle class, male organizational experts who shadowed them, were in part enacting their own social/emotional biographies. For example, we learn that Frederick Winslow Taylor, architect of the minutely regulated factory of the 1930s, had a youth preoccupied with order, control and parsimony, rooted clearly in the puritanical strictures of his family. This extended to fastidious analyses of his sporting activities, country walks, sleeping position, and even the organization of his dancing (e.g. Kakar 1970; Morgan 1986). It is perhaps no accident that his influential 'scientific management' is emotionally inert. Likewise, Henry Ford's highly conservative upbringing, again reflecting the era, probably assisted him viewing his extraordinary production line with quiet pride – rather than a likely source of harsh alienation for those who had to work on it (Jardin 1970; Zaleznik and Kets de Vries 1975).

In the 1960s and 1970s organization theory, reflecting a new liberalism in the West, took a significant step towards the democratization of work (Likert 1961; Argyris 1964). Interest turned to the 'psychological needs' of employees, from security to self-actualization (Maslow 1943; Herzberg 1966). The benefits, or otherwise, of employee participation in decision-making were a key topic in organizational and social psychology, and 'quality of working life' became an international movement in social science (Warr and Wall 1975; Lawler 1976). This set the agenda for current principles of human resource management, where human beings and their subjectivity are placed more firmly at the centre of the organizational stage. Yet, on close examination, it is clear that the people depicted are rather like the splintered characters in a computer game. As I have concluded elsewhere,

> the people presented are emotionally anorexic. They have 'dissatisfactions' and 'satisfactions', they may be 'alienated' or 'stressed', they will have 'preferences', 'attitudes' and 'interests'. Often these are noted as variable for managerial control. (Fineman 1993a: 9)

I will briefly elaborate two key strands of this viewpoint: job satisfaction and stress. Intuitively, job satisfaction connotes emotional processes or 'being' feelings such as of joy, enthusiasm, pleasure, pride, happiness, delight and fulfilment. But these have not been the focus of job satisfaction researchers. In the main, as already discussed, they have defined job satisfaction as a global outcome attitude towards work, or a job facet, measured on investigator-prescribed scales. Despite the voluminous material on job satisfaction, which proceeds like a juggernaut through job attitude research, it offers a poor insight into the essential emotionalities of working (Sandelands 1988; Pekrun and Frese 1992; Fineman 1994).

Stress can be criticized on similar grounds. It is a diffuse, non-specific, global negative state (Pekrun and Frese 1992; Selye 1956; 1976). In the 1960s and 1970s stress formulation was rooted firmly within the stimulus–response tradition of psychology. The individual's level of stress could, was the contention, be measured in relation to specific, predefined, life events or 'stressors' (Dohrenwend and Dohrenwend 1974; Rabkin and Struening 1976), where stress indices included self-reports of behaviour, anxiety and physical health. Since that period social psychological renditions of stress are quarrelled over, but the models presented have very similar elements: objective stressor, self-reported stress, physical symptoms, individual/social moderators (e.g. Cooper 1991).

It is clear that many emotions do characterize the experience of stress, such as anger, anxiety, sadness, despair, depression and disappointment. Stressed people undoubtedly *feel* their distress or illness. Significantly, some writers (e.g. Lazarus 1993) are now arguing for a *rapprochement* between theories of emotion and those of stress. Lazarus's central point is that the stress responses should be seen in terms of a number of different emotional states, each of which is related to particular ways that individuals appraise and cope with their circumstances. Such an approach asserts a separation between appraisal, the cognitive act, and emotion – a point to which we shall return.

EMOTIONALITY: ISSUES OF DEFINITION AND FORM

The backcloth to emotion so far presented covers various uses and variations of the concept in work and organizational life. How can emotion best be conceptualized and refined for understanding organizational processes? The field is confusing, and different terms are used interchangeably. However, there are some important distinctions that can be made (see Oakley 1993; Hochschild 1983; Frijda et al. 1991; Ratner 1989). The first relates to *feelings*. A feeling is essentially the subjective experience – which is at the heart of most definitions of emotion. To feel means we are aware 'in' ourselves of some bodily state, perturbation, or more diffuse psychological change. Some feelings can be in part determined by early life experiences and expectations – sources of which we may be unaware.

Next, *emotions* are the personal displays of *affected*, or 'moved', 'agitated' states – such as of joy, love, fear, anger, sadness, shame, embarrassment. They acquire their meaning, their social currency, from the cultural setting – national, local and organizational (Ratner 1989; Lutz and White 1986; Fineman 1993a). While we may be physiologically 'wired' in ways that permit emotional (and feeling) processes, the arousal requires the use of culturally shared communicative signs – body movements, facial expressions, cognitive labels, language nuances – to achieve its understanding, social significance and meaning (Ekman 1985; Sugrue 1982).

Emotion episodes and private feeling do not always correspond. One can 'be' angry without feeling angry. Indeed, an actor's anger outburst might *feel* to him/her as fairly neutral, pleasurable or even exciting. Given the performance element of emotions, they can be seen to fulfil a strategic purpose in interpersonal relations: a display of anger to bring out a change; a look of despair to attract attention. This requires some level of dramatic skill (Harré 1986; Gallois 1993; Hopfl and Linstead 1993; Ekman 1984; Mangham and Overington 1987).

Emotions are also situational, where particular displays of emotion are attached to specific social encounters: there may be an appropriate emotion to show when 'caught by a police officer for speeding', or when 'at a party'. The emotion norms may be even more prototypical and role-bound, such as for 'mother', 'father', 'boss', 'subordinate', 'man' or 'woman' (Zurcher 1982; Kemper 1981; Geertz 1973; Shott 1979; Hearn 1993; Parkin 1993; Hochschild 1975; 1990). Implicit and explicit emotion rules are moulded and transmitted in our ethnic groups, families, religions and workplaces, bolstered by the extensive influence of the media (Denzin 1990; Fineman 1993a). The messages often have a double imperative of the sort: 'these are the emotions you ought to be showing; these are the feelings you should be feeling.' Emotion 'work' is entailed in ensuring that private feelings are suppressed or re-presented to achieve the socially acceptable emotional face. Emotional 'labour' is the buying of an employee's emotional demeanour; the individual is being paid to 'look nice', smile, be caring, be polite (Hochschild 1975; 1990; 1993; Wharton 1993).

Feelings and emotions are processes which are the quintessence of humanness, social functioning and social order. Feelings connect us with our realities; they provide an experiential, personal readout on how we are doing, where we 'are', what we want, what we might do next. In this sense most feelings are mobile; we interact with them, work them over. We have feelings about our feelings, guided by existing social scripts or stocks of knowledge, e.g. 'how should I really feel in these circumstances?', 'need I feel so upset by this?' (Rosenberg 1990; Fischer and Frijda 1992). We may sometimes 'fall victim' to our feelings, especially when they are of the consuming, passionate sort such as hate or love. Or we may get stuck in feeling traps, a recursiveness such as being anxious about being anxious (Scheff 1990). Feelings are Janus faced, both a necessary part of personal perception and something of which to be wary (Franks and Gecas 1992).

Feelings of Work

Do we know what doing work *feels* like? As earlier suggested, the research in this area has a distal quality, remote from the self-referentiality of feelings that essentially constitute the doing of work, management, or organizing. Some writers argue that there are certain sorts of feelings that are flow-related experiences, absorbing the self and free from self-judgements of the sort: 'can I do this job?', 'how well am I doing?' (Czikszent-mihalyi 1977; Frese et al. 1991). The activity is the work and the work is the activity; people are 'lost' in their work. The feelings are *of* me, but not *about* me. Feelings of work are a form of acquaintance knowledge not typically found in social science. It refers to the sense of goodness, tedium, irritation, gloom, excitement, fear or surge that working evokes, and the kind of adaptations and shifts that people make as a result of such feelings. There is a serenade of motions that can be intrinsically pleasurable to people in aesthetic occupations, such as dancing, designing, decorating, painting and pottery (Sandelands and Buckner 1989; Frese 1990). Surgeons, computer programmers, mathematicians are reputed to report similar feelings of deep involvement.

A conundrum in specifying and accounting for work feelings is whether we can 'know' them somehow free from the implicit values of culture or linguistic form. This is both a methodological and a philosophical puzzle. The very reporting of one's feelings in words, or other symbols, offers a translation of the 'raw' experience. And talk about feelings mirrors the value and language system to which the individual belongs. The Chinese, for example, will talk far less than Americans about emotions, focusing more on the body (Lutz and White 1986). But a question

remains as to whether experiencing the experience in the first place requires some learned symbolic form, some language in the head, to make even the most inchoate sensation worthy of personal attention (Bedford 1986; Oakley 1993).

THE MYTH OF THE RATIONAL ORGANIZATION ACTOR?

Rational assumptions on human conduct continue to shape a whole range of organizational/management issues, from advice books on decision-making (Leigh 1993; Magee 1991) and optimum incentive and reward systems (Friedman 1990) to the 'best' leadership styles (Rabey 1994). Rationality is thought of as the unique property of human beings to be able to make decisions which will maximize their gains in relation to specific goals. They will do this by careful search and assessment of information, and then adopt an optimum means to achieve their goals. Rationality is essentially a thinking, cognitive, process of cool calculation. Impulsive, emotional, desiring qualities are antithetical to rationality and cognition, a duality rooted deeply in traditional Western philosophy and science (Franks and Gecas 1992; Putnam and Mumby 1993). But as our discussion so far implies, emotionality has been gaining pace, and place, in organizational analysis. So can we still talk meaningfully of the rational organizational actor?

The emotion challenge to rationality comes in three fairly distinct forms: (i) that emotions will *interfere* with rationality; (ii) that emotional processes can *serve* rationality; and more radically, (iii) that emotions and cognitions are inextricably *entwined*, that rationality is a myth. An articulation of these three positions reveals both the breadth of the controversy on where emotions should be best positioned in organizational studies, and the kind of understandings that different perspectives provide.

Emotions Interfere with Rationality

A number of writers have pointed out that people at work can fail to think 'straight' when feeling threatened (Argyris 1990). They may be trapped in escalating commitment to the wrong course of action, pouring more and more resources into defending a lost cause, such as the US involvement in the Vietnam War (Schwenk 1986; Staw 1981). Such 'irrational' responses may be explained by people's needs to justify their previous decisions and to appear consistent in their behaviour (Staw and Ross 1987). Essentially these are psychologically defensive reactions, a phenomenon of special interest to clinical organizational analysts, especially followers of traditional Freudian personality theory (Diamond 1993; de Board 1978; Miller 1993; Kets de Vries l991a; Schwartz 1990). Their argument runs as follows.

Organizational actors fail to act rationally because what they see is not necessarily a veridical reading of what is 'there'. It is distorted by the actors' imported needs and desires, especially unconscious fears. Anxiety, envy, shame and guilt can shape organizational interactions and structures in ways of which participants are unaware. Such emotionalized thinking twists reality, confuses the appraisal of options, and undermines organizational effectiveness and health. Because of this, negative feelings are suspect and to be handled with care. Eliot Jaques, a psychoanalytic writer on organizations, counsels chief executives to express feelings only 'within the specified limits', and preferably 'outside the company' (1989: 41). The feelings should be 'treated' along the lines that a psychoanalyst would treat an individual patient. People in work organizations place each other in roles and relationships which correspond exactly to the unconscious positioning of 'objects' in adult psychoanalysis (Hinshelwood 1987).

The organization is placed on the couch, so to speak (Diamond and Allcorn 1985; Hirschhorn 1988). Kets de Vries (1991b) speaks of decoding the emotional components of the 'organizational text' through a historical analysis of aspirations, fears, and goals. Special attention is paid to interpretation of transference – where attitudes developed early in life are repeated in the present. So, for example, a person may react to an autocratic boss with the negative feelings previously experienced for an autocratic parent or teacher. The feelings for these past characters are 'transferred' to the boss, and acted out accordingly (Baum 1991).

Evidence of the operation of unconscious emotional processes is taken from a broad range of organizational behaviours – individual and group. While such behaviours have an internal rationality, in the sense that they serve actors' anxieties and fears, they can obstruct the organizational rationality of optimizing task behaviour and achieving organizational goals. Kets de Vries and Miller (1984; 1987) and Lapierre (1991) explore leadership. They suggest that there are unconscious fantasies underlying the actions of many organizational leaders – such as an ever-lurking threat, the need to be in control, and the need to be centre-stage. The centre-stageness can be supported by followers' needs and anxieties. A leader's vision of the problems with the organization awakens an awareness in the follower of his or her personal needs or problems. As the connection between the two tightens, the leader's presence, influence and opinions are progressively accepted without question. In this manner the follower's anxieties can be transferred to the leader (Kets de Vries 1990; Bryman 1992). Such is the relational basis of charismatic leadership, which flourishes in stressful times (House 1977).

Executives will wish to gratify these 'neurotic' desires through their management styles. Kets de Vries and Miller (1984; 1991) muster case studies which purport to show that top executives' fears and fantasies are reflected in the emotional tone and behaviour of the whole organization. Paranoid, depressive, or schizoid executives create respectively suspicious, pessimistic or bewildered employees. This rationale is most persuasive when applied to small, centrally controlled organizations with a dominant chief executive (Miller and Toulouse 1986). It should be borne in mind that cause–effect links in such analyses (as indeed in many psychodynamic interpretations) are open to question. The executives' anxiety could be a response to their work groups' inability to cope. Similarly with authoritarians. Leaders with 'authoritarian' personalities, according to Freudian conceptualization (Adorno et al. 1950), are the products of status-anxious parents who enforce harsh disciplinarian rules on their offspring, creating fear of failure, hostility and anxiety. When repressed from consciousness these feelings re-emerge as strongly conservative, aggressive behaviours. Industrial and military leaders marked with authoritarianism are noted for their irrational behaviour – blindness to warning signals, inability to admit their own mistakes, and stifling work style (Dixon 1976; Hosking and Morley 1991; Jackall 1988).

Psychodynamics, Politics and Work Group Emotions

Political behaviour in organizations is the strategic mobilization of self-interest – a complex web of individual interpretations and agendas (Lawler and Bacharach 1983; Pfeffer 1978). Politics may seem anything but rational in terms of the *manifest* goals and purposes of an organization. People will 'buy' friends, divide enemies, nurture protective coalitions, diminish another's success (Zaleznik 1970; Eagle and Newton 1981). A realist interpretation of such behaviours is that they represent what organizations essentially are about, an inevitable feature of organizing. A psychoanalytic perspective is different. Politics stem from individuals' unconscious fears concerning their identity, security and self-worth. They generally sap the organization's productive energy by consolidating irrationality, but they are not immutable.

Politics, as expressed in the irrationalities of work group behaviour, have been put under the psychoanalytic microscope. Working in groups can pose a basic threat to personal identity as well as being a source of identity (Winnicott 1965; Rycroft 1968). It can raise feelings of vulnerability, embarrassment, and fear corresponding to the tensions and dramas of early family life (Weinberg and Mauksch 1991). Wilfred Bion (1959) has identified three distinct emotional, unspoken, 'basic assumptions' of ingroup activity: dependency, pairing, fight/flight. Group processes are constantly changing the dominance of one emotional state over another as feelings of security, insecurity and threats to identity ebb and flow. The emotional agendas can, at the least, deflect the group from its task; at worst they can swamp the group. Bion seeks to improve the work effectiveness and rationality of the group by assisting it to increase its psychoanalytic insight – a mark of the 'sophisticated' group. Diamond and Allcorn (1987) take a similar tack, aiming to create an 'intentional work group' which has skills of 'double-loop learning' – the ability to re-examine the assumptions by which it operates (after Argyris 1990).

Under shared threat, such as retrenchment, management cutbacks, or leadership changes, the group as a whole may react in unison with regressive, child-like behaviours: for example, by refusing to cooperate with management, becoming aggressive, or being excessively dependent on a hero figure as a potential 'saviour' (Diamond and Allcorn 1987). Such reactions feel safe because that is exactly the kind of protection they once afforded in early life. But, in psychoanalytic terms, excessive reliance on these defences insulates the group from the colder realities that it will need to face up to if it is to preserve its functional integrity, if not very survival, in the organization.

Social Defences as Institutionalized Irrationality

Irrationality can become institutionalized in organizations. Unconsciously motivated feelings and primitive anxieties are collectively transferred and dramatized as systems of 'social defences' in the design and operation of work routines and structures (Hinshelwood 1987; Jaques 1951). Menzies-Lythe's (1988; 1991) work in a London teaching hospital offers a powerful illustration of social defences in operation. Menzies-Lythe approached the alarming waste of good students in the hospital as if they were presenting symptoms. Following Melanie Klein's (1959) thoughts on ego defences, she observed that work routines protected the student nurses from the anxiety of the work itself:

> Their work involves carrying out tasks which, by ordinary standards, are distasteful, disgusting and frightening. Intimate physical contact with patients arouses strong libidinal and erotic wishes and impulses which may be difficult to control. The work situation arouses very strong and mixed feelings in the nurse: pity, compassion and love; guilt and anxiety; hatred and resentment of patients who arouse these strong feelings; envy of the care given to the patient. (Menzies-Lythe 1988: 46)

The way work was organized ensured non-feeling, numbed, mechanical caring – minimal emotional contact with the patients. Procedures included keeping the nurse and patient apart as far as possible through rotas and specific tasks on a large number of patients; the depersonalization of patients, who were known by their bed number or disease type; a rhetoric of coping and detachment, e.g. 'a good nurse doesn't get too involved and doesn't mind moving'; checks and counterchecks to dissipate the burden of anxiety about a final decision on a patient; and rituals such as precise task lists, regularly repeated, which induced thoughtlessness and helped nurses avoid anxiety. Nurses would regularly wake patients to give them drugs, even when it was better for patient care to let them sleep. Such defences helped evade anxiety – but it froze coping. And it was for this reason that some nurses left. They found the routines too restrictive, denying them the close patient contact that they desired for their professional development and personal satisfaction.

Social defences have been demonstrated by a number of psychodynamic organizational researchers. Jaques's (1951) early study of factory communication showed how sub-groups interacted, but did not communicate. Suspicion, hostility and guilt prevailed across management and workers, splits based on primitive defences.

In screening people from anxiety, social defences can interfere with activities or precautions which avert accidents or disasters. Indeed, they can increase the very probability of an accident happening. To act safely requires a sense of vulnerability to injury. If this vulnerability is projected elsewhere – 'the system will handle it', 'it's a foolproof machine', 'it's the safety officer's job' – the precautionary anxiety can no longer play its self-alerting role (Hirschhorn and Young 1991). This is one explanation why eminently rational security notices of the sort 'what to do in case of an emergency' often have such little impact. The fatal explosion of the American space shuttle *Challenger* in 1986 has been interpreted along these lines by Schwartz (1988) and Hirschhorn (1988). Far from being a bit of technological misfortune, the failure can be attributed to NASA officials mythologizing the glory and invulnerability of the machine they had created. This made psychodynamic sense given the overwhelming technical complexities and political pressures of a launch at that time, but the wishful thinking obscured warning signs that the shuttle's booster seals might fail.

The psychoanalytic writers cited in this section offer a picture of an objective, rational organizational world that is obfuscated by the unwitting defensive reactions of anxious, emotional actors. Uprooting the 'demon of irrationality' (Gay 1988: xvii) is the interventionist's task. Examples of 'healthy', rational, organizations are hard to spot in this literature, which tends to focus on the diseased 'patient'. And indeed, there are some despairing critics within the genre who point to (a) a failure of their professional community to free organizations from social defence routines, and (b) the inadequacy of traditional, clinical, psychoanalysis when applied to organizational outcomes and results. Psychoanalysis claims to transform and heal through its *process*; organizational performance indicators are at best a very rough guide to psychological health. The couch is, perhaps, a little at sea (Gould 1991; Menzies-Lythe 1991).

Emotions Serve Rationality

People at work do not always follow rationally 'optimal' processes or paths in their own decisions, or conform to managerially defined rationalities. Relevant information can be missed in making decisions. Hunches, acts of faith, gut feelings, idiosyncratic preferences unlock a problem or change the course of events. A rational actor has to contend with the information to hand. And because there are simply too many possible alternatives for a person to evaluate, rationality must be 'subjective' and 'bounded' (Simon 1957). We thus move to a model of sufficing rationality. The actor has to make do and, in making do, emotions will show the way. The actor is not the victim of his or her feelings. On the contrary, without emotions even an approximation to rationality could not be achieved.

Emotions and feelings are, according to this perspective, necessary appendages to reason (Mumby and Putnam 1992). Cognitions will follow their own paths, but emotions stop them getting lost. Particular emotions can serve rationality in particular ways. So Frank (1993) and Hirshleifer (1993) suggest that negative emotions, such as anger, serve to ensure the credibility of threats, while love and affection ensure the credibility of promises to cooperate. Emotions block actions that are irrational in a narrow time frame, but are rational when more distant consequences are considered. Emotions allow us to act in ways compatible with our long-term interests.

Artificial intelligence experiments show that emotion is necessary for task-oriented cognition – to make judgements about what is relevant or irrelevant for problem solution (Dennett 1978; de Sousa 1987). It allows us to decide what is worth thinking about, and what is relevant and irrelevant once we start thinking. Franks and Gecas relate the following tale to make the point:

> when a computerized robot was put into a wagon with a bomb and told to figure out what to do before the bomb exploded at a prescribed time, it sat paralyzed from the preliminary stage of figuring out whether the distance between the wagon and China and the price of tea in New York were relevant to the problem. (1992: 10)

Or, as Minsky (1986) suggests, the question is not whether intelligent machines can have any emotions, but whether machines can be intelligent without emotions.

Emotions and Rationality Entwine

The central tenet of this position is that rational self-interest is thoroughly imbued with emotion. The two cannot be separated and the weighing of means and ends is overwhelmingly emotional. Many rational organizational strategies are pursued on highly emotional grounds, and much of what we describe as rational is in fact emotional (Kemper 1993; de Sousa 1987). We have feelings about what we want, and what we want is infused with feelings; and that is intrinsic, not residual, to individual, interpersonal and group functioning (Smith and Berg 1987a; 1987b). In further advancing this argument, some writers insist that emotion cannot exist outside the thought/symbolic processes of language, so the cognitive/affective distinction cannot be sustained (e.g. Harré 1986; Gallois 1993; Sarbin 1986; Abu-Lughod and Lutz 1990).

Once the emotion/cognition duality is broken down in this manner, the rational actor cannot exist. The setting of goals, the selection and use of information, and the benefits gained, involve myriad emotionalized/feeling adjustments, 'readings' and personal judgement calls. The whole process may be driven by some overriding emotion: anger with a competitor pushes a retaliatory executive to considerably over-stretch his department, regardless of consequences; fear of upsetting a powerful supplies director leads a manager to reject a considerably cheaper outside rate for some components.

In sum, the combined assault on rationality from the three perspectives leaves us with a compelling case that emotions matter a great deal in organizational behaviour, and that rationality is, at the least, a problematic concept. As researchers of emotion have tended to Balkanize into disciplinary pockets, cross-fertilization of perspectives has been very slight (Kemper 1990). So we find that the recent surge in sociological interest in emotions, which underpins the 'entwinement' hypothesis on rationality, rarely asks the historical questions that the psychoanalysts raise. The latter may be criticized for promulgating a psychology about 'windowless encapsulated individuals' (Elias 1978), but the former rarely acknowledge that individuals carry a personal past which can exert its own special emphasis on the social meaning-making process. Separating the dancer from the dance may well be extremely short-sighted (Sarbin 1986; Franks and Gecas 1992); separating the dancer from past dances could be a sin of equivalent order.

EMOTIONS AND ORGANIZATIONAL ORDER

The way social order is maintained in organizations has been characterized as a feat of social construction. Actors interpret their situations and seek to 'make sense' through negotiating meanings, some temporary, some less so, with their fellow workers (Berger and Luckmann 1966; Weick 1979). This is regarded as a cognitive process, conducted by thinking, meaning-seeking souls who invent and invoke social rules to help them on their way. Weick (1993) recently refines these cognitive dynamics to focus on the 'commitments' between actors which bind particular interpretations and organizational policies. But Weick does not reveal what makes a commitment a commitment, or where the different strengths of commitment come from or feel like – such as being driven by fear, or by loyalty, pride or affection. Different commitments reflect different emotional contracts – with others and with self – and this determines the commitments' potency. Cognitive processes alone are an insufficient explanation of organizational order (Pfeffer 1982).

Certain emotions are central to the nature of organizational order and control, providing the springs to self-regulation that social enterprises require to function. The ability to feel shame, embarrassment or guilt is pivotal in this respect. As Wentworth and Ryan note, such emotions 'put the sensed *imperative* into social duties, the *ought* into morality, the *feeling* into respect, the *sting* into conscience, the *deference* necessary for social hierarchies' (1992: 38). And, arguably, displaying such emotions without feeling them is one route to moral bankruptcy and organizational decay (Scheff 1988; 1990; Shott 1979; Oakley 1993). These emotions are nurtured in the processes of socialization in a nation's culture, and fine-tuned in specific work organizations. They are, broadly speaking, emotions which concern how we think others are seeing us, and how our performances are judged. Cooley (1922) spoke appealingly of the 'looking glass self', suggesting that people routinely monitor their presentation of self: positive feelings lead to pride, negative feelings lead to embarrassment. While embarrassment may be intrinsic to certain social orders, so too is the taboo on its outward expression – especially in Western societies where it is seen to reflect social incompetence (Goffman 1967; Harrington 1992).

Anticipation of embarrassment can, therefore, ensure that behaviour in organizations holds to certain normative codes such as deference patterns to superiors, views not to express in particular settings, confidences not to break, dress codes, modes of speech, ways to deal with 'outsiders' or customers. Furthermore, when embarrassment *is* felt people will attempt to repress or deny the feeling to prevent it leaking into emotional display. This can grow to monomaniac proportions in some institutions, such as the British government system. Deep within unwritten rules of British party politics is the expectation that a party, especially the ruling one, should avoid public embarrassment at all costs (Flam 1990). Consequently an elaborate public relations machinery and language are used to filter, smooth over, or redefine potential or actual embarrassing moments. In the commercial world it not uncommon for companies to relish a competitor's discomfort as it struggles to disguise an embarrassing revelation on 'unorthodox conduct'.

The social codes of shame and guilt are more deeply rooted than embarrassment. They are tied intimately to moral conduct. If people are unable to anticipate shame or guilt before they act in particular ways, then moral codes are rendered invalid (Callahan 1988). The field of 'business ethics' (e.g. Walton 1988) rests on the assumption that moral behaviour is important, but problematic, for the organizational actor. Business ethics research focuses on an important feature of organizational behaviour, but attention to the emotional underpinnings is minimal, leaving the field in an affective vacuum.

Typically, the literature portrays ethical issues as practical decision problems with a 'bite' – because of the harm that can accrue to innocent others. Decisions may involve lying, deceit, fraud, evasion or negligence – disapproved of in many cultures. But ethical monitoring and control go beyond just the pragmatics of harm. They reach into the emotional springs that get people thinking 'harmfully' in the first place.

There is evidence that corporations develop values that, in effect, determine their own moralities. Corporate ideology replaces wider moral codes, and it is held in place by fear of unemployment, demotion, non-promotion, humiliation, and/or appeals to loyalty or achievement (Flam 1993; Smith 1990; Jackall 1988). As Kunda (1992) notes of a high technology company, its employees lack the foundations of a moral framework that enables them to evaluate corporate activities. The social consequences of the company's technology are glossed over by words like 'innovation', 'productivity', and 'profit', 'with their connotations of inevitability and rightness'. Similarly, Jackall reports a manager's pithy assertion on his own organization:

> What is right in the corporation is not what's right in a man's home or in his church. What is right in the corporation is what the guy above wants from you. That's what morality is in the corporation. (1988: 109)

Shame is still a possible feeling in this form of corporate morality, but shame linked to the organization's own 'moral', committed, community – in isolation, or opposition, to the broader community in which it exists (Schwartz 1990). It is an organizational representation of Stanley Milgram's (1974) experimental demonstration of the extraordinary power of locally contrived rules and regulations to subvert people's normal moral standards. Many of Milgram's subjects felt more anxious about resisting the experimenter's authoritative exhortations to injure a fellow human being (and they believed they actually did) than about not following their own feelings of repulsion at this act. In this manner organizational actors can be relatively impervious to wider social censure: on, say, marketing health damaging products to a country which has weak public health controls; exploiting a poorly organized workforce; or creating significant environmental damage. The shameful employee is the one who breaks the organization's normative codes, as is evidenced in the decisive way that whistleblowers are sidelined and ejected from the corporation (Miceli and Near 1991; Jackall 1988).

EMOTIONALIZING ORGANIZATIONAL CULTURE

Organizational culture is a major carrier of social order. Organizational cultures and subcultures bond people emotionally, while also defining the nature, form and legitimacy of their emotionality. And cultures are susceptible to manipulation (Collins 1990; Pfeffer 1982; Fineman 1993a; Aldrich 1992).

Skilled emotion managers, often charismatic chief executives or consultants, have mobilized employee feelings by exhortation. So consultant Tom Peters urges managers to 'be enthralled by the product', and 'to laugh, cry and smile' to be effective (1989: 39–41). In a high technology company, top managers speak of 'trying to make it fun to work here, make it challenging and exciting, make you feel you can make important contributions' (Kunda 1992: 65). The evocation of feelings of loyalty, 'family', and shared fate can stir primitive bonding when the drama is well scripted and the props appropriate – as was the performance of Jan Carlzon, president of Sweden's domestic airline. He stood on a tall ladder in a huge aircraft hanger, surrounded by his assembled workforce, ingenuously placing the organization's fate in their 'valued' hands (Carlzon 1987). Other companies, known for their 'strong' cultures, inspire new recruits and reinvigorate old ones through a careful social programme to keep alive the managerial vision of collective feelings and purpose. Many such events blur the division between work and non-work (Van Maanen 1986; Van Maanen and Kunda 1989; Peven 1968). A marketing director of a direct-sales perfumery describes her reactions to such indoctrination:

> They ended the presentation with the words, 'Tomorrow will be the same as today unless you do something about it now! Can you afford not to?' It was that that ensnared me into the positive thinker's nirvana. For a nominal fee I was soon on the road to building my dream and, whether I had a dream or not, I was soon to acquire one. . . . Parisienne provided me with an ideal opportunity to build my own business with no financial risk (and) to feel valued, recognized and rewarded.

> Once caught on the roundabout, many people become so involved that their whole life revolves around their team. Their friends are the people they recruit. Their social life revolves around company meetings. These are always fun events – bright lights, loud music, razzamataz. For many people whose work life is routine, perhaps mundane, working in such an atmosphere of glitz becomes addictive. (Hopfl and Linstead 1993: 82–3)

The emotional medicine can be potent. Seidenberg (1975) reports how IBM employees have shown more pride at seeing the company flag on the corporate offices than seeing their national flag. With such strong programming there is little room for doubters or the disaffected. If they cannot sincerely fall into line they must feign enthusiasm, or leave.

Culturalizing Stress

The managerial prerogative over emotionality can also extend to determining the organizational place for negative feelings, especially those associated with stress. Stress has not normally been addressed as an organizational cultural phenomenon, although its psychological processes have been well documented (e.g. Selye 1956; Cooper 1991; Cooper and Payne 1978; Cox et al. 1981).

Stress has become extraordinarily diffused and popularized over the last decade or so. The discourse on 'stress the disease' and its 'control' has been co-opted by managers, along with a range of health-care professionals (Giddens 1991; Murphy 1984; Newton 1989). It would be rare indeed to find a student of management who has not been exposed to a textbook rendition on the personal and organizational dangers of excessive stress, despite the evidence that suggests some stress ('eustress') can have positive, energizing qualities (Selye 1956). Indeed, stress has acquired something of the status of a cultural symbol in organizations, representing the plight of individuals who are at once damaged by the work/organization and responsible for their own predicament (Barley and Knight 1992; Abbott 1990; Newton et al. 1995). This point is nicely captured by Allinson et al.'s view of why stress counselling is needed in the workplace:

> Many employees are grimly beginning to acknowledge the fact that the stability (in the sense of freedom from constant change) is a thing of the past, but this in itself is not helping them to cope any better. (1989: 385–6)

Company-based stress management programmes are fast expanding (Murphy 1987; 1988). The initial seduction lies in their compatibility with a 'caring' management style, where feelings *are* the concern of 'enlightened employers'. The presenting rhetoric is of the sort: 'We all get stress feelings from time to time, which can be an unhappy state of affairs. It is understandable, and help is at hand to assist you coping.' Most companies emphasize the liability of stress: a highly stressed, or burned out, worker is unreliable, one of the 'walking wounded' (Kunda 1992). In this way, stress is a dangerous personal weakness. Supervisors are trained to spot the symptoms in their staff and to intervene.

Managerial self-interest is not far from the surface in such interventions. Matteson and Ivancevich proclaim that the issue of labour costs is a 'compelling' reason for stress management courses, 'viewed from virtually any perspective' (1982: 770). A reduction of labour costs, turnover, sickness, and absence, and an increase in productivity, are the promises (Barley and Knight 1992; Allinson et al. 1989). Individualizing stress in this manner circumvents a company's responsibility for dealing more structurally with stress. It is the individual's coping that has to improve. But the partiality of this position can be contested, reinforcing the view that stress can be culturally embedded and politically driven. For example, Neale et al. (1982) compared management and union perspectives on stress, noting union rejection of the view that workers needed to learn to change their perceptions of job pressures to reduce stress (an axiom of cognitive appraisal theories of stress). On the contrary, argued the union, more relaxed styles would follow if demands and deadlines, job-loss threats and speed-ups were diminished to a more acceptable level.

Stress rhetorics can become a vocabulary for organizing, penetrating a major part of the cultural space of an organization or occupation. In the semi-professions, such as nursing and social work, it can build solidarity. Barley and Knight (1992) suggest that an 'interpretive contagion' occurs in these settings. The occupational social network sanctions stress talk because it represents a shared feeling about over-demanding work and excessive pressures. Consequently, the support community does not ameliorate stress as advocated in traditional stress research. It heightens it, at least presentationally. Sometimes contagion will be indirect, but signalling a tacit acceptability of stress. For example, in a study of a social work agency Fineman (1985) observed that workers would rarely admit their stresses to one another, and hardly ever to their supervisors – whom they believed would disapprove of such 'weakness' and use it against them. But non-verbal, public, expressions of stress were rampant: harassed looks, sighs, tense movements, shouting and smoking. 'Going sick' was prevalent and hardly ever questioned by management. Privately, staff acknowledged that more often than not, such sickness meant stress.

RIGIDIFYING EMOTIONAL ENACTMENTS

Corporately prescribed emotions can be fine-tuned. The checkout clerk at a supermarket is instructed that 'a friendly smile is a must', or is rewarded with a gift ranging from $25 to a new car if 'caught' being friendly to mystery shoppers (Czepiel et al. 1985; Rafaeli and Sutton 1987; 1989). McDonald's 'Hamburger University' instructs its managers to ensure that 'all-American' traits are displayed by its counter staff: 'sincerity, enthusiasm, confidence and a sense of humor' (Boas and Chain 1976). And Walt Disney World advises its new employees about the way they must appear:

> First we *practice a friendly smile* at all times with our guests and among ourselves. Second, we use friendly courteous phrases. 'May I help you' . . . 'Thank you' . . . 'Have a nice day' . . . 'Enjoy the rest of your stay', and many others are all part of our working vocabulary. (Walt Disney Productions 1982: 6)

Interactive style is stripped of its usual improvization. Affective demeanour, precise words, and sometimes physical posture, are scripted for short bursts of friendliness or courtesy. Some parts of the insurance sales business have developed such programming with awesome precision so that 'positive mental attitude' (PMA) can be exuded by its sales agents (Leidner 1991). 'Negative thinking' is wiped out with scripts for all occasions; radiated enthusiasm and an ever-present smile is *de rigueur*. Leidner describes an insurance company where it is reputed that even non-English-speaking agents in the USA can perform the scripts. They learn them phonetically.

Emotion is taken as a resource that a company needs to get the job done, what Mills (1956) calls the 'personality market'. There have been behaviouristic studies which relate emotional demeanour to work performance, such as in nurses (Ostner and Beck-Gernsheim 1979), cocktail waitresses who get better tips (Tidd and Lockard 1978), conmen (Sutherland 1937) and poker players (Hayano 1982). Women who have recently become prostitutes are preferred by clients for their emotional openness; long-term prostitutes display emotions more superficially (Girtler 1985). Recent work by Rafaeli and Sutton (1987; 1989) and Rafaeli (1989) continues this tradition, examining the emotions workers convey in order to satisfy role and performance expectation. In a study of supermarket cashiers the researchers measured eye contact, smiling, thanking, pleasantness and attending as 'expressed positive emotions' and discovered, perhaps unsurprisingly, that the busier the cashier, the fewer the positive emotions. They also found that sex of supermarket clerks, their form of dress and the presence of other clerks or customers, influenced the display of positive emotion.

The segmentation of emotional display, as exemplified in these studies, is aimed at managerial and productivity concerns. The inquiries fail to engage significantly with private feelings or the social/negotiative subtleties of workplace emotion. Hochschild's (1983) seminal depth study of flight attendants was rather different in orientation. She identified 'feeling rules' in an American airline's recruitment and training systems. Flight attendants' grooming and personal attitudes had to be in accord with such rules. Encounters with customers had to be met with warmth and smiles. And the smiles were to be 'inside-out' ones – really felt and meant. The turmoil of passenger service, the time pressures, the spillages, the provocative customers, the angry customers, the sexualized remarks, all had to be received with understanding and a smile.

For some this was hard work, *emotional labour*. They strove through 'deep acting' to take the company's message to heart and to 'really feel' what they were presenting. They became emotionally encapsulated in their job role, and some reported confusion about their self-image and sexuality. Others took the job to be all about acting, or face work (Goffman 1959); they resisted the corporation's attempts at deeper programming. So the smile, the laughter, the sympathy, would be switched on and off as and when necessary. The act, though, could break down under pressure when feelings of anger, irritation or rebellion could surface. A key incident illustrates:

> A young businessman said to a flight attendant, 'Why aren't you smiling?' She put her tray back on the food cart and said, 'I'll tell you what. You smile first, then I'll smile.' The businessman smiled at her. 'Good,' she replied. 'Now freeze and hold that for fifteen hours'. (Hochschild 1983: 127)

The act can go stale, a sentiment amplified by another flight attendant in a British study:

> You try saying 'hello' to 300 people and sound as though you mean it towards the end. Most of us make a game of it. Someone – probably a manager – said 'This business is all about interpersonal transactions.' He was wrong. It's all about bullshit. If life is a cabaret, this is a bloody circus. (Hopfl 1991: 5–6)

Hochschild's research points up the psychological damage of a high degree of emotional labour – when feeling rules, coupled with hierarchical surveillance, become oppressive. Because of this, the very existence of emotional labour has been regarded as pernicious, and some argue for a radical reformulation of organizing where implicit feeling rules prevail, based on mutual relatedness (Mumby and Putnam 1992). While this may be a laudable goal, the stereotyping of emotional labour tends to overstate its negativity. The 'play' or 'drama' between server and served can be mutually rewarding, echoing views of Homans (1958) and Thibaut and Kelly (1959). Rather like a tease, or game, both parties are trying to look 'convincing' while neither fully believes in the emotions presented. The fun is in pulling off a good performance – in the aircraft, shop, restaurant, theme park, or wherever (Fineman 1993a). Indeed, Wouters's (1989) work with flight attendants presents a decidedly less bleak picture than Hochschild's. And Leidner's (1991) insurance agents were not at all fazed about their emotional programming: sales commission was all.

There has been considerable interest in refining and developing the emotional labour concept. Hochschild herself expands it to include the 'knowing about, and assessing as well as managing emotions, other people's as well as one's own' (Hochschild 1993: x). So a manager's emotional labour will involve assessing others' feelings in everyday supervision, as well as in more exceptional times – like disputes and emergencies. It will also involve regulating own feelings and those of others, such as in counselling and 'motivating'. Emotional labour tends to be most onerous in jobs with low autonomy, and in some boundary-spanning roles where people represent their companies to outsiders (Wharton 1993).

Most studies of emotional labour take a tightly contained view of organizational actors; they are disconnected from other life roles and from their historical and psychodynamic context (Wharton and Erickson 1993; James 1989; 1993). The virtue of a wider analysis is revealed in studies on the legacy effects of periods of unemployment. Both family and prior employment experiences help explain why some people struggle with their feelings of commitment to a new job or employer. They act out a positive and harmonious role at work to 'look right' to management in order to protect their job and family security. Privately they feel especially nervous and insecure about committing themselves – because of being let down by a previous employer (Constantas 1994; Fineman 1987). One of Constantas's re-employed unskilled workers expressed his new difficulty in 'play acting':

> It's not only that you've got to crawl [to management], but you can never express yourself negatively, having to pretend and look as though you're working hard. (1994: 231)

The more a person *wants* to wrap his or her identity in the job, the more he or she will embrace any 'necessary' emotional labour – a fair exchange for what the organization has to offer (Ashford and Humphrey 1993; Kunda 1992). Emotional labour is built into many professional jobs, where the doctor, nurse, lawyer, banker and so forth is, in effect, paid to be 'serious', 'concerned', 'sympathetic', 'objective' or 'detached'. Such presented images become part of the professional mystique with which clients collude (Hosking and Fineman 1990). If the mask cracks the professional relationship is threatened – such as the doctor who gets very upset in front of a patient; the nurse who shouts at a nervous patient; the lawyer who over-identifies with a client; or the banker who seems too frivolous. Emotional labour for these people can be a burdensome and lonely affair, self-monitored until something goes drastically wrong.

Emotional labourers can be part of a network, or hierarchy, which determines who conveys what emotional messages to whom. For example, the bad news on a failed promotion or redundancy is sidelined by a supervisor to a personnel officer. James (1993) aptly shows more subtle divisions of emotional labour, formal and informal, in the way a diagnosis of cancer is disclosed to a patient and her relatives. Although the broad context and hierarchical tone are set by the consultant surgeon in charge of the case, disclosure in fact is an unfolding product of emotion work between the patient, relatives, nurses and junior doctors. In *ad hoc* and opportunistic fashion they negotiate boundaries of acceptability, emotional tolerance and information.

Gender is also a factor in emotional labour. Gender and emotion discourses are often closely interrelated (Chodorow 1979; Hearn and Parkin 1987; Lutz 1990). In the patriarchy of many work organizations, men, by virtue of positional status and power, are more able to impose their understanding and valuation of emotionality on other men and women, to the extent that emotional labour has been accused of being the product of a quiet male conspiracy about the role of emotion in organizational affairs (Mumby and Putnam 1992; Putnam and Mumby 1993). A similar reasoning can apply to categorizations of 'women's work' and 'men's work', which usually contain assumptions about the emotional performance or stability of the sexes.

EMOTIONALIZED ZONES

Some writers have argued the benefits of aggregating an organization's feeling states and emotion norms for broad predictions of different organizational behaviours (Staw and Sutton 1993; Isen and Baron 1991). However, this can run the risk of over-homogenizing important differences. One can envisage a cultural map of an organization which charts the various settings and locations, or *zones*, which have come to 'permit' different types of emotional expression. These are not randomly distributed but exist in relation to each other, sometimes counterbalancing, sometimes complementing. Each relies on socially constructed, culturally transmitted *implicit* feeling rules, and together they generate a series of sub-cultural swirls of emotional meaning and conduct (Martin 1992; Aldrich 1992).

If we return to the cabin of an aircraft, the galley is a place where it is possible for flight attendants to drop their public mask, if they wish. In low voice, by facial expression, they can reveal to each other some of their feelings about their service encounters, the management, or whatever (Hochschild 1983). These sorts of compensatory, even cathartic, acts are permissible in the school staff room, behind the kitchen door of a restaurant, in a closed police car, in a doctor's rest room, and so forth (Goffman 1956; 1959; Gabriel 1988; Hearn 1993). Such settings offer workers an amnesty from their normal emotional labours, a chance to enjoy self-expression through a different set of emotional codes. So academics round a lunch table vent their despair about the students they have just 'suffered'. 'Safe' settings such as these provide fertile territory for power-coded humour and stories, a symbolic attack on those (especially bosses) whose normal status protects them from open criticism; this is what Clark (1990) describes as a renegotiation of social place.

Some emotionalized zones may be more temporarily defined, but just as significant in the patchwork of emotional cultures. Corridors, company car parks, lobby areas and washrooms are places where confidences are exchanged, formal stances dropped, 'real feelings' expressed, persuasion exercised, and old camaraderies reinforced. Turner (1969) speaks of 'liminal episodes' between formally structured events, when language and behaviour become more playful and fraternal. An organizational example would be the quick, informal debriefings and interpretation checking that take place during breaks in, and between, meetings. In Kunda's ethnography of an engineering company, such periods were used to voice the unofficial line on top management – that 'bullshit that comes from above' (1992: 158).

ISSUES AND DIRECTIONS FOR ORGANIZATIONAL EMOTION

A major challenge to our understanding of emotion in organizations is to soften the disciplinary lines. Encouragingly, we are now hearing voices raised in that direction from within the separate disciplines (e.g. Oatley 1992; Kemper 1990). However, the translation of such an ethos into organizational studies is only just beginning.

If we are to see more theoretical convergence, this present review suggests some propositions to consider:

● Organizational actors will carry with them an emotional history, which includes both conscious and unconscious traces of previous emotion work. The emotionalities of organizing and culture will both reflect and be influenced by these, and they may be better construed as important 'givens' rather than aberrations or oddities.

● The social context not only defines the meaning and place of emotions, but also defines its legitimacy. This will reflect the social times as well as the specific organization. Emotion can become highly politicized in this process, as is the case of stress, and the value placed on work as a source of 'well-being' or 'happiness'.

● In-context research means that emotions should not be divorced from the actor/task activity, or from other social roles and related experiences. 'Tasks' and 'emotion' take on their meaning and affective significance within the actor's phenomenological and 'doing' universe.

We can, as I have indicated elsewhere (Fineman 1993b), focus this type of thinking in a number of ways, as exemplified in the following sections.

What Are the Emotionalities of Working and Organizing?

Currently we have surprisingly little insight into real-time feelings and emotions as they unfold, interact, form and reform. We might expect a blend of flow-type experiences, private feelings and emotional performances as organizational life proceeds. Such basic, and engaging, descriptive data are missing in the haste to predefine and isolate specific emotions in advance of a study. While the driving feelings (fear, anger, passion, worry, shame) no doubt saturate some work experiences and performances, more often we pass through a range of mundane feelings which set the trajectories and character of a working day. And these feelings will become redefined and reformed as some of them are told and retold in the various social groupings of work (Rime et al. 1991).

We need a social science of the prosaic, the fleeting, as well as of the loud emotions. Methodologies of subjectivity and observation are required, such as introspections, 'live' diaries, deep ethnography, participant observation – and possibly less conventional media (Ellis and Bochner 1992; Ronai 1992). The foundational role of such research cannot be over-emphasized. We should not atomize and quantify emotions before we know what we have to atomize and quantify.

Feelings and Action Lines

Within the above picture, there will be *doing* along with the feeling. Perhaps this means doing *x* instead of *y*, staying longer than intended with a particular colleague, missing a meeting, going home early, returning often to the coffee machine.

Tightly defined studies could track particular prototypical organizational decisions, or decision arenas – such as in personnel selection, budget allocation, the purchase of new equipment, layoffs, environmental protection. Such studies could be revealing at a number of levels. They could trace the political effect of emotions as different emotional performances, such as anger, hurt and pride, are used strategically to influence outcomes. Some channels of possible actions will be closed off to avoid embarrassment, or for fear of exposure; others will be opened to retain feelings of solidarity and warmth. This would be an excellent test-bed for those interested in the way 'rationality' in organizations operates, and how more subtle emotional agendas (personal fears and threats, desire for recognition, envy) are employed, or woven into, decisional processes.

Ethical questions can arise with certain decisions, such as on layoffs, promotions and environmental protection. What is the emotional substructure of the organizational values that shape these considerations? What social defence mechanisms operate? Does a stirring of guilt or shame ever happen, and if so (or if not) what difference does it make to the outcomes? At present, mainstream research into business ethics is almost an emotion-free zone. Yet, as Solomon observes, 'without such emotions there can be no ethics, no business ethics, whatever the rules, policies, the corporate codes and fine speeches from company headquarters' (1991: 197).

Emotionalized Zones

With a more sociological eye we can explore the ways organizations divide in emotional architecture and emotion work. How do office spaces (open plan, cellular, closed doors, open doors) come to feel safe or risky for different types of emotional presentation or the sharing of intimacies? How do meeting places and structures of all sorts come to be socially defined as 'right' or 'wrong' for certain forms of emotionality? Are they linked to the organization's power and status differentials? Is their degree of perceived privateness or publicness important (Parkin 1993)? Is there, as I have suggested earlier, a necessary complementarity in these processes? And if there is, are people generally unhappier working in organizations where emotionalized zones are restricted or restrictive? In such circumstances people have nowhere to 'go' to test out, work on, redefine or refine their feelings. They have to rely heavily on themselves and their feelings *of* work, and/or on others outside of the organization. In this sense, the doing of emotion work and the social regulation of feeling are both intrapsychic and socially located phenomena.

Managerial Control of Emotions

In the last decade or so we have witnessed an acceleration in the institutionalization of managerial control over emotional display. What was once intuitive 'good sense' to the effective shopkeeper or door-to-door salesman is now a commodity which is subjected to the full rigours of corporate training and control. Deliberate hierarchical control of emotions – where positive, 'smiling', ones are inculcated and negative 'stress' ones are pathologized – presents a compelling picture of a late twentieth century form of Taylorism. Most social psychological studies of emotion operate with the material 'as given', regardless. So, if smiling and niceness can be elevated and more sincere, to link better with managerial and market purpose, so be it (e.g. Staw and Sutton 1993; Baron 1993). By way of contrast, some writers regard this response as both collusive and regressive (Hochschild 1983; Kemper 1990; Flam 1993). Enhancing service efficiency or corporate loyalty by selecting and training people for the 'right' feelings and emotional gloss is akin to emotional eugenics. Human beings are diminished – and often exploited because many have little choice but to comply. Perhaps justifiably, this scenario has become something of a bogy in the sociology of emotions because of its manipulative aura and the distress it can cause. But, as signalled in this review, there is a less seedy side to such endeavours, and also a more pluralistic/negotiative one – as emotional regulation moves between actors of different status and power. Such processes merit further investigation.

Nevertheless, there is evidence that 'have a nice day', or the McDonaldization of industry, is gaining an ever-tightening grip, especially on the increasing world market in casual labour (Ritzer 1993). There has been little constructively critical response to this from the organizational sciences, with the exception of a few writers who urge employees to resist emotional enculturation and to encourage employers to think more in terms of the advantages of employee self-formation and owned feelings (Willmott 1993; Putnam and Mumby 1993). As students and researchers of emotion we can, perhaps, prod, educate, and shout more in unison if managerial control of emotions is edging towards a new authoritarianism. It also requires disengagement from activities which tacitly support or collude with the worst elements of such ventures. But most importantly, we need to offer imaginative organizational designs which place emotionality, in both its manageable *and* unmanageable forms, nearer the centre of the organizational stage.

REFERENCES

Abbott, A. (1990) 'Positivism and interpretation in sociology: lessons for sociologists from the history of stress research', *Sociological Forum*, 5: 435–58.

Abramis, D.J. (1987) 'Fun at work: does it matter?' Paper presented at 95th Annual Convention of the American Psychological Association, New York.

Abu-Lughod, L. and Lutz, C.A. (1990) 'Introduction: emotion and the politics of everyday life', in C.A. Lutz and L. Abu-Lughod (eds), *Language and the Politics of Emotion*. Cambridge: Cambridge University Press.

Adorno, T.W., Frenkel-Brunswick, E., Levinson, D.J. and Sanford, R.N. (1950) *The Authoritarian Personality*. New York: W.W. Norton.

Aldrich, H.E. (1992) 'Incommensurable paradigms? Vital signs from three perspectives', in M. Reed and M. Hughes (eds), *Rethinking Organization*. London: Sage.

Allinson, P., Cooper, C.L. and Reynolds, P. (1989) 'Stress counselling in the workplace: the Post Office experience', *The Psychologist*, 2(9): 384–8.

Argyle, M. and Martin, M. (1991) 'The psychological causes of happiness', in F. Stack, M. Argyle and N. Schwarz (eds), *Subjective Well-Being*. Oxford: Pergamon Press.

Argyris, C. (1964) *Integrating the Individual and the Organization*. New York: Wiley.

Argyris, C. (1990) *Overcoming Organizational Defenses*. Boston: Allyn and Bacon.

Ashford, B.E. and Humphrey, R.H. (1993) 'Emotional labor in service roles: the influence of identity', *Academy of Management Review*, 18(1): 88–115.

Barley, S.R. and Knight, D.B. (1992) 'Towards a cultural theory of stress complaints', *Research in Organizational Behavior*, 14: 1–48.

Baron, R. (1993) 'Affect and organizational behavior: when and why feeling good (or bad) matters', in J.K. Murningham (ed.), *Social Psychology in Organizations: Advances in Theory and Research*. Englewood Cliffs, NJ: Prentice-Hall.

Baum, H. S. (1991) 'How bureaucracy discourages responsibility', in M.F.R. Kets de Vries (ed.), *Organizations on the Couch: Clinical Perspectives on Organizational Behavior and Change*. San Francisco: Jossey-Bass.

Bedford, E. (1986) 'Emotions, and statements about them', in R. Harré and R. Finlay Jones (eds), *The Social Construction of Emotions*. Oxford: Blackwell.

Berger, P. and Luckmann, T. (1966) *The Social Construction of Reality*. New York: Doubleday.

Bion, W.R. (1959) *Experiences in Groups*. New York: Basic Books.

Bloom, L. and Beckwith, R. (1989) 'Talking with feeling: integrating affective and linguistic expression in early language development', *Cognition and Emotion*, 3: 313–42.

Boas, M. and Chain, S. (1976) *Big Mac: the Unauthorized Story*. New York: Dutton.

Brayfield, A.H. and Rothe, H.F. (1951) 'An index of job satisfaction', *Journal of Applied Psychology*, 35: 307–11.

Brief, A. and Motowidlo, S.J. (1986) 'Prosocial organizational behaviors', *Academy of Management Review*, 11: 710–25.

Bryman, A. (1992) *Charisma and Leadership in Organizations*. London: Sage.

Callahan, E. (1988) 'The role of emotion in ethical decision making', *Hastings Center Report*, June/July: 9–14.

Carlzon, J. (1987) *Moments of Truth*. New York: Harper and Row.

Carnevale, P.J.D. and Isen, A.M. (1986) 'The influence of positive affect and visual access on the discovery of integrative solutions in bilateral negotiation', *Journal of Applied Psychology*, 71: 672–8.

Chodorow, N. (1979) *The Reproduction of Mothering: Psychoanalysis and the Sociology of Gender*. Berkeley, CA: University of California Press.

Clark, C. (1990) 'Emotions and micropolitics in everyday life: some patterns and paradoxes of "place"', in T.D. Kemper (ed.), *Research Agendas in the Sociology of Emotions*. Albany, NY: State University of New York Press.

Collins, R. (1990) 'Stratification, emotional energy, and the transient emotions', in T.D. Kemper (ed.), *Research Agendas in the Sociology of Emotions*. Albany, NY: State University of New York Press.

Constantas, A. (1994) 'Employment, unemployment, re-employment: a social psychological study'. Unpublished doctoral thesis, Faculty of Social and Political Sciences, University of Cambridge.

Cooley, C.H. (1922) *Human Nature and the Social Order*. New York: Scribners.

Cooper, C.L. (1991) 'Stress in organizations', in M. Smith (ed.), *Analyzing Organizational Behaviour.* Houndmills, Basingstoke: Macmillan.

Cooper, C. and Payne, R. (1978) *Stress at Work.* New York: Wiley.

Cox, T., Hunter, L.C. and Mulvey, C. (1981) *Stress.* London: Macmillan.

Czepiel, J.A., Solomon, M.E. and Surprenent, C.F. (1985) *The Service Encounter.* Lexington, MA: Lexington Books.

Czikszentmihalyi, M. (1977) *Beyond Boredom and Freedom.* San Francisco: Jossey-Bass.

de Board, R. (1978) *The Psychoanalysis of Organisations: a Psychoanalytic Approach to Behaviour of Groups and Organisations.* London: Tavistock.

de Sousa, R. (1987) *The Rationality of Emotion.* Cambridge, MA: MIT Press.

Dennett, D.C. (1978) *Brainstorms: Philosophical Essays on Mind and Psychology.* Cambridge, MA: MIT Press.

Denzin, N. (1990) 'On understanding emotion: the interpretive-cultural agenda', in T.D. Kemper (ed.), *Research Agendas in the Sociology of Emotions.* Albany, NY: State University of New York Press.

Diamond, M.A. (1993) *The Unconscious Life of Organizations: Interpreting Organizational Identity.* Westport, CT: Quorum Books.

Diamond, M.A. and Allcorn, S. (1985) 'Psychological barriers to personal responsibility', *Organizational Dynamics*, 12(4): 66–77.

Diamond, M.A. and Allcorn, S. (1987) 'The psychodynamics of regression in work groups', *Human Relations*, 40(8): 525–43.

Dixon, N.F. (1976) *On the Psychology of Military Incompetence.* London: Jonathan Cape.

Dohrenwend, B.S. and Dohrenwend, B.P. (eds) (1974) *Stressful Life Events.* New York: Wiley.

Donahue, W.A. and Ramesh, C.R. (1992) 'Negotiator–opponent relationships', in L.L. Putnam and M. Roloff (eds), *Communication and Negotiation.* Newbury Park, CA: Sage.

Eagle, J. and Newton, P.M. (1981) 'Scapegoating in small groups', *Human Relations*, 34: 283–301.

Ekman, P. (1984) 'Expression and the nature of emotion', in K.R. Scherer and P. Ekman (eds), *Approaches to Emotion.* Hillsdale, NJ: Erlbaum.

Ekman, P. (1985) *Telling Lies.* New York: Norton.

Elias, N. (1978) *The Civilizing Process. Vol. 1: The History of Manners*, translated by Jephcott. New York: Urizen Books.

Ellis, C. and Bochner, A.P. (1992) 'Telling and performing personal stories: the constraints of choice in abortion', in C. Ellis and M.G. Flaherty (eds), *Investigating Subjectivity.* Newbury Park, CA: Sage.

Fineman, S. (1985) *Social Work Stress and Intervention.* Aldershot: Gower.

Fineman, S. (1987) 'Back to employment: wounds and wisdom', in D. Fryer and P. Ullah (eds), *Unemployed People.* Milton Keynes: Open University Press.

Fineman, S. (1993a) 'Organizations as emotional arenas', in S. Fineman (ed.), *Emotion in Organizations.* London: Sage.

Fineman, S. (1993b) 'An emotion agenda', in S. Fineman (ed.), *Emotion in Organizations.* London: Sage.

Fineman, S. (1994) 'Organizing and emotion: towards a social construction', in M. Parker and J. Hassard (eds), *Towards a New Theory of Organizations.* London: Routledge.

Fischer, A.H. and Frijda, N.H. (1992) 'The emotion process as a whole: a response to Greenwood', *New Ideas in Psychology*, 10(1): 23–7.

Fishbein, M. and Ajzen, I. (1975). *Belief, Attitude and Behavior.* Reading, MA: Addison-Wesley.

Flam, H. (1990) 'Emotional "man". II: Corporate actors as emotion-motivated emotion managers', *International Sociology*, 5(2): 225–34.

Flam, H. (1993) 'Fear, loyalty and greedy organizations', in S. Fineman (ed.), *Emotion in Organizations.* London: Sage.

Frank, R.H. (1993) 'The strategic role of the emotions', *Rationality and Society*, 5(3): 160–94.

Franks, D.D. and Gecas, V. (1992) *Social Perspectives on Emotion: a Research Annual*, vol 1. Greenwich, CT: JAI Press.

Frese, M. (1990) 'Work and emotion', in F. Frey and I. Udis (eds), *The Image of Work.* Bern: Huber.

Frese, M., Fritz, A. and Stolte, W. (1991) 'Psychological aspects of the work of software developers', in M. Frese, C. Kasten, C. Skarpelis and B. Zang-Scheucher (eds), *Software for the Work of Tomorrow.* Bonn: Arbeit und Technik.

Friedman, B. (1990) *Effective Staff Incentives.* London: Kogan Page.

Frijda, N., Mesquita, B., Sonnemans, J. and Van Goosen, S. (1991) 'The duration of affective phenomena, or emotions, sentiments and passions', in K.T. Strongman (ed.), *International Review of Studies on Emotion*, vol. 1. New York: Wiley.

Gabriel, Y. (1988) *Working Lives in Catering.* London: Routledge.

Gallois, C. (1993) 'The language and communication of emotion: universal, interpersonal, or intergroup?', *American Behavioral Scientist*, 36(3): 309–38.

Gay, P. (1988) *Freud: a Life for our Time.* New York: Newton.

Geertz, C. (1973) *The Interpretation of Cultures.* New York: Basic Books.

George, J.M. (1990) 'Personality, affect, and behavior in groups', *Journal of Applied Psychology*, 76: 299–307.

George, J.M. (1991) 'State or trait: effects of positive mood on prosocial behavior at work', *Journal of Applied Psychology*, 76: 299–307.

Gerth, H.H. and Mills, C.W. (1958) *From Max Weber: Essays in Sociology.* New York: Oxford University Press.

Giddens, A. (1991) *Modernity and Self-Identity*. Cambridge: Polity Press.

Girtler, R. (1985) *Prostitution: Sexuality as Business*. Munich: Heyne.

Goffman, E. (1956) 'Embarrassment and social organization', *American Journal of Sociology*, 62: 264–71.

Goffman, E. (1959) *The Presentation of Self in Everyday Life*. New York: Doubleday Anchor.

Goffman, E. (1967) *Interaction Ritual*. Garden City, NY: Doubleday.

Gould, L.J. (1991) 'Using psychoanalytic frameworks for organizational analysis', in M.F.R. Kets de Vries (ed.), *Organizations on the Couch: Clinical Perspectives on Organizational Behavior and Change*. San Francisco: Jossey-Bass.

Guba, E.G. (1958) 'Morale and satisfaction: a study in past–future time perspective', *Administrative Science Quarterly*, 3: 195–209.

Harré, R. (1986) 'The social construction of emotions', in R. Harré and R. Finlay Jones (eds), *The Social Construction of Emotions*. Oxford: Blackwell.

Harrington, C.L. (1992) 'Talk about embarrassment: exploring the taboo-repression-denial hypothesis', *Symbolic Interaction*, 15(2): 203–25.

Harrison, R. (1987) *Organization Culture and Quality of Service: a Strategy for Releasing Love in the Workplace*. London: Association for Management Education and Development.

Hayano, D.M. (1982) *Poker Faces*. Berkeley: University of California Press.

Hearn, J. (1993) 'Emotive subjects: organizational men, organizational masculinities and the (de)construction of "emotions"', in S. Fineman (ed.), *Emotion in Organizations*. London: Sage.

Hearn, J. and Parkin, W. (1987) *'Sex' at 'Work': the Power and Paradox of Organization Sexuality*. Brighton: Wheatsheaf.

Hersey, R. (1951) *Zest for Work*. New York: Harper.

Herzberg, F. (1966) *Work and the Nature of Man*. Chicago: World Publishing Company.

Hinshelwood, R.D. (1987) *What Happens in Groups*. London: Free Association Books.

Hirschhorn, L. (1988) *The Workplace Within: Psychodynamics of Organizational Life*. Cambridge, MA: MIT Press.

Hirschhorn, L. and Young, D.R. (1991) 'Dealing with the anxiety of working: social defenses as coping strategy', in M.F.R. Kets de Vries (ed.), *Organizations on the Couch: Clinical Perspectives on Organizational Behavior and Change*. San Francisco: Jossey-Bass.

Hirshleifer, J. (1993) 'The affections and the passions: their economic logic', *Rationality and Society*, 5(3): 185–202.

Hochschild, A. (1975) 'The sociology of feelings and emotions: selected possibilities', in M. Millman and R. Kanter (eds), *Another Voice*. Garden City, New York: Anchor.

Hochschild, A. (1983) *The Managed Heart*. Berkeley, CA: University of California Press.

Hochschild, A. (1990) 'Ideology and emotion management: a perspective and path for future research', in T.D. Kemper (ed.), *Research Agendas in the Sociology of Emotions*. Albany, NY: State University of New York Press.

Hochschild, A. (1993) 'Preface', in S. Fineman (ed.), *Emotion in Organizations*. London: Sage.

Homans, G.C. (1958) 'Social behavior and exchange', *American Journal of Sociology*, 63: 597–606.

Hopfl, H. (1991) 'Nice jumper Jim!: dissonance and emotional labour in a management development programme'. Paper presented at 5th European Congress – The Psychology of Work and Organizations, Rouen, 24–27 March.

Hopfl, H. and Linstead, S. (1993) 'Passion and performance: suffering and the carrying of organizational roles', in S. Fineman (ed.), *Emotion in Organizations*. London: Sage.

Hoppock, R. (1935) *Job Satisfaction*. New York: Harper.

Hosking, D. and Fineman, S. (1990) 'Organizing processes', *Journal of Management Studies*, 27(6): 583–604.

Hosking, D. and Morley, I.E. (1991) *A Social Psychology of Organizing*. New York: Harvester Wheatsheaf.

House, R.J. (1977) 'A 1976 theory of charismatic leadership', in J.G. Hunt and I.L. Larson (eds), *Leadership: the Cutting Edge*. Carbondale, IL: Southern Illinois University Press.

Howard, N. (1993) 'The role of emotions in multi-organizational decision-making', *Journal of the Operational Research Society*, 44(6): 613–23.

Iaffaldano, M.T. and Muchinsky, P.M. (1985) 'Job satisfaction and job performance: a meta analysis', *Psychological Bulletin*, 97: 251–73.

Isen, A.M. and Baron, R.A. (1991) 'Positive affect as a factor in organizational behavior', *Research in Organizational Behavior*, 13: 1–53.

Jackall, R. (1988) *Moral Mazes: the World of Corporate Managers*. New York: Oxford University Press.

James, N. (1989) 'Emotional labour: skill and work in the social regulation of feeling', *Sociological Review*, 37(1): 15–24.

James, N. (1993) 'Divisions of emotional labour: disclosure and cancer', in S. Fineman (ed.), *Emotion in Organizations*. London: Sage.

James, W. (1884) 'What is emotion?', *Mind*, 9: 188–205.

Jaques, E. (1951) *The Changing Culture of a Factory*. London: Tavistock.

Jaques, E. (1989) *Requisite Organization*. Cason Hall.

Jardin, A. (1970) *The First Henry Ford: a Study of Personality and Business Leadership*. Cambridge, MA: MIT Press.

Judge, T.A. and Watanabe, S. (1993) 'Another look at

the job-satisfaction/life-satisfaction relationship', *Journal of Applied Psychology*, 78(6): 939–48.

Kakar, S. (1970) *Frederick Taylor: a Study of Personality and Innovation*. Cambridge, MA: MIT Press.

Kemper, T.D. (1981) 'Social constructionist and positivist approaches to the sociology of emotions', *American Journal of Sociology*, 87: 336–62.

Kemper, T.D. (1990) 'Foundations of social relational determinants of emotions', in T.D. Kemper (ed.), *Research Agendas in the Sociology of Emotions*. New York: State University of New York Press.

Kemper, T.D. (1993) 'Reasons in emotions or emotions in reason', *Rationality and Society*, 5(3): 275–82.

Kets de Vries, M.F.R. (1990) *Prisoners of Leadership*. New York: Wiley.

Kets de Vries, M.F.R (ed.) (1991a) *Organizations on the Couch: Clinical Perspectives on Organizational Behavior and Change*. San Francisco: Jossey-Bass.

Kets de Vries, M.F.R. (1991b) 'Introduction', in M.F.R. Kets de Vries (ed.), *Organizations on the Couch: Clinical Perspectives on Organizational Behavior and Change*. San Francisco: Jossey-Bass.

Kets de Vries, M.F.R. and Miller, D. (1984) *The Neurotic Organization*. San Francisco: Jossey-Bass.

Kets de Vries, M.F.R. and Miller, D. (1987) 'Interpreting organizational texts', *Journal of Management Studies*, 24(3): 233–43.

Kets de Vries, M.F.R. and Miller, D. (1991) 'Leadership styles and organizational cultures: the shaping of neurotic organizations', in M.F.R. Kets de Vries (ed.), *Organizations on the Couch: Clinical Perspectives on Organizational Behavior and Change*. San Francisco: Jossey-Bass.

Klein, M. (1959) 'Our adult world and its roots in infancy', *Human Relations*, 12: 291–303.

Kunda, G. (1992) *Engineering Culture: Control and Commitment in a High-Tech Corporation*. Philadelphia: Temple University Press.

Lakoff, G. and Johnson, M. (1980) *Metaphors We Live By*. Chicago: University of Chicago Press.

Landy, F.J. (1985) *Psychology of Work Behavior*. Homewood, IL: Dorsey Press.

Lapierre, L. (1991) 'Exploring the dynamics of leadership', in M.F.R. Kets de Vries (ed.), *Organizations on the Couch: Clinical Perspectives on Organizational Behavior and Change*. San Francisco: Jossey-Bass.

Lawler, E.E. (1976) 'Should quality of work life be legislated?', *Personnel Administration*, January: 17–21.

Lawler, E.J. and Bacharach, S.B. (1983) 'Political action and alignments in sociology', *Research in the Sociology of Organizations*, 2: 83–107.

Lazarus, R.S. (1993) 'From psychological stress to the emotions', *Annual Review of Psychology*, 44: 1–21.

Leeper, R.W. (1965) 'Some needed developments in the motivational theory of emotions', in D. Levine (ed.), *Nebraska Symposium on Motivation*. Nebraska: University of Nebraska Press. pp. 25–122.

Leidner, R. (1991) 'Serving hamburgers and selling insurance: gender, work and identity in interactive service jobs', *Gender and Society*, 5(2): 154–77.

Leigh, A. (1993) 'Perfect decision'. London: Pitman.

Likert, R. (1961) *New Patterns of Management*. New York: McGraw-Hill.

Locke, E.A. (1976) 'The nature and causes of job satisfaction', in M.D. Dunnette (ed.), *Handbook of Industrial and Organizational Psychology*. Chicago: Rand McNally.

Lutz, C.A. (1990) 'Engendered emotion: gender, power, and the rhetoric of emotional control in American discourse', in C.A. Lutz and L. Abu-Lughod (eds), *Language and the Politics of Emotion*. Cambridge: Cambridge University Press.

Lutz, C.A. and White, G. (1986) 'The anthropology of emotions', *Annual Review of Anthropology*, 15: 405–36.

Magee, J.E. (1991) 'Decision trees for decision making', reprinted in *Harvard Business Review Paperback: The Logic of Business Decision Making*. Harvard: Harvard Business Publications.

Mangham, I.L. and Overington, M.A. (1987) *Organizations as Theatre*. Chichester: Wiley.

Martin, J. (1992) *Cultures in Organizations: Three Perspectives*. New York: Oxford University Press.

Maslow, A.H. (1943) 'A theory of human motivation', *Psychological Review*, 50: 370–96.

Matteson, M.T. and Ivancevich, J.M. (1982) 'The how, what and why of stress management training', *Personnel Journal*, 61: 768–74.

Menzies-Lythe, I. (1988) *Containing Anxiety in Institutions: Selected Essays*. London: Free Association Books.

Menzies-Lythe, I. (1991) 'Changing organizations and individuals: psychoanalytic insights for improving organizational health', in M.F.R. Kets de Vries (ed.), *Organizations on the Couch: Clinical Perspectives on Organizational Behavior and Change*. San Francisco: Jossey-Bass.

Miceli, M.P. and Near, J.P. (1991) 'Whistleblowing as an organizational process', *Research in the Sociology of Organizations*, 9: 139–200.

Milgram, S. (1974) *Obedience to Authority*. New York: Harper and Row.

Miller, D. and Toulouse, J.M. (1986) 'Chief executive personality and corporate strategy and structure in small firms', *Management Science*, 32: 1389–409.

Miller, E. (1993) *From Dependency to Autonomy*. London: Free Association Books.

Mills, C.W. (1956) *White Collar*. New York: Oxford University Press.

Minsky, M. (1986) *The Society of the Mind*. New York: Simon and Schuster.

Morgan, G. (1986) *Images of Organization*. Beverly Hills, CA: Sage.

Mumby, D.K. and Putnam, L.L. (1992) 'The politics

of emotion: a feminist reading of bounded rationality', *Academy of Management Review*, 17(3): 465–86.

Munsterberg, H. (1912) *Psychology and Business Life*. Leipzig: Barth.

Murphy, L.R. (1984) 'Occupational stress management: a review and appraisal', *Journal of Occupational Psychology*, 57: 1–15.

Murphy, L.R. (1987) 'A review of organizational stress management research: methodological considerations', in J.M. Ivancevich and D.C. Ganster (eds), *Job Stress: from Theory to Suggestion*. New York: Haworth.

Murphy, L.R. (1988) 'Workplace interventions for stress reduction and prevention', in C.L. Cooper and R. Payne (eds), *Causes, Coping and Consequences of Stress at Work*. Chichester: Wiley.

Neale, M.S., Singer, J.A., Schwartz, G.E. and Schwartz, J. (1982) 'Conflicting perspectives on stressor reduction in occupational settings: a systems approach to their resolution'. Unpublished paper, Department of Psychology, Yale University.

Newton, A. (1989) 'Occupational stress and coping with stress: a critique', *Human Relations*, 42: 441–61.

Newton, T., Handy, J. and Fineman, S. (1995) *'Managing' Stress: Emotion and Power at Work*. London: Sage.

O'Reilly, C.R. (1991) 'Organizational behaviour', *Annual Review of Psychology*, 42: 427–58.

Oakley, J. (1993) *Morality and the Emotions*. London: Routledge.

Oatley, K. (1992) 'Human emotions: function and dysfunction', *Annual Review of Psychology*, 43: 55–85.

Ortony, A., Clore, G. and Collins, A. (1988) *The Cognitive Structure of Emotion*. Cambridge: Cambridge University Press.

Ostner, I. and Beck-Gernsheim, E. (1979) *Empathic Helping as Profession*. Frankfurt: Campus.

Park, O.H., Sims, H. and Motowildo, S.J. (1986) 'Affect in organizations: how feelings and emotions influence managerial judgment', in H.P. Sims, D.A. Gioia and Associates (eds), *The Thinking Organization*. San Francisco: Jossey-Bass.

Parkin, W. (1993) 'The public and the private: gender, sexuality and emotion', in S. Fineman (ed.), *Emotion in Organizations*. London: Sage.

Pekrun, R. and Frese, M. (1992) 'Emotions in work and achievement', in C.L. Cooper and I.T. Robertson (eds), *International Review of Industrial and Organizational Psychology*, vol. 7. Chichester: Wiley.

Peters, T. (1989) *Leadership and Emotion*. California: TPG Communications.

Peters, T. and Austin, N. (1985) *A Passion for Excellence*. New York: Random House.

Peven, D. (1968) 'The use of religious revival techniques to indoctrinate personnel', *Sociological Quarterly*, 9(1): 97–106.

Pfeffer, J. (1978) 'The micropolitics of organizations', in M.W. Meyer and Associates (eds), *Environments and Organizations*. San Francisco: Jossey-Bass.

Pfeffer, J. (1982) *Organizations and Organization Theory*. Marshfield, MA: Pitman.

Plutchik, R. (1970) 'Emotions, evolution and adaptive processes', in M.D. Arnold (ed.), *Feelings and Emotions: the Loyola Symposium*. New York: Academic Press. pp. 3–24.

Putnam, L. and Mumby, D.K. (1993) 'Organizations, emotion and the myth of rationality', in S. Fineman (ed.), *Emotion in Organizations*. London: Sage.

Rabey, G. (1994) *In Charge*. London: Pitman.

Rabkin, J.G. and Struening, E.L. (1976) 'Life events, stress and illness', *Science*, 194: 1013–20.

Rafaeli, A. (1989) 'When clerks meet customers: a test of variables relating to emotional expression on the job', *Journal of Applied Psychology*, 74: 385–93.

Rafaeli, A. and Sutton, R.I. (1987) 'Expression of emotion as part of the work role', *Academy of Management Review*, 12(1): 23–37.

Rafaeli, A. and Sutton, R.I. (1989) 'The expression of emotion in organizational life', *Research in Organizational Behavior*, 11: 1–42.

Ratner, C. (1989) 'A social constructionist critique of the naturalistic theory of emotion', *The Journal of Mind and Behavior*, 10(3): 211–30.

Rime, B., Mesquita, B., Phillipott, P. and Boca, S. (1991) 'Beyond the emotional event: six studies on the social sharing of emotion', *Journal of Cognition and Emotion*, 5(5/6): 435–65.

Ritzer, G. (1993) *The McDonaldization of Society*. Thousand Oaks, CA: Pine Forge Press.

Roethlisberger, F.J. and Dickson, W.J. (1939) *Management and the Worker*. New York: Wiley.

Ronai, C.R. (1992) 'The reflexive self through narrative: a night in the life of an erotic dancer/researcher', in C. Ellis and M.G. Flaherty (eds), *Investigating Subjectivity*. Newbury Park, CA: Sage.

Rosenberg, M. (1990) 'Reflexivity and emotions', *Social Psychology Quarterly*, 53(1): 3–12.

Rycroft, C.A. (1968) *A Critical Dictionary of Psychoanalysis*. New York: Penguin Books.

Sandelands, L.E. (1988) 'The concept of work feeling', *Journal for the Theory of Social Behavior*, 18(4): 437–57.

Sandelands, L.E. and Buckner, G.C. (1989) 'Of art and work: aesthetic experience and the psychology of work feelings', *Research in Organizational Behavior*, 11.

Sarbin, T.R. (1986) 'Emotion and act: roles and rhetoric', in R. Harré and R. Finlay Jones (eds), *The Social Construction of Emotions*. Oxford: Blackwell.

Scheff, T.J. (1988) 'Shame and conformity: the defence-emotion system', *American Sociological Review*, 53: 395–406.

Scheff, T.J. (1990) *Microsociology: Discourse. Emotion and Social Structure*. Chicago: University of Chicago Press.

Schwartz, H.S. (1988) 'The symbol of the space shuttle

and the degeneration of the American dream', *Journal of Organizational Change Management*, 1(2): 5–20.

Schwartz, H.S. (1990) *Narcissistic Process and Corporate Decay: the Theory of the Organizational Ideal*. New York: New York University Press.

Schwenk, C.R. (1986) 'Information, cognitive biases, and commitment to a course of action', *Academy of Management Review*, 11: 298–310.

Seidenberg, R. (1975) *Corporate Wives – Corporate Casualties?* New York: Doubleday, Anchor.

Selye, H. (1956) *The Stress of Life*. New York: McGraw-Hill.

Selye, H. (1976) 'Forty years of stress research: principal remaining problems and misconceptions', *Canadian Medical Association Journal*, 115: 53–6.

Shott, S. (1979) 'Emotion and social life: a symbolic interactionist analysis', *American Journal of Sociology*, 84(6): 1317–35.

Simon, H. (1957) *Administrative Behavior*. New York: Macmillan.

Smith, K.K. and Berg, D.N. (1987a) 'A paradoxical conception of group dynamics', *Human Relations*, 40(10): 633–58.

Smith, K.K. and Berg, D.N. (1987b) *Paradoxes of Group Life: Understanding Conflict. Paralysis and Movement in Group Dynamics*. San Francisco: Jossey-Bass.

Smith, N.C. (1990) *Morality and the Market*. London: Routledge.

Smith, P.C., Kendall, L.M. and Hulin, C.L. (1969) *The Measurement of Satisfaction in Work and Retirement*. Chicago: Rand McNally.

Solomon, R.C. (1991) 'Business ethics, literacy, and the education of emotions', in R.E. Freeman (ed.), *Business Ethics: The State of the Art*. New York: Oxford University Press.

Spielberger, C.D. (1966) 'Theory and research on anxiety', in C.D. Spielberger (ed.), *Anxiety and Behavior*. New York: Academic Press.

Staw, B.M. (1981) 'The escalation of commitment to a course of action', *Academy of Management Review*, 6: 577–87.

Staw, B.M. and Ross, J. (1987) 'Understanding escalations situations: antecedents, prototypes and solutions', in B.M. Staw and L.L. Cummings (eds), *Research in Organizational Behavior*, 9. Greenwich, CT: JAI Press.

Staw, B.M. and Sutton, R.I. (1993) 'Macro organizational psychology', in J.K. Murningham (ed.), *Social Psychology in Organizations: Advances in Theory and Research*. Englewood Cliffs, NJ: Prentice-Hall.

Stearns, P.N. (1989) 'Suppressing unpleasant emotions: the development of a twentieth-century American', in A.E. Barnes and P.N. Stearns (eds), *Social History and Issues in Human Consciousness*. New York/London: NY University Press.

Stearns, P.N. (1993) 'Girls, boys and emotions: redefinitions and historical change', *The Journal of American History*, 80(1): 36–74.

Stein, N.L. and Trabasso, T. (1992) 'The organization of emotional experience: creating links among emotion, thinking, language and intentional action', *Cognition and Emotion*, 6: 225–44.

Strongman, K.T. (1978) *The Psychology of Emotion*. Chichester: Wiley.

Sugrue, N. (1982) 'Emotions as property and context for negotiation', *Urban Life*, 11(3): 280–92.

Sutherland, E.H. (1937) *The Professional Thief*. Chicago: University of Chicago Press.

Terkel, S. (1975) *Working*. Harmondsworth: Penguin.

Thibaut, J.W. and Kelly, H.H. (1959) *The Social Psychology of Groups*. New York: Wiley.

Tidd, K.L. and Lockard, J.S. (1978) 'Monetary significance of the affiliative smile', *Bulletin of the Psychonomic Society*, 11: 344–6.

Turner, V. (1969) *The Ritual Process*. Chicago: Aldine.

Van Maanen, J. (1986) 'Power in the bottle', in S. Srivasta (ed.), *Executive Power*. San Francisco: Jossey-Bass.

Van Maanen, J. and Kunda, G. (1989) '"Real feelings": emotional expression and organizational culture', *Research in Organizational Behavior*, 11: 43–103.

Vroom, V. (1964) *Work and Motivation*. New York: Wiley.

Wallraff, G. (1985) *Lowest of the Low*. London: Methuen.

Walt Disney Productions (1982) *Your Role in the Walt Disney World Show*. Orlando, FL: Walt Disney Productions.

Walton, C.C. (1988) *The Moral Manager*. Grand Rapids and Philadelphia: Harper and Row.

Warr, P.B. (1971) 'Attitudes, actions and motives', in P.B. Warr (ed.), *Psychology at Work*. Harmondsworth: Penguin.

Warr, P.B. and Wall, T. (1975) *Work and Well-Being*. Harmondsworth: Penguin.

Weick, K.E. (1979) *The Social Psychology of Organizing*. Reading, MA: Addison-Wesley.

Weick, K.E. (1993) 'Sensemaking in organizations: small structures with large consequences', in J.K. Murningham (ed.), *Social Psychology in Organizations: Advances in Theory and Research*. Englewood Cliffs, NJ: Prentice-Hall.

Weinberg, R.B. and Mauksch, L.B. (1991) 'Examining family-of-origin influences in life at work', *Journal of Marital and Family Therapy*, 17: 233–42.

Wentworth, W.M. and Ryan, J.R. (1992) 'Balancing body, mind and culture: the place of emotion in social life', in D.D. Franks and V. Gecas (eds), *Social Perspectives on Emotion: a Research Annual*, vol 1. Greenwich, CT: JAI Press.

Wharton, A.S. (1993) 'The affective consequences of service work: managing emotions on the job', *Work and Occupations*, 20(2): 205–32.

Wharton, A.S. and Erickson, R.J. (1993) 'Managing emotions on the job and at home: understanding the consequences of multiple emotional roles', *Academy of Management Review*, 18(3): 457–86.

Willmott, H. (1993) 'Strength is ignorance; slavery is freedom: managing culture in modern organizations', *Journal of Management Studies*, 30(4): 515–52.

Winnicott, D.W. (1965) *The Maturational Processes and the Facilitating Environment*. New York: International Universities Press.

Wouters, C. (1989) 'The sociology of emotions and flight attendants: Hochschild's "managed heart"', *Theory, Culture and Society*, 6(1): 95–123.

Zajonc, R.B., Murphy, S.T. and Inglehart, M. (1989) 'Feelings and facial efference: implications of the vascular theory of emotion', *Psychological Review*, 96: 395–416.

Zaleznik, A. (1970) 'Power and politics in organizational life', *Harvard Business Review*, 48: 47–60.

Zaleznik, A. and Kets de Vries, M. (1975) *Power and the Corporate Mind*. Boston: Houghton Mifflin.

Zurcher, L. (1982) 'The staging of emotion: a dramaturgical analysis', *Symbolic Interactionism*, 5(1): 1–22.

3.4

Exploring the Aesthetic Side of Organizational Life

PASQUALE GAGLIARDI

THE TANGIBLE ORGANIZATION

I was brought up not just by my mother but also by the colours registered by my eyes, by the noises that prompted reactions of alertness or of calm, by the smell of fragrance and danger, by the habit of distinguishing good and bad more through sampling than through opinions, through the variants of touch born out of wishes or prompted by desires.[1]
(Crovi 1993: 1)

Students of organizations usually conceive, describe and interpret them as (utilitarian) forms of social aggregation. We have always been accustomed to associating the idea of organization with the image of people who make decisions, act and interact, each performing different tasks, more or less specialized and more or less linked, between them and with a collective task or purpose. If you ask a manager to describe the company for which he or she works he or she will probably draw you an organization chart, that is, nothing other than a graphic and summary representation of a set of socio-professional roles and of relations between these roles.

At one time I used to view organizations in a similar corporate way. My perspective changed as a result of some field work during which I asked a workman assigned to an old lathe to describe his company to me. In reply he said:

For me, this company is that damned gate I come through every morning, running if I'm late, my grey locker in the changing-room, this acrid smell of iron filings and grease – can't you smell it yourself? – the smooth surface of the pieces I've milled – I instinctively rub my fingers over them before

putting them aside – and . . . yes! that bit of glass up there, in front, where sometimes – there you are – I spot a passing cloud.

Maybe my respondent had a poetic soul and felt things that the majority of corporate actors do not feel, though I don't believe that is so. I think he was merely more aware than most that our experience of the real is first and foremost sensory experience of a physical reality, while he was less concerned to supply an intellectualized version of his firm. For him it was obviously above all a *place*, a physical and *tangible* reality.

He had grasped the elementary truth that the physical setting is not a naked container for organizational action (Strati 1990), but a context that *selectively* solicits – and hence, so to speak, 'cultivates' – all our senses. This context refines some of our perceptive capacities (perhaps at the expense of others), enabling us to grasp minimal gradations in the intensity of a stimulus, and accustoms us to certain sensations till we become 'fond' of them, even if those same sensations may well be unpleasant in other contexts and for other people.

The physical setting can be natural (as the rectangle of sky of my informant) but in contemporary organizations – generally receptive towards any technical expedient that may improve efficiency – it is in large measure strewn with *artifacts*. An artifact may be defined as '(a) a *product* of human action which exists independently of its creator, (b) *intentional*, it aims, that is, at solving a problem or satisfying a need, (c) *perceived by the senses*, in that it is endowed with its own corporality or physicality' (Gagliardi 1990a: 3).

The study of corporate artifacts and space has emerged in recent years as one of the more interesting new currents in the general approach whereby organizations are studied as cultures.[2] Seemingly, the object of this type of study is what in the tradition of anthropological research is defined as the material culture of a social group. In that tradition, though, material culture has been generally considered *an* element (although secondary and accessory) of the cultural system, and the objects in which the material culture is expressed have often been considered worthy only of scrupulous classification. Even the study of the artistic production of traditional societies, which – as Forge (1973) observes – was an object of particular interest on the part of pioneers of anthropology such as Haddon and Boas, has vanished from the agenda of anthropologists with the spread and development of field-work techniques.

The choice of certain researchers of organizational culture to devote themselves to the study of artifacts springs not from the desire to become specialists in a secondary or superficial 'aspect' or 'element' of the cultural system – however fascinating it may be – but from the awareness that the study of artifacts and of physical reality enables one to approach a basic human experience: aesthetic experience.

The term 'aesthetic' (from the Greek *aisthànomai* 'perceive, feel with the senses') is used here in the general sense, to refer to all types of sense experience and not simply to experience of what is socially described as 'beautiful' or defined as 'art'. In the general sense I employ it, aesthetic experience includes:

1   a form of *knowledge: sensory* knowledge[3] (different from *intellectual* knowledge), often unconscious or tacit and ineffable, i.e. not translatable into speech
2   a form of *action: expressive*, disinterested action shaped by impulse and by a mode of feeling rather than by the object (the opposite of *impressive* action aimed at practical ends) (Witkin 1974)
3   a form of *communication* (different from *speech*) which can take place to the extent that expressive actions – or the artifacts which these produce – become the object of sensory knowledge and hence a way of passing on and sharing particular ways of feeling or ineffable knowledge.

When I call the aesthetic experience 'basic', I intend the adjective also in the literal sense of the term, to indicate, that is, that the aesthetic experience is *the basis* of other experiences and forms of cognition which constitute the usual object of organizational studies and that it therefore implies that aesthetic experiences have

a profound influence on the life and performance of the organization. Despite the basic grounds that aesthetic experience provides for the sense of organization life it is an aspect generally ignored in organizational literature. The few isolated exceptions (Jones et al. 1988; Ramirez 1991; Sandelands and Buchner 1989; Strati 1990; 1992) constitute early – sometimes timid – attempts at exploring an issue that awaits and deserves in-depth investigation.

Considering the novelty of the theme and the fact that knowledge that is still to be produced cannot be systematized, the main aim of this chapter is to be mould-breaking, future-oriented and agenda-setting. In order to break the mould we have to analyse and transcend the inveterate reluctance of social scientists – and of organization people in particular, be they practitioners or scholars – to deal with things and with aesthetics. Here one needs a critical analysis of some of the implicit assumptions dominant in the world of social and organizational research. Having done this I shall lay the basis for a consistent conceptual framework. Having provided an appropriate language, the discussion of aesthetic experience in organizations need not rely on antiquated interpretative categories. Categories such as 'motivator factors' or 'intrinsic satisfaction' rightly have been challenged for their contemporary lack of depth by writers such as Sandelands and Buchner (1989) as shallow, inconsequential and trite in revealing the depth of sensations and feelings in the workplace.

Aesthetics, conceived as a single discipline in the terms of philosophy, does not prove adequate for the task proposed. One must, as ever in interesting organization studies, be catholic in one's use of sources. Points of view and analytic categories drawn from such diverse disciplines as the theory of knowledge, cultural anthropology, the psychology of perception, neuro-psychology, the sociology of art, the history of art, and others, turn out to be necessary. A glance at the references to this chapter will give the reader some idea of the wide range of disciplines invoked in the efforts so far made to grasp the hidden regularities of phenomena that remain, in many ways, ungraspable.

THE REASONS FOR NEGLECT: DOMINANT VIEWS OF SOCIAL AND ORGANIZATIONAL KNOWLEDGE

Every culture habituates those who share in it. Habituation takes the form of fundamental polarities that express oppositions or complementarities between extremes that shape the perception, analysis and structure of experience.

A series of paired terms, close and partly over-lapping, well rooted in modern Western culture, are of particular importance for my proposed analysis: art/science, intuitive knowledge/logico-scientific knowledge, play (or leisure)/work, beauty/utility, expressivity/instrumentality, contemplation/activity. These distinctions do not reflect – as many believe – an order inherent in reality. On the contrary, such distinctions are culturally determined and derive from visions and conceptions inspired by the utilitarian rationalism which became rooted and wide-spread in the West from the second half of the eighteenth century. These conceptions are, at the same time, cause and effect, reflection and justification of the industrial revolution. More generally they are grounded in that profound cultural transformation which we usually iden-tify with the advent of 'modernity' and which Max Weber defined as the disenchantment of the world.

The scientific revolution and the perfecting of the cognitive framework of the natural sciences achieved by Newton divided the study of the *primary qualities* of the physical world – objective, universal and subject to the language of mathematics – from its *secondary qualities*, which are the object of subjective experiences, sensory and inexact. 'Special aesthetics', mean-ing the study of beauty, arise at the moment when the *beautiful* is definitively split off and distinguished from the *useful* and practical, when the moment of *activity*, connected with the exercise of the *cognitive faculties* of the intellect and its productions (science and technology), is conceptually and socially split off from the moment of *contemplation* and of the *imagination* linked to the fruition of the beautiful and of art (Carmagnola 1994). These oppositions/divisions did not exist – or did not have the same force and the same consequence – before the eight-eenth century: in the Renaissance (as in the Graeco-Hellenistic civilization which inspired humanism) art and technique, functionality and beauty were hardly separable, either concep-tually or in the organization of social life, and Hamilton (1942) suggests that the extraordinary level reached by those civilizations was the outcome of this integration.

With the advent of modernity the aforemen-tioned distinctions hardened. New hierarchies took unequivocal shape among the values referred to by such polarities. Work and pro-duction became more important than leisure and play,[4] activity than contemplation, utility than beauty. Above all – for what interests us here – logico-scientific (objective) knowledge estab-lished itself definitively as a superior form of knowledge over aesthetico-intuitive (subjective) knowledge. The aesthetic was demoted to the 'secondary sphere of consumption, of spare time, of the useless'[5] (Carmagnola 1994: 129).

In the old scholastic treatises logic was con-sidered the art of demonstration, while elo-quence (or rhetoric) was held to be the art of persuasion. In the first the capacity to convince the hearer depends on objective features of the discourse, in the second on subjective qualities of the speaker and on his style, that is to say, on the formal properties – i.e. sensorially and emotion-ally perceptible – of his speech, which in their turn appeal to subjective characteristics and perceptual attitudes in the hearer. Rhetoric was often represented in the treatises by the image of an open hand and logic by that of a fist (Howell, cited in Mamiani 1992). This symbolization gave clear expression to the idea that the progress of knowledge is the fruit of an oscillation between two diverse forms of knowledge and commu-nication of equal worth and dignity. But, starting with Newton, the sage became more and more identified with the scientist whose reports *had to be* the outcome of cold observa-tion, stripped of any stylistic stratagem and divested of the charm of imagination. Modernity has thus inherited from the eighteenth-century scientific revolution a closed fist – or at least the idea of the superiority of the closed fist over the open hand – and hence a conception of science 'clenched in its processes of demonstration'[6] (Mamiani 1992: 225). This conception is still dominant in the social sciences also, despite the fact that efforts – among which those of Polanyi (1966) and of Brown (1977) are outstanding – to establish an aesthetic view of social knowledge, combining the rigorous outlook of scientific realism with the creative potentiality of Roman-tic idealism, have found more than a handful of enthusiastic supporters. The problem is that, apart from affirmations of principle, not much has been done to work out the methodological implications of these attempts at synthesis.

If formal organizations are the social artifacts which best embody the rationalistic and utilitar-ian ideal of modernity, it should not surprise us that those who deal with organizations – be they practitioners or academics – are irresistibly attracted to the pragmatic, serious, rationalist half of the paired terms mentioned above. How-ever open-minded organizational scholars may be, the fact remains that the knowledge that they produce is aimed at practitioners. Their episte-mology, implicit or explicit, will thereby tend to reflect the worldview and theory of knowledge of those in whose eyes they strive to be credible: it is a question, so to speak, of cognitive and cultural attunement (Barley et al. 1988). This explains, in my view, why even among students of organizational cultures, interest in the study of artifacts and of the aesthetic dimension is comparatively limited, despite the fact that the founding principles of this line of study included from the start the legitimacy of a form of understanding of corporate life different from and alternative to that of rational cognition, one which Ebers (1985) specifically defined as 'the poetic mode'.

When one moves from the *forms* of knowledge to the *objects* of social knowledge (that is to say, if we pass from the question of epistemology to the question of ontology), we come up against the idiosyncratic tendency of social scientists, and organizational ones in particular, to shuttle between people – as subjects of relationships – and their mental products, between the 'thinker' and the 'thought', excluding from their visual field and interests material things (the 'product', so to speak) (Ammassari 1985). Here, too, we can see, on the one hand, the influence of Descartes's idea of the self as the subject of thought capable of self-consciousness, and on the other the influence of the rooted distinction between mind and body, with the evident assumption of the superiority of the former over the latter. However, as Latour (1992a) has brilliantly observed, material things are the missing masses who knock insistently at the doors of sociology. To neglect to analyse them and observe only human action is like limiting one's gaze to half of the court during a tennis match: the observed movements seem to have no meaning. For Latour (1992a; 1992b), in fact, the development of technology in modern society makes it possible to delegate a growing number of action programmes to non-human subjects, to things which while being often stationary and lacking any trace of 'machinery' – as for example an indicator board – are machines in the more general sense of the term. They, in fact, incorporate activity that could be – or that was previously – performed by human beings, they condition human beings, they interact with them and are conditioned by them, in a chain of delegations and transfers – or translations, as Latour calls them – which have conscious human beings at one extreme, efficient and tenacious machines at the other, and the power of symbols and signals halfway between.

From a different standpoint, but one close to that of Latour, we can also say that ideas and things, thought and action, spirit and matter do not belong to separate and non-communicating worlds. On the contrary, things can represent the *materialization of ideas* (Czarniawska-Joerges and Joerges 1995) and thus can generate in their turn ideas that tend to materialize themselves, in a process that only when it is captured in its entirety makes possible an understanding of the *nature* and the *forms* of social and organizational change.

THE RELEVANCE OF ARTIFACTS FOR THE STUDY OF ORGANIZATIONAL CULTURES

The need for the study of artifacts is particularly striking for those embarking on the exploration of organizations as cultures – that is to say, as symbolic systems of meaning – for at least two reasons.

In the first place, we can reasonably conjecture, as I have elsewhere claimed (Gagliardi 1990a), that artifacts do not constitute secondary and superficial manifestations of deeper cultural phenomena (Schein 1984), but are themselves – so to speak – primary cultural phenomena which influence corporate life from two distinct points of view: (a) artifacts make materially possible, help, hinder, or even prescribe organizational *action*; (b) more generally, artifacts influence our *perception* of reality, to the point of subtly shaping beliefs, norms and cultural values.

In the second place, if one is concerned with organizational symbolism, one must not forget that symbols are *concretions of sense*, and things constitute their more usual and natural abode. To the extent to which, as I said at the beginning, material reality is the vehicle through which ineffable or tacit knowledge – which generally escapes the control of the mind – is communicated, the study of things enables us to aim directly at the heart of a culture, or at what the subjects do not wish – and above all *cannot* – communicate, at least in words. Various authors (Meyerson 1991; Van Maanen 1979; Whyte 1961) have stated that the things most interesting to know about people are those which they take for granted or find difficulty in expressing and discussing openly: that about which the actors lie, or do not manage to be sincere even when they want, is in fact very often what is most central to them and can thus explain important aspects of their behaviour and social relations. So, corporate artifacts can function as 'clues' to ways of seeing and 'feeling' very distant from the rationalizations offered by the actors, sometimes entirely in good faith, when faced with a questionnaire or an interviewer, or during participant observation itself.

In other words, artifacts make it possible to rescue *the sense beyond the action* (Monaci 1991). Without wanting to resuscitate Dilthey and German historicism – and the stress on 'understanding' (*verstehen*) rather than on 'explanation' (*erklären*) – but taking over Weber's filtered version, one may say that as social scientists we are interested in grasping the uniformities in action and in the reasons behind it, taking as our starting-point the socially elaborated meanings of the actors. Up to now the study of action – that is to say of manifest behaviour – and of conscious intentions has been the principal mode of access to systems of meaning. This emphasis on behaviour has been judged a form of short-sightedness in the social sciences (Laughlin and Stephens 1980), and for some time now the necessity has been stressed of providing a more rigorous reformulation of the whole problem of meaning, with the hope that new ways of exploring it will emerge (Foster 1980). The study of artifacts can constitute an answer to this need. It is therefore time to turn our attention to things and to the experience that the actors have of them in society and in organizations.

This experience can be analysed on two different levels, as subjective experience and as social fact. In the first case the aim is to explore the psychological dynamics entailed by our relationship with things; in the second case it is a matter of reconstructing the meaning and the impact of artifacts and of physical reality on the life of an organization and, in general, of a social group.

THE MEANING OF THINGS

The things of the world have the function of stabilizing human life, and their objectivity lies in the fact that ... men, their ever-changing nature notwithstanding, can retrieve their sameness, that is, their identity, by being related to the same chair and the same table. (Arendt 1958: 137)

The most careful study of transactions between people and things is that by Csikszentmihalyi and Rochberg-Halton (1981), which puts together a series of reflections deriving from psychological theories with empirical data gathered during some ethnographic research conducted in the tradition of the Chicago School of urban sociology. Two observations – central to the authors' argument – deserve to be looked at here since they provide a convincing psychological reason for some of the regularities observable in organizational life and can serve as important elements in the conceptual framework that I am trying to construct. The first observation concerns the relationship between things and the development of the self, the second the interactive nature of our relationships with objects.

If it is easy to concede that the things we *create*, which we *use* and with which we *surround* ourselves 'reflect' our personality, it is more difficult to acknowledge – Csikszentmihalyi and Rochberg-Halton observe – that often they are *part of* or an *extension of the self*, not in a metaphorical or mystical sense but in a factual and concrete sense. Depth psychology has from time past shown the importance of the 'object'

and of 'objectual' investment in the construction of personal identity, referring generally, however, to relationships with other people and not to relationships with inanimate objects. But people invest psychic energy both in other people and in ideas or things. Things – as compared to people and ideas – have the singular property of restituting to the self a feedback that is steadily and immediately perceptible to the senses. Even the feedback from our investment in ideas or people comes to us unquestionably through material signs and things: if, for example, we seek confirmation of our identity as thinkers through the working out of ideas, it is only the *written page* in front of us – it is only the *materialized* idea – which reassures us about our capacity to pursue such aims. Only the sight, the feel, the smell of printing ink from the newly published book unequivocally tell us that we are capable of exercising those particular forms of control of external reality with which our identity as writers is bound up.

Things thus incorporate our intentions of control, and the self develops out of feedback to acts of control. In things reside the traces and memories of our past, the witness to our present experiences, our desires and our dreams for the future. Things tell us constantly who we are, what it is that differentiates us from others and what it is that we have in common with others. And in many cases it is difficult to trace out the boundary between our bodily identity and external physical reality: a judge is not a judge, does not feel himself such and is not perceived as such without his robes; a woman feels herself beautiful because she has an elegant dress; and for all of us the possibility of driving nonchalantly down a narrow street depends on the fact that we have learned to 'feel' the car as an extension of our bodily schema.

Inanimate objects that on first view seem often to be only the outcome of our projects or the ground of our dominion, have in reality an 'active' role which has been brought out by various writers and analysed from various points of view. Scarry states that 'the object is only a fulcrum or lever across which the force of creation moves back onto the human site and remakes the makers' (1985: 307). It has been said that artifacts are pathways of action (Gagliardi 1990a) in the sense that they structure sensory experience and enlarge or narrow the range of behaviour that is materially *possible*. But they can even embody – as Latour (1992a) has shown in his analysis of, for example, the impact of an automated door-closer on human behaviour – a programme of action which prescribes a *specific* piece of behaviour. Finally, given that in all objects, even the most practical, it is difficult to separate function from symbolic meaning, the 'power' of the object derives from its capacity – as a symbol – of *awakening* sensations, feelings and reasons for acting. The stimulating and creative role of an inanimate symbol shows itself in a special way when it stands not for something else that *exists*, but for something else that *might exist*, in which case it is not a symbol *of* reality but a symbol *for* reality. This meaning of things, Csikszentmihalyi and Rochberg-Halton note, is not exclusively the outcome of a projection of categories of thought by the knowing subject. In other words the meaning of things does not depend only on the structure of the mind: it is equally determined by the intrinsic and sensible properties that things have (which make them fitted to convey specific meanings) and by the experience which the circumstances foster of them, even beyond (in the case of artifacts) the intentions of their creator.

The interactive nature of our relationship with things has also been described by Witkin (1974) – with particular regard to artistic creation – as a reverberative process, a continual shuttling between the impulse which shapes the expressive action and the material means through which the impulse expresses itself, till one becomes the echo of the other. Alluding to the same dynamics, Fabbri (1992: 38) has even spoken of a 'malignity' in objects, which constitute in their irreducible materiality and otherness 'a radical challenge to subjectivity which wearies itself, fades in the attempt to interpret their dumbness'.[7]

THE CORPORATE LANDSCAPE

Men must feed themselves, wrest from nature the conditions for their survival; and can do so only by taking account of the environment that characterizes their habitat. History shows us, however, that their productive practices are not necessarily in functional accord with this environment, but are equally determined by rites, symbols, ideas – in brief, by a worldview. A pure productive practice does not exist; every productive practice is immediately a symbolic practice of appropriation of the world; every productive practice is a way of responding, fitted to a determined environment, to the basic biological requirement, but in so far as that is already culturally formulated. And the signature through which an environment testifies to this *cultural requirement of survival* is called landscape.[8] (Duby 1986: 29)

Material reality, which performs such an important role in the construction and development of the individual self, is equally decisive, perhaps more so, for the collective identity of an organization. If, in fact, the existence of a consciousness of self which does not seek confirmation in the external world is theoretically admissible – in extreme and pathological forms of solipsism – the existence of a social self which is not *publicly* objectivized in forms which survive the coming and going of individual people and generations, and which embody a *sharable* vision of reality, is conceptually unthinkable (Arendt 1958).

In an organization, ends are pursued, energies invested and ideas made concrete in machines, products and places. All this is done through productive practices which – as Duby says in the passage just cited – are never pure productive practices but are always also symbolic practices, combinations of expressive disinterested (aesthetic) actions and of impressive actions aimed at practical results. Actions, like thoughts and speeches, are contingent signs, destined to vanish if they are not reified. Only things last. A brilliant idea left out of the minutes of a meeting can be irretrievably lost. And students of strategic management learned long ago to identify the real strategy of an organization by the choices irreversibly incorporated in its concrete investments or disinvestments, in the renovated building, in the plant that is set up or dismantled.

In order to think and act, especially when they must reciprocally coordinate, organizational actors need an intelligible world. Things are the visible counterparts of this intelligibility, they indicate rational categories and hierarchies of values, and in this sense they collectively constitute an important system of communication, alternative to language, as we shall see more clearly below. Above all, things make it possible to pin down meanings, and contain their fluctuations. As Douglas and Isherwood (1979) have observed, verbal rituals, spoken and not recorded, vanish into the air, and hardly contribute to the demarcation of the field of interpretation. For this reason rituals make use of things, and the more costly the ritual accoutrements the stronger and more striking is the intention to fix the meaning for the future.

The instantaneous perception of things is linked with our idea of *space*. Just as new things are being incessantly created, others are multiplying and spreading, while still others are discarded. They reveal patterns of invention, repetition, and selection, cycles of stability and change, chaos and order: from things emerge the form which the collective identity has taken on over *time* (Kubler 1962). The physical setting of an organization (with its formal qualities, i.e. sensorially perceptible qualities) is thus the most faithful portrayal of its cultural identity, and artifacts – to the extent that they adumbrate a view of the world (and of the self in the world), in the dual sense of how one believes *it is* and of how one *would like it to be* – constitute a vital force for the evolution of the organization as culture.

The worldview that the physical setting offers daily and uninterruptedly to the unconscious perception of members constitutes at the same time indelible testimony about the past and a guide for the future. Thus it contains an implicit promise of immortality for the collective self, a public declaration that the organization will survive as a super-individual and impersonal reality (Sievers 1990). The concern of French presidents to link the construction of grandiose monuments to their time in office unequivocally expresses their desire to contribute and define the *form over time* of 'Frenchness'. On a smaller scale, the president of an industrial association – whose mandate was only three years – told me that all his predecessors (and he himself was following their example) had been concerned to leave behind some indelible trace of their brief occupation of the post by physically changing the shape of the presidential floor: thus waiting rooms, meeting rooms and offices changed form and aspect, shrinking and growing alternately, every time offering subtly different conceptions of a microcosm of roles and relations.

In light of the considerations set out so far, we can state that the supreme manifestation of a culture is the landscape, that is to say, a *natural* reality which has inscribed within itself a *cultural* code. This code is in the first place an aesthetic code. The argument for this latter affirmation requires some reflection on the relations existing between *ideas/concepts* and *images/forms*, *identity* and *style*, systems of *meanings* and systems of *sensations*.

To translate an idea into an image (or vice versa) entails passing from the conceptual abstract order to the formal concrete order, expressing, that is, a logical relationship between representations of the *mind* in terms of relations between formal elements perceptible to the *senses*. In a visual image these relations are spatial and chromatic, in an auditory perception they are temporal relations between sonic stimuli of different pitch and intensity, and so on. Every cultural system seems to have structural correspondences between its ontological or deontological codes and its aesthetic codes, that is to say, between systems of beliefs and of values on the one hand, and specific patterns of relation/combination between formal elements on the other. Hauser (1952), for example, studied the connection between the geometric style, the stability of institutions and the autocracy of forms of government in the culture of neolithic peasantry, while Vernant (1969) studied the relationship between the structuring of space and

political organization in ancient Greece, and Panofsky (1974) studied the relationship between Gothic architecture and scholastic philosophy. Coming to artistic movements closer to our time, considerable interest has been shown in the relation between Italian Futurism and fascism (De Maria 1973). Croce (1924), for example, claims that the conceptual source of fascism is to be found in Futurism and its trumpeted values of determination, aggressivity, thirst for the new, the rejection of tradition, the exaltation of force, youth and modernity. Like Croce, the leaders of the movement themselves (Marinetti 1924) stressed the links between Futurist ideology – the Futurist notion of the function of art in society – and fascist ideology, especially in its original revolutionary elements. But it is also possible to set out detailed structural correspondences between these ideologies and the Futurist aesthetic codes. For example, the exaltation of dynamism finds its correspondence in the paradoxical efforts of Boccioni (1912) to represent movement in sculpture despite the fixity of the material. Again, the idea that Futurist art (and fascism) had to destroy society and re-create it on new foundations has its counterpart in the tendency of the Futurist painters to burst the boundaries of their traditional space through the materiality of their pigments, the stridency of their colours, and the striving to make the canvas three-dimensional (Fael 1993).

In the same way, translating a particular conception of ourselves into concrete behaviour entails passing from an abstract definition of our *identity* to the adoption of a *style*, a word which we usually associate with an aesthetic – in the broad sense – experience. This problem is well known to those who are concerned with corporate identity, and who seek to translate particular conceptions of the collective self into subtle formal variants of elements – graphic, spatial, chromatic – that are sensorially perceptible.

There is a widely held opinion, even among anthropologists and historians of art (Firth 1973), that artifacts are the illustration of a *pre-existing* worldview, and that therefore the translations of which I have been speaking are always one-directional: from abstract thought to concrete manufactured object. But it is difficult to say whether it is ideas which produce forms or forms which generate ideas. I have from the start expressed my leaning towards considering aesthetic experience *basic*, if for no other reason than that it takes place *before* (and often *without*) the intellect's conferring of unity on the data of sensory experience through concepts (Gagliardi 1990a). Artifacts – according to Goldwater's (1973) thesis as taken over by Geertz (1983) – convey their own messages, often untranslatable into ideas, at least to the same extent as they demonstrate existing conceptions. In this sense, the relation between systems of meanings and systems of sensations is probably circular in nature.

Students of organizational cultures who have a cognitivist bias (that is, students who are primarily interested in mental representations of cultures) often use the expression 'vision of reality' metaphorically to indicate a 'conception' of reality. I am suggesting that we use the expression literally, to look at the corporate landscape as a materialization of a worldview, and strive to interpret the aesthetic code written into the landscape as a privileged pathway to the quiddity of a culture.

A land becomes landscape – it is aestheticized, so to speak – in two different ways, working that is *in situ* (in the physical place) and also *in visu* (into the eye) (Roger 1991). The first way consists of writing the aesthetic code directly onto the physicality of the place, populating it with artifacts; the second consists in educating the eye, in furnishing it with schemata of perception and taste, models of vision, 'lenses' through which to look at reality.

The two modalities described are equally important in the processes of socialization. The first – the writing of the aesthetic code into the physicality of place – is easily observed by those who do not belong to the culture in question, even if it is not always easy to interpret. Every landscape has a scenographic element, meaning that it is 'constructed to be seen'. This setting displays and hides, provides backgrounds and close-ups, sequences and articulations. Often the setting constitutes a real visual metaphor (just as a caricature does): it prompts one to interpret a factory as a cathedral, a pathway as a labyrinth, a ministry as a monastery (Larsen and Schultz 1990).

The second mode of aestheticization of a physical place – the writing of the aesthetic code into the eye – is very much more difficult to grasp: it is a matter, in fact, of managing to see things materially 'through the eyes' of the natives. The importance of the education of the eye in a culture has been stressed by Worth (Worth and Adair 1972; Worth 1981), who speaks of the anthropology of visual communications and distinguishes it from visual anthropology, indicating by the former the study of *a way of seeing* – and hence a way of photographing, filming, portraying, putting on show – as a culturally determined phenomenon, and by the latter the ethnographer's use of film or photographs to record cultural phenomena in images which replace or fill out the written report (Dabbs 1982; Van Maanen 1982). For Worth, a way of seeing is a way of choosing and combining in images aspects and fragments of the real, expressing in this way one's conception of the world and of one's role in the world. In contrast to Arnheim's (1969) objectivist standpoint, Worth denies that the natural world presents an intrinsic order to the eye: it is the eye which projects onto the world an image of order. Visual communication thus presupposes the sharing of conventions between those who transmit and those who receive a message, a shared education of the eye: looking from close to and not from a distance, looking at the details and not the whole, the form more than the colour, and so on. Even a setting which selects and combines elements for the specific purpose of exhibiting them can hence be looked at from many points of view, and it is this which often makes interpretation difficult for the outsider.

The idea that the particular conception of the order which is in force in a culture is the reflection of sense experiences that are either inevitable or possible in that culture (and, conversely, the idea that every landscape is the materialization of a particular conception of the order of things) seems well worth exploring in the world of organizations, which base their social legitimacy on their instrumentality as regards specific ends and which *should* consequently tend to be *ordered* on the basis of criteria of instrumental rationality. How do pragmatic exigencies and the aesthetic code combine to determine the organizational order? How does the aesthetic code of an organization arise and change? What relationship is there between the aesthetic code and the idealized image of the collective identity? What relationship is there between the structure of the physical setting – the form of the corporate landscape – and the corporate structure – the form of the social organization? Can the form of the social organization reflect a conscious ideal of beauty (Ramirez 1991)? These questions indicate fascinating areas for research to which it would be worthwhile devoting far greater resources and energies than those that have so far been invested.

AESTHETIC EXPERIENCES AND ORGANIZATIONAL CONTROL

Beauty is a ray of light that from the first good
    derives
and into appearances then divides . . .
Into the senses it comes and then the wits,
and shows in one forms scattered and split apart:
it feeds and does not sate, and creates from part
to part desire for itself and hope of bliss.[9]

Galeazzo di Tarsia, *Canzoniere*

As tangible reality the organization offers itself not only to the eye but to all the possible forms of sensory knowledge, even if not all the senses – or not all to the same extent – are solicited by the diverse artifacts which populate the different organizations. It is also true that – in the human species – not all the senses are equally developed or have the same completeness, the same perceptive potential, as sight. Nevertheless, the dynamics described with reference to vision are very likely common to all the forms of sense experience: every organizational culture educates the sense of taste, of smell, of touch, of hearing, as well as of sight.

The wealth of associative and reactive capacities that people accumulate through living in a specific physical-cultural setting forms a set of patterns of classification, interpretation and reaction to perceptual stimuli that I propose to call 'sensory maps' (Gagliardi 1990a), distinguishing them from 'cognitive maps' (Weick 1979). Cognitive maps can be conscious or unconscious but are 'knowable'; sensory maps are learned instinctively through intuitive and imitative processes over which the mind exercises no control, and integrated automatically into life daily.

A corporate culture, then, is recognizable not only by the specificity of its beliefs – the 'logos' that pertains to *cognitive* experience – and of its values – the 'ethos' that pertains to *moral* experience – but also by the specificity of its 'pathos' – the particular way of perceiving and 'feeling' reality – that belongs to aesthetic experience. A concept analogous to that of 'pathos' was formulated by Kubler (1962), in his claim that cultural artifacts are bearers of a central *pattern of sensibility*. Works of art, as things made to be contemplated and admired, reveal this pattern in a special way since action is guided in them only by the expressive impulse, by the way of 'feeling', and therefore need take no account of practical exigencies, as happens instead with other cultural artifacts.

In organizations whose purpose is profit the central pattern of sensibility is difficult to recognize precisely because expressive disinterested action – and the disinterested enjoyment of it, in its ongoing process or in its outcome – has no legitimate place in them: anything gratuitous can't help but be considered waste or play in a social group which demands to be judged on its efficiency and which strives to appear efficient, if not to be so. It is the reverse in not-for-profit (e.g. voluntary) organizations in which, without renouncing instrumental rationality, the 'disinterested' action of members, central to the definition of the collective identity, is set higher on the scale of values: it is more likely that expressivity is permitted or fostered, and the

pattern of sensibility is more immediately and easily recognizable. But in the majority of economically oriented organizations the pattern of sensibility lodges in the folds of impressive actions, corrects the formal scansion of objects and space dictated by practical purposes. Sometimes it stands out clearly – like a lapse in the collective unconscious – in a detail or an object, apparently insignificant and useless, but which instead synthesizes the aesthetic code of a culture, the distinctive 'way of feeling' of its members.

At the opposite extreme, in organizations in which the specific result of the coordinated action of the members is an artistic product, the socialization of a new member is essentially and expressly education to the group pattern of sensibility. The expression of the pattern is not only legitimate but indispensable for organizational action, and communication between the members comes about almost exclusively on the aesthetic level. The most obvious example of such a situation is that of a chamber orchestra which – like the Orpheus Chamber Orchestra – plays without a conductor. Our admiration and astonishment in cases of the kind express our recognition of the power and mystery of ineffable communication. Yet, at levels certainly less refined and where the outcome is less startling, one may presume that there can be no organization which does not make recourse to it, given that the aesthetic is a fundamental component of every human experience: the more the pathos is distinctive and idiosyncratic, the more it constitutes a special bond between members and can turn into an extraordinary resource for coordination.

These latter observations introduce a topic I have already alluded to here and there in the preceding pages – in particular when discussing the relationships between systems of meanings and systems of sensations – but one which merits systematic treatment of its own: the essential characteristics of sensory knowledge and aesthetic communication that differentiate them from intellectual knowledge and communication through the language of words. Various commonplaces and assumptions – related to the dominant views of knowledge discussed in the second section – here invite critical scrutiny.

In the first place, as Langer (1967; 1969) has cogently demonstrated, words constitute merely one of the systems that we employ in symbolizing, a system which owes its supremacy to the natural availability of words, to their cheapness and their readiness to be combined. But it is untrue that the language of words is the expression of knowledge and that other systems of symbolization are mere expression of emotions and of feelings: there is an infinity of things that we *know* and that we cannot say in words, and in the very moment that the mind confers unity on experience through concepts formulable in words, it *reduces* it irremediably. The language of words, in its literal and merely denotative function, is the most excellent of tools for exact reasoning, but its weakness lies in *discursiveness,* in the linear order of words, strung one after the other like beads on a rosary. By contrast, aesthetic communication – based on purely sensory contact with the forms – makes use of a system of symbolization that Langer calls *presentational*: the object is presented directly and holistically, in such a way that its elements – which do not have a fixed and independent meaning like words in a dictionary – are grasped in a single act of perception and understood simultaneously by virtue of their reciprocal relations and of their relation with the global structure of the object.[10]

Discursive language is the vehicle of a *knowledge by description*: it permits us to say one thing at a time. Presentational language is the vehicle of a *knowledge by acquaintance*: it permits us to say more – even contradictory – things simultaneously and without the filter of abstraction. But precisely in this intimacy without mediations, so to speak, lies the richness and ambiguity of aesthetic communication, its capacity to break the schemata and penetrate ineffable reality, its surprising, stunning, moving character, its being – as Bruner (1962: 108) says – 'a play of impulses at the fringe of awareness'. In this sense, aesthetic knowledge is an intuitive knowledge of the *possible*, rather and more than of the *true*, and aesthetic communication is not so much the account of that which has happened as the prompting of that which might happen or might be (Bottiroli 1993).

The *cognitive* potential of the aesthetic experience – bound up with its character of ambiguity, globality, unresolved tension – has been explored by Rochberg-Halton (1979a; 1979b). The approach of this author is based on Dewey's (1934) distinction between 'recognition' – the interpretation of the object based on pre-existent schemes and stereotypes – and 'perception' – the capacity to embrace the object while letting its qualities modify previously formed mental schemes and habits. Perception thus understood is constitutive of aesthetic experience, and the source of psychological development and learning. The conclusion, seemingly paradoxical, is that: 'Aesthetic experiences, which are often considered subjective and hence inessential by social scientists, thus actually may be one of the essential ways we learn to become *objective,* in the sense of coming to recognize the pervasive qualities of the environment in their own terms' (Csikszentmihalyi

and Rochberg-Halton 1981: 178). The idea of the 'superiority' of aesthetic knowledge is implicit in the approach of Dewey and Rochberg-Halton, as it is, for that matter, in the vision of a neo-positivist philosopher such as Polanyi (1966), for whom to know intellectually is to discover what one already knew unconsciously and tacitly at the subliminal level of perception of the body.

I said at the start that I would be using the term 'aesthetic experience' to include every type of sense experience and not only experiences that are socially defined as 'beautiful' or as 'art'. But it is clear that not every form of sense experience presents the above-mentioned features with the same intensity. The pleasure linked to perceptual surprise, the emotion, the learning, depend on at least three factors. The first is the capacity of the object perceived – be it a work of nature or a work of art – to surprise by the novelty of its form. The second is the specific 'pathos' – or pattern of sensibility – that the subject has learned by living in a particular physical-cultural setting and which he/she shares with the other members of that culture: in relation to features of this pattern an event or an object may leave us indifferent or it may reawaken our senses, it may cause pleasure or disgust, it may attract or repulse us. The third is the subjective and contingent willingness to embrace the quality of the object: a natural spectacle already seen more than once will move and surprise us as if we were seeing it for the first time only when we find the time to contemplate it and are willing to perceive it in a new way. From what I have said it follows that the feeling for beauty is a cultural product – like artifacts – and that any event or object has the potential to provide intense aesthetic emotion.

In short, one may agree with Vickers (1982) that we have two different modes of knowledge open to us, both of which we use in our efforts to understand the world in which we live. One mode relies largely on analysis, calculation, and logic, entails abstraction and the manipulation of elements – without concern for the form in which they are combined – and is completely describable. The other mode relies more on synthesis and recognition of the global context, entails recognition or creation of the form – without concern for the elements which constitute it – and is not completely describable. As we know, logico-rational knowledge and aesthetico-intuitive knowledge are both aspects of the neo-cortical development that distinguishes the human species from other mammals and appear to be linked with the specialization of the hemispheres of the brain. The right hemisphere appears to synthesize the perceptual input into holistic images (visual, olfactory, tactile, auditory) maintaining the interrelations between the elements in perception, while the left hemisphere codifies verbal information, processing it serially through hierarchical categories (Dimond and Beaumont 1974).

I have referred already to the importance of aesthetic experiences in relation to certain major organizational issues: in particular, I pointed to the role of artifacts in the formation of a concrete collective identity and in fostering the identification of members. We have also seen how the concept of corporate pathos enables us to considerably expand both our notion of communication media and our understanding of the mechanisms of coordination among inter-dependent activities. The argument just put forward on the differential features of sensory knowledge *vis-à-vis* intellectual knowledge in my view enables us to see in a new light another crucial organizational question, that of control. Organization theory has for some time been stressing the influence of *informative premises* – logical and ideological – in determining the nature of decisions, and hence of organizational action. If the force of sensory knowledge and communication is in part due to the fact that it escapes the control of the mind, the importance taken on by the characteristics of the context and of *perceptual premises* in determining the effective course of events in corporate life becomes evident. For this reason I proposed (Gagliardi 1990a) adding to the three levels of control identified by Perrow (1972) – (1) direct orders, (2) programmes and procedures, (3) influence of the ideological premises of the action – a fourth level corresponding to the possibility of influencing the sensory premises of choices and behaviour. I shall look briefly at some studies that validate this suggestion and, at the same time, exemplify lines of research that could fruitfully be taken further.

Sassoon (1990) has analysed the links existing between colour codes and the formation of ideological thought, showing how shades of colour can express with extraordinary immedi-ateness and efficacy variations in ideological vectors and in the social meaning of artifacts. It will be interesting to investigate empirically how these semantic correspondences – which seem at least in part to be cross-cultural in so far as they are bound up with universal bio-psychological experiences – translate themselves into the specific cultural codes of a society, and what use individual organizations make of these codes (to what extent they embrace them, invert them or adapt them) in relation to their own 'character' and to their own distinctive ideology (Selznick 1957).

In a study of a telecommunications company (Gagliardi 1991) the presence of a 'decomposi-tional-sequential' archetype was identified that perhaps constituted an analogical extension of the procedure used in telegraphic transmission, the original concern of the company. This archetype was primarily recognizable in the structuring of space: the building, laid out only horizontally, had been expanded with successive additions of parts which tended to be single elements themselves, without the pre-existing or the whole ever being questioned. This formal pattern led one to interpret – or expressed the tendency to interpret – the interdependence between the parts exclusively in terms of a unilateral sequentiality, and influenced the division of tasks, the structure of internal communications, the articulation of plans and projects: tasks were extremely fragmented, communications flowed exclusively one way, plans for action tended to be broken down into successive phases minutely specified without any appeal to forms of parallel planning and mechanisms of mutual adjustment. The most obvious use of this archetype was the way in which a global plan for corporate restructuring was conducted: the areas into which the company was divided were restructured *one after another*, and no move was made to pass to the subsequent one until the previous one had been defined in detail.

In another case (Gagliardi 1989) it was possible to interpret the failure of an expensive and massive programme aimed at sensitizing the staff of a bank – the purpose was to instil the value of 'service to the customer' – through an analysis of the perceptual conditioning exerted daily on employees by physical objects and structures: the thickness of the walls, the monumental character of the entrance – extremely lofty, but largely blocked by a steel grill – the luxurious carpets and tapestry in the management offices, and so on. Each of these elements – and all as a set – solicited feelings of solidity, comfort, safety on the one hand, and feelings of independence and superiority over the world outside on the other, rendering in fact barely credible the ambition to invert the image of dominance that the artifacts embodied. This example, like the previous, suggests a need to re-examine the way in which corporate planning and planned corporate change have so far been conceptualized, concentrating more attention on the interplay of physical, symbolic and social structures (Gagliardi 1992).

As final examples, mention must be made of a study by Witkin (1990) and an essay of Rosen et al. (1990). Witkin explored in particularly careful fashion the subtle relationship between the stylistic qualities of artifacts and the sen-suous experience of members of an organization, showing how the design of artifacts can be an instrument of control in bureaucratic organizations. Through an analysis of the formal characteristics of a corporate micro-setting – the boardroom of a large company – he shows how a physical place can foster certain sensations and hinder others, induce a two-dimensional rather than three-dimensional vision of reality, even deliberately suppress 'sensuous values that are centred in the being of the individual as a living subject' (1990: 334). Rosen et al. instead analysed from the macro point of view the dialectical relation between the organization of labour and the structuring of space on the one hand, and the way in which bureaucratic ideology concretely shapes social life on the other. Both these studies prompt further exploration (from a critical and emancipatory standpoint) of the way in which the corporate stage is conceived, constructed, and invested with meaning.

EXPLORING THE CORPORATE PATHOS

'... the resources of science are far from being exhausted. I think that an evening in that study would help me much.'

'An evening alone!'

'I propose to go up there presently . . . I shall seat in that room and see if its atmosphere brings me inspiration. I am a believer in the *genius loci*. You smile, friend Watson. Well, we shall see.'

Conan Doyle, *The Valley of Fear*

The reader who has followed to this point, if he/she has become persuaded of the importance of aesthetic knowledge, action and communication in organizational life, will be asking now how it is possible to investigate this particular form of human and social experience. One of the first questions he/she will probably come up with is whether this new object can be known using the logico-analytical methods traditionally used in the practice of organizational studies or whether the choice of aesthetic experience as object necessarily implies the recourse by the enquirer to aesthetico-intuitive forms of understanding (Strati 1992). One might ask, in other words: can we study the products of the right cerebral hemisphere with the left hemisphere, or is only the right hemisphere capable of really knowing what it itself produces?

Put in these terms, the dilemma is not easily solved. If everything I have said about the incommensurability of the two realms, about the richness of the aesthetic experience and about its ineffability, is plausible, the deployment of analytical methods and of discursive language will be intrinsically reductive, and we will not even be certain that our speeches even partially reflect tacit knowledge. Whether we ask corporate actors to tell us of their aesthetic experiences, or whether it is we ourselves as researchers who interpret them, we will always be dealing with 'espoused' theories which may not in any way coincide with the secret regularities of expressive action. If, on the other hand, we strive to 'feel' as the natives feel, we shall have understood more but we will be unable to transfer to others this 'knowledge by acquaintance' without ourselves employing forms of aesthetic communication. But perhaps this is to ask too much of intellectuals by profession: it is probable that those who have artistic gifts and vocation do not take up organizational studies. At all the international conferences organized over the last fifteen years on organizational culture, the call for papers has prompted out-of-the-way, unorthodox, creative forms of communication, but – with some rare, often disconcerting, exceptions – these have never gone beyond the use of slides that more often contained words than images.

The dilemma that I have posed is as old as the criticism of art: either one describes the work of art, pointing to its analytically observable formal canons – rhythm, sequences, proportions, correspondences – which usually in no way help 'to feel' the work, or one deploys an evocative, allusive, poetic language intended to transfer to the listener the aesthetic emotion experienced by the critic. It is this that leads many people to claim that the great critics are great artists in their turn. This view is very close to that of those who maintain that linguistic invention and aesthetico-literary qualities go a long way to explain the success of scientific theories, at least in the human and social sciences (Geertz 1988). But our problem is how to realistically develop in researchers the ability and the bent which will enable them to investigate aesthetic experiences through modalities appropriate to their nature without having to renounce the transference, and hence the accumulation, of their acquired knowledge, and without requiring them to have innate and marked artistic gifts.

As Bateson and Mead stated in their introduction to *Balinese Character: A Photographic Analysis* (the most comprehensive and ambitious visual ethnography ever carried out), our effort should be 'to translate aspects of culture never successfully recorded by the scientist, although often caught by the artist, into some form of communication sufficiently clear and sufficiently unequivocal to satisfy the requirements of scientific enquiry' (1942: xi). The work of Bateson and Mead is an interesting example of how pictures can be used to illustrate patterns of culture analytically described in the text: the authors used the pictures as records *about* culture rather than records *of* culture, as research tools rather than research material (Worth 1981). However, their more or less implicit assumption that the camera can tell us the 'aesthetic truth' about the social system studied is seriously undermined by the post-modernist critique of traditional 'realist' ethnography and documentary photography: pictures are created social artifacts, to be interpreted by learning the system of conventions used by their makers to imply meanings; as such, they tell us more about the picture-makers than about what is pictured (Harper 1994).

In my view, even in exploring the pathos of an organization it is not a matter of the sole and unconditional employment of a particular form of knowledge and communication. As the scholastic philosophers claimed, knowledge progresses through a systematic shuttling between intuition and rationalization, tacit and conscious knowledge, hand open and hand closed, alternately, with the regularity of breathing. It is a matter, therefore, of employing one or the other form of knowledge and of communication, one or the other cerebral hemisphere, according to the relevance that each may assume in the diverse phases of the research process, and according to the heuristic value of one method *vis-à-vis* the other (that is, according to how much we win or lose in terms of understanding).

There is no doubt that the sole way of *coming to grips with* the pathos of an organization without the filter of the actors' rationalizations, and without the ethnocentric danger of attributing to the organization studied the pattern of sensibility we have assimilated in our own culture (Iwanska 1971), is that of *sharing in the aesthetic experiences* of the natives by immersing ourselves in their perceptual context and allowing ourselves to be imbued by sense experience (Gagliardi 1990a). If we split the process whereby a phenomenon is studied into three main phases – observation, interpretation, report – it is essential in the first phase to abandon oneself to what Kant calls 'passive intuition', and it is not difficult to do so. It is done spontaneously and effortlessly by those who – venturing into a physical and symbolic terrain – are prepared to stay, as the newcomers. If we are interested in exploring the pathos of an organization, we must thus initially act 'as if we are there to stay'. As I have more than once remarked, artifacts constitute the main empirical correlate of pathos. It is to them we shall mostly devote our attention, and faced with any object – even those which appear to have an exclusively practical function – we shall ask not what purpose they serve but what sensations they rouse in us, and record these sensations in the roughest and most immediate possible form in a

new column of the field notes that we are inured to keeping as ethnographers.

The idea of Worth and Adair (1972) of asking natives to film for us, thus concretely showing their 'way of seeing' the world, or Meyer's (1991) notion of asking informants to answer questions with images, figure, diagrams and other visual displays, suggest that there are alternative ways of getting at ineffable knowledge. These proposals, of great interest in my opinion, aim at enriching our field of observation by adding to artifacts already *existing* artifacts produced *on the spot* at the request of the ethnographer. If on the one hand what is produced is certainly influenced by the informant's relationship with the researcher and from his/her eventual desire to lie about himself/herself and the organization to which he/she belongs, on the other hand the possibility of observing the expressive action as it takes place can offer new and diverse opportunities for intuition.

Whether it is a matter of existing artifacts or ones produced on the spot, it is important to resist the structuralist temptation to interpret them as if they had an intrinsic semiotic status, as if they were a system of signs interpretable on the basis of a self-evident grammar accessible to all (Hodder 1994). Just as for verbal language a more complex linguistic model is required to explain poetry, so visual language requires a model more complex than one that can account for an unequivocal system of signs (Forge 1973). Objects, let us remember, are mainly vectors of symbols: they can say many, even contradictory, things, simultaneously, and their meaning oscillates in an ambiguous range, an interweaving of the intentions that motivated their *production* and the conditions of their *reception*, i.e. the sensory and emotive experiences that the artifacts awaken in a specific spatial and temporal context (Semprini 1992). It is a question, true enough, of grasping a code, a syntactic principle, a pattern: but, whatever one wants to call it, it is irremediably local.

Gaining an awareness of the local pattern of sensibility is the most difficult part of the task, not least because it must be done *in good time*. We must in fact manage to 'give a name' to our sensations before we become too inured to the aesthetic climate of the setting and while we are still capable of appreciating the specificity of the stimuli to which we are exposed. There is, in other words, a magical moment, short-lived I believe, in which one can hope to lead out the 'play of impulses at the fringe of awareness' of which Bruner (1962: 108) speaks *beyond* that fringe, translating one's sensations into thoughts without too much betraying them. In the interpretative phase it is then essential to solicit and keep in tension *both* forms of knowledge, achieving that balancing of emotion and reflection, empathy and analytic detachment that is perhaps in general – even when the focus of research is not the pathos of the organization – the essence of ethnographic work. As Whyte has said of his Cornerville study,

> The parts of the study that interest me most depended upon an intimate familiarity with people and situations. . . . This familiarity gave rise to the basic ideas in this book. I did not develop these ideas by any strictly logical processes. They dawned on me out of what I was seeing, hearing, doing – and feeling. They grew out of an effort to organize a confusing welter of experience. . . . I had to balance familiarity with detachment, or else no insights would have come. There were fallow periods when I seemed to be just marking time. Whenever life flowed so smoothly that I was taking it for granted, I had to try to get outside of my participating self and struggle again to explain the things that seemed obvious. (1955: 357)

How may it be possible to develop this ability in the researcher? In the first place, we must admit that to some extent it requires a capacity for self-reflection that cannot be acquired if one does not have a minimum of talent and natural bent. For the rest, the best training is to 'try one's hand' under the guidance of able people. There are no recipes or handbooks, and the only really useful literature in my opinion are autobiographical reports on ethnographic research such as the splendid appendix to *Street Corner Society* from which the quotation above is taken.

Finally, the drafting of the report will rigorously follow logico-analytical methods, but it will be useful if at least in part – and without any pretence to the production of literary artifacts aimed at communicating only or mainly on the aesthetic plane – a little 'eloquence' goes along with the 'logic' and visual reporting with the verbal reporting: we shall be more certain of not having lost too much along the road, the long journey whereby knowledge is generated and passed on. And perhaps we shall learn, little by little, to share a richer, more unitary and decidedly more attractive conception of organizational knowledge.

NOTES

1 The translation is my own.
2 The Standing Conference on Organizational Symbolism – an independent work group within the European Group for Organizational Studies (EGOS) – devoted its Third International Conference (Milan 1987) to 'The Symbolics of Corporate Artifacts'. A selection of those papers which concentrated on all the elements that go to make up the physical setting of corporate life – buildings, objects, images, forms – has been published in an edited book (Gagliardi 1990b).
3 In Baumgarten's definition, aesthetics are the *scientia cognitionis sensitivae* (the science of sensory cognition).
4 Huizinga (1964) has claimed that the eighteenth century is that which took itself and the whole of creation most seriously.
5 My translation.
6 My translation.
7 My translation.
8 My translation.
9 Translated by Michael Sullivan.
10 Langer's distinction between discursive and presentational language corresponds to that of Goodman (1976) between *articulated* language – in which the characters, as the letters of the alphabet, are separate and differentiated without ambiguity, with a univocal correspondence between syntactic and semantic unity – and the *dense/exemplificatory* language – in which the inverse procedure to notation is followed, i.e. one goes not from the label to the object but from the object to the label.

REFERENCES

Ammassari, P. (1985) 'I fondamentali problemi di metodologia della ricerca sociale', *Studi di Sociologia*, 23: 176–93.

Arendt, H. (1958) *The Human Condition*. Chicago: University of Chicago Press.

Arnheim, R. (1969) *Visual Thinking*. Los Angeles: University of California Press.

Barley, S.R., Meyer, G.W. and Gash, D. (1988) 'Cultures of culture: academic practitioners, and the pragmatics of normative control', *Administrative Science Quarterly*, 33(1): 24–60.

Bateson, G. and Mead, M. (1942) *Balinese Character: a Photographic Analysis*. New York: New York Academy of Science.

Boccioni, U. (1912) *Manifesto tecnico della scultura futurista*, 11 aprile.

Bottiroli, G. (1993) *Retorica. L'intelligenza figurale nell'arte e nella filosofia*. Torino: Bollati Boringhieri.

Brown, R.H. (1977) *A Poetic for Sociology*. Cambridge: Cambridge University Press.

Bruner, J. (1962) *Essays for the Left Hand*. Cambridge, MA: Harvard University Press.

Carmagnola, F. (1994) 'Non sapere di sapere'. Unpublished manuscript.

Croce, B. (1924) 'Fatti politici e interpretazioni storiche', *La Stampa*, 15 maggio.

Crovi, R. (1993) *La valle dei cavalieri*. Milano: Arnoldo Mondadori Editore.

Csikszentmihalyi, M. and Rochberg-Halton, E. (1981)

The Meaning of Things. Cambridge: Cambridge University Press.

Czarniawska-Joerges, B. and Joerges, B. (1995) 'Winds of organizational change', in S. Bacharach, P. Gagliardi and B. Mundell (eds), *Studies of Organizations in the European Tradition*. Greenwich, CT: JAI Press.

Dabbs, J.M. (1982) 'Making things visible', in J. Van Maanen, J.M. Dabbs and R.R. Faulkner (eds), *Varieties of Qualitative Research*. Beverly Hills, CA: Sage.

De Maria, L. (ed.) (1973) *Per conoscere Marinetti e il futurismo*. Milano: Mondadori.

Dewey, J. (1934) *Art as Experience*. New York: Minton, Balch.

Dimond, S.J. and Beaumont, J.G. (1974) 'Experimental studies of hemisphere function in the human brain', in S.J. Dimond and J.G. Beaumont (eds), *Hemisphere Function in the Human Brain*. New York: Wiley.

Douglas, M. and Isherwood, B. (1979) *The World of Goods*. New York: Basic Books.

Duby, G. (1986) *Il sogno della storia*. Milano: Garzanti.

Ebers, M. (1985) 'Understanding organizations: the poetic mode', *Journal of Management*, 11(2): 51–62.

Fabbri, P. (1992) 'Dalla parte del maligno', interview by M. Ciampa, *Leggere*, 40.

Fael, A. (1993) 'Le arti visive e il futurismo (manifesti, cinema, teatro)'. Unpublished dissertation, University of Milan.

Firth, R. (1973) 'Tikopia art and society', in A. Forge (ed.), *Primitive Art and Society*. London and New York: Oxford University Press. pp. 25–48.

Forge, A. (1973) 'Introduction', in A. Forge (ed.), *Primitive Art and Society*. London and New York: Oxford University Press. pp. xiii–xxii.

Foster, M.L. (1980) 'The growth of symbolism in culture', in M.L. Foster and S.H. Brandes (eds), *Symbol as Sense: New Approaches to the Analysis of Meaning*. New York: Academic Press.

Gagliardi, P. (1989) 'Instillare il valore del servizio al cliente: problemi di coerenza tra comunicazioni esplicite e implicite'. Unpublished research report.

Gagliardi, P. (1990a) 'Artifacts as pathways and remains of organizational life', in P. Gagliardi (ed.), *Symbols and Artifacts: Views of the Corporate Landscape*. Berlin and New York: de Gruyter. pp. 3–38.

Gagliardi, P. (ed.) (1990b) *Symbols and Artifacts: Views of the Corporate Landscape*. Berlin and New York: de Gruyter.

Gagliardi, P. (1991) 'Archetipi culturali e sviluppo organizzativo'. Unpublished research report.

Gagliardi, P. (1992) 'Designing organizational settings: the interplay between physical, symbolic and social structures', in R. Eisendle and E. Miklautz (eds), *Produktkulturen: Dynamik und Bedeutungswandel des Konsums*. Frankfurt/New York: Campus. pp. 67–77.

Geertz, C. (1983) *Local Knowledge: Further Essays in Interpretive Anthropology*. New York: Basic Books.

Geertz, C. (1988) *Works and Lives: the Anthropologist as Author*. Cambridge: Polity Press.

Goldwater, R. (1973) 'Art history and anthropology: some comparisons of methodology', in A. Forge (ed.), *Primitive Art and Society*. London and New York: Oxford University Press. pp. 1–10.

Goodman, N. (1976) *Languages of Art: an Approach to a Theory of Symbols*. Cambridge: Hackett.

Hamilton, E. (1942) *The Greek Way*. New York: Norton.

Harper, D. (1994) 'On the authority of the image. Visual methods at the crossroads', in N.K. Denzin and Y.S. Lincoln (eds), *Handbook of Qualitative Research*. Thousand Oaks, CA: Sage. pp. 403–12.

Hauser, A. (1952) *The Social History of Art*. New York.

Hodder, I. (1994) 'The interpretation of documents and material culture', in N.K. Denzin and Y.S. Lincoln (eds), *Handbook of Qualitative Research*. Thousand Oaks, CA: Sage. pp. 393–402.

Huizinga, J. (1964) *Homo ludens*. Milano: Il Saggiatore.

Iwanska, A. (1971) 'Without art', *British Journal of Aesthetics*, 11(4): 402–11.

Jones, M.O., Moore, M.D. and Snyder, R.C. (eds) (1988) *Inside Organizations: Understanding the Human Dimension*. Newbury Park, CA: Sage.

Kubler, G. (1962) *The Shape of Time*. New Haven and London: Yale University Press.

Langer, S.K. (1967) *Mind: an Essay on Human Feeling*. Baltimore: Johns Hopkins University Press.

Langer, S.K. (1969) *Philosophy in a New Key: a Study in the Symbolism of Reason, Rite, and Art*. Cambridge, MA: Harvard University Press.

Larsen, J. and Schultz, M. (1990) 'Artifacts in a bureaucratic monastery', in P. Gagliardi (ed.), *Symbols and Artifacts: Views of the Corporate Landscape*. Berlin and New York: de Gruyter. pp. 281–302.

Latour, B. (1992a) 'Where are the missing masses? Sociology of a few mundane artifacts', in W. Bijker and J. Law (eds), *Shaping Technology-Building Society: Studies in Sociotechnical Change*. Cambridge, MA: MIT Press. pp. 225–59.

Latour, B. (1992b) 'Technology is society made durable', in J. Law (ed.), *A Sociology of Monsters: Essays on Power, Technology and Domination*. London: Routledge. pp. 103–31.

Laughlin, C.D. and Stephens, C.D. (1980) 'Symbolism, canalization, and structure', in M.L. Foster and S.H. Brandes (eds), *Symbol as Sense: New Approaches to the Analysis of Meaning*. New York: Academic Press. pp. 323–63.

Mamiani, M. (1992) 'La retorica della certezza: il metodo scientifico di Newton e l'interpretazione dell'Apocalisse', in M. Pera and W.R. Shea (eds), *L'arte della persuasione scientifica*. Milano: Guerini e Associati. pp. 207–26.

Marinetti, F.T. (1924) *Futurismo e fascismo*. Foligno: Campitelli.

Meyer, A.D. (1991) 'Visual data in organizational research', *Organization Science*, 2(2): 218–36.

Meyerson, D.E. (1991) 'Acknowledging and uncovering ambiguities in cultures', in P.J. Frost, L.F. Moore, M.R. Louis, C.C. Lundberg and J. Martin (eds), *Reframing Organizational Culture*. Newbury Park, CA: Sage. pp. 254–70.

Monaci, M. (1991) 'Il valore euristico dello studio degli artefatti'. Unpublished manuscript.

Panofsky, E. (1974) *Architecture gothique et pensée scolastique*. Paris: Editions de Minuit.

Perrow, C. (1972) *Complex Organizations: a Critical Essay*. Glenview, IL: Scott, Foresman.

Polanyi, M. (1966) *The Tacit Dimension*. Garden City, NY: Doubleday.

Ramirez, R. (1991) *The Beauty of Social Organization*. Munich: ACCEDO.

Rochberg-Halton, E. (1979a) 'The meaning of personal art objects', in J. Zuzanek (ed.), *Social Research and Cultural Policy*. Waterloo, Ontario: Otium.

Rochberg-Halton, E. (1979b) 'Cultural signs and urban adaptation: the meaning of cherished household possessions'. Unpublished PhD dissertation, University of Chicago.

Roger, A. (1991) 'Il paesaggio occidentale', *Lettera internazionale*, 30: 38–43.

Rosen, M., Orlikowski, W.J. and Schmahmann, K.S. (1990) 'Building buildings and living lives: a critique of bureaucracy, ideology and concrete artifacts', in P. Gagliardi (ed.), *Symbols and Artifacts: Views of the Corporate Landscape*. Berlin and New York: de Gruyter. pp. 69–84.

Sandelands, L.E. and Buchner, G.C. (1989) 'Of art and work: aesthetic experience and the psychology of work feelings', in L.L. Cummings and B.M. Staw (eds), *Research in Organizational Behavior*, vol. 11. Greenwich, CT: JAI Press. pp. 105–31.

Sassoon, J. (1990) 'Colors, artifacts, and ideologies', in P. Gagliardi (ed.), *Symbols and Artifacts: Views of the Corporate Landscape*. Berlin and New York: de Gruyter. pp. 169–84.

Scarry, E. (1985) *The Body in Pain*. Oxford: Oxford University Press.

Schein, E.H. (1984) 'Coming to a new awareness of organizational culture', *Sloan Management Review*, 25(4): 3–16.

Selznick, P. (1957) *Leadership in Administration*. Evanston, IL: Harper and Row.

Semprini, A. (1992) 'Oggetti, soggetti, testi. Aspetti semiotici della relazione oggettuale', in A. Borsari (ed.), *L'esperienza delle cose*. Genova: Marietti. pp. 61–79.

Sievers, B. (1990) 'The diabolization of death: some thoughts on the obsolescence of mortality in organization theory and practice', in J. Hassard and D. Pym (eds), *The Theory and Philosophy of Organizations: Critical Issues and New Perspectives*. London: Routledge.

Strati, A. (1990) 'Aesthetics and organizational skill', in B. A. Turner (ed.), *Organizational Symbolism*. Berlin: de Gruyter. pp. 207–22.

Strati, A. (1992) 'Aesthetic understanding of organizational life', *Academy of Management Review*, 17(3): 568–81.

Van Maanen, J. (1979) 'The fact of fiction in organizational ethnography', *Administrative Science Quarterly*, 24: 539–50.

Van Maanen, J. (1982) 'Fieldwork on the beat', in J. Van Maanen, J.M. Dabbs and R.R. Faulkner (eds), *Varieties of Qualitative Research*. Beverly Hills, CA: Sage.

Vernant, J.P. (1969) *Mythe et pensée chez les Grecs*. Paris: Maspero.

Vickers, G. (1982) 'Razionalità e intuizione', in J. Wechsler (ed.), *L'estetica nella scienza*. Roma: Editori Riuniti. pp. 173–99.

Weick, K. (1979) 'Cognitive processes in organizations', in L.L. Cummings and B.M. Staw (eds), *Research in Organizational Behavior*, vol. 1. Greenwich, CT: JAI Press. pp. 41–74.

Whyte, W.F. (1955) *Street Corner Society*. Chicago: University of Chicago Press.

Whyte, W.F. (1961) *Men at Work*. Homewood, IL: Dorsey Press.

Witkin, R.W. (1974) *The Intelligence of Feeling*. London: Heinemann.

Witkin, R.W. (1990) 'The aesthetic imperative of a rational-technical machinery: a study in organizational control through the design of artifacts', in P. Gagliardi (ed.), *Symbols and Artifacts: Views of the Corporate Landscape*. Berlin and New York: de Gruyter. pp. 325–38.

Worth, S. (1981) *Studying Visual Communication*. Philadelphia: University of Pennsylvania Press.

Worth, S. and Adair, J. (1972) *Through Navajo Eyes: an Exploration in Film Communication and Anthropology*. Bloomington, IN: Indiana University Press.

3.5

Images of Time in Work and Organization

JOHN HASSARD

This chapter examines how time and temporality have been portrayed in studies of work and organization. The chapter is developed in three sections. In the first, we outline some of the key images of time to emerge from social philosophy and social theory. This short section draws contrasts between images which emanate from two key time metaphors, the line and the cycle.

In the second section, we examine the main images of time to emerge from the history of industrial capitalism. While initially the focus is upon those linear time images which stem from the progressive intensification and commodification of the labour process, subsequently this section is qualified by time images which reflect the circularity of cultural reproduction in the workplace. In this analysis, an examination of the homogeneous time-reckoning systems of Taylorism is complemented by examples of heterogeneous time-reckoning from ethnographic studies of work and occupations.

Finally, in the third section, we address structural issues of time and organization. We argue that the structure of social time, and ultimately of organizations, is based on three temporal factors: sychronization, sequencing, and rate of activity. Following a discussion of the notion of career as a normative 'time chart' for organization members, the chapter assesses the three main time problems that organizations must solve: the reduction of temporal uncertainty; inter-unit conflicts of interest over temporal matters; and the inevitable scarcity of time. The chapter shows how, in a very real sense, organizations owe their existence to the need for collectivities to solve these problems.

IMAGES OF TIME

To develop a sociologically informed analysis of time, we will first construct a conceptual framework. To achieve this, we draw upon some of the main images of time in social philosophy and upon two of the main time metaphors in social theory. These concerns are then brought together in the main body of the chapter, which analyses how these various temporal images are employed in studies of work and organization.

Social Philosophy

In philosophy, there is a long and sophisticated tradition of temporal analysis. The concept of time has, as Jaques (1982: xi) notes, been of central concern to philosophers for over 2,000 years. Debate is found at a number of abstract levels, ranging from ontological concerns with time and existence to epistemological concerns with time and understanding. It is a tradition which has yielded a wealth of abstract, complex, yet unresolved questions (see Gale 1968). Although a detailed analysis of such questions is beyond our scope, we can note some of the main issues which confront the philosopher of time. To achieve this, we turn to the excellent introduction to temporal philosophy presented by Heath (1956).

Heath introduces the philosophy of time by asking three questions central to discussions in the field. First, at the level of ontology, he asks whether we should regard time as an objective 'fact' located 'out there' in the external world, or as a subjective 'essence' which is constructed via a 'network of meanings'; that is, should we think of time as real and concrete or as essential and abstract? Second, he asks whether we should think of time as homogeneous (where time units are equivalent) or as heterogeneous (where time units are experienced differentially); is time atomistic and divisible or continuous and infinite? And third, he asks whether time can be measured, and if so, whether we can have more than one valid time; should time be regarded as a 'unitary quantitative commodity' or as a 'manifold qualitative experience'?

It can be argued that the ways in which we answer these questions will determine how we conceptualize time in relation to the analysis of work and organization. Heath's antinomies represent basic constructs for interpreting the nature of time in formal institutions. Moreover, they provide a set of tools for dissecting sociological concepts relating to temporal issues of organization, and lay analytical foundations for associated research perspectives.

Metaphor

Sociologists have argued that metaphor is another powerful tool for social analysis (Manning 1979; Pinder and Moore 1979; Tinker 1986). In particular, it has become popular to use metaphors, or other related tropes, when illustrating the imagery of sociological concepts (see Lakoff and Johnson 1980). Morgan (1986), for example, has shown the power of metaphor for interpreting work organizations as 'systems', 'machines', 'dramas', 'organisms', and even 'psychic prisons'.

Although the literature on the philosophy of time is replete with metaphoric images (see Gale 1968), thus far only a few generic metaphors have evolved to conceptualize what is, like organization, an abstract and elusive notion (see Jacques 1982). Of those that have evolved, the most sociologically illuminating have been the 'cycle' and the 'line'.

Cyclic Time

For the metaphor of cycle, one of the most sophisticated analyses has been that provided by Eliade (1959). Eliade describes how the cycle was the basic time metaphor of what he calls 'archaic man' (or 'pre-Christian man'). He suggests that for archaic man events unfolded in an ever recurring rhythm; his sense of time was developed out of his struggle with the seasons; his time horizon was defined by the 'myth of the eternal return'. In contrast, Eliade argues that when 'Christian man' abandoned this bounded world for a direct, linear progression to redemption and

salvation, for the first time he found himself exposed to the dangers inherent in the historical process. Since then humankind has tried to master history and to bring it to a conclusion; as, for example, Marx and Hegel sought to do. In the modern world, we seek refuge in various forms of faith in order to rationalize a historical process that seems to have neither beginning nor end (Eliade 1959; see also Park 1980; Fabian 1983).

Linear Time

A complementary analysis is developed by de Grazia (1972) in his assessment of the linear time metaphor. De Grazia suggests similarly that, whereas primitive concepts of time are dominated by the metaphor of the cycle, for modern societies Christian beliefs give the image of time as a straight line – as a testing pathway from sin on earth, through redemption, to eternal salvation in heaven. He argues that in the evolution of modern culture the idea of irreversibility has replaced that of eternal return. The distinguishing feature of ultimate progression has led the way to a new linear concept of time, and with it a sense of firm beginning. For example, in book II of his *Confessions*, Augustine broke the circle of Roman time. In contrast to Herodotus and his notion of the cycle of human events, Augustine dispelled 'false circles' and instead purported the straight line of human history. Although *anno Domini* chronology became widespread only during the eighteenth century, history began to be dated from the birth of Jesus Christ.

TIME, INDUSTRIALISM AND THE WORKPLACE

For us, the linear metaphor is important because of its link with a further concept, time as a commodity of the industrial process. This link is central to the development of what we shall term the linear-quantitative tradition of temporal imagery in industrial sociology.

The Linear-Quantitative Tradition

During the rise of industrial capitalism this sense of unilinearity was to find time equated with value (E.P. Thompson 1967; Nyland 1986; Thrift 1990). Time, like the individual, became a commodity of the production process, for in the crucial equation linking acceleration and accumulation, a human value could be placed upon time. Surplus value could be accrued through extracting more time from labourers than was required to produce goods having the value of their wages (Marx 1976). The emphasis was upon formality and scarcity. The images came from Newton and Descartes: time was real, uniform and all-embracing; it was a mathematical phenomenon; it could be plotted as an abscissa.

In this tradition, modern industrial cultures adopt predominantly linear time perspectives. Here, the past is unrepeatable, the present is transient, and the future is infinite and exploitable. Time is homogeneous: it is objective, measurable, and infinitely divisible; it is related to change in the sense of motion and development; it is quantitative. Whereas in modern theology linear time has as its conclusion the promise of eternity, in the mundane, secular activities of industrialism temporal units are seen as finite. Time is a resource that has the potential to be consumed by a plethora of activities. In advanced societies time scarcity makes events become more concentrated and segregated, with special 'times' being given over for various forms of activities. Time is experienced not only as a sequence but also as a boundary condition. As the functionalist sociologist Wilbert Moore stated, time becomes 'a way of locating human behaviour, a mode of fixing the action that is particularly appropriate to circumstances' (1963a: 7).

By uniting the ideas of linearity and value we begin to see time as a limited good: its scarcity enhances its worth. Lakoff and Johnson (1980) crystallize this idea by citing three further metaphors to illustrate the dominant conception of linear time: time is money; time is a limited resource; time is a valuable commodity. Graham (1981), likewise, suggests that time and money are increasingly exchangeable commodities: time is one means by which money can be appropriated, in the same way as money can be used to buy time; money increases in value over time, while time can be invested now to yield money later.

This quantitative, commodified image of time thus emerges as primarily a by-product of industrialism. Mumford (1934: 14) for instance has emphasized how 'the clock, not the steam engine [was] the key machine of the industrial age'. He argues that rapid developments in synchronization were responsible for organizations of the industrial revolution being able to display such high levels of functional specialization. Large production-based firms required considerable segmentation of both parts and processes in time and space. Such specialization set requirements for extensive time/space coordination at both intra- and inter-organizational levels. As high levels of coordination needed high levels of planning, so sophisticated temporal schedules were necessary to provide a satisfactory degree of predictability. The basis of fine prediction became that of sophisticated measurement, with efficient organization becoming synonymous with detailed temporal assessments of productivity. As the machine became the focal point of work, so time schedules became the central feature of planning. During industrialism the clock was *the* instrument of coordination and control. The time period replaced the task as the focal unit of production (Mumford 1934; see also Landes 1983).

In another landmark study, E.P. Thompson (1967) argues that industrialism sees a crucial change in the employment relation, as it is now time rather than skill or effort that becomes of paramount concern. In large-scale manufacturing, the worker becomes subject to extremely elaborate and detailed forms of time discipline (E.P. Thompson 1967; see also McKendrick 1962). Whereas prior to industrialism 'nearly all craftsmen were self employed, working in their own homes with their tools, to their own hours' (Wright 1968: 16), with the factory system came temporal rigidification. Before the industrial revolution the prime characteristic of work was its irregularity. Periods of intense working were followed by periods of relative inactivity. There was the tradition of 'St Monday', with Mondays often being taken as a casual day like Saturday and Sunday; most of the work was done in the middle of the week (Reid 1976). Similarly, the length of the working day was irregular and determined largely by the time of the year. E.P. Thompson's quote from Hardy complements his analysis well: 'Tess . . . started her way up the dark and crooked lane or street not made for hasty progress; a street laid out before inches of land had value, and when one-handed clocks sufficiently subdivided the day' (1967: 56).

The linear-quantitative tradition thus emphasizes how, in contrast to the task-oriented experience of most historical and developing economies, under industrial capitalism not only have the great majority of workers become subject to rigidly determined time schedules, but they have also become remunerated in terms of temporal units: that is, paid by the hour, day, week, month, or year. The omnipresence of the factory clock brought with it the idea that one is exchanging time rather than skill: selling labour-time rather than labour. Under industrial capitalism, workers are forced to sell their time by the hour (see Gioscia 1972).

Out of this form of analysis industrial sociology came to view modern conceptions of time as hegemonic structures whose essences are precision, control, and discipline. In industrial societies, the clock becomes the dominant machine of productive organization; it provides

584 HANDBOOK OF ORGANIZATION STUDIES

the signal for labour to commence or halt activity. Workers must consult the time-clock before they begin working. Although life in modern societies is structured around times allocated for many different activities, it is always production that takes preference: 'Man is synchronised to work, rather than technology being synchronised to man' (de Grazia 1972: 439). Time is given first to production; other times must be fitted around the margins of the production process. Ideal productive organizations are those having temporal assets which are highly precise in their structuring and distribution. As technological determinism dominates modern perceptions of time, so correct arithmetical equations are seen as the solutions to time problems: there are finite limits and optimal solutions to temporal structuring. The basic rule is that a modern productive society is effective only if its members follow a highly patterned series of temporal conventions; each society's productive day must be launched precisely on time. In this process, clock-time holds advantages for capital as it is both visible and standardized. It has two strengths in particular: it provides a common organizing framework to synchronize activities, and it commodifies labour as a factor of production (Clark 1982; Hassard 1990).

It is indeed from this scenario that, for industrial sociology, Frederick W. Taylor was to emerge as the heir to Adam Smith's pin factory, and thus to become the high priest of rational time use. It is in the manuals of industrial engineers following Taylor (1911) that were found the logical conclusions to the ideas of Smith, Ricardo and Babbage. Scientific management, and the time and motion techniques that were its legacy, established by direct administrative authority what the machine accomplished indirectly, namely fine control of human actions. In Taylorism we reach the highpoint in separating labour from the varied rhythms experienced in craft or agricultural work: clock rhythms replace fluctuating rhythms; machine-pacing replaces self-pacing; labour serves technology.

Thus, for modern industrial societies, the linear conception of time became 'commodified' due to a major change in economic development; that is, when time was discovered as a factor in production. Time was a value that could be translated into economic terms: 'it became the medium in which human activities, especially economic activities, could be stepped up to a previously unimagined rate of growth' (Nowotny 1976: 330). Time was a major symbol for the production of economic wealth. No longer was it merely given, and reproducible through cultural notions of the 'eternal return',

but it represented instead an economic object whose production is symbolized. Under industrial capitalism, timekeepers were the new regulators and controllers of work; they quantified and transformed activity into monetary value. When time became a valuable commodity its users were obliged to display good stewardship; time was scarce and must be used rationally (see Julkunnen 1977; Thrift 1990).

The Neglect of Qualitative Time-Reckoning

The linear-quantitative thesis is powerful because it describes how, under industrial capitalism, time became an object for consumption. Time becomes reified and given commodity status so that relative surplus value can be extracted from the labour process. The emphasis is upon time as a boundary condition of the employment relation. Time is an objective parameter rather than an experiential state (Fabian 1983).

However, the standard linear-quantitative thesis is one needing qualification. When taken up by industrial sociologists, especially those concerned with labour process analysis, it is often used to overstate the quantitative rationality of production practices and understate the qualitative construction of temporal meanings (Starkey 1988). There is a tendency, for example, to gloss over the fact that the industrial world is not simply composed of machine-paced work systems, but includes a wealth of work processes based on self-paced production.

Although temporal flexibility has recently been associated with new structural forms of employment (see Atkinson 1984; Pollert 1988), in the more subtle sense of social construction, it has long remained widespread in boundary spanning organizational functions, such as sales, marketing, R&D, and corporate planning. Moreover, while professional roles retain flexible, event-based task trajectories, also many non-professional occupations operate within irregular, if not totally self-determined, temporal patterns. As Moore (1963b: 29ff) pointed out some years ago, examples here include the emergency services, police, and maintenance crews. Further, event-based temporal trajectories have long been commonplace within Britain's large service economy, while new forms of employment systems have violated the tradition of selling labour-time in the homogeneous sense of eight hours a day, five days a week, fifty weeks a year. An example of this increasing heterogeneity in work-time arrangements is the 'no-hours' contract in retailing, where an employee can (in theory) decline to accept the work schedules offered by management.

We can begin to question, therefore, whether the linear-quantitative thesis should be applied so readily as the basis for explaining the nature of time at work. Whereas writers sympathetic to Braverman's (1974) structuralist thesis suggest that progressive temporal commodification accompanies increased deskilling, other writers note that employers' time-structuring practices are far more complex and less deterministic than mainstream labour process theory implies (see Clark 1982; Clark et al. 1984; Starkey 1988; Hassard 1990).

Clark (1982: 18), for instance, suggests that 'the claim that commodified time has to be transposed into a highly fractionated division of labour through Taylorian recipes is naive.' Drawing upon socio-technical theory, he offers examples of 'rational' task designs that are not anticipated by the Marxian theory of the 'porous day' (see also Clark et al. 1984). For example, in socio-technical systems a major key to improving productivity, and also the quality of working life, is to permit temporal autonomy. Here, much time-structuring is taken away from the 'planners' and handed over to the 'executors', that is, to the semi-autonomous work group or work cell.

Indeed many of the scenarios that emerge from an unrestrained linear-quantitative thesis require scrutiny. The standard image is of homogeneous activities being measured in microseconds in order to form some optimal, aggregate, standardized production output. However, production line ethnographies (e.g. by Roy 1960; Cavendish 1982; Kamata 1982) have documented how this image ignores the power of work groups, on even the most externally determined task processes, to construct their own time-reckoning systems. Whilst in comparison to other forms of organization the temporal inventories of manufacturing are exact, they remain of bounded rationality when we consider contingencies such as effort, technical failure, market demand and withdrawals of labour.

For contemporary market-based organizations, time inventories are by no means so finite and determined as the so-called 'rational' models would portray. Stability and the deployment of long-term time horizons are luxuries rarely available within the conditions of chaos and turbulence which characterize the 'postmodern' organizational world (see Clegg 1990; Hassard 1993). Despite the emergence of technologies designed to ensure temporal stability (e.g. robotics, flexible manufacturing systems, computer integrated manufacturing), most industrial time-structuring sees production processes subject to the fallible judgements of planners and supervisors. In everyday practice,

time systems are rarely a set of optimal solutions to mechanical problems: temporal strategies are factors which seldom equate with ideal calculations. Bounded rationality still characterizes decision-making linked to production management. Firms which have sought to eliminate temporal porosity, through attempting to realize computer integrated manufacturing, have often reverted to less technologically sophisticated operating systems (e.g. cellular manufacturing) when faced with the difficulties experienced in achieving database integrity for their own operations and adequate electronic data interchange with suppliers and customers.

Towards Cyclic-Qualitative Time Analysis

It can be argued, therefore, that working time is a much richer phenomenon than is portrayed in mainstream industrial sociology. Dominant perspectives such as functionalism and structuralism mostly fail to capture the complexity of industrial temporality. Such paradigms concentrate either on delineating ideal-types of temporal structuring, or on suggesting that working time reflects the social relations of capitalist production.

However, in contrast to the wealth of sociological studies which reflect elements of the linear-quantitative tradition (see Table 1), studies of temporal experience are few. The qualitative dimension of working time is understated, and research evidence is found only in occasional pieces of ethnography. To conduct research into working time, it can be argued that we need qualitative as well as quantitative approaches: we need methods which access intersubjective features as well as structural ones; methods which describe subjective as well as objective features of time-structuring.

In developing such a qualitative approach we are not, however, as ill-equipped as we might think. The identification of qualitative tools has been a major theme in both the French and the American traditions in the sociology of time (see

Table 1 *Two paradigms for working time*

Linear-quantitative paradigm emphasizes:	Cyclic-qualitative paradigm emphasizes:
Realism	Nominalism
Determinism	Voluntarism
Linearity	Circularity
Homogeneity	Heterogeneity
Nomothesis	Ideography
Quantity	Quality

Hassard 1990). In the French tradition, the writings of Hubert (1905), Hubert and Mauss (1909), Mauss (1966), and Durkheim (1976) all emphasize the 'rhythmical' nature of social life through developing a notion of 'qualitative' time; that is, an appreciation of time far removed from writers who present it as simply measurable duration. Hubert (1905), for example, defined time as a symbolic structure representing the organization of society through its temporal rhythms, this being a theme also developed by Durkheim who analysed the social nature of time (Isambert 1979). Durkheim focused on time as a collective phenomenon, as a product of collective consciousness (see Pronovost 1986). For Durkheim, all members of a society share a common temporal consciousness; time is a social category of thought, a product of society. In Durkheim we find a macro-level exposition of the concept of social rhythm. Collective time is the sum of temporal procedures which interlock to form the cultural rhythm of a given society. Durkheim argues that: 'The rhythm of collective life dominates and encompasses the varied rhythms of all the elementary lives from which it results; consequently, the time that is expressed dominates and encompasses all particular durations' (1976: 69). For Durkheim, time is derived from social life and becomes the subject of collective representations. It is fragmented into a plethora of temporal activities which are reconstituted into an overall cultural rhythm that gives it meaning (see Pronovost 1986).

In the American tradition, Sorokin and Merton (1937) also highlight this qualitative nature of social time. In so doing, they draw not only on Durkheim, but also, and significantly, on the works of early cultural anthropologists, such as Codrington (1891), Hodson (1908), Nilsonn (1920), Best (1922) and Kroeber (1923). This synthesis allows Sorokin and Merton to identify qualitative themes at both micro and macro levels. Whilst, at the micro level, they emphasize the discontinuity, relativity and specificity of time – 'social time is qualitatively differentiated' – they also suggest, like Durkheim, that: 'units of time are often fixed by the rhythm of collective life' (1937: 615).

Indeed, they take this position a step further. Whereas Evans-Pritchard (1940) in his studies of the Nuer illustrated how certain activities give significance to social time, Sorokin and Merton adopt a position more characteristic of the sociology of knowledge. They argue that meaning comes to associate an event with its temporal setting, and that the recognition of specific periods is dependent on the degree of significance attributed to them. Drawing on Gurdon's (1914) anthropology, they argue that 'systems of time reckoning reflect the social activities of the group' (1937: 620). They show that the concept of qualitative time is important not only for primitive societies, but also for modern industrial states. They suggest that: 'Social time is qualitative and not purely quantitative. . . . These qualities derive from the beliefs and customs common to the group. . . . They serve to reveal the rhythms, pulsations, and beats of the societies in which they are found' (1937: 623).

Finally, perhaps the most ambitious attempt to outline the qualitative nature of social time has been made by Gurvitch (1964). In a sophisticated, if at times rather opaque, thesis, Gurvitch offers a typology of eight 'times' to illustrate the temporal complexity of modern, class-bound society (i.e. enduring, deceptive, erratic, cyclical, retarded, alternating, pushing forward, explosive). He illustrates how cultures are characterized by a *mélange* of conflicting times, and how social groups are constantly competing over a choice of 'appropriate' times. Like earlier writers, Gurvitch distinguishes between the micro-social times characteristic of groups and communities, and the macro-social times characteristic of, for example, systems and institutions. He makes constant reference to a plurality of social times, and notes how in different social classes we find differences of time scales and levels. He suggests that through analysing time at the societal level we can reveal a double time scale operating – with on the one hand the 'hierarchically ordered and unified' time of social structure, and on the other the 'more flexible time of the society itself' (1964: 391).

This literature suggests, then, that modern societies – as well as primitive ones – hold pluralities of qualitative time-reckoning systems, and that these are based on combinations of duration, sequence and meaning. Unlike with homogeneous time-reckoning, there is no uniformity of pace and no quantitative divisibility or cumulation of units. The emphasis is on cultural experience and sense-making, on creating temporal meanings rather than responding to temporal structures. The goal is to explain the cyclical and qualitative nature of social time.

Cyclic-Qualitative Studies in the Workplace

Having introduced elements of a cyclic-qualitative paradigm for work-time *thought*, we will now overlay this with evidence from a cyclic-qualitative paradigm for work-time *research*. In this section, the tone of the analysis changes, from theoretical discussion to empirical description, as we present field studies which develop this approach, research which reflects cyclic and qualitative elements of time at work (see Table 1).

Although the paradigm is at present a nascent one, and as such there are relatively few fieldwork studies to consult, we can nevertheless trace four clear examples. We review Roy's (1960) account of time-structuring amongst factory workers, Ditton's (1979) analysis of the time strategies of bakers, Cavendish's (1982) portrayal of time battles on the assembly line, and Clark's (1978; 1982) attempts to link temporal experience with organization structure. Although these studies represent essentially isolated and unconscious attempts at paradigm building, they are important in that they move toward a nominalist ontology, produce explanations from ideographic data, and illustrate how time-structuring can be voluntarist as well as determinist. Above all, they describe how our everyday understanding of work is based on the experience and construction of recurrent 'event-times' (Clark 1982). As such, these cases offer examples on which to build an ethnographic, cyclic-qualitative paradigm for work-time research.

Roy: Banana Time

Of the above accounts, Roy's is probably the best known. In what has become a classic paper in industrial sociology, he outlines how workers who are subject to monotonous tasks make their experiences bearable by putting meaning into their (largely meaningless) days. In Roy's machine shop, the work was both long (twelve-hour day, six-day week) and tedious (simple machine operation). He describes how he nearly quit the work immediately when first confronted with the combination of the 'extra-long work-day, the infinitesimal cerebral excitement, and the extreme limitation of physical movement' (1960: 207). It was only on discovering the 'game of work' which existed within the shop that the job became bearable. The group in which he worked had established its own event-based, time-reckoning system for structuring the day, although it was one which took some time to understand. As the working day stretched out infinitely, the group punctuated it with several 'times', each of which was the signal for a particular form of social interaction. The regularity of 'peach time', 'banana time', 'window time', 'pick up time', 'fish time' and 'coke time', together with the specific themes (variations on 'kidding' themes and 'serious' themes) which accompanied each time, meant that instead of the day being endless *durée* it was transformed into a series of regular social activities. In place of one long time horizon,

the day contained several short horizons. Roy explains that after his initial discouragement with the meagreness of the situation, he gradually began to appreciate how

> interaction was there, in constant flow. It captured attention and held interest to make the long day pass. The twelve hours of 'click, – move die, – click, – move die' became as easy to endure as eight hours of varied activity in the oil fields or eight hours of playing the piece work game in a machine shop. The 'beast of boredom' was gentled to the harmlessness of a kitten. (1960: 215)

Ditton: Baking Time

Ditton's (1979) analysis of the time perceptions of bakery workers is in the same tradition. Like Roy, he describes the social construction of time, and how workers develop 'consummatory acts to manage the monotony of time . . . breaking endless time down into digestible fragments to make it psychologically manageable' (1979: 160). He illustrates how time is both handled differently and experienced differently according to the type of work being done. For example, in the bakery there were two main production lines – the 'big (loaf) plant' and the 'small (roll) plant' – each with a range of tasks. Whereas in the big plant the work was physically more difficult ('hot, hard and heavy'), it was preferred because the number and speed of events made the day pass quickly. In contrast, life on the small plant was made bearable only because slower production meant there were more opportunities to 'manipulate' time.

In the bakery study, not only do we see (as in Roy's study) the use of event-based time-reckoning to give meaning to the day, but further how such time-reckoning is strategic. Ditton shows not only how management and workforce possess different time strategies but, furthermore, how these are linked, directly, to their differing time orientations. Ditton distinguishes between the linear time orientation of management and the cyclic time orientation of workers. Management is consumed by the linearity of clock-time: with the calculation and division of duration, and with the unending rhythm of the machinery. Workers, on the other hand, use their knowledge of event cycles in order to control time. The bakers possessed a whole repertoire of 'unofficial instrumental acts' for exercising control over the pace of the line. Ditton's work is aimed, specifically, at showing how these acts were appropriated in five main ways, that is, as strategies for 'making time', 'taking time twice', 'arresting time', 'negotiating time', and 'avoiding time'. In the bakery, individual work roles were evaluated according to their potential for manipulating time to a worker's advantage.

Cavendish: Doing Time

Cavendish (1982) is another to show the strategic importance of time in the workplace. In her account of women assembly workers 'doing time', she portrays time as fundamental to a global struggle between capital and labour. As time was what the assemblers were paid for, sharp distinctions were made between 'our time and their time'. Time obedience was the crucial discipline that management had to enforce, with skirmishes over clocking-off being more than just symbolic:

> they were real attempts by them to encroach on our time and, by us, to resist such encroachments . . . UMEC counted the minutes between 4.10 and 4.15 in lost UMO's, and every day the last few minutes before lunch and before the end of the afternoon were tense – each side tried to see what it could get away with. (1982: 117)

Like Roy and Ditton, Cavendish outlines how working time is not only an objective boundary condition, but also a subjective state; time was experienced differently according to the social situations the work group faced. Indeed working on the line 'changed the way you experienced time altogether . . . the minutes and hours went very slowly but the days passed very quickly once they were over, and the weeks rushed by' (1982: 117). There was a general consensus amongst the women as to the speed at which time was passing: 'Everyone agreed whether the morning was fast or slow, and whether the afternoon was faster or slower than the morning' (1982: 112). Similar to Roy's machine operatives, the women at UMEC developed time 'rituals', which served both to 'make the day go faster and divide up the week . . . all the days were the same, but we made them significant by their small dramas' (1982: 115).

However, while Cavendish, like Roy, shows how such events gave work days a sense of temporal structure, she delves deeper into the phenomenology of the situation and makes us aware of the personal time strategies within the network of meaning. In the interstices between rituals/events, or simply during periods when time seemed unusually burdensome, the women would devise personal strategies for 'getting through' the day. Cavendish explains how:

> Sometimes 7.30 to 9.10 seemed like several days itself, and I would redivide it up by starting on my sandwiches at 8 am. I would look at the clock when we'd already been working for ages, and find it was still only 8.05, or, on very bad days 7.50. . . . Then I redivided the time into half hours, and ten-minute periods to get through, and worked out how many UMO's I'd have done in ten minutes, twenty minutes and half an hour. (1982: 113)

Group members would adopt different strategies for getting through these periods: 'Arlene was deep in memories, and Alice sang hymns to herself. Grace always found something to laugh about, and Daphne watched everything that went on' (1982: 115). In general, older workers were better at 'handling' time. In particular, the older women were adept at 'going inside', or deciding to cut off from chatting in order to pass the time by day-dreaming.

In Cavendish's account organizational time was also reckoned differently according to the day of the working week. She notes how Monday was a good day time-wise, because it was the first day of the week and everyone was fresh ('it seemed a long time since Friday'), and because the group could catch up on the weekend's news. Tuesday, however, was a 'very bad day' because it wasn't special in any sense. On Wednesday the supervisor came around with the bonus points which would form part of the basis for Thursday's pay. This made Wednesday bearable; first, because the bonus points gave the group a vehicle for ritual discussion, and second because, as the points were related to the pay packet, it gave the impression that it was 'almost Thursday', and thus near to the end of the week: 'By Wednesday lunchtime, people would say half the week was over and we could see our way to Friday afternoon.' Although Thursday was pay day, it could be experienced as a long day. This was mainly because the pay slips arrived in the first half of the morning. However, the pay slips often served as a vehicle to give the group 'a few minutes interest', especially if one of the packets had been calculated incorrectly. Friday, although being the last day of the week, was also a slow day as there were few external incidents to supplement the group's own daily rituals. Apart from the horizon of subsidized fish and chips at lunchtime, the day was a long haul to finishing at 4.10. At the end of the afternoon the women always tried to spin out the last break by an extra five minutes, so there was only half an hour or so to finishing time.

Clark: the Temporal Repertoire

Finally, some of the most innovative of case work in this area has been by Clark (1978; 1982), who in studies of two contrasting industries – sugar beet processing and hosiery manufacture – illustrates how temporal differentiation represents a crucial link between a firm's culture and its structure. One of the few writers to make this link, Clark argues that in depicting organizations in a static mode sociologists have failed to consider how structures 'vary rhythmically' (1978: 406). Following Kuznets (1933), Sorokin (1943) and Etzioni (1961), he suggests that all large firms experience periodic differences in the intensity of production or service, and that these changes bring differences to the organization's character and culture.

In sugar beet production, Clark notes how the time frame 'contains two sharply contrasting sets of recurring activities' (1978: 12). He notes the marked differences in activities and attitudes between the period of sugar beet processing ('100–20 days after 26 September') and the rest of the year ('when the factory is dismantled and rebuilt by the labour force') (1978: 12). Clark highlights the cultural rhythms that ebb and flow during these two periods: he illustrates the excitement at the commencement of the 'campaign' ('26 September onwards'); how 'start-up' is full of anticipation; and how processing seems to change the relationships between the men and their families. Clark also notes, however, that as the campaign 'matures' the workforce becomes somewhat alienated from the work, the corollary being open expressions of control by management. Indeed, by January the workforce comes to welcome the second major transitional period, when, after the processing is completed, the men are dispersed to relatively self-regulating groups with distinct tasks.

In seeking a concept with which to analyse this 'structural and cultural flexibility' Clark (1982) draws upon the anthropology of Gearing (1958) and the notion of the 'structural pose'. The structural pose is a concept which denotes: the set of rules for categorizing a recurring situation; the type of social actors required for the situation; and the forms of action that should be employed. Gearing located four main structural poses in the organization of the Cherokee Indian village of the eighteenth century. He gave the example of the cue of the red flag which, although ostensibly representing the signal for conducting warfare against another village, also acted as the signal for organizing the village on a clan basis under the council of elders, and for allocating specific roles among the village community. He insists, however, that the concept does not simply imply a set of organizing procedures, for the same pose can be evoked for situations which, although of a qualitatively different nature, are deemed to require similar structural responses (for example, playing ball against another village).

For organizations, Clark uses the concept to denote how similar sequences fit several occasions. Structural poses are the tacit rules of conduct shared by those familiar with relationships between the organization's structure and culture; they are keys to anticipation and inter-subjectivity, and are founded on experience; they are blueprints which suggest the actions to take in response to certain sets of circumstances.

This is well demonstrated in Clark's second study, concerning a marketing group within a large hosiery firm, and how it drew on its structural poses to account for, and react to, a major seasonal shift in fashion and demand. The case involved a comparison between two of the firm's marketing departments and how each handled this major shift. The two groups were from different divisions and located in different parts of the country. With regard to personnel, while one division (Acorn) was composed mainly of experienced staff, the other (Harp) comprised marketing managers new to the industry. Clark shows how, of these groups, only the Acorn team were able to anticipate and handle the change satisfactorily. They were able to respond to the situation by 'activat[ing] a structural arrangement by which employees in various parts of the firm were redesignated as members of an innovation group' (1982: 31). In contrast, the Harp team, who in the short four-year history of the site had only experienced seasons of expanded production, interpreted the poor sales figures as being merely the result of a bad season:

> It was some time before they realized that a major shift in style was unfolding. When they did realize, they had neither the credibility nor the capability to achieve the appropriate collateral structure for innovation. It was not in the structural repertoire of Harp Mill. (1982: 31)

Clark argues that organizations possess whole repertoires of structural poses based on the premise of temporal recursiveness. In developing such repertoires, employees are able to account for the recurrent, but varying, rhythms of the organization, and thus for its heterogeneous time-reckoning system. Clark's marketing study, in particular, illustrates the links between temporal experience, structural differentiation and strategic time-reckoning. It indicates how organizations, over time, develop mechanisms for activating new structures from their repertoires in order to deal with anticipated events in the environment. Instead of the case turning on the linear, clock-time metaphor, it highlights the importance of cyclic, event-based trajectories.

ORGANIZATIONS, CAREERS AND TEMPORAL STRUCTURING

Having examined images of time in work and industrialism, we now consider temporal aspects of organization. We describe how individuals learn time discipline through membership of formal organizations such as the family and the school, institutions which prepare them for the organization demanding the greatest time discipline of all, the workplace. We also note how on gaining entry into a workplace, individuals embark upon a 'career', a process which sees them constantly evaluated in time-related terms. The focus shifts, subsequently, to the study of 'organizations in themselves'. The ontological emphasis changes as organizations are portrayed as systems which have time problems of their own. We look specifically at the temporal resources of work organizations, and assess the difficulties such institutions face in controlling temporal assets. In so doing, we draw upon the works of Moore (1963b), Lauer (1980), and McGrath and Rotchford (1983) to describe the measures organizations take for resolving problems of scheduling, allocation and synchronization.

Coming to Terms with Organization

Time is an inherent quality of human life. The sheer nature of existence prompts awareness of temporal differences between, for example, hunger and satisfaction, comfort and pain, and waking and dreaming. We first place structure on existence by assimilating times which have a natural and physiological basis.

Despite the potency of such natural times, we must remember that many of our physiological times become linked, inextricably, to social times. As an infant is unable to sustain life unaided, its physical well-being becomes dependent not only on its capacity to demand, but also on the willingness of those responsible for it to meet such demands. Given the nature of this relationship, the infant has no other choice than to allow the timing of demands to be regulated by social convention. Gradually needs become influenced by social constraints which dictate the 'correct' times for feeding, drinking, sleeping etc. As the process of physical development is joined by social development, so the infant begins to appreciate time as a vehicle which brings it within the orbit of human organization.

So that individuals may function adequately in society, they must, therefore, come to terms with the temporality which underlies social organization. Although physiological time needs persist throughout life, and while there are limits to the social ingenuity which can be placed upon their structuring, nevertheless social convention comes in time to regulate their satisfaction. The dominance of the physiological as the basis for action is seen to moderate and

then to decline as the individual matures. Physiological demand gives way to social performance; biological decree succumbs to social negotiation. While our sense of temporality is founded on the biology of the human organism, it becomes refined and ordered by participation in society and culture. In maturation, individuals learn to organize temporal experience in accordance with particular social and cultural processes.

For the infant, the temporal parameters of its actions become modified from their basis in physiological need to a new locus in the normative structures of an organization, the family. The development of social relations with parents and siblings signals that experience has become increasingly controlled, and that the infant has grasped a sense of organization. The acceptance of normative constraints sees physiological needs – for multiple feeds, or for sleeping during the middle of the day – deferred in favour of alternative possibilities, such as play. Through time, the infant becomes aware of how its actions are organized into formal patterns by agents in its environment.

This familiarization with the temporal structures of the family in turn prepares the child for a further, more formal, encounter with organization, the school. It is at school that the child experiences a more rigid temporal discipline, from the fixed lengths of daily and weekly attendance, to the formal separation of activities. The school day is segmented into precise temporal units, with each unit devoted to a specific topic or task. The child learns that school has a primary claim on time. Children learn that the school's organization of time must be accepted as legitimate, even when the school extends its temporal influence beyond its physical boundaries, as for example in the assignment of homework.

Above all, the formal time-structuring of the school prepares the individual for the institution demanding the greatest time discipline of all, the work organization. Joining a formal work organization represents the final stage in conditioning the individual to an 'organized' time consciousness. While earlier we noted how in most primitive and developing economies work systems either are, or have been, primarily task-oriented, in modern economies they are time-oriented. In the factory or office employees are held to minimum temporal standards: their work day is characterized by known temporal parameters and constraints. Through the combination of minute specialization and fine measurement, employees become subject not merely to temporal cycles based on the week, day or hour, but to ones defined by minutes or even seconds.

Externality and Specialization

Our analysis begins to suggest that while individuals experience time as natural and inherent, and while subjective awareness of time becomes expressed in the construction of intersubjective temporal meanings, nevertheless, in modern society pressures for synchronization force time sense to become objectified and constrained. In order to be organized, individuals must subscribe to times which are rational but external.

As societies have become increasingly complex, work organizations become primary claimants of social time. In modern societies the formal, external organization has replaced the family as the main locus of time-structuring. As the family has lost many of its functions to outside agencies, it has likewise relinquished claims on its members' time. Familial functions have been surrendered in line with greater specialization around distinct foreign agencies. Social functions have become the province of organizations such as the state, the factory, the shop and the school. Notable here has been the externalization of child education, and the removal from the home of the main forms of economic production. Despite a qualified return to homeworking, the only significant productive functions which remain in the home are those of cooking, cleaning, child care, laundry and shopping.

In the wake of this specialization, family members devote their time, typically, to performing one particular role within a single place of work. Modern employment practice has demanded that we acquire expertise in one specific field. It demands that we develop skills relevant to a particular 'career'. As individuals have since long exchanged 'organic utility' for 'mechanistic specialization' (Laslett 1965), so their worth has become checked against a linear, external and generic social instrument, the career 'ladder'. Increasingly, success or failure is judged on one criterion, the timing of personal accomplishments.

The Career

The career has become the dominant model for contemporary employment. As a concept it has become engrained into everyday common sense and culture. When Western adults meet for the first time, the question they ask – 'What do you do?' – begs an answer that is singular, functional and career-oriented; it begs an answer that is status-loaded and linear; an answer that can be indexed directly to the wider social structure.

The notion of career is thus central to an assessment of the social position: it is the definer *par excellence* of the individual's progress in organized society; it is the central element in the list of social times which regulate biographies and determine personal worth. Society determines a normative time chart for its members, and it is according to this chart that we construct appropriate timetables and schedules for living. So important are these timetables that individuals construct their biographies no longer simply by passing through states determined by nature, but more importantly by reference to the sophisticated, normative structures of social life. An individual's biography is evaluated according to the rate and sequence with which he or she passes through what Glaser and Strauss (1965) term 'status passages': that is, through stages which relate the various positions and identities available in society.

The career thus charts how an individual has passed through a socially recognized and meaningful sequence of related events. As Hughes (1971: 137) puts it, the career is 'the moving perspective in which the person sees his life as a whole and interprets the meaning of his various attributes, actions, and the things which happen to him'. Through time, individuals develop a perspective in which their careers are endowed with particular meanings and values. As the person passes from one stage to another, this perspective serves as a basis for assessment. Careers give the individual an acute sense of social time, and we think of ourselves in terms of a career path which includes the states of past, present and future. As we move from status to status, from organization to organization, we become sensitive to our relative position on the ladder of social biography. We ask: are we living too rapidly or not rapidly enough? Is the pace of our biography concordant with the ideal? The career timetable is socially sanctioned and based on a normative assessment of achievement; it prescribes the normal time for a person to pass from position to position. Individuals who are seen to progress at a rate faster or slower than normal risk being identified as age deviates. Anyone who departs from age-related normalcy is likely to be attributed with extraordinary skills, qualities or characteristics.

In modern societies, then, the relationship between age and career has become highly structured and formalized. Many organizations, starting with the school, provide detailed inventories which compare age with skill in order to arrive at selection. In large work organizations careers become interpreted in terms of age–grade relationships. Qualifications notwithstanding, an individual may simply be deemed too young or too old for higher office.

Organizations and Temporal Structuring

We now turn to the time problems faced by organizations as entities in themselves. Given the dominant conception of time in Western culture as scarce, valuable, homogeneous, linear and divisible, and given the dominant characteristics of work organizations as functional, specialized, formalized and rational, organizations are confronted with three key time problems: the reduction of temporal uncertainty, the resolution of conflicts over temporal activities, and the allocation of scarce temporal resources (McGrath and Rotchford 1983). In attempting to solve these problems, three temporal needs emerge: the need for time schedules (for reliable predictions of the points in time at which specific actions will occur), the need for synchronization (for temporal coordination among functionally segmented parts and activities), and the need for time allocations (for distributing time so that activities will consume it in the most efficient and rational way) (Moore 1963b). In this section, we analyse the relationships between these various problems and needs.

Uncertainty and Control

For a structural analysis of temporal uncertainty, J.D. Thompson's (1967) classic text on organizational design, *Organizations in Action*, represents a valuable first model (see Clark 1982; McGrath and Rotchford 1983). In this work, Thompson contrasts problems of temporal structuring with those of organizational structuring. In focusing upon the changing nature of organizational environments, he brings out the difficulties encountered when organizations seek to establish stable and efficient time structures. Thompson illustrates not only problems which stem from temporal uncertainty, but also those which arise when we apply generic solutions such as scheduling, synchronization and allocation.

A main theme of Thompson's analysis is that organizations have a technical core that requires protection against uncertainty. To operate successfully, an organization must comprehend, and as far as possible control, the numerous environmental forces which impinge on its activities. Whereas this may seem a straightforward task for organizations operating in stable environments, Thompson notes that for those operating in dynamic ones there is a need to protect the technical core through: 'buffering to absorb the uncertainty', 'smoothing and levelling to reduce the amount of uncertainty', and 'anticipating and adapting the environmental uncertainty so that it can be treated as a constant constraint within the organization

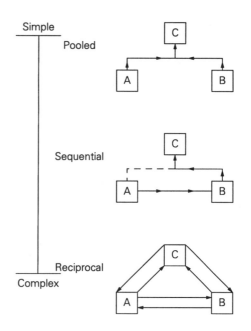

Figure 1   *Types of task interdependence in organization design*

functions'. It is these strategies which make the interaction of organization and environment more predictable, because they reduce the uncertainty over the availability and timing of resources. In particular, it is these processes which illustrate the importance of efficient scheduling; for they suggest ways of resolving temporal uncertainty by increasing the predictability of when some event will occur and/or when some product will be available.

In developing this argument, Thompson outlines three types of intra-organizational interdependence, each of which, he suggests, requires a different type of coordination (see Figure 1). First, he talks of 'pooled interdependence', where all organization units contribute to and are supported by the organization as a whole, and where coordination is achieved by employing standardized units and regulations. Second, he discusses 'sequential interdependence', where the outputs of one unit form inputs to another, and where coordination is achieved through planning. And third, he talks of 'reciprocal interdependence', where the outputs of one unit are inputs to all other units, and where coordination is achieved through ongoing mutual adjustment among units. His argument is that for organizations to operate efficiently these interdependencies must be coordinated rationally. Organizations must group units by type of interdependence into layers and departments. The purpose of such grouping is to minimize the costs associated with communication and decision/effort times. Groupings must be made first on the basis of reciprocally interdependent units, because they involve the greatest communication and decision/effort time. The second most time-costly to coordinate are sequentially interdependent units, so they have the next priority in hierarchical and departmental grouping. And, finally, as the pooled interdependent units are the least time-costly to coordinate, they are grouped only after the reciprocal and sequentially interdependent positions have been arranged.

Thompson suggests, therefore, that the major imperative in organizational structuring is the desire to minimize communication and decision/effort times. He argues that coordination through the standardized rules of pooled interdependence requires 'less frequent decisions and a smaller volume of communication during a specific period of operations than does planning, and planning calls for less decision and communication than does mutual adjustment' (1967: 56). Through this analysis, we see that a major reason why decision and communication activities incur costs is that they consume time: they use up scarce temporal resources.

Conflict over Activities

For our second problem – conflict over activities – we consider how functionally segmented actions can be coordinated through specialization and interpersonal norms.

In dealing with the coordination of segmented activities, we are concerned with questions of synchronization rather than with scheduling. We are concerned with: (a) the temporal patterning of an actor's multiple actions, (b) the temporal patterning of the actor's actions in relation to those of other actors, and (c) the temporal patterning of an actor's actions in relation to other objects or events (e.g. the timing of a machine, the activities of another unit). Such patterning is a problem in that it points to a need to operate within an elaborate set of procedures and norms.

As Weber (1947) described, the logic of organization is such that the larger and more complex an organization becomes, the greater functional specialization it will display. As functional specialization requires the synchronization of various parts and activities, the greater the need for temporal coordination of the various activities among the various parts. However, while the logic of specialization demands that each individual performs one function efficiently, this is at the cost of performing a number of functions overall. As activities become increasingly specialized, and in turn as their location in a temporal pattern becomes increasingly fixed,

the greater the pressure to apply principles of formalization, or even to automate the whole activity. The irony here is that while the need for increased synchronization is a direct consequence of functional specialization, what is needed to accomplish this, the coordination of workers on individual tasks, violates one of the premises on which functional specialization is based, the interchangeability of parts.

Nevertheless, not all of an organization's activities are reducible to such tight specifications, nor is all temporal organizing so mechanical. There indeed remain many organizational activities which require the synchronizing of individuals – as subjective actors – as well as of processes. While these activities require temporal coordination, this is achieved not so much by mechanistic specialization, but by the organic process of developing implicit working norms.

Norms develop during interaction in order to synchronize the activities of participants. As failure to synchronize activities can be a major cost to both productive efficiency and group satisfaction, time norms emerge in order to reduce such costs. As we move from dyadic interaction to the activities of larger groups, synchronization of norms becomes all the more important, because the temporal and spatial needs of such large, complex systems become more demanding.

As norms take on an increasingly critical role, there is pressure to make them explicit. Eventually implicit regulatory norms become translated into explicit rules, regulations and standard operating procedures, with these formalized sets of expectations being associated with specific 'positions' or 'roles' in the organizational network. In the process of organizational growth, the norms by which actors regulate their actions become mere subsets of the role expectations extant in the formal organizational structure. No longer are behaviours indexed to particular individuals, groups and situations; instead they are objectified on to particular functions. It is the role which acts, not the actor. Positions which are formalized in the shape of recognized organizational procedures allow for expertise only within an established framework of regulations. Normative procedures become control devices which operate in the service of smooth temporal coordination; they effect explicit synchronization between the various activities of the organization's members (see Clark 1982: 22).

Scarcity

For the third problem, 'scarcity', we are concerned with matching productive activities to limited time allocations; that is, with 'the efficient assignment of temporal resources to tasks, hence the assignment of priorities or values to the tasks and assignment of responsibility for those tasks to staff' (McGrath and Rotchford 1983: 85). Our goals here are twofold: at the macro level, to balance temporal resources between units; and at the micro level, to obtain optimal matches between an employee's available time and the number of actions to be performed.

While in the next section we discuss scarcity issues at the macro level, we are concerned here with problems arising at the micro level. In particular we note how the matching of time and activities forms the basis for an employee's role/load problems, a form of stress which results from a perceived scarcity of time relative to the requirements of tasks to be performed. Role overload is an almost inevitable consequence of the interaction between Western time culture and modern forms of organization. This reflects the interaction of functional specialization, temporal and spatial segregation, synchronization, and fine time measurement. In modern societies, adults are likely to divide their time between many spatially, functionally and temporally segregated organizations, in relation, for example, to work, the family, recreation and religion. These sophisticated time allocations, and the temporal precision that comes with them, can become double-edged. While on the one hand this makes synchronization within narrow time tolerances more feasible, on the other the ability to account for increasingly precise time allocations gives individuals scope to pack activities more tightly into their roles. This can have the effect of increasing: the perceived scarcity of time in each role, the precision required for synchronizing between roles, and the strains on the boundaries between roles.

Solving Time Problems in Organizations

We finally describe some of the tactics which organizations use to cope with time scarcity. In particular we examine three ways of coping with tight temporal constraints: by adjusting the specific time locations of activities, by redistributing peak-time loads over other phases of time cycles, and by trying to recover time that would otherwise be lost (see McGrath and Rotchford 1983).

Altering Time Locations

For the first of the tactics, adjusting the specific time locations of activities, we refer to instances in which organizations need ways of freeing activities from their fixed locations in 'real' time.

For example, the most pressing time problem for employees is the pressure to do two or more things simultaneously; or, in other words, the pressure imposed by multiple, conflicting demands either within one role or across two or more roles. The only solution to this problem is through time relocation: through having one or more of these events extracted from its location and rescheduled.

While some events are relatively amenable to temporal relocations, and can easily be extracted from context – processes which can be easily separated from related processes – others cannot be so readily extracted, and depend instead on being enacted at a specific place and time. While such temporal conflicts are not easily remedied, and while such problems must generally be solved by assigning priorities, nevertheless, technological developments have provided partial solutions. Video-taping, for example, has meant that we can record certain activities in real time and then react to them when convenient. This enables rescheduling, whereas previously the only viable solution would have been through prioritizing.

A related problem concerns the need for parts of activities to be accomplished in a fixed, temporally coordinated sequence. As work activities tend to be structured linearly, so that the sequence covers a substantial period of real time, this can be problematic in two ways: (a) because the total time required may not allow the task sequence to be accomplished quickly enough, or (b) because the individual may not be able to commit sufficient time, at a given time, to the whole process. For these situations, methods are required for uncoupling the sequence linkages between substages of the task, so that constituent subtasks can be accomplished in temporal isolation.

For the first problem, large tasks are often subdivided into substages which are then executed in temporal parallel. Although this does not save time, in the sense of the hours used, it serves to get the whole task completed sooner in real time, even though a price may be paid in terms of the detailed coordination of the separately executed parts. Similarly, for the latter problem, a large task may be divided into several small segments that can be accomplished over a wide stretch of real time. For example, when prioritizing tasks, organizations often arrange for certain jobs to be accomplished only when no urgent work is at hand, such as maintenance, safety and renovation.

Distributing Time Loads

For the second coping strategy, redistributing peak-time loads, we are concerned with the reallocation of activities in order to make better use of the system capacity as a whole. In other words, we wish to operate more effectively by either increasing capacity during periods of low load or increasing capability during periods of high load.

In practice, the former often involves experiments in 'inverse pricing', or attempts to encourage demand during unfashionable or low-load periods. Common methods for accomplishing this are, for example, offering 'off-peak' rates for electricity, telephones, transport and advertising; 'off-season' rates for holidays and flights; and 'end-of-season' prices for clothes and sporting equipment.

During periods of high demand, organizations simply provide more capability, notably by getting more staff-hours devoted to peak-load activities. As markets have become more volatile, organizations have also started to balance loads by distinguishing between core and peripheral workforces, again so as to buffer against uncertainty. In order to balance staff demands with market demands, organizations have recruited a greater percentage of employees on short, fixed-term contracts, which offer little protection under employment law. Similarly, because firms wish to keep labour costs to a minimum, recent decades have seen a growth in agencies supplying temporary, predominantly female, labour for generic tasks at short notice, a practice commonly referred to as 'temping'.

Reclaiming Time

The techniques above reflect strategies for avoiding time waste in work systems. However, despite our desire to eliminate temporal waste, the very logic of modern organization – functional specialization and temporal segregation – means that certain pieces of time are inevitably lost. As specialization and segregation encourage planning in ever more precise temporal divisions, so the very fact of slicing work into smaller intervals means that slivers of time are lost in the process.

Other arenas of 'wasted' time are those of travelling and waiting. While in one sense these sections of time are 'filled', in that they are dedicated to specific purposes, to most of us they represent intervals which are empty. As such, they are time spaces open to development. Many commuters for instance use up travelling time by writing reports, dictating letters, or simply reading work-related literature. For others, travelling to work now represents an opportunity to conduct business with the office or with customers direct, through the use of car or other portable phones.

Finally, and related to the above, is the double use of time that is filled not with waiting, but with activity. Time can sometimes be 'saved' by the purposeful combining of activities which, while different in nature, are oriented towards the same functional end. Examples of these are the working lunch and the executive golf game. The aim of both is to enhance business dealings by making the interaction between the parties less formal.

CONCLUSIONS

In the early sections of the chapter, we outlined how industrial sociologists have portrayed the dominant image of time as objective, measurable, highly valued and scarce. The emphasis is upon rationality and homogeneity, and the view that time is quantifiable and evenly distributed. We accept that employment defines the pivotal time around which all other social times are structured. As economic performance is assessed by the number of hours it takes to produce certain goods, time is given a commodity image. A corollary of this is the portrayal of work organizations as marvels of synchronicity; contemporary production systems, with their fine arithmetic assembly operations, are held to be the most rational of technologies: they, more than anything, epitomize quantitative time-reckoning.

However, in concentrating upon quantitative time, industrial sociologists have overlooked the importance of qualitative time. Stress has been placed on time-structuring rather than experience. The focus has been upon how time is formally patterned in task systems rather than the way it is 'interpreted' in task execution. In concentrating upon temporal structuring, and thus in treating time as a hard, objective, and homogeneous facility, we have neglected how it is experienced as a soft, subjective and heterogeneous abstraction.

Indeed, from the complex relationships linking production systems, labour and the environment, there emerge whole ranges of time patterns and rhythms. New employees learn these rhythms gradually, through experiencing how the character of work changes according to the particular time period being endured. While most work roles are structured according to a formal inventory of activities, new recruits discover the meaning of work by reference to an informal typology of events. Tasks are categorized not only in relation to explicit work schedules, but also according to the group's own personal and social constructs. As we noted in Ditton's study, time is one of the major criteria here. The experience of work is inextricably linked to the way time is socially constructed.

Thus, we have argued that industrial sociology needs research which accesses not only the concrete facts of time-structuring, but also the subjective essences of temporal meanings. While the discipline's conceptions of time are based, predominantly, on metaphors of linearity, rationality and quantification, we have illustrated how these images are overstated; they proffer a truncated awareness of time by ignoring the subjective and irrational features of time at work. By turning to the French and American traditions in the sociology of time, we have suggested that at the interface of sociology, philosophy, and anthropology lies a position more sensitive to temporal heterogeneity – a position capable of illuminating the cyclical and qualitative features of working time.

In the third section of the chapter, we have analysed the complex relationship between time and organization. As we enter the world of affairs, we find that a major function of socialization is the structuring of our time sense within formal institutions. Notable here is the process whereby school and workplace teach us rigid time disciplines; they segment activities into precise temporal units, and condition us to an 'organized' time consciousness. This conditioning sees us subscribe to times which are external and specialized, times which are technocratic. In the West, the external and highly specialized organization has become not only the main regulator of social time, but also its primary claimant.

In organized society, we structure our actions according to what we feel are 'proper' social times. We base our temporal understanding on practices we learn from the environment. In dealing with sophisticated social structures, we develop ways of expressing our needs for coordinated acts. To reproduce order, we create common definitions and assumptions in regard to the location of events in time. In particular, we form common understandings of synchronization, sequence and rate. Given the increasing scope of human communication – and thus the problem of dealing with a plurality of times – we seek means by which diverse groups can adjust their actions to meet the challenges of mutual dependence: we require general temporal agreements so that we can relate processes in ways which avoid activities becoming conflictual. This is especially necessary in situations where actions must be regulated in order to give scope for each to fulfil its potential.

Temporal structuring is thus at the heart of organization. When organizations are designed or changed, temporal factors are of primary concern. As the logic of organization is such that with increased size comes greater specialization, time emerges as a central feature of structuring. Time is basic to resolving problems of environmental uncertainty, conflicts over activities, and the allocation of scarce resources. Synchronization, sequence and rate are critical factors when we seek predictions of when specific actions will occur relative to others; when we attempt to coordinate functionally segmented parts and activities; and when we want to distribute time so that activities consume it in the most efficient manner. In competitive markets, organizations are driven to find new ways of reducing communication and decision/effort times. They seek new techniques for reducing levels of conflict between activities, and in particular for effecting superior coordination, through meshing sophisticated specialization with appropriate cultural/normative values.

REFERENCES

Atkinson, J. (1984) 'Manpower strategies for flexible organizations', *Personnel Management*, August: 28–31.

Best, E. (1922) 'The Maori division of time', *Dominion Museum Monograph*, 4.

Braverman, H. (1974) *Labor and Monopoly Capital: the Degradation of Work in the Twentieth Century*. New York and London: Monthly Review Press.

Cavendish, R. (1982) *Women on the Line*. London: Routledge & Kegan Paul.

Clark, P.A. (1978) 'Temporal innovations and time structuring in large organizations', in J.T. Fraser, N. Lawrence and D. Park (eds), *The Study of Time*, vol. 3. New York: Springer-Verlag.

Clark, P.A. (1982) 'A review of the theories of time and structure for organisational sociology'. Working paper no. 248, Management Centre, University of Aston.

Clark, P.A., Hantrais, L., Hassard, J.S., Linhart, D. and Starkey, K.P. (1984) 'The porous day and *temps choisi*'. Paper presented at the Third Annual Organization and Control of the Labour Process Conference, Aston University, UK.

Clegg, S. (1990) *Modern Organizations: Organization Studies in the Postmodern World*. London: Sage.

Codrington, R.H. (1891) *The Melanesians*. Oxford.

de Grazia, S. (1972) 'Time and work', in H. Yaker, H. Osmond and F. Cheek (eds), *The Future of Time*. New York: Anchor Books.

Ditton, J. (1979) 'Baking time', *Sociological Review*, 27: 157–67.

Durkheim, E. (1976) *The Elementary Forms of the Religious Life*, 2nd edn. London: George Allen & Unwin.

Eliade, M. (1959) *Cosmos and History: the Myth of the Eternal Return*. New York: Harper & Row.

Etzioni, A. (1961) *A Comparative Analysis of Complex Organizations.* New York: Free Press.

Evans-Pritchard, E.E. (1940) *The Nuer.* Oxford: Oxford University Press.

Fabian, J. (1983) *Time and the Other: How Anthropology Makes its Object.* New York: Columbia University Press.

Gale, R. (ed.) (1968) *The Philosophy of Time: a Collection of Essays.* Sussex: Harvester.

Gearing, E. (1958) 'The structural poses of the 18th century Cherokee villages', *American Anthropologist,* 60: 1148–57.

Gioscia, V. (1972) 'On social time', in H. Yaker, H. Osmond and F. Cheek (eds), *The Future of Time.* New York: Anchor Books.

Glaser, B.G. and Strauss, A. (1965) 'Temporal aspects of dying', *American Journal of Sociology,* 71: 48–59.

Graham, R.J. (1981) 'The perception of time in consumer research', *Journal of Consumer Research,* 7: 335–42.

Gurdon, P.T.R. (1914) *The Khasis.* London.

Gurvitch, G. (1964) *The Spectrum of Social Time.* Dordrecht: D. Reidel.

Hassard, J. (1990) 'Introduction', in J. Hassard (ed.), *The Sociology of Time.* London: Macmillan.

Hassard, J. (1993) *Sociology and Organization Theory: Positivism, Paradigms and Postmodernity.* Cambridge: Cambridge University Press.

Heath, L.R. (1956) *The Concept of Time.* Chicago: University of Chicago Press.

Hodson, T.C. (1908) *The Meitheis.* London.

Hubert, H. (1905) 'Étude sommaire de la représentation du temps dans la religion et la magie', *Annuaire de l'École Pratique des Hautes Études,* 1–39.

Hubert, H. and Mauss, M. (1909) *Mélanges d'histoire des religions.* Paris: Alcan.

Hughes, E.C. (1971) *The Sociological Eye.* New York: Aldine.

Isambert, F.-A. (1979) 'Henri Hubert et la sociologie du temps', *Revue Française de Sociologie,* 20: 183–204.

Jaques, E. (1982) *The Form of Time.* London: Heinemann.

Julkunnen, R.A. (1977) 'A contribution to the categories of social time and the economies of time', *Acta Sociologica,* 20: 5–24.

Kamata, S. (1982) *Life in the Passing Lane: an Insider's Account of Life in a Japanese Auto Factory.* London: Counterpoint.

Kroeber, A.L. (1923) *Anthropology.* New York.

Kuznets, S. (1933) *Seasonal Variations in Industry and Trade.* New York: National Bureau of Economic Research.

Lakoff, G. and Johnson, M. (1980) *Metaphors We Live By.* Chicago: University of Chicago Press.

Landes, D.S. (1983) *Revolution in Time: Clocks and the Making of the Modern World.* Cambridge, MA: Belknap Press of Harvard University Press.

Laslett, P. (1965) *The World We Have Lost.* London: Methuen.

Lauer, R.H. (1980) *Temporal Man.* New York: Praeger.

McGrath, J.E. and Rotchford, N.L. (1983) 'Time and behaviour in organizations', *Research in Organizational Behaviour,* 5: 57–101.

McKendrick, N. (1962) 'Josiah Wedgwood and the factory discipline', *The Historical Journal,* 4: 30–5.

Manning, P. (1979) 'Metaphors of the field', *Administrative Science Quarterly,* 24: 660–71.

Marx, K. (1976) *Capital* (1867), vol. 1. Harmondsworth: Penguin.

Mauss, M. (1966) *Sociologie et anthropologie.* Paris: Presses Universitaires de France.

Moore, W.E. (1963a) *Man, Time and Society.* New York: Wiley.

Moore, W.E. (1963b) 'The temporal structure of organizations', in E.A. Tiryakian (ed.), *Sociological Theory, Values and Sociocultural Change.* New York: Free Press.

Morgan, G. (1986) *Images of Organization.* New York: Sage.

Mumford, L. (1934) *Technics and Civilisation.* New York: Harcourt, Brace & World.

Nilsonn, P. (1920) *Primitive Time Reckoning.* London: Oxford University Press.

Nowotny, H. (1976) 'Time structuring and time measurement', in J.T. Fraser and N. Lawrence (eds), *The Study of Time,* vol. 2. New York: Springer.

Nyland, C. (1986) 'Capitalism and the history of work-time thought', *British Journal of Sociology,* 37: 513–34. Reprinted as Chapter 8 in J. Hassard (ed.), *The Sociology of Time.* London: Macmillan, 1990.

Park, D. (1980) *The Image of Eternity: Roots of Time in the Physical World.* Amherst, MA: University of Massachussetts Press.

Pinder, C. and Moore, L. (1979) 'The resurrection of taxonomy to aid the development of middle range theories of organization behaviour', *Administrative Science Quarterly,* 24: 99–118.

Pollert, A. (1988) 'The flexible firm: fixation or fact?', *Work, Employment and Society,* 2: 281–316.

Pronovost, G. (1986) 'Time in a sociological and historical perspective', *International Social Science Journal,* 107: 5–18.

Reid, D.A. (1976) 'The decline of Saint Monday', *Past and Present,* 71: 76–101.

Roy, D.F. (1960) 'Banana time: job satisfaction and informal interaction', *Human Organization,* 18: 156–68. Reprinted as Chapter 9 in J. Hassard (ed.), *The Sociology of Time.* London: Macmillan, 1990.

Sorokin, P.A. (1943) *Sociocultural Causality, Space and Time.* Durham, NC: Duke University Press.

Sorokin, P.A. and Merton, R.K. (1937) 'Social time: a methodological and functional analysis', *American Journal of Sociology,* 42: 615–29.

Starkey, K.P. (1988) 'Time and the labour process: a theoretical and empirical analysis'. Paper presented at the Labour Process Conference, Aston University, UK.

Taylor, F.W. (1911) *Principles of Scientific Management*. New York: Harper.

Thompson, E.P. (1967) 'Time, work-discipline and industrial capitalism', *Past and Present*, 38: 56–97.

Thompson, J.D. (1967) *Organizations in Action*. New York: McGraw-Hill.

Thrift, N. (1990) 'Owners' time and own time: the making of a capitalist time consciousness 1300–1800', in J. Hassard (ed.), *The Sociology of Time*. London: Macmillan.

Tinker, T. (1986) 'Metaphor or reification?', *Journal of Management Studies*, 23: 363–84.

Weber, M. (1947) *The Theory of Social and Economic Organization*. Glencoe, IL: Free Press.

Wright, L. (1968) *Clockwork Man*. London: Elek.

3.6

The Organizational Culture War Games: a Struggle for Intellectual Dominance

JOANNE MARTIN AND PETER FROST

The childhood war game of King of the Mountain is preferably played on a sandy beach so no one will get hurt. One king's temporary triumph at the top of a sand pile is rapidly superseded by the reign of another would-be monarch (boy or girl), until the succession of short-lived victories and the plethora of defeats leaves the pile flattened. Sometimes the tide washes away the traces of the struggle and sometimes children (usually a fresh army) rebuild the pile and start the game anew. Other children refrain from playing King of the Mountain, preferring to build their own castles in the sand.

Organizational culture researchers, like other organizational behavior scholars, generally (but not always) use conventional structures for reviewing literature. Intellectual differences of opinion are usually handled with the indirection and tact that sometimes can help scholars to co-exist in a close-knit field and continue to have cordial intellectual exchanges. The most frequently used strategy is silence, whereby a paper or book focuses predominantly on one point of view, simply by not citing competing perspectives or by relegating them to the margins (for example, in a parenthetical aside, a separate chapter in a book, or a footnote). This popular strategy permits the full exploration and delineation of the favoured point of view, while not creating a need to criticize, or even draw attention to other perspectives. A variant on this silence/marginalization approach is the review which cites a wider range of perspectives, but focuses primarily on the perspective the author personally prefers (and of course, no public record is left of these more conflictful encounters). Whether silence, marginalization, or tactful

understatement is used, these commonly utilized strategies mask intellectual disagreements, so one is forced to attend to silences and 'read between the lines' of what is published in order to decipher what fundamental issues are causing discord.

The culture literature is unusual, however, in that these norms of silencing, marginalizing, and minimizing intellectual disagreements have sometimes been broken, usefully, in a number of publications which argue openly for one point of view in preference to other, extensively described alternatives. Reviews of the cultural literature which fit this description include, for example, Alvesson and Berg (1992), Calás and Smircich (1987), Czarniawska-Joerges (1992), Frost et al. (1991), Jeffcutt (forthcoming), Kunda (1991), Linstead and Grafton-Small (1992), Martin (1992), Schultz (1994), Smircich and Calás (1987), Stablein and Nord (1985), Sypher et al. (1985), Turner (1986), and Willmott (1993). Fundamental disagreements about epistemology, methodology, political ideology, and theory, which might have been handled only in 'subterranean' outlets such as blind reviews, have been openly argued in the cultural literature. We therefore have a textual record of overt conflict that can be quite informative and enlightening. Such critiques can challenge taken-for-granted certainties and inspire new ideas.

The seriousness of these intellectual differences makes it difficult to review the results of research in this area, for there is chaos rather than order, conflict rather than consensus, and little sense of a cumulative building of what would be generally recognized as advances in knowledge. These problems are compounded because so many cultural researchers, for good reasons, prefer qualitative methodology, developing context-specific descriptions of cultures rather than collecting the quantitative data that lend themselves more obviously to systematic meta-analyses and the development of empirically based theoretical generalizations. For all these reasons, cultural research epitomizes the lack of paradigm consensus in our field, an attribute that some worry about because it may inhibit the cumulation of knowledge, harm the reputation of our field, or draw attention to textual analysis rather than the material conditions of work (e.g. Donaldson 1989; Pfeffer 1993; Reed 1990). Other organizational scholars welcome paradigm proliferation, so evident in the cultural arena, as a spur to creativity and the proliferation of previously silenced viewpoints (e.g. Burrell and Morgan 1979; Van Maanen 1995).

Whether one welcomes or avoids overt conflicts about fundamental issues, it is clear that any review of organizational culture research must respond to the existence of these disagreements. Rather than telling a conventional, chronological tale of linear progress toward greater knowledge, we have decided to experiment with one of several possible alternative structures for this review, portraying research in this domain as a struggle for intellectual dominance among the proponents of various theories, methodological preferences, epistemologies, and political orientations (e.g. Burrell and Morgan 1979; Kuhn 1970). We use a metaphor to structure our description of this struggle for dominance: the organizational culture 'war games' or, more specifically, a game of 'king of the mountain'. This chapter reviews organizational culture research as if this field began, without history, in approximately 1970. We cite some intellectual predecessors of particular points of view, but less as contributors of the history of an idea and more as totems invoked to legitimate certain points of view, drawing attention to the exclusion of other viewpoints with equally venerable intellectual lineage. We chose to constrain the historical depth of this review because of space limitations and because excellent treatments of the history of the organizational culture 'chaos' – a phrase variously attributed to Turner (1990) and Calás and Smircich (1987) – are available (e.g. Alvesson and Berg 1992; Jeffcutt forthcoming b; Ouchi and Wilkins 1985; Pettigrew 1979; Smircich and Calás 1987; Schultz 1994; Turner 1990).

The game of king of the mountain has several attributes that make it a useful metaphor for our purposes. First, some players choose not to play the game, preferring to build their own castles in the sand. This allows description of isolationist contributions to the literature, as when advocates of one point of view cite only work in their own tradition, while ignoring or marginalizing competing perspectives. (Although even isolationist strategies can be construed as a play in the game for intellectual dominance.) Coalitions in king of the mountain games usually evolve spontaneously, without much conscious coordination; the goal is to depose the current king and when that is accomplished, the coalition often dissolves, only to reconstitute itself in a somewhat different form when a new king takes over. 'Attacks' often take the form of a solo climbing to the top of the sand pile, rather than someone deliberately and aggressively pulling rivals down. Finally, it is important to say that we, as authors of this review, do not see ourselves as innocent, distant, or dispassionate adult observers, watching children play. We have, for better or worse, been fully involved players in the game, sometimes consciously, sometimes not.

Although we believe using the war games metaphor is a useful way to describe the struggle for intellectual dominance within organizational culture studies, it is undeniable that this metaphor, like any other metaphor, brings some issues into focus while obscuring others – particularly those which are congruent with a linear, positivistic view of hypothesis-testing theory development (see Pinder and Bourgeois 1982). The war games metaphor can unfortunately de-emphasize isolationist intellectual strategies, leave an impression of intentional coordination when coincidence or independent simultaneity would be more accurate descriptions, and describe as an aggressive 'attack' what was intended to be a non-aggressive, almost isolationist description of an intellectual position. In short, the war games metaphor reads aggressive competition in, when none may be intended. However (in accord with, for example, Morgan 1983a) we believe that any less obviously metaphorical framework would also, inevitably, draw attention to some aspects of an intellectual domain, rather than others, and distort, to some extent, what is included in an account to improve its narrative flow and support its point of view. We will endeavor to minimize these problems as we write around the war games metaphor, but we, like others who eschew an explicitly metaphorical structure, cannot avoid them completely.

Moving from the structure of this review to its tone, we sought a tone that is relaxed, playful in the postmodern tradition, and sometimes ironic. However, such a tone should not be interpreted as a sign of disrespect for the work we are describing. We hope that this metaphor and tone will permit us to generate some new insights about the cultural research that has and has not been done. Furthermore, we would welcome a lessening of the deleterious effects of a struggle for dominance. It is our hope that looking at organizational culture research as a struggle for dominance will illuminate what is worthwhile and insightful about all the competing points of view, not in a Panglossian desire for harmony and resolution, but in a clear-eyed call for the worth of trying to understand the importance of the differences that cause these conflicts to recur. The less time we spend fighting for dominance and the more time we spend trying to understand reasons for differences, the deeper our understandings may become.

This story of the culture wars takes place in a broader societal context. We begin the telling of this story in the 1970s and 1980s – decades when increasing attention was paid to sources of cultural difference, for example among ethnic groups, races, genders, and regions. For example, in Europe, in the wake of the European Common Market, moves to reduce the salience of national boundaries brought regional and ethnic differences to the fore. In the US, Canada, and Australia, some minorities (such as African-Americans, French-speaking Canadians, and various indigenous peoples) challenged claims of nationally shared values (see, for example, Schlesinger's (1992) *The Disuniting of America*). In some US universities, the phrase 'culture wars' refers to debates about multiculturalism on campus and in the curriculum; the 'great books' tradition of education was criticized for being centered on the writings of a few dead white Western men, a charge that was hotly resisted in the name of quality (e.g. Bloom 1987). After these debates, it was no longer sufficient to simply add a slogan 'we value diversity' to a list of values presumably shared by all. Valuing diversity was now defined to entail learning about difference, understanding it deeply, and facilitating its flourishing, without the traditional (at least in the US) pressures towards assimilation to a more dominant view.

THE REVOLUTIONARY VANGUARD

There are many ways to tell the history of the renaissance of interest in culture in the late 1970s, but most organizational accounts cite the successes of Japanese management and the perceived failures of traditional organizational analysis as catalysts for awakening managerial interest in corporate culture (e.g. Turner 1990: 85–6). For example:

> The dearth of practical additions to old ways of thought was painfully apparent. It was never so clear as in 1980, when US managers, beset by

obvious problems of stagnation, leaped to adopt Japanese management practices, ignoring the cultural difference, so much wider than even the vast expanse of the Pacific would suggest . . . The theorists from academe, we found, were wrestling with the same concerns. Our timing was good. The state of theory is in refreshing disarray. (Peters and Waterman 1982: 4–5)

Many members of the revolutionary vanguard of cultural researchers were highly critical of mainstream organizational research, which, at that time, emphasized quantitative, normal science in both the US (where it has long been the tradition) and the UK (where the Aston Studies were gaining momentum). They declared this approach to be arid and fruitless because it was overly reliant on a rational model of human behavior, a structural approach to questions of corporate strategy, and a love of numerical analysis. Business education based on such research, they argued, created a generation of managers who knew more about managing spreadsheets than people:

> A buried weakness in the analytic approach to business decision making is that people analyze what can be most readily analyzed, spend more time on it, and more or less ignore the rest. As Harvard's John Steinbruner [1974] observes, 'If quantitative precision is demanded, it is gained, in the current state of things, only by so reducing the scope of what is analyzed that most of the important problems remain external to the analysis.' (1982: 44)

Members of the revolutionary vanguard, whether or not they advocated the use of qualitative methods, shared a conviction that a cultural framework would permit them to broaden the kinds of organizational phenomena they studied. For example:

> My interest in culture stemmed from a feeling of excitement: that through the cultural lens we could bring to the top of the agenda, in a constructive way, the emotional side of organizational life. I felt that our approaches to organizations were quite antiseptic and lifeless in many ways. Also I saw that we could begin to look at the texture of organizational life, again in ways that had been brushed aside/dismissed/discounted in the mainstream of research. It was now potentially ok to do qualitative research, to be playful and experimental, to collect, study, and learn from the stories, events, dramas, and tedium in organizations. It was a liberation from seemingly purely technical, engineered approaches to studying organizations. I experienced a sense of the fun and the theoretical potential of looking at organizations that way . . . We took risks and invented things that we would not likely have thought about in the previous era. (Frost 1995)

At these first stages of the cultural revolution, hope was in the air, new insights seemed likely, and the possibility of an organizational theory that was at once more broad and more useful was a heady tonic for many.

VALUE ENGINEERING AND THE INTEGRATION PERSPECTIVE

At this point, the game of king of the mountain had not yet begun. It was as if children drifted to the beach and began to play in the sand, at first without much interaction or coordination. Although publication dates can be misleading, and (as will be the case throughout this chapter) it is difficult to choose which of many exemplars to cite, many of the first widely influential culture publications were managerially oriented and written for a popular audience. Critics later labeled this cultural approach 'value engineering',[1] because these authors had the temerity to argue that effective cultural leaders could create 'strong' cultures, built around their own values. Perhaps the most popular was Peters and Waterman's (1982) *In Search of Excellence: Lessons from America's Best-Run Companies.* This anecdote-filled, lively book began with many of the same premises outlined and quoted above. The key to corporate financial success, according to Peters and Waterman, was a strongly unified culture. Top managers could build such a culture by articulating a set of values and then reinforcing those values, again and again, with formal policies, informal norms, stories, rituals, and jargon. In time, and with consistency, those values would become shared – with enthusiasm – by all employees. This would set up a domino effect: higher commitment, greater productivity, and ultimately, more profits. These seductive promises, complete with advice about how to create a 'strong' (meaning unitary) culture, were popularized in other books written primarily for executive and MBA audiences (e.g. Deal and Kennedy 1982; Ouchi 1981; Pascale and Athos 1981; see Fitzgerald 1988 for a rebuttal to some of these claims). Not surprisingly, culture quickly became the hottest product on the consulting market.

The value engineers touched a responsive chord in many managerially oriented academic researchers who shared the perception that organizational research had become dead-ended, boring, and/or too distant from the practical concerns of business. A flurry of culture research appeared (e.g. Enz 1988; Ott 1989; Ouchi and Jaeger 1978; Pennings and Gresov 1986; Pfeffer 1981; Pondy et al. 1983; Sathe

1985; Sergiovanni and Corbally 1984). These studies define culture as an internally consistent package of cultural manifestations that generates organization-wide consensus, usually around some set of shared values. In these cultural portraits all is clear; culture is 'an area of meaning carved out of a vast mass of meaninglessness, a small clearing of lucidity in a formless, dark, always ominous jungle' (Berger 1967: 23; quoted in Wuthnow et al. 1984: 26). Within the domain that is considered the culture, there is virtually no ambiguity (e.g. Schein 1991). Subcultures are noted only as a secondary consideration (if at all). Very little deep, collective conflict is acknowledged. Studies which share these characteristics (consistency, organization-wide consensus, and clarity) have been termed 'integration' research (Martin 1992). Many, *but not all,* integration studies have value engineering overtones, claiming that culture can be managed or that 'strong' cultures can lead to improved financial performance. Reviews which include a description of some of the historical roots of the integration literature are Ott (1989), Ouchi and Wilkins (1985), Schultz (1994), and Trice and Beyer (1993).

The integration perspective conceptualizes cultural change as an organization-wide cultural transformation, whereby an old unity is replaced – hopefully – by a new one; in the interim, conflict and ambiguity may occur, but these are interpreted as evidence of the deterioration of culture before a new unity is established (e.g. Clark 1972; Greenwood and Hinings 1988; Jonsson and Lundin 1977; Selznick 1957). For example, Schein (1985) describes several organizational leaders who articulate their personal values and apparently generate harmonious and universal commitment to those values, reaping benefits of high morale and smoothly coordinated task performance. When dissent appears or ambiguities emerge, these anomalies are explained as evidence of individual deviance, insufficiently homogeneous employee selection procedures, poor socialization of new employees, a weak culture, a temporary period of confusion during a time of cultural realignment, or – in the case of ambiguity – as a domain of organizational life that is not part of its culture (Schein 1991). The bottom line is that homogeneity, harmony, and a unified culture are achievable.

Other good examples of integration studies include Barley's (1983) study of how funeral directors manipulated a variety of physical artifacts (e.g. changing the sheets on a death bed, washing and putting make-up on a corpse, closing the corpse's eyes) to create the illusion that death is life-like. Pettigrew (1979) described how headmasters used rituals, stories, and jargon to generate commitment to their schools.

McDonald (1991) described how uniforms, slogans, posters, a charismatic leader, well-defined rituals, and a strong work ethic combined to create a sense of excitement and a commitment to excellence among volunteers and employees of a temporary organization, the Los Angeles Olympic Organizing Committee.[2] These are generalist cultural studies, that is, in addition to formal practices, rules and structures they describe and interpret informal practices (such as norms about appropriate behavior or proper decision-making procedures), as well as organizational stories, rituals, specialized jargon, and physical artifacts, such as decor, dress norms, machinery, architecture. In contrast to 'generalist' cultural studies, 'specialist' cultural studies focus on only a single cultural manifestation. Examples of specialist integration studies include Dandridge (1986) on ceremonies, Martin et al. (1983) on organizational stories, and Trice and Beyer (1984) on rituals. Specialist research done within the integration perspective assumes that the manifestations of a culture are consistent with each other, and thus sometimes, without adequate evidence, asserts that a single manifestation represents the culture as a whole (e.g. Martin et al. 1983).

ASSEMBLING THE TROOPS: THE DIFFERENTIATION PERSPECTIVE

Roughly at the same time as the flood of integration research began to appear, another group of scholars, mostly working independently, were drawn to some but not all the ideas expressed by the revolutionary vanguard. They too thought that mainstream organizational theory and research needed revitalization. They too thought that a renaissance of interest in organizational culture would bring an interdisciplinary creativity into the field, expanding the types of issues being studied and the kinds of methods considered valid.

Some of the members of this second group of cultural scholars had done work considered by many to be marginal to the managerial, quantitative emphases common to much mainstream organizational theory and research. Like many of the advocates of the integration viewpoint, some of this second group of scholars were qualitative researchers, who were excited because now ('at last' in the US) ethnographic research would have a home in organizational studies and qualitative case studies would be appreciated for their richly detailed, context-specific insights, rather than being dismissed as 'a nice story about an *N* of one'. Some scholars in this second group were also hopeful that

cultural work would generate alternatives to the managerial orientation that had been dominant for so long; now the opinions and interests of lower-level employees would be more fully represented. These and other deviants, dissidents, and disenchanted organizational scholars seeking a fresh perspective were attracted to cultural studies. Because culture itself was so vaguely defined, because it lacked a clear and commonly accepted theoretical framework, and because so many of these scholars prided themselves individually on their iconoclastic openness to new ideas, this 'rag-tag' collection of marginals soon generated an impressive body of work that shared some common characteristics, labeled here and elsewhere (e.g. Martin and Meyerson 1988) as the differentiation perspective.

Differentiation studies developed commonalities without much intentional coordination (although meetings, such as the 1984 Vancouver Conference on Organizational Culture and the annual gatherings of the Standing Conference on Organizational Symbolism, did provide some opportunities for contact and interchange among a wide range of cultural researchers). These commonalities emerged from a disparate set of intellectual traditions and, as outlined in the next section of this chapter, this *de facto* alliance was shaky, soon to be threatened by dissension. In the terms of the king of the mountain game, it was as if children playing independently on the beach began to notice each other, eventually moving together to play in a parallel fashion: an unstable coalition at best.

Differentiation studies, like integration studies, stress the ideational aspects of culture, such as values, cognitions (meanings), symbolism (including aesthetics), and/or emotions – topics which were being neglected in mainstream organizational research. Rather than defining culture in purely ideational terms, however, differentiation studies preferred a less ethereal, more material approach that included within the definition of culture practical/structural considerations such as pay, task responsibilities, hierarchical reporting relationships, formal policies and procedures – in short, any organizational practice formal enough to be written down. Most differentiation studies seem to assume that a good study of a culture should be generalist rather than specialist, that is, it should include a wide range of cultural manifestations.

Such generalist breadth was not enough; a good cultural study also had to have depth, to 'penetrate the front' presented to strangers (e.g. Gregory 1983), and to observe conflicts, the unresolved, the shameful, what causes ambivalence – the chinks in the armor through which deeper, more complex considerations become visible. This emphasis on depth of understanding produced cultural accounts that were sensitive to inconsistencies between stated attitudes and actual behavior, between formal practices and informal norms, between one story and another, and – most important – between the interpretations of one person and another (e.g. Van Maanen and Barley 1984; Van Maanen and Kunda 1989). Differences in perception and opinion were associated with status, tasks, jobs, seniority, sex, occupation, race, and ethnicity – often coalescing into overlapping, nested subcultures (e.g. Louis 1985). Although Rosen (1991) rightly observes that true ethnographies of organizational cultures are rare, the best differentiation ethnographies are highly complex, full of nuance, open to conflict, pervaded by inconsistencies and ambivalences: a complex richness that indeed fulfilled many of the hopes of the cultural vanguard (e.g. Jaques 1951; Kunda 1991; Rosen 1985; Van Maanen 1991; Young 1989). These studies are bold, empirically well-supported challenges to the integration assumption that organizational culture can be a unitary monolith composed of clear values and interpretations perceived, enacted, and shared by all employees, in an organization-wide consensus.

In addition, differentiation research showed that the subcultures within an organization can reflect, and be partially determined by, cultural groupings in the larger society. For example, functional subcultures within a firm can reflect occupational subcultures that cross firm boundaries, as when accountants appear to be the 'same everywhere' (e.g. Gregory 1983). From this perspective, cultural change is localized within one or more subcultures, alterations tend to be incremental, and innovations are triggered primarily by pressures from an organization's environment (e.g. Meyerson and Martin 1987). That environment is likely to be segmented, so different subcultures within the same organization experience different kinds and rates of change. Thus, from a differentiation viewpoint, an organizational culture is not unitary; it is a *nexus* where environmental influences intersect, creating a nested, overlapping set of subcultures within a permeable organizational boundary (Martin 1992: 111–14).

Examples show the texture of this kind of cultural work. Christensen and Kreiner (1984) drew on several case studies to distinguish different aspects of cultures in organizations: the firm's external 'aura' (what economists refer to as its reputation in the market); its 'corporate culture' (the values and goals espoused by its top management – not necessarily accepted or even noticed by lower-level employees); and 'cultures in work' (reflecting the everyday working lives of

groups of employees who share tasks). Rosen (1985) focused on the discordance between the espoused values of an advertising agency's top management and the reactions of various subcultures of employees, as they attended an annual company breakfast ritual. Van Maanen (1991) studied subcultures at Disneyland, as operators of various rides and concessions stands arranged themselves in a status hierarchy, harassed obnoxious customers, and ignored their supervisors. Bartunek and Moch (1991) described the non-too-enthusiastic reactions of various subcultures (in-house consulting staff, management of local plants, line employees, and machinists) to a management-initiated 'quality of working life' intervention. Young (1989) observed women working on an assembly line, describing their fission into two subcultures reflecting differences in age, marital status, and task assignments. A few researchers have delineated the difficulties women and minorities have in 'fitting into' corporate cultures dominated by white men (e.g. Bell 1990; Cox 1993; Kanter 1977; Mills 1992). Other studies consistent with a differentiation approach, broadly defined, include Brunsson (1985), Riley (1983), and Van Maanen (1986).

These studies have in common a willingness to acknowledge inconsistencies (i.e. attitudes versus behavior, formal policies versus actual practices, etc). They see consensus as occurring only within subcultural boundaries. They acknowledge conflicts of interest, for example, between top management and other employees or within a top management group. These studies describe whatever inconsistencies and subcultural differences they find in clear terms: there is little ambiguity here, except in the interstices between subcultures. Thus, inconsistency, subcultural consensus, and subcultural clarity are the hallmark characteristics of differentiation research (Martin 1992).

DISSENSION IN THE RANKS OF THE DIFFERENTIATION PERSPECTIVE

Although differentiation studies share the common characteristics described above, these commonalities mask important distinctions (for an extended discussion of this issue, see Alvesson 1993; Alvesson and Berg 1992).[3] For example, there is an important distinction between pluralism (the delineation of differences within a whole) and the awareness of power and conflicts of interest that come with a more critical perspective (i.e. Knights and Willmott 1987; Lucas 1987; Mumby 1988; Reed 1985; Riley 1983). There is a fundamental difference between the 'describe reality' tone of a historical-hermeneutic orientation (e.g. Agar 1986; Garfinkel 1967; Goffman 1967; Spradley 1979) and the challenge to the status quo represented by critical theories, for example what Habermas (1975) terms an emancipatory point of view (for a more extensive discussion of critical theory and related issues, see Chapter 1.7 by Alvesson and Deetz in this volume). In Burrell and Morgan's (1979) terminology, some of these issues stem from differences between the interpretative and the radical humanist paradigms. Putnam et al.'s (1993) debate between ethnography and critical theory outlines some of these differences in orientation, and Stablein and Nord's (1985) review classifies organizational culture research according to the extent to which it represents an emancipatory point of view.

Clues to where differentiation studies stand on these issues can most easily be found in their theoretical introductions, rather than in the content of their descriptions of particular subcultures. Studies that stem from a more critical, rather than interpretative or pluralistic, tradition tend to cite some common intellectual predecessors to legitimate their theoretical orientation and anti-management tone. These include organizational scholars open to the insights of Marxist/critical theory (e.g. Burawoy 1979; Burrell and Morgan 1979; Deetz 1992; Perrow 1979; Reed 1985), occupational research in the tradition of the Chicago School of sociology (e.g. Becker et al. 1961; Hughes 1958; Manning 1977), and some early qualitative studies of organizations that included a focus on lower-level employees (e.g. Crozier 1964; Jaques 1951).

These intellectual predecessors share a concern with the everyday working lives of people of relatively low status, a focus which is congruent with a relatively leftist political ideology that challenges the top management's views and delineates the negative consequences of the status quo on those who are relatively disadvantaged. In this context, it is surprising to note that few differentiation studies, even those written from a critical theory viewpoint, go beyond the delineation of subcultural differences to examine processes of organizational change that might, for example in a grass roots collective action, benefit those who are at the bottom of an organizational hierarchy. Although several literatures are relevant to these questions of change (for example, research on social movements, unions, and sabotage), these issues have received relatively little attention to date from cultural researchers.

Thus, the differentiation perspective includes at least two subdivisions that have developed in distinctive ways from differing intellectual traditions. One documents pluralism within a culture, usually utilizing ethnographic methods and a hermeneutic epistemology, offering a single, presumably 'accurate' interpretation of what was observed without fundamentally challenging a managerial perspective (i.e. Barley et al. 1988; Louis 1985; Martin and Siehl 1983). The other adds a critical, anti-management reading of the data (empirical examples include Rosen 1985; Van Maanen 1991; Young 1989). In some critical studies, sometimes even the pluralist sensitivity to difference that is the foundation of all differentiation research is underemphasized, while critique of the hegemony of management takes precedence. Thus, these differences in intellectual orientation within the differentiation classification can sometimes blur the boundaries of the category. Some differentiation scholars, particularly those working from a critical theory perspective, have been concerned about delineating these differences within their ranks (see Alvesson and Berg 1992 and Alvesson 1993, for example), while others have directed their attention to criticizing integration research. Now the battle lines had been drawn and the attack was about to begin.

LET THE GAME BEGIN: THE ATTACK OF THE DIFFERENTIATION ADVOCATES

Literally hundreds of integration studies were published in the 1980s. In the vast majority of these publications, consultants and academics had adopted the language of cultural studies and transformed it into a barely recognizable variant (some would say, travesty). Suddenly 'strong' unitary cultures had become the latest 'new' answer to managers' desires for greater control over their employees and greater profitability for their firms (Barley et al. 1988). Differentiation scholarship, of both pluralistic and critical varieties, had been outflanked by a value engineering perspective; the integration view had become king of the mountain. Advocates of the differentiation viewpoint were, needless to say, not pleased by these developments and they regrouped and then counter-attacked on several different fronts.

Some noted that in spite of efforts to distinguish practitioner-oriented integrationist writings from academic integrationist studies, the boundaries between these two categories were permeable (for example, many academics consulted and many consultants had fine academic credentials); more importantly, they shared a managerial emphasis (Barley et al. 1988; Jeffcutt forthcoming) and came to similar conclusions: organizational cultures were supposedly characterized by consistency, organization-wide consensus, and clarity. Some noted such commonalities with contempt, as evidence that these integration studies had 'sold out' to the managerial perspective that dominated mainstream organizational research (see also Van Maanen and Kunda 1989: 92):

> The companies studied are the cream of America's corporate crop, and range from IBM to McDonald's hamburgers. The dedication and quasi-religious commitment which the new manager seeks to instill into his employees sometimes sits a little oddly with the nature of the company goal: it may be inspiring to hear of sales staff risking their life in a snow storm to ensure that the company goal of regular delivery of supplies is maintained, but when the reader learns that the product is a high-salt, high-calorie junk food, doubts about whether some of this shining dedication is perhaps misplaced begin to arise. (Turner 1986: 108)

Calás and Smircich (1987), noting the overwhelming numbers of integration studies being published, declared that the cultural revolution was in danger of becoming 'dominant, but dead'. As Calás and Smircich had hoped, this fear was premature. Many of those who were not willing to give up the fight to dethrone the integration view utilized a methodological critique, a move that ultimately had the effect of partially cross-cutting the integration/differentiation battle lines and bringing different issues to the front.

THE METHODOLOGY BATTLE

The methodology battle was particularly fierce because underlying these method preferences were firmly held epistemological beliefs (e.g. Burrell and Morgan 1979). Although some skirmishes in this battle took place out in the open, most were more like guerrilla warfare, taking place in a series of out-of-sight maneuvers; the methods battle affected an editor's choice of journal reviewers for a culture article, a 'blind' reviewer's verdict about the merits of a particular manuscript, and even the content of letters from external reviewers in tenure cases. Of course, such out-of-sight maneuvers left few published traces that can be quoted here, without breaking norms of confidentiality and blind review. Nevertheless, we personally can testify that these non-public fights were, and are, fiercely contested. The stakes were high, at least in academic terms. Viewing culture from the differentiation perspective and studying it using qualitative methods can be a risky career strategy, particularly in the US where the field is dominated by managerial interests, integrationist theoretical preconceptions, and quantitative methods.

Some qualitative researchers were disappointed by this reaction. They responded by citing texts justifying their methods choices and outlining the fundamentals of good qualitative research methodology (some helpful texts include Agar 1986; Blau 1965; Glaser and Strauss 1967; Schein 1987; Van Maanen et al. 1982). Even among advocates of qualitative methods for studying culture there were strident disagreements, most of which surfaced in less public places, like journal reviews. The purist ethnographers criticized short-term and/or interview-based qualitative studies as being 'smash and grab' ethnographies.[4] If a researcher was to truly 'penetrate the front' of cultural members, he or she had to, they argued, adopt 'true' ethnographic methods. This meant spending months or even years as a participant-observer in order to see things from an insider's 'emic' perspective (e.g. Gregory 1983). Anything less was worthy of being classified, at best, as exploratory pilot testing, anecdotal examples to illustrate ideas based on more solid evidence – in short, probably not worth mentioning, in print (see Sutton 1994 for a frank discussion of these issues).

Other cultural researchers, perhaps in response to criticisms of qualitative methods, developed quantitative measures of cultural phenomena, drawing primarily on techniques used in organizational climate research (Schneider 1990). Quantitative culture studies are generally 'specialist' in that they focus on only one kind of cultural manifestation – usually a measure of agreement with a series of espoused (rather than enacted) values or a self-report of behavioral norms (e.g. 'People in my work group are generally more cooperative than competitive'), measured using seven-point scales or more innovative techniques, such as adjective sorting tasks (e.g. O'Reilly et al. 1991).

There are several problems with these quantitative approaches. Specialist studies should not (although integration studies often do) assume or assert that the one kind of manifestation is consistent with or representative of the culture as a whole (see Martin et al. 1983 as an illustration of this problem). Additionally, respondents may not be aware that their espoused values are not being consistently enacted (e.g. Argyris and Schon 1978). They may fear that researchers' promises of anonymity will not be kept, endangering their jobs, and so may give misleading answers that are reflective of top management's expressed preferences, rather than actual behavior, thus creating an illusion of organizational consensus. To manage the impression given to researchers, respondents may give answers that seem socially desirable or that reflect their current levels of job satisfaction (high or low).

Furthermore, this kind of quantitative measure may give a misleading representation of a culture because the researcher has generated the alternatives that the respondents are evaluating. Most importantly, such quantitative studies are likely to provide empirical support for integrationist assumptions, if responses that do not reflect organization-wide consensus are excluded from discussion and analysis – as not part of the 'culture'. Significantly, other questionnaire-based specialist studies have used broader, random samples of respondents, across status levels, and have found evidence of subcultural differentiation (pockets of ignorance of and resistance to managerial values), rather than organization-wide consensus (Kilmann 1985; Rousseau 1990).

Some integration studies, which use specialist quantitative (questionnaire) measures of culture, have claimed to have found evidence of a link to financial performance (Denison 1990; Gordon 1985; Ouchi and Johnson 1978). Other specialist quantitative studies (for example, a content analysis of espoused managerial values in annual reports has been used as a measure of 'culture') conclude that valid empirical confirmation of a link to financial performance has not yet been found and is unlikely to be found, given the many non-cultural determinants of financial performance and the difficulty of developing adequately generalist measures of the cultures of large numbers of firms (see Siehl and Martin 1990 for a review of the research on this issue).

Advocates of ethnographic methods, from both the integration and differentiation perspectives, have been particularly critical of specialist studies which by definition lack the richly detailed, context-specific understandings that emerge from generalist ethnographic cultural portraits (e.g. Schein 1987; Smircich 1983; Smircich and Morgan 1982; Van Maanen et al. 1982), especially those with a longitudinal focus (e.g. Pettigrew 1985a; 1985b). Ethnographers also have disapproved of an exclusive focus on espoused values or self-reported behavioral norms. Because such a superficial focus cannot 'penetrate the front' of people's desires to present themselves in a favourable light, it is far inferior to the depth made accessible by long-term participant-observation. In organizational contexts, behavior is often constrained by managerial preferences or career ambitions and cannot be assumed to reflect an employee's true attitudes. Many ethnographers had thought that the cultural movement would provide respect, particularly in the US where qualitative methods had been so disparaged. Many of these qualitative researchers were disappointed that this domain of organizational research, like all the others, was in danger of being taken over by the number crunchers, a reaction that was expressed, in public forums, by the usual strategies of silence and marginalization; in more private arenas, such as 'blind reviews', the negative reaction was more pronounced and many researchers felt it was difficult to get their work recognized due to methods preferences of reviewers and editors (see, for example, Rousseau 1994).

The result was a strident debate over the merits of qualitative and quantitative methods for studying culture (for a particularly clear discussion of the underlying issues, although not within the context of this particular body of literature, see Blau 1965; Daft 1980; Light 1979), with some researchers advocating matching particular conventional methods with particular conceptual problems (e.g. McGrath 1982; Rousseau 1990), while others preferred an uneasy, but possibly innovative hybrid mix of the two approaches (e.g. Martin 1990a). For example, one such hybrid qualitative-quantitative approach to studying culture involved a two-step procedure (Martin et al. 1985). An open-ended, structured interview protocol was used to collect qualitative, context-specific event histories, generated by employees themselves, using such questions as: 'Describe the ten incidents that made your company what it is today. Give details. For each event, tell us what meanings this event holds for you personally and for the company as a whole.' These open-ended responses were then quantitatively content-analyzed, to measure subcultural or organization-wide agreement about what happened, to delineate which employees' actions were considered important, and which interpretations of the meanings of these events were shared. Such hybrid methods represent an uneasy compromise between quite different epistemologies. The qualitative/quantitative debates among cultural researchers continue (see the edited volumes by Schneider 1990, and Hassard and Pym 1990, for some recent salvos in this battle). Given the deep differences that underlie these disputes, agreement is unlikely.

Taken as a whole, qualitative cultural studies do not provide consistent, convincing support for the premises of either the integration or the differentiation perspectives. For those who thought quantitative research could resolve the conflict between these two viewpoints, the contradictory empirical record caused confusion: how could conscientious culture researchers come to such different conclusions? Was it the case simply that integration research generally focused on organizations where organization-wide consensus existed, while differentiation research picked organizations where subcultures prevailed? This was unlikely, given that integration studies dismissed evidence of non-unitary cultures as examples of weak or failed integration (e.g.

Schein 1991), while differentiation research often failed to look for or report organization-wide agreement.

At this point, the conflict escalated, as advocates of each viewpoint accused each other of theoretical and methodological tautology, whether or not they used quantitative methods. Integration studies were accused (for examples from the literature, see Martin 1992: 65–7) of engaging in a kind of tautology because they defined culture as consistent and clear, then included in their cultural portraits only those manifestations which seemed to have consistent and clear interpretations. They defined culture (or a 'strong' culture) as organization-wide agreement with values espoused by top management, but their sampling procedures were seldom either random or stratified to include all levels of the hierarchy. Instead, integration studies tended to study those cultural members who were particularly articulate informants, or those who were most likely to have views similar to top managers (i.e. high-ranking and upwardly mobile managers, professionals such as accountants or engineers, or loyal lower-ranking members selected by management). Unfortunately, integration studies seldom hesitated to generalize from such limited subject samples to the culture of the whole organization.

Even studies which refrained from these non-standard sampling procedures found organization-wide consensus by excluding from their cultural portraits (as 'not part of the culture' or 'evidence of a weak culture') all aspects of the culture that generated conflicting or ambiguous interpretations (see Schein 1991 for a cogent defense of this position). Not surprisingly, the portraits of culture that emerged from these research designs were entirely consistent with integrationist theoretical preconceptions: each 'strong' culture was a monolith where every manifestation reinforced the values of top management, employees complied with managerial directives, and preferences were assumed to share these values, and there was, apparently, only one interpretation of the meaning of events shared by all. These studies were designed so integration research would find what it was looking for.

Advocates of the integration point of view did not take all this criticism without fighting back. They accused differentiation research of also being tautological (for examples, see Martin 1992: 106–8). Differentiation studies, these critics argued, defined cultural manifestations as inconsistent, and then included in their cultural portraits those manifestations that fit these definitions. Differentiation studies were accused of seeking subcultural differentiation, by using focused, non-random samples of lower-level employees and ignoring (or not searching for) evidence of values shared on an organization-wide basis. Integration critics claimed that, if differentiation studies had only had sufficiently astute clinical and ethnographic skills, they would have understood that, at a deep enough level, fundamental assumptions (for example, about the nature of time) are shared by all or most members of an organization (e.g. Schein 1985; 1994). Of course, when such widely shared, deep assumptions are found, they may in fact be part of a society's culture, and not appropriately studied at the organizational level of analysis (Martin 1992: 53–6). And so it goes on: the openly combative exchanges in public, as well as the more private and less visible forms of battle, continue.

This academic battle about methodology and theory shows some considerable indifference to the fates of actual people in real organizations (see Donaldson 1989: 250 for an articulate version of this criticism); even differentiation research, ostensibly so concerned about the fate of the disadvantaged and oppressed, contributes little so far to understanding how to make people's organizational lives better. Outside academia, in corporations the stakes are high. Managers do not generally care about the hair splitting disputes of academics, but they do care, deeply, about the considerable expense and unwanted consequences of ill-thought-out cultural change interventions. Many executives, consultants, and lower-level employees dismiss culture as 'yesterday's fad', and predictably have turned elsewhere to find another 'quick fix' for corporate ills.

The theoretical and methodological disputes described above have caused chaos in the field of cultural studies. In the struggle to be king of the mountain, skirmishes are constant among proponents of various epistemologies, methodologies, intellectual heritages, publication norms, and even different career paths (e.g. US versus European). Everyone is out to prove what they already believe in. It is not clear what has been learned, who is more correct, or even what methods could convincingly resolve these differences of opinion. In fact, for reasons explained in the next two sections of this review, such disputes may not be resolvable. In the short term, however, the confusion caused by the methods battle created an opening for other parties to enter the battlefield.

A New Contender: the Fragmentation Perspective

These new parties to the conflict each tried to redraw the battle lines so that their point of view would emerge triumphant – the king of the mountain. The first of these new contenders has been termed the fragmentation perspective (Martin 1992), as it is positioned as the third logical possibility on the dimensions that are the focus of the integration versus differentiation struggle. According to the advocates of the fragmentation view, the relationships among the manifestations of a culture are neither clearly consistent nor clearly inconsistent; instead, the relationships are complex, containing elements of contradiction and confusion. Similarly, consensus is not organization-wide nor is it specific to a given subculture. Instead, consensus is transient and issue-specific, producing short-lived affinities among individuals that are quickly replaced by a different pattern of affinities, as a different issue draws the attention of cultural members (e.g. Kreiner and Schultz 1993). In such an ephemeral environment, culture is no longer a clearing in a jungle of meaninglessness. Now, culture is the jungle itself. According to the fragmentation point of view, the essence of any culture is ambiguity, which pervades all (e.g. Feldman 1991; Meyerson 1991). Clarity, then, is a dogma of meaningfulness and order propagated by management to create an illusion of clarity where there is none (e.g. Levitt and Nass 1989).

Lack of consistency, lack of consensus, and ambiguity are the hallmarks of a fragmentation view of culture. In a fragmentation account, power is diffused broadly at all levels of the hierarchy and throughout the organization's environment. Change is a constant flux, rather than an intermittent interruption in an otherwise stable state. Because change is largely triggered by the environment or other forces beyond an individual's control, fragmentation studies of change offer few guidelines for those who would normatively control the change process.

For example, Feldman (1989) studied policy analysts in a large government bureaucracy. They spent their days writing policy reports that might never be read and, in any case, were unlikely to influence the formation of a policy. In such a context, ambiguities became a protective cloud that prevented a clear analysis of the meaning(lessness) of the analysts' work. In Meyerson's (1991) studies of social workers, ambiguity pervaded an occupation whose practitioners had to operate in a world where the objectives of social work were unclear, the means to those goals were not specified, and sometimes it wasn't even clear when an intervention had been successful or even what success in this context might have meant. Meyerson concluded that to study the culture of this occupation – while excluding ambiguity from the realm of what is defined as cultural – would have been dramatically incomplete, even

misleading. Weick (1991) offered a fragmentation view of a foggy airport in Tenerife, as pilots, controllers, and cockpit crews struggled to make themselves understood across barriers of status, language, and task assignment. In this context, pervasive ambiguity was not benign: hundreds of lives were lost as two jumbo jets collided in the fog.

AN ATTEMPT TO REDRAW THE BATTLE LINES: A META-THEORETICAL MOVE

What had been a war among two perspectives was now a war among many: among the integration, differentiation, and fragmentation views; between the qualitative and quantitative advocates; and between the critical theorists and their more interpretative colleagues. The game of king of the mountain was now being played in earnest; all of these contenders were competing for supremacy, although each was arguing for the use of different playing rules. Rather than going for a minor victory (a fourth perspective), the next obvious move in the king of the mountain game was to create a meta-theory that would encompass all three perspectives.

Martin (1992) outlined the problems of methodological tautology discussed above and argued that such tautologies were also evident in fragmentation research. Fragmentation studies focused on contexts (airports literally in the fog) and occupations (policy analyst, social worker) that were particularly ambiguous and then wrote cultural portraits emphasizing those ambiguities. Both fragmentation and differentiation studies tended to focus on a wide range of cultural manifestations, making it less likely that all manifestations would have consistent interpretations. Thus, integration, differentiation, and fragmentation researchers defined culture in a particular way and then designed studies which made it more likely they would find what they were looking for. This problem of tautology explained, to a large extent, why three traditions of research on ostensibly the same topic could produce such conflicting empirical records. (Indeed, some have argued that similar tautological problems characterize all of organizational research; see Morgan 1983b).

However, the fact remains that evidence congruent with each perspective had been found. Martin (1992) argues that it is not only that advocates of the various perspectives have sought and found cultural contexts that fit their preconceptions; in addition, *any* organizational culture contains elements congruent with all three perspectives. If any organization is studied in enough depth, some issues, values, and objectives will be seen to generate organization-wide consensus, consistency, and clarity (an integration view). At the same time, other aspects of an organization's culture will coalesce into subcultures that hold conflicting opinions about what is important, what should happen, and why (a differentiation view). Finally, some problems and issues will be ambiguous, in a state of constant flux, generating multiple, plausible interpretations (a fragmentation view). A wide range of organizational contexts have been examined using the three-perspective framework, including studies of a temporary educational organization for unemployed women in England, a newly privatized bank in Turkey, truants from an urban high school in the US, and Peace Corps/Africa volunteers (Baburoglu and Gocer 1991; Enomoto 1993; Jeffcutt forthcoming; Meyerson and Martin 1987). Implicit in the three-perspective framework is the assumption that these social scientific viewpoints are subjectively imposed on the process of collecting and interpreting cultural data. Often one perspective, labeled the 'home' viewpoint, is easy for cultural members and researchers to acknowledge, while the other two perspectives can be more difficult to access. It is therefore a misunderstanding to conclude that a particular organization has a culture that is best characterized by one of the three perspectives. Rather, any culture at any point in time will have some aspects congruent with all three perspectives (e.g. Frost et al. 1991; Martin 1992; Meyerson and Martin 1987).

The three-perspective framework is a meta-theory, which claims to encompass and thereby surpass prior, more narrow theories by moving to a higher level of abstraction, claiming that, when a cultural context is viewed from all three perspectives, a deeper understanding will emerge. Presumably, because the three-perspective theory is more inclusive and thereby possibly more insightful, it supposedly deserves to dominate other approaches to understanding cultures in organizations. This is a classic attempt to redraw the lines of battle and so become 'king of the mountain', and as such, it arouses considerable antagonism.

Obviously, this approach does have limitations. To paraphrase and quote arguments made elsewhere (Martin 1992: 192), this tripartite classification scheme is based on a series of undeconstructed dichotomies that position the perspectives in opposition to one another. It ignores aspects of theories and studies that straddle boundaries among the perspectives (see, especially, rich ethnographies such as Kunda 1991 and Pettigrew 1985b), omits unclassifiable research or relegates it to marginalized places in the text, and reserves treatment of issues that

transcend these categories for separate parts of the text (for example, see the discussion above of the differences between the critical theory and interpretative traditions or the qualitative versus quantitative methods debates). Most importantly, by using these tripartite categories to classify studies, the perspectives are reified and individual studies are pigeonholed, thereby diminishing the uniqueness of their contributions. Such a use of categories is common social scientific practice, and not unique to this particular attempt to build a meta-theory, but it does have harmful effects on the ways knowledge gets created and scholarly work is and is not evaluated (e.g. Gagliardi 1990; Turner 1989). And these criticisms are mild compared to the postmodern critiques of meta-theories outlined in the next section of this review.

To summarize the results of the last few battles described above: in spite of (or perhaps because of) the confusion caused by these disputes, the last decade of cultural research has produced a variety of insightful, innovative studies that might not have been completed within the narrower orthodoxies of theory and method that have constrained other kinds of organizational inquiry. Cultural studies have brought epistemological and methodological variety to the field, introduced ideas from other disciplines, and (speaking now of qualitative generalist work) offered richly detailed, context-specific descriptions of organizational life. Now, however, cultural research faces a new and formidable challenge: postmodernists have entered the culture wars. The postmodernists' bid to be king of the mountain has a very different tone than the modernist traditions of cultural research described so far. If the postmodernists are successful, cultural researchers will admit that it is impossible, ever, to know, or represent, the truth about a culture.

THE END OF THEORY: A POSTMODERN ROUT OF ALL ARMIES FROM THE FIELD OF BATTLE?

It is beyond the mandate of this chapter to discuss postmodernism at length (readers should consult Chapter 1.7 by Alvesson and Deetz) but, nonetheless, we are able to discuss its implications for and contributions to the work on organizational culture. Postmodernism is the most profound, potentially disruptive, and possibly insightful development in cultural studies to date (e.g. Calás and Smircich 1987; Czarniawska-Joerges 1992; Jeffcutt forthcoming; Linstead and Grafton-Small 1991). There is not just one postmodernism: it is a discourse, rather than a unified theory, in part because it has attracted such a diverse group of advocates, including architects, philosophers, and literary critics. Some postmodernists have been accused of fascism, while others are leftist refugees from the political activism of the 1960s. In all these varieties, postmodernism challenges ideas which are the foundation of modern science: rationality, order, clarity, realism, truth, and intellectual progress (e.g. Baudrillard 1983; Derrida 1976; Foucault 1976; Grafton-Small and Linstead 1987; Lyotard 1984). When contrasted to postmodern ideas, modernist cultural scholarship is seen to share some preconceptions. For example, modern cultural studies (even those written from differentiation and fragmentation perspectives) attempt to provide coherent accounts – to order the disorder that is organizational life. Carrying this emphasis on order one step further, integration studies offer a portrait of unity, harmony, and in many instances, the promise of cultural control.

In contrast, postmodern accounts draw attention to disorder and offer a multiplicity of contradictory interpretations, making integration studies particularly suspect from a postmodern viewpoint. The relationship between the signifier and the signified, between an image and the original experience it was once produced to represent, is from a postmodern viewpoint attenuated, complex, and in part arbitrary (Alvesson and Berg 1992: 220). This arbitrariness should not be confused with the more tepid, manageable ambiguities, irrationalities, and randomness that are the focus of fragmentation research.

The key difference is that while ambiguity implies a surplus of meaning attached to a particular object, i.e., a somewhat unclear, fuzzy, vague, obscure or enigmatic relation, arbitrariness implies a capricious or willful relationship that cannot be determined by any rule or principle. While an ambiguous relationship means that there is a way of understanding and capturing this relationship and of understanding the inherent way in which the signifier represents the signified, an arbitrary relationship makes no such assumptions. (Alvesson and Berg 1992: 220)

Modern cultural scholarship, particularly that which uses ethnographic methods, attempts to cut through superficial cultural manifestations and interpretations to uncover a deeper reality, revealing knowledge that is closer to the truth. Modern scholarship is careful to draw distinctions among the objective truth about reality, the subjectivity of a researcher-author, and a text. These distinctions, however, are not inviolable. For example, modernist studies sometimes explore the flaws of an imperfect relationship

between reality and data (which presumably can be improved by more rigorous ethnographic or quantitative methods). Modern scholars also sometimes acknowledge a flawed relationship between presumably objective data and their imperfect representation in a text (which presumably can be improved by clearer, more 'transparent' writing). More rarely, a modernist author may engage in self-reflexivity concerning the effects of his or her individualized subjectivity on a text (e.g. Kunda 1991; Van Maanen 1988). Such introspection is usually confined to the margins of a text (an introduction, and anecdote, or an appendix). Such marginalization enables the modern author, in the main body of the text, to maintain the impersonal, supposedly objective style and language that sustain scientific credibility by making the individualized subjectivity of the author invisible (e.g. Clifford and Marcus 1986; Geertz 1988).

In contrast, from a postmodern point of view, reality is a serious of fictions and illusions (Alvesson and Berg 1992; Arac 1986; Clifford and Marcus 1986; Geertz 1988). A text is not a closed system; it reflects the subjective views of its author, those who read it, and those whose views are quoted, included, suppressed, or excluded (e.g. Hassard and Parker 1993; Linstead and Grafton-Small 1992). This focus on representational issues, such as the ways impersonal language reinforces the authority of an author, undermines any claim that a text can represent the objective truth about a reality that is 'out there' – separable from the text (e.g. Cooper and Burrell 1988; Jeffcutt 1995; Smircich 1995). Truth therefore becomes 'a matter of credibility rather than an objective condition' (Alvesson and Berg 1992: 223; Van Maanen 1988). This focus on textual analysis (rather than collective change efforts or data collection) is justified from a postmodern point of view because there is nothing outside or beyond the text (e.g. Moi 1985; Weedon 1987).

Whereas modern scholars argue about what the truth is or what methods or modes of engagement would bring research closer to truth, postmodernists use analytic techniques such as deconstruction to reveal strategies used to represent truth claims in a text, for example, how: an author establishes his or her credibility; particular data are selected and interpreted (to the exclusion of other, equally valid data and interpretations); uncertainties are hidden; opposing meanings are suppressed or omitted; and unintended and suppressed viewpoints emerge in the margins of a text (such as footnotes, asides, metaphors, etc.). (For introductions to and examples of deconstruction, see Calás and Smircich 1991; Czarniawska-Joerges 1992; Ferguson 1993; Flax 1990; Martin 1990b; Weedon 1987.) Reading in these ways, between the lines of a text, silences become eloquent and the false certainties inherent in language (such as the clarities of a dichotomy) are exposed.

Postmodernist cultural scholars use textual analysis to interrogate, disrupt, and overturn claims to truth or theoretical superiority (e.g. Gagliardi 1991; Jeffcutt 1995). Their goal is not to establish a better theory of culture (this would perpetuate the struggle for intellectual dominance of the field, as described for example by Kuhn 1970), but rather to challenge the foundations of modern cultural scholarship (Alvesson and Berg 1992; Smircich and Calás 1987). For example:

> Not surprisingly, postmodern theorizing is adamantly disdainful of meta-theories, labeling them 'narratives of transcendence' because each claims to be better than its predecessors – more abstract and yet also closer to 'the' empirical 'truth.' Lyotard, for example, views meta-theories as totalitarian attempts, by those who are or wish to become dominant, to provide all-encompassing world views that silence diversity of opinion. Postmodern scholars argue that attempts to create meta-theories are misguided and futile; fragmentation and multiplicity will flourish, in spite of attempts to make particular meta-theories dominant. (Martin 1992: 193)

For this reason, postmodern analyses often take the form of critiques or parodies (e.g. Calás and Smircich 1988; Willmott 1993) – carnivalesque writing that steadfastly maintains a marginalized position. Such writing attempts to 'overturn a disciplinary and prejudicial order through the articulation of ambiguity and contradiction from the margin' but does not seek 'to co-ordinate this difference into a fresh hierarchy through the articulation of a superior vision of progress' (Jeffcutt forthcoming a: 18–19).

Given the postmodern disdain for attempts to legitimize claims of theoretical supremacy, a postmodern history of cultural research would not be a linear tale of progress, with new insights learned and old errors abandoned. Postmodernism, if taken seriously, makes the structure and form of a traditional handbook or review chapter an impossibility. Instead, postmodernism, in accord with Kuhn's (1970) views of paradigm revolutions, views the history of research on a topic as a struggle for intellectual dominance. Each new development, whether theoretical or methodological, is seen as an attempt to declare superiority over prior efforts.

This handbook chapter has been structured around some of these ideas, using the metaphor of culture wars and a war game (king of the mountain) to describe developments in this field

as struggles for intellectual dominance, rather than linear advancements in the progression toward greater knowledge. The various moves in the culture wars, outlined in the first sections of this chapter, are described as if these modernist culture scholars were saying 'My approach is deeper, more complex, or more inclusive than yours' (ethnography, a longitudinal approach, or the three-perspective framework); or 'My approach is more responsive to the needs of business than yours' (the integration framework); or 'Look what you have been ignoring' (the fragmentation perspective). Such claims of superiority have in common the implication that each view is, somehow, closer to the truth about a culture. All are attempts to impose order and meaning.

A postmodern critique would deconstruct these attempts to establish dominance in a hierarchical order. For example, such a critique would show how all these modern studies refrain from fully exploring the inherent and inescapable limitations of textual representation. Rather than perpetuating the king of the mountain game, where each new theory or meta-theory attempts to dominate other current contenders, postmodernism apparently abandons claims of linear progress and superior insight. Postmodernism is an attempt to rout all contenders from the field of battle and change the terms of engagement in the culture wars: no longer are we discussing ways to 'penetrate the front' of cultural members and get closer to some truth; now truth is impossible to represent.

A VICTORY FOR POSTMODERNISM OR MORE OF THE SAME?

Many academics have dismissed postmodernism on grounds that it is esoteric, reactionary, apolitical, too relativistic, or nihilistic (e.g. Okin 1994; Reed 1990). This reaction has been particularly strong among some empirical, relatively positivistic culture researchers, perhaps because postmodernism represents a deep challenge to basic tenets of the scientific method: rationality, order, truth, and progress. Modernist cultural scholars, rather than seeing only the threat that the burgeoning postmodern literature represents, could try to learn from and use some aspects of postmodern thinking (see, for example, Clegg 1990; Hassard and Parker 1993; and Chapter 1.7 on postmodernism in this volume). For example, postmodernism offers a way of escaping the cycles of disillusionment that trouble relationships between cultural scholars and practitioners, whereby each attempt at theoretical innovation is oversimplified and transformed into yet another managerial panacea – an easy answer to managers' endless desire to use 'quick fix' remedies to attain greater productivity or profitability. Such easy answers are doomed, ultimately, to fall short of their advance press and be labeled a failure, only to start the cycle again (e.g. Calás and Smircich 1990). Indeed, some have said that organizational culture represents just such a failed managerial fad. Could deconstruction make this cycle visible and be a tool to prevent its recurrence?

In addition, cultural researchers have invested a considerable amount of time and effort trying to combat the unitary assumptions of the integration perspective (i.e. Gregory 1983; Lucas 1987; Martin and Siehl 1983; Turner 1986; Van Maanen and Kunda 1989; Young 1989). Every careful ethnography or quantitative study that tries to challenge integrationist assumptions is countered quickly by yet another assertion that any culture can be a haven of homogeneity and harmony – a place where management's values are shared by all, and an employee's major task is simply to find a culture where he or she will 'fit in'. Could this cycle be short-circuited by postmodernism, so that researchers could devote their time and energy to deeper and more important cultural questions?

A postmodern approach could most certainly offer insight into the representational strategies that make cultural accounts more like fiction than, supposedly, like science (e.g. Calás 1987; Jermier 1992; Van Maanen 1988). Our cultural texts could become more self-reflexive and we could seek, as anthropologists are now doing, new, polyphonic ways of writing about culture that allow multiple voices to be heard and de-constructed, without transforming the researcher into a transcriber who has given informants total control of and responsibility for the text (Clifford and Marcus 1986).

As Alvesson and Berg (1992) observe, such 'benefits' would not represent a major change in modern cultural research strategies and they would not fully acknowledge the depth of the challenge to the scientific method that would follow from a full acceptance of postmodern ideas. Common criticisms of postmodernism (e.g. nihilistic, relativist, apolitical, esoteric, etc.) could be redefined as problems in postmodernism that cultural scholars might be able to help solve. Not only might this reorientation represent a contribution to problems that many postmodernists have been struggling with; it might also open the minds of modern cultural – and more broadly organizational – scholars to the value of postmodern insights.

For example, some scholars are seeking clear ways of explaining postmodern ideas to a broader range of organizational researchers (at the risk of being accused of oversimplification and other intellectual crimes and misdemeanors) (e.g. Boje and Dennehy 1993; Clegg 1990; Cooper and Burrell 1988; Hassard and Parker 1993). Some are trying to align postmodern insights with activist social change agendas, focusing on small wins and the likelihood of ambiguous and random outcomes as more attainable, less romanticized views of what kinds of organizational change are possible in contemporary circumstances (e.g. Arac 1986; Bergquist 1993; Letiche 1991; Simons and Billig 1994). Still others (e.g. Ferguson 1993; Flax 1990; Okin 1994) are struggling with ways to reconcile the indeterminism of postmodernism with ideological certainties (for example, from moral philosophy and feminism) in order to avoid problems of ethical relativism. The insights from all these lines of inquiry could enrich cultural studies in helpful ways.

SOME LESSONS OF WAR

One striking aspect of the culture literature, at this point in its development, is that none of the cultural approaches outlined in this chapter have gone very far in helping improve the lives of people who work in organizations. Integration studies have perhaps gone the farthest, although this research seems aimed primarily at aiding managers without acknowledging conflicts of interest with other constituencies, such as lower-level employees. Some differentiation research, several ethnographies, and studies in the critical theory tradition have effectively chronicled the views and material conditions of work of non-management employees, but these studies say less about how to fix the problems they describe so eloquently. The fragmentation perspective and symbolic approaches also offer description and analysis, but relatively few tools for action. Postmodern organizational scholars have not, so far, taken as their mission helping employees take action, although such work is starting to emerge (e.g. Letiche 1991). Of course, not all cultural researchers have, as part of their agendas, the goal of helping others to improve their working lives. For those that do, we can draw on this analysis of the culture wars to see what might be learned and applied.

If managers, employee representatives, and other stakeholders in and around organizations paid attention to the culture literature and studied the debates as we have represented them here, they might at first blush throw up their hands and dismiss culture as a fad or as unimportant. Alternatively, they might fixate on one or the other theoretical viewpoint, borrowing only a subset of the available ideas about culture. We would predict, in the latter case, that most managers would want to create and control a unified and strong culture that would maximize productivity and performance, trying to manage cultural change in a controlled and predictable manner. If unreflective, they would draw primarily from the integration perspective, given its prevalence in publications written for executives and MBAs. Rather than relying on the integration literature, some employees might find differentiation research, with its emphasis on intergroup conflict, to be more attuned to their goals (for example, achieving job security, fair wages, equity, resistance to change). They might also be interested in differentiation ideas about cultural control, particularly when there is a perceived need for a unified resistance (e.g. to a management initiative) or a need to understand what management is thinking as it pushes its agenda. Other stakeholders, such as customers, legislators, shareholders, and environmentalists, may view an organizational arena as being fragmented and conflict-ridden, rather than highly integrated. Alternatively, those 'outsiders' with a skeptical eye may view cultures as purely symbolic representations used by managers and employees to influence outcomes in self-serving ways. This last view may be closer to a postmodern perspective on culture than any of the others.

The aspirations of these various stakeholders differ, as group members struggle to accomplish outcomes they believe serve their interests. This is neither good nor bad. If we take the position that understanding culture is important, and that having such understandings available to all stakeholders is a basis for more informed and just efforts to make organizations more profitable and humane, then sharing the intellectual 'spoils' of the culture wars with everyone may be a useful undertaking. We think that trying to make sense of the ideas, insights, prescriptions, and the like that are currently reported in the various literatures might improve the chances of reflective, informed, and creative approaches to working and living with culture. Some examples are as follows:

First, practitioners tend to oversimplify the meaning of organizational culture as they borrow, adapt, or are fed the latest theory of organizational culture. This produces a high probability of a failed adaptation of culture to organizational issues, especially those related to improving productivity and performance. This, in turn, leads to disillusionment and dismissal of the cultural approach as a fad. Analysis of common oversimplifications of cultural theories and representative failed attempts at cultural

change (e.g. Bartunek and Moch 1991) can be particularly useful in this regard.

Second, no one theory or collection of theories about culture can conclusively claim superiority over others. One is better off adopting a multiperspective framework that assumes that, in any organizational setting, there will be some values, interpretations, and practices that generate organization-wide consensus, some that cause conflict, and some that are not clear. At any point in time, a subset of these will be easily visible (a 'home' perspective of a researcher or an employee), while other perspectives will be harder to see. To the extent that it is possible to work with culture to attain collectively desired ends, actions and processes will have to take into account these different, co-existing cultural possibilities. Accepting this proposition means that culture 'users' will have to understand and accept that there is no 'happy acculturated forever after' ending to change attempts. In all likelihood, there is no 'forever after' in the script. At best, there may be some combination of agreement, dispute, and confusion that can be stitched together by human agency, as managers and others move the action along, accomplish some objective, and then regroup around subsequent problems, issues, and opportunities.

Third, in attempting to manage change, it may be useful to try to accomplish collective objectives in a way that incorporates the postmodernist treatment of 'reality' as a series of fictions and illusions. In particular, if one understands that the culture theorist (or consultant) who promotes a perspective on organizational culture is providing a fictional account of the phenomenon (and plays a part in the story as well), then one is empowered to treat the 'story' with caution – preferably to rewrite, or better yet co-write, the script for the setting he or she is in. The application of theories of culture to organizational issues then becomes a joint venture between the theorist and those who work with the story or stories. This approach is likely to incorporate more improvisation and reflexivity than is usually the case when cultural theories are applied to managing organizational issues.

Fourth, at the same time, some stories about culture are more compelling than others and some are more influential than others (particularly if they are rooted in the values of those with power). Consequently, a useful additional source of value to a cultural theory – as story/representation – can be its deconstruction. While the tools of deconstruction may be outside the grasp of the typical organizational practitioner, they need not necessarily remain so. This may be a challenge that postmodernists can take on in the interests of helping improve the human condition in the work place (see Boje and Dennehy 1993; Clegg 1990). Application of deconstructive techniques might be used to help reconstruct a theory, strategy, action plan, or story in ways that would be more useful to a wider array of interested stakeholders.

Fifth, if truth is a matter of credibility rather than an objective condition (e.g. Alvesson and Berg 1992: 223), then management of change by practitioners (not necessarily only managers) becomes a matter of developing credible scripts and framing issues to bridge different understandings, rather than imposing or inserting a new set of values in a situation. There is likely to be much more emphasis on dialogue, process, co-creation, and finding ways to build credibility for such activities and outcomes than is typically prescribed by most cultural theories.

Sixth, wars don't typically end: they are settled for a time and then they flare up in new forms, perhaps with new armies, new 'would-be kings'. Other wars start up in different situations. We expect this to continue in the culture arena. What this might mean for change agents is a willingness to remain alert to the existence and nature of the wars, to learn from the 'dispatches' from the front lines, and to factor these messages into their plans and strategies for change. One cannot assume a 'settled once and for all' script, any more than a 'forever after' one.

Finally, the intentions and actions of members of groups sometimes identified as having strong cultures (e.g. 'the managers', 'the workers') might be better understood, and their cultural roles in organizations more effectively identified, if we treated them as less homogeneous, more multidimensional in their intentions, and more tentative and experimental in their actions. If, as we suspect, the organizations that people negotiate have, simultaneously, elements of integration, conflict, power, uncertainty, and 'truth construction', then there is exciting and challenging work to be done. Cultural researchers need to figure out what this means for their definitions, theories, investigations, and practices.

AND SO IT GOES

We have no illusions about the creation of a unifying theory. If players in the cultural war games, now struggling for a place at the top of the sand mountain, have the courage and curiosity to talk with the 'enemies' and to suspend disbelief about who and what is 'right', we think that the resulting *rapprochement* might forge some creative new alliances to take the field of organizational culture into some fruitful areas of inquiry.

We were originally drawn to culture as an emancipating way of approaching organizational phenomena, and as a metaphor for revitalizing organizational theory. Culture seemed to allow us to move away from the constricting aspects – the 'boxes' – of our theories, methods, and usual ways of doing things at a time when this change seemed to be needed, helpful, empowering, and energizing. We suspect many others felt the same way. It was astonishing to us, however, to see how quickly this apparently open conceptual terrain became cluttered – in part, by ourselves – with maps, boxes, categorizations and so forth. Many of these quickly became reified and served as ammunition in the emerging cultural wars. ('In search of excellence' rapidly became 'the ingredients of excellence'. Other formulations suffered similar fates.)

During these war years, many of the most playful, inquiring, irreverent and inventing voices left the cultural field or played less frequently on it. Culture became a part of the hegemony within organizational theory and practice, even turning up on the tables of contents of handbooks. This Quixotic victory had the paradoxical effect of 'deadening' culture's effect on open inquiry, a point made most eloquently by Smircich and Calás as long ago as 1987.

Perhaps this is the fate of all innovative endeavours. They either die out or, if success strikes, they become coopted and routinized so they can be used in organizations (Daft and Bradshaw 1980; Frost and Egri 1991). Such developments are not all negative since we must have ways to preserve creative and useful ideas and practices. Our point is that these preserved insights become 'truth ammunition' in the struggle for dominance. In contrast, we need some mechanisms to foster 'free-range' thinking that has the capacity to learn from and about the wars, but also can be used to negotiate peace – depicting alternative worlds where wars are not the only or the preferred way to study culture. We believe that efforts are needed to balance or even unbalance the culture wars mentality, counteracting the tendency for theories and methods to become constraining boxes that impede 'free-range' inquiry.

Several things have to happen, in our opinion, if we are to have such alternatives to war. First, we need to identify and nurture exemplars of 'unboxed' thinking who can and do write about organizational life without succumbing to the war games mentality. We suspect that such individuals come to their subject with the same degree of passion for understanding that characterizes the best of the warriors in the game. Some of our 'unboxed' exemplars develop their ideas in ways that inform, without creating reifiable categories. Their work moves others to develop their own insights without seeming to engender imitation or a need for strict adherence to any particular formulation of 'truth'. Such works often are characterized by the ambiguity of their concepts, forcing readers and the authors themselves back on their assumptions; what emerges is playful, provocative, and, at best, upending. For us, such 'unboxed' exemplars include James March, Barry Turner, and Karl Weick.

Other exemplary authors seem to join the war games but not take sides. Somehow they remain 'unhooked' from the struggle for dominance, delivering their broadsides without aiming to throw their support behind any of the factions. They speak with eloquence and fire, from the margins, serving to draw the battle lines outward, creating an opportunity for a reexamination of the premise for the war in the first place. We suspect that these exemplars may play in other games, but they do not seem interested in becoming monarchs. From our point of view, Gideon Kunda, Linda Smircich, Marta Calás, Walter Nord, Steve Linstead, Antonio Strati, Sylvia Gherardi, Robert Grafton-Small, and John Van Maanen are exemplars of this manner of engagement – although they and others may not see them this way.

We also need champions for peace who will articulate and set the stage for alternatives to the dominance game. The innovation literature is replete with evidence of the importance of individuals willing and able to champion new ideas, protect the innovators, and find ways to ensure that new ideas get implemented (Chakrabarti 1974; Frost and Egri 1991; Howell and Higgins 1990). This is a role open to all, but perhaps it will be most tempting to those who are new to the game, not yet having invested themselves in winning and losing battles, and as yet less tainted by the field's usual ways of doing scholarly business. Other champions of peace may be insiders looking out – battle-hardened veterans who have come, the hard way, to see the futility of war. Such champions of peace, working on the fringes of the battlefield, may share some of the characteristics of the tempered radical (Meyerson and Scully 1995): that is, they may have values different from those in the mainstream of the organizational scene, but may wish to contribute to the well-being of the whole while finding a way to stay true to their personal vision and values. Perhaps, increasingly, more of us will become champions of peace.

We also believe there is a need for appreciative approaches to cultural work that feature critique that is fair and tough minded, rather than biased and destructive (e.g. Cooperrider 1986; Gergen 1990; Harman 1990; Mirvis 1990; Vickers 1968). Such critique would seek to inform, to build and improve, even to help dismantle when this seems appropriate. Such critique would seek to advance a field, rather than a particular point of view, focusing on ideas and issues rather than individuals. The goal would be to preserve rather than attack the dignity of individual researchers, so time, effort, and emotion would not have to be spent repairing and defending damaged egos and positions. The challenge is to create institutionalized practices which would, systematically and continuously, develop and sustain such an appreciative orientation to discourse; the keys lie in the arenas of manuscript review, doctoral training, conference settings, and the like. Appreciative critique is a tough skill to learn and tougher still to teach and model, as evidenced, for example, in our struggle to chronicle the culture wars while retaining an appreciative tone and some fidelity to our own convictions.

This review is, partially, a plea for more imaginative and courageous attempts to turn the culture field away from warlike endeavors. We do not believe that wars will vanish from the intellectual landscape and we know that not all changes flowing from wars are negative. They sometimes clear the air and fresh ideas emerge. We do think, however, that competition for dominance is costly in terms of lost ideas and silenced or disillusioned people. The 'king of the mountain' approach – whether the conflict is overt or advocates of opposing views ignore each other – is not the only way to structure cultural inquiry and it may not be the best. Undoubtedly, some readers will say: 'There's a war (game) to be played; let's get on with it!' Others will say: 'I choose not to play and will pursue my own path.' We say: 'Let's find a way or ways to focus as much energy as we can to keep the study of culture free of destructive conflict, so we can collectively imbue it with characteristics that will invite us all to do our best work, to share that work with excitement and passion, and to keep the search for understanding and application rich and open.'

Notes

We wish to express our thanks to Cynthia Hardy for her thoughtful, insight-giving advice and guidance. Her patience with us was limitless. Our thanks go too to our reviewers who provided feedback that helped us immeasurably. We were the beneficiaries of the kind of constructive, appreciative critique from all three colleagues that we advocate in this chapter as the norm for discourse in a war-free environment. And we are also grateful for the assistance of Karen Harlos and Vivien Clark.

1 We do not know the origins of this term, but it was first drawn to our attention as the title of the annual meeting theme of the Standing Conference on Organizational Symbolism, held in Montreal, Canada, in 1986.

2 Although the scope of this review does not include studies of national cultures performed by organizational scholars, it is worth noting that these studies tend to use an integration framework to describe national cultures in unitary terms. For example, Lincoln and Kallberg (1985) implicitly adopt an integration perspective for the study of international cultures, describing US and Japanese cultures as internally homogeneous, characterized by consistency, consensus, and clarity.

3 In this section particularly, we are grateful for the suggestions of an anonymous reviewer, although errors and omissions remain our own responsibility.

4 This felicitous phrase was, we believe, coined by Robert Sutton.

REFERENCES

Agar, M. (1986) *Speaking of Ethnography*. Beverly Hills, CA: Sage.

Alvesson, M. (1993) *Cultural Perspectives on Organizations*. Cambridge: Cambridge University Press.

Alvesson, M. and Berg, P. (1992) *Corporate Culture and Organizational Symbolism*. Berlin: Walter de Gruyter.

Arac, J. (ed.) (1986) *Postmodernism and Politics*. Minneapolis: University of Minnesota Press.

Argyris, C. and Schon, D. (1978) *Organizational Learning: a Theory of Action Perspective*. Reading, MA: Addison-Wesley.

Baburoglu, O. and Gocer, A. (1991) 'The impact of privatization on the organizational culture: the Sumerbank's case'. Paper presented at the International Conference on Organizational Symbolism and Corporate Culture, Copenhagen.

Barley, S. (1983) 'Semiotics and the study of occupational and organizational cultures', *Administrative Science Quarterly*, 28: 393–414.

Barley, S., Meyer, G. and Gash, D. (1988) 'Cultures of culture: academics, practitioners, and the pragmatics of normative control', *Administrative Science Quarterly*, 33: 24–61.

Bartunek, J. and Moch, M. (1991) 'Multiple constituencies and the quality of working life intervention at FoodCom', in P. Frost, L. Moore, M. Louis, C. Lundberg and J. Martin (eds), *Reframing Organizational Culture*. Newbury Park, CA: Sage. pp. 104–14.

Baudrillard, J. (1983) *Simulations*. New York: Semiotext(e).

Becker, H., Geer, B., Hughes, E. and Strauss, A. (1961) *Boys in White: Student Cultures in Medical School*. Chicago: University of Chicago Press.

Bell, E. (1990) 'The bicultural life experience of career-oriented black women', *Journal of Organizational Behavior*, 11: 459–78.

Berger, P. (1967) *The Sacred Canopy*. Garden City, NY: Doubleday.

Bergquist, W. (1993) *The Postmodern Organization: Mastering the Art of Irreversible Change*. San Francisco: Jossey-Bass.

Blau, P. (1965) 'The comparative study of organizations', *Industrial and Labour Relations Review*, 28: 323–38.

Bloom, A. (1987) *The Closing of the American Mind*. New York: Simon and Schuster.

Boje, D. and Dennehy, R. (1993) *Managing in the Postmodern World: America's Revolution against Exploitation*. Dubuque, IA: Kendall-Hunt.

Brunsson, N. (1985) *The National Organization*. New York: Wiley.

Burawoy, M. (1979) *Manufacturing Consent: Changes in the Labor Process under Monopoly Capitalism*. Chicago: University of Chicago Press.

Burrell, G. and Morgan, G. (1979) *Sociological Paradigms and Organizational Analysis*. London: Heinemann.

Calás, M. (1987) 'Organizational science/fiction: the postmodern in the management disciplines'. Unpublished doctoral dissertation, Amherst, MA: University of Massachusetts.

Calás, M. and Smircich, L. (1987) 'Post-culture: is the organizational culture literature dominant but dead?'. Paper presented at the International Conference on Organizational Symbolism and Corporate Culture, Milan.

Calás, M. and Smircich, L. (1988) 'Reading leadership as a form of cultural analysis', in J. Hunt, B. Baliga, H. Dachler and A. Schriesheim (eds), *Emerging Leadership Vistas*. Lexington, MA: Lexington Books. pp. 201–26.

Calás, M. and Smircich, L. (1990) 'Thrusting towards more of the same', *Academy of Management Review*, 15: 698–705.

Calás, M. and Smircich, L. (1991) 'Voicing seduction to silence leadership', *Organizational Studies*, 12: 567–601.

Chakrabarti, A. (1974) 'The role of the champion in product innovation', *California Management Review*, 17: 58–62.

Christensen, S. and Kreiner, K. (1984) 'On the origin of organizational cultures'. Paper presented at the International Conference on Organizational Symbolism and Corporate Culture, Lund, Sweden.

Clark, B. (1972) 'The organizational saga in higher education', *Administrative Science Quarterly*, 17: 178–84.

Clegg, S. (1990) *Modern Organizations: Organization Studies in a Postmodern World*. London: Sage.

Clifford, J. and Marcus, G. (eds) (1986) *Writing*

Culture: the Poetics and Politics of Ethnography. Berkeley, CA: University of California Press.

Cooper, R. and Burrell, G. (1988) 'Modernism, postmodernism, and organizational analysis', *Organization Studies*, 9: 91–112.

Cooperrider, D. (1986) *Appreciative Inquiry: a Method for Understanding and Enhancing Organizational Innovation.* Ann Arbor, MI: University Microfilms International.

Cox, T. (1993) *Cultural Diversity in Organizations: Theory, Research, and Practice.* San Francisco: Berrett-Koehler.

Crozier, M. (1964) *The Bureaucratic Phenomenon.* Chicago: University of Chicago Press.

Czarniawska-Joerges, B. (1992) *Exploring Complex Organizations: a Cultural Perspective.* Newbury Park, CA: Sage.

Daft, R. (1980) 'The evolution of organization analysis in *ASQ*, 1959–1979', *Administrative Science Quarterly*, 25: 623–36.

Daft, R. and Bradshaw, P. (1980) 'The process of horizontal differentiation: two models', *Administrative Science Quarterly*, 25: 441–56.

Dandridge, T. (1986) 'Ceremony as an integration of work and play', *Organization Studies*, 7: 159–70.

Deal, T. and Kennedy, A. (1982) *Corporate Cultures: the Rites and Rituals of Corporate Life.* Reading, MA: Addison-Wesley.

Deetz, S. (1992) *Democracy in an Age of Corporate Colonization: Developments in Communication and the Politics of Everyday Life.* New York: State University of New York Press.

Denison, D. (1990) *Corporate Culture and Organizational Effectiveness.* New York: Wiley.

Derrida, J. (1976) *Speech and Phenomenon.* Evanston, IL: Northwestern University Press.

Donaldson, L. (1989) 'Redirections in organizational analysis', *Australian Journal of Management*, 14: 243–54.

Enomoto, E. (1993) 'In-school truancy in a multiethnic urban high school examined through organizational culture lenses'. PhD dissertation, University of Michigan.

Enz, C. (1988) 'The role of value congruity in intraorganizational power', *Administrative Science Quarterly*, 33: 284–304.

Feldman, M. (1989) *Order without Design: Information Processing and Policy Making.* Stanford, CA: Stanford University Press.

Feldman, M. (1991) 'The meanings of ambiguity: learning from stories and metaphors', in P. Frost, L. Moore, M. Louis, C. Lundberg and J. Martin (eds), *Reframing Organizational Culture.* Newbury Park, CA: Sage. pp. 145–56.

Ferguson, K. (1993) *The Man Question: Visions of Subjectivity in Feminist Theory.* Berkeley, CA: University of California Press.

Fitzgerald, T. (1988) 'Can change in organizational culture really be managed?', *Organizational Dynamics*, 17: 5–15.

Flax, J. (1990) *Thinking Fragments: Psychoanalysis, Feminism, and Postmodernism in the Contemporary West.* Berkeley, CA: University of California Press.

Foucault, M. (1976) *The Archeology of Knowledge*, translated by E. Smith. New York: Harper and Row.

Frost, P. (1995) Personal communication.

Frost, P. and Egri, C. (1991) 'The political process of innovation', in L. Cummings and B. Staw (eds), *Research in Organizational Behavior.* Greenwich, CT: JAI Press. pp. 229–95.

Frost, P., Moore, L., Louis, M., Lundberg, C. and Martin, J. (1991) *Reframing Organizational Culture.* Newbury Park, CA: Sage.

Gagliardi, P. (ed.) (1990) *Symbols and Artifacts: Views of the Corporate Landscape.* Hawthorne, NY: Walter de Gruyter.

Gagliardi, P. (1991) 'Reflections on reframing organizational culture'. Paper presented at the International Conference on Organizational Symbolism and Corporate Culture, Copenhagen.

Garfinkel, H. (1967) *Studies in Ethnomethodology.* Englewood Cliffs, NJ: Prentice-Hall.

Geertz, C. (1988) *Works and Lives: the Anthropologist as Author.* Stanford, CA: Stanford University Press.

Gergen, K. (1990) 'Affect and organization in postmodern society', in S. Srivastava, D. Cooperrider and Associates (eds), *Appreciative Management and Leadership.* San Francisco: Jossey-Bass. pp. 153–74.

Glaser, B. and Strauss, A. (1967) *The Discovery of Grounded Theory.* Chicago, IL: Aldine.

Goffman, I. (1967) *Interaction Ritual.* New York: Anchor Books.

Gordon, G. (1985) 'The relationship of corporate culture to industry sector and corporate performance', in R. Kilmann, M. Saxton, R. Serpa and Associates (eds), *Gaining Control of the Corporate Culture.* San Francisco: Jossey-Bass. pp. 103–25.

Grafton-Small, R. and Linstead, S. (1987) 'Theory as artifact'. Paper presented at the International Conference on Organizational Symbolism and Corporate Culture, Milan.

Greenwood, R. and Hinings, C. (1988) 'Organizational design types, tracks and the dynamics of strategic change', *Organization Studies*, 9: 293–316.

Gregory, K. (1983) 'Native-view paradigms: multiple cultures and culture conflicts in organizations', *Administrative Science Quarterly*, 28: 359–76.

Habermas, J. (1975) *Legitimation Crisis*, translated by T. McCarthy. Boston: Beacon Press.

Harman, W. (1990) 'Shifting context for executive behavior: signs of change and revaluation', in S. Srivastava, D. Cooperrider and Associates (eds), *Appreciative Management and Leadership.* San Francisco: Jossey-Bass. pp. 37–54.

Hassard, J. and Parker, M. (eds) (1993) *Postmodernism and Organizations.* London: Sage.

Hassard, J. and Pym, D. (eds) (1990) *The Theory and*

Philosophy of Organizations: Critical Issues and New Perspectives. London: Routledge.

Howell, J. and Higgins, C. (1990) 'Champions of technological innovation', *Administrative Science Quarterly*, 35: 317–41.

Hughes, E. (1958) *Men and Their Work*. New York: Free Press.

Jaques, E. (1951) *The Changing Culture of a Factory: a Study of Authority and Participation in an Industrial Setting*. London: Tavistock. New York: Dryden Press, 1952.

Jeffcutt, P. (1995) 'The interpretation of organization: a contemporary analysis and critique', *Journal of Management Studies*, 31: 225–50.

Jeffcutt, P. (forthcoming) *Culture and Symbolism in Organizational Analysis*. Newbury Park, CA: Sage.

Jermier, J. (1992) 'Literary methods and organizational science: reflections on "When the sleeper wakes"', in P. Frost and R. Stablein (eds), *Doing Exemplary Research*. Newbury Park, CA: Sage.

Jonsson, S. and Lundin, R. (1977) 'Myths and wishful thinking as management tools', in P. Nystrom and W. Starbuck (eds), *Studies in Management Sciences. Vol. 5: Prescriptive Models of Organizations*. Amsterdam: North Holland. pp. 157–70.

Kanter, R. (1977) *Men and Women of the Corporation*. New York: Anchor Press.

Kilmann, R. (1985) *Beyond the Quick Fix: Managing Five Tracks to Organizational Success*. San Francisco: Jossey-Bass.

Knights, D. and Willmott, H. (1987) 'Organizational culture as management strategy: a critique and illustration', *International Studies of Management and Organization*, 13: 40–63.

Kreiner, K. and Schultz, M. (1993) 'Informal collaboration in R&D: the formation of networks across organizations', *Organization Studies*, 14: 189–209.

Kuhn, T. (1970) *The Structure of Scientific Revolutions*, 2nd edn (1st edn 1962). Chicago: University of Chicago Press.

Kunda, G. (1991) *Engineering Culture: Control and Commitment in a High-Tech Corporation*. Philadelphia: Temple University Press.

Letiche, H. (1991) 'Postmodernism goes practical'. Paper presented at the International Conference on Organizational Symbolism and Corporate Culture, Copenhagen.

Levitt, B. and Nass, C. (1989) 'The lid on the garbage can: institutional constraints on decision making in the technical core of college-text publishers', *Administrative Science Quarterly*, 34: 190–207.

Light, D. Jr (1979) 'Surface data and deep structure: observing the organization of professional training', *Administrative Science Quarterly*, 24: 551–60.

Lincoln, J. and Kallberg, A. (1985) 'Work organization and workforce commitment: a study of plants and employees in the U.S. and Japan', *American Sociological Review*, 50: 738–60.

Linstead, S. and Grafton-Small, R. (1991) 'No visible means of support: ethnography and the end of deconstruction'. Paper presented at the International Conference on Organizational Symbolism and Corporate Culture, Copenhagen.

Linstead, S. and Grafton-Small, R. (1992) 'On reading organizational culture', *Organization Studies*, 13: 331–55.

Louis, M. (1985) 'An investigator's guide to workplace culture', in P. Frost, L. Moore, M. Louis, C. Lundberg and J. Martin (eds), *Organizational Culture*. Beverly Hills, CA: Sage. pp. 73–94.

Lucas, R. (1987) 'Political-cultural analysis of organizations', *Academy of Management Review*, 12: 144–56.

Lyotard, J. (1984) *The Postmodern Condition*. Minneapolis: University of Minnesota Press.

Manning, P. (1977) *Police Work: the Social Organization of Policing*. Cambridge, MA: MIT Press.

Martin, J. (1990a) 'Breaking up the mono-method monopolies in organizational analysis', in J. Hassard and D. Pym (eds), *The Theory and Philosophy of Organizations*. New York: Routledge. pp. 30–43.

Martin, J. (1990b) 'Deconstructing organizational taboos: the suppression of gender conflict in organizations', *Organizational Science*, 1: 339–59.

Martin, J. (1992) *Cultures in Organizations: Three Perspectives*. New York: Oxford University Press.

Martin, J. and Meyerson, D. (1988) 'Organizational cultures and the denial, channeling, and acknowledgement of ambiguity', in L. Pondy, R. Boland, and H. Thomas (eds), *Managing Ambiguity and Change*. New York: Wiley. pp. 93–125.

Martin, J. and Siehl, C. (1983) 'Organizational culture and counter culture: an uneasy symbiosis', *Organizational Dynamics*, 12: 52–64.

Martin, J., Feldman, M., Hatch, M. and Sitkin, S. (1983) 'The uniqueness paradox in organizational stories', *Administrative Science Quarterly*, 28: 438–53.

Martin, J., Sitkin, S. and Boehm, M. (1985) 'Founders and the elusiveness of a cultural legacy', in P. Frost, L. Moore, M. Louis, C. Lundberg and J. Martin (eds), *Organizational Culture*. Beverly Hills, CA: Sage. pp. 99–124.

McDonald, P. (1991) 'The Los Angeles Olympic Organizing Committee: developing organizational culture in the short run', in P. Frost, L. Moore, M. Louis, C. Lundberg and J. Martin (eds), *Reframing Organizational Culture*. Newbury Park, CA: Sage. pp. 26–38.

McGrath, J. (1982) 'Dilemmatics: the study of research choices and dilemmas', in J. McGrath, J. Martin and R. Kulka, *Judgment Calls in Research*. Newbury Park, CA: Sage. pp. 69–102.

Meyerson, D. (1991) '"Normal" ambiguity? A glimpse of an occupational culture', in P. Frost, L. Moore, M. Louis, C. Lundberg and J. Martin (eds), *Reframing Organizational Culture*. Newbury Park, CA: Sage. pp. 131–44.

Meyerson, D. and Martin, J. (1987) 'Cultural change: an integration of three different views', *Journal of Management Studies*, 24: 623–47.

Meyerson, D. and Scully, M. (1995) 'Tempered radicalism and the politics of ambivalence and change', *Organizational Science*, 6: 585–600.

Mills, A. (1992) 'Organization, gender, and culture', in A. Mills and P. Tancred (eds), *Gendering Organizational Analysis*. Newbury Park, CA: Sage. pp. 93–111.

Mirvis, P. (1990) 'Merging of heart and mind in crisis management', in S. Srivastava, D. Cooperrider and Associates (eds), *Appreciative Management and Leadership*. San Francisco: Jossey-Bass. pp. 55–90

Moi, T. (1985) *Sexual/Textual Politics: Feminist Literary Theory*. New York: Methuen.

Morgan, G. (1983a) 'More on metaphor: why we cannot control tropes in administrative science', *Administrative Science Quarterly*, 28: 601–7.

Morgan, G. (ed.) (1983b) *Beyond Method: Strategies for Social Research*. Beverly Hills, CA: Sage.

Mumby, D. (1988) *Communication and Power in Organizations: Discourse, Ideology and Domination*. Norwood, NJ: Ablex.

Okin, S. (1994) 'Gender and relativism'. Unpublished manuscript, Stanford University.

O'Reilly, C., Chatman, J. and Caldwell, D. (1991) 'People and organizational culture: a Q-sort approach to assessing person–organization fit', *Academy of Management Journal*, 34: 487–516.

Ott, J. (1989) *The Organizational Culture Perspective*. Pacific Grove, CA: Brooks & Cole.

Ouchi, W. (1981) *Theory Z: How American Business Can Meet the Japanese Challenge*. Reading, MA: Addison-Wesley.

Ouchi, W. and Jaeger, A. (1978) 'Type Z organization: stability in the midst of mobility', *Academy of Management Review*, 3: 305–14.

Ouchi, W. and Johnson, J. (1978) 'Types of organizational control and their relationship to emotional well-being', *Administrative Science Quarterly*, 23: 293–317.

Ouchi, W. and Wilkins, A. (1985) 'Organizational culture', *Annual Review of Sociology*, 11: 457–83.

Pascale, R. and Athos, A. (1981) *The Art of Japanese Management: Applications for American Executives*. New York: Simon and Schuster.

Pennings, J. and Gresov, C. (1986) 'Technoeconomic and structural correlates of organizational culture: an integrative framework', *Organization Studies*, 7: 317–34.

Perrow, C. (1979) *Complex Organizations: A Critical Essay*. Glenview, IL: Scott, Foresman & Co.

Peters, T. and Waterman, R. (1982) *In Search of Excellence: Lessons from America's Best-Run Companies*. New York: Harper & Row.

Pettigrew, A. (1979) 'On studying organizational cultures', *Administrative Science Quarterly*, 24: 570–81.

Pettigrew, A. (1985a) 'Examining change in the long-term context of culture and politics', in J. Pennings and Associates (eds), *Organizational Strategy and Change*. San Francisco: Jossey-Bass. pp. 269–318.

Pettigrew, A. (1985b) *The Awakening Giant: Continuity and Change in ICI*. Oxford: Blackwell.

Pfeffer, J. (1981) 'Management as symbolic action: the creation and maintenance of organizational paradigms', in B. Staw and L. Cummings (eds), *Research in Organizational Behavior*. Greenwich, CT: JAI Press. pp. 1–52.

Pfeffer, J. (1993) 'Barriers to the advance of organizational science: paradigm development as a dependent variable', *Academy of Management Review*, 18: 599–620.

Pinder, C. and Bourgeois, V. (1982) 'Controlling tropes in administrative science', *Administrative Science Quarterly*, 27: 641–52.

Pondy, L., Frost, P., Morgan, G. and Dandridge, T. (eds) (1983) *Organizational Symbolism*. Greenwich, CT: JAI Press.

Putnam, L., Bantz, C., Deetz, S., Mumby, D. and Van Maanen, J. (1993) 'Ethnography versus critical theory: debating organizational research', *Journal of Management Inquiry*, 2: 221–35.

Reed, M. (1985) *Redirections in Organizational Analysis*. London: Tavistock.

Reed, M. (1990) 'From paradigms to images: the paradigm warrior turns postmodernist guru', *Personnel Review*, 19: 35–40.

Riley, P. (1983) 'A structurationist account of political cultures', *Administrative Science Quarterly*, 28: 414–37.

Rosen, M. (1985) 'Breakfast at Spiro's: dramaturgy and dominance', *Journal of Management*, 11: 31–48.

Rosen, M. (1991) 'Coming to terms with the field: understanding and doing organizational ethnography', *Journal of Management Studies*, 28: 1–24.

Rousseau, D. (1990) 'Assessing organizational culture: the case for multiple methods', in B. Schneider (ed.), *Organizational Climate and Culture*. San Francisco: Jossey-Bass. pp. 153–92.

Rousseau, D. (1994) 'A fresh start for organizational culture research', *Contemporary Psychology*, 39: 194–5.

Sathe, V. (1985) *Culture and Related Corporate Realities: Text, Cases, and Readings on Organizational Entry, Establishment, and Chance*. Homewood, IL: Irwin.

Schein, E. (1985) *Organizational Culture and Leadership*. San Francisco: Jossey-Bass.

Schein, E. (1987) *The Clinical Perspective in Field Work*. Newbury Park, CA: Sage.

Schein, E. (1991) 'What is culture?', in P. Frost, L. Moore, M. Louis, C. Lundberg and J. Martin (eds), *Reframing Organizational Culture*. Newbury Park, CA: Sage. pp. 243–53.

Schein, E. (1994) 'Book review: Martin: *Cultures in Organizations: Three Perspectives*', *Administrative Science Quarterly*, 39: 339–42.

Schlesinger, A. (1992) *The Disuniting of America*. New York: Norton.

Schneider, B. (ed.) (1990) *Organizational Climate and Culture*. San Francisco: Jossey-Bass.

Schultz, M. (1994) *On Studying Organizational Cultures: Diagnosis and Understanding*. Berlin: De Gruyter.

Selznick, P. (1957) *Leadership and Administration*. Evanston, IL: Row & Peterson.

Sergiovanni, T. and Corbally, J. (eds) (1984) *Leadership and Organizational Culture*. Urbana, IL: University of Illinois Press.

Siehl, C. and Martin, J. (1990) 'Organizational culture: a key to financial performance?', in B. Schneider (ed.), *Organizational Climate and Culture*. San Francisco: Jossey-Bass. pp. 241–81.

Simons, H. and Billig, M. (eds) (1994) *After Postmodernism: Ideology Critique*. Thousand Oaks, CA: Sage.

Smircich, L. (1983) 'Concepts of culture and organizational analysis', *Administrative Science Quarterly*, 28: 339–58.

Smircich, L. (1995) 'Writing organizational tales: reflections on three books on organizational culture', *Organizational Science*, 6: 232–7.

Smircich, L. and Calás, M. (1987) 'Organizational culture: a critical assessment', in F. Jablin, L. Putnam, K. Roberts and L. Porter (eds), *Handbook of Organizational Communication*. Beverly Hills, CA: Sage. pp. 228–63.

Smircich, L. and Morgan, G. (1982) 'Leadership: the management of meaning', *Journal of Applied Behavioral Science*, 18: 257–73.

Spradley, J. (1979) *The Ethnographic Interview*. New York: Holt, Rinehard & Winston.

Stablein, R. and Nord, W. (1985) 'Practical and emancipatory interests in organizational symbolism: a review and evaluation', *Journal of Management*, 11: 13–28.

Steinbruner, J.D. (1974) *The Cybernetic Theory of Decision: New Dimensions of Political Analyses*. Princeton, NJ: Princeton University Press.

Sutton, R. (1994) 'The virtues of closet qualitative research'. Unpublished manuscript, Stanford University.

Sypher, B., Applegate, J. and Sypher, H. (1985) 'Culture and communication in organizational contexts', in W. Gudykundst, L. Stewart and S. Ting-Toomey (eds), *Communication, Culture, and Organizational Process*. Newbury Park, CA: Sage. pp. 13–29.

Trice, H. and Beyer, J. (1984) 'Studying organizational cultures through rites and ceremonials', *Academy of Management Review*, 9: 653–69.

Trice, H. and Beyer, J. (1993) *The Cultures of Work Organizations*. Englewood Cliffs, NJ: Prentice-Hall.

Turner, B. (1986) 'Sociological aspects of organizational symbolism', *Organizational Studies*, 7: 101–15.

Turner, B. (ed.) (1989) *Organizational Symbolism*. Hawthorne, NY: Walter de Gruyter.

Turner, B. (1990) 'The rise of organizational symbolism', in J. Hassard and D. Pym (eds), *The Theory and Philosophy of Organizations: Critical Issues and New Perspectives*. London: Routledge. pp. 83–96.

Van Maanen, J. (1986) 'Power in the bottle: drinking patterns and social relations in a British police agency', in S. Srivastava (ed.), *Executive Power*. San Francisco: Jossey-Bass. pp. 204–39.

Van Maanen, J. (1988) *Tales of the Field*. Chicago: University of Chicago Press.

Van Maanen, J. (1991) 'The smile factory: work at Disneyland', in P. Frost, L. Moore, M. Louis, C. Lundberg and J. Martin (eds), *Reframing Organizational Culture*. Newbury Park, CA: Sage. pp. 58–76.

Van Maanen (1995) 'Style as theory', *Organizational Science*, 6: 133–43.

Van Maanen, J. and Barley, S. (1984) 'Occupational communities: culture and control in organizations', in B. Staw and L. Cummings (eds), *Research in Organizational Behavior*, vol. 6. Greenwich, CT: JAI Press. pp. 287–366.

Van Maanen, J. and Kunda, G. (1989) '"Real feelings": emotional expression and organizational culture', in L. Cummings and B. Staw (eds), *Research in Organizational Behavior*, vol. 11. Greenwich, CT: JAI Press. pp. 43–103.

Van Maanen, J., Dabbs, J. and Faulkner, R. (1982) *Varieties of Qualitative Research*. Newbury Park, CA: Sage.

Vickers, G. (1968) *Value Systems and Social Process*. New York: Basic Books.

Weedon, C. (1987) *Feminist Practice and Poststructuralist Theory*. New York: Basil Blackwell.

Weick, K. (1991) 'The vulnerable system: an analysis of the Tenerife air disaster', in P. Frost, L. Moore, M. Louis, C. Lundberg and J. Martin (eds), *Reframing Organizational Culture*. Newbury Park, CA: Sage. pp. 117–30.

Willmott, H. (1993) 'Strength is ignorance; slavery is freedom: managing culture in modern organizations', *Journal of Management Studies*, 30: 515–52.

Wuthnow, R., Hunter, J., Bergesen, A. and Kurzweil, E. (1984) *Cultural Analysis*. Boston: Routledge & Kegan Paul.

Young, E. (1989) 'On the naming of the rose: interests and multiple meanings as elements of organizational culture', *Organization Studies*, 10: 187–206.

3.7

Some Dare Call It Power

CYNTHIA HARDY AND STEWART R. CLEGG

Historically, the precursors of modern 'organization' consisted of the medieval guild structure – a simple tripartite structure (Offe 1976). One entered the organization at the base as an apprentice. Having served one's time as an apprentice, during which the rudiments of the knowledge base appropriate to the guild were learned and practised, one became a journeyman. A journeyman plied his trade peripatetically, honing his skill and knowledge with new masters as he travelled, and, if fortunate, slowly acquiring some capital.[1] With capital and the right connections, established during the apprenticeship and the journey, journeymen might one day become masters in their own right. The master oversaw everything: if not masters of the universe, they would at least profess monopoly mastery over a licensed sphere of skills in a particular locale, and thus enjoy a parochial mastery. Of course, conditions would vary from workshop to workshop: some masters would be excellent guides to the apprentice, passing on skill, knowledge and learning generally. Others might be petty tyrants, incapable of creating learning other than through fear. Within the general form, different personalities, to use a contemporary concept, would infuse the relationship with a different ethos.

Guild structures were task-continuous status structures, in which obedience to a wide range of technical rules was required from all individuals (Offe 1976). Superordinates differed from subordinates 'merely in terms of greater mastery of the rules and greater ability, knowledge and experience in production' (1976: 25). Here, power clearly derived from ownership and control of the means of production, supported by the power of surveillance. Important too was knowledge, with power also deriving from

knowledge of the means of production – from 'mastery'.

Modern organizations did not so much evolve from guild structures as pass them by. They grew not out of the absolutist soil of mercantile feudalism, with its monopolies in trade and industry, so much as in its interstices, where, frequently, the displaced and dispossessed carved out artisanal and industrial niches for themselves (Hall 1986). As organizations grew larger, skills became increasingly fragmented and specialized, and positions became more functionally differentiated. Strategies were developed to steer a common path for the organization by centralizing power and enveloping the potentially troublesome and plural sources of identity that had arisen with the division of labour. Modern organizations were thus designed to function as if they were a unitary organism. It is because they are composed of a multitude of unique components that this design is promoted against, or in spite of, their non-unitary form.

These are 'task-discontinuous status structures' (Offe 1976). Unlike the guilds, the status structure and the functional structure are no longer mapped precisely on to each other in a universal sphere of organization knowledge. Tasks are fragmented, skills are diverse, and knowledge is differentially codified, held and valued. Typically, according to labour process theorists (e.g. Braverman 1974), knowledge is divided between that which is more valued, which is generally more esoteric, abstract and related to mental rather than manual labour, and that which is less valued, more mundane and related to manual labour. Implicit in these distinctions is the notion of contemporary organization. Some jobs have been designated as supervisory, while other posts exist to execute orders derived from superordinates. Hence power is structured into organization design.

In such a design, the issue of 'organization obedience' is central to the discussion of power (e.g. Mintzberg 1983; Hamilton and Biggart 1985; also see Etzioni 1961; Weber 1978; Assad 1987; Kieser 1987). Power has typically been seen as the ability to get others to do what you want them to, if necessary against their will (Weber 1978), or to get them to do something they otherwise would not (Dahl 1957). This seemingly simple definition, which presents the negative rather than the positive aspects of power, has been challenged, amended, critiqued, extended, and rebuffed over the years but, nonetheless, remains the starting point for a remarkably diverse body of literature.

But that is where the synergy and convergence end. There are, in fact, a multitude of different voices that speak to power. The result has been a variety of contradictory conceptualizations. The confusion has been exacerbated because the two loudest voices to emerge – the functionalist and the critical (to use simple categorizations) – rarely communicate with each other. The former has adopted a managerialist orientation whose underlying assumptions are rarely articulated, much less critiqued. The result has been an apparently pragmatic concept, easy to use but also easy to abuse. The latter has confronted issues of domination and exploitation head on but appears increasingly to be less relevant to those seeking to achieve collective action.

The aim of this chapter is to explore these different voices increasingly heard in the literature on power and to forge a reconceptualization of power as the medium necessary for responsible, collective action. The first section explores the historical development of these two voices. It discusses the broader heritage of Marx and Weber concerning power, followed by the early management work on power. The second section shows how subsequent developments built on the respective approaches, in many respects drawing them further apart. An analysis of more recent work shows how the different voices have continued to grow apart.

THE FOUNDING VOICES

This section examines some of the key work that provided the foundations for the current work on power and politics in organizations. Broadly speaking, the impetus came from two, quite different directions. The older tradition stems from the work of Marx and Weber. Obviously, with such a parentage, this body of work has

focused on the existence of conflicting interests and has examined power as domination. As a result, it has addressed how power becomes embedded in organizational structures in a way that serves certain, but not all, interest groups. The second tradition developed more centrally within the field of organization studies itself. In contrast to the work on power and interests, this body of work has taken for granted the way in which power is distributed in formal organizational structure and, instead, examined how groups acquire and wield power *not* granted to them under official arrangements.

Power and Interests in Organizations

One approach to the way in which power is structured into organization design has derived from work on class structures (see Clegg and Dunkerley 1980: 463–82 for a discussion of the key literature). In as much as conceptions of interests depict the arena of organizational life in terms of the leitmotif of 'class' and its social relations, they will be attuned to the general conditions of economic domination and subordination in organizations, as theorists of the left from Marx onwards have defined them (see, for instance, Carchedi 1987: 100 for an identification of these conditions).

Marx (1976) argued that class interests are structurally predetermined, irrespective of other bases of identity. They follow from the relations concerning the ownership and control of the means of production. While relations concerning production, property, ownership and control have inscribed the key social relations of capitalist modernity (Clegg and Dunkerley 1980; Clegg et al. 1986), few scholars accept this deterministic view today.[2] The first writer to render Marx's view more complex was Weber, who considered relations *in* production as well as relations *of* production.

Weber acknowledged that power was derived from owning and controlling the means of production, but he argued that it was not reducible exclusively to the dichotomous categories of ownership and non-ownership of the means of production, as proposed by Marx. From Weber's perspective, power also derived from the *knowledge* of operations as much as from ownership. Organizations could be differentiated in terms of people's ability to control the methods of production, as influenced by technical relations of production, and embedded in diverse occupational identities from which grew the subjective life-world of the organization. In this way, Weber emphasized the forms of identification and representation of which organizational members actually made use, rather than simply assumed that their view of the world was merely a 'false' consciousness.

Weber's insights indicated that all organizational members had some creativity, discretion and agency to use power (although some more than others). In the view of Marx and much subsequent theory, there is little room for discretion and its opportunities for strategic agency. Economic conditions regulate the context in which labour is sold and capital raised and, at the outset, two classes are defined: those who possess capital and those who do not. The latter own only their own creative, differentially trained and disciplined capacities that they are obliged to sell on the labour market. But, once sold to bureaucratic organizations (Clegg 1990), labour has the opportunity to use those capacities creatively in 'certain social relationships or carry out forms of social action within the order governing the organization' (Weber 1978: 217). So, by factoring in the differential possibilities for creativity, it becomes clear that organizational members have some control over their disposition to exercise power, both to challenge and to reproduce the formal organization structure in which differential powers are vested, legitimated and reproduced. Thus organizational 'structures of dominancy' do not depend solely on economic power for their foundation and maintenance (1978: 942).

In this way, labour power represents a capacity embodied in a person who retains discretion over the application of that capacity. From the employer's point of view, the employee represents a capacity to labour which must be realized: these are the conditions of effective management. Standing in the way of realization is the embodiment of potential power in the capacities of the people hired, who may be more or less willing to work as subjects ruled by managerial discretion and control. Always, because of embodiment, the people hired as labour will retain ultimate discretion over themselves, what they do, and how they do it. Consequently, a potential source of resistance resides in this inescapable and irreducible embodiment of labour power.

The gap between the capacity to labour and its effective realization implies power and the organization of control. The depiction of this gap is the mainstay of some Marxian traditions of analysis, particularly of alienation (Schacht 1971; Geyer and Schweitzer 1981; Mézáros 1970; Gamble and Walton 1972). Management is forever seeking new strategies and tactics through which to deflect discretion. The most effective and economical are thought to be those that substitute self-discipline for the discipline of an external manager. Less effective but historically more prolific, however, have been the attempts of organizations to close the discretionary gap through the use of rule systems, the mainstay of Weberian analyses of organizations as bureaucracies. Such rule systems seek to regulate meaning to control relations in organizations through the structure of formal organization design. Thus, a hierarchy is prescribed within which legitimate power is circumscribed.

In summary, this founding research focused on the way in which power derived from owning and controlling the means of production, a power that was reinforced by organizational rules and structures. Weber's work provided for more room for strategic manoeuvre than Marxian views. As a result, workers had options and possibilities to challenge the power that controlled them. However, as we shall see, these options proved to be far from easy to exercise due to more sophisticated strategies on the part of dominant groups.

Power and Hierarchy in Organizations

As the section above demonstrates, power in organizations necessarily concerns the hierarchical structure of offices and their relation to each other. Particularly (but not exclusively) the field of management has tended to label such power as 'legitimate' power.[3] One consequence of the widespread, if implicit, acceptance of the hierarchical nature of power has been that social scientists have rarely felt it necessary to explain why it is that power should be hierarchical. In other words, in this stream of research, the power embedded in the hierarchy has been viewed as 'normal' and 'inevitable' following from the formal design of the organization. As such, it has been largely excluded from analyses which have, instead, focused on 'illegitimate' power, i.e. power exercised outside formal hierarchical structures and the channels that they sanction.

One of the earliest management studies of such power was that of Thompson (1956), who researched two USAF bomber wings. The work of the USAF personnel was characterized by highly developed technical requirements in the operational sphere, for both aircrew and ground crew. While the aircrew possessed greater formal authority than the ground crew, the latter were in a highly central position within the workflow of the USAF base relative to the more autonomous aircrew. The aircrew depended upon the ground crew for their survival and safety, which conferred a degree of power on the latter not derived from the formal design of the base relations. Thompson attributed the power of the ground crew to their technical competency *vis-à-vis* the flight security of the planes and the strategic position it accorded them because of the centrality of concerns for the aircrew's safety.

Other writers confirmed Thompson's (1956) view that it was the technical design of tasks and their interdependencies that best explained the operational distribution of power, rather than the formal prescriptions of the organization design. Dubin (1957: 62), for example, noted how some tasks will be more essential to the functional interdependence of a system than will others, and the way in which some of these may be the exclusive function of a specific party. Mechanic (1962) built on this argument, extending it to all organizations, saying that such technical knowledge generally might be a base for organization power. In this way, researchers began to differentiate between formally prescribed power and 'actual' power, which was also regarded as illegitimate.

> research workers have seldom regarded actual power ... [but] have stressed the rational aspects of organization to the neglect of unauthorized or illegitimate power. (Thompson 1956: 290)

Other researchers were to echo this distinction as they followed in Thompson's footsteps. Bennis et al. (1958: 144) made a distinction between 'formal' and 'informal' organization. In the formal organization there resides 'authority', a potential to influence based on position; while in the informal organization there exists power, 'the actual ability of influence based on a number of factors including, of course, organizational position'.

Another important study was carried out by Crozier (1964), which focused on maintenance workers in a French state-owned tobacco monopoly. Their job was to fix machine breakdowns referred to them by production workers. The production workers, at the technical core of the organization, were highly central to the workflow centred bureaucracy that characterized the organization. The maintenance workers were marginal, at least in the formal representation of the organization design. In practice, however, the story was very different.

The production workers were paid on a piece-rate system in a bureaucracy designed on scientific management principles. Most workers were effectively 'deskilled'. The bureaucracy was a highly formal, highly prescribed organization: there was very little that was not planned and regulated, except for the propensity of the machines to break down, and thus diminish the bonus that the production workers could earn. Hence, to maintain their earnings the production workers needed the machines to function, which made them extraordinarily dependent on the maintenance workers. Without their expertise, breakdowns could not be rectified or bonus rates

protected. Consequently, the maintenance workers had a high degree of power over the other workers in the bureaucracy because they controlled the remaining source of uncertainty.

Management and the production workers were aware of this and had attempted to remedy the situation through preventive maintenance. But manuals disappeared and sabotage sometimes occurred. The maintenance workers were indefatigable in defence of their relative autonomy, privilege and power. Through a skilled capacity, the result of their technical knowledge, they could render the uncertain certain. The price of restoring normalcy was a degree of autonomy and relative power, enjoyed and defended by the maintenance workers, well in excess of that formally designed for them.

Crozier's (1964) study was a landmark. He had taken an under-explicated concept – power – and had attached it to the central concept of the emergent theory of the firm – uncertainty. A central feature of organizations as conceptualized in the 'behavioural theory of the firm' (Cyert and March 1963) was that they attempted to behave as if they were systems. Yet, they did so in an uncertain environment. The ability to control that uncertainty thus represented a potential source of power.

After Crozier (1964) the field developed rapidly. A theory emerged, called the 'strategic contingencies theory of intra-organizational power' (Hickson et al. 1971), which built on these ideas. At the core was the idea that power was related to uncertainty, or at least to its control. More formal survey methods were used, instead of grounded research, in which a series of hypothetical scenarios were presented for evaluation by departmental managers. In this way, those functionally specific personnel were identified who used esoteric technical knowledge to control uncertainty and thus increase their power relative to the formally designed hierarchy.

The change in methodology helped produce a formal functionalist model. The organization was conceptualized as comprising four functional sub-systems or sub-units. The sub-units were interdependent, but some were more or less dependent, and produced more or less uncertainty for others. What connected them in the model was the major task element of the organization, which was conceptualized as 'coping with uncertainty'. The theory ascribed the balance of power between the sub-units to imbalances in how these interdependent sub-units coped with this uncertainty. Thus the system of sub-units was opened up to environmental inputs, which were the initial source of uncertainty. Sub-units were characterized as more or less specialized and differentiated by the functional division of labour, and were related by an essential need to reduce uncertainty and achieve organizational goals: 'to use differential power to function within the system rather than to destroy it' (1971: 217).

According to this model, power is defined in terms of 'strategic contingency'. Strategically contingent sub-units are the most powerful, because they are the least dependent on other sub-units and can cope with the greatest systemic uncertainty, given that the sub-unit is central to the organization system and not easily substitutable. The theory assumes that the sub-units are unitary and cohesive in nature whereas, in fact, they are more likely to be hierarchical, with a more or less problematic culture of consent and dissent. To be unitary, some internal mechanisms of power must exist to allow such a representation to flourish, silence conflicting voices, and over-rule different conceptions of interests, attachments, strategies and meanings. The theory assumes that management definitions prevail but research suggests this is not always the case (Collinson 1994). Nor can we assume that management itself will necessarily be a unitary or cohesive category. For it to speak with one voice usually means that other voices have been marginalized or silenced. In other words, the strategic contingencies theory provides very little about these aspects of power because it does not challenge existing patterns of legitimacy.

Similar to the strategic contingencies view of power, in terms of theoretical approach, is the resource dependency view. It derives from the social psychological literature that Emerson (1962) developed and which was implicit in Mechanic's (1962) study of the power of lower-level participants. Examples include French and Raven (1968), Pettigrew (1973), Pfeffer and Salancik (1974) and Salancik and Pfeffer (1974). Information (Pettigrew 1973), uncertainty (Crozier 1964), expertise, credibility, stature and prestige (Pettigrew 1973), access to and contacts with higher echelon members and the control of money, rewards and sanctions (French and Raven 1968; Benfari et al. 1986) have all been identified as bases of power. All resource lists are infinite, however, since different phenomena become resources in different contexts. Without a total theory of contexts, which is impossible, one can never achieve closure on what the bases of power are. They might be anything, under the appropriate circumstances.

Possessing scarce resources is not enough in itself, however, to confer power. Actors have to be aware of their contextual pertinence and control and use them accordingly (Pettigrew 1973). This process of mobilizing power is known as politics (Pettigrew 1973; Hickson et al. 1986), a term whose negative connotations have

helped to reinforce the mainstream view that power used outside formal authoritative arrangements was illegitimate and dysfunctional. It was the dichotomous nature of power and authority that created the theoretical space for the contingency and dependency approaches. The concept of power was thus reserved primarily for exercises of discretion by organization members which were not sanctioned by their position in the formal structure. Such exercises are premised on an illegitimate or informal use of resources; while the legitimate system of authority, on the other hand, is taken for granted and rendered non-problematic.

Two Voices Compared

The comparison of this early work on power reveals two diverging streams of research. The former, developed from and sustained by the work of Marx and Weber, adopted a critical look at the processes whereby power was legitimated in the form of organizational structures. For these researchers, power was *domination*, and actions taken to challenge it constituted *resistance* to domination (see Barbalet 1987). The mainstream management work saw power quite differently: existing organizational arrangements were structures not of domination but of formal, legitimate, functional *authority*. Power was, effectively, resistance but of an illegitimate, dysfunctional kind. In other words, in studying 'power', the founding voices speak to different phenomena, and from quite different value positions. The Marxist/Weberian tradition equated power with the structures by which certain interests were dominated; while the management theorists defined power as those actions that fell outside the legitimated structures, and which threatened organizational goals.

VARIATIONS ON TWO THEMES

Subsequent work was designed to enhance and extend these foundational ideas. In so doing, it served to widen the gulf that had already grown between the two voices that had appeared. These voices were directed principally at their own constituencies, not at bridging the gulf through dialogue across the divide.

Strategies of Domination: Manufacturing Consent

The various constituent parts of the critical literature began to probe the means of domination in more detail. The heritage left by Weber provided a theoretical basis for reflecting on resistance by subordinate groups. But, why was there so little resistance and why did these groups so often consent to their own subjugation? Equally puzzling was the prevalence of passivity, which was so much more marked than revolutionary fervour. Marx had predicted that the individual acts of resistance to their exploitation would meld into a revolutionary challenge to existing power structures by the proletariat who peopled the base of most large, complex organizations. Yet, clearly, such dreams of a proletarian class consciousness had failed to materialize.

One writer who addressed this issue, through a somewhat circuitous route, was Steven Lukes (1974). He traced the developments in the study of power made in the political sciences. Early studies had typically focused exclusively on the decision-making process (e.g. Dahl 1957; 1961; Polsby 1963; Wolfinger 1971). Researchers analyzed key decisions that seemed likely to illustrate the power relations prevailing in a particular community. The object was to determine who made these decisions. If the same groups were responsible for most decisions, as some researchers had suggested, the community could be said to be ruled by an elite. The researchers found, in contrast, that different groups prevailed in decision-making. Such a community was termed *pluralist* and it was hypothesized that America as a whole could be considered a pluralist society.

Some writers began to question the pluralist assumption that decision-making processes were accessible, and non-participation reflected satisfaction. Doubt about the 'permeability' of the US political system was prompted by the civil rights movement and the backlash to the Vietnam War (Parry and Morriss 1975). The pluralists were criticized for their failure to recognize that interests and grievances might remain inarticulate, unarticulated, and outside the decision-making arena. Consequently, conflict might well exist even if it was not directly observable (e.g. Gaventa 1980; Saunders 1980). The focus on formal decision-making was also criticized because of its assumption that access to it was equally available to all organizational members.

Researchers started to examine how full and equal participation was constrained. Schattschneider argued non-participation might be due to:

the suppression of options and alternatives that reflect the needs of the non participants. It is not necessarily true that people with the greatest needs participate in politics most actively – whoever decides what the game is about also decides who gets in the game. (1960: 105)

Building on this insight, Bachrach and Baratz (1962; 1963; 1970) developed the concept of a second face of power – a process whereby issues could be excluded from decision-making, confining the agenda to 'safe' questions. A variety of barriers are available to the more powerful groups to prevent subordinates from fully participating in the decision-making process through the invocation of procedures and political routines. The use of these mechanisms has been termed non-decision-making, because it allows the more powerful actors to determine outcomes from behind the scenes. This work highlights the fact that power is not exercised solely in the taking of key decisions, and that visible decision-makers are not necessarily the most powerful.

Lukes (1974) argued that Bachrach and Baratz's model did not go far enough because it continued to assume that some form of conflict was necessary to stimulate the use of non-decision-making power. Their focus was very much upon 'issues' about which 'decisions' were made, albeit 'non-decisions' (Ranson et al. 1980: 8). Lukes maintained, however, that power could be used to prevent conflict by shaping

[people's] perceptions, cognitions, and preferences in such a way that they accept their role in the existing order of things, either because they can see or imagine no alternative to it, or because they view it as natural and unchangeable, or because they value it as divinely ordained and beneficial. (1974: 24)

The study of power could not, according to Lukes, be confined to observable conflict, the outcomes of decisions, or even suppressed issues. It must also consider the question of political quiescence: why grievances do not exist; why demands are not made; and why conflict does not arise, since such *inaction* may also be the result of power. We may, then, be 'duped, hoodwinked, coerced, cajoled or manipulated into political inactivity' (Saunders 1980: 22).

It was this use of power that helped sustain the dominance of elite groups and reduced the ability of subordinate interests to employ the discretionary power they possessed:

Power is most effective and insidious in its consequences when issues do not arise at all, when actors remain unaware of their sectional claims, that is, power is most effective when it is unnecessary. (Ranson et al. 1980: 8)

In this third dimension, Lukes focused attention on the societal and class mechanisms which perpetuated the status quo. These relate to Gramsci's concept of ideological hegemony (Clegg 1989a) – where 'a structure of power relations is fully legitimized by an integrated system of cultural and normative assumptions'

(Hyman and Brough 1975: 199). According to this view, the ability to define reality is used by dominant classes to support and justify their material domination, thus preventing challenges to their position.

Another stream of research on this issue came from labour process theorists (e.g. Braverman 1974; Burawoy 1979; Edwards 1979), who examined the day-to-day minutiae of power and resistance, built around the 'games' that characterize the rhythms of organizational life (Burawoy 1979). Studies (e.g. Edwards 1979) also considered the historical patterns that structure the overall context of power, from simple, direct control premised on surveillance; through technical control based on the dominance of the employee by the machine, and particularly the assembly line; to fully fledged bureaucratic control – Weber's rule by rules. This tradition focuses on the dialectics of power and resistance in relation to phenomena such as gender, technology, ethnicity, managerial work and other aspects of the structuration of work and its organizational context (Knights and Willmott 1985; 1989; Knights and Morgan 1991; Knights and Murray 1992; Kerfoot and Knights 1993).

More recently, the notion of 'organizational outflanking' (Mann 1986: 7) has been used to provide another answer to the question of why the dominated so frequently consent to their subordination. Rather than seeing this phenomenon as either denial on the part of the oppressed or outwitting on the part of the elite, this view focuses on the relative collective powers of the participants. Organizational outflanking can be thought of in at least two related ways. One of these concerns the absence of knowledgeable resources on the part of the outflanked. The other concerns precisely what it is that the organizationally outflanked may know only too well.

First, let us consider the absence of knowledge: ignorance. Frequently those who are relatively powerless remain so because they are ignorant of the ways of power: ignorant, that is, of matters of strategy such as assessing the resources of the antagonist, of routine procedures, rules, agenda setting, access, informal conduits as well as formal protocols, the style and substance of power. It is not that they do not know the rules of the game so much as that they might not even recognize the game, let alone know its rules. Ignorance also often extends to a lack of knowledge of other powerless agencies with whom one might construct an alliance. Here resistance remains an isolated occurrence, easily surmounted and overcome. As long as resistance remains uncoordinated it can easily be dealt with by

defeat, exile or incorporation, even though the antagonists might easily outweigh the protagonists if they could only connect. One step further from isolation is division. Time and space may be ordered and arranged to minimize interaction or even render one group of subordinates invisible to another (Barnes 1988: 101). Complex divisions of labour may achieve this as may the extreme experience of competition. Examples of the latter might be the arrangement of concerted action within an organization in such a way that it is experienced in individual rather than collective terms, through competitive individual bonus systems of payment or through other mechanisms for constructing an egocentric environment.

Secondly, organizational outflanking on the basis of knowledge operates in so far as individuals, who may know what is to be done, also know that the costs of doing so outweigh the chances of success or the benefits of succeeding. The necessity of dull compulsion in order to earn one's living, the nature of busy work, arduous exertion and ceaseless activity as routinely deadening, compulsory and invariable: such techniques of power may easily discipline the blithest of theoretically free spirits when the conditions of that freedom become evident. In this way, outflanking works against certain groups either because they do not know enough to resist – or because they know rather too much concerning the futility of such action.

Strategies of Management: Defeating Conflict

The mainstream management literature took a different approach: instead of concerning itself with the use of power to prevent conflict, it focused almost exclusively on the use of power to defeat conflict. In fact definitions explicitly linked power to situations of conflict that arise when groups and individuals seek to preserve their vested interests (e.g. Pettigrew 1973; 1985; MacMillan 1978; Pfeffer 1981a; 1992; Narayaran and Fahey 1982; Gray and Ariss 1985; Schwenk 1989).

> From the definition of power, it is clear that political activity is activity which is undertaken to overcome some resistance or opposition. Without opposition or contest within the organization, there is neither the need nor the expectation that one would observe political activity. (Pfeffer 1981a: 7)

These definitions evoke the idea of a 'fair fight' where one group (usually senior management) is forced to use power to overcome the opposition of another (perhaps intransigent unions or dissident employees). Such a view is reinforced by the definition of politics in terms of illegiti- macy. A common definition of politics in the management literature is the unsanctioned or illegitimate use of power to achieve unsanc- tioned or illegitimate ends (e.g. Mintzberg 1983; 1984; also see Mayes and Allen 1977; Gandz and Murray 1980; Enz 1988). It clearly implies that this use of power is dysfunctional and aimed at thwarting initiatives intended to benefit the organization for the sake of self-interest.

> Distilled to its essence, therefore, politics refers to individual or group behaviour that is informal, ostensibly parochial, typically divisive, and above all, in the technical sense, illegitimate – sanctioned neither by formal authority, accepted ideology, nor certified expertise (though it may exploit any one of those). (Mintzberg 1983: 172, emphasis removed)

These definitions ignore the question: in *whose* eyes is power deemed illegitimate, unsanctioned, or dysfunctional? Legitimacy is usually defined in terms of the 'organization', when writers really mean the organizational elites, i.e. senior management. Thus managerial interests are equated with organizational needs, and the possibility that managers, like any other group, might seek to serve their own vested interests is largely ignored (e.g. Watson 1982).

Existing organizational structures and systems are not neutral or apolitical but structurally sedimented phenomena. There is a history of struggles already embedded in the organization. The organization is a collective life-world in which traces of the past are vested, recur, shift and take on new meanings. In Weber's terms organizations already incorporate a 'structure of dominancy' in their functioning. Authority, structure, ideology, culture, and expertise are invariably saturated and imbued with power but the mainstream tradition has taken the struc- tures of power vested in formal organization design very much for granted. The focus is on the exercise of power within a given structure of dominancy. Such an approach focuses only on surface politics and misrepresents the balance of power. It attributes far too much power to subordinate groups who are chastised for using it; while the hidden ways in which senior managers use power behind the scenes to further their position by shaping legitimacy, values, technology and information are conveniently excluded from analysis. This narrow definition (see Frost 1987) obscures the true workings of power and depoliticizes organizational life (Clegg 1989a). It paints an ideologically con- servative picture that implicitly advocates the status quo and hides the processes whereby organizational elites maintain their dominance (Alvesson 1984). Mechanisms of domination such as leadership, culture and structure are

usually treated in this mainstream literature as neutral, inevitable, or objective and, hence, unproblematic (Clegg 1989a; 1989b; also see Ranson et al. 1980; Deetz 1985; Knights and Willmott 1992; Willmott 1993).

Thus the functionalist perspective has equated power with illegitimate, dysfunctional, self- interested behaviour. These definitions have raised an interesting question concerning what happens when there is no conflict: does power simply cease to exist or does it turn into something else? If so, what does it become? Clearly, according to this work, only 'bad guys' use power; the 'good guys' use something else, although the literature is not clear on exactly what. This issue becomes even more proble- matic when the broader management literature is factored into the equation. Much of this work does not focus on power *per se* and, so, does not bother to define it. Nevertheless, power is an integral part of the discussion. For example, work on leadership advocates the use of charisma by managers. Writers assume (usually implicitly) that managers will automatically use it responsibly to achieve organizational objec- tives, even though much of what we know about charismatic power comes from studying such leaders as Hitler, Mussolini, and Pol Pot! So, adding up the streams of functional, managerial work the assumption is that managers use power (or something like it) responsibly in pursuit of organizational goals, while everyone else uses it irresponsibly to resist those objectives. Potential abuses of power by dominant groups are downplayed, while those who challenge managerial prerogatives are automatically discredited by the label 'political'. In this way, ethical issues associated with the use of power are shielded from view, rendering this approach ill-equipped to deal with matters of abuse and exploitation.

In summary, work carried out in the 1970s sought to refine the bases laid down by the founding figures. In each case, however, they built on each body of work separately; little was done in the way of bridging. This is partly due to the apparent reluctance of many management researchers to refer to the broader body of social sciences of which they are a part, and the seeming indifference of sociologists and political scientists to the study of organizational, rather than societal or class, processes.

A Bridge Too Far?

A few studies did offer the prospect of bridging the two worlds. However, as the following discussion demonstrates, their ideas were not

readily adopted by the larger body of functionalist literature, which remained committed to
existing conceptualizations. At the same time,
developments in the critical field were devoted
explicitly to rejecting functionalism, not accommodating it. As will be discussed, these developments were also to challenge many of the
modernist assumptions embedded in the critical
literature.

Managing Meaning: the
Creation of Legitimacy

One issue that did, finally, attract attention
within the management literature was power
as legitimation (Astley and Sachdeva 1984).
Political scientists had long recognized the
advantages of creating legitimacy for existing
institutions, thereby avoiding the necessity of
using more coercive, visible forms of power
(Lipset 1959; Schaar 1969; Roelofs 1976; Rothschild 1979). Legitimacy can also be created for
individual actions, thus reducing the chances of
opposition to them. Edelman (1964; 1971; 1977)
pointed out that power is mobilized not only to
achieve physical outcomes, but also to give those
outcomes meanings – to legitimize and justify
them. Political actors use language, symbols,
and ideologies to placate or arouse the public.

> Political analysis must then proceed on two levels
> simultaneously. It must examine how political
> actions get some groups the tangible things they
> want from government and at the same time it must
> explore what these same actions mean to the mass
> public and how it is placated or aroused by them. In
> Himmelstrand's terms, political actions are both
> instrumental and expressive. (Edelman 1964: 12)

In this way, in the manner described by Lukes's
(1974) third dimension of power, the process of
legitimation prevents opposition from arising.
    The advantages of creating legitimacy had not
gone completely unnoticed, even in organization
studies.

> Stable organizing power requires legitimation. To be
> sure, men can be made to work and to obey com-
> mands through coercion, but the coercive use of
> power engenders resistance and sometimes active
> opposition. Power conflicts in and between societies
> are characterized by resistance and opposition, and
> while the latter occur in organizations, effective
> operations necessitate that they be kept at a
> minimum there and, especially, that members do
> not exhibit resistance in discharging their daily
> duties but perform them and comply with directives
> willingly. (Blau 1964: 199–200)

The functionally oriented management literature
had, however, largely ignored this issue.

One writer who attempted to draw legitimation processes into the management fold was
Pettigrew (1977). His work on the management
of meaning explicitly addressed how legitimacy
was created.

> Politics concerns the creation of legitimacy for
> certain ideas, values and demands – not just action
> performed as a result of previously acquired
> legitimacy. The management of meaning refers to
> a process of symbol construction and value use
> designed both to create legitimacy for one's own
> demands and to 'de-legitimize' the demands of
> others. (1977: 85)

He acknowledged that political actors define
success not always in terms of winning in the
face of confrontation (where there must always
be a risk of losing), but sometimes in terms of
their ability to section off spheres of influence
where their domination is perceived as legitimate
and thus unchallenged (Ranson et al. 1980;
Frost 1988). In this way, power is mobilized to
influence behaviour indirectly by giving outcomes and decisions certain meanings, by
legitimizing and justifying them.
    Pfeffer (1981a; 1981b) considered a similar use
of power when he distinguished sentiment
(attitudinal) from substantive (behavioural) outcomes of power. The latter depend largely on
resource dependency considerations, while the
former refer to the way people feel about the
outcomes and are mainly influenced by the
symbolic aspects of power, such as the use of
political language, symbols and rituals. Pfeffer
(1981a) argued there is only a weak relationship
between symbolic power and substantive outcomes: that symbolic power is only used *post hoc*
to legitimize outcomes already achieved by
resource dependencies. In this way, Pfeffer
stops short of acknowledging that power can
be used to prevent conflict and opposition. In
fact, there is an inconsistency in Pfeffer's
arguments: if symbolic power is effective
enough to 'quiet' opposition *ex post*, why not
use it *ex ante* to prevent opposition from arising
in the first place? The only factor preventing
Pfeffer from reaching this conclusion is his
refusal to acknowledge the existence of power in
situations other than those characterized by
conflict and opposition (1981a: 7).
    The work of these writers and others (e.g.
Clegg 1975; Gaventa 1980; Ranson et al. 1980;
Hardy 1985) offered an opportunity to merge
the management 'school' with the more critical
work on domination. The bridge was never
made, however, for a number of reasons. First,
the idea of using power to manage meaning and
create legitimacy was never taken up to any
great extent by North American and other
mainstream, functionalist writers, who continued

to focus on dependency and define power in terms of conflict and illegitimacy (e.g. Mayes and Allen 1977; MacMillan 1978; Gandz and Murray 1980; Narayaran and Fahey 1982; Mintzberg 1983; Gray and Ariss 1985; Pettigrew 1985; Enz 1988; Schwenk 1989; Pfeffer 1992). Pfeffer's (1981a) prevarication is, in fact, indicative of the entire field. The idea of managers using power in this way threatens to open up a can of worms for a perspective grounded in managerialism. Rather than delve into the power hidden in and mobilized through apparently neutral structures, cultures, and technologies, the vast majority of researchers preferred to continue to view these constructs as apolitical management tools. For example, most mainstream writers on organizational culture have gone to considerable lengths to avoid any association with power and politics (see Smircich 1983; Izraeli and Jick 1986; Mumby 1988). Cultural change is presented in neutral terms that suggest that it is to everyone's advantage (see Willmott 1993). Weiss and Miller (1987) explore this issue in an interesting exposé of how widely cited articles have 'doctored' the definitions of ideology to avoid any political connotations. (Also see Beyer et al. 1988 and Weiss and Miller 1988 for the resulting debate on the matter.)

A second barrier to bridge building was the fact that a new stream of work was rapidly moving to challenge sovereign views of power and, in so doing, questioned not only the functional perspective, but also the modernist assumptions that underlay much of the critical theory, as the following sections discuss.

Power and Discipline

The rule systems that made up Weber's bureaucracy have, more recently, been reinterpreted under the auspices of 'disciplinary practices' derived from Foucault (1977).[4] Writers influenced by this tradition refer to 'micro-techniques' of power. Unlike rule systems, these techniques are not ordinarily thought of in terms of the causal concept of power (the notion of someone getting someone else to do something that they would not otherwise do). Rather than being causally observable social episodes, they represent ways in which both individual and collectively organized bodies become socially inscribed and normalized through the routine aspects of organizations. In this way, power is embedded in the fibre and fabric of everyday life. At the core are practices of 'surveillance', which may be more or less mediated by instrumentation. Historically, the tendency is for a greater instrumentation as surveillance moves from a literal supervisory gaze to more complex forms of observation, reckoning and comparison. Surveillance, whether personal, technical, bureaucratic or legal, ranges through forms of supervision, routinization, formalization, mechanization, legislation and design that seek to effect increasing control of employee behaviour, dispositions and embodiment. Surveillance is not only accomplished through direct control. It may happen as a result of cultural practices of moral endorsement, enablement and suasion, or as a result of more formalized technical knowledge, such as the computer monitoring of keyboard output or low-cost drug-testing systems.

The effectiveness of disciplinary power in the nineteenth century was linked to the emergence of new techniques of discipline appropriate for more impersonal, large-scale settings in which the *Gemeinschaft* conditions whereby each person knew their place no longer prevailed (see Bauman 1982; Foucault 1977). Previous localized, moral regulation, premised on the transparency of the person to the gaze of the community, was no longer viable. So, new forms of state institution emerged in which new forms of control were adopted, and later copied by the factory masters. No grand plan caused these institutions to adopt similar forms of disciplinary technique. The process is perhaps best seen in terms of the pressures of institutional innovation (Meyer and Rowan 1977; DiMaggio and Powell 1983). People copied what was already available; hence they created their own world in isomorphic likeness of key features they already knew.

Machiavelli once observed that 'Men nearly always follow the tracks made by others and proceed in their affairs by imitation, even though they cannot entirely keep to the tracks of others or emulate the prowess of their models' (1961: 49). This view captures much of the sense of contemporary institutional theory, an organization theory with clear parallels to Foucault's (1977) work (see Scott 1987). Disciplinary techniques had been readily available in the monastic milieu of religious vocation, the military, institutional forms of schooling, poor houses, etc. Their effectiveness had been established during the past two centuries. Practices of institutional isomorphism thus tended to reproduce similar relations of meaning and membership as the basis for social integration in other organizations. Because certain forms of technique were already available and known they had a certain legitimacy which enabled them to be more widely dispersed than they might otherwise have been (e.g. Meyer and Rowan 1977).

Such forms of control, whether direct and personal or more mediated and instrumented, changed commonly held notions of private individual space. In the medieval monastery there was very little. As industrialization developed from 'putting out' to the 'factory system' the definition of this space was transformed in secular organization life as well. At a more general level, one may be dealing with the development of disciplines of knowledge shaped almost wholly by the 'disciplinary gaze' of surveillance, as Foucault (1977) suggests was the case of much nineteenth century social science, particularly branches of social welfare, statistics and administration. Organizationally, the twentieth century development of the personnel function under the 'human relations' guidance of Mayo (1975) may be seen to have had a similar tutelary role (see Clegg 1979; Ray 1986). Individual or collective bodies may be discriminated and categorized through diverse tactics of ratiocination. Mechanisms are often local, diverse and uncoordinated. They form no grand strategy. Yet, abstract properties of people, goods and services can be produced that are measurable, gradeable, assessable in an overall anonymous strategy of discipline.

In this way, then, sovereign notions of power (which underlay both modernist and functionalist approaches) were challenged. Power was no longer a convenient, manipulable, deterministic resource. Instead, all actors operated within an existing structure of dominancy – a prevailing web of power relations – from which the prospects of escape were limited for dominant and subordinate groups alike. Previously, power had been characterized in a number of ways but each required one to 'take sides'. For the functionalists, their side was that of the managers: resistance to their power was illegitimate. For the critical theorists, resistance was a good thing: it was an opportunity for creative human agency, particularly that associated with subjugated identities such as workers, women, ethnic minorities, to reassert itself against domination. An implicit morality was in play in both perspectives, and each was an affront to the other. Foucault's views and those directly influenced by him were different. Power does not involve taking sides, identifying who has more or less of it, as much as seeking to describe its strategic role – how it is used to translate people into characters who articulate an organizational morality play. Much of this work adopts a principled indifference to the sentiments attached to those parts; instead the thrust is strategic, descriptive and empirical.

Power and Gender in Organizations

Work on gender helped support the view that power in the organization should be represented as a total, rather than partial, picture. Early contributions on the role of women in organizations were Kanter's (1975; 1977) and Janet Wolff's (1977) articles. Kanter's case studies were probably the first ever to take gender seriously, in terms of the numbers, power and opportunities open to men and women in the corporation. Both as members of the organization and in the supporting roles that women play outside organizations as 'company wives', women were systematically subjected to power that was frequently implicit, tacit and unconscious. Wolff's (1977) article was concerned less with the tacit hegemony within organizations and more with the ways in which women's positions in organizations were inseparable from their broader social role. This perspective was to be developed later in the work of Gutek and Cohen (1982) who coined the idea of 'sex role spillover', the carrying over of societally defined gender-based roles into the workplace, whereby the sex roles associated with the demographically dominant gender become incorporated into the work roles. The armed forces and nursing are probably the best examples of polar opposites in this respect.

By the 1970s, scholars were increasingly aware of the gender blindness not only of organizations but also of organization studies (see Mills and Tancred 1992 for a brief overview). Major works were reassessed in terms of how their contribution to the literature was often premised on unspoken assumptions about gender or unobserved and unremarked sampling decisions or anomalies in gender terms (Acker and Van Houton 1974). For example, Crozier's (1964) maintenance workers were all men while the production workers were all women. As Hearn and Parkin (1983) were to demonstrate, this blindness was symptomatic of the field as a whole, not any specific paradigm within it.

A peculiar irony attaches to this, as Pringle (1989) was to develop. Gender and sexuality are extremely pervasive aspects of organizational life. In major occupational areas, such as secretaries and receptionists for example, organizational identity is defined through gender and the projection of forms of emotionality, and indeed sexuality, implicated in it. The mediation of, and resistance to, the routine rule enactments of organizations are inextricably tied in with gender since not only is behaviour defined as organizationally appropriate or inappropriate, but its appropriateness is characterized in gendered terms. Neatness, smartness, demureness take on gendered dimensions (Mills 1988; 1989; Mills and Murgatroyd 1991). Rather than challenging these taken-for-granted assumptions, the gender bias inherent in the study of organizations has helped to preserve the status quo. How else could the vantage point and privileges of white, usually Anglo-Saxon, normally American, males have been taken for granted for so long (Calás and Smircich 1992)?

Functionality attaches to dominant ideologies: presumably that is why they dominate (Abercrombie et al. 1980). Repression is not necessarily an objective or a prerequisite, but often is simply a by-product of an ideology that maximizes the organization's ability to act. Masculinist ideology has long been dominant in the majority of organizations. Certain male identities constituted in socially and economically privileged contexts routinely will be more strategically contingent for organizational decision-making, and for access to and success in hierarchically arranged careers (Heath 1981). But, organizations do not produce actions that are masculinist, so much as masculinism produces organizations that take masculinist action. Often they do this without anyone even being explicitly aware of it. In such a case the decisions that characterize organizational action will be a result, not a cause, of ideology. Organizations may be the arenas in which gender politics play out, and, as such, suitable places for treatment through anti-discriminatory policies. But, such 'solutions' may address only the symptoms and not the causes of deep seated gender politics. Attacking their organizational expression may suppress these symptoms but it is unlikely to cure the body politic, behind which there is a history of living, being and (dis)-empowering in a gendered world that is tacit, taken for granted and constitutive of the very sense of that everyday life-world.

Power and Identity in Organizations

People's identities are not only tied up in their gender or sexuality, any more than in the type of labour power that they sell to an organization. People in organizations are signifiers of meaning. As such they are subjects of regimes of both specific organizational signification and discipline, usually simultaneously. Identities premised on the salience of extra-organizational issues such as ethnicity, gender, class, age and other phenomena provide a means of resistance to organizational significations and discipline by forming limits on the discretion of organizational action. Who may do what, how, where, when and in which ways are customarily and, sometimes, legally specific identities, which are prescribed or proscribed for certain forms of practice. Embodied identities will only be salient in as much as they are socially recognized and organizationally consequent.[5]

Accordingly organizations are structures of patriarchal domination, ethnic domination and

so on. Clearly such matters are contingent: most organizations may be structures of class, gender, or ethnic dominancy but not all *necessarily* are. Too much hinges on other aspects of organization identity left unconsidered. In specific organizational contexts, for example, the general conditions of economic or class domination may not necessarily be the focus of resistance or struggle. More specific loci of domination may be organizationally salient; after all, divisions of labour are embodied, gendered, departmentalized, hierarchized, spatially separated and so on.

As a result, organizations are locales in which negotiation, contestation and struggle between organizationally divided and linked agencies are routine occurrences. Divisions of labour are both the object and the outcome of struggle. All divisions of labour within any employing organization are necessarily constituted within the context of various contracts and conditions of employment. Hence the employment relationship of economic domination and subordination is the underlying sediment over which other organization practices are stratified and overlaid, often in quite complex ways. This complexity of organizational locales renders them subject to multivalent powers rather than monadic sites of total control: contested terrains rather than total institutions. It is in these struggles that power and resistance are played out in dramatic scenes that those approaches influenced by Foucault (1977) seem best able to appreciate, because they are not predisposed to know in advance who the victorious and vanquished *dramatis personae* should be. Rather, the emphasis is on the play of meaning, signification and action through which all organization actors seek to script, direct and position all others. In this way, the fragility of unified interest 'groups' is emphasized and the simplistic nature of pluralistic (much less dualistic) approaches to power relations is countered.

Power and Resistance

Any superordinate member of a complex organization is only one relay in a complex flow of authority up, down and across organization hierarchies. Ideally, according to functionalist views, such relays should be without resistance; there should be no 'problem' of obedience. Rarely, if ever, is this the case as organization researchers have long known (Coch and French 1948). Consequently, obedience cannot be guaranteed, despite the search for a secular equivalent to divinely inspired obeisance because of the complexity and contingency of human agency. Instead, resistance is pervasive as organizational actors use their discretion. It is the ability to exercise discretion, to have chosen this rather than that course of action, which characterizes power, both on the part of power holders, those who are its subjects, and on the part of those who are its objects.

Important implications flow from the relationship between power, resistance and discretion. Power will always be inscribed within contextual 'rules of the game' which both enable and constrain action (Clegg 1975). Action can only ever be designated as such-and-such an action by reference to the rules which identify it. Those rules can never be free of surplus or ambiguous meaning: they can never provide for their own interpretation. Issues of interpretation are always implicated in the processes whereby agencies make reference to and signify rules (Wittgenstein 1968; Garfinkel 1967; Clegg 1975; Barnes 1986). 'Ruling' is thus an activity: it is accomplished by some agency as a constitutive sense-making process whereby attempts are made to fix meaning. Both rules and games necessarily tend to be the subject of contested interpretation and, although some players may have the advantage of also being the referee, there is always discretion and therein lies the possibility of resistance.

Here we confront the central paradox of power: the power of an agency is increased in principle by that agency delegating authority; the delegation of authority can only proceed by rules; rules necessarily entail discretion; and discretion potentially empowers delegates. From this arises the tacit and taken-for-granted basis of organizationally negotiated order, and on occasion its fragility and instability, as has been so well observed by Strauss (1978). Matters must be rendered routine and predictable if negotiation is to remain an unusual and out of the ordinary state of affairs. Thus freedom of discretion requires disciplining if it is to be a reliable relay. Whether this is achieved through what Foucault referred to as 'disciplinary' or some other mode of practice is unimportant. In any event, discipline occurs not so much by prohibition and intervention in states of affairs, but through the knowledgeable construction of these states of affairs which enables subordinates to minimize the sanctions directed at them by superordinates.

> [Actors] must recognize that the output of appropriate action which they produce is what minimizes the input of coercion and sanctioning which they receive. (Barnes 1988: 103)

In this way, power is implicated in authority and constituted by rules; rules embody discretion and provide opportunities for resistance; and, so, their interpretation must be disciplined, if new powers are not to be produced and existing powers transformed. In fact, given the inherent indexicality of rule use, things will never be wholly stable, even though they may appear so historically (Laclau and Mouffe 1985). Resistance to discipline is thus irremediable because of the power/rule constitution as a nexus of meaning and interpretation which, because of indexicality, is always open to being refixed. So, although the term 'organization' implies stabilization of control – of corporate and differential membership categories across space and across time – this control is never total. Indeed, it is often the contradictions in the evolution of regimes of control that explain their development (Clegg and Dunkerley 1980). Resistance and power thus comprise a system of power relations in which the possibilities of, and tensions between, both domination and liberation inevitably exist (Sawicki 1991: 98). Politics is a struggle both to achieve and to escape from power (Wrong 1979; Hindess 1982; Barbalet 1985; Clegg 1994a). The definitional distinction between power and resistance signifies 'qualitatively different contributions to the outcome of power relations made by those who exercise power over others, on the one hand, and those subject to that power, on the other' (Barbalet 1985: 545). In other words, according to this view, power is substantively different from resistance.

This view involves a reconceptualization from the duality of power (domination) or resistance (liberation) that had existed in sociological literature (e.g. Giddens 1979; 1982). It challenges the views of sovereign power which, at their furthest reach, embraced the fiction of supreme 'super-agency' while denying authentic sovereignty to others: an overarching A imposing its will on the many Bs. Concepts of the ruling class, ruling state and ruling culture or ideology overwhelmed the consciousness of subjects, thereby creating false consciousness (and explaining the absence of Marx's revolutionary predictions). In this way, writers like Lukes (1974) accepted the problematic of 'hegemony' (Gramsci 1971) or 'dominant ideology' (Abercrombie et al. 1980) and presumed to know, unproblematically, what the interests of the oppressed really were. The practical implications of these analyses were clear: good theory would replace bad theory; good theory would enable the realization of real interests.

Foucault (1980) sounded the death-knell of sovereign power with his distrust of the very notion of ideology. Criticisms concerning the empirical problems in *measuring* real interests (e.g. Benton 1981) were replaced by a more fundamental challenge. Foucault regarded ideology as a term of 'falsehood' whose relational opposition to a 'true' concept of 'science' can never be too far away. By demonstrating that the 'truths' and 'falsehoods' of particular discourses have been constituted historically, he showed that no assumption of reality can exist as anything more than its representation in language. Language cannot *mask* anything, it simply *represents* possibilities. Claims to know the real interests of any group, other than through the techniques of representation used to assert them, cannot survive this reconceptualization of power.

Power/Knowledge and Emancipation

The recognition that resistance was implicated by power has not led to an acknowledgement of enhanced prospects for emancipation. The space and ambiguity in which resistance is fostered do not lead to a transformation of prevailing power relations; they only reinforce those power relations. This is the sobering implication of the Foucauldian-influenced tradition. The death of the sovereign subject was accompanied by the killing of originating sources of action: none were to inhabit the poststructural world.

The pervasiveness of power relations makes them difficult to resist. Prevailing discourses are experienced as fact, which makes alternatives difficult to conceive of, let alone enact. Indeed, resistance often serves only to reinforce the existing systems of power (Clegg 1979; Knights and Willmott 1989; Knights and Morgan 1991). In addition, the production of identity confers a positive experience on individuals which leads to the reproduction of the power relations, not their transformation (Knights and Willmott 1989; Knights and Morgan 1991). Finally, while all actors are, to some extent, captured in the prevailing web of power relations (Deetz 1992a; 1992b), those advantaged by it are, usually, in the best position to develop strategies (such as outflanking, managing meaning, manipulating culture, choosing technology, etc.) that will protect their position.

Another blow to emancipation came from Foucault's attack on modernist assumptions that with knowledge comes 'truth', i.e. a situation free from power. Instead, argued Foucault, with knowledge only comes more power.

> Truth isn't outside power, or lacking in power: contrary to a myth whose history and functions would repay further study, truth isn't the reward of free spirits, the child of protracted solitude, nor the privilege of those who have succeeded in liberating themselves. Truth is a thing of this world: it is produced only by virtue of multiple forms of constraint. And it induces regular effects of power. Each society has its regime of truth, its 'general' politics of truth: that is, the type of discourse which

it accepts and makes function as true; the mechanisms and instances which enable one to distinguish true and false statements, the means by which each is sanctioned; and the techniques and procedures accorded value in the acquisition of truth; the status of those who are charged with saying what counts as true. (1980: 131)

In other words, salvation does not lie in understanding. The modernist idea that demystifying processes and structures of domination would help the subjugated to escape from them was shaken to its roots.

Despite the protestations of those who contend that Foucault's work is compatible with the idea of resistance (e.g. Smart 1985; 1986; 1990; Sawicki 1991; Alvesson and Willmott 1992), opponents argue, with equal fervour, that his work is antithetical to notions of liberation and emancipation (e.g. Hoy 1986; Said 1986; Walzer 1986; White 1986; Ashley 1990). These writers argue that the Foucauldian attack on agency removes the possibility of using power for particular objectives, especially the possibility of the powerless achieving empowerment. Whatever the result of this debate, one outcome is sure: opposing camps have engaged in a highly theoretical, intellectual struggle concerning matters of ontology and epistemology (Clegg 1989a; Nord and Doherty 1994).

> The debate is polarized around two apparently conflicting epistemological positions: modernism with its belief in the essential capacity of humanity to perfect itself through the power of rational thought and postmodernism with its critical questioning, and often outright rejection, of the ethnocentric rationalism championed by modernism. (Cooper and Burrell 1988: 2)

What is ignored in this absorbing – but somewhat esoteric – discourse are the practical matters of overcoming barriers to collective action and devising concrete strategies of resistance (Nord and Doherty 1994).

Thus those with the greatest case for emancipation have been largely ignored. The functionalist literature does not consider them to have a cause: the power embedded in organizational structures and processes is not power, much less domination. Those who dare to challenge it are irresponsible and irrational, if not downright subversive. The critical literature that derived its focus from its concern with underprivileged groups (e.g. Freire 1992) has, with the loss of faith in Marxist formulae, distanced itself from its former constituents. Once the struggles of resistance occupied a central place; now they revolve around sterile debates conducted in obfuscatory language.[6]

FROM CACOPHONY TO CHORUS?

Researchers have long noted the confusion that exists concerning the definition of power. It is no wonder when we consider the many different voices that have spoken on power. Depending on who is studying it, what they are studying, and why they are studying it, these voices are often looking at different phenomena or, at the very least, looking at the same phenomenon through very different lenses. Power has been both the independent variable causing outcomes such as domination, and the dependent variable, in this case the outcome of dependency. Power has been viewed as functional in the hands of managers who use it in the pursuit of collective, organizational goals, and dysfunctional in the hands of those who challenge those goals and seek to promote self-interest. Power has been viewed as the means by which legitimacy is created and as the incarnation of illegitimate action. Power has been equated with the formal organizational arrangements in which legitimacy is embedded, and as the informal actions that influence organizational outcomes. It has been seen as conditional on conflict and as a means to preempt conflict. It has been defined as a resource that is consciously and deliberately mobilized in the pursuit of self-interest – a resource that has failed to be used by those (such as women and workers) whose self-interest has been ascribed to them – and as a system of relations that knows no interest, but from which some groups inadvertently benefit. It has been seen as an intentional act to which causality can be clearly attributed, and as an unintentional, unpredictable game of chance. The study of power has meant a behavioural focus for some researchers, and attitudinal or hegemonic factors for others. Power has been berated for being repressive, and lauded for being productive. Small wonder, then, that there is little agreement!

This range of conceptualizations has, in general, coalesced around two very different streams of research, each of which has little to say to the other and each of which defends its own borders, thereby influencing the process of social inquiry. In the functionalist approach, power is a political 'disorganizing' tool used by opponents of managers. Sometimes, power is used by managers but only to repel these illegitimate attacks. This body of work adopts an unquestioning managerial perspective, and assumes that power is a malleable, useful resource, which is 'good' when used by managers and 'bad' when used against them. The alternative, critical approach has viewed power as a means of domination and resistance to it as an emancipatory tool. Starting out with a modernist perspective, it has recently been struggling to incorporate postmodernist ideas. Ironically, the power/knowledge concept of Foucault has robbed this body of work of much of its emancipatory power, and many writers (e.g. Alvesson and Willmott 1992; Knights and Vurdubakis 1994) seem to be struggling to give the postmodern adaptation back its modernist edge. The majority of the work is, however, highly theoretical, often ignoring the practicalities of developing strategies for resistance and liberation.

Perhaps it is time for both functionalists and critical theorists to pause. Maybe the practical, ethically situated and socially contexted uses of power need thinking through? The quotidian round of organization life has its own drama, its own theatricality, its own epistemologies, ontologies and methods, as Callon and Latour (1981) have demonstrated. It is not only through the moral play of functional legitimacy and illegitimacy versus critical opprobrium and approval that power is analyzed. The time is ripe to treat all forms of power play, including its theorizing, as moves in games that enrol, translate and treat others in various ways, in various situated moralities, according to various codes of honour and dishonour which constitute, maintain, reproduce and resist various forms and practices of power under their rubric. There is no reason to think that all games will necessarily share one set of rules, or be capable of being generated from the same deep and underlying rule set. Power requires understanding in its diversity even as it resists explanation in terms of a singular theory.

A theory of power does not, and cannot, exist other than as an act of power in itself – in attempting to rule out other understandings of phenomena in favour of a universalistic explanation, as Hobbes recognized almost at the outset. Such a power theory of power is unreflexive: it cannot account for itself, and any theory of power that cannot account for its own power cannot account for very much at all. This is the hermeneutic circle within which post-Foucauldian approaches to power leave us. The door marked 'general theory of power', whether fashioned critically or conventionally, seems to lead us back into a reduced version of the circle with a perspective that renders many organizational phenomena invisible or unimportant, particularly the concerns of the people whose lives frame the circle. One way out of this impasse is to explore the circle more completely and to investigate the relations and meanings that constitute it, by listening more carefully to the voices that normally populate it (e.g. Forester 1989) and unmasking the researcher who enters it.

This approach advocates more empirical study of local struggles, focusing not on a monolithic conception of power, but on the strategic concerns raised by Machiavelli (1961) or the war of manoeuvre highlighted by Gramsci (1971). We can learn much about power by deliberately selecting 'transparent' examples that illuminate the processes we wish to explore (Eisenhardt 1989). In this way, we can expose the variety of marginalized voices by, for example, examining how different women in different cultural and social situations are affected by different aspects and manifestations of gender discrimination (see Sawicki 1991; Kerfoot and Knights 1993). We can deconstruct prevalent disciplinary practices as in accounting (e.g. Knights and Collinson 1987). We can reveal how organizational practices contribute to the subjectivity and subjugation of employees (e.g. Knights and Willmott 1992); or contrast the characteristics of a Foucauldian web of power with existing conceptualizations of sovereign power, as in the case of fragmented refugee systems (Hardy 1994). We can amplify previously silent voices or herald voices of resistance. In so doing, we may privilege certain discourses (resulting in a temporary elitism: see Chapter 1.7 by Alvesson and Deetz in this volume) but, nonetheless, a space is claimed for voices that might otherwise be lost. By listening to the stories that people tell, we learn about how certain voices come to be silenced and how resistant subjects are constituted (Clegg 1994b).

We must also acknowledge the researcher's arrival within the circle, not as a neutral observer, but as an implicated participant. This requires a greater awareness of who the researcher is and where he or she comes from. Researchers must make clear how they access and interpret 'subjectivities' and outline methodological protocols (Collinson 1994; Clegg 1994a). We must expose both our analytic interpretations and our theoretical assumptions to the same kind of analysis. In this way we are in a position to identify the 'danger' of particular practices whether in the situation under study or in the very act of studying itself. For Foucault, freedom lay in bringing to light the anonymous historical processes through which any and all subjectivity is constructed, in questioning and reevaluating our inherited identities and values, and in challenging received interpretations of them (Sawicki 1991). By exposing ourselves and our work to this kind of genealogical analysis (e.g. Knights and Morgan 1991), we become more aware of how we are also prisoners in a web of power that we have helped to create.

NOTES

The authors acknowledge the Social Sciences and Humanities Research Council of Canada, the University of Western Sydney, Macarthur and McGill University for their support and Walt for the title.

1 In the early days of the guild structure the use of the masculine gender would have been less acceptable, but, as Rowbotham (1975: 1) notes, 'Separate organisations developed to protect the masters, and the terms of entry became formalised. It was consequently more difficult for journeymen's wives to be formally involved in the workshops, or for the master's wife to supervise the apprentices, and less customary for widows to take over from their husbands.' Thus, the emergence of power in pre-modern organizations had a gender bias built into its historical development; women were progressively screened out from the emergent organization form.

2 Marxist models have been premised on a series of capitalist/worker polarities, e.g. exploitation versus non-exploitation; productive versus non-productive; wage-earners versus revenue receivers (Carchedi 1977). Class was assumed to be the most salient base for identity. Recent empirical research in this tradition suggests that associational aspects of society, such as personal support for sports clubs, are more important (Baxter et al. 1991). Consequently, the empirical grounds for attaching credence to Marxist analyses of organization power as principally class power seem poorly grounded. Instead, the means of production are considered to be only one part of the picture: interests are variable, and dependent on organizational mechanisms of representation and outflanking (Mann 1986).

3 As interpreted from the Weberian concept of *Herrschaft* by Parsons (Henderson and Parsons 1947).

4 The concept is derived from Foucault but is implicit in Weber (1978) and labour process theory (see Littler and Salaman 1982).

5 Forms of embodiment such as age, gender, sexuality, ethnicity, religiosity and handicap are particularly recognizable as bases which serve to locate practices for stratifying organization members: this is evidenced by their being the precise target of various anti-discrimination laws.

6 Obviously, researchers do directly consider subjects of oppression and their work has produced claims, for example, that womanhood and ethnicity are new universal subjects of oppression. Such studies do, however, run into the 'old' problem of imputation of interests to subjects whose empirical behaviour confounds the interest assumption. In this direction lie new quagmires of morality, signposted as 'political correctness'.

REFERENCES

Abercrombie, N., Hill, S. and Turner, B.S. (1980) *The Dominant Ideology Thesis*. London: Allen and Unwin.

Acker, J. and Van Houton, D. (1974) 'Differential

recruitment and control: the sex structuring of organizations', *Administrative Science Quarterly*, 119(2): 152–63.

Alvesson, M. (1984) 'Questioning rationality and ideology: on critical organization theory', *International Studies of Management and Organizations*, 14(1): 61–79.

Alvesson, M. and Willmott, H. (1992) 'On the idea of emancipation in management and organization studies', *Academy of Management Review*, 17(3): 432–64.

Ashley, D. (1990) 'Habermas and the completion of the "project of modernity"', in B.S. Turner (ed.), *Theories of Modernity and Post Modernity*. London: Sage. pp. 88–107.

Assad, T. (1987) 'On ritual and discipline in medieval Christian monasteries', *Economy and Society*, 16(2): 159–203.

Astley, W. Graham and Sachdeva, Paramjit S. (1984) 'Structural sources of intraorganizational power: a theoretical synthesis', *Academy of Management Review*, 9(1): 104–13.

Bachrach, P. and Baratz, M.S. (1962) 'The two faces of power', *American Political Science Review*, 56: 947–52.

Bachrach, P. and Baratz, M.S. (1963) 'Decisions and nondecisions: an analytical framework', *American Political Science Review*, 57: 641–51.

Bachrach, P. and Baratz, M.S. (1970) *Power and Poverty*. London: Oxford University Press.

Barbalet, J.M. (1985) 'Power and resistance', *British Journal of Sociology*, 36(4): 531–48.

Barbalet, J.M. (1987) 'Power, structural resources and agency', *Perspectives in Social Theory*, 8: 1–24.

Barnes, B. (1986) 'On authority and its relationship to power', in J. Law (ed.), *Power, Action and Belief: a New Sociology of Knowledge?*, *Sociological Review Monograph*, 32. London: Routledge and Kegan Paul. pp. 180–95.

Barnes, B. (1988) *The Nature of Power*. Cambridge: Polity Press.

Bauman, Z. (1982) *Memories of Class: the Pre-History and After-Life of Class*. London: Routledge and Kegan Paul.

Baxter, J., Emmison, M. and Western J. (eds) (1991) *The Class Structure of Australia*. Sydney: Macmillan.

Benfari, R.C., Wilkinson, H.E. and Orth, C.D. (1986) 'The effective use of power', *Business Horizons*, 29(3): 12–16.

Bennis, W.G., Berkowitz, N., Affinito, M. and Malone, M. (1958) 'Authority, power and the ability to influence', *Human Relations*, 11(2): 143–56.

Benton, T. (1981) '"Objective" Interests and the Sociology of Power', *Sociology*, 15(2): 161–84.

Beyer, J.M., Dunbar, R.L.M. and Meyer, A.D. (1988) 'Comment: the concept of ideology in organizational analysis', *Academy of Management Review*, 13(3): 489–99.

Blau, P. (1964) *Exchange and Power in Social Life*. New York: Wiley.

Braverman, H. (1974) *Labor and Monopoly Capital*. New York: Monthly Review Press.

Burawoy, M. (1979) *Manufacturing Consent*. Chicago: Chicago University Press.

Calás, M.B. and Smircich, L. (1992) 'Using the "F" word: feminist theories and the social consequences of organizational research', in A. Mills and P. Tancred (eds), *Gendering Organization Analysis*. London: Sage. pp. 222–34.

Callon, M. and Latour, B. (1981) 'Unscrewing the Big Leviathan: how actors macrostructure reality and sociologists help them to do so', in K.D. Knorr-Cetina and A. Cicourel (eds), *Advances in Social Theory and Methodology: Towards an Integration of Micro- and Macro-sociologies*. London: Routledge and Kegan Paul. pp. 227–303.

Carchedi, G. (1977) *On the Economic Identification of Social Classes*. London: Routledge and Kegan Paul.

Carchedi, G. (1987) *Class Analysis and Social Research*. Oxford: Blackwell.

Clegg, S.R. (1975) *Power, Rule and Domination*. London: Routledge.

Clegg, S.R. (1979) *The Theory of Power and Organization*. London: Routledge and Kegan Paul.

Clegg, S.R. (1989a) *Frameworks of Power*. London: Sage.

Clegg, S.R. (1989b) 'Radical revisions: power, discipline and organizations', *Organization Studies*, 10(1): 97–115.

Clegg, S.R. (1990) *Modern Organizations: Organization Studies for the Postmodern World*. London: Sage.

Clegg, S.R. (1994a) 'Power relations and the constitution of the resistant subject', in J.M. Jermier, W.R. Nord and D. Knights (eds), *Resistance and Power in Organizations: Agency, Subjectivity and the Labour Process*. London: Routledge.

Clegg, S.R. (1994b) 'Weber and Foucault: social theory for the study of organizations', *Organization*, 1(1): 149–78.

Clegg, S.R. and Dunkerley, D. (1980) *Organization, Class and Control*. London: Routledge and Kegan Paul.

Clegg, S.R., Boreham, P. and Dow, G. (1986) *Class, Politics and the Economy*. London: Routledge and Kegan Paul.

Coch, L. and French, J.R.P. Jr (1948) 'Overcoming resistance to change', *Human Relations*, 1: 512–32.

Collinson, D. (1994) 'Strategies as resistance: power, knowledge and subjectivity', in J.M. Jermier, W.R. Nord and D. Knights (eds), *Resistance and Power in Organizations: Agency, Subjectivity and the Labour Process*. London: Routledge.

Cooper, R. and Burrell, G. (1988) 'Modernism, postmodernism and organizational analysis: an introduction', *Organization Studies*, 9(1): 91–112.

Crozier, M. (1964) *The Bureaucratic Phenomenon.* Chicago: University of Chicago Press.

Cyert, R.M. and March, J.G. (1963) *A Behavioral Theory of the Firm.* Englewood Cliffs, NJ: Prentice-Hall.

Dahl, R. (1957) 'The concept of power', *Behavioral Science*, 20: 201–15.

Dahl, R. (1961) *Who Governs: Democracy and Power in an American City.* New Haven, CT: Yale University Press.

Deetz, S. (1985) 'Critical-cultural research: new sensibilities and old realities', *Journal of Management*, 11(2): 121–36.

Deetz, S. (1992a) *Democracy in an Age of Corporate Colonization: Developments in Communication and the Politics of Everyday Life.* Albany, NY: State University of New York.

Deetz, S. (1992b) 'Disciplinary power in the modern corporation', in M. Alvesson and H. Willmott (eds), *Critical Management Studies.* London: Sage. pp. 21–45.

DiMaggio, P.J. and Powell, W.W. (1983) 'The iron cage revisited: institutional isomorphism and collective rationality in organizational fields', *American Sociological Review*, 48: 147–60.

Dubin, R. (1957) 'Power and union-management relations', *Administrative Science Quarterly*, 2: 60–81.

Edelman, M. (1964) *The Symbolic Uses of Politics.* Champaign, IL: University of Illinois Press.

Edelman, M. (1977) *Political Language.* London: Academic Press.

Edwards, R. (1979) *Contested Terrain.* New York: Basic Books.

Eisenhardt, K.M. (1989) 'Building theories from case study research', *Academy of Management Review*, 14: 532–50.

Emerson, R.M. (1962) 'Power–dependence relations', *American Sociological Review*, 27(1): 31–41.

Enz, C.A. (1988) 'The role of value congruity in intraorganizational power', *Administrative Science Quarterly*, 33: 284–304.

Etzioni, A. (1961) *A Comparative Analysis of Organizations.* New York: Free Press.

Forester, J. (1989) *Planning in the Face of Power.* Berkeley, CA: University of California Press.

Foucault, M. (1977) *Discipline and Punish: the Birth of the Prison.* Harmondsworth: Penguin.

Foucault, M. (1980) *Power/Knowledge.* New York: Pantheon.

Freire, P. (1992) *Pedagogy of the Oppressed.* New York: Continuum.

French, J.R.P. and Raven, B. (1968) 'The bases of social power', in D. Cartwright and A. Zander (eds), *Group Dynamics.* New York: Harper and Row.

Frost, P.J. (1987) 'Power, politics and influence', in F.M. Tablin, L.L. Putnam, K.H. Roberts and L.W. Porter (eds), *Handbook of Organizational Communications: an Interdisciplinary Perspective.* London: Sage.

Frost, P.J. (1988) 'The role of organizational power and politics in human resource management', in G.R. Ferris and K.M. Rowland (eds), *International Human Resources Management.* Greenwich, CT: JAI Press.

Gamble, A. and Walton, P. (1972) *From Alienation to Surplus Value.* London: Croom Helm.

Gandz, J. and Murray, V.V. (1980) 'The experience of workplace politics', *Academy of Management Journal*, 23(2): 237–51.

Garfinkel, H. (1967) *Studies in Ethnomethodology.* Englewood Cliffs, NJ: Prentice-Hall.

Gaventa, J. (1980) *Power and Powerlessness: Quiescence and Rebellion in an Appalachian Valley.* Oxford: Clarendon Press.

Geyer, R.F. and Schweitzer, D. (1981) *Alienation: Problems of Meaning, Theory and Method.* London: Routledge and Kegan Paul.

Giddens, A. (1979) *Central Problems in Social Theory.* London: Macmillan.

Giddens, A. (1982) 'A reply to my critics', *Theory, Culture and Society*, 1(2): 107–13.

Gramsci, A. (1971) *Selections from the Prison Notebooks.* London: Lawrence & Wishart.

Gray, Barbara and Ariss, Sonny S. (1985) 'Politics and strategic change across organizational life cycles', *Academy of Management Review*, 10(4): 707–23.

Gutek, B.A. and Cohen, A. (1982) 'Sex ratios, sex role spillover, and sex at work: a comparison of men's and women's experiences', *Human Relations*, 40(2): 97–115.

Hall, J.A. (1986) *Powers and Liberties: the Causes and Consequences of the Rise of the West.* Harmondsworth: Penguin.

Hamilton, G.G. and Biggart, N.W. (1985) 'Why people obey: theoretical observations on power and obedience in complex organizations', *Sociological Perspectives*, 28(1): 3–28.

Hardy, C. (1985) 'The nature of unobtrusive power', *Journal of Management Studies*, 22(4): 384–99.

Hardy, C. (1994) 'Understanding interorganizational domains: the case of refugee systems', *Journal of Applied Behavioural Science.*

Hearn, J. and Parkin, P.W. (1983) 'Gender and organizations: a selective review and a critique of a neglected area', *Organization Studies*, 4(3): 219–42.

Heath, A. (1981) *Social Mobility.* Glasgow: Fontana.

Henderson, A.M. and Parsons, T. (eds) (1947) *Max Weber: the Theory of Social and Economic Organization.* New York: Oxford University Press.

Hickson, D.J., Butler, R.J., Cray, D., Mallory, G.R. and Wilson, D.C. (1986) *Top Decisions: Strategic Decision-Making in Organizations.* San Francisco: Jossey-Bass.

Hickson, D.J., Hinings, C.A., Lee, C.A., Schneck, R.E. and Pennings, J.M. (1971) 'A strategic contingencies theory of intraorganizational power', *Administrative Science Quarterly*, 16(2): 216–29.

Hindess, B. (1982) 'Power, interests and the outcomes of struggles', *Sociology*, 16(4): 498–511.

Hoy, D.C. (1986) 'Power, repression, progress: Foucault, Lukes, and the Frankfurt School', in David Couzens Hoy (ed.), *Foucault: a Critical Reader*. Basil Blackwell. pp. 123–47.

Hyman, R. and Brough, I. (1975) *Social Values and Industrial Relations*. Oxford: Basil Blackwell.

Izraeli, D.M. and Jick, T.D. (1986) 'The art of saying no: linking power to culture', *Organization Studies*, 7(2): 171–92.

Kanter, R.M. (1975) 'Women in organizations: sex roles, group dynamics, and change strategies', in A. Sargent (ed.), *Beyond Sex Roles*. St Paul, MN: West.

Kanter, R.M. (1977) *Men and Women of the Corporation*. New York: Basic Books.

Kerfoot, D. and Knights, D. (1993) 'Management, masculinity and manipulation: from paternalism to corporate strategy in financial services in Britain', *Journal of Management Studies*, 30(4): 659–77.

Kieser, A. (1987) 'From asceticism to administration of wealth: medieval monasteries and the pitfalls of rationalization', *Organization Studies*, 8(2): 103–24.

Knights, D. and Collinson, D. (1987) 'Disciplining the shop floor: a comparison of the disciplinary effects of managerial psychology and financial accounting', *Accounting, Organizations and Society*, 457–77.

Knights, D. and Morgan, G. (1991) 'Strategic discourse and subjectivity: towards a critical analysis of corporate strategy in organizations', *Organization Studies*, 12(3): 251–73.

Knights, D. and Murray, F. (1992) 'Politics and pain in managing information technology: a case study from insurance', *Organization Studies*, 13(2): 211–28.

Knights, D. and Vurdubakis, T. (1994) 'Power, resistance and all that', in J.M. Jermier, W.R. Nord and D. Knights (eds), *Resistance and Power in Organizations: Agency, Subjectivity and the Labour Process*. London: Routledge.

Knights, D. and Willmott, H. (1985) 'Power and identity in theory and practice', *Sociological Review*, 33(1): 22–46.

Knights, D. and Willmott, H. (1989) 'Power and subjectivity at work: from degradation to subjugation in social relations', *Sociology*, 23(4): 535–58.

Knights, D. and Willmott, H. (1992) 'Conceptualizing leadership processes: a study of senior managers in a financial services company', *Journal of Management Studies*, 29(6): 761–82.

Laclau, E. and Mouffe, C. (1985) *Hegemony and Socialist Strategy*. London: Verso.

Lipset, S.M. (1959) 'Some social requisites of democracy: economic development and political legitimacy', *American Political Science Review*, 53: 69–105.

Littler, C.R. and Salaman, G. (1982) 'Bravermania and beyond: recent theories of the labour process', *Sociology*, 16: 251–69.

Lukes, S. (1974) *Power: a Radical View*. London: Macmillan.

Machiavelli, N. (1961) *The Prince*. Harmondsworth: Penguin.

MacMillan, I.C. (1978) *Strategy Formulation: Political Concepts*. St Paul, MN: West.

Mann, M. (1986) *The Sources of Social Power. Vol. 1: A History of Power from the Beginning to A.D. 1760*. Cambridge: Cambridge University Press.

Marx, K. (1976) *Capital*. Harmondsworth: Penguin.

Mayes, B.T. and Allen, R.W. (1977) 'Toward a definition of organizational politics', *Academy of Management Review*, 2: 674–8.

Mayo, E. (1975) *The Social Problems of an Industrial Civilization*. London: Routledge and Kegan Paul.

Mechanic, D. (1962) 'Sources of power of lower participants in complex organizations', *Administrative Science Quarterly*, 7(3): 349–64.

Meyer, J.W. and Rowan, B. (1977) 'Institutionalized organizations: formal structure as myth and ceremony', *American Journal of Sociology*, 83(2): 340–63.

Mézáros, I. (1970) *Marx's Theory of Alienation*. London: Merlin.

Mills, A.J. (1988) 'Organization, gender and culture', *Organization Studies*, 9(3): 351–69.

Mills, A.J. (1989) 'Gender, sexuality and organization theory', in J. Hearn, D.L. Sheppard, P. Tancred-Smith and G. Burrell (eds), *The Sexuality of Organizations*. London: Sage. pp. 29–44.

Mills, A.J. and Murgatroyd, S.J. (1991) *Organizational Rules: a Framework for Understanding Organizations*. Milton Keynes: Open University Press.

Mills, A.J. and Tancred, P. (1992) *Gendering Organization Analysis*. London: Sage.

Mintzberg, H. (1983) *Power In and Around Organizations*. Englewood Cliffs, NJ: Prentice-Hall.

Mintzberg, H. (1984) 'Power and organizational life cycles', *Academy of Management Review*, 9(2): 207–24.

Mumby, D.K. (1988) *Communication and Power in Organizations: Discourse, Ideology and Domination*. Norwood, NJ: Ablex.

Narayanan, V.K. and Fahey, L. (1982) 'The micro-politics of strategy formulation', *Academy of Management Review*, 7(1): 25–34.

Nord, W.R. and Doherty, E.M. (1994) 'Towards an assertion perspective for empowerment: blending employee rights and labor process theories'. Unpublished paper: College of Business Administration University of South Florida.

Offe, C. (1976) *Industry and Inequality*, translated and with an introduction by J. Wickham. London: Edward Arnold.

Parry, G. and Morriss, P. (1975) 'When is a decision not a decision?', in L. Crewe (ed.), *British Political Sociology Yearbook*, vol. 1. London: Croom Helm.

Pettigrew, A.M. (1973) *The Politics of Organizational Decision Making*. London: Tavistock.

Pettigrew, A.M. (1977) 'Strategy formulation as a political process', *International Studies of Management and Organizations*, 7(2): 78–87.

Pettigrew, A.M. (1985) *The Awakening Giant: Continuity and Change in Imperial Chemical Industries.* Oxford: Basil Blackwell.

Pfeffer, J. (1981a) *Power in Organizations.* Marshfield, MA: Pitman.

Pfeffer, J. (1981b) 'Management as symbolic action', in L.L. Cummings and B.M. Staw (eds), *Research in Organizational Behavior*, vol. 3. Greenwich, CT: JAI Press. pp. 1–52.

Pfeffer, J. (1992) 'Understanding power in organizations', *California Management Review*, 35: 29–50.

Pfeffer, J. and Salancik, G. (1974) 'Organizational decision making as a political process', *Administrative Science Quarterly*, 19: 135–51.

Polsby, N.W. (1963) *Community Power and Political Theory.* New Haven, CT: Yale University Press.

Pringle, R. (1989) 'Bureaucracy, rationality, and sexuality: the case of secretaries', in J.D. Hearn, D.L. Sheppard, P. Tancred-Sherriff and G. Burrell (eds), *The Sexuality of Organizations.* London: Sage.

Ranson, S., Hinings, R. and Greenwood, R. (1980) 'The structuring of organizational structure', *Administrative Science Quarterly*, 25(1): 1–14.

Ray, C. (1986) 'Social innovation at work: the humanization of workers in twentieth century America'. PhD, University of California, Santa Cruz.

Roelofs, H.M. (1976) *Ideology and Myth in American Politics.* Boston: Little, Brown.

Rothschild, J. (1979) 'Political legitimacy in contemporary Europe', in B. Denitch (ed.), *Legitimation of Regimes.* Beverly Hills, CA: Sage.

Rowbotham, S. (1975) *Hidden from History: 300 Years of Women's Oppression and the Fight Against It.* Ringwood, Vic.: Pelican.

Said, E.W. (1986) 'Foucault and the imagination of power', in David Couzens Hoy (ed.), *Foucault: a Critical Reader.* Oxford: Basil Blackwell. pp. 149–55.

Salancik, G. and Pfeffer, J. (1974) 'The bases and use of power in organizational decision making', *Administrative Science Quarterly*, 19: 453–73.

Saunders, P. (1980) *Urban Politics: a Sociological Interpretation.* Harmondsworth: Penguin.

Sawicki, J. (1991) *Disciplining Foucault.* London: Routledge.

Schaar, J.H. (1969) 'Legitimacy in the modern state', in P. Green and S. Levinson (eds), *Power and Community.* New York: Pantheon.

Schacht, R. (1971) *Alienation.* London: Allen and Unwin.

Schattschneider, E.F. (1960) *The Semi-Sovereign People.* New York: Holt, Rinehart and Winston.

Schwenk, C.R. (1989) 'Linking cognitive, organizational and political factors in explaining strategic change', *Journal of Management Studies*, 26(2): 177–88.

Scott, W.R. (1987) 'The adolescence of institutional theory', *Administrative Science Quarterly*, 32(4): 493–511.

Smart, B. (1985) *Michel Foucault.* London: Tavistock.

Smart, B. (1986) 'The politics of truth and the problem of hegemony', in David Couzens Hoy (ed.), *Foucault: a Critical Reader.* Oxford: Basil Blackwell. pp. 157–73.

Smart, B. (1990) *Theories of Modernity and Post Modernity*, edited by B.S. Turner. London: Sage.

Smircich, L. (1983) 'Concepts of culture and organizational analysis', *Administrative Science Quarterly*, 28: 339–58.

Strauss, A. (1978) *Negotiations.* San Francisco: Jossey-Bass.

Thompson, J.D. (1956) 'Authority and power in identical organizations', *American Journal of Sociology*, 62: 290–301.

Walzer, M. (1986) 'The politics of Michel Foucault', in David Couzens Hoy (ed.), *Foucault: a Critical Reader.* Oxford: Basil Blackwell. pp. 51–68.

Watson, T.J. (1982) 'Group ideologies and organizational change', *Journal of Management Studies*, 19(3): 259–75.

Weber, M. (1978) *Economy and Society: an Outline of Interpretive Sociology*, 2 vols, edited by G. Roth and C. Wittich. Berkeley, CA: University of California Press.

Weiss, R.M. and Miller, L.E. (1987) 'The concept of ideology in organizational analysis: the sociology of knowledge or the social psychology of beliefs?', *Academy of Management Review*, 12(1): 104–16.

Weiss, R.M. and Miller, L.E. (1988) 'Response: ideas, interests, and the social science of organizations', *Academy of Management Review*, 13(3): 490–4.

White, S.K. (1986) 'Foucault's challenge to critical theory', *American Political Science Review*, 80(2): 419–32.

Willmott, H. (1993) 'Strength is ignorance: slavery is freedom: managing culture in modern organizations', *Journal of Management Studies*, 30(4): 515–52.

Wittgenstein, L. (1968) *Philosophical Investigations*, translated by G.E.M. Anscombe. Oxford: Blackwell.

Wolff, J. (1977) 'Women in organizations', in S. Clegg and D. Dunkerley (eds), *Critical Issues in Organizations.* London: Routledge and Kegan Paul. pp. 7–20.

Wolfinger, R.E. (1971) 'Nondecisions and the study of local politics', *American Political Science Review*, 65: 1063–80.

Wrong, D. (1979) *Power: its Forms, Bases and Uses.* Oxford: Blackwell.

3.8

Normal Science, Paradigms, Metaphors, Discourses and Genealogies of Analysis

GIBSON BURRELL

LIFE IN THE 1960S

In the 1960s the field of organizational analysis was deceptively simple. The figure of Max Weber bestrode the terrain like a colossus and it was within his shadow that almost all the work was carried out. The simplicities of the period were widespread and involved assumptions about the centrality of modernity, the institutional superiority of bureaucratic structures and the need for measurement of Weber's ideal type construct. The rise of contingency theory had done nothing to question these assumptions, for theory was still to be tested by collecting data, usually of a quantitative kind, utilizing standard positivistic methods in the search for managerially relevant conclusions.

The writers on organizations of this period, in which the growth of the welfare and warfare state had created something of a movement towards corporatism, saw their role as being that of scientization of the field and adding administrative science to the list of managerially relevant fields like operational science and economics. Their subject matter – the organization – was gaining an importance from major societal changes to do with bureaucratization. And Weber, whose writings promised a protected future to his professional audience, was a graven image before which these analysts bowed.

Sociologists, of course, had long recognized that the complexities of Weber's thought could not be reduced to such simplicities. His style was one in which he was always careful to show how provisional, partial and tentative his thoughts were. His concept of *verstehen* also raised uncomfortable issues, for it pointed to the tradition of German Idealism of and for which the Anglophone organization theorists had little sympathy or understanding. So even as organizational analysis formed around a hagiographic image of Weber, it ignored those parts of his fecund writing which the Parsonians wished consciously or unconsciously to suppress.

There is little space here to evaluate the importance of the Pareto Circle at Harvard University but their impact upon organization theory can be easily underestimated. This group met as a dining club in the early 1930s and included the names of many eminent personages who collectively called themselves by the name of Vilfredo Pareto, the 'Marx of the bourgeoisie'. Parsons, Merton, Mayo, Homans, Roethlisberger and Chester Barnard all belonged to this inner circle of major figures in organization theory. In seeking to reject the influence of Marx they turned to other European social theorists. Whilst Pareto served this purpose in the early 1930s, it was Weber who came to the rescue in the post World War II period (Ray and Reed 1994).

This is not to say that Parsons was not an extremely able social theorist, or that he was ignorant of the German Idealist tradition, or that he wilfully misrepresented Weber's ideas any more than most. It is more to say that in seeking to form an administrative science, unity, homogeneity and coherence were emphasized at the expense of fracture, fissure and difference. In the Parsonians' discussion of the work of Max Weber, his original philosophical and political tensions are almost totally ignored. Moreover, their analysis of organizations could be held up as in no need of Marx or leftist ideas. Weber, or more accurately right Weberianism, provided the perfect defence of bureaucratic rule and the importance of the administrative function (Mouzelis 1975). Meanwhile, the relevance of left Weberianism was ignored along with the concept of *verstehen*. Thus, almost from the outset, a unified organization theory began to dissolve in front of our eyes. No sooner had a modified Weber been presented as the patron saint of organizational analysis than the vandals began to daub the holy figure with the graffiti of political and methodological disaffection.

Administrative science then is no stranger to fractured lines of analysis. The Weber who was politically of the left and intellectually idealist had been ignored in much of the classic work. As soon as *this* Weber had been resurrected, the project of organization theory, almost at its moment of conception, became fought over. Organization theory, from that day on, was 'contested terrain'.

Such a view of organizational analysis suggests that contestation over political, epistemological and methodological grounds was present even in the heyday of the Aston Studies, the launch of *Administrative Science Quarterly* (*ASQ*) and the rise of contingency theory. Whilst the leading figures did not shout out their concerns about its coherence – indeed one might argue that 'leading' figures only become so because they never voice any doubt in public about the integral nature of their project – such coherence had to be asserted rather than demonstrated to audiences which were not yet aware. Bruno Latour (1982) has shown us that for a field of science to be successful, an actor network tends to be developed, and whether the area does or does not develop to full fruition in practice depends upon hard work and political nous amongst its leading lights.

Thus one can forgive the first organization theorists some of their myopia for it served a highly important political purpose. However, the notion of a golden age is always suspect, for when we look back we can see not only a much smaller field but one in which the powerful agreed to ignore fundamental problems in addressing fundamental issues. The power the group gained came more from a widespread external recognition of its 'explanandum' rather than its 'explanans'. In other words, lots of influential people thought administration was an important phenomenon to be explained (the *explanandum*) irrespective of the explanatory framework being used which was both positivistic and structural (its *explanans*). So long as the problematic nature of the phenomenon was being addressed, therefore, it was almost im-

material how any putative solutions were reached. Thus the real difficulty for organizational analysis was, and still is, how to convince the influential that we are addressing a vitally important explanandum – from *their* point of view. If we see ourselves as 'servants of power' (Baritz 1962) then having the ear of the powerful is a crucial issue on which our political and economic fortunes hang. What explanans we possess is, by and large, of interest only to ourselves.

Yet this present piece is not about the explanandum of our discipline; rather it concerns itself with our explanans at the most basic levels. Here, paradigms, frameworks, cognitive maps, theoria etc. are the words (and sometimes even concepts) that we use to describe how we approach and confront our subject matter. But if we look at organization theory in the last few years of the century we see that it shows more of a fractured visage than it did thirty years ago. What we faced in the 1960s was an agreement of sorts that the focus of our attention had to be the large bureaucratic organization within a modern society. With agreement on the explanandum, difficulties over what was the explanans retreated. We lived in a golden age because the object of our desires was fixed.

This golden age of modernism gradually has given way to a situation in which it is not agreement and identity that are celebrated but difference and heteroglossia (Cooper and Burrell 1988). In the mainstream areas of organization theory today it would be foolish to maintain that postmodernism has been embraced with any affection, but a gradual awareness of the avantgarde relevance of the work of Michel Foucault and Jacques Derrida, for example, has slowly dawned. This chapter will attempt to show the undermining effect upon our explanandum of which postmodernism is capable – as long as we note here that, such is the centrality of dispute and of speaking with many voices to 'postmodernism', neither Foucault nor Derrida would accept that label as a classifier for their own work. Moreover in the struggle between those twin Greek gods, Apollo and Dionysius, whilst Apollo had dominated the 1960s and 1970s, Dionysius has made something of a comeback in the last fifteen years. And with this Bacchic rise, phallocentric as it is, it becomes possible to speak of desire and the body rather than thought and the mind.

How then to describe the fractured present? In the spirit of the authors about to be discussed, let us search for another deep-seated myth regarding human knowledge and, on finding it, use it metaphorically to understand our discipline. The myth that usefully springs to mind here is found not in Greek mythology but in the Bible. Like all myths its significance is capable of multi-layered analysis, but one effort which the reader might find helpful is to be found in George Steiner's *After Babel: Aspects of Language and Translation* (1975).

THE TOWER OF BABEL

In Genesis, the story is told that God became unhappy with humanity in the shape of the builders of the temple at Babel (Babylon). Their temple is so high and their aims so transparent as to rival God in his power that God decides to spread them to the four corners of the Earth in a diaspora which leaves builder unable to speak unto builder. The diaspora of the builders is motivated by God's desire to ensure their deliberate division into many warring encampments. The speaking of many languages comes only *after* the abandonment of the work on the same edifice. What is important is the shared project, not the shared language. The babel of voices comes from the cessation of the shared task and not vice versa.

What organization studies lack today is a shared language and a shared project. How then does this fit in with the much used notion of 'the project of modernity' and the role of organization studies within it? The answer of course is that modernity in its late or postmodern phases *questions* bureaucratic organization and its legitimacy almost as much as it was interrogated in those far-off premodern times before industrialization. With the explanandum of our activities in retreat, is it any wonder that our explanans, too, suffers from a lack of confidence?

Pfeffer (1993) in a recent piece of provocation has argued that organization theory needs to be much more disciplined, centralized and controlled by a small elite grouping if it is to have any future at all in the groves of academe. Although he does not use the metaphor of Babel there is a clear idea of a disparate, fragmented field ripe for hostile take-over from those without, who are better organized and centrally commanded. Thus this particular chapter will consider three elements within the structure of the field. The first is the nature of the fragmentation of our discipline into schools of thought and a corresponding lack of a universally recognized elite in control; the second is the resultant lack of shared explanans; and the third is the cause of both – the shifting nature of the administrative enterprise itself. Of course these are interconnected but let us concentrate upon one at a time.

The Diaspora of the Builders

The builders of organization theory do not live in a single city. The discipline is global in its sites of production. For example, the transatlantic nature of much of organization theory has long been recognized. The importation into the USA of Weber's intellectual remains is but one form of traffic. The reverse importation back into Europe of organizational principles developed on the railways of the eastern seaboard itself merely reflected the importation of French ideas on discipline and linearity into West Point Academy somewhat earlier (Hoskin and MacVe 1986). Yet in each import and export, small changes are necessarily made to customize the intellectual product for particular markets. Something is added. Something else is removed. Thus the European concerns with property, with serfdom, with the absence of land for the masses, with aristocracy and monarchy, with the sheer weight of tradition, are not as vibrant and alive in the USA from the outset. What is seen in the arena of administration when we look carefully is the confrontation of the New World by the Old. How can they possibly have the same views about how to administer the people within their domain? Hence, just as Weber is partially lost in both translation and transatlantic passage, the builders of organization theory rely upon and use different assumptions about the nature of the social and psychological world – depending upon which side of the North Atlantic they happen to be standing at the relevant moment.

However, lest the accusation of hemisphericentrism be levelled against this chapter, allow me to quickly point out that much current work of interest is being carried out in the southern hemisphere and around a larger ocean than the Atlantic. It was on one night in May 1985 that air traffic above the Pacific became denser than that over the Atlantic for the first time, and this shift in global trade is also quite recognizable in intellectual exchanges. The Atlantic no longer represents the undisputed geopolitical centre of organization theory as it once did.

Now the existence of this North Atlantic Theory of Organization (NATO) does not mean that the original builders ever shared a *complete* identity of approach. What they did share however was a post-war consensus in which welfarism brought in by post-war governments was fused with Keynesian economics, a distrust of the USSR and Euro-communism, types of organizational restructuring brought about by US consultancy firms, huge defence spending and supposed attempts to keep unemployment down. All of these features relied upon large centrally planned and coordinated activities in which American ideas, just like the American military, predominated. For, as has been recently pointed out, the D-Day landings represented the first successful invasion of European soil since the East had succumbed to one of the pashas in the late fourteenth century. Five hundred years of European predominance had given way to an invasion of capital, ideas and military hardware from the West. Organization theory, delicately placed in the framework of a German sociologist as it was, nevertheless was an American re-import.

Organization theory was and to some extent still is built around this inter-continental inter-mingling. And like all products of interchange it invites attempts to understand the way in which it operates.

Key to the issue is the centrality of science in our ways of looking at administration and organizational behaviour. Science begins by placing the perpetually dynamic into a field of stasis. *Ceteris paribus* clauses, the experiment and the laboratory are all ways of stabilizing the real world's perpetual flow. There is the terrible example of a 4,900-year-old bristlecone pine tree in Wyoming being cut down by an impatient researcher because his tree corer would not work. The oldest living thing on the planet was killed in order to find out how old it was (Zwicky 1992). The creation of stasis, the better to hold the scientific victim steady so that it might be anatomically examined, is a long one. We must look, perhaps, at the range of conceptualizations within organization theory as ways of enforcing anatomizing stasis upon the dynamics of organizational life. They are notions of and for stasis through which the mobile, the dynamic, the restless are forced to offer themselves up unto the gaze of the observer. Concepts are the ultimate form of the panopticon (Foucault 1977). By classifying and marking their victims, concepts perform an imprisoning act of considerable sophistication. But much more than incarceration takes place. Once immobilized, the body of thought becomes subject to inscription. Concepts inscribe their marks upon the body of the literature and, in the process of marking with cuts and incisions, they leave a trail of lesions behind which all can follow. The deeper cuts are those which make the biggest impression upon those that read off the significance of the author's (re)marks for themselves. But these impressive cuts ultimately spell death and immobility. At the very least the subject is wounded by the deepest and most incisive inscriptions.

Paradigms, metaphors, discourses and genea-logies are all incised lesions on the body of organizational life. Analysis of almost any kind requires the death or at least the mutilation of that which is analysed. To identify anything as an explanandum is to offer it up for execution. To alight upon anything as an explanans is to provide at the very least a fearsome weapon of mutilation. Thus words, especially in the form of conceptualizations, serve to imprison, immobi-lize, and injure that which they seek to address.

No Agreement over the Explanans

Just as the builders came to 'fall out' over the terms and methods to be used in the construc-tion of the tower, so too in organization theory is there very little agreement over the *types* of conceptualizations to be used, never mind the actual conceptualization itself. The moments of force for dissolution, of course, are there in the area right from the start. As has been argued, it would be foolish to imagine the existence of some coherent structure which came to the point of incipient collapse. All that happened in the late 1960s was that the reality of fragmentation became clearer when it became glaringly obvious that one particular group of contingency theorists had, hitherto, shouted down the other voices on the far side of the structure. The idea that one voice could drown out the rest is an attractive one to the pulmonarily gifted but it is a dream which can never be realized fully. There will, thank goodness, always be the voices of dissent and the clamour of alternatives vying for aural space. What we had in the 1960s was merely the period of hushed opposition before the volume of babble rose. Different explana-tions of differently conceived problems quickly came to prominence as the numbers of academics employed in the arena of organization theory increased. The demographic changes in the academic population are significant but should not be seen as the cause of fragmenta-tion. They merely made it more visible.

The Shifting Nature of the Enterprise

In the same way as the demographics of the academic population affected the nature of the fragmentary dynamics within organization theory, so too did the changes occurring within the population of organizations in which our interest had centred. Privatization, franchising, the break-up of the large corporations into quasi-independent entities, the attacks upon bureaucracy, the attacks upon the middle manager and so on, all meant that the expla-nandum itself was changing. The mode of organization was altering to the extent that markets and networks were starting to take the place of those bureaucracies of which Weber had been a major theorist. Whilst very few thought, or more accurately think, that bureaucracy is 'dead', clearly it is in retreat to some extent across the developed world. Thus, it is possible to say that the diaspora of theoreticians has been matched by the diaspora of the isomorphic organizational form. There is no easy silhouetting here, for there is no close identity between those, for example, who study the voluntary sector and those who use a particular managerial stance. The lines of fissure do not match up. The fragmentation is much worse than that.

THE PROCRUSTEAN BED OF THEORY

Given all these lines of fissure and the desperate need, under modernity, for academics to claim an understanding of the world, it is little wonder that the theoreticians have attempted to 'fix' the organizational world and, by reducing its dynamics to a static classificatory system, imprison it. We must now, at last, turn to the ways in which the stabilizers have attempted to offer momentary glimpses of a world in flux. In this they have forced organizational analysis on to a procrustean bed on which it groans and squirms because it is not the right size to fit the cramping framework into which it is being pressed. Yet the forcing goes on. Each of the terms to be addressed below forces the subject into an understandable and simplifying framework. This, after all, is what science does. But we must realize that what every concept does is to exclude as well as include, to ignore as well as concentrate upon, to consign to obscurity as well as bring into the limelight. Concepts stretch the point. And nowhere more than in the concept of 'paradigm'.

THE ORIGINS OF PARADIGM THINKING

At the beginning of this century, German science and philosophy were seen as being in a state of chaos. The external view which emphasized the power of these thought systems was not shared by the likes of Carnap, Neurath and the Viennese positivists or by the Berlin School of logical empiricists. They all sought to overcome the well accepted situation of heterogeneity and fragmentation by offering a vision of a common language for science which would lead eventually to a unified science. Their unified science, to the outsider's eye, looks uncommonly like mathematics but for them this way lay progress. Neurath and Carnap proposed a central work which would achieve such a goal. *The Foundations of the Unity of Science: Toward an International Encyclopaedia of Unified Science* was begun in 1938 and by 1962 included in its programme a key text for those interested in the notion of paradigms. This was Thomas Kuhn's *The Structure of Scientific Revolutions* (1962).

The appearance of this particular book in this particular project is heavily ironic perhaps, because Kuhn's book is seen by many as offering a defence of non-unified science. However, for reasons that we will examine shortly, it is not all that clear that Kuhn is totally committed to the beneficial impact of a lack of unity in science. As Gioia and Pitre (1993) show, Carnap, a great unificationist, welcomed the appearance of the book in the series he was editing. Gioia and Pitre (1993) suggest that

> The irony of including Kuhn's putatively radical work in the Neurath et al. series may be only apparent. Although Kuhn's work typically is cited as a milestone in the downfall of logical empiricism, its actual opposition to post World War II empiricism is – arguably – overstated.

Nevertheless, what Kuhn achieved in *The Structure of Scientific Revolutions* did not sit well with the then contemporary views on scientific progress and how this was to be explained. In developing the concept of 'normal science', Kuhn argued that the evidence on progress in the physical sciences, particularly in the grand works of synthesis by Newton and then Einstein, did not fit with the inductivist or falsificationist views of science. Science does not proceed by the facts revealing themselves to clever thinkers or by scientists attempting to falsify their own hypotheses in every experiment. Kuhn sees science as developing through political tensions being resolved in the scientific community in a cycle which begins with the challenge of youth, then resistance from the powerful, the death of the powerful, their replacement by the ageing young who then come to dominate, and finally the challenge yet again of new youth. Hence the life cycles of individuals and the path of scientific progress are heavily intertwined. It requires the death of the old for the new to come to fruition. Thus there is a cyclical relation between normal science and revolutionary science with one giving way to the other, repetitively.

Science, then, is not a linear pathway of falsifiable hypotheses. Rather, for Kuhn, it is a series of discontinuous periods of 'normal science' and revolutionary change. Established ways of seeing the world are replaced, throughout history, by tremendous upheavals in thought. These changes are so expansive that the old ways of thinking are totally incompatible with the new. To embrace the new is to undertake a conversion experience. By no means are all scientists in the field willing to contemplate this move from a comfortable stability. The new view of the world – an Einsteinian one rather than a Newtonian one, for example – creates a new structure, a new set of community agendas, a revolutionary new set of social arrangements, a new paradigm which revolutionizes our understanding. The full enormity of this revolution in thinking can only be seen if the scientist undergoes a '*Gestalt* switch'.

'Paradigm', as used in Kuhn (1962), is a word which excited many in the philosophy of science but fascinated others from elsewhere. Masterman (1970), in a widely quoted article, shows that Kuhn uses the term in over twenty different ways in *The Structure of Scientific Revolutions*. However in the second edition, written in 1970, Kuhn maintained – in a much watered-down version of the radicalism of the first – that he preferred the term 'disciplinary matrix' to 'paradigm'. For in the intervening period Kuhn's work had enjoyed the time honoured fate of all important work. It was subjected to detailed and critical analysis. A conference organized by Imre Lakatos, the leading sophisticated falsificationist of the period, attacked the Kuhnian position with gusto and, unsurprisingly, found it had weaknesses. In the face of this, by the end of the 1960s Kuhn had retreated to a less radical position. Since 1970, this retreat has continued and reached the stage where he could say in 1982 that 'paradigms' did not preclude full communication across the revolutionary divide, and by 1990 he argued that understanding across barriers could not be ruled out (Gioia and Pitre 1993).

Howard Sankey (1993) has engaged in a full discussion of Kuhn's changing position on paradigms and persuasively argues for the view that Kuhn's work may be divided into three phases. These are 'the early position', 'the transitional phase' and 'the later position'. He argues, in a section worth quoting at length, that

Kuhn's treatment of incommensurability divides into early and late positions, separated by a transitional stage. Originally Kuhn's notion of incommensurability involved semantical, observational and methodological differences between global theories or paradigms. His initial discussion suggested that proponents of incommensurable theories are unable to communicate and that there is no recourse to neutral experience or objective standards to adjudicate between theories. In subsequent efforts to clarify his position he restricted incommensurability to semantic differences and assimilated it to Quinean indeterminacy of translation. During this intermediate stage Kuhn's treatment of the issues tended to be incomplete, often resulting in cursory discussion. However, in recent years he has begun to develop his position in more refined form. His present view is that there is

translation failure between a localized cluster of indefined terms within the language of theories. (1993: 760)

Arguably, the problem of the incommensurability of paradigms remains at the very core of the continuing issue of the relevance, existence, or future of organizational paradigms. If one paradigm could be easily translated into another then the question becomes one of how and when the total dominance of the numerically stronger encampment will take place. If the approaches of the smaller, less politically strong, groups can be so easily incorporated into the language of the dominant orthodoxy then their language, their culture, their very existence are unlikely to be secure. This notion of survival then, and the metaphors of death and destruction attendant upon it, are quite crucial. For those who argue for the existence of paradigm incommensurability, there is a real tendency to think that any course of action predicated upon a belief in translation rules will result, sooner or later, in the take-over – the over-running – of their position by hostile forces. The functionalist orthodoxy, irrespective of its advantages in numbers, resources and institutional position, is very good at translating concerns, ideas and approaches originating from 'outside' into its own terms. Think of the way in which 'alienation' becomes transmogrified as a concept. The words remain the same. The content, ideology and political significance are stripped out, however, leaving behind the word but not its signification.

ORGANIZATIONAL PARADIGMS

On both sides of the Atlantic, the notion of 'paradigms' in organizational analysis has received much attention in the last fifteen years. It is not clear, as we have already noted, in *The Structure of Scientific Revolutions* (1962; 1970) what is meant precisely by a 'paradigm', for Kuhn uses the term in at least twenty different ways in his analysis of the breakdown of Newtonian physics. However, the term revolves around the idea of 'classic laws' and 'modes of community life'. This is to say that the paradigm marks out, in an agreed and deep-seated sense, a way of seeing the world and how it should be studied, and that this view is shared by a group of scientists who live in a community marked by a common conceptual language, who seek to build upon a shared conceptual edifice and who are possessed of a very defensive political posture to outsiders.

Social scientists alighted on the Kuhnian approach with great enthusiasm in the late

1960s and early 1970s and began to see their own disciplines in this 'paradigmatic' way (Friedrichs 1970; Ritzer 1975). This fitted in well with the notion of a crisis in post-war social science and the possibility of a new, indeed revolutionary, science overthrowing the old ideas developed by the ageing yet still powerful figures who dominated their fields. Kuhnianism, in many of its forms, appealed to the young.

The ways in which 'paradigm' as a term came into organizational analysis were various, but the book published in 1979 by Burrell and Morgan articulated the procrustean approach to stabilizing the field in a somewhat extreme form. And it is probable that its extremism in fixing and stabilizing the subject matter of organization theory explains some of its impact. They identified four 'paradigms' which were necessarily formed by the adoption of a position with regard to two key conceptual dimensions. Given that sociology and organization theory are uncontentiously parts of social science, they argued, any statement that is made in these areas of a theoretical nature has to make assumptions about both the nature of society and the nature of science. If it does not do this, either unconsciously or consciously, then it is not making a social scientific statement. Burrell and Morgan attempted to identify the nature of these assumptions on two axes which when placed at right angles create four 'mutually exclusive' paradigms. This mapping, for such it is, is presented as Figures 1 and 2.

As soon as the book appeared, it was subjected to a sustained critique, much of it focusing on the impossibility of forcing both social theory and organization theory into four static categories. Whilst the term 'procrustean bed' was not widely utilized in the critique, many commentators objected to the forced over-simplifications of the schema. Clegg (1982), for example, said that this fixing of complexity by using a 2×2 matrix was typical of functional approaches to the subject matter and, whilst the book claimed to be able to identify and encourage alternatives to functionalism, it had fallen into the self-same trap of conservatism. Much attention was paid to the concept of paradigm itself and the ways in which it diverged from the 'view' (sic) that Kuhn had of the term. The component dimensions of the subjective–objective dichotomy, as outlined in Figure 2, were also attacked as was the supposed misuse of the term 'ontology'. What critics found most disturbing, however, was the notion of paradigm incommensurability to which Burrell and Morgan had clung so tenaciously. Here the idea that paradigm could not speak unto paradigm was taken so far as to suggest that the concepts and terms and methods of one

paradigm were not translatable into those used by another paradigm. The absence of translation rules was presumed by Burrell and Morgan to lead to the mutual exclusivity of paradigms. They argued that since the meta-theoretical assumptions of the paradigms differed there could be no translation rules which would be totally effective. The commentators, however, argued in favour of the possibility of some translation being available and in this assertion, as we have seen, there is certainly some support from Kuhn himself in his later publications.

What Burrell and Morgan's book may have succeeded in doing was to highlight the breakdown of the field of organization theory into warring encampments and to demonstrate that functionalist approaches, whilst popular, politically superior and common, were by no means the only possible avenues open to organizational analysis. The text articulated and legitimated to some extent the voices of those who did not share the functionalist orientation. Notice here that the argument within *Sociological Paradigms and Organizational Analysis* is not that functionalism is representative of a normal science in our discipline and that it will be replaced eventually and inevitably by another single approach after a period of revolution (à la Kuhn). Rather it is argued that the normal state of organizational science is pluralistic. This does not mean that organizational analysis is 'immature' or is awaiting its normal science phase with bated breath. It is simply that a plurality of legitimate and competing perspectives is to be expected in all sciences but especially in the social ones.

Despite the criticisms levelled against Burrell and Morgan and despite some pressure from the publishers, the authors did not produce a second edition. They had seen the way in which writers modify their work in response to criticism and the tendency for this type of modification to resemble a watering down of radical arguments. They eschewed the opportunity to respond to the critics for this simple if dubious reason of maintaining 'purity'.

The present author dares to believe that the book stands as a piece written at a time when functionalism was in decline but the legitimacy of alternative perspectives was still in doubt. It provided the means for some organization analysts to embrace other frames of reference and not worry too much about the orthodoxy. However, the legitimacy of the other paradigms today is by no means assured. If one looks at radical structuralism, for example, then its vitality and some might even say its viability have certainly been thrown into doubt since the late 1980s. On the other hand, the functionalist orthodoxy – which is not the same thing at all as normal science – remains very well entrenched.

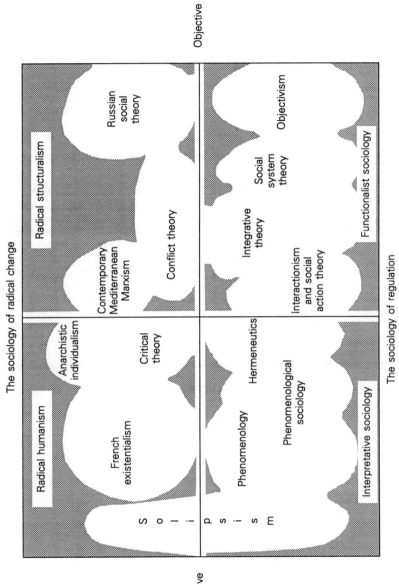

Figure 1   *The four sociological paradigms*

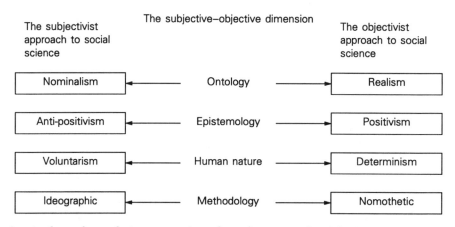

Figure 2   *A scheme for analysing assumptions about the nature of social science*

As we have already seen, the dimension which really irritates the functionalists in the area most especially, but also tends to concern all those who believe in the values of debate, argument and compromise, is the notion of incommensurability. For it hits at the very core of the widely held belief in rational academic debate and discourse. What the proponents of the thesis of paradigm commensurability fail to understand is that one of the few lessons of history, in things epistemological, is that despite the best endeavours of many able minds the dream of translation remains just that. One does not have to fully embrace the work, for example, of Hofstede (1991) to believe that culture affects perspectives on organizations, but it is clear to some nevertheless that culture does have consequences, not only making language often difficult to learn but implying that its nuances are rarely if ever to be understood by a nonnative. Wittgenstein said much the same in the famous aphorism 'meaning is use'. Here in that most eloquent yet enigmatic phrase is the assertion that if you don't use a language on a regular basis then you cannot fully understand how it is used by natives.

The problem of the incommensurability of paradigms remains at the very centre of the issue of organizational paradigms. There is one group – the 'paradigm warriors' is the name by which they are sometimes called – who continue to advocate the notion of incommensurability (e.g. Jackson and Carter 1993). For them, the separation of the approaches taken within the paradigm from those without is of crucial importance because what this isolationism (Reed 1985) does is to ensure for the internal membership, in the short term at least, the survival of that approach and, more importantly perhaps, of the ideological standpoint from which it is made. The belief in incommensur-

ability then has its origins in politics as well as in epistemology. The attacks upon 'paradigm warriors' which depend for their force on issues based upon logic, linguistic theory and discourse analysis (e.g. Willmott 1993) fail to recognize this. These criticisms also fail to appreciate that not only is discourse about power but concomitantly power without discourse is much weaker. Dialogue is a weapon of the powerful.

Much of what one reads today about normal science and paradigms is concerned with some Habermasian injunction to engage in speech and to talk through one's problems. Much of what one reads is predicated upon the university culture of debate, argumentation and dialogue. The presentation of ideas is often seen as separate from the intellectual force of one's argument (which partly explains the inability of many scholars to lecture effectively) yet it is very obvious that the latter is heavily dependent upon convincing the audience of the utility of the thought contained in the presentation. It is almost impossible to escape from these conventions, for as I sit here writing this paragraph I am concerned to convince you, the reader, that what I am saying is worth listening to. Universities rely upon the goodwill of those who try to speak (or more often write) to others in convincing terms. Thus the threat to this universal notion of truth was and is too much for some to bear.

A hostile response to the concept of paradigm closure in organization theory has come from Lex Donaldson (1985), whose aptly named text *In Defence of Organization Theory* attempts *inter alia* to refute the arguments contained in *Sociological Paradigms and Organizational Analysis* (Burrell and Morgan 1979). Donaldson argues that structural functionalism has never been in a state of crisis and in fact has been very well able to deal with new theoretical and practical issues when they arise. He maintains that core functionalist concepts are very sound both conceptually and philosophically. He argues for a revamped contingency theory which would carry the field any day in the face of the insubstantial work carried out by the critics of functionalism. The editors of the journal *Organization Studies* devoted a whole issue to the Donaldson piece in 1988 and invited a number of scholars to talk about 'offence or defence' (cf. Hassard 1993: 71). Donaldson's triumphalism at this time was not easy to understand because for many the debate highlighted the existence of paradigms and their potency in explaining different philosophical positions. To Donaldson it showed the opposite. But perhaps this difference is in the nature of paradigm thinking itself!

At about the same time, Reed (1985) also discussed these issues, but by no means from the same position as Donaldson. Nor however should it be assumed that he came close to accepting the arguments for paradigm closure. His book *Redirections in Organizational Analysis* ends with a discussion of what these redirections for the discipline might actually look like. Four possibilities were outlined: integrationism, isolationism, imperialism and pluralism. The first refers to the hope for eclectic reconciliation; the second to the strategy of paradigm separatism; the third to the success of one theoretical position over another; and the fourth to that which Reed personally advocates, which involves the rejection of any one overarching approach and the promulgation of the notion of 'let a thousand flowers bloom'.

In a similar vein, Hassard (1993: 74–5) argues more recently that we now face a crisis.

> The crisis is deepened by the fact that the notion of paradigm heterodoxy is often joined by one of paradigm closure. Writers who specify a range of paradigm candidates often add that these various communities are incommensurable with one another. Professional practice in different traditions is based on philosophies which are antithetical; scientists from different paradigms do not debate, they talk through one another. This is a problem in that paradigm incommensurability seems to infer [*sic*] an extreme form of sociological relativism. If scientists cannot debate how can progress be signalled?

If this has any validity to it as an assertion then we must, perforce, concern ourselves with the recent attempts to engage in the widest debates possible concerning scientific progress. In other words, the widespread retreat from incommensurability needs to be chronicled in some depth. And here the work of Gareth Morgan is central both for his contribution to the discipline and for

the symbolic nature of his work. For we see in his progress the European/North-American tension clearly expressed.

METAPHORS

The notion of metaphor has been around as an analytical device for centuries and is clearly signalled by Vico, for example, to be of considerable importance. Within social science as a whole, a number of writers sought, in the postwar period, to elevate the notion to a high place in the lexicon of devices for understanding that are open to us. However, in organization theory the metaphor approach came to be used primarily because of Morgan's (1988) book *Images of Organization*.

Gareth Morgan has attempted to move organization theory in the direction of more pluralist perspectives and since arriving in North America has gone on to do much to extend the range of approaches more or less acceptable within orthodox organization theory. His doctorate, completed at the University of Lancaster, identified the importance of metaphor as a way of seeing the world within each of the four paradigms identified in Burrell and Morgan (1979). On his move to North America there was a concomitant and very marked shift in his intellectual position. Metaphor become the vehicle through which paradigms become actualized in the minds of the theorist and Morgan sought to identify the dominant ones active within each paradigm. Thus we are presented with a variety of metaphors which inform the analysis of organizations in the 1980s. Morgan's thesis contained a quarter of a million words and within it he pointed out that metaphors are but one of the tropes or figures of speech which we need to recognize. The saliency of synecdoche, metonymy and irony is intriguingly mentioned but the follow-up book to *Images of Organization* on each of these has yet to appear. The book which did appear was a beautifully crafted piece which 'attempts to develop the more practical implications of the basic ideas' (1988: 345). It thus shortens considerably the arguments within the thesis; indeed, many of the major conceptual items are to be found in the footnotes rather than in the body of the text. It might be argued that the impact of this book was greater than that of *Sociological Paradigms and Organizational Analysis* (*SPOA*), for not only was it written in a non-technical way but it opened up the 'paradigm' concept by quite clearly turning its back on incommensurability.

Morgan articulates, in the final sections of the text, an integrating metaphor of binocular vision whereby, it is argued, two metaphors taken together can provide a better picture of the reality under investigation than a single metaphor. In the same way as two eyes are superior to one, then two metaphors are better than a single one. But how metaphors can be processed by the equivalent of the visual regions of the brain is left unexplored. The assumption is made – rather than defended – that metaphors are not incompatible. On the contrary they can supposedly be synthesized into a superior binocular vision.

The other implicit metaphor which underpins the book is typical of the mid 1980s. It is that of the *supermarket* of ideas. It is clear that incommensurability is no longer central to Morgan's ideas because within organization studies, metaphors can be picked off the supermarket shelf at will. Of course they bring with them all kinds of assumptions but these are merely part of the product. Had Burrell and Morgan used the same metaphor in 1979 then the equivalent position within *SPOA* would have been that whole sections of the hypermarket were out of bounds to shoppers by dint of the shoppers' refusal to enter areas where there was nothing of interest to them. The meat, baby food, pet food and alcohol sections would all have been ignored by paradigm equivalents of vegetarians, the childless and so on. But when writing by himself for an American audience, Morgan told readers of *Images of Organization* that, if they so wished, nothing was out of bounds and they could roam at will in the market for and of ideas. They were welcomed as consumers. Whilst incommensurability within *SPOA* had meant that the message there and at that time was entirely different, for functionalists were told that they could not get their acquisitive hands on genuine 'green' products in that textual hypermarket, in *Images of Organization* the store was thrown open to them to plunder and pillage as they saw fit. They were licensed by the book to roam in stereotypical North American tourist fashion. Once again, the search for a good deal suppressed any concerns that translation from domestic to overseas languages would not be possible. Nothing could be kept from 'the tourist gaze' (Urry 1990).

This opening up of ideas, the powerful and persuasive way in which the book was written, and the distancing within the book from the segregating limitations of *SPOA*, had a tremendous impact. Of course, critics pointed out that metaphors are also static concepts and that the development of new ones (stolen often from the natural sciences which in turn take their ideas from classical literature, e.g. chaos) does little to escape from the presupposition that they are ways of organizing, capturing and fixing

thought. There is clear evidence, too, of the importance of Stephen Pepper's (1948) work on world hypotheses for Morgan at this stage, for Pepper's influence is much more obvious than that of Thomas Kuhn. Of course, we should not underestimate the sophistication of the way in which the ideas are expressed in the text, for Morgan demonstrates his erudition in the literature very clearly. Many courses were and still are taught using this framework, and the wealth of examples contained within it and their intrinsic interest for our discipline make *Images of Organization* a very important book for the 1980s. Just as Morgan hoped, its influence in teaching has been considerable, for the text and the notion of metaphors generally has become a key organizing principle for many courses.

MEANWHILE, BACK IN EUROPE

The development of Morgan's position was carefully watched by his ex-colleagues in Lancaster where there was a ready willingness to attribute his obvious intellectual movement to cultural and institutional pressures. Talk at this time, in the very early 1980s, was of the impending and longed-for demise of the Thatcher government and, less certainly, of the work of the French philosopher Michel Foucault. We had been introduced to his ideas, originally in the form of the book *Discipline and Punish* (1977), by Bob Cooper. My personal reaction to reading that text was akin to confronting a major *Gestalt* shift in which the patterning of the world became seen through new and improved lenses. For Morgan the future was binoculars: in Lancaster it was panopticons, something made apparent in 1984, when a piece written on Foucault's contribution to organizational analysis was submitted to *ASQ*. I treasure its referees' comments to this day, for all three questioned the relevance of 'an unknown French philosopher' and asked 'what could an American audience learn' from such thought. My understanding of the importance of the North Atlantic Ocean as a divide as well as a communication route was firmly fixed at this moment. Yet it is perhaps a relevant question which the next section will attempt to answer.

FOUCAULT'S PENDULUM

Although this raises important issues about the relevance of authors in comprehending their own work, it is arguable that the corpus of Foucault's work can only be fully understood in terms of the personal and intellectual context in which he found himself. The centrality of the human body to his writings and the notion of pleasure – and of pain – appear to place him at some distance from the study of organizations. In *Discipline and Punish*, however, he specifically addresses the issue of contingency and organizational goals when he claims that all organizations resemble prisons. Thus the themes of the body, power and pleasure in organized and well disciplined contexts are ones which illuminate the study of organizations with an intensity of perspicacity. He had much distaste for classificatory schemata and attempted to avoid being labelled himself. Yet, of course, he is vulnerable to such devices.

Foucault, it is authoritatively said, was one of the first French citizens to die of AIDS. His untimely death in 1984 did nothing to stem the burgeoning interest in his articulation of his intellectual approaches. Note that the plural term has to be used here, for it is clear that Foucault's hatred of being labelled, boxed in and categorized affected his own body and his own body of work. He sought to evade fixed terms as best he could and changed his own intellectual position constantly. His movement from what are called the 'archaeological' to the 'genealogical' orientations will be discussed a little later, but it must be recognized that we, ourselves, are fixing in time and space, within a relatively crude classification, ideas from an intellectual of considerable stature that are essentially dynamic. This makes his work uncannily difficult for Anglophone audiences to fully appreciate, for it transgresses many of our assumptions. Yet his work is directly relevant to organization studies for he concentrates, in his later work particularly, on issues in which our discipline is traditionally interested. At first sight, however, such are the difficulties in comprehending his ideas that their relevance for all of social science and not just organization theory needs careful articulation. To do so requires more space than is available here, so the reader is referred to Dreyfus and Rabinow's (1982) lucid text on Foucault's work. Certain key points, nevertheless, need some attention here.

Archaeology and Discourse

Whilst the metaphor of the careful uncovering of history and historical artefacts has influenced many social scientists with the appeal of its sedimentary imagery, Foucault does not, in his early work, adopt a crude structuralism in his discussion of archaeology. For him, discourse analysis is that method which 'the archaeologist' performs upon the past, seeing within history the precise codes of knowledge which have lain there awaiting our discovery. Any archaeologists of knowledge must distantiate themselves from the past and seek to be objective, but they realize very quickly and very clearly that our present period itself contains discourses. Our codes of understanding today are therefore discourses too, subject to the same rules of articulation as those located in the past. Our contemporary discourses are subject to the same inflexibilities and problems as any theories emanating from the Middle Ages. Discourse is put as far away from its social setting as possible in this early work of Foucault and, acting as the archaeologist, he attempts to discover the rules which govern its own self-regulation. To do this, he enlisted the help of a rather short-lived notion – that of the 'episteme'. The episteme unites the set of discursive practices which exist at any one time so that in any given epoch one will find that a particular episteme predominates. Modernity then becomes characterized by the episteme, put crudely and genderly, in which Man invents himself. This episteme required a catastrophic upheaval, an 'archaeological mutation', which signalled that the Classical Age had come to an end before it could struggle into existence itself. Since it first struggled for life it has succeeded in coming to dominate the epoch.

In his book *The Archaeology of Knowledge* (1972), Foucault takes his method to new-found depths of analysis. In the text he is interested in 'serious speech acts', mindful that the context in which this sort of discursive practice takes place is crucial for understanding profound differences in meaning. Ludwig Wittgenstein had obviously noted this tendency too and this interpretation had an important effect upon Thomas Kuhn. But Foucault is relatively silent on the whole issue of paradigms as 'language games'. Dreyfus and Rabinow (1982: 60) conclude that this silence is because he misunderstood the notion and its Kuhnian intent. The silence may also have been a result of his unwillingness to confront ideas from outside a particular realm of his *own* discourse. He was to say later in life that he had not read Habermas's work on discourse when this, too, would seem to have been a useful exercise. Certainly, he was not ignorant of the existence of such literature.

But what of the relevance of the archaeological method to organization studies? Before we attempt to show this, perhaps it would be helpful to also consider Foucault's work on genealogy.

Genealogy

Once he had dispensed with the archaeological method, Foucault turned to genealogy. Dreyfus and Rabinow (1982: 106) ask, rhetorically, 'what is genealogy?' The answer, they say, is

> genealogy opposes itself to traditional historical method: its aim is to 'record the singularity of events outside of any monotonous finality'. . . . For the genealogist there are no fixed essences, no underlying laws, no metaphysical finalities. Genealogy seeks out discontinuities where others have found continuous development. It finds recurrences and play where others found progress and seriousness. It records the past of mankind to unmask the solemn hymns of progress. Genealogy avoids the search for depth. Instead it seeks the surfaces of events, small details, minor shifts and subtle contours.

Thus the search for the modernist goals of hidden meaning, for truth, for the meanings of the unconscious rests on a failure to recognize that these are shams. Foucault says that we should shun these sorts of activities for there are no essences which we can uncover. Thus, Plato is the archenemy to the genealogist, whereas, of course, Nietzsche is the central, heroic figure. The foundations of morality are to be found not in ideal truth but in *pudenda origo* with their lowly origins. History is about lies not truth. It is about a struggle for domination acted out in a play of wills. But there is no one who is responsible for the emergence of any event; for the genealogist there is no individual or any collectivity who can move history. For we all live in the interstice created by this play of dominations. And all that we see is all that there is.

This is important for it firmly suggests that the relativism of human conceptualizations of truth, beauty and virtue needs to be recognized. These are ever changing notions and are not located in something essential. Even the human body is not to be understood as something with an essence which has stood the test of time over millennia. Just the opposite. It is a notion which has undergone many changes. And the human body was to be one of Foucault's major concerns. In *Discipline and Punish* (1977), Foucault reversed the priority of archaeology to genealogy by privileging the latter. The genealogist is portrayed as a diagnostician who concentrates on the relationship between power, knowledge and the body. At this point, Foucault turns organization theory around by focusing on the body as the locale where minute social practices meet the large scale organization of power. The organization of the body and its pleasure become a prime area for theoretical and practical debate. Whilst not taking Merleau-Ponty's notion of *le corps propre* – the lived body as opposed to the physical body – to heart, Foucault does explore the way in which

> the body is also directly involved in a political field. . . . Power relations have an immediate hold upon it; they invest it, mark it, train it, torture it, force it to carry out tasks, to perform ceremonies, to emit signs. (1977: 25)

This wonderful passage prefigures his interest in the political technology of the body which, it is claimed, has the greatest significance for Western society (Shilling 1993: 75–82). But we should not assume that this analysis suggests that it is *the state* which is the key to understanding power-knowledge and the body. In fact, Foucault does not believe that the state plays a major role in this at all. Rather it is in institutions, like prisons, asylums, schools, factories and barracks, that one finds the loci of power. The metaphor of the prison is central here for all these types of institutions are claimed to be imprisoning, and in a famous section of *Discipline and Punish* Foucault articulates the importance of Bentham's Panopticon as marking the search for the 'ultimate managerial tool'. Here the bodies of inmates are subject to the disciplinary technologies of close surveillance, the gaze and the process of 'normalization'. What Foucault does is to open up the analysis of organizations to new notions in which the body plays a central role as a target for a plethora of disciplinary technologies located within organizational forms which all bear an uncanny resemblance to prisons. Power comes from the knowledge of the body which develops in the minds and comes into the hands of 'the judges of normality'. These are organizationally based professionals who are key parts of the 'somatic society' (Turner 1992: 12).

Foucault and Organizational Analysis

Whilst the concern for metaphors drove the teaching of courses in many programmes, the Foucaldian legacy – for by 1984, after his death, this is all we had – drove considerable amounts of research (for example, Hollway 1991; Townley 1994; Rose 1990). Of course, it would be foolish to say that many academics embraced this particular French philosopher with any relish, for his work, as we have said, is difficult to pin down and is theoretically challenging. Yet within organization studies, attempts have been made to elevate surveillance to a primary focus of attention and, almost weekly, new analyses of panopticism appear which show the relevance of Foucault to the mid 1990s through his concentration on power-knowledge. Yet archaeological and genealogical methods are not in much favour in many areas of the discipline.

Table 1 *Two analytical approaches found in Foucault's writings*

The same	and	The different
The archaeological method Uncover those rules which regulate and govern social practices, and which are unknown to the actors involved		*The genealogical method* Record the singularity of surface events, looking at the meaning of small details, minor shifts and subtle contours
It is possible to achieve some partial distancing from these institutional bonds by a bracketing of 'accepted truth'		There are no fixed essences or underlying laws. There is discontinuity and arbitrariness. Since the world is as it appears, one seeks out the 'superficial secrets'
Act as an 'excavator', revealing depth and interiority		Act as a recorder of accidents, chance and lies. Oppose the search for depth and interiority

Warner's (1994) recent review of organizational behaviour pays no attention to his work whatsoever.

Table 1 attempts to place these two very different approaches developed by Foucault alongside each other. What this oversimplification does is to show that the genealogical approach is much more in tune with postmodernism whereas, perhaps, the archaeological method stands much more in tune with modernism. Foucault turned his back on discourse analysis, saying that: 'I confused it too much with systematicity, the theoretical form, or something like a paradigm'. Genealogy stands much more happily with postmodernism, we might therefore argue. For us to label his later work as 'postmodern' would be fair perhaps but we must note that he explicitly rejected this epithet, preferring instead to claim that any classification scheme, any labelling device was itself part of a field of power-knowledge in which the speaker as well as the one spoken about became subject to disciplining. This is why he is difficult to classify as a thinker because almost any work that he did was self-consciously opposed to the piece which preceded it. Movement allowed the evasion of capture.

The whole issue of the links between postmodernism and organizational analysis will be picked up in a later section, but first we must, albeit all too briefly, consider the work of Jacques Derrida whose contribution to social science in this period was also of considerable import. Derrida is only one of a number of French writers in the last fifteen years who have attempted to shift social theory away from the certainties of the 1960s. The reasons for this concentration in France of intellectuals sympathetic to the embraces of postmodernism cannot be addressed here, but the Anglophone derision for 'Parisian fashions' is very indicative of a hostility to theorizing and a concern to protect naive empiricism from the depredations of the

slavering theoretician. Derrida is chosen here merely to symbolize this type of work. He is a cipher for a movement which we watch from afar. For him, social life is made up of texts which are constantly read in very different ways so that our understandings are continually being broken down and reassembled. Just as Foucault seeks to avoid imprisonment for his ideas, Derrida argues that at least a *double* reading of any text is possible. Fixity is no longer tenable.

Derrida's notion of deconstructionism has proved to be a powerful stimulus to postmodern forms of thought. It asserts a rather different way of thinking about and 'reading' texts. Whilst under modernism it was believed that the medium and the message were tightly interconnected, Derrida sees these as 'continually breaking apart and reattaching in new combinations'. Texts are the way in which writers and readers come to understand the world and each new level of understanding produces new texts which are added to the textual weave. Intertextual weaving comes to have a life of its own for we write things of which we know naught and our words cannot convey what we mean. Language works through us, not the other way round. So, for the deconstructionist, one text dissolves into another, one text is located within another, one text is built upon another. Thus the objective of deconstructionism is to break the power of the author to claim the primacy of a particular narrative or to impose meanings upon the reader. All fixed systems of representation become seen as merely illusory and as capable of at least a *double* reading (Cooper 1989: 492–501).

The key form of discourse in postmodernism is the collage or montage. The inherent heterogeneity of this form of cultural work means that both producers and consumers of the artefact participate in its meaning generation. This is profoundly democratic, based as it is upon popular conceptualizations of the product within the audience, but of course the very in-coherence of many conceptualizations does allow for mass-market manipulation. The montage is vulnerable to recombinatory meanings which are never fixed and never stable but often they may well be exploitative and imprisoning.

POSTMODERNISM AND ORGANIZATIONAL ANALYSIS

Those certainties of the post World War II world which supposedly confronted the organization theorists of the 1960s relied for much of their solid existence upon a belief in the pillars of modernism. Science and technology were seen as determinate of a future which, since it grew directly from what was in front of our eyes, was knowable for those observers located in the present. Time was linear and tomorrow was likely to be better than today. Bureaucracy, rationality and effectiveness were unquestioned as the elements upon which organizations relied for their legitimacy. Contingencies were merely those elements which interfered with the operation of well tried and tested principles of organization design and functioning. Contingency 'theory', a misnomer perhaps, articulated in good practical and relevant terms the questions of 'how' to organize. At this time, although the evidence was clearer then than it is today, few saw the defining organizational form of the whole twentieth century to be the death camps of Auschwitz.

Modernism is about the death camps in a fairly uncontentious way even though its apologists seek to distance the likes of Auschwitz from the achievements of the modernist society, based as it is supposedly upon critical enquiry and the pursuit of truth. Ritzer's (1993) book *The McDonaldization of Society* shows how the high achievements of modernity such as the Big Mac are still heavily redolent of the mechanized death of large numbers of creatures; in this case, cattle. But we also know that French soldiers in World War I went to almost certain death at the front, baaing like sheep; we know that the trains into Auschwitz were made up of cattle trucks; and we know that the efficiencies of the Ford motor plants relied heavily upon lessons learnt and technology drawn from the abattoirs of Chicago. The attainments of the organized world of modernism are, in fact, built upon the flesh and bones of the dead and the methods of their speedy and cheap execution.

This may offend those who wish to speak only of the achievements of modern society. Yet if we forget that alongside this fashionable and sanitized view lies a much darker picture – a vision of death, pain and torture – then we lose some of the sense of emnity to modernism that the postmodernists have sought to engender.

Now this is not to say that Foucault or Derrida have written at length on the limitations of modernism, but there is clear implication in their epistemologies that the old certainties have gone. 'All that is solid melts into air' may well be a refrain with which they would have an affinity. The *fin de siècle* has brought with it the usual concerns for the century whose end we are witnessing.

FIN DE SIÈCLE POSTMODERNISM AND THE FUTURE

The end of each century brings with it two zeros on the number of the year. Only this century brings in a new millennium with the requisite three zeros. The cabbalistic significance of this is clear to almost all of us, for a new millennium will surely bring new modes of thinking. Each end of a century allows us to look back at the accomplishments and failings of the previous one hundred years. Every *fin de siècle* brings with it disappointment and relief for the passing of that era. If we look to the last years of the nineteenth century we see that modernism and the modern world were just appearing (Mestrovic 1993). The large organizations of the robber barons were gaining a foothold and there was talk in New York, Paris, London and St Petersburg of a moral crisis in which the old values were being challenged by the breakdown in the normative structure of the society. This breakdown was linked in the minds of most commentators to the vast economic restructuring which was taking place in many parts of the globe.

Today, globalization is talked about and even analysed but there is also a cabbalistic sense (*à la* Nostrodamus) of the breakdown of the old order. The nation-state, the bureaucratic organization, the scientific method, the natural world are all concepts which are under threat after a century of superiority. 'Superiority' of course does not mean that these notions have not always been contested. It is more important for us to recognize that it is the fact that they are questioned widely by the powerful (rather than by groups of intellectuals) which makes for the significance of the questioning of these core values. But the powerful do seek narratives which the populace will buy into, in ways which explain their own subordinate role and that of their 'superiors'. The dominant ideology is meant for general consumption (Abercrombie et al. 1983).

So the concepts which have been elaborated in this piece do not fit in well with the needs of the dominant ideology. Paradigms rather than a paradigm, metaphors rather than a complete narrative, discourse rather than a shared language, genealogy rather than the historical method, deconstruction rather than the authority of an author, all that is solid melts into air rather than one-minute management. All of these suggest that we should be uncertain. All of these suggest that knowledge is politicized. All of these suggest that our understandings are limited by our conceptualizations and metatheory.

If the 1960s concerned theorizing and its practical utility then we might understand why so few courses in management education today manage to escape from the literature of this golden age of certainty. The literature of this period – the so-called classics – is precisely classical because that age in which it flowered has gone. Today we are much more circumspect about what, if anything, we know. Then, in principle all was knowable. 'Would that it were again' is the heartfelt plea of many a contemporary organization theorist.

However, the *fin de siècle* has created new uncertainties for us. Beware of chaos theory and catastrophe theory for they tell us that it is possible to understand major changes by using mathematics, so they are by no means symptomatic of the forces for uncertainty. In fact these theories, despite their titles, are the last vestiges of modernity. That chaotic and catastrophic changes are in principle understandable would have been the everyday view of the heroic figures in 1960s organization theory. No, the uncertainties in our theories are to do with the failure of science to sell its narrative of being a form of knowledge superior to all others in delivering the goods. As a cargo cult of the twentieth century it was remarkably successful but new narratives and new epistemologies now seem more necessary than ever.

For science seems to have run out of steam. What do we put in its place? Poetry, literature, art? Can these deliver the goods? Well, of course, whatever *these* forms of knowledge produce, it is unlikely to look the same as the performativity conscious (Lyotard 1983) artefacts of the twentieth century. In the classic tension between the *Geisteswissenschaften* and the *Naturwissenschaften*, surely it is not simply a matter of one achieving re-ascendancy over the other? Of course it is not that simple. But in that antinomy there is an exceptionally good place to attempt to build organization theory for the new millennium. It is deep within *premodernity*, where we will also find a good time at which to begin an innovative approach to the future of our discipline.

For example, if we were to look to the body and the way in which it has been conceptualised since medieval times we would see the 'anatomizing urge' being developed. The body, seen as being made up of organs, becomes the dominant metaphor for arranging how those tasks of administration might be carried out – that is to say, organized. Thus we are reliant upon the wounding imperative of the surgeon's knife for the incisiveness of our thought. We anatomize constantly and ask our students in their apprenticeship to do the same to case studies, situations and texts. The cutting edge is the place to be. Whilst one can only point to the significance of the anatomical urge, if one was to spend some time looking at Foucault, Derrida and some other social theorists one would find that they are highly resistant to the notion of incision and surgical separation. What remains for organization theory is the task of theorizing the body in such a way as to allow anatomization and yet encourage the understanding of visceral morphological flows. Organization theory in the next century may well attempt to 'shape shift' itself through understanding the premodern concept of the body before it became subject to organizing anatomy, through articulating a way forward from the simple dichotomies of the discipline which rely upon the oblique slash (/) to separate the indivisible, and through embracing the fluidity, flows and liquidity of the human body as being relevant to how we organize. In doing so, much that is new to us can be learned from Foucault and from Derrida. Unifying the body and *différance* may well be one way forward which reunites us in a common cause. This may not be the building of the Tower but it might be a premodern start for these postmodern times.

REFERENCES

Abercrombie, N., Hill, S. and Turner, B.S. (1983) *The Dominant Ideology Thesis*. London: Routledge.

Burrell, G. and Morgan, G. (1979) *Sociological Paradigms and Organizational Analysis*. London: Heinemann.

Clegg, S. (1982) 'Review of Burrell and Morgan (1979)', *Organization Studies*, 3(4).

Cooper, R. (1989) 'Modernism, postmodernism and organizational analysis: the contribution of Jacques Derrida', *Organization Studies*, 10(4): 479–602.

Cooper, R. and Burrell, G. (1988) 'Modernism, postmodernism and organizational analysis: an introduction', *Organization Studies*, 10(4): 479–502.

Donaldson, L. (1985) *In Defence of Organization Theory*. Cambridge: Cambridge University Press.

Dreyfus, Hubert and Rabinow, P. (1982) *Michel Foucault: beyond Structuralism and Hermeneutics*. Brighton: Harvester.

Foucault, M. (1972) *The Archaeology of Knowledge.* London: Tavistock.

Foucault, M. (1977) *Discipline and Punish.* Harmondsworth: Penguin.

Friedrichs, R. (1970) *A Sociology of Sociology.* Free Press.

Gioia, D. and Pitre, E. (1993) 'Paradigms lost', *Organization Studies.*

Hassard, J. (1993) *Sociology and Organization Theory.* Cambridge: Cambridge University Press.

Hofstede, G. (1991) *Cultures and Organizations.* Maidenhead: McGraw-Hill.

Hollway, W. (1991) *Work Psychology and Organizational Behaviour.* London: Sage.

Hoskin, K. and MacVe, R. (1986) 'Accounting and the examination', *Accounting, Organizations and Society,* 105–36.

Jackson, N. and Carter, P. (1993) 'Paradigm wars': a response to Hugh Willmott', *Organizational Studies,* 14(5): 727–30.

Kuhn, T.S. (1962) *The Structure of Scientific Revolutions.* Chicago: University of Chicago Press.

Kuhn, T.S. (1970) *The Structure of Scientific Revolutions,* 2nd edn. Chicago: University of Chicago Press.

Latour, B. (1982) *Science in Action.* Milton Keynes: Open University Press.

Lyotard, J.P. (1983) *The Postmodern Condition.* Manchester: Manchester University Press.

Masterman, H. (1970) 'The nature of a paradigm', in I. Lakatos and A. Musgrave (eds), *Criticism and the Growth of Knowledge.* Cambridge: Cambridge University Press. pp. 59–89.

Mestrovic, S. (1993) *The Coming Fin de Siècle.* London: Routledge.

Morgan, G. (1988) *Images of Organization.* London: Sage.

Mouzelis, N. (1975) *Organisation and Bureaucracy,* 2nd edn. London: Routledge.

Pfeffer, J. (1993) 'Barriers to the advance of organizational science: paradigm development as a dependent variable', *Academy of Management Review,* 18(4): 599–620.

Ray, L. and Reed, M. (eds) (1994) *Organizing Modernity.* London: Routledge.

Reed, M. (1985) *Redirections in Organizational Analysis.* London: Tavistock.

Ritzer, G. (1975) *Sociology: a Multiple Paradigm Science.* Allyn & Bacon.

Ritzer, G. (1993) *The McDonaldization of Society.* Newbury Park: Pine Forge.

Rose, N. (1990) *Governing the Soul: the Shaping of the Private Self.* London: Routledge.

Sankey, H. (1993) 'Kuhn's changing concept of incommensurability', *British Journal of the Philosophy of Science,* 44: 759–74.

Shilling, C. (1993) *The Body and Social Theory.* London: Sage.

Steiner, G. (1975) *After Babel: Aspects of Language and Translation.*

Townley, B. (1994) *Reframing Human Resource Management.* London: Sage.

Turner, B. (1992) *Regulating Bodies.* London: Routledge.

Urry, J. (1990) *The Tourist Gaze.* Cambridge: Polity Press.

Warner, M. (1994) 'Organizational behaviour revisited', *Human Relations,* 47(10): 1151–66.

Willmott, H. (1993) 'Paradigm gridlock: a reply', *Organization Studies,* 14(5): 727–30.

Zwicky, J. (1992) *Lyric Philosophy.* Toronto: University of Toronto Press.

3.9

The Owl of Minerva: Reflections on Theory in Practice

RICHARD MARSDEN AND BARBARA TOWNLEY

The relationship between 'theory' and 'practice' is perhaps the most central issue of the whole *Handbook*. It raises many questions: 'Why do we have an area of work devoted to organization studies?', 'What is it for?', 'What does it do?', 'Whom does it address?', and 'How does it relate to what people ordinarily do at work in organizations?' These are difficult questions, especially since the *Handbook* aims to address a diverse, global audience, and it is as well that they are left until the end of this book.

Let us begin with the common-sense understanding of theory and practice. Although it has long been surpassed by developments in the philosophy of social science, most lay people (and not a few organizational analysts) subscribe to this view and, for this reason alone, it must be taken seriously. According to this view, 'theory' refers to the world of thought and reflection, while 'practice' refers to the world of action, of doing things. Theory and practice are construed as distinct. The second is typically considered more real and is usually the arbiter of the first: 'That may be OK in theory, but how would it work in practice?' Theory is construed pejoratively as impractical, unrealistic or 'academic'. Practice is construed as the antithesis of theory, as atheoretical. Practitioners often pride themselves on their immunity from theory and some academics pride themselves on their distance from the practical world.

This philosophically naive view has long been demolished, of course, by philosophers of social science, who have demonstrated conclusively that the most innocent observation of what is 'out there' is conceptually mediated by the ideas in our head (Keat and Urry 1975; Sayer 1992).

Everyone, not just academics, theorizes about the causes and consequences of the social world and acts on this basis. Most practices operationalize some theory, however implicit, vague and contradictory it may be. Indeed, 'practice' is a theoretical construct and theorizing itself is a practice. But if the common-sense understanding of theory and practice is wrong, the nature of the alternative is much less certain. In this case, what is the relationship between the theorizing of academics and the practice of those constituting organizations? Before exploring this question, we must make some preliminary points.

Clearly, there is a variety of organizational practices. While the management of work is normally the focus of organization theory, this has recently been broadened to include the practices that constitute and organize sexuality (Burrell 1984; Hearn and Parkin 1987; Hearn et al. 1989), gender (Mills and Tancred-Sheriff 1992), emotion (Rafaeli and Sutton 1989; Mumby and Putnam 1992; Fineman 1993), pleasure (Burrell 1992), war and famine (Jones 1994), and time and space (Harvey 1989). Evidently, there is considerable disagreement over what 'organization' is and how it can and should be studied and acted upon.

Although we tend to speak of the generic 'organization theory', just as there is no one organizational practice so there is an assortment of theories that draw attention to some things and shadow others. 'The zoological garden of organizational theorists is crowded with a bewildering variety of specimens,' says Perrow (1980: 259), 'we are not even looking at the same beast.' Organization is a crystal viewed through a kaleidoscope of theories.

Just as there is a variety of practices and theories, so there is a variety of conceptions of practice and theory. Organization studies participates in the debate over what exists 'out there' (practice or ontology) and how it can be known (theory or epistemology) and the nature of their interrelationship (Keat and Urry 1975). Are organizations objective, tangible, empirical things or are they more elusive, intersubjective constructs? Similarly, is theory a framework for organizing observation, a synonym for hypothesis or explanation, or is it a conceptualized real object (Sayer 1992)?

For these reasons, 'organization', 'theory', and 'practice' are among the most contested concepts in the human and social sciences. So what? Who cares? Why does it matter?

Organization theory matters because it not only reflects the practice of organization, in ways we shall explain, but also helps constitute that practice. One of the ways it does this is by favouring the practices of some groups over others. Organization theory is essentially a theory of, and mostly for, management; it has much less to say of and for those who are managed. The conflict over theories of organization matters, then, because it is a contest over the future shaping of organizations and the tangible lives of those who comprise them. This politics of organizations is reflected in the academic politics of theory. As Wolin puts it: 'Theories are not like explorations where a flag is planted for the first time. They are, in the revealing language frequently employed, "attacks" upon another theory. They contest ground that is already held and so they must not only establish their own legitimacy but delegitimate the prevailing theory and its practitioners' (1981: 402). Within organization studies, the most notable legitimation struggle is between advocates and opponents of a positivist organization theory, between 'normal' and 'contra' organization science (Donaldson 1985; 1988; Hinings 1988; Clegg 1988; Marsden 1993a).

Superimposed on the normal versus contra organization science debate is a pervasive belief that modes of organizing and modes of knowing are fundamentally changing. The object before us ('organization') may be a moving target and our analytical tools of understanding ('theory') may need reformulating. This is the modernism versus postmodernism controversy. This is no academic debate. The belief that the past is no longer an adequate guide to the future is the central message of some influential prescriptions for today's managers: Peters's *Liberation Management* (1992), Senge's *The Fifth Discipline* (1990), Hammer and Champy's *Reengineering the Corporation* (1993) and Osborne and Gaebler's *Reinventing Government* (1993).

Hammer and Champy tell us: 'Adam Smith's world and its ways of doing business are yesterday's paradigm' (1993: 17, 47). Tradition, apparently, counts for nothing. Osborne and Gaebler lament: 'we're struggling to figure out a new way . . . so far there is no theory guiding it. People don't have a real clear idea of why past practices aren't working or what a new model might be. So they can't learn from success or failure; there's no theoretical framework people can use to integrate their experiences' (1993: 321). These books reflect a belief that there is a fundamental transformation going on in organizational practices and the way in which they are managed, and urge managers to break with the past. We must begin again, afresh, anew. What does this tell us of the relationship between organization theory and practice? Do these books herald the dissolution of the modern organizational form, Weber's bureaucratic organization, and the creation of the postmodern organization?

If the owl of Minerva flies only at dusk, perhaps the apparent twilight of modernity can illuminate our understanding of the past and, on this basis, we can better assess the claim that it is no longer an accurate guide to the future. To this end, we begin by reevaluating the work of two of modernity's most powerful analysts, Marx and Weber, for organization studies has developed within and against their legacy. This development has been shaped by disagreements over the question: can organizations be studied in the same way as nature (Donaldson 1985)? For this reason, we build on this account of Marx and Weber by describing the development of first normal and then contra organization science and consider their practical implications. We conclude that rather than choose between normal and contra organization science, it is more productive to investigate the nature of the object *over* which they disagree.

BACK TO THE FUTURE: MARX, WEBER AND ORGANIZATION

The normal science of organization needs little introduction. It builds on the belief that organizations are hard, empirical things capable of being studied using scientific techniques (Donaldson 1985). Normal science typically presents a teleological history of its own conceptual formation and leaves the impression that things could not possibly be other than they are (Kuhn 1970). The origins of organization studies are normally traced to Weber, who is construed as an advocate of the modern bureaucratic corporation as a model of capitalist efficiency. He is equally well known as a critic of Marx. Weber's work was coopted, within American sociology, in the Cold War against the Soviet Union and it became taken for granted, since so few read their work, that Weber and Marx are antithetical and that Marx has little to say on 'organization': 'Marx not only left no theory of organization, he left little room for one to develop' (Clegg and Higgins 1987: 209). The collapse of the Soviet Union, and its satellite states, seemed to reinforce the popular belief that 'Marxism is Wrong, and Thankfully, Dead' (Buss 1993) and to legitimate the evangelical fervour with which the market is celebrated during the current intensification of the globalization of capital (Peck and Richardson 1991). There is no alternative, it would seem. Practically and theoretically it is important to scrutinize this prevailing view.

To explore an alternative practical future, we want to sketch an alternative conceptual past by dragging organization studies out of the shadow of 'Weber versus Marx'. This is a good time to rethink this textbook cliché. The revolts in Europe during 1989 were a practical critique both of regimes constructed in Marx's name and of Weber's thoughts on the indestructibility of bureaucratic power. Marx and Weber are theorists of modernity *par excellence*. The twilight of modernity can help us better understand their work and this is a basis on which to develop an understanding of *post*modernity. Understanding of Marx and Weber is constantly revised and there is now a basis for reexamining their relationship (Löwith 1993; Sayer 1991). As Sayer puts it, what they agree upon is more important than what divides them and 'provides a basis, perhaps, for going beyond both' (1991: 3). Together, Marx and Weber have much to teach us about organization, capitalism and modernity.

Marx: the Problem of Modernity

The hallmark of modernity is the creation of 'man', 'I', the abstract citizen. Since modernity preoccupies many organization theorists today (Clegg 1990; Hassard and Parker 1993), it is worth recalling that this is the problem with which Marx *began* 150 years ago in his critique of the first philosopher of modernity, Hegel (Marx 1843). He construes this problem as the dissolution of feudalism's fixed, personal relations of dependency into the abstract, atomized monads of civil society:

> they crowd by one another as though they had nothing in common, nothing to do with one another, and their only agreement is the tacit one,

that each keeps to his own side of the pavement, so as not to delay the opposing streams of the crowd, while it occurs to no man to honour another with so much as a glance. The brutal indifference, the unfeeling isolation of each in his private interest becomes the more repellant and offensive, the more these individuals are crowded together, within a limited space. And, however much one may be aware that this isolation of the individual, *this narrow self-seeking is the fundamental principle of our society everywhere*, it is nowhere so shamelessly barefaced, so self-conscious as just here in the crowding of the great city. This dissolution of mankind into monads of which each one has a separate principle and a separate purpose, the world of atoms, is here carried out to its utmost extreme. (Engels 1969: 58, our emphasis)

These words by Engels, describing life on the streets of London, were written as Marx scrutinized Hegel's concept of the state – the source, incidentally, of the concept of bureaucracy (Albrow 1992). They describe Marx's initial explicandum: the 'narrow self-seeking' of the alienated monad of modernity. The disorganization of life on the streets in 'civil society' is the problem Marx set out to explain, not the organization of life in the factory. This atom or monad is no fiction or philosophical nicety, but a palpable reality on the streets – then *and now*. We can extend Engels's description to include the atomized users of the information superhighway, the narcissistic individuals described by Lasch (1979) and Callinicos's 'sinister, centreless, chaos', a 'violent, illiterate mass lobotomized by television, all coherent understanding lost as, their attention span dwindling, they hop from channel to channel' (1989: 144). Given the contemporary salience of this problem of modernity and the belief that Marx has little to contribute to our understanding, it is worth reflecting on Marx's attempted explanation and its relevance to understanding 'organization'.

Marx reasons thus: modern 'Man' is produced by the dissolution of feudalism and the development of new forms of organizing production. The further back in history we delve, the more we find that the individual is dependent on others, a member of a greater whole. Paradoxically, the 'isolated' individual's semblance of independence is a product of modern, developed social relations. The human being is 'an animal which can individuate itself only in the midst of society' (1858: 84). We must, therefore, explain the 'alien powers' controlling this apparently free and independent monad, i.e. show how it is 'already *determined* by society' (1858: 248, Marx's emphasis). Marx seeks an explanation of these 'alien powers' in the 'anatomy' of civil society (1859: 20), by which he means 'the material foundation, the skeletal structure as it were, of its organization' (1858: 110). Marx construes civil society as the surface of an object, a product of a process taking place beneath it, which he explains in terms of the 'moving unity' and 'inner necessity' of the elements comprising 'the inner organization of the capitalist mode of production' (1864: 831). The name of this 'inner structure' and 'complicated social process' (1864: 830) – which 'actually conceals the inner connection behind the utter indifference, isolation, and alienation' of the problematic 'abstract private person' – is *capital*.

The *primum mobile* of capitalist production is the creation of a surplus by organizing labour into a productive power or 'force'. This is 'the absolute motive and content' of the capitalist's activity (1866: 990). For Marx, the organization of labour into a productive power and the dissolution of feudalism's fixed, personal relations of dependency into the abstract, atomized monads of 'civil society' are sides of the same process. Capitalism and modernity are internally related, facets of the same nexus of production relations. The same process that organizes people into a productive power within the factory creates the atomized monads of modernity on the streets. Whatever explains how labour is organized into a productive power, objectifies or 'subsumes' it as the 'force' of capital, will also explain how people are rendered the 'abstract' monads of civil society. The problem with Marx's model of capital is that while he establishes the necessity for the organization of labour into a productive power for capital, he does not explain how this organization is achieved. Put simply: he explains the 'why' (the motive) of organization, but not the 'how' (the means).

Weber: without Regard for Persons

Weber and Marx agree that society is dominated by capitalism and that its distinctiveness lies in the organization of production, and they are both interested in the contrast between earlier personalized and modern impersonal modes of domination. The concept linking them is Weber's 'rationalization': the calculation between end, means and the results of social action through the application of impersonal rules. Capitalism, says Weber, has produced 'a rational organization of labour, which nowhere previously existed' (cited in Sayer 1991: 93). Rationalization works by eliminating from business those human, emotional elements that escape calculation:

> Precision, speed, unambiguity, knowledge of the files, continuity, discretion, unity, strict subordination, reduction of friction and of material and personal costs – these are raised to the optimum point in the strictly bureaucratic administration. . . . Bureaucratization offers above all the optimum possibility for carrying through the principle of specializing administrative functions according to purely objective considerations. . . . The 'objective' discharge of business primarily means a discharge of business according to calculable rules and '*without regard for persons*'. (cited in Bauman 1989: 14, our emphasis)

Bureaucratic administration is rational not only because of its impersonal formalism and its machine-like efficiency but also, and most fundamentally, because it is based on knowledge and technical expertise. Rationalization is a process of domination based on seemingly apolitical techniques.

The rationalization of economic activity is part of a broader process of rationalization, which affects the state, church, army and university, subsumed by Weber under the concept of bureaucratization. Rationalization, then, is a multiplicity of distinct, but interrelated, processes with different historical sources, developing at different rates and furthering different interests. Rationalization, rather than capitalism *per se*, is the root of the modern world. Capitalism did not create rationalization, rather rationalization facilitated the development of capitalism. 'Capitalism is but one theatre among others in which the drama of rationality is played out' (Sayer 1991: 134). It is for this reason that Weber is circumspect in prescribing remedies for capitalism's problems. Since Weber is often portrayed as an enthusiastic exponent of rationalization, it is worth stressing that he finds administration 'without regard for persons' deeply morally and politically problematic. Rationalization enhances efficiency, but it also dehumanizes, and the tension between formal and substantive rationality is an important cause of social problems.

Far from opposing Marx's analysis, Weber complements, broadens and extends it. Rationalization is the mode of organization Marx does not explain, the mode of acting of capital, the mode of calculating of the monad of modernity, *Homo economicus*. Weber theorizes about the essential conditions of rational calculation: the nexus linking wage labour, private property, technology, law, the market and the state.

The Creation of Organization

The work of Marx and Weber is the stage upon which practitioners perform. The practical stimulus to the study of organization came from men, such as Ure, Gilbreth, Taylor, Ford, Fayol, Barnard and Urwick, who wanted to recruit social science to the task of efficiently organizing labour into a productive power for capital. They set the prevailing conception of practice for organization studies: management. The imperative for the study of 'organization' came from the marginalist 'revolution' against Marx and the resultant neo-classical economics.[1] Whereas, for Marx, the abstract individual of modernity is the phenomenon to be explained, neo-classical economics accepts it as given. It abstracts individuals from their social context to form *Homo economicus* and abstracts material things from the social relations that produced them to form the 'economy'. It then develops an *a priori* model of rational economic action between these abstractions. This double abstraction expels from economic analysis 'power' and 'social relations', the nature of the employment relationship and the organization of work. Economics delegates these problems to complementary, but subordinate, disciplines that developed within the theoretical space of economists' implicit social ontology. Organization studies is one such discipline. This theoretical imperative combined with the influence of practical theorists, such as Barnard (1938), to define the object of knowledge of organization studies as control and coordination within the corporation. The privately owned, rationalized corporation is the organizational nucleus of modernity/capitalism and the implicit model for organization studies (Gortner et al. 1987; Leblebici and Salancik 1989; Sandelands and Srivatsan 1993).

Just as economics abstracts from social relations of production to form 'the firm', so organization theory abstracts from them to form its analogue, 'the organization', the apparently concrete and self-evident object of normal organization science. 'The organization' is an abstraction from the individuals, and the social relations among them, who constitute this modern form of social life. In the abstraction of 'organization' from 'society' the corporation's connections with the social relations that constitute this form of private property are conceptually severed. The conceptual exclusion of society from organization is the basis for the internal/external metaphor usually applied to the organization/society relationship: a *physical* metaphor suggestive of walls and fences quite unsuited to social realities, but apt for the boundary of private property. This conceptual severing militates against recognition of the causal connections between the behaviour of people within organizations and this broader social relationship structuring their interactions, between life in the factory and life in the home and on the streets.

NORMAL ORGANIZATION SCIENCE

Organization Theory: the First Generation

The initial practical imperative to organization theory, then, was a desire to develop knowledge of and for management so as to help organize labour into a productive power or force for capital. The abstraction of corporations from the relations of exclusion that constitute this form of private property retained the structure of property rights, underwriting management's right to direct production and appropriate its product. This structure of rights is theorized in economics as capitalist rationality, and propagated in an ideology that construes management as allocating resources on the basis of an impartial interpretation of market signals. This abstracted structure is 'formal' organization: it is what is supposed to happen, because economic theory tells us it will and management ideology tells us it should. The underside of property rights and managerial authority, workers' indirect or negative control – basically their power to say 'no!' – is what actually happens and is labelled 'informal' (Clegg and Dunkerley 1980).

Organization was initially defined as a formal system oriented towards the achievement of a goal. The presumption was that theorists of organization can advise managers on how to efficiently realize organizational goals. The practical problem posed by the discovery of behaviour inconsistent with this formal structure of rights, the informal systems of 'human relations' codified in the work of Mayo and colleagues at the Harvard Business School (Roethlisberger and Dickson 1949), is how to motivate individual workers by addressing their psychological needs. Despite their differences, however, theorists of both formal and informal organization share an interest in diagnosing the causes of inefficiency within organizations and in prescribing how they can be made more efficient by ascertaining the conditions under which the attainment of goals is promoted or hindered (Etzioni 1959: 43).

The sociological framework within which organization studies developed during the twentieth century was provided by Parsons's translation and interpretation of Weber. Weber's model of bureaucracy, in particular, has been the point of departure for most theoretical and empirical work on organizations. According to Parsons's interpretation, encouraged by the nuances of his translation of the German original and influenced by Malinowski, under whom he studied at the London School of Economics during the 1930s, Weber's concerns were leadership rather than domination, coordination not conflict and control (Weiss 1983). Through the influence of Parsons, and his students, a belief developed that Weber's writing on bureaucracy is a description of and prescription for an efficient modern organization. 'Bureaucracy is seen as an epitome of rationality and of efficient implementation of goals and provision of services' (Eisenstadt 1959: 303). In this fashion, the ideal type of bureaucracy became 'ideally rational' and 'perfectly efficient'. The belief spread that formal bureaucracy is the most efficacious means of organizational goal attainment. Once organizational goals are known, criteria for the assessment of organizational effectiveness can be derived. Given the notorious difficulty of reading Weber, this Parsonian interpretation prevailed. Merton, a student of Parsons at Harvard during the 1930s, and his students, Blau, Gouldner, Selznick and Sills, produced the seminal early works on the sociology of organizations.

The Scientification of Organization Theory

The tacit assumption of this theory of and for management was that knowledge can best serve managers if it is true. During the late 1950s and 1960s, science became the adjudicator of the truth of knowledge and positivism became the adjudicator of science. The more scientific is knowledge, the truer it must be, and the more true, the more practically useful it must be. 'Good theory is practical precisely because it advances knowledge in a scientific discipline, guides research towards crucial questions, and enlightens the profession of management' (Van de Ven 1989: 486). For this reason, the scientification overtook the first wave of organization studies. This intended science of organization is described in the first (1956) issue of *Administrative Science Quarterly*. This envisaged the development of an applied administrative science that would serve managers, much as the physical sciences serve engineers, and as the biological sciences serve physicians. Henceforth, organization studies was shaped as an applied science. Its particular positivist understanding of the practice of science became the organizing principle of research into organization.

Mainstream texts embodied this vision. The diffuse amalgam of applied psychology, sociology and human relations geared towards problem solving, characteristic of the first generation of organization theorists, was transformed into a preoccupation with scientific method, i.e., 'careful sampling, precise measurement, and sophisticated design and analysis in the test of hypotheses derived from tentative general laws' (Behling 1980: 483). By 1980, it could be said that 'research methods similar to those used in the natural sciences have long been the norm in organizational behaviour and organization theory. . . . The authors of mainstream texts in organization behaviour and organization theory accept the natural science model of good research' (1980: 483). The parameters of legitimate enquiry in the field were defined by the intersection between a particular understanding of Weber and a particular understanding of science. 'One might describe organization theory as that discipline which moves between the discussion of what Max Weber's writings can be made to mean and the exploration of what computers can be made to say' (Perry 1992: 85). These two influences are synthesized in the Aston Studies, perhaps the most thorough and comprehensive example of this mode of research.

The Aston Studies

The basis of the Aston approach is set out in Pugh et al.'s (1963) 'A conceptual scheme for organizational analysis': 'the main problem for the researcher has been how to use Weberian concepts in analysis with data on a real functioning organization' (1963: 294). The key tasks Pugh et al. set themselves have done much to shape subsequent organization theory: (a) to 'isolate the conceptually distinct elements that go into Weber's formulation of bureaucracy', (b) to translate 'the insights of Weber into a set of empirically testable hypotheses' (1963: 298), and (c) to postulate 'a conceptual framework for analyzing the structure and functioning of organizations, which will serve as a predictive instrument' (1963: 315). The study examined the interdependence of three conceptually distinct levels of analysis of behaviour in organizations: individual personality and behaviour; group composition and interaction; organizational structure and functioning (1963: 292).

The Aston approach translated theoretical concepts into measurable independent and dependent variables. 'Structure' was construed as a set of variables capable of empirical verification, which were then related to contextual variables such as size, ownership and control, charter and technology. The contextual variables were taken to be independent variables for the study of organizational structure and functioning (the dependent variables). The relationships between independent and dependent variables were examined using multivariate regression analysis. The discovery: the operation of an organization (its 'behaviour') is contingent on a wide range of variables. Bureaucracy is not a unitary concept. There is no one best way to organize. 'Organizational effectiveness is contingent on a "match" between internal structure and characteristics of the organization's task and environment' (Cheng and McKinley 1983: 87). Contingency theory 'emphasizes the multivariate nature of organizations and attempts to understand how organizations operate under varying conditions and in specific circumstances' (Kast and Rosenzweig, cited in Shepard and Houghland 1978: 413–14). Research into the contingencies between organizational structure and its environment is intended to produce a coherent model for guiding decision-making by managers. But let us note: 'The project deals with what is officially expected should be done, and what is in practice allowed to be done; it does not include what is actually done, that is, what "really" happens in the sense of behavior beyond that instituted in organizational forms' (Pugh et al. 1968: 69). We might want to ask, what is practical or scientific about 'knowledge of things which do not actually happen' (Clegg and Dunkerley 1980: 226)?

Theories of Organization

Having abstracted individuals and organizations from the social relations that constitute them, normal organization science must then go about reestablishing the connections it has methodologically severed: between the individual and the organization, and between the organization and its environment.

Individual and Organization

Much organization theory focuses on the individual and considers the tension between the formal and the informal aspects of organization, between what is supposed to happen and what actually happens. This is the task of expectancy theory, goal setting, needs theory and job design, political theories of organizations, and leadership theory. The problem is how to integrate individuals into the authority structure of the organization: in particular, how can they be motivated? From a focus on the individual, theory broadened to include organizational constraints on individuals, i.e. on social relations *within* organizations. This is the task of exchange-based and informational influence, social learning theory, role theory, retrospective rationality. This theoretical focus on the individual is the counterpart of the methodological individualism of neo-classical economics and Weberian sociology. It also complements the individualism at the heart of American culture which is evident today in the vogue of 'unlimited power' and the 'science' of personal

achievement (Robbins 1986): 'Yes, you can do, have, achieve, and create anything you want out of life.'

Organization and Environment

The issue here is how organizations adapt to their external 'environments', 'the organization's source of inputs and sink of outputs' (Pennings 1975: 393). The external environment is normally the market. Theories of the organization–environment relationship aim to advise managers of how to interpret market signals and translate them into efficient modes of organization. This is the task of the market failures approach, structural contingency theory, population ecology, resource dependency and organization economics. Population ecology, for example, focuses on how environments 'select' the most robust organization by examining populations of organizations and their wider 'ecology'. 'It is competitive pressure which drives the ecological theoretical system as surely as it does the more obviously economically indebted contributions to organization analysis' (Clegg 1990: 77).

The Nature of Theorizing and the Divorce of Theory from Practice

Although theories of organization differ over the variables they consider and over their hypotheses about the nature of functional relationships between them, they share an underlying belief in the nature of organizations and how they can be known. Organizations are taken to be empirical, concrete things. Concepts are abstracted from these observables and operationalized through the construction of scales, indices and factors. Statistical inferences are made upon differences between variables. As Burrell and Morgan (1979: 163) note, 'there is scarcely an organizational variable which has not been measured in some form or even correlated with itself in the objectivist search for "significant" relationships which eventually will prove to be "determinate".' General laws are inferred from the statistical manipulation of differences between factors. These inferences and laws are developed into an ordering theoretical framework.

This positivist concept of science, institutionalized through the Aston School, severs the connection between organization theory and practice by emphasizing testing at the expense of the creation of theory (Weick 1989). Positivism has little to say about theory creation or discovery because it assumes discovery and proof are sides of the same process and because it assumes that the only logical reason for proposing a hypothesis is that certain considerations lead one to think it is true (Hanson 1958). But these assumptions are wrong. Typically, a hypothesis is proven long after its creation, by different people. Positivist accounts of scientific method begin with the hypothesis as given; they say nothing about the process of discovery in science. The emphasis on hypothesis testing impedes understanding of the creation of theory and severs the link between real problems and their putative explanations.

Normal organization science does not examine the relationship between problems and explanations but examines that between independent and dependent variables. Research methods, rather than the problems and needs of managers, workers and policy makers, drive research (Boyacigiller and Adler 1991: 270). The original problems that stimulated the creation of organization studies fade into the past and problems are now derived from review essays and statistical models. Organizational scientists are so caught up in the science of hypothesis testing that often the practical utility of this 'theorizing' is lost from sight. A striking number of books and articles deal solely with 'theory'. This divorce between organizational theory and practice is institutionalized in the division of labour between the two journals of the Academy of Management: *Academy of Management Journal* (practice) and *Academy of Management Review* (theory).

Normal Science's Implicit Concept of Practice

Although normal organization science is replete with references to organizational 'members', it has never given equal weight to workers and managers. It is very much a theory of, and for, management. Indeed, 'organization' and 'management' have evolved in tandem. An important practical dimension of this body of theory is its implicit understanding of managers, workers and the employment relationship between them.

Much of organization studies assumes that management is the agency of organization. It is 'the organ of society specifically charged with making resources productive, that is, with the responsibility for organized economic advance, [this] reflects the base spirit of the modern age' (Drucker 1954, cited in Scott 1979: 23). Managers are guardians of rationality, interpreting market signals for the good of all. 'Management is . . . the enterprise that makes resources productive, and thereby, it acts as an agency of human betterment' (1979: 23). Senior executives exercise their 'strategic choice' over

how the organization is to be managed. Organization theories concur on the nature of practice; they differ only on the advice they would provide to managers.

Managers are leaders with a high degree of discretion and influence over the organizations within which they work. 'These leaders can implement new ideas and discoveries uncovered by organization theory and research' (Cheng and McKinley 1983: 85). Managers have discretion because their authority makes employees malleable. The employee is an instrument of management and can be programmed to obey its instructions (Kilduff 1993: 21).

Business is driven by management decisions. The more correct the decisions, the more successful the corporation and the economy. These decisions can be improved by management education and training. The more systematic, analytical, logical and informed the decision, the better it will be and the greater the economic success. Scientific knowledge of organization and management can be translated into information and techniques that are relevant to the practitioner. For example, if managers know the contingent relationships between their organization's structure and environment they will be in a better position to manage. 'If greater efficiency is desired, the theory suggests increasing the formalization of rules; if greater job satisfaction is desired, the theory suggests decreasing the stratification of rewards' (Hage 1965: 319).

Finally, normal organization science is imprinted with an American orientation (Boyacigiller and Adler 1991: 265). Most management schools and academic management journals are American and the majority of management academics are American trained (1991: 267). Normal science assumes that the post-war economic success of the United States has been caused, in large part, by its conception of management and business and that the experiences of the post-war United States are applicable globally. 'Cultural values of the United States underlie and have fundamentally framed management research, thus imbuing organizational science with implicit, and yet inappropriate, universalism' (1991: 262). For example, normal organization science assumes that property and management rights are beyond dispute and that individuals are largely free of external, structural constraints. The atomization of civil society, which Marx first identified as a problem, is celebrated as a virtue in the name of freedom of the individual. The authority of science confirmed the validity of America's concept of management and ownership and imbued organization science with a false universality. Indeed the US conception of management and organization is ascendant; it is active in the creation of business schools in Britain and in the former Soviet bloc. The globalization of capital goes hand in hand with the globalization of North American organization theory and practice.

CONTRA ORGANIZATION SCIENCE

A systematic critique of normal organization science developed during the 1970s, spurred on by developments in epistemology and ontology which undermined the prevailing positivist conception of the practice of science which is active in the study of organization (Burrell and Morgan 1979). Over the past twenty years, this critique stimulated an assortment of theories of organizations which oppose normal organization science. They share an attempt to restore what rationalization has attempted to remove practically and what normal science attempts to obscure theoretically: those human characteristics of organization which escape calculation – human affectivity. In this section, we describe the line of argument traced by these contra organization theories and reflect on their practical significance.

The Interpretative Paradigm

Silverman's (1968; 1970) early work proved pivotal in the development of contra organization science because it articulated a dissatisfaction many were feeling about much organization theory and offered the basis of an alternative (Clegg 1975: viii). Drawing on Weber's concept of social action, the phenomenology of Goffman, Schutz and Berger and Luckman, the ethnomethodology of Cicourel, and the empirical work of Gouldner, Silverman argued against the managerialism, functionalism and 'abstracted empiricism' of normal organization science. Formal theorists, he argued, reify management objectives as the goals of the 'organization'. This error of reification creates a distinction between formal and informal organization, or between what management says should happen and the contra goals of their subordinates, which normal organization science understands as a distinction between rationality and non-rationality.

Silverman's alternative, the 'action frame of reference', is less a theory and more 'a method of analyzing social relations within organizations' (1970: 147) or, as he later acknowledges, a set of questions that might guide empirical research (Silverman 1991). This alternative is based on the belief that organizations are distinct from natural phenomena because they are socially constructed out of 'meanings which define social reality' (1970: 127). Organizations must be explained by grasping the meanings which cause people to act, and this requires an entirely different set of techniques to those practised by positivist organization researchers.

The action frame of reference proved influential in the following ways. First, by stressing the socially constructed nature of organizations, Silverman deconstructed the unitary 'organizational goals' of normal organization science to reveal the possibility of a plurality of competing goals of rival groups within organizations. Second, it shifted attention from what people are supposed to do and what they say they do to what they *actually* do. This method for generating theory provided a welcome alternative to the emphasis on theory testing of positivist organization theory and stimulated ideographic research of organizations, which attempt 'to make explicit the implicit structure and meaning of human experience' (Sanders 1982: 353; Morgan and Smircich 1980). Finally, the action frame of reference countered the managerialism of formal organization theory by aligning itself with social change, for, if organizations are creations rather than natural given entities, they can be changed by social intervention.

The Critique of Empiricism and the Radical Concept of Power

The rediscovery of the construction of social reality complemented the critique of empiricist epistemology, which reconstituted the social sciences in Britain during the 1970s, and the ensuing understanding that what we see is mediated by the conceptual framework of the observer. These two influences combined to make organizations less tangible and organization theory more uncertain. The critique of empiricism affected organization theory by changing the understanding of 'power'. It widened the scope of enquiry to latent, unobservable conflict and to the role of ideology in shaping perceptions and preferences contrary to the real interests of those who hold them, and stimulated work on the 'radical' concept of power: '*A* exercises power over *B* when *A* affects *B* in a manner contrary to *B's* interests' (Lukes 1974: 34). The radical concept of power, in terms of objective interests and subjective misconceptions, owes much to base/superstructure interpretations of Marx. Objective interests are located in the economic base; subjective perception of these interests is obscured by an ideological superstructure. For this reason, the radical concept of power and the concept of ideology are mutually supportive. The then influential Marxian analysis of their conflicting real interests pointed to an imperative, at the point of production, for capital to control labour and for labour to resist that control.

The radical concept of power was worked through organizational analysis, principally by Clegg and his various collaborators (Clegg 1975; Clegg and Dunkerley 1977; 1980). This radicalization of organization theory coincided with the discovery of the 'labour process' in Braverman (1974). Radical organization theory became subsumed under the vogue of labour process analysis; workplace relations and labour process became synonymous; and such was the strength of association between 'control' and 'labour process' that 'control of the labour process' was construed as the *modus operandi* of the workplace for a generation of radical scholars and formed the theoretical object of radical organization theory (Clegg and Dunkerley 1980: 1). And this despite the word 'control' scarcely appearing in Braverman (1974). Nevertheless, 'control' reconceptualized organizational analysis, industrial relations and labour history, even touching accounting and management studies, blurring their disciplinary boundaries and creating a common theoretical object. This, essentially Marxian, analysis drove contra theoretical and empirical studies of organization during the 1980s.

The organon of control broadened understanding of organizational practice, beyond the customary focus on management, to include the interests and practices of workers. It argued that to understand what happens within organizations we must situate them in their political and economic context and it thereby challenged the *cordon sanitaire* erected by positivism around organizations and organization theory. 'Control' added impetus to the developing split between organization theory and the sociology (or political economy) of organizations. Given the connection between the radical concept of power and the concept of ideology, normal organization science was construed as ideological and politically conservative because it hinders recognition of the nature of power. Its emphasis on real interests encourages explanation of organizations in terms of the motives of the people who constitute them. Finally, it changed understanding of the role of the academic from neutral observer to partisan. One must choose whose interests to serve, the controllers or the controlled.

'Control' was but the beginning of a broader attempt by critics of normal organization science to explain what positivism attempts to mask and to restore what rationalization attempts to eliminate: human affectivity. The concern with control and resistance extended to other previously neglected aspects of organization, such as pleasure (Burrell 1992), sexuality (Hearn and Parkin 1987; Hearn et al. 1989), gender (Mills 1988; Mills and Tancred-Sheriff 1992), emotion (Fineman 1993) and feelings (Albrow 1992). The intended practice of this diverse body of theory is social change via the rehumanization and repoliticization of modern organizational forms of life. This approach entails quite different criteria for assessing the performance of organizations. As Frost (1980: 501) argues: 'people operating in organizational arenas may be damaged, compromised, and even destroyed by what they experience in those arenas . . . [and] organizations often do *not* serve the individuals and groups that administrators claim are the primary recipients of organizational energy and resources.' Organizational forms should be reconstructed to enhance creativity and fulfilment.

Conceiving organizations in terms of control remains the core of contra organization studies, but it has been clear for some time that this approach has run out of steam (Knights and Willmott 1990). Its potential for further development is restricted by the limitations of its basis in traditional Marxism, the radical concept of power and the critique of empiricist epistemology. In the following sections, we explain how attempts to transcend these limitations have considerably broadened the scope of contra organization science.

From Traditional Marxism to Foucault

The radical formulation of power, in terms of control versus resistance, is regularly confounded by empirical evidence, which consistently shows that managers are seldom interested in control *per se* and that workers are often complicit in the practices that radical analysis suggests they should be resisting (Burawoy 1979; Cressey and MacInnes 1980; Storey 1983; 1985; Edwards 1986). The radical concept of power certainly improves upon the earlier concepts, but criticisms of 'control' suggest that a residuum needs explaining: the coexistence, within production, of creation and alienation, empowerment and repression, cooperation and resistance. 'Calm surfaces with barely a political ripple disturbing them, just as much as scenes of heroic struggle to the political death, are something to be explained, not something to be taken for granted' (Clegg 1989: 111). Power is not *either* resistance *or* consensus, but *both*.

The problem of 'control' is firmly rooted in the problem of traditional Marxism. It is partly for this reason that Marxists have struggled for years to develop an alternative to the base/

superstructure metaphor and its 'erroneous, simplistic, and unexplored assumptions not only about the nature of the state and the workplace but also about the relationship between the two' (Burawoy 1984: 27). This theoretical problem is compounded by the seeming lack of a viable practical alternative to the organization of work criticized by Marxists, and by the revolts against Soviet state bureaucracies during 1989 (Remnick 1994; Yakovlev 1993).

Within this context, Foucault's implicit critique of traditional Marxism and of the practices of the Soviet bloc has proven attractive to some organizational analysts (Burrell 1988; Townley 1994). The first thing to note is that Foucault's work developed in reaction to traditional Marxism's implicit, radical concept of power and its corollaries, real interests and ideology, base and superstructure. Foucault does not deny the reality of control and subordination: he claims only that power is more complex than prohibition and that an understanding of power cannot be deduced from an imputed motive. The failure to analyze how power is exercised, 'concretely and in detail', in favour of deducing its existence from a motive, is a criticism Foucault levels at 'traditional' Marxists who, he says, worry more about the definition of class than the nature of the struggle: 'orthodox Marxists could ignore organizational questions as they waited for capitalism to collapse' (Clegg and Higgins 1987: 203). Foucault's concern is less with the why, more with the how of power. He shows how the exercise of power simultaneously generates forms of knowledge: 'knowledge follows the advances of power, discovering new objects of knowledge over all the surface on which power is exercised' (1977: 204). Organizations are both architectures of power and apparatuses of knowledge; discipline is both a system of correction and a system of knowledge. Disciplines are organizing devices central to the operation of power. Through the organization of time, space and movement, disciplines operate simultaneously on the population and the individual, enabling both to be directed (Foucault 1980). Their effect is simultaneously to totalize and to individualize. They are 'tiny, everyday, physical mechanisms', methods of controlling the operation of the body that work through exploring, breaking down and rearranging its operation (1977: 137–8). As Foucault points out, the body has been a neglected dimension of work on power. Marxists, in particular, have a 'terrible tendency to occlude the question of the body, in favour of consciousness and ideology' (1980: 59).

Foucault's conception of power has several implications. By showing how mechanisms of disciplinary power are simultaneously instruments for the formation and accumulation of knowledge, Foucault dissolves the traditional, positivist distinction between power and knowledge (or practice and theory). We should, says Foucault, 'abandon a whole tradition that allows us to imagine that knowledge can exist only where the power relations are suspended and that knowledge can develop only outside its injunctions, its demands and interests' (1977: 27). Power and knowledge, conceived by positivism as independent, are internally related sides of the same social relation, and known by the conceptual shorthand, 'power-knowledge'. Just as for Marx capital alienates while it produces, for Foucault power constrains while it creates and enables. Foucault's approach is, then, an implicit critique of conceptions of power solely in terms of negation and repression of the actions of others – A getting B to do something he or she would not or should not do, in other words, 'control'. Marxist and liberal conceptions share an economism, says Foucault. Liberals regard power as a property of rights which are bestowed by a protective state and which one can possess like a commodity. Marxists simply replace the benign with the malign state, juridic with economic subjects. As for Marx (1867: 990), power for Foucault is a machinery in which everyone is caught, 'those who exercise power just as much as those over whom it is exercised'. This underlying realist ontology redirects attention towards the everyday, the normal: 'Rather than A getting B to do something B would not otherwise do, social relations of power typically involve both A and B doing what they *ordinarily* do' (Isaac 1987: 96).

Like Marx, Foucault is concerned not with what people imagine or conceive, but with what they actually do. Foucault's empirical enquiries revealed to him that power relations 'go right down into the depths of society . . . they are not localized in the relationship between the state and its citizens or on the frontier between classes' (1977: 27). Thus he urges us to study power at 'the point where power reaches into the very grain of individuals, touches their bodies and inserts itself into their actions and attitudes, their discourses, learning processes and everyday lives' (1980: 39). We should adopt an 'ascending' analysis, starting with the infinitesimal mechanisms of power and showing how they have been incorporated and colonized by more general state mechanisms and cloaked in its theory of power and system of rights. Thus we should study techniques rather than institutions; practices rather than intentions; webs of power rather than classes or groups; knowledge rather than ideology; in short, the way power is exercised, concretely and in detail, a relatively neglected area in studies of production relations (Townley 1994).

From the Critique of Empiricism to the Relativism of Postmodernism

The viability of the 'control' approach to the study of organization is also limited by the apparent difficulty in finding a suitable alternative to the empiricism and positivism which it so severely criticized. Recognition of the impossibility of theory-neutral observation undermined confidence in empirical work, lest it be tainted with 'empiricism', and encouraged a retreat into the relative safety of 'theory'. A mistaken belief that observation is conceptually determined led to a rejection of the possibility of any sort of science of organizations. These two influences facilitated the development of a diverse amalgam of ideas known as postmodernism, during the 1980s, which questioned the validity of modern science and the notion of objective knowledge or truth (Cooper and Burrell 1988; Clegg 1990; Power 1990; Gergen 1992; Parker 1992).

The debate on postmodernism has two interrelated arguments. According to the first, we are experiencing a fundamental change in the way society, particularly our experience of space and time, is organized. According to the second, we are experiencing a fundamental change in how we know things. These two arguments are usually distinguished by reference to the former as postmoder*nity* and the latter as postmodern*ism*. Postmodernity, or the search for the postmodern organization, analyzes the changes occurring in organizational forms and focuses 'on what agents actually do in accomplishing the constitutive work involved in organizations' (Clegg 1990: 13). Stressed, in particular, is the move away from the dominant organizational form described by Weber. The latter's ideal typical model of a hierarchical, bureaucratic organizational form was based on a division of labour from which was derived several characteristics which typified modern organizations. Briefly, division of labour underscores task discontinuity, specialization and functional separation, with the result that organizational forms are characterized by stratification, hierarchization and coordination through an impersonalized formalization of rules. Emphasis is placed on standardization and coordination is centralized. Contractual arrangements and credentials negotiate social and personal relations. Organized for mass markets, these ways of organizing no longer appear relevant for today's market conditions. Postmodernity rejects these

central tenets of organizing and is identified in many cases by their polar opposites. Hence, rather than differentiation based on strict divisions of labour, observers identify a blurring of boundaries, de-differentiation (Clegg 1990). The postmodern organization is characterized by flexibility. It purports to empower employees. Supervision stresses the importance of trust and the internalized recognition of and adherence to the organization's missions and goals.

The debates between modernism and postmodernism reflect broader epistemological differences, though these too are reflected and incorporated into debates on the postmodern organizational form. In essence, modernism is identified with the Enlightenment project, that is, progress through the application of reason, and social development by advances in science and technology. Emphasis is placed on the importance of government, administration and planning, on the ordering of social relations (Cooper and Burrell 1988). The dominant metaphor is of society as a machine. Indeed, 'organization' is very much a modernist metaphor. What is 'out there' is susceptible to enquiry and the formulation of scientific laws. Language is a mechanism or tool that gives access to the outside world and is reflective of external order. Once acquired, knowledge gives greater agency to individuals who are then able to impose greater order or control on that which they survey. Postmodernists reject these assumptions. They deny grand narratives. They reject the view that language is unconditionally tied to its external referent. For postmodernists, meaning is not a relationship between word and object, but is derived from a system of language. This renders the meaning of words unstable and indeterminate and fundamentally affects understanding of how we know things.

What has all this got to do with organization analysis? The understanding of meaning as relational has undermined the dichotomous thinking or dualisms that inform normal organizational science, for example, inside/outside, organization/environment. The rejection of universal truths has emphasized the importance of local and specific knowledge and increased sensitivity to difference and incommensurability. Postmodernism emphasizes difference, ambivalence, internal contradictions and mutual dependence. For postmodernists, the world is not a stage, but a text to be read and interpreted. Understanding organizations is a process of textual interpretation, not knowledge building. Multiple and conflicting readings may be held simultaneously. The counterpart of the belief that there is no one best way of knowing things is a rejection of the belief that there is a one best way of doing things. Whilst postmodernism has stimulated critique, it is criticized for its relativism, nihilism and conservatism. It seems to deny the belief in the progress of reason, in the capacity of humanity to perfect itself through the power of rational thought. It offers no firm foundation for political action. 'The Enlightenment is dead, Marxism is dead, the working class movement is dead . . . and the author does not feel very well either' (Neil Smith, in Harvey 1989: 325).

NORMAL AND CONTRA ORGANIZATION SCIENCE: ASSESSMENT AND ALTERNATIVE

In assessing the relative merits of normal and contra organizational science, 'we must be aware of the near certainty that "the" field looks different to the beholder depending not only on his/her own personal predilections, but also on his/her country' (Lammers 1990: 187). Organization studies continues to be dominated by the hegemony of a positivist orthodoxy, based in the United States. European, largely British, critics have made little impact in North America, where 'organization theory . . . is positivistic and geared to a general organization design framework' (Hinings 1988: 6). Contra organization science is not a powerful force because critics of the science of organization have failed to develop a viable alternative to the positivism they have so severely criticized. They seem to have retreated into theory and adopted a hopeless relativism of incommensurable paradigms. 'If paradigms are characterized as incommensurable or metaphors as infinitely exchangeable, then a relativistic discipline is defined in which there are no secure grounds for selecting, using or valuing one approach over another' (Brown 1992: 76; Jackson and Carter 1991). If there is no right or wrong, just different points of view, contra organization science undermines its own foundations as a political force. As each criticism is voiced and a neglected area of study is identified, they are incorporated into the orthodoxy as one more phenomenon to be explained, one more variable to be measured. As Clegg puts it, 'Anything could be a contingency, such that as new objections – "culture", "power" – are raised to existing contingency frameworks, they can be incorporated within them by contingency entrepreneurs' (1988: 11). This allows criticisms to be 'dealt with as conceptual and theoretical additions to existing frameworks . . . for the most part . . . critiques are taken to mean adjustments to existing positions' (Hinings 1988: 6).

Rather than choose between normal and contra organization science, which is something

of a futile and sterile debate (Donaldson 1985; *Organization Studies* Symposium 1988), it is more productive to think of them as documenting the two faces of modernity: efficiency and dehumanization. Let us explain by indicating some connections between the work of Marx, Weber and Foucault.

Although it is fashionable to disregard Marx, Harvey makes a compelling case that what we currently recognize as postmodernity is the disruptive effect on political-economic practices and organizational forms caused by a 'general speed-up in the turnover times of capital' (1989: 285) and its consequent time–space compression. The effects of capital, in the modern world, are surely beyond doubt, but the mechanisms by which capital acts remain elusive. Capital is best understood as the social DNA of the cells that constitute society. It is both a social structure (relations of production) and a complicated social process (mode of production), depending on whether it is regarded statically or dynamically (Marsden 1993b). These organizational cells are not a microcosm of the social body; they constitute the social body, just as actual cells constitute actual bodies. It might be objected that this analogy with DNA leads to an unduly deterministic concept of capital. But this would be to misunderstand both DNA and capital. DNA is not the inert, predictably stable molecule it is often taken to be. It is a metabolic molecule, an integral part of the cell and responsive to what happens around it (Rennie 1993). Capital is analogous to DNA because it is the primary, self-replicating genetic material from which action is produced and is present in nearly all social organisms.[2] As to how capital works, we think this question can best be answered by exploring the connections between Weber and Foucault and their respective models of rationalization and disciplinary power (O'Neill 1987; Gordon 1987; Clegg 1994). Just as, for Marx, capital alienates while it produces, organizes life within the workplace and atomizes life in civil society, so, for Foucault, power simultaneously empowers and represses, and, for Weber, rationalization simultaneously increases efficiency and dehumanizes. It is a question not of either/or, but of understanding the dialectic between these two faces of modernity/capitalism. We think this is the most pressing problem facing organization studies.

The most salutary demonstration of the reality of the dialectic between efficiency and dehumanization is not the modern corporation, beloved of organization theorists, but Bauman's (1989) remarkable account of the logic of events developing in Germany – ironically, as Parsons was translating and interpreting Weber – which culminated in the Holocaust. The Holocaust is normally regarded as a grotesque aberration from the progress of modernity, explicable only in terms of the evil actions of abnormal people. Bauman's thesis is that, to the contrary, it was conducted, in the main, by normal people using the following principles of organizing.

First, transform human subjects into objects of power and knowledge by transcribing them into a set of quantitative measures. This dehumanizes them, cancels their moral demands and allows them to be treated with ethical indifference.

Second, elevate formal above substantive rationality and apply to these objects routine bureaucratic procedures: means–ends calculus, budget balancing and universal rule application. In this way, modern, bureaucratically organized power is able to 'induce actions functionally indispensable to its purposes while jarringly at odds with the vital interests of the actors' (1989: 122).

Third, allow rationalization to create social distance between causes and effects, intentions and consequences, perpetrators and victims. There is an inverse ratio between readiness to cruelty and proximity to its victims: 'the more rational is the organization of action, the easier it is to cause suffering – and remain at peace with oneself' (1989: 155).

Fourth, at each stage, place the ruled in a position of choice, however invidious, and allow them to participate in the decisions that adversely affect them. In this fashion, the rationality of their choice becomes a weapon of the rulers. The victims of the Holocaust deployed their rationality to the end: to kill fewer is less odious than to kill more, sacrifice some in order to save many (1989: 140).

If these principles seem familiar it is because they lie behind the knowledges and techniques found in modern workplaces and taught in today's business schools. The Holocaust illuminates the rationality of all modern modes of organizing, however benign or innocuous they may seem: 'Most bureaucrats composed memoranda, drew up blueprints, talked on the telephone, and participated in conferences. They could destroy a whole people by sitting at their desk' (Hilberg, cited in Bauman 1989: 24). As social relations are rationalized and technically perfected, 'so is the capacity and the efficiency of the social production of inhumanity' (1989: 154). The Holocaust was rule 'without regard for persons' *in extremis*.

The unfolding of this logic of power depends on its context: the exercise of the capacity to act is always negotiated and is contingent on political skill, the motives of people and the circumstances of its deployment. But lest we think we are immune to this moral blindness:

it is helpful to think of the workers of an armament plant who rejoice in the 'stay of execution' of their factory thanks to big new orders, while at the same time honestly bewailing the massacres visited upon each other by Ethiopians and Eritreans; or to think how it is possible that the 'fall in commodity prices' may be universally welcomed as good news while 'starvation of African children' is equally universally, and sincerely, lamented. (1989: 24)

'The owl of Minerva', we are told, 'spreads its wings only with the falling of the dusk' (Hegel 1967: 13). Perhaps only in the twilight of modernity can we fully comprehend its nature. If the practices that made the Holocaust possible are not pathological, but normal, what does this tell us about modernity? We contend that modernity is Janus-faced: it enriches and impoverishes, empowers and represses, organizes life within the workplace and atomizes life in civil society on the streets and in homes, enhances efficiency and dehumanizes. This dialectic points to the tension between formal and substantive rationality, between means to an end and ends and values in themselves, a tension evident within social conflicts and present within each of us.

'Reason' alone cannot be the arbiter of organizational practice. 'The belief that the messiness of the human world is but a temporary and repairable state, sooner or later to be replaced by the orderly and systematic rule of reason' is an illusion (Bauman 1993: 32). When we rule without regard for persons, anything becomes morally permissible. The locus of the theory–practice relationship must be an ethical interrogation of experience, how one conducts oneself, one's daily practices *vis-à-vis* others.

If ethics is at the heart of all organizational practices, then the role of social science is muted. It may allow us to understand and explain action, but it cannot tell us what to do. Endemic conflicts over ends or values cannot be resolved through the acquisition of more knowledge. We need to recognize and debate issues of responsibility, choice and values, upon which organizing is based, and ask the central question: 'What shall we do and how shall we live?' (Weber, quoting Tolstoy, cited in Sayer 1991: 150).

NOTES

1 The following paragraphs draw on Marsden (1993a).

2 The analogy between capital and DNA is not as fanciful as it might at first seem. The discovery of the structure of the DNA molecule by Crick and Watson verified Darwin's theory of natural selection. Darwin's theory of natural selection and Marx's theory of

capital are parallel: 'Just as Darwin discovered the law of evolution in organic nature, so Marx discovered the law of evolution in human history' (from Engels's address at Marx's funeral, cited in Colp 1982: 470). Marx 'read, and then reread, Darwin's *The Origin of Species* in the early 1860s, looking for some natural-scientific basis for his own political and social conceptions' (1982: 461). There can be no doubt that Marx viewed 'the development of the economic formation of society . . . as a process of natural history' (1867: 92). He studied the cell form of society, 'very simple and slight in content', but more difficult to study than the 'complete body' or 'organism' (1867: 90).

REFERENCES

Albrow, M. (1992) '*Sine ira et studio* – or do organizations have feelings?', *Organization Studies*, 13(3): 313–29.

Barnard, C. (1938) *The Functions of the Executive*. Cambridge, MA: Harvard University Press.

Bauman, Z. (1989) *Modernity and the Holocaust*. Cambridge/Oxford: Polity/Blackwell.

Bauman, Z. (1993) *Postmodern Ethics*. Oxford: Blackwell.

Behling, O. (1980) 'The case for the natural science model for research in organizational behavior and organization theory', *Academy of Management Review*, 5(4): 483–90.

Boyacigiller, N.A. and Adler, Nancy J. (1991) 'The parochial dinosaur: organizational science in a global context', *Academy of Management Review*, 16(2): 262–90.

Braverman, H. (1974) *Labor and Monopoly Capital: the Degradation of Work in the Twentieth Century*. New York: Monthly Review Press.

Brown, C. (1992) 'Organization studies and scientific authority', in M. Reed and M. Hughes (eds), *Rethinking Organization: New Directions in Organization Theory and Analysis*. London: Sage.

Burawoy, M. (1979) *Manufacturing Consent: Changes in the Labor Process under Monopoly Capitalism*. Chicago: University of Chicago Press.

Burawoy, M. (1984) 'The contours of production politics', in C. Bergquist (ed.), *Labor in the Capitalist World Economy*. London: Sage. pp. 23–47.

Burrell, G. (1984) 'Sex and organizational analysis', *Organization Studies*, 5(2): 97–118.

Burrell, G. (1988) 'Modernism, post modernism and organizational analysis. 2: The contribution of Michel Foucault', *Organization Studies*, 9(2): 221–35.

Burrell, G. (1992) 'The organization of pleasure', in M. Alvesson and H. Willmott (eds), *Critical Management Studies*. London: Sage. pp. 66–89.

Burrell, G. and Morgan, G. (1979) *Sociological Paradigms and Organisational Analysis*. London: Heinemann.

Buss, T.F. (1993) 'Marxism is wrong, and thankfully, dead', *Academy of Management Review*, 18(1): 10–11.

Callinicos, A. (1989) *Against Postmodernism: a Marxist Critique*. Cambridge: Polity.

Cheng, J.L.C. and McKinley, William (1983) 'Toward an integration of organization research and practice: a contingency study of bureaucratic control and performance in scientific settings', *Administrative Science Quarterly*, 28: 85–100.

Clegg, S.R. (1975) *Power, Rule and Domination: a Critical and Empirical Understanding of Power in Sociological Theory and Organizational Life*. London: Routledge.

Clegg, S.R. (1988) 'The good, the bad and the ugly', *Organization Studies*, 9(1): 7–13.

Clegg, S.R. (1989) 'Radical revisions: power, discipline and organizations', *Organization Studies*, 10(1): 97–115.

Clegg, S.R. (1990) *Modern Organizations: Organization Studies in the Postmodern World*. London: Sage.

Clegg, S.R. (1994) 'Weber and Foucault: social theory for the study of organizations', *Organization*, 1(1): 149–78.

Clegg, S.R. and Dunkerley, D. (eds) (1977) *Critical Issues in Organizations*. London: Routledge and Kegan Paul.

Clegg, S.R. and Dunkerley, D. (1980) *Organization, Class and Control*. London: Routledge.

Clegg, S.R. and Higgins, W. (1987) 'Against the current: organizational sociology and socialism', *Organization Studies*, 8(3): 201–21.

Coase, R.H. (1937) 'The nature of the firm', *Economica*, 4: 386–405.

Colp, R. (1982) 'The myth of the Darwin–Marx letter', *History of Political Economy*, 14(4): 461–82.

Cooper, R. and Burrell, G. (1988) 'Modernism, postmodernism and organizational analysis: an introduction', *Organization Studies*, 9(1): 91–112.

Cressey, P. and MacInnes, J. (1980) 'Voting for Ford: industrial democracy and the control of labour', *Capital and Class*, 11: 5–33.

Donaldson, L. (1985) *In Defence of Organization Theory: a Reply to the Critics*. London: Cambridge University Press.

Donaldson, L. (1988) 'In successful defence of organization theory: a routing of the critics', *Organization Studies*, 9(1): 28–32.

Edwards, P.K. (1986) *Conflict at Work: a Materialist Analysis of Workplace Relations*. Oxford: Blackwell.

Eisenstadt, S.N. (1959) 'Bureaucracy, bureaucratization, and debureaucratization', *Administrative Science Quarterly*, 4(3): 302–20.

Engels, F. (1969) *The Condition of the Working Class in England: from Personal Observation and Authentic Sources*. London: Grafton.

Etzioni, A. (1959) 'Authority structure and organizational effectiveness', *Administrative Science Quarterly*, 4(1): 43–67.

Fineman, S. (1993) *Emotion in Organization*. London and New York: Sage.

Foucault, M. (1977) *Discipline and Punish: the Birth of the Prison*. London and Harmondsworth: Penguin.

Foucault, M. (1980) *Power/Knowledge*. New York: Pantheon.

Frost, P. (1980) 'Toward a radical framework for practicising organization science', *Academy of Management Review*, 5(4): 501–7.

Gergen, K. (1992) 'Organization theory in the postmodern era', in M. Reed and M. Hughes (eds), *Rethinking Organization: New Directions in Organization Theory and Analysis*. London: Sage. pp. 207–26.

Gordon, C. (1987) 'The soul of the citizen: Max Weber and Michel Foucault on rationality and government', in S. Whimster and S. Lash (eds), *Max Weber: Rationality and Modernity*. London: Allen & Unwin.

Gortner, H.F., Mahler, J. and Nicholson, J.B. (1987) *Organization Theory: a Public Perspective*. Chicago: Dorsey Press.

Hage, J. (1965) 'An axiomatic theory of organizations', *Administrative Science Quarterly*, 10: 289–32.

Hammer, M. and Champy, J. (1993) *Reengineering the Corporation: a Manifesto for Business Revolution*. New York: Harper.

Hanson, N.R. (1958) 'The logic of discovery', *Journal of Philosophy*, 55(25): 1073–89.

Harvey, D. (1989) *The Condition of Postmodernity*. Oxford: Blackwell.

Hassard, J. and Parker, M. (eds) (1993) *Postmodernism and Organizations*. London: Sage.

Hearn, J. and Parkin, W. (1987) *'Sex' at 'Work': the Power and Paradox of Organisation Sexuality*. Brighton: Wheatsheaf.

Hearn, J., Sheppard, D.L., Tancred-Sheriff, P. and Burrell, G. (1989) *The Sexuality of Organization*. London: Sage.

Hegel, F. (1967) *Philosophy of Right*. Oxford: Oxford University Press.

Hinings, C.R. (1988) 'Defending organization theory: a British view from North America', *Organization Studies*, 9(1): 2–7.

Isaac, J.C. (1987) *Power and Marxist Theory: a Realist View*. Ithaca, NY: Cornell University Press.

Jackson, N. and Carter, P. (1991) 'In defence of paradigm incommensurability', *Organization Studies*, 12(1): 109–27.

Jones, S. (1994) 'Many worlds – or, *Là ne sont pas des morts*', *Organization*, 1(1): 203–15.

Keat, R. and Urry, J. (1975) *Social Theory as Science*. London: Routledge & Kegan Paul.

Kilduff, M. (1993) 'Deconstructing organizations', *Academy of Management Review*, 18(1): 13–31.

Knights, D. and Willmott, H. (1990) *Labour Process Theory*. London: Macmillan.

Kuhn, T.S. (1970) *The Structure of Scientific Revolutions*. Chicago: University of Chicago Press.

Lammers, C.J. (1990) 'Sociology of organizations around the globe: similarities and differences between American, British, French, German and Dutch brands', *Organization Studies*, 11(2): 179–205.

Lasch, C. (1979) *The Culture of Narcissism*. New York: Warner.

Leblebici, H. and Salancik, Gerald R. (1989) 'The rules of organizing and the managerial role', *Organization Studies*, 10(3): 301–25.

Löwith, K. (1993) *Max Weber and Karl Marx*. London and New York: Routledge.

Lukes, S. (1974) *Power: a Radical View*. London: Macmillan.

Marsden, R. (1993a) 'The politics of organizational analysis', *Organization Studies*, 14(1): 93–124.

Marsden, R. (1993b) 'Marx, realism and Foucault: an enquiry into the problem of industrial relations theory'. Unpublished PhD thesis, University of Warwick.

Marx, K. (1843) 'Contribution to the critique of Hegel's philosophy of right', in Karl Marx and Frederick Engels (1975–), *Collected Works*, vol. 3. New York: International Publishers.

Marx, K. (1858) *Grundrisse Notebooks: Foundations of the Critique of Political Economy* (rough draft). Harmondsworth: Penguin, 1973.

Marx, K. (1859) *A Contribution to the Critique of Political Economy*. Moscow: Progress, 1970.

Marx, K. (1864) *Capital: a Critique of Political Economy. Vol. 3: The Process of Capitalist Production as a Whole*, edited by F. Engels. New York: International Publishers, 1967.

Marx, K. (1866) 'Results of the immediate process of production', Appendix to Marx 1867.

Marx, K. (1867) *Capital: a Critique of Political Economy. Vol. 1: The Process of Capitalist Production*. Harmondsworth: Penguin, 1976.

Mills, A.J. (1988) 'Organization, gender and culture', *Organization Studies*, 9(3): 351–69.

Mills, A.J. and Tancred-Sheriff, P. (1992) *Gendering Organizational Analysis*. London: Sage.

Morgan, G. and Smircich, Linda (1980) 'The case for qualitative research', *Academy of Management Review*, 5(4): 491–500.

Mumby, D.K. and Putnam, L.L. (1992) 'The politics of emotion: a feminist reading of bounded rationality', *Academy of Management Review*, 17: 465–86.

O'Neill, J. (1987) 'The disciplinary society: from Weber to Foucault', *British Journal of Sociology*, 37(1): 42–60.

Organization Studies Symposium (1988) 9(1).

Osborne, D. and Gaebler, T. (1993) *Reinventing Government: How the Entrepreneurial Spirit is Transforming the Public Sector*. London: Penguin, Plume.

Parker, M. (1992) 'Post-modern organizations or postmodern organization theory?', *Organization Studies*, 13(1): 1–17.

Peck, M.J. and Richardson, Thomas J. (1991) *What is to be Done? Proposals for the Soviet Transition to the*

Market. New Haven and London: Yale University Press.

Pennings, J.M. (1975) 'The relevance of the structural-contingency model for organizational effectiveness', *Administrative Science Quarterly*, 20: 393–410.

Perrow, C. (1980) 'Zoo story, or life in the organizational sandpit', in G. Salaman and K. Thompson (eds), *Control and Ideology in Organizations*. Cambridge, MA: MIT Press. pp. 259–77.

Perry, N. (1992) 'Putting theory in its place: the social organization of organizational theorizing', in M. Reed and M. Hughes (eds), *Rethinking Organization: New Directions in Organization Theory and Analysis*. London: Sage. pp. 85–101.

Peters, T. (1992) *Liberation Management: Necessary Disorganization for the Nanosecond Nineties*. New York: Fawcett Columbine.

Power, M. (1990) 'Modernism, postmodernism and organization', in J. Hassard and D. Pym (eds), *The Theory and Philosophy of Organizations: Critical Issues and New Perspectives*. London: Routledge. pp. 109–24.

Pugh, D.S., Hickson, D.J., Hinings, C.R., Macdonald, K.M., Turner, C. and Lupton, T. (1963) 'A conceptual scheme for organizational analysis', *Administrative Science Quarterly*, 8: 289–315.

Pugh, D.S., Hickson, D.J., Hinings, C.R. and Turner, C. (1968) 'Dimensions of organization structure', *Administrative Science Quarterly*, 13: 65–105.

Rafaeli, A. and Sutton, R. (1989) 'The expression of emotion in organizational life', *Research in Organizational Behavior*, 11: 1–42.

Remnick, D. (1994) *Lenin's Tomb: the Last Days of the Soviet Empire*. New York: Vintage.

Rennie, J. (1993) 'DNA's new twists', *Scientific American*, March: 122–32.

Robbins, A. (1986) *Unlimited Power*. New York: Fawcett Columbine.

Roethlisberger, F.J. and Dickson, W.J. (1949) *Management and Morale*. Cambridge, MA: Harvard University Press.

Sandelands, L.E. and Srivatsan, V. (1993) 'The problem of experience in the study of organizations', *Organization Studies*, 14(1): 1–22.

Sanders, P. (1982) 'Phenomenology: a new way of viewing organizational research', *Academy of Management Review*, 7(3): 353–60.

Sayer, A. (1992) *Method in Social Science*. London: Routledge.

Sayer, D. (1991) *Capitalism and Modernity: An Excursus on Marx and Weber*. London and New York: Routledge.

Scott, W.G. (1979) 'Organicism: the moral anesthetic of management', *Academy of Management Review*, 4(1): 21–8.

Senge, P.M. (1990) *The Fifth Discipline: the Art and Practice of the Learning Organization*. New York and London: Doubleday.

Shepard, J.M. and Houghland, James G. Jr (1978) 'Contingency theory: "complex man" or "complex organization"', *Academy of Management Review*, 413–27.

Silverman, D. (1968) 'Formal organizations or industrial sociology: towards a social action analysis of organizations', *Sociology*, 2(2): 221–38.

Silverman, D. (1970) *The Theory of Organizations: a Sociological Framework*. London: Heinemann.

Silverman, D. (1991) 'On throwing away ladders: re-writing the theory of organisations. Towards a new theory of organizations'. Paper presented at the Towards a New Theory of Organization Conference, University of Keele.

Storey, J. (1983) *Managerial Prerogative and the Question of Control*. London: Routledge and Kegan Paul.

Storey, J. (1985) 'The means of management control', *Sociology*, 19(2): 193–211.

Townley, B. (1994) *Reframing Human Resource Management: Power, Ethics and the Subject at Work*. London: Sage.

Van de Ven, A.H. (1989) 'Nothing is quite so practical as a good theory', *Academy of Management Review*, 14(4): 486–9.

Weick, K.E. (1989) 'Theory construction as disciplined imagination', *Academy of Management Review*, 14(4): 516–31.

Weiss, R.M. (1983) 'Weber on bureaucracy: management consultant or political theorist?', *Academy of Management Review*, 8(2): 242–8.

Wolin, S.S. (1981) 'Max Weber: legitimation, method, and the politics of theory', *Political Theory*, 9(3): 401–24.

Yakovlev, A. (1993) *The Fate of Marxism in Russia*. New Haven and London: Yale University Press.

Conclusion: Representations

STEWART R. CLEGG AND CYNTHIA HARDY

Earlier in this *Handbook*, we made initial reference to the metaphor of 'mapping the terrain'. As Stablein (Chapter 3.1) reminds us, it was John Van Maanen (1979) who stressed that the map is not the territory. As Magritte implied in much of his art (see, for instance, *La Représentation*, 1937), there remains a fundamental difference between the means of representation and the represented image.

A painter 'maps' onto a canvas, quite self-consciously painting a lifelike representation of a familiar object, such as a pipe. Yet, of course, the object represented in the painting is not 'the pipe': it always remains a representation of a pipe. A painter paints a painting of a map, perfect in every detail. It is not 'the map': it always remains a representation of a map that is itself a representation of something else: not just any terrain, any territory, but the landscape outside. Looking through the gallery window, we compare the painting to the landscape. We notice that it resembles neither the painting of the map, nor the map itself. As we step through the gallery door, the landscape is even less like the two-dimensional picture as we hear the traffic and smell the fresh breeze coming off the harbour, mingled with the scent of the bush, eucalyptus and wattle, as well as the Gitanes and perfume of the nearby French tourists.

How beautiful this scene, how quintessentially Australian, we say to each other. 'C'est un cliché,' we hear. One of us understands: 'Pardon?' 'Cet endroit, ce panorama nous rappelle des films de Godard, de Truffaut. C'est élégant, c'est chic. Il y a un milieu étranger ici, une ambiance française transposée dans un autre hémisphère comme une scène cadrée par Sydney Harbour.' A conversation begins: someone translates; old Warner Brothers movies are mentioned; 'des hommages' of Godard and Truffaut are discussed; we argue movies; we speak 'franglais'; we move to a café and compare it, contrast it, to Le Café de Paris, Le Café de Flore, 'non, aucune ressemblance'. Thus this mixture of French, English, Canadian, Australian translates, interprets, converses, learns and fills the spaces that the map 'represents'.

So, when we map we miss. We miss the gap between representation and image represented. We miss the contrivance of the representational practices that produce the effect of representation. We miss the point if we think that what we see is what we see. What we see is a representation of a phenomenon, with technical, aesthetic, experiential presence and absence. What we miss is what we don't see. We don't see the history that produces this structuring of space and time, this representational mismatch of spaces, environments, activities, sounds, symbols, scents and sights. But, to draw on the other metaphor framing this book, conversations help us understand what we don't see. Conversations help us see the figures in the landscape, moving through it, retreating to its margins, filling it with their voices, their anxieties, their emotions, their feelings, their beauty and the ghosts that haunt them: their ancestors, both literal and real.

Organization theory is no exception. It, like any other representational practice, is nothing less, nothing more, nothing other than its practices of representation. No objective grounds exist from which to criticize any one genre of representation from another. In the art of life (as well as the life of art) we can relate to any representation, even if only in recoil. Any representation can be related to other, earlier, later, alternative representations, especially when ostensibly the same thing.

Voice: [*entering from off-stage*] The same thing? What do you mean? Is it like music? I know that you like music because I hear music playing in the background. Something about 'snowdrops on kittens' isn't it, by John Coltrane? Isn't this the same as 'My Favourite Things' sung by Julie Andrews in *The Sound of Music*?

Author 1: I guess that you're talking to me since I'm the jazz buff. Well, I think that I'd have to say, not really. Don't you think there is a difference between this version by Coltrane and the song by Julie Andrews?

Voice: Yes, but doesn't the difference between these two versions of 'My Favourite Things' make one more real, less fake and more true to the original? Isn't there a genuine article, that all other representations should seek to emulate?

Author 1: No. 'My Favourite Things' ceases to exist as anything other than its representations once it is represented.

Voice: This is all very well. I know we started talking about music, or at least I did, but where does that get us?

Author 2: That's right. What are we talking about music for? It's just some background, music while we work. So, let's get back to the real work. In any case, organization studies are closer to science than art, aren't they?

Author 1: It depends. It depends on precisely what sense of 'science', what sense of 'art', what sense of being 'closer', what sense of 'getting somewhere', and, most importantly, the translation between them . . .

Author 2: No, this isn't a book about music, it's a book about organization studies. So, let's get back to the chapter. Forget your jazz obsessions.

REPRESENTING THE SUBJECT(S) IN ORGANIZATION STUDIES

The individual chapters have spoken. To make sense of the diversity of approaches, topics and arguments of the preceding pages of this *Handbook* is no easy task. Yet, someone has to do it. This privilege falls, in time honoured tradition, to the editors. Unlike more traditional approaches, however, we do *not* attempt to summarize in detail the large number of themes that emerge from the various contributions. Instead, we construct our own interpretation, trying to make sense in our own terms, of particular threads woven around the theme of representation. We initiate here a conversation that explores representation, one which draws upon and is inspired by the narratives in this book, which focuses on how the individual and organizational subjects that comprise our

research are represented in organization studies, and what this means for the researcher as subject.

The precarious 'position' of the subject is a major concern of research in organization studies. Obviously, postmodern approaches have drawn attention to the risks associated with placing the 'individual' at the centre of our intellectual universe. The postmodern subject is not a stable constellation of essential characteristics, but a socially constituted, socially recognized, category of analysis. As the status of the research subject is challenged so, too, is that of the researcher. No longer all-knowing, all-seeing, objective or omnipotent, the researcher must re-examine his or her role in the research process and the production of 'knowledge'. But it is not only postmodern work that is critically re-examining the subject. More mainstream approaches are also questioning who the 'subject' is, what constitutes an 'organization', and what role the 'researcher' plays, as the chapters in this book clearly demonstrate. For example, concerns with 'agency' occupy institutional theorists, psychological approaches, and leadership theorists; managers of 'diversity' debate the social construction of gender, ethnicity and race; global and ecological approaches draw our attention to subjects far removed from our normal span and scope of attention. Contingency theorists, organizational economists and strategists alike note the problematic conceptualization of 'the' organization as it dissipates into cyberspace, permeates its own boundaries, and is razed, inverted and collapsed into flat, empowered hierarchy-less structures. Other theorists struggle with the role of 'science': why we cannot find a foolproof recipe to facilitate organizational learning and innovation; how we should apply theories of cognition and decision-making to practice; what is the best way to study organizational phenomena; what constitute data and how we can analyze them. Thus the subject, in its varying and precarious forms, preoccupies, in different ways, the diverse areas and scholars of organization studies.

In these conclusions, we develop three particular themes concerning the subject. First, we discuss how the enterprising subject is represented in organization studies. By this, we refer to the new organization forms described in the introduction. We argue that they raise important questions that are only partially addressed in organization studies. We offer some of our ideas for a new research agenda to take us into the next century. Next, we take a closer look at the individual subject as represented in organization studies. We argue that *all* the different approaches to research that exist in organization studies run the risk of losing sight of the people who constitute that research; even those researchers who focus on one group of subjects often lose sight of others. Consequently academics from neither normal nor contra science have served this constituency terribly well and we show how future research might look to a resuscitated subject.

Finally, we look back on how we represent ourselves, in our research, our theorizing, our writing. We challenge the separateness of the identities that we have constructed for ourselves, particularly those that separate 'theory' from 'practice'. The nature of all identity is contingent upon discursive practices: theorists theorize according to the conditions of particular discursive processes; they specify the theory/practice relation also within the conditions of particular discursive practices. While the paradigm debate has drawn attention to the discursive basis of theory and theorizing, rather less attention has been focused on the relationship between theory and practice. Consequently, we lack a reflexive account of this most vital relationship in organization theory. We believe that it is the intersection of the different identities that make up organization studies which offers great potential in this regard. It is here that new conversations can arise and new conversationalists can emerge – although not just any old conversation will do. The *Handbook* that you are reading thus serves as a manifesto: a promotion of conversations that will facilitate greater reflexive awareness.

THE ENTERPRISING SUBJECT

Organizations, despite the assumptions of overly structuralist frameworks, are not essences that exist outside of the configuration of changing times and spaces. We can afford to ignore neither the emergence of new organizational forms, discussed in detail in the introduction to this book, nor the broader changes in which they are embedded such as those noted in this book by Reed, Egri and Pinfield, and Parker. These changes generate a series of new research questions to which research in organization studies must respond if it is to link to and inform practice. Some of the answers or, at least, the beginnings of answers are to be found in the chapters of this *Handbook*. However, it is also clear that considerable gaps remain. In this section, we offer our ideas, by no means an exhaustive list, about some of the directions that future research might take. They include a greater understanding of: collaboration and trust in interorganizational relations; the problematic nature of change in interorganizational net-

works; the limits to power in interorganizational networks; the new skills needed in the enterprising organization; the changing nature of resistance; the question of whether it is still 'a man's world' and the impact feminist theory has had on organization research and practice; the body as subject; and the impact that organizational changes have had on the body.

Collaboration and Trust in Interorganizational Relations

Obviously, in the light of new arrangements emerging between organizations, more work adopting an interorganizational level of analysis would seem helpful. Researchers can no longer afford to concentrate exclusively on individual organizations: what goes on outside the organization obviously influences what goes on inside, as the boundaries that define 'the' organization become both more permeable and more questionable, and the organization is defined only empirically rather than ontologically *a priori*. Obviously, approaches such as population ecology, organizational economics and institutional theory already adopt an interorganizational level of analysis that allows them to address some of these questions. Nonetheless, important issues still remain to be explored which, as we will discuss here, would benefit from different research approaches.

For example, many new organizational forms depend upon collaboration with other organizations rather than competition between them. Collaboration often depends upon trusting relationships between partners. Organizational economics has directly considered the issue of trust, as Barney and Hesterly illustrate in Chapter 1.4, noting that trust serves to reduce uncertainty and the likelihood of cheating in ways that contracts cannot. Such work draws on definitions of trust that revolve around predictable behaviour: trust is linked to an assessment by an actor that another actor will act in a certain way (e.g. Luhmann 1979; Barber 1983; Lewis and Weigert 1985; Gambetta 1988). According to this view, we make predictions (or have expectations) concerning the behaviour of others. If we are confident that our predictions will come to pass, we trust these others. Trust thus reduces complexity by ensuring that the social system is based on mutual expectations about actors' future behaviour, encouraging social actors to select specific options of social action and reaction. The basic function of coordinating social interaction is achieved, and cooperation, rather than opportunistic behaviour, is the result (see Lane and Bachmann 1995).

Such approaches have a number of limitations, however. In general, they pay little attention to how trust is created (Perrow 1993; Hardy and Phillips 1995a). Typically, trust has been conceptualized retrospectively, often by writers (e.g. Ring and Van de Ven 1992) drawing on the work of Granovetter (1985) who focus on the social relations within which business transactions are embedded. In other words, trust exists as a result of frequent interactions and previous trusting relationships (e.g. Dasgupta 1988). Reliance on trust by organizations can thus be expected to emerge between business partners only when they have successfully completed transactions in the past and they perceive one another as complying with norms of equity (Ring and Van de Ven 1992: 489). But the tautology of this statement begs the question: how do partners achieve a trusting relationship *in the first place*?

Writers have tended to assume that partners collaborate voluntarily, and share common goals and equal power. Such conditions may characterize some collaborative ventures but certainly not all (e.g. Westley and Vredenburg 1991). Many collaborative initiatives bring together stakeholders with different goals, values and ideologies (Blumer 1971; Rainey 1983; Laumann and Knoke 1987; Waddock 1989; Pasquero 1991). In such a situation, creating trust is a problematic process and a broader research agenda is necessary to flesh out the dynamics of building trust. For example, more work on the institutional aspects of trust (e.g. Zucker 1986) may help to reveal the ways in which trust and trustworthiness are signalled in different settings. This approach to trust illuminates the importance of *shared* meanings that are necessary if partners are to signal trust and trustworthiness to each other.

Accordingly, a sociological approach (rather than one associated with transaction cost economics or game theory) might conceptualize trust as a communicative, sense-making process, highlighting interpretative, communicative, sense-making activities (Berger and Luckmann 1967; Schutz 1970; Geertz 1973) which then translate into action (e.g. Collins 1981). Such work might also be enriched by insights from narrative theory and discourse analysis, as well as ethnomethodological studies. In this way, we stand to learn more about the theoretical and practical issues involved in collaboration between parties with more or less different aims, languages, cultures, power; more about what works, and what does not, in setting up collaborative relationships (e.g. Huxham 1995).

There is also room for more critical analyses of collaboration since existing work has been noticeably mute on questions relating to power (Fox 1974; Knights et al. 1993). All too often, collaboration is assumed to be beneficial for participants as well as other stakeholders (e.g. Gray 1989: Alter 1990; Knoke 1990; Nathan and Mitroff 1991; Alter and Hage 1993). Joint ventures (Harrigan 1985) and alliances (Kanter 1990) are advanced on the grounds that they reduce uncertainty, acquire resources, and solve problems (e.g. Emery and Trist 1965; Astley 1984). Research on network organizations (e.g. Powell 1990; Alter and Hage 1993) argues that they provide goods and services in ways more effective than either markets or hierarchies. Other research on interorganizational relations also promotes cooperation under the rubric of conformity (Oliver 1991), integration (Knoke 1990), and coordination (Rogers and Whetten 1981). But in adopting these structural-functionalist perspectives, such work on collaboration has ignored the role that power and interests play in collaborative relationships.

> [Studies] have tended to be 'heavy' on notions of negotiations and trust between members of the network and exceptionally 'light' on domination and power relations ... networks continue to be portrayed as interdependent relationships based on reciprocity and mutual trust where self interest is sacrificed for the communal good. (Knights et al. 1993: 979)

Domination lurks in collaborative relationships as much as in competitive ones, and we cannot afford to ignore the less savoury aspects of these new organizational forms. We cannot ignore that power can be hidden behind the façade of 'trust' and the rhetoric of 'collaboration', and used to promote vested interests through the manipulation of and capitulation by weaker partners (Hardy and Phillips 1995a).

Power is in fact, a 'functional equivalent' of trust in ensuring predictability in coordination (Luhmann 1979; Lane and Bachmann 1995).

> 'We've got to trust them' means in fact: 'We don't trust them but feel constrained to submit to their discretion.' This simply describes, of course, a power relationship. (Fox 1974: 95)

Many of the complexities of interorganizational interactions are resolved, not by trust, but 'by implicit or explicit power relations *among* firms' (Granovetter 1985: 502). But predictability and interorganizational coordination based on power are unlikely to lead to the synergy and creativity associated with more trusting forms of collaboration (Fox 1974; see Hardy and Phillips 1995a; 1995b). Trust means taking risks, being vulnerable in order to achieve something that cannot be achieved otherwise. In this way, partners are able to 'see different aspects of a problem [and] can constructively explore their differences and search for solutions that go beyond their own limited vision of what is possible' (Gray 1989: 5).

> [Trusting] participants share certain ends of values; bear each other a diffuse sense of long-term obligations; offer each other spontaneous support without narrowly calculating the cost or anticipating any equivalent short-term reciprocation; communicate freely and honestly; are ready to repose their fortunes in each other's hands; and give each other the benefit of any doubt that may arise with respect to goodwill and motivation. (Fox 1974: 368)

Power, on the other hand, operates through submission, socialization and indoctrination (Fox 1974). It may lead to cooperation and, certainly, may be convenient from the dominant partner's point of view (Warren et al. 1974; Rose and Black 1985; Hasenfeld and Chesler 1989). But such 'spurious' trust (Fox 1974) is unlikely to produce the synergistic creativity that more reciprocal collaboration is hoped to promote.

There is, then, a substantive difference between cooperation achieved through power differentials that render some partners *unable* to engage in opportunistic behaviour, and a willingness to *voluntarily sacrifice* the benefits of opportunistic behaviour in order to cooperate with a trusted partner. Moreover, building trust does not and, in fact, should not preclude conflict since it is through conflict that things get changed. Otherwise, 'when the power position of one firm is obviously dominant, the other is apt to capitulate early so as to cut its losses. Such capitulation may not involve explicit confrontation if there is a clear understanding of what the other side requires' (Granovetter 1985: 502; also see Thorelli 1986). More critical studies of collaboration would, then, help to counteract the structuralist and functionalist approaches found in organizational economics, strategic management and institutional theory and provide more insight into these complex processes.

Change in Interorganizational Networks

Another potential agenda item for future research emerges from an important gap in the work of institutional theorists: how do institutional fields change and what role do interorganizational relationships, specifically forms of collaboration, play in that process? An institutional field is defined as 'those organizations that, in the aggregate, constitute a recognized area of institutional life' (DiMaggio and Powell 1983: 148). It encompasses a set of social orders or patterns where departures from the pattern are counteracted in a regulated fashion, by repeti-

tively activated, socially constructed controls, by some set of rewards and sanctions (Jepperson 1991: 145). Structures become institutionalized when they 'owe their survival to relatively self-activating processes' (1991: 145). Thus institutional theory, as Tolbert and Zucker point out in Chapter 1.6, emphasizes conformity rather than adaptation and downplays agency and interest (Oliver 1991). Accordingly, it is weak on explaining change, especially changes that are not embraced by dominant organizations, changes that are sharply contested, and changes that delegitimate the institutional order of the field (DiMaggio 1988: 12).

Some theorists have proposed a role for institutional 'entrepreneurs' (DiMaggio 1988), people who possess sufficient resources to take advantage of the contradictions that aid deinstitutionalization (Oliver 1992) and that might arise from political, functional, or social pressures. Entrepreneurs need not be private individuals. For instance, in some European countries, like Norway and Denmark, the state has played an important role in creating institutional isomorphism around the network form; but how important is the state as an institutional entrepreneur in other contexts, and how does this importance vary by country (e.g. see Weiss 1988)?

But, in explaining deinstitutionalization, institutional theorists often present causes in the form of deterministic, reified environmental or technological forces: the trigger of change is not problematized. It is as if the hand of god (or, failing god, technology) magically reaches down. But both god and technology (Barley 1986) have to be socially and collectively recognized in the first place. Interorganizational networks, fields and domains are not objective structures but processes of social construction (Warren 1967; Warren et al. 1974; Altheide 1988; McGuire 1988) whereby social order is negotiated (Strauss et al. 1963; Gray 1989; Nathan and Mitroff 1991).

> [Interorganizational d]omains are cognitive as well as organizational structures . . . one can only too easily fall into the trap of thinking of them as objectively given, quasi-permanent fixtures in the social fabric rather than ways we have chosen to construe various facets of it. (Trist 1983: 273)

As a result, when theorists do consider agency, they present a picture in which change can be championed only by actors with power, such as institutional entrepreneurs who may only rarely define their interests in terms of the transformation rather than the reproduction of the status quo. Writers argue, somewhat plaintively, that the powerless must acquire power to influence the domain (e.g. Gricar and Brown 1981), at the same time as pointing out that powerful groups are usually reluctant to give power away. If this is the case, how can relatively powerless groups ever acquire power and influence the domain in the face of the defensive manoeuvres of more powerful adversaries? What strategies of power and resistance are most likely to succeed in particular contexts (Clegg 1995)?

Consequently, considerable scope exists to apply critical, cultural, textual, and ethnomethodological approaches to the field of interorganizational relations (e.g. Knights et al. 1993; Clegg and Palmer 1996) to reveal 'power operating in structures of thinking and behaviour that previously seemed devoid of power relations' (White 1986: 421). In this way, work that draws more attention to how the relations of power and domination pervade new organizational forms might intersect with more 'mainstream' work which has, perhaps too readily, but not always inappropriately, attributed both benefit and benevolence to collaboration.

The Limits to Power

Lest we get carried away with the 'power of power', it is important to remember that many of the relations in which 'new' organizations engage are not contained within their grasp as legally fictive individuals. Organizations do more than negotiate contracts of employment with individuals; they engage in sub-contracting, build alliances, formalize linkages, or informalize them, with other organizations. As networks expand and markets intrude more into organizations, hierarchies recede in importance, and control takes on a very different form. Accordingly, as Hardy and Clegg point out in Chapter 3.7, existing models of power need modification: both 'mainstream' and 'critical' approaches are inadequate to deal with the complexity of power in these interorganizational relations. Both models emphasize a sovereign view where one agent exercises power over another: the former through the possession of critical resources; the latter through domination and hegemony. Neither is appropriate to situations where individual actors are unable to exert systematic control, such as in complex interorganizational networks (Hardy 1995).

New organizational 'realities' thus make for a complex challenge: old certainties concerning power require radical overhaul. If research is to inform practice, actors need to know more about the dynamics of the complex networks through which power flows instead of preoccupying themselves with the possession of information, expertise, rewards and punishments, and other 'critical' resources. Foucauldian insights seem particularly relevant. Power is no longer adequately considered as a manipulable, deterministic resource but must be viewed as a web of relations in which all actors operate and from which the prospects of escape are limited for dominant and subordinate groups alike. Comprehending how new identities are created by interorganizational networks helps to pinpoint tensions that might undermine those relationships (Knights et al. 1993). Yet, as these power networks constrain, they also enable: the fragmentation of power structures offers space for colonization even by the weaker players (Hardy 1994). There is scope, then, for change, based on a productive, facilitative side of power. Viewing power as a solely negative phenomenon, as critical theorists tend to do, does not do justice to the obvious collaborative efforts that have made breakthroughs and achieved objectives that no individual organization could have achieved alone.

Being Green?

One arena where collaboration is particularly pertinent concerns the environment and the management of the global commons, as Egri and Pinfield make clear in Chapter 2.11. It involves forging very different types of relationships between public and private institutions at local, national and international levels, and redefining public and private institutional roles for the protection of global and local commons. Yet, such initiatives have met with limited success. As Egri and Pinfield point out, interorganizational collaboration to establish new sociopolitical systems of governance is easier said than done, especially when parties are unequal and/or different in terms of philosophical values, resources, power and influence, and particularly as we take into account the global scale of these issues and the degradation inflicted on Third World lifestyles and opportunities.

We cannot, however, afford to ignore the magnitude of the environmental challenges we face. They force us to confront the future of our times: the impact of actions taken now and decisions made now for aeons to come. Time is not merely elapsed time, or even the temporal present, that phenomenological moment of coming-to-be and passing away. Time projects; time lives now in the future, in our genes, our maturation and degeneration, our children and our children's children, and in the world that time, and its custodians in the here and now, bequeath to the future. The future is not unaccountable: although its costs may be evaded in the here and now, they cannot be avoided forever.

The ultimate purpose of business is not, or should not be, simply to make money. Nor is it merely a system of making and selling things. The promise of business is to increase the general well-being of humankind through service, a creative invention and ethical philosophy. Making money is, on its own terms, totally meaningless, an insufficient pursuit for the complex and decaying world we live in. We have reached an unsettling and portentous turning point in industrial civilization. It is emblematic that the second animal ever to be 'patented' is a mouse with no immune system that will be used to research diseases of the future, and that mother's milk would be banned by the food safety laws of industrialized nations if it were sold as a packaged good. What's in the milk besides milk and what's suppressing our immune system is literally industry – its by-products, wastes, and toxins. Facts like this lead to an inevitable conclusion. Businesspeople must either dedicate themselves to transforming commerce to a restorative undertaking or march society to the undertaker. . . . Quite simply, our business practices are destroying life on earth. . . . The land, water, air, and sea have been functionally transformed from life-supporting systems into repositories for waste. (Paul Hawken 1993: 1–3)

Business views may be rapidly changing in this arena, but they still lag behind, deviate from, and in some cases directly confront the more radical approaches described in Egri and Pinfield's chapter. While more radical critics attack even initiatives like the Brundtland Report and the United Nations Conference on Environment and Development's (UNCED) Agenda 21 as environmentally *destructive* rather than sustainable, the business approach, by and large, has been to redefine green issues. Through 'mainstreaming' and repackaging, the environmental 'problem' has been transformed into a series of business 'opportunities'. For example, according to recent debates in *Fortune* magazine, the natural environment should receive recognition as a key stakeholder in organizations, through advocacy representation at board level. For many organizations, as for example the Body Shop, being perceived to be green has become an important source of competitive advantage. From this perspective, green organizations are smart organizations: the values of green culture have been downgraded into a major, but manageable, pressure to adopt processes that add value in the light of new concerns.

For some, then, the environmental movement is a source of mischief, an irritation, an unnecessary constraint on economic and community activities or, for the more entrepreneurial, a market opportunity; to others it is a sacred cause, a fundamentally constitutive element of the human condition. No wonder there are no easy answers. Yet, if we are to protect our ecological environment, we will require international collaboration of a scale and degree difficult to imagine (Gray 1995). Reason enough, then, for a harder, closer look at the possibilities for and limits to collaboration in interorganizational, international, intercultural settings.

New Skills in the Enterprising Organization

What of management *inside* these new organization forms? Whatever the advantages concerning synergy, flexibility, reduced costs and lower investment, they do not come without a price. To be successful, managers must learn to work across, and eventually dismantle, traditional organizational boundaries; develop trust in outsiders; and provide ways of linking different companies together in effective alliances that may span the breadth of the world. Managers can expect to encounter considerable difficulty in mastering these challenges. According to Eccles and Nohria (1993), decentralization and flexibility have remained elusive goals for more than fifty years: calls for an end to hierarchy, which can be traced back to the 1920s, have yet to be realized. If managers cannot break down interdepartmental barriers, how can they expect to work across interorganizational boundaries, particularly when they traverse international frontiers and bring together diverse cultures?

Internally, these new forms of organization demand a very different skill set from both employee and researcher. The nuances of collaborative power are as relevant here as in the external arena. These organizations must learn quickly and continuously, as stressed by Weick and Westley in Chapter 2.10 (also see Dodgson 1993). Influential consultants urge that competitive edge attaches to those organizations that succeed in doing so (Kanter 1989; Senge 1990; Garrat 1987). Research suggests that it is the differential ability of smaller organizations to learn, particularly with regard to technological opportunities, that has been responsible for a changing pattern of competitive relationships between large and small organizations in favour of the latter (Rothwell 1992). The extent to which smaller, more competitive firms can also be more ecologically responsible than larger organizations remains to be seen, and is a worthwhile research topic. Does an increase in size mean a greater capacity to act ecologically through access to more resources, or does bureaucratization limit the capacity to be responsive? Are such ethical concerns better transmitted through hierarchy or some other means? We don't know: research is overdue.

Weick and Westley in Chapter 2.10, and Dougherty in Chapter 2.9, point out some of the difficulties that organizations encounter in trying to learn and innovate: despite countless articles on organizational learning and even more on innovation, we still cannot identify, much less guarantee, the organizational practices that bring about these goals. These authors point to overly simplistic theorizing as one cause of the problem. Organizational learning and innovation rest on *maintaining* the tensions that occur between disorganizing and organizing; forgetting and remembering; increasing and decreasing variety; between the inside and the outside; the old and the new; determining and emerging; freedom and responsibility. Too often, it seems, research emphasizes one side of the equation at the expense of the other; while practice has yet to develop the capacities for action that individuals need to manage these tensions. These authors also suggest how, by conceptualizing learning and innovation as sense-making, communicative activities that are grounded in specific linguistic and cultural settings, we might learn more about how identities can be established, which allow individuals to manage the tensions in creative ways.

Thus, communication in, around and across organizations becomes crucial:

> excellent communication is possible within the small compartment where multi-order feedback leads to great creativity. Mutual understanding is high, shared values predominate. There is a common language for communication, there are common criteria for judgement. Strong ties of affection and trust develop between the small number of people involved. They get to know each other well, and share the experience of working together to achieve shared goals. (Fairtlough 1993: 5)

Fairtlough's (1994) Celltech experience recommends the minimization of hierarchy and the maximization of integrative 'compartments', an analogy that he takes from molecular biology. If two kinds of molecule cooperate they can improve their accuracy of replication at least tenfold; if they stay closely associated, they can evolve together and the scientist can aid this joint evolution by putting the two kinds of molecule in a compartment that keeps the compatible variants together and apart from other similar molecules. Once established, compartments start to compete with each other in a Darwinian fashion. Create compartments similarly within organizations, he recommends, where all barriers to discourse, functional, technical and hierarchical, are minimized (Fairtlough 1994).

Compartments need order in the creative flux and to achieve this managers need to have something akin to the creative genius of a Carla Bley, able to work not only to their own charts but also to those of collaborators (in her case, musicians like Steve Swallow, Charlie Haden and the Music Liberation Orchestra), comprehending the whole and seeing interrelationships, involving people in the ensemble and improvising with others, to maintain the dynamic from the focal point outwards, never losing the groove, but extemporizing around it. As Putnam, Phillips and Chapman imply in Chapter 2.7, organizational communication in such a model adopts metaphors that emphasize collaboration and improvisation rather than carefully scripted texts.

Leadership under such circumstances, rather than being the prerequisite of a charismatic leader, may instead be something best nurtured by group processes. 'Managers' and 'leaders' of tomorrow's organizations may look much the same (as discussed by Bennis 1993: 10; and by Bryman in Chapter 2.2). A 'climate of trust' based on competence, congruity and constancy, the creation of meaning and the ability to learn from mistakes, becomes imperative; there is stress on a healthy and empowering environment, and the strategic importance of flatter, flexible, adaptive, decentralized and learning systems and organizations (Bennis 1993). Management develops more affinity with activities of listening, learning and launching conversations (e.g. Westley 1990) rather than commanding and controlling. In such arenas, our understanding of groups, cognition and decision-making (as discussed in the chapters by Shulman (2.6), Miller et al. (2.3) and Tenbrunsel et al. (2.4)) requires modification to take into account these changed organizational contexts. While these ideas are not particularly new, the momentum for their adoption in both research and practice is increasing.

New Forms of Resistance

In the past, while formal structures of imperative command, crystallized as bureaucracy, could aspire to control all that was within the reach of the organization, that control could never be total. The many 'vicious circles' of attempts at control by management led to increased employee resistance, as recorded from Gouldner (1954) onwards (see Clegg and Dunkerley 1980). New organizational forms and the radical changes in information technology that underpin them give cause for both hope and concern. As Reed points out in Chapter 1.1, as new forms of control open up, so too do new opportunities for resistance.

> There is much talk of a neo-Taylorite strategy of organizational control as the economic and political

driving force behind contemporary technological change. . . . Yet, a more nuanced reading would seem to suggest that the new sites of struggle and circuits of power opening up around advanced technologies make predictions about long-term trends in power structures more difficult.

When the most important relations that the organization enters into are outside its grasp as a legally fictive individual, control is particularly incomplete, and efforts to achieve it particularly inappropriate. As networks expand and as markets intrude into organizations, intraorganizational hierarchies, and control premised on them, recede in importance. As organizations seek value through the strength of their ties to other organizations, attempts at imperative managerial control become intrusive and inappropriate. Control through networks, particularly where there is considerable complexity and a short span of product life-cycles, means that emergent 'windows of opportunity' require rapid and widespread sharing of knowledge rather than its concealment from competitors.

Much as in the external arena, the internal organizational experience of changed conditions is neither good nor bad; neither dominating nor empowering; neither constraining nor enabling. Or perhaps, to be more accurate, it is all of these. For example, the move towards 'employee empowerment' places considerable emphasis on unobtrusive controls. Selection, socialization and socializing become means whereby individuals are 'conditioned' to accept organizational goals (Stewart 1989; Barker 1993; Parker 1993). Peer pressure is substituted for managerial directives and teams are used to reinforce managerial control through the language of the team effort (Parker and Slaughter 1988; Deetz 1992; Barker 1993; Parker 1993). Dissenters, if they are not fired, may be marginalized as uncooperative, or in need of additional education or training (O'Connor 1993). A critical approach renders these political dynamics more visible (see Leiba and Hardy 1994).

> the assembly line and traditional scientific management methods have actually found a new life in the team concept idea . . . in which a kind of worker empowerment takes place, but only insofar as it conforms to an even more carefully regimented shop floor regime. Indeed, rather than taking a step forward toward a new era of industrial democracy, the new participatory management schemes constitute an intensification, not an abandonment, of the essence of classical Taylorism. (Parker 1993: 250)

However, to dismiss employees involved in these initiatives as simple-minded victims does them a disservice. The changed organizational environment also offers an improvement in the quality of working life for some, if not all, employees. Instead of dismissing empowerment, critical researchers might consider how to make organizations *more* empowering, for example, by examining how the wealth created through empowerment should be distributed; how support can be provided for those employees, previously successful in hierarchical organizations, who find it difficult to adjust; how empowerment affects lower-level managers who stand to lose power; how employees can be protected from the use of empowerment as an excuse for layoffs. 'Mainstream' work, on the other hand, might take a closer look at some of its assumptions and learn about some of the drawbacks of being a player enmeshed in an interorganizational network or immersed in an empowerment, team building program (see Leiba and Hardy 1994). Again, considerable potential is to be found in the intersection of approaches.

Is It Still a Man's, Man's, Man's World?

The bureaucratic game was clear: play the rules, deny any identity that defined itself against the rules. Try to keep that identity, and be labelled a 'maverick'. Who has not learned these painful lessons one way or another, at school, at work, in the army, the church, or the university? Modern organizations, modern management, modern life were built on these disciplines. And these disciplines were not disinterested in a gender sense. When Weber (1947) wrote on the nature of 'vocation', which he saw as an essential ethical commitment of and for modernity, he wrote of the need to do one's duty, to act 'manfully'. Evidently, for Weber, it was a man's world. Is this still the case?

The postmodern organization, that which is consciously designed to be more flexible, flat and creative than the military models of modern management, centres attention on the growing importance of highly skilled, highly motivated, knowledge-based workers. Almost every authority mentions this as the critical ingredient for future business success. Reich (1992) identifies the rise of what he calls the 'symbolic analyst'. Drucker insists: 'The social centre of gravity has shifted to the knowledge worker. All developed countries are becoming . . . knowledge societies' (1990: 167). That such pieties might seem a revelation, as Drucker intends, is an ironical indictment of the era of modernist management that Taylor (1911) formally inaugurated with his *Scientific Management*.

Scientific management, it will be recalled, sought to structure and restrict the distribution of knowledge in organizations, redesigning it as a hierarchical rather than convivial tool. The wish was always stronger than the reality. Of necessity, it has always been the case that developed societies were 'knowledge societies'. No complex organization can last long that does not have recourse to, in some ways, the tacit knowledge of its workforce, even where jobs within it had been formally 'deskilled'. Drucker notes that in contemporary organizations the tendency will be not to deskill but to consciously enhance 'skill formation'. This context means a very different experience for organizational members which must be matched by very different approaches to research.

Perhaps one area where the differences loom large concerns the role of women in the organization. The ranks of management in many countries, but certainly not all, are becoming staffed with more women than in the past; also the substantive content of management activity is taking a less 'masculine' form than in older, military-derived models. That these were not the exclusive preserve of men is evident. Consider traditionally 'feminine' occupations such as nursing, where, although the employees were principally women, the organizational model derived from the male world of the military, with its bureaucratized ranks, uniforms, distinctions and command structure (Clegg and Chua 1990). The masculinist model was capable of imposition irrespective of the gendered ranks.

Older models of management derived from the military, through public sector bureaucracies (Weber 1978) and engineering practice (Taylor 1911). In these organizations, serried ranks loomed large in the male imagination as members strove to advance through them. The organization's wishes were their imperatives; its commands the inscriptions that shaped their working lives, even as they resisted them. Hierarchy was huge, pervasive, formidable, foreboding; sometimes it was uniformed and titled. Even when not militaristically attired it denoted endless divisions in the ranks of humanity: different organization entry points, different car parks, different cafeterias, different washrooms, bathrooms or toilets, different modes of address, different obsequies and indignations, different ranks and stations in life. Hierarchy humiliated some as it elevated others. It rewarded those who scrambled for its ladders while punishing those who found themselves with snakes. Hierarchy hurt like hell for those at the receiving end of it and made life sweet for those who succoured its desire for order, obedience, discipline.

It was, in James Brown's immortal words, 'a man's world'. The male members at the base of the bureaucratic pyramid felt the weight of the hierarchy every day, pressing down on them. Quite definite and different functions attached to women, those of comfort, emotional support and femininity.

This is a man's world, this is a man's world,
but it wouldn't be nothing, nothing,
without a woman or a girl

You see, man makes the cars, that take us over the road,
man made the train, to carry the heavy load
man made the electric light, to take us out of the dark
man made the boat for the water, like Noah made the Ark

This is a man's, man's, man's world,
but it wouldn't be nothing, nothing,
without a woman or a girl

Man thinks about a little bitty baby girls and a baby boys,
man makes them happy, 'cos man makes them toys
And after man makes everything, everything he can
You know that man makes money, to buy some other man

This is a man's world,
but it wouldn't be nothing, nothing, not one little thing, without a woman or a girl

(from James Brown, 'It's a Man's, Man's, Man's World', Intersong Ltd 1966)

While organization studies has certainly moved towards a greater appreciation of issues such as gender, race, ethnicity and culture, as Calás and Smircich make clear in Chapter 1.8, many of the changes to 'feminize' management involve not a transformation of organizational practices but rather a reform. Similarly, Nkomo and Cox show in Chapter 2.5 that for many researchers and practitioners, the challenge presented by a more racioethnically disparate workforce is how to 'manage' such diversity within the confines of current management practice and prevailing research paradigms and methodologies. They draw our attention to the need to understand identity as a complex, multifaceted, and transient construct; to appreciate that individuals have multiple identities; that identities intersect to create an amalgamated identity; that identities are socially, historically, culturally and organizationally constructed, and subject to contradictions, revisions, and change. A social construction view, which emphasizes the processes through which identity distinctions emerge and become salient to individuals and groups in organizations, has much to offer. Calás and Smircich remind us how the way in which we conduct our research, and the theory on which we draw, not only targets particular solutions but also defines the 'problem' in particular ways.

Consequently, more critical work promises a substantial revision to the research agenda in the areas of diversity, gender, culture, feeling and emotion in organizations, as the chapters by Nord and Fox, Martin and Frost, Calás and Smircich, Nkomo and Cox, Fineman, Gagliardi, and Hassard suggest in their various ways. First, it offers a way to document the experience of recently emerging voices, such as those gendered, coloured, emotional, aesthetic subjects in both organizations and organization studies. Second, by adopting a broader, more sensitive appreciation of the people who make up the organizations we study, we may derive greater insight into the new management practices required as global, interorganizational networks span not only different organizations but also different cultures and countries; where organizations incorporate not just a man's world, but worlds of different genders, ethnicities and cultures. Issues of gender, race, ethnicity, emotion, aesthetics and culture become far more apparent when those within organizations must nurture, group, collaborate, and engage in different ways of being, thinking, feeling and doing. Finally, we must also remember that many of the practitioners raised in a (white, authoritarian, logical, rational) man's world will find these new practices difficult. Critical research provides the opportunity to address the needs, and the emotions, of those struggling to maintain their own identities in the face of demands from 'new' organizational members, 'new' management styles, and 'new' strategic mandates.

The Subject and the Body

All social change leaves its imprint on the human body. The agricultural revolution of the late eighteenth century saw an improvement in yield, the productivity of the land, technology and distribution, all of which led to a healthier and more robust population, one that the industrial revolution bent into new shapes and new rhythms with new technologies. From the outset, observers of organizations were aware of these transformations. Marx (1975) spends much of *Capital* discussing the effects of capitalist industrialization on the bodies and subjectivity of the new class of English wage workers. Gramsci (1971) discusses the effects of what he refers to as 'Fordism' and 'Americanism' on the psycho-physiological constitution of workers, as does Weber (1978) in his reflections on the impact of Taylorism. But by the same token, one feature of bureaucracy that Weber did not stress in his ideal type was the impact of bureaucracy on the bodies and subjectivities of those that comprised it. Strange that this should be so: given that the Prussian army, with its regimented units and its goose-stepping soldiers, with their erect carriage and precise drill, polished brass and ordered uniforms, was above all else a machine for making many subjectivities and many bodies into the embodiment of one will, one Germany.

Although these goose-stepping soldiers belong to another era, it is one so constitutive of modernity that, even today, we hardly sense its strangeness, except perhaps to remark on the military bearing of a person, or the discipline of a parade ground (except when consciously mocked and ironicized, as in Monty Python's 'Ministry for Silly Walks'). Ranks of soldiers and other occupations honed on the military model (police force/service, nurses, firecrews, flight attendants, boy scouts, girl guides, security guards, gym instructors, strict tempo bands and orchestras, for instance) hardly affront our notions of 'naturalness' even today (Dandekker 1990). But, while the organizational body may still display some elements of these past models in the use of titles, ranks, uniforms, dress codes, bearing and demeanour, and other elements of embodied organizational life, the postmodern organizational world increasingly witnesses these signs of the body disappearing into cyberspace.

Bodies used to be embedded in specific organizational contexts. One worked here, in this organization; shopped there, in this store; travelled this physical and familiar route; saw these pedestrians (and street children and homeless people, depending where one drives) every day. No more. One writer of these pages types in a hotel room in Berlin, on a portable computer, in spaces between presentations at a conference on 'Culture and Identity: City, Nation and World'. Soon the text will hurtle through cyberspace to the desktop of his co-author, who will read, write, add, subtract, and transmit the revisions back to her colleague, by now back in his office on a third continent.

We live in cyberspace but our bodies remain grounded. The 'encompassing world of computer technology . . . supports an admixture of codes of observing, commentating, imagining and fictionalizing to construct and support the immediate space in which human relations occur' (Rojek 1995: 147). The technologies of the self are massively elaborated. Once, action at a distance was possible only through literacy and adequate postal delivery systems; then the telephone extended the range and shortened the time of communication, although still at some cost. The fax reduced the cost greatly; while the internet, e-mail and the world-wide web have heightened immediacy and established disembedded communication as an organizational norm. Routinely, organization members deal with others who are invisible, unknown in any direct sense, unmediated in presence, and who exist only as signs. In cyberspace, global integration and immediacy become possible through an encrypted, coded and encoded form of discourse between multiple persons, adopting multiple identities, plural statuses. In cyberspace no paramount determination exists of identities and statuses. This is its defining, postmodern characteristic (1995: 149).

In addition, as Rojek (1995: 153) argues, nations have become more tightly coupled and interdependent because of the globalization of the economy (see Chapter 2.12 by Parker). Recession or crisis in one economy affects other economies. Economic risks can no longer be insulated nationally. The tightly coupled integration of culture, nature and technology also has global, and not merely national, implications. The diminution of Brazilian rainforest, the catastrophe at Chernobyl, the *Exxon Valdez* oilspill in Alaska, are all testament to the impact of contemporary cultures of technology on the natural environment. Perrow (1984) argues that some technologies are inherently risky, because they cannot be designed as a part of loosely coupled systems in which disaster in one subsystem does not immediately lead to systemic catastrophe. Hence, some writers believe we live increasingly in high risk societies, where risk is now 'uncontainable, unlimited and uncompensatable' and where 'Life has become more dependent upon contingencies which no one can control' (Rojek 1995: 152, 153; Perrow 1984). Accordingly, we are advised not to continue to behave as if we can control contingencies that, patently, we cannot (Perrow 1984).

Other writers, like Bauman (1992), show the changing nature of contingencies over time. In the past, tradition stabilized conditions of contingency: place, family, and religion were the personal correlates of organizational contingencies for the individual, determining the individual's life-chances; blind forces work through subjects, individuals in the one case, organizations in the other, who are oblivious to their fate. Then modernity changed individuals, suggests Bauman: the life course was no longer a matter of destiny. Rather it became a question of contingent power relations: hence, Marx and Engels (1965) were able to compose a 'Manifesto' that believed that individual destinies were shaped by class relations and that fate could be overthrown by a class reflexively aware of its own formation and demographic density in a society.

Well, today there are hardly any Marxists left. History, not being subject to the grand narratives imagined for it, dealt the Marxist project a death-blow from which it would never recover. Today, the contingencies are no longer structured. Instead, postmodern theorists stress not the collective, but the plastic, free-floating and highly individually contingent structure of identities in societies. Order is precarious. Risk is pervasive. Individual security is not achieved by modern organization but threatened by it.

It is organizations that pollute the planet, cause economic disasters through contingent calculations, and inadvertently infect the security of our bodies with toxic wastes and contaminated blood supplies. In a postmodern world, one that recognizes the illusion in the power of class consciousness or the global rationality of organizations, there is scope for reflexive emancipation. One can become free to doubt, to disbelieve, to be sceptical of claims to overarching rationality. The partiality and value-embeddedness of all claims to 'rationality' become more evident in both everyday and theoretical life. These are our conditions of existence now.

Whereas we used to live 'in' the here and now, today we live in the heres, the nows, the pasts, and the futures, virtually and simultaneously. Imagine Disneyland, if you will. Dressed in character as Huckleberry Finn, a nineteenth century voice narrates a history in which you, and the other tourists on the boat, are asked to participate. The props to the performance are modern, involving electrically engineered simulacra of alligators and other creatures. Back on land, with different visual effects, you step into the imagined future of EPCOT (one from which, when one checks the sponsors, all risk has been evacuated), a reality in which you are asked to suspend disbelief. Out of the compound and back in the hotel fantasy suite of your choice, you plug into a 'star wars' video game set in a different future from the one you have just 'witnessed'. Later you settle down to watch the video movie *Blade Runner*, and begin to doubt the more palatable futures of which you were earlier a part, which were imagined for you. The dark side of Disneyland is only an unscripted moment away, an ironic subterfuge to another scripted text, an alternative narrative to the sense made for you in one here and now.

Start making sense. Stop being here where you are told you are.

The post-chip generation are the first to be able to 'be' anytime, any place, to connect anywhere that is wired. Being there and being here are now coterminous as one sits in front of one's terminal and engages in immediate and virtually instantaneous communication. This person works in Chicago but the transmission of her decisions to 'buy' or 'sell' affects the lives of people in a peasant community in Mexico who have never imagined her, while she, who perhaps could imagine them, chooses not to. Simultaneity brings disparate elements of the world into immediate, but mediated and unknown, interconnection, achieved by organizational and technological mastery of the universe, and expressed in signs that communicate, inform and connect virtually anywhere with anywhere else. Yet, in globalized terms, knowledge is not power. The world that watches CNN knows of the latest famine or war but knowing it cannot prevent it. And as the post-chip generation colonizes time and space, generation X lives in a more narrow, delimited, confining present with little to do, nowhere new to go, and little sense of nihilistic outrage left to flaunt.

Nor are the bodies of the post-chip generation immune to this 'brave new world'. Sitting at the terminal, year in, year out, one ages, one's sight suffers, repetitive strain impairs one's movement, the back gives up, the paunch grows. Contact lenses can fix the eyesight; the paunch that comes from physical passivity can be liposuctioned away; as we age, the bald scalp may be bewigged with a hairpiece 'undetectable in normal everyday use, so smart in winter or summer', or hair can be transplanted; breasts can be augmented, penises can be extended, and, when the ageing process can no longer be resisted, our organs can be 'donated' to improve, sustain, save the lives of others. The body is no longer a reliable ground of identity.

Think of Michael Jackson, whom cosmetic surgery has made a virtual person, for as long as he exists. His continuing claim to fame, notwithstanding his 'desacralization' through accusations of child molestation (Rojek 1995), is of considerable organizational consequence for his recording company, Sony, which owns and produces those aspects of his image that are organizationally manufactured for goal-oriented purposes. Even those aspects of that image not manufactured by Sony, such as the allegations of child molestation, have been appropriated by other organizational interests, such as the sleazy mass circulation tabloids. His identities are an effect of diverse organizational practices. They cease to exist in any 'authentic' sense.

Dead stars are safer: the costs are sunk, they cannot sue or misbehave, and 'necro-fever' can be manufactured, reproduced and repackaged without risk. Thus Elvis lives! And performs in a cabaret or bar near you, suggests Rojek (1995: 160–4). Certainly that is true in Las Vegas. One can hardly move without bumping into Elvis: singing; car-washing; marrying; tour-guiding: Elvis everywhere and nowhere. The dead star is the perfect sign of postmodern corporeality:

always absent, never attainable, a contrived image from some choice moment of youth and beauty, frozen for all time, never there, always here. Forever young. Forever dead. Forever.

In the postmodern cybernetic world, you are who you want to be, what you want to be, and your interlocutors have to take your word for it. The body disappears in cyberspace so that one knows the other only through their signs. Trust or cheat? Does it matter if you meet only in cyberspace? In this world of representations, the self-evident boundedness of 'nature' from 'society' dissolves. We can no longer believe the claims to a big truth. Truth has its histories, truth is contingent, truth is in our imagination. The subject seems to disappear, rather like the Cheshire Cat, with just its traces remaining.

In the past, much of organization life and interorganization life was premised on face-to-face interaction between peers and between immediate subordinates and superiors (although face-to-face communication between members of vastly different strata was rare, at least in large complex organizations). Now these relationships can flourish in the absence of any interpersonal basis, as linkages form through cyberspace. Where once trust could be established through intimacy, where surveillance was immediate, does the disappearing body now elude managerial control?

Great hopes are expressed daily in the business press for the post-internet organizational world. But, in these pages are warning signs. How will the informal organization, so vital to formal organization, be shaped in a virtual world? Which communicative competencies can flourish in cyberspace and which cannot? What are the implications of the absence of subtle, tacit and embodied clues to meaning and context that are present in more face-to-face communication? Are there contexts where mediated communication can still be followed up with more direct access? New competencies will be required to navigate this cyberscape, both within and across organizations, that presently we know little about.

The disappearance of the body from an immediate, physical workspace shared with others has been interpreted in different ways. Some suggest that as cyberspace grows, control shrinks; others suggest that cyberspace offers the potential for more sophisticated controls. On the one hand, we have the recent collapse of Baring Brothers, which has been attributed to risky and insufficiently scrutinized trading in cyberspace on far-flung options markets. Information flowed back and forth between the head office in London and the trading desk in Singapore, but managers apparently failed to register the implicit clues embedded in this disembodied, electronic language. On the other hand, we hear stories of managers who, having e-mailed employees at 9.05, await the return messages to see who is at their desk. This 'brave new world' reawakens memories of the factory 'time-clock', showing a potential for Foucauldian disciplinary controls exerted through pervasive electronic media. Yet, where there is control, there is resistance, as hackers hack into computers and code crackers crack sophisticated passwords. The struggle simply moves to a new arena, takes on a new dimension as 'displaced' employees lose the luxury of even cleaning out their offices; today, it may be done for them, in case they sabotage complex computer systems. Or the scope of e-mail communication is narrowed down as it is 'hijacked' by employees to express their concerns and complaints to an organization-wide audience (e.g. Romm and Pliskin 1995). Thus, the emergence and expansion of cyberspace carry no clear meaning, bring about no clear outcome: how it is used, abused, not used, depends upon the social context in which it is embedded.

THE RESUSCITATED SUBJECT

The body of the individual subject might disappear from sight into cyberspace, or fluctuate and oscillate under the 'pornographic' gaze of the organization (Hopfl and Sinclair 1995), but who the individual is, and what the individual might be, cannot be 'bleached' away. Those signs of identity, frequently washed away by organization studies, require a renewed theoretical gaze. In this section, we focus on the human, rather than the organizational, subject, as we consider the individual, groups of individuals, individuals in various forms of relationships, who comprise and surround the organizations that we study.

In the past, research, based on both normal and contra traditions, has often lost sight of this subject, as we will show here by exploring two paradoxes. To examine the normal science tradition, we use the example of the Aston Studies to illuminate the paradox of translation. We argue that only by silencing the individual subject, in this case managers, were the Aston Studies able to achieve the successful series of translations which helped constitute this body of work as 'science'. But, ironically, this resounding silence also prevented the final translation: that of theory into practice. To investigate the contra tradition, we draw on the modernist/postmodernist debate to explore the paradox of meaning, in which we illuminate the incongruous tendencies of postmodern work to marginalize and

draw attention away from the subject at the very moment it tries to acknowledge it. While we argue that all genres of research *risk* condemning the individual subject to the margins, we do not suggest that *all* research actually succumbs to this tendency. As many of the chapters in this book show, we can envision possible futures where the individual subject might be resuscitated in various ways.

The Paradox of Translation

While resisting generalization, the chapters in this book indicate that the development of organization studies has differed somewhat between North America and Europe (see Burrell in Chapter 3.8 and Marsden and Townley in Chapter 3.9). In North America, Parsons's interpretation of Weber resulted in a view of bureaucracy as the ideal type of modern organization (see Weiss 1983). Notable studies, such as those of Merton (1957) and Gouldner (1954), developed this theme. Coupled with Taylorist traditions and Fordist practices, a functional approach to 'management' theory flourished. In Europe, on the other hand, a traditional interest in class structure created a space for a more radical interpretation of Weber: one that focused on the domination of structures, rules, and procedures in modern life, and also drew from Marx (see Braverman 1974; Clegg 1975; Burawoy 1979; Clegg and Dunkerley 1980; Clegg 1990; Thompson and McHugh 1990).

There is thus an irony in that one of Europe's main contributions to organization theory in the 1960s was the Aston School, considered by Marsden and Townley to be the archetypal example of normal science and functionalism. Although geographically located in the UK, intellectually the Aston School could have been anywhere. The members of the school make much of the camaraderie forged in a basement in Birmingham (Pugh and Hickson 1976) but, when one inspects their work for signs of regional imprinting, none are visible. As a conception it was immaculately clean of any signs of its own place of genesis. Consequently, bearing the sign of nowhere it was rapidly to travel almost everywhere, as the word spread through the prestigious pages of the *Administrative Science Quarterly*, and became the keystone, the very centre, of claims to the existence of an orthodox consensus in organization studies.[1]

The Aston Studies were successful precisely *because* of their lack of distinguishing features. Their portability, their universal appeal, facilitated the translation process that ensured their widespread acceptance.[2] According to students of scientific practice (e.g. Callon 1986; Latour

1987; 1993) what makes a science is less the moral basis of its practices and more the quality of its translations. Those of the Aston Group were exemplary. The Aston Studies constructed a set of concerns from texts ranging from the classics of Weber and Taylor to those of their contemporaries, which were then translated into the concerns of managers in local enterprises in the British West Midlands. Reiterative translations proceeded apace in the basement 'laboratory', where the already translated concerns of such matters as 'spans of control' were translated once more, with great ingenuity, into dimensions of standardization, routinization and the like. Researchers then translated these dimensions into simple instructions that collectively formed their questionnaire, the results of which were translated by factor analysis into universal attributes of all organizations everywhere. The research process translated whatever subjectivities were found in the field into an instrumentalized intersubjectivity: a research design capable of representing any organization as if it were a variation on any other organization. Such was the audacity of the research process.

Unlike the artful construction of a laboratory setting, where the scientists can reconstruct the experiment, note any changes, and map any theoretical contingencies, the Aston researchers were forced to deal with a 'living' organization, whose members had an agency quite unlike that of microbes and chemicals trapped in a test tube (although Callon 1986 warns us about making a false dichotomy between natural and social entities). These managers and employees could change the substance of the environment that the researchers had taken so much trouble to translate; they could encroach on the translation process.[3] The Aston translation process arrested this agency and prevented managerial discretion from contaminating the results: only the researchers knew which organizations were in the study, and they preserved them in the analytical formaldehyde of 'formalization', 'standardization', 'centralization', 'routinization' and 'configuration'. Aston froze one image of these organizations in a timeless and motionless frame (Starbuck 1981). Outside this frame, however, had the camera continued rolling, it would have been shooting 'truth twenty-four times a second' (Godard 1963).[4]

By such strategies, then, the Aston Studies silenced the managers of the organizations they studied, denying any agency or intent they had. The process of consultation with the managers reminds us of a similar consultation conducted by Dom Casmurro:

> I got hold of old books, dead books, books dead and buried, opened them and compared them,

seeking out the text and the meaning in order to discover the common origin of the pagan oracle and the biblical message. I even had recourse to the maggots in the books to ask what there was in the text they had eaten.

> 'My dear sir', replied a long, fat maggot, 'we know absolutely nothing about the texts we eat. We do not choose what we eat, neither do we like or detest what we eat. We just eat.'

> I could get nothing more from him. And all the others, as if by mutual consent, repeated the same story. Perhaps this discreet silence concerning the eaten texts was just another way of devouring again what had already been eaten. (de Assis 1992: 40)

By marginalizing the agency of their managers, however, the Aston researchers were never able to complete fully their translation. Translation into practice, as far as we are aware, never occurred and the Aston Studies have never been a blueprint for organization design. So, the Aston Studies, and other work in their mould, failed to translate research into practice, despite their supposed managerialist orientation.

> This positivist concept of science, institutionalized through the Aston School, severs the connection between organization theory and practice by emphasizing testing at the expense of the creation of theory (Weick 1989). Positivism has little to say about theory creation or discovery because it assumes discovery and proof are sides of the same process and because it assumes that the only logical reason for proposing a hypothesis is that certain considerations lead one to think it is true. (Marsden and Townley in Chapter 3.9)

The success of the translation process was also its weakness. What it could not do was arrest the gnawing of other 'maggots' not enrolled in its program, both organizational participants and academic observers, who presumed to interpret, not just to be translated, who wished to create new translations, to challenge existing translations. In retrospect, the Aston project failed because it could not resolve the contradictions of translation contained within it and particularly, the contradictions posed by managerial agency. It ignores the subject,[5] as does much research of the functionalist, positivist genre.

The Paradox of Meaning

Normal science, of which Aston is a particularly illuminating example, is not the only branch of organizational studies that silences the subject. By drawing on the modernist/postmodernist debate, a debate that engages many of our authors (e.g. Alvesson and Deetz, Reed, Marsden and Townley, Burrell, Hardy and Clegg), we can explore another paradox, that of meaning. Postmodernism announced the death of meaning by showing the meaning of 'non-meaning', as Eduardo Ibarra-Colado reminded us when commenting on an earlier version of this text. In this section we discuss the implications of this paradox for the subject, showing that postmodernist approaches have, by informing our understanding of the subject, often silenced the very voices they sought to amplify.

Postmodernist writers have not been the only ones to struggle with the loss of meaning. For example, Gouldner's critique of technology revealed the loss of meaning that modernity had wrought through its institutionalization. At the centre of Gouldner's intellectual universe was an ontology of modernism (Lee 1994: 7), one which signalled a subjective idealism that privileged those who critiqued technology, a project central to Gouldner's (1976) later thought. In this respect, Gouldner was unequivocally modern and his reaction typical of prevailing radical North American disillusionment (Lee 1994: 9). European modernist thought signalled similar disenchantment. For example, the Habermasian tradition made similar assumptions about reflexivity (Steffy and Grimes 1986). Such approaches seek not so much to transcend modernism as to elevate it to a 'critical' or 'high' modernism (Jencks 1989), using the idea of pure communicative competence to forge a new world free of unwarranted domination and distortion: the Enlightenment echoes of Kantian reason resound with clarity.

In the postmodern tradition, however, the loss of meaning was a very different matter. Whereas radical modernists tried to *salvage* meaning through such means as Gouldner's critique of technology, writers in French semiology, such as Lefebvre (1971), announced the *death* of meaning through the domination of the symbol by the sign. Here was a postsubjectivist world that followed the uncoupling of the signifiers and the signified. In this world, meaning, no longer fixed, floats free: the self as subject no longer controls its own fate, while the sign as object controls everyone. The 'freedom' of the speaking subject is illusory. The Durkheimian 'social facticity' of language is reasserted as the subject is reconceived as spoken rather than speaking. It is language that speaks: subjects are simply its conduits, its mediated bearers.[6]

Postmodernist writers in organization studies responded to the challenges presented by the loss of meaning and the decentring of the subject[7] by focusing on reflexivity. Marcus (1994: 569) identifies different forms of reflexivity. Of particular interest here is reflexivity that takes the form of 'self-critique and personal quest, playing on the subjective, the experiential, and

the idea of empathy' (1994: 569); reflexivity that emphasizes the intertextual, diverse field of representations involved in any project and the fact that we operate in a complex matrix of already existing alternative representations; reflexivity that reminds us of the positioning of the gendered, coloured, classed subject. Such reflexivity is intended to address both 'crises' brought about by postmodern thinking: a legitimation crisis, which cast doubt on assumptions that 'qualified, competent observers can with objectivity, clarity, and precision report on their own observations of the social world, including the observations of others' (Denzin and Lincoln 1994a: 11); and a representation crisis, which challenged the 'belief in a real subject, or real individual, who is present in the world and able, in some form, to report on his or her experiences' (1994a: 12).

Such reflexivity which, as we stated in our introduction, aims to find 'ways of seeing which act back on and reflect existing ways of seeing', has been pursued in organization studies in a variety of ways. One approach, for example, has been through the link between theory and practice. Hassard (1993: 19) argues that 'the essence of theory is not its database but its intelligibility.' But the question inevitably arises: intelligible for whom? Hassard does not answer this question directly, but he does argue that the successful communication of a theory's intelligibility lies in its usefulness. In this way, continues Hassard, theory and practice become inseparable and, as academics, we should continuously absorb 'other cultural intelligibilities into our own' (1993: 19) to promote and enhance this interaction, and avoid the problem of privileging one discourse over another.

> [This tenet is] central to anyone who aspires to write from within a distinctively postmodern paradigm. The notion of an expert writing from within an institution in social scientific language is one that cannot be sustained if postmodernism is accepted. (Parker 1992: 12)

In this way, postmodernism supposedly achieves reflexivity through the critical examination of the assumptions that underlie 'the nature of the relation between author, text and reader' (1992: 12).

The reader might include subjects who experience the phenomena under investigation, generating input to the research process; or subjects who act on the analysis and theories provided by the researcher, consuming the output of the research process. Yet terms like 'author', 'text' and 'reader' focus our attention on what an academic (the author) writes, in academic journals and books (the text), which are usually read by other academics (the reader) rather than by either practitioners or those purportedly 'studied'. The linguistics reveal an elitist approach which is not uncharacteristic of the practice of postmodern research: readers might recall the use of deconstructionism as a technique in the hands of elitist, indeed fascist, thinkers such as Heidegger. That such elitism is still evident, even though the impulses to serve a particular ideology have vanished, should not surprise us.

Many postmodernist writers tend, then, to render their work intelligible primarily for other researchers and academics, rather than other subjects, such as those 'studied'. Postmodernist researchers often distance themselves from those who experience and consume the phenomena around which they construct their academic endeavours. One reason for this distance is, as Marsden and Townley (Chapter 3.9) point out, the fact that not much empirical research is being done. Ironically, the fragility and vulnerability of the 'researcher as subject' highlighted by this type of perspective dissuades scholars from taking on that role. It appears easier to avoid research altogether if it involves messing with the subjectivities of others who are non-academics.

> Recognition of the impossibility of theory-neutral observation undermined confidence in empirical work, lest it be tainted with 'empiricism', and encouraged a retreat into the relative safety of 'theory'. (Marsden and Townley in Chapter 3.9)

Instead of conducting empirical work, scholars are urged to spend their time with other scholars. For example, Burrell (1994) asks us to be less like social science researchers (carrying out empirical work) and more like philosophers. To do so, we should interact more with 'professional' philosophers, despite what Burrell sees as the likely painful consequences.

> To confront a professional philosopher is to confront one's own ignorance. Nevertheless, the embarrassment must be endured. . . . As social scientists, we need to be more like philosophers; as people locked into empiricism we should be more excited by the transcendental; as pursuers of practice we should be more utopian in what we advocate. (1994: 15)

In this way, the written text creates knowledge, at its best informed by 'professional' philosophers (who, presumably, are better at philosophizing than the amateurs in organizational studies), while other subjects remain unnamed and nameless. In this regard, as Parker notes, reflexivity appears to be the area where postmodernist literature has been least successful.

> If the real world does not exist in anything other than discourse, then is the act of writing one interpretation of a discourse a worthwhile pursuit? The problems of (fictional) individuals in (mythical) organizations are safely placed behind philosophical double-glazing and their cries are treated as interesting example of discourse. (1992: 11)

The conservative role of modern universities, not only those steeped in 'tradition' as Bourdieu and Passeron (1977) note, also makes itself evident in the postmodern 'caste of intellectuals' (Derrida 1978; Cooper 1989). Caste work consists of taboos as to who can do what, where, when, with what, and to whom. At the pinnacle stand the scholars, producers of articulate texts published as scholarly words, read and reviewed by professedly articulate colleagues creating a self-contained and hermetically sealed community. The pollution of everyday life is kept at textual length; opportunities for listening and learning from those who experience and consume the process that empirical research creates are kept away. This elite cult of postmodernism preserves its own caste by excluding, and thus minimizing, the reflexivity of others: it requires a truncated reflexivity, one that involves the death of subjectivity other than that of the privileged author.

Maintaining consistency between 'doing' research and the tenets of postmodern theory is particularly difficult because of the significant relationship between author and text; yet the ethos of postmodernism means that it is particularly important to do so. Little wonder, then, that many researchers avoid this dilemma by eschewing field work altogether. By subscribing to a reflexivity that is the preserve of a largely formalist, formulaic and limited theoretical conversation, these high caste scholars not only free themselves from the chore of rendering their theories intelligible to individuals who might find it difficult to decipher the words of a postmodern text, let alone derive any meaning from it; they also absolve themselves of the responsibility for doing so.

Critical forms of modernism also distance themselves from the subject. We would argue that both critical modernist and postmodernist writers find their espoused philosophies breaking down when confronted by actual subjects in the flesh rather than merely those in the text. For example, in contrasting Paulo Freire's philosophy and teaching method, Taylor (1993) found the latter undermined the former by being anti-dialogic and manipulative, partly as a result of the practical and logistical difficulties involved in translating a thought into action in a way consistent with the underpinning philosophy. It is, it appears, one thing to write a coherent philosophical position, it is another to act on its terms.

Neither critical theory nor postmodernism has, then, bridged theory and practice with any degree of confidence. In fact, both approaches have denied the very thing they most revere. The postmodern tradition simultaneously reclaims and marginalizes the subject. The identity of those subjects, so carefully constructed through postmodern analysis and insight, is then stripped away, as writers seek the safety of philosophical theorizing. The voices of the unnamed subjects, who experience and consume the research process, still to the sounds of silence. Similarly the emancipatory ideals of critical theory fade (see Alvesson and Willmott 1992a; 1992b; Martin and Frost in Chapter 3.6 in this volume). The practicalities of resistance and emancipation are often ignored by both post-modernists and critical theorists and, when these matters are discussed, it is often in such general-ized, theoretical, esoteric terminology that it offers little help to many of those who might benefit from it (see Chapters 1.7 by Alvesson and Deetz, and 3.7 by Hardy and Clegg; also Clegg 1989; Parker 1992; Nord and Doherty 1994).

In this regard, postmodernism and critical theory are not unlike the positivism they seek to resist. All marginalize and silence the people of whom they talk: the one by reducing them to meaningless statistics in which they cannot see themselves, the other by excluding them through esoteric jargon in which they cannot speak themselves.

Subject Silence

Pity the poor subject: neglected for so long in organization studies, particularly where issues of gender, culture and ethnicity were involved; homogenized by functionalist assumptions in the mainstream of analysis; and pronounced dead on arrival in positions as diverse as Aston (Pugh and Hickson 1976) and 'structural Marxism' (Althusser 1972).

In organization studies, we have seen how postmodern, critical and normal science have the potential to neglect the subject. In fact, research by its very nature tends to privilege the researcher at the expense of the subject (although some theories privilege more than others). Academics are schooled in 'articulating' (or not) their thoughts and fears, and in presenting their views thoughtfully, rationally, and logically. Articulation soon overwhelms the 'exclamation' that communicates the experience of what the subject believes, sees, feels, and senses. Exclamation is translated and channelled into requisite, articulate categories provided by

the well-trained researcher. Yet, as Fugelsang (1973) also points out, exclamation is 'genuine' because it refers to sensations, feelings, experi-ences unfiltered through the control mechanism of 'second thoughts'; while articulation is often concealing and influenced by systematized thinking (see Taylor 1993).

Most research agendas, both normal and contra, call for ever more careful and sophisti-cated articulation, reducing further the limited legitimacy attached to exclamation. Therein lies the dilemma. As Burrell (Chapter 3.8) points out, analysis 'requires the death or at least the mutilation of that which is analysed'. As researchers 'develop' their understanding, they seem to become further removed from the subjects, less able to engage in conversation with them.

Normal scientists issue edicts and predictions about appropriate behaviour, as measured by highly sophisticated, quantitative analyses and experimental paraphernalia, from the safety of their laboratories. Subjects to them are like rats in a maze (or maggots in a book). The theor-eticians who populate much of the critical theory and postmodernist genre engage with the subject mainly in terms of their own subjectivity, pre-ferring the haven of the library in which to engage in endless debate about the meaning (for themselves) of what they do. Those of the post-modern persuasion rarely give advice any more; critical theorists do, but only to those they deem to be oppressed. Advice is the *raison d'être* of the practitioner-oriented proselytizers, who preach at their subjects from the pulpit of commerce. They tell them how to be bigger, better, brighter than the rest, but remain oblivious to the costs of their recommendations to individuals both inside and outside the organization.

Everyone ignores someone. The philosophers ignore everyone; the functionalists ignore work-ers; critical theorists ignore managers (even oppressed managers because, in the view of many of these theorists, there is no such thing). Even ethnographers distance themselves, return-ing from elsewhere as 'lionized' field workers with 'stories about strange people' (Denzin and Lincoln 1994a: 7) or 'cultural romantics' who (mis)represent deviants as heroes (1994a: 9). Those who do not distance themselves may get so close to the subject as to 'go native' and become one of them. Part of them, unable to see past them, these researchers ignore the power structures that created not only the subject but also themselves, researcher-as-subject (see Chap-ter 1.7 by Alvesson and Deetz; see also Denzin and Lincoln 1994a). Even when, for example in qualitative research (Denzin and Lincoln 1994a), attempts have been made to let the subject speak, we talk about or for them, 'taking over their voice' (Denzin 1994: 503). The perspective of the articulate, scientifically trained, insightful researcher is privileged (Jeffcutt 1994; Marcus 1994).

> I am waiting for them to stop talking about the 'Other', to stop even describing how important it is to be able to speak about difference. It is not just important what we speak about, but how and why we speak. Often this speech about the 'Other' is also a mask, an oppressive talk hiding gaps, absences, that space where our words would be if we were speaking, if there were silences, if we were there. This 'we' is that 'us' who inhabit the marginal space that is not a site of domination but a place of resistance. Enter that space. Often this speech about the 'Other' annihilates, erases: 'no need to hear your voice when I can talk about you better than you can speak about yourself. No need to hear your voice. Only tell me about your pain. I want to know your story. And then I will tell it back to you in a new way. Tell it back to you in such a way that it has become mine, my own. Rewriting you. I write myself anew. I am still author, authority. I am still the colonizer, the speaking subject, and you are now at the centre of my talk. Stop'. (hooks 1989: 151–2; quoted in Fine 1994: 70)

This is especially true, as Calás and Smircich point out in Chapter 1.8 (also see Slater 1992), of those subjects associated with the 'developing' world. Even with the best of post-colonial intentions, this project is fraught with difficulty because we lack the tools to carry it out. Research so far has tended either to romanticize these subjects or to focus on the relationship between them and their oppressors. While such work may provide new insight there is an obvious risk of contamination. The challenge is to find an original space untouched by the power of the colonizers: no mean achievement. Another question that Calás and Smircich ask is: who deconstructs the West? While deconstruction is itself a Western practice, a 'return match' would at least offer some interesting insights.

For example, because of globalization, we can only explain postmodernity in 'advanced' societies by understanding 'other' societies. Globalism itself involves two dynamic movements that are always in tension: the modernist advance of information technology and communications facilitates a process of world integration dominated by economic and political fluxes; while the re-emergence of localism and nationalism, and a return of cultural and religious essentialism, focus attention on so-called 'traditional' societies. In the latter societies, a 'modernist' façade, articulated and constituted by a political and economic elite, often hides an unmodern interior. While a powerful minority displays the trappings of modernity, the majority inhabits a space somewhere between the traditions of premodernity and the chaos of postmodernity, the latter often imposed by modernist institutions such as the World Bank, the UN, and the IMF. In this sense, such societies are postmodern because they have never been modern; while the postmodernity of 'advanced' societies is really a peculiarly modern condition. We might also benefit from imagining the transition from premodernity, through modernity, to postmodernity not simply as an economic or a technological process, but as a personal experience, as an individual connects with both organization and society. 'Civilization' processes are a complex web of structural constraint and subjective constitution. Our analyses have tended to bear witness to the organizational attributes of these dynamics, such as new organizational forms and technological developments, and we have much to learn about the role of subjective experience.[8]

Thus, many different types of researchers and theorizers privilege certain information, either through not listening in the first place (by not engaging in 'empirical' work or by engaging in unfettered empiricism); or by discounting and discouraging the genuine in favour of the manufactured, exclamation instead of articulation, the emic over the etic (Taylor 1993; Denzin 1994). Ironically, by problematizing the researcher, we have drawn all the attention to her; as she engages increasingly in forms of experimental writing to achieve reflexivity – such as fiction, narratives of the self, performance science, polyvocal texts, responsive readings, aphorisms, comedy and satire, visual presentations, mixed genres (Richardson 1994) – the creative and literary skills to entertain become paramount. The living, breathing, thinking, acting subject defers to the playwright, the novelist and perhaps, if we come full circle, the puppeteer.

Subject Speak

By exposing the privilege that the articulate voices of academia currently have, we hope to reclaim some privilege for those willing to exclaim their experiences. In this way, not only might these voices secure an opportunity to speak; we might also listen. In other words, conversations *between* researcher and researched might emerge. As we mentioned earlier, while all forms of research run the risk of forgetting the subject, all have the potential for recall. Accordingly some writers *have* listened by focusing all their attention on the subject, the person, in all of the gendered, culturated and identity-laden senses in which subjectivity might manifest itself.

No longer embedded in any sense of the authenticity, integrity and individuality of a heroic and world-ordering subject, this subject is merely a sign. Feminist scholars, in particular, have adopted this view to explore the signs of the increasingly fragmented times, and the increasingly insecure and fragmented subjectivities that these times constitute and frame.

Such writers are well represented in this *Handbook*. Consider Calás and Smircich (Chapter 1.8), who explore a variety of different ways in which the female subject has achieved a voice in organization studies and beyond; Nkomo and Cox (Chapter 2.5), who put the spotlight on the whole range of ethnic diversity; Egri and Pinfield (Chapter 2.11), who acknowledge the costs borne by inhabitants of less developed countries by our consumerism and materialism, while noting that individuals from radically different spiritual traditions know a lot more about caring for our natural environment than we do. Other chapters have put the subject back in the frame in a different way by taking pictures that would not normally be taken, to reveal different facets of our identity. Not for Fineman, Gagliardi, Hassard and Weick and Westley the mugshot of rational 'man'; instead, by highlighting the way in which people feel about organizations, what they sense of the corporate landscape, how they deal with moments of boredom, or moments of humour, they achieve a three-dimensional picture.

The subject may not speak loudly from a paper on population ecology, contingency theory or organizational economics but, even here, there is scope for researchers to reconnect with the people they study. Certainly the concerns of contingency theory, organizational ecology, and organizational economics are not so far removed from the real world: what manager or employee is unaffected by organizational effectiveness and performance, by organizational founding and failure, by change and inertia, by transaction costs? Consider Donaldson's (1995) arguments against branches of normal science that he believes to be 'anti-management'; the call from Tenbrunsel et al. (Chapter 2.4) for organizational behaviour to provide managers with new skills and levers for change; the observation by Tolbert and Zucker (Chapter 1.6) that institutional theory has increased its interest in the role of the institutional entrepreneur; Barney and Hesterley's perceptions (Chapter 1.4) concerning how the firm can be managed, why some organizations outperform others, and how firms can cooperate; Shulman's insights (Chaper 2.6) into the effective working of groups. There are many ways, then, to reconnect with the inhabitants of the organizations we study (and without whom

many of us would be unemployed). While all types of research run the risk of losing the subject, they also all have the potential to relocate the subject, as Nord and Fox (Chapter 1.5) have found in their work.

Some approaches that connect with the subject do so from a managerial perspective. A number of contributors in this book confront managerial challenges head on: Bryman (Chapter 2.2) tackles how managers are or might become leaders; Whipp (Chapter 2.1) shows some of our understanding about how managers might and do make strategy; Miller, Hickson and Wilson (Chapter 2.3) explore some of the different ways in which managers take decisions; Eden and Huxham (Chapter 3.2) show how action research can help managers bring about change; Roberts and Grabowski (Chapter 2.8) discuss the challenges presented by technological development. Weick and Westley (Chapter 2.10) and Dougherty (Chapter 2.9), respectively examine how managers might help their organizations learn and innovate; Egri and Pinfield (Chapter 2.11) offer insights into how managers might become better custodians of the biosphere; Parker (Chapter 2.12) shows how managers might confront some of the challenges associated with globalization.

Other writers, notably those from critical and postmodern traditions, tend to eschew such managerialist stances, ignoring managers as a legitimate constituency (Alvesson and Willmott 1992b; Nord and Jermier 1992). For example, in this book, Hassard (Chapter 3.5) discusses time as boredom experienced by workers; but one could just as easily discuss the oppressive effects of time experienced as pressure and stress, from the perspective of managers, perhaps by revisiting the work of Mintzberg (1973) or Stewart (1967). Managers as subjects seem to disappear under the gaze of the critical and the postmodern, or appear only as the 'bad' guys.

Resistance to manager as subject undoubtedly occurs, at least partly, through the fear of managerialist hijacking and a wish to avoid the unthinking managerialism of some texts. There are good reasons for such resistance, as Martin and Frost argue in Chapter 3.6. Culture was a theme quickly taken up by managerialist researchers, and turned into a more effective managerial tool – even, some would say, instrument of oppression (Hollway 1991; Willmott 1993). There is always the risk that, as the field gets richer and more 'sophisticated', and we bring in more and more aspects of situated humanity, we also increase the possibilities and probability of manipulation. Foucault's link between power and knowledge is apposite: generating more knowledge can create more opportunities for manipulation. Knowledge is not the antidote of power. Another good reason to resist unthinking managerialism is, ironically, its lack of success in helping managers. Thus in simplifying the concept of culture, an ineffective, faddish recipe has been concocted.

What is needed is respect for the subjects – not just managers, not just employees, but all subjects – and an awareness of those subjects who abuse the power they have. For example, Bryman (Chapter 2.2) turns our attention to how leadership is constituted not just by the practices of leaders but also through its consumption by followers (also see Linstead and Grafton-Small 1992). Dougherty's discussions (Chapter 2.9) of the organizational tensions that must be managed in the case of innovation involves not just managers but all employees. Weick and Westley (Chapter 2.10) show that organizations exist in the way that all members experience them. Egri and Pinfield (Chapter 2.11) discuss how interest groups from a variety of different backgrounds might help bring about new, more effective ways of sustaining our natural environment. In other words, managers are a legitimate constituency (Nord and Jermier 1992), but rarely are they the *only* constituency: there are all the various employees, buyers, suppliers, customers, shareholders, governments, communities, propertied, moneyed, dispossessed, poverty-stricken individuals contributing to, affected by, ignored by the organizations we study. Thus we need a greater appreciation for multiple constituencies, although that places enormous demands on research, not least how to recognize the relevant constituencies, especially those that have been marginalized and excluded, and how to design research that can accommodate them.

There are as many categories of subject as there are stakeholders in organizations and organization theories and, to resuscitate the subjects, we need to be willing to follow them into the circle of research that we construct. This means a number of things. First, we need an enhanced awareness of the relationship of the researchers to those subjects under investigation, something which is not to be dismissed as a postmodern whim. 'Normal' scientists may strive for objectivity, but discussion within any scientific community acknowledges how underlying assumptions and positions affect research results (see, for example, Chapter 2.4 by Tenbrunsel et al.). Managerially oriented work that does not question its motives and assumptions is severely hamstrung (see Chapter 2.1 by Whipp). Second, we need to *listen* to what all subjects have to say in both conceiving and executing research (Forrester 1989).

Letting people in organizations speak for themselves by conducting ethnographic studies is a vital means

of moderating 'totalizing' accounts of management and organization. (Alvesson and Willmott 1992a: 454)

However, we need to do more than just listen since listening alone simply reinforces the status and power of the intellectual (even if he or she is willing to leave the safety of the library or laboratory and venture into the world outside). Consequently, we need to engage in *conversations* between researcher and researched in which both parties may learn and from which explicitly political and coercive elements have been purged (e.g. Bowen and Power 1993; Forrester 1989). Drawing on narrative theory, we can see that the aim of such conversations is to open up multiple narratives with multiple meanings; resist conventional narratives; not marginalize those narratives that do not conform to the accepted protocols (Cobb 1993). Such conversations are not necessarily comfortable: they destabilize; they offer ambiguity and ambivalence, not coherence and closure. And they certainly make research a lot tougher to carry out.

To be responsive to new narratives is important in research because narratives produce identities: as stories are elaborated, persons are coopted into identities they did not author and cannot transform. So, narratives are political in that they establish positions from which persons must speak and from which consequences in the material world flow. Narratives are never totally coherent: there is always also some degree of 'autopoetic organization' (self-regulation) that stabilizes, at least momentarily, the interpretation of the narrative. The structure of that narrative delimits the possible range of interpretations which in turn increases its coherence. This is problematic because it limits actions and privileges certain definitions of the problem (Cobb 1993). But, if narratives can be opened, people are less likely to be pressganged into forced roles or confined in straitjacket identities. If culture is produced by all organizational members, and leadership is constituted by followers as much as leaders, then surely research is produced and consumed by all subjects in its circle.

Let us remember that, despite all the strictures that postmodern analysis places on autonomous actors, subjects are not passive receptacles, sites of nothing more than history writ subjectively. As de Certeau (1984: 32) has pointed out, consumption is as much a feature of (post)-modern life as production. If those who read an academic text help to constitute it, those who experience everyday life help to constitute both it and their role in it. De Certeau draws on examples as diverse as TV audiences which, treated as inert statistical data, have to be transformed into a 'lexicon of user practices' because researchers are forced to ask 'what do consumers *make* of the images that pass before their eyes?'; as well as native Indians in South America, who neither rejected nor accepted the dominant order that Spanish law imposed on them, but made it 'function in another register' through procedures of consumption that allowed them to maintain their difference 'in the very space that the occupier was organizing'. To see the subject as historically constituted is still to see the subject, and to acknowledge the limits of its being also acknowledges the possibilities of its emancipation (Laclau 1988).

> What we have rejected is the idea that humanist values have the metaphysical status of an essence and that they are, therefore, prior to any concrete history and society. However, this is not to deny their validity; it only means that their validity is constructed by means of particular discursive and augmentative practices. ... It is within this discursive plurality that 'humanist values' are constructed and expanded. And we know well that they are always threatened: racism, sexism, class discrimination, always limit the emergence and full validity of humanism. To deny to the 'human' the status of essence is to draw attention to the historical conditions that have led to its emergence and to make possible, therefore, a wider degree of realism in the fight for the full realization of those values. (Laclau and Mouffe 1987: 102)

As Nord and Fox point out in Chapter 1.5, the individual has *not* disappeared.

By examining how the subject is constituted by events and processes beyond any immediate or complete control, the distance between researcher and subject is decreased, not increased. To understand how he or she is constituted and created in this world of uncertainties is not to claim victim status, however, but to show the possibilities for action. To combine listening with learning transforms reflexivity from elite privilege to a property of a system (see Lash and Urry 1994). Created and re-created in these flows are spaces and signs, significations and semiotics, symbols and selves. Postmodernism in this empirical mode involves analysis of different forms and trajectories of different types of mobile subjects and objects through circuits of power framed by meaning, space and time. Some subjects are more reflexive than others because of specific configurations of space and time which flow through them, but they are not confined to supposedly specialized, articulate researchers.

This is not to romanticize the subject, or to yearn nostalgically for the return of mind over matter. As Denzin and Lincoln (1994a: 11) point out in the introduction to their handbook, organization studies must adapt to the challenges posed by the representation crisis: the concepts of the aloof researcher and the knowing subject must be abandoned. This does not preclude action- and activist-oriented research, or social criticism and critique. It means 'reading' theory; searching for local rather than grand narratives; engaging in struggle rather than revolution; listening and learning; understanding style and rhetoric; attending to language and meaning; being aware of our temporal, spatial, emotional involvement in the research enterprise, and starting up conversations. Future research might, then, select more diverse subjects from which to learn, such as managers *and* workers, men *and* women, black *and* white, Asian *and* Caucasian, the developed *and* the developing world. Through exploring diverse subjectivities, we are more likely to avoid stereotypical categorizations, and to meld theory and practice from both (different) managerial and emancipatory positions (Alvesson and Willmott 1992b).

It is through listening and learning, through the fusion of insight gained from experience with insight offered by theory, that one is likely to achieve reflexivity. Theorizing helps us see beyond experience to the webs of power and language that entrap and produce 'experience'. It prevents submergence (Freire 1992) in the dark prisons where experience often resides. However, as academics we must also directly confront the subjects for whom we purport to speak. It is in this nexus of theory and experience that reflexivity is most potent.

Bringing such agency back into focus does matter to organization studies. As Peter Frost suggested to us, when reading an earlier draft of these conclusions, organization theorists have been only too adept at developing and teaching theories and creating intellectual movements that scoffed at, dismissed or eliminated agency. We all know these approaches: contingency perspectives, where it is only 'size that matters'; population ecology perspectives, where only niches matter and not the people who may help to fill them; postmodernism, where only the discourses speak and the agency of those spoken through is given the status of little more than a ventriloquist's dummy. If we believe that nothing can be done, that we don't make a difference, we put the chains on ourselves and leave the controllers, the oppressors, whomsoever, to eliminate whatever agency they desire. Isn't this, after all, the intellectual position that is most conducive to tyranny? Hence, to resist tyranny let us resuscitate the subject, breathe life back into those stilled lips, disturb the somnolent and death-like state, shatter metaphorical bottles of analytic formaldehyde.

THE SUBJECT: MAKING SENSE OF ORGANIZATION STUDIES

In the first section, we examined the organization of the enterprising subject, pointing out that it was often far ahead of the attempts of organization studies to represent it. In the second section, we described how the individual subject, who is often unrepresented or misrepresented in organization studies, fades away. In this section, we explore a third subject: organization studies themselves, how we represent ourselves and whether we can reflexively account for that representation. In this way, we contemplate our identities as researchers of organizations.

As we have already suggested, reflexivity comes from conversations that take place at the intersections: between researcher and researched; between different theories; between theorizing and practice. In particular, we wish to draw attention to the relationship *between* theory and practice. Theory, practice and the relationship between them are contingent upon discursive practices: theorists not only theorize, they also specify the relationship between theory and practice within the conditions of particular discursive practices. No calibration of this relationship can stand outside of those discourses that constitute or oppose particular representations. Thus our identity as organization studies researchers depends partly on our understanding of the relation of theory and practice; and any reflexive understanding of our identity hinges on our understanding of the limits to this relationship. While the debates between the paradigms and between modernism and postmodernism highlight the need for more reflexive forms of theorizing, they have not devoted similar attention to the vital relationship between theory and practice.

Some writers have simply opted out from conversations between research and practice. Write what you will and damn the consequences: it matters not whether practitioners understand or even read it. Those that opt out of practitioner discourse may well have interesting things to say, but, by definition, rarely will they concern the relationship of theory to practice: the relationship of a theory to other theories perhaps, but not necessarily to practice other than that of other theorists. The relevancies of these researchers are rarely attuned to the relevancies of practitioners, in part because the latter change more rapidly as a result of situational, competitive pressures, whereas the former are concerned with maintaining existing investments in intellectual capital. So, having built up an expertise in a particular area, academics have a real interest in saving it from extinction, even if their focus sometimes runs counter to or lags behind what is happening in the organizational marketplace external to their knowledge interests. Thus does the organizational world change irrespective of what we think we know of it.

Other writers do focus on the link between theory and practice, making prescriptions to denote what organizational practice should be. But they tend, knowingly or unknowingly, to rely on privileged analysis, unreflective of the power implications that this involves. For example, prescriptions often conjure up a medical model by referring to the state of the organization's health, and providing prognoses for survival or morbidity. These functionalist approaches tend to founder on the organicism imported with this model: there is no *a priori* organic entity, whose health corresponds to that of the body in medical discourse, outside the representational aspirations of those theorists and consultants seeking to prescribe. So, while the liver and the arteries cannot debate the appropriate prescription for their health, the constituent parts of organizations usually do – and rarely agree. As a result, any representation tends to take sides, even as it comforts itself with the illusion that it does not.

Some representations tend to listen to the best resourced voices, the dominant coalitions (Cyert and March 1963) that purport to speak for the organization. This leads to unreflective recommendations. As Lukes (1974: 34) remarked in another context, 'talk of interests provides a licence for the making of normative judgements of a moral and political character.' Critical or radical perspectives take a different but equally privileged stance when they base their judgements, not on what privileged members of the organization say they want, but on what the researcher thinks underprivileged members ought to want (see the discussion on 'real' interests in e.g. Lukes 1974; Benton 1981; Knights and Willmott 1982; Clegg 1989).

Hence prescriptive theorists presume to know the interests of either a reification, the organization as a unitary phenomenon, or a particular group of individuals within it. What they cannot easily do is to articulate prescription within the context of a contested conception of what, and whose, these interests really are, other than through protocols that are empirically fashionable, by chasing after the chimera of the current vogue. How does one avoid becoming subordinated to such power, either established or resistant, in such a situation? The answer is that one cannot. But one can cast a more reflective eye over the relationship between theory and practice. For example, from what place of privilege can theory speak if not one rooted in the views existing within the organization? If prescriptive theorizing is rooted in the organization, whose image of the organization prevails? Should theory seek, through its prescriptions, to create an illusion of order or represent actual dissonance and dissent? Should it identify with those interests that are currently organizationally dominant or with some emergent or dominated interest?

We do not believe that there are easy answers to these questions but we do believe that they should be asked. In this way, we find that we need neither fear, nor hide behind, infinite relativism. Or, to be more accurate, relativism is not the issue. We may no longer have the means to judge one theory, one representation against another in any absolute terms, but, there again, it was ever an illusion to think otherwise (commensurability arguments not withstanding). What we can do, and do indeed do, is promote representations that have a greater reflexive awareness of what they map *and* what they miss.

In this section we explore how greater reflexivity might be achieved. We first contrast two broad approaches, or identities, in organization studies: those that emphasize organization and structure; and those that emphasize people and culture. We then show how identity is consolidated through distance and difference, not just between different theoretical identities but also between identities that revolve around theory or practice. Instead of separation, we argue for conversation, especially at the intersection of the practical and theoretical. The approaches covered in this *Handbook*, if they stand alone, risk becoming too encoded in their own constitution and, therefore, unreflexive. In establishing their own identity, they must also be open to other identities, theories and practices.

Identities in Organization Studies

The chapters, despite their differences, agree on two key issues. First, organizations exist as empirical objects, even though there may be little agreement as to which features are most salient to their interpretation and explanation. Second, at the centre of organizations, and also surrounding them, are the people who comprise them, found them, work in them, benefit from them, are disadvantaged by them. Starting from these simple data – 'organizations' and 'people' – two vantage points, two identities, present themselves.

Some chapters stress organization structure and downplay the agency of the people: for example, contingency theory, population ecology, economic approaches, and much of institutional theory. Structure refers to organization patterning, based on some transcendent organizing principle, like natural selection, goodness of fit or efficiency. There may be disagreements on how to prioritize the conceptualization of structure but not on the prioritization *per se*. Other chapters emphasize people and their cultures, the centrality of actors and action to organizational life. One thinks of the chapters on critical theory, postmodernism, power, emotion, aesthetics. For some researchers, cultures bind people together, unifying them in common frames of meaning and practice; for others, cultures demarcate and define differences between people.

These more or less structuralist or culturalist perspectives represent broad identities within organization studies, built around the dialectics of inclusion and exclusion; relevance and irrelevance; legitimacy and illegitimacy. They are rooted in discourses that address the analytical constitution of what is taken to be the 'real' world of organizations since we cannot presume any ontology of organization, as Stablein reminds us in Chapter 3.1. Thus different identities lead to different conclusions. For structuralists, the organizational world is characterized principally by economic configuration and issues, by integration, convergence and divergence. For culturalists, organizational realities exhibit primarily the interlinkage of different cultural dimensions that do not necessarily stop at the organization boundary: they may come into the organization from elsewhere; once there they may travel, nomadically, anywhere. Theorists of each persuasion will look for, and find, quite different relevancies. Structuralists stress key elements that function independently and have a variable effect on other, dependent phenomena: the relation of size to bureaucracy, for instance, or the relation of transaction costs to the form that carries the exchange. Culturalists attend to issues of social construction, meaning and its security or fragility.

The constructions of these identities comprise three crucial moments: differentiation; the settlement of self-reference or self-image; the recognition of others (Therborn 1995: 229). Differentiation takes place through the social construction of a boundary, for instance when contingency theorists demarcate themselves from population ecologists. Drawing boundaries facilitates the creation of a self-image and, in turn, makes it easier to recognize others, outsiders, aliens, enemies. The more clearly the opponents in the struggle can be seen, the more different that they appear, the earlier and the stronger a separate identity emerges.

Threats to identity tend to lead to a re-inforcement and narrowing of boundaries, heightening separation and difference.

> In situations of unusual uncertainty or adversity, entrepreneurs of mistrust, of more narrow boundaries of identity, should, *ceteris paribus*, be expected to be more successful than proponents of trust and open boundaries. (1995: 229–300)

Thus paradigm warriors have sought to strengthen barricades and fortify positions, making it difficult to argue, reflexively, that the barricades are neither exhaustive of the possible options nor capable of resolving issues within the entrenched positions. In such conditions of adversity and uncertainty, there have been entre-preneurs of mistrust aplenty, who have differ-entiated identities very effectively: radical structuralists and radical humanists, functional-ists and interpretativists, critical and institutional theorists, contingency entrepreneurs and popula-tion ecologists. Differentiation achieved; self-image established; others recognized, repelled, rejected.

We dispute neither the existence of these identities, nor the importance of self-image in carving out space for different forms of research and theory. Our objective is to challenge their separateness. We advocate the recognition of others in ways that promote the possibility of conversation. Consequently, neither structuralist nor culturalist approaches are adequate, because, as must be evident now, neither accounts for the other, and each only focuses on some aspects of the phenomenal world that the other does not focus on at all. Both structure and culture are active, not inert: there is both structuration and enculturation at work in the phenomenal world. Both shape organizational action as a species of social action and are, in turn, shaped by it. Similarly, the organizational world as we 'know' it is an effect of the knowl-edge interests, protocols, and practices of researchers, students, and consultants – as well as those of the people who constitute the phenomenal aspects of the organizational reality under study. Fundamentalists on one side would argue for the determination of lay knowledge by expert knowledge; while those on another would say lay concerns are paramount. Rather than saying that our knowledge of organizations is either wholly 'real' (an effect only of the knowl-edge interests, protocols, and practices of organization members and stakeholders) or wholly 'unreal' (an effect only of the knowledge interests, protocols, and practices of the mem-bers of organization studies communities), we prefer to see the two positions as standing in relation to, and marked by conversations between, each other.

Conversations

Our aim in editing this *Handbook*, as we said in the introduction to the volume, is to capture and stimulate conversations.

> How aspects of organizations are represented, the means of representation, the features deemed salient, those features glossed, and those features ignored, these are not attributes of the organization. They are an effect of the reciprocal interaction of multiple conversations: those that are professionally organized, through journals, research agendas, citations and networks, and those that take place in the empirical world of organizations. The dynamics of reciprocity in this mutual interaction can vary: for some the conversations of practice inform those of the profession; for others profes-sional talk dominates practice; for still others, practice and profession sustain each other.

The terms through which organizations achieve representation are always an effect of theoretical privilege afforded certain ways of seeing, certain terms of discourse, and their conversational enactment. The work of this book is to construct a space in which conversation between theor-etically self-privileging discourses becomes an option that researchers can pursue reflexively, where theoretical identities can be affirmed *and* differences can be negotiated, not just differ-entiation from other theoretical positions but also within conditions of self-identification.

Conversation, whether located in the organiz-ation of an academic specialism, or applied in the actions that constitute the analytical subject of such specialisms, is a public phenomenon. Conversation is intersubjective, shared and embedded within distinct local practices. By definition, no theoretical work ever floats free, hovering high above the plains of mundane knowledge, soaring over the peaks and gullies of societal interests. There are no ways in which theory can sever itself from the conditions of its own existence. While some forms of theory may claim autonomy, it is important to see the dangers therein. For example, much of the work from a feminist perspective resists autonomy and disinterestedness precisely because such disin-terest led to the neglect of the feminine part of the world: a disinterested, autonomous discourse of organization theory unreflexively reproduced largely non-gendered or masculinist views of and practices in the organizational world. Viewed from the position of the neglected interests, disinterest looks a lot like the particularism of those represented and the slighting of those not.

Thus a general and guiding theoretical point emerges. Those theoretical positions able to account, reflexively, for their own theorizing, *as well as* whatever it is that they theorize about, will be clearest about their own identity, and the extent to which it is partial or formed in dialogue with other positions. The recognition of the 'other' is crucial: self-regarding behaviour in the absence of recognition of and by others is of no value in itself. On these criteria, it is not the alleged 'disinterestedness' of a position that makes it worthwhile, but the degree of reflexivity that it exhibits in relation to the conditions of its own existence. Severing the conversational elements that nurtured the theory in the first place and which link it to practice makes it harder to attain this reflexivity. Thus we argue for the grounding of theoretical claims in local and specific circumstances, rather than their radical and rapid translation out of them. In an organizational world that is part of the social, which is inscribed with the materiality of words and the indeterminacy of meaning, such conversational stretch is essential. Otherwise the paradigm closes, conversational practice becomes monologue, and reflexivity declines accordingly.

Theoretical positions can be judged according to three criteria. The first criteria of differentiation relates to the ways in which theories separate themselves from the practices of 'individual(s)' in the 'organization(s)' that sustain them. The reference here is to the individual in both the 'concrete' organization and the theoretical organization of knowledge. How does the epistemology of a theoretical position translate to the practical knowledge of those researching and those being researched? Are these knowledges mediated? If so, on whose terms? The second set of criteria refers to the supply and demand of reference images, the ways in which theory knows itself to be the type of theory that it is, and is not. How does the theory reflexively recognize itself, achieve its epistemological self-recognition? How narrow or broad is its discourse? The third set of criteria refers to the extent of pluralist positive and negative recognition: not only the patterns of self-citation within discursive communities (e.g. population ecology citing population ecology) but also recognition, both negative and positive, from theoretical 'others'. In our opinion, forms of theoretical representation that cannot meet these criteria should be viewed with suspicion: they are unreflexive about their existence, a lack of reflexivity that augers ill for their relation to knowledges in and of the organizational world.

We have elaborated a means for discrimination, using ideas about the relative autonomy and reflexivity of theories. But that is not all. We can also exercise discretion and judgement concerning individual representations. There is an aesthetic dimension to all human activity, theorizing included. Aesthetics refers to the investigation and appreciation of beauty, especially, but not exclusively, in the arts. It refers to the beauty of scientific prose as much as to literary endeavour. If the text does not please it will not be pleasurable: why should one endure experiences that lack aesthetic style if, elsewhere, one can find more aesthetic wit, elegance and refinement, or whatever aesthetic calculus one chooses? In this way, argue writers like Zald (1994) organizational studies can be reconfigured at the intersection of both science and humanities.

> Humanistic disciplines render behaviour in specific time and societal contexts – not time as a generalised measurement of distance between events, but particular time sequences in which specific events are embedded. Secondly, humanistic disciplines are concerned with substantive meaning – how particular objects and symbols relate to each other; the roots and background by which symbols, high and low, have achieved their meaning and transformation. Third, humanistic disciplines have been concerned with the coherence and transformation of high culture, of the symbols and meaning systems of intellectuals and artists and how if at all these systems relate to other societal institutions. Finally, the humanities have been interested not only in the substantive meaning of symbolic forms, but their presentational form: rhetorical and narrative devices and artistic styles have been of interest, as well as their impact upon social institutions and social change. (Zald 1994: 518)

Part of the postmodern ethic concerns the aestheticization of everyday life, where everything is explained in terms of 'culture' and 'style wars' (Rojek 1995: 165). The modernist differentiation of the world into high and low culture, separating ethics, politics and economics into unrelated spheres, is past, a spent force. With postmodernization, signs signify everywhere. No space remains innocent of meaning, of style, of ambiguity, of irony. In matters of style, appearance and reference are everything. Scratch the surface and one should find nothing deeper. The surface is already complex enough.

Aesthetics is no mere privileged realm of heightened senses. We live in it and are affronted by its absence everyday. Beautiful, playful, deconstructive and ironic images pervade all of everyday life: the billboards on the freeway, the narrative codes of current soaps, even children's television programmes such as 'The Simpsons', all display signs of reflexive, ironic postmodernity. It saturates our senses from the media that extend and reflect our immediate sociability, just as it covers our disinclination to face the unaesthetics of everyday life: the despair, misery and ugliness of poverty, risk, hunger and disease. We can, then, develop competencies for aesthetic judgement. In the world of the humanities, the artists, the musicians, the actors, directors, writers, audience, spectators, and patrons, are hardly devoid of appreciation and criticism. One song may capture a mood better than another; a play may fail to make the social commentary it intended; one book may read more fluidly, more persuasively, more cleverly than another; a photograph may see something a painting does not. Thus aesthetics raises moral and ethical questions. Bauman (1992) suggests that in an economy of signs, a world where the materiality of things pales before their signification, people are less actors working out well-rehearsed scripts, and more morally competent subjects. Such moral competence extends to aesthetics: 'the propensity of actors to believe that something is right and good is intimately connected with judgements of beauty' (Rojek 1995: 169). And what is considered beautiful is a matter of knowledge which, we know, can never be innocent of power (Foucault 1977).

Nor are aesthetic judgements separate from the organizational practices that surround and support them. We can all make a sensible assessment of both Julie Andrews and John Coltrane in their different renditions of 'My Favourite Things'. Our agency is no less touched by the improvisational beauty of John Coltrane's 'My Favourite Things' than it is unmoved by the banality of Julie Andrews's rendition. Yet, the expression of this agency is not merely a matter of style, of taste, of aesthetics, as we have been at pains to document in this conclusion. It is constructed organizationally through the impact of organizational developments: before the invention of the long-playing record, if one had not heard Coltrane in performance, his improvisation would have remained nothing other than a memory trace. The technology did not exist to capture it. Today, in the age of the microchip, both Coltrane and Andrews are accessible on compact or laser disks, on personal stereos that we carry to and from work, use while working, listen to while working out.

To bring agency back in, in our postmodern times, does not necessarily lead to a fixed, embodied human or organizational subject, to a definite sense of *the* person, *the* organization in the sight of organization studies. The developments that make the headlines in the daily papers or on the television news; the developments that fill the spaces created by the convergence of media and communications industries; the developments that mark our international, multicultural, global village, reveal both the possibilities of and limits to agency. The information superhighway; the internet; biotechnology; new forms of organizations and of employment; deregulation; the dissolution and creation of

trading blocs; the breakup of states; conditions like AIDs; genocide and ethnic cleansing; worldwide displacements of refugees; these are signs of a more ambiguous, less certain world, a world of mobile bodies, fluid subjects and emergent identities. The subject is there, the subjects are there: sometimes difficult to see; sometimes fractured into multiple places and times; sometimes strong enough to struggle; sometimes helpless; sometimes aware, sometimes not; sometimes aesthetically pleasing, sometimes deliberately disturbing.

All subjects construct their subjectivity; yet no subject is omnipotent since no subject can ever determine the reception of their subjectivity. The subject is product of neither an empiricist canvas, recorded as seen, nor a theoretician's palette, mixed and used at will. Subjects organize themselves and seek to organize the judgements of others. The signs of the subject jostle for our attention – an attention that is socially organized through hierarchies of judgement. So, while the subject is ever present, the signs of the subject are ever changing because of diverse representations, both lay and professional. The subject as a simple sign is unlikely to reappear, as professional discourse becomes more reflexive and as the world becomes more complex, as we have sketched in this chapter.

So, the subject is always there. But where? In what style of being 'there'? The subject is never 'there', capturable by some fixed and simple grid, any more than the grid of the city map captures the complexities and possibilities of the landscape outside the gallery window. Step outside and the signs multiply, and become more complex. There is always more than one means of capture and more than one sense of the captive. 'A *picture* held us captive. And we could not get ouside it, for it lay in our language and language seemed to repeat it to us inexorably. . . . Language is like a labyrinth of paths. You approach from *one* and know your way about; you approach the same place from another side and no longer know your way about' (Wittgenstein 1972: 116, 203). The *Handbook of Organization Studies* contains many such paths in the form of the chapters that comprise it; but we believe that it is the conversations between them, the *wholeness* of the book, that offer the prospects of escape, so that no single picture holds us captive.

And in the End . . .

Wittgenstein (1972: 527) said that 'understanding a sentence is much more akin to understanding a theme in music than one may think.' And so we shall return to music, once more, to compose a conclusion. *Abbey Road* defined one version of 'the end' and, playing with its sense, we can say: 'and in the end, the sense you take is equal to the sense you make'.

> *Voice*: [*interrupting the narrative*] Do you mean that we have no way of determining truth or falsity in organization studies, other than through what people do, their forms of life?
>
> *Authors*: No, come to think of it, maybe issues of truth and falsehood are never absolute. Truth is not a thing but a process for producing something that passes as the truth. It has its politics, its aesthetics, its practices of representation and translation, just like any other discourse. The truths of organization studies do not stand apart, like a touchline referee, from the game that they represent. They are part of a game in which there are many players, not all of them academics.
>
> *Voice*: So there is nothing to get hung about, no point being hung up on 'normal science' or 'critical theory', on 'modern' or 'postmodern' perspectives?
>
> *Authors*: They are that, just perspectives, we see different things with them, different facets of that which is represented. They are voices in a conversation but they are not the conversation. Energy and vitality derive from the difference rather than the similarity, the contrasts and the contradictions rather than the agreement. We can use that energy to learn more about what we do, who we are, what we can achieve, and where we have failed.
>
> *Voice*: The *Handbook* functions as a whole then, not in its parts, but in the tensions and contradictions between them, in the creative space between sharp edges and those moments of ambiguity, uncertainty and anomie to which their interrelation gives rise?
>
> *Authors*: Yes, that's it!
>
> *Voice*: That raises some interesting questions. Perhaps you should address them; maybe in another book?
>
> Authors: No way!
>
> *Voice*: Why do you say this? [*Pause. Reflection. Silence for 20 seconds.*]
>
> *Authors*: [*haltingly*] Look, the point is, there is a moment when, how should we say, 'whereof one cannot speak, thereof one must be silent', right? Stop making sense?
>
> *Voice*: What do you mean?
>
> *Authors*: Leave it to the readers.

NOTES

We acknowledge the substantive suggestions made by Walter Nord, Peter Frost, John Gray, Eduardo Ibarra-Colado and Sue Jones on an earlier draft of this chapter.

1 Some writers, like Gibson Burrell in Chapter 3.8 in this book, argue that the unity of the Aston era was illusory since very different approaches to research existed elsewhere in Britain as well as further afield (also see Zald 1994). While Burrell does not shy away from such contradiction others yearn for more unity, seeing the current fragmentation as atypical and, in many cases, to be resisted (e.g. Donaldson 1985; 1995; Reed 1985). Whatever the interpretation, some things seem clear. In North America, by and large, functionalism ruled the field, earning itself the appellation of 'dominant orthodoxy' (at least in the eyes of the unorthodox); while in Europe, the functionalism characterized by the Aston School was challenged by the rise of other schools of thought, methods of inquiry, and styles of research (see Hofstede 1995). It was in this context that, in 1979, Burrell and Morgan wrote *Sociological Paradigms and Organizational Analysis*, which mapped out four approaches to organization theory depending on underlying assumptions concerning the nature of our world and the nature of knowledge (see the introduction and Burrell's chapter for more details).

2 One might be tempted to attribute Aston's success to its adherence to Popperian principles (e.g. Donaldson 1985), but Popper's philosophy of science stems from his interpretation of the history of scientific progress, not from the empirical study of what scientists actually do. We are sceptical of using a non-empirical basis for a defence of empiricism (Law 1986) and suggest that empirical observation is a more appropriate defence of orthodoxy than historical speculation. Contemporary studies that have empirically examined what scientists do when they do science (e.g. Latour 1987) find that they do something quite different to Popper's recommendations and, as this discussion demonstrates, Aston is no exception.

3 Consider the problems caused to Callon's (1986) scientists when their anonymous subjects exercised discretion in a scientifically inconvenient way.

4 What the Aston researchers forgot, paradoxically, is that by preserving anonymity, the organizational members preserved untrammelled agency as far as their particular organization was concerned. In other words, once the researchers had left, the managers and employees were free to choose this technology, that design, change this, institutionalize that, without anyone ever knowing.

5 The Aston methodology not only silenced organizational members, but also tried to muzzle other researchers. The success of its translation provided a one-dimensional discourse within which debate could take place, but always in the terms set by that discourse. In science, when narratives become too one-dimensional, science ceases to be interesting. Nothing much is left to be said; the field-setting is a secret; only the processes of its translation are open to inspection; only its initial translators are able to revisit the field to reaffirm their translation, thus always being capable of delivering variation on the same meaning. The field can

be approached only as it is already translated, already mediated, already arrested. What dull science!

6 These themes of French structuralism and poststructuralism are debated widely in most fields of the humanities and social sciences (Lane 1971; Weedon 1987) but have remained marginal in organizational studies (but see Clegg 1989 for a case where they have not). Here, the notions of 'structure' and 'structuralism' have had far more circumscribed meanings, as in the contribution of Blau and Schoenherr (1971) or Pugh and Hickson (1976): while the debate centres resolutely on organizational structure, it does so in decidedly 'objectivist' terms.

7 Even writers from functionalist, normal science traditions have wrestled with the disappearance of the subject. Their response, however, has been one of nostalgia: the search for subject-centred reason in an embrace of the certainty of 'organization', if not of self. Enlightenment according to such approaches rarely concerned the individual and the personal: it encompassed only the technical. The embrace of method dissolved all traces of its ontogenesis, including the irony and parentheses embedded in Weber's original conception of modern organization. The tragic self locked in the 'iron cage' of bureaucracy, a little cog striving to be a bigger cog, disappeared. Instead, a contingent version of the 'iron cage' has been reconstructed: the machinery remains the same, but with a few more gears added: now it is geared up to cope with the environment, with technology, with size. With all its optional features, the basic model T survives well into the latter half of the twentieth century, although it no longer has a driver, despite attempts to reinstate choice (e.g. Child 1972). As ever more dedicated engineers toil to achieve its perfection (e.g. Donaldson 1985), they empty the organization and, with no driver, no self, no meaning, the refinement of engineering excellence becomes its own form of subjectivity. As the organization, as subject-object, becomes an increasingly empty symbol, social engineering takes a firmer hold. From the time when the Hawthorne Studies challenged time and motion (see Reed in Chapter 1.1), still more gears have been added to *rebuild* meaning, passion, commitment, indeed vocation, through empowerment, participation, charisma, chaos, quality, excellence and the like. Ironically, this new organization science is a perfect example of those 'sensualists without spirit' that Weber (1947) warned against. The technicians are out of the cage; their subjectivity designs its representations, becoming embodied in pure objectivism.

8 We are grateful to Eduardo Ibarra-Colado for his contribution to these arguments.

REFERENCES

Alter, C. (1990) 'An exploratory study of conflict and coordination in interorganizational service delivery systems', *Academy of Management Journal*, 33: 478–502.

Alter, C. and Hage, J. (1993) *Organizations Working Together*. Newbury Park, CA: Sage.

Altheide, D.L. (1988) 'Mediating cutbacks in human services: a case study in the negotiated order', *The Sociological Quarterly*, 29(3): 339–45.

Althusser, L. (1972) *For Marx*. London: NLB.

Alvesson, M. and Willmott, H. (1992a) 'On the idea of emancipation in management and organization studies', *Academy of Management Review*, 17(3): 432–64.

Alvesson, M. and Willmott, H. (eds) (1992b) *Critical Management Studies*. London: Sage.

Astley, W.G. (1984) 'Toward an appreciation of collective strategy', *Academy of Management Review*, 9(3): 526–35.

Barber, B. (1983) *The Logic and Limits of Trust*. New Brunswick, NJ: Rutgers University Press.

Barker, J.R. (1993) 'Tightening the iron cage: concertive control in self-managing teams', *Administrative Science Quarterly*, 38: 408–37.

Barley, S.R. (1986) 'Technology as an occasion for structuring: evidence from observations of CT scanners and the social order of radiology departments', *Administrative Science Quarterly*, 31: 78–108.

Bauman, Z. (1992) *Intimations of Postmodernity*. London: Routledge.

Bennis, W.G (1993) *An Invented Life: Reflections on Leadership and Change*. Reading, MA: Addison-Wesley.

Benton, T. (1981) '"Objective" interests and the sociology of power', *Sociology*, 15(2): 161–84.

Berger, P.L. and Luckmann, T. (1967) *The Social Construction of Reality: a Treatise on the Sociology of Knowledge*. Garden City, NY: Anchor Books.

Blau, P.M. and Schoenherr, R.A. (1971) *The Structure of Organizations*. New York: Basic Books.

Blumer, H. (1971) 'Social problems as collective behaviour', *Social Problems*, 19: 298–306.

Bourdieu, P. and Passeron, J.-C. (1977) *Reproduction in Education, Society and Culture*. London: Sage.

Bowen, M.G. and Power, F.C. (1993) 'The moral manager: communicative ethics and the *Exxon Valdez* disaster', *Business Ethics Quarterly*, 3(2): 97–116.

Braverman, H. (1974) *Labour and Monopoly Capital*. Chicago: University of Chicago Press.

Burawoy, M. (1979) *Manufacturing Consent*. Chicago: Chicago University Press.

Burrell, G. (1994) 'Modernism, postmodernism and organizational analysis 4: the contribution of Jürgen Habermas', *Organization Studies*, 15(1): 1–19.

Burrell, G. and Morgan, G. (1979) *Sociological Paradigms and Organizational Analysis: Elements of the Sociology of Corporate Life*. London: Heinemann. Aldershot: Arena, 1994.

Callon, M. (1986) 'Some elements of a sociology of translation: domestication of the scallops and the fishermen of St Briene Bay', in J. Law (ed.), *Power, Action and Belief: a Sociology of Knowledge?* Sociological Review Monograph 32. London: Routledge.

Child, J. (1972) 'Organization structure, environment and performance: the role of strategic choice', *Sociology*, 6: 1–22.

Clegg, S.R. (1975) *Power, Rule and Domination.* London and Boston: Routledge & Kegan Paul.

Clegg, S.R. (1989) *Frameworks of Power.* London: Sage.

Clegg, S.R. (1990) *Modern Organizations: Organization Studies in the Postmodern World.* London: Sage.

Clegg, S.R. (1995) 'Power and the resistant subject', in J.M. Germier, W. Nord and D. Knights (eds), *Resistance and Power in Organizations: Agency, Subjectivity and the Labour Process.* London: Routledge.

Clegg, S.R. and Chua, W.F. (1990) 'Professional closure: the case of British nursing', *Theory and Society*, 19: 135–72.

Clegg, S.R. and Dunkerley, D. (1980) *Organization, Class and Control.* London and Boston: Routledge and Kegan Paul.

Clegg, S.R. and Palmer, G. (eds) (1996) *The Politics of Mangement.* London: Sage.

Cobb, S. (1993) 'Empowerment and mediation: a narrative perspective', *Negotiation Journal*, July: 245–61.

Collins, R. (1981) 'On the microfoundations of macrosociology', *American Journal of Sociology*, 86(5): 984–1013.

Cooper, R. (1989) 'Modernism, postmodernism and organisational analysis. The contribution of Jacques Derrida', *Organization Studies*, 10(4): 479–502.

Cyert, R.M. and March, J.G. (1963) *A Behavioural Theory of the Firm.* Englewood Cliffs, NJ: Prentice-Hall.

Dandekker, C. (1990) *Surveillance, Power and Modernity.* Cambridge: Polity Press.

Dasgupta, P. (1988) 'Trust as a commodity', in D. Gambetta (ed.), *Trust: Making and Breaking Cooperative Relations.* Oxford: Basil Blackwell.

de Assis, M. (1992) *Dom Cassmurro*, translated from the Portuguese and with an introduction by R.L. Scott-Buccleuch. London: Peter Owen.

de Certeau, M. (1984) *The Practice of Everyday Life.* Berkeley, CA: University of California Press.

Deetz, S. (1992) *Democracy in an Age of Corporate Colonization: Developments in Communication and the Politics of Everyday Life.* Albany, NY: State University of New York.

Denzin, N.K. (1994) 'The art and politics of interpretation', in N.K. Denzin and Y.S. Lincoln (eds), *Handbook of Qualitative Research.* London: Sage. pp. 500–15.

Denzin, N.K. and Lincoln, Y.S. (1994a) 'Entering the field of qualitative research', in N.K. Denzin and Y.S. Lincoln (eds), *Handbook of Qualitative Research.* London: Sage. pp. 1–18.

Denzin, N.K. and Lincoln, Y.S. (1994b) 'The fifth moment', in N.K. Denzin and Y.S. Lincoln (eds), *Handbook of Qualitative Research.* London: Sage. pp. 575–85.

Derrida, J. (1978) *Writing and Différance.* Chicago: University of Chicago Press.

DiMaggio, P.J. (1988) 'Interest and agency in institutional theory', in L.G. Zucker (ed.), *Institutional Patterns and Organizations: Culture and Environment.* Cambridge, MA: Ballinger. pp. 3–22.

DiMaggio, P.J. and Powell, W.P. (1983) 'The iron cage revisited: institutional isomorphism and collective rationality in organisational fields', *American Sociological Review*, 48: 147–60.

Dodgson, M. (1993) 'Organisational learning: a review of some literatures', *Organization Studies*, 14(3): 375–94.

Donaldson, L. (1985) *In Defence of Organization Theory: a Reply to the Critics.* Cambridge: Cambridge University Press.

Donaldson, L. (1995) *American Anti-Management Theories of Organization: a Critique of Paradigm Proliferation.* Cambridge and New York: Cambridge University Press.

Drucker, P.F. (1990) *Innovation.* Boston, MA: Harvard Business School.

Eccles, R. and Nohria, N. (1993) *Beyond the Hype.* Cambridge, MA: Harvard Business School.

Emery, F.E. and Trist, E.L. (1965) 'The causal texture of organisational environments', *Human Relations*, 18: 21–32.

Fairtlough, G. (1993) 'Innovation and biotechnology'. Paper presented to the Science Policy Research Unit, University of Sussex, 19 February.

Fairtlough, G. (1994) *Creative Compartments: a Design For Future Organisation.* London: Adamantine.

Fine, M. (1994) 'Working the hyphens: reinventing self and other in qualitative research', in N.K. Denzin and Y.S. Lincoln (eds), *Handbook of Qualitative Research.* London: Sage.

Forrester, J. (1989) *Planning in the Age of Power.* Berkeley, CA: University of California Press.

Foucault, M. (1977) *Discipline and Punish.* New York: Pantheon.

Fox, A. (1974) *Beyond Contract: Work, Power and Trust Relations.* London: Faber & Faber.

Freire, P. (1992) *Pedagogy of the Oppressed.* New York: Continuum.

Fugelsang, A. (1973) *Applied Communication in Developing Countries.* Uppsala: Dag Hammarskjöld Foundation.

Gambetta, D. (ed.) (1988) *Trust: Making and Breaking Cooperative Relations.* Oxford: Blackwell.

Garrat, R. (1987) *The Learning Organization.* London: Fontana/Collins.

Geertz, C. (1973) *The Interpretation of Cultures.* New York: Harper Collins.

Godard, J.-L. (1963) *Les Carabiniers.* Rome-Paris Films/Les Films Marceau.

Gouldner, A.W. (1954) *Patterns of Industrial Bureaucracy*. New York: Free Press.

Gouldner, A.W. (1976) *The Dialectic of Ideology and Technology: The Origins of Grammar, and the Future of Ideology*. London: Macmillan.

Gramsci, A. (1971) *Selections from the Prison Notebooks*. London: Lawrence & Wishart.

Granovetter, M. (1985) 'Economic action and social structure: the problem of embeddedness', *American Journal of Sociology*, 91: 481–510.

Gray, B. (1989) *Collaborating: Finding Common Ground For Multiparty Problems*. San Francisco: Jossey-Bass.

Gray, B. (1995) 'The development of global environmental regimes: organizing in the absence of authority'. Paper presented at the Second International Workshop of Multi-Organizational Partnerships: Working Together Across Organizational Boundaries, Glasgow, June.

Gricar, B.G. and Brown, L.D. (1981) 'Conflict, power and organization in a changing community', *Human Relations*, 34.

Hardy, C. (1994) 'Understanding interorganizational domains: the case of refugee systems', *Journal of Applied Behavioral Science*, 30(3): 278–96.

Hardy, C. (1995) 'Power and the production of a refugee: refugee systems as systems of Foucauldian power'. Paper presented at a Meeting of APROS (Asian–Pacific Researchers on Organization Studies), University of Western Sydney, Macarthur, Campbelltown, New South Wales, Australia.

Hardy, C. and Phillips, N. (1995a) 'Overcoming illusions of trust: towards a communicative theory of trust and power', *McGill Working Papers*, Montreal, Canada.

Hardy, C. and Phillips, N. (1995b) 'Overcoming illusions: combining trust and power'. Paper presented at the Second International Workshop on Multi-Organizational Partnerships, University of Strathclyde, Glasgow, Scotland.

Harrigan, K.R. (1985) *Strategies for Joint Ventures*. Lexington, MA: D.C. Heath/Lexington Books.

Hasenfeld, Y. and Chesler, M.A. (1989) 'Client empowerment in the human services: personal and professional agenda', *Journal of Applied Behavioural Science*, 25(4): 499–521.

Hassard, J. (1993) *Sociology and Organization Theory: Positivism, Paradigms and Postmodernity*. London: Sage.

Hawken, P. (1993) *Ecology of Commerce*. London: Harper Collins.

Hofstede, G. (1995) 'Keynote presentation' to EGOS (European Group on Organization Studies), Istanbul, Turkey, July.

Hollway, W. (1991) *Work Psychology and Organizational Behaviour: Managing the Individual at Work*. London: Sage.

hooks, b. (1989) *Talking Back: Thinking Feminist Thinking Black*. Boston: South End.

Hopfl, H. and Sinclair, J. (1995) 'Representations,

technology and the pornographic gaze'. Paper presented at SCOS (Standing Conference on Organizational Symbolism), Turku, Finland.

Huxham, C. (1995) *Creating Collaborative Advantage*. London: Sage.

Jeffcutt, P. (1994) 'From interpretation to representation in organizational analysis: postmodernism, ethnography and organizational symbolism', *Organization Studies*, 15(2): 241–74.

Jencks, C. (1989) *What is Post-Modernism?*, 3rd edn. New York: Academy Editions, St Martin's Press.

Jepperson, R.L. (1991) 'Institutions, institutional effects, and institutionalism', in W.W. Powell and P.J. DiMaggio (eds), *The New Institutionalism in Organizational Analysis*. Chicago: University of Chicago Press.

Kanter, R.M. (1989) *When Giants Learn to Dance*. Sydney: Allen & Unwin.

Kanter, R.M. (1990) 'When giants learn cooperative strategies', *Planning Review*, 18(1): 15–25.

Knights, D. and Willmott, H. (1982) 'Power, values and relations: a comment on Benton', *Sociology*, 16(4): 578–85.

Knights, D., Murray, F. and Willmott, H. (1993) 'Networking as knowledge work: a study of strategic interorganizational development in the financial services industry', *Journal of Management Studies*, 30(6): 975–95.

Knoke, D. (1990) *Organizing for Collective Action*. Berlin: de Gruyter.

Laclau, E. (1988) 'Politics and the limits of modernity', in A. Ross (ed.), *Universal Abandon: the Politics of Postmodernism*. Minneapolis: University of Minnesota Press. pp. 63–82.

Laclau, E. and Mouffe, C. (1987) *Hegemony and Socialist Strategy: towards a Radical Democratic Politics*. London: Verso.

Lane, C. and Bachmann, R. (1995) 'Risk, trust and power: the social constitution of supplier relations in Britain and Germany'. Working paper WP5, Centre for Business Research, University of Cambridge.

Lane, M. (ed.) (1971) *Structuralism: a Reader*. London: Jonathan Cape.

Lash, S. and Urry, G. (1994) *Economies of Signs and Space*. London: Sage.

Latour, B. (1987) *Science in Action: How to Follow Scientists and Engineers through Society*. Cambridge, MA: Harvard University Press.

Latour, B. (1993) *We Have Never Been Modern*. Hemel Hempstead: Harvester Wheatsheaf.

Laumann, E.O. and Knoke, D. (1987) *The Organizational State*. Madison: University of Wisconsin Press.

Law, J. (1986) *Power, Action and Belief: a Sociology of Knowledge?* Sociological Review Monograph 32. London: Routledge.

Lee, R.L.M. (1994) 'Modernization, postmodernism and the Third World', *Current Sociology*, 42(2): 1–66.

Lefebvre, H. (1971) *Everyday Life in the Modern World*. New York: Harper & Row.

Leiba, S. and Hardy, C. (1994) 'Employee empowerment: a seductive misnomer?', in C. Hardy (ed.), *Managing Strategic Action: Mobilizing Change*. London: Sage.

Lewis, J.D. and Weigert, A. (1985) 'Trust as a social reality', *Social Forces*, 43(4): 967–85.

Linstead, S. and Grafton-Small, R. (1992) 'On reading organisation culture', *Organization Studies*, 13(3): 331–56.

Luhmann, N. (1979) *Trust and Power*. Chichester: Wiley.

Lukes, S. (1974) *Power: a Radical View*. London: Macmillan.

Marcus, G.E. (1994) 'What comes (just) after "Post"? The case of ethnography', in N.K. Denzin and Y.S. Lincoln (eds), *Handbook of Qualitative Research*. London: Sage. pp. 563–74.

Marx, K. (1975) 'A contribution to Hegel's philosophy of right', in L. Coletti (ed.), *Karl Marx: Early Writings*. Harmondsworth: Penguin. pp. 243–58.

Marx, K. and Engels, F. (1965) 'The Communist Manifesto', in L.S. Fleur (ed.), *Marx & Engels: Basic Writings on Politics and Philosophy*. London: Fontana. pp. 43–82.

McGuire, J.B. (1988) 'A dialectical analysis of interorganizational networks', *Journal of Management*, 14(1): 109–24.

Merton, R.K. (1957) 'Bureaucratic structure and personality', in R.K. Merton (ed.), *Social Theory and Social Structure*. Glencoe, IL: Free Press.

Mintzberg, H. (1973) *The Nature of Managerial Work*. New York: Harper & Row.

Nathan, M.L. and Mitroff, I.I. (1991) 'The use of negotiated order theory as a tool for the analysis and development of an interorganizational field', *Journal of Applied Behavioral Science*, 27: 163–80.

Nord, W.R. and Doherty, E.M. (1994) 'Towards an assertion perspective for empowerment: blending employee rights and labor process theories'. Unpublished paper, College of Business Administration, University of South Florida.

Nord, W.R. and Jermier, J.M. (1992) 'Critical social science for managers? Promising and perverse possibilities', in M. Alvesson and H. Willmott (eds), *Critical Management Studies*. London: Sage. pp. 202–22.

O'Connor, E.S. (1993) 'Paradoxes of participation: a textual analysis of case studies documenting employee involvement efforts'. Paper presented at the Academy of Management, Atlanta, August.

Oliver, C. (1991) 'Strategic responses to institutional processes', *Academy of Management Review*, 16: 145–79.

Oliver, C. (1992) 'The antecedents of deinstitutionalisation', *Organization Studies*, 13: 563–88.

Parker, M. (1992) 'Post-modern organisations or postmodern organisation theory?', *Organization Studies*, 13: 1–13.

Parker, M. (1993) 'Industrial relations myth and shop-floor reality: the 'team' concept in the auto industry', in N. Lichtenstein and J.H. Howell (eds), *Industrial Democracy in America*. Cambridge: Cambridge University Press.

Parker, M. and Slaughter, J. (1988) 'Managing by stress: the dark side of the team concept', *ILR Report*, 26(1): 19–23.

Pasquero, J. (1991) 'Supraorganizational collaboration: the Canadian environmental experiment', *Journal of Applied Behavioral Science*, 27(1): 38–64.

Perrow, C. (1984) *Normal Accidents*. New York: Basic Books.

Perrow, C. (1993) 'Small-firm networks', in N. Nohria and R.G. Eccles (eds), *Networks and Organizations: Structure, Form and Action*. Cambridge, MA: Harvard Business School.

Pettigrew, A.M. (1992) 'On studying managerial elites', *Strategic Management Journal*, 13: 163–82.

Powell, W.W. (1990) 'Neither market nor hierarchy: network forms of organisation', in B. Staw and L.L. Cummings (eds), *Research in Organisational Behaviour*, vol. 12. Greenwich, CT: JAI Press. pp. 295–336.

Pugh D.S. and Hickson, D.J. (1976) *Organizational Structure in its Context: the Aston Programme I*. Farnborough: Saxon House.

Rainey, H.G. (1983) 'Public agencies and private firms: incentive structures, goals, and individual roles', *Administration and Society*, 15(2): 207–42.

Reed, M. (1985) *Redirections in Organisational Analysis*. London: Tavistock.

Reich, R.B. (1992) *The Works of Nations: Preparing Ourselves for 21st Century Capitalism*. New York: Vintage Books.

Richardson, L. (1994) 'Writing: a method of inquiry', in N.K. Denzin and Y.S. Lincoln (eds), *Handbook of Qualitative Research*. London: Sage. pp. 516–29.

Ring, P.S. and Van de Ven, A.H. (1992) 'Structuring cooperative relationships between organizations', *Strategic Management Journal*, 13: 483–98.

Rogers, D.L. and Whetten, D.A. (eds) (1981) *Interorganizational Coordination*. Ames, IA: Iowa State University Press.

Rojek, C. (1995) *Decentring Leisure: Rethinking Leisure Theory*. London: Sage.

Romm, C.T. and Pliskin, N. (1995) 'Using e-mail to achieve political objectives: a case study'. Paper presented at the APROS Regional Meeting on Power and Politics, University of Western Sydney, Macarthur, Sydney.

Rose, S.M. and Black, B.L. (1985) *Advocacy and Empowerment: Mental Health Care in the Community*. Boston: Routledge & Kegan Paul.

Rothwell, J.D. (1992) *In Mixed Company: Small Group Communication*. Fort Worth, TX: Harcourt Brace Jovanovich.

Schutz, Alfred (1970) *On Phenomenology and Social Relations*. Chicago, IL: University of Chicago Press.

Senge, P.M. (1990) *The Fifth Discipline: the Art and*

Practice of the Learning Organization. New York: Doubleday/Currency.

Slater, D. (1992) 'Theories of development and politics of the post-modern: exploring a border zone', *Development and Change*, 3: 283–319.

Starbuck, W.H. (1981) 'A trip to view the elephants and the rattlesnakes in the garden of Aston: the Aston program perspective', in A. Van de Ven and W. Joyce (eds), *Perspectives on Organisation Design and Behaviour*. New York: Wiley.

Steffy, B.D. and Grimes, A.J. (1986) 'A critical theory of organization science', *Academy of Management Review*, 11(2): 322–36.

Stewart, R. (1967) *Managers and their Jobs: a Study of the Similarities and Differences in the Ways Managers Spend their Time*. London: Macmillan.

Stewart, T.A. (1989) 'New ways to exercise power', *Fortune*, 6 November: 48–53.

Strauss, A., Schatzman, L., Bucher, R., Ehrlich, D. and Satshin, M. (1963) 'The hospital and its negotiated order', in E. Friedson (ed.), *The Hospital in Modern Society*. Chicago: Free Press. pp. 147–69.

Taylor, F.W. (1911) *The Principles of Scientific Management*. New York: W.W. Norton.

Taylor, P.V. (1993) *The Texts of Paulo Freire*. Milton Keynes: Open University Press.

Therborn, G. (1995) *European Modernity and Beyond: the Trajectory of European Societies 1945–2000*. London: Sage.

Thompson, P. and McHugh, D. (1990) *Work Organisations: a Critical Introduction*. London: Macmillan.

Thorelli, H.B. (1986) 'Networks: between markets and hierarchies', *Strategic Management Journal*, 7: 37–51.

Trist, E. (1983) 'Referent organizations and the development of interorganizational domains', *Human Relations*, 36(2): 269–84.

Van Maanen, J. (1979) 'Reclaiming qualitative methods for organisational research: a preface', *Administrative Science Quarterly*, 24(4): 520–6.

Waddock, S.A. (1989) 'Understanding social partnerships: an evolutionary model of partnership organizations', *Administration and Society*, 21: 78–100.

Warren, R. (1967) 'The interorganisational field as a focus for investigation', *Administrative Science Quarterly*, 12: 396–419.

Warren, R., Rose, S. and Bergunder, A. (1974) *The Structure of Urban Reform*. Lexington, MA: D.C. Heath.

Weber, M. (1947) *The Theory of Social and Economic Organization*. New York: Free Press.

Weber, M. (1978) *Economy and Society*. Berkeley, CA: University of California Press.

Weedon, C. (1987) *Feminist Practice and Poststructuralist Theory*. Oxford: Blackwell.

Weick, K.E. (1989) 'Theory construction as a disciplined imagination', *Academy of Management Review*, 14: 516–31.

Weiss, L. (1988) *Creating Capitalism: the State and Small Business since 1945*. Oxford: Blackwell.

Weiss, R.M. (1983) 'Weber on bureaucracy: management consultant or political theorist?', *Academy of Management Review*, 8(2): 242–8.

Westley, F.R. (1990) 'Middle managers and strategy: microdynamics of inclusion', *Strategic Management Journal*, 11: 337–51.

Westley, F.R. and Vredenburg, H. (1991) 'Strategic bridging: the collaboration between environmentalists and business in the marketing of green products', *Journal of Applied Behavioral Science*, 27: 65–90.

White, S.K. (1986) 'Foucault's challenge to critical theory', *American Political Science Review*, 80(2): 419–32.

Willmott, H. (1993) 'Strength is ignorance; slavery is freedom: managing culture in modern organizations', *Journal of Management Studies*, 30(4): 515–52.

Wittgenstein, L. (1972) *Philosophical Investigations*. Oxford: Blackwell.

Zald, M.N. (1994) 'Organization studies as a scientific and humanistic enterprise: toward a reconceptualization of the foundations of the field', *Organization Science*, 4(4): 513–28.

Zucker, L.G. (1986) 'Production of trust: institutional sources of economic structure 1884–1920', in *Research in Organizational Behaviour*. Greenwich, CT: JAI Press. pp. 53–111.

Index